# LaunchPad PSYCHOLOGY

## LaunchPad for PSYCHOLOGY, Third Canadian Edition

Available July 2014 at *http://www.worthpublishers.com/launchpad/schacter3ecanadian*

Each chapter in LaunchPad for PSYCHOLOGY, **Third Canadian Edition,** features a collection of activities carefully chosen to help master the major concepts. The site serves students as a comprehensive online study guide, available any time, with opportunities for self-quizzing with instant feedback, exam preparation, and further exploration of topics from the textbook. For instructors, all units and activities can be instantly assigned, and students' results and analytics are collected in the Gradebook.

## FOR STUDENTS

- Full e-Book of *PSYCHOLOGY*, Third Canadian Edition
- LearningCurve Quizzing
- Student Video Activities
- Interactive Flashcards
- PsychInvestigator
- PsychSim 5.0 by Thomas Ludwig, Hope College
- *Scientific American* Newsfeed

## FOR INSTRUCTORS

- Gradebook
- Presentation Slides
- iClicker Questions
- Electronic Figures, Photographs, and Tables
- Correlation of *PSYCHOLOGY*, Third Canadian Edition, to MCAT 2015 Topics

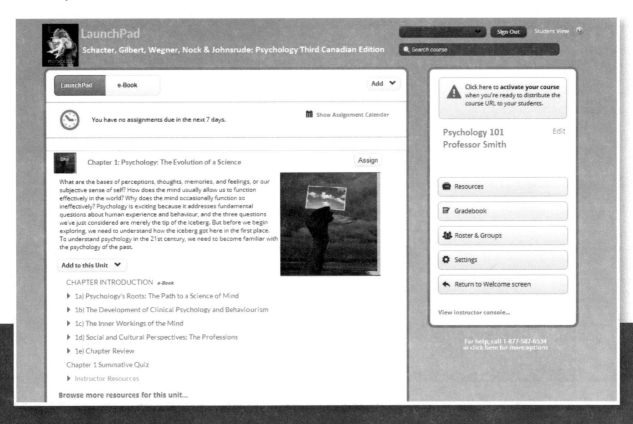

# PSYCHOLOGY

# PSYCHOLOGY

### THIRD CANADIAN EDITION

## DANIEL L. SCHACTER
HARVARD UNIVERSITY

## DANIEL T. GILBERT
HARVARD UNIVERSITY

## DANIEL M. WEGNER
HARVARD UNIVERSITY

## MATTHEW K. NOCK
HARVARD UNIVERSITY

## INGRID JOHNSRUDE
UNIVERSITY OF WESTERN ONTARIO

**WORTH PUBLISHERS**

A Macmillan Higher Education Company

**Senior Vice President, Editorial and Production:** Catherine Woods
**Publisher:** Kevin Feyen
**Senior Acquisitions Editor:** Daniel DeBonis
**Senior Development Editors:** Valerie Raymond; Eileen Jung, First Folio Resource Group Inc.
**Editorial Assistants:** Katie Garrett; Loretta Johnson, First Folio Resource Group Inc.
**Marketing Manager:** Lindsay Johnson
**Associate Director of Market Research:** Carlise Stembridge
**Executive Media Editor:** Rachel Comerford
**Director of Development for Print and Digital Products:** Tracey Kuehn
**Associate Managing Editor:** Lisa Kinne
**Project Editor:** Robert Errera
**Production Manager:** Sarah Segal
**Photo Editors:** Cecilia Varas; Maria DeCambra & Associates
**Photo Researchers:** Elyse Rieder; Maria DeCambra & Associates
**Chapter Opener Researcher:** Lyndall Culbertson
**Art Director and Cover Designer:** Babs Reingold
**Text Designers:** Babs Reingold and Lyndall Culbertson
**Layout Designer:** Paul Lacy
**Illustration Coordinator:** Matthew McAdams
**Illustrations:** Evelyn Pence, Jackie Heda, Matthew McAdams, Matt Holt, Christy Krames,
            Don Stewart, and Todd Buck
**Cover Photograph:** © Lois Greenfield
**Composition:** Tom Dart, First Folio Resource Group Inc.
**Printing and Binding:** RR Donnelley

**Chapter Opener Credits:** p. xxiv, Yagi Studio/Getty Images; p. 38, photosindia/Getty Images;
p. 78, Cary Wolinsky/Getty Images; p. 128, Andrew Geiger; p. 176, Chad Baker/Getty Images;
p. 220, David Johnston/Getty Images; p. 264, Gandee Vasan/Getty Images; p. 312, Image
Source/age fotostock; p. 350, Kalium/age fotostock; p. 394, Christopher Wilson; p. 424, Tooga/
Getty Images; p. 470, Copyright Karim Parris; p. 506, Tim Macpherson/Getty Images;
p. 548, © Fotosearch/age fotostock; p. 582, © easyFotostock/age fotostock; p. 626, © 2008 Lívia
Fernandes/Getty Images

ISBN-13: 978-1-4292-3721-5
ISBN-10: 1-4292-3721-X

Worth Publishers
41 Madison Avenue
New York, NY 10010
www.worthpublishers.com

*We dedicate this edition to the memory of Dan Wegner, our co-author, colleague, and deeply missed friend.*

# About the Authors

**Daniel Schacter** is William R. Kenan, Jr., Professor of Psychology at Harvard University. Dan received his B.A. degree from the University of North Carolina at Chapel Hill. He subsequently developed a keen interest in amnesic disorders associated with various kinds of brain damage. He continued his research and education at the University of Toronto, where he received his Ph.D. in 1981. He taught on the faculty at Toronto for the next 6 years before joining the psychology department at the University of Arizona in 1987. In 1991, he joined the faculty at Harvard University. His research explores the relationship between conscious and unconscious forms of memory, the nature of distortions and errors in remembering, and the ways in which we use memory to imagine future events. Many of Schacter's studies are summarized in his 1996 book, *Searching for Memory: The Brain, The Mind, and The Past*, and his 2001 book, *The Seven Sins of Memory: How the Mind Forgets and Remembers,* both winners of the APA's William James Book Award. Schacter has also received a number of awards for teaching and research, including the Harvard-Radcliffe Phi Beta Kappa Teaching Prize, the Warren Medal from the Society of Experimental Psychologists, and the Award for Distinguished Scientific Contributions from the American Psychological Association. In 2013, he was elected to the National Academy of Sciences.

**Daniel Gilbert** is Edgar Pierce Professor of Psychology at Harvard University. Dan received his his B.A. from the University of Colorado at Denver and his Ph.D. from Princeton University. From 1985 to 1996 he taught at the University of Texas, Austin, and in 1996 he joined the faculty of Harvard University. He has received the American Psychological Association's Distinguished Scientific Award for an Early Career Contribution to Psychology, the Diener Award for Outstanding Contributions to Social Psychology, and has won teaching awards that include the Phi Beta Kappa Teaching Prize and the Harvard College Professorship. His research focuses on how and how well people think about their emotional reactions to future events. He is the author of the international best seller *Stumbling on Happiness*, which won the Royal Society's General Prize for best popular science book of the year, and he is the co-writer and host of the PBS television series, *This Emotional Life*.

**Daniel Wegner** was the John Lindsley Professor of Psychology in Memory of William James at Harvard University. He received his B.S. in 1970 and Ph.D. in 1974, both from Michigan State University. He began his teaching career at Trinity University in San Antonio, TX, before receiving his appointments at the University of Virginia in 1990 and then Harvard University in 2000. He was a Fellow of the American Academy of Arts and Sciences and also the recipient of the William James Award from the Association for Psychological Science, the Award for Distinguished Scientific Contributions from the American Psychological Association, and the Distinguished Scientist Award from the Society of Experimental Social Psychology. His research focused on thought suppression and mental control, transactive memory in relationships and groups, and the experience of conscious will. His work on thought suppression and consciousness served as the basis of two popular books, *White Bears and Other Unwanted Thoughts* and *The Illusion of Conscious Will,* both of which were named *Choice* Outstanding Academic Books. He died in 2013.

NICOLAS GUEVARA

**Matthew Nock** is a Professor of Psychology at Harvard University. Matt received his B.A. from Boston University (1995) and his Ph.D. from Yale University (2003), and he completed his clinical internship at Bellevue Hospital and the New York University Child Study Center (2003). Matt joined the faculty of Harvard University in 2003 and has been there ever since. While an undergraduate, Matt became very interested in the question of why people do things to intentionally harm themselves, and he has been conducting research aimed at answering this question ever since. His research is multidisciplinary in nature and uses a range of methodological approaches (e.g., epidemiologic surveys, laboratory-based experiments, and clinic-based studies) to better understand how these behaviours develop, how to predict them, and how to prevent their occurrence. He has received multiple teaching awards at Harvard, four early career awards recognizing his research, and in 2011 was named a MacArthur Fellow.

PHOTO BY ERIC BROUSSEAU

**Ingrid Johnsrude** is Professor of Psychology at the University of Western Ontario where she is also the Research Chair at the Brain and Mind Institute and School of Communication Sciences and Disorders. Previously, she was Associate Professor of Psychology and Canada Research Chair in Cognitive Neuroscience at Queen's University where she directed the Cognitive Neuroscience of Communication and Hearing (CoNCH) lab. Ingrid received her B.Sc. from Queen's University (1989), and her M.Sc. and Ph.D. from McGill University (1992, 1997), where she was supervised by internationally renowned psychologist, Brenda Milner. After earning her doctorate, she spent time in the United Kingdom as a postdoctoral fellow at University College London and then as an Investigator Scientist in Cambridge, before returning to Queen's to join the faculty there. During her time in England, she contributed to a paper showing that taxi drivers in London with extensive navigation experience have larger hippocampi than the general population, revealing one of the ways that experience can alter the structure of the human brain. This finding, notable for both the content of the study and the pioneering methods used, is a common example in introductory psychology texts. Ingrid's principal area of investigation is the neural basis of understanding speech, and she leads experiments examining how utterances are transformed into acoustic signals and then into meaning via a variety of cognitive processes. Her investigations span multiple levels—from understanding the brain structures involved in hearing and comprehension to observing the ways listeners deal with challenges such as background noise.

# Brief Contents

Preface .................................................................................................. xix

1  Psychology: Evolution of a Science ........................................ 1

2  Methods in Psychology ............................................................. 39

3  Neuroscience and Behaviour ................................................... 79

4  Sensation and Perception ......................................................... 129

5  Consciousness ............................................................................ 177

6  Memory ......................................................................................... 221

7  Learning ........................................................................................ 265

8  Emotion and Motivation ........................................................... 313

9  Language and Thought .............................................................. 351

10  Intelligence .................................................................................. 395

11  Development ................................................................................ 425

12  Personality ................................................................................... 471

13  Social Psychology ...................................................................... 507

14  Stress and Health ....................................................................... 549

15  Psychological Disorders .......................................................... 583

16  Treatment of Psychological Disorders ................................ 627

Glossary ......................................................................................... G-1

References ..................................................................................... R-1

Name Index ................................................................................... NI-1

Subject Index ................................................................................ SI-1

# Contents

Preface......................................................................................xix

> **Chapter 1**  Psychology: Evolution of a Science.............................1

THE REAL WORLD **The Perils of Procrastination**  4

Psychology's Roots: The Path to a Science of Mind........................5
  Psychology's Ancestors: The Great Philosophers  5
  From the Brain to the Mind: The French Connection  6
  Structuralism: Applying Methods from Physiology to Psychology  7
  Titchener Brings Structuralism to the United States  9
  James and the Functional Approach  10
  THE REAL WORLD **Improving Study Skills**  10

The Development of Clinical Psychology.................................13
  The Path to Freud and Psychoanalytic Theory  13
  Influence of Psychoanalysis and the Humanistic Response  15

The Search for Objective Measurement: Behaviourism Takes Centre Stage.........16
  Watson and the Emergence of Behaviourism  16
  OTHER VOICES **Is Psychology a Science?**  17
  B. F. Skinner and the Development of Behaviourism  18

Return of the Mind: Psychology Expands.................................20
  The Pioneers of Cognitive Psychology  20
  Technology and the Development of Cognitive Psychology  22
  The Brain Meets the Mind: The Rise of Cognitive Neuroscience  24
  The Adaptive Mind: The Emergence of Evolutionary Psychology  25

Beyond the Individual: Social and Cultural Perspectives.........................27
  The Development of Social Psychology  27
  The Emergence of Cultural Psychology  28
  CULTURE & COMMUNITY **Analytic and Holistic Styles in Western and Eastern Cultures**  30

The Profession of Psychology: Past and Present.........................31
  Psychologists Band Together: Psychological Associations  31
  What Psychologists Do: Research Careers  33
  HOT SCIENCE **Psychology as a Hub Science**  34

> **Chapter 2**  Methods in Psychology...............................................39

Empiricism: How to Know Stuff.........................................40
  The Scientific Method  40
  The Art of Looking  42

Observation: Discovering What People Do.................................43
  Measurement  43
  CULTURE & COMMUNITY **Best Place to Fall on Your Face**  45
  Descriptions  47

Explanation: Discovering Why People Do What They Do..........................................51
   Correlation   51
   Causation   54
   THE REAL WORLD "Oddsly" Enough   61
   Drawing Conclusions   62
   HOT SCIENCE Do Violent Movies Make Peaceful Streets?   64
   Thinking Critically about Evidence   66

The Ethics of Science: First, Do No Harm.............................................................70
   Respecting People   70
   Respecting Animals   72
   Respecting Truth   73
   OTHER VOICES Can We Afford Science?   75

Chapter 3   Neuroscience and Behaviour.....................................................79

Neurons: The Origin of Behaviour........................................................................80
   Components of the Neuron   80
   Major Types of Neurons   82
   Neurons Specialized by Location   83

The Electrochemical Actions of Neurons: Information Processing........................84
   Electric Signalling: Conducting Information within a Neuron   84
   Chemical Signalling: Transmission between Neurons   87

The Organization of the Nervous System...............................................................92
   Divisions of the Nervous System   92
   Components of the Central Nervous System   94

Structure of the Brain...........................................................................................95
   The Hindbrain   96
   The Midbrain   96
   The Forebrain   97
   Brain Plasticity   103
   THE REAL WORLD Brain Plasticity and Sensations in Phantom Limbs   104

The Development and Evolution of Nervous Systems............................................106
   Prenatal Development of the Central Nervous System   106
   Evolutionary Development of the Central Nervous System   107
   Genes, Epigenetics, and the Environment   108
   HOT SCIENCE Epigenetics and the Persisting Effects of Early Experiences   112

Investigating the Brain........................................................................................114
   Studying the Damaged Brain   114
   Studying the Brain's Electrical Activity   118
   Using Brain Imaging to Study Structure and to Watch the Brain in Action   119
   THE REAL WORLD Brain Death and the Vegetative State   123
   OTHER VOICES Neuromyths   124

**Chapter 4** Sensation and Perception ......................................................... 129

Sensation and Perception Are Distinct Activities ................................. 130
Psychophysics   131
Measuring Thresholds   132
Signal Detection   133
Sensory Adaptation   134

Vision I: How the Eyes and the Brain Convert Light Waves to Neural Signals.... 135
Sensing Light   136
Perceiving Colour   140
The Visual Brain   141

Vision II: Recognizing What We Perceive .............................................. 144
Attention: The "Glue" That Binds Individual Features into a Whole   144
THE REAL WORLD Multitasking   146
Recognizing Objects by Sight   146
Perceiving Depth and Size   150
Perceiving Motion and Change   153
OTHER VOICES Hallucinations and the Visual System   156
CULTURE & COMMUNITY Does Culture Influence Change Blindness?   157

Audition: More Than Meets the Ear ....................................................... 158
Sensing Sound   158
The Human Ear   159
Perceiving Pitch   160
Localizing Sound Sources   161
Hearing Loss   162
THE REAL WORLD Music Training: Worth the Time   163

The Body Senses: More Than Skin Deep ................................................ 164
Touch   164
Pain   165
Body Position, Movement, and Balance   167

The Chemical Senses: Adding Flavour .................................................. 168
Smell   167
HOT SCIENCE Taste: From the Top Down   170
Taste   171

**Chapter 5** Consciousness .................................................................... 177

Conscious and Unconscious: The Mind's Eye, Open and Closed ........... 178
The Mysteries of Consciousness   178
The Nature of Consciousness   181
HOT SCIENCE Disorders of Consciousness   185
The Unconscious Mind   189
THE REAL WORLD Anyone for Tennis?   192

Sleep and Dreaming: Good Night, Mind ............................................... 194
Sleep   194
Dreams   200
CULTURE & COMMUNITY What Do Dreams Mean to Us around the World?   203

Drugs and Consciousness: Artificial Inspiration.................................................205
Drug Use and Abuse   206
Types of Psychoactive Drugs   209

Hypnosis: Open to Suggestion ...................................................................214
Induction and Susceptibility   214
Hypnotic Effects   215
OTHER VOICES The Blink of an Eye   217

Chapter 6 Memory .................................................................................221

Encoding: Transforming Perceptions into Memories.................................223
Semantic Encoding   223
Visual Imagery Encoding   224
Organizational Encoding   225
Encoding of Survival-Related Information   226

Storage: Maintaining Memories over Time.................................................228
Sensory Storage   228
Short-Term Storage and Working Memory   229
Long-Term Storage   230
HOT SCIENCE Sleep on It   233
Memories, Neurons, and Synapses   234

Retrieval: Bringing Memories to Mind.................................................236
Retrieval Cues: Reinstating the Past   236
Consequences of Retrieval   237
Separating the Components of Retrieval   239
CULTURE & COMMUNITY Does Culture Affect Childhood Amnesia?   240

Multiple Forms of Memory: How the Past Returns .................................241
Explicit and Implicit Memory   242
Semantic and Episodic Memory   244
THE REAL WORLD Is Google Hurting our Memories?   248

Memory Failures: The Seven Sins of Memory .................................249
1. Transience   249
2. Absentmindedness   250
3. Blocking   252
4. Memory Misattribution   253
5. Suggestibility   255
6. Bias   256
7. Persistence   257
Are the Seven Sins Vices or Virtues?   259
OTHER VOICES Early Memories   261

Chapter 7 Learning .................................................................................265

Classical Conditioning: One Thing Leads to Another.................................267
The Development of Classical Conditioning: Pavlov's Experiments   267
The Basic Principles of Classical Conditioning   268
THE REAL WORLD Understanding Drug Overdoses   270
Conditioned Emotional Responses: The Case of Little Albert   272
A Deeper Understanding of Classical Conditioning   273

**Operant Conditioning: Reinforcements from the Environment**............................277
The Development of Operant Conditioning: The Law of Effect   277
B. F. Skinner: The Role of Reinforcement and Punishment   278
CULTURE & COMMUNITY Are There Cultural Differences in Reinforcers?   281
The Basic Principles of Operant Conditioning   282
A Deeper Understanding of Operant Conditioning   288
HOT SCIENCE Dopamine and Reward Learning in Parkinson's Disease   292

**Observational Learning: Look at Me**..........................................................295
Observational Learning in Humans   295
Observational Learning in Animals   297
Neural Elements of Observational Learning   299

**Implicit Learning: Under the Radar**..........................................................300
Cognitive Approaches to Implicit Learning   301
Implicit and Explicit Learning Use Distinct Neural Pathways   303

**Learning in the Classroom**.......................................................................304
Techniques for Learning   304
Testing Aids Attention   306
Control of Learning   307
OTHER VOICES Online Learning   308

**Chapter 8**   **Emotion and Motivation**..................................................313

**Emotional Experience: The Feeling Machine**............................................314
What Is Emotion?   314
The Emotional Body   316
The Emotional Brain   319
The Regulation of Emotion   320

**Emotional Communication: Msgs w/o Wrds**..............................................322
Communicative Expression   323
HOT SCIENCE The Body of Evidence   325
Deceptive Expression   326
OTHER VOICES I Used to Get Invited to Poker Games...   329
CULTURE & COMMUNITY Is It What You Say or How You Say It?   330

**Motivation: Getting Moved**......................................................................331
The Function of Emotion   331
Instincts and Drives   333
What the Body Needs   334
THE REAL WORLD Jeet Jet?   338
What the Mind Wants   342

**Chapter 9**   **Language and Thought**....................................................351

**Language and Communication: From Rules to Meaning**..........................352
The Complex Structure of Human Language   353
Language Development   355
Theories of Language Development   359

Language Development and the Brain.............................................362
  Broca's Area and Wernicke's Area of the Brain   362
  Involvement of the Right Cerebral Hemisphere   363
  Bilingualism and the Brain   363
  OTHER VOICES Canada's Future Has to Be Bilingual   364
  Can Other Species Learn Human Language?   365

Language and Thought: How Are They Related?.......................367
  Language and Colour Processing   367
  Language and the Concept of Time   368

Concepts and Categories: How We Think...................................369
  Psychological Theories of Concepts and Categories   369
  Concepts, Categories, and the Brain   371

Decision Making: Rational and Otherwise...............................374
  The Rational Ideal   374
  The Irrational Reality   374
  CULTURE & COMMUNITY Does Culture Influence Optimism Bias?   378
  Why Do We Make Decision-Making Errors?   378
  Decision Making and the Brain   380

Problem Solving: Working It Out...............................................382
  Means–Ends Analysis   382
  Analogical Problem Solving   383
  Creativity and Insight   384
  HOT SCIENCE Sudden Insight and the Brain   386

Transforming Information: How We Reach Conclusions ...........388
  Practical, Theoretical, and Syllogistic Reasoning   388
  THE REAL WORLD From Zippers to Political Extremism: An Illusion of Understanding   390
  Reasoning and the Brain   391

Chapter 10  Intelligence...............................................................395

How Can Intelligence Be Measured? ......................................396
  The Intelligence Quotient   397
  The Intelligence Test   398
  THE REAL WORLD Look Smart   400

What Is Intelligence?................................................................401
  A Hierarchy of Abilities   401
  The Middle-Level Abilities   403

Where Does Intelligence Come From?.....................................407
  Genetic Influences on Intelligence   407
  Environmental Influences on Intelligence   411
  HOT SCIENCE Dumb and Dumber?   414
  Genes and Environments   415

Who Is Most Intelligent?..........................................................416
  Individual Differences in Intelligence   416
  Group Differences in Intelligence   417
  Improving Intelligence   420
  OTHER VOICES How Science Can Build a Better You   421

**Chapter 11** Development .................................................. 425

Prenatality: A Womb with a View ............................... 426
Prenatal Development  427
Prenatal Environment  428
OTHER VOICES Men, Who Needs Them?  429

Infancy and Childhood: Becoming a Person .............. 431
Perceptual and Motor Development  431
Cognitive Development  433
HOT SCIENCE A Statistician in the Crib  435
THE REAL WORLD Walk This Way  442
Social Development  442
Moral Development  447

Adolescence: Minding the Gap ................................... 452
The Protraction of Adolescence  453
Sexuality  455
Parents and Peers  458

Adulthood: Change We Cannot Believe In .................. 460
Changing Abilities  460
HOT SCIENCE The End of History Illusion  460
Changing Goals  463
Changing Roles  465
OTHER VOICES You Are Going to Die  467

**Chapter 12** Personality .......................................... 471

Personality: What It Is and How It Is Measured ........ 472
Describing and Explaining Personality  472
Measuring Personality  473

The Trait Approach: Identifying Patterns of Behaviour ...... 476
Traits as Behavioural Dispositions and Motives  476
The Search for Core Traits  477
HOT SCIENCE Personality on the Surface  479
Traits as Biological Building Blocks  480
THE REAL WORLD Are There "Male" and "Female" Personalities?  481

The Psychodynamic Approach: Forces That Lie beneath Awareness ...... 484
The Structure of the Mind: Id, Ego, and Superego  485
Psychosexual Stages and the Development of Personality  487

The Humanistic–Existential Approach: Personality as Choice ...... 488
Human Needs and Self-Actualization  488
Personality as Existence  489

The Social-Cognitive Approach: Personalities in Situations ...... 490
Consistency of Personality across Situations  491
Personal Constructs  491
CULTURE & COMMUNITY Does Your Personality Change According to which Language You are Speaking or Who You Are Speaking With?  492
Personal Goals and Expectancies  493

The Self: Personality in the Mirror.................................................494
  Self-Concept  495
  Self-Esteem  498
  OTHER VOICES Does the Study of Personality Lack ... Personality?  503

▶ Chapter 13 Social Psychology ................................................507

Social Behaviour: Interacting with People ...............................508
  Survival: The Struggle for Resources  508
  HOT SCIENCE Mouse Over  516
  Reproduction: The Quest for Immortality  517
  THE REAL WORLD Making the Move  519
  Breaking up: When the Costs Outweigh the Benefits  525

Social Influence: Controlling People ........................................526
  The Hedonic Motive: Pleasure Is Better Than Pain  527
  CULTURE & COMMUNITY Free Parking  528
  The Approval Motive: Acceptance Is Better Than Rejection  528
  OTHER VOICES 91% of All Students Read This Box and Love It  531
  The Accuracy Motive: Right Is Better Than Wrong  533

Social Cognition: Understanding People ...................................537
  HOT SCIENCE The Wedding Planner  538
  Stereotyping: Drawing Inferences from Categories  538
  Attribution: Drawing Inferences from Actions  543

▶ Chapter 14 Stress and Health ................................................549

Sources of Stress: What Gets to You .........................................550
  Stressful Events  550
  Chronic Stressors  551
  HOT SCIENCE Can Discrimination Cause Stress and Illness?  552
  Perceived Control over Stressful Events  553

Stress Reactions: All Shook Up ..................................................553
  Physical Reactions  554
  Psychological Reactions  558

Stress Management: Dealing with It ...........................................561
  Mind Management  561
  Body Management  563
  Situation Management  565
  CULTURE & COMMUNITY Oh, Canada, Our (New) Home and (Non-)Native Land...  566

The Psychology of Illness: Mind over Matter............................568
  Psychological Effects of Illness  569
  Recognizing Illness and Seeking Treatment  569
  THE REAL WORLD This Is Your Brain on Placebos  571
  Somatic Symptom Disorders  572
  On Being a Patient  572
  Patient–Practitioner Interaction  573

The Psychology of Health: Feeling Good ..................................... 574
Personality and Health   574
Health-Promoting Behaviours and Self-Regulation   576
OTHER VOICES False Hopes and Overwhelming Urges   579

Chapter 15  Psychological Disorders ................................. 583

Defining Mental Disorders: What Is Abnormal? ....................... 584
Conceptualizing Mental Disorders   585
Classifying Mental Disorders   586
Causation of Disorders   587
CULTURE & COMMUNITY What Do Mental Disorders Look Like in Different Parts
   of the World?   589
A New Approach to Understanding Mental Disorders: RDoC   590
THE REAL WORLD How Are Mental Disorders Defined and Diagnosed?   592
Dangers of Labelling   592

Anxiety Disorders: When Fears Take Over ................................. 593
Phobic Disorders   594
Panic Disorder   595
Generalized Anxiety Disorder   596

Obsessive-Compulsive Disorder: Trapped in a Loop ................ 598

Post-traumatic Stress Disorder: Troubles after a Trauma ......... 599

Depressive and Bipolar Disorders: At the Mercy of Emotions ... 601
Depressive Disorders   601
Bipolar Disorder   604

Schizophrenia and Other Psychotic Disorders: Losing the
Grasp on Reality ....................................................................... 607
Symptoms and Types of Schizophrenia   607
Biological Factors   609
Psychological Factors   611
OTHER VOICES Successful and Schizophrenic   613

Disorders of Childhood and Adolescence: Difficulties during Development ...... 614
Autism Spectrum Disorder   614
HOT SCIENCE Optimal Outcome in Autism Spectrum Disorder   615
Attention-Deficit/Hyperactivity Disorder   616
Conduct Disorder   616

Personality Disorders: Going to Extremes .............................. 618
Types of Personality Disorders   618
Antisocial Personality Disorder   619

Self-Harm Behaviours: When the Mind Turns against Itself ..... 621
Suicidal Behaviour   621
Non-suicidal Self-Injury   622

**Chapter 16** Treatment of Psychological Disorders...........................627

Treatment: Getting Help to Those Who Need It.......................................628
  Why Many People Fail to Seek Treatment   629
  THE REAL WORLD Types of Psychotherapists   630
  Approaches to Treatment   631
  CULTURE & COMMUNITY Treatment of Psychological Disorders around the World   632

Psychological Treatments: Healing the Mind through Interaction.......................633
  Psychodynamic Therapy   633
  Humanistic and Existential Therapies   636
  Behavioural and Cognitive Therapies   637
  HOT SCIENCE "Rebooting" Psychological Treatment   642
  Group Treatments: Healing Multiple Minds at the Same Time   643

Medical and Biological Treatments: Healing the Mind by
Physically Altering the Brain .......................................646
  Antipsychotic Medications   646
  THE REAL WORLD Treating Severe Mental Disorders   647
  Anti-anxiety Medications   649
  Antidepressants and Mood Stabilizers   649
  Herbal and Natural Products   651
  Combining Medication and Psychotherapy   652
  OTHER VOICES Diagnosis: Human   653
  Biological Treatments Beyond Medication   654

Treatment Effectiveness: For Better or for Worse .......................................656
  Treatment Illusions   657
  Treatment Studies   658
  Which Treatments Work?   659

Glossary.......................................................................................G-1

References....................................................................................R-1

Name Index...................................................................................NI-1

Subject Index................................................................................SI-1

# Preface

Why are you reading the preface? The book really gets going in about 10 pages, so why are you here instead of there? Are you the kind of person who cannot stand the idea of missing something? Are you trying to justify the cost of the book by consuming every word? Did you just open to this page out of habit? Are you starting to think that maybe you made a big mistake?

For as long as we can remember, we have been asking questions like these about ourselves, about our friends, and about anyone else who did not run away fast enough. Our curiosity about why people think, feel, and act as they do drew each of us into our first psychology course, and though we remember being swept away by the lectures, we do not remember much about our textbooks. That is probably because those textbooks were little more than colourful encyclopedias of facts, names, and dates. Little wonder that we sold them back to the bookstore the moment we finished our final exams.

When we became psychology professors, we did the things that psychology professors often do: We taught classes, we conducted research, and we wore sweater vests long after they stopped being fashionable. We also wrote stuff that people truly enjoyed reading, and that made us wonder why no one had ever written an introductory psychology textbook that students truly enjoyed reading. After all, psychology is the single most interesting subject in the known universe, so why should a psychology textbook not be the single most interesting object in a student's backpack? We could not think of a reason, so we sat down and wrote the book that we wished we had been given as students. The first American edition of *Psychology* was published in 2008, and the reaction to it was nothing short of astounding. We had never written a textbook before, so we did not know exactly what to expect, but never in our wildest dreams did we imagine that we would *win the Pulitzer Prize!*

Which was good, because we did not. But what did happen was even better: We started getting letters and emails from students all over the country who just wanted to tell us how much they liked reading our book. They liked the content, of course, because as we may have already mentioned, psychology is the single most interesting subject in the known universe. But they also liked the fact that our textbook did not *sound* like a textbook. It was not written in the stodgy voice of the announcer from one of those nature films that we all saw in seventh grade biology ("Behold the sea otter, nature's furry little scavenger"). Rather, it was written in *our* voices—the same voices in which we talk to our students, our spouses, our kids, and our pets. We made a conscious effort to tell the *story* of psychology—to integrate topics rather than just list them, to illustrate ideas rather than just describe them. We realized that because science is such a complicated and serious business, some teachers might think that a science textbook should be complicated and serious too. We did not see it that way. We think writing is the art of making complicated things seem simple and of making serious things seem fun. The students who sent us nice letters seemed to agree (even if the Pulitzer Prize committee did not).

The last edition of our book was a hit—so why have we replaced it? Two reasons. First, we got tired of being asked about the two guys in checkerboard leotards who were cavorting on the cover. They are gone now, and we are only going to say this one more time: No, they were not any of us, and yes, they probably did use superglue. The second and somewhat more important reason for bringing out a new edition is

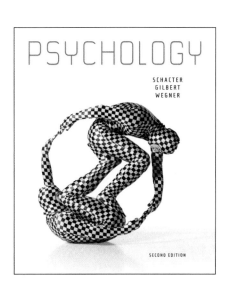

PSYCHOLOGY

SCHACTER
GILBERT
WEGNER

SECOND EDITION

that things change. Science changes (psychologists know all sorts of things about the mind and the brain that they didn't know just a few years ago), the world changes (when we wrote the first edition, no one had heard of an iPad or Barack Obama), and we change (our research and reading gave us new perspectives on psychological issues, and our writing and teaching showed us new ways to help students learn). With all of these changes happening around us and to us, we felt that our book should change as well and now we are adding a Canadian edition, which is based on the third edition. So we are calling this edition the Third Canadian Edition.

# Changes in the Third Edition

## New focus on critical thinking

As sciences uncover new evidence and develop new theories, scientists change their minds. Some of the facts that students learn in a science course will still be facts a decade later, and others will require qualification or will turn out to have just been plain wrong. That's why students not only need to learn the facts but also how to *think* about facts—how to examine, question, and weigh the evidence that scientists produce. We emphasize this sort of critical thinking throughout our text, of course, but in this edition, we have included a new section dedicated entirely to helping students think about the mistakes human beings make when they try to consider evidence (see "Thinking Critically about Evidence" in Chapter 2: Methods in Psychology, page 66). We hope this section will help students learn how to use empirical evidence to develop well-grounded beliefs—not only about psychological science but also about the stuff of their everyday lives.

## New section "Learning in the Classroom"

Like other psychology textbooks, the first two editions of our text provided in-depth coverage of many different kinds of learning, ranging from classical conditioning to observational learning. This edition still does this. But strangely enough, the Learning chapters in most psychology texts, including the previous two editions of this text, have not said much about the very kind of learning that is most relevant to our readers: learning in the classroom. We think that it is about time to change this puzzling state of affairs, and so we have. Chapter 7 now includes a new section on learning in the classroom that summarizes some of the exciting recent developments in this area, including evaluation of the most effective study techniques, insights into cognitive illusions that can mislead us into studying ineffectively, research on how to improve attention and learning during lectures, and discussion of the prospects for online learning. The Learning chapter should be relevant to the lives of students, and we have done our best to make it so.

## New research

A textbook should give students a complete tour of the classics, of course, but it should also take them out dancing on the cutting edge. We want students to realize that psychology is not a museum piece—it is not just a collection of past events but also of current events—and that this young and evolving science has a place for them if they want it. So we have packed the third edition with information about what is happening in the field today. Not only have we included more than 400 new citations, but we have also featured some of the hottest new findings in the "Hot Science" boxes that you will find in every chapter.

| Chapter Number | Hot Science |
|---|---|
| 1 | Psychology as a Hub Science, p. 34 |
| 2 | Do Violent Movies Make Peaceful Streets?, p. 64 |
| 3 | Epigenetics and the Persisting Effects of Early Experiences, p. 112 |
| 4 | Taste: From the Top Down, p. 170 |
| 5 | Disorders of Consciousness, p. 185 |
| 6 | Sleep on It, p. 233 |
| 7 | Dopamine and Reward Learning in Parkinson's Disease, p. 292 |
| 8 | The Body of Evidence, p. 325 |
| 9 | Sudden Insight and the Brain, p. 386 |
| 10 | Dumb and Dumber?, p. 414 |
| 11 | A Statistician in the Crib, p. 435 |
| 11 | The End of History Illusion, p. 460 |
| 12 | Personality on the Surface, p. 479 |
| 13 | Mouse Over, p. 516 |
| 13 | The Wedding Planner, p. 538 |
| 14 | Can Discrimination Cause Stress and Illness?, p. 552 |
| 15 | Optimal Outcome in Autism Spectrum Disorder, p. 615 |
| 16 | "Rebooting" Psychological Treatment, p. 642 |

## Fully updated coverage of *DSM-5*

One area where there has been lots of new research—and lots of big changes—is in the study of psychological disorders. As you will learn, psychologists use a manual called the *Diagnostic and Statistical Manual of Mental Disorders* (*DSM*) to make decisions about which behaviours should be formally considered "disordered." For instance, we all get sad from time to time, but when should extreme sadness be classified as a psychological disorder that should be treated? The *DSM* answers questions like this. After nearly 20 years of using the fourth edition of the *DSM* (*DSM-IV*), the field of psychology now has an updated fifth edition (*DSM-5*), which was just published in 2013. Psychologists have learned a lot about psychological disorders over the past 20 years, and this third edition of our book contains updated information about how psychologists think about, define, and classify psychological disorders.

## New organization

We have rearranged our table of contents to better fit our changing sense of how psychology is best taught. Specifically, we have moved the chapter on Stress and Health forward so that it now appears before the chapters on Psychological Disorders and Treatment of Psychological Disorders. We think this change improves the flow of the book in several ways. First, as you will learn, the experience of stress has a lot to do with interpersonal events and how we respond to them, information that you will have just learned about in the chapters on Personality and Social Psychology. Second, current models of psychological disorders view them as resulting from an interaction of some underlying predisposition (e.g., genetic or otherwise) and stressful life events. Such models will be much more intuitive if you first learn about the body's stress response. Third, this chapter has information about health-promoting behaviours that could come in handy during exam season—and so better to tell you about them before the end of the semester!

## New Other Voices feature

Long before psychologists appeared on Earth, the human nature business was dominated by poets, playwrights, pundits, philosophers, and several other groups beginning with P. Those folks are still in that business today, and they continue to have deep and original insights into how and why people behave as they do. In this edition, we decided to invite some of them to share their thoughts with you via a new feature that we call Other Voices. In every chapter, you will find a short essay by someone who has three critical qualities: (a) They think deeply, (b) they write beautifully, and (c) they know things we do not. For example, you will find essays by leading journalists such as David Brooks, Ted Gup, Tina Rosenberg, David Ewing Duncan, and Lisa Willemse; leading educators such as Robert Rothon; renowned legal scholar Elyn Saks; and eminent scientists such as biologist Greg Hampikian and computer scientist Daphne Koller. And just to make sure we are not the only psychologists whose voices you hear, we have included essays by Tim Wilson, Chris Chabris, Daniel Simons, V. S. Ramachandran, Stephen Porter, and Charles Fernyhough. Every one of these amazing people has something important to say about human nature, and we are delighted that they have agreed to say it in these pages. Not only do these essays encourage students to think critically about a variety of psychological issues, but they also demonstrate both the relevance of psychology to everyday life and the growing importance of our science in the public forum.

| Chapter Number | Other Voices |
|---|---|
| 1 | Is Psychology a Science?, p. 17 |
| 2 | Can We Afford Science?, p. 75 |
| 3 | Neuromyths, p. 124 |
| 4 | Hallucinations and the Visual System, p. 156 |
| 5 | The Blink of an Eye, p. 217 |
| 6 | Early Memories, p. 261 |
| 7 | Online Learning, p. 308 |
| 8 | I Used to Get Invited to Poker Games …, p. 329 |
| 9 | Canada's Future Has to Be Bilingual, p. 364 |
| 10 | How Science Can Build a Better You, p. 421 |
| 11 | Men, Who Needs Them?, p. 429 |
| 11 | You Are Going to Die, p. 467 |
| 12 | Does the Study of Personality Lack … Personality?, p. 503 |
| 13 | 91% of All Students Read This Box and Love It, p. 531 |
| 14 | False Hopes and Overwhelming Urges, p. 579 |
| 15 | Successful and Schizophrenic, p. 613 |
| 16 | Diagnosis: Human, p. 653 |

## New Changing Minds questions

What can 784 introductory psychology professors agree about? They can agree that students usually come into their first psychology class with a set of beliefs about the field and that most of these beliefs are wrong. With the help of the wonderful people at Worth Publishers (they made us say that), we conducted a survey of 784 introductory psychology teachers and asked them to name their students' most common misconceptions about psychology. We then created the Changing Minds questions you will see at the end of every chapter. These questions ask you first to think about an everyday situation in which a common misconception might arise, and then to use the science you have just learned to overcome that misconception. We hope these exercises will prepare you to apply what you learn—and maybe even change some minds about psychology (thereby justifying our corny title).

> ### CHANGING MINDS
>
> 1. One of the MPPs from your province is supporting legislation that would impose heavy fines on aggressive drivers who run red lights. One of your classmates thinks this is a good idea. "The textbook taught us a lot about punishment and reward. It's simple. If we punish aggressive driving, its frequency will decline." Is your classmate right? Might the new law backfire? Might another policy be more effective in promoting safe driving?

A Changing Minds question from Chapter 13.

## Additional Student Support

### Practice

> *Cue questions* encourage critical thinking and help identify the most important concepts in every major section of the text.
> *Bulleted summaries* follow each major section to reinforce key concepts and make it easier to study for the test.

*gathering scientific information by un...*

**How do people respond when they know they are being observed?**

several opponents at once (Erffmeye...

A cue question from Chapter 2.

> *A Key Concept Quiz* at the end of each chapter offers students the opportunity to test what they know.

> *Critical thinking questions* are offered throughout the chapters within a number of the photograph captions, offering the opportunity to apply various concepts.

## Practical Application

What would the facts and concepts of psychology be without real-world application? Throughout this edition of the text, we provide lots of examples of how the material presented in this book applies to things that you will experience in the real world. For instance, each chapter contains a The Real World box that applies concepts from inside the book to your life outside the book. (We like this idea so much we even included a box in the Preface!) In addition, because culture influences just about everything we do—from how we perceive lines to how long we will stand in them—this edition continues to celebrate the rich diversity of human beings both in Culture & Community boxes and throughout the text, as detailed on the next page.

CLEMENT PHILIPPE/ARTERRA PICTURE LIBRARY/ALAMY

According to the theory of natural selection, inherited characteristics that provide a survival advantage tend to spread throughout the population across generations. Why might sensory adaptation have evolved? What survival benefits might it confer to a small animal trying to avoid predators? To a predator trying to hunt prey?

Critical thinking questions in a photo caption from Chapter 4.

## THE REAL WORLD

# Join the Club!

Once upon a time, Western science was the hobby of wealthy European gentlemen. Fortunately, the face of this field has changed profoundly since its early days and continues to progress even now.

In fact, social changes have led to openness and diversity in psychology more swiftly and completely than in most other fields of study. In 2006, for example, while women were only poorly represented in engineering and the physical sciences, they received more than 71% of all new Ph.D. degrees in psychology (Burrelli, 2008). As you can see in the accompanying figure, although women are earning a growing proportion of Ph.D.s in all fields, they are now a whopping majority in psychology. Meanwhile, psychology Ph.D.s to Hispanic, African American, and Native American students have more than doubled from 1985 to 2005, and those to Asians and Pacific Islanders have tripled (National Science Foundation, 2008). It is now the future, and in this future, psychology is the science of everyone.

COURTESY UNIVERSITY OF MISSOURI PSI CHI & PSYCHOLOGY CLUB

Signs of the openness of psychology are all around. Just take a look at some of the students in undergraduate psychology clubs. Psychology students now are far more often women than men (77%) (Planty et al., 2008), and there is substantial representation of minority groups in psychology everywhere you look. Like its clubs, the study of psychology is open and welcoming to people of any age, sex, sexual orientation, race, different ability, colour, religion, or national or ethnic origin. Please join us!

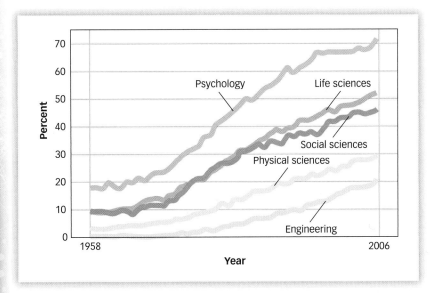

◄ The proportion of new Ph.D.s earned by women in the United States has grown faster in psychology than in other fields (Burrelli, 2008). This trend is echoed in Canada (King, 2008).

| Chapter Number | The Real World |
|---|---|
| 1 | The Perils of Procrastination, p. 4 |
| 1 | Improving Study Skills, p. 10 |
| 2 | "Oddsly" Enough, p. 61 |
| 3 | Brain Plasticity and Sensations in Phantom Limbs, p. 104 |
| 3 | Brain Death and the Vegetative State, p. 123 |
| 4 | Multitasking, p. 146 |
| 4 | Music Training: Worth the Time, p. 163 |
| 5 | Anyone for Tennis?, p. 192 |
| 6 | Is Google Hurting Our Memories?, p. 248 |
| 7 | Understanding Drug Overdoses, p. 270 |
| 8 | Jeet Jet?, p. 338 |
| 9 | From Zippers to Political Extremism: An Illusion of Understanding, p. 390 |
| 10 | Look Smart, p. 400 |
| 11 | Walk This Way, p. 442 |
| 12 | Are There "Male" and "Female" Personalities?, p. 481 |
| 13 | Making the Move, p. 519 |
| 14 | This is Your Brain on Placebos, p. 571 |
| 15 | How Are Mental Disorders Defined and Diagnosed?, p. 592 |
| 16 | Types of Psychotherapists, p. 630 |
| 16 | Treating Severe Mental Disorders, p. 647 |

| Chapter Number | Culture & Community |
|---|---|
| 1 | Analytic and Holistic Styles in Western and Eastern Cultures, p. 30 |
| 2 | Best Place to Fall on Your Face, p. 45 |
| 4 | Does Culture Influence Change Blindness?, p. 157 |
| 5 | What Do Dreams Mean to Us around the World?, p. 203 |
| 6 | Does Culture Affect Childhood Amnesia?, p. 240 |
| 7 | Are There Cultural Differences in Reinforcers?, p. 281 |
| 8 | Is It What You Say or How You Say It?, p. 330 |
| 9 | Does Culture Influence Optimism Bias?, p. 378 |
| 12 | Does Your Personality Change According to the Language You Are Speaking or Who You Are Speaking With?, p. 492 |
| 13 | Free Parking, p. 528 |
| 14 | Oh Canada, Our (New) Home and (Non-)Native Land ..., p. 566 |
| 15 | What Do Mental Disorders Look Like in Different Parts of the World?, p. 589 |
| 16 | Treatment of Psychological Disorders around the World, p. 632 |

## The Psychology of Men and Women

Aggression and biology, pp. 509–510
Alcohol
  myopia, pp. 208–209
  pregnancy, pp. 428–430
Attraction, pp. 518–519
Beauty standards of, pp. 521–522
Biological sex/gender, pp. 453–457
Body image, pp. 335–336
Child-rearing
  attachment and, pp. 443–446
  day care, pp. 444, 447
Dating, pp. 517–518
Dieting, pp. 337–338
Eating disorders, pp. 333–339
Freud's views, pp. 13–14, 487–488
Gender and social connectedness, p. 465
Happiness, p. 463
Hormones, pp. 453–454
Hostility and heart disease, p. 558
Jealousy, p. 26
Life expectancy, p. 464
Life satisfaction, p. 463
Marriage, pp. 465–466
Mating preferences
  biological, pp. 517–518
  cultural, pp. 517–518
Menarche, p. 453
Moral development, pp. 453–454
Personality, pp. 479, 481
Pheromones, p. 171
Physical development, pp. 450–454
Pregnancy
  health of mother and child, pp. 428–430
  teen, p. 457
Psychological disorders, depression, p. 602
panic disorder, p. 596
Rape, p. 211
Relationships, pp. 524–525
Sex
  avoiding risks, p. 340
  motivation for, pp. 339–340
  and teens, pp. 338–340
Social connectedness, pp. 566–568
Stereotyping, p. 538
Stress, coping, pp. 561–563
Suicide, pp. 621–622
Talkativeness, pp. 475–476
Women in psychology, pp. 31–32

## Culture and Multicultural Experience

Aggression and culture,
pp. 511–512
  and geography, p. 511
  groups, p. 514
Aging population,
pp. 460–467
Alcohol, binge drinking,
p. 209
Attachment style,
pp. 444–445
Attractiveness, p. 520
Autism, pp. 439, 614–615
Body ideal, p. 521
Brain death, p. 123
Conformity, pp. 528–529
Cultural norms,
pp. 528–529
Cultural psychology,
  definition, pp. 28–30
Culture, discovering,
pp. 440–441
Deaf culture, pp. 356, 439
Depression, pp. 601–604
Development
  adolescence, protracted,
  pp. 453–455

attachment, pp. 443–444
child-rearing, pp. 445–446
cognitive development,
pp. 433–435
counting ability, p. 440
moral development,
pp. 446–449
Dreams, meaning of,
pp. 201–203
Drugs, psychological effects
of, pp. 646–654
Eating disorders,
pp. 335–339
Expression, display rules,
p. 326
Expression, universality,
pp. 323–324
False memories,
pp. 255–256
Family therapy, p. 643
Freedom, p. 528
Helpfulness, p. 45
Homosexuality
  genes, p. 456
  pheromones, p. 171
  views on, pp. 455–456

Hunger, pp. 334–335
Implicit learning, aging,
p. 302
Intelligence, pp. 406–407,
417–421
  age, pp. 410–412
  cultural aspects,
  pp. 406–407
  education on,
  pp. 414–415
  generational, pp. 412–413
  socioeconomic factors
  and, pp. 399–400, 410,
  413–415
  testing bias, pp. 417–419
Intrinsic motivation, p. 442
Language
  bilingualism, pp. 363–365
  memory retrieval, p. 236
  and personality,
  pp. 491–492
  structure, pp. 353–355
  and thought, pp. 367–368
Life expectancy, p. 465
Marijuana laws,
pp. 213–214

Marriage, pp. 524–526
Mating preferences,
pp. 518–524
Minorities in psychology,
pp. 31–32
Movie violence, p. 64
Norms, pp. 528–529
Obesity, p. 577
Observational learning,
pp. 295–297
Parent and peer relation-
ships, pp. 458–459
Perceptual illusions,
pp. 20–21
Prejudice and stereotyping,
p. 28
Psychoanalysis,
pp. 634–635
Psychological disorders
  antisocial personality disorder, pp. 619–620
  eating disorders,
  pp. 335–339
  outlook on in different cultures, pp. 585, 589
  schizophrenia,
  pp. 607–609

Psychotherapy, p. 633
Racism
  civil rights, p. 28
  stress, p. 552
Reasoning, p. 388
Research ethics, pp. 70–74
Sensory branding, p. 129
Stereotype threat, p. 541
Stereotyping, p. 538
Stress
  adjusting to a new culture,
  p. 566
  chronic, p. 552
  poverty and inequality,
  p. 557
Subliminal perception,
p. 191
Suicide, pp. 621–622
Taste preference,
pp. 170–172
Teen pregnancy, p. 457
Threat reaction, p. 559
Tone of voice and meaning,
p. 330

## Preparing for the MCAT 2015

A complete correlation of the MCAT psychology topics with this book's contents is available for download from the Resources area of LaunchPad at http://www.worthpublishers.com/launchpad/schacter3ecanadian. In addition, since the MCAT represents a global standard for assessing the ability to reason about scientific information, the Test Bank for Psychology, Third Canadian Edition, features a new set of data-based questions for each chapter, which are designed to test students' quantitative reasoning. These questions are available for preview in LaunchPad.

| MCAT 2015: Categories in Sensation and Perception | SGWNJ, *Psychology*, Third Canadian Edition, Correlations | |
|---|---|---|
| Content Category 6A: Sensing the environment | Section Title | Page Number(s) |
| **Sensory Processing** | Sensation and Perception | 129–173 |
| Sensation | Sensation and Perception | 129–173 |
| • Thresholds | Measuring Thresholds | 132–133 |
| • Weber's Law | Measuring Thresholds | 132–133 |
| • Signal detection theory | Signal Detection | 133–134 |
| • Sensory adaptation | Sensory Adaptation | 134–135 |
| • Sensory receptors | Sensation and Perception Are Distinct Activities | 130–132 |
| • Sensory pathways | The Visual Brain | 141–143 |
| | Touch and Pain | 164–167 |
| | Body Position, Movement, and Balance | 167 |
| | Smell and Taste | 168–173 |
| • Types of sensory receptors | Vision I: How the Eyes and the Brain Convert Light Waves to Neural Signals | 135–143 |
| | The Human Ear | 158–160 |
| | The Body Senses: More Than Skin Deep | 164–167 |
| | Smell and Taste | 168–173 |

| MCAT 2015: Categories in Sensation and Perception | SGWNJ, *Psychology*, Third Canadian Edition, Correlations | |
|---|---|---|
| **Content Category 6A: Sensing the environment** | **Section Title** | **Page Number(s)** |
| **Vision** | Vision I and Vision II | 135–155 |
| Structure and function of the eye | The Human Eye | 137–138 |
| Visual processing | Vision I | 135–143 |
| • Visual pathways in the brain | From the Eye to the Brain | 139–141 |
| • Parallel processing | The Visual Brain | 141–144 |
| • Feature detection | Studying the Brain's Electrical Activity | 118–119 |
| | The Visual Brain | 141–143 |
| **Hearing** | Audition: More Than Meets the Ear | 157–162 |
| Auditory processing | Perceiving Pitch | 160 |
| • Auditory pathways in the brain | Perceiving Pitch | 160 |
| Sensory reception by hair cells | The Human Ear | 158–160 |
| **Other Senses** | The Body Senses: More Than Skin Deep | 163–166 |
| | The Chemical Senses: Adding Flavour | 167–172 |
| Somatosensation | Touch | 164–165 |
| • Pain perception | Pain | 165–167 |
| Taste | Taste | 170–173 |
| • Taste buds/chemoreceptors that detect specific chemicals | Taste | 170–173 |
| Smell | Smell | 168–171 |
| • Olfactory cells/chemoreceptors that detect specific chemicals | Smell | 168–169 |
| • Pheromones | Smell | 171 |
| • Olfactory pathways in the brain | Smell | 168–171 |
| Kinesthetic sense | Body Position, Movement, and Balance | 167 |
| Vestibular sense | Body Position, Movement, and Balance | 167 |
| **Perception** | Sensation and Perception | 129–173 |
| Perception | Sensation and Perception Are Distinct Activities | 130–135 |
| • Bottom-up/Top-down processing | Pain | 165–167 |
| | Smell | 168–171 |
| • Perceptual organization (e.g., depth, form, motion, constancy) | Vision II: Recognizing What We Perceive | 144–156 |
| • Gestalt principles | Principles of Perceptual Organization | 148–149 |

# About the Canadian Edition

In writing the Canadian edition, we retained all the unique features of the first American edition textbook, and included the essential and updated coverage of the third American edition. Building on this third edition, our goal was to create a textbook that would engage Canadian students by situating the content in Canadian and international contexts, replacing American examples with those of relevance for both Canadian and other international students. This is why we call it the third Canadian edition. Current Canadian and international data replace American data and statistics where appropriate. We highlight the remarkable scientific accomplishments of Canadian scientists in psychology and neuropsychology, drawing upon Canadian issues. Finally, we have included photographs and figures that reflect the Canadian context and Canadian research.

To illustrate how we have incorporated a Canadian perspective, we highlight some of the specific information included across different chapters.

> In our introductory chapter on the evolution of psychology (Chapter 1), we discuss the development of the field in Canada, highlighting Canadian pioneers, such as James Mark Baldwin, Donald Olding Hebb, Brenda Milner, and Wilder Penfield. Besides the American Psychological Association, we include

descriptions of other Canadian psychological organizations, such as the Canadian Psychological Association, the Canadian Society for Brain, Behaviour and Cognitive Science, and the Canadian Association of Neuroscience.

> In the chapter on research methods (Chapter 2), we include greater details on the fundamentals of conducting research and data evaluation, using Canadian data in our explanations. Most importantly, we include TriCouncil ethical guidelines, and the Canadian Psychological Association code of ethics that all Canadian psychologists are to follow whether in conducting research or dealing with clients.

> When discussing neuroscience and behaviour (Chapter 3), we start with relevant Canadian examples to illustrate the issue of sports-related head trauma and chronic traumatic encephalopathy. We also highlight the contributions of internationally renowned neurosurgeon Wilder Penfield in mapping the somatosensory and motor cortex. McGill researcher Michael Meaney's work demonstrating that maternal caretaking behaviour has a profound influence on the stress response in offspring is profiled in the Hot Science box.

> In Sensation and Perception (Chapter 4), we highlight research from the University of Western Ontario on the neural pathways for vision or visual streams. We also describe University of Toronto researcher Glenn Schellenberg's study on the link between music education and IQ scores.

> In the chapter on consciousness (Chapter 5), we highlight a case study by researchers at the University of Western Ontario who use fMRI technology to determine the level of consciousness in brain-damaged patients with disorders of consciousness.

> In Memory (Chapter 6), we cover the seminal research on levels of processing by Fergus Craik and Endel Tulving, from University of Toronto, which has been so influential in our understanding of how humans encode information. In this chapter, we discuss Brenda Milner's discovery, through her early work with Henry Molaison (H.M.), of the role of the hippocampus in long-term memory.

> In the chapter on Learning (Chapter 7), we discuss some of McMaster University researcher Shepard Siegel's work on classical conditioning and how it can be used to explain how drug overdoses occur with experienced drug abusers. We also describe research at McGill University with rats that demonstrates how operant conditioning occurs.

> In Emotion and Motivation (Chapter 8), we discuss the issue of eating disorders from a Canadian perspective and the research of University of British Columbia researcher Stephen Porter on lie detection.

> In the chapter on language and thought (Chapter 9), we discuss the future of bilingualism in Canada.

> In the chapter on intelligence (Chapter 10), we use athleticism as a model for intelligence, and Canadian hockey player, Hayley Wickenheiser, as an example. By examining Wickenheiser's athletic abilities we question how intelligence is measured and thus discuss in detail intelligence testing and measurement methods. We also describe the work of University of British Columbia researcher Mark Holder on emotional intelligence.

> In Development (Chapter 11), we highlight Canadian statistics on health-related issues. McGill University research sheds light on the relationship between reflexes and motor development. We describe work by Canadian researcher Tomáš Paus that show how areas of the brain develop with age.

> The chapter on personality (Chapter 12) describes a study by University of British Columbia researchers on personality, language, and behaviour.

> Social Psychology (Chapter 13) includes research on the frustration-aggression hypothesis by University Calgary researchers. We also discuss the research conducted at McGill University on attraction and relationship maintenance.

> Stress and Health (Chapter 14) includes a study on Canadian immigration and health patterns, and statistics relating to health issues.

> In the chapter on psychological disorders (Chapter 15), we look at the incidence rates of psychological disorders in Canada. We also look at alternative disorder evaluation protocols.

> In Treatment of Psychological Disorders (Chapter 16), we examine treatment rates and strategies available to Canadians and the ethics code for the treatment of patients.

# Media and Supplements

## LaunchPad with LearningCurve Quizzing

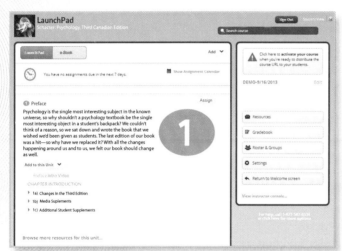

### A comprehensive web resource for teaching and learning psychology

LaunchPad combines Worth Publishers' award-winning media with an innovative platform for easy navigation. For students, it is the ultimate online study guide, with rich interactive tutorials and videos, as well as an e-Book and the LearningCurve adaptive quizzing system. For instructors, LaunchPad is a full course space where class documents can be posted, quizzes are easily assigned and graded, and students' progress can be assessed and recorded. Whether you are looking for the most effective study tools or a robust platform for an online course, LaunchPad is a powerful way to enhance your class.

LaunchPad for *Psychology*, Third Canadian Edition, includes all the following resources:

LaunchPad to Accompany *Psychology*, Third Canadian Edition, can be previewed and purchased at http://www.worthpublishers.com/launchpad/schacter3ecanadian.

*Psychology*, Third Canadian Edition, and LaunchPad can be ordered together with
ISBN-10: 1-4641-9363-0 /
ISBN-13: 978-1-4641-9363-7.

> The design of the **LearningCurve** quizzing system is based on the latest findings from learning and memory research. It combines adaptive question selection, immediate and valuable feedback, and a gamelike interface to engage students in a learning experience that is unique to them. Each LearningCurve quiz is fully integrated with other resources in LaunchPad through the Personalized Study Plan, so students will be able to review using Worth's extensive library of videos and activities. And state-of-the-art question analysis reports allow instructors to track the progress of individual students as well as their class as a whole.

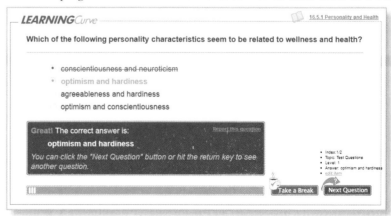

> **New! Data Visualization Exercises** offer students practice in understanding and reasoning about data. In each activity, students interact with a graph or visual display of data and must think like a scientist to answer the accompanying questions. These activities build quantitative reasoning skills and offer a deeper understanding of how science works.

> **An interactive e-Book** allows students to highlight, bookmark, and scribble in their own notes on the e-Book page, just as they would with a printed textbook. Google-style searching and in-text glossary definitions make the text ready for the digital age.

> **Student Video Activities** include more than 100 engaging video modules that instructors can easily assign and customize for student assessment. Videos cover classic experiments, current news footage, and cutting-edge research, all of which are sure to spark discussion and encourage critical thinking.

> **PsychInvestigator: Laboratory Learning in Introductory Psychology** is a series of activities that model a virtual laboratory and are produced in association with Arthur Kohn, Ph.D., of Dark Blue Morning Productions. Students are introduced to core psychological concepts by a video host and then participate in activities that generate real data and lead to some startling conclusions! Like all activities in LaunchPad, PsychInvestigator activities can be assigned and automatically graded.

> The award-winning tutorials in Tom Ludwig's (Hope College) **PsychSim 5.0** and **Concepts in Action** provide an interactive, step-by-step introduction to key psychological concepts.

> **The *Scientific American* Newsfeed** delivers weekly articles, podcasts, and news briefs on the very latest developments in psychology from the first name in popular science journalism.

## Additional Student Supplements

> The **CourseSmart e-Book** offers the complete text of *Psychology*, Third Canadian Edition, in an easy-to-use format. Students can choose either to purchase the CourseSmart e-Book as an online subscription or to download it to a personal computer or a portable media player, such as a smart phone or iPad. The CourseSmart e-Book for *Psychology*, Third Canadian Edition, can be previewed and purchased at **www.coursesmart.com.**

> **Pursuing Human Strengths: A Positive Psychology Guide** by Martin Bolt of Calvin College is a perfect way to introduce students to both the amazing field of positive psychology as well as their own personal strengths.

> **The Critical Thinking Companion for Introductory Psychology,** by Jane S. Halonen of the University of West Florida and Cynthia Gray of Beloit College, contains both a guide to critical thinking strategies as well as exercises in pattern recognition, practical problem solving, creative problem solving, scientific problem solving, psychological reasoning, and perspective-taking.

> Worth Publishers is proud to offer several readers of articles taken from the pages of *Scientific American*. Drawing on award-winning science journalism, the ***Scientific American* Reader to Accompany Psychology, Third Edition, by Daniel L.**

---

**Take advantage of our most popular supplements!**

Worth Publishers is pleased to offer cost-saving packages of *Psychology*, Third Canadian Edition, with our most popular supplements. Below is a list of some of the most popular combinations available for order through your local bookstore.

*Psychology*, 3rd Canadian Ed. & LaunchPad Access Card
ISBN-10: 1-4641-9363-0 / ISBN-13: 978-1-4641-9363-7

*Psychology*, 3rd Canadian Ed. & iClicker 2
ISBN-10: 1-4641-9366-5 / ISBN-13: 978-1-4641-9366-8

*Psychology*, 3rd Canadian Ed. & *Scientific American* Reader
ISBN-10: 1-4641-9364-9 / ISBN-13: 978-1-4641-9364-4

*Psychology*, 3rd Canadian Ed. & *Psychology and the Real World*
ISBN-10: 1-4641-9365-7 / ISBN-13: 978-1-4641-9365-1

**Schacter, Daniel T. Gilbert, Daniel M. Wegner, and Matthew K. Nock** features pioneering and cutting-edge research across the fields of psychology. Selected by the authors themselves, this collection provides further insight into the fields of psychology through articles written for a popular audience. These articles are available for the Third Canadian Edition.

> ***Psychology and the Real World: Essays Illustrating Fundamental Contributions to Society*** is a superb collection of essays by major researchers that describe their landmark studies. Published in association with the not-for-profit FABBS Foundation, this engaging reader includes Elizabeth Loftus's own reflections on her study of false memories, Eliot Aronson on his cooperative classroom study, and Daniel Wegner on his study of thought suppression. A portion of all proceeds is donated to FABBS to support societies of cognitive, psychological, behavioural, and brain sciences.

## Course Management

> Worth Publishers supports multiple Course Management Systems with enhanced cartridges for upload into Blackboard, eCollege, Angel, Desire2Learn, Sakai, and Moodle. Cartridges are provided free upon adoption of *Psychology*, Third Canadian Edition, and can be downloaded from Worth's online catalog at www.worthpublishers.com.

## Assessment

> The **Computerized Test Bank** powered by Diploma includes a full assortment of test items from author Chad Galuska of the College of Charleston. Each chapter features over 200 multiple-choice, true/false, and essay questions to test students at several levels of Bloom's taxonomy. The new edition also features a new set of data-based reasoning questions to test advanced critical thinking skills in a manner similar to the MCAT. All the questions are matched to the outcomes recommended in the 2013 APA Guidelines for the Undergraduate Psychology Major. The accompanying grade book software makes it easy to record students' grades throughout a course, to sort student records, to view detailed analyses of test items, to curve tests, to generate reports, and to add weights to grades.

> The **iClicker** Classroom Response System is a versatile polling system developed by educators for educators that makes class time more efficient and interactive. iClicker allows you to ask questions and instantly record your students' responses, take attendance, and gauge students' understanding and opinions. iClicker is available at a 10% discount when packaged with *Psychology*, Third Canadian Edition.

## Presentation

> **Interactive Presentation Slides** are another great way to introduce Worth's dynamic media into the classroom without lots of advance preparation. Each presentation covers a major topic in psychology and integrates Worth's high quality videos and animations for an engaging teaching and learning experience. These interactive presentations are complimentary to adopters of *Psychology*, Third Canadian Edition, and are perfect for technology novices and experts alike.

> The **Instructor's Resources** by Jeffrey Henriques of The University of Wisconsin-Madison features a variety of materials that are valuable to new and veteran teachers alike. In addition to background on the chapter reading and suggestions for in-class lectures, the manual is rich with activities to engage students in different modes of learning. The Instructor's Resources can be downloaded at http://www.worthpublishers.com/launchpad/schacter3ecanadian.

> **The Worth Video Anthology for Introductory Psychology** includes over 300 unique video clips to bring lectures to life. Provided complimentary to adopters of *Psychology*, Third Canadian Edition, this rich collection includes clinical footage, interviews, animations, and news segments that vividly illustrate topics across the psychology curriculum.

> **Faculty Lounge** is an online forum provided by Worth Publishers where teachers can find and share favourite teaching ideas and materials, including videos, animations, images, PowerPoint slides, news stories, articles, web links, and lecture activities. Sign up to browse the site or upload your favorite materials for teaching psychology at www.worthpublishers.com/facultylounge.

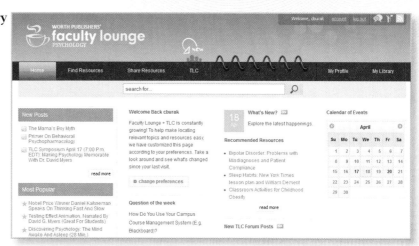

## Acknowledgments

Despite what you might guess by looking at our photographs, we all found partners who were willing to marry us. We thank Susan McGlynn, Marilynn Oliphant, Keesha Nock, and Mark Wolforth for that particular miracle and also for their love and support during the time when we were busy writing this book.

Although ours are the names on the cover, writing a textbook is a team sport, and we were lucky to have an amazing group of professionals in our dugout. We greatly appreciate the contributions of Martin M. Antony, Mark Baldwin, Michelle A. Butler, Patricia Csank, Denise D. Cummins, Ian J. Deary, Howard Eichenbaum, Sam Gosling, Paul Harris, Catherine Myers, Shigehiro Oishi, Arthur S. Reber, Morgan T. Sammons, Dan Simons, Alan Swinkels, Richard M. Wenzlaff, and Steven Yantis.

We are grateful for the editorial, clerical, and research assistance we received from Molly Evans and Mark Knepley.

In addition, we would like to thank our core supplements authors. They provided insight into the role our book can play in the classroom and adeptly developed the materials to support it. Chad Galuska, Jeff Henriques, and Russ Frohardt, we appreciate your tireless work in the classroom and the experience you brought to the book's supplements.

We would like to thank the faculty who reviewed the manuscript. These teachers showed a level of engagement we have come to expect from our best colleagues.

For the Canadian edition, we thank:

George Alder
*Simon Fraser University*

Karen Brebner
*St. Francis Xavier University*

Stan Cameron
*Centennial College*

Karla Emeno
*University of Ontario Institute of Technology*

Gerald Goldberg
*York University*

Peter Graf
*University of British Columbia*

Mark Holder
*University of British Columbia–Okanagan*

Tru Kwong
*Mount Royal University*

Laura Loewen
*Okanagan College*

Michael MacGregor
*University of Saskatchewan*

Stacey MacKinnon
*University of Prince Edward Island*

Colleen MacQuarrie
*University of Prince Edward Island*

Neil McGrenaghan
*Humber College*

Rick Mehta
*Acadia University*

Lisa Sinclair
*University of Winnipeg*

Michael Souza
*University of British Columbia*

Paul Valliant
*Laurentian University*

Ena Vukatana
*University of Calgary*

Bruce Walker
*Humber College*

Kristian Weihs
*Seneca College*

Leslie Wright
*Dalhousie University*

For the American edition, we thank:

Eileen Achorn
*University of Texas, San Antonio*

Jim Allen
*SUNY Geneseo*

Randy Arnau
*University of Southern Mississippi*

Benjamin Bennett-Carpenter
*Oakland University*

Stephen Blessing
*University of Tampa*

Kristin Biondolillo
*Arkansas State University*

Jeffrey Blum
*Los Angeles City College*

Richard Bowen
*Loyola University of Chicago*

Nicole Bragg
*Mt. Hood Community College*

Jennifer Breneiser
*Valdosta State University*

Michele Brumley
*Idaho State University*

Josh Burk
*College of William and Mary*

Jennifer Butler
*Case Western Reserve University*

Richard Cavasina
*California University of Pennsylvania*

Amber Chenoweth
*Kent State University*

Stephen Chew
*Samford University*

Chrisanne Christensen
*Southern Arkansas University*

Sheryl Civjan
*Holyoke Community College*

Jennifer Dale
*Community College of Aurora*

Jennifer Daniels
*University of Connecticut*

Joshua Dobias
*University of New Hampshire*

Dale Doty
*Monroe Community College*

Julie Evey-Johnson
*University of Southern Indiana*

Valerie Farmer-Dugan
*Illinois State University*

Diane Feibel
*University of Cincinnati, Raymond Walters College*

Jocelyn Folk
*Kent State University*

Chad Galuska
*College of Charleston*

Afshin Gharib
*Dominican University of California*

Jeffrey Gibbons
*Christopher Newport University*

Adam Goodie
*University of Georgia*

John Governale
*Clark College*

Patricia Grace
*Kaplan University Online*

Sarah Grison
*University of Illinois at Urbana-Champaign*

Deletha Hardin
*University of Tampa*

Jason Hart
*Christopher Newport University*

Lesley Hathorn
*Metropolitan State College of Denver*

Mark Hauber
*Hunter College*

Jacqueline Hembrook
*University of New Hampshire*

Allen Huffcutt
*Bradley University*

Mark Hurd
*College of Charleston*

Linda Jackson
*Michigan State University*

Jennifer Johnson
*Rider University*

Lance Jones
*Bowling Green State University*

Linda Jones
*Blinn College*

Katherine Judge
*Cleveland State University*

Don Kates
*College of DuPage*

Martha Knight-Oakley
*Warren Wilson College*

Ken Koenigshofer
*Chaffey College*

Neil Kressel
*William Patterson University*

Josh Landau
*York College of Pennsylvania*

Fred Leavitt
*California State University, East Bay*

Tera Letzring
*Idaho State University*

Karsten Loepelmann
*University of Alberta*

Ray Lopez
*University of Texas at San Antonio*

Jeffrey Love
*Penn State University*

Greg Loviscky
*Penn State, University Park*

Lynda Mae
*Arizona State University at Tempe*

Caitlin Mahy
*University of Oregon*

Gregory Manley
*University of Texas at San Antonio*

Karen Marsh
*University of Minnesota at Duluth*

Robert Mather
*University of Central Oklahoma*

Wanda McCarthy
*University of Cincinnati at Clermont College*

Daniel McConnell
*University of Central Florida*

Robert McNally
*Austin Community College*

Dawn Melzer
*Sacred Heart University*

Dennis Miller
*University of Missouri*

Mignon Montpetit
*Miami University*

Todd Nelson
*California State University at Stanislaus*

Margaret Norwood
*Community College of Aurora*

Aminda O'Hare
*University of Kansas*

Melissa Pace
*Kean University*

Brady Phelps
*South Dakota State University*

Raymond Phinney
*Wheaton College*

Claire St. Peter Pipkin
*West Virginia University, Morgantown*

Christy Porter
*College of William and Mary*

Douglas Pruitt
*West Kentucky Community and Technical College*

Elizabeth Purcell
*Greenville Technical College*

Gabriel Radvansky
*University of Notre Dame*

Celia Reaves
*Monroe Community College*

Diane Reddy
*University of Wisconsin, Milwaukee*

Cynthia Shinabarger Reed
*Tarrant County College*

David Reetz
*Hanover College*

Tanya Renner
*Kapi'olani Community College*

Anthony Robertson
*Vancouver Island University*

Nancy Rogers
*University of Cincinnati*

Wendy Rote
*University of Rochester*

Larry Rudiger
*University of Vermont*

Sharleen Sakai
*Michigan State University*

Matthew Sanders
*Marquette University*

Phillip Schatz
*Saint Joseph's University*

Vann Scott
*Armstrong Atlantic State University*

Colleen Seifert
*University of Michigan at Ann Arbor*

Wayne Shebilske
*Wright State University*

Elisabeth Sherwin
*University of Arkansas at Little Rock*

Lisa Shin
*Tufts University*

Kenith Sobel
*University of Central Arkansas*

Genevieve Stevens
*Houston Community College*

Mark Stewart
*American River College*

Holly Straub
*University of South Dakota*

Mary Strobbe
*San Diego Miramar College*

William Struthers
*Wheaton College*

Lisa Thomassen
*Indiana University*

Jeremy Tost
*Valdosta State University*

Laura Turiano
*Sacred Heart University*

Jeffrey Wagman
*Illinois State University*

Alexander Williams
*University of Kansas*

John Wright
*Washington State University*

Dean Yoshizumi
*Sierra College*

Keith Young
*University of Kansas*

We are especially grateful to the extraordinary people of Worth Publishers. They include senior vice president Catherine Woods and publisher Kevin Feyen, who provided guidance and encouragement at all stages of the project; our acquisitions editor, Dan DeBonis, who managed the project with intelligence, grace, and good humour; our development editors, Valerie Raymond and Mimi Melek; director of development for print and digital products Tracey Kuehn; project editor Robert Errera; production manager Sarah Segal; and editorial assistant Katie Garrett, who through some remarkable alchemy turned a manuscript into a book; our art director Babs Reingold; layout designer Paul Lacy; photograph editor Cecilia Varas; and photograph researcher Elyse Rieder, who made that book an aesthetic delight; our media editor Rachel Comerford; and production manager Stacey Alexander, who guided the development and creation of a superb supplements package; our marketing manager Lindsay Johnson; and associate director of market development Carlise Stembridge, who served as tireless public advocates for our vision. For the Canadian edition, we would like to thank the team at First Folio Resource Group Inc. for editorial and production services, and Maria DeCambra & Associates for photograph editing and research. Thank you one and all. We look forward to working with you again.

Daniel L. Schacter

Daniel T. Gilbert

Matthew K. Nock

Ingrid S. Johnsrude

# Psychology: Evolution of a Science

THE REAL WORLD The Perils of
Procrastination

▲ Psychology's Roots: The Path to a
Science of Mind
Psychology's Ancestors: The Great
Philosophers
From the Brain to the Mind: The French
Connection
Structuralism: Applying Methods from
Physiology to Psychology
Titchener Brings Structuralism to the United
States
James and the Functional Approach
THE REAL WORLD Improving Study Skills

▲ The Development of Clinical
Psychology
The Path to Freud and Psychoanalytic Theory
Influence of Psychoanalysis and the
Humanistic Response

▲ The Search for Objective Measurement:
Behaviourism Takes Centre Stage
Watson and the Emergence of Behaviourism
OTHER VOICES Is Psychology a Science?
B. F. Skinner and the Development of
Behaviourism

▲ Return of the Mind: Psychology
Expands
The Pioneers of Cognitive Psychology
Technology and the Development of
Cognitive Psychology
The Brain Meets the Mind: The Rise of
Cognitive Neuroscience
The Adaptive Mind: The Emergence of
Evolutionary Psychology

▲ Beyond the Individual: Social and
Cultural Perspectives
The Development of Social Psychology
The Emergence of Cultural Psychology
CULTURE & COMMUNITY Analytic and
Holistic Styles in Western and Eastern
Cultures

▲ The Profession of Psychology:
Past and Present
Psychologists Band Together: Psychological
Associations
What Psychologists Do: Research Careers
HOT SCIENCE Psychology as a Hub Science

A LOT WAS HAPPENING IN 1860. In the United Province of Canada, the cornerstone of the Canadian Parliament buildings was laid in Ottawa, and the Cariboo gold rush was about to begin in British Columbia. In the United States Abraham Lincoln had just been elected president and a woman named Anne Kellogg had just given birth to a child who would one day grow up to invent the cornflake. But none of this mattered very much to William James, a bright, taciturn, 18-year-old who had no idea what to do with his life. He loved to paint and draw, but worried that he was not talented enough to become a serious artist. He had enjoyed studying biology in school but doubted that a naturalist's salary would ever allow him to get married and have a family of his own. So, like many young people who are faced with difficult decisions about their futures, William abandoned his dreams and chose to do something in which he had little interest but of which his family heartily approved. Alas, within a few months of arriving at Harvard Medical School, his lack of interest in medicine blossomed into a troubling lack of enthusiasm, and so with a bit of encouragement from the faculty, he put his medical studies on hold to join a biological expedition to the Amazon. The adventure failed to focus his wandering mind (although he learned a great deal about leeches), and when he returned to medical school, both his physical and mental health began to deteriorate. It was clear to everyone that William James was not the sort of person who should be put in charge of a scalpel and a bag of drugs.

Had James become an artist, a biologist, or a physician, we would probably remember nothing about him today. Fortunately for us, he was a deeply confused young man who could speak five languages, and when he became so depressed that he was once again forced to leave medical school, he decided to travel around Europe, where at least he knew how to talk to people. He spent much of his time in what is now Germany, which at that time was a leading centre for scientific enquiry, especially in the field of

Throughout his youth, William James (1842–1910) seemed seriously mixed up. He began university as a chemistry major, then switched to anatomy, then set sail on a biological expedition to the Amazon, and then travelled to Europe, where he became interested in the new science of psychology. Luckily for us, he stuck with it for a while.

physiology. As he talked and listened, he learned about a new science called *psychology* (from a combination of the Greek *psyche* [soul] and *logos* [to study]). He saw that this developing field, in which physiology, medicine, and philosophy merged, was taking a modern, scientific approach to age-old questions about human nature. Such questions had become painfully familiar to him during his personal search for meaning, but only poets and philosophers had ever before offered answers to them (Bjork, 1983; Simon, 1998). Excited about the new discipline, James returned to America and quickly finished his medical degree. But he never practised medicine and never intended to do so. Rather, he became a professor at Harvard University and devoted the rest of his life to psychology. His landmark book, *The Principles of Psychology*, is still widely read and remains one of the most influential books ever written on the subject (James, 1890).

**A LOT HAS HAPPENED SINCE THEN.** Abraham Lincoln has become the subject of an Oscar award-winning film, the gold rush has been replaced in the West by the oil sands development, and the Kellogg Company sells about $9 billion worth of cornflakes every year. If William James (1842–1910) were alive today, he would be amazed by all of these things. But he would probably be even more amazed by the intellectual advances that have taken place in the science that he helped create.

Psychology is *the scientific study of mind and behaviour*. The **mind** refers to *the private inner experience of perceptions, thoughts, memories, and feelings,* an ever-flowing stream of consciousness. **Behaviour** refers to *observable actions of human beings and nonhuman animals,* the things that we do in the world, by ourselves or with others. As you will see in the chapters to come, psychology is an attempt to use scientific methods to address fundamental questions about mind and behaviour that have puzzled people for millennia. The answers to these questions would have astonished William James. Let us take a look at three key examples:

**1.** *What are the bases of perceptions, thoughts, memories, and feelings, or our subjective sense of self?*

For thousands of years, philosophers tried to understand how the objective, physical world of the body was related to the subjective, psychological world of the mind. Today, psychologists know that all of our subjective experiences arise from the electrical and chemical activities of our brains. As you will see throughout this book, some of the most exciting developments in psychological research focus on how our perceptions, thoughts, memories, and feelings are related to activity in the brain. Psychologists and neuroscientists are using new technologies to explore this relationship in ways that would have seemed like science fiction only 20 years ago.

For example, the technique known as *functional magnetic resonance imaging* (fMRI) allows scientists to scan a brain to determine which parts are active when a person reads a word, sees a face, learns a new skill, or remembers a personal experience. In one study, the brains of both professional and novice pianists were scanned as they made complex finger movements, like those involved in piano playing. The results showed that professional pianists have *less* activity than novices in the parts of the brain that guide these finger movements (Krings et al., 2000). This suggests that extensive practice at the piano changes the brains of professional pianists and that the regions controlling finger movements operate more efficiently for them than they do for novices. You will learn more about this in the Memory and Learning chapters and see in the coming chapters how studies using fMRI and related techniques are transforming many different areas of psychology.

DAVID COOPER/TORONTO STAR VIA GETTY IMAGES

Montreal-born Oscar Peterson (1925–2007) is considered to be one of the greatest jazz pianist of all time. His career spanned more than 60 years. Compared to those of a novice piano player, the brain regions that controlled Oscar's fingers were relatively *less* active when he played.

**2.** *How does the mind usually allow us to function effectively in the world?*

Scientists sometimes say that form follows function; that is, if we want to understand *how* something works (e.g., an engine or a thermometer), we need to know what it is working *for* (e.g., powering vehicles or measuring temperature). As William James often noted, "Thinking is for doing," and the function of the mind is to help us do those things that sophisticated animals have to do in order to prosper, such as acquire food, shelter, and mates. Psychological processes are said to be *adaptive,* which means that they promote the welfare and reproduction of organisms that engage in those processes. Perception allows us to recognize our families, see predators before they see us, and avoid stumbling into oncoming traffic. Language allows us to organize our thoughts and communicate them to others, which enables us to form social groups and cooperate. Memory allows us to avoid solving the same problems over again every time we encounter them and to keep in mind what we are doing and why. Emotions allow us to react quickly to events that have life or death significance, and they enable us to form strong social bonds. The list goes on and on.

Given the adaptiveness of psychological processes, it is not surprising that people with deficiencies in these processes often have a pretty tough time. The neurologist Antonio Damasio (1994) described the case of Elliot, a middle-aged husband and father with a good job, whose life was forever changed when surgeons discovered a tumour in the middle of his brain. The surgeons were able to remove the tumour and save his life, and for a while Elliot seemed just fine. But then odd things began to happen. At first, Elliot seemed more likely than usual to make bad decisions (when he could make decisions at all), and as time went on, his bad decisions became truly dreadful ones. He could not prioritize tasks at work because he could not decide what to do first, and when he did, he got it wrong. Eventually he was fired, so he pursued a series of risky business ventures—all of which failed—and he lost his life's savings. His wife divorced him, he married again, and his second wife divorced him too.

So what ruined Elliot's life? The neurologists who tested Elliot were unable to detect any decrease in his cognitive functioning. His intelligence was intact, and his ability to speak, think, and solve logical problems was every bit as sharp as it ever was. But as they probed further, they made a startling discovery: Elliot was no longer able to experience emotions. For example, Elliot did not experience any regret or anger when his boss gave him the pink slip and showed him the door, he did not experience anxiety when he poured his entire bank account into a foolish business venture, and he did not experience any sorrow when his wives packed up and left him. Most of us have wished from time to time that we could be as stoic and unflappable as that; after all, who needs anxiety, sorrow, regret, and anger? The answer is that we all do.

**3.** *Why does the mind occasionally function so ineffectively in the world?*

The mind is an amazing machine that can do a great many things quickly. We can drive a car while talking to a passenger while recognizing the street address while remembering the name of the song that just came on the radio. But like all machines, the mind often trades accuracy for speed and versatility. This can produce "bugs" in the system, causing occasional malfunctions in our otherwise efficient mental processing. One of the most fascinating aspects of psychology is that we are *all* prone to a variety of errors and illusions. Indeed, if thoughts, feelings, and actions were error free, then human behaviour would be orderly, predictable, and dull, which it clearly is not. Rather, it is endlessly surprising, and its surprises often derive from our ability to do precisely the wrong thing at the wrong time.

Emotions are adaptive. For example, fear leads many animals to freeze so that their enemies cannot see them—as it did to these young women who were touring a "haunted house" in Niagara Falls.

**psychology**
The scientific study of mind and behaviour.

**mind**
The private inner experience of perceptions, thoughts, memories, and feelings.

**behaviour**
Observable actions of human beings and nonhuman animals.

Consider a few examples from diaries of people who took part in a study concerning mental errors in everyday life (Reason & Mycielska, 1982, pp. 70–73):

> I meant to get my car out, but as I passed the back porch on my way to the garage, I stopped to put on my boots and gardening jacket as if to work in the yard.

> I put some money into a machine to get a stamp. When the stamp appeared, I took it and said, "Thank you."

> On leaving the room to go to the kitchen, I turned the light off, although several people were there.

If these lapses seem amusing, it is because, in fact, they are. But they are also potentially important as clues to human nature. For example, notice that the person who bought a stamp said, "Thank you," to the machine and not, "How do I find the subway?" In other words, the person did not just do *any* wrong thing; rather, he did something that would have been perfectly correct in a real social interaction. As each of these examples suggests, people often operate on "autopilot," or behave automatically, relying on well-learned habits that they execute without really thinking. When we are not actively focused on what we are saying or doing, these habits may be triggered inappropriately. William James (1890) thought that the influence of habit could help explain the seemingly bizarre actions of "absent-minded" people: "Very absent-minded persons," he wrote in *The Principles of Psychology,* "on going into their

THE REAL WORLD

# The Perils of Procrastination

William James understood that the human mind and behaviour are fascinating in part because they are not error free. The mind's mistakes interest us primarily as paths to achieving a better understanding of mental activity and behaviour, but they also have practical consequences. Let us consider a malfunction that can have significant consequences in your own life: procrastination.

At one time or another, most of us have avoided carrying out a task or put it off to a later time. The task may be unpleasant, difficult, or just less entertaining than other things we could be doing at the moment. For university students, procrastination can affect a range of academic activities, such as writing an essay or preparing for a test. Academic procrastination is not uncommon: Over 70 percent of university students report that they engage in some form of procrastination (Schouwenburg, 1995). Although it is fun to hang out with your friends tonight, it is not so much fun to worry for 3 days about your impending history exam or try to study at 4:00 a.m. the day of the test. Studying now, or at least a little bit each day, robs procrastination of its power over you.

Some procrastinators defend the practice by claiming that they tend to work best under pressure or by noting that as long as a task gets done, it does not matter all that much if it is completed just before the deadline. Is there any merit to such claims, or are they just feeble excuses for counterproductive behaviour?

A study of 60 undergraduate psychology students provided some intriguing answers (Tice & Baumeister, 1997). At the beginning of the semester, the instructor announced a due date for a final essay and told students that if they could not meet the date, they would receive an extension to a later date. About a month later, students completed a scale that measures tendencies toward

procrastination. At that same time, and then again during the last week of class, students recorded health symptoms they had experienced during the past week, the amount of stress they had experienced during that week, and the number of visits they had made to a health care centre during the previous month.

Students who scored high on the procrastination scale tended to turn in their papers late. One month into the semester, these procrastinators reported less stress and fewer symptoms of physical illness than did nonprocrastinators. But at the end of the semester, the procrastinators reported more stress and more health symptoms than did the nonprocrastinators, and also reported more visits to the health centre. The procrastinators also received lower grades on their essays and on course exams. More recent studies have found that higher levels of procrastination are associated with poorer academic performance (Moon & Illingworth, 2005) and higher levels of psychological distress (Rice, Richardson, & Clark, 2012). Therefore, in addition to making use of the tips provided in The Real World box on increasing study skills (pp. 10–11), it would seem wise to avoid procrastination in this course and others.

bedroom to dress for dinner have been known to take off one garment after another and finally get into bed" (p. 115).

James understood that the mind's mistakes are as instructive as they are intriguing, and modern psychology has found it quite useful to study them. Things that are whole and unbroken hum along nicely and do their jobs while leaving no clue about how they do them. Cars gliding down the expressway might as well be magic carpets as long as they are working properly because we have no idea what kind of magic is moving them along. It is only when automobiles break down that we learn about their engines, water pumps, and other fine pieces and processes that normally work together to produce the ride. Breakdowns and errors are not just about destruction and failure, they are pathways to knowledge. (See The Real World box for an example common to us all: procrastination.) In the same way, understanding lapses, errors, mistakes, and the occasionally puzzling nature of human behaviour provides a vantage point for understanding the normal operation of mental life and behaviour. The story of Elliot, whose behaviour broke down after he had brain surgery, is an example that highlights the role that emotions play in guiding normal judgment and behaviour.

Psychology is exciting because it addresses fundamental questions about human experience and behaviour, and the three questions we have just considered are merely the tip of the iceberg. Think of this book as a guide to exploring the rest of the iceberg. But before we don our parkas and grab our pick axes, we need to understand how the iceberg got here in the first place. To understand psychology in the twenty-first century, we need to become familiar with the psychology of the past.

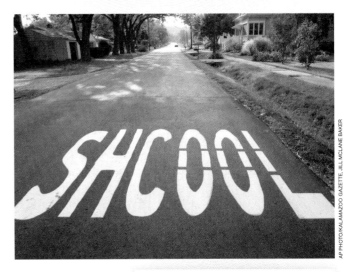

Mistakes can teach us a lot about how people think … or fail to think, as the case may be.

# Psychology's Roots: The Path to a Science of Mind

When the young William James interrupted his medical studies to travel in Europe during the late 1860s, he wanted to learn about human nature. But he confronted a very different situation than a similarly curious student would confront today, largely because psychology did not yet exist as an independent field of study. As James cheekily wrote, "The first lecture in psychology that I ever heard was the first I ever gave" (quoted in Perry, 1996, p. 228). Of course, that does not mean no one had ever thought about human nature before. For 2000 years, thinkers with scraggly beards and poor dental hygiene had pondered such questions and, in fact, modern psychology acknowledges its deep roots in philosophy. We will begin by examining those roots and then describe some of the early attempts to develop a scientific approach to psychology by relating the mind to the brain. Next, we will see how psychologists divided into different camps (or schools of thought): *Structuralists* tried to analyze the mind by breaking it down into its basic components, and *functionalists* focused on how mental abilities allow people to adapt to their environments.

How do young children learn about the world? Plato believed that certain kinds of knowledge are innate, whereas Aristotle believed that the mind is a blank slate on which experiences are written.

## Psychology's Ancestors: The Great Philosophers

The desire to understand ourselves is not new. Greek thinkers such as Plato (428 BCE–347 BCE) and Aristotle (384 BCE–322 BCE) were among the first to struggle with fundamental questions about how the mind works (Robinson, 1995). Greek philosophers debated many of the questions that psychologists continue to debate today. For example, are cognitive

**nativism**
The philosophical view that certain kinds of knowledge are innate or inborn.

**philosophical empiricism**
The view that all knowledge is acquired through experience.

**phrenology**
A now defunct theory that specific mental abilities and characteristics, ranging from memory to the capacity for happiness, are localized in specific regions of the brain.

abilities and knowledge inborn, or are they acquired only through experience? Plato argued in favour of **nativism,** *the philosophical view that certain kinds of knowledge are innate or inborn.* Children in every culture figure out early on that sounds can have meanings that can be arranged into words, which then can be arranged into sentences. Before a child is old enough to poop in the proper place, he or she has already mastered the fundamentals of language without any formal instruction. Is the propensity to learn language "hardwired" (something that children are born with)? Or does the ability to learn language depend on the child's experience? Aristotle believed that the child's mind was a *tabula rasa* (blank slate) on which experiences were written, and he argued for **philosophical empiricism,** *the view that all knowledge is acquired through experience.*

Although few, if any, modern psychologists believe that nativism or empiricism is entirely correct, the issue of just how much "nature" and "nurture" explain any given behaviour is still a matter of controversy. In some ways, it is quite amazing that ancient philosophers were able to articulate so many of the important questions in psychology and offer many excellent insights into their answers without any access to scientific evidence. Their ideas came from personal observations, intuition, and speculation. Although they were quite good at arguing with one another, they usually found it impossible to settle their disputes because their approach provided no means of testing their theories. As you will see in the Methods chapter, the ability to test a theory is the cornerstone of the scientific approach and the basis for reaching conclusions in modern psychology.

> What fundamental question has puzzled philosophers for millennia?

## From the Brain to the Mind: The French Connection

We all know that the brain and the body are physical objects that we can see and touch and that the subjective contents of our minds—our perceptions, thoughts, and feelings—are not. Inner experience is perfectly real, but where in the world is it? French philosopher René Descartes (1596–1650) argued that body and mind are fundamentally different things—that the body is made of a material substance, whereas the mind (or soul) is made of an immaterial or spiritual substance. But if the mind and the body are different things made of different substances, then how do they interact? How does the mind tell the body to put its foot forward, and when the body steps on a rusty nail, why does the mind say "ouch"? This is the problem of *dualism,* or how mental activity can be reconciled and coordinated with physical behaviour.

Descartes suggested that the mind influences the body through a tiny structure near the bottom of the brain known as the pineal gland. He was largely alone in this view because other philosophers at the time either rejected his explanation or offered alternative ideas. For example, British philosopher Thomas Hobbes (1588–1679) argued that the mind and body are not different things at all; rather, the mind *is* what the brain *does*. From Hobbes's perspective, looking for a place in the brain where the mind meets the body is like looking for the place in a television where the picture meets the flat panel display.

> What were early explanations for dualism?

The German physician Franz Joseph Gall (1758–1828) also thought that brains and minds were linked, but by size rather than by glands. He examined the brains of animals and of people who had died of disease, or as healthy adults, or as children, and observed that mental ability often increases with larger brain size and decreases with damage to the brain. These aspects of Gall's findings were generally accepted (and the part about brain damage still is today). But Gall went far beyond his evidence to develop a psychological theory known as **phrenology,** *a now defunct theory that specific mental abilities and characteristics, ranging from memory to the capacity*

© THOM LANG/CORBIS

René Descartes believed that the physical body was a container for the non-physical thing called the mind. Centuries later, the philosopher Gilbert Ryle (1949) argued that Descartes was wrong, that there is no "ghost in the machine," and that all mental activity is simply the result of the physical activity of the brain. Most modern scientists reject Descartes's "dualism" and embrace Ryle's "scientific materialism."

*for happiness, are localized in specific regions of the brain* (see **FIGURE 1.1**). The idea that different parts of the brain are specialized for specific psychological functions turned out to be right; as you will learn later in the book, a part of the brain called the *hippocampus* is intimately involved in memory, just as a structure called the *amygdala* is intimately involved in fear. But phrenology took this idea to an absurd extreme. Gall asserted that the size of bumps or indentations on the skull reflected the size of the brain regions beneath them and that by feeling those bumps, one could tell whether a person was friendly, cautious, assertive, idealistic, and so on. What Gall did not realize was that bumps on the skull do not necessarily reveal anything about the shape of the brain underneath.

Phrenology made for a nice parlour game and gave young people a good excuse for touching each other, but in the end it amounted to a series of strong claims based on weak evidence. Not surprisingly, his critics were galled (so to speak), and they ridiculed many of his proposals. Despite an initially large following, phrenology was quickly discredited (Fancher, 1979).

While Gall was busy playing bumpologist, French scientists were beginning to link the brain and the mind in a more convincing manner. Biologist Marie Jean Pierre Flourens (1794–1867) was appalled by Gall's far-reaching claims and sloppy methods, so he conducted experiments in which he surgically removed specific parts of the brain from dogs, birds, and other animals and found (not surprisingly!) that their actions and movements differed from those of animals with intact brains.

French surgeon Pierre Paul Broca (1824–1880) worked with a patient who had suffered damage to a small part of the left side of the brain (now known as *Broca's area*). The patient, Monsieur Leborgne, was virtually unable to speak and could utter

> **How did work involving patients with brain damage help demonstrate the mind–brain connection?**

only the single syllable "tan." Yet the patient understood everything that was said to him and was able to communicate using gestures. Broca had the crucial insight that damage to a specific part of the brain impaired a specific mental function, clearly demonstrating that the brain and mind are closely linked. This was important in the nineteenth century because at that time many people accepted Descartes's idea that the mind is separate from, but interacts with, the brain and the body. Broca and Flourens, then, were the first to demonstrate that the mind is grounded in a material substance, namely, the brain. Their work jump-started the scientific investigation of mental processes.

## Structuralism: Applying Methods from Physiology to Psychology

Another birthplace of psychology was Germany. In the middle of the nineteenth century, German scientists who were trained in the field of **physiology,** *the study of biological processes, especially in the human body*, were making discoveries fundamental to the new field of psychology. Physiologists had developed methods that allowed them to measure such things as the speed of nerve impulses, and some of them had begun to use these methods to measure mental abilities. William James was drawn to the work of two such physiologists: Hermann von Helmholtz (1821–1894) and Wilhelm Wundt (1832–1920). "It seems to me that perhaps the time has come for psychology to begin to be a science," wrote James in a letter written in 1867 during his visit to Berlin. "Helmholtz and a man called Wundt at Heidelberg are working at it." What attracted James to the work of these two scientists?

◄ Figure **1.1** **Phrenology** Franz Joseph Gall (1758–1828) developed a theory called phrenology, which suggested that psychological capacities (such as the capacity for friendship) and traits (such as cautiousness and mirth) were located in particular parts of the brain. The greater the number of these capacities and traits a person had, the larger the corresponding bumps on the skull.

MARY EVANS PICTURE LIBRARY/
THE IMAGE WORKS

APIC/GETTY IMAGES

M. Leborgne was nicknamed "Tan" because it was the only word he could say. When he died in 1861, Paul Broca dissected his brain and found a lesion in the left hemisphere which, he concluded, had been responsible for Leborgne's loss of speech. Today, Leborgne's brain lives in a jar at the Musée Dupuytren in Paris, France. And to this day, no one knows his first name.

**physiology**
The study of biological processes, especially in the human body.

## Helmholtz Measures the Speed of Responses

A brilliant experimenter with a background in both physiology and physics, Helmholtz had developed a method for measuring the speed of nerve impulses in a frog's leg, which he then adapted to the study of human beings. Helmholtz trained participants to respond when he applied a **stimulus**—*sensory input from the environment*—to different parts of the leg. He recorded his participants' **reaction time,** or *the amount of time taken to respond to a specific stimulus,* after applying the stimulus. Helmholtz found that people generally took longer to respond when their toe was stimulated than when their thigh was stimulated, and the difference between these reaction times allowed him to estimate how long it took a nerve impulse to travel to the brain. These results were astonishing to nineteenth-century scientists because, at that time, just about everyone thought that mental processes occurred instantaneously. When you move your hands in front of your eyes, you do not feel your hands move a fraction of a second before you see them. The real world does not appear like one of those late-night movies in which the video and the audio are off by just a fraction of a second. Scientists assumed that the neurological processes underlying mental events *must* be instantaneous for everything to be so nicely synchronized, but Helmholtz showed that this was not true. In so doing, he also demonstrated that reaction time could be a useful way to study the mind and the brain. Helmholtz also made fundamental contributions to our understanding of colour vision and perception of sound.

> **What was the useful application of Hemholtz's results?**

By measuring a person's reaction times to different stimuli, Hermann von Helmholtz (1821–1894) estimated the length of time it takes a nerve impulse to travel to the brain.

HULTON ARCHIVE/GETTY IMAGES

## Wundt and the Development of Structuralism

Although Helmholtz's contributions were important, historians generally credit the official emergence of psychology to Helmholtz's research assistant, Wilhelm Wundt (1832–1920) (Rieber, 1980). In 1867, at the University of Heidelberg, Wundt taught what was probably the first course in physiological psychology, which led to the publication of his book, *Principles of Physiological Psychology,* in 1874. Wundt called the book "an attempt to mark out [psychology] as a new domain of science" (Fancher, 1979, p. 126). In 1879, at the University of Leipzig, Wundt opened the first laboratory exclusively devoted to psychological studies, and this event marked the official birth of psychology as an independent field of study. The new lab was full of graduate students carrying out research on topics assigned by Wundt, and it soon attracted young scholars from all over the world who were eager to learn about the new science that Wundt had developed.

Wundt believed that scientific psychology should focus on analyzing **consciousness,** *a person's subjective experience of the world and the mind.* Consciousness encompasses a broad range of subjective experiences. We may be conscious of sights, sounds, tastes, smells, bodily sensations, thoughts, or feelings. As Wundt tried to figure out a way to study consciousness scientifically, he noted that chemists try to understand the structure of matter by breaking down natural substances into basic elements. So he and his students adopted an approach called **structuralism,** *the analysis of the basic elements that constitute the mind.* This approach involved breaking down consciousness into elemental sensations and feelings, and you can do a bit of structuralism right now without leaving your chair.

> **How did the work of chemists influence early psychology?**

Consider the contents of your own consciousness. At this very moment you may be aware of the meaning of these words, the visual appearance of the letters on the page, the key ring pressing uncomfortably against your thigh, your feelings of excitement or boredom (probably excitement), the smell of curried chicken salad, or the nagging

**stimulus**
Sensory input from the environment.

**reaction time**
The amount of time taken to respond to a specific stimulus.

**consciousness**
A person's subjective experience of the world and the mind.

**structuralism**
The analysis of the basic elements that constitute the mind.

**introspection**
The subjective observation of one's own experience.

question of whether the War of 1812 really deserves its own overture. At any given moment, all sorts of things are swimming in the stream of consciousness, and Wundt tried to analyze them in a systematic way using the method of **introspection,** *the subjective observation of one's own experience.* In a typical experiment, observers (usually students) were presented with a stimulus (usually a colour or a sound) and then asked to report their introspections. The observers described the brightness of a colour or the loudness of a tone. They reported on their "raw" sensory experience, rather than on their interpretations of that experience. For example, an observer presented with this page would not report seeing words on the page (which counts as an interpretation of the experience), but instead might describe a series of black marks, some straight and others curved, against a bright white back-ground. Wundt also attempted to carefully describe the feelings associated with ele-mentary perceptions. For example, when Wundt listened to the clicks produced by a metronome, some of the patterns of sounds were more pleasant than others. By analyzing the relation between feelings and perceptual sensations, Wundt and his students hoped to uncover the basic structure of conscious experience.

Wilhelm Wundt (1832–1920), far right, founded the first laboratory devoted exclusively to psychology at the University of Leipzig in Germany. He sought to understand consciousness by breaking it down into its basic parts, including individual sensations and feelings.

ARCHIVES OF THE HISTORY OF AMERICAN PSYCHOLOGY

Wundt tried to provide objective measurements of conscious processes by using reac-tion time techniques similar to those first developed by Helmholtz. Wundt used reaction times to examine a distinction between the perception and interpretation of a stimulus. His research participants were instructed to press a button as soon as a tone sounded. Some participants were told to concentrate on perceiving the tone before pressing the button, whereas others were told to concentrate only on pressing the button. Those people who concentrated on the tone responded about one tenth of a second more slowly than those told to concentrate only on pressing the button. Wundt reasoned that both fast and slow participants had to register the tone in consciousness (perception), but only the slower participants also had to interpret the significance of the tone and press the button. The faster research participants, focusing only on the response they were to make, could respond automatically to the tone because they did not have to engage in the additional step of interpretation (Fancher, 1979). This type of experimen-tation broke new ground by showing that psychologists could use scientific techniques to disentangle even subtle conscious processes. In fact, as you will see in later chapters, reaction time procedures have proven extremely useful in modern research.

## Titchener Brings Structuralism to the United States

The pioneering efforts of Wundt's laboratory launched psychology as an independent science and profoundly influenced the field for the remainder of the nineteenth cen-tury. Many European and American scholars journeyed to Leipzig to study with Wundt. Among the most eminent was British-born Edward Titchener (1867–1927), who stud-ied with Wundt for 2 years in the early 1890s. Titchener then moved to the United States and set up a psychology laboratory at Cornell University (where, if you would like to see it, his brain is still on display in the psychology department). Titchener brought some parts of Wundt's approach to America, but he also made some changes (Brock, 1993; Rieber, 1980). For instance, whereas Wundt emphasized the relationship between elements of consciousness, Titchener focused on identifying the basic elements them-selves, using introspection. In his textbook, *An Outline of Psychology* (1896), Titchener put forward a list of more than 44 000 elemental qualities of conscious experience, most of them visual (32 820) or auditory (11 600) (Schultz & Schultz, 1987).

The influence of the structuralist approach gradually faded, due mostly to the introspective method. Science requires replicable observations; we could never

Titchener was not the first to try to identify the elements of conscious experience. As this drawing shows, seventeenth-century physician and artist Robert Fludd tried to do the same thing—and was about equally successful.

HULTON ARCHIVE/GETTY IMAGES

determine the structure of DNA or the life span of a dust mite if every scientist who looked through a microscope saw something different. Alas, even trained observers provided conflicting introspections about their conscious experiences ("I see a cloud that looks like a duck"—"No, *I* think that cloud looks like a horse"), thus making it difficult for different psychologists to agree on the basic elements of conscious experience. Indeed, some psychologists had doubts about whether it was even possible to identify such elements through introspection alone. One of the most prominent skeptics was someone you have already met: a young man with a bad attitude and a useless medical degree named William James.

> **What are the problems with the introspective method?**

## James and the Functional Approach

James returned from his European tour inspired by the idea of approaching psychological issues from a scientific perspective. He received a teaching appointment at Harvard, in Boston, Massachusetts (primarily because the president of the university was a neighbour and family friend) and his position at Harvard enabled him to purchase laboratory equipment for classroom experiments. As a result, James taught the first course at a North American university to draw on the new experimental psychology developed by Wundt and others (Schultz & Schultz, 1987).

James agreed with Wundt on some points, including the importance of focusing on immediate experience and the usefulness of introspection as a technique (Bjork, 1983),

# Improving Study Skills

**THE REAL WORLD**

To get the most out of taking this course, you should begin by doing something that might seem a bit strange: Make it hard on yourself. But by making it hard on yourself in the right way, you will end up making the course easier and take away a lot more from it than you would otherwise. What do we mean by making it hard on yourself? Our minds do not work like video cameras, passively recording everything that happens and then faithfully storing the information. In order to retain new information, you need to take an active role in learning, by doing such things as rehearsing, interpreting, and testing yourself. These activities initially might seem difficult, but in fact they are what psychologists call *desirable difficulties* (Bjork & Bjork, 2011): Making it more difficult by actively engaging during critical phases of learning will increase your retention and ultimately result in improved performance. Here are some specific suggestions:

● **Rehearse.** One useful type of active manipulation is rehearsal: repeating to-be-learned information to yourself. Psychologists have found that a particularly effective strategy is called spaced rehearsal, where you repeat information

to yourself at increasingly long intervals. For example, suppose that you want to learn the name of a person you have just met named Eric. Repeat the name to yourself right away, wait a few seconds and think of it again, wait a bit longer (maybe 30 seconds) and bring the name to mind once more, then rehearse the name again after a minute and once more after 2 or 3 minutes. Making rehearsal gradually more difficult will improve retention; studies show that this type of rehearsal improves long-term learning more than rehearsing the name without any spacing between rehearsals (Landauer & Bjork, 1978). You can apply this technique to names, dates, definitions, and many other kinds of information, including concepts presented in this textbook.

● **Interpret.** Simple rehearsal can be beneficial, but one of the most important lessons from psychological research is that we acquire information most effectively when we think about its meaning and reflect on its significance. In fact, we do not even have to try to remember something if we think deeply enough about what we want to remember; the act of

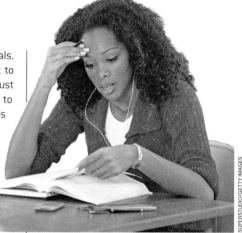

▲ Anxious feelings about an upcoming exam may be unpleasant, but as you have probably experienced yourself, they can motivate much-needed study.

reflection itself will virtually guarantee good memory. For example, suppose that you want to learn the basic ideas behind Skinner's approach to behaviourism (see page 18). Ask yourself the following kinds of questions: How did behaviourism differ from previous approaches in psychology? How would a behaviourist like Skinner think about psychological issues that interest you, such as whether a mentally disturbed individual should be held responsible for committing a crime, or what factors would contribute to your but he disagreed with Wundt's claim that consciousness could be broken down into separate elements. James believed that trying to isolate and analyze a particular moment of consciousness (as the structuralists did) distorted the essential nature of consciousness. Consciousness, he argued, was more like a flowing stream than a bundle of separate elements. So James decided to approach psychology from a different perspective entirely and developed an approach known as **functionalism,** *the study of the purpose mental processes serve in enabling people to adapt to their environment.* In contrast to structuralism, which examined the structure of mental processes, functionalism set out to understand the functions those mental processes served. (See The Real World box for some strategies to enhance one of those functions—learning.)

James's thinking was inspired by the ideas in Charles Darwin's (1809–1882) recently published book on biological evolution, *On the Origin of Species by Means of Natural Selection* (1859). Darwin proposed the

> **How does functionalism relate to Darwin's theory of natural selection?**

principle of **natural selection:** *The features of an organism that help it survive and reproduce are more likely than other features to be passed on to subsequent generations.* From this perspective, James reasoned, mental abilities must have evolved because they were adaptive, that is, because they helped people solve problems and increased their chances of survival. Like other animals, people have always needed to avoid predators, locate food, build shelters, and attract mates. Applying Darwin's principle of natural selection, James (1890) reasoned that consciousness must serve an important biological function and the task for psychologists was to

**functionalism**
The study of the purpose mental processes serve in enabling people to adapt to their environment.

**natural selection**
Charles Darwin's theory that the features of an organism that help it survive and reproduce are more likely than other features to be passed on to subsequent generations.

---

choice of a major subject or career path? In attempting to answer such questions, you will need to review what you have learned about behaviourism and then relate it to other things you already know about. This may seem like a demanding activity, but it is much easier to remember new information when you can relate it to something you already know. The Critical Thinking questions that are sprinkled throughout the text will help you to reflect on and interpret the material, and a happy consequence of that activity is that you will be more likely to remember the information that the questions engage you to think about.

- **Build.** Think about and review the information you have acquired in class on a regular basis. Begin soon after class, and then try to schedule regular "booster" sessions. Do not wait until the last second to cram your review into one sitting; as discussed in the Rehearse section, research shows that spacing out review and repetition leads to longer-lasting recall.
- **Test.** Do not just look at your class notes or this textbook; test yourself on the material as often as you can. As you will learn in the Memory and Learning chapters, research also shows that actively

testing yourself on information you have acquired helps you to later remember that information more than just looking at it again. Testing yourself can also guard against a common pitfall. You may think that you have learned the material because it seems familiar to you after having reviewed it several times, but just because the material seems familiar, that does not necessarily mean that you have learned it well enough to answer a test question. Testing yourself will alert you to when you need to study more, even when the information seems familiar. The Cue Questions that you will encounter throughout the text (highlighted by green question marks, as you will see just above this box) are designed to test you and thereby increase learning and retention. Be sure to use them. The Learning Curve study aid will also help you to test and learn (see the Preface for further discussion of Learning Curve).

- **Hit the main points.** Take some of the load off your memory by developing effective note-taking and outlining skills. Students often scribble down vague and fragmentary notes during lectures, figuring that the notes will be good enough

to jog memory later. But when the time comes to study, they have forgotten so much that their notes are no longer clear. Realize that you cannot write down everything an instructor says, and try to focus on making detailed notes about the main ideas, facts, and people mentioned in the lecture.

- **Organize.** The act of organizing an outline in a way that clearly highlights the major concepts will force you to reflect on the information in a way that promotes retention and will also provide you with a helpful study guide to promote self-testing and review. Again, this activity may seem difficult or demanding at first, but it will result in improved retention and ultimately will make learning easier for you.
- **Sleep on it.** We have stressed the importance of making it hard on yourself, but this final item is an easy one: get some sleep. As you will learn in the Hot Science box in the Memory chapter, research shows that sleep helps to form lasting memories. In fact, research shows that sleep does a particularly good job of increasing memory for important, meaningful material. So be sure to enlist sleep as an ally in studying and test preparation.

YURI KADOBNOV/AFP/GETTY IMAGES

You do not have to look at this photograph for more than a half-second to know that Vladimir Putin, the President of Russia, is not feeling very happy. William James suggested that your ability to read emotional expressions in an instant serves an important function that promotes your survival and well-being.

© KAREN HUNT/CORBIS

G. Stanley Hall (1844–1924) believed that as they develop, children retrace the evolutionary history of our species, starting out as "mental cavemen" and ending up as … well, us.

understand what those functions are. Wundt and the other structuralists worked in laboratories, and James believed that such work was limited in its ability to tell us how consciousness functioned in the natural environment. Wundt, in turn, believed that James did not focus enough on new findings from the laboratory that he and the structuralists had begun to produce. Commenting on *The Principles of Psychology,* Wundt conceded that James was a topflight writer but disapproved of his approach: "It is literature, it is beautiful, but it is not psychology" (Bjork, 1983, p. 12).

The rest of the world did not agree, and James's functionalist psychology quickly gained followers, especially in North America where Darwin's ideas were influencing many thinkers. G. Stanley Hall (1844–1924), who studied with both Wundt and James, set up the first psychology research laboratory in North America at Johns Hopkins University in 1881. Hall's work focused on development and education, and was strongly influenced by evolutionary thinking (Schultz & Schultz, 1987).

Hall believed that, as children develop, they pass through stages that repeat the evolutionary history of the human race. Thus, the mental capacities of a young child resemble those of our ancient ancestors, and children grow over a lifetime in the same way that a species evolves over aeons.

The efforts of James, Hall, and others set the stage for functionalism to develop as a major school of psychological thought in North America. Psychology departments that embraced a functionalist approach started to spring up at major universities and, in a struggle for survival that would have made Darwin proud, functionalism became more influential than structuralism had ever been. By the 1920s, functionalism was the dominant approach to psychology in North America.

James Mark Baldwin (1867–1934) established the first psychology laboratory in Canada in 1889, at the University of Toronto. Baldwin was a student of Wundt's. He was only in Toronto for 4 years, but his two daughters were born there. Their birth inspired his experimental research, which, in Canada and afterwards, focused on infant development. Hall and Baldwin were the first *developmental psychologists*—those concerned with how organisms develop psychologically as they grow and age. Baldwin's ideas strongly influenced the thinking of other developmental psychologists who you will learn about later in this course, like Jean Piaget.

## IN SUMMARY

▶ Philosophers have pondered and debated ideas about human nature for millennia but, given the nature of their approach, they did not provide empirical evidence to support their claims.

▶ Some of the earliest successful efforts to develop a science linking mind and behaviour came from the French scientists Marie Jean Pierre Flourens and Paul Broca, who showed that damage to the brain can result in impairments of behaviour and mental functions.

▶ Hermann von Helmholtz furthered the science of the mind by developing methods for measuring reaction time.

▶ Wilhelm Wundt is credited with the founding of psychology as a scientific discipline. His structuralist approach focused on analyzing the basic elements of consciousness. Wundt's student, Edward Titchener, brought structuralism to the United States.

▶ William James applied Darwin's theory of natural selection to the study of the mind. His functionalist approach focused on how mental processes serve to enable people to adapt to their environments.

▶ The first psychological research laboratories in North America were established by G. Stanley Hall (Hopkins University) and James Mark Baldwin (University of Toronto).

# The Development of Clinical Psychology

At about the same time that some psychologists were developing structuralism and functionalism in the laboratory, other psychologists working in the clinic were beginning to study people with psychological disorders. They began to realize that one can often understand how something works by examining how it breaks, and their observations of mental disorders influenced the development of psychology.

## The Path to Freud and Psychoanalytic Theory

French physicians Jean-Martin Charcot (1825–1893) and Pierre Janet (1859–1947) reported striking observations when they interviewed patients who had developed a condition known then as **hysteria,** *a temporary loss of cognitive or motor functions, usually as a result of emotionally upsetting experiences.* Hysterical patients became blind, paralyzed, or lost their memories, even though there was no known physical cause of their problems. However, when the patients were put into a trancelike state through the use of hypnosis (an altered state of consciousness characterized by suggestibility), their symptoms disappeared: Blind patients could see, paralyzed patients could walk, and forgetful patients could remember. After coming out of the hypnotic trance, the patients forgot what had happened under hypnosis and again showed their symptoms. The patients behaved like two different people in the waking versus hypnotic states.

These peculiar disorders were ignored by Wundt, Titchener, and other laboratory scientists, who did not consider them a proper subject for scientific psychology (Bjork, 1983). But William James believed they had important implications for understanding the nature of the mind (Taylor, 2001). He thought it was important to capitalize on these mental disruptions as a way of understanding the normal operation of the mind. During our ordinary conscious experience we are only aware of a single "me" or "self," but the aberrations described by Charcot, Janet, and others suggested that the brain can create many conscious selves that are not aware of each other's existence (James, 1890, p. 400). These striking observations also fuelled the imagination of a young physician from Vienna, Austria, who studied with Charcot in Paris in 1885. His name was Sigmund Freud (1856–1939).

After his visit to Charcot's clinic in Paris, Freud returned to Vienna, where he continued his work with hysteric patients. (The word *hysteria*, by the way, comes from the Latin word *hyster* [womb]. It was once believed that only women suffered from hysteria, which was thought to be caused by a "wandering womb.") Working with physician Joseph Breuer (1842–1925), Freud began to make his own observations of hysteric patients and develop theories to explain their strange behaviours and symptoms. Freud theorized that many of the patients' problems could be traced to the effects of painful childhood experiences that the person could not remember, and he suggested that the powerful influence of these seemingly lost memories revealed the presence of an unconscious mind. According to Freud, the **unconscious** is *the part of the mind that operates outside of conscious awareness but influences conscious thoughts, feelings, and actions.* This idea led Freud to develop **psychoanalytic theory,** *an approach that emphasizes the importance of*

**How was Freud influenced by work with hysteric patients?**

**hysteria**
A temporary loss of cognitive or motor functions, usually as a result of emotionally upsetting experiences.

**unconscious**
The part of the mind that operates outside of conscious awareness but influences conscious thoughts, feelings, and actions.

**psychoanalytic theory**
An approach that emphasizes the importance of unconscious mental processes in shaping feelings, thoughts, and behaviour.

In this photograph, Sigmund Freud (1856–1939) sits by the couch reserved for his psychoanalytic patients, where they would be encouraged to recall past experiences and bring unconscious thoughts into awareness.

**psychoanalysis**
A therapeutic approach that focuses on bringing unconscious material into conscious awareness to better understand psychological disorders.

*unconscious mental processes in shaping feelings, thoughts, and behaviours.* From a psychoanalytic perspective, it is important to uncover a person's early experiences and to illuminate a person's unconscious anxieties, conflicts, and desires. Psychoanalytic theory formed the basis for a therapy that Freud called **psychoanalysis,** which focuses on *bringing unconscious material into conscious awareness to better understand psychological disorders.* During psychoanalysis, patients recalled past experiences ("When I was a toddler, I was frightened by a masked man on a black horse") and related their dreams and fantasies ("Sometimes I close my eyes and imagine not having to pay for this session"). Psychoanalysts used Freud's theoretical approach to interpret what their patients said.

In the early 1900s, Freud and a growing number of followers formed a psychoanalytic movement. Carl Gustav Jung (1875–1961) and Alfred Adler (1870–1937) were prominent in the movement, but both were independent thinkers, and Freud apparently had little tolerance for individuals who challenged his ideas. Soon enough, Freud broke off his relationships with both men so that he could shape the psychoanalytic movement himself (Sulloway, 1992). Psychoanalytic theory became quite controversial (especially in America) because it suggested that understanding a person's thoughts, feelings, and behaviour required a thorough exploration of the person's early sexual experiences and unconscious sexual desires. In those days these topics were considered far too racy for scientific discussion.

Most of Freud's followers, like Freud himself, were trained as physicians and did not conduct psychological experiments in the laboratory (although early in his career, Freud did do some nice laboratory work on the sexual organs of eels). By and large, psychoanalysts did not hold positions in universities and developed their ideas in isolation from the research-based approaches of Wundt, Titchener, James, Hall, Baldwin, and others. One of the few times that Freud met with the leading academic psychologists was at a conference that G. Stanley Hall organized at Clark University in Massachusetts in 1909. It was there that William James and Sigmund Freud met for the first time. Although James worked in an academic setting and Freud worked with clinical patients, both men believed that mental aberrations provide important clues into the nature of mind.

This famous psychology conference, held in 1909 at Clark University, was organized by G. Stanley Hall and brought together many notable figures, such as William James and Sigmund Freud. Both men are circled, with James on the left.

## Influence of Psychoanalysis and the Humanistic Response

Most historians consider Freud to be one of the most influential thinkers of the twentieth century, and the psychoanalytic movement influenced everything from literature and history to politics and art. Within psychology, psychoanalysis had its greatest impact on clinical practice, but that influence has been considerably diminished over the past 40 years.

This is partly because Freud's vision of human nature was a dark one, emphasizing limitations and problems rather than possibilities and poten-

**Why are Freud's ideas less influential today?**

tials. He saw people as hostages to their forgotten childhood experiences and primitive sexual impulses, and the inherent pessimism of his perspective frustrated those psychologists who had a more optimistic view of human nature. In America, the years after World War II were positive, invigorating, and upbeat: Poverty and disease were being conquered by technology, the standard of living of ordinary Americans was rising sharply, and people were landing on the moon. The era was characterized by the accomplishments—not the foibles—of the human mind, and Freud's viewpoint was out of step with the spirit of the times.

Freud's ideas were also difficult to test, and a theory that cannot be tested is of limited use in psychology or other sciences. Although Freud's emphasis on unconscious processes has had an enduring impact on psychology, psychologists began to have serious misgivings about many aspects of Freud's theory.

It was in these times that psychologists such as Abraham Maslow (1908–1970) and Carl Rogers (1902–1987) pioneered a new movement called **humanistic psychology,** *an approach to understanding human nature that emphasizes the positive potential of human beings.* Humanistic psychologists focused on the highest aspirations that people had for themselves. Rather than viewing people as prisoners of events in their remote pasts, humanistic psychologists viewed people as free agents who have an inherent need to develop, grow, and attain their full potential. This movement reached its peak in the 1960s when a generation of "flower children" found it easy to see psychological life as a kind of blossoming of the spirit. Humanistic therapists sought to help people realize their full potential; in fact, they called them *clients* rather than *patients*. In this relationship, the therapist and the client (unlike the psychoanalyst and the patient) were on equal footing. The development of the humanistic perspective was one more reason why Freud's ideas eventually became less influential.

Humanistic psychology offered a positive view of human nature that matched the zeitgeist of the 1960s.

### IN SUMMARY

▶ Psychologists have often focused on patients with psychological disorders as a way of understanding human behaviour. Clinicians such as Jean-Martin Charcot and Pierre Janet studied unusual cases in which patients acted like different people while under hypnosis, raising the possibility that each of us has more than one self.

▶ Through his work with hysteric patients, Sigmund Freud developed psychoanalysis, which emphasized the importance of unconscious influences and childhood experiences in shaping thoughts, feelings, and behaviour.

▶ Happily, humanistic psychologists offered a more optimistic view of the human condition, suggesting that people are inherently disposed toward growth and can usually reach their full potential with a little help from their friends.

**humanistic psychology**
An approach to understanding human nature that emphasizes the positive potential of human beings.

**behaviourism**
An approach that advocates that psychologists restrict themselves to the scientific study of objectively observable behaviour.

# The Search for Objective Measurement: Behaviourism Takes Centre Stage

Our discussion of the development of clinical psychology into the 1960s took us a little ahead of ourselves—we need to turn our attention back a few decades to understand some other important developments.

The schools of psychological thought that had developed by the early twentieth century—structuralism, functionalism, and psychoanalysis—differed substantially from one another. But they shared an important similarity: Each tried to understand the inner workings of the mind by examining conscious perceptions, thoughts, memories, and feelings or by trying to elicit previously unconscious material, all of which were reported by participants in experiments or patients in a clinical setting. In each case it proved difficult to establish with much certainty just what was going on in people's minds, due to the unreliable nature of the methodology. As the twentieth century unfolded, a new approach developed as psychologists challenged the idea that psychology should focus on mental life at all. This new approach was called **behaviourism,** which *advocated that psychologists restrict themselves* to *the scientific study of objectively observable behaviour.* (See Other Voices: Is Psychology a Science? for a modern discussion of the science of psychology.) Behaviourism represented a dramatic departure from previous schools of thought.

## Watson and the Emergence of Behaviourism

John Broadus Watson (1878–1958) believed that private experience was too idiosyncratic and vague to be an object of scientific inquiry. Science required replicable, objective measurements of phenomena that were accessible to all observers, and the introspective methods used by structuralists and functionalists were far too subjective for that. So instead of describing conscious experiences, Watson proposed that psychologists focus entirely on the study of behaviour—what people *do*, rather than what people *experience*—because behaviour can be observed by anyone and it can be measured objectively. Watson thought that a focus on behaviour would put a stop to the endless philosophical debates in which psychologists were currently entangled, and it would encourage psychologists to develop practical applications in such areas as business, medicine, law, and education. The goal of scientific psychology, according to Watson, should be to predict and to control behaviour in ways that benefit society.

Why would someone want to throw the mind out of psychology? This may seem excessive, until you notice that Watson studied the behaviour of animals such as rats and birds. In such studies, inferring a mind is a matter of some debate. Shall we say that dogs have minds, for instance, but leave out pigeons? If we include pigeons, what about worms? Animal behaviour specialists staked out claims in this area. In 1908, Margaret Floy Washburn (1871–1939) published *The Animal Mind,* in which she reviewed what was then known about perception,

> **How did behaviourism help psychology advance as a science?**

learning, and memory in different animal species. She argued that nonhuman animals, much like human beings, have conscious mental experiences (Scarborough & Furumoto, 1987). Watson reacted to this claim with venom. Because we cannot ask pigeons about their private, inner experiences (well, we can ask, but they never tell us), Watson decided that the only way to understand how animals learn and adapt was to focus solely on their behaviour, and he suggested that the study of human beings should proceed on the same basis.

Watson was influenced by the work of Russian physiologist Ivan Pavlov (1849–1936), who carried out pioneering research on the physiology of digestion. In the course of that work, Pavlov noticed something interesting about the dogs he was

ARCHIVES OF THE HISTORY OF AMERICAN PSYCHOLOGY

In 1894, Margaret Floy Washburn (1871–1939), a student of Edward Titchener at Cornell, became the first woman to receive a Ph.D. in psychology. Washburn went on to a highly distinguished career, spent mainly in teaching and research at Vassar College in Poughkeepsie, New York. Washburn wrote an influential book, *The Animal Mind,* developed a theory of consciousness, and contributed to the development of psychology as a profession.

# OTHER VOICES

## Is Psychology a Science?

**Timothy Wilson**
Timothy D. Wilson is a professor of psychology at the University of Virginia, and the author of several popular books, including *Redirect: The Surprising New Science of Psychological Change* (2011).

PHOTO BY JEN FARIELLO, COURTESY TIMOTHY D. WILSON

Nobody can dispute that you are taking a course in psychology, but are you taking a science course? Some critics maintain that psychology fails to meet accepted criteria for what constitutes a science. Timothy Wilson, a psychology professor at the University of Virginia, took on the critics by drawing from an appropriate source: the scientific literature (Wilson, 2012).

Once, during a meeting at my university, a biologist mentioned that he was the only faculty member present from a science department. When I corrected him, noting that I was from the Department of Psychology, he waved his hand dismissively, as if I were a Little Leaguer telling a member of the New York Yankees that I too played baseball.

There has long been snobbery in the sciences, with the "hard" ones (physics, chemistry, biology) considering themselves to be more legitimate than the "soft" ones (psychology, sociology). It is thus no surprise that many members of the general public feel the same way. But of late, skepticism about the rigors of social science has reached absurd heights. The U.S. House of Representatives recently voted to eliminate funding for political science research through the National Science Foundation. In the wake of that action, an opinion writer for the *Washington Post* suggested that the House did not go far enough. The NSF should not fund any research in the social sciences, wrote Charles Lane, because "unlike hypotheses in the hard sciences, hypotheses about society usually cannot be proven or disproven by experimentation."

Lane's comments echoed ones by Gary Gutting in the Opinionator blog of the *New York Times*. "While the physical sciences produce many detailed and precise predictions," wrote Gutting, "the social sciences do not. The reason is that such predictions almost always require randomized controlled experiments, which are seldom possible when people are involved."

This is news to me and the many other social scientists who have spent their careers doing carefully controlled experiments on human behaviour, inside and outside the laboratory. What makes the criticism so galling is that those who voice it, or members of their families, have undoubtedly benefited from research in the disciplines they dismiss.

Most of us know someone who has suffered from depression and sought psychotherapy. He or she probably benefited from therapies such as cognitive behavioural therapy that have been shown to work in randomized clinical trials.

Problems such as child abuse and teenage pregnancy take a huge toll on society. Interventions developed by research psychologists, tested with the experimental method, have been found to lower the incidence of child abuse and reduce the rate of teenage pregnancies.

Ever hear of stereotype threat? It is the double jeopardy that people face when they are at risk of confirming a negative stereotype of their group. When African American students take a difficult test, for example, they are concerned not only about how well they will do but also about the possibility that performing poorly will reflect badly on their entire group. This added worry has been shown time and again, in carefully controlled experiments, to lower academic performance. But fortunately, experiments have also showed promising ways to reduce this threat. One intervention, for example, conducted in a middle school, reduced the achievement gap by 40%.

If you know someone who was unlucky enough to be arrested for a crime he did not commit, he may have benefited from social psychological experiments that have resulted in fairer lineups and interrogations, making it less likely that innocent people are convicted.

An often-overlooked advantage of the experimental method is that it can demonstrate what does not work. Consider three popular programs that research psychologists have debunked: Critical Incident Stress Debriefing, used to prevent post-traumatic stress disorders in first responders and others who have witnessed horrific events; the D.A.R.E. anti-drug program, used in many schools throughout America; and Scared Straight programs designed to prevent at-risk teens from engaging in criminal behaviour.

All three of these programs have been shown, with well-designed experimental studies, to be ineffective or, in some cases, to make matters worse. And as a result, the programs have become less popular or have changed their methods. By discovering what does not work, social scientists have saved the public billions of dollars.

To be fair to the critics, social scientists have not always taken advantage of the experimental method as much as they could. Too often, for example, educational programs have been implemented widely without being adequately tested. But increasingly, educational researchers are employing better methodologies. For example, in a recent study, researchers randomly assigned teachers to a program called My Teaching Partner, which is designed to improve teaching skills, or to a control group. Students taught by the teachers who participated in the program did significantly better on achievement tests than did students taught by teachers in the control group.

Are the social sciences perfect? Of course not. Human behaviour is complex, and it is not possible to conduct experiments to test all aspects of what people do or why. There are entire disciplines devoted to the experimental study of human behaviour, however, in tightly controlled, ethically acceptable ways. Many people benefit from the results, including those who, in their ignorance, believe that science is limited to the study of molecules.

Wilson's examples of psychological investigations that have had beneficial effects on society are excellent, but perhaps even more important is his point that much of psychology is based on carefully controlled experimentation using randomization procedures that the critics apparently believe—mistakenly—cannot be applied to the study of human beings. The next chapter in this textbook is devoted to explaining how psychologists apply the scientific method to the study of the mind and behaviour. It should come as no surprise to learn that your textbook authors believe that psychology is indeed a science. But what *kind* of science is psychology? (See the Hot Science box, "Psychology as a hub science," for one approach to this question.) Should psychology strive to come up with general laws like those of physics, or try to make precise predictions like those made by so-called hard sciences? Should psychologists focus on laboratory experimentation or spend more effort attempting to study behaviour in everyday life? What methods seem most promising to you as tools for psychological investigations? There is room for debate about what kind of science psychology is and should be; we hope that you think about these questions as you read this book.

**response**
An action or physiological change elicited by a stimulus.

studying (Fancher, 1979). Not only did the dogs salivate at the sight of food; they also salivated at the sight of the person who fed them. The feeders were not dressed in Purina suits, so why should the mere sight of them trigger a basic digestive response in the dogs? To answer this question, Pavlov developed a procedure in which he sounded a tone every time he fed the dogs, and after a while he observed that the dogs would salivate when they heard the tone alone. In Pavlov's experiments, the sound of the tone was a stimulus (sensory input from the environment) that influenced the salivation of the dogs, which was a **response:** *an action or physiological change elicited by a stimulus.* Watson and other behaviourists made these two notions the building blocks of their theories, which is why behaviourism is sometimes called *stimulus–response* (S–R) psychology.

Watson applied Pavlov's techniques to human infants. In a famous and controversial study, Watson and his student Rosalie Rayner taught an infant known as "Little Albert" to have a strong fear of a harmless white rat (and other white furry animals and toys) that he had previously not feared. Why would they do such a thing? You will learn more about this study in the Learning chapter, but the short answer is this: Watson believed that human behaviour is powerfully influenced by the environment, and the experiments with Little Albert provided a chance to demonstrate such influence at the earliest stage of life. Neither Watson nor later behaviourists believed that the environment was the *only* influence on behaviour (Todd & Morris, 1992), but they did think it was the most important one. Consistent with that view, Watson became romantically involved with someone prominent in his environment: Rosalie Rayner. He refused to end the affair when confronted by colleagues, and the resulting scandal forced Watson to leave his position at Johns Hopkins University. He found work in a New York advertising agency, where he applied behaviourist principles to marketing and advertising (which certainly involves manipulating the environment to influence behaviour!). Watson also wrote popular books that exposed a broad general audience to the behaviourist approach (Watson, 1924, 1928). The result of all these developments—Pavlov's work in the laboratory, Watson and Rayner's applications to humans, and Watson's practical applications to daily life—was that by the 1920s, behaviourism had become a dominant force in scientific psychology.

## B. F. Skinner and the Development of Behaviourism

In 1926 Burrhus Frederick Skinner (1904–1990) finished his undergraduate degree, and could not decide what to do with his life. He aspired to become a writer, and his interest in literature led him indirectly to psychology. Skinner wondered whether a novelist could portray a character without understanding why the character behaved as he or she did, and when he came across Watson's books, he knew he had the answer. Skinner completed his Ph.D. studies in psychology at Harvard (Wiener, 1996) and began to develop a new kind of behaviourism. In Pavlov's experiments, the dogs had been passive participants that stood around, listened to tones, and drooled. Skinner recognized that in everyday life, animals do not just stand there—they do something! Animals *act* on their environments in order to find shelter, food, or mates, and Skinner wondered if he could develop behaviourist principles that would explain how they *learned* to act in those situations.

Skinner built what he called a *conditioning chamber* but what the rest of the world would forever call a *Skinner box*. The box has a lever and a food tray, and a hungry rat could get food delivered to the tray by pressing the lever. Skinner observed that when a rat was put in the box, it would wander around, sniffing and exploring, and would usually press the bar by accident, at which point a food pellet would drop into the tray. After that happened, the rate of bar pressing would increase

> **What did Skinner learn by observing the behaviour of hungry rats?**

Inspired by Watson's behaviourism, B. F. Skinner (1904–1990) investigated the way an animal learns by interacting with its environment. Here, he demonstrates the Skinner box, in which rats learn to press a lever to receive food: The lever press is the learned behaviour and the food is the reinforcement that increases the frequency of future lever pressing.

NINA LEEN/TIME LIFE PICTURES/GETTY IMAGES

dramatically and remain high until the rat was no longer hungry. Skinner saw evidence for what he called the principle of **reinforcement,** which states that *the consequences of a behaviour determine whether it will be more or less likely to occur again.* The concept of reinforcement became the foundation for Skinner's new approach to behaviourism (see the Learning chapter), which he formulated in a landmark book, *The Behavior of Organisms: An Experimental Analysis* (Skinner, 1938).

Skinner set out to use his ideas about reinforcement to help improve the quality of everyday life. He was visiting his daughter's Grade 4 class when he realized that he might be able to improve classroom instruction by breaking a complicated task into small bits and then using the principle of reinforcement to teach children each bit (Bjork, 1993). He developed automatic devices known as *teaching machines* that did exactly that (Skinner, 1958). The teaching machine asked a series of increasingly difficult questions that built on the students' answers to the simpler ones. To learn a complicated mathematics problem, for instance, students would first be asked an easy question about the simplest part of the problem. They would then be told whether the answer was right or wrong, and if a correct response was made, the machine would move on to a more difficult question. Skinner thought that the satisfaction of knowing they were correct would be reinforcing and help students learn.

If Grade 4 students and rats could be successfully trained, then why stop there? In the controversial books, *Beyond Freedom and Dignity* (1971) and *Walden II* (1948/1986), Skinner laid out his vision of a utopian society in which behaviour was controlled by the judicious application of the principle of reinforcement (Skinner, 1971). In those books, he put forth the simple but stunning claim that our subjective sense of free will is an illusion and that when we think we are exercising free will, we are actually responding to present and past patterns of reinforcement. We do things in the present that have been rewarding in the past, and our sense of "choosing" to do them is nothing more than an illusion. In this, Skinner echoed the sentiments of philosopher Benedict Spinoza (1632–1677), who several centuries earlier had noted that "men are deceived in thinking themselves free, a belief that consists only in this, that they are conscious of their actions and ignorant of the causes by which they are determined. As to their saying that human actions depend on the will, these are mere words without any corresponding idea" (1677/1982, p. 86).

Skinner argued that his insights could be used to increase human well-being and solve social problems. Not surprisingly, that claim sparked an outcry from critics who believed that Skinner was giving away one of our most cherished attributes—free will—and calling for a repressive society that manipulated people for its own ends. The criticism even extended to *TV Guide,* which featured an interview with Skinner and called his ideas "the taming of mankind through a system of dog obedience schools for all" (Bjork, 1993, p. 201). Given the nature of Skinner's ideas, the critics' attacks were understandable—he had seriously underestimated how much people cherish the idea of free will—but in the sober light of hindsight, they were clearly overblown. Skinner did not want to turn society into a "dog obedience school" or strip people of their personal freedoms. Rather, he argued that an understanding of the principles by which behaviour is generated could be used to increase the social welfare, which is precisely what happens when a government launches advertisements to encourage citizens to eat healthy or quit smoking. The result of all the controversy, however, was that Skinner's fame reached a level rarely attained by psychologists. A popular magazine that listed the 100 most important people who ever lived ranked Skinner just 39 points below Jesus Christ (Herrnstein, 1977).

**? Which of Skinner's claims provoked an outcry?**

**reinforcement**
The consequences of a behaviour determine whether it will be more or less likely to occur again.

Skinner's well-publicized questioning of such cherished notions as free will led to a rumour that he had raised his own daughter in a Skinner box. This urban legend, while untrue, likely originated from the climate-controlled, glass-encased crib that he invented to protect his daughter from the cold Minnesota winter. Skinner marketed the crib under various names, including the "Air-crib" and the "Heir Conditioner," but it failed to catch on with parents.

BETTMANN/CORBIS

IN SUMMARY

▶ Behaviourism advocated the study of observable actions and responses, and held that inner mental processes were private events that could not be studied scientifically. Ivan Pavlov and John B. Watson studied the association between a stimulus and a response, and emphasized the importance of the environment in shaping behaviour.

▶ Influenced by Watson's behaviourism, B. F. Skinner developed the concept of reinforcement using a Skinner box. He demonstrated that animals and humans repeat behaviours that generate pleasant results and avoid performing those that generate unpleasant results. Skinner extended Watson's contentions about the importance of the environment in shaping behaviour by suggesting that free will is an illusion and that the principle of reinforcement can be used to benefit society.

# Return of the Mind: Psychology Expands

Watson, Skinner, and the behaviourists dominated psychology from the 1930s to the 1950s. Psychologist Ulric Neisser recalled the atmosphere when he was a student in the early 1950s:

> Behaviorism was the basic framework for almost all of psychology at the time. It was what you had to learn. That was the age when it was supposed that no psychological phenomenon was real unless you could demonstrate it in a rat. (quoted in Baars, 1986, p. 275)

Behaviourism would not dominate the field for much longer, however, and Neisser himself would play an important role in developing an alternative perspective. Why was behaviourism replaced? Although behaviourism allowed psychologists to measure, predict, and control behaviour, it did this by ignoring some important things. First, it ignored the mental processes that had fascinated psychologists such as Wundt and James and, in so doing, found itself unable to explain some very important phenomena, such as how children learn language. Second, it ignored the evolutionary history of the organisms it studied and was thus unable to explain why, for example, a rat could learn to associate nausea with food much more quickly than it could learn to associate nausea with a tone or a light. As we will see, the approaches that ultimately replaced behaviourism met these kinds of problems head-on.

## The Pioneers of Cognitive Psychology

Even at the height of behaviourist domination, there were a few revolutionaries whose research and writings were focused on mental processes. German psychologist Max Wertheimer (1880–1943) focused on the study of **illusions,** *errors of perception, memory, or judgment in which subjective experience differs from objective reality.* In one

What do you see when you look at this image? Why do you see more than just random markings?

of Wertheimer's experiments, a person was shown two lights that flashed quickly on a screen, one after the other. One light was flashed through a vertical slit, the other through a diagonal slit. When the time between two flashes was relatively long (one fifth of a second or more), an observer would see that it was just two lights flashing in alternation. But when Wertheimer reduced the time between flashes to around one twentieth of a second, observers saw a single flash of light moving back and forth (Fancher, 1979; Sarris, 1989). Wertheimer reasoned that the perceived motion could not be explained in terms of the separate elements that cause the illusion (the two flashing lights) but instead that the moving flash of light is perceived as a *whole* rather than as the sum of its two parts. This unified whole, which in German is called *Gestalt,* makes up the perceptual experience. Wertheimer's interpretation of the illusion led to the development of **Gestalt psychology,** *a psychological approach that emphasizes that we often perceive the whole rather than the sum of the parts.* In other words, the mind imposes organization on what it perceives, so people do not see what the experimenter actually shows them (two separate lights); instead, they see the elements as a unified whole (one moving light).

> **Why might people not see what an experimenter actually showed them?**

Another pioneer who focused on the mind was Sir Frederic Bartlett (1886–1969), a British psychologist interested in memory. Bartlett was dissatisfied with existing research, especially the research of German psychologist Hermann Ebbinghaus (1850–1909), who had performed groundbreaking experiments on memory in 1885 (described in the Memory chapter). Serving as his own research subject, Ebbinghaus tried to discover how quickly and how well he could memorize and recall meaningless information, such as the three-letter nonsense syllables *dap, kir,* and *sul.* Bartlett believed that it was more important to examine memory for the kinds of information people actually encounter in everyday life, so he gave people stories to remember and carefully observed the kinds of errors they made when they tried to recall them at a later time (Bartlett, 1932). Bartlett discovered many interesting things that Ebbinghaus could never have learned with his nonsense syllables. For example, he found that research participants often remembered what *should* have happened or what they *expected* to happen rather than what actually *did* happen. These and other errors led Bartlett to suggest that memory is not a photographic reproduction of past experience and that our attempts to recall the past are powerfully influenced by our knowledge, beliefs, hopes, aspirations, and desires.

Jean Piaget (1896–1980) was a Swiss psychologist who studied the perceptual and cognitive errors of children in order to gain insight into the nature and development of the human mind. For example, in one of his tasks, Piaget gave a 3-year-old a large and a small mound of clay and told the child to make the two mounds equal. Then Piaget broke one of the clay mounds into smaller pieces and asked the child which mound now had more clay. Although the amount of clay remained the same, of course, 3-year-olds usually said that the mound that was broken into smaller pieces was bigger, but

**illusions**
Errors of perception, memory, or judgment in which subjective experience differs from objective reality.

**Gestalt psychology**
A psychological approach that emphasizes that we often perceive the whole rather than the sum of the parts.

BILL ANDERSON/SCIENCE SOURCE

Jean Piaget (1896–1980) studied and theorized about the developing mental lives of children. How were his methods a marked departure from the methods of the behaviourists?

This 1950s computer was among the first generation of digital computers. How was the computer analogy helpful in the early days of cognitive psychology?

Kurt Lewin argued that people react to the world as they see it and not to the world as it is.

by the age of 6 or 7, they no longer made this error. As you will see in the Development chapter, Piaget theorized that younger children lack a particular cognitive ability that allows older children to appreciate the fact that the mass of an object remains constant even when it is divided. For Piaget, errors such as these provided key insights into the mental world of the child (Piaget & Inhelder, 1969).

German psychologist Kurt Lewin (1890–1947) was also a pioneer in the study of thought at a time when thought had been banished from psychology. Lewin (1936) argued that a person's behaviour in the world could be predicted best by understanding the person's subjective experience of the world. A television soap opera is a meaningless series of unrelated physical movements unless one thinks about the characters' experiences (how Karen feels about Bruce; what Van was planning to say to Kathy about Emily; whether Linda's sister, Nancy, will always hate their mother for meddling in her marriage; etc.). Lewin realized that it was not the stimulus, but rather the person's *construal* of the stimulus, that determined the person's subsequent behaviour. A pinch on the cheek can be pleasant or unpleasant depending on who administers it, under what circumstances, and to which set of cheeks. Lewin used a special kind of mathematics called *topology* to model the person's subjective experience, and although his topological theories were not particularly influential, his attempts to model mental life and his insistence that psychologists study how people construe their worlds would have a lasting impact on psychology.

But, aside from a handful of pioneers such as these, psychologists happily ignored mental processes until the 1950s, when something important happened: the computer. The advent of computers had enormous practical impact, of course, but it also had an enormous conceptual impact on psychology. People and computers differ in important ways, but both seem to register, store, and retrieve information, leading psychologists to wonder whether the computer might be useful as a model for the human

> How did the advent of computers change psychology?

mind. Computers are information-processing systems, and the flow of information through their circuits is clearly no fairy tale. If psychologists could think of mental events—such as remembering, attending, thinking, believing, evaluating, feeling, and assessing—as the flow of information through the mind, then they might be able to study the mind scientifically after all. The emergence of the computer led to a re-emergence of interest in mental processes all across the discipline of psychology, and spawned a new approach called **cognitive psychology,** *the scientific study of mental processes, including perception, thought, memory, and reasoning.*

## Technology and the Development of Cognitive Psychology

Although the contributions of psychologists such as Wertheimer, Bartlett, Piaget, and Lewin provided early alternatives to behaviourism, they did not depose it. That job required the Army. During World War II, the military turned to psychologists to help understand how soldiers could best learn to use new technologies, such as radar. Radar operators had to pay close attention to their screens for long periods while trying to decide whether blips were friendly aircraft, enemy aircraft, or flocks of wild geese in need of a good chasing (Ashcraft, 1998; Lachman, Lachman, & Butterfield, 1979).

How could radar operators be trained to make quicker and more accurate decisions? The answer to this question clearly required more than the swift delivery of pellets to the radar operator's food tray. It required that those who designed the equipment think about and talk about cognitive processes, such as perception, attention, identification, memory, and decision making. Behaviourism solved the problem by denying it, so some psychologists decided to deny behaviourism and forge ahead with a new approach.

British psychologist Donald Broadbent (1926–1993) was among the first to study what happens when people try to pay attention to several things at once. For instance,

**What did psychologists learn from pilots during World War II?**

Broadbent observed that pilots cannot attend to many different instruments at once and must actively move the focus of their attention from one to another (Best, 1992). Broadbent (1958) showed that the limited capacity to handle incoming information is a fundamental feature of human cognition and that this limit could explain many of the errors that pilots (and other people) made. At about the same time, American psychologist George Miller (1956) pointed out a striking consistency in our capacity limitations across a variety of situations: We can pay attention to, and briefly hold in memory, about seven (give or take two) pieces of information. Cognitive psychologists began conducting experiments and devising theories to better understand the mind's limited capacity, a problem that behaviourists had ignored.

As you have already read, the invention of the computer in the 1950s had a profound impact on psychologists' thinking. A computer is made of hardware (e.g., chips and disk drives today; magnetic tapes and vacuum tubes a half-century ago) and software (stored on optical disks today; on punch cards a half-century ago). If the brain is roughly analogous to the computer's hardware, then perhaps the mind was roughly analogous to a software program. This line of thinking led cognitive psychologists to begin writing computer programs to see what kinds of software could be made to mimic human speech and behaviour (Newell, Shaw, & Simon, 1958).

Ironically, the emergence of cognitive psychology was also energized by the appearance of B. F. Skinner's (1957) book, *Verbal Behaviour,* which offered a behaviourist analysis of language. A linguist at the Massachusetts Institute of Technology (MIT), Noam Chomsky (b. 1928), published a devastating critique of the book in which he argued that Skinner's insistence on observable behaviour had caused him to miss some of the most important features of language. According to Chomsky, language relies on mental rules that allow people to understand and produce novel words and sentences. The ability of even the youngest child to generate new sentences that he or she had never heard before flew in the face of the behaviourist claim that children learn to use language by reinforcement. Chomsky provided a clever, detailed, and thoroughly cognitive account of language that could explain many of the phenomena that the behaviourist account could not (Chomsky, 1959).

These developments during the 1950s set the stage for an explosion of cognitive studies during the 1960s. Cognitive psychologists did not return to the old introspective procedures used during the nineteenth century, but instead developed new and ingenious methods that allowed them to study cognitive processes. The excitement of the new approach was summarized in a landmark book, *Cognitive Psychology,* written by someone you met earlier in this chapter, Ulric Neisser. Neisser's (1967) book provided a foundation for the development of cognitive psychology, which grew and thrived in the years that followed.

**cognitive psychology**
The scientific study of mental processes, including perception, thought, memory, and reasoning.

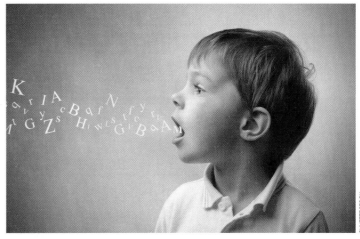

Noam Chomsky (b. 1928) pointed out that even young children generate sentences they have never heard before, and therefore could not possibly be learning language by reinforcement. This critique of Skinner's theory signalled the end of behaviourism's dominance in psychology and helped spark the development of cognitive psychology.

SHUTTERSTOCK

**behavioural neuroscience**
An approach to psychology that links psychological processes to activities in the nervous system and other bodily processes.

# The Brain Meets the Mind:
# The Rise of Cognitive Neuroscience

If cognitive psychologists studied the software of the mind, they had little to say about the hardware of the brain. And yet, as any computer scientist knows, the relationship between software and hardware is crucial: Each element needs the other to get the job done. Our mental activities often seem so natural and effortless—noticing the shape of an object, using words in speech or writing, recognizing a face as familiar—that we fail to appreciate the fact that they depend on intricate operations carried out by the brain. This dependence is revealed by dramatic cases in which damage to a particular part of the brain causes a person to lose a specific cognitive ability. Recall that in the nineteenth century, French physician Paul Broca described a patient who, after damage to a limited area in the left side of the brain, could not produce words, even though he could understand them perfectly well. As you will see later in the book, damage to other parts of the brain can also result in syndromes that are characterized by the loss of specific mental abilities (e.g., prosopagnosia, in which the person cannot recognize human faces) or by the emergence of bizarre behaviour or beliefs (e.g., Capgras syndrome, in which the person believes that a close family member has been replaced by an imposter). These striking—sometimes startling—cases remind us that even the simplest cognitive processes depend on the brain.

Karl Lashley (1890–1958), a psychologist who studied with John B. Watson, conducted a famous series of studies in which he trained rats to run mazes, surgically removed parts of their brains, and then measured how well they could run the maze again. Lashley hoped to find the precise spot in the brain where *learning* occurred. Alas, no one spot seemed to uniquely and reliably eliminate learning (Lashley, 1960). Rather, Lashley simply found that the more of the rat's brain he removed, the more poorly the rat ran the maze. Lashley was frustrated by his inability to identify a specific site of learning, but his efforts inspired other scientists to take up the challenge. They developed a research area called *physiological psychology*. Today, this area has grown into **behavioural neuroscience,** *an approach to psychology that links psychological processes to activities in the nervous system and other bodily processes.* To learn about the relationship between brain and behaviour, behavioural neuroscientists observe animals' responses as the animals perform specially constructed tasks, such as running through a maze to obtain food rewards. The neuroscientists can record electrical or chemical responses in the brain as the task is being performed, or later remove specific parts of the brain to see how performance is affected.

Of course, experimental brain surgery cannot ethically be performed on human beings; thus, psychologists who want to study the human brain often have to rely on nature's cruel and inexact experiments. Birth defects, accidents, and illnesses often cause damage to particular brain regions and, if that damage disrupts a particular ability, then psychologists deduce that the region is involved in producing the ability. For example, in the Memory chapter you will learn about a patient whose memory was virtually eliminated by damage to a specific part of the brain, and you will see how this tragedy provided scientists with remarkable clues about how memories are stored (Scoville & Milner, 1957). Fortunately in the late 1980s, technological breakthroughs led to the development of noninvasive brain scanning techniques that made it possible for psychologists to watch what happens inside a human brain as a person performs a task such as reading, imagining, listening, and remembering. Brain scanning is an invaluable tool because it allows us to observe the brain in action and to see which parts are involved in which operations (see the Neuroscience and Behaviour chapter).

For example, researchers used scanning technology to identify the parts of the brain in the left hemisphere that are involved in specific aspects of language, such as understanding or producing words (Peterson et al., 1989). Later scanning studies showed that people who are deaf from birth, but who learn to communicate using

American Sign Language (ASL), rely on regions in the right hemisphere (as well as the left) when using ASL. In contrast, people with normal hearing who learned ASL after puberty seemed to rely only on the left hemisphere when using ASL (Newman et al., 2002). These findings suggest that although both spoken and signed language usually rely on the left hemisphere, the right hemisphere also can become involved—but only for a limited period (perhaps until puberty). The findings also provide a nice example of how psychologists can now use scanning techniques to observe people with various kinds of cognitive capacities and use their observations to unravel the mysteries of the mind and the brain (see **FIGURE 1.2**). In fact, there is a name for this area of research. **Cognitive neuroscience** is the *field of study that attempts to understand the links between cognitive processes and brain activity* (Gazzaniga, 2000).

> **What have we learned by watching the brain at work?**

## The Adaptive Mind: The Emergence of Evolutionary Psychology

Psychology's renewed interest in mental processes and its growing interest in the brain were two developments that led psychologists away from behaviourism. A third development also pointed them in a different direction. Recall that one of behaviourism's key claims was that organisms are blank slates on which experience writes its lessons, and hence any one lesson should be as easily written as another. But in experiments conducted during the 1960s and 1970s, psychologist John Garcia and his colleagues showed that rats can learn to associate nausea with the smell of food much more quickly than they can learn to associate nausea with a flashing light (Garcia, 1981). Why should this be? In the real world of forests, sewers, and garbage cans, nausea is usually caused by spoiled food and not by lightning, and although these particular rats had been born in a laboratory and had never left their cages, millions of years of evolution had prepared their brains to learn the natural association more quickly than the artificial one. In other words, it was not only the rat's learning history but the rat's *ancestors'* learning histories that determined the rat's ability to learn.

Although that fact was at odds with the behaviourist doctrine, it was the credo for a new kind of psychology. **Evolutionary psychology** *explains mind and behaviour in terms of the adaptive value of abilities that are preserved over time by natural selection.* Evolutionary psychology has its roots in Charles Darwin's theory of natural selection, which, as we saw earlier, holds that the features of an organism that help it survive and reproduce are more likely than other features to be passed on to subsequent generations.

**cognitive neuroscience**
The field of study that attempts to understand the links between cognitive processes and brain activity.

**evolutionary psychology**
A psychological approach that explains mind and behaviour in terms of the adaptive value of abilities that are preserved over time by natural selection.

ROGER RESSMEYER/CORBIS

◄ Figure **1.2** **PET Scans of Healthy and Alzheimer's Brains** PET scans are one of a variety of brain imaging technologies that psychologists use to observe the living brain. The four brain images on the top each come from a person suffering from Alzheimer's disease; the four on the bottom each come from a healthy person of similar age. The red and green areas reflect higher levels of brain activity compared to the blue areas, which reflect lower levels of activity. In each image, the front of the brain is on the top and the back of the brain is on the bottom. You can see that the person with Alzheimer's disease, compared with the healthy person, shows more extensive areas of lowered activity toward the front of the brain.

HULTON ARCHIVE/GETTY IMAGES

In 1925, schoolteacher John Scopes was arrested for teaching students about Darwin's theory of evolution. Today, that theory is the centrepiece of modern biology—and of evolutionary psychology.

This theory inspired the functionalist approaches of William James and G. Stanley Hall because it led them to focus on how mental abilities help people to solve problems and therefore increase their chances of survival. But it is only since the publication in 1975 of *Sociobiology,* by the biologist E. O. Wilson, that evolutionary thinking has had an identifiable presence in psychology. That presence is steadily increasing (Buss, 1999; Pinker, 1997a, 1997b; Tooby & Cosmides, 2000). Evolutionary psychologists think of the mind as a collection of specialized "modules" that are designed to solve the human problems our ancestors faced as they attempted to eat, mate, and reproduce over millions of years. According to evolutionary psychology, the brain is not an all-purpose computer that can do or learn one thing just as easily as it can do or learn another; rather, it is a computer that was built to do a few things well and everything else not at all. It is a computer that comes with a small suite of built-in applications that are designed to do the things that previous versions of that computer needed to have done.

Consider, for example, how evolutionary psychology treats the emotion of jealousy. All of us who have been in romantic relationships have experienced jealousy, if only because we noticed our partner noticing someone else. Jealousy can be a powerful, overwhelming emotion that we might wish to avoid but, according to evolutionary psychology, it exists today because it once served an adaptive function. If some of our hominid ancestors experienced jealousy and others did not, then the ones who experienced it might have been more likely to guard their mates and threaten their rivals and thus may have been more likely to reproduce their "jealous genes" (Buss, 2000, 2007; Buss & Haselton, 2005).

Critics of the evolutionary approach point out that many traits of modern humans and other animals probably evolved to serve different functions than those they currently serve. For example, biologists believe that the feathers of birds probably evolved initially to perform such functions as regulating body temperature or capturing prey and only later served the entirely different function of flight. Likewise, people are reasonably adept at learning to drive a car, but nobody would argue that such an ability is the result of natural selection; the learning abilities that allow us to become skilled car drivers must have evolved for purposes other than driving cars.

Complications such as these have led the critics to wonder how evolutionary hypotheses can ever be tested (Coyne, 2000; Sterelny & Griffiths, 1999). We do not have a record of our ancestors' thoughts, feelings, and actions, and fossils will not provide much information about the evolution of mind and behaviour. Testing ideas about the evolutionary origins of psychological phenomena is indeed a challenging task, but not an impossible one (Buss et al., 1998; Pinker, 1997a, 1997b).

Start with the assumption that evolutionary adaptations should also increase reproductive success. So, if a specific trait or feature has been favoured by natural selection, it should be possible to find some evidence of this in the numbers of offspring that are produced by the trait's bearers. Consider, for instance, the hypothesis that men tend to have deep voices because women prefer to mate with baritones rather than sopranos. To investigate this hypothesis, researchers studied a group of modern hunter-gatherers, the Hadza people of Tanzania. Consistent with the evolutionary hypothesis, they found that the pitch of a man's voice did indeed predict how many children he would have, but the pitch of a woman's voice did not (Apicella, Feinberg, & Marlowe, 2007). This kind of study provides evidence that allows evolutionary psychologists to test their ideas. Not every evolutionary hypothesis can be tested, of course, but evolutionary psychologists are becoming increasingly inventive in their attempts.

What evidence suggests that some traits can be inherited?

© JUNIORS BILDARCHIV GMBH/ALAMY

Behaviourists explain behaviour in terms of organisms learning to make particular responses that are paired with reinforcement (and to avoid responses that are paired with punishment). Evolutionary psychology focuses on how abilities are preserved over time if they contribute to an organism's ability to survive and reproduce. How might a proponent of each approach explain the fact that a rat placed in an unfamiliar environment will tend to stay in dark corners and avoid brightly lit open areas?

## IN SUMMARY

▶ Psychologists such as Max Wertheimer, Frederic Bartlett, Jean Piaget, and Kurt Lewin defied the behaviourist doctrine and studied the inner workings of the mind. Their efforts, as well as those of later pioneers such as Donald Broadbent, paved the way for cognitive psychology to focus on inner mental processes such as perception, attention, memory, and reasoning.

▶ Cognitive psychology developed as a field due to the invention of the computer, psychologists efforts to improve the performance of the military, and Noam Chomsky's theories about language.

▶ Cognitive neuroscience attempts to link the brain with the mind by studying individuals with brain damage (connecting the area damaged with the loss of specific abilities) and individuals without brain damage, using brain scanning techniques.

▶ Evolutionary psychology focuses on the adaptive function that minds and brains serve and seeks to understand the nature and origin of psychological processes in terms of natural selection.

# Beyond the Individual:
# Social and Cultural Perspectives

The picture we have painted so far may vaguely suggest a scene from some 1950s science-fiction film in which the protagonist is a living brain that thinks, feels, hopes, and worries while suspended in a vat of pink jelly in a basement laboratory. Although psychologists often do focus on the brain and the mind of the individual, they have not lost sight of the fact that human beings are fundamentally social animals who are part of a vast network of family, friends, teachers, and co-workers. Trying to understand people in the absence of that fact is a bit like trying to understand an ant or a bee without considering the function and influence of the colony or hive. People are the most important and most complex organisms that we ever encounter; thus it is not surprising that our behaviour is strongly influenced by their presence—or their absence. The two areas of psychology that most strongly emphasize these facts are social and cultural psychology.

## The Development of Social Psychology

**Social psychology** is *the study of the causes and consequences of sociality.* As this definition suggests, social psychologists address a remarkable variety of topics. Historians trace the birth of social psychology to an experiment conducted in 1895 by psychologist and bicycle enthusiast Norman Triplett, who noticed that cyclists seemed to ride faster when they rode with others. Intrigued by this observation, he conducted an experiment that showed that children reeled in a fishing line faster when tested in the presence of other children than when tested alone. Triplett was not trying to improve the fishing abilities of children, of course, but rather was trying to show that the mere presence of other people can influence performance on even the most mundane kinds of tasks.

Social psychology's development began in earnest in the 1930s and was driven by several historical events. The rise of Nazism led many of Germany's most talented scientists to immigrate to America, and among them were psychologists such as Solomon Asch (1907–1996) and Kurt Lewin. These psychologists had been strongly influenced by Gestalt psychology, which you will recall held that "the whole is greater than the sum of its parts," and though the Gestaltists had been talking about the visual

**social psychology**
The study of the causes and consequences of sociality.

perception of objects, these psychologists felt that the phrase also captured a basic truth about the relationship between social groups and the individuals who constitute them. Philosophers had speculated about the nature of sociality for thousands of years, and political scientists, economists, anthropologists, and sociologists had been studying social life scientifically for some time. But these German émigrés were the first to generate theories of social behaviour that resembled the theories generated by natural scientists and, more importantly, they were the first to conduct experiments to test their social theories. For example, Lewin (1936) adopted the language of mid-century physics to develop a "field theory" that viewed social behaviour as the product of "internal forces" (such as personality, goals, and beliefs) and "external forces" (such as social pressure and culture), whereas Asch (1946) performed laboratory experiments to examine the "mental chemistry" that allows people to combine small bits of information about another person into a full impression of that person's personality.

> **How did historical events influence the development of social psychology?**

Other historical events also shaped social psychology in its early years. For example, the Holocaust brought the problems of conformity and obedience into sharp focus, leading psychologists such as Asch (1956) and others to examine the conditions under which people can influence each other to think and act in inhuman or irrational ways. The civil rights movement and the rising tensions between African Americans and white Americans led psychologists such as Gordon Allport (1897–1967) to study stereotyping, prejudice, and racism, and to shock the world of psychology by suggesting that prejudice was the result of a perceptual error that was every bit as natural and unavoidable as an optical illusion (Allport, 1954). Allport argued that the same perceptual processes that allow us to efficiently categorize elements of our social and physical world allow us to erroneously categorize entire groups of people. Social psychologists today study a wider variety of topics (from social memory to social relationships) and use a wider variety of techniques (from opinion polls to neuroimaging) than did their forebears, but this field of psychology remains dedicated to understanding the brain as a social organ, the mind as a social adaptation, and the individual as a social creature.

AP PHOTO/AHN YOUNG-JOON

Social psychology studies how the thoughts, feelings, and behaviours of individuals can be influenced by the presence of others. Members of the Reverend Sun Myung Moon's Unification Church are often married to one another in ceremonies of 10 000 people or more; in some cases couples do not know each other before the wedding begins. Social and religious movements such as this have the power to sway individuals.

## The Emergence of Cultural Psychology

North Americans and Western Europeans are sometimes surprised to realize that most of the people on the planet are members of neither culture. Although we are all more alike than we are different, there is nonetheless considerable diversity within the human species in social practices, customs, and ways of living. Culture refers to the values, traditions, and beliefs that are shared by a particular group of people. Although we usually think of culture in terms of nationality and ethnic groups, cultures can also be defined by age (youth culture), sexual orientation (gay culture), religion (Jewish culture), or occupation (academic culture). **Cultural psychology** is *the study of how cultures reflect and shape the psychological processes of their members* (Shweder & Sullivan, 1993). Cultural psychologists study a wide range of phenomena, ranging from visual perception to social interaction, as they seek to understand which of these phenomena are universal and which vary from place to place and time to time.

Perhaps surprisingly, one of the first psychologists to pay attention to the influence of culture was someone recognized today for pioneering the development of experimental psychology, Wilhelm Wundt. He believed that a complete psychology would have to combine a laboratory approach with a broader cultural perspective (Wundt,

**cultural psychology**
The study of how cultures reflect and shape the psychological processes of their members.

1900–1920). But Wundt's ideas failed to spark much interest from other psychologists, who had their hands full trying to make sense of results from laboratory experiments and formulating general laws of human behaviour. Outside of psychology, anthropologists such as Margaret Mead (1901–1978) and Gregory Bateson (1904–1980) attempted to understand the workings of culture by travelling to far-flung regions of the world and carefully observing child-rearing patterns, rituals, religious ceremonies, and the like. Such studies revealed practices—some bizarre from a North American perspective—that served important functions in a culture, such as the painful ritual of violent body mutilation and bloodletting in mountain tribes of New Guinea, which initiates young boys into training to become warriors (Mead, 1935/1968; Read, 1965).

Yet, at the time, most anthropologists paid as little attention to psychology as psychologists did to anthropology. Cultural psychology only began to emerge as a strong force in psychology during the 1980s and 1990s, when psychologists and anthropologists began to communicate with each other about their ideas and methods (Stigler, Shweder, & Herdt, 1990).

> **How did anthropologists influence psychology in the 1980s?**

It was then that psychologists rediscovered Wundt as an intellectual ancestor of this area of the field (Jahoda, 1993).

Physicists assume that $E = mc^2$ whether the $m$ is located in Moosejaw, Moscow, or the Orion Nebula. Chemists assume that water is made of hydrogen and oxygen, and that it was made of hydrogen and oxygen in 1609 as well. The laws of physics and chemistry are assumed to be universal, and for much of psychology's history, the same assumption was made about the principles that govern human behaviour (Shweder, 1991). *Absolutism* holds that culture makes little or no difference for most psychological phenomena, that "honesty is honesty and depression is depression, no matter where one observes it" (Segall, Lonner, & Berry, 1998, p. 1103). And yet, as any world traveller knows, cultures differ in exciting, delicious, and frightening ways, and things that are true of people in one culture are not necessarily true of people in another. John Berry (of Queen's University) and his colleagues maintain that *relativism* holds that psychological phenomena are likely to vary considerably across cultures and should be viewed only in the context of a specific culture (Berry et al., 1992). Although depression is observed in nearly every culture, the symptoms associated with it vary dramatically from one place to another. For example, in Western cultures there is greater emphasis on cognitive symptoms such as worthlessness, whereas in Eastern cultures there is greater focus on somatic symptoms such as fatigue and body aches (Draguns & Tanaka-Matsumi, 2003).

The symptoms of some mental disorders can be reported differently across different cultures. Cultural psychology studies the similarities and differences in psychological processes that arise between people living in different cultures.

Today, most cultural psychologists fall somewhere between these two extremes. Most psychological phenomena can be influenced by culture, some are completely determined by it, and others seem to be entirely unaffected. For example, the age of a person's earliest memory differs dramatically across cultures (MacDonald, Uesiliana, & Hayne, 2000), whereas judgments of facial attractiveness do not (Cunningham et al., 1995). As noted when we discussed evolutionary psychology, it seems likely that the most universal phenomena are those that are closely associated with the basic biology that all human beings share. Conversely, the least universal phenomena are those rooted in the varied socialization practices that different cultures evolve. Of course, the only way to determine whether a phenomenon is variable or constant across cultures is to design research to investigate these

> **Why are psychological conclusions so often relative to the person, place, or culture described?**

# CULTURE & COMMUNITY

### Analytic and Holistic Styles in Western and Eastern Cultures

The study of cultural influences on mind and behaviour has increased dramatically over the past decade. An especially intriguing line of research has revealed differences in how the world is viewed by people from Western cultures such as North America and Europe, and Eastern cultures such as China, Japan, Korea, and other Asian countries. One of the most consistently observed differences is that people from Western cultures tend to adopt an *analytic* style of processing information, focusing on an object or person without paying much attention to the surrounding context, whereas people from Eastern cultures tend to adopt a *holistic* style that emphasizes the relationship between an object or person and the surrounding context (Nisbett & Miyamoto, 2005).

This difference is illustrated nicely by a study in which American and Japanese participants performed a novel task, called the *framed-line test*, which assesses how well an individual incorporates or ignores contextual information when making a judgment about a simple line stimulus (Kitayama et al., 2003). As shown in the accompanying figure, participants saw a line inside a square. They were asked to draw the line again in a new square, either to exactly the same length as the original stimulus (the absolute task), or so that the length of the line in the new square was in the same proportion to the height of its frame as the length of the original line relative to the height of the original frame (the relative task). The absolute task engages analytic processing, whereas the relative task draws on holistic processing. The researchers found that American participants living in the United States were more accurate on the absolute task than on the relative task, whereas Japanese participants living in Japan were more accurate on the relative task than on the absolute task. Interestingly, Americans living in Japan performed more like Japanese participants, and Japanese living in the United States performed more like American participants. While we do not yet know how long it takes for a culture to produce a shift from an analytic style to a holistic style or vice versa, research on cultural influences continues to develop rapidly and we are even beginning to obtain some clues about how differences between individuals from Eastern and Western cultures are realized in the brain (Kitayama & Uskul, 2011).

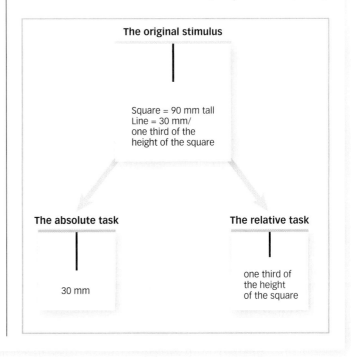

The original stimulus

Square = 90 mm tall
Line = 30 mm/
one third of the
height of the square

The absolute task

30 mm

The relative task

one third of
the height
of the square

possibilities, and cultural psychologists do just that (Cole, 1996; Segall et al., 1998). We will highlight the work of cultural psychologists throughout the text and in Culture & Community boxes like the one in this section concerning cultural differences in analytic and holistic styles of processing information.

## IN SUMMARY

▶ Social psychology recognizes that people exist as part of a network of other people and examines how individuals influence and interact with one another. Social psychology was pioneered by German émigrés, such as Kurt Lewin, who were motivated by a desire to address social issues and problems.

▶ Cultural psychology is concerned with the effects of the broader culture on individuals and with similarities and differences among people in different cultures. Within this perspective, absolutists hold that culture has little impact on most psychological phenomena, whereas relativists believe that culture has a powerful effect.

▶ Together, social and cultural psychology help expand the discipline's horizons beyond just an examination of individuals. These areas of psychology examine behaviour within the broader context of human interaction.

# The Profession of Psychology: Past and Present

If ever you find yourself on an airplane with an annoying seatmate who refuses to let you read your magazine, there are two things you can do. First, you can turn to the person and say in a calm and friendly voice, "Did you know that I am covered with strange and angry bacteria?" If that seems a bit extreme, you might instead try saying, "Did you know that I am a psychologist, and I am forming an evaluation of you as you speak?" as this will usually eliminate the problem without getting you arrested. The truth is that most people do not really know what psychology is or what psychologists do, but they do have some vague sense that it is not wise to talk to one. Now that you have been briefly acquainted with psychology's past, let us consider its present by looking at psychology as a profession. We will look first at the origins of psychology's professional organizations, next at the contexts in which psychologists tend to work, and finally at the kinds of training required to become a psychologist.

## Psychologists Band Together: Psychological Associations

You will recall that when we last saw William James, he was wandering around the greater Boston area, expounding the virtues of the new science of psychology. In July 1892, James and five other psychologists travelled to Clark University to attend a meeting called by G. Stanley Hall. Each worked at a large university where they taught psychology courses, performed research, and wrote textbooks. Although they were too few to make up a jury or even a respectable hockey team, these seven men decided that it was time to form an organization that represented psychology as a profession, and on that day the American Psychological Association (APA) was born. The seven psychologists could scarcely have imagined that today their little club would grow to have more than 150 000 members from all over the world. Although all of the original members were employed by universities or colleges, today academic psychologists make up only 20 percent of the membership, whereas nearly 70 percent of the members work in clinical and health-related settings. Because the APA is no longer as focused on academic psychology as it once was, the American Psychological Society (APS) was formed in 1988 by 450 academic psychologists who wanted an organization that focused specifically on the needs of psychologists carrying out scientific research. The APS, renamed the Association for Psychological Science in 2006, grew quickly, attracting 5000 members within 6 months; today it numbers nearly 12 000 psychologists. Although many Canadians belong to both the APA and the APS, Canada also has the Canadian Psychological Association (CPA; like the APA) and the Canadian Society for Brain, Behaviour and Cognitive Science (CSBBCS) for psychologists oriented toward scientific research. Finally, the Canadian Association for Neuroscience–association canadienne de neuroscience (CAN-ACN) is a rapidly growing society of neuroscientists, including many psychologists.

### The Growing Role of Women and Minorities

In 1892, the APA had 31 members, all of whom were white and all of whom were male. Today, about half of all CPA and APA members are women, and the percentage of non-white members continues to grow. Surveys of recent Ph.D. (doctor of philosophy) recipients reveal a picture of increasing diversification in the field. The proportion of women receiving Ph.D.s in psychology increased from only 15 percent in 1950 to 70 percent in 2010

How has the face of psychology changed as the field has evolved?

Donald Olding Hebb (1904–1985) was a Canadian psychologist whose work has had a profound impact on cognitive neuroscience. He studied how brain cells (neurons) contribute to psychological processes. Hebb suggested, in a nutshell, that "neurons that fire together, wire together." This famous rule is now widely considered one of the most important cellular mechanisms of learning and memory. Although Hebb made the suggestion in 1949, the biological techniques required to observe it were not available until the late 1960s.

Brenda Milner (b. 1918) is a Canadian psychologist, best known for her discovery of the critical importance of a specific part of the brain, the hippocampus, to memory. She studied patients with removals of different parts of the brain (usually to relieve seizure disorders), in order to understand how the different regions contribute to human cognition and behaviour.

Wilder Graves Penfield (1891–1976) during his life was called "the greatest living Canadian." He was a neurosurgeon who pioneered the surgical treatment of epilepsy, by carefully removing in each patient the specific part of the brain causing seizures. In the process, he was able to create the first detailed functional maps of the human brain—locating the regions responsible for feeling touch on different parts of the body, for moving different parts of the body, and for understanding and producing language. He relied on Hebb and Milner to evaluate the psychological effects of the surgeries that he conducted.

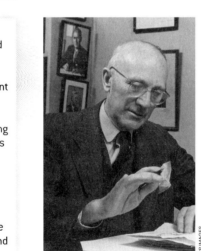

and the proportion of racial minorities receiving Ph.D.s in psychology grew from a very small number to 24 percent during that same period. Clearly, psychology is increasingly reflecting the diversity of North American society.

## Psychology in Canada

The development of psychology in Canada paralleled that in Europe and in the United States. As you read earlier, the first psychology laboratory in Canada was established by James Mark Baldwin, a student of Wundt's, in 1889, at the University of Toronto. Although Baldwin did not stay in Toronto, his laboratory was expanded by August Kirschmann, another student of Wundt's, around the turn of the twentieth century. Although at most other universities psychology was considered a field of philosophy, by 1926, psychology was established enough at the University of Toronto to became an independent department. McGill University also had an independent psychology department from 1922. Elsewhere, after 1940, independent psychology departments began springing up at Canadian universities.

One of the first graduate students in the new Department of Psychology at McGill University was Donald Olding Hebb (1904–1985) from Chester, Nova Scotia. Hebb was working as a school principal, and pursued a master's thesis at McGill part-time. He fell in love with physiological psychology (as cognitive neuroscience was then called) and applied to do a Ph.D. in the United States with Karl Lashley, who you met earlier in this chapter. After obtaining his Ph.D. (he studied the effects of being reared in darkness on the development of vision in rats), he applied to work with Wilder Penfield, and moved back to Montreal in 1937. Penfield was one of the most famous neurosurgeons in the world. He founded the Montreal Neurological Institute in the 1920s, and there he pioneered the surgical removal of brain tissue to relieve seizure disorders—his approach became known as "the Montreal procedure." Hebb wanted to study the effects on psychological processes of the very specific brain removals that Penfield was producing. By 1948, Hebb was Chair of the Department of Psychology at McGill, and in 1949 he published his landmark book *The Organization of Behaviour* in which he lays out his theory of the neural basis of learning. As you will learn in Chapter 6, this theory was extraordinarily prescient, and Hebb's ideas are now the basis of our understanding of how the physical structure of the brain changes with experience.

Brenda Milner, a Cambridge-trained psychologist, came to Canada in 1944. Her husband, Peter, was an engineer, who had been invited to help develop Canada's first nuclear reactors. Brenda enrolled as a Ph.D. student with Hebb, and worked with Penfield's patients, studying how the removals of specific parts of the brain affected perception and memory. She has remained in Montreal ever since. Over her long career, she has made several fundamental contributions to our understanding of how human thinking and behaviour depend on different parts of the brain. She is probably best known for the discovery of the brain basis of long-term memory—a topic that you will learn more about in the chapter on Memory.

# What Psychologists Do: Research Careers

Before describing what psychologists do, it should be noted that most people who major in psychology do not go on to become psychologists. Psychology has become a major academic, scientific, and professional discipline with links to many other disciplines and career paths (see the Hot Science box). That being said, what should you do if you *do* want to become a psychologist, and what should you fail to do if you desperately want to avoid it? You can become a "psychologist" by a variety of routes, and the people who call themselves psychologists may hold a variety of different degrees. Typically, students finish university and enter graduate school in order to obtain a Ph.D. in some particular area of psychology (e.g., social, cognitive, developmental). During graduate school, students generally gain exposure to the field by taking classes and learn to conduct research by collaborating with their professors. Although William James was able to master every area of psychology because the areas were so small during his lifetime, today a student can spend the better part of a decade mastering just one.

After receiving a Ph.D., you can go on for more specialized research training by pursuing a postdoctoral fellowship under the supervision of an established researcher in his or her area, or apply for a faculty position at a college or university or a research position in government or industry. Academic careers usually involve a combination of teaching and research, whereas careers in government or industry are typically dedicated to research alone.

## The Variety of Career Paths

As you saw earlier, research is not the only career option for a psychologist. Most people who call themselves psychologists neither teach nor do research but, rather, they assess or treat people with psychological problems. Most of these *clinical psychologists* work in private practice, often in partnerships with other psychologists or with psychiatrists (who have earned an M.D., or medical degree, and are allowed to prescribe medication). Other clinical psychologists work in hospitals or medical schools, some have faculty positions at universities or colleges, and some combine private practice with an academic job. Many clinical psychologists focus on specific problems or disorders, such as depression or anxiety, whereas others focus on specific populations such as children, ethnic minority groups, or older adults (see **FIGURE 1.3**). *Counselling psychologists* assist people in dealing with work or career issues and changes or help people deal with common crises such as divorce, the loss of a job, or the death of a loved one. Counselling psychologists may have a Ph.D. or an M.A. (master's degree) in counselling psychology or an M.S.W. (Master of Social Work).

> **?**
> In what ways does psychology contribute to society?

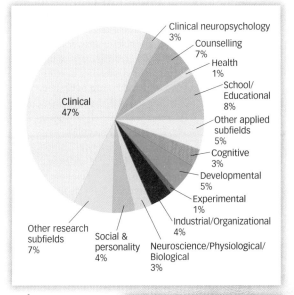

▲ Figure 1.3 **The Major Subfields in Psychology**
Psychologists are drawn to many different subfields in psychology. Here are the percentages of people receiving Ph.D.s in various subfields. Clinical psychology makes up almost half of the doctorates awarded in psychology.

*Note:* The numbers do not add up to 100% due to rounding.

*Source:* 2004 Graduate Study in Psychology. Compiled by APA Research Office.

A person earning a Ph.D. in psychology can go on to a wide range of fields, like these three: a practising clinical psychologist, a science and health journalist for a major news outlet, and a behavioural scientist for an international affairs consulting firm.

**Michael Friedman**

**Shirley Wang**

**Betsy Stevens**

# Psychology as a Hub Science

This chapter describes how psychology emerged as a field of study, and the Other Voices box on page 17 illustrates some of the ways in which psychology is indeed a *scientific* field of study. But where does psychology stand in relation to other areas of science? That is, how big a field is it? What links does it have to other scientific disciplines? What fields (if any) are influenced by psychological science? With recent advances in computing and electronic record keeping, researchers are now able to answer these questions by literally creating maps of science. Information about scientific articles, the journals in which they are published, and the frequency and patterns with which articles in one field are cited by articles in another field, is now fully electronic and available online (in the Science Citation and Social Science Citation Indexes). Researchers can use this information to learn about the interconnectedness of different scientific disciplines.

As an example, in an article called "Mapping the Backbone of Science," Kevin Boyack and his colleagues (2005) used data from more than 1 million articles, with over 23 million references, published in more than 7000 journals to create a map showing the similarities and interconnectedness of different areas of science based on how frequently journal articles from different disciplines cite each other.

The results are fascinating. As shown in the figure on the left, seven major fields, or "hub sciences," that link with and influence smaller subfields emerged in the data: math, physics, chemistry, earth sciences, medicine, *psychology*, and social science. The organization of the hubs is interesting to note. As you can see in the figure on the left, psychology sits between medicine and social studies, whereas physics sits

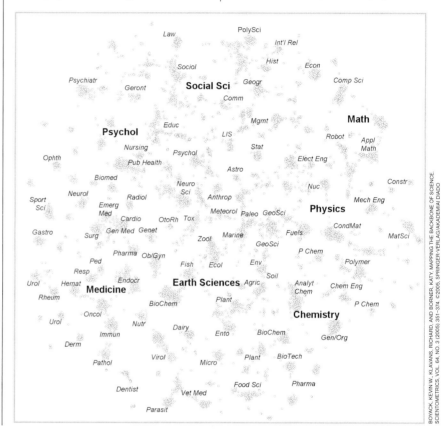

BOYACK, KEVIN W., KLAVANS, RICHARD, AND BORNER, KATY. MAPPING THE BACKBONE OF SCIENCE. SCIENTOMETRICS, VOL. 64, NO. 3 (2005) 351–374. ©2005, SPRINGER-VERLAG/AKADEMIAI DIADO

Psychologists are also quite active in educational settings. *School psychologists,* offer guidance to students, parents, and teachers. A similar proportion of APA members focus on issues in the workplace. Psychologists who work in business or industry are known as *industrial/organizational psychologists.* They may be involved in assessing potential employees, finding ways to improve productivity, or helping staff and management to develop effective planning strategies for coping with change or anticipated future developments. Of course, this brief list does not begin to cover all the different career paths that someone with training in psychology might take. For instance, sports psychologists help athletes improve their performance, forensic psychologists assist lawyers and courts, and consumer psychologists help companies develop and advertise new products. Indeed, we cannot think of any major enterprise that *does not* employ psychologists.

Even this brief and incomplete survey provides a sense of the wide variety of contexts in which psychologists operate. You can think of psychology as an international community of professionals devoted to advancing scientific knowledge; assisting people with psychological problems and disorders; and trying to enhance the quality of life in work, school, and other everyday settings.

between mathematics and chemistry. The location of subfields also matches with what you might expect: public health and neurology fall between psychology and medicine, statistics between psychology and math, and economics between social science and math.

Studies like this one provide an informative picture of how different areas of science relate to each other historically (i.e., the citations in that study dated back many years). But science is dynamic and constantly changing and so an important question is: What does the science look like right now (while you are in school and deciding which classes to take and what career path to follow)? In another study, data from more than 6 million citations, found in over 6000 journals was used to create a map of citation patterns focusing only on citations to articles published in a recent 5-year period (in this case from 2000–2004) (Rosvall & Bergstrom, 2008). In that analysis, psychology again emerged as a major scientific hub (see the figure on the left). The largest scientific fields, in order, are molecular and cell biology, medicine, physics, neuroscience, ecology and evolution, economics, geosciences, psychology, and chemistry. Psychological research has strong links (based on the frequency of citations of work in journals in each field) with neuroscience, psychiatry, education, sociology, business and marketing, medicine, and ecology and evolution. More recent and larger studies continue to support the overall structure of these maps of science (Börner et al., 2012).

Studies like these are useful to university administrators, funding agencies, and also to students to help them understand the relationships between different academic departments and how the scientific work of one field relates to the scientific field more broadly. They also show the reach of psychology to other disciplines and support the idea that knowledge about psychology has relevance for many related disciplines and career paths. Good thing you are taking this class!

ROSVALL, MARTIN AND BERGSTROM, CARL T, MAPS OF RANDOM WALKS ON COMPLEX NETWORKS REVEAL COMMUNITY STRUCTURE. PNAS, JAN 29, 2008, VOL. 105, NO 2, PP. 1118–1123. © 2008 NATIONAL ACADEMY OF SCIENCES, U.S.A.

## IN SUMMARY

▶ The American Psychological Association (APA) has grown dramatically since it was formed in 1892 and now includes over 150 000 members working in clinical, academic, and applied settings. Psychologists are also represented by professional organizations such as the Association for Psychological Science (APS), which focuses on scientific psychology, and in Canada by the Canadian Psychological Association (CPA), the Canadian Society for Brain Behaviour and Cognitive Sciences (CSBBCS), and the Canadian Association for Neuroscience—association canadienne de neuroscience (CAN-ACN).

▶ Psychology in Canada developed similarly to psychology elsewhere. By the 1920s, the University of Toronto and McGill University had stand-alone departments of psychology and, by the 1940s, these were beginning to appear at other Canadian universities.

▶ Psychologists prepare for research careers through graduate and postdoctoral training, and work in a variety of applied settings, including schools, clinics, and industry.

# Chapter Review

## KEY CONCEPT QUIZ

1. In the 1800s, French biologist Marie Jean Pierre Flourens and surgeon Paul Broca conducted research that demonstrated a connection between
   a. animals and humans.
   b. the mind and the brain.
   c. brain size and mental ability.
   d. skull indentations and psychological attributes.

2. What was the subject of the famous experiment conducted by Hermann von Helmholtz?
   a. reaction time
   b. childhood learning
   c. phrenology
   d. functions of specific brain areas

3. Wilhelm Wundt is credited with
   a. coining the phrase "philosophical empiricism."
   b. setting the terms for the nature–nurture debate.
   c. the founding of psychology as a scientific discipline.
   d. conducting the first psychological experiment.

4. Wundt and his students sought to analyze the basic elements that constitute the mind, an approach called
   a. consciousness.
   b. introspection.
   c. structuralism.
   d. objectivity.

5. ___ helped establish functionalism as a major school of psychological thought in North America.
   a. William James
   b. René Descartes
   c. Franz Joseph Gall
   d. Edward Titchener

6. The functional approach to psychology was inspired by
   a. Darwin's *On the Origin of Species by Means of Natural Selection.*
   b. James's *The Principles of Psychology.*
   c. Wundt's *Principles of Physiological Psychology.*
   d. Titchener's *An Outline of Psychology.*

7. To understand human behaviour, French physicians Jean-Martin Charcot and Pierre Janet studied people
   a. who appeared to be completely healthy.
   b. with psychological disorders.
   c. with damage in particular areas of the brain.
   d. who had suffered permanent loss of cognitive and motor function.

8. Building on the work of Charcot and Janet, Sigmund Freud developed
   a. psychoanalytic theory.
   b. the theory of hysteria.
   c. humanistic psychology.
   d. physiological psychology.

9. The psychological theory that emphasizes the positive potential of human beings is known as
   a. structuralism.
   b. psychoanalytic theory.
   c. humanistic psychology.
   d. functionalism.

10. Behaviourism involves the study of
    a. observable actions and responses.
    b. the potential for human growth.
    c. unconscious influences and childhood experiences.
    d. human behaviour and memory.

11. The experiments of Ivan Pavlov and John Watson centred on
    a. perception and behaviour.
    b. stimulus and response.
    c. reward and punishment.
    d. conscious and unconscious behaviour.

12. Who developed the concept of reinforcement?
    a. B. F. Skinner
    b. Ivan Pavlov
    c. John Watson
    d. Margaret Floy Washburn

13. The study of mental processes such as perception and memory is called
    a. behavioural determinism.
    b. Gestalt psychology.
    c. social psychology.
    d. cognitive psychology.

14. During World War II, cognitive psychologists discovered that many of the errors pilots make are the result of
    a. computer errors in processing detailed information.
    b. limited human cognitive capacity to handle incoming information.
    c. pilot inattention to incoming information.
    d. lack of behavioural training.

15. The use of scanning techniques to observe the brain in action and to see which parts are involved in which operations helped the development of
    a. evolutionary psychology.
    b. cognitive neuroscience.
    c. cultural psychology.
    d. cognitive accounts of language formation.

16. Central to evolutionary psychology is the ___ function that minds and brains serve.
    a. emotional
    b. adaptive
    c. cultural
    d. physiological

17. Social psychology differs most from other psychological approaches in its emphasis on
    a. human interaction.
    b. behavioural processes.
    c. the individual.
    d. laboratory experimentation.

18. Cultural psychology emphasizes that
    a. all psychological processes are influenced to some extent by culture.
    b. psychological processes are the same across all human beings, regardless of culture.

c. culture shapes some, but not all psychological phenomena.

d. insights gained from studying individuals from one culture will only rarely generalize to individuals from other cultures, who have different social identities and rituals.

**19.** Donald Hebb

a. studied with Wundt in the first psychology laboratory.

b. was a famous Canadian neurosurgeon.

c. was a student of William James.

d. was interested in how the brain changes as a result of learning.

**20.** Brenda Milner

a. discovered the brain basis of long-term memory.

b. studied with Karl Lashley.

c. operated on patients with seizure disorders.

d. studied "Little Albert" with J. B. Watson.

## KEY TERMS

behaviour (p. 3)

behavioural neuroscience (p. 24)

behaviourism (p. 16)

cognitive neuroscience (p. 25)

cognitive psychology (p. 23)

consciousness (p. 8)

cultural psychology (p. 28)

evolutionary psychology (p. 25)

functionalism (p. 11)

Gestalt psychology (p. 21)

humanistic psychology (p. 15)

hysteria (p. 13)

illusions (p. 21)

introspection (p. 8)

mind (p. 3)

nativism (p. 6)

natural selection (p. 11)

philosophical empiricism (p. 6)

phrenology (p. 6)

physiology (p. 7)

psychoanalysis (p. 14)

psychoanalytic theory (p. 13)

psychology (p. 3)

reaction time (p. 8)

reinforcement (p. 19)

response (p. 18)

social psychology (p. 27)

stimulus (p. 8)

structuralism (p. 8)

unconscious (p. 13)

## CHANGING MINDS

**1.** One of your classmates says that she is only taking this class because it is required for her education major. "Psychology is all about understanding mental illness and treatment. I don't know why I have to learn this stuff when I'm going to be a teacher, not a psychologist." Why should your friend reconsider her opinion? What subfields of psychology are especially important for a teacher?

**2.** One of your friends confesses that he really enjoys his psychology courses, but he has decided not to major in psychology. "You have to get a graduate degree to do anything with a psychology major," he says, "and I don't want to stay in school for the rest of my life. I want to get out there and work in the real world." Based on what you have read in this chapter about careers in psychology, what might you tell him?

**3.** On May 6, you spot a news item announcing that it is the birthday of Sigmund Freud, "the father of psychology." How accurate is it to call Freud the "father of psychology"? Having read about psychology's subfields, are there other people who are as important, or more important, than Freud?

**4.** One of your classmates flipped ahead in the book, and noticed that there is a lot of material—including an entire chapter—on the brain. "I don't see why we have to learn so much biology," he says. "I want to be a school counsellor, not a brain surgeon. I don't need to understand the parts of the brain or chemical reactions in order to help people." How are the brain and the mind connected? In what specific ways might knowing about the brain help us to understand the mind?

**5.** Another classmate is very unsettled after reading about B. F. Skinner's claim that free will is an illusion. "Psychology always tries to treat human beings like lab rats, whose behaviour can be manipulated. I have free will, and I decide what I'm going to do next." What would you tell your friend? Does an understanding of the basic principles of psychology allow us to predict every detail of what individual humans will do?

## ANSWERS TO KEY CONCEPT QUIZ

1. b; 2. a; 3. c; 4. c; 5. a; 6. a; 7. b; 8. a; 9. c; 10. a; 11. b; 12. a; 13. d; 14. b; 15. b; 16. b; 17. a; 18. c; 19. d; 20. a.

Need more help? Additional resources are located in Launchpad at:

www.worthpublishers.com/launchpad/schacter3ecanadian

# Methods in Psychology

▲ **Empiricism: How to Know Stuff**
The Scientific Method
The Art of Looking

▲ **Observation: Discovering What People Do**
Measurement
**CULTURE & COMMUNITY** Best Place to Fall on Your Face
Descriptions

▲ **Explanation: Discovering Why People Do What They Do**
Correlation
Causation
**THE REAL WORLD** "Oddsly" Enough
Drawing Conclusions
**HOT SCIENCE** Do Violent Movies Make Peaceful Streets?
Thinking Critically about Evidence

▲ **The Ethics of Science: First, Do No Harm**
Respecting People
Respecting Animals
Respecting Truth
**OTHER VOICES** Can We Afford Science?

*Y*OU CAN HEAL YOUR LIFE HAS sold over 35 million copies. Its author, Louise Hay, suggests that everything that happens to us is a result of the thoughts we choose to think. She claims that she cured herself of cancer simply by changing her thoughts, and says that others can learn to do the same by buying her books, CDs, and DVDs, and by attending her seminars. In a recent television interview, Hay explained how she knows that her technique is effective.

**Interviewer:** How do you know what you are saying is right?

**Hay:** Oh, my inner ding.

**Interviewer:** Ding?

**Hay:** My inner ding. It speaks to me. It feels right or it does not feel right. Happiness is choosing thoughts that make you feel good. It is really very simple.

**Interviewer:** But I hear you saying that even if there were no proof for what you believed, or even if there were scientific evidence against it, it would not change.

**Hay:** Well, I do not believe in scientific evidence, I really do not. Science is fairly new. It has not been around that long. We think it is such a big deal, but it is, you know, it is just a way of looking at life.

Louise Hay says she does not "believe" in scientific evidence, but what could that possibly mean? After all, if Hay's techniques really do cure cancer, then even she would have to expect cancer victims who practise her techniques to have a higher rate of remission than cancer victims who do not. That is not "a way of looking at life." It is just plain, old-fashioned, common sense—exactly the kind of common sense that lies at the heart of science.

Science tells us that the only way to know for sure whether a claim is true is to go out and have a look. But that sounds easier than it is. For example, where would you look to see whether Louise Hay's claims are true? Would you go to one of her seminars and ask people in the audience whether or not they would been healed? Would you examine the medical records of people who had and had not bought her books? Would you invite people to sign up for a class that teaches her techniques and then wait to see how many got cancer? All of these things sound reasonable, but the fact is that none of them would be particularly informative. There are a few good ways to

Louise Hay says she does not believe in scientific evidence and instead trusts her "inner ding."

MICHELE ASSELIN/
CONTOUR BY GETTY IMAGES

39

**empiricism**
The belief that accurate knowledge can be acquired through observation.

**scientific method**
A procedure for finding truth by using empirical evidence.

**theory**
A hypothetical explanation of a natural phenomenon.

test claims like Louise Hay's and a whole lot of bad ways, and in this chapter you will learn to tell one from the other. Scientists have developed powerful tools for determining when an inner ding is right and when it is wrong, and it is these tools that make science special. As the philosopher Bertrand Russell (1945, p. 527) wrote, "It is not *what* the man of science believes that distinguishes him, but *how* and *why* he believes it." That, it turns out, goes for women of science too.

**WE WILL START BY EXAMINING THE GENERAL PRINCIPLES THAT GUIDE** scientific research and distinguish it from every other way of knowing. Next, we will see that the methods of psychology are meant to answer two basic questions: *What* do people do? and *Why* do they do it? Psychologists answer the first question by observing and measuring, and they answer the second question by looking for relationships between the things they measure. We will see that scientific research allows us to draw certain kinds of conclusions and not others, and we will see that most people have problems thinking critically about scientific evidence. Finally, we will consider the unique ethical questions that confront scientists who study humans and nonhuman animals.

# Empiricism: How to Know Stuff

When ancient Greeks sprained their ankles, caught the flu, or accidentally set their togas on fire, they had to choose between two kinds of doctors: dogmatists (from *dogmatikos,* meaning "belief"), who thought that the best way to understand illness was

to develop theories about the body's functions, and empiricists (from *empeirikos,* meaning "experience"), who thought that the best way to understand illness was to observe sick people. The rivalry between these two schools of medicine did not last long because the people who went to see dogmatists tended to die, which was bad for business. Today we use the word *dogmatism* to describe the tendency for people to cling to their assumptions, and the word **empiricism** to describe *the belief that accurate knowledge can be acquired through observation.* The fact that we can answer questions about the natural world by examining it may seem painfully obvious to you, but this painfully obvious fact has only recently gained wide acceptance. For most of human history, people trusted authority to answer important questions, and it is only in the last millennium (and especially in the past three centuries) that people have begun to trust their eyes and ears more than their elders.

BETTMANN/CORBIS

The astronomer Galileo Galilei (1564–1642) was excommunicated and sentenced to prison for sticking to his own observations of the solar system rather than accepting the teachings of the church. In 1597 he wrote to his friend and fellow astronomer Johannes Kepler (1571–1630), "What would you say of the learned here, who, replete with the pertinacity of the asp, have steadfastly refused to cast a glance through the telescope? What shall we make of this? Shall we laugh, or shall we cry?" As it turned out, the answer was *cry.*

## The Scientific Method

Empiricism is the essential element of the **scientific method,** which is *a procedure for finding truth by using empirical evidence.* In essence, the scientific method suggests that when we have an idea about the world—about how bats navigate, or where the moon came from, or why people cannot forget traumatic events—we should gather empirical evidence relevant to that idea and then modify the idea to fit with the evidence. Scientists usually refer to an idea of this kind as a **theory,** which is *a hypothetical explanation of a natural phenomenon.* We might theorize that bats navigate by making sounds and then listening for the echo, that the moon was formed when a small planet collided with the Earth, or that the brain

> **What is the scientific method?**

responds to traumatic events by producing chemicals that facilitate memory. Each of these theories is an explanation of how something in the natural world works.

When scientists set out to develop a theory, they generally follow *the rule of parsimony*, which says that the *simplest* theory that explains all the evidence is the best one. Parsimony comes from the Latin word *parcere*, meaning "to spare," and the rule is often credited to the fourteenth-century logician William Ockham, who wrote "Plurality should not be posited without necessity." Ockham was not suggesting that nature is simple or that complex theories are wrong. He was merely suggesting that it makes sense to *start* with the simplest theory and then make the theory more complicated only if one must. Part of what makes $E = mc^2$ such a lovely theory is that it expresses all the necessary information in exactly three letters and one number.

We want our theories to be as simple as possible, but we also want them to be right. How do we decide if a theory is right? Theories make specific predictions about what we should observe in the world. For example, if bats really do navigate by making sounds and then listening for echoes, then we should observe that deaf bats cannot navigate. That "should statement" is technically known as a **hypothesis,** which is *a falsifiable prediction made by a theory*. The word *falsifiable* is a critical part of that definition. Some theories, such as "God created the universe," simply do not specify what we should observe if they are true, and thus no observation can ever falsify them. Because these theories do not give rise to hypotheses, they can never be the subject of scientific investigation. That does not mean they are wrong—it just means that we cannot evaluate them by using the scientific method.

So what happens when we test a hypothesis? Albert Einstein is reputed to have said that, "No amount of experimentation can ever prove me right, but a single experiment can prove me wrong." Why should that be? Well, just imagine what you could possibly learn about the navigation-by-sound theory if you observed a few bats. If you saw the deaf bats navigating every bit as well as the hearing bats, then the navigation-by-sound theory would instantly be proved wrong; but if you saw the deaf bats navigating more poorly than the hearing bats, your observation would be *consistent* with the navigation-by-sound theory but would not prove it. After all, even if you did not see a deaf bat navigating perfectly today, it is still possible that someone else did, or that you will see one tomorrow.

**Why can theories be proven wrong but not right?**

**hypothesis**
A falsifiable prediction made by a theory.

Classical thinkers like Euclid and Ptolemy believed that our eyes work by emitting rays that travel to the objects we see. Ibn al-Haytham (965 CE–1039 CE) reasoned that if this were true, then when we open our eyes it should take longer to see something far away than something nearby. And guess what? It does not. And with that single observation, a centuries-old theory vanished—in the blink of an eye.

SCIENCE SOURCE/
COLOURIZATION BY:
MARY MARTIN

SEFANO BIANCHETTI/CORBIS

INTERFOTO/ALAMY

Scientists once believed that all combustible objects contain an element called *phlogiston* that is released during burning. But in 1779, the chemist Antoine Lavoisier (1734–1794) demonstrated that when metals such as mercury are burned, they do not get lighter, as the phlogiston theory said they must. Pictured here are Lavoisier (*left*) and his theory-killing apparatus (*right*).

We cannot observe every bat that has ever been and will ever be, which means that even if the theory was not disproved by your observation there always remains some chance that it will be disproved by some other observation. When evidence is consistent with a theory, it increases our confidence in it, but it never makes us completely certain. The next time you see a newspaper headline that says "Scientists prove theory X correct," you are hereby authorized to roll your eyes.

The scientific method suggests that the best way to learn the truth about the world is to develop theories, derive hypotheses from them, test those hypotheses by gathering evidence, and then use that evidence to modify the theories. But what exactly does gathering evidence entail?

## The Art of Looking

For centuries, people rode horses. And for centuries when they got off their horses they sat around and argued about whether all four of a horse's feet ever leave the ground at the same time. Some said yes, some said no, and some said they really wished they could talk about something else for a change. In 1877, Eadweard Muybridge invented a technique for taking photographs in rapid succession, and his photographs showed that when horses gallop, all four feet do indeed leave the ground. And that was that. Never again did two riders have the pleasure of a flying horse debate because Muybridge had settled the matter, once and for all time.

Frames 2 and 3 of this historic photo by Eadweard Muybridge (1830–1904) show that horses can indeed fly, albeit briefly and only in coach.

But why did it take so long? After all, people had been watching horses gallop for quite a few years, so why did some say that they clearly saw the horse going airborne while others said that they clearly saw at least one hoof on the ground at all times? Because as wonderful as eyes may be, there are a lot of things they cannot see and a lot of things they see incorrectly. We cannot see germs but they are very real. Earth looks perfectly flat but it is imperfectly round. As Muybridge knew, we have to do more than just look if we want to know the truth about the world. Empiricism is the right approach, but to do it properly requires an **empirical method,** *a set of rules and techniques for observation.*

In many sciences, the word *method* refers primarily to technologies that enhance the powers of the senses. Biologists use microscopes and astronomers use telescopes because the things they want to observe are invisible to the naked eye. Human behaviour, on the other hand, is quite visible, so you might expect psychology's methods to be relatively simple. In fact, the empirical challenges facing psychologists are among the most daunting in all of modern science, thus psychology's empirical methods are among the most sophisticated in all of modern science. These empirical challenges arise because people have three qualities that make them unusually difficult to study:

> *Complexity:* No galaxy, particle, molecule, or machine is as complicated as the human brain. Scientists can describe the birth of a star or the death of a cell in exquisite detail, but they can barely begin to say how the 500 million interconnected neurons that constitute the brain give rise to the thoughts, feelings, and actions that are psychology's core concerns.

**What makes human beings especially difficult to study?**

> *Variability:* In almost all the ways that matter, one *E. coli* bacterium is pretty much like another. But people are as varied as their fingerprints. No two individuals ever do, say, think, or feel exactly the same thing under exactly the same circumstances, which means that when you have seen one, you have most definitely not seen them all.

**empirical method**
A set of rules and techniques for observation.

> *Reactivity:* An atom of cesium-133 oscillates 9 192 631 770 times per second regardless of whether anyone is watching. But people often think, feel, and act one way when they are being observed and a different way when they are not. When people know they are being studied, they do not always behave as they otherwise would.

The fact that human beings are complex, variable, and reactive presents a major challenge to the scientific study of their behaviour, and psychologists have developed two kinds of methods that are designed to meet these challenges head-on: *methods of observation,* which allow them to determine what people do, and *methods of explanation,* which allow them to determine why people do it. We will examine both of these methods in the sections that follow.

## IN SUMMARY

▶ Empiricism is the belief that the best way to understand the world is to observe it firsthand. It is only in the last few centuries that empiricism has come to prominence.

▶ Empiricism is at the heart of the scientific method, which suggests that our theories about the world give rise to falsifiable hypotheses, and that we can thus make observations that test those hypotheses. The results of these tests can disprove our theories but cannot prove them.

▶ Observation does not just mean "looking." It requires a method. The methods of psychology are special because, more than most other natural phenomena, human beings are complex, variable, and reactive.

LEONARD MCCOMBE/GETTY IMAGES

In the 1930s, the Hawthorne Plant, a factory for telephone parts outside of Chicago, commissioned a study to examine whether a change in shop-floor lighting would improve worker's productivity. And indeed, when the lighting was made brighter, productivity increased. However, when the lighting was dimmed, productivity also increased! It did not matter what was changed: productivity always went up (for a short time). In general, people behave differently when they know they are being watched compared to when they do not—this phenomenon is now known as the Hawthorne effect.

# Observation: Discovering What People Do

To *observe* means to use one's senses to learn about the properties of an event (e.g., a storm or a parade) or an object (e.g., an apple or a person). For example, when you observe a round, red apple, your brain is using the pattern of light that is coming into your eyes to draw an inference about the apple's identity, shape, and colour. That kind of informal observation is fine for buying fruit but not for doing science. Why? First, casual observations are notoriously unstable. The same apple may appear red in the daylight and crimson at night or spherical to one person and elliptical to another. Second, casual observations cannot tell us about all of the properties that might interest us. No matter how long and hard you look, you will never be able to discern an apple's crunchiness or pectin content simply by watching it.

Luckily, scientists have devised techniques that allow them to overcome these problems. In the first section (Measurement), we will see how psychologists design instruments and then use them to make measurements. In the second section (Descriptions), we will see what psychologists do with their measurements once they have made them.

## Measurement

For most of human history, people had no idea how old they were because there was no simple way to keep track of time—or weight, or volume, or density, or temperature, or anything else, for that matter. Today we live in a world of rulers, clocks, calendars, odometers, thermometers, and mass spectrometers. Measurement is not just a basic part of science, it is a basic part of modern life. But what exactly does measurement

**What two things does measurement require?**

**operational definition**
A description of a property in concrete, measurable terms.

**instrument**
Anything that can detect the condition to which an operational definition refers.

**validity**
The goodness with which a concrete event defines a property.

**reliability**
The tendency for an instrument to produce the same measurement whenever it is used to measure the same thing.

**power**
An instrument's ability to detect small magnitudes of the property.

**demand characteristics**
Those aspects of an observational setting that cause people to behave as they think someone else wants or expects.

**naturalistic observation**
A technique for gathering scientific information by unobtrusively observing people in their natural environments.

require? Whether we want to measure the intensity of an earthquake, the distance between molecules, or the attitude of a registered voter, we must always do two things—*define* the property we wish to measure and then find a way to *detect* it.

## Defining and Detecting

The last time you said, "just give me a second," you probably did not know you were talking about atomic decay. Every unit of time has an **operational definition,** which is *a description of a property in concrete, measurable terms.* The operational definition of a second is *the duration of 9 192 631 770 cycles of microwave light absorbed or emitted by the hyperfine transition of cesium-133 atoms in their ground state undisturbed by external fields* (which takes roughly 6 seconds just to say). To actually count the cycles of light emitted as cesium-133 decays requires an **instrument,** which is *anything that can detect the condition to which an operational definition refers.* An instrument known as a "cesium clock" can count cycles of light, and when it counts 9 192 631 770 of them, one second has officially passed.

The steps we take to measure a physical property are the same steps we take to measure a psychological property. For example, if we wanted to measure a person's intelligence, or shyness, or happiness, we would have to start by generating an operational definition of that property—that is, by specifying some concrete, measurable event that indicates it. For example, we might define happiness as *the frequency with which a person smiles.* Once we do, we just need a smile-detecting instrument, such as a computer-assisted camera or maybe just a human eye. Having an operational definition that specifies a measurable event and an instrument that measures that event are the keys to scientific measurement.

## Validity, Reliability, and Power

There are many ways to define and detect a property such as happiness, so which ways are best? The most important feature of an operational definition is **validity,** *the goodness with which a concrete event defines a property.*

For example, the concrete event called *frequency of smiling* is a valid way to define the property called *happiness* because, as we all know, people tend to smile more often when they feel happy. Do they eat more or talk more or spend more money? Well, maybe. But maybe not. And that is why food consumption or verbal output or financial expenditures would probably be regarded by most people as invalid measures of happiness (though perfectly valid measures of something else). Validity is to some extent in the eye of the beholder, but most beholders would agree that the frequency of smiles is a more valid way to operationally define happiness than is frequency of eating, talking, or spending.

> What are the properties of a good operational definition and a good instrument?

What then is the most important feature of an instrument? Actually, there are two. First, a good instrument has **reliability,** which is *the tendency for an instrument to produce the same measurement whenever it is used to measure the same thing.* For example, if a person smiles just as much on Tuesday as on Wednesday, then a smile-detecting instrument should produce identical results on those two days. If it produced different results (i.e., if the instrument detected differences that were not actually there), it would lack reliability. Second, a good instrument has **power,** which is *an instrument's ability to detect small magnitudes of the property.* If a person smiled just *slightly* more often on Tuesday than on Wednesday, then a good smile-detector should produce different results on those 2 days. If it produced the same result (i.e., if it failed to detect a small difference that was actually there), then it would lack power (see **FIGURE 2.1**).

▼ Figure 2.1 **Measurement** There are two steps in the measurement of a property.

| Define the Property | Detect the Property |
|---|---|
| Generate an operational definition that has validity | Design an instrument that has reliability and power |

## Demand Characteristics

Once we have a valid definition and a reliable and powerful instrument, are we *finally* ready to measure behaviour? Yes, as long as we want to measure the behaviour of an amoeba or a raindrop or anything else that does not care if we are watching it. But if we want to measure the behaviour of a human being, then we still have some work to do, because while we are trying to discover how people normally behave, normal people will be trying to behave as they think we want or expect them to. **Demand characteristics** are *those aspects of an observational setting that cause people to behave as they think someone else wants or expects.* We call these demand characteristics because

> **How do people respond when they know they are being observed?**

they seem to "demand" or require that people say and do certain things. When someone you love asks, "Do these jeans make me look fat?" the right answer is always no, and if you

Are most people prejudiced against people with disabilities? People rarely admit to being prejudiced when asked, and they generally will not behave in prejudiced ways if someone is watching. So how could you measure prejudice in a way that minimized demand characteristics?

have ever been asked this question, then you have experienced demand. Demand characteristics make it hard to measure behaviour as it typically unfolds.

One way that psychologists avoid the problem of demand characteristics is by observing people without their knowledge. **Naturalistic observation** is *a technique for gathering scientific information by unobtrusively observing people in their natural environments.* For example, naturalistic observation has shown that the biggest groups leave the smallest tips in restaurants (Freeman et al., 1975), that hungry shoppers buy the most impulse items at the grocery store (Gilbert, Gill, & Wilson, 2002), that golfers are most likely to cheat when they play several opponents at once (Erffmeyer, 1984), that men do not usually approach the most beautiful woman at a singles' bar (Glenwick, Jason, & Elman, 1978), and that Olympic athletes smile more when they win the bronze medal than the silver medal (Medvec, Madey, & Gilovich, 1995). Each of these conclusions is the result of measurements made by psychologists who observed people who did not know they were being observed. It seems unlikely that the same observations could have been made if the diners, shoppers, golfers, singles, and athletes had realized that they were being scrutinized.

Unfortunately, naturalistic observation is not always a viable solution to the problem of demand characteristics. First, some of the things psychologists want to observe simply do not occur naturally. If we wanted to know whether people who have undergone sensory deprivation perform poorly on motor tasks, we would have to hang around the shopping mall for a very long time before a few dozen blindfolded people with earplugs just happened to wander by and start typing. Second, some of the things that psychologists want to observe can only be gathered from direct interaction with a person, for example, by administering a survey, giving tests, conducting an interview, or hooking someone up to a machine. If we wanted to know how often people worry about dying, how accurately they can remember their high school graduations, how quickly they can solve a logic puzzle, or how much electrical activity their brains produce when they feel jealous, then simply watching them from the bushes will not do.

Luckily, there are other ways to avoid demand characteristics. For instance, people are less likely to be influenced by demand characteristics when they cannot be

## CULTURE & COMMUNITY

### Best Place to Fall on Your Face

Robert Levine of California State University–Fresno sent his students to 23 large international cities for an observational study in the field. Their task was to observe helping behaviours in a naturalistic context. In two versions of the experiment, students pretended to be either blind or injured while trying to cross a street, while another student stood by to observe whether anyone would come to help. A third version involved a student dropping a pen to see if anyone would pick it up.

The results showed that people helped in all three events fairly evenly within cities, but there was a wide range of response between cities. Rio de Janeiro, Brazil, came out on top as the most helpful city in the study with an overall helping score of 93 percent. Kuala Lampur, Malaysia, came in last with a score of 40 percent, and New York City placed next to last with a score of 45 percent. On average, Latin American cities ranked as most helpful (Levine, Norenzayan, & Philbrick, 2001).

THINKSTOCK

One way to avoid demand characteristics is to measure behaviours that people are unable or unlikely to control. For example, our pupils contract when we are bored (*left*) and dilate when we are interested (*right*), which makes pupillary dilation a useful measure of a person's level of engagement in a task.

identified as the originators of their actions, and psychologists often take advantage of this fact by allowing people to respond privately (e.g., by having them complete questionnaires when they are alone) or anonymously (e.g., by not collecting personal information, such as the person's name or address). Another technique that psychologists often use to avoid demand characteristics is to measure behaviours that cannot easily be demanded. For instance, a person's behaviour cannot be influenced by demand characteristics if that behaviour is not under the person's voluntary control. You may not want a psychologist to know that you are extremely interested in the celebrity gossip magazine that he or she has asked you to read, but you cannot prevent your pupils from dilating, which is what they do when you are engaged. Behaviours are also unlikely to be influenced by demand characteristics when people do not know that the demand and the behaviour are related. For example, you may vwant the psychologist to believe that you are concentrating hard on the *Wall Street Journal* article that he or she has asked you to read, but you probably do not realize that your blink rate slows when you are concentrating, thus you probably will not fake a slow blink.

One of the best ways to avoid demand characteristics is to keep the people who are being observed from knowing the true purpose of the observation. When people are "blind" to the purpose of an observation, they cannot behave the way they think they should behave because they do not *know* how they should behave. For instance, if you did not know that a psychologist was studying the effects of music on mood, you would not feel obligated to smile when music was played. This is why psychologists typically do not reveal the true purpose of an observation to the people who are being observed until the study is over.

Why is it important for subjects to be "blind"?

Of course, people are clever and curious, and when psychologists do not tell them the purpose of their observations, people generally try to figure it out for themselves. That is why psychologists sometimes use *cover stories,* or misleading explanations that are meant to keep people from discerning the true purpose of an observation. For example, if a psychologist wanted to know how music influenced your mood, he or she might falsely tell you that the purpose of the study was to determine how quickly people can do logic puzzles while music plays in the background. (We will discuss the ethical implications of deceiving people later in this chapter.) In addition, the psychologist might use *filler items,* or pointless measures that are designed to mislead you about the true purpose of the observation. So, for example, the psychologist might ask you a few questions whose answers are of real interest to him or her (How happy are you right now?), as well as a few questions whose answers are not (Do you like cats more or less than dogs?). This makes it difficult for you to guess the true purpose of the observation from the nature of the questions you were asked.

## Observer Bias

The people being observed are not the only ones who can make measurement a bit tricky. In one study, students in a psychology class were asked to measure the speed with which a rat learned to run through a maze (Rosenthal & Fode, 1963). Some students were told that their rat had been specially bred to be "maze-dull" (i.e., slow to learn a maze) and others were told that their rat had been specially bred to be "maze-bright" (i.e., quick to learn a maze). Although all the rats were actually the same breed, the students who *thought* they were measuring the speed of a maze-dull rat reported that their rats took longer to learn the maze than did the students who *thought* they were measuring the speed of a maze-bright rat. In other words, the measurements revealed precisely what the students expected them to reveal.

Why did this happen? First, *expectations can influence observations.* It is easy to make errors when measuring the speed of a rat, and our expectations often determine the kinds of errors we make. Does putting one paw over the finish line count as learning the maze? If the rat falls asleep, should the stopwatch be left running or should the rat be awakened and given a second chance? If a rat runs a maze in 18.5 seconds, should that number be rounded up or rounded down before it is recorded in the log book? The answers to these questions may depend on whether one thinks the rat is bright or dull. The students who timed the rats probably tried to be honest, vigilant, fair, and objective, but their expectations influenced their observations in subtle ways that they could neither detect nor control. Second, *expectations can influence reality.* Students who expected their rats to learn quickly may have unknowingly done things to help that learning along for example, by muttering, "Oh no!" when the bright rat looked the wrong direction or by petting the dull rat less affectionately. (We will discuss both of these phenomena more extensively in the Social Psychology chapter.)

> **Why is it important for experimenters to be "blind"?**

Observers' expectations, then, can have a powerful influence on both their observations and on the behaviour of those whom they observe. Psychologists use many techniques to avoid these influences, and one of the most common is the **double-blind** observation, which is *an observation whose true purpose is hidden from both the observer and the person being observed.* For example, if the students had not been told which rats were bright and which were dull, then they would not have *had* any expectations about their rats, thus their expectations could not have influenced their measurements. That is why it is common practice in psychology to keep the observers as blind as the participants. For example, measurements are often made by research assistants who do not know what is being studied or why, and who therefore do not have any expectations about what the people being observed will or should do. Indeed, studies nowadays are often carried out by the world's blindest experimenter— a computer—which can present information to people and measure their responses while having no expectations at all.

"It was more of a 'triple-blind' test. The patients didn't know which ones were getting the real drug, the doctors didn't know, and, I'm afraid nobody knew."

S. HARRIS/CARTOONSTOCK.COM

## Descriptions

You now know how to generate a valid operational definition, how to design a reliable and powerful instrument, and how to use that instrument while avoiding demand characteristics and observer bias. Suppose you use this knowledge to conduct an experiment. You now have a big page filled with numbers—and if you are like most people, a big page filled with numbers just does not seem very informative. Do not worry, most psychologists feel the same way, and that is why they have two techniques for making sense of big pages full of numbers: graphic representations and descriptive statistics.

### Graphic Representations

A picture may be worth a thousand words, but it is worth a million digits. As you will learn in the Sensation and Perception chapter, vision is our most sophisticated sense, and human beings typically find it easier to understand things when they are represented visually than numerically or verbally. Psychologists are people too, and they often create graphic representations of the measurements they collect. The most

**double-blind**
An observation whose true purpose is hidden from both the observer and the person being observed.

► Figure **2.2** **Frequency Distributions** This graph shows how a hypothetical group of men and women scored on a test of fine motor skills. Test scores are listed along the horizontal axis, and the frequency with which each score was obtained is represented along the vertical axis.

common kind is the **frequency distribution,** which is *a graphic representation of measurements arranged by the number of times each measurement was made.* **FIGURE 2.2** shows a pair of frequency distributions that represent the hypothetical performances of a group of men and women who took a test of fine motor skills (i.e., the ability to manipulate things with their hands). Every possible test score is shown on the horizontal axis. The number of times (or the *frequency* with which) each score was observed is shown on the vertical axis. Although a frequency distribution can have any shape, a common shape is the *bell curve,* which is technically known as the *Gaussian distribution* or the **normal distribution,** which is *a mathematically defined distribution in which the frequency of measurements is highest in the middle and decreases symmetrically in both directions.* The mathematical definition of the normal distribution is not important. (Well, for you anyway. For statisticians it is slightly more important than breathing.) What is important for you is what you can easily see for yourself: The normal distribution is symmetrical (i.e., the left half is a mirror image of the right half), has a peak in the middle, and trails off at both ends.

> What is a frequency distribution?

The picture in Figure 2.2 reveals—in a single optical gulp—what a page full of numbers never can. For instance, the shape of the distributions instantly tells you that most people have moderate motor skills, and that only a few have exceptionally good or exceptionally bad motor skills. You can also see that the distribution of men's scores is displaced a bit to the left of the distribution of women's scores, which instantly tells you that women tend to have somewhat better motor skills than men. And finally, you can see that the two distributions have a great deal of overlap, which tells you that although women tend to have better motor skills than men, there are still plenty of men who have better motor skills than plenty of women.

On average, men are taller than women, but there are still many women (like Nicole Kidman) who are taller than many men (like her husband, Keith Urban).

**frequency distribution**
A graphical representation of measurements arranged by the number of times each measurement was made.

**normal distribution**
A mathematically defined distribution in which the frequency of measurements is highest in the middle and decreases symmetrically in both directions.

## Descriptive Statistics

A frequency distribution depicts every measurement and thus provides a full and complete picture of those measurements. But sometimes a full and complete picture is just too much information. When you ask a friend how she is, you do not want her to show you a frequency distribution of her happiness scores on each day of the previous 6 months. You want a brief summary statement that captures the essential information that such a graph would provide (e.g., "I have been doing pretty well," or, "I have been having some ups and downs lately"). In psychology, brief summary statements that capture the essential information from a frequency distribution are called *descriptive statistics.* There are two important kinds of descriptive statistics: those that describe the *central tendency* of a frequency distribution and those that describe the *variability* in a frequency distribution.

Descriptions of *central tendency* are statements about the value of the measurements that *tend* to lie near the *centre* or midpoint of the frequency distribu-

What are the two major kinds of descriptive statistics?

tion. When a friend says that she is "doing pretty well," she is describing the central tendency (or approximate location of the midpoint) of the fre-quency distribution of her happiness over time (see **FIGURE 2.3**). The three most common descriptions of central tendency are: the **mode** (*the value of the most frequently observed measurement*); the **mean** (*the average value of all the measurements*); and the **median** (*the value that is in the middle, i.e., greater than or equal to half the measurements and less than or equal to half the measurements*). **FIGURE 2.4** shows how each of these descriptive statistics is calculated. When you hear a descriptive statistic such as "the average university undergraduate sleeps 8.3 hours per day," you are hearing about the central tendency of a frequency distribution (in this case, the mean).

In a normal distribution, the mean, median, and mode all have the same value, but when the distribution is not normal, these three descriptive statistics can differ. For example, imagine that you measured the net worth of 40 university professors, and Mark Zuckerberg (a co-founder of Facebook). The frequency distribution of your measurements would not be normal, but *positively skewed*. As you can see in **FIGURE 2.5** (on the next page), the mode and the median of a positively skewed distribution are much lower than the mean because the mean is more strongly influenced by the value of a single extreme measurement (which, in case you have been sleeping for the last few years, would be the net worth of Mark Zuckerberg). When distributions become skewed, the mean gets dragged off toward the tail, the mode stays home at the hump, and the median goes to live between the two. When distributions are skewed, a single

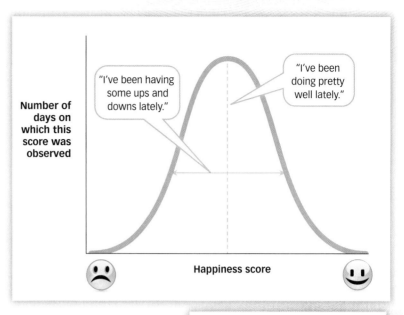

▲ Figure **2.3** **Two Kinds of Descriptive Statistics** Descriptive statistics are used to describe two important features of a frequency distribution: central tendency (Where do most of the scores lie?) and variability (How much do the scores differ from one another?).

**mode**
The value of the most frequently observed measurement.

**mean**
The average value of all the measurements.

**median**
The value that is in the middle, that is, greater than or equal to half the measurements and less than or equal to half the measurements.

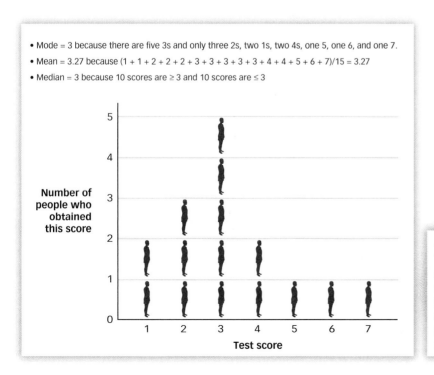

- Mode = 3 because there are five 3s and only three 2s, two 1s, two 4s, one 5, one 6, and one 7.
- Mean = 3.27 because (1 + 1 + 2 + 2 + 2 + 3 + 3 + 3 + 3 + 3 + 4 + 4 + 5 + 6 + 7)/15 = 3.27
- Median = 3 because 10 scores are ≥ 3 and 10 scores are ≤ 3

◀ Figure **2.4** **Some Descriptive Statistics** This frequency distribution shows the scores of 15 individuals on a 7-point test. Descriptive statistics include measures of central tendency (such as the mean, median, and mode) and measures of variability (such as the range and the standard deviation).

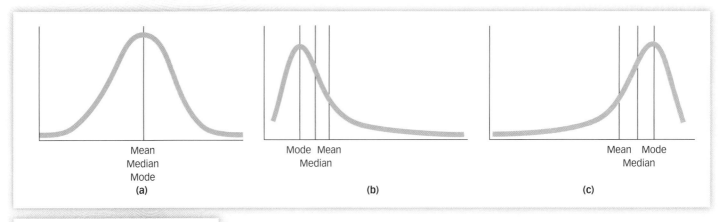

Mean
Median
Mode
(a)

Mode Mean
Median
(b)

Mean Mode
Median
(c)

▲ Figure 2.5 **Skewed Distributions** When a frequency distribution is (a) normal, the mean, median, and mode are all the same, but when it is (b) positively skewed or (c) negatively skewed, these three measures of central tendency are quite different.

measure of central tendency can paint a misleading picture of the measurements. For example, the average net worth of the people you measured is probably about a billion dollars each, but that statement makes the university professors sound a whole lot richer than they are. You could provide a much better description of the net worth of the people you measured if you also mentioned that the median net worth is $300 000 and that the modal net worth is $288 000. Indeed, you should always be suspicious when you hear some new fact about "the average person" but do not hear anything about the shape of the frequency distribution.

Whereas descriptions of central tendency are statements about the location of the measurements in a frequency distribution, descriptions of variability are statements about the extent to which the measurements differ from each other. When a friend says that she has been "having some ups and downs lately," she is offering a brief summary statement that describes how measurements of her happiness taken at different times tend to differ from one another. The simplest description of variability is the **range,** which is *the value of the largest measurement in a frequency distribution minus the value of the smallest measurement.* When the range is small, the measurements do not vary as much as when the range is large. The range is easy to compute, but like the mean it can be dramatically affected by a single measurement. If you said that the net worth of people you had measured ranged from $40 000 to $14 billion, a listener might get the impression that these people were all remarkably different from each other when, in fact, they were all quite similar save for one very rich guy in California.

When Mark Zuckerberg walks into a room he dramatically increases the mean income of the people in it, but does little to the median, and nothing at all to the mode. Facebook is trying to fix that.

Other descriptions of variability are not quite as susceptible to this problem. For example, the **standard deviation** is *a statistic that describes the average difference between the measurements in a frequency distribution and the mean of that distribution.* In other words, on average, how far are the measurements from the centre of the distribution? As **FIGURE 2.6** shows, two frequency distributions can have the same mean, but very different ranges and standard deviations. For example, studies show that men and women have the same mean IQ, but that men have a larger range and standard deviation, which is to say that a man is more likely than a woman to be much more or much less intelligent than the average person of his or her own sex.

**What are two measures of variability?**

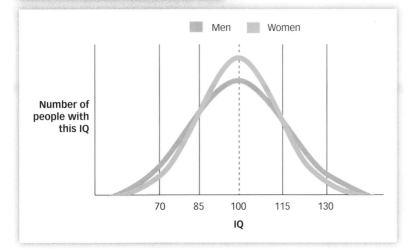

▼ Figure 2.6 **IQ of Men and Women** Men and women have the same average IQ, but men are more variable than women.

Men   Women

Number of people with this IQ

70   85   100   115   130

IQ

## IN SUMMARY

▶ Measurement involves defining a property in terms of a concrete condition, and then constructing a measure that can detect that condition. A good measure is valid (the concrete conditions it measures are conceptually related to the property of interest), reliable (it produces the same measurement whenever it is used to measure the same thing), and powerful (it can detect the concrete conditions when they actually exist).

▶ When people know they are being observed, they may behave as they think they should. Demand characteristics are features of a setting that suggest to people that they should behave in a particular way. Psychologists try to reduce or eliminate demand characteristics by observing participants in their natural habitats or by hiding their expectations from the participant. Observer bias is the tendency for observers to see what they expect to see or cause others to behave as they expect them to behave. Psychologists try to eliminate observer bias by making double-blind observations.

▶ Psychologists often describe the measurements they make with a graphic representation called a frequency distribution, which often has a special shape known as the normal distribution. They also describe their measurements with descriptive statistics; the most common are descriptions of central tendency (such as mean, median, and mode) and descriptions of variability (such as range and standard deviation).

**range**
The value of the largest measurement in a frequency distribution minus the value of the smallest measurement.

**standard deviation**
A statistic that describes the average difference between the measurements in a frequency distribution and the mean of that distribution.

# Explanation: Discovering Why People Do What They Do

It would be interesting to know whether happy people are healthier than unhappy people. However, it would be even more interesting to know why. Does happiness make people healthier? Does being healthy make people happier? Does being wealthy make people healthy and happy? These are the kinds of questions scientists often wish to answer, and scientists have developed some clever ways of using their measurements to do just that. In the first section (Correlation), we will examine techniques that can tell us whether two things are related. In the second section (Causation), we will examine techniques that can tell us whether the relationship between two things is causal. In the third section (Drawing Conclusions), we will see what kinds of conclusions these techniques do—and do not—allow us to draw. Finally, in the fourth section (Thinking Critically about Evidence), we will discuss the difficulty that most of us have thinking critically about scientific evidence.

## Correlation

How much sleep did you get last night? Now, how many capital cities around the world can you name? If you asked a dozen university students those two questions, you would probably find that the students who got a good night's sleep are better capital city namers than are students who pulled an all-nighter. A pattern of responses like the one shown in **TABLE 2.1** would probably lead you to conclude that sleep deprivation causes memory problems. But on what basis did you draw that conclusion? How did you manage to use measurement to tell you not only about *how much* sleeping and remembering had occurred among the students you measured, but also about the *relationship* between sleeping and remembering?

> Table 2.1

**Hypothetical Data Showing the Relationship between Sleep and Memory**

| Participant | Hours of Sleep | No. of Capital Cities Named |
|---|---|---|
| A | 0 | 11 |
| B | 0 | 17 |
| C | 2.7 | 16 |
| D | 3.1 | 21 |
| E | 4.4 | 17 |
| F | 5.5 | 16 |
| G | 7.6 | 31 |
| H | 7.9 | 41 |
| I | 8 | 40 |
| J | 8.1 | 35 |
| K | 8.6 | 38 |
| L | 9 | 43 |

## Patterns of Variation

Measurements tell us about the properties of objects and events. We can learn about the relationships between those objects and events by comparing the *patterns of variation in a series of measurements*. When you asked university students questions about sleep and capital cities, you actually did three things:

> First, you measured a pair of **variables,** which are *properties whose values can vary across individuals or over time*. (When you took your first algebra course you were probably horrified to learn that everything you would been taught in elementary school about the distinction between letters and numbers was a lie, that mathematical equations could contain Xs and Ys as well as 7s and 4s, and that the letters are called *variables* because they can have different values under different circumstances. Same idea here.) You measured one variable (number of hours slept) whose value could vary from *0 to 24*, and you measured a second variable (number of capital cities named) whose value could vary from *0 to 196.*

> **How can we tell if two variables are correlated?**

> Second, you did this again. And then again. And then again. That is, you made a *series* of measurements rather than making just one.

> Third and finally, you tried to discern a pattern in your series of measurements. If you look at the second column of Table 2.1, you will see that it contains values that vary as your eyes move down the column. That column has a particular *pattern of variation*. If you compare the third column with the second, you will notice that the patterns of variation in the two columns are synchronized: in this case, both increase as you move from top to bottom (see **FIGURE 2.7**). This synchrony is known as a *pattern of covariation* or a **correlation** (as in "co-relation"). Two variables are said to "covary" or be "correlated" when *variations in the value of one variable are synchronized with variations in the value of the other*. As the values in the second column vary from small to large, the values in the third column do the same.

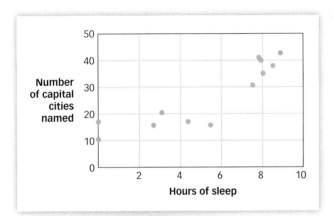

▲ Figure **2.7** **Pattern between Amount of Sleep and Memory** The graph shows the pattern in the data of Table 2.1 between hours of sleep and number of capital cities named.

By looking for synchronized patterns of variation, we can use measurement to discover the relationships between variables. Indeed, this is the only way anyone has *ever* discovered the relationship between variables, which is why most of the facts you know about the world can be thought of as correlations. For example, you know that people who smoke generally die younger than people who do not, but this is just a shorthand way of saying that as the value of *cigarette consumption* increases, the value of *longevity* decreases. Correlations not only describe the world as it is, they also allow us to predict the world as it will be. For example, given the correlation between smoking and longevity, you can predict with some confidence that a young person who starts smoking today will probably not live as long as a young person who does not start. In short, when two variables are correlated, knowledge of the value of one variable allows us to make predictions about the value of the other variable.

### Measuring the Direction and Strength of a Correlation

If you predict that a well-rested person will have a better memory than a sleep-deprived person, you will be right more often than wrong. But you will not be right in every single instance. Statisticians have developed a way to estimate how accurate such predictions are likely to be by measuring the *direction* and *strength* of the correlation on which the predictions are based.

Direction is easy to measure because the direction of a correlation is either positive or negative. A positive correlation exists when two variables have a "more-is-more" or

**variable**
A property whose value can vary across individuals or over time.

**correlation**
Two variables are said to "covary" or be "correlated" when variations in the value of one variable are synchronized with variations in the value of the other.

1

1

"less-is-less" relationship. So, for example, when we say that *more sleep* is associated with *more memory* or that *less sleep* is associated with *less memory,* we are describing a positive correlation. Conversely, a negative correlation exists when two variables have a "more-is-less" or "less-is-more" relationship. When we say that *more cigarette smoking* is associated with *less longevity* or that *less cigarette smoking* is associated with *more longevity,* we are describing a negative correlation.

The direction of a correlation is easy to measure, but the strength is a little more complicated. The **correlation coefficient** is *a mathematical measure of both the direction and strength of a correlation* and it is symbolized by the letter $r$ (as in "relationship"). Like most measures, the correlation coefficient has a limited range. What does that mean? Well, if you were to measure the number of hours of sunshine per day in your hometown, that number could range from 0 to 24. Numbers such as $-7$ and 36.8 would be meaningless. Similarly, the value of $r$ can range from $-1$ to 1, and numbers outside that range are meaningless. What, then, do the numbers *inside* that range mean?

> **How can correlations be measured?**

> If every time the value of one variable increases by a fixed amount the value of the second variable also increases by a fixed amount, then the relationship between the variables is called a *perfect positive correlation* and $r = 1$ (see **FIGURE 2.8a**). For example, if every 30-minute increase in sleep was associated with a 2-capital-city increase in memory, then sleep and memory would be *perfectly positively correlated.*

> If every time the value of one variable increases by a fixed amount the value of the second variable *decreases* by a fixed amount, then the relationship between the variables is called a *perfect negative correlation* and $r = -1$ (see **FIGURE 2.8b**). For example, if every 30-minute increase in sleep was associated with a 2-capital-city decrease in memory, then sleep and memory would be *perfectly negatively correlated.*

> If every time the value of one variable increases by a fixed amount the value of the second variable neither increases nor decreases systematically, then the two variables are said to be *uncorrelated* and $r = 0$ (see **FIGURE 2.8c**). For example, if a 30-minute increase in sleep was sometimes associated with an increase in memory, sometimes associated with a decrease in memory, and sometimes associated with no change in memory at all, then sleep and memory would be uncorrelated.

Perfect correlations are extremely rare in real life. As you will learn in the Consciousness chapter, sleep really does enhance memory performance, but the relationship is not perfect. It is not as though every 18 minutes of sleep buys you exactly

Researchers have found a positive correlation between mental illness and smoking. Can you think of three reasons why this correlation might exist?

▼ Figure 2.8 **Three Kinds of Correlations** These figures illustrate correlations between variables: (a) a perfect positive correlation ($r = 1$), (b) a perfect negative correlation ($r = -1$), and (c) no correlation ($r = 0$).

$r = 1$
**(a)** Perfect Positive Correlation

$r = -1$
**(b)** Perfect Negative Correlation

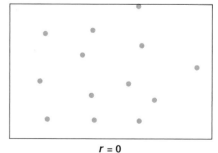

$r = 0$
**(c)** No Correlation

▶ Figure **2.9** **Positive Correlations of Different Strengths** These graphs illustrate different degrees of positive correlation between two variables. When there are few exceptions to the rule X = Y, then the correlation is strong and r is closer to 1 (see Figure 2.8a). When there are many exceptions to this rule, the correlation is weak and r is closer to 0 (see Figure 2.8c). Negative correlations can be just as strong as positive correlations. The only difference is that for positive correlations, greater values of X are associated with greater values of Y and for negative correlations, greater values of X are associated with lesser values of Y.

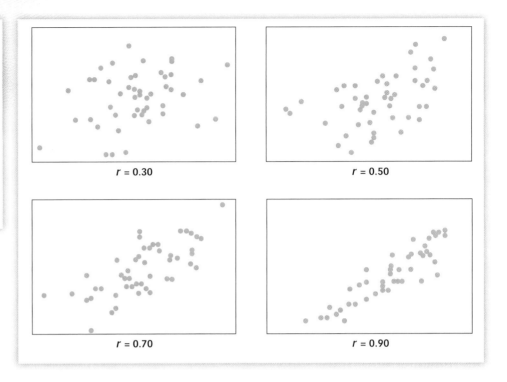

r = 0.30

r = 0.50

r = 0.70

r = 0.90

one third of a remembered capital city! Sleep and memory are *positively* correlated (i.e., as one increases, the other also increases), but they are *imperfectly* correlated, thus r will lie somewhere between 0 and 1. But where? That depends on how many exceptions there are to the "X more minutes of sleep = Y more capital cities remembered" rule. If there are only a few exceptions, then r will lie much closer to 1 than to 0. But as the number of exceptions increases, then the value of r will begin to move toward 0.

**FIGURE 2.9** shows four cases in which two variables are positively correlated but have different numbers of exceptions and, as you can see, the number of exceptions changes the value of r quite dramatically. Two variables can have a perfect correlation (r = 1 as in Figure 2.8a), a strong correlation (e.g., r = 0.90), a moderate correlation (e.g., r = 0.70), or a weak correlation (e.g., r = 0.30). The correlation coefficient, then, is a measure of both the *direction* and *strength* of the relationship between two variables. The sign of r (plus or minus) tells us the direction of the relationship and the absolute value of r (between 0 and 1) tells us about the number of exceptions and hence how confident we can be when using the correlation to make predictions.

> What does it mean for a correlation to be strong?

It is not always easy to detect causal relationships accurately. For centuries, people sacrificed their enemies without realizing that doing so does not actually cause rain, and they smoked cigarettes without realizing that doing so actually does cause illness.

## Causation

We observe correlations all the time: between automobiles and pollution, between bacon and heart attacks, between sex and pregnancy. **Natural correlations** are *the correlations observed in the world around us*, and although such observations can tell us whether two variables have a relationship, they cannot tell us what *kind* of relationship these variables have. For example, many studies have found a positive correlation between the amount of violence to which a child is exposed through media such as television, movies, and video games

THE GRANGER COLLECTION

APIC/GETTY IMAGES

(variable $X$) and the aggressiveness of the child's behaviour (variable $Y$) (Anderson & Bushman, 2001; Anderson et al., 2003; Huesmann et al., 2003). The more media violence a child is exposed to, the more aggressive that child is likely to be. These variables clearly have a relationship—they are imperfectly positively correlated—but why?

## The Third-Variable Problem

One possibility is that exposure to media violence ($X$) causes aggressiveness ($Y$). For example, media violence may teach children that aggression is a reasonable way to vent anger and solve problems. A second possibility is that aggressiveness ($Y$) causes children to be exposed to media violence ($X$). For example, children who are naturally aggressive may be especially likely to seek opportunities to play violent video games or watch violent movies. A third possibility is that a *third variable* ($Z$) causes children to be aggressive ($Y$) and to be exposed to media violence ($X$), neither of which is causally related to the other. For example, lack of adult supervision ($Z$) may allow children to get away with bullying others and to get away with watching television shows that adults would normally not allow. If so, then being exposed to media violence ($X$) and behaving aggressively ($Y$) may not be causally related to each other at all and may instead be the independent effects of a lack of adult supervision ($Z$). In other words, the relation between aggressiveness and exposure to media violence may be a case of **third-variable correlation,** which means that *two variables are correlated only because each is causally related to a third variable.* **FIGURE 2.10** shows three possible causes of any correlation.

> **What is third-variable correlation?**

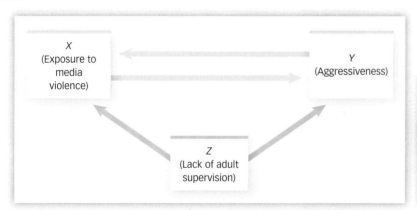

◄ Figure **2.10** **Causes of Correlation**
If $X$ (exposure to media violence) and $Y$ (aggressiveness) are correlated, then there are at least three possible explanations: $X$ causes $Y$, $Y$ causes $X$, or $Z$ (some other factor, such as lack of adult supervision) causes both $Y$ and $X$, neither of which causes the other.

How can we determine by simple observation which of these three possibilities best describes the relationship between exposure to media violence and aggressiveness? Take a deep breath. The answer is: *We cannot.* When we observe a natural correlation, the possibility of third-variable correlation can never be dismissed. But do not take this claim on faith. Let us try to dismiss the possibility of third-variable correlation and you will see why such efforts are always doomed to fail.

The most straightforward way to determine whether a third variable, such as lack of adult supervision ($Z$), causes both exposure to media violence ($X$) and aggressive behaviour ($Y$) is to eliminate differences in adult supervision ($Z$) among a group of children and see if the correlation between exposure ($X$) and aggressiveness ($Y$) is eliminated too. For example, we could observe children using the **matched samples technique,** which is *a technique whereby the participants in two groups are identical in terms of a third variable* (see **FIGURE 2.11** on the next page). For instance, we could measure only children who are supervised by an adult exactly $Q$ percent of the time, thus ensuring that every child who was exposed to media

> **What is the difference between matched samples and matched pairs?**

**natural correlation**
A correlation observed in the world around us.

**third-variable correlation**
Two variables are correlated only because each is causally related to a third variable.

**matched samples technique**
A technique whereby the participants in two groups are identical in terms of a third variable.

► Figure **2.11** **Matched Sample and Pairs**
Both the (a) matched samples technique and the (b) matched pairs technique ensure that children in the exposure and no-exposure groups have the same amount of adult supervision on average, and thus any differences we observe between the groups cannot be due to differences in adult supervision.

| Matched Sample | | Matched Pairs | |
|---|---|---|---|
| **Exposure** | **No Exposure** | **Exposure** | **No Exposure** |
| 48% | 48% | 20% | 20% |
| 48% | 48% | 91% | 91% |
| 48% | 48% | 33% | 33% |
| | | **Mean = 48%** | **Mean = 48%** |

PHOTOS © PHOTODISC

GEORGE MARKS/GETTY IMAGES

BETTMANN/CORBIS

In 1949, Dr. Benjamin Sandler a physician from North Carolina, United States, noticed a correlation between the incidence of polio and ice cream consumption, and concluded that sugar made children susceptible to the disease. Public health officials issued warnings. As it turned out, a third variable—warm weather—caused both an increase in disease (viruses become more active in the summer) and an increase in ice cream consumption.

**matched pairs technique**
A technique whereby each participant is identical to one other participant in terms of a third variable.

**third-variable problem**
The fact that a causal relationship between two variables cannot be inferred from the naturally occurring correlation between them because of the ever-present possibility of third-variable correlation.

**experiment**
A technique for establishing the causal relationship between variables.

violence had exactly the same amount of adult supervision as every child who was not exposed. Alternatively, we could observe children using the **matched pairs technique,** which is *a technique whereby each participant is identical to one other participant in terms of a third variable*. We could measure children who have different amounts of adult supervision, but we could make sure that for every child we measure who is exposed to media violence and is supervised $Q$ percent of the time, we also observe a child who is not exposed to media violence and is supervised $Q$ percent of the time, thus ensuring that children who are and are not exposed to media violence have the same amount of adult supervision *on average*. Regardless of which technique we used, we would know that children who were and were not exposed to media violence had equal amounts of adult supervision on average. So if those who were exposed are on average more aggressive than those who were not exposed, we can be sure that lack of adult supervision was not the cause of this difference.

So we solved the problem, right? Well, not exactly. The matched samples technique and the matched pairs techniques can be useful, but neither eliminates the possibility of third-variable correlation entirely. Why? Because even if we used these techniques to dismiss a *particular* third variable (such as lack of adult supervision), we would not be able to dismiss *all* third variables. For example, as soon as we finished making these observations, it might suddenly occur to us that emotional instability could cause children to gravitate toward violent television or video games and to behave aggressively. Emotional instability would be a new third variable ($Z$) and we would have to design a new test to investigate whether it explains the correlation between exposure ($X$) and aggression ($Y$). Unfortunately, we could keep dreaming up new third variables all day long without ever breaking a sweat, and every time we dreamed one up, we would have to rush out and do a new test using matched samples or matched pairs to determine whether *this* third variable was the cause of the correlation between exposure and aggressiveness.

Are you starting to see the problem? There are a humongous number of third variables, so there are a humongous number of reasons why $X$ and $Y$ might be correlated.

And because we cannot perform a humongous number of studies with matched samples or matched pairs, we cannot be absolutely sure that the correlation we observe between X and Y is evidence of a causal relationship between them. The **third-variable problem** refers to the fact that *a causal relationship between two variables cannot be inferred from the naturally occurring correlation between them because of the ever-present possibility of third-variable correlation.* In other words, if we care about causality, then naturally occurring correlations just will not tell us what we really want to know. Luckily, another technique will.

## Experimentation

The matched pairs and matched samples techniques eliminate a single difference between two groups: for example, the difference in adult supervision between groups of children who were and were not exposed to media violence. The problem is that they only eliminate one difference and a

> What are the two main features of an experiment?

humongous number remain. If we could just find a technique that eliminated *all* of the humongous number of differences then we *could* conclude that exposure and aggression are causally related. If exposed kids were more aggressive than unexposed kids, and if the two groups did not differ in *any* way except for that exposure, then we could be sure that their level of exposure had caused their level of aggression.

In fact, scientists have a technique that does exactly that. It is called an **experiment,** which is *a technique for establishing the causal relationship between variables.* The best way to understand how experiments eliminate all the differences between groups is by examining their two key features: *manipulation* and *random assignment.*

## Manipulation

The most important thing to know about experiments is that you already know the most important thing about experiments because you have been doing them all your life. Imagine that you are surfing the web on a laptop when all of a sudden you lose your wireless connection. You suspect that another device—say, your roommate's new cell phone—has somehow bumped you off the network. What would you do to test your suspicion? Observing a natural correlation would not be much help. You could carefully note when you did and did not have a connection and when your roommate did and did not use his cell phone, but even if you observed a correlation between these two variables you still could not conclude that the cell phone was *causing* you to lose your network connection. After all, if your roommate was afraid of loud noises and called his mommy for comfort whenever there was an electrical storm, and if that storm zapped your router and crashed your wireless network, then the storm (Z) would be the cause of both your roommate's cell phone usage (X) and your connectivity problem (Y).

So how could you test your suspicion? Well, rather than *observing* the correlation between cell phone usage and connectivity, you could try to *create* a correlation by intentionally making a call on your roommate's cell phone, hanging up,

(a)　　　(b)

Where should you put the "buy now" button on a web page? Developers often create two versions of their web pages. Some visitors see one version, some see the other, and the developer measures the number of clicks that each version elicits. Developers call this "A/B Testing," but scientists just call it experimentation.

How do you determine whether eating 4 kg of poutine would make you sick? You eat it one day, do not eat it the next, and see which day you barf. That is manipulation! By the way, in 2012, Joey Chestnut won the World Poutine Eating Championship by consuming 19 boxes (almost 5 kg) of poutine in 10 minutes. He accomplished this by mashing the poutine in his fist, and stuffing it in his mouth. That is manipulation too!

**manipulation**
Changing a variable in order to determine its causal power.

**independent variable**
The variable that is manipulated in an experiment.

**experimental group**
The group of people who are exposed to a particular manipulation, as compared to the control group, in an experiment.

**control group**
The group of people who are not exposed to the particular manipulation, as compared to the experimental group, in an experiment.

**dependent variable**
The variable that is measured in a study.

**self-selection**
A problem that occurs when anything about a person determines whether he or she will be included in the experimental or control group.

making another call, hanging up again, and observing changes in your laptop's connectivity as you did so. If you observed that "laptop connection off" only occurred in conjunction with "cell phone on" then you could conclude that your roommate's cell phone was the *cause* of your failed connection, and you could sell the phone on eBay and then lie about it when asked. The technique you intuitively used to solve the third-variable problem is called **manipulation,** which involves *changing a variable in order to determine its causal power.* Congratulations! You are now officially a manipulator.

Manipulation is a critical ingredient in experimentation. Until now, we have approached science like polite dinner guests, taking what we were offered and making the best of it. Nature offered us children who differed in how much violence they were exposed to and who differed in how aggressively they behaved, and we dutifully measured the natural patterns of variation in these two variables and computed their correlations. The problem with this approach is that when all was said and done, we still did not know what we really wanted to know, namely, whether these variables had a causal relationship. No matter how many matched samples or matched pairs we observed, there was always another third variable that we had not yet dismissed. Experiments solve this problem. Rather than *measuring* exposure and *measuring* aggression and then computing the correlation between these two naturally occurring variables, experiments require that we *manipulate* exposure in exactly the same way that you manipulated your roommate's cell phone. In essence, we need to systematically switch exposure on and off in a group of children and then watch to see whether aggression goes on and off too.

There are many ways to do this. For example, we might ask some children to participate in an experiment, then have half of them play violent video games for an hour and make sure the other half does not. Then, at the end of the hour, we could measure the children's aggression and compare the measurements across the two groups. When we compared these measurements, we would essentially be computing the correlation between a variable that we manipulated (exposure) and a variable that we measured (aggression). Because we *manipulated* rather than *measured* exposure, we would never have to ask whether a third variable (such as lack of adult supervision) caused children to experience different levels of exposure. After all, we already *know* what caused that to happen. *We* did!

Experimentation involves three critical steps (and several ridiculously confusing terms):

> First, we perform a manipulation. We call *the variable that is manipulated* the **independent variable** because it is under our control, and thus it is "independent" of what the participant says or does. When we manipulate an independent variable (such as exposure to media violence), we create at least two groups of participants: an **experimental group,** which is *the group of people who are exposed to a particular manipulation,* and a **control group,** which is *the group of people who are not exposed to that particular manipulation.* (Another way to design an experiment would be to test every participant in the experiment twice—once when they have experienced the manipulation and once when they have not. Such a design is efficient, but it is not possible for every experimental question.)

> Second, having manipulated one variable (exposure), we now measure another variable (aggression). We call *the variable that is measured* the **dependent variable** because its value "depends" on what the person being measured says or does.

> Third and finally, we look to see whether our manipulation of the independent variable produced changes in the dependent variable. **FIGURE 2.12** (on the next page) shows exactly how manipulation works.

What are the three main steps in doing an experiment?

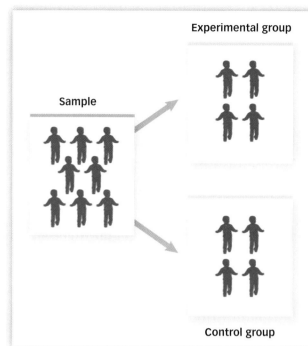

**Experimental group**

| Exposed to media violence? | Aggression |
|---|---|
| Yes | High |
| Yes | High |
| Yes | High |
| Yes | High |

**Sample**

| Exposed to media violence? | Aggression |
|---|---|
| No | Low |
| No | Low |
| No | Low |
| No | Low |

**Control group**

◄ Figure **2.12** **Manipulation** The independent variable is exposure to media violence and the dependent variable is aggression. Manipulation of the independent variable results in an experimental group and a control group. When we compare the behaviour of participants in these two groups, we are actually computing the correlation between the independent variable and the dependent variable.

## Random Assignment

Once we have manipulated an independent variable and measured a dependent variable, we have done one of the two things that experimentation requires. The second thing is a little less intuitive but equally important. Imagine that we began our exposure and aggression experiment by finding a group of children and asking each child whether he or she would like to be in the experimental group or the control group. Imagine that half the children said that they would like to play violent video games and the other half said they would rather not. Imagine that we let the children do what they wanted to do, measured aggression some time later, and found that the children who had played the violent video games were more aggressive than those who had not. Would this experiment allow us to conclude that playing violent video games causes aggression? Definitely not—but *why* not? After all, we switched exposure on and off like a cell phone, and we watched to see whether aggression went on and off too. So where did we go wrong?

We went wrong when we let the children decide for themselves whether or not they would play violent video games. After all, children who ask to play

There is no evidence that Louise Hay's techniques can cure cancer. But even if cancer victims who bought her books *did* show a higher rate of remission than those who did not, there would *still* be no evidence because buyers are self-selected and thus may differ from non-buyers in countless ways.

**Why can we not allow people to select the condition of the experiment in which they will participate?**

such games are probably different in many ways from those who ask not to. They may be older, or stronger, or smarter—or younger, weaker, or dumber—or less often supervised or more often supervised. The list of possible differences goes on and on. The whole point of doing an experiment was to divide children into two groups that differed *in only one way,* namely, in terms of their exposure to media violence. The moment we let the children decide for themselves whether they would be in the experimental group or the control group, we had two groups that differed in countless ways, and any of those countless differences could have been a third variable that was responsible for any differences we may have observed in their measured aggression. **Self-selection** is *a problem that occurs when anything about a person determines whether he or she will be included in the experimental*

Do strawberries taste better when dipped in chocolate? If you dip the big juicy ones and do not dip the small dry ones, then you will not know if the chocolate is what made the difference. But if you randomly assign some to be dipped and others not to be dipped, and if the dipped ones taste better on average, then you will have demonstrated scientifically what every 3-year-old already knows.

*or control group.* Just as we cannot allow nature to decide which of the children in our study is exposed to media violence, we cannot allow the children to decide either. Okay, then who decides?

The answer to this question is a bit spooky: *No one does.* If we want to be sure that there is one and only one difference between the children in our study who are and are not exposed to media violence, then their inclusion in the experimental or control groups must be *randomly determined.* If you flipped a coin and a friend asked what had *caused* it to land heads up, you would correctly say that *nothing* had. This is what it means for the outcome of a coin flip to be random. Because the outcome of a coin flip is random, we can put coin flips to work for us to solve the problem that self-selection creates. If we want to be sure that a child's inclusion in the experimental or control group was not caused by nature, was not caused by the child, and was not caused by *any* of the countless third variables we could name if we only had the time to name them, then all we have to do is let it be caused by the outcome of a coin flip—which itself has no cause! For example, we could walk up to each child in our experiment, flip a coin, and, if the coin lands heads up, assign the child to play violent video games. If the coin lands heads down, then we could assign the child to play no violent video games. **Random assignment** is a *procedure that lets chance assign people to the experimental or the control group.*

> Why is random assignment so useful and important?

What would happen if we assigned children to groups with a coin flip? As **FIGURE 2.13** shows, the first thing we would expect is that about half the children would be assigned to play violent video games and about half would not. Second—and *much* more important—we could expect the experimental group and the control group to have roughly equal numbers of supervised kids and unsupervised kids, roughly equal numbers of emotionally stable and unstable kids, roughly equal numbers of big kids and small kids, of active kids, fat kids, tall kids, funny kids, and kids with blue hair named Larry McSweeny. In other words, we could expect the two groups to have roughly equal numbers of kids who are anything-you-can-ever-name-and-everything-you-cannot! Because the kids in the two groups will be the same *on average* in terms of height, weight, emotional stability, adult supervision, and every other variable in the

► Figure **2.13** **Random Assignment** Children with adult supervision are shown in orange and those without adult supervision are shown in blue. The independent variable is exposure to media violence and the dependent variable is aggression. Random assignment ensures that participants in the experimental and the control groups are on average equal in terms of all possible third variables. In essence, it ensures that there is no correlation between a third variable and the dependent variable.

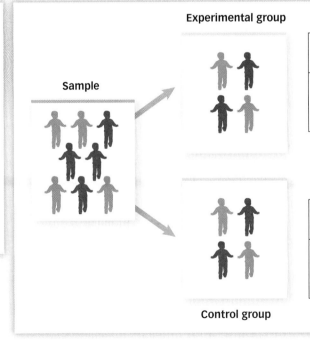

**Sample**

**Experimental group**

| Exposed to media violence? | Adult supervision? | Aggression |
| --- | --- | --- |
| Yes | Yes | High |
| Yes | No | High |
| Yes | Yes | High |
| Yes | No | High |

**Control group**

| Exposed to media violence? | Adult supervision? | Aggression |
| --- | --- | --- |
| No | Yes | Low |
| No | No | Low |
| No | Yes | Low |
| No | No | Low |

known universe *except the one we manipulated*, we can be sure that the variable we manipulated (exposure) was the one and only cause of any changes in the variable we measured (aggression). Because exposure was the *only* difference between the two groups of children when we started the experiment, it *must* be the cause of any differences in aggression we observe at the end of the experiment.

**random assignment**
A procedure that lets chance assign people to the experimental or control group.

## Significance

Random assignment is a powerful tool but, like a lot of tools, it does not work every time you use it. If we randomly assigned children to watch or not watch televised violence, we could expect the two groups to have roughly equal numbers of supervised and unsupervised kids, roughly equal numbers of emotionally stable and unstable kids, and so on. The key word in that sentence is *roughly*. When you flip a coin 100 times, you can expect it to land heads up *roughly* 50 times. But every once in a while, 100 coin flips will produce 80 heads, or 90 heads, or even 100 heads, by sheer chance alone. This does not happen often, of course, but it does happen. Because random assignment is achieved by using a randomizing device such as a coin, every once in a long while the coin will assign more unsupervised, emotionally unstable kids to play violent video games and more supervised, emotionally stable kids to play none. When

## THE REAL WORLD

## "Oddsly" Enough

A recent Gallup survey found that 53 percent of university graduates believe in extrasensory perception, or ESP. Very few psychologists share that belief. What makes them such a skeptical lot is their understanding of the laws of probability.

Consider the case of The Truly Amazing Coincidence. One night you dream that a panda is piloting an airplane over the Indian Ocean, and the next day you tell a friend, who says, "Wow, I had exactly the same dream!" One morning you wake up humming an old Radiohead tune (probably "Paranoid Android") and an hour later you hear it playing in the mall. You and your roommate are sitting around watching television when suddenly you turn to each other and say in perfect unison, "Want pizza?" Coincidences like these might make anyone believe in supernatural mental weirdness.

Well, not anyone. The Nobel laureate Luis Alvarez was reading the newspaper one day and a particular story got him thinking about an old friend whom he had not seen in years. A few minutes later, he turned the page and was shocked to see the very same friend's obituary. But before concluding that he had an acute case of ESP Alvarez decided to use probability theory to determine just how amazing this coincidence really was.

First he estimated the number of friends an average person has, and then he estimated how often an average person thinks about each of those friends. With these estimates in hand, he did a few simple calculations and determined the likelihood that someone would think about a friend 5 minutes before learning about that friend's death. The odds were astonishing. In a country the size of the United States, for example, Alvarez predicted that this amazing coincidence should happen to 10 people every day (Alvarez, 1965). Another Nobel laureate disagreed. He put the number closer to 80 people a day (Charpak & Broch, 2004)!

"In 10 years there are 5 million minutes," says statistics professor Irving Jack. "That means each person has plenty of opportunity to have some remarkable coincidences in his life" (quoted in Neimark, 2004). For example, 28 million Canadians dream for about two hours every night (that is 56 million hours of dreaming!), so it is not surprising that two people sometimes have the same dream, or that we sometimes dream about something that actually happens the next day. As mathematics professor John Allen Paulos (quoted in Neimark, 2004) put it, "In reality, the most astonishingly incredible coincidence

*"Idaho! What a coincidence—I'm from Idaho."*

imaginable would be the complete absence of all coincidence."

If all of this seems surprising to you, then you are not alone. Research shows that people routinely underestimate the likelihood of coincidences happening by chance (Diaconis & Mosteller, 1989; Falk & McGregor, 1983; Hintzman, Asher, & Stern, 1978). If you want to profit from this fact, assemble a group of 24 or more people and bet anyone that at least 2 of the people share a birthday. The odds are in your favour, and the bigger the group, the better the odds. In fact, in a group of 35, the odds are 85 percent. Happy fleecing!

Scientists take a solemn oath to wear this T-shirt under their clothing at all times.

this happens, random assignment has failed—and when random assignment fails, the third-variable problem rises up out of its grave like a guy with a hockey mask and a grudge. When random assignment fails, we cannot conclude that there is a causal relationship between the independent and dependent variables.

How can we tell when random assignment has failed? Unfortunately, we cannot tell for sure. But we can calculate the *odds* that random assignment has failed each time we use it. It is not important for you to know how to do this calculation, but it is important for you to understand how psychologists interpret its results. Psychologists perform this calculation every time they do an experiment, and they do not accept the results of those experiments unless the calculation tells them that if random assignment had failed, then there is less than a 5 percent chance that they would have seen those particular results.

When there is less than a 5 percent chance that a result would happen if random assignment had failed, then that result is said to be *statistically significant*. You have already learned about descriptive statistics, such as mean, median, mode, range, and standard deviation. There is another kind of statistics—called *inferential statistics*—that tells scientists what kinds of conclusions or inferences they can draw from observed differences between the experimental and control groups. For example, *p* (for "probability") is an inferential statistic that tells psychologists the likelihood that random assignment failed in a particular experiment. When psychologists report that $p < 0.05$, they are saying that according to the inferential statistics they calculated, the odds that their results would have occurred if random assignment had failed are less than 5 percent, and given that those results did occur, a failure of random assignment is unlikely to have happened. Therefore, differences between the experimental and control groups were unlikely to have been caused by a third variable.

## Drawing Conclusions

If we applied all the techniques discussed so far, we could design an experiment that had a very good chance of establishing the causal relationship between two variables. That experiment would have **internal validity,** which is *an attribute of an experiment that allows it to establish causal relationships.* When we say that an experiment is internally valid, we mean that everything *inside* the experiment is working exactly as it must in order for us to draw conclusions about causal relationships. But what exactly are those conclusions? If our imaginary experiment revealed a difference between the aggressiveness of children in the exposed and unexposed groups, then we could conclude that media violence *as we defined it* caused aggression *as we defined it* in the people *whom we studied.* Notice those phrases in italics. Each corresponds to an important restriction on the kinds of conclusions we can draw from an experiment, so let us consider each in turn.

### Representative Variables

The results of any experiment depend, in part, on how the independent and dependent variables are defined. For instance, we are more likely to find that exposure to media violence causes aggression when we define exposure as "watching 2 hours of gory axe murders" rather than "watching 10 minutes of football," or when we define aggression as "interrupting another person" rather than "smacking someone silly with a tire iron." The way we define variables can have a profound influence on what we find, so which of these is the *right* way?

One answer is that we should define variables in an experiment as they are defined in the real world. **External validity** is *an attribute of an experiment in which variables have been defined in a normal, typical, or realistic way.* It seems pretty clear that the kind of aggressive behaviour that concerns teachers and parents lies somewhere between an interruption and an assault, and that the kind of media violence to which children

**internal validity**
An attribute of an experiment that allows it to establish causal relationships.

**external validity**
An attribute of an experiment in which variables have been defined in a normal, typical, or realistic way.

are typically exposed lies somewhere between sports and torture. If the goal of an experiment is to determine whether the kinds of media violence to which children are typically exposed causes the kinds of aggression with which societies are typically concerned, then external validity is essential. When variables are defined in an experiment as they typically are in the real world, we say that the variables are *representative* of the real world.

External validity sounds like such a good idea that you may be surprised to learn that most psychology experiments are externally *invalid*—and that most psychologists do not mind. The reason for this is that psychologists are rarely trying to learn about the real world by creating tiny replicas of it in their laboratories. Rather, they are usually trying to learn about the real world by using experiments to test hypotheses derived from theories, and externally invalid experiments can often do that quite nicely (Mook, 1983).

> **Why is external validity unnecessary?**

RADIUS IMAGES/ALAMY

AP PHOTO/KEYSTONE, TIPRESS/SAMUEL GOLAY

Does piercing make a person more or less attractive? The answer, of course, depends entirely on how you operationally define *piercing*.

To see how, consider an example from physics. Physicists have a theory stating that heat is the result of the rapid movement of molecules. This theory gives rise to a hypothesis, namely, that when the molecules that constitute an object are slowed, the object should become cooler. Now imagine that a physicist tested this hypothesis by performing an experiment in which a laser was used to slow the movement of the molecules in a rubber ball, whose temperature was then measured. Would you criticize this experiment by saying, "Sorry, but your experiment teaches us nothing about the real world because in the real world, no one actually uses lasers to slow the movement of the molecules in rubber balls"? Let us hope not. The physicist's theory (molecular motion causes heat) led to a hypothesis about *what would happen in the laboratory* (slowing the molecules in a rubber ball should cool it), and the events that the physicist manipulated and measured in the laboratory served to test the theory. Similarly, a well-thought-out theory about the causal relationship between exposure to media violence and aggression should lead to hypotheses about how children in a laboratory will behave after watching a violent movie, and thus their reaction to the movie serves to test the theory. If children who watched *Iron Man 3* were more likely to push and shove each other on their way out of the laboratory, then any theory that says that media violence cannot influence aggression has just been proved wrong.

In short, theories allow us to generate hypotheses about what can, must, or will happen under particular circumstances, and experiments are usually meant to create those circumstances, test the hypotheses, and thereby provide evidence for or against the theories that generated them. Experiments are not usually meant to be miniature versions of everyday life, and thus external invalidity is not necessarily a problem (see the Hot Science box, Do Violent Movies Make Peaceful Streets?).

## Representative People

Our imaginary experiment on exposure to media violence and aggression would allow us to conclude that exposure as we defined it caused aggression as we defined it in the people *whom we studied.* That last phrase represents another important restriction on the kinds of conclusions we can draw from experiments.

Who are the people whom psychologists study? Psychologists rarely observe an entire **population,** which is *a complete collection of people*, such as the population of

**population**
A complete collection of participants who might possibly be measured.

## HOT SCIENCE

# Do Violent Movies Make Peaceful Streets?

In 2000, the American Academy of Pediatrics and five other American public health organizations issued a joint statement warning about the risks of exposure to media violence. They cited evidence from psychological experiments in which children and young adults who were exposed to violent movie clips showed a sharp increase in aggressive behaviour immediately afterward. They noted that "well over 1000 studies ... point overwhelmingly to a causal connection between media violence and aggressive behaviour."

Given the laboratory results, we might expect to see a correlation in the real world between the number of people who see violent movies in theatres and the number of violent crimes. When economists Gordon Dahl and Stefano Della Vigna (2009) analyzed crime statistics and box office statistics, they found just such a correlation—except that it was negative! In other words, on evenings when more people went to the theatre to

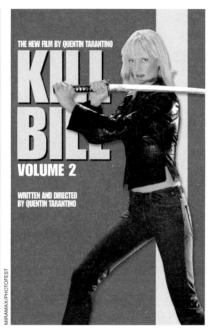

watch violent movies, there were *fewer* violent crimes. Why? The researchers suggested that violent movies are especially appealing to the people who are most likely to commit violent crimes. Because those people are busy watching movies for a few hours, violent crime drops. In other words, blood-and-bullet movies take criminals off the street by luring them to the theatre!

Laboratory experiments clearly show that exposure to media violence *can* cause aggression. But as the movie theatre data remind us, experiments are a tool for establishing the causal relationships between variables and are not meant to be miniature versions of the real world, where things are ever so much more complex.

◀ The movie *Kill Bill 2* premiered on April 16, 2004 in North America to an audience of over 8 million. Does this mean that writer and director Quentin Tarantino deterred 8 million potential crimes that day?

**sample**
A partial collection of people drawn from a population.

**case method**
A procedure for gathering scientific information by studying a single individual.

**random sampling**
A technique for choosing participants that ensures that every member of a population has an equal chance of being included in the sample.

Jay Greenburg was just 15 years old when his first CD was released—a recording of the London Symphony Orchestra performing his fifth Symphony.

human beings (about 7 billion), the population of Canadians (about 35 million), or the population of Canadians with Down syndrome (about 35 000). Rather, they observe a **sample,** which is *a partial collection of people drawn from a population.* How big can a sample be? The size of a population is signified by the uppercase letter $N$, the size of a sample is signified by the lowercase letter $n$, so $0 < n < N$. If you read this as an emoticon it means ... oh well, never mind.

In most studies $n$ is closer to 0 than to $N$, and in some cases $n = 1$. For example, sometimes single individuals are so remarkable that they deserve close study, and when psychologists study them they use the **case method,** which is *a procedure for gathering scientific information by studying a single individual.* We can learn a lot about memory by studying someone like Akira Haraguchi, who can recite the first 100 000 digits of pi; about consciousness by studying someone like Henry Molaison, whose ability to look backward and forward in time was destroyed by damage to his brain; about intelligence and creativity by studying someone like former child prodigy Jay Greenburg, whose musical compositions have been recorded by the Julliard String Quartet and the London Symphony Orchestra. Cases such as these are interesting in their own right, but they also provide important insights into how the rest of us work.

Of course, most of the psychological studies you will read about in the other chapters of this book included samples of ten, a hundred, a thousand, or a few thousand people. So how do psychologists decide which people to include in their samples? One way to select a sample from a population is by **random sampling,** which is *a technique for choosing participants that ensures that every member of a population has an equal chance of being included in the sample.* When we randomly sample participants from a population, the sample is said to be *representative* of the population. This allows us to *generalize* from the sample to the population—that is, to conclude that what we observed in our sample would also have been observed if we had measured the entire population. You probably already have solid intuitions about the importance of random

> **What is the difference between a population and a sample?**

sampling. For example, if you stopped at a farm stand to buy a bag of cherries and the farmer offered to let you taste a few that he had handpicked from the bag, you would be reluctant to generalize from that sample to the population of cherries in the bag. But if the farmer invited you to pull a few cherries from the bag at random, you would probably be willing to take those cherries as representative of the cherry population.

Random sampling sounds like such a good idea that you might be surprised to learn that most psychological studies involve nonrandom samples—and that most psychologists do not mind. Indeed, virtually every participant in every psychology experiment you will ever read about was a volunteer, and most were university students who were significantly younger, smarter, healthier, wealthier, and whiter than the average human. About 96 percent of the people whom psychologists study come from countries that have just 12 percent of the world's population, and 70 percent come from the United States alone (Henrich, Heine, & Norenzayan, 2010).

> **If random sampling is good, why is it not necessary?**

So why do psychologists sample nonrandomly? They have no choice. Even if there were a computerized list of all the world's human inhabitants from which we could randomly choose our research participants, how would we ever *find* the 72-year-old Bedouin woman whose family roams the desert so that we could measure the electrical activity in her brain while she watched cartoons? How would we convince the 3-week-old infant in New Delhi to complete a lengthy questionnaire about his political beliefs? Most psychology experiments are conducted by professors and graduate students at colleges and universities in the Western hemisphere, and as much as they might *like* to randomly sample the population of the planet, the practical truth is that they are pretty much stuck studying the folks who volunteer for their studies.

So how can we learn *anything* from psychology experiments? Surely the failure to sample randomly is a fatal flaw? No, it is not, and there are three reasons why. First, sometimes the similarity of a sample and a population does not matter. If one pig flew over the CN Tower just one time, it would instantly disprove the traditional theory of porcine locomotion. It would not matter if all pigs flew or if any other pigs flew. If one did, then that is enough. An experimental result can be illuminating even when the sample is not typical of the population.

> **Why is nonrandom sampling a nonfatal flaw?**

Second, when the ability to generalize an experimental result *is* important, psychologists perform new experiments that use the same procedures but on different samples. For example, after measuring how a nonrandomly selected group of Canadian children behaved after playing violent video games, we might try to replicate our experiment with Japanese children, or with Canadian teenagers, or with deaf adults. In essence, we could treat the attributes of our sample, such as culture and age and ability, as independent variables, and we could do experiments to determine whether these attributes influenced our dependent variable. If the results of our study were replicated in these other samples, then we would be more confident (but never completely confident) that the results describe a basic human tendency. If the results do not replicate, then we would learn something about the influence of culture or age or ability on aggressiveness. Replicating research with new samples drawn from different populations is a win–win strategy: No matter what happens, we learn something interesting.

Third, sometimes the similarity of the sample and the population is simply a reasonable starting assumption. Instead of asking, "Do I have a compelling reason to believe that my sample is representative of the population?" we could instead ask, "Do I have a compelling reason not to?" For example, few of us would be willing to take an experimental medicine if a nonrandom sample of seven participants took it and died. Indeed, we would probably refuse the medicine even if the seven participants were mice. Although these nonrandomly sampled participants were different from us

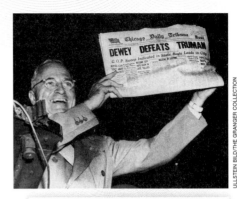

Nonrandom sampling can lead to errors. In the American presidential election of 1948, the *Chicago Tribune* mistakenly predicted that Thomas Dewey would beat Harry Truman. Why? Because polling was done by telephone, and Dewey Republicans were more likely to have telephones than were Truman Democrats.

in many ways (including tails and whiskers), most of us would be willing to generalize from their experience to ours because we know that even mice share enough of our basic biology to make it a good bet that what harms them can harm us too. By this same reasoning, if a psychology experiment demonstrated that some Canadian children behaved violently after playing violent video games, we might ask whether there is a compelling reason to suspect that Ecuadorian University students or middle-aged Australians would behave any differently. If the answer was yes, then experiments would provide a way for us to investigate that possibility.

## Thinking Critically about Evidence

In 1620, Sir Francis Bacon published a book called *Novum Organum* in which he described a new method for discovering the truth about the natural world. Today, his so-called Baconian Method is more simply known as the scientific method, and that method has allowed human beings to learn more in the last four centuries than in all the previous centuries combined.

This mouse died after drinking the green stuff. Want to drink the green stuff? Why not? You are not a mouse, are you?

As you have seen in this chapter, the scientific method allows us to produce empirical evidence. But empirical evidence is only useful if we know how to think about it, and the fact is that most of us do not. Using evidence requires *critical thinking*, which involves asking ourselves tough questions about whether we have interpreted the evidence in an unbiased way, and whether the evidence tells not just the truth, but the *whole* truth. Research suggests that most people have trouble doing both of these things, and that educational programs designed to teach or improve critical thinking skills are not particularly effective (Willingham, 2007). Why do people have so much trouble thinking critically?

Consider the armadillo. Some animals freeze when threatened, and others duck, run, or growl. Armadillos jump. This natural tendency served armadillos quite well for millennia because for millennia the most common threat to an armadillo's well-being was a rattlesnake. Alas, this natural tendency serves armadillos rather poorly today because when they wander onto a Texas highway and are threatened by a speeding car, they jump up and hit the bumper. This is a mistake no armadillo makes twice.

Human beings also have natural tendencies that once served them well but no longer do. Our natural and intuitive ways of thinking about evidence, for example, worked just fine when we were all hunter-gatherers living in small groups on the African savannah. But now most of us live in large-scale, complex societies, and these natural ways of thinking interfere with our ability to reason in the modern world. Sir Francis Bacon understood this quite well. In the very same book in which he developed the scientific method, he argued that two ancient and all-too-human tendencies—to see what we expect or want to see and to ignore what we cannot see—are the enemies of critical thinking.

Sir Francis Bacon (1561–1626) is credited with having devised the scientific method, which he used until he died from pneumonia, which he caught while studying the effects of low temperatures on the preservation of meat.

### We See What We Expect and Want

When two people are presented with the same evidence, they often draw different conclusions. Sir Francis Bacon knew why. "The human understanding, once it has adopted opinions… draws everything else to support and agree with them," thus our "first conclusion colours and brings into conformity with itself all that come after." In other words, our pre-existing beliefs colour our view of new evidence, causing us to see what we expect to see. As such, evidence often seems to confirm what we believed all along.

This tendency has been widely documented in psychological science. For instance, participants in one study (Darley & Gross, 1983) learned about a little girl named Hannah. One group of participants was told that Hannah came from an affluent family and another group was told that Hannah came from a poor family. All participants were then shown some evidence about Hannah's academic abilities (specifically, they watched a video of Hannah taking a reading test) and were then asked to rate Hannah. Although the video was exactly the same for all participants, those who believed that Hannah was affluent rated her performance more positively than did those who believed that Hannah was poor. What is more, both groups of participants defended their conclusions by citing evidence from the video! Experiments like this one suggest that when we consider evidence, what we see depends on what we *expected* to see.

Our beliefs are not the only things that colour our views of evidence. Those views are also coloured by our preferences and prejudices, our ambitions and aversions, our hopes and needs and wants and dreams. As Bacon noted, "The human understanding is not a dry light, but is infused by desire and emotion which give rise to wishful science. For man prefers to believe what he wants to be true."

Research suggests that Bacon was right about this as well. For example, participants in one study (Lord, Ross, & Lepper, 1979) were shown some scientific evidence about the effectiveness of the death penalty. Some of the evidence suggested that the death penalty deterred crime, and some suggested it did not. What did participants make of this mixed bag of evidence? Participants who originally supported the death penalty became even *more* supportive, and participants who originally opposed the death penalty became even *more* opposed. In other words, when presented with exactly the same evidence, participants saw what they *wanted* to see and ended up feeling even more sure about their initial views. Subsequent research has shown that the same pattern emerges when professional scientists are asked to rate the quality of scientific studies that either confirm or disconfirm what they want to believe (Koehler, 1993).

Exactly how do beliefs and desires shape our view of the evidence? People hold different kinds of evidence to different standards. When evidence confirms what we

**How do our beliefs and desires shape the way we think about evidence?**

believe or want to believe, we tend to ask ourselves, "*Can* I believe it?" and our answer is usually yes; but when evidence disconfirms what we believe or want to believe, we tend to ask ourselves, "*Must* I believe it?" and the answer is often no (Gilovich, 1991). *Can* you believe that people with university degrees are happier than people without them? Yes! There are plenty of surveys showing that just such a relationship exists and a reasonable person who studied the evidence could easily defend this conclusion. Now, *must* you believe it? Well, no. After all, those surveys did not measure every single person on Earth, did they? And if the survey questions had been asked differently they might well have produced different answers, right? A reasonable person who studied the evidence could easily conclude that the relationship between education and happiness is not yet clear enough to warrant an opinion.

Our beliefs and desires also influence *which* evidence we consider in the first place. Most people surround themselves with others who believe what they believe and want what they want, which means that our friends and families are much more likely to validate our beliefs and desires than to challenge them. Studies also show that when given the opportunity to search for evidence, people preferentially search for evidence that confirms their beliefs and fulfills their desires (Hart et al., 2009). What is more, when people find evidence that confirms their beliefs and fulfills their desires, they tend to stop looking, but when they find evidence that does the opposite, they keep searching for more evidence (Kunda, 1990).

What all of these studies suggest is that evidence leaves room for interpretation, and that is the room in which our beliefs and desires spend most of their time. Because it is so easy to see what we expect to see or to see what we want to see, the first step in critical thinking is simply to doubt your own conclusions. One of the best ways to reduce your own certainty is to seek out people who doubt you and listen carefully to what they have to say. Scientists go out of their way to expose themselves to criticism by sending their papers to the colleagues who are most likely to disagree with them or by presenting their findings to audiences full of critics, and they do this in large part so they can achieve a more balanced view of their own conclusions. If you want to be happy, take your friend to lunch; if you want to be right, take your enemy.

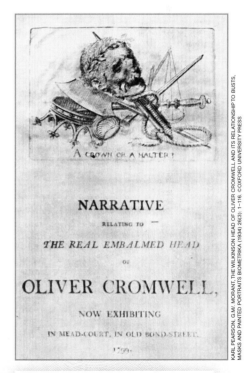

KARL PEARSON, G.M. MORANT, THE WILKINSON HEAD OF OLIVER CROMWELL AND ITS RELATIONSHIP TO BUSTS, MASKS AND PAINTED PORTRAITS BIOMETRIKA (1934) 26(3): 1–116. ©OXFORD UNIVERSITY PRESS

In 1650, the Lord Protector of England, Oliver Cromwell, wrote to the Church of Scotland and said, "I beseech you, in the bowels of Christ, think it possible that you may be mistaken," and his colourful plea is today known as *Cromwell's rule*, which advises us to be less sure than we are, no matter how sure we are! After Cromwell died, his embalmed head changed hands for nearly 200 years. It was donated to Sidney Sussex College, Cambridge University (UK) in 1960.

AMANDA EDWARDS/GETTY IMAGES

No matter how well the contestants perform, Jeopardy host Alex Trebek always seems like the smartest guy on the stage. But would you still get that impression if contestants were given an opportunity to ask him a few questions?

## We Consider What We See and Ignore What We Do not

In another part of his remarkable book, Sir Francis Bacon recounted an old story about a man who visited a Roman temple. The priest showed the man a portrait of several sailors who had taken religious vows and then miraculously survived a shipwreck, and suggested that this was clear evidence of the power of the gods. The visitor paused a moment and then asked precisely the right question: "But where are the pictures of those who perished after taking their vows?" According to Bacon, most of us never think to ask this kind of question. We consider the evidence we can see and forget about the evidence we cannot. Bacon claimed that "little or no attention is paid to things invisible" and he argued that this natural tendency was "the greatest impediment and aberration of the human understanding."

Bacon was right when he claimed that people rarely consider what they cannot see. For example, participants in one study (Newman, Wolff, & Hearst, 1980) played a game in which they were shown a set of trigrams, which are three-letter combinations such as *SXY*, *GTR*, *BCG*, and *EVX*. On each trial, the experimenter pointed to one of the trigrams in the set and told the participants that *this* trigram was the special one. The participants' job was to figure out what made the special trigram so special. How many trials did it take before participants figured it out? It depended on the trigram's special feature. For half the participants, the special trigram was always the one that contained the letter *T*, and participants in this condition needed to see about 34 sets of trigrams before they figured out that the presence of *T* was what made the trigram special. But for the other half of the participants, the special trigram was always the one that *lacked* the letter *T*. How many trials did it take before participants figured it out? They *never* figured it out. Never. What this study shows is that we naturally consider the evidence we see and rarely, if ever, consider the evidence we do not.

The tendency to ignore missing evidence can cause us to draw all kinds of erroneous conclusions. Consider a study in which participants were randomly assigned to play one of two roles in a game (Ross, Amabile, & Steinmetz, 1977). The "quizmasters" were asked to make up a series of difficult questions, and the "contestants" were asked to answer them. If you give this a quick try, you will discover that it is very easy to generate questions that you can answer but that most other people cannot. For example, think of the last city you visited. Now give someone the name of the hotel you stayed in and ask them what street it is on. Very few will know.

So participants who were cast in the role of quizmaster asked lots of clever-sounding questions and participants who were cast in the role of contestant gave lots of wrong answers. Now comes the interesting part. Quizmasters and contestants played this game while another participant—the observer—watched. After the game was over, the observer was asked to make some guesses about what the players were like in their everyday lives. The results were clear: observers consistently concluded that the quizmaster was a more knowledgeable person than the contestant! Observers *saw* the quizmaster asking sharp questions and *saw* the contestant saying "Um, gosh, I do not know," and observers considered this evidence. What they failed to consider was the evidence they did *not* see. Specifically, they failed to consider what would have happened if the person who had been assigned to play the role of quizmaster had instead been assigned to play the role of contestant, and vice versa. If that had happened, then surely the contestant would have been the one asking clever questions and the quizmaster would have been the one struggling to answer them. Bottom line? If the first step in critical thinking is to doubt what you do see, then the second step is to consider what you do not.

> **Why is it important to consider unseen evidence?**

## The Skeptical Stance

Winston Churchill once said that democracy is the worst form of government, except for all the others. Similarly, science is not an infallible method for learning about the world; it is just a whole lot less fallible than the other methods. Science is a human enterprise, and humans make mistakes. They see what they expect to see, they see what they want to see, and they rarely consider what they cannot see at all.

What makes science different than most other human enterprises is that science actively seeks to discover and remedy its own biases and errors. Scientists are constantly striving to make their observations more accurate and their reasoning more rigorous, and they invite anyone and everyone to examine their evidence and challenge their conclusions. As such, science is the ultimate democracy—one of the only institutions in the world in which the lowliest nobody can triumph over the most celebrated someone. When an unknown Swiss patent clerk named Albert Einstein challenged the greatest physicists of his day, he did not have a famous name, a fancy degree, powerful friends, or a fat wallet. He just had evidence. And he prevailed for one reason: His evidence was right.

So think of the remaining chapters in this book as a report from the field—a description of the work that psychological scientists have done as they stumble toward knowledge. These chapters tell the story of the men and women who have put their faith in Sir Francis Bacon's method and used it to pry loose small pieces of the truth about who we are, how we work, and what we are all doing here together on the third stone from the sun. Read it with interest, but also with skepticism. Some of the things we are about to tell you simply are not true; we just do not yet know which things they are. We invite you to think critically about what you read here, and everywhere else. Now, let the doubting begin.

## IN SUMMARY

▶ To determine whether two variables are causally related, we must first determine whether they are related at all. This can be done by measuring each variable many times and then comparing the patterns of variation within each series of measurements. If the patterns covary, then the variables are correlated. Correlations allow us to predict the value of one variable from knowledge of the value of the other. The direction and strength of a correlation are measured by the correlation coefficient ($r$).

▶ Even when we observe a correlation between two variables, we cannot conclude that they are causally related because there are an infinite number of third variables that might be causing them both. Experiments solve this third-variable problem by manipulating an independent variable, randomly assigning participants to the experimental and control groups that this manipulation creates, and measuring a dependent variable. These measurements are then compared across groups. If inferential statistics show that there was less than a 5 percent chance that random assignment failed, then differences in the measurements across groups are assumed to have been caused by the manipulation.

▶ An internally valid experiment establishes a causal relationship between variables as they were operationally defined and among the participants whom they included. When an experiment mimics the real world, it is externally valid. Most psychology experiments are not attempts to mimic the real world, but to test hypotheses derived from theories.

▶ Thinking critically about evidence is difficult because people have a natural tendency to see what they expect to see, to see what they want to see, and to consider what they see but not what they do not.

# The Ethics of Science: First, Do No Harm

Somewhere along the way, someone probably told you that it is not nice to treat people like objects. And yet, it may seem that psychologists do just that by creating situations that cause people to feel fearful or sad, to do things that are embarrassing or immoral, and to learn things about themselves and others that they might not really want to know. Do not be fooled by appearances. The fact is that psychologists go to great lengths to protect the well-being of their research participants, and they are bound by a code of ethics that is as detailed and demanding as the professional codes that bind physicians, lawyers, and accountants. That code requires that psychologists show respect for people, for animals, and for the truth. Let us examine each of these obligations in turn.

## Respecting People

During World War II, Nazi doctors performed truly barbaric experiments on human subjects, such as removing organs or submerging them in ice water just to see how long it would take them to die. When the war ended, the international community developed the Nuremberg Code of 1947 and then the Declaration of Helsinki in 1964, which spelled out rules for the ethical treatment of human subjects. Unfortunately, not everyone obeyed them. For example, from 1942 to 1952, the Canadian federal government conducted food and nutrition experiments on malnourished Cree communities in Northern Manitoba, and later at six Aboriginal residential schools. Some children received foods with vitamins and minerals, while others did not. At the time, no one in the communities was aware why some children were being fed products made with vitamin-enriched flour, while others were being fed broth, bread, and lard. Dental health care—even the use of fluoride—was restricted, since cavities and gum disease were both considered important measures of nutritional status, and dental interventions might interfere with the the results of the study (Mosby, 2013). Essentially the Canadian government was complicit in a set of experiments conducted on some of Canada's most vulnerable people without their consent, and in which the risks far outweighed any potential benefit of the research.

Over time, the basic tenets of the Declaration of Helsinki have become increasingly enshrined in national legislation and regulations. In Canada, all research involving human persons or tissue is covered by the Tri-Council Policy Statement (TCPS): Ethical Conduct for Research Involving Humans. The "tri-council" refers to the three federal research agencies: Canadian Institute of Health Research, Natural Science and Engineering Research Council of Canada, and Social Sciences and Humanities Research Council. The TCPS describes the core principles, based on respect for human dignity, that all research involving human subjects should follow. First, research should show *respect for persons* and their right to make decisions for and about themselves without undue influence or coercion. Second, research should show *concern for welfare*, which means that it should attempt to maximize benefits and reduce risks to the participant. Third, research should be *just*, which means that it should distribute benefits and risks equally to participants without prejudice toward particular individuals or groups.

> **What are three features of ethical research?**

The man at this bar is upset. He just saw another man slip a drug into a woman's drink and he is alerting the bartender. What he does not know is that all the people at the bar are actors and that he is being filmed for the television show *What Would You Do?* Was it ethical for ABC to put this man in such a stressful situation without his consent? And how did men who did not alert the bartender feel when they turned on their televisions months later and were confronted by their own shameful behaviour?

© AMERICAN BROADCASTING COMPANIES, INC.

The specific ethical code that psychologists follow incorporates these basic principles and expands them. (You can find the American Psychological Association's *Ethical Principles of Psychologists and Code of Conduct* [2002] at http://www.apa.org/ethics/code/index.aspx and The Canadian Psychological Association's *Canadian Code of Ethics for Psychologists* [2000], which is very similar, at http://www.cpa.ca/aboutcpa/committees/ethics/codeofethics/.) Here are a few of the most important rules that govern the conduct of psychological research:

> *Informed consent*: Participants may not take part in a psychological study unless they have given **informed consent,** which is *a written agreement to participate in a study made by an adult who has been informed of all the risks that participation may entail*. This does not mean that the person must know everything about the study (e.g., the hypothesis), but it does mean that the person must know about anything that might potentially be harmful or painful. If people cannot give informed consent (e.g., because they are minors or are mentally incapable), then informed consent must be obtained from their legal guardians. And even after people give informed consent, they always have the right to withdraw from the study at any time without penalty.

> *Freedom of consent*: Psychologists may not coerce participation. Coercion not only means physical and psychological coercion but monetary coercion as well. It is unethical to offer people large amounts of money to persuade them to do something that they might otherwise decline to do. University students may be invited to participate in studies as part of their training in psychology, but they are ordinarily offered the option of learning the same things by other means.

> *Protection for vulnerable persons*: Psychologists must take every possible precaution to protect their research participants from physical or psychological harm. If there are two equally effective ways to study something, the psychologist must use the safer method. If no safe method is available, the psychologist may not perform the study.

> *Risk–benefit analysis*: Although participants may be asked to accept small risks, such as a minor shock or a small embarrassment, they may not even be *asked* to accept large risks, such as severe pain, psychological trauma, or any risk that is greater than the risks they would ordinarily take in their everyday lives. Furthermore, even when participants are asked to take small risks, the psychologist must first demonstrate that these risks are outweighed by the social benefits of the new knowledge that might be gained from the study.

> *Deception*: Psychologists may only use deception when it is justified by the study's scientific, educational, or applied value and when alternative procedures are not feasible. They may never deceive participants about any aspect of a study that could cause them physical or psychological harm or pain.

> *Debriefing*: If a participant is deceived in any way before or during a study, the psychologist must provide a **debriefing,** which is *a verbal description of the true nature and purpose of a study*. If the participant was changed in any way (e.g., made to feel sad), the psychologist must attempt to undo that change (e.g., ask the person to do a task that will make him or her happy) and restore the participant to the state he or she was in before the study.

> *Confidentiality*: Psychologists are obligated to keep private and personal information obtained during a study confidential.

These are just some of the rules that psychologists must follow. But how are those rules enforced? Almost all psychology studies are done by psychologists who work at colleges and universities. These institutions have research ethics boards (REBs) that

**informed consent**
A written agreement to participate in a study made by an adult who has been informed of all the risks that participation may entail.

**debriefing**
A verbal description of the true nature and purpose of a study.

are composed of instructors and researchers, university staff, and laypeople from the community (e.g., business leaders or members of the clergy). If the research is federally funded (as much research is), then the law requires that the REB consist of at least five people, including an ethics expert, a legal expert, and a community member who is not affiliated with the institution. A psychologist may conduct a study only after the REB has reviewed and approved it.

As you can imagine, the code of ethics and the procedure for approval are so strict that many studies simply cannot be performed anywhere, by anyone, at any time. For example, psychologists would love to know how growing up without exposure to language affects a person's subsequent ability to speak and think, but they cannot ethically manipulate that variable in an experiment. They can only study the natural correlations between language exposure and speaking ability, and so may never be able to firmly establish the causal relationships between these variables. Indeed, there are many questions that psychologists will never be able to answer definitively because doing so would require unethical experiments that violate basic human rights.

## Respecting Animals

Not all research participants have human rights because not all research participants are human. Some are chimpanzees, rats, pigeons, or other nonhuman animals. The Canadian Council on Animal Care (CCAC) is the national organization responsible for establishing standards for the ethical use and care of animals in research. It describes the special rights of these nonhuman participants, and provides guidelines that all research must follow. The Three Rs tenet (Replacement, Reduction, and Refinement) guides the ethical use of animals in science, ensuring appropriate consideration of the animals' comfort, health, and humane treatment.

> **What steps must psychologists take to protect nonhuman subjects?**

> *Replacement:* Researchers have to prove that there is no alternative to using animals in research and that the use of animals is justified by the scientific or clinical value of the study.

> *Reduction:* Researchers must use the fewest number of animals possible to achieve the research.

> *Refinement:* Procedures must be modified to minimize discomfort, infection, illness, and pain of animals. This requires that animals be treated humanely, with comfortable housing and the ability to satisfy their basic instincts, (for example, mice have to make nests), and appropriate administration of painkillers.

These rules are good—but are they good enough? Some people do not think so. For example, philosopher Peter Singer (1975) argued that all creatures capable of feeling pain have the same fundamental rights, and that treating nonhumans differently than humans is a form of speciesism that is every bit as abhorrent as racism or sexism. Singer's philosophy has inspired groups such as People for the Ethical Treatment of Animals to call for an end to all research involving nonhuman animals. Unfortunately, it has also inspired some groups to attack psychologists who legally conduct such research. As two researchers (Ringach & Jentsch, 2009, p. 11417) recently reported:

> We have seen our cars and homes firebombed or flooded, and we have received letters packed with poisoned razors and death threats via e-mail and voicemail. Our families and neighbors have been terrorized by angry mobs of masked protesters who throw

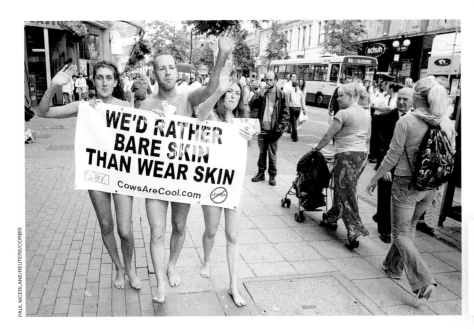

Some people consider it unethical to use animals for clothing or research. Others see an important distinction between these two purposes.

rocks, break windows, and chant that "you should stop or be stopped" and that they "know where you sleep at night." Some of the attacks have been cataloged as attempted murder. Adding insult to injury, misguided animal-rights militants openly incite others to violence on the Internet, brag about the resulting crimes, and go as far as to call plots for our assassination "morally justifiable."

Where do most people stand on this issue? The majority of Canadians consider it morally acceptable to use non-human animals in research and say they would reject a governmental ban on such research (Gallup poll: Kiefer, 2003). Indeed, most Canadians eat meat, wear leather, and support the rights of hunters, which is to say that most Candians see a sharp distinction between animal and human rights. Science is not in the business of resolving moral controversies, and every individual must draw his or her own conclusions about this issue. But whatever position you take, it is important to note that only a small percentage of psychological studies involve animals, and only a small percentage of those studies cause animals pain or harm. Psychologists mainly study people, and when they do study animals, they mainly study their behaviour.

"What if these guys in white coats who bring us food are, like, studying us and we're part of some kind of big experiment?"

## Respecting Truth

Research ethics boards ensure that data are collected ethically. But once the data are collected, who ensures that they are ethically analyzed and reported? No one does. Psychology, like all sciences, works on the honour system. No authority is charged with monitoring what psychologists do with the data they have collected, and no authority is charged with checking to see if the claims they make are true. You may find that a bit odd. After all, we do not use the honour system in stores ("Take the television set home and pay us next time you are in the neighborhood"), banks ("No need to look up your account, just tell me how much money you want to withdraw"), or courtrooms ("If you say you are innocent, well then, that is good enough for me"), so why would we expect it to work in science? Are scientists more honest than everyone else?

ERIK VAN DER BURGT/VERBEELD/REDUX

In 2012, psychologist Diederik Stapel was found to have committed massive fraud over the course of many years. He was fired from his job as a professor and dozens of published scientific articles were retracted.

Definitely! Okay, we just made that up. But the honour system does not depend on scientists being especially honest, but on the fact that science is a community enterprise. When scientists claim to have discovered something important, other scientists do not just applaud, they start studying it too. When physicist Jan Hendrik Schön announced in 2001 that he had produced a molecular-scale transistor, other physicists were deeply impressed—that is, until they tried to replicate his work and discovered that Schön had fabricated his data (Agin, 2007). Schön lost his job and his doctoral degree was revoked, but the important point is that such frauds cannot last long because one scientist's conclusion is the next scientist's research question. This does not mean that all frauds are uncovered swiftly: psychologist Diederik Stapel lied, cheated, and made up his data for decades before people became suspicious enough to investigate (Levelt Committee, Noort Committee, Drenth Committee, 2012). But it does mean that the *important* frauds are uncovered eventually. The psychologist who fraudulently claims to have shown that chimps are smarter than goldfish may never get caught because no one is likely to follow up on such an obvious finding, but the psychologist who fraudulently claims to have shown the opposite will soon have a lot of explaining to do.

What exactly are psychologists on their honour to do? At least three things. First, when they write reports of their studies and publish them in scientific journals, psychologists are obligated to report truthfully on what they did and what they found. They cannot fabricate results (e.g., claiming to have performed studies that they never really performed) or fudge results (e.g., changing records of data that were actually collected), and they cannot mislead by omission (e.g., by reporting only the results that confirm their hypothesis and saying nothing about the results that do not). Second, psychologists are obligated to share credit fairly by including as co-authors of their reports the other people who contributed to the work, and by mentioning in their reports the other scientists who have done related work. And third, psychologists are obligated to share their data. The Canadian Psychological Association's code of ethics states that ethical psychologists "not interfere with the free and open exchange of psychological knowledge and theory between themselves, their students, colleagues, and the public." The fact that anyone can check up on anyone else is part of why the honour system works as well as it does.

> **What are psychologists expected to do when they report the results of their research?**

## IN SUMMARY

▶ Research ethics boards ensure that scientific research that uses human subjects is based on the principles of respect for persons, beneficence, and justice.

▶ Psychologists are obligated to uphold these principles by getting free informed consent from participants, protecting participants from harm, weighing benefits against risks, avoiding deception, and keeping information confidential.

▶ Psychologists are obligated to respect the rights of animals and treat them humanely.

▶ Psychologists are obligated to tell the truth about their studies, to share credit appropriately, and to grant others access to their data.

# OTHER VOICES

## Can We Afford Science?

**David Brooks** is a columnist for the *New York Times*, a commentator on *CNN*, and the author of several popular books on behavioural science.

PHOTO: ©JOSH HANER/ COURTESY OF THE NEW YORK TIMES

Who pays for all the research described in textbooks like this one? The answer is you. By and large, scientific research is funded by governmental agencies, such as the Natural Sciences and Engineering Research Council (NSERC), which give scientists grants (also known as money) to do particular research projects that the scientists proposed. Of course, this money could be spent on other things, for example, feeding the poor, housing the homeless, caring for the ill and elderly, and so on. Does it make sense to spend taxpayer dollars on psychological science when some of our fellow citizens are cold and hungry?

American journalist and author David Brooks (2011) argued that research in the behavioural sciences in not an expenditure—it is an investment that pays for itself, and more. Although he is describing the American situation, his words are equally relevant in Canada. Here is what he had to say:

Over the past 50 years, we've seen a number of gigantic policies produce disappointing results—policies to reduce poverty, homelessness, drop-out rates, single-parenting and drug addiction. Many of these policies failed because they were based on an overly simplistic view of human nature. They assumed that people responded in straightforward ways to incentives. Often, they assumed that money could cure behaviour problems.

Fortunately, today we are in the middle of a golden age of behavioral research. Thousands of researchers are studying the way actual behavior differs from the way we assume people behave. They are coming up with more accurate theories of who we are, and scores of real-world applications. Here's one simple example:

When you renew your driver's license, you have a chance to enroll in an organ donation program. In countries like Germany and the U.S., you have to check a box if you want to opt in. Roughly 14 percent of people do. But behavioral scientists have discovered that how you set the defaults is really important. So in other countries, like Poland or France, you have to check a box if you want to opt out. In these countries, more than 90 percent of people participate.

This is a gigantic behavior difference cued by one tiny and costless change in procedure.

Yet in the middle of this golden age of behavioral research, there is a bill working through [the American] Congress that would eliminate the National Science Foundation's Directorate for Social, Behavioral and Economic Sciences. This is exactly how budgets should not be balanced—by cutting cheap things that produce enormous future benefits.

Let's say you want to reduce poverty. We have two traditional understandings of poverty. The first presumes people are rational. They are pursuing their goals effectively and do not need much help in changing their behavior. The second presumes that the poor are afflicted by cultural or psychological dysfunctions that sometimes lead them to behave in shortsighted ways. Neither of these theories has produced much in the way of effective policies.

Eldar Shafir of Princeton and Sendhil Mullainathan of Harvard have recently, with federal help, been exploring a third theory, that scarcity produces its own cognitive traits.

A quick question: What is the starting taxi fare in your city? If you are like most upper-middle-class people, you do not know. If you are like many struggling people, you do know. Poorer people have to think hard about a million things that affluent people do not. They have to make complicated trade-offs when buying a carton of milk: If I buy milk, I can't afford orange juice. They have to decide which utility not to pay.

These questions impose enormous cognitive demands. The brain has limited capacities. If you increase demands on one sort of question, it performs less well on other sorts of questions.

Shafir and Mullainathan gave batteries of tests to Indian sugar farmers. After they sell their harvest, they live in relative prosperity. During this season, the farmers do well on the I.Q. and other tests. But before the harvest, they live amid scarcity and have to think hard about a thousand daily decisions. During these seasons, these same farmers do much worse on the tests. They appear to have lower I.Q.'s. They have more trouble controlling their attention. They are more shortsighted. Scarcity creates its own psychology.

Princeton students don't usually face extreme financial scarcity, but they do face time scarcity. In one game, they had to answer questions in a series of timed rounds, but they could borrow time from future rounds. When they were scrambling amid time scarcity, they were quick to borrow time, and they were nearly oblivious to the usurious interest rates the game organizers were charging. These brilliant Princeton kids were rushing to the equivalent of payday lenders, to their own long-term detriment.

Shafir and Mullainathan have a book coming out next year, exploring how scarcity—whether of time, money or calories (while dieting)—affects your psychology. They are also studying how poor people's self-perceptions shape behavior. Many people do not sign up for the welfare benefits because they are intimidated by the forms. Shafir and Mullainathan asked some people at a Trenton soup kitchen to relive a moment when they felt competent and others to recount a neutral experience. Nearly half of the self-affirming group picked up an available benefits package afterward. Only 16 percent of the neutral group did.

People are complicated. We each have multiple selves, which emerge or don't depending on context. If we're going to address problems, we need to understand the contexts and how these tendencies emerge or do not emerge. We need to design policies around that knowledge. Cutting off financing for this sort of research now is like cutting off navigation financing just as Christopher Columbus hit the shoreline of the New World.

What do you think? Is Brooks right? Is psychological science a wise use of public funds, or is it a luxury that we simply cannot afford?

# Chapter Review

## KEY CONCEPT QUIZ

1. The belief that accurate knowledge can be acquired through observation is
   a. parsimony.
   b. dogmatism.
   c. empiricism.
   d. scientific research.

2. Which of the following is the best definition of a hypothesis?
   a. empirical evidence
   b. a scientific investigation
   c. a falsifiable prediction
   d. a theoretical idea

3. The methods of psychological investigation take _____ into account because when people know they are being studied, they do not always behave as they otherwise would.
   a. reactivity
   b. complexity
   c. variability
   d. sophistication

4. When a measure produces the same measurement whenever it is used to measure the same thing, it is said to have
   a. validity.
   b. reliability.
   c. power.
   d. concreteness.

5. Aspects of an observational setting that cause people to behave as they think they should are called
   a. observer biases.
   b. reactive conditions.
   c. natural habitats.
   d. demand characteristics.

6. In a double-blind observation
   a. the participants know what is being measured.
   b. people are observed in their natural environments.
   c. the purpose is hidden from both the observer and the person being observed.
   d. only objective, statistical measures are recorded.

7. Which of the following describes the average value of all the measurements in a particular distribution?
   a. mean
   b. median
   c. mode
   d. range

8. What does a correlation coefficient show?
   a. the value of one specific variable
   b. the direction and strength of a correlation
   c. the efficiency of the relevant research method
   d. the degree of natural correlation

9. When two variables are correlated, what keeps us from concluding that one is the cause and the other is the effect?
   a. the possibility of third-variable correlation
   b. random assignment of control groups
   c. the existence of false-positive correlation
   d. correlation strength is impossible to measure accurately

10. A researcher administers a questionnaire concerning attitudes toward global warming to people of both sexes and of all ages who live all across the country. The dependent variable in the study is the _____ of the participants.
    a. age
    b. gender
    c. attitudes toward global warming
    d. geographic location

11. The characteristic of an experiment that allows conclusions about causal relationships to be drawn is called
    a. external validity.
    b. internal validity.
    c. random assignment.
    d. self-selection.

12. An experiment that operationally defines variables in a realistic way is said to be
    a. externally valid.
    b. controlled.
    c. operationally defined.
    d. statistically significant.

13. Research suggests that people are usually
    a. open to seeing both sides of an issue.
    b. able to reason without emotion.
    c. able to arrive at conclusions based solely on facts.
    d. none of the above.

14. When people find evidence that confirms their beliefs, they often
    a. tend to stop looking.
    b. seek evidence that disconfirms their conclusions.
    c. seek evidence that presents both sides.
    d. talk to their colleagues.

15. What are psychologists ethically required to do when reporting research results?
    a. to report findings truthfully
    b. to share credit for research
    c. to make data available for further research
    d. All of the above.

## KEY TERMS

case method (p. 64)

control group (p. 58)

correlation (p. 52)

correlation coefficient (p. 53)

debriefing (p. 71)

demand characteristics (p. 44)

dependent variable (p. 58)

double-blind (p. 47)

empirical method (p. 42)

empiricism (p. 40)

experiment (p. 56)

experimental group (p. 58)

external validity (p. 62)

frequency distribution (p. 48)

hypothesis (p. 41)

independent variable (p. 58)

informed consent (p. 71)

instrument (p. 44)

internal validity (p. 62)

manipulation (p. 58)

matched pairs technique (p. 56)

matched samples technique (p. 55)

mean (p. 49)

median (p. 49)

mode (p. 49)

natural correlation (p. 55)

naturalistic observation (p. 44)

normal distribution (p. 48)

operational definition (p. 44)

population (p. 63)

power (p. 44)

random assignment (p. 61)

random sampling (p. 64)

range (p. 51)

reliability (p. 44)

sample (p. 64)

scientific method (p. 40)

self-selection (p. 58)

standard deviation (p. 51)

theory (p. 40)

third-variable correlation (p. 55)

third-variable problem (p. 56)

validity (p. 44)

variable (p. 52)

## CHANGING MINDS

1. Back in Psychology: Evolution of a Science, you read about B. F. Skinner, who studied the principle of reinforcement, which states that the consequences of a behaviour determine whether it will be more or less likely to occur in the future. So, for example, a rat's rate of lever pressing will increase if it receives food reinforcement after each lever press. When you tell a classmate about this principle, she only shrugs. "That's obvious. Anyone who's ever owned a dog knows how to train animals. If you ask me, psychology is just common sense. You don't have to conduct scientific experiments to test things that everyone already knows are true." How would you explain the value of studying something that seems like "common sense"?

2. You are watching television with a friend when a news program reports that a research study has found that people in Europe who work longer hours are less happy than those who work shorter hours, but in the United States it is the other way around: Americans who work long hours are happier (Okulicz-Kozaryn, 2011). "That's an interesting experiment," he says. You point out that the news only said it was a research study, not an experiment. What would have to be true for it to be an experiment? Why are all research studies not experiments? What can you not learn from this study that you *could* learn from an experiment?

3. After the first test, your professor says she has noticed a strong positive correlation between the location of students' seats and their test scores: "The closer students sit to the front of the room, the higher their scores on the test," she says. After class, your friend suggests that the two of you should sit up front for the rest of the semester to improve your grades. Having read about correlation and causation, should you be skeptical? What are some possible reasons for the correlation between seating position and good grades? Could you design an experiment to test whether sitting up front actually causes good grades?

4. A classmate in your criminal law class suggests that mental illness is a major cause of violent crimes in Canada. As evidence, he mentions a highly publicized murder trial in which the defendant was diagnosed with schizophrenia. What scientific evidence would he need to support this claim?

5. You ask your friend if he wants to go to the gym with you. "No," he says, "I never exercise." You tell him that regular exercise has all kinds of health benefits, including greatly reducing the risk of heart disease. "I don't believe that," he replies, "I had an uncle who got up at 6 a.m. every day of his life to go jogging, and he still died of a heart attack at age 53." What would you tell your friend? Does his uncle's case prove that exercise really does not protect against heart disease after all?

## ANSWERS TO KEY CONCEPT QUIZ

1. c; 2. c; 3. a; 4. b; 5. d; 6. c; 7. a; 8. b; 9. a; 10. c; 11. b; 12. a; 13. d; 14. a; 15. d.

WWW

Need more help? Additional resources are located in Launchpad at:

*www.worthpublishers.com/launchpad/schacter3ecanadian*

# 3

# Neuroscience and Behaviour

▲ Neurons: The Origin of Behaviour
  Components of the Neuron
  Major Types of Neurons
  Neurons Specialized by Location

▲ The Electrochemical Actions of
  Neurons: Information Processing
  Electric Signalling: Conducting
    Information within a Neuron
  Chemical Signalling: Transmission
    between Neurons

▲ The Organization of the Nervous
  System
  Divisions of the Nervous System
  Components of the Central Nervous
    System

▲ Structure of the Brain
  The Hindbrain
  The Midbrain
  The Forebrain
  Brain Plasticity
  THE REAL WORLD Brain Plasticity and
    Sensations in Phantom Limbs

▲ The Development and Evolution of
  Nervous Systems
  Prenatal Development of the Central
    Nervous System
  Evolutionary Development of the Central
    Nervous System
  Genes, Epigenetics, and the Environment
  HOT SCIENCE Epigenetics and
    the Persisting Effects of Early
    Experiences

▲ Investigating the Brain
  Studying the Damaged Brain
  Studying the Brain's Electrical Activity
  Using Brain Imaging to Study Structure
    and to Watch the Brain in Action
  THE REAL WORLD Brain Death and the
    Vegetative State
  OTHER VOICES Neuromyths

N THE SUMMER OF 2011, THREE National Hockey League players died within a few months of each other. Wade Belak, the oldest of the three, was born in Saskatoon in 1976. He was drafted into the NHL when he was 17 and played for six teams over his career, including the Quebec Nordiques and the Toronto Maple Leafs. He died accidentally (the police treated it as a suicide) in a Toronto apartment, leaving behind a wife and two young daughters. He was 35. Derek Boogaard, another native of Saskatchewan and the son of a Mountie, played for the Minnesota Wild and the New York Rangers. He was 28 years old when he died of a drug overdose, having mixed powerful painkillers and alcohol on a night out with friends. Rick Rypien, from Blairmore, Alberta, was the youngest of the three. He spent some time with the Regina major junior team and then with a minor professional team in Manitoba. When he was 22, he joined the Vancouver Canucks and played six seasons with them. He took his own life in his home in Crowsnest Pass, Alberta—he was 27.

What did these three young men have in common, besides their passion for hockey? They were all "enforcers," players who are expected to use aggressive methods such as fighting and checking, to respond to violence against their team members, especially star players and goalies. They had all suffered blows to the head and concussions in their hockey careers. Both Rypien and Belak suffered from clinical depression and Boogaard battled an addiction to painkillers, as well as depression.

Postmortem analysis of Boogaard's brain revealed the presence of a condition known as chronic traumatic encephalopathy (CTE), a form of progressive brain damage that has been linked to repeated concussions (McKee et al., 2012). Although their brains were not examined, CTE is strongly suspected to have played a role in the deaths of Belak and Rypien as well, and is a confirmed diagnosis in three other deceased professional hockey players. CTE has been confirmed in the brains of over 20 professional football players, and has also been observed after repeated head injuries in boxing, wrestling, and rugby (Costanza et al., 2011; Daneshvar et al., 2011; Lahkan & Kirchgessner, 2012; McKee et al., 2012).

CTE is associated with an array of cognitive and emotional deficits in afflicted individuals, including inability to concentrate, memory loss, irritability, and depression, usually beginning within a decade after repeated concussions and worsening

Derek Boogaard, a professional hockey player for the New York Rangers, died of a drug overdose in 2011 at the age of 28. After his death, his brain was observed to be reduced in size, with fluid-filled spaces where brain tissue should be. This is characteristic of chronic traumatic encephalopathy, CTE, a progressive degenerative disease caused by repeated blows to the head.

**neurons**
Cells in the nervous system that communicate with one another to perform information-processing tasks.

with time (McKee et al., 2009). CTE is not confined to aging or retired athletes. A recent study found evidence of CTE in a 17-year-old football player who died as a result of multiple head injuries (McKee et al., 2012). Fortunately, there is growing awareness of CTE and its consequences, which is leading professional sports organizations, as well as universities, schools, and others involved in youth sports, to take steps to address the problem.

The symptoms of CTE, and the havoc they can wreak in the lives of affected individuals and their families, are stark reminders that our psychological, emotional, and social well-being depend critically on the health and integrity of the brain. The consequences of CTE also highlight that understanding neuroscience is not just an academic exercise confined to scientific laboratories: The more we know about the brain, and the more people who know it, the better our chances of finding solutions to problems such as CTE.

**IN THIS CHAPTER, WE WILL CONSIDER HOW THE BRAIN WORKS,** what happens when it does not, and how both states of affairs determine behaviour. First, we will introduce you to the basic unit of information processing in the brain, the neuron. The electrical and chemical activities of neurons are the starting point of all behaviour, thought, and emotion. Next, we will consider the anatomy of the central nervous system, focusing especially on the brain, including its overall organization, key structures that perform different functions, and its evolutionary development. Finally, we will discuss methods that allow us to study the brain and clarify our understanding of how it works. These include methods that examine the damaged brain and methods for scanning the living and healthy brain.

# Neurons: The Origin of Behaviour

An estimated 1 billion people watch the final game of World Cup soccer every 4 years. That is a whole lot of people, but to put it in perspective, it is still only a little over 14 percent of the estimated 7 billion people currently living on Earth. A more impressive number might be the 30 billion viewers who tune in to watch any of the World Cup action over the course of the tournament. But a really, really big number is inside your skull right now, helping you make sense of these big numbers you are reading about. There are approximately *100 billion* nerve cells in your brain that perform a variety of tasks to allow you to function as a human being.

Humans have thoughts, feelings, and behaviours that are often accompanied by visible signals. Consider how you might feel on your way to meet a good friend. An observer might see a smile on your face or notice how fast you are walking; internally, you might mentally rehearse what you will say to your friend and feel a surge of happiness as you approach her. All those visible and experiential signs are coordinated by the activity of your brain cells. The anticipation you have, the happiness you feel, and the speed of your feet are the result of information processing in your brain. All of your thoughts, feelings, and behaviours spring from cells in the brain that take in information and produce some kind of output trillions of times a day. These cells are **neurons,** *cells in the nervous system that communicate with one another to perform information-processing tasks.*

## Components of the Neuron

During the 1800s, scientists began to turn their attention from studying the mechanics of limbs, lungs, and livers to studying the harder-to-observe workings of the brain. Philosophers wrote poetically about an "enchanted loom" that mysteriously wove a tapestry of behaviour, and many scientists confirmed the metaphor (Corsi, 1991). To those scientists, the brain looked as though it were composed of a continuously connected lattice of fine threads, leading to the conclusion that it was one big woven

ED RESCHKE/GETTY IMAGES

▲ Figure **3.1 Golgi-Stained Neurons**
Santiago Ramón y Cajal used a Golgi stain (like the one shown here) to highlight the appearance of neurons. He was the first to see that each neuron is composed of a body with many threads extending outward toward other neurons. He also saw that, surprisingly, the threads of each neuron do not actually touch other neurons.

web of material. However, in the late 1880s, Spanish physician Santiago Ramón y Cajal (1852–1934) learned about a new technique for staining neurons in the brain (DeFelipe & Jones, 1988). The stain highlighted the appearance of entire cells, revealing that they came in different shapes and sizes (see **FIGURE 3.1** on the previous page).

Cajal discovered that neurons are complex structures composed of three basic parts: the cell body, the dendrites, and the axon (see **FIGURE 3.2**). Like cells in all organs of the body, neurons have a **cell body** (also called the *soma*), the largest component of the neuron that *coordinates the information-processing tasks and keeps the cell alive*. Functions such as protein synthesis, energy production, and metabolism take place here. The cell body contains a *nucleus*, which houses chromosomes that contain our DNA, or the genetic blueprint of who we are. The cell body is surrounded by a porous cell membrane that allows some molecules to flow into and out of the cell.

Unlike other cells in the body, neurons have two types of specialized extensions of the cell membrane that allow them to communicate: dendrites and axons. **Dendrites** *receive information from other neurons and relay it to the cell body*. The term *dendrite* comes from the Greek word for "tree"; indeed, most neurons have many dendrites

**cell body (or soma)**
The part of a neuron that coordinates information-processing tasks and keeps the cell alive.

**dendrite**
The part of a neuron that receives information from other neurons and relays it to the cell body.

▼ Figure **3.2** **Components of a Neuron** A neuron is made up of three parts: a cell body that houses the chromosomes with the organism's DNA and maintains the health of the cell; dendrites that receive information from other neurons; and an axon that transmits information to other neurons, muscles, and glands.

---

---

**axon**
The part of a neuron that carries information to other neurons, muscles, or glands.

**myelin sheath**
An insulating layer of fatty material.

**glial cells**
Support cells found in the nervous system.

**synapse**
The junction or region between the axon of one neuron and the dendrites or cell body of another.

**sensory neurons**
Neurons that receive information from the external world and convey this information to the brain.

**motor neurons**
Neurons that carry signals from the spinal cord to the muscles to produce movement.

that look like tree branches. The **axon** *carries information to other neurons, muscles, or glands*. Axons can be very long, even stretching up to a metre from the base of the spinal cord down to the big toe.

In many neurons, the axon is covered by a **myelin sheath,** *an insulating layer of fatty material*. The myelin sheath is composed of **glial cells** (named for the Greek word for "glue"), which are *support cells found in the nervous system*. Although there are 100 billion neurons busily processing information in your brain, there are 10 to 50 times that many glial cells serving a variety of functions. Some glial cells digest parts of dead neurons, others provide physical and nutritional support for neurons, and others form myelin to insulate the axon. An axon insulated with myelin can more efficiently transmit signals to other neurons, organs, or muscles. In fact, with *demyelinating diseases,* such as multiple sclerosis, the myelin sheath deteriorates, slowing the transmission of information from one neuron to another (Schwartz & Westbrook, 2000). This leads to a variety of problems, including loss of feeling in the limbs, partial blindness, and difficulties in coordinated movement and cognition (Butler, Corboy, & Filley, 2009).

> **Which components of a neuron allows it to communicate?**

Cajal also observed that the dendrites and axons of neurons do not actually touch each other. There is a small gap or cleft between the axon of one neuron and the dendrites or cell body of another. This gap is part of the **synapse,** *the junction or region between the axon of one neuron and the dendrites or cell body of another* (see **FIGURE 3.3**). Many of the 100 billion neurons in your brain have a few thousand synaptic junctions, so it should come as no shock that most adults have 100 to 500 trillion synapses. As you will read shortly, the transmission of information across the synapse is fundamental to communication between neurons, a process that allows us to think, feel, and behave.

## Major Types of Neurons

There are three major types of neurons, each performing a distinct function: sensory neurons, motor neurons, and interneurons. **Sensory neurons** *receive information from the external world and convey this information to the brain.* They have receptors on their dendrites that receive signals for light, sound, touch, taste, and smell. For example, sensory neurons' endings in our eyes are sensitive to light. **Motor neurons** *carry signals from the spinal cord to the muscles to produce movement.* These neurons often have long axons that can stretch to muscles at our extremities. However,

> **How do the three types of neurons work together to transmit information?**

▼ Figure **3.3** **The Synapse** The synapse is the junction between the dendrites of one neuron and the axon or cell body of another. Notice that neurons do not actually touch one another: There is a small synaptic space between them across which information is transmitted.

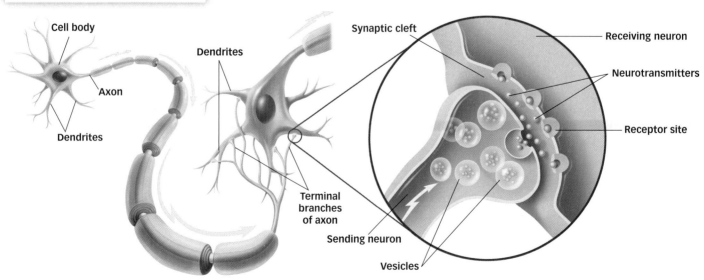

most of the nervous system is composed of the third type of neuron, **interneurons,** which *connect sensory neurons, motor neurons, or other interneurons*. Some interneurons carry information from sensory neurons into the nervous system, others carry information from the nervous system to motor neurons, and still others perform a variety of information-processing functions within the nervous system. Interneurons work together in small circuits to perform simple tasks, such as identifying the location of a sensory signal, and much more complicated ones, such as recognizing a familiar face.

**interneurons**
Neurons that connect sensory neurons, motor neurons, or other interneurons.

## Neurons Specialized by Location

Besides specialization for sensory, motor, or connective functions, neurons are also somewhat specialized depending on their location (see **FIGURE 3.4**). For example, *Purkinje cells* are a type of interneuron that carries information from the cerebellum to the rest of the brain and spinal cord. These neurons have dense, elaborate dendrites that resemble bushes. *Pyramidal cells*, found in the cerebral cortex, have a triangular cell body and a single, long dendrite among many smaller dendrites. *Bipolar cells*, a type of sensory neuron found in the retinas of the eyes, have a single axon and small dendrites that feed into a single long dendrite that connects to the cell body. The brain processes different types of information, so a substantial amount of specialization at the cellular level has evolved to handle these tasks.

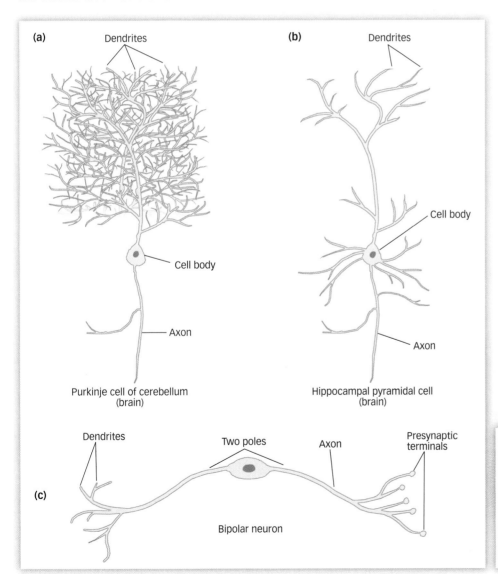

(a) Dendrites — Cell body — Axon
Purkinje cell of cerebellum (brain)

(b) Dendrites — Cell body — Axon
Hippocampal pyramidal cell (brain)

(c) Dendrites — Two poles — Axon — Presynaptic terminals
Bipolar neuron

◄ Figure **3.4** **Types of Neurons** Neurons have a cell body, an axon, and at least one dendrite. The size and shape of neurons vary considerably, however. The Purkinje cell has an elaborate treelike assemblage of dendrites (*a*). Pyramidal cells have a triangular cell body and a single, long dendrite with many smaller dendrites (*b*). Bipolar cells have only one dendrite and a single axon (*c*).

IN SUMMARY

▶ Neurons are the building blocks of the nervous system: They process information received from the outside world, communicate with one another, and send messages to the body's muscles and organs.

▶ Neurons are composed of three major parts: the cell body, the dendrites, and the axon.
    ▶ The cell body contains the nucleus, which houses the organism's genetic material.
    ▶ Dendrites receive sensory signals from other neurons and transmit this information to the cell body.
    ▶ Each axon carries signals from the cell body to other neurons or to muscles and organs in the body.

▶ Neurons do not actually touch. They are separated by a small gap or cleft, which is part of the synapse across which signals are transmitted from one neuron to another.

▶ Glial cells provide support for neurons, usually in the form of the myelin sheath, which coats the axon to facilitate the transmission of information. In demyelinating diseases, the myelin sheath deteriorates.

▶ Neurons are differentiated according to the functions they perform. The three major types of neurons include sensory neurons (e.g., bipolar neurons), motor neurons, and interneurons (e.g., Purkinje cells).

# The Electrochemical Actions of Neurons: Information Processing

Our thoughts, feelings, and actions depend on neural communication, but how does it happen? The communication of information within and between neurons proceeds in two stages:

> *Conduction* is the movement of an electric signal within a neuron, from the dendrites to the cell body, then throughout the axon.

> *Transmission* is movement of electric signals from one neuron to another over the synapse.

Together, these stages are what scientists generally refer to as the *electrochemical action* of neurons.

## Electric Signalling: Conducting Information within a Neuron

The neuron's cell membrane has small pores that act as channels to allow small electrically charged molecules, called *ions*, to flow in and out of the cell. It is this flow of ions across the neuron's cell membrane that creates the conduction of an electric signal within the neuron. How does it happen?

### The Resting Potential: The Origin of the Neuron's Electrical Properties

Neurons have a natural electric charge called the **resting potential,** *the difference in electric charge when the neuron is at rest* (Kandel, 2000). When first discovered by biologists in the 1930s, the resting

British biologists Alan Hodgkin and Andrew Huxley discovered the resting potential in the summer of 1939, while studying marine invertebrates—sea creatures that lack a spine, such as clams, squid, and lobsters (Stevens, 1971). Hodgkin and Huxley worked with the squid giant axon because it is 100 times larger than the biggest axon in humans. They inserted a thin wire into the squid axon so that it touched the jellylike fluid inside. Then they placed another wire just outside the axon in the watery fluid that surrounds it. They found a substantial difference between the electric charges inside and outside the axon, which they called the resting potential.

MAREVISION/AGEFOTOSTOCK/GETTY IMAGES

potential was measured at about about −70 mV. This is a much smaller charge than a typical battery, for example a 9-V battery has 9000 mV (Klein & Thorne, 2007).

The resting potential arises from the difference in concentrations of ions inside and outside the neuron's cell membrane (see **FIGURE 3.5a**). Ions can carry a positive (+) or a negative (−) charge. In the resting state, there is a high concentration of a positively charged ion, potassium (K⁺), as well as negatively charged protein ions (A⁻), *inside* the neuron's cell membrane compared to outside it. By contrast, there is a high concentration of positively charged sodium ions (Na⁺) and negatively charged chloride ions (Cl⁻) *outside* the neuron's cell membrane.

The concentration of K⁺ inside and outside a neuron is controlled by channels in the cell membrane that allow K⁺ ions to flow in and out of the neuron. In the resting

> What difference between the inside and outside of the neuron's cell membrane creates the resting potential?

state, the channels that allow K⁺ ions to flow freely across the cell membrane are open, while channels that allow the flow of Na⁺ (and A⁻, and Cl⁻) are generally closed. Because of the naturally higher concentration of K⁺ ions *inside* the neuron, some K⁺ molecules move out of the neuron through the open channels, leaving the inside of the neuron with a charge of about −70 mV relative to the outside. Like a dam that holds back a river until the floodgates are released, resting potential is potential energy, because it creates the environment for a possible electrical impulse.

**resting potential**
The difference in electric charge when the neuron is at rest.

▼ Figure **3.5** **The Resting and Action Potentials** Neurons have a natural electric charge called a resting potential. Electric stimulation causes an action potential.

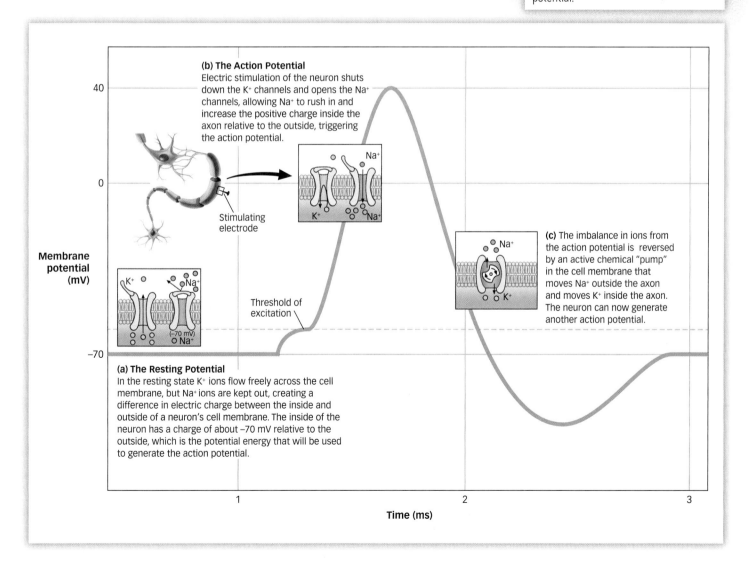

## The Action Potential: Sending Signals across the Neuron

The neuron maintains its resting potential most of the time. However, the biologists working with the giant squid axon (see photograph on page 84) noticed that when they stimulated the axon with a brief electric shock, it resulted in the conduction of an electric impulse down the length of the axon producing a signal (Hausser, 2000; Hodgkin & Huxley, 1939). This electric impulse is called an **action potential,** *an electric signal that is conducted along the length of a neuron's axon to a synapse.*

The action potential occurred only when the electric shock reached a certain level, or *threshold*. When the shock was below this threshold, the researchers recorded only tiny signals, which dissipated rapidly. When the shock reached the threshold, a much larger signal, the action potential, was observed. Interestingly, increases in the electric shock above the threshold did *not* increase the strength of the action potential. The action potential is *all or none*: Electric stimulation below the threshold fails to produce an action potential, whereas electric stimulation at or above the threshold always produces the action potential. The action potential always occurs with exactly the same characteristics and at the same magnitude regardless of whether the stimulus is at or above the threshold.

> Why is an action potential an all-or-nothing event?

The biologists working with the giant squid axon observed another surprising property of the action potential: They measured a peak charge of about +40 mV, which is well above zero. This suggests that the mechanism driving the action potential could not simply be the loss of the −70 mV resting potential because this would have only brought the charge back to zero. So why does the action potential reach a value above zero?

The action potential occurs when there is a change in the state of the axon's membrane channels. Remember, during the resting potential, the channels that allow K⁺ to flow out are open. However, when an electric charge is raised to the threshold value, these channels briefly shut down, and channels that allow the flow of *positively* charged sodium ions (Na⁺) are opened (see **FIGURE 3.5b**). We have seen already that Na⁺ is typically much more concentrated outside the axon than inside. When the channels open, those positively charged ions (Na⁺) flow inside, increasing the positive charge inside the axon relative to that outside. This flow of Na⁺ into the axon pushes the action potential to its maximum value of +40 mV.

After the action potential reaches its maximum, the membrane channels return to their original state, and K⁺ flows out until the axon returns to its resting potential. This leaves a lot of extra Na⁺ ions inside the axon and a lot of extra K⁺ ions outside the axon. During this period when the ions are imbalanced, the neuron cannot initiate another action potential, so it is said to be in a **refractory period,** *the time following an action potential during which a new action potential cannot be initiated.* The imbalance in ions is eventually reversed by an active chemical "pump" in the cell membrane that moves Na⁺ outside the axon and moves K⁺ inside the axon (the pump does not operate during the action potential; see **FIGURE 3.5c**).

So far we have described how the action potential occurs at one point in the neuron. But how does this electric charge move down the axon? It is a domino effect. When an action potential is generated at the beginning of the axon, it spreads a short distance, which generates an action potential at a nearby location on the axon. That action potential also spreads, initiating an action potential at another nearby location, and so on, thus conducting the charge down the length of the axon. This simple mechanism ensures that the action potential travels the full length of the axon and that it maintains its full intensity at each step, regardless of the distance travelled.

The myelin sheath facilitates the conduction of the action potential. Myelin does not cover the entire axon; rather, it clumps around the axon with little break points

Like the flow of electricity when you turn on a light, the action potential is all or none. Either the switch is turned on or the room remains dark. Similarly, either the electrical stimulation in the neuron reaches the threshold to fire an action potential, or no action potential is generated.

**action potential**
An electric signal that is conducted along a neuron's axon to a synapse.

**refractory period**
The time following an action potential during which a new action potential cannot be initiated.

**terminal buttons**
Knoblike structures that branch out from an axon.

**neurotransmitters**
Chemicals that transmit information across the synapse to a receiving neuron's dendrites.

**receptors**
Parts of the cell membrane that receive the neurotransmitter and initiate or prevent a new electric signal.

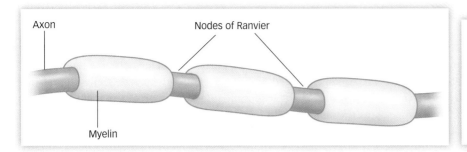

Axon
Nodes of Ranvier
Myelin

◀ Figure **3.6** **Myelin and Nodes of Ranvier** Myelin is formed by a type of glial cell, and it wraps around a neuron's axon to speed the movement of the action potential along the length of the axon. Breaks in the myelin sheath are called the nodes of Ranvier. The electric impulse appears to jump from node to node, thereby speeding the conduction of information down the axon.

between clumps, looking kind of like sausage links. These breakpoints are called the *nodes of Ranvier,* after French pathologist Louis-Antoine Ranvier, who discovered them (see **FIGURE 3.6**). When an electric current passes down the length of a myelinated axon, the charge seems to "jump" from node to node rather than having to traverse the entire axon (Poliak & Peles, 2003). This process is called *saltatory conduction*, and it helps speed the flow of information down the axon.

## Chemical Signalling: Transmission between Neurons

When the action potential reaches the end of an axon, you might think that it stops there. After all, the synaptic space between neurons means that the axon of one neuron and the neighbouring neuron's dendrites do not actually touch one another.

> **How does a neuron communicate with another neuron?**

However, the electric charge of the action potential triggers a chemical signal that can cross the relatively small space of the synaptic cleft.

Axons usually end in **terminal buttons,** *knoblike structures that branch out from an axon.* A terminal button is filled with tiny *vesicles*, or "bags," that contain **neurotransmitters,** *chemicals that transmit information across the synapse to a receiving neuron's dendrites.* The dendrites of the receiving neuron contain **receptors,** *parts of the cell membrane that receive neurotransmitters and either initiate or prevent a new electric signal.*

As K⁺ and Na⁺ flow across a cell membrane, they move the sending neuron, or *presynaptic neuron*, from a resting potential to an action potential. The action potential travels down the length of the axon to the terminal buttons, where it stimulates the release of neurotransmitters from vesicles into the synapse. These neurotransmitters float across the synapse and bind to receptor sites on a nearby dendrite of the receiving neuron, or *postsynaptic neuron*. A new action potential is initiated in that neuron, and the process continues down that neuron's axon to the next synapse and the next neuron. This electrochemical action, called *synaptic transmission* (see **FIGURE 3.7**), allows neurons to communicate with one another and ultimately underlies your thoughts, emotions, and behaviour.

Now that you understand the basic process of how information moves from one neuron to another, we can refine things a bit. You will recall that a given neuron may make a few thousand synaptic connections with other neurons, so what tells the dendrites which of the neurotransmitters flooding into the synapse to receive? One answer is that neurons tend to form pathways in the brain that are characterized by specific types of neurotransmitters; one neurotransmitter might be prevalent in one part of

▼ Figure **3.7** **Synaptic Transmission** (1) The action potential travels down the axon and (2) stimulates the release of neurotransmitters from vesicles. (3) The neurotransmitters are released into the synapse, where they float over to bind with receptor sites on a dendrite of a postsynaptic neuron, initiating a new action potential. The neurotransmitters are cleared out of the synapse by (4) reuptake into the sending neuron, (5) being broken down by enzymes in the synapse, or (6) binding to autoreceptors on the sending neuron.

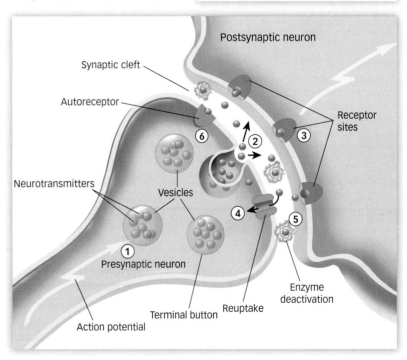

Postsynaptic neuron
Synaptic cleft
Autoreceptor
Receptor sites
Neurotransmitters
Vesicles
Presynaptic neuron
Action potential
Terminal button
Reuptake
Enzyme deactivation

the brain, whereas a different neurotransmitter might be prevalent in a different part of the brain.

A second answer is that neurotransmitters and receptor sites act like a lock-and-key system. Just as a particular key will only fit in a particular lock, so, too, will only some neurotransmitters bind to specific receptor sites on a dendrite. The molecular structure of the neurotransmitter must "fit" the molecular structure of the receptor site.

So what happens to the neurotransmitters left in the synapse after the chemical message is relayed to the postsynaptic neuron? Something must make neurotransmitters stop acting on neurons; otherwise, there would be no end to the signals that they send. Neurotransmitters leave the synapse through three processes (see Figure 3.7). First, *reuptake* occurs when neurotransmitters are reabsorbed by the terminal buttons of the presynaptic neuron's axon. Second, neurotransmitters can be destroyed by enzymes in the synapse in a process called *enzyme deactivation*; specific enzymes break down specific neurotransmitters. Finally, neurotransmitters can bind to the receptor sites called *autoreceptors* on the presynaptic neurons. Autoreceptors detect how much of a neurotransmitter has been released into a synapse and signal the neuron to stop releasing the neurotransmitter when an excess is present.

## Types and Functions of Neurotransmitters

Given that different kinds of neurotransmitters can activate different kinds of receptors, like a lock and key, you might wonder how many types of neurotransmitters are floating across synapses in your brain right now. Today we know that some 60 chemicals play a role in transmitting information throughout the brain and body, and differentially affect thought, feeling, and behaviour, but a few major classes seem particularly important. We will summarize those here, and we will discuss some of these neurotransmitters again in later chapters.

> **Acetylcholine (ACh)** is *a neurotransmitter involved in a number of functions, including voluntary motor control*. Acetylcholine is found in neurons of the brain and in the synapses where axons connect to muscles and body organs, such as the heart. Acetylcholine activates muscles to initiate motor behaviour, but it also contributes to the regulation of attention, learning, sleeping, dreaming, and memory (Gais & Born, 2004; Hasselmo, 2006; Wrenn et al., 2006). Alzheimer's disease, a medical condition involving severe memory impairments (Salmon & Bondi, 2009), is associated with the deterioration of ACh-producing neurons.

> **Dopamine** is *a neurotransmitter that regulates motor behaviour, motivation, pleasure, and emotional arousal*. Because of its role in basic motivated behaviours, such as seeking pleasure or associating actions with rewards, dopamine plays a role in drug addiction (Baler & Volkow, 2006). High levels of dopamine have been linked to schizophrenia (Winterer & Weinberger, 2004), whereas low levels have been linked to Parkinson's disease.

> **Glutamate** is the *major excitatory neurotransmitter in the brain,* meaning that it enhances the transmission of information between neurons. **GABA (gamma-aminobutyric acid),** in contrast, is *the primary inhibitory neurotransmitter in the brain*, meaning that it tends to stop the firing of neurons. Too much glutamate, or too little GABA, can cause neurons to become overactive, causing seizures.

> Two related neurotransmitters influence mood and arousal: norepinephrine and serotonin. **Norepinephrine** is *particularly involved in states of vigilance, or a heightened awareness of dangers in the environment* (Ressler & Nemeroff, 1999). **Serotonin** is *involved in the regulation of sleep and wakefulness, eating, and aggressive behaviour* (Dayan & Huys, 2009; Kroeze & Roth, 1998). Because both neurotransmitters affect mood and arousal, low levels of each have been associated with mood disorders (Tamminga et al., 2002).

---

**acetylcholine (ACh)**
A neurotransmitter involved in a number of functions, including voluntary motor control.

**dopamine**
A neurotransmitter that regulates motor behaviour, motivation, pleasure, and emotional arousal.

**glutamate**
The major excitatory neurotransmitter in the brain.

**GABA (gamma-aminobutyric acid)**
The primary inhibitory neurotransmitter in the brain.

**norepinephrine**
A neurotransmitter that is particularly involved in states of vigilance, or heightened awareness of dangers in the environment.

**serotonin**
A neurotransmitter that is involved in the regulation of sleep and wakefulness, eating, and aggressive behaviour.

**endorphins**
Chemicals that act within the pain pathways and emotion centres of the brain.

**agonists**
Drugs that increase the action of a neurotransmitter.

**antagonists**
Drugs that block the function of a neurotransmitter.

> **Endorphins** *are chemicals that act within the pain pathways and emotion centres of the brain* (Keefe et al., 2001). The term *endorphin* is a contraction of *endo*genous m*orphine,* and that is a pretty apt description. Morphine is a synthetic drug that has a calming and pleasurable effect; an endorphin is an internally produced substance that has similar properties, such as dulling the experience of pain and elevating moods. The "runner's high" experienced by many athletes as they push their bodies to painful limits of endurance can be explained by the release of endorphins in the brain (Boecker et al., 2008).

> How do neurotransmitters create the feeling of runner's high?

Sandra Wallenhorst of Germany began a 180-km bicycle ride, just one part of the 2009 Ironman World Championship in Hawaii. When athletes such as Wallenhorst engage in extreme sports, they may experience subjective highs that result from the release of endorphins—chemical messengers acting in emotion and pain centres that elevate mood and dull the experience of pain.

Each of these neurotransmitters affects thought, feeling, and behaviour in different ways, so normal functioning involves a delicate balance of each. Even a slight imbalance—too much of one neurotransmitter or not enough of another—can dramatically affect behaviour. These imbalances sometimes occur naturally: For example, changes in both the serotonin and dopamine systems may be a cause of some of the symptoms of schizophrenia, including hallucinations. Other times a person may actively seek to cause imbalances. People who smoke, drink alcohol, or take drugs, legal or not, are altering the balance of neurotransmitters in their brains. The drugs LSD and mescaline both produce an increase in dopamine and serotonin neurotransmission, which may be related to their hallucinatory effects.

## How Drugs Mimic Neurotransmitters

Many drugs that affect the nervous system operate by increasing, interfering with, or mimicking the manufacture or function of neurotransmitters (Cooper, Bloom, & Roth, 2003; Sarter, 2006). **Agonists** are *drugs that increase the action of a neurotransmitter.* **Antagonists** are *drugs that block the function of a neurotransmitter.* Some drugs alter a step in the production or release of the neurotransmitter, whereas others have a chemical structure so similar to a neurotransmitter that the drug is able to bind to that neuron's receptor. If, by binding to a receptor, a drug activates the neurotransmitter, it is an agonist; if it blocks the action of the neurotransmitter, it is an antagonist (see **FIGURE 3.8** on the next page).

For example, the drug L-dopa was developed to treat Parkinson's disease, a movement disorder characterized by tremors and difficulty initiating movement, caused by the loss of neurons that use the neurotransmitter dopamine. Dopamine is created in neurons by a modification of a molecule called L-dopa. Ingesting L-dopa will elevate the amount of L-dopa in the brain and spur the surviving neurons to produce more dopamine. In other words, L-dopa acts as an agonist for dopamine. The use of L-dopa has been reasonably successful in the alleviation of Parkinson's disease symptoms (Muenter & Tyce, 1971; Schapira et al., 2009). However, the effectiveness of L-dopa typically decreases when used over a long

> How does L-dopa alleviate symptoms of Parkinson's disease?

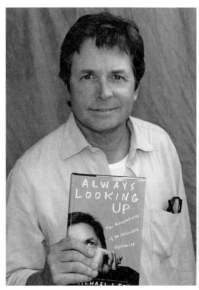

Canadian actor Michael J. Fox vividly described his struggles with Parkinson's disease in his 2009 memoir. Fox's visibility has increased public awareness of the disease and spurred greater efforts toward finding a cure.

▲ Figure **3.8 The Actions of Agonist and Antagonist Drugs** Agonist and antagonist drugs can enhance or interfere with synaptic transmission at every point in the process: in the production of neurotransmitters, in the release of neurotransmitters, at the autoreceptors, in reuptake, in the postsynaptic receptors, and in the synapse itself.

period of time, so that many longtime users experience some symptoms of the disease. The Canadian actor Michael J. Fox, who was diagnosed with Parkinson's disease in 1991 and takes L-dopa, described the simple act of trying to brush his teeth in his memoir:

Grasping the toothpaste is nothing compared to the effort it takes to coordinate the two-handed task of wrangling the toothbrush and strangling out a line of paste onto the bristles. By now, my right hand has started up again, rotating at the wrist in a circular motion, perfect for what I am about to do. My left hand guides my right hand up to my mouth, and once the back of the Oral-B touches the inside of my upper lip, I let go. It is like releasing the tension on a slingshot and compares favorably to the most powerful state-of-the-art electric toothbrush on the market. With no off switch, stopping means seizing my right wrist with my left hand, forcing it down to the sink basin, and shaking the brush loose as though disarming a knife-wielding attacker. (Fox, 2009, pp. 2–3)

Many other drugs, including some street drugs, alter the actions of neurotransmitters. Let us look at a few more examples.

*Amphetamine* is a popular drug that stimulates the release of norepinephrine and dopamine. In addition, both amphetamine and *cocaine* prevent the reuptake of norepinephrine, serotonin, and dopamine. The combination of increased release of norepinephrine, serotonin, and dopamine and prevention of their reuptake floods the synapse with those neurotransmitters, resulting in increased activation of their receptors. Both of these drugs therefore are strong agonists, although the psychological effects of the two drugs differ somewhat because of subtle distinctions in where and how they act on the brain. Norepinephrine and dopamine play a critical role in mood control, such that increases in either neurotransmitter result in euphoria, wakefulness, and a burst of energy. However, norepinephrine also increases heart rate. An overdose of amphetamine or cocaine can cause the heart to contract so rapidly that heartbeats do not last long enough to pump blood effectively, leading to fainting and sometimes death.

*Prozac*, a drug commonly used to treat depression, is another example of a neurotransmitter agonist. Prozac blocks the reuptake of the neurotransmitter *serotonin*, making it part of a category of drugs called *selective serotonin reuptake inhibitors*, or *SSRIs* (Wong, Bymaster, & Engleman, 1995). By blocking reuptake, more of the neurotransmitter remains in the synapse longer and produces greater activation of serotonin receptors. Serotonin elevates mood, which can help relieve depression (Mann, 2005).

An antagonist with important medical implications is a drug called *propranolol*, one of a class of drugs called *beta blockers* that obstruct a receptor site for norepinephrine in the heart. Because norepinephrine cannot bind to these receptors when propranolol is present, heart rate slows down, which is helpful for disorders in which the heart beats too fast or irregularly. Beta blockers are also prescribed to reduce the agitation, racing heart, and nervousness associated with stage fright (Mills & Dimsdale, 1991). (For additional discussion of antianxiety and antidepression drug treatments, see the Treatment of Psychological Disorders chapter.)

## IN SUMMARY

▶ The conduction of an electric signal within a neuron happens when the resting potential is reversed by an electric impulse called an action potential. An action potential is generated in a neuron when that neuron's membrane has been sufficiently depolarized. The action potential acts like a signal, travelling down the axon of the cell in which it was generated, triggering the release of neurotransmitters so that the signal is communicated to postsynaptic neurons.

▶ The neuron's resting potential is due to a difference in electric charge across the neuron's cell membrane. This charge difference arises because in the resting state, positively charged potassium ions ($K^+$) can move freely across the membrane, whereas positively charged sodium ions ($Na^+$) are kept out of the cell.

▶ If electric signals reach a threshold, this initiates an action potential, an all-or-none signal that moves down the entire length of the axon. The action potential occurs when $K^+$ channels in the axon membrane close and $Na^+$ channels open, allowing the $Na^+$ ions to flow inside the axon. After the action potential has reached its maximum, a chemical pump reverses the imbalance in ions, returning the neuron to its resting potential. For a brief refractory period, the action potential cannot be re-initiated. Once it is initiated, the action potential spreads down the axon, appearing to jump across the nodes of Ranvier to the synapse.

▶ Communication between neurons takes place through synaptic transmission, where an action potential triggers release of neurotransmitters from the terminal buttons of the presynaptic (sending) neuron's axon, which travel across the synapse to bind with receptors in the postsynaptic (receiving) neuron's dendrite.

▶ Neurotransmitters bind to dendrites on specific receptor sites. Neurotransmitters leave the synapse through reuptake, through enzyme deactivation, and by binding to autoreceptors.

▶ Some of the major neurotransmitters are acetylcholine (ACh), dopamine, glutamate, GABA, norepinephrine, serotonin, and endorphins.

▶ Drugs can affect behaviour by acting as agonists by facilitating or increasing the actions of neurotransmitters, or as antagonists by blocking the action of neurotransmitters. Recreational drug use can have an effect on brain function.

**nervous system**
An interacting network of neurons that conveys electrochemical information throughout the body.

**central nervous system (CNS)**
The part of the nervous system that is composed of the brain and spinal cord.

**peripheral nervous system (PNS)**
The part of the nervous system that connects the central nervous system to the body's organs and muscles.

**somatic nervous system**
A set of nerves that conveys information between voluntary muscles and the central nervous system.

▼ Figure 3.9 **The Human Nervous System**
The nervous system is organized into the peripheral and central nervous systems. The peripheral nervous system is further divided into the autonomic and somatic nervous systems.

# The Organization of the Nervous System

We have seen how individual neurons communicate with each other. What is the bigger picture? Neurons work by forming circuits and pathways in the brain, which in turn influence circuits and pathways in other areas of the body. Without this kind of organization and delegation, neurons would be churning away with little purpose. Neurons are the building blocks that form *nerves*, or bundles of axons and the glial cells that support them. The **nervous system** is *an interacting network of neurons that conveys electrochemical information throughout the body.* In this section, we will look at the major divisions and components of the nervous system.

## Divisions of the Nervous System

There are two major divisions of the nervous system: the central nervous system and the peripheral nervous system (see **FIGURE 3.9**). The **central nervous system (CNS)** is *composed of the brain and spinal cord.* The central nervous system receives sensory information from the external world, processes and coordinates this information, and sends commands to the skeletal and muscular systems for action. At the top of the CNS rests the brain, which contains structures that support the most complex perceptual, motor, emotional, and cognitive functions of the nervous system. The spinal cord branches down from the brain; nerves that process sensory information and relay commands to the body connect to the spinal cord.

The **peripheral nervous system (PNS)** *connects the central nervous system to the body's organs and muscles.* The peripheral nervous system is itself composed of two major subdivisions, the somatic nervous system and the autonomic nervous system. The **somatic nervous system** is *a set of nerves that conveys information between voluntary muscles and the central nervous system.* Humans have conscious control over this system and use it to perceive, think, and coordinate their behaviours. For example, reaching for your morning cup of coffee involves the elegantly orchestrated

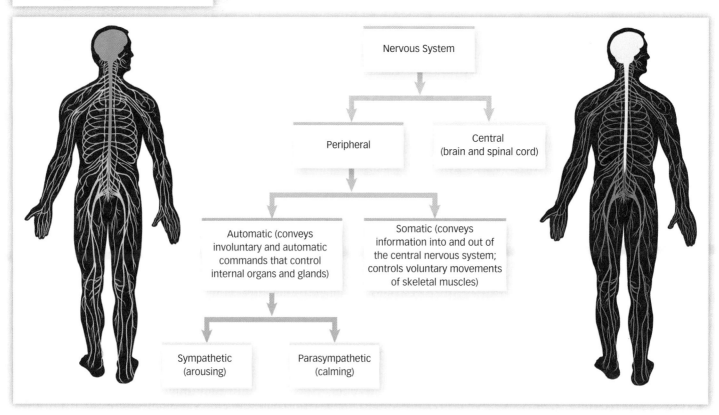

activities of the somatic nervous system: Information from the receptors in your eyes travels to your brain, registering that a cup is on the table; signals from your brain travel to the muscles in your arm and hand; feedback from those muscles tells your brain that the cup has been grasped, and so on.

In contrast, the **autonomic nervous system (ANS)** is *a set of nerves that carries involuntary and automatic commands that control blood vessels, body organs, and glands.* As suggested by its name, this system works on its own to regulate bodily systems, largely outside of conscious control. The ANS has two major subdivisions, the sympathetic nervous system and the parasympathetic nervous system. Each exerts a different type of control on the body. The **sympathetic nervous system** is *a set of nerves*

> **What triggers the increase in your heart rate when you feel threatened?**

*that prepares the body for action in challenging or threatening situations* (see **FIGURE 3.10**). For example, imagine that you are walking alone late at night and frightened by footsteps behind you in a dark alley. Your sympathetic nervous system kicks into action at this point: It dilates your pupils to let in more light, increases your heart rate and respiration to pump more oxygen to muscles, diverts blood flow to your brain and muscles, and activates sweat glands to cool your body. To conserve energy, the sympathetic nervous system inhibits salivation and bowel movements, suppresses the body's immune responses, and suppresses responses to pain and injury. The sum total of these fast, automatic responses is that they increase the likelihood that you can escape.

**autonomic nervous system (ANS)**
A set of nerves that carries involuntary and automatic commands that control blood vessels, body organs, and glands.

**sympathetic nervous system**
A set of nerves that prepares the body for action in challenging or threatening situations.

**Sympathetic nervous system**

- Dilates pupil
- Relaxes bronchi
- Accelerates heartbeat
- Inhibits digestive activity
- Stimulates glucose release
- Stimulates secretion of epinephrine/norepinephrine
- Relaxes bladder
- Stimulates ejaculation in male

**Parasympathetic nervous system**

- Contracts pupil
- Constricts bronchi
- Slows heartbeat
- Stimulates digestive activity
- Stimulates gallbladder
- Contracts bladder
- Allows blood flow to sex organs

◄ Figure **3.10** **Sympathetic and Parasympathetic Systems** The autonomic nervous system is composed of two subsystems that complement each other. Activation of the sympathetic system serves several aspects of arousal, whereas the parasympathetic nervous system returns the body to its normal resting state.

**parasympathetic nervous system**
A set of nerves that helps the body return to a normal resting state.

**spinal reflexes**
Simple pathways in the nervous system that rapidly generate muscle contractions.

The **parasympathetic nervous system** *helps the body return to a normal resting state*. When you are far away from your would-be attacker, your body does not need to remain on red alert. Now the parasympathetic nervous system kicks in to reverse the effects of the sympathetic nervous system and return your body to its normal state. The parasympathetic nervous system generally mirrors the connections of the sympathetic nervous system. For example, the parasympathetic nervous system constricts your pupils, slows your heart rate and respiration, diverts blood flow to your digestive system, and decreases activity in your sweat glands.

As you might imagine, the sympathetic and parasympathetic nervous systems coordinate to control many bodily functions. One example is sexual behaviour. In men, the parasympathetic nervous system engorges the blood vessels of the penis to produce an erection, but the sympathetic nervous system is responsible for ejaculation. In women, the parasympathetic nervous system produces vaginal lubrication, but the sympathetic nervous system underlies orgasm. In both men and women, a successful sexual experience depends on a delicate balance of these two systems; in fact, anxiety about sexual performance can disrupt this balance. For example, sympathetic nervous system activation caused by anxiety can lead to premature ejaculation in males and lack of lubrication in females.

## Components of the Central Nervous System

Compared to the many divisions of the peripheral nervous system, the central nervous system may seem simple. After all, it has only two elements: the brain and the spinal cord. But those two elements are ultimately responsible for most of what we do as humans.

The spinal cord often seems like the brain's poor relation: The brain gets all the glory and the spinal cord just hangs around, doing relatively simple tasks. Those tasks, however, are pretty important: They keep you breathing, respond to pain, and move your muscles, allowing you to walk. What is more, without the spinal cord, the brain would not be able to put any of its higher processing into action.

> What important functions does the spinal cord perform on its own?

Do you need your brain to tell you to pull your hand away from a hot stove? For some very basic behaviours such as this, the spinal cord does not need input from the brain at all. Connections between the sensory inputs and motor neurons in the spinal cord mediate **spinal reflexes,** *simple pathways in the nervous system that rapidly generate muscle contractions*. If you touch a hot stove, the sensory neurons that register pain send inputs directly into the spinal cord (see **FIGURE 3.11**). Through just a few synaptic connections within the spinal cord, interneurons relay these sensory inputs to motor neurons that connect to your arm muscles and direct you to quickly retract your hand.

▼ Figure **3.11** **The Pain Withdrawal Reflex** Many actions of the central nervous system do not require the brain's input. For example, withdrawing from pain is a reflexive activity controlled by the spinal cord. Painful sensations (such as the heat of fire) travel directly to the spinal cord via sensory neurons, which then issue an immediate command to motor neurons to retract the hand.

Interneuron

Sensory neuron

Motor neuron

Spinal cord

Sensory receptors

More elaborate tasks require the collaboration of the spinal cord and the brain. The peripheral nervous system sends messages from sensory neurons through the spinal cord into the brain. The brain sends commands for voluntary movement through the spinal cord to motor neurons, whose axons project out to skeletal muscles. Damage to the spinal cord severs the connection from the brain to the sensory and motor neurons that are essential to sensory perception and movement. The location of the spinal injury often determines the extent of the abilities that are lost. As you can see in **FIGURE 3.12** (on the next page), different regions of the spinal cord control different systems of the body. Individuals with damage at a particular level of the spinal cord lose sensations of touch and pain in body parts below the level of the injury, as well as a loss of motor control of the muscles in the same areas. A spinal injury higher up the cord usually predicts a much poorer prognosis, such as quadriplegia (loss of sensation and motor control over all limbs), breathing through a respirator, and lifelong immobility.

The late actor Christopher Reeve, who starred as Superman in four *Superman* movies, damaged his spinal cord in a horseback riding accident in 1995, resulting in loss of sensation and motor control in all of his body parts below the neck. Despite great efforts over several years, Reeve made only modest gains in his motor control and sensation, highlighting the extent to which we depend on communication from the brain through the spinal cord to the body, and showing how difficult it is to compensate for the loss of these connections (Edgerton et al., 2004). Sadly, Christopher Reeve died at age 52 in 2004 from complications due to his paralysis. On a brighter note, researchers are making progress in understanding the nature of spinal cord injuries and how to treat them by focusing on how the brain changes in response to injury (Blesch & Tuszynski, 2009; Dunlop, 2008), a process that is closely related to the concept of brain plasticity that we will examine later in this chapter.

## IN SUMMARY

▶ Neurons make up nerves, which in turn form the human nervous system.

▶ The nervous system is divided into the peripheral and the central nervous systems. The peripheral nervous system connects the central nervous system with the rest of the body, and it is itself divided into the somatic nervous system and the autonomic nervous system.

▶ The somatic nervous system, which conveys information into and out of the central nervous system, controls voluntary muscles, whereas the autonomic nervous system automatically controls the body's organs.

▶ The autonomic nervous system is further divided into the sympathetic and parasympathetic nervous systems, which complement each other in their effects on the body. The sympathetic nervous system prepares the body for action in threatening situations, and the parasympathetic nervous system returns it to its normal state.

▶ The central nervous system is composed of the spinal cord and the brain. The spinal cord can control some basic behaviours such as spinal reflexes without input from the brain.

## Structure of the Brain

The human brain weighs in at about 1.4 kg. You already know that its neurons and glial cells are busy humming away, giving you potentially brilliant ideas, consciousness, and feelings. But which neurons in which parts of the brain control which functions? To answer that question, neuroscientists had to find a way of describing the brain that allows researchers to communicate with one another. It can be helpful to talk about areas of the brain from "bottom to top," noting how the different regions are specialized for different kinds of tasks. In general, simpler functions are performed at the "lower levels" of the brain, whereas more complex functions are performed at successively "higher" levels (see **FIGURE 3.13** on the next page). Or, as you will see shortly, the brain can also be approached in a

▼ Figure 3.12 **Regions of the Spinal Cord** The spinal cord is divided into four main sections; each controls different parts of the body. Damage higher on the spinal cord usually means greater impairment.

C1 — CERVICAL NERVES
C2 — Head and neck
C3
C4 — Diaphragm
C5 — Deltoids, biceps
C6 — Wrist extenders
C7 — Triceps
T1 — Hand
T2
T3 — THORACIC NERVES
T4
T5 — Chest muscles
T6
T7
T8
T9 — Abdominal muscles
T10
T11
T12
L1 — LUMBAR NERVES
L2
L3 — Leg muscles
L4
L5 — SACRAL NERVES
S1
S2 — Bowel, bladder
S3
S4 — Sexual function
S5

OMIKRON/SCIENCE SOURCE

The human brain weighs only 1.4 kg but its accomplishments are staggering.

Forebrain

Midbrain

Hindbrain

▲ Figure **3.13** **The Major Divisions of the Brain** The brain can be organized into three parts, moving from the bottom to the top, from simpler functions to the more complex: the hindbrain, the midbrain, and the forebrain.

Canadian Olympic medallist Charles Hamelin relies on his cerebellum to execute graceful, coordinated motions on the ice. The cerebellum, part of the hindbrain, helps direct the smooth action of a variety of motor behaviours.

STREETER LECKA/GETTY IMAGES

"side-by-side" fashion: Although each side of the brain is roughly analogous, one half of the brain specializes in some tasks that the other half does not. Although these divisions make it easier to understand areas of the brain and their functions, keep in mind that none of these structures or areas in the brain can act alone: They are all part of one big, interacting, interdependent whole.

Let us look first at the divisions of the brain, and the responsibilities of each part, moving from the bottom to the top. Using this view, we can divide the brain into three parts: the hindbrain, the midbrain, and the forebrain (see Figure 3.13).

## The Hindbrain

If you follow the spinal cord from your tailbone to where it enters your skull, you will find it difficult to determine where your spinal cord ends and your brain begins. That is because the spinal cord is continuous with the **hindbrain,** *an area of the brain that coordinates information coming into and out of the spinal cord.* The hindbrain looks like a stalk on which the rest of the brain sits, and it controls the most basic functions of life: respiration, alertness, and motor skills. The structures that make up the hindbrain include: the medulla, the reticular formation, the cerebellum, and the pons (see **FIGURE 3.14** on the next page).

The **medulla** is *an extension of the spinal cord into the skull that coordinates heart rate, circulation, and respiration.* Beginning inside the medulla and extending upward is a small cluster of neurons called the **reticular formation,** which *regulates sleep, wakefulness, and levels of arousal.* In one early experiment, researchers stimulated the reticular formation of a sleeping cat. This caused the animal to awaken almost instantaneously and remain alert. Conversely, severing the connections between the reticular formation and the rest of the brain caused the animal to lapse into an irreversible coma (Moruzzi & Magoun, 1949). The reticular formation maintains the same delicate balance between alertness and unconsciousness in humans. In fact, many general anesthetics work by reducing activity in the reticular formation, rendering the patient unconscious.

Behind the medulla is the **cerebellum,** *a large structure of the hindbrain that controls fine motor skills.* (*Cerebellum* is Latin for "little brain," and the structure does look like a small replica of the brain.) The cerebellum orchestrates the proper sequence of movements when we ride a bike, play the piano, or maintain balance while walking and running. It contributes to the fine-tuning of behaviour: smoothing our actions to allow their graceful execution rather than initiating the actions (Smetacek, 2002). The initiation of behaviour involves other areas of the brain; as you will recall, different brain systems interact and are interdependent with one another.

> Which part of the brain helps to orchestrate movements that keep you steady on your bike?

The last major area of the hindbrain is the **pons,** *a structure that relays information from the cerebellum to the rest of the brain.* (*Pons* means "bridge" in Latin.) Although the detailed functions of the pons remain poorly understood, it essentially acts as a relay station or bridge between the cerebellum and other structures in the brain.

## The Midbrain

Sitting on top of the hindbrain is the *midbrain,* which is relatively small in humans. As you can see in **FIGURE 3.15** (on the next page), the midbrain contains two main structures: the tectum and the tegmentum. The **tectum** *orients an organism in the*

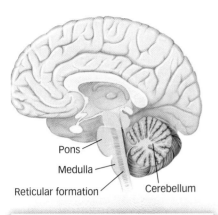

▲ Figure 3.14 **The Hindbrain** The hindbrain coordinates information coming into and out of the spinal cord and controls the basic functions of life. It includes the medulla, the reticular formation, the cerebellum, and the pons.

▲ Figure 3.15 **The Midbrain** The midbrain is important for orientation and movement. It includes structures such as the tectum and tegmentum.

*environment.* The tectum receives stimulus input from the eyes, ears, and skin and moves the organism in a coordinated way toward the stimulus. For example, when you are studying in a quiet room and you hear a *click* behind and to the right of you, your body will swivel and orient to the direction of the sound; this is your tectum in action.

The **tegmentum** is *involved in movement and arousal*; it also helps to orient an organism toward sensory stimuli. The midbrain may be relatively small, but it is a central location of neurotransmitters involved in arousal, mood, and motivation and the brain structures that rely on them (White, 1996). You could survive if you had only a hindbrain and a midbrain. The structures in the hindbrain would take care of all the bodily functions necessary to sustain life, and the structures in the midbrain would orient you toward or away from pleasurable or threatening stimuli in the environment. But this would not be much of a life. To understand where the abilities that make us fully human come from, we need to consider the last division of the brain.

## The Forebrain

When you appreciate the beauty of a poem, detect the sarcasm in a friend's remark, plan to go skiing next winter, or notice the faint glimmer of sadness on a loved one's face, you are enlisting the forebrain. The *forebrain* is the highest level of the brain—literally and figuratively—and controls complex cognitive, emotional, sensory, and motor functions. The forebrain itself is divided into two main sections: the cerebral cortex and the subcortical structures.

The **cerebral cortex** is *the outermost layer of the brain, visible to the naked eye, and divided into two hemispheres.* The **subcortical structures** are *areas of the forebrain housed under the cerebral cortex near the centre of the brain* (see **FIGURE 3.16** on the next page). We will have much more to say about the two hemispheres of the cerebral cortex and the functions they serve in the next section, fittingly saving the highest level of the brain for last. First, we will examine the subcortical structures.

### Subcortical Structures

The subcortical (beneath the cortex) structures are nestled deep inside the brain, where they are quite protected. If you imagine sticking an index finger in each of your ears and pushing inward until they touch, that is about where you would find the thalamus, hypothalamus, pituitary gland, limbic system, and basal ganglia (see

**hindbrain**
An area of the brain that coordinates information coming into and out of the spinal cord.

**medulla**
An extension of the spinal cord into the skull that coordinates heart rate, circulation, and respiration.

**reticular formation**
A brain structure that regulates sleep, wakefulness, and levels of arousal.

**cerebellum**
A large structure of the hindbrain that controls fine motor skills.

**pons**
A brain structure that relays information from the cerebellum to the rest of the brain.

**tectum**
A part of the midbrain that orients an organism in the environment.

**tegmentum**
A part of the midbrain that is involved in movement and arousal.

**cerebral cortex**
The outermost layer of the brain, visible to the naked eye and divided into two hemispheres.

**subcortical structures**
Areas of the forebrain housed under the cerebral cortex near the centre of the brain.

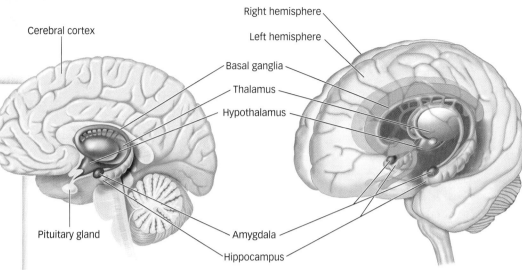

Right hemisphere

Left hemisphere

Cerebral cortex

Basal ganglia

Thalamus

Hypothalamus

Amygdala

Hippocampus

Pituitary gland

► Figure **3.16** **The Forebrain** The fore brain is the highest level of the brain and is critical for complex cognitive, emotional, sensory, and motor functions. The forebrain is divided into two parts: the cerebral cortex and the underlying subcortical structures. The cerebral cortex, the outermost layer of the brain, is divided into two hemispheres, connected by the corpus callosum (see Figure 3.18). The subcortical structures include the thalamus, hypothalamus, pituitary gland, amygdala, and hippocampus.

Figure 3.16). Each of these subcortical structures plays an important role in relaying information throughout the brain, as well as performing specific tasks that allow us to think, feel, and behave as humans. Here we will give you a brief introduction to each, and you will read more about many of these structures in later chapters.

**Thalamus, Hypothalamus, and Pituitary Gland.** The thalamus, hypothalamus, and pituitary gland, located in the centre of the brain, interact closely with several other brain structures. They relay signals to and from these structures and also help to regulate them.

The **thalamus** *relays and filters information from the senses and transmits the information to the cerebral cortex.* The thalamus receives inputs from all the major senses except smell, which has direct connections to the cerebral cortex. The thalamus acts as a kind of computer server in a networked system,

> How is the thalamus like a computer?

The thalamus receives inputs from all the major senses except smell. You can thank your thalamus when you see the red apple, feel its smoothness in your hand, hear the crunch as you bite into it, and taste its sweetness.

ISTOCK/THINKSTOCK

taking in multiple inputs and relaying them to a variety of locations (Guillery & Sherman, 2002). However, unlike the mechanical operations of a computer ("send input A to location B"), the thalamus actively filters sensory information, giving more weight to some inputs and less weight to others. The thalamus also closes the pathways of incoming sensations during sleep, providing a valuable function in *not* allowing information to pass to the rest of the brain.

The **hypothalamus,** located below the thalamus (*hypo-* is Greek for "under"), *regulates body temperature, hunger, thirst, and sexual behaviour.* Although the hypothalamus is a tiny area of the brain, clusters of neurons in the hypothalamus oversee a wide range of basic behaviours, keeping body temperature, blood sugar levels, and metabolism within an optimal range for normal human functioning. Lesions to some areas of the hypothalamus result in overeating, whereas lesions to other areas leave an animal with no desire for food at all, highlighting that the hypothalamus plays a key role in regulating food intake (Berthoud & Morrison, 2008). Also, when you think about sex, messages from your cerebral cortex are sent to the hypothalamus to trigger the release of hormones. Finally, electric stimulation of some areas of the hypothalamus in cats can produce hissing and biting, whereas stimulation of other areas in the hypothalamus can produce what appears to be intense pleasure for an animal (Siegel et al., 1999). McGill University researchers James Olds and Peter Milner found that a small electric current delivered to a certain region of a

**thalamus**
A subcortical structure that relays and filters information from the senses and transmits the information to the cerebral cortex.

**hypothalamus**
A subcortical structure that regulates body temperature, hunger, thirst, and sexual behaviour.

rat's hypothalamus was extremely rewarding for the animal (Olds & Milner, 1954). In fact, when allowed to press a bar attached to the electrode to initiate their own stimulation, rats would do so several thousand times an hour, often to the point of exhaustion!

Located below the hypothalamus is the **pituitary gland,** *the "master gland" of the body's hormone-producing system, which releases hormones that direct the functions of many other glands in the body.* The hypothalamus sends hormonal signals to the pituitary gland, which in turn sends hormonal signals to other glands to control stress, digestive activities, and reproductive processes. For example, when a baby suckles its mother's breast, sensory neurons in her breast send signals to her hypothalamus, which then signals her pituitary gland to release a hormone called *oxytocin* into the bloodstream (McNeilly et al., 1983). Oxytocin, in turn, stimulates the release of milk from reservoirs in the breast. The pituitary gland is also involved in the response to stress. When we sense a threat, sensory neurons send signals to the hypothalamus, which stimulates the release of adrenocorticotropic hormone (ACTH) from the pituitary gland. ACTH, in turn, stimulates the adrenal glands (above the kidneys) to release hormones that activate the sympathetic nervous system (Selye & Fortier, 1950). As you read earlier in this chapter, the sympathetic nervous system prepares the body to either meet the threat head-on or flee from the situation.

**The Limbic System.** The hypothalamus also is part of the **limbic system,** *a group of forebrain structures including the hypothalamus, the hippocampus, and the amygdala, which are involved in motivation, emotion, learning, and memory* (Maclean, 1970; Papez, 1937). The limbic system is where the subcortical structures meet the cerebral cortex.

The **hippocampus** (from Latin for "sea horse," due to its shape) is *critical for creating new memories and integrating them into a network of knowledge so that they can be stored indefinitely in other parts of the cerebral cortex.* Individuals with damage to the hippocampus can acquire new information and keep it in awareness for a few seconds, but as soon as they are distracted, they forget the information and the experience that produced it (Scoville & Milner, 1957; Squire, 2009). This kind of disruption is limited to everyday memory for facts and events that we can bring to consciousness; memory of learned habitual routines or emotional reactions remains intact (Squire, Knowlton, & Musen, 1993). As an example, people with damage to the hippocampus can remember how to drive and talk, but they cannot recall where they have recently driven or a conversation they have just had. You will read more about the hippocampus and its role in creating, storing, and combining memories in the Memory chapter.

The **amygdala** (from Latin for "almond," also due to its shape), located at the tip of each horn of the hippocampus, *plays a central role in many emotional processes, particularly the formation of emotional memories* (Aggleton, 1992). The amygdala attaches significance to previously neutral events that are associated with fear, punishment, or reward (LeDoux, 1992). As an example, think of the last time something scary or unpleasant happened to you: A car came barrelling toward you as you started walking into an intersection or a ferocious dog leaped out of an alley as you passed by. Ordinarily, these stimuli—a car or a dog—are fairly neutral; you do not have a panic attack every time you walk by a used car lot. But after a scary experience, the emotional significance attached to events involving those stimuli is the work of the amygdala (McGaugh, 2006). When we are in emotionally arousing situations, the amygdala stimulates the hippocampus to remember many details surrounding the situation (Kensinger & Schacter, 2005). For example, people who lived through the terrorist attacks of September 11, 2001 remember vivid details about where they were, what they were doing, and how they felt when they heard the news, even years later (Hirst et al., 2009). In particular, the amygdala seems to be especially involved in encoding events as *fearful* (Adolphs et al., 1995; Sigurdsson et al., 2007). We will

> **Why are you likely to remember details of a traumatic event?**

**pituitary gland**
The "master gland" of the body's hormone-producing system, which releases hormones that direct the functions of many other glands in the body.

**limbic system**
A group of forebrain structures including the hypothalamus, the hippocampus, and the amygdala, which are involved in motivation, emotion, learning, and memory.

**hippocampus**
A structure critical for creating new memories and integrating them into a network of knowledge so that they can be stored indefinitely in other parts of the cerebral cortex.

**amygdala**
A part of the limbic system that plays a central role in many emotional processes, particularly the formation of emotional memories.

A haunted house is designed to stimulate your amygdala, but only a little.

**basal ganglia**
A set of subcortical structures that direct intentional movements.

**corpus callosum**
A thick band of nerve fibres that connects large areas of the cerebral cortex on each side of the brain and supports communication of information across the hemispheres.

**occipital lobe**
A region of the cerebral cortex that processes visual information.

**parietal lobe**
A region of the cerebral cortex whose functions include processing information about touch.

DONNA RANIERI

Crumpling a newspaper allows the same amount of surface area to fit into a much smaller space, just like the wrinkles and folds in the cortex allow a great deal of brain power to fit inside the human skull.

▶ Figure **3.17** **Cerebral Cortex and Lobes**
The four major lobes of the cerebral cortex are the occipital lobe, the parietal lobe, the temporal lobe, and the frontal lobe. The smooth surfaces of the cortex are called gyri and the indentations are called sulci.

have more to say about the amygdala in the Emotion and Motivation chapter. For now, keep in mind that a group of neurons the size of a lima bean buried deep in your brain help you to laugh, weep, or shriek in fright when the circumstances call for it.

**The Basal Ganglia.** There are several other structures in the subcortical area, but we will consider just one more. The **basal ganglia** are *a set of subcortical structures that direct intentional movements.* The basal ganglia are located near the thalamus and hypothalamus; they receive input from the cerebral cortex and send outputs to the motor centres in the brain stem. One part of the basal ganglia, the *striatum,* is involved in the control of posture and movement. As we saw in the excerpt from Michael J. Fox's book, people who suffer from Parkinson's disease typically show symptoms of uncontrollable shaking and sudden jerks of the limbs and are unable to initiate a sequence of movements to achieve a specific goal. This happens because the dopamine-producing neurons in the substantia nigra (found in the tegmentum of the midbrain) have become damaged (Dauer & Przedborski, 2003). The undersupply of dopamine then affects the striatum in the basal ganglia, which in turn leads to the visible behavioural symptoms of Parkinson's.

So, what is the problem in Parkinson's: the jerky movements, the ineffectiveness of the striatum in directing behaviour, the botched interplay of the substantia nigra and the striatum, or the underproduction of dopamine at the neuronal level? The answer is all of the above. This unfortunate disease provides a nice illustration of two themes regarding the brain and behaviour. First, barely visible actions at the level of neurons in the brain can produce substantial effects at the level of behaviour. Second, the interaction of hindbrain, midbrain, and forebrain structures shows how the various regions are interdependent.

## The Cerebral Cortex

Our tour of the brain has taken us from the very small (neurons) to the somewhat bigger (major divisions of the brain) to the very large: the cerebral cortex. The cortex is the highest level of the brain, and it is responsible for the most complex aspects of perception, emotion, movement, and thought (Fuster, 2003). It sits over the rest of the brain, like a mushroom cap shielding the underside and stem, and it is the wrinkled surface you see when looking at the brain with the naked eye.

The smooth surfaces of the cortex—the raised part—are called *gyri* (*gyrus* if you are talking about just one), and the indentations or fissures are called *sulci* (*sulcus* when singular). Sulci and gyri represent a triumph of evolution. The cerebral cortex occupies roughly the area of a newspaper page. Fitting that much cortex into a human skull is a tough task. But if you crumple a sheet of newspaper, you will see that the same surface area now fits compactly into a much smaller space. The cortex, with its wrinkles and folds, holds a lot of brainpower in a relatively small package that fits comfortably inside the human skull (see **FIGURE 3.17**). The functions of the cerebral cortex can be understood at three levels: the separation of the cortex into two hemispheres, the functions of each hemisphere, and the role of specific cortical areas.

Frontal lobe    Parietal lobe

Occipital lobe

Temporal lobe    Sulci    Gyri

**Organization across Hemispheres.** The first level of organization divides the cortex into the left and right hemispheres. The two hemispheres are more or less symmetrical in their appearance and, to some extent, in their functions. However, each hemisphere controls the functions of the opposite side of the body. This is called *contralateral control*, meaning that your right cerebral hemisphere perceives stimuli from and controls movements on the left side of your body, whereas your left cerebral hemisphere perceives stimuli from and controls movement on the right side of your body.

The cerebral hemispheres are connected to each other by *commissures*, bundles of axons that make possible communication between parallel areas of the cortex in each half. The largest of these commissures is the **corpus callosum,** which *connects large areas of the cerebral cortex on each side of the brain and supports communication of information across the hemispheres* (see **FIGURE 3.18**). This means that information received in the right hemisphere, for example, can pass across the corpus callosum and be registered, virtually instantaneously, in the left hemisphere.

**Organization within Hemispheres.** The second level of organization in the cerebral cortex distinguishes the functions of the different regions within each hemisphere of the brain. Each hemisphere of the cerebral cortex is divided into four areas, or *lobes*: From back to front, these are the occipital lobe, the parietal lobe, the temporal lobe, and the frontal lobe, as shown in Figure 3.17. We will examine the functions of these lobes in more detail in later chapters, noting how scientists have used a variety of techniques to understand the operations of the brain. For now, here is a brief overview of the main functions of each lobe.

The **occipital lobe,** located at the back of the cerebral cortex, *processes visual information*. Sensory receptors in the eyes send information to the thalamus, which in turn sends information to the primary areas of the occipital lobe, where simple features of the stimulus are extracted, such as the location and orientation of an object's edges (see the Sensation and Perception chapter for more details). These features are then processed into a more complex "map" of the stimulus onto the occipital cortex, leading to comprehension of what is being seen. As you might imagine, damage to the primary visual areas of the occipital lobe can leave a person with partial or complete blindness. Information still enters the eyes, which work just fine. But without the ability to process and make sense of the information at the level of the cerebral cortex, the information is as good as lost (Zeki, 2001).

The **parietal lobe,** located in front of the occipital lobe, carries out functions that include *processing information about touch*. The parietal lobe contains the *somatosensory cortex*, a strip of brain tissue running from the top of the brain down to the sides (see **FIGURE 3.19** on the next page). Within each hemisphere, the somatosensory cortex represents the skin areas on the contralateral surface of the body. Each part of the somatosensory cortex maps onto a particular part of the body. If a body area is more sensitive, a larger part of the somatosensory cortex is devoted to it. For example, the part of the somatosensory cortex that corresponds to the lips and tongue is larger than the area corresponding to the feet. The somatosensory cortex can be illustrated as a distorted figure, called a *homunculus* ("little man"), in which the body parts are rendered according to how much of the somatosensory cortex is devoted to them (Penfield & Rasmussen, 1950). This map of the body in the brain was developed by Montreal neurosurgeon Wilder Penfield and his colleagues by stimulating the brains of their patients who were awake during surgery, and recording where the patient reported feeling a sensation (Penfield & Rasmussen, 1950). Penfield mapped both the somatosensory and motor cortex, and his maps are still used today. Directly in front of the somatosensory cortex, in the frontal lobe, is a parallel strip of brain tissue called the

> **Why is the part of the somatosensory cortex relating to the lips bigger than the area corresponding to the feet?**

▲ Figure **3.18** **Cerebral Hemispheres** Top view of the brain with part of the right cerebral hemisphere pulled away to expose the corpus callosum (indicated by the arrow).

VIDEOSURGERY/SCIENCE SOURCE

The homunculus is a rendering of the body in which each part is shown in proportion to how much of the somatosensory cortex is devoted to it.

© THE NATURAL HISTORY MUSEUM/THE IMAGE WORKS

Motor cortex
Hip
Knee
Arm
Wrist Trunk
Elbow Ankle
Hand Foot
Toes
Fingers
Thumb
Brow
Eye
Face
Lips
Jaw
Tongue
Esophagus
**Section of left hemisphere**

Sensory cortex
Trunk Leg
Head
Arm Neck Foot
Elbow
Forearm Toes
Hand Genitals
Thumb
Eye
Nose
Face
Lips
Teeth
Gums
Jaw
Tongue
Pharynx
**Section of left hemisphere**

▶ Figure **3.19** **Somatosensory and Motor Cortices** The motor cortex, a strip of brain tissue in the frontal lobe, represents and controls different skin and body areas on the contralateral side of the body. Directly behind the motor cortex, in the parietal lobe, lies the somatosensory cortex. Like the motor cortex, the somatosensory cortex represents skin areas of particular parts on the contralateral side of the body.

*motor cortex*. Like the somatosensory cortex, different parts of the motor cortex correspond to different body parts. The motor cortex initiates voluntary movements and sends messages to the basal ganglia, cerebellum, and spinal cord. The motor and somatosensory cortices, then, are like sending and receiving areas of the cerebral cortex, taking in information and sending out commands as the case might be.

The **temporal lobe,** located on the lower side of each hemisphere, is *responsible for hearing and language.* The *primary auditory cortex* in the temporal lobe is analogous to the somatosensory cortex in the parietal lobe and the primary visual areas of the occipital lobe: It receives sensory information from the ears based on the frequencies of sounds (Recanzone & Sutter, 2008). Secondary areas of the temporal lobe then process the information into meaningful units, such as speech and words. The temporal lobe also houses the visual association areas that interpret the meaning of visual stimuli and help us recognize common objects in the environment (Martin, 2007).

The **frontal lobe,** which sits behind the forehead, has *specialized areas for movement, abstract thinking, planning, memory, and judgment.* As you just read, it contains the motor cortex, which coordinates movements of muscle groups throughout the body. Other areas in the frontal lobe coordinate thought processes that help us manipulate information and retrieve memories, which we can use to plan our behaviours and interact socially with others. In short, the frontal cortex allows us to do the kind of thinking, imagining, planning, and anticipating that sets humans apart from most other species (Schoenemann, Sheenan, & Glotzer, 2005; Stuss & Benson, 1986; Suddendorf & Corballis, 2007).

> What types of thinking occur in the frontal lobe?

**temporal lobe**
A region of the cerebral cortex responsible for hearing and language.

**frontal lobe**
A region of the cerebral cortex that has specialized areas for movement, abstract thinking, planning, memory, and judgment.

**association areas**
Areas of the cerebral cortex that are composed of neurons that help provide sense and meaning to information registered in the cortex.

**Organization within Specific Lobes.** The third level of organization in the cerebral cortex involves the representation of information within specific lobes in the cortex. There is a hierarchy of processing stages from primary areas that handle fine details of information all the way up to **association areas,** which are *composed of neurons that help provide sense and meaning to information registered in the cortex.* For example, neurons in the primary visual cortex are highly specialized: Some detect features of the environment that are in a horizontal orientation, others detect movement, and still others process information about human versus nonhuman forms. Secondary areas interpret the information extracted by these primary areas (shape, motion, etc.) to make sense of what is being perceived; in this case, perhaps a large cat leaping toward your face. Similarly, neurons in the primary auditory cortex register sound frequencies, but it is the association areas of the temporal lobe that allow you to turn those noises into the meaning of your friend screaming, "Look out for the cat!" Association areas, then, help stitch together the threads of information in the various parts of the cortex to produce a meaningful understanding of what is being registered in the brain.

A striking example of this property of association areas comes from the discovery of the mirror-neuron system. **Mirror neurons** are *active when an animal performs a behaviour, such as reaching for or manipulating an object, and are also activated when the animal observes another animal performing the same behaviour*. Mirror neurons are found in the frontal lobe (near the motor cortex) and in the parietal lobe (Rizzolatti & Craighero, 2004; Rizzolatti & Sinigaglia, 2010). They have been identified in birds, monkeys, and humans, and their name reflects the function they serve. Neuroimaging studies with humans have shown that mirror neurons are active when people watch someone perform a behaviour, such as grasping in midair. But they are more highly activated when that behaviour has some purpose or context, such as grasping a cup to take a drink (Iacoboni et al., 2005), and seem to be related to recognizing the goal someone has in carrying out an action and the outcome of the action, rather than to the particular movements a person makes while performing that action (Hamilton & Grafton, 2006, 2008; Iacoboni, 2009; Rizzolatti & Sinigaglia, 2010). In the Learning chapter we will find out more about the role of mirror neurons in learning.

AP PHOTO/DAVID LONGSTREATH

Finally, neurons in the association areas are usually less specialized and more flexible than neurons in the primary areas. As such, they can be shaped by learning and experience to do their job more effectively. This kind of shaping of neurons by environmental forces allows the brain flexibility, or plasticity, our next topic.

When one animal observes another engaging in a particular behaviour, some of the same neurons become active in the observer as well as in the animal exhibiting the behaviour. These mirror neurons seem to play an important role in social behaviour.

## Brain Plasticity

The cerebral cortex may seem like a fixed structure, one big sheet of neurons designed to help us make sense of our external world. Remarkably, though, sensory cortices are not fixed. They can adapt to changes in sensory inputs, a quality researchers call *plasticity* (i.e., the ability to be molded). As an example, if you lose your middle finger in an accident, the part of the somatosensory area that represents that finger is initially unresponsive (Kaas, 1991). After all, there is no longer any sensory input going from that location to that part of the brain. You might expect the left middle-finger neurons

?

**What does it mean to say that the brain is plastic?**

of the somatosensory cortex to wither away. However, over time, that area in the somatosensory cortex becomes responsive to stimulation of the fingers *adjacent* to the missing finger. The brain is plastic: Functions that were assigned to certain areas of the brain may be capable of being reassigned to other areas of the brain to accommodate changing input from the environment (Feldman, 2009). This suggests that sensory inputs "compete" for representation in each cortical area. (See The Real World box for a striking illustration of phantom limbs.)

Plasticity does not only occur to compensate for missing digits or limbs, however. An extraordinary amount of stimulation of one finger can result in that finger "taking over" the representation of the part of the cortex that usually represents other, adjacent fingers (Merzenich et al., 1990). For example, concert pianists have highly

**mirror neurons**
Neurons that are active when an animal performs a behaviour, such as reaching for or manipulating an object, and are also activated when the animal observes another animal performing the same ◄ behaviour.

**THE REAL WORLD**

# Brain Plasticity and Sensations in Phantom Limbs

ong after a limb is amputated, many patients continue to experience sensations where the missing limb would be, a phenomenon called *phantom limb syndrome*. Patients can feel their missing limbs moving, even in coordinated gestures such as shaking hands. Some even report feeling pain in their phantom limbs. Why does this happen? Some evidence suggests that phantom limb syndrome may arise in part because of plasticity in the brain.

Researchers stimulated the skin surface in various regions around the face, torso, and arms while monitoring brain activity in amputees and non-amputated volunteers (Ramachandran & Blakeslee, 1998; Ramachandran, Brang, & McGeoch, 2010; Ramachandran, Rodgers-Ramachandran, & Stewart, 1992). Brain imaging techniques displayed the somatosensory cortical areas activated when the skin was stimulated. This allowed the researchers to map how touch is represented in the somatosensory cortex for different areas of the body. For example, when the face was touched, the researchers could determine which areas in the somatosensory cortex were most active; when the torso was stimulated, they could see which areas responded, and so on.

Brain scans of the amputees revealed that stimulating areas of the face and upper arm activated an area in the somatosensory cortex that previously would have been activated by a now-missing hand. Stimulating the face or arm produced phantom limb sensations in the amputees; they reported "feeling" a sensation in their missing limbs.

Brain plasticity can explain these results (Pascual-Leone et al., 2005). The cortical representations for the face and the upper arm normally lie on either side of the representation for the hand. The somatosensory areas for the face and upper arm were larger in amputees and had taken over the part of the cortex normally representing the hand. Indeed, the new face and arm representations were now contiguous with each other, filling in the space occupied by the hand representation. Some of these new mappings were quite concise. For example, in some amputees, when specific areas of the facial skin were activated, the patient reported sensations in just *one finger* of the phantom hand!

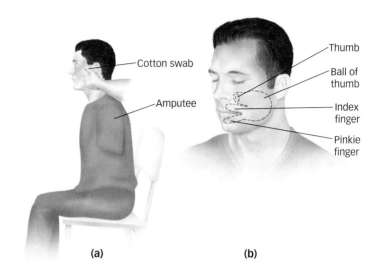

**(a)** **(b)**

▲ **Mapping Sensations in Phantom Limbs** (*a*) Researchers lightly touch an amputee's face with a cotton swab, eliciting sensations in the "missing" hand. (*b*) Touching different parts of the cheek can even result in sensations in particular fingers or the thumb of the missing hand.

This and related research suggest one explanation for a previously poorly understood phenomenon. How can a person "feel" something that is not there? Brain plasticity, an adaptive process through which the brain reorganizes itself, offers an answer (Flor, Nikolajsen, & Jensen, 2006). The brain established new mappings that led to novel sensations.

This idea also has practical implications for dealing with the pain that can result from phantom limbs (Ramachandran & Altschuler, 2009). Researchers have used a "mirror box" to teach patients a new mapping to increase voluntary control over their phantom limbs. For example, a patient would place his intact right hand and phantom left hand in the mirror box such that when looking at the mirror, he sees his right hand reflected on the left—where he has placed his phantom—creating the illusion that the phantom has been restored. The phantom hand thus appears to respond to motor commands given by the patient, and with practice the patient can become better at "moving" the phantom in response to voluntary commands. As

a result, when feeling the excruciating pain associated with a clenched phantom hand, the patient can now voluntarily unclench the hand and reduce the pain. This therapeutic approach based on brain plasticity has been applied successfully to a variety of patient populations (Ramachandran & Altschuler, 2009). In one of the most striking applications of this approach, researchers used mirror box therapy with survivors of the destructive 2010 earthquake in Haiti who were experiencing phantom limb pain after amputation of lower limbs (Miller, Seckel, & Ramachandran, 2012). Seventeen of the 18 amputees in that study reported a significant reduction in experienced pain following mirror box therapy.

▲ A mirror box creates the illusion that the phantom limb has been restored.

developed cortical areas for finger control: The continued input from the fingers commands a larger area of representation in the somatosensory cortices in the brain. Consistent with this observation, recent research indicates greater plasticity within the motor cortex of professional musicians compared with nonmusicians, perhaps reflecting an increase in the number of motor synapses as a result of extended practice (Rosenkranz, Williamon, & Rothwell, 2007). Similar findings have been obtained with quilters (who have highly developed areas for the thumb and forefinger, which are critical to their profession) and taxi drivers (who have overdeveloped brain areas in the hippocampus that are used during spatial navigation) (Maguire, Woollett, & Spiers, 2006).

Plasticity is also related to a question you might not expect to find in a psychology text: How much exercise have you been getting lately? While we expect that you are spending countless happy hours reading this text, we also hope that you have been finding enough time for physical exercise. A large of number of studies in rats and other nonhuman animals indicate that physical exercise can increase the number of synapses and even promote the development of new neurons in the hippocampus (Hillman, Erickson, & Kramer, 2008; van Praag, 2009). Recent studies with people have begun to document beneficial effects of cardiovascular exercise on aspects of brain function and cognitive performance (Colcombe et al., 2004, 2006). Although these effects tend to be seen most clearly in older adults (okay, so it is time for your textbook authors to get on a treadmill), benefits have also been documented throughout the life span (Hertig & Nagel, 2012; Hillman et al., 2008; Roig et al., 2012). In fact, some researchers believe that this kind of activity-dependent brain plasticity is relevant to treating spinal cord injuries (which, as we saw, have a devastating impact on people's lives), because understanding how to maximize plasticity through exercise and training may help to guide rehabilitation efforts (Dunlop, 2008). It should be clear by now that the plasticity of the brain is not just an interesting theoretical idea; it has potentially important applications to everyday life (Bryck & Fisher, 2012).

Everyday forms of exercise, such as running, can benefit not only your heart, but also your brain.

MARK ANDERSEN/ GETTY IMAGES

## IN SUMMARY

▶ The brain can be divided into the hindbrain, midbrain, and forebrain.

▶ The hindbrain generally coordinates information coming into and out of the spinal cord with structures such as the medulla, the reticular formation, the cerebellum, and the pons. These structures respectively coordinate breathing and heart rate, regulate sleep and arousal levels, coordinate fine motor skills, and communicate this information to the cortex.

▶ The midbrain structures generally coordinate functions such as orientation to the environment and movement and arousal toward sensory stimuli.

▶ The forebrain generally coordinates higher-level functions, such as perceiving, feeling, and thinking. The forebrain houses subcortical structures, such as the thalamus, hypothalamus, limbic system (including the hippocampus and amygdala), and basal ganglia; all these structures perform a variety of functions related to motivation and emotion. Also in the forebrain, the cerebral cortex, composed of two hemispheres with four lobes each (occipital, parietal, temporal, and frontal), performs tasks that help make us fully human: thinking, planning, judging, perceiving, and behaving purposefully and voluntarily.

▶ The human brain is amazingly plastic. Neurons in the brain can be shaped by experience and the environment.

# The Development and Evolution of Nervous Systems

The human brain is surprisingly imperfect. Far from being a single, elegant machine—the enchanted loom the philosophers wrote so poetically about—the human brain is instead a system comprised of many distinct components that have been added at different times during the course of evolution. The human species has retained what worked best in earlier versions of the brain, then added bits and pieces to get us to our present state through evolution.

To understand the central nervous system, it is helpful to consider two aspects of its development. Prenatal development (growth from conception to birth), reveals how the nervous system develops and changes within each member of a species. Evolutionary development reveals how the nervous system in humans evolved and adapted from other species.

## Prenatal Development of the Central Nervous System

The nervous system is the first major bodily system to take form in an embryo (Moore, 1977). It begins to develop within the 3rd week after fertilization, when the embryo is still in the shape of a sphere. Initially, a ridge forms on one side of the sphere and then builds up at its edges to become a deep groove. The ridges fold together and fuse to enclose the groove, forming a structure called the *neural tube*. The tail end of the neural tube will remain a tube, and as the embryo grows larger, it forms the basis of the spinal cord. The tube expands at the opposite end, so that by the 4th week the three basic levels of the brain are visible. During the 5th week, the forebrain and hindbrain further differentiate into subdivisions. During the 7th week and later, the forebrain expands considerably to form the cerebral hemispheres.

> **What are the stages of development of the embryonic brain?**

As the embryonic brain continues to grow, each subdivision folds onto the next one and begins to form the structures easily visible in the adult brain (see **FIGURE 3.20**). The hindbrain forms the cerebellum and medulla, the midbrain forms the tectum and the tegmentum, and the forebrain subdivides further, separating the thalamus and hypothalamus from the cerebral hemispheres. Over time, the cerebral hemispheres undergo the greatest development, ultimately covering almost all the other subdivisions of the brain.

The *ontogeny* of the brain (how it develops within a given individual) is pretty remarkable. In about half the time it takes you to complete a 15-week semester, the basic structures of the brain are in place and rapidly developing, eventually allowing a newborn to enter the world with a fairly sophisticated set of abilities. In comparison, the *phylogeny* of the brain (how

▼ Figure **3.20** **Prenatal Brain Development** The more primitive parts of the brain, the hindbrain and midbrain, develop first, followed by successively higher levels. The cerebral cortex with its characteristic fissures does not develop until the middle of the pregnancy. The cerebral hemispheres undergo most of their development in the final trimester.

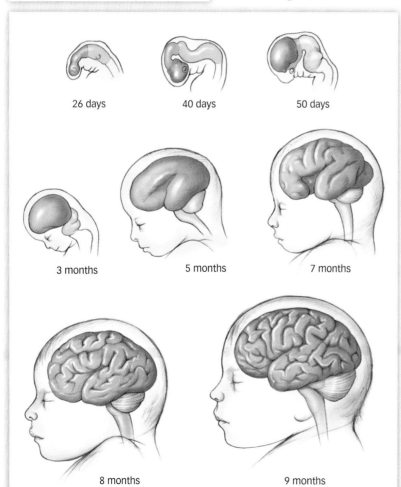

26 days  40 days  50 days

3 months  5 months  7 months

8 months  9 months

it developed within a particular species) is a much slower process. However, it, too, has allowed humans to make the most of the available brain structures, enabling us to perform an incredible array of tasks.

## Evolutionary Development of the Central Nervous System

The central nervous system evolved from the very simple one found in simple animals to the elaborate nervous system in humans today. Even the simplest animals have sensory neurons and motor neurons for responding to the environment (Shepherd, 1988). For example, single-celled protozoa have molecules in their cell membrane that are sensitive to food in the water. Those molecules trigger the movement of tiny threads called *cilia*, which help propel the protozoa toward the food source. The first neurons appeared in simple invertebrates, such as jellyfish; the sensory neurons in the jellyfish's tentacles can feel the touch of a potentially dangerous predator, which prompts the jellyfish to swim to safety. If you are a jellyfish, this simple neural system is sufficient to keep you alive. The first central nervous system worthy of the name, though, appeared in flatworms. The flatworm has a collection of neurons in the head—a simple kind of brain— that includes sensory neurons for vision and taste and motor neurons that control feeding behaviour. Emerging from the brain is a pair of tracts that form a spinal cord.

Flatworms do not have much of a brain, but then again, they do not need much of a brain. The rudimentary brain areas found in simple invertebrates eventually evolved into the complex brain structures found in humans.

BLICKWINKEL/ALAMY

During the course of evolution, a major split in the organization of the nervous system occurred between invertebrate animals (those without a spinal column) and vertebrate animals (those with a spinal column). In all vertebrates, the central nervous system is organized into a hierarchy: The lower levels of the brain and spinal cord execute simpler functions, while the higher levels of the nervous system perform more complex functions. As you saw earlier, in humans, reflexes are accomplished in the spinal cord. At the next level, the midbrain executes the more complex task of orienting toward an important stimulus in the environment. Finally, a more complex task, such as imagining what your life will be like 20 years from now, is performed in the forebrain (Addis, Wong, & Schacter, 2007; Schacter, Addis, et al., 2012; Szpunar, Watson, & McDermott, 2007).

The forebrain undergoes further evolutionary advances in vertebrates. In lower vertebrate species such as amphibians (frogs and newts), the forebrain consists only of small clusters of neurons at the end of the neural tube. In higher vertebrates, including reptiles, birds, and mammals, the forebrain is much larger, and it evolves in two different patterns. Reptiles and birds have almost no cerebral cortex. By contrast, mammals have a highly developed cerebral cortex, which develops multiple areas that serve a broad range of higher mental functions. This forebrain development has reached its peak—so far—in humans (**FIGURE 3.21**).

The human brain, then, is not so much one remarkable thing; rather, it is a succession of extensions from a quite serviceable foundation. Like other species, humans have a hindbrain, and as in those species, it performs important tasks to keep us alive. For some species, that is sufficient. All flatworms need to do to ensure their species' survival is eat, reproduce, and stay alive a reasonable length of time. But as the human brain evolved, structures in the midbrain and forebrain developed to handle the increasingly complex demands of the environment. The forebrain of a bullfrog is about as differentiated as

▼ Figure **3.21 Development of the Forebrain** Reptiles and birds have almost no cerebral cortex, whereas mammals such as rats and cats do have a cerebral cortex, but their frontal lobes are proportionately much smaller than the frontal lobes of humans and other primates. How might this explain the fact that only humans have developed complex language, computer technology, and calculus?

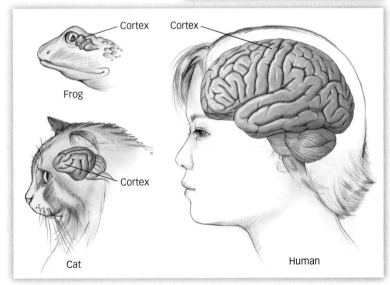

it needs to be to survive in a frog's world. The human forebrain, however, shows substantial refinement, which allows for some remarkable, uniquely human abilities: self-awareness, sophisticated language use, abstract reasoning, and imagining, among others.

There is intriguing evidence that the human brain evolved more quickly than the brains of other species (Dorus et al., 2004). Researchers compared the sequences of 200 brain-related genes in mice, rats, monkeys, and humans and discovered a collection of genes that evolved more rapidly among primates. What is more, they found that primate brains not only evolved quickly compared to those of other species, but the brains of the particular primates who eventually became humans evolved even more rapidly. These results suggest that in addition to the normal adaptations that occur over the process of evolution, the genes for human brains took particular advantage of a variety of mutations (changes in a gene's DNA) along the evolutionary pathway (Vallender, Mekel-Bobrov, & Lahn, 2008). These results also suggest that the human brain is still evolving—becoming bigger and more adapted to the demands of the environment (Evans et al., 2005; Mekel-Bobrov et al., 2005).

> Are our brains still evolving?

Genes may direct the development of the brain on a large, evolutionary scale, but they also guide the development of an individual and, generally, the development of a species. Let us take a brief look at how genes and the environment contribute to the biological bases of behaviour.

## Genes, Epigenetics, and the Environment

Is it genetics (nature) or the environment (nurture) that reigns supreme in directing a person's behaviour? The emerging picture from current research is that both nature *and* nurture play a role in directing behaviour, and the focus has shifted to examining the interaction of the two rather than the absolute contributions of either alone (Gottesman & Hanson, 2005; Rutter & Silberg, 2002; Zhang & Meaney, 2010).

### What Are Genes?

A **gene** is *the major unit of hereditary transmission.* Historically, the term *gene* has been used to refer to two distinct but related concepts. The initial, relatively abstract concept of a gene referred to units of inheritance that specify traits such as eye colour. More recently, genes have been defined as sections on a strand of DNA (deoxyribonucleic acid) that code for the protein molecules that affect traits. Genes are organized into large threads called **chromosomes,** *strands of DNA wound around each other in a double-helix configuration* (see **FIGURE 3.22** on the next page). The DNA in our chromosomes produces protein molecules through the action of a molecule known as messenger RNA (ribonucleic acid; mRNA), which communicates a copy of the DNA code to cells that produce proteins. Chromosomes come in pairs, and humans have 23 pairs each. These pairs of chromosomes are similar but not identical: You inherit one of each pair from your father and one from your mother. There is a twist, however: The selection of *which* of each pair is given to you is random.

Perhaps the most striking example of this random distribution is the determination of sex. In mammals, the chromosomes that determine sex are the X and Y chromosomes; females have two X chromosomes, whereas males have one X and one Y chromosome. You inherited an X chromosome from your mother because she has only X chromosomes to give. Your biological sex, therefore, was determined by whether you received an additional X chromosome or a Y chromosome from your father.

As a species, we share about 99 percent of the same DNA (and almost as much with other apes), but there is a portion of DNA that varies across individuals. Children share more of this variable portion of DNA with their parents than with more distant

**gene**
The major unit of hereditary transmission.

**chromosomes**
Strands of DNA wound around each other in a double-helix configuration.

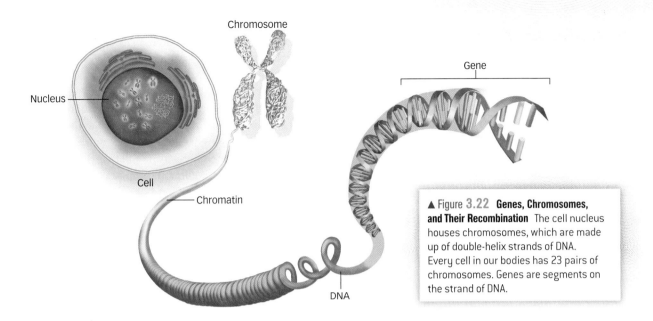

▲ Figure **3.22** **Genes, Chromosomes, and Their Recombination** The cell nucleus houses chromosomes, which are made up of double-helix strands of DNA. Every cell in our bodies has 23 pairs of chromosomes. Genes are segments on the strand of DNA.

relatives or with nonrelatives: They share half their genes with each parent, a quarter of their genes with their grandparents, an eighth of their genes with cousins, and so on. The probability of sharing genes is called *degree of relatedness.* The most genetically related people are *monozygotic twins*

> **Why do dizygotic twins share 50% of their genes, just like siblings born separately?**

(also called *identical twins*), who develop from the splitting of a single fertilized egg and therefore share 100 percent of their genes. *Dizygotic twins* (*fraternal twins*) develop from two separate fertilized eggs and share 50 percent of their genes, the same as any two siblings born separately.

Many researchers have tried to determine the relative influence of genetics on behaviour. One way to do this is to compare a trait shown by monozygotic twins with that same trait among dizygotic twins. This type of research usually enlists twins who were raised in the same household, so that the impact of their environment (their socioeconomic status, access to education, parental child-rearing practices, and environmental stressors) remains relatively constant. Finding that monozygotic twins have a higher presence of a specific trait suggests a genetic influence (Boomsma, Busjahn, & Peltonen, 2002).

Monozygotic twins (*left*) share 100 percent of their genes, whereas dizygotic twins (*right*) share 50 percent of their genes, the same as other siblings. Studies of monozygotic and dizygotic twins help researchers estimate the relative contributions of genes and environmental influences on behaviour.

As an example, the likelihood that the dizygotic twin of a person who has schizophrenia (a mental disorder we will discuss in greater detail in the Psychological Disorders chapter) will *also* develop schizophrenia is 27 percent. However, this statistic rises to 50 percent for monozygotic twins. This observation suggests a substantial genetic influence on the likelihood of developing schizophrenia. Monozygotic twins share 100 percent of their genes and, if one assumes environmental influences are relatively consistent for both members of the twin pair, the 50 percent likelihood can be traced to genetic factors. That sounds frighteningly high … until you realize that the remaining 50 percent probability must be due to environmental influences. In short, genetics can contribute to the development, likelihood, or onset of a variety of traits. But a more complete picture of genetic influences on behaviour must always take the environmental context into consideration. Genes express themselves within an environment, not in isolation.

## A Role for Epigenetics

The idea that genes are expressed within an environment is central to an important and rapidly growing area of research known as **epigenetics:** *environmental influences that determine whether or not genes are expressed, or the degree to which they are expressed, without altering the basic DNA sequences that constitute the genes themselves.* To understand how epigenetic influences work, it is useful to think about DNA as analogous to a script for a play or a movie. The biologist Nessa Carey (2012) offers the example of Shakespeare's *Romeo and Juliet*, which was made into a movie back in 1936 starring classic actors Leslie Howard and Norma Shearer, and in 1996 starring Leonardo DiCaprio and Claire Danes. Shakespeare's script formed the basis of both films, but the directors of the two films used the script in different ways, and the actors in the two films gave different performances. Thus, the final products departed from Shakespeare's script and were different from one another, even though Shakespeare's original script still exists. Something similar happens with epigenetics: Depending on the environment, a gene can be expressed or not without altering the underlying DNA code.

The environment can influence gene expression through **epigenetic marks,** *chemical modifications to DNA that can turn genes on or off.* You can think of epigenetic marks as analogous to notes that the movie directors made on Shakespeare's script that determined how the script was used in a particular film. There are two widely studied epigenetic marks:

> **DNA methylation** refers to *adding a methyl group to DNA.* There are special enzymes, referred to as *epigenetic writers,* whose role is to add methyl groups to DNA. Although adding a methyl group does not alter the basic DNA sequence, it switches off the methylated gene (see **FIGURE 3.23** on the next page). This process is roughly analogous to Claire Danes's director making notes that instruct her to ignore a certain portion of the Shakespeare script. That portion of the script—like the switched-off gene—is still there, but its contents are not expressed.

> **Histone modification** involves *adding chemical modifications to proteins called histones that are involved in packaging DNA.* We tend to visualize DNA as the free-floating double helix shown in Figure 3.22, but DNA is actually tightly wrapped around groups of histone proteins, as shown in Figure 3.23. However, whereas DNA methylation serves to switch genes off, histone modification can either switch genes off or turn them on. But just like DNA methylation, histone modifications influence gene expression without altering the underlying DNA sequence (Carey, 2012).

You may have wondered whether Claire Danes's performance in *Romeo and Juliet* prepared her to play Carrie in *Homeland* (come to think of it, Carrie's relationship

**epigenetics**
Environmental influences that determine whether or not genes are expressed, or the degree to which they are expressed, without altering the basic DNA sequences that constitute the genes themselves.

**epigenetic marks**
Chemical modifications to DNA that can turn genes on or off.

**DNA methylation**
Adding a methyl group to DNA.

**histone modification**
Adding chemical modifications to proteins called histones that are involved in packaging DNA.

Chromosome

Gene

Methyl group

Nucleus

Cell

Chromatin

Gene

DNA

DNA

Histone tail

DNA winding around histones

▲ Figure **3.23** **Epigenetics** Studies suggest that DNA methylation and histone modification play a key role in the long-lasting effects of early life experiences for both rodents and humans.

with Brody bears some resemblance to Shakespeare's doomed lovers). But what is the relevance of epigenetics to the brain and to psychology? It turns out to be more relevant than anyone suspected until the past decade or so. Experiments with rats and mice have shown that epigenetic marks left by DNA methylation and histone modifcation play a role in learning and memory (Bredy et al., 2007; Day & Sweatt, 2011; Levenson, & Sweatt, 2005). Several studies (including recent research with humans) have linked epigenetic changes with responses to stress (Zhang & Meaney, 2010). For example, studies of nurses working in high-stress versus low-stress environments found differences between the two groups in DNA methylation (Alasaari et al., 2012). Subjective levels of stress in a sample of 92 Canadian adults, as well as physiological signs of stress, were correlated with levels of DNA methylation (Lam et al., 2012). Another study reported a link between DNA methylation and early life experience, with differences observed between individuals who grew up in relatively affluent households versus those who grew up in poverty, even when controlling for such factors as current socioeconomic status (Lam et al., 2012). Similar findings were reported in a separate study of 40 British adults (Borghol et al., 2012). These observations fit well with an important line of research described in the Hot Science box, showing that DNA methylation and histone modifications play a key role in the long-lasting effects of early experiences for both rodents and humans.

## The Role of Environmental Factors

Genes set the range of possibilities that can be observed in a population, but the characteristics of any individual within that range are determined by environmental factors and experience. The genetic capabilities that another species might enjoy, such as breathing underwater, are outside the range of *your* possibilities, no matter how much you might desire them.

With these parameters in mind, behavioural geneticists use calculations based on relatedness to compute the heritability of behaviours (Plomin et al., 2001). **Heritability** is *a measure of the variability of behavioural traits among individuals that can be accounted for by genetic factors.* Heritability is calculated as a proportion, and its numerical value (index) ranges from 0 to 1.00. A heritability of 0 means that genes do not contribute to individual differences in the behavioural trait; a heritability of 1.00 means that genes are the *only* reason for the individual differences. As you might guess,

**heritability**
A measure of the variability of behavioural traits among individuals that can be accounted for by genetic factors.

**HOT SCIENCE**

# Epigenetics and the Persisting Effects of Early Experiences

An exciting series of studies show that epigenetic processes play a critical role in the long-lasting effects of early life experiences. Much of this work has come from the laboratory of Michael Meaney and his colleagues at McGill University, beginning with research on maternal behaviours in rats and recently extending to the persisting effects of childhood abuse.

Let us first consider early work from Meaney's lab that provides critical background (Francis et al., 1999; Liu et al., 1997). This work was based on the finding that there are notable differences in the mothering styles of rats: Some mothers spend a lot of time licking and grooming their young pups (high LG mothers), whereas others spend little time doing so (low LG mothers). The researchers found that pups of high LG mothers are much less fearful as adults when placed in stressful situations than the adult pups of low LG mothers. Perhaps this simply reflects the effects of a genetic profile shared by the mother and her pups? Not so. Meaney and colleagues demonstrated that when the offspring of low LG mothers are raised by high LG mothers, they act just like the natural (genetic) offspring of the high LG mothers, and vice versa. These effects were accompanied by physiological changes. When placed in fear-inducing situations, adult rats raised by the high LG mothers showed lower levels of several stress-related hormones than adult rats that had been raised by low LG mothers. Regardless of who their biological mother was there was also increased evidence of hippocampal serotonin in the adult pups of LG mothers; as you learned earlier in this chapter, increased levels of serotonin are associated with elevated mood. In other words, the high LG pups grow up to become "chilled out" adults. But exactly how did these effects persist from infancy to adulthood? This is where epigenetics come in. The increased serotonin response produced by high LG mothers triggers a decrease in DNA methylation of the glucocorticoid receptor gene (see the Stress & Health chapter for a discussion of glucocorticoids and stress), which leads to greater expression of the gene and a corresponding ability to respond more

calmly to stress (Weaver et al., 2004). The rats raised by low LG mothers showed relatively increased DNA methylation of the glucocorticoid receptor gene, which leads to reduced expression of the gene and a corresponding inability to respond calmly to stress. Because DNA methylation can be very stable over time, these studies with rats provide the foundation for more recent studies with humans showing a role for epigenetics in the persisting effects of a highly disturbing experience: childhood abuse.

Meaney's group examined hippocampal samples taken from the brains of 24 men who had committed suicide around the age of 35 (McGowan et al., 2009). (The hippocampus plays a role in response to stress and has the highest concentration glucocorticoid receptions in the entire brain.) Twelve of those men had a history of childhood abuse and 12 did not. The researchers compared their hippocampal samples to a separate control group of 12 men who had died suddenly at around the same age but had no history of abuse and had not committed suicide. Strikingly, they found evidence for increased levels of DNA methylation at the hippocampal glucocorticoid receptor gene in the 12 men who had suffered childhood abuse and committed suicide compared with the 12 men in the control group. But they found no such differences between the 12 men who committed suicide but had not been abused and the 12 men in the control group. Increased DNA methylation reduced expression of the glucocorticoid receptor gene in the 12 victims of childhood abuse, just as in the adult pups of low LG mothers. Although this research does not tell us whether or how differences in DNA

▲ Rodent pups raised by mothers who spend a lot of time licking and grooming them are less fearful as adults in stressful situations.

JUNIORS BILDARCHIV GMBH/ALAMY

methylation were related to the behaviours of the abused and non-abused men when they were alive, it does point toward similar epigenetic effects of adverse early experiences in rats and humans.

Studies suggest that the effects of early experience are not restricted to a single gene, but occur more broadly. A more recent study of rats from Meaney's lab demonstrates hundreds of DNA methylation differences in the hippocampus of the offspring of high and low LG mothers (McGowan et al., 2011). New analyses of hippocampal samples from abused suicide victims also reveal widespread DNA methylation differences between the abused sample and a control group of non-abused individuals (Suderman et al., 2012). Although there were also methylation differences between rats and humans that probably reflect a combination of environmental and biological differences between the two species (Suderman et al., 2012), the overall pattern of results suggests a broad role for epigenetic influences in understanding the effects of early experiences on subsequent development and behaviour (Meaney & Ferguson-Smith, 2010).

| **High LG Mother** | **Low LG Mother** |
|---|---|
| Increased serotonin in the hippocampus | Decreased serotonin in the hippocampus |
| Decrease in DNA methylation of glucocorticoid receptor gene (related to stress) | Increase in DNA methylation of glucocorticoid receptor gene (related to stress) |
| Greater expression of the gene | Reduced expression of the gene |
| ↓ | ↓ |
| Pups grow to be "chilled out" adults with better regulated stress response | Pups grow into adults with less ability to respond calmly to stress |

scores of 0 or 1.00 occur so infrequently that they serve more as theoretical limits than realistic values; almost nothing in human behaviour is completely due to the environment or owed *completely* to genetic inheritance. Scores between 0 and 1.00, then, indicate that individual differences are caused by varying degrees of genetic and environmental contributions—a little stronger influence of genetics here, a little stronger influence of the environment there, but each always within the context of the other (Moffitt, 2005; Zhang & Meaney, 2010).

For human behaviour, almost all estimates of heritability are in the moderate range, between 0.30 and 0.60. For example, a heritability index of 0.50 for intelligence indicates that half of the variability in intelligence test scores is attributable to genetic influences and the remaining half is due to environmental influences. Smart parents often (but not always) produce smart children; genetics certainly plays a role. But smart and not-so-smart children attend good or not-so-good schools, practise their piano lessons with more or less regularity, study or not study as hard as they might, have good and not-so-good teachers and role models, and so on. Genetics is only half the story in intelligence. Environmental influences also play a significant role in predicting the basis of intelligence (see the Intelligence chapter).

**Are abilities, such as intelligence and memory, inherited through our genes?**

*"The title of my science project is 'My Little Brother: Nature or Nurture.'"*

Heritability has proven to be a theoretically useful and statistically sound concept in helping scientists understand the relative genetic and environmental influences on behaviour. However, there are four important points about heritability to bear in mind. First, remember that *heritability is an abstract concept*: It tells us nothing about the *specific* genes that contribute to a trait. Second, *heritability is a population concept*: It tells us nothing about an individual. Heritability provides guidance for understanding differences across individuals in a population rather than abilities within an individual.

Third, *heritability is dependent on the environment*. Just as behaviour occurs within certain contexts, so do genetic influences. For example, intelligence is not an unchanging quality: People are intelligent within a particular learning context, a social setting, a family environment, a socioeconomic class, and so on. Heritability, therefore, is meaningful only for the environmental conditions in which it was computed, and heritability estimates may change dramatically under other environmental conditions. Finally, *heritability is not fate*. It tells us nothing about the degree to which interventions can change a behavioural trait. Heritability is useful for identifying behavioural traits that are influenced by genes, but it is not useful for determining how individuals will respond to particular environmental conditions or treatments.

## IN SUMMARY

▶ Examining the development of the nervous system over the life span of an individual (its ontogeny) and across the time within which a species evolves (its phylogeny) presents further opportunities for understanding the human brain.

▶ The nervous system is the first system that forms in an embryo, starting as a neural tube, which forms the basis of the spinal cord. The neural tube expands on one end to form the hindbrain, midbrain, and forebrain, each of which folds onto the next structure.

▶ Within each of these areas, specific brain structures begin to differentiate. The forebrain shows the greatest differentiation and, in particular, the cerebral cortex is the most developed in humans.

*(continued)*

► Nervous systems evolved from simple collections of sensory and motor neurons in simple animals, such as flatworms, to elaborate centralized nervous systems found in mammals.

    ► The evolution of the human nervous system can be thought of as a process of refining, elaborating, and expanding structures present in other species.

    ► Reptiles and birds have almost no cerebral cortex. By contrast, mammals have a highly developed cerebral cortex.

    ► The human brain appears to have evolved more quickly compared to other species to become adapted to a more complex environment.

► The gene, or the unit of hereditary transmission, is built from strands of DNA in a double-helix formation that is organized into chromosomes.

► Humans have 23 pairs of chromosomes; half come from each parent.

    ► A child shares 50 percent of his or her genes with each parent.

    ► Monozygotic twins share 100 percent of their genes, whereas dizygotic twins share 50 percent, the same as any other siblings. Because of their genetic relatedness, twins are often participants in genetic research.

► The study of genetics indicates that both genes and the environment work together to influence behaviour. Genes set the range of variation in populations within a given environment, but they do not predict individual characteristics; experience and other environmental factors play a crucial role as well.

► Epigenetics refers to environmental influences that determine whether or not genes are expressed, without altering the basic DNA sequences that constitute the genes themselves. Epigenetic marks such as DNA methylation and histone modification influence whether specific genes are switched on or off. Epigenetic influences have been shown to play a critical role in persisting effects of early experiences in rodents and humans.

# Investigating the Brain

So far, you have read a great deal about the nervous system: how it is organized, how it works, what its components are, and what those components do. But one question remains largely unanswered: *How* do we know all of this? Anatomists can dissect a human brain and identify its structures, but they cannot determine which structures play a role in producing which behaviours by dissecting a nonliving brain.

Scientists use a variety of methods to understand how the brain affects behaviour. Let us consider three of the main ones: studying people with brain damage; studying the brain's electrical activity; and using brain imaging to study brain structure and watch the brain in action. Let us examine each of these ways of investigating the brain.

## Studying the Damaged Brain

To understand the normal operation of a process better, it is instructive to understand what happens when that process fails. Much research in neuroscience correlates the loss of specific perceptual, motor, emotional, or cognitive functions with specific areas of brain damage (Andrewes, 2001; Kolb & Whishaw, 2003). By studying these instances, neuroscientists can theorize about the functions those brain areas normally perform. The modern history of neuroscience can be dated to the work of Paul Broca (see the Psychology: Evolution of a Science chapter). In 1861,

Broca described a patient who had lost the capacity to produce spoken language (but not the ability to understand language) due to damage in a small area in the left frontal lobe. In 1874, Carl Wernicke (1848–1905) described a patient with an impairment in language comprehension (but not the ability to produce speech) associated with damage to an area in the upper-left temporal lobe. These areas were named, respectively, *Broca's area* and *Wernicke's area* (see Figure 9.3 in the Language and Thought chapter), and they provided the earliest evidence that the brain locations for speech production and speech comprehension are separate and that for most people, the left hemisphere is critical to producing and understanding language (Young, 1990).

> **How have brain disorders been central to the study of specific areas of the brain?**

## The Emotional Functions of the Frontal Lobes

As you have already seen, the human frontal lobes are a remarkable evolutionary achievement. However, psychology's first glimpse at some functions of the frontal lobes came from a rather unremarkable fellow; so unremarkable, in fact, that a single event in his life defined his place in the annals of psychology's history (Macmillan, 2000). Phineas Gage was a muscular 25-year-old railroad worker. On September 13, 1848, in Cavendish, Vermont, he was packing an explosive charge into a crevice in a rock when the powder exploded, driving a 1-m, 6-kg iron rod through his head at high speed (Harlow, 1848). As **FIGURE 3.24** shows, the rod entered through his lower left jaw and exited through the middle top of his head. Incredibly, Gage lived to tell the tale. But his personality underwent a significant change.

Before the accident, Gage had been mild mannered, quiet, conscientious, and a hard worker. After the accident, however, he became irritable, irresponsible, indecisive, and given to profanity. The sad decline of Gage's personality and emotional life nonetheless provided an unexpected benefit to psychology. His case study was the first to allow researchers to investigate the hypothesis that the frontal lobe is involved in emotion regulation, planning, and decision making. Furthermore, because the connections between the frontal lobe and the subcortical structures of the limbic system were affected, scientists were able to understand better how the amygdala, hippocampus, and related brain structures interacted with the cerebral cortex (Damasio, 2005).

COLLECTION OF JACK AND BEVERLY WILGUS

▲ Figure 3.24 **Phineas Gage** Phineas Gage's traumatic accident allowed researchers to investigate the functions of the frontal lobe and its connections with emotion centres in the subcortical structures. The likely path of the metal rod through Gage's skull is reconstructed here.

## The Distinct Roles of the Left and Right Hemispheres

You will recall that the cerebral cortex is divided into two hemispheres, although typically the two hemispheres act as one integrated unit. Sometimes, though, disorders can threaten the ability of the brain to function, and the only way to stop them is with radical methods. This is sometimes the case for people who suffer from severe, intractable epilepsy. Seizures that begin in one hemisphere cross the corpus callosum (the thick band of nerve fibres that allows the two hemispheres to communicate) to the opposite hemisphere and start a feedback loop that results in a kind of firestorm in the brain. To alleviate the severity of the seizures, surgeons can sever the corpus

KEYSTONE/HULTON ARCHIVE/GETTY IMAGES

Roger Wolcott Sperry (1913–1994) received the Nobel Prize in Physiology in 1981 for his pioneering work investigating the independent functions of the cerebral hemispheres.

▼ Figure **3.25** **Split-Brain Experiment** When a person with a split brain is presented with the picture of a ring on the right and that of a key on the left side of a screen, she can verbalize *ring* but not *key* because the left hemisphere "sees" the ring and language is usually located in the left hemisphere. She would be able to choose a key with her left hand from a set of objects behind a screen. She would not, however, be able to pick out a ring with her left hand because what the left hemisphere "sees" is not communicated to the left side of her body.

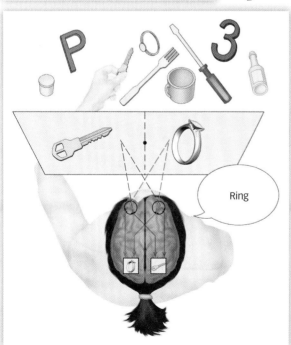

Ring

callosum in a procedure called a *split-brain procedure*. The result is that a seizure that starts in one hemisphere is isolated in that hemisphere because there is no longer a connection to the other side. This procedure helps people with epilepsy, but also produces some unusual, if not unpredictable, behaviours.

Nobel laureate Roger Sperry (1913–1994) was intrigued by the observation that the everyday behaviour of people who had their corpus collosum severed did not seem to be affected by the operation. Did this mean that the corpus callosum played no role at all in behaviour? Sperry thought that this conclusion was premature, reasoning that casual observations of everyday behaviours could easily fail to detect impairments that might be picked up by sensitive tests. To evaluate this idea experimentally, Sperry and his colleagues first showed that when the corpus callosum was severed in cats, learning was not transferred from one hemisphere to the other (Sperry, 1964). Later, Sperry designed several experiments that investigated the behaviours of people with split brains and, in the process, revealed a great deal about the independent functions of the left and right hemispheres (Sperry, 1964). Normally, any information that initially enters the left hemisphere is also registered in the right hemisphere and vice versa: The information comes in and travels across the corpus callosum, and both hemispheres understand what is going on (see **FIGURE 3.25**). But in a person with a split brain, information entering one hemisphere stays there. Without an intact corpus callosum, there is no way for that information to reach the other hemisphere. Sperry and his colleagues used this understanding of lateralized perception in a series of experiments. For example, they had a person with a split brain look at a spot in the centre of a screen and then projected a stimulus either on the left side of the screen (the left visual field) or the right side of the screen (the right visual field), isolating the stimulus to the opposite hemisphere (see Figure 4.10 in the Sensation and Perception chapter for more details about how information from one visual field enters the opposite hemisphere).

**What role does the corpus callosum play in behaviour?**

The hemispheres themselves are specialized for different kinds of tasks. You just learned about Broca's and Wernicke's areas, which revealed that language processing is largely a left-hemisphere activity. So imagine that some information came into the left hemisphere of a person with a split brain, and she was asked to describe verbally what it was. No problem: The left hemisphere has the information, it is the "speaking" hemisphere, so she should have no difficulty verbally describing what she saw. But suppose she were asked to reach behind the screen with her left hand and pick up the object she just saw. Remember that the hemispheres exert contralateral control over the body, meaning that the left hand is controlled by the right hemisphere. But this person's right hemisphere has no clue what the object was because that information was received in the left hemisphere and was unable to travel to the right hemisphere! So, even though she saw the object and could verbally describe it, she would be unable to use the right hemisphere to perform other tasks regarding that object, such as correctly selecting it from a group with her left hand (see Figure 3.25).

Of course, information presented to the right hemisphere would produce complementary deficits. In this case, she might be presented with a familiar object in her left hand (e.g., a key), be able to demonstrate that she knew what it was (by using the key to mime unlocking a door), yet be unable to verbally describe what she was holding. In this case, the information in the right hemisphere is unable to travel to the left hemisphere, which controls the production of speech.

Furthermore, suppose a person with a split brain was shown the unusual face in **FIGURE 3.26**. This is called a *chimeric face,* and it is assembled from half-face components of the full faces also shown in the figure. When asked to indicate which face was presented, she would indicate that she saw *both* faces because information about the face on the left is recorded in the right hemisphere and information about the face on the right is recorded in the left hemisphere (Levy, Trevarthen, & Sperry, 1972).

These split-brain studies reveal that the two hemispheres perform different functions and can work together seamlessly as long as the corpus callosum is intact. Without a way to transmit information from one hemisphere to the other, information remains in the hemisphere it initially entered and we become acutely aware of the different functions of each hemisphere. Of course, a person with a split brain can adapt to this by simply moving her eyes a little so that the same information independently enters both hemispheres. Split-brain studies have continued over the past few decades and continue to play an important role in shaping our understanding of how the brain works (Gazzaniga, 2006).

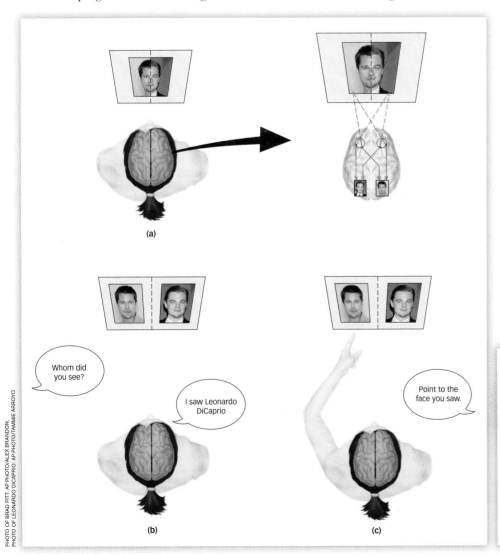

(a)

(b)

(c)

◀ Figure **3.26 Chimeric Faces and the Split Brain** (*a*) When a person with a split brain views a chimeric face of Brad Pitt and Leonardo DiCaprio, her left hemisphere is aware only of Leonardo DiCaprio and her right hemisphere sees only Brad Pitt. (*b*) When asked whom she sees, she answers, "Leonardo DiCaprio," because speech is controlled by the left hemisphere. (*c*) When asked to point to the face she saw with her left hand, she points to Brad Pitt because her right hemisphere is only aware of the left half of the picture.

▲ Figure 3.27 **EEG** The electro-encephalograph (EEG) records electrical activity in the brain. Many states of consciousness, such as wakefulness and stages of sleep, are characterized by particular types of brain waves.

## Studying the Brain's Electrical Activity

A second approach to studying the link between brain structures and behaviour involves recording the pattern of electrical activity of neurons. An **electroencephalograph (EEG)** is *a device used to record electrical activity in the brain.* Typically, electrodes are placed on the outside of the head, and even though the source of electrical activity in synapses and action potentials is far removed from these wires, the electric signals can be amplified several thousand times by the EEG. This provides a visual record of the underlying electrical activity, as shown in **FIGURE 3.27**. Using this technique, researchers can determine the amount of brain activity during different states of consciousness. For example, as you will read in the Consciousness chapter, the brain shows distinctive patterns of electrical activity when awake versus asleep; in fact, there are even different brain-wave patterns associated with different stages of sleep. EEG recordings allow researchers to make these fundamental discoveries about the nature of sleep and wakefulness (Dement, 1978). The EEG can also be used to examine the brain's electrical activity when awake individuals engage in a variety of psychological functions, such as perceiving, learning, and remembering.

> How does the EEG record electrical activity in the brain?

A different approach to recording electrical activity resulted in a more refined understanding of the brain's division of responsibilities, even at a cellular level. Nobel laureates David Hubel and Torsten Wiesel used a technique that inserted electrodes into the occipital lobes of anesthetized cats and observed the patterns of action potentials of individual neurons (Hubel, 1988). Hubel and Wiesel amplified the action potential signals through a loudspeaker so that the signals could be heard as clicks as well as seen on an oscilloscope. While flashing lights in front of the animal's eye, Hubel and Wiesel recorded the resulting activity of neurons in the occipital cortex. What they discovered was not much of anything: Most of the neurons did not respond to this kind of general stimulation. This was frustrating to them. Hubel (1988, p. 69) recalled years later that "we tried everything short of standing on our heads to get it to fire," but then they began to notice something interesting.

Nearing the end of what seemed like a failed set of experiments, they projected a glass slide that contained a black dot in front of the cat's eyes and heard a brisk flurry of clicks as the neurons in the cat's occipital lobe fired away! Observing carefully, they realized that the firing did not have anything to do with the black dot, but instead was produced by a faint but sharp shadow cast by the edge of the glass slide. They discovered that neurons in the primary visual cortex are activated whenever a contrast between light and dark occurs in part of the visual field, seen particularly well when the visual stimulus was a thick line of light against a dark background. In this case, the shadow caused by the edge of the slide provided the kind of contrast that prompted particular neurons to respond. They then found that each neuron responded vigorously only when presented with a contrasting edge at a particular orientation. Since then, many studies have shown that neurons in the primary visual cortex represent particular features of visual stimuli, such as contrast, shape, and colour (Zeki, 1993).

These neurons in the visual cortex are known as *feature detectors* because they selectively respond to certain aspects of a visual image. For example, some neurons fire only when detecting a vertical line in the middle of the visual field, other neurons fire when a line at a 45° angle is perceived, and still others in response to wider lines, horizontal lines, lines in the periphery of the visual field, and so on (Livingstone & Hubel, 1988). The discovery of this specialized function for neurons was a huge leap forward in our understanding of how the visual cortex works. Feature detectors

Canadian David Hubel (*left,* 1926–2013) and Swede Torsten Wiesel (*right,* b. 1924) received the Nobel Prize in Physiology in 1981 for their work on mapping the visual cortex.

identify basic dimensions of a stimulus ("slanted line ... other slanted line ... horizontal line"); those dimensions are then combined during a later stage of visual processing to allow recognition and perception of a stimulus ("Oh, it is a letter *A*").

Other studies have identified a variety of features that are detected by sensory neurons. For example, some visual processing neurons in the temporal lobe are activated only when detecting faces (Kanwisher, 2000; Perrett, Rolls, & Caan, 1982). Damage to this area results in an inability to perceive faces. These complementary observations (showing that the type of function that is lost or altered when a brain area is damaged corresponds to the kind of information processed by neurons in that cortical area) provide the most compelling evidence linking the brain to behaviour.

## Using Brain Imaging to Study Structure and to Watch the Brain in Action

The third major way that neuroscientists can peer into the workings of the human brain has only become possible within the past several decades. EEG readouts give an overall picture of a person's level of consciousness, and single-cell recordings shed light on the actions of particular clumps of neurons. The ideal of neuroscience, however, has been the ability to see the brain in operation during behaviour. This goal has been steadily achieved thanks to a wide range of *neuroimaging techniques* that use advanced technology to create images of the living, healthy brain (Posner & Raichle, 1994; Raichle & Mintun, 2006). *Structural brain imaging* provides information about the basic structure of the brain and allows clinicians or researchers to see abnormalities in brain structure. *Functional brain imaging*, in contrast, provides information about the activity of the brain when people perform various kinds of cognitive or motor tasks.

### Structural Brain Imaging

One of the first neuroimaging techniques developed was the *computerized axial tomography (CT) scan*. In a CT scan, a scanner rotates a device around a person's head and takes a series of X-ray photographs from different angles. Computer programs then combine these images to provide views from any angle. CT scans show different densities of tissue in the brain. For example, the higher-density skull looks white on a CT scan, the cortex shows up as grey, and the least dense fissures and ventricles in the brain look dark (see **FIGURE 3.28**). CT scans are used to locate lesions or tumours, which typically appear darker because they are less dense than the cortex.

*Magnetic resonance imaging (MRI)* uses a strong magnetic field to line up the nuclei of specific molecules in the brain tissue. Brief, but powerful, pulses of radio waves cause the nuclei to rotate out of alignment. When a pulse ends, the nuclei snap back in line with the magnetic field and give off a small amount of energy in the process.

**electroencephalograph (EEG)**
A device used to record electrical activity in the brain.

◀ Figure **3.28** **Structural Imaging Techniques (CT and MRI)** CT (*left*) and MRI (*right*) scans are used to provide information about the structure of the brain and can help to spot tumours and other kinds of damage. Each scan shown here provides a snapshot of a single slice in the brain. Note that the MRI scan provides a clearer, higher-resolution image than the CT scan (see the text for further discussion of how these images are constructed and what they depict).

Different molecules have unique energy signatures when they snap back in line with the magnetic field, so these signatures can be used to reveal brain structures with different molecular compositions. MRI produces pictures of soft tissue at a better resolution than a CT scan, as you can see in Figure 3.28. These techniques give psychologists a clearer picture of the structure of the brain and can help localize brain damage (as when someone suffers a stroke), but they reveal nothing about the functions of the brain.

*Diffusion tensor imaging (DTI)* is a newer type of MRI that is used to visualize white matter pathways, which are fibre bundles that connect both nearby and distant brain regions to one another. DTI measures the rate and direction of diffusion or movement of water molecules along white matter pathways. Because the diffusion of water molecules follows the direction of the pathway, information about the direction in which water molecules diffuse can be used to determine where a white matter pathway goes. Scientists can use measures based on the rate and direction of diffusion to assess the integrity of a white matter pathway, which is very useful in cases of neurological and psychological disorders (Thomason & Thompson, 2011).

Because DTI provides information about pathways that connect brain areas to one another, it is a critical tool in mapping the connectivity of the human brain, and plays a central role in an ambitious undertaking known as the Human Connectome Project. This is a collaborative effort funded by the American National Institutes of Health beginning in 2009 that involves a collaboration among several groups of researchers in the United States and a group in the United Kingdom. The main goal of the project is to provide a complete map of the connectivity of neural pathways in the brain: the human connectome (Toga et al., 2012). A unique and exciting feature of the Human Connectome Project is that the researchers have made available some of their results at their website (www.humanconnectomeproject.org), which include fascinating colourful images of some of the connection pathways they have discovered.

DTI allows researchers to visualize white matter pathways in the brain, the fibre bundles that play an important role by connecting brain regions to one another.

## Functional Brain Imaging

Functional brain imaging techniques show researchers much more than just the structure of the brain by allowing them to watch the brain in action. These techniques rely on the fact that activated brain areas demand more energy for their neurons to work. This energy is supplied through increased blood flow to the activated areas. Functional imaging techniques can detect such changes in blood flow. In *positron emission tomography (PET)*, a harmless radioactive substance is injected into a person's bloodstream. Then the brain is scanned by radiation detectors as the person performs perceptual or cognitive tasks, such as reading or speaking. Areas of the brain that are activated during these tasks demand more energy and greater blood flow, resulting in a higher amount of radioactivity in that region. The radiation detectors record the level of radioactivity in each region, producing a computerized image of the activated areas (see **FIGURE 3.29** on the next page). Note that PET scans differ from CT scans and MRIs in that the image produced shows activity in the brain while the person performs certain tasks. So, for example, a PET scan of a person speaking would show activation in Broca's area in the left frontal lobe.

For psychologists, the most widely used functional brain imaging technique nowadays is *functional magnetic resonance imaging (fMRI)*, which detects the difference between oxygenated hemoglobin and deoxygenated hemoglobin when exposed to magnetic pulses. Hemoglobin is the molecule in the blood that carries oxygen to our tissues, including the brain. When active neurons demand more energy and blood flow, oxygenated hemoglobin concentrates in the active areas; fMRI detects the oxygenated hemoglobin and provides a picture of the level of activation in each brain area

**PET scan**

◄ Figure **3.29** **Functional Imaging Techniques (PET and fMRI)**
PET and fMRI scans provide information about the function of the brain by revealing which brain areas become more or less active in different conditions. The PET scan [*directly above*] shows areas in the left hemisphere [Broca's area, left; lower parietal–upper temporal area, right] that become active when people hold in mind a string of letters for a few seconds. The red areas in the fMRI scans [*all views to the left*] indicate activity in the auditory cortex of a person listening to music.

(see Figure 3.29). Just as MRI was a major advance over CT scans, *functional* MRI represents a similar leap in our ability to record the brain's activity during behaviour. Both fMRI and PET allow researchers to localize changes in the brain very accurately. However, fMRI has a couple of advantages over PET. First, fMRI does not require any exposure to a radioactive substance. Second, fMRI can localize changes in brain activity across briefer periods than PET, which makes it more useful for analyzing psychological processes that occur extremely quickly, such as reading a word or recognizing a face. With PET, researchers often have to use experimental designs different from those they would use in the psychology laboratory in order to adapt to the limitations of PET technology. With fMRI, researchers can design experiments that more closely resemble the ones they carry out in the psychology laboratory.

**What does an fMRI track in an active brain?**

Functional MRI can also be used to explore the relationship of brain regions with one another, using a recently developed technique referred to as *resting-state functional connectivity*. As implied by the name, this technique does not require participants to perform a task; they simply rest quietly while fMRI measurements are made. Functional connectivity measures the extent to which spontaneous activity in different brain regions is correlated over time; brain regions whose activity is highly correlated are thought to be functionally connected with one another (Lee, Smyser, & Shimony, 2013). Functional connectivity measures have been used extensively in recent years to identify brain *networks*; that is, sets of brain regions that are closely connected to one another (Yeo et al., 2011). For example, functional connectivity helped to identify the *default network* (Gusnard & Raichle, 2001), a group of interconnected regions in the frontal, temporal, and parietal lobes that is involved in internally focused cognitive activities, such as remembering past events, imagining future events, daydreaming, and mind wandering (Andrews-Hanna, 2012; Buckner, Andrews-Hanna, & Schacter, 2008) (see chapters on Memory and Consciousness). Functional connectivity, along with DTI (which measures structural connectivity), is used in studies conducted by the Human Connectome Project, and will contribute important information to the map of the human connectome.

## Insights from Functional Imaging

PET and fMRI provide remarkable insights into the types of information processing that take place in specific areas of the brain. For example, when a person performs a simple perceptual task, such as looking at a circular checkerboard, the primary visual areas are activated. As you have read, when the checkerboard is presented to the left visual field, the right visual cortex shows activation, and when the checkerboard is presented to the right visual field, the left visual cortex shows activation (Fox et al., 1986). Similarly, when people look at faces, fMRI reveals strong activity in a region located near the border of the temporal and occipital lobes called the *fusiform gyrus* (Kanwisher, McDermott, & Chun, 1997). When this structure is damaged, people experience problems with recognizing faces—even faces of friends and family they have known for years—although they do not have problems with their eyes and can recognize visual objects other than faces (Mestry et al., 2012). Finally, when people perform a task that engages emotional processing (e.g., looking at sad pictures), researchers observe significant activation in the amygdala, which you learned earlier is linked with emotional arousal (Phelps, 2006). There is also increased activation in parts of the frontal lobe that are involved in emotional regulation; in fact, in the same areas that were most likely damaged in the case of Phineas Gage (Wang et al., 2005).

You will recall from the Methods in Psychology chapter that at the heart of the scientific method is the relationship between ideas and evidence. There is no statute of limitations on scientific investigation. In this case, these modern brain imaging techniques confirm the theories derived from studies of brain damage from over 100 years ago. When Broca and Wernicke reached their conclusions about language production and language comprehension, they had little more to go on than some isolated cases and good hunches. PET scans have since confirmed that different areas of the brain are activated when a person is listening to spoken language, reading words on a screen, saying words out loud, or thinking of related words. This suggests that different parts of the brain are activated during these related but distinct functions. Similarly, it was pretty clear to the physician who examined Phineas Gage that the location of Gage's injuries played a major role in his drastic change in personality and emotionality. fMRI scans have since confirmed that the frontal lobe plays a central role in regulating emotion. It is always nice when independent methods (in these instances, very old case studies and very recent technology) arrive at the same conclusions. As you will also see at various points in the text, brain imaging techniques such as fMRI are also revealing new and surprising findings, such as the insights described in The Real World box (Brain Death and the Vegetative State).

Although the insights that we are obtaining from fMRI are exciting, it is important that we do not get too carried away with them, as sometimes happens in media depictions of fMRI results (Marcus, 2012). Consider, as an example, the topic of memory accuracy and distortion. Using experimental paradigms that you will learn about in the chapter on Memory, fMRI studies have shown that activity in some parts of the brain is greater during the retrieval of accurate rather than inaccurate memories (Schacter & Loftus, 2013). Does that mean we are ready to use fMRI in the courtroom to determine whether a witness is recounting an accurate memory or an inaccurate memory? Schacter and Loftus argued that the answer to this question is an emphatic no. For example, we do not yet know whether the results of laboratory fMRI studies of memory, which typically use simple materials like words or pictures, generalize to the kinds of complex everyday events that are relevant in the courtroom. Furthermore, evidence that fMRI can distinguish accurate from inaccurate memories comes from studies in which brain activity is averaged across a *group* of participants. But in the courtroom we need to determine whether an *individual* is

> **Why should we avoid jumping to conclusions based on fMRI results?**

## THE REAL WORLD

# Brain Death and the Vegetative State

n 1981, the President's Commission for the Study of Ethical Problems in Medicine and Biomedical and Behavioural Research defined brain death as the *irreversible loss of all functions of the brain*. Contrary to what you may think, brain death is not the same as being in a coma or being unresponsive to stimulation. Indeed, even a flatline EEG does not indicate that all brain functions have stopped; the reticular formation in the hindbrain, which generates spontaneous respiration and heartbeat, may still be active.

Brain death came to the forefront of national attention in the case of Terri Schiavo, a woman who had been kept alive on a respirator for nearly 15 years in a Florida nursing home. She died on March 31, 2005, after the feeding tube that sustained her was removed. A person like Schiavo is commonly referred to as *brain dead*, but such an individual is more accurately described as being in a *persistent vegetative state*. Does a persistent vegetative state qualify as "life"? Consider this: Neuroimaging research has found evidence that people diagnosed as being

in a vegetative state show signs of intentional mental activity (Monti, 2012). In one study, researchers used fMRI to observe the patterns of brain activity in a 25-year-old woman with severe brain injuries as the result of a traffic accident. When the researchers spoke ambiguous sentences ("The creak came from a beam in the ceiling") and unambiguous sentences ("There was milk and sugar in his coffee"), fMRI revealed that the activated areas in the woman's brain were comparable to those areas activated in the brains of normal volunteers (Owen et al., 2006). What is more, when the woman was instructed to imagine playing a game of tennis and then imagine walking through the rooms of her house, the areas of her brain that showed activity were again indistinguishable from those brain areas in normal, healthy volunteers.

The researchers suggested that these findings are evidence for, at least, conscious understanding of spoken commands and, at best, a degree of intentionality in an otherwise vegetative person. The patient's brain activity while "playing tennis" and

"walking through her house" revealed that she could both understand the researchers' instructions and willfully complete them. A more recent fMRI study that used these and related mental imagery tasks in a much larger sample found evidence for willful modulation of brain activity in 5 of 54 patients with disorders of consciousness (Monti et al., 2010). Other recent studies have revealed evidence of normal cerebral responses to language and complex sounds in 2 out of 3 patients in a vegetative state (Fernandez-Espejo et al., 2008), stronger emotional responding to familiar rather than unfamiliar voices in a single patient (Eickhoff et al., 2008), and willful attempts to execute a command to move a specific hand in another patient (Cruse et al., 2012a). Although it is too early to tell how these and other research findings may impact decisions regarding the brain and when life ends (Laureys et al., 2006), scientists and physicians are now engaged in intensive discussions concerning their ethical and clinical implications (Bernat, 2009; Monti, 2012; Monti, Coleman, & Owen, 2009).

remembering accurately or not, and there is little evidence yet that fMRI can answer that question. More generally, it is important to think carefully about how fMRI evidence is obtained before leaping to conclusions about how that evidence can be used in everyday life.

## Transcranial Magnetic Stimulation

We noted earlier that scientists have learned a lot about the brain by studying the behaviour of people with brain injuries. But, although brain damage may be related to particular patterns of behaviour, that relationship may or may not be causal. Experimentation is the premier method for establishing causal relationships between variables, but scientists cannot ethically cause brain damage in human beings, thus they have not been able to establish causal relationships between particular kinds of brain damage and particular patterns of behaviour. Functional neuroimaging techniques such as fMRI do not help on this point because they do not provide information about when a particular pattern of brain activity causes a particular behaviour.

Fortunately, scientists have discovered a way to mimic brain damage with a benign technique called *transcranial magnetic stimulation* (TMS) (Barker, Jalinous, & Freeston, 1985; Hallett, 2000). If you have ever held a magnet under a piece of paper and used it to drag a pin across the paper's surface, you know that magnetic fields can pass through insulating material. The human skull is no exception. TMS delivers a magnetic pulse that passes

Transcranial magnetic stimulation (TMS) activates and deactivates regions of the brain with a magnetic pulse, temporarily mimicking brain damage.

©BSIP SA/ALAMY IMAGES

through the skull and deactivates neurons in the cerebral cortex for a short period. Researchers can direct TMS pulses to particular brain regions (essentially turning them off) and then measure temporary changes in the way a person moves, sees, thinks, remembers, speaks, or feels. By manipulating the state of the brain, scientists can perform experiments that establish causal relationships.

# OTHER VOICES

## Neuromyths

**Christopher Chabris** and **Daniel Simons**

Christopher Chabris is an associate professor of psychology at Union College and Daniel Simons is a professor of psychology at the University of Illinois. Chabris and Simons co-authored *The Invisible Gorilla: And Other Ways Our Intuitions Deceive Us* (2010).

PHOTOS: (*LEFT*) MATT MILLESS; (*RIGHT*) COURTESY DANIEL J. SIMONS

You have no doubt often heard the phrase "we only use 10 percent of our brains," and perhaps you have wondered whether there is anything to it. Chabris and Simons (2012) discussed this and other statements about the brain that they believe to be merely myths, based in part, on a recent study by Sanne Dekker and her colleagues (2012).

Pop quiz: Which of these statements is false?

1. We use only 10% of our brain.
2. Environments rich in stimuli improve the brains of preschool children.
3. Individuals learn better when they receive information in their preferred learning style, whether auditory, visual, or kinesthetic.

If you picked the first one, congratulations. The idea that we use only 10 percent of our brain is patently false. Yet it so permeates popular culture that, among psychologists and neuroscientists, it is known as the "10% myth." Contrary to popular belief, the entire brain is put to use—unused neurons die and unused circuits atrophy. Reports of neuroimaging research might perpetuate the myth by showing only a small number of areas "lighting up" in a brain scan, but those are just areas that have more than a base line level of activity; the dark regions are not dormant or unused.

Did you agree with the other two statements? If so, you fell into our trap. All three statements are false—or at least not substantiated by scientific evidence. Unfortunately, if you got any of them wrong, you are hardly alone.

These "neuromyths," along with others, were presented to 242 primary and secondary school teachers in the Netherlands and the United Kingdom as part of a study by Sanne Dekker and colleagues at VU University Amsterdam and Bristol University, and just published in the journal *Frontiers in Psychology*. They found that 47% of the teachers believed the 10% myth. Even more, 76%, believed that enriching children's environments will strengthen their brains.

This belief might have emerged from evidence that rats raised in cages with amenities like exercise wheels, tunnels, and other rats showed better cognitive abilities and improvements in brain structure compared with rats that grew up isolated in bare cages. But such experiments show only that a truly impoverished and unnatural environment leads to poorer developmental outcomes than a more natural environment with opportunities to play and interact. It follows that growing up locked in a closet or otherwise cut off from human contact will impair a child's brain development. It does not follow that "enriching" a child's

environment beyond what is already typical (e.g., by constant exposure to "Baby Einstein"-type videos) will boost cognitive development.

The myth about learning styles was the most popular: 94% of the teachers believed that students perform better when lessons are delivered in their preferred learning style. Indeed, students do have preferences about how they learn; the problem is that these preferences have little to do with how effectively they learn.

Our own surveys of the U.S. population have found even more widespread belief in myths about the brain. About two-thirds of the public agreed with the 10% myth. Many also believed that memory works like a video recording or that they can tell when someone is staring at the back of their head.

Ironically, in the Dekker group's study, the teachers who knew the most about neuroscience also believed in the most myths. Apparently, teachers who are (admirably) enthusiastic about expanding their knowledge of the mind and brain have trouble separating fact from fiction as they learn. Neuromyths have so much intuitive appeal, and they spread so rapidly in fields like business and self-help, that eradicating them from popular consciousness might be a Sisyphean task. But reducing their influence in the classroom would be a good start.

If for some perverse reason you wanted to annoy the instructor of your psychology course, you probably could do no better than to claim that "we use only 10 percent of our brains." Even though, as pointed out by Chabris and Simon (2012), a surprisingly high proportion of elementary and secondary schoolteachers in the Netherlands and the United Kingdom subscribe to this myth, we do not know any psychologists teaching courses like the one you are taking who would endorse it, and we hope that there are none. How did the myth get started? Nobody really knows. Some think it may have arisen from a quotation by the great psychologist William James ("We are making use of only a small part of our possible mental and physical resources") or that it possibly owes to Albert Einstein's attempt to make sense of his own massive intellect (Boyd, 2008).

The key point for our purposes is that when you hear such bold claims made, say by a friend who heard it from somebody else, it is time for you to put into action the kinds of critical thinking skills that we are focusing on in this text, and start asking questions: What is the evidence for the claim? Is there a specific study or studies that your friend can name to provide evidence in support of the claim? Are the studies published in peer-reviewed scientific journals? What kind of sample was used in the study? Is it large enough to support a clear conclusion? Has the finding been replicated? Tall tales like the 10 percent myth do not stand much chance of surviving for long if claims for their existence are met head on with critical thinking.

In the Methods in Psychology chapter you learned about the difference between correlation and causation, and that even if two events are correlated, it does not necessarily mean that one causes the other. Suppose a researcher designs an experiment in which participants view words on a screen and are asked to pronounce each word aloud, while the researcher uses fMRI to examine brain activity. First, what areas of the brain would you expect to show activity on fMRI while participants complete this task? Second, can the researcher now safely conclude that those brain areas are required for humans to perform word pronunciation?

For example, in an early study using TMS, scientists discovered that magnetic stimulation of the visual cortex temporarily impairs a person's ability to detect the motion of an object without impairing the person's ability to recognize that object (Beckers & Zeki, 1995). This intriguing discovery suggests that motion perception and object recognition are accomplished by different parts of the brain, but moreover, it establishes that activity in the visual cortex *causes* motion perception. More recent research has revealed that applying TMS to the specific part of the visual cortex responsible for motion perception also impairs the accuracy with which people reach for moving objects (Schenk et al., 2005) or for stationary objects when there is motion in the background of a visual scene (Whitney et al., 2007). These findings indicate that the visual motion area plays a crucial role in guiding actions when we are responding to motion in the visual environment.

Rather than relying solely on observational studies of people with brain injuries or the snapshots provided by fMRI or PET scans, researchers can also manipulate brain activity and measure its effects. Scientists have also begun to combine TMS with fMRI, allowing them to localize precisely where in the brain TMS is having its effect (Caparelli, 2007). Studies suggest that TMS has no harmful side effects (Anand & Hotson, 2002; Pascual-Leone et al., 1993), and this new tool has changed the study of how our brains create our thoughts, feelings, and behaviours.

## IN SUMMARY

▶ There are three major approaches to studying the link between the brain and behaviour:

  ▶ Observing how perceptual, motor, intellectual, and emotional capacities are affected following brain damage. By carefully relating specific psychological and behavioural disruptions to damage in particular areas of the brain, researchers can better understand how the brain area normally plays a role in producing those behaviours.

  ▶ Examining global electrical activity in the brain and the activity patterns of single neurons. The patterns of electrical activity in large brain areas can be examined from outside the skull using the electroencephalograph (EEG). Single-cell recordings taken from specific neurons can be linked to specific perceptual or behavioural events, suggesting that those neurons represent particular kinds of stimuli or control particular aspects of behaviour.

  ▶ Using brain imaging to scan the brain as people perform different perceptual or intellectual tasks. Correlating energy consumption in particular brain areas with specific cognitive and behavioural events suggests that those brain areas are involved in specific types of perceptual, motor, cognitive, or emotional processing.

# Chapter Review

1. Which of the following is NOT a function of a neuron?
   a. processing information
   b. communicating with other neurons
   c. nutritional provision
   d. sending messages to body organs and muscles

2. Signals from other neurons are received and relayed to the cell body by
   a. the nucleus.
   b. dendrites.
   c. axons.
   d. glands.

3. Signals are transmitted from one neuron to another
   a. across a synapse.
   b. through a glial cell.
   c. by the myelin sheath.
   d. in the cell body.

4. Which type of neuron receives information from the external world and conveys this information to the brain via the spinal cord?
   a. sensory neuron
   b. motor neuron
   c. interneuron
   d. axon

5. An electric signal that is conducted along the length of a neuron's axon to the synapse is called
   a. a resting potential.
   b. an action potential.
   c. a node of Ranvier.
   d. an ion.

6. The chemicals that transmit information across the synapse to a receiving neuron's dendrites are called
   a. vesicles.
   b. terminal buttons.
   c. postsynaptic neurons.
   d. neurotransmitters.

7. The _____ automatically controls the organs of the body.
   a. autonomic nervous system
   b. parasympathetic nervous system
   c. sympathetic nervous system
   d. somatic nervous system

8. Which part of the hindbrain coordinates fine motor skills?
   a. the medulla
   b. the cerebellum
   c. the pons
   d. the tegmentum

9. What part of the brain is involved in movement and arousal?
   a. the hindbrain
   b. the midbrain
   c. the forebrain
   d. the reticular formation

10. The _____ regulates body temperature, hunger, thirst, and sexual behaviour.
    a. cerebral cortex
    b. pituitary gland
    c. hypothalamus
    d. hippocampus

11. What explains the apparent beneficial effects of cardiovascular exercise on aspects of brain function and cognitive performance?
    a. the different sizes of the somatosensory cortices
    b. the position of the cerebral cortex
    c. specialization of association areas
    d. neuron plasticity

12. During the course of embryonic brain growth, the _____ undergoes the greatest development.
    a. cerebral cortex
    b. cerebellum
    c. tectum
    d. thalamus

13. The first true central nervous system appeared in
    a. flatworms.
    b. jellyfish.
    c. protozoa.
    d. early primates.

14. Genes set the _____ in populations within a given environment.
    a. individual characteristics
    b. range of variation
    c. environmental possibilities
    d. behavioural standards

15. Identifying the brain areas that are involved in specific types of motor, cognitive, or emotional processing is best achieved through
    a. recording patterns of electrical activity.
    b. observing psychological disorders.
    c. psychosurgery.
    d. brain imaging.

## KEY TERMS

| | | | |
|---|---|---|---|
| acetylcholine (ACh) (p. 88) | DNA methylation (p. 110) | interneurons (p. 83) | receptors (p. 86) |
| action potential (p. 86) | dopamine (p. 88) | limbic system (p. 99) | refractory period (p. 86) |
| agonists (p. 88) | electroencephalograph (EEG) (p. 119) | medulla (p. 97) | resting potential (p. 85) |
| amygdala (p. 99) | endorphins (p. 88) | mirror neurons (p. 103) | reticular formation (p. 97) |
| antagonists (p. 88) | epigenetic marks (p. 110) | motor neurons (p. 82) | sensory neurons (p. 82) |
| association areas (p. 102) | epigenetics (p. 110) | myelin sheath (p. 82) | serotonin (p. 88) |
| autonomic nervous system (ANS) (p. 93) | frontal lobe (p. 102) | nervous system (p. 92) | somatic nervous system (p. 92) |
| axon (p. 82) | GABA (gamma-aminobutyric acid) (p. 88) | neurons (p. 80) | spinal reflexes (p. 94) |
| basal ganglia (p. 100) | gene (p. 108) | neurotransmitters (p. 86) | subcortical structures (p. 97) |
| cell body (or soma) (p. 81) | glial cells (p. 82) | norepinephrine (p. 88) | sympathetic nervous system (p. 93) |
| central nervous system (CNS) (p. 92) | glutamate (p. 88) | occipital lobe (p. 100) | synapse (p. 82) |
| cerebellum (p. 97) | heritability (p. 111) | parasympathetic nervous system (p. 94) | tectum (p. 97) |
| cerebral cortex (p. 97) | hindbrain (p. 97) | parietal lobe (p. 100) | tegmentum (p. 97) |
| chromosomes (p. 108) | hippocampus (p. 99) | peripheral nervous system (PNS) (p. 92) | temporal lobe (p. 102) |
| corpus callosum (p. 100) | histone modification (p. 110) | pituitary gland (p. 99) | terminal buttons (p. 86) |
| dendrite (p. 81) | hypothalamus (p. 98) | pons (p. 97) | thalamus (p. 98) |

## CHANGING MINDS

1. While watching late-night television, you come across an infomercial for all-natural BrainGro. "It's a well-known fact that most people use only 10 percent of their brain," the spokesman promises, "but with BrainGro you can increase that number from 10 percent to 99 percent!" Why should you be skeptical of the claim that we use only 10 percent of our brains? What would happen if a drug actually increased neuronal activity by ten-fold?

2. Your friend has been feeling depressed and has gone to a psychiatrist for help. "He prescribed a medication that's supposed to increase serotonin in my brain. But my feelings depend on me, not on a bunch of chemicals in my head," she said. What examples could you give your friend to convince her that hormones and neurotransmitters really do influence our cognition, mood, and behaviour?

3. A classmate has read the section in this chapter about the evolution of the central nervous system. "Evolution is just a theory," he says. "Not everyone believes in it. And, even if it's true that we're all descended from monkeys, that doesn't have anything to do with the psychology

of humans alive today." What is your friend misunderstanding about evolution? How would you explain to him the relevance of evolution to modern psychology?

4. A news program reports on a study (Hölzel et al., 2011) in which people who practised meditation for about 30 minutes a day for 8 weeks showed changes in their brains, including increases in the size of the hippocampus and the amygdala. You tell a friend, who is skeptical. Your friend says "The brain doesn't change like that. Basically, the brain you're born with is the brain you're stuck with for the rest of your life." Why is your friend's statement wrong? What are several specific ways in which the brain does change over time?

5. A friend of yours announces that he has figured out why he is bad at math. "I read it in a book," he says. "Left-brained people are analytical and logical, but right-brained people are creative and artistic. I'm an art major, so I must be right-brained, and that's why I'm not good at math." Why is your friend's view too simplistic?

## ANSWERS TO KEY CONCEPT QUIZ

1. c; 2. b; 3. a; 4. a; 5. b; 6. d; 7. a; 8. b; 9. b; 10. c; 11. d; 12. a; 13. a; 14. b; 15. d.

Need more help? Additional resources are located in Launchpad at:

www.worthpublishers.com/launchpad/schacter3ecanadian

# 4

# Sensation and Perception

▲ **Sensation and Perception Are Distinct Activities**
Psychophysics
Measuring Thresholds
Signal Detection
Sensory Adaptation

▲ **Vision I: How the Eyes and the Brain Convert Light Waves to Neural Signals**
Sensing Light
Perceiving Colour
The Visual Brain

▲ **Vision II: Recognizing What We Perceive**
Attention: The "Glue" That Binds Individual Features into a Whole
THE REAL WORLD Multitasking
Recognizing Objects by Sight
Perceiving Depth and Size
Perceiving Motion and Change
OTHER VOICES Hallucinations and the Visual System
CULTURE & COMMUNITY Does Culture Influence Change Blindness?

▲ **Audition: More Than Meets the Ear**
Sensing Sound
The Human Ear
Perceiving Pitch
Localizing Sound Sources
Hearing Loss
THE REAL WORLD Music Training: Worth the Time

▲ **The Body Senses: More Than Skin Deep**
Touch
Pain
Body Position, Movement, and Balance

▲ **The Chemical Senses: Adding Flavour**
Smell
HOT SCIENCE Taste: From the Top Down
Taste

N THE 1930S, A YOUNG ARCHITECT and designer named Donald Deskey won a competition to design the interiors for Radio City Music Hall in New York City. His design was met with immediate acclaim and enabled Deskey to create his own graphic design firm. In 1946, he helped to create the box design for Procter & Gamble's revolutionary new laundry detergent, Tide, which used, for the first time, synthetic compounds rather than plain old soap (Hine, 1995). Although extremely familiar to us today, in 1946 the bold, blue lettered "Tide" emblazoned on bull's-eye rings of yellow and orange marked the first use of eye-catching Day-Glo colours on a commercial product, and this mix of type and graphics was unlike any product design that anyone had seen before. The product would be impossible to miss on store shelves, and as admirers of the design observed, "it was the box itself that most dynamically conveyed the new product's extraordinary power" (Dyer, Dalzell, & Olegario, 2004). Tide went to market in 1949 and Procter & Gamble never looked back.

Nowadays we are used to seeing advertisements that feature exciting, provocative, or even sexual images to sell products. In television commercials these images are accompanied by popular music that advertisers hope will evoke an overall mood favourable to the product. The notion is that the sight and sound of exciting things will become associated with what might be an otherwise drab product. This form of advertising is known as *sensory branding* (Lindstrom, 2005). The idea is to exploit all the senses to promote a product or a brand. Sensory branding goes beyond sight and sound by enlisting smell, taste, and touch as well as vision and hearing. That new-car smell you anticipate while you take a test drive? It is a manufactured fragrance sprayed into the car, carefully tested to evoke positive feelings among potential buyers. Bang and Olufsen, a Danish high-end stereo manufacturer, carefully designed its remote control units to have a certain distinctive "feel" in a user's hand. Singapore Airlines, which has consistently been rated "the world's best airline," has actually patented the smell of their airplane cabins (it is called Stefan Floridian Waters).

These companies, just like Procter & Gamble back in 1946, recognize the power of sensation and perception to shape human experience and behaviour.

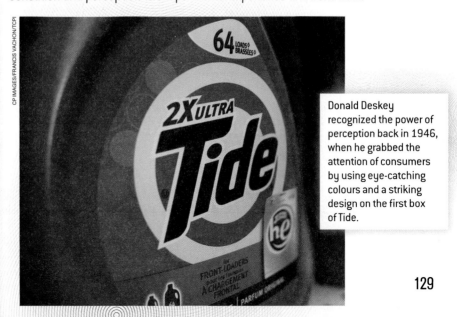

Donald Deskey recognized the power of perception back in 1946, when he grabbed the attention of consumers by using eye-catching colours and a striking design on the first box of Tide.

IN THIS CHAPTER WE WILL EXPLORE KEY INSIGHTS INTO THE NATURE of sensation and perception. These experiences are basic to survival and reproduction; we would not last long without the ability to accurately make sense of the world around us. Indeed, research on sensation and perception is the basis for much of psychology, a pathway toward understanding more complex cognition and behaviour such as memory, emotion, motivation, or decision making. Yet sensation and perception also sometimes reveal various kinds of illusions that you might see at a science fair or in a novelty shop: reminders that the act of perceiving the world is not as simple or straightforward as it might seem.

We will look at how physical energy in the world around us is encoded by our senses, sent to the brain, and enters conscious awareness. Vision is predominant among our senses; correspondingly, we will devote a fair amount of space to understanding how the visual system works. Then we will discuss how we perceive sound waves as words or music or noise, followed by the body senses, emphasizing touch, pain, and balance. We will end with the chemical senses of smell and taste, which together allow you to savour the foods you eat. But before doing any of that, we will provide a foundation for examining all of the sensory systems by reviewing how psychologists measure sensation and perception in the first place.

## Sensation and Perception Are Distinct Activities

To us, sensation and perception appear to be one seamless event. However, they are two distinct activities.

> **Sensation** is *simple stimulation of a sense organ*. It is the basic registration of light, sound, pressure, odour, or taste as parts of your body interact with the physical world.

> After a sensation registers in your central nervous system, **perception** takes place at the level of your brain: *the organization, identification, and interpretation of a sensation in order to form a mental representation*.

As an example, your eyes are coursing across these sentences right now. The sensory receptors in your eyeballs are registering different patterns of light reflecting off the page. Your brain, however, is integrating and processing that light information into the meaningful perception of words, such as *meaningful, perception,* and *words*. Your eyes—the sensory organ—are not really seeing words; they are simply encoding different lines and curves on a page. Your brain—the perceptual organ—is transforming those lines and curves into a coherent mental representation of words and concepts.

If all of this sounds a little peculiar, it is because, from the vantage point of your conscious experience, it *seems* as if you are reading words directly. If you think of the discussion of brain damage in the Neuroscience and Behaviour chapter, you will recall that sometimes a person's eyes can work just fine, yet the individual is still "blind" to faces she has seen for many years (p. 122). Damage to the visual processing centres in the brain can interfere with the interpretation of information coming from the eyes: The senses are intact, but perceptual ability is compromised. Sensation and perception are related—but separate—events.

How do sensory receptors communicate with the brain? It all depends on the process of **transduction,** which occurs *when sensors in the body convert physical signals from the environment into encoded neural signals sent to the central nervous system*. In vision, light reflected from surfaces provides the eyes with information about the shape, colour, and position of objects. In audition, vibrations (from

> What role does the brain play in what we see and hear?

You can enjoy a tempting ice cream sundae even if you do not know that its sweet taste depends on a complex process of transduction, in which molecules dissolved in saliva are converted to neural signals processed by the brain.

© ISTOCKPHOTO.COM/FOTOFLARE

vocal cords or a guitar string, perhaps) cause changes in air pressure that propagate through space to a listener's ears. In touch, the pressure of a surface against the skin signals its shape, texture, and temperature. In taste and smell, molecules dispersed in the air or dissolved in saliva reveal the identity of substances that we may or may not want to eat. In each case physical energy from the world is converted to neural energy inside the central nervous system (see **TABLE 4.1**). We will discuss in more detail how transduction works with each of the five primary senses—vision, hearing, touch, taste, and smell—in separate sections later in this chapter.

## Psychophysics

Knowing that perception takes place in the brain, you might wonder if two people see the same colours in the sunset when looking at the evening sky. It is intriguing to consider the possibility that our basic perceptions of sights or sounds might differ fundamentally from those of other people. How can we measure such a thing objectively? Measuring the physical energy of a stimulus, such as the wavelength of a light, is easy enough: You can probably buy the necessary instruments online to do that yourself. But how do you quantify a person's private, subjective *perception* of that light?

**sensation**
Simple stimulation of a sense organ.

**perception**
The organization, identification, and interpretation of a sensation in order to form a mental representation.

**transduction**
What takes place when sensors in the body convert physical signals from the environment into encoded neural signals sent to the central nervous system.

**Table 4.1**

### Transduction

The five senses convert physical energy from the world into neural energy, which is sent to the brain.

| Sense | Sensory Input | Conversion into Neural Energy |
|---|---|---|
| Vision | Light reflected from surfaces (for example, from a leaf) provides the eyes with information about the shape, colour, and positions of objects. | (See Figure 4.4 for a more detailed view.) |
| Audition (hearing) | Vibrations (from a guitar string, perhaps) cause changes in air pressure that move through space to the listener's ears. | (See Figure 4.24 for a more detailed view.) |
| Touch | Pressure of a surface against the skin signals its shape, texture, and temperature. | (See Figure 4.27 for a more detailed view.) |
| Taste and Smell | Molecules dispersed in the air or dissolved in saliva reveal the identity of substances that we may or may not want to eat. | (See Figures 4.28 and 4.30 for more detailed views.) |

**psychophysics**
Methods that measure the strength of a stimulus and the observer's sensitivity to that stimulus.

**absolute threshold**
The minimal intensity needed to just barely detect a stimulus in 50 percent of the trials.

**just noticeable difference (JND)**
The minimal change in a stimulus that can just barely be detected.

A few early psychologists, such as Edward Titchener, tried using introspection to measure perceptual experiences (see the Psychology: Evolution of a Science chapter). They failed miserably at this task. After all, two people may both describe their experience of the sunset in the same words ("orange" and "beautiful"), but neither can directly perceive the other's experience of the same event. In the mid-1800s, German scientist and philosopher Gustav Fechner (1801–1887) developed a new approach to measuring sensation and perception called **psychophysics:** *methods that measure the strength of a stimulus and the observer's sensitivity to that stimulus* (Fechner, 1860/1966). In a typical psychophysics experiment, researchers ask people to make a simple judgment—whether or not they saw a flash of light, for example. The psychophysicist then relates the measured stimulus, such as the brightness of the light flash, to each observer's yes-or-no response.

> **Why should a psychophysicist measure more than the strength of a stimulus?**

## Measuring Thresholds

Psychophysicists begin the measurement process with a single sensory signal to determine precisely how much physical energy is required for an observer to become aware of a sensation. The simplest quantitative measurement in psychophysics is the **absolute threshold,** *the minimal intensity needed to just barely detect a stimulus in 50 percent of the trials*. A *threshold* is a boundary. The doorway that separates the inside from the outside of a house is a threshold, as is the boundary between two psychological states (awareness and unawareness, for example). In finding the absolute threshold for sensation, the two states in question are *perceiving* and *not perceiving* some stimulus. **TABLE 4.2** (on the next page) lists the approximate sensory thresholds for each of the five senses.

To measure the absolute threshold for detecting a sound, for example, an observer sits in a soundproof room wearing headphones linked to a computer. The experimenter presents a pure tone (the sort of sound made by striking a tuning fork) using the computer to vary the loudness or the length of time each tone lasts and recording how often the observer reports hearing that tone under each condition. The outcome of such an experiment is graphed in **FIGURE 4.1.** Notice from the shape of the curve that the transition from *not hearing* to *hearing* is gradual rather than abrupt.

If we repeat this experiment for many different tones, we can observe and record the thresholds for tones ranging from very low to very high pitch. It turns out that people tend to be most sensitive to the range of tones corresponding to human conversation. If the tone is low enough, such as the lowest note on a pipe organ, most humans cannot hear it at all; we can only feel it. If the tone is high enough, we likewise cannot hear it, but dogs and many other animals can.

The absolute threshold is useful for assessing how sensitive we are to faint stimuli, but the human perceptual system is better at detecting *changes* in stimulation than the simple onset or offset of stimulation. When parents hear their infant's cry, it is useful to be able to differentiate the "I am hungry" cry from the "I am cranky" cry from the "something is biting my toes" cry. The **just noticeable difference (JND)** is *the minimal change in a stimulus that can just barely be detected*. This is another kind of threshold: the difference threshold.

The JND is not a fixed quantity; rather, it depends on how intense the stimuli being measured are and on the particular sense being measured. Consider measuring the JND for a bright light. An observer in a dark room is shown a light of fixed intensity, called the *standard* (S), next to a comparison light that is slightly brighter or dimmer

▲ Figure **4.1  Absolute Threshold** Some of us are more sensitive than others, and we may even detect sensory stimulation below our own absolute threshold. Absolute threshold is graphed here as the point where the increasing intensity of the stimulus enables an observer to detect it on 50 percent of the trials. As its intensity gradually increases, we detect the stimulation more frequently.

than the standard. When S is very dim, observers can see even a very small difference in brightness between the two lights: The JND is small. But if S is bright, a much larger increment is needed to detect the difference: The JND is larger.

When calculating a difference threshold, it is the proportion between stimuli that is important. This relationship was first noticed in 1834 by German physiologist Ernst

> **What is the importance of proportion to the measurement of *just noticeable difference*?**

Weber (Watson, 1978). Fechner applied Weber's insight directly to psychophysics, resulting in a formal relationship called **Weber's law:** *The just noticeable difference of a stimulus is a constant proportion despite variations in intensity.* As an example, if you picked up a 20-g envelope, then a 40-g envelope, you would probably notice the difference between them. But if you picked up a 2-kg package, then a 2.02-kg package, you would probably detect no difference at all between them.

## Signal Detection

Measuring absolute and difference thresholds requires a critical assumption: that a threshold exists! But much of what scientists know about biology suggests that such a discrete, all-or-none change in the brain is unlikely. Humans do not suddenly and rapidly switch between perceiving and not perceiving; in fact, recall that the transition from *not sensing* to *sensing* is gradual (see Figure 4.1). The very same physical stimulus, such as a dim light or a quiet tone, presented on several different occasions, may be perceived by the same person on some occasions but not on others. Remember, an absolute threshold is operationalized as perceiving the stimulus 50 percent of the time, which means the other 50 percent of the time it might go undetected.

Our accurate perception of a sensory stimulus, then, can be somewhat haphazard. Whether in the psychophysics lab or out in the world, sensory signals face a lot of

> **How accurate and complete are our perceptions of the world?**

competition, or *noise,* which refers to all the other stimuli coming from the internal and external environment. Memories, moods, and motives intertwine with what you are seeing, hearing, and smelling at any given time. This internal "noise" competes with your ability to detect a stimulus with perfect, focused attention. Other sights, sounds, and smells in the world at large also compete for attention; you rarely have the luxury of attending to just one stimulus apart from everything else. As a consequence of noise, you may not perceive everything that you sense, and you may even perceive things that you have not sensed. If you have ever been in the shower while eagerly anticipating a telephone call, you know how easy it is to "hear" a ringing telephone in the noise of the rushing water!

An approach to psychophysics called **signal detection theory** holds that *the response to a stimulus depends both on a person's sensitivity to the stimulus in the presence of noise and on a person's decision criterion.* That is, observers consider the sensory evidence evoked by the stimulus and compare it to an internal decision

**Table 4.2**

**Approximate Sensory Thresholds**

| Sense | Absolute Threshold |
|---|---|
| Vision | A candle flame 48 km away on a clear, dark night |
| Hearing | A clock's tick 6 m away when all is quiet |
| Touch | A fly's wing falling on the cheek from 1 cm away |
| Smell | A single drop of perfume diffused through an area equivalent to the volume of six rooms |
| Taste | 5 mL of sugar dissolved in 7.5 L of water |

*Source:* Adapted from Galanter (1962).

**Weber's law**
The just noticeable difference of a stimulus is a constant proportion despite variations in intensity.

**signal detection theory**
The response to a stimulus depends both on a person's sensitivity to the stimulus in the presence of noise and on a person's response criterion.

Crowds of people such as this one in a parade present our visual system with a challenging signal detection task.

criterion (Green & Swets, 1966; Macmillan & Creelman, 2005). If the sensory evidence exceeds the criterion, the observer responds by saying, "Yes, I detected the stimulus," and if it falls short of the criterion, the observer responds by saying, "No, I did not detect the stimulus." The four outcomes are summarized in **FIGURE 4.2**.

Signal detection theory allows researchers to quantify an observer's response in the presence of noise. In a signal detection experiment, a stimulus, such as a dim light, is randomly presented or not. If you have ever taken an eye exam that checks your peripheral vision, you have an idea about this kind of setup: Lights of varying intensity are flashed at various places in the visual field, and your task is to respond anytime you see one. Observers in a signal detection experiment must decide whether they saw the light or not. If the light is presented and the observer correctly responds yes, the outcome is a *hit*. If the light is presented and the observer says no, the result is a *miss*. However, if the light is *not* presented and the observer nonetheless says it was, a *false alarm* has occurred. Finally, if the light is *not* presented and the observer responds no, a *correct rejection* has occurred: The observer accurately detected the absence of the stimulus.

Signal detection theory proposes a way to measure *perceptual sensitivity* (how effectively the perceptual system represents sensory events) separately from the observer's decision-making strategy. It explicitly takes into account observers' response tendencies, such as liberally saying yes when there is any hint of a stimulus or conservatively reserving identifications only for obvious instances of the stimulus. Even when one person says yes much more often than another, both may be equally accurate in distinguishing between the presence or absence of a stimulus.

Signal detection theory has practical applications at home, school, work, and even while driving. For example, a radiologist may have to decide whether a mammogram shows that a woman has breast cancer. The radiologist knows that certain features, such as a mass of a particular size and shape, are associated with the presence of cancer. But noncancerous features can have a very similar appearance to cancerous ones. The radiologist may decide on a strictly liberal criterion and check every possible case of cancer with a biopsy. This decision strategy minimizes the possibility of missing a true cancer but leads to many unnecessary biopsies. A strictly conservative criterion will cut down on unnecessary biopsies but will miss some treatable cancers.

As another example, imagine that police are on the lookout for a suspected felon who they have reason to believe will be at a crowded soccer match. Although the law enforcement agency provided a fairly good description (white, 1.8 m (6 feet) tall, sandy brown hair, beard, glasses) there are still thousands of people to scan. Rounding up all men between 1.6 m (5′5″) and 2 m (6′5″) would probably produce a hit (the felon is caught) but at the expense of an extraordinary number of false alarms (many innocent people are detained and questioned).

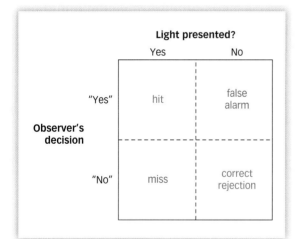

These different types of errors have to be weighed against one another in setting the decision criterion. Signal detection theory offers a practical way to choose among criteria that permit decision makers to take into account the consequences of hits, misses, false alarms, and correct rejections (McFall & Treat, 1999; Swets, Dawes, & Monahan, 2000). For an example of a common everyday task that can interfere with signal detection, see The Real World box.

▲ Figure **4.2** **Signal-Detection Experiment Outcomes** This table represents the four possible outcomes of a signal-detection experiment. Either a signal is or is not present, and the observer can either detect it ("yes") or not.

## Sensory Adaptation

When you walk into a bakery, the aroma of freshly baked bread overwhelms you, but after a few minutes the smell fades. If you dive into cold water, the temperature is shocking at first, but after a few minutes you get used to it. When you wake up in the middle of the night for a drink of water, the bathroom light blinds you, but after a few minutes you no longer squint. These are all examples of **sensory adaptation:** *Sensitivity to prolonged stimulation tends to decline over time as an organism adapts to current conditions.*

Sensory adaptation is a useful process for most organisms. Imagine what your sensory and perceptual world would be like without it. When you put on your jeans in the

> **What conditions have you already adapted to today? Sounds? Smells?**

morning, the feeling of rough cloth against your bare skin would be as noticeable hours later as it was in the first few minutes. The stink of garbage in your apartment when you first walk in would never dissipate. If you had to be constantly aware of how your tongue feels while it is resting in your mouth, you would be driven to distraction. Sensory adaptation is generally due to neural fatigue—the cells that are firing to signal the stimulus get tired after a time, and stop firing—but as far as your body is concerned, the signal has stopped. If the cells have a chance to rest, they will signal again as strongly as ever. So after the smell of freshly baked bread has faded, if you leave the bakery for a few minutes, and then re-enter the bakery, the smell should be just as strong as it was at first, before fading again. Another phenomenon, called *habituation,* also results in sensations fading with time. But habituation is due to learning. If you move to an apartment on a busy street with a lot of traffic noise, your sleep might be disturbed for a few nights. But soon you are sleeping soundly again. Your perceptual system has learned to disregard the noise. You will learn more about habituation in the Learning chapter.

According to the theory of natural selection, inherited characteristics that provide a survival advantage tend to spread throughout the population across generations. Why might sensory adaptation have evolved? What survival benefits might it confer to a small animal trying to avoid predators? To a predator trying to hunt prey?

## IN SUMMARY

▶ Sensation and perception are critical to survival. Sensation is the simple stimulation of a sense organ, whereas perception organizes, identifies, and interprets sensation at the level of the brain.

▶ All of our senses depend on the process of transduction, which converts physical signals from the environment into neural signals carried by sensory neurons into the central nervous system.

▶ In the nineteenth century, researchers developed psychophysics, an approach to studying perception that measures the strength of a stimulus and an observer's sensitivity to that stimulus. Psychophysicists have developed procedures for measuring an observer's absolute threshold, or the smallest intensity needed to just barely detect a stimulus, and the just noticeable difference (JND), or the smallest change in a stimulus that can just barely be detected.

▶ Signal detection theory allows researchers to distinguish between an observer's perceptual sensitivity to a stimulus and criteria for making decisions about the stimulus.

▶ Sensory adaptation occurs because sensitivity to unchanging stimulation tends to decline over time due to neural fatigue.

# Vision I: How the Eyes and the Brain Convert Light Waves to Neural Signals

You might be proud of your 20/20 vision, even if it is corrected by glasses or contact lenses. 20/20 refers to a measurement associated with a Snellen chart, named after Hermann Snellen (1834–1908), the Dutch ophthalmologist who developed it as a means of assessing **visual acuity,** *the ability to see fine detail;* it is the smallest line of letters that a typical person can read from a distance of 20 feet (6 m).

**sensory adaptation**
Sensitivity to prolonged stimulation tends to decline over time as an organism adapts to current conditions.

**visual acuity**
The ability to see fine detail.

Though controversial for other reasons, research has shown that action-shooter games improve attention and even basic visual acuity (Green & Bavelier, 2007; Li et al., 2009).

But if you dropped into the Birds of Prey Ophthalmologic Office, your visual pride would wither. Hawks, eagles, owls, and other raptors have much greater visual acuity than humans: in many cases, about 5 times greater (meaning that what the normal human can just see from 4 feet (1.2 m) away can be seen by these birds at a distance of 20 feet away), or the equivalent of 20/4 vision. Your sophisticated visual system has evolved to transduce visual energy in the world into neural signals in the brain. Humans have sensory receptors in their eyes that respond to wavelengths of light energy. When we look at people, places, and things, patterns of light and colour give us information about where one surface stops and another begins. The array of light reflected from those surfaces preserves their shapes and enables us to form a mental representation of a scene (Rodieck, 1998). Understanding vision, then, starts with understanding light.

## Sensing Light

Visible light is simply the portion of the electromagnetic spectrum that we can see, and it is an extremely small slice (see **FIGURE 4.3**). You can think about light as waves of energy. Like ocean waves, light waves vary in height and in the distance between their peaks, or *wavelengths*. There are three properties of light waves, each of which has a physical dimension that produces a corresponding psychological dimension (see **TABLE 4.3** on the next page). In other words, light does not need a human to have the properties it does: Length, amplitude, and purity are properties of the light waves themselves. What humans perceive from those properties are colour, brightness, and saturation.

> The *length* of a light wave determines its hue, or what humans perceive as colour.

> The intensity or *amplitude* of a light wave—how high the peaks are—determines what we perceive as the brightness of light.

> *Purity* is the number of distinct wavelengths that make up the light. Purity corresponds to what humans perceive as saturation, or the richness of colours.

### The Human Eye

Eyes have evolved as specialized organs to detect light. **FIGURE 4.4** (on the next page) shows the human eye in cross-section. Light that reaches the eyes passes first through a clear, smooth outer tissue called the *cornea,* which bends the light wave and sends it through the *pupil,* a hole in the coloured part of the eye. This coloured part is the *iris,* which is a translucent, doughnut-shaped muscle that controls the size of the pupil and hence the amount of light that can enter the eye.

► Figure **4.3 Electromagnetic Spectrum** The sliver of light waves visible to humans as a rainbow of colours from violet-blue to red is bounded on the short end by ultraviolet rays, which honeybees can see, and on the long end by infrared waves, upon which night-vision equipment operates. Someone wearing night-vision goggles, for example, can detect another person's body heat in complete darkness. Light waves are minute, but the scale along the bottom of this chart offers a glimpse of their varying lengths, measured in nanometres (nm). (1 nm = 1 billionth of a metre)

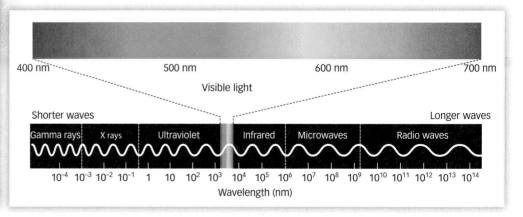

▶ Table 4.3

### Properties of Light Waves

| Physical Dimension | | Psychological Dimension |
|---|---|---|
| Length 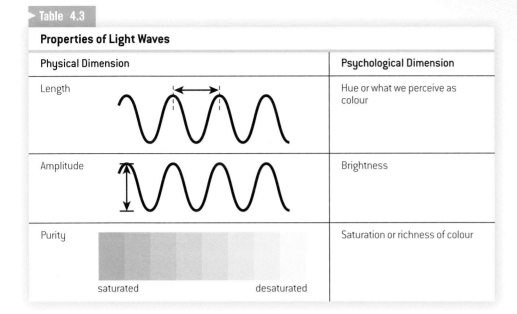 | | Hue or what we perceive as colour |
| Amplitude | | Brightness |
| Purity<br>saturated　　　desaturated | | Saturation or richness of colour |

Immediately behind the iris, muscles inside the eye control the shape of the *lens* to bend the light again and focus it onto the **retina,** *light-sensitive tissue lining the back of the eyeball.* The muscles change the shape of the lens to focus objects at different distances, making the lens flatter for objects that are far away or rounder for nearby objects. This is called **accommodation,** *the process by which the eye maintains a clear image on the retina.* **FIGURE 4.5a** (on the next page) shows how accommodation works.

If your eyeballs are a little too long or a little too short, the lens will not focus images properly on the retina. If the eyeball is too long, images are focused in front of

> **How do eyeglasses actually correct vision?**

the retina, leading to nearsightedness (*myopia*), which is shown in **FIGURE 4.5b** (on the next page). If the eyeball is too short, images are focused behind the retina, and the result is farsightedness (*hyperopia*), as shown in **FIGURE 4.5c** (on the next

page). Eyeglasses, contact lenses, and surgical procedures can correct either condition. For example, eyeglasses and contacts both provide an additional lens to help focus light more appropriately, and procedures such as LASIK physically reshape the eye's existing lens.

**retina**
Light-sensitive tissue lining the back of the eyeball.

**accommodation**
The process by which the eye maintains a clear image on the retina.

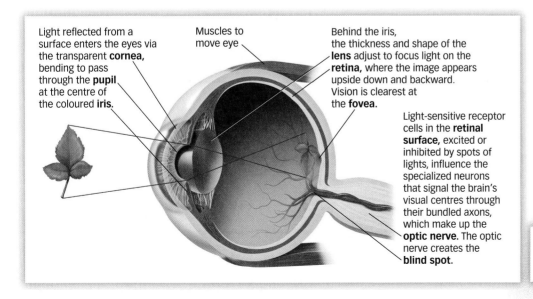

Light reflected from a surface enters the eyes via the transparent **cornea,** bending to pass through the **pupil** at the centre of the coloured **iris.**

Muscles to move eye

Behind the iris, the thickness and shape of the **lens** adjust to focus light on the **retina,** where the image appears upside down and backward. Vision is clearest at the **fovea.**

Light-sensitive receptor cells in the **retinal surface,** excited or inhibited by spots of lights, influence the specialized neurons that signal the brain's visual centres through their bundled axons, which make up the **optic nerve.** The optic nerve creates the **blind spot.**

◄ Figure **4.4** **Anatomy of the Human Eye** Specialized organs of the eye evolved to detect light. ◄

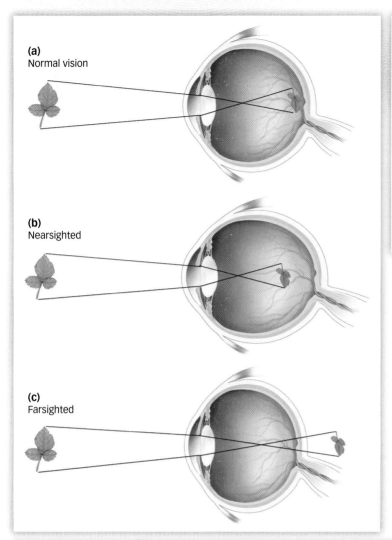

**(a)**
Normal vision

**(b)**
Nearsighted

**(c)**
Farsighted

◀ Figure **4.5** **Accommodation**  Inside the eye, the lens changes shape to focus nearby or faraway objects on the retina. People with normal vision focus the image on the retina at the back of the eye, both for near and far objects (*a*). Nearsighted people see clearly what's nearby, but distant objects are blurry because light from them is focused in front of the retina, a condition called *myopia* (*b*). Farsighted people have the opposite problem: Distant objects are clear, but those nearby are blurry because their point of focus falls beyond the surface of the retina, a condition called *hyperopia* (*c*).

▼ Figure **4.6** **Close-up of the Retina**  The surface of the retina is composed of photoreceptor cells, the rods and cones, beneath a layer of transparent neurons, the bipolar and retinal ganglion cells (RGCs), connected in sequence. The axon of a retinal ganglion cell joins with all other RGC axons to form the optic nerve. Viewed close up in this cross-sectional diagram is the area of greatest visual acuity, the fovea, where most colour-sensitive cones are concentrated, allowing us to see fine detail as well as colour. Rods, the predominant photoreceptors activated in low-light conditions, are distributed everywhere else on the retina.

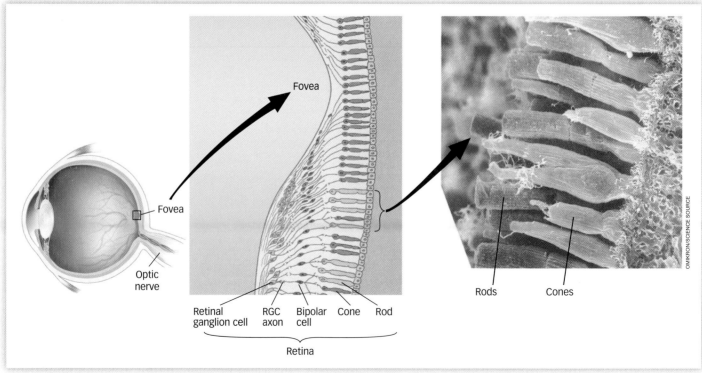

Fovea

Optic nerve

Fovea

Retinal ganglion cell   RGC axon   Bipolar cell   Cone   Rod

Retina

Rods   Cones

OMIKRON/SCIENCE SOURCE

## From the Eye to the Brain

How does a wavelength of light become a meaningful image? The retina is the interface between the world of light outside the body and the world of vision inside the central nervous system. Two types of *photoreceptor cells* in the retina contain light-sensitive pigments that transduce light into neural impulses. **Cones** *detect colour, operate under normal daylight conditions, and allow us to focus on fine detail.* **Rods** *become active under low-light conditions for night vision* (see **FIGURE 4.6** on the previous page).

Rods are much more sensitive photoreceptors than cones, but this sensitivity comes at a cost. Because all rods contain the same photopigment, they provide no information about colour and sense only shades of grey. Think about this the next time you wake up in the middle of the night and make your way to the bathroom for a drink of water. Using only the moonlight from the window to light your way, do you see the

> **What are the major differences between rods and cones?**

room in colour or in shades of grey? Rods and cones differ in several other ways as well, most notably in their numbers. About 120 million rods are distributed more or less evenly around each retina except in the very centre, the **fovea,** *an area of the retina where vision is the clearest and there are no rods at all.* The absence of rods in the fovea decreases the sharpness of vision in reduced light, but it can be overcome. For example, when amateur astronomers view dim stars through their telescopes at night, they know to look a little off to the side of the target so that the image will not fall on the rod-free fovea, but on some other part of the retina that contains many highly sensitive rods.

In contrast to rods, each retina contains only about 6 million cones, which are densely packed in the fovea and much more sparsely distributed over the rest of the retina, as you can see in Figure 4.6. This distribution of cones directly affects visual acuity and explains why objects off to the side, in your *peripheral vision,* are not so clear. The light reflecting from those peripheral objects is less likely to land in the fovea, making the resulting image less clear. The more fine detail encoded and represented in the visual system, the clearer the perceived image. The process is analogous to the quality of photographs taken with a 6-megapixel digital camera versus a 2-megapixel camera. (See the photographs of money below.)

The retina is thick with cells. As seen in Figure 4.6, the photoreceptor cells (rods and cones) form the innermost layer. They are beneath a layer of transparent neurons, the bipolar and retinal ganglion cells. The *bipolar cells* collect neural signals from the rods and cones and transmit them to the outermost layer of the retina, where neurons called *retinal ganglion cells (RGCs)* organize the signals and send them to the brain.

The bundled RGC axons—about 1.5 million per eye—form the *optic nerve,* which leaves the eye through a hole in the retina. Because it contains neither rods nor cones and therefore has no mechanism to sense light, this hole in the retina creates a **blind spot,** *a location in the visual field that produces no sensation on the retina.* Try the demonstration in **FIGURE 4.7** (on the next page) to find the blind spot in each of your own eyes.

MIKE SONNENBERG/ISTOCKPHOTO

The full-colour image on the left is what you would see if your rods and cones are fully at work. The greyscale image on the right is what you would see if only your rods are functioning.

**cones**
Photoreceptors that detect colour, operate under normal daylight conditions, and allow us to focus on fine detail.

**rods**
Photoreceptors that become active under low-light conditions for night vision.

**fovea**
An area of the retina where vision is the clearest and there are no rods at all.

**blind spot**
A location in the visual field that produces no sensation on the retina.

FIRST FOLIO RESOURCE GROUP INC.

The image on the *left* was taken at a higher resolution than the image on the *right*. The difference in quality is analogous to light falling on the fovea versus the periphery of the retina.

▲ Figure **4.7** **Blind Spot Demonstration** To find your blind spot, close your left eye and stare at the cross with your right eye. Hold the book 15 to 30 cm away from your eyes and move it slowly toward and away from you until the dot disappears. The dot is now in your blind spot and not visible. At this point the vertical lines may appear as one continuous line because the visual system fills in the area occupied by the missing dot. To test your left eye's blind spot, turn the book upside down and repeat with your right eye closed.

## Perceiving Colour

Sir Isaac Newton pointed out around 1670 that colour is not something "in" light. In fact, colour is nothing but our perception of wavelengths from the spectrum of visible light (see Figure 4.3). We perceive the shortest visible wavelengths as deep purple. As wavelengths increase, the colour perceived changes gradually and continuously to blue, then green, yellow, orange, and, with the longest visible wavelengths, red. This rainbow of hues and accompanying wavelengths is called the *visible spectrum,* illustrated in **FIGURE 4.8**.

You will recall that all rods are ideal for low-light vision but bad for distinguishing colours. Cones, by contrast, come in three types; each type is especially sensitive to either red (long-wavelength), green (medium-wavelength), or blue (short-wavelength) light. Red, green, and blue are the primary colours of light; colour perception results from different combinations of the three basic elements in the retina that respond to the wavelengths corresponding to the three primary colours of light. For example, lighting designers add primary colours of light together, such as shining red and green spotlights on a surface to create a yellow light, as shown in **FIGURE 4.9**. Notice that in the centre of the figure, where the red, green, and blue lights overlap, the surface looks white. This demonstrates that a white surface really is reflecting all visible wavelengths of light.

The fact that three types of cones in the retina respond preferentially to different wavelengths (corresponding to blue, green, or red light) means that the pattern of responding across the three types of cones provides a unique code for each colour. In fact, researchers can "read out" the wavelength of the light entering the eye by working backward from the relative firing rates of the three types of cones (Gegenfurtner &

▶ Figure **4.8** **Seeing in Colour** We perceive a spectrum of colour because objects selectively absorb some wavelengths of light and reflect others. Colour perception corresponds to the relative activity of the three types of cones. Each type is most sensitive to a narrow range of wavelengths in the visible spectrum—short (bluish light), medium (greenish light), or long (reddish light). Rods, represented by the white curve, are most sensitive to the medium wavelengths of visible light but do not contribute to colour perception.

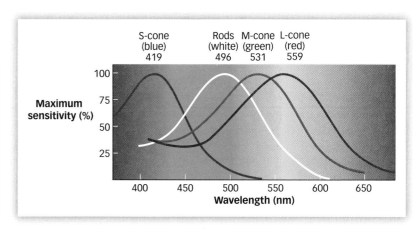

▶ Figure **4.9** **Colour Mixing** The millions of shades of colour that humans can perceive are products not only of a light's wavelength, but also of the mixture of wavelengths a stimulus absorbs or reflects. Coloured spotlights work by causing the surface to reflect light of a particular wavelength, which stimulates the red, blue, or green photopigments in the cones. When all visible wavelengths are present, we see white.

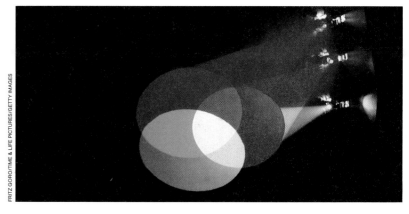

Kiper, 2003). A genetic disorder in which one of the cone types is missing—and, in some very rare cases, two or all three—causes a *colour deficiency.* This trait is sex-linked, affecting men much more often than women.

Colour deficiency is often referred to as *colour blindness,* but in fact, people missing only one type of cone can still distinguish many colours, just not as many as someone who has the full complement of three cone types. You can create a kind of temporary colour deficiency by exploiting the idea of sensory adaptation. Just like the rest of your body, cones need an occasional break too. Staring too long at one colour fatigues the cones that respond to that colour, producing a form of sensory adaptation that results in a *colour afterimage.* To demonstrate this effect for yourself, follow these instructions for **FIGURE 4.10:**

Many people (including about 8 to 10 percent of all males) inherit conditions in which either the "red" or the "green" photoreceptors do not transduce light properly. Such people have difficulty distinguishing hues that to typical individuals appear as red or green. Unfortunately, in Canada, traffic signals use red and green lights to indicate whether cars should stop or go through an intersection. Why do drivers with red–green colour blindness not risk auto accidents every time they approach an intersection?

> Stare at the yellow patch for about 1 minute. Try to keep your eyes as still as possible.

> After a minute, look to the right of the yellow patch. You should see a vivid colour aftereffect that lasts for a minute or more. Pay particular attention to the colour in the afterimage.

Were you puzzled that the yellowish patch produces a bluish afterimage? This result reveals something important about colour perception. The explanation stems from the **colour-opponent system,** where *pairs of visual neurons work in opposition:* blue-sensitive cells against yellow-sensitive (as in Figure 4.10) and red-sensitive cells against green-sensitive (Hurvich & Jameson, 1957). The colour-opponent system explains colour aftereffects. When you view a colour, let us say, green, the cones that respond most strongly to green become fatigued over time. Now, when you stare at a white or grey patch, which reflects all the colours equally, the green-sensitive cones respond only weakly compared with the still-fresh red-sensitive cones, which fire strongly. The result? You perceive the patch as tinted red or magenta.

**What happens when the cones in your eyes get fatigued?**

▲ Figure **4.10** **Colour Afterimage Demonstration** Follow the accompanying instructions in the text, and sensory adaptation will do the rest. When the afterimage fades, you can get back to reading the chapter.

## The Visual Brain

Streams of action potentials containing information encoded by the retina (neural impulses) travel to the brain along the optic nerve. Half of the axons in the optic nerve that leave each eye come from retinal ganglion cells (RGCs) that code information in the right visual field, whereas the other half code information in the left visual field. These two nerve bundles link to the left and right hemispheres of the brain, respectively (see FIGURE 4.11 on the next page). The optic nerve travels from each eye to the *lateral geniculate nucleus (LGN),* located in the thalamus. As you will recall from the Neuroscience and Behaviour chapter, the thalamus receives inputs from all of the senses except smell. From there, the visual signal travels to the back of the brain, to a location called **area V1,** the *part of the occipital lobe that contains the primary visual cortex.* Here the information is systematically mapped into a representation of the visual scene.

**What is the relationship between the right and left eyes, and the right and left visual fields?**

**colour-opponent system**
Pairs of visual neurons that work in opposition.

**area V1**
The part of the occipital lobe that contains the primary visual cortex.

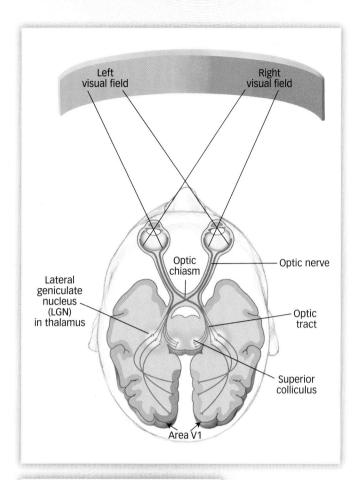

▲ Figure 4.11 **Visual Pathway from Eye through Brain** Objects in the right visual field stimulate the left half of each retina, and objects in the left visual field stimulate the right half of each retina. The optic nerves, one exiting each eye, are formed by the axons of retinal ganglion cells emerging from the retina. Just before they enter the brain at the optic chiasm, about half the nerve fibres from each eye cross. The left half of each optic nerve (representing the right visual field) runs through the brain's left hemisphere via the thalamus, and the right half of each optic nerve (representing the left visual field) travels this route through the right hemisphere. So, information from the right visual field ends up in the left hemisphere and information from the left visual field ends up in the right hemisphere.

**visual form agnosia**
The inability to recognize objects by sight.

## Neural Systems for Perceiving Shape

One of the most important functions of vision involves perceiving the shapes of objects; our day-to-day lives would be a mess if we could not distinguish individual shapes from one another. Imagine not being able to reliably differentiate between a warm doughnut with glazed icing and a straight stalk of celery and you will get the idea; breakfast could become a traumatic experience if you could not distinguish shapes. Perceiving shape depends on the location and orientation of an object's edges. It is not surprising, then, that area V1 is specialized for encoding edge orientation. As you also read in the Neuroscience and Behaviour chapter, neurons in the visual cortex selectively respond to bars and edges in specific orientations in space (Hubel & Wiesel, 1962, 1998). In effect, area V1 contains populations of neurons, each "tuned" to respond to edges oriented at each position in the visual field. This means that some neurons fire when an object in a vertical orientation is perceived, other neurons fire when an object in a horizontal orientation is perceived, still other neurons fire when objects in a diagonal orientation of 45° are perceived, and so on (see **FIGURE 4.12** on the next page). The outcome of the coordinated response of all these feature detectors contributes to a sophisticated visual system that can detect where a doughnut ends and celery begins.

## Pathways for What, Where, and How

Two functionally distinct pathways, or *visual streams,* project from the occipital cortex to visual areas in other parts of the brain (see **FIGURE 4.13** on the next page):

> The *ventral* (below) *stream* travels across the occipital lobe into the lower levels of the temporal lobes and includes brain areas that represent an object's shape and identity, in other words, what it is, essentially a "what" pathway (Kravtiz et al., 2013; Ungerleider & Mishkin, 1982).

> The *dorsal* (above) *stream* travels up from the occipital lobe to the parietal lobes (including some of the middle and upper levels of the temporal lobes), connecting with brain areas that identify the location and motion of an object, in other words, where it is (Kravtiz et al., 2011). Because the dorsal stream allows us to perceive spatial relations, researchers originally dubbed it the "where" pathway (Ungerleider & Mishkin, 1982). Neuroscientists from the University of Western Ontario later argued that because the dorsal stream is crucial for guiding movements, such as aiming, reaching, or tracking with the eyes, the "where" pathway should more appropriately be called the "how" pathway (Milner & Goodale, 1995).

What are the main jobs of the ventral and dorsal streams?

How do we know there are two pathways? The most dramatic evidence comes from studying the impairments that result from brain injuries to each of the areas.

For example, a woman known as D.F. suffered permanent damage to a large region of the lateral occipital cortex, an area in the ventral stream (Goodale et al., 1991). Her ability to recognize objects by sight was greatly impaired, although her ability to recognize objects by touch was normal. This suggests that her *visual representation* of objects, and not her *memory* for objects, was damaged. D.F.'s brain damage belongs to a category called **visual form agnosia,** *the inability to recognize*

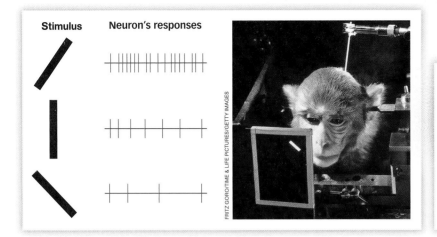

◄ Figure **4.12 Single-Neuron Feature Detectors** Area V1 contains neurons that respond to specific orientations of edges. Here a single neuron's responses are recorded (*below left*) as the monkey views bars at different orientations (*below right*). This neuron fires continuously when the bar is pointing to the right at 45°, less often when it is vertical, and not at all when it is pointing to the left at 45°.

◄ Figure **4.13 Visual Streaming** One interconnected visual system forms a pathway that courses from the occipital visual regions into the lower temporal lobe. This ventral pathway enables us to identify what we see. Another interconnected pathway travels from the occipital lobe through the upper regions of the temporal lobe into the parietal regions. This dorsal pathway allows us to locate objects, to track their movements, and to move in relation to them.

*objects by sight* (Goodale & Milner, 1992, 2004). Oddly, although D.F. could not recognize objects visually, she could accurately *guide* her actions by sight, as demonstrated in **FIGURE 4.14.** When D.F. was scanned with fMRI, researchers found that she showed normal activation of regions within the dorsal stream during guided movement (James et al., 2003).

Conversely, other people with brain damage to the parietal lobe, a section of the dorsal stream, have difficulty using vision to guide their reaching and grasping movements (Perenin & Vighetto, 1988). However, their ventral streams are intact, meaning they recognize what objects are.

We can conclude from these two patterns of impairment that the ventral and dorsal visual streams are functionally distinct; it is possible to damage one while leaving the other intact. Still, the two streams must work together during visual perception in order to integrate "what" and "where," and researchers are starting to examine how they interact. One intriguing possibility is suggested by recent fMRI research indicating that some regions within the dorsal stream are sensitive to properties of an object's identity, responding differently, for example, to line drawings of the same object in different sizes or viewed from different vantage points (Konen & Kastner, 2008; Sakuraba et al., 2012). This may be what allows the dorsal and ventral streams to exchange information and thus integrate the "what" and "where" (Farivar, 2009; Konen & Kastner, 2008).

▼ Figure **4.14 Testing Visual Form Agnosia** When researchers asked D.F. to orient her hand to match the angle of the slot in the testing apparatus, she was unable to comply (*left*). However, when asked to insert a card into the slot at various angles (*right*), D.F. accomplished the task virtually to perfection.

## IN SUMMARY

► Light passes through several layers in the eye to reach the retina. Two types of photoreceptor cells in the retina transduce light into neural impulses: cones, which operate under normal daylight conditions and sense colour; and rods, which are active under low-light conditions for night vision. The neural impulses are sent along the optic nerve to the brain.

► The retina contains several layers, and the outermost consists of retinal ganglion cells (RGCs) that collect and send signals to the brain. Bundles of RGCs form the optic nerve.

► Light striking the retina causes a specific pattern of response in each of three cone types that are critical to colour perception: short-wavelength (bluish) light, medium-wavelength (greenish) light, and long-wavelength (reddish) light. The overall pattern of response across the three cone types results in a unique code for each colour.

► Information encoded by the retina travels to the brain along the optic nerve, which connects to the lateral geniculate nucleus (LGN) in the thalamus and then to the primary visual cortex, area V1, in the occipital lobe.

► Two functionally distinct pathways project from the occipital lobe to visual areas in other parts of the brain. The ventral stream travels into the lower levels of the temporal lobes and includes brain areas that represent an object's shape and identity. The dorsal stream goes from the occipital lobes to the parietal lobes, connecting with brain areas that identify the location and motion of an object.

# Vision II: Recognizing What We Perceive

Our journey into the visual system has already revealed how it accomplishes some pretty astonishing feats. But the system needs to do much more in order for us to be able to interact effectively with our visual worlds. Let us now consider how the system links together individual visual features into whole objects, allows us to recognize what those objects are, organizes objects into visual scenes, and detects motion and change in those scenes. Along the way we will see that studying visual errors and illusions provides key insights into how these processes work.

## Attention: The "Glue" That Binds Individual Features into a Whole

Specialized feature detectors in different parts of the visual system analyze each of the multiple features of a visible object: orientation, colour, size, shape, and so forth. But how are different features combined into single, unified objects? What allows us to perceive so easily and correctly that the young man in the photograph is wearing a red shirt and the young woman is wearing a yellow shirt? How come we do not see free-floating patches of red and yellow, or even incorrect combinations, such as the young man wearing a yellow shirt and the young woman wearing a red shirt? These questions refer to what researchers call the **binding problem** in perception, *how features are linked together so that we see unified objects in our visual world rather than free-floating or miscombined features* (Treisman, 1998, 2006).

## Illusory Conjunctions: Perceptual Mistakes

In everyday life, we correctly combine features into unified objects so automatically and effortlessly that it may be difficult to appreciate that binding is ever a problem at all. However, researchers have discovered errors in binding that reveal important clues

**binding problem**
How features are linked together so that we see unified objects in our visual world rather than free-floating or miscombined features.

We correctly combine features into unified objects; so, for example, we see that the young man is wearing a red shirt and the young woman is wearing a yellow shirt.

FUSE/PUNCHSTOCK

about how the process works. One such error is known as an **illusory conjunction,** *a perceptual mistake where features from multiple objects are incorrectly combined.* In a pioneering study of illusory conjunctions, Anne Treisman and Hilary Schmidt (1982) briefly showed study participants visual displays in which black digits flanked coloured letters, then instructed them first to report the black digits and second to describe the coloured letters. Participants frequently reported illusory conjunctions, claiming to have seen, for example, a blue *A* or a red *X* instead of the red *A* and the blue *X* that had actually been shown (see **FIGURE 4.15a** and **b**). These illusory conjunctions were not just the result of guessing; they occurred more frequently than other kinds of errors, such as reporting a letter or colour that was not present in the display (see **FIGURE 4.15c**). Illusory conjunctions look real to the participants, who were just as confident they had seen them as they were about the actual coloured letters they perceived correctly.

> How does the study of illusory conjunctions help us understand the role of attention in feature binding?

Why do illusory conjunctions occur? Treisman and her colleagues have tried to explain them by proposing a **feature-integration theory** (Treisman, 1998, 2006; Treisman & Gelade, 1980; Treisman & Schmidt, 1982), which holds that *focused attention is not required to detect the individual features that comprise a stimulus,* such as the colour, shape, size, and location of letters, *but is required to bind those individual features together.* From this perspective, attention provides the "glue" necessary to bind features together, and illusory conjunctions occur when it is difficult for participants to pay full attention to the features that need to be glued together. For example, in the experiments we just considered, participants were required to process the digits that flank the coloured letters, thereby reducing attention to the letters and allowing illusory conjunctions to occur. When experimental conditions are changed so that participants can pay full attention to the coloured letters, and they are able to correctly bind their features together, illusory conjunctions disappear (Treisman, 1998; Treisman & Schmidt, 1982).

## The Role of the Parietal Lobe

The binding process makes use of feature information processed by structures within the ventral visual stream, the "what" pathway (Seymour et al., 2010) (see Figure 4.13). But because binding involves linking together features processed in distinct parts of the ventral stream at a particular spatial location, it also depends critically on the parietal lobe in the dorsal stream, the "where" pathway (Robertson, 1999). For example, Treisman and others studied R.M., who had suffered strokes that destroyed both his left and right parietal lobes. Although many aspects of his visual function were intact, he had severe problems attending to spatially distinct objects. When presented with stimuli such as those in Figure 4.15, R.M. perceived an abnormally large number of illusory conjunctions, even when he was given as long as 10 seconds to look at the displays (Friedman-Hill, Robertson, & Treisman, 1995; Robertson, 2003). More recent studies of persons with similar brain injuries suggest that damage to the upper and posterior portions of the parietal lobe is likely to produce similar problems (Braet & Humphreys, 2009; McCrea, Buxbaum, & Coslett, 2006). These same parietal regions are activated in healthy individuals when they perform the kind of visual feature binding that persons with parietal lobe damage are unable to perform (Shafritz, Gore, & Marois, 2002), as well as when they search for conjunction features (Corbetta et al., 1995; Donner et al., 2002).

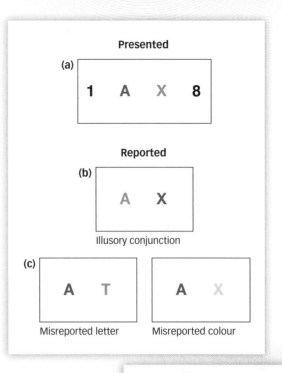

▲ Figure **4.15 Illusory Conjunctions** Illusory conjunctions occur when features such as colour and shape are combined incorrectly. For example, when participants are shown a red *A* and blue *X*, they sometimes report seeing a blue *A* and red *X*. Other kinds of errors, such as a misreported letter (e.g., reporting *T* when no *T* was presented) or misreported colour (reporting green when no green was presented) occur rarely, indicating that illusory conjunctions are not the result of guessing (based on Robertson, 2003).

**illusory conjunction**
A perceptual mistake where features from multiple objects are incorrectly combined.

**feature-integration theory**
The idea that focused attention is not required to detect the individual features that comprise a stimulus, but is required to bind those individual features together.

THE REAL WORLD

# Multitasking

By one estimate, using a cell phone while driving makes having an accident four times more likely (McEvoy et al., 2005). In response to highway safety experts and statistics such as this, provincial and territorial legislatures are passing laws that restrict, and sometimes ban, using mobile phones while driving. You might think that is a fine idea … for everyone else on the road. But surely *you* can manage to punch in a number on a phone, carry on a conversation, or maybe even text-message while simultaneously driving in a safe and courteous manner. Right? In a word, *wrong*.

The issue here is *selective attention*, or perceiving only what is currently relevant to you. Perception is an active, moment-to-moment exploration for relevant or interesting information, not a passive receptacle for whatever happens to come along. Talking on a cell phone while driving demands that you juggle two independent sources of sensory input—vision and audition—at the same time. This is problematic because research has found that when attention is directed to audition, activity in visual areas decreases (Shomstein & Yantis, 2004).

This kind of *multitasking* creates problems when you need to react suddenly while driving. Researchers have tested experienced drivers in a highly realistic driving simulator, measuring their response times to brake lights and stop signs while they listened to the radio or carried on phone conversations about a political issue, among other tasks (Strayer, Drews, & Johnston, 2003). These experienced drivers reacted significantly more slowly during phone conversations than during the other tasks. This is because a phone conversation requires memory retrieval, deliberation, and planning, and often carries an emotional stake in the conversation topic. Tasks such as listening to the radio require far less attention.

The tested drivers became so engaged in their conversations that their minds no longer seemed to be in the car. Their slower braking response translated into an increased stopping distance that, depending on the driver's speed, would have resulted in a rear-end collision. Whether the phone was handheld or hands-free made little difference, and similar results have been obtained in field studies of actual driving (Horrey & Wickens, 2006). This suggests that laws requiring drivers to use hands-free phones may have little effect on reducing accidents. Even after extensive practice at driving while using a hands-free cell phone in a simulator, the distruptive effects of cell phone use were still observed (Cooper & Strayer, 2008). The situation is even worse when text messaging is involved: Compared with a no-texting control condition, when either sending or receiving a text message in the simulator, drivers spent dramatically less time looking at the road, had a much harder time staying in their lane, missed numerous lane changes, and had greater difficulty maintaining an appropriate distance behind the car ahead of them (Hosking, Young, & Regan, 2009). A recent review concluded that the impairing effect of texting while driving is comparable to that of alcohol consumption and greater than that of smoking marijuana (Pascual-Ferrá, Liu, & Beatty, 2012).

Interestingly, people who report that they multitask frequently in everyday life have difficulty in laboratory tasks that require focusing attention in the face of distractions compared with individuals who do not multitask much in daily life (Ophir, Nass, & Wagner, 2009). So how well do we multitask in a couple of tonnes of metal hurtling down the highway? Not very much—you would do well to keep your eyes on the road and not on the phone.

SHOMSTEIN & YANTIS, 2004

Superior temporal lobe    Fusiform gyrus

(a)                        (b)

▲ **Shifting Attention** Participants received fMRI scans as they performed tasks that required them to shift their attention between visual and auditory information. (*a*) When focusing on auditory information, a region in the superior (upper) temporal lobe involved in auditory processing showed increased activity (yellow/orange). (*b*) In striking contrast, a visual region, the fusiform gyrus, showed decreased activity when participants focused on auditory information (blue).

## Recognizing Objects by Sight

Take a quick look at the letters in the illustration on the next page. Even though they are quite different from one another, you probably effortlessly recognized them as all being examples of the letter G. Now consider the same kind of demonstration using your best friend's face. Suppose one day your friend gets a dramatic new haircut—or adds glasses, hair dye, or a nose ring. Even though your friend now looks strikingly different, you still recognize that person with ease. Just like the variability in Gs, you somehow are able to extract the underlying features of the face that allow you to accurately identify your friend.

This thought exercise may seem trivial, but it is no small perceptual feat. If the visual system were somehow stumped each time a minor variation occurred in an object being perceived, the inefficiency of it all would be overwhelming. We would have to process information effortfully just to perceive our friend as the same person from one meeting to another, not to mention labouring through the process of knowing when a *G* is really a *G*. In general, though, object recognition proceeds fairly smoothly, in large part due to the operation of the feature detectors we discussed earlier.

How do feature detectors help the visual system get from a spatial array of light hitting the eye to the accurate perception of an object in different circumstances, such as your friend's face? Some researchers argue for a *modular view*, that specialized brain areas, or modules, detect and represent faces or houses or even body parts. Using fMRI to examine visual processing in healthy young adults, researchers found a subregion in the temporal lobe that responds most strongly to faces compared to just about any other object category, whereas a nearby area responds most strongly to buildings and landscapes (Kanwisher, McDermott, & Chun, 1997). This view suggests we not only have feature detectors to aid in visual perception but also "face detectors," "building detectors," and possibly other types of neurons specialized for particular types of object perception (Downing et al., 2006; Kanwisher & Yovel, 2006). Other researchers argue for a more *distributed representation* of object categories. In this view, it is the pattern of activity across multiple brain regions that identifies any viewed object, including faces (Haxby et al., 2001). Each of these views explains some data better than the other one, and researchers continue to debate their relative merits.

Another perspective on this issue is provided by experiments designed to measure precisely where seizures originate; these experiments have also provided insights on how single neurons in the human brain respond to objects and faces (Suthana & Fried, 2012). For example, in a study by Quiroga and his colleagues (2005), electrodes were placed in the temporal lobes of people who suffer from epilepsy. Then the volunteers were shown photographs of faces and objects as the researchers recorded their neural responses. The researchers found that neurons in the temporal lobe respond to specific objects viewed from multiple angles and to people wearing different clothing and facial expressions and photographed from various angles. In some cases, the neurons also respond to the words for these same objects. For example, neurons that responded to photographs of the Sydney Opera House also responded when the words *Sydney Opera* were displayed, but not when the words *Eiffel Tower* were displayed.

Taken together, these experiments demonstrate the principle of **perceptual constancy:** *Even as aspects of sensory signals change, perception remains consistent.* Recall our discussion of difference thresholds early in this chapter. Our perceptual systems are sensitive to relative differences in changing stimulation and make allowances for varying sensory input. This general principle helps explain why you still recognize your friend despite changes in hair colour or style or the addition of facial jewellery. It is not as though your visual perceptual system

**How do we recognize our friends, even when they are hidden behind sunglasses?**

**perceptual constancy**
A perceptual principle stating that even as aspects of sensory signals change, perception remains consistent.

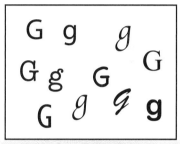

A quick glance and you recognize all these letters as *G*, but their varying sizes, shapes, angles, and orientations ought to make this recognition task difficult. What is it about the process of object recognition that allows us to perform this task effortlessly?

Our visual systems allow us to identify people as the same individual even when they change such features as hair style and skin colour. Despite the extreme changes in these two photographs, you can probably tell that they both show Johnny Depp.

responds to a change with, "Here's a new and unfamiliar face to perceive." Rather, it is as though it responds with, "Interesting … here's a deviation from the way this face usually looks." Perception is sensitive to changes in stimuli, but perceptual constancies allow us to notice the differences in the first place.

## Principles of Perceptual Organization

Before object recognition can even kick in, the visual system must perform another important task: grouping the image regions that belong together into a representation of an object. The idea that we tend to perceive a unified, whole object rather than a collection of separate parts is the foundation of Gestalt psychology, which you read about in the Psychology: Evolution of a Science chapter. Gestalt principles characterize many aspects of human perception. Among the foremost are the Gestalt *perceptual grouping rules,* which govern how the features and regions of things fit together (Koffka, 1935). Here's a sampling (see **FIGURE 4.16** on the next page):

> *Simplicity*: A basic rule in science is that the simplest explanation is usually the best so, when confronted with two or more possible interpretations of an object's shape, the visual system tends to select the simplest or most likely interpretation. In **FIGURE 4.16a** we see an arrow.

> *Closure*: We tend to fill in missing elements of a visual scene, allowing us to perceive edges that are separated by gaps as belonging to complete objects. In **FIGURE 4.16b** we see an arrow despite the gaps.

> *Continuity*: Edges or contours that have the same orientation have what the Gestalt psychologists called *good continuation*, and we tend to group them together perceptually. In **FIGURE 4.16c** we perceive two crossing lines instead of two V shapes.

> *Similarity*: Regions that are similar in colour, lightness, shape, or texture are perceived as belonging to the same object. In **FIGURE 4.16d** we perceive three columns—a column of circles flanked by two columns of triangles.

> *Proximity*: Objects that are close together tend to be grouped together. In **FIGURE 4.16e** we perceive three groups or "clumps" of 5 or 6 dots each, not just 16 dots.

> *Common fate*: Elements of a visual image that move together are perceived as parts of a single moving object. In **FIGURE 4.16f** the series of flashing lights in the road sign are perceived as a moving arrowhead.

## Separating Figure from Ground

Perceptual grouping is a powerful aid to our ability to recognize objects by sight. Grouping involves visually separating an object from its surroundings. In Gestalt terms, this means identifying a *figure* apart from the (back)*ground* in which it resides. For example, the words on this page are perceived as figural: They stand out from the ground of the sheet of paper on which they are printed. Similarly, your instructor is perceived as the figure against the backdrop of all the other elements in your classroom. You certainly can perceive these elements differently, of course: The words *and* the paper are all part of a thing called *a page*, and your instructor *and* the classroom can all be perceived as *your learning environment*. Typically, though, our perceptual systems focus attention on some objects as distinct from their environments.

Size provides one clue to what is figure and what is ground: Smaller regions are likely to be figures, such as tiny letters on a big sheet of paper. Movement also helps: Your instructor is (we hope) a dynamic lecturer, moving around in a static environment. Another critical step toward object recognition is *edge assignment*. Given an edge, or boundary, between figure and ground, which region does that edge belong

**template**
A mental representation that can be directly compared to a viewed shape in the retinal image.

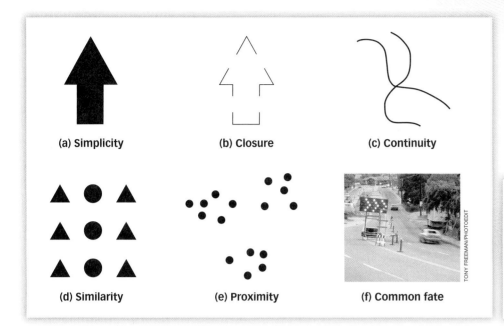

(a) Simplicity  (b) Closure  (c) Continuity

(d) Similarity  (e) Proximity  (f) Common fate

TONY FREEMAN/PHOTOEDIT

◄ Figure **4.16** **Perceptual Grouping Rules** Principles first identified by Gestalt psychologists and now supported by experimental evidence demonstrate that the brain is predisposed to impose order on incoming sensations. One neural strategy for perception involves responding to patterns among stimuli and grouping like patterns together.

to? If the edge belongs to the figure, it helps define the object's shape, and the background continues behind the edge. Sometimes, though, it is not easy to tell which is which.

Edgar Rubin (1886–1951), a Danish psychologist, capitalized on this ambiguity and developed a famous illusion called the *Rubin vase* or, more generally, a *reversible figure–ground relationship*. You can view this "face–vase" illusion in **FIGURE 4.17** in two ways, either as a vase on a black background or as a pair of silhouettes facing each other. Your visual system settles on one or the other interpretation and fluctuates between them every few seconds. This happens because the edge that would normally separate figure from ground is really part of neither: It equally defines the contours of the vase as it does the contours of the faces. Evidence from fMRIs shows, quite nicely, that when people are seeing the Rubin image as faces, there is greater activity in the face-selective region of the temporal lobe we discussed earlier than when they are seeing it as a vase (Hasson et al., 2001).

## Theories of Object Recognition

Researchers have proposed two broad explanations of object recognition, one based on the object as a whole and the other on its parts.

▲ Figure **4.17** **Ambiguous Edges** This is how Rubin's classic reversible figure–ground illusion works: Fixate your eyes on the centre of the image and your perception will alternate between a vase and facing silhouettes, even as the sensory stimulation remains constant.

> According to *image-based object recognition* theories, an object you have seen before is stored in memory as a **template,** *a mental representation that can be*

**What is an important difference between template and parts-based theory of object recognition?**

*directly compared to a viewed shape in the retinal image* (Tarr & Vuong, 2002). Your memory compares its templates to the current retinal image and selects the template that most closely matches the current image (recall the different forms

of the letter G on p. 147). Image-based theories are widely accepted, yet they do not explain everything about object recognition. For one thing, correctly matching images to templates suggests that you would have to have one template for cups in a normal orientation, another template for cups on their side, another for cups upside down, and so on. This makes for an unwieldy and inefficient system and therefore one that is unlikely to be effective, yet seeing a cup on its side rarely perplexes anyone for long.

**(a) Geons**

1    2

3    4    5

**(b) Objects**

▲ Figure **4.18** **An Alphabet of Geometric Elements** Parts-based theory holds that objects such as those shown in (b) are made up of simpler 3-D components called *geons*, shown in (a), much as letters combine to form different words.

**monocular depth cues**
Aspects of a scene that yield information about depth when viewed with only one eye.

> *Parts-based object recognition* theories propose instead that the brain deconstructs viewed objects into a collection of parts (Marr & Nishihara, 1978). One important parts-based theory contends that objects are stored in memory as structural descriptions: mental inventories of object parts along with the spatial relations among those parts (Biederman, 1987). The parts inventories act as a sort of "alphabet" of geometric elements called *geons* that can be combined to make objects, just as letters are combined to form words (see **FIGURE 4.18**). Parts-based object recognition does not require a template for every view of every object, and so avoids some of the pitfalls of image-based theories. But parts-based object recognition does have major limitations. Most importantly, it allows for object recognition only at the level of categories and not at the level of the individual object. Parts-based theories offer an explanation for recognizing an object such as a face, for example, but are less effective at explaining how you distinguish between your best friend's face and a stranger's face.

Each set of theories has strengths and weaknesses, making object recognition an active area of study in psychology. Researchers are developing hybrid theories that attempt to exploit the strengths of each approach (Peissig & Tarr, 2007).

## Perceiving Depth and Size

Objects in the world are arranged in three dimensions—length, width, and depth—but the retinal image contains only two dimensions, length and width. How does the brain process a flat, 2-D retinal image so that we perceive the depth of an object and how far away it is? The answer lies in a collection of *depth cues* that change as you move through space. Monocular and binocular depth cues all help visual perception (Howard, 2002).

### Monocular Depth Cues

**Monocular depth cues** are *aspects of a scene that yield information about depth when viewed with only one eye.* These cues rely on the relationship between distance and size. Even with one eye closed, the retinal image of an object you are focused on grows smaller as that object moves farther away, and larger as it moves closer. Our brains routinely use these differences in retinal image size, or *relative size,* to perceive distance.

This works particularly well in a monocular depth cue called *familiar size.* Most adults, for example, fall within a familiar range of heights (perhaps 1.5–2.1 m tall), so retinal image size alone is usually a reliable cue to how far away they are. Our visual system automatically corrects for size differences and attributes them to differences in distance. **FIGURE 4.19** (on the next page) demonstrates how strong this mental correction for familiar size is.

In addition to relative size and familiar size, there are several more monocular depth cues, such as those shown in Figure 4.20 on the next page.

> *Linear perspective,* which describes the phenomenon that parallel lines seem to converge as they recede into the distance (see **FIGURE 4.20a**).

> *Texture gradient,* which arises when you view a more or less uniformly patterned surface because the size of the pattern elements, as well as the distance between them, grows smaller as the surface recedes from the observer (see **FIGURE 4.20b**).

> *Interposition,* which occurs when one object partly blocks another (see **FIGURE 4.20c**). You can infer that the blocking object is closer than the blocked

THE PHOTO WORKS

◀ Figure **4.19** **Familiar Size and Relative Size** When you view images of people, such as the people in the left-hand photograph, or of things you know well, the object you perceive as smaller appears farther away. With a little image manipulation, you can see in the right-hand photograph that the relative size difference projected on your retinas is far greater than you perceive. The image of the person in the blue vest is exactly the same size in both photographs.

object. However, interposition by itself cannot provide information about how far apart the two objects are.

> *Relative height* in the image depends on your field of vision (see **FIGURE 4.20d**). Objects that are closer to you are lower in your visual field, whereas faraway objects are higher.

## Binocular Depth Cues

We can also obtain depth information through **binocular disparity,** *the difference in the retinal images of the two eyes that provides information about depth.* Because our eyes are slightly separated, each registers a slightly different view of the world.

SUPERSTOCK

**(a) Linear perspective**

AGE FOTOSTOCK/SUPERSTOCK

**(b) Texture gradient**

ALTRENDO IMAGES/GETTY IMAGES

**(c) Interposition**

ROB BLAKERS/LONELY PLANET/GETTY IMAGES

**(d) Relative height**

◀ Figure **4.20** **Pictorial Depth Cues** Visual artists rely on a variety of monocular cues to make their work come to life. You can rely on cues such as linear perspective (*a*), texture gradient (*b*), interposition (*c*), and relative height (*d*) in an image to infer distance, depth, and position, even if you are wearing an eye patch.

► Figure **4.21** **Binocular Disparity** We see the world in three dimensions because our eyes are a distance apart and the image of an object falls on the retinas of each eye at a slightly different place. In this two-object scene, the images of the square and the circle fall on different points of the retina in each eye. The disparity in the positions of the circle's retinal images provides a compelling cue to depth.

Your brain computes the disparity between the two retinal images to perceive how far away objects are, as shown in **FIGURE 4.21**. Viewed from above in the figure, the images of the more distant square and the closer circle each fall at different points on each retina.

Binocular disparity as a cue to depth perception was first discussed by Sir Charles Wheatstone in 1838. Wheatstone went on to invent the stereoscope, essentially a holder for a pair of photographs or drawings taken from two horizontally displaced locations. (Wheatstone did not lack for original ideas; he also invented the accordion and an early telegraph and coined the term *microphone*.) When viewed, one by each eye, the pairs of images evoked a vivid sense of depth. The View-Master toy is the modern successor to Wheatstone's invention, and 3-D movies are based on this same idea.

The View-Master (*left*) has been a popular toy for decades. It is based on the principle of binocular disparity: Two images taken from slightly different angles (*right*) produce a stereoscopic effect.

## Illusions of Depth and Size

We all are vulnerable to *illusions,* which, as you will remember from the Psychology: Evolution of a Science chapter, are errors of perception, memory, or judgment in which subjective experience differs from objective reality (Wade, 2005). The relation between size and distance has been used to create elaborate illusions that depend on fooling the visual system about how far away objects are. All these illusions depend on the same principle: When you view two objects that project the same retinal image size, the object you perceive as farther away will be perceived as larger. One of the most famous illusions is the *Ames room,* constructed by the American ophthalmologist Adelbert Ames in 1946. The room is trapezoidal in shape rather than square: Only two sides are parallel (see **FIGURE 4.22a** on the next page). A person standing in one corner of an Ames room is physically twice as far away from the viewer as a person standing in the other corner. But when viewed with one eye through the small peephole placed in one wall, the Ames room looks square because the shapes of the windows and the flooring tiles are carefully crafted to *look* square from the viewing port (Ittelson, 1952).

The visual system perceives the far wall as perpendicular to the line of sight so that people standing at different positions along that wall appear to be at the same distance, and the viewer's judgments of their sizes are based directly on retinal image size. As a result, a person standing in the right corner appears to be much larger than a person standing in the left corner (see **FIGURE 4.22b**).

**binocular disparity**
The difference in the retinal images of the two eyes that provides information about depth.

(a)

(b)

(B) PHIL SCHERMEISTER/CORBIS

▲ Figure **4.22** **The Amazing Ames Room**
(*a*) A diagram showing the actual proportions of the Ames room reveals its secrets. The sides of the room form a trapezoid with parallel sides but a back wall that is way off square. The uneven floor makes the room's height in the far back corner shorter than the other. Add misleading cues such as specially designed windows and flooring, position the room's occupants in each far corner and you are ready to lure an unsuspecting observer. (*b*) Looking into the Ames room through the viewing port with only one eye, the observer infers a normal size–distance relationship— that both people are the same distance away. But the different image sizes they project on the retina leads the viewer to conclude, based on the monocular cue of familiar size, that one person is very small and the other is very large.

## Perceiving Motion and Change

You should now have a good sense of how we see what and where objects are, a process made substantially easier when the objects stay in one place. But real life, of course, is full of moving targets. Objects change position over time: Birds fly and horses gallop; rain and snow fall; and trees bend in the wind. Understanding how we perceive motion and why we sometimes fail to perceive change can bring us closer to appreciating how visual perception works in everyday life.

### Motion Perception

To sense motion, the visual system must encode information about both space and time. The simplest case to consider is an observer who does not move trying to perceive an object that does.

As an object moves across an observer's stationary visual field, it first stimulates one location on the retina, and then a little later it stimulates another location on the retina. Neural circuits in the brain can detect this change in position over time and respond to specific speeds and directions of motion (Emerson, Bergen, & Adelson, 1992). A region in the middle of the temporal lobe referred to as *MT* (part of the dorsal stream we discussed earlier) is specialized for the visual perception of motion (Born & Bradley, 2005; Newsome & Paré, 1988), and brain damage in this area leads to a deficit in normal motion perception (Zihl, von Cramon, & Mai, 1983).

Of course, in the real world, rarely are you a stationary observer. As you move around, your head and eyes move all the time, and motion perception is not as simple. The motion-perception system must take into account the position and movement of your eyes, and ultimately of your head and body, in order to perceive the motions of objects correctly and allow you to approach or avoid them. The brain accomplishes this by monitoring your eye and head movements and "subtracting" them from the motion in the retinal image.

Motion perception, like colour perception, operates in part on opponent processes and is subject to sensory adaptation. A motion aftereffect called the *waterfall illusion* is analogous to colour aftereffects. If you stare at the downward rush of a waterfall for several seconds, you will experience an upward motion aftereffect when you then look at stationary objects near the waterfall such as trees or rocks. What is going on here?

The process is similar to seeing green after staring at a patch of red. Motion-sensitive neurons are connected to motion detector cells in the brain that encode

Colour perception and motion perception both rely partially on opponent processing, which is why we fall prey to illusions such as colour aftereffects and the waterfall illusion.

motion in opposite directions. A sense of motion comes from the difference in the strength of these two opposing sensors. If one set of motion detector cells is fatigued through adaptation to motion in one direction, then the opposing sensor will take over. The net result is that motion is perceived in the opposite direction. Evidence from fMRIs indicates that when people experience the waterfall illusion while viewing a stationary stimulus, there is increased activity in region MT, which plays a key role in motion perception (Tootell et al., 1995).

The movement of objects in the world is not the only event that can evoke the perception of motion. The successively flashing lights of a traffic diversion sign can evoke a strong sense of motion because people perceive a series of flashing lights as a whole, moving object (see Figure 4.16*f*). This *perception of movement as a result of alternating signals appearing in rapid succession in different locations* is called **apparent motion.**

> **How can flashing lights on a traffic sign give the impression of movement?**

Video technology and animation depend on apparent motion. Motion pictures flash 24 still frames per second (fps). A slower rate would produce a much choppier sense of motion; a faster rate would be a waste of resources because we would not perceive the motion as any smoother than it appears at 24 fps.

## Change Blindness and Inattentional Blindness

Motion involves a change in an object's position over time, but objects in the visual environment can change in ways that do not involve motion (Rensink, 2002). You might walk by the same clothing store window every day and notice when a new suit or dress is on display or register surprise when you see a friend's new haircut. Intuitively, we feel that we can easily detect changes to our visual environment. However, our comfortable intuitions have been challenged by experimental demonstrations of **change blindness,** which occurs *when people fail to detect changes to the visual details of a scene* (Rensink, 2002; Simons & Rensink, 2005). Strikingly, change blindness occurs even when major details of a scene are changed—changes that we incorrectly believe that we could not miss (Beek, Levin, & Angelone, 2007). For example, participants in one study were shown a movie in which a young blond man sits at a desk, gets up and walks away from the desk, and exits from the room (Levin and Simons, 1997). The scene then shifted outside the room, where the young man made a phone call. This all sounds straightforward, but unknown to the participants, the man sitting at the desk was not the same person as the man who made the phone call. Although both are young, blond, and wearing glasses, they were clearly different people. Still, two-thirds of the participants failed to notice the change.

It is one thing to create change blindness by splicing a film, but does change blindness also occur in live interactions? Another study tested this idea by having an experimenter ask a person on a university campus for directions (Simons & Levin, 1998). While they were talking, two men walked between them holding a door that hid a second experimenter (see **FIGURE 4.23** on the next page). Behind the door, the two experimenters traded places, so that when the men carrying the door moved on, a different person was asking for directions than the one who had been there just a second or two earlier. Remarkably, only 7 of 15 participants reported noticing this change.

**apparent motion**
The perception of movement as a result of alternating signals appearing in rapid succession in different locations.

**change blindness**
When people fail to detect changes to the visual details of a scene.

**inattentional blindness**
A failure to perceive objects that are not the focus of attention.

(a)    (b)    (c)

Although it is surprising that people can be blind to such dramatic changes, these findings once again illustrate the importance of focused attention for visual perception (see the discussion of feature-integration theory, p. 145). Just as focused attention is critical for binding together the features of objects, it is also necessary for detecting changes to objects and scenes (Rensink, 2002; Simons & Rensink, 2005). Change blindness is most likely to occur when people fail to focus attention on the changed object (even though the object is registered by the visual system) and is least likely to occur for items that draw attention to themselves (Rensink, O'Regan, & Clark, 1997).

> How can a failure of focused attention explain change blindness?

The role of focused attention in conscious visual experience is also dramatically illustrated by the closely related phenomenon of **inattentional blindness,** *a failure to perceive objects that are not the focus of attention.* Imagine the following scenario. You are watching a circle of people passing around a basketball, somebody dressed in a gorilla costume walks through the circle, and the gorilla stops to beat his chest before moving on. It seems inconceivable that you would fail to notice the gorilla, right? Think again. Simons and Chabris (1999) filmed such a scene, using two teams of three players each who passed the ball to one another as the costumed gorilla made his entrance and exit. Participants watched the film and were asked to track the movement of the ball by counting the number of passes made by one of the teams. With their attention focused on the moving ball, approximately half the participants failed to notice the chest-beating gorilla.

This has interesting implications for a world in which many of us are busy texting and talking on our cell phones while carrying on other kinds of everyday business. We have already seen that using cell phones has negative effects on driving (see The Real World: Multitasking). Ira Hyman and colleagues (2010) asked whether cell phone use contributes to inattentional blindness in everyday life. They recruited a clown to ride a unicycle around a large square in the middle of Western Washington University campus. On a pleasant afternoon, the researchers asked 151 students who had just walked through the square whether they saw the clown. Seventy-five percent of the students who were using cell phones failed to notice the clown, compared with less than 50 percent who were not using cell phones. Using cell phones draws on focused attention, resulting in increased inattentional blindness and emphasizing again that our conscious experience of the visual environment is restricted to those features or objects selected by focused attention.

▲ Figure **4.23** **Change Blindness** The white-haired man was giving directions to one experimenter (*a*), who disappeared behind the moving door (*b*), only to be replaced by another experimenter (*c*). Like many other people, the man failed to detect a seemingly obvious change.

Simons, D. J., & Levin, D. T. (1998). Failure to detect changes to people during a real-world interaction. *Psychonomic Bulletin & Review, 5*(4), 644–649. Figure provided by Daniel Simons.

University students who were using their cell phones while walking through campus failed to notice the unicycling clown more frequently than students who were not using their cell phones.

HYMAN ET AL., 2009

## OTHER VOICES

# Hallucinations and the Visual System

We rely on our perceptual systems to provide reliable information about the world around us. Yet we have already seen that perception is prone to various kinds of illusions. Even more striking, our perceptual systems are capable of creating hallucinations: perceptions of sights, sounds, or other sensory experiences that do not exist in the world outside us. As discussed by the perceptual psychologist V. S. Ramachandran in an interview with the *New York Times,* reported in an article written by Susan Kruglinski, vivid visual hallucinations can even occur in low vision or even blind individuals with severe damage to their retinas.

One day a few years ago, Doris Stowens saw the monsters from Maurice Sendak's "Where the Wild Things Are" stomping into her bedroom. Then the creatures morphed into traditional Thai dancers with long brass fingernails, whose furious dance took them from the floor to the walls to the ceiling.

Although shocked to witness such a spectacle, Ms. Stowens, 85, was aware that she was having hallucinations, and she was certain that they had something to do with the fact that she suffered from the eye disease macular degeneration.

"I knew instantly that something was going on between my brain and my eyes," she said.

Ms. Stowens says that ever since she developed partial vision loss, she has been seeing pink walls and early American quilts floating through the blind spots in her eyes several times each week.

In fact, Ms. Stowens's hallucinations are a result of Charles Bonnet syndrome, a strange but relatively common disorder found in people who have vision problems. Because the overwhelming majority of people with vision problems are more than 70 years old, the syndrome, named after its eighteenth-century Swiss discoverer, is mostly found among the elderly. And because older people are more susceptible to cognitive deterioration, which can include hallucinations or delusions, Charles Bonnet (pronounced bon-NAY) is easily misdiagnosed as mental illness. Many patients who have it never consult a doctor, out of fear that they will be labelled mentally ill.

"It is not a rare disorder," said Dr. V. S. Ramachandran, a neurologist at the University of California at San Diego, who has written about the syndrome. "It's quite common. It's just that people don't want to talk about it when they have it."

Researchers estimate that 10 to 15 percent of people whose eyesight is worse than 20/60 develop the disorder. Any eye disease that causes blind spots or low vision can be the source, including cataracts, glaucoma, diabetic retinopathy and, most commonly, macular degeneration. The hallucinations can vary from simple patches of color or patterns to lifelike images of people or landscapes to phantasms straight out of dreams. The hallucinations are usually brief and nonthreatening, and people who have the syndrome usually understand that what they are seeing is not real....

In some ways, researchers say, the hallucinations that define the syndrome are similar to the phenomenon of phantom limbs, where patients still vividly feel limbs that have been amputated, or phantom hearing, where a person hears music or other sounds while going deaf. In all three cases, the perceptions are caused by a loss of the sensory information that normally flows unceasingly into the brain.

In the case of sight, the primary visual cortex is responsible for taking in information, and also for forming remembered or imagined images. This dual function, Dr. Ramachandran and other experts say, suggests that normal vision is in fact a fusion of incoming sensory information with internally generated sensory input, the brain filling in the visual field with what it is used to seeing or expects to see. If you expect the person sitting next to you to be wearing a blue shirt, for example, you might, in a quick sideways glance, mistakenly perceive a red shirt as blue. A more direct gaze allows for more external information to correct the misperception.

"In a sense, we are all hallucinating all the time," Dr. Ramachandran said. "What we call normal vision is our selecting the hallucination that best fits reality."

With extensive vision loss, less external information is available to adjust and guide the brain's tendency to fill in sensory gaps. The results may be Thai dancers or monsters from a children's book....

Charles Bonnet syndrome was first described over 250 years ago by Bonnet, a Swiss scientist whose own blind grandfather experienced hallucinations like those reported by Ms. Stowens. However, neurologists and others have only recently begun to study the syndrome. Can you make some sense of this syndrome based on what you have learned about the visual system? How can someone who sees poorly or cannot see at all have intense visual experiences? What brain processes could be responsible for these kinds of visual hallucinations? Some clues come from neuroimaging studies of people who experience visual hallucinations, which have shown that specific types of hallucinations are accompanied by activity in parts of the brain responsible for the particular content of the hallucinations (Allen et al., 2008). For example, facial hallucinations are accompanied by activity in a part of the temporal lobe known to be involved in face processing. Our understanding of the visual system beyond the retina can provide some insight into how and why blind individuals experience visual hallucinations.

# CULTURE & COMMUNITY

## Does Culture Influence Change Blindness?

The experiments discussed in this section of the chapter show that change blindness is dramatic and occurs across a range of situations. But the evidence for change blindness that we have considered comes from studies using participants from Western cultures, mainly Americans. Would change blindness occur in individuals from other cultures? If so, is there any reason to suspect that it would work differently across cultures? Think back to the Culture & Community box from the Psychology: Evolution of a Science chapter, where we discussed evidence showing that people from Western cultures rely on an *analytic* style of processing information (i.e., they tend to focus on an object without paying much attention to the surrounding context), whereas people from Eastern cultures tend to adopt a *holistic* style (i.e., they tend to focus on the relationship between an object and the surrounding context) (Kitayama et al., 2003; Nisbett & Miyamoto, 2005).

With this distinction in mind, Masuda and Nisbett (2006) noted that previous studies of change blindness, using mainly American participants, had shown that participants are more likely to detect changes in the main or focal object in a scene, and less likely to detect changes in surrounding context. They hypothesized that individuals from an Eastern culture would be more focused on, and therefore likely to notice, changes in surrounding context than individuals from a Western culture. To test their prediction, they conducted three experiments examining change detection in American (University of Michigan) and Japanese (Kyoto University) university students using still photographs and brief movie-type vignettes (Masuda & Nisbett, 2006). In each experiment, they made changes either to the main or focal object in a scene, or to the surrounding context (e.g., objects in the background of a scene).

The results of the experiments were consistent with predictions: Japanese students detected more changes to contextual information than did American students, whereas American students detected more changes to focal objects than did Japanese students. These findings extend earlier reports that people from Eastern and Western cultures see the world differently, with Easterners focusing more on the context in which an object appears and Westerners focusing more on the object itself.

## IN SUMMARY

▶ Illusory conjunctions occur when features from separate objects are mistakenly combined. According to feature-integration theory, attention provides the glue necessary to bind features together. The parietal lobe is important for attention and contributes to feature binding.

▶ Some regions in the occipital and temporal lobes respond selectively to specific object categories, supporting the modular view that specialized brain areas represent particular classes of objects such as faces, houses, or body parts.

▶ The principle of perceptual constancy holds that even as sensory signals change, perception remains consistent. Gestalt principles of perceptual grouping, such as simplicity, closure, and continuity, govern how the features and regions of things fit together.

▶ Image-based and parts-based theories each explain some, but not all, features of object recognition.

▶ Depth perception depends on: monocular cues, such as familiar size and linear perspective; binocular cues, such as retinal disparity; and motion-based cues, which are based on the movement of the head over time.

▶ We experience a sense of motion through the differences in the strengths of output from motion-sensitive neurons. These processes can give rise to illusions such as apparent motion.

▶ Change blindness and inattentional blindness occur when we fail to notice visible and even salient features of our environment, emphasizing that our conscious visual experience depends on focused attention.

**pitch**
How high or low or somewhere in between, a sound is.

**loudness**
A sound's intensity.

**timbre**
A listener's experience of sound quality or resonance.

# Audition: More Than Meets the Ear

Vision is based on the spatial pattern of light hitting the retina. The sense of hearing, by contrast, is all about *sound waves*: changes in air pressure unfolding over time. Plenty of things produce sound waves: the collision of a tree hitting the forest floor, the impact of two hands clapping, the vibration of vocal cords during a stirring speech, the resonance of a bass guitar string during a thrash metal concert. Understanding auditory experience requires understanding how we transform changes in air pressure into perceived sounds.

## Sensing Sound

Striking a tuning fork produces a *pure tone,* a simple sound wave that first increases air pressure and then creates a relative vacuum. This cycle repeats hundreds or thousands of times per second as sound waves travel outward in all directions from the source. Just as there are three dimensions of light waves corresponding to three dimensions of visual perception, so, too, there are three physical dimensions of a sound wave. Frequency, amplitude, and complexity determine what we hear as the pitch, loudness, and quality of a sound (see **TABLE 4.4** on the next page).

> The *frequency* of the sound wave, or its wavelength, depends on how often the peak in air pressure passes the ear or a microphone, measured in cycles per second, or hertz (Hz). Changes in the physical frequency of a sound wave are perceived by humans as changes in **pitch,** which is *how high* (like a tinkling bell) *or low* (like the sound of a double bass) *or somewhere in between, a sound is.*

> The *amplitude* of a sound wave refers to its height, relative to the threshold for human hearing (which is set at zero decibels, or dBs). Amplitude corresponds to **loudness,** or *a sound's intensity.* To give you an idea of amplitude and intensity, the rustling of leaves in a soft breeze is about 20 dB, normal conversation is measured at about 40 dB, shouting produces 70 dB, a Nickelback concert is about 130 dB, and the sound of the space shuttle taking off 1.6 km away registers at 160 dB or more. That is loud enough to cause permanent damage to the auditory system and is well above the pain threshold; in fact, any sounds above 85 dB can be enough to cause hearing damage, depending on the length and type of exposure.

> Differences in the *complexity* of sound waves, or their mix of frequencies, correspond to **timbre,** *a listener's experience of sound quality or resonance.* Timbre (pronounced "TAM-ber") offers us information about the nature of sound. The same note played at the same loudness produces a perceptually different experience depending on whether it was played on a flute versus a trumpet, a phenomenon due entirely to timbre. Many natural sounds also illustrate the complexity of wavelengths, such as the sound of bees buzzing, the tonalities of speech, or the babbling of a brook. Unlike the purity of a tuning fork's hum, the drone of cicadas is a clamor of many different sound frequencies.

> **Why does one note sound so different on a flute and a trumpet?**

Most sounds—such as voices, music, trees rustling in the wind, the screech of brakes, the purring of a cat—are composed of not one, but many different frequency components. Although you perceive the mixture (the cat's purr, for example, not the

▶ Table 4.4

**Properties of Sound Waves**

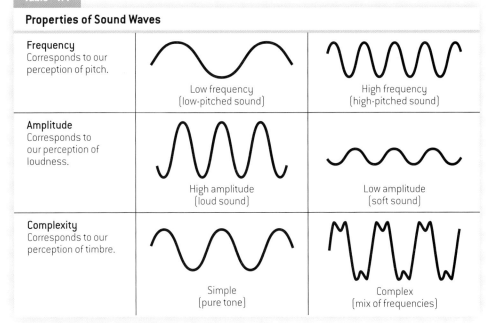

| Frequency<br>Corresponds to our<br>perception of pitch. | Low frequency<br>(low-pitched sound) | High frequency<br>(high-pitched sound) |
|---|---|---|
| Amplitude<br>Corresponds to<br>our perception of<br>loudness. | High amplitude<br>(loud sound) | Low amplitude<br>(soft sound) |
| Complexity<br>Corresponds to our<br>perception of timbre. | Simple<br>(pure tone) | Complex<br>(mix of frequencies) |

206 Hz component in the purr), the first thing the ear does to a sound is to analyze it—break it down into its separate component frequencies. The psychological attributes of pitch, loudness, and timbre are then "built up" by the brain from the separate frequency components that are represented in the inner ear, just like visual perceptions are "built up" from the spatial pattern of activity on the retina. The focus in our discussion of hearing, then, is on how the auditory system encodes and represents sound frequency (Kubovy, 1981).

## The Human Ear

How does the auditory system convert sound waves into neural signals? The process is very different from the visual system, which is not surprising given that light is a form of electromagnetic radiation, whereas sound is a physical change in air pressure over time: Different forms of energy require different processes of transduction. The human ear is divided into three distinct parts, as shown in **FIGURE 4.24** (on the next page). The *outer ear* collects sound waves and funnels them toward the *middle ear,* which transmits the vibrations to the *inner ear,* embedded in the skull, where they are transduced into neural impulses.

The outer ear consists of the visible part on the outside of the head (called the *pinna*); the auditory canal; and the eardrum, an airtight flap of skin that vibrates in response to sound waves gathered by the pinna and channelled into the canal. The middle ear, a tiny, air-filled chamber behind the eardrum, contains the three smallest bones in the body, called *ossicles.* Named for their appearance as hammer, anvil, and stirrup, the ossicles fit together into a lever that mechanically transmits and intensifies vibrations from the eardrum to the inner ear.

The inner ear contains the spiral-shaped **cochlea** (Latin for "snail"), *a fluid-filled tube that is the organ of auditory transduction.* The cochlea is divided along its length by the **basilar membrane,** *a structure in the inner ear that undulates when vibrations from the ossicles reach the cochlear fluid* (see **FIGURE 4.25**). Its wavelike movement stimulates thousands of tiny **hair cells,** *specialized auditory receptor neurons embedded in the*

"The ringing in your ears—I think I can help."

LEO CULLUM/THE NEW YORKER COLLECTION/CARTOONBANK.COM

**? How do hair cells in the ear enable us to hear?**

**cochlea**
A fluid-filled tube that is the organ of auditory transduction.

**basilar membrane**
A structure in the inner ear that undulates when vibrations from the ossicles reach the cochlear fluid.

**hair cells**
Specialized auditory receptor neurons embedded in the basilar membrane.

▶ Figure **4.24 Anatomy of the Human Ear** The pinna funnels sound waves into the auditory canal to vibrate the eardrum at a rate that corresponds to the sound's frequency. In the middle ear, the ossicles pick up the eardrum vibrations, amplify them, and pass them along by vibrating a membrane at the surface of the fluid-filled cochlea in the inner ear. Here fluid carries the wave energy to the auditory receptors that transduce it into electrochemical activity, exciting the neurons that form the auditory nerve, leading to the brain.

◀ Figure **4.25 Auditory Transduction** Inside the cochlea (shown here as though it were uncoiling) the basilar membrane undulates in response to wave energy in the cochlear fluid. Waves of differing frequencies ripple varying locations along the membrane, from low frequencies at its tip to high frequencies at the base, and bend the embedded hair cell receptors at those locations. The hair cell motion generates impulses in the auditory neurons, whose axons form the auditory nerve that emerges from the cochlea.

*basilar membrane.* The hair cells then release neurotransmitter molecules, initiating a neural signal in the auditory nerve that travels to the brain. You might not want to think that the whispered "I love you" that sends chills up your spine got a kick start from lots of little hair cells wiggling around, but the mechanics of hearing are what they are!

## Perceiving Pitch

From the inner ear, action potentials in the auditory nerve travel to the thalamus and ultimately to an area of the cerebral cortex called **area A1,** *a portion of the temporal lobe that contains the primary auditory cortex* (see **FIGURE 4.26** on the next page). For most of us, the auditory areas in the left hemisphere analyze sounds related to language and those in the right hemisphere specialize in rhythmic sounds and music. There is also evidence that the auditory cortex is composed of two distinct streams, roughly analogous to the dorsal and ventral streams of the visual system. Spatial ("where") auditory features, which allow you to locate the source of a sound in space, are handled by areas toward the back (caudal) part of the auditory cortex,

**area A1**
A portion of the temporal lobe that contains the primary auditory cortex.

whereas nonspatial ("what") features, which allow you to identify the sound, are handled by areas in the lower (ventral) part of the auditory cortex (Recanzone & Sutter, 2008). Note: All of hearing, including perceiving "where," depends on "temporal aspects."

Neurons in area A1 respond well to simple tones, and successive auditory areas in the brain process sounds of increasing complexity (see Figure 4.26, inset) (Rauschecker & Scott, 2009; Schreiner, Read, & Sutter, 2000; Schreiner & Winer, 2007). The human ear is most sensitive to frequencies around 1000 to 3500 Hz. But how is the frequency of a sound wave encoded in a neural signal? Our ears have evolved two mechanisms to encode sound-wave frequency, one for high frequencies and one for low frequencies.

> The **place code,** used mainly for high frequencies, refers to the process by which *different frequencies stimulate neural signals at specific places along the basilar membrane.* In a series of experiments carried out from the 1930s to the 1950s, Nobel laureate Georg von Békésy (1899–1972) used a microscope to observe the basilar membrane in the inner ear of cadavers that had been donated for medical research (Békésy, 1960). Békésy found that the movement of the basilar membrane resembles a travelling wave (see Figure 4.25). The frequency of the stimulating sound determines the wave's shape. When the frequency is low, the wide, floppy tip (*apex*) of the basilar membrane moves the most; when the frequency is high, the narrow, stiff end (*base*) of the membrane moves the most. The movement of the basilar membrane causes hair cells to bend, initiating a neural signal in the auditory nerve. Axons fire the strongest in the hair cells along the area of the basilar membrane that moves the most, and the brain uses information about which axons are the most active to help determine the pitch you "hear."

> A complementary process handles lower frequencies. A **temporal code** *registers relatively low frequencies (up to about 5000 Hz) via the firing rate of action potentials entering the auditory nerve.* Action potentials from the hair cells are synchronized in time with the peaks of the incoming sound waves (Johnson, 1980). If you imagine the rhythmic *boom-boom-boom* of a bass drum, you can probably also imagine the *fire-fire-fire* of action potentials corresponding to the beats. This process provides the brain with very precise information about pitch that supplements the information provided by the place code. The firing rate of individual neurons is only of limited relevance, since typically information is coded across groups of cells—not just one.

**How does the frequency of a sound wave relate to what we hear?**

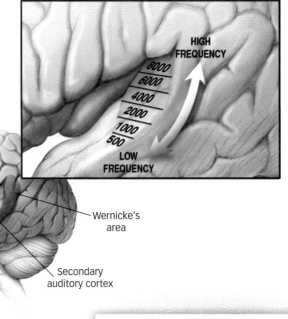

▲ Figure 4.26 **Primary Auditory Cortex** Area A1 is folded into the temporal lobe beneath the lateral fissure in each hemisphere. The left hemisphere auditory areas govern speech in most people. A1 cortex has a topographic organization (*inset*), with lower frequencies mapping toward the front of the brain and higher frequencies toward the back, mirroring the organization of the basilar membrane along the cochlea (see Figure 4.25).

## Localizing Sound Sources

Just as the differing positions of our eyes give us stereoscopic vision, the placement of our ears on opposite sides of the head gives us stereophonic hearing. The sound arriving at the ear closer to the sound source is louder than the sound in the farther ear, mainly because the listener's head partially blocks sound energy. This loudness difference decreases as the sound source moves from a position directly to one side (maximal difference) to straight ahead (no difference).

**place code**
The process by which different frequencies stimulate neural signals at specific places along the basilar membrane.

**temporal code**
The cochlea registers relatively low frequencies (up to about 5000 Hz) via the firing rate of action potentials entering the auditory nerve.

Another cue to a sound's location arises from timing: Sound waves arrive a little sooner at the near ear than at the far ear. The timing difference can be as brief as a few microseconds but, together with the intensity difference, it is sufficient to allow us to perceive the location of a sound. When the sound source is ambiguous, you may find yourself turning your head from side to side to localize it. By doing this, you are changing the relative intensity and timing of sound waves arriving in your ears and collecting better information about the likely source of the sound. Turning your head also allows you to use your eyes to locate the source of the sound—and your visual system is much better at pinpointing the location of things than your auditory system is.

## Hearing Loss

Broadly speaking, hearing loss has two main causes. *Conductive hearing loss* arises because the eardrum or ossicles are damaged to the point that they cannot conduct sound waves effectively to the cochlea. The cochlea itself, however, is normal, making this a kind of "mechanical problem" with the moving parts of the ear: the hammer, anvil, stirrup, or eardrum. In many cases, medication or surgery can correct the problem. Sound amplification from a hearing aid also can improve hearing through conduction via the bones around the ear directly to the cochlea.

> **Sound amplification helps in the case of which type of hearing loss?**

*Sensorineural hearing loss* is caused by damage to the cochlea, the hair cells, or the auditory nerve, and it happens to almost all of us as we age. Sensorineural hearing loss can be heightened in people regularly exposed to high noise levels (such as rock musicians or jet mechanics). Simply amplifying the sound does not help because the hair cells can no longer transduce sound waves. In these cases a *cochlear implant* may offer some relief.

A cochlear implant works when a microphone picks up sounds and sends them to a small speech-processing computer worn on the user's belt or behind the ear. The electric signals from the speech processor are transmitted to an implanted receiver, which sends the signals via electrodes to the cochlea, where the signals directly stimulate the auditory nerve.

A cochlear implant is an electronic device that replaces the function of the hair cells (Waltzman, 2006). The external parts of the device include a microphone and speech processor, about the size of a USB key, worn behind the ear, and a small, flat, external transmitter that sits on the scalp. The implanted parts include a receiver just inside the skull and a thin wire containing electrodes inserted into the cochlea to stimulate the auditory nerve. Sound picked up by the microphone is transformed into electric signals by the speech processor, which is essentially a small computer. The signal is transmitted to the implanted receiver, which activates the electrodes in the cochlea. Cochlear implants are now in routine use and can improve hearing to the point where speech can be understood.

Marked hearing loss is commonly experienced by people as they grow older, but is rare in an infant. However, infants who have not yet learned to speak are especially vulnerable because they may miss the critical period for language learning (see the Learning chapter). Without auditory feedback during this time, normal speech is nearly impossible to achieve, but early use of cochlear implants has been associated with improved speech and language skills for hearing-impaired children (Hay-McCutcheon et al., 2008). Efforts are under way to introduce cochlear implants to children as young as 12 months old or younger to maximize their chances of normal language development (DesJardin, Eisenberg, & Hodapp, 2006; Holman et al., 2013). (For research on the importance of music and brain development, see The Real World box.)

**THE REAL WORLD**

# Music Training: Worth the Time

Did you learn to play an instrument when you were younger? Maybe for you, music was its own reward (or maybe not). For anyone who practised mostly to keep Mom and Dad happy, there is good news. Musical training has a range of benefits. Let us start with the brain. Musicians have greater plasticity in the motor cortex compared with nonmusicians (Rosenkranz et al., 2007); they have increased grey matter in motor and auditory brain regions compared with nonmusicians (Gaser & Schlaug, 2003; Hannon & Trainor, 2007); and they show differences in brain responses to musical stimuli compared with nonmusicians (Pantev et al., 1998). But musical training also extends to auditory processing in nonmusical domains (Kraus & Chandrasekaran, 2010). Musicians, for example, show enhanced brain responses when listening to speech compared with nonmusicians (Parbery-Clark et al., 2012). Musicians also exhibit an improved ability to detect speech when it is presented in a noisy background (Parbery-Clark, Skoe, & Kraus, 2009). This effect has been demonstrated in children, young adults, and even older adults, who typically have serious problems perceiving speech in a noisy environment (Parbery-Clark et al., 2011)

Remembering to be careful not to confuse correlation with causation, you may ask: Do differences between musicians and nonmusicians reflect the effects of musical training, or do they reflect individual differences, perhaps genetic ones, that lead some people to become musicians in the first place? Maybe people blessed with enhanced brain responses to musical or other auditory stimuli decide to become musicians *because* of their natural abilities. Recent experiments support a causal role for musical training. One study demonstrated structural brain differences in auditory and motor areas of elementary schoolchildren after 15 months of musical

THINKSTOCK

training (learning to play piano), compared with children who did not receive musical training (Hyde et al., 2009). Furthermore, brain changes in the trained group were associated with improvements in motor and auditory skills. Another study compared two groups of 8-year-old children, one group with 6 months of musical training and the other with 6 months of painting training. Musical training produced changes in the brain's electrical responses to musical and speech stimuli, and those changes were correlated with enhanced performance on both musical and speech perception tasks (Moreno et al., 2009). And when students were randomly assigned to music or drama lessons, those who received music lessons showed an increase in IQ scores after training relative to those taking drama (Schellenberg, 2004). More recent musical training studies have also documented benefits for speech perception (François et al., 2013), and indicate that neural changes produced by musical training in childhood persist into adulthood (Skoe & Kraus, 2012).

We have yet to know all the reasons why musical training has such broad effects on auditory processing, but one likely contributor is that learning to play an instrument demands attention to precise details of sounds (Kraus & Chandrasekaran, 2010). Future studies will no doubt pinpoint additional factors, but the research to date leaves little room for doubt that your hours of practice were indeed worth the time.

## IN SUMMARY

▶ Perceiving sound depends on three physical dimensions of a sound wave: The frequency of the sound wave determines the pitch; the amplitude determines the loudness; and differences in the complexity, or mix, of frequencies determines the sound quality or timbre.

▶ Auditory pitch perception begins in the ear, which consists of an outer ear that funnels sound waves toward the middle ear, which in turn sends the vibrations to the inner ear, which contains the cochlea. Action potentials from the inner ear travel along an auditory pathway through the thalamus to the primary auditory cortex (area A1) in the temporal lobe.

▶ Auditory perception depends on both a place code and a temporal code. Our ability to localize sound sources depends critically on the placement of our ears on opposite sides of the head.

▶ Some hearing loss can be overcome with hearing aids that amplify sound. When hair cells are damaged, a cochlear implant is a possible solution.

**haptic perception**
The active exploration of the environment by touching and grasping objects with our hands.

# The Body Senses: More Than Skin Deep

Vision and audition provide information about the world at a distance. By responding to light and sound energy in the environment, these "distance" senses allow us to identify and locate the objects and people around us. In comparison, the body senses, also called *somatosenses* (*soma* from the Greek for "body"), are up close and personal. **Haptic perception** is *the active exploration of the environment by touching and grasping objects with our hands.* We use sensory receptors in our muscles, tendons, and joints as well as a variety of receptors in our skin to get a feel for the world around us (see **FIGURE 4.27**).

## Touch

Touch begins with the transduction of skin sensations into neural signals. Four types of receptors located under the skin's surface enable us to sense pressure, texture, pattern, or vibration against the skin (see Figure 4.27). The receptive fields of these specialized cells work together to provide a rich tactile (from Latin, "to touch") experience when you explore an object by feeling it or attempting to grasp it. In addition, *thermoreceptors,* nerve fibres that sense cold and warmth, respond when your skin temperature changes. All these sensations blend seamlessly together in perception, of course, but detailed physiological studies have successfully isolated the parts of the touch system (Hollins, 2010; Johnson, 2002).

This rather unimposing geodesic dome sits on the floor of the Exploratorium, a world-renowned science museum in San Francisco, California. Called the Tactile Dome, it was created in 1971 by August Coppola (brother of director Francis Ford Coppola and father of actor Nicolas Cage) and Carl Day, who wanted to create an environment in which only haptic perception could be used. The inside of the dome is pitch black; visitors must crawl, wiggle, slide, and otherwise navigate the unfamiliar terrain using only their sense of touch. How would you feel being in that environment for an hour or so?

There are three important principles regarding the neural representation of the body's surface. First, the left half of the body is represented in the right half of the brain and vice versa. Second, just as more of the visual brain is devoted to foveal vision where acuity is greatest, more of the tactile brain is devoted to parts of the skin surface that have greater spatial resolution. Regions such as the fingertips and lips are very good at discriminating fine spatial detail, whereas areas such as the lower back are quite poor at that task. Think back to the homunculus you read about in the Neuroscience and Behaviour chapter; you will recall that different locations on the body project sensory signals to different locations in the somatosensory cortex in the parietal lobe. Third, there is mounting evidence for a distinction between "what" and "where" pathways in touch analogous to similar distinctions we have already considered for vision and audition. The "what"

> Why might it be important to use fingertips and lips to discriminate spatial detail?

▶ Figure 4.27 **Touch Receptors**
Specialized sensory neurons form distinct groups of haptic receptors that detect pressure, temperature, and vibrations against the skin. Touch receptors respond to stimulation within their receptive fields, and their long axons enter the brain via the spinal or cranial nerves. Pain receptors populate all body tissues that feel pain; they are distributed around bones and within muscles and internal organs as well as under the skin surface. Both types of pain receptors (the fibres that transmit immediate, sharp pain sensations quickly and those that signal slow, dull pain that lasts and lasts) are free nerve endings.

Skin surface

Texture and pattern receptors

Pain receptor (free nerve endings)

Pressure receptor

Low-frequency vibrating receptor

Duct of sweat gland

Fat cells

High-frequency vibrator receptor

EXPLORATORIUM

system for touch provides information about the properties of surfaces and objects; the "where" system provides information about a location in external space that is being touched or a location on the body that is being stimulated (Lederman & Klatzky, 2009). fMRI evidence suggests that the "what" and "where" touch pathways involve areas in the lower and upper parts of the parietal lobe, respectively (Reed, Klatzky, & Halgren, 2005).

Touch information can have a powerful effect on our decisions and judgments. For example, recent research has shown that merely touching an object that we do not already own can increase our feeling of ownership and lead us to value the object more highly than when we view it but do not touch it (Peck & Shu, 2009); the longer we touch an object, the more highly we value it (Wolf, Arkes, & Muhanna, 2008). You might keep this "mere touch" effect in mind next time you are in a shop and considering buying an expensive item. Retailers are probably aware of this effect: During the 2003 holiday shopping season the office of the Illinois state attorney general warned shoppers to be cautious in stores that encouraged them to touch the merchandise (Peck & Shu, 2009).

CKDJ/CORBIS

Be warned for your next shopping trip: Touching the merchandise can lead you to value it more highly than just looking at it.

## Pain

Does the possibility of a life free from pain seem appealing? Although pain is arguably the least pleasant of sensations, this aspect of touch is among the most important for survival: Pain indicates damage or potential damage to the body. Without the ability to feel pain, we might ignore infections, broken bones, or serious burns. Congenital insensitivity to pain, a rare inherited disorder that specifically impairs pain perception, is more of a curse than a blessing: Children who experience this disorder often mutilate themselves (e.g., biting into their tongues or gouging their skin while scratching) and are at increased risk of dying during childhood (Nagasako, Oaklander, & Dworkin, 2003).

Too little pain is bad, but so is too much: Chronic pain is pain without apparent biological value, that has persisted after the time it takes tissue to heal (usually 3 months). It is estimated to afflict about 20 percent of the population (Ospina & Harstall, 2003; Breivik et al., 2006). A large European survey found that, of those afflicted with chronic pain, 60 percent had suffered for more than 2 years, and 20 percent had lost their job because of their pain condition. Chronic pain has an enormous effect on quality of life, and consumes a large fraction of health care resources in Canada and elsewhere (Breivik et al., 2006). As Ron Melzack from McGill University and Patrick Wall said in their book *The Challenge of Pain* (1988): "Every human being has a right to freedom from pain to the extent that our knowledge permits health professionals to achieve this goal. … Pain … is more than an intriguing puzzle. It is a terrible problem that faces all humanity and urgently demands a solution"(pp. x, 13).

Tissue damage is transduced by pain receptors, the free nerve endings shown in Figure 4.27. Researchers have distinguished between fast-acting *A-delta fibres,* which transmit the initial sharp pain one might feel right away from a sudden injury, and slower *C fibres,* which transmit the longer-lasting, duller pain that persists after the initial injury. If you were running barefoot outside and stubbed your toe against a rock, you would first feel a sudden stinging pain transmitted by A-delta fibres that would die down quickly, only to be replaced by the throbbing but longer-lasting pain carried by C fibres. Both the A-delta and C fibres are impaired in cases of congenital insensitivity to pain, which is one reason why the disorder can be life threatening.

As you will remember from the chapter on Neuroscience and Behaviour, the pain withdrawal reflex is coordinated by the spinal cord. No brainpower is required when you touch a hot stove; you retract your hand almost instantaneously. But neural signals for pain—such as wrenching your elbow as you brace yourself from falling—travel to two distinct areas in the brain and evoke two distinct psychological experiences

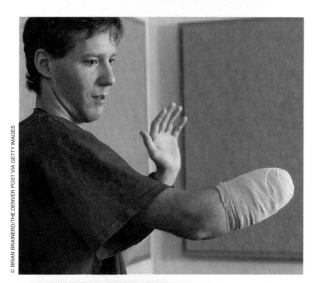

Aron Ralston was hiking in a remote canyon in the Western United States when tragedy struck. A 454-kg boulder pinned him in a 1-m-wide space for 5 days, eventually leaving him no choice but to amputate his own arm with a pocketknife. He then applied a tourniquet, rappelled down the canyon, and hiked out to safety. Ralston has written a memoir about his ordeal, appropriately called *Between a Rock and Hard Place*—this was turned into the 2010 movie *127 Hours*. Ralston's story, and others like it, illustrate that the extent of an injury is not perfectly correlated with the amount of pain felt. Although self-amputation is undoubtedly excruciating, luckily in this case it was not debilitating.

**referred pain**
Feeling of pain when sensory information from internal and external areas converges on the same nerve cells in the spinal cord.

**gate-control theory of pain**
A theory of pain perception suggesting that signals arriving from pain receptors in the body can be stopped, or gated, by interneurons in the spinal cord via feedback from two directions.

(Treede et al., 1999). One pain pathway sends signals to the somatosensory cortex, identifying where the pain is occurring and what sort of pain it is (sharp, burning, dull). The second pain pathway sends signals to the motivational and emotional centres of the brain, such as the hypothalamus and amygdala, and to the frontal lobe. This is the aspect of pain that is unpleasant and motivates us to escape from or relieve the pain.

Pain typically feels as if it comes from the site of the tissue damage that caused it. If you burn your finger, you will perceive the pain as originating there. But we have pain receptors in many areas besides the skin: around bones and within muscles and internal organs as well. When pain originates internally, in a body organ, for example, we actually feel it on the surface of the body. This kind of **referred pain** occurs when *sensory information from internal and external areas converges on the same nerve cells in the spinal cord.* One common example is a heart attack: Victims often feel pain radiating from the left arm rather than from inside the chest.

Pain intensity cannot always be predicted solely from the extent of the injury that causes the pain (Keefe, Abernathy, & Campbell, 2005). For example, *turf toe* sounds like the mildest of ailments; it is pain at the base of the big toe as a result of bending or pushing off repeatedly, as a runner or football player might do during a sporting event. This small-sounding injury in a small area of the body can nonetheless sideline an athlete for a month with considerable pain. On the other hand, you have probably heard a story or two about someone treading bone-chilling water for hours on end, or dragging their shattered legs a kilometre down a country road to seek help after a tractor accident, or performing some other incredible feat despite searing pain and extensive tissue damage. Pain type and pain intensity show a less-than-perfect correlation, a fact that has researchers intrigued.

One influential account of pain perception, the **gate-control theory of pain,** holds that *signals arriving from pain receptors in the body can be stopped, or gated, by interneurons in the spinal cord via feedback from two directions* (Melzack & Wall, 1965). Pain can be gated by the skin receptors, for example, by rubbing the affected area. Rubbing your stubbed toe activates neurons that "close the gate" to stop pain signals from travelling to the brain. Pain can also be gated from the brain by modulating the activity of pain-transmission neurons. This neural feedback is elicited not by the pain itself, but rather by activity deep within the thalamus.

> Why does rubbing an injured area sometimes help alleviate pain?

The neural feedback comes from a region in the midbrain called the *periaqueductal grey* (PAG). Under extreme conditions, such as high stress, naturally occurring endorphins can activate the PAG to send inhibitory signals to neurons in the spinal cord that then suppress pain signals to the brain, thereby modulating the experience of pain. The PAG is also activated through the action of opiate drugs, such as morphine.

A different kind of feedback signal can *increase* the sensation of pain. This system is activated by events such as infection and learned danger signals. When we are quite ill, what might otherwise be experienced as mild discomfort can feel quite painful. This pain facilitation signal presumably evolved to motivate people who are ill to rest and avoid strenuous activity, allowing their energy to be devoted to healing.

Although some details of the gate-control theory of pain have been challenged, a key concept underlying the theory—that perception is a two-way street—has broad implications. The senses feed information such as pain sensations to the brain, a pattern termed *bottom-up control* by perceptual psychologists. The brain processes this sensory data into perceptual information at successive levels to support movement, object recognition, and eventually more complex cognitive tasks, such as memory and planning. But there is ample evidence that the brain exerts plenty of control over what we sense as well. Visual illusions and the gestalt principles of filling in, shaping up, and rounding out what is not really there provide some examples. This kind of *top-down control* also explains how the brain influences the experience of touch and pain.

## Body Position, Movement, and Balance

It may sound odd, but one aspect of sensation and perception is knowing where parts of your body are at any given moment. Your body needs some way to sense its position in physical space other than moving your eyes constantly to visually check the location of your limbs. Sensations related to position, movement, and balance depend on stimulation produced within our bodies. Receptors in the muscles, tendons, and joints signal the position of the body in space, whereas information about balance and head movement originates in the inner ear.

Sensory receptors provide the information we need to perceive the position and movement of our limbs, head, and body. These receptors also provide feedback about whether we are performing a desired movement correctly and how resistance from held objects may be influencing the movement. For example, when you swing a baseball bat, the weight of the bat affects how your muscles move your arm as well as the change in sensation when the bat hits the ball. Muscle, joint, and tendon feedback about how your arms actually moved can be used to improve performance through learning.

Maintaining balance depends primarily on the **vestibular system,** *the three fluid-filled semicircular canals and adjacent organs located next to the cochlea in each inner ear* (see Figure 4.24). The semicircular canals are arranged in three perpendicular orientations and studded with hair cells that detect movement of the fluid when the head moves or accelerates. The bending of the hair cells generates activity in the vestibular nerve which is then conveyed to the brain. This detected motion enables us to maintain our balance, or the position of our bodies relative to gravity (Lackner & DiZio, 2005).

Vision also helps us keep our balance. If you see that you are swaying relative to a vertical orientation, such as the contours of a room, you move your legs and feet to keep from falling over. Psychologists have experimented with this visual aspect of balance by placing people in rooms that can be tilted forward and backward (Bertenthal, Rose, & Bai, 1997; Lee & Aronson, 1974). If the room tilts enough—particularly when small children are tested—people will topple over as they try to compensate for what their visual system is telling them. When a mismatch between the information provided by visual cues and vestibular feedback occurs, motion sickness can result. Remember this discrepancy the next time you try reading in the back seat of a moving car!

> **Why is it so hard to stand on one foot with your eyes closed?**

**vestibular system**
The three fluid-filled semicircular canals and adjacent organs located next to the cochlea in each inner ear.

MIKE HEWITT/GETTY IMAGES

Hitting a ball with a bat or racket provides feedback as to where your arms and body are in space, as well as how the resistance of these objects affects your movement and balance. Successful athletes, such as Milos Raonic, have particularly well-developed body senses.

## IN SUMMARY

▶ Sensory receptors on the body send neural signals to locations in the somatosensory cortex, a part of the parietal lobe, which the brain translates as the sensation of touch.

▶ The experience of pain depends on signals that travel along two distinct pathways. One sends signals to the somatosensory cortex to indicate the location and type of pain, and another sends signals to the emotional centres of the brain that result in unpleasant feelings that we wish to escape. The experience of pain varies across individuals, which is explained by bottom-up and top-down aspects of the gate-control theory of pain.

▶ Balance and movement depend primarily on the vestibular system, but are also influenced by vision.

**olfactory receptor neurons (ORNs)**
Receptor cells that initiate the sense of smell.

# The Chemical Senses: Adding Flavour

Somatosensation is all about physical changes in or on the body: Vision and audition sense energetic states of the world—light and sound waves—and touch is activated by physical changes in or on the body surface. The last set of senses we will consider share a chemical basis to combine aspects of distance and proximity. The chemical senses of *olfaction* (smell) and *gustation* (taste) respond to the molecular structure of substances floating into the nasal cavity as you inhale or dissolving in saliva. Smell and taste combine to produce the perceptual experience we call *flavour*.

## Smell

Olfaction is the least understood sense and the only one directly connected to the forebrain, with pathways into the frontal lobe, amygdala, and other forebrain structures (recall from the Neuroscience and Behaviour chapter that the other senses connect first to the thalamus). This mapping indicates that smell has a close relationship with areas involved in emotional and social behaviour. Smell seems to have evolved in animals as a signaling sense for the familiar: a friendly creature, an edible food, or a sexually receptive mate.

Countless substances release odours into the air, and some of their *odorant molecules* make their way into our noses, drifting in on the air we breathe. Situated along the top of the nasal cavity shown in **FIGURE 4.28** is a mucous membrane called the *olfactory epithelium,* which contains about 10 million **olfactory receptor neurons (ORNs)**, *receptor cells that initiate the sense of smell.* Odorant molecules bind to sites on these specialized receptors, and if enough bindings occur, the ORNs send action potentials into the olfactory nerve (Dalton, 2003).

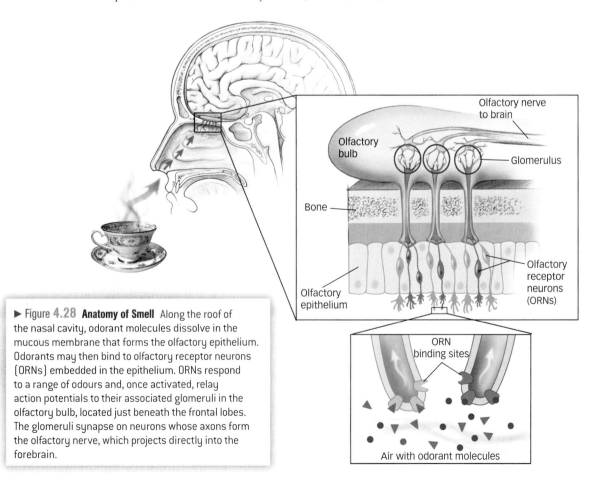

▶ Figure **4.28** **Anatomy of Smell** Along the roof of the nasal cavity, odorant molecules dissolve in the mucous membrane that forms the olfactory epithelium. Odorants may then bind to olfactory receptor neurons (ORNs) embedded in the epithelium. ORNs respond to a range of odours and, once activated, relay action potentials to their associated glomeruli in the olfactory bulb, located just beneath the frontal lobes. The glomeruli synapse on neurons whose axons form the olfactory nerve, which projects directly into the forebrain.

Each olfactory neuron has receptors that bind to some odorants but not to others, as if the receptor is a lock and the odorant is the key (see Figure 4.28). Groups of ORNs send their axons from the olfactory epithelium into the **olfactory bulb,** *a brain structure located above the nasal cavity beneath the frontal lobes.* Humans possess about 350 different ORN types that permit us to discriminate among some 10 000 different odorants through the unique patterns of neural activity each odorant evokes. This setup is similar to our ability to see a vast range of colours based on only a small number of retinal receptor cell types or to feel a range of skin sensations based on only a handful of touch receptor cell types.

**How many scents can humans smell?**

Some dogs have as many as 100 times more ORNs than humans do, producing a correspondingly sharpened ability to detect and discriminate among millions of odours. Nevertheless, humans are sensitive to the smells of some substances in extremely small concentrations. For example, a chemical compound that is added to natural gas to help detect gas leaks can be sensed at a concentration of just 0.0003 part per million. By contrast, acetone (nail polish remover), something most people regard as pungent, can be detected only if its concentration is 15 parts per million or greater.

The olfactory bulb sends outputs to various centres in the brain, including the parts that are responsible for controlling basic drives, emotions, and memories. Odour perception includes both information about the identity of an odour, which involves relating olfactory inputs to information stored in memory (Stevenson & Boakes, 2003), as well as our emotional response to whether it is pleasant or unpleasant (Khan et al., 2007). Which of these processes occurs first? When you walk into a house and encounter the wonderful smell of freshly baked chocolate chip cookies, does your positive emotional response come before you identify the smell or vice versa? According to the *object-centred approach,* information about the identity of the "odour object" is quickly accessed from memory and then triggers an emotional response (Stevenson & Wilson, 2007). According to the *valence-centred approach,* the emotional response comes first and provides a basis for determining the identity of the odour (Yeshrun & Sobel, 2010). Recent attempts to distinguish between these two views support that odour perception is guided first by memory and then by emotion (Olofsson et al., 2012).

The relationship between smell and emotion explains why smells can have immediate, strongly positive or negative effects on us. If the slightest whiff of an apple pie baking brings back fond memories of childhood or the unexpected sniff of vomit mentally returns you to a particularly bad party you once attended, you have the idea. Thankfully, sensory adaptation is at work when it comes to smell, just as it is with the other senses. Whether the associations are good or bad, after just a few minutes the smell fades. Smell adaptation makes sense: It allows us to detect new odours that may require us to act, but after that initial evaluation has occurred, it may be best to reduce our sensitivity to allow us to detect other smells.

Our experience of smell is determined not only by bottom-up influences, such as odorant molecules binding to sites on ORNs, but also by top-down influences, such as our previous experiences with an odour (Gottfried, 2008). Consistent with this idea, people rate the identical odour as more pleasant when it is paired with an appealing verbal label such as *cheddar cheese* rather than an unappealing one such as *body odour* (de Araujo et al., 2005; Herz & von Clef, 2001). fMRI evidence indicates that brain regions involved in coding the pleasantness of an experience, such as the orbiotofrontal cortex, respond more strongly to the identical odour when people think it is cheddar cheese than when they think it is a body odour (de Araujo et al., 2005) (see the Hot Science box, Taste: From the Top Down, for a related finding concerning taste perception).

**olfactory bulb**
A brain structure located above the nasal cavity beneath the frontal lobes.

Taste and smell both contribute to what we perceive as flavour. This is why smelling the bouquet of a wine is an essential part of the wine-tasting ritual. The experience of wine tasting is also influenced by cognitive factors, such as knowledge of a wine's price.

RADIUS IMAGES/
JUPITER IMAGES

**HOT SCIENCE**

# Taste: From the Top Down

I n 2008, the publication of a book titled *The Wine Trials* (Goldstein & Herschkowitsch, 2008) ruffled the feathers of more than a few wine connoisseurs. The book was based on an article in which the authors and several colleagues analyzed the results of 6175 observations gathered during 17 blind wine tastings involving wines of varying prices, organized by lead author and food critic Robin Goldstein (Goldstein et al., 2008). The results suggested that, if anything, tasters liked the more expensive wines slightly *less* than the more inexpensive ones.

Although these findings will not encourage ordinary wine drinkers to spend a large amount of money on their next wine purchase, they leave open the question of whether knowing a wine's price affects enjoyment of it. Similar to olfaction, our experience of taste is partly determined by bottom-up influences, such as the patterns of activity in the five taste receptor types that are evoked by food molecules, but it is also influenced by top-down factors, such as knowing what brand we are eating or drinking.

To investigate the effects of a top-down influence (price knowledge) on the enjoyment of wine and associated brain activity, researchers used fMRI to scan 20 participants while they drank different wines or a control solution (Plassman et al., 2008). The participants were told that they would be sampling five different cabernet sauvignons, that the different wines would

be identified by their price, and that they should rate how much they liked each wine. The participants did not know, however, that only three different wines were actually presented, and that two critical wines were presented twice. One critical wine was presented once at its actual price ($5) and once marked-up to a high price ($45); the other critical wine was also presented once at its actual price ($90) and once at a marked-down price ($10). This design allowed the researchers to compare ratings and brain activity for the identical wine when participants thought it was expensive or cheap.

Results revealed that during scanning, participants reported liking both wines better when they were accompanied by a high price than by a low price. For the fMRI analysis, the researchers focused on the activity of the medial orbitofrontal cortex (mOFC), a part of the brain located deep inside the frontal lobe that is known to be involved in coding the pleasantness of an experience (Kuhn & Gallinat, 2012). The level of mOFC activity was closely correlated with subjective ratings of taste pleasantness in a previous fMRI study (Kringelbach et al., 2003). As shown in the accompanying figure, there was greater mOFC activity for both wines in the high price condition than in the low price condition.

These results demonstrate clearly that taste experience and associated neural activity can be affected by top-down influences such as price knowledge. Related

work has shown that other top-down influences, such as expectations, can also affect both taste experience and brain responses (Nitschke et al., 2006). Consider a recent fMRI study in which researchers manipulated whether participants expected that a liquid they were about to taste would be sweet or tasteless (Veldhuizen et al., 2011). On most trials, the participants' expectations were met: They were cued to expect a sweet or a tasteless liquid and then received the type of liquid indicated by the cue. On some trials, though, their expectations were violated: They were cued to expect a sweet or a tasteless liquid and then received the opposite. When expectations were violated either by receiving a sweet or a tasteless stimulus, activity in a number of brain regions showed increased activity, reflecting in part a general "surprise" response. However, a part of the brain's taste system known as the *anterior insula* showed the most activity when the unexpected stimulus contained the sweet taste, thus indicating that top-down influences can affect a part of the brain known to be involved in the experience of taste.

The results of these studies should provide some comfort to wine drinkers who are willing to pay for expensive brands. Even if they cannot tell the difference from cheaper brands under blind tasting conditions, just knowing that they are drinking an expensive wine should make for an enjoyable experience.

Smell may also play a role in social behaviour. Humans and other animals can detect odours from **pheromones,** *biochemical odorants emitted by other members of its species that can affect the animal's behaviour or physiology.* Parents can distinguish the smell of their own children from other people's children. An infant can identify the smell of its mother's breast from the smell of other mothers. Pheromones also play a role in reproductive behaviour in insects and in several mammalian species, including mice, dogs, and primates (Brennan & Zufall, 2006). Can the same thing be said of human reproductive behaviour?

Studies of people's preference for the odours of individuals of the opposite sex have produced mixed results, with no consistent tendency for people to prefer them over other pleasant odours. Recent research, however, has provided a link between sexual orientation and responses to odours that may constitute human pheromones. Researchers used positron emission tomography (PET) scans to study the brain's response to two odours, one related to testosterone, which is produced in men's sweat, and the other related to estrogen, which is found in women's urine. The testosterone-based odour activated the hypothalamus (a part of the brain that controls sexual behaviour; see the Neuroscience and Behaviour chapter) in heterosexual women but not in heterosexual men, whereas the estrogen-based odour activated the hypothalamus in heterosexual men but not in heterosexual women. Strikingly, homosexual men responded to the two chemicals in the same way as heterosexual women did: The hypothalamus was activated by the testosterone- but not estrogen-based odour (Savic, Berglund, & Lindstrom, 2005) (see **FIGURE 4.29**). Other common odours unrelated to sexual arousal were processed similarly by all three groups. A follow-up study with lesbians showed that their responses to the testosterone- and estrogen-based odours were largely similar to those of heterosexual men (Berglund, Lindstrom, & Savic, 2006). Taken together, the two studies suggest that some human pheromones are related to sexual orientation.

**pheromones**
Biochemical odorants emitted by other members of its species that can affect an animal's behaviour or physiology.

**taste buds**
The organ of taste transduction.

◀ Figure 4.29 **Smell and Social Behaviour** In a PET study, heterosexual women, homosexual men, and heterosexual men were scanned as they were presented with each of several odours. During the presentation of a testosterone-based odour (4,16-androstadien-3-one, [AND]), there was significant activation in the hypothalamus for heterosexual women (*left*) and homosexual men (*centre*) but not for heterosexual men (*right*) (Savic et al., 2005).

## Taste

One of the primary responsibilities of the chemical sense of taste is identifying things that are bad for you—as in poisonous and lethal. Many poisons are bitter, and we avoid eating things that nauseate us for good reason, so taste aversions have a clear adaptive significance. Some aspects of taste perception are genetic, such as an aversion to extreme bitterness, and some are learned, such as an aversion to a particular food that once caused nausea. In either case, the direct contact between a tongue and possible foods allows us to anticipate whether something will be harmful or palatable.

**Why is the sense of taste an evolutionary advantage?**

The tongue is covered with thousands of small bumps, called *papillae,* which are easily visible to the naked eye. Within each papilla are hundreds of **taste buds,** *the* *organ of taste transduction* (see **FIGURE 4.30**). The mouth contains 5000 to 10 000 taste buds fairly evenly distributed over the tongue, roof of the mouth, and upper throat (Bartoshuk & Beauchamp, 1994; Halpern, 2002). Each taste bud contains 50 to 100 taste receptor cells. Taste perception fades with age (Methven et al., 2012): On average, people lose half their taste receptors by the time they turn 20. This may help to explain why young children seem to be "fussy eaters," since their greater number of taste buds brings with it a greater range of taste sensations.

The human eye contains millions of rods and cones, the human nose contains some 350 different types of olfactory receptors, but the taste system contains just five main types of taste receptors, corresponding to five primary taste sensations: salt, sour, bitter, sweet, and umami (savoury). The first four are quite familiar, but *umami* may not be. In fact, perception researchers are still debating its existence. The umami receptor was discovered by Japanese scientists who attributed it to the tastes evoked by foods containing a high concentration of protein, such as meats and cheeses (Yamaguchi, 1998). If you are a meat eater and you savour the feel of a steak topped with butter or a cheeseburger as it sits in your mouth, you have an idea of the umami sensation.

Each taste bud contains several types of taste receptor cells whose tips, called *microvilli,* react with *tastant molecules* in food. Salt taste receptors are most strongly activated by sodium chloride (table salt). Sour receptor cells respond to acids, such as vinegar or lime juice. Bitter and sweet taste receptors are more complex. Some 50 to 80 distinct binding sites in bitter receptors are activated by an equal number of different bitter-tasting chemicals. Sweet receptor cells likewise can be activated by a wide range of substances in addition to sugars.

Although umami receptor cells are the least well understood, researchers are homing in on their key features (Chandrashekar et al., 2006). They respond most strongly to glutamate, an amino acid in many protein-containing foods. Recall from the Neuroscience and Behaviour chapter, glutamate acts as a neurotransmitter; in fact, it is a major excitatory neurotransmitter. The food additive *monosodium glutamate (MSG)*, which is often used to flavour Asian foods, particularly activates umami receptors. Some people develop headaches or allergic reactions after eating MSG.

Fussy eater or just too many taste buds? Our taste perception declines with age: We lose about half of our taste receptors by the time we are 20 years old. That can make childhood a time of either savoury delight or a sensory overload of taste.

LESLIE BANKS/ISTOCKPHOTO

▼ Figure **4.30** **A Taste Bud** Taste buds stud the bumps (papillae) on the tongue, shown here, as well as the back, sides, and roof of the mouth (*a*). Each taste bud contains a range of receptor cells that respond to varying chemical components of foods called *tastants* (*b*). Tastant molecules dissolve in saliva and stimulate the microvilli that form the tips of the taste receptor cells (*c*). Each taste bud contacts the branch of a cranial nerve at its base.

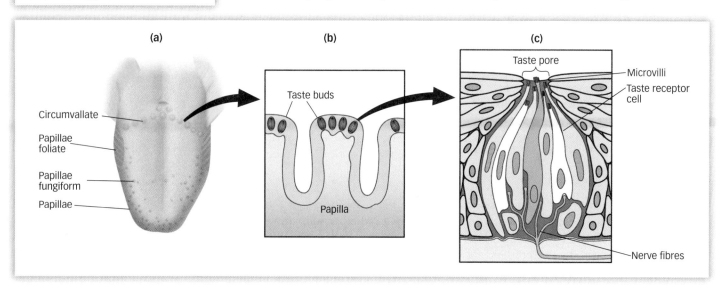

(a)  (b)  (c)

Circumvallate
Papillae foliate
Papillae fungiform
Papillae

Taste buds

Papilla

Taste pore
Microvilli
Taste receptor cell
Nerve fibres

Of course, the variety of taste experiences greatly exceeds the five basic receptors discussed here. Any food molecules dissolved in saliva evoke specific, combined patterns of activity in the five taste receptor types. Although we often think of taste as the primary source for flavour, in fact, taste and smell collaborate to produce this complex perception. As any wine connoisseur will attest, the full experience of a wine's flavour cannot be appreciated without a finely trained sense of smell. Odorants from substances outside your mouth enter the nasal cavity via the nostrils, and odorants in the mouth enter through the back of the throat. This is why wine aficionados are taught to pull air in over wine held in the mouth: It allows the wine's odorant molecules to enter the nasal cavity through this "back door." (The taste of wine can also be influenced by cognitive factors, as illustrated in the Hot Science box.)

You can easily demonstrate the contribution of smell to flavour by tasting a few different foods while holding your nose, preventing the olfactory system from detecting their odours. If you have a head cold, you probably already know how this turns out. Your favourite spicy burrito or zesty pasta probably tastes as bland as can be.

"We would like to be genetically modified to taste like Brussels sprouts."

Taste experiences also vary widely across individuals. About 50 percent of people report a mildly bitter taste in caffeine, saccharine, certain green vegetables, and other substances, whereas roughly 25 percent report no bitter taste. Members of the first group are called *tasters* and members of the second group are called *nontasters*. The remaining 25 percent of people are *supertasters*, who report that such substances, especially dark green vegetables, are extremely bitter, to the point of being inedible (Bartoshuk, 2000). Children start out as tasters or supertasters, which could help explain their early tendency toward fussiness in food preference. However, some children grow up to become nontasters. Because supertasters tend to avoid fruits and vegetables that contain tastes they experience as extremely bitter, they may be at increased health risk for diseases such as colon cancer. On the other hand, because they also tend to avoid fatty, creamy foods, they tend to be thinner and may have decreased risk of cardiovascular disease (Bartoshuk, 2000). Genetic factors contribute to individual differences in taste perception (Kim et al., 2003), but much remains to be learned about the specific genes that are involved (Hayes et al., 2008; Reed, 2008).

## IN SUMMARY

▶ Our experience of smell, or olfaction, is associated with odorant molecules binding to sites on specialized olfactory receptors, which converge at the glomerulus within the olfactory bulb. The olfactory bulb in turn sends signals to parts of the brain that control drives, emotions, and memories, which helps to explain why smells can have immediate and powerful effects on us.

▶ Smell is also involved in social behaviour, as illustrated by pheromones, which are related to reproductive behaviour and sexual responses in several species.

▶ Sensations of taste depend on taste buds, which are distributed across the tongue, roof of the mouth, and upper throat, and on taste receptors that correspond to the five primary taste sensations of salt, sour, bitter, sweet, and umami.

▶ Taste experiences vary widely across individuals and, like olfactory experiences, depend in part on cognitive influences.

# Chapter Review

## KEY CONCEPT QUIZ

1. Sensation involves _____ , whereas perception involves _____ .
   a. organization; coordination
   b. stimulation; interpretation
   c. identification; translation
   d. comprehension; information

2. What process converts physical signals from the environment into neural signals carried by sensory neurons into the central nervous system?
   a. representation
   b. identification
   c. propagation
   d. transduction

3. The smallest intensity needed to just barely detect a stimulus is called
   a. proportional magnitude.
   b. absolute threshold.
   c. just noticeable difference.
   d. Weber's law.

4. The world of light outside the body is linked to the world of vision inside the central nervous system by the
   a. cornea.
   b. lens.
   c. retina.
   d. optic nerve.

5. Light striking the retina, causing a specific pattern of response in the three cone types, leads to our ability to see
   a. motion.
   b. colours.
   c. depth.
   d. shadows.

6. In which part of the brain is the primary visual cortex, where encoded information is systematically mapped into a representation of the visual scene?
   a. the thalamus
   b. the lateral geniculate nucleus (LGN)
   c. the fovea
   d. area V1

7. Our ability to visually combine details so that we perceive unified objects is explained by
   a. feature-integration theory.
   b. illusory conjunction.
   c. synesthesia.
   d. ventral and dorsal streaming.

8. The idea that specialized brain areas represent particular classes of objects is
   a. the modular view.
   b. attentional processing.

   c. distributed representation.
   d. neuron response.

9. The principle of _____ holds that even as sensory signals change, perception remains consistent.
   a. apparent motion
   b. signal detection
   c. perceptual constancy
   d. closure

10. Image-based and parts-based theories both involve the problem of
    a. motion detection.
    b. object identification.
    c. separating figure from ground.
    d. judging proximity.

11. What kind of cues are relative size and linear perspective?
    a. motion-based
    b. binocular
    c. monocular
    d. template

12. What does the frequency of a sound wave determine?
    a. pitch
    b. loudness
    c. sound quality
    d. timbre

13. The placement of our ears on opposite sides of the head is crucial to our ability to
    a. localize sound sources.
    b. determine pitch.
    c. judge intensity.
    d. recognize complexity.

14. The location and type of pain we experience is indicated by signals sent to
    a. the amygdala.
    b. the spinal cord.
    c. pain receptors.
    d. the somatosensory cortex.

15. What best explains why smells can have immediate and powerful effects?
    a. the involvement in smell of brain centres for emotions and memories
    b. the vast number of olfactory receptor neurons we have
    c. our ability to detect odours from pheromones
    d. the fact that different odorant molecules produce varied patterns of activity

# KEY TERMS

absolute threshold (p. 132)

accommodation (p. 137)

apparent motion (p. 154)

area A1 (p. 160)

area V1 (p. 141)

basilar membrane (p. 159)

binding problem (p. 144)

binocular disparity (p. 152)

blind spot (p. 139)

change blindness (p. 154)

cochlea (p. 159)

colour-opponent system (p. 141)

cones (p. 139)

feature-integration theory (p. 145)

fovea (p. 139)

gate-control theory of pain (p. 166)

hair cells (p. 159)

haptic perception (p. 164)

illusory conjunction (p. 145)

inattentional blindness (p. 154)

just noticeable difference (JND)
(p. 132)

loudness (p. 158)

monocular depth cues (p. 150)

olfactory bulb (p. 169)

olfactory receptor neurons (ORNs)
(p. 168)

perception (p. 131)

perceptual constancy (p. 147)

pheromones (p. 171)

pitch (p. 158)

place code (p. 161)

psychophysics (p. 132)

referred pain (p. 166)

retina (p. 137)

rods (p. 139)

sensation (p. 131)

sensory adaptation (p. 135)

signal detection theory (p. 133)

taste buds (p. 171)

template (p. 148)

temporal code (p. 161)

timbre (p. 158)

transduction (p. 131)

vestibular system (p. 167)

visual acuity (p. 135)

visual form agnosia (p. 142)

Weber's law (p. 133)

# CHANGING MINDS

1. A friend of yours is taking a class in medical ethics. "We discussed a tough case today," she says. "It's to do with a patient who's been in a vegetative state for several years, and the family has to decide whether to take him off life support. The doctors say he has no awareness of himself or his environment, and he's never expected to recover. But when light is shined in his eyes, his pupils contract. That shows he can sense light, so he has to have some ability to perceive his surroundings, doesn't he?" Without knowing any of the details of this particular case, how would you explain to your friend that a patient might be able to sense light but not perceive it? What other examples from the chapter could you use to illustrate the difference between sensation and perception?

2. In your philosophy class, the professor discusses the proposition that "perception is reality." From the point of view of philosophy, reality is the state of things that actually exists, whereas perception is how they

appear to the observer. What does psychophysics have to say about this issue? What are three ways in which sensory transduction can alter perception, causing perceptions that may differ from absolute reality?

3. A friend comes across the story of an American soldier, Leroy Petry, who received the Medal of Honor (a prestigious American military award) for saving the lives of two of his men. The soldiers were in a firefight in Afghanistan when a live grenade landed at their feet; Petry picked up the grenade and tried to toss it away from the others, but it exploded, destroying his right hand. According to the news report, Petry did not initially feel any pain; instead, he set about applying a tourniquet to his own arm while continuing to shout orders to his men as the firefight continued. "That's amazingly heroic," your friend says, "but that bit about not feeling the pain—that's crazy. He must just be so tough that he kept going despite the pain." What would you tell your friend? How can the perception of pain be altered?

# ANSWERS TO KEY CONCEPT QUIZ

1. b; 2. d; 3. b; 4. c; 5. b; 6. d; 7. a; 8. a; 9. c; 10. b; 11. c; 12. a; 13. a; 14. d; 15. a.

# 5

# Consciousness

▲ **Conscious and Unconscious:**
**The Mind's Eye, Open and Closed**
The Mysteries of Consciousness
The Nature of Consciousness
**HOT SCIENCE** Disorders of
Consciousness
The Unconscious Mind
**THE REAL WORLD** Anyone for Tennis?

▲ **Sleep and Dreaming:**
**Good Night, Mind**
Sleep
Dreams
**CULTURE & COMMUNITY** What Do
Dreams Mean to Us around
the World?

▲ **Drugs and Consciousness:**
**Artificial Inspiration**
Drug Use and Abuse
Types of Psychoactive Drugs

▲ **Hypnosis: Open to Suggestion**
Induction and Susceptibility
Hypnotic Effects
**OTHER VOICES** The Blink of an Eye

U NCONSCIOUSNESS IS SOMETHING YOU DO NOT REALLY appreciate until you need it. Belle Riskin needed it one day on an operating table, when she awoke just as doctors were pushing a breathing tube down her throat. She felt she was choking, but she could not see, breathe, scream, or move. Unable to even blink an eye, she could not signal to the surgeons that she was conscious. "I was terrified. Why is this happening to me? Why can't I feel my arms? I could feel my heart pounding in my head. It was like being buried alive, but with somebody shoving something down your throat," she explained later. "I knew I was conscious, that something was going on during the surgery. I had just enough awareness to know I was being intubated" (Groves, 2004).

How could this happen? Anesthesia for surgery is supposed to leave the patient unconscious, "feeling no pain," and yet, as in this case, in about one in every 1000–2000 surgeries (Sandin et al., 2000) the patient regains consciousness at some point and even remembers the experience. Some patients remember pain; others remember the clink of surgical instruments in a pan or the conversations of doctors and nurses. This is not how modern surgery is supposed to go, but the problem arises because muscle-relaxing drugs are used to keep the patient from moving involuntarily and making unhelpful contributions to the operation. Then, when the drugs that are given to induce unconsciousness fail to do the job, the patient with extremely relaxed muscles is unable to show or tell doctors that there is a problem.

Waking up in surgery sounds pretty rough all by itself, but this could cause additional complications. The conscious patient could become alarmed and emotional during the operation, spiking blood pressure and heart rate to dangerous levels. Awareness also might lead to later emotional problems. Fortunately, new methods of monitoring wakefulness by measuring the electrical activity of the brain are being developed. One system uses sensors attached to the patient's head and gives readings on a scale from 0 (*no electrical activity in the brain*) to 100 (*fully alert*), providing a kind of "consciousness meter."

MASTERFILE

When it is time for surgery, it is great to be unconscious.

Anesthesiologists using this index deliver anesthetics to keep the patient in the recommended range of 40–60 for general anesthesia during surgery; they have found that this system reduces postsurgical reports of consciousness and memory of the surgical experience (Myles et al., 2004), and that letting patients fall below 45 on this index for prolonged periods increases the risk of negative postoperative outcomes, including death (Kertai et al., 2010). One of these devices in the operating room might have helped Belle Riskin settle into the unconsciousness she so dearly needed.

**MOST OF THE TIME, OF COURSE, CONSCIOUSNESS IS SOMETHING WE CHERISH.** How else could we experience a favourite work of art, the familiar lyrics of an old song, the taste of a sweet, juicy peach, or the touch of a loved one's hand? **Consciousness** is *a person's subjective experience of the world and the mind.* Although you might think of consciousness as simply "being awake," the defining feature of consciousness is *experience,* which you have when you are awake or when having a vivid dream. Conscious experience is essential to what it means to be human. The anesthesiologist's dilemma in trying to monitor Belle Riskin's consciousness is a stark reminder, though, that it is impossible for one person to experience another's consciousness. Your consciousness is utterly private, a world of personal experience that only you can know.

How can this private world be studied? We will begin by examining consciousness directly, trying to understand what it is like and how it compares with the mind's *unconscious* processes. Then we will examine its departures from normal by exploring altered states: sleep and dreams, intoxication with alcohol and other drugs, hypnosis and meditation, and disorders of consciousness resulting from brain damage. Like the traveller who learns the meaning of *home* by roaming far away, we can learn the meaning of *consciousness* by exploring its exotic variations.

# Conscious and Unconscious: The Mind's Eye, Open and Closed

What does it feel like to be you right now? It probably feels as though you are somewhere inside your head, looking out at the world through your eyes. You can feel your hands on this book, perhaps, and notice the position of your body or the sounds in the room when you orient yourself toward them. If you shut your eyes, you may be able to imagine things in your mind, even though all the while thoughts and feelings come and go, passing through your imagination. But where are "you," really? And how is it that this theatre of consciousness gives you a view of some things in your world and your mind but not others? The theatre in your mind does not have seating for more than one, making it difficult to share what is on your mental screen with your friends, a researcher, or even yourself in precisely the same way a second time. We will look first at the difficulty of studying consciousness directly, examine the nature of consciousness (what it is that can be seen in this mental theatre), and then explore the unconscious mind (what is *not* visible to the mind's eye).

## The Mysteries of Consciousness

Other sciences, such as physics, chemistry, and biology, have the great luxury of studying *objects,* things that we all can see. Psychology studies objects, too, looking at people and their brains and behaviours, but it has the unique challenge of also trying to make sense of *subjects.* Physicists are not concerned with what it is like to be a neutron, but psychologists hope to understand what it is like to be a human; that is,

**consciousness**
A person's subjective experience of the world and the mind.

they seek to understand the subjective perspectives of the people whom they study. Psychologists hope to include an understanding of **phenomenology**, *how things seem to the conscious person*, in their understanding of mind and behaviour. After all, consciousness is an extraordinary human property. But including phenomenology in psychology brings up mysteries pondered by great thinkers almost since the beginning of thinking. Let us look at two of the more vexing mysteries of consciousness: the problem of other minds and the mind–body problem.

> What are the great mysteries of consciousness?

**phenomenology**
How things seem to the conscious person.

**problem of other minds**
The fundamental difficulty we have in perceiving the consciousness of others.

## The Problem of Other Minds

One great mystery is called the **problem of other minds,** *the fundamental difficulty we have in perceiving the consciousness of others.* How do you know that anyone else is conscious? They tell you that they are conscious, of course, and are often willing to describe in depth how they feel, how they think, what they are experiencing, and how good or how bad it all is. But perhaps they are just *saying* these things. There is no clear way to distinguish a conscious person from someone who might do and say all the same things as a conscious person but who is *not* conscious. Philosophers have called this hypothetical nonconscious person a *zombie*, in reference to the living-yet-dead creatures of horror films (Chalmers, 1996). A philosopher's zombie could talk about experiences ("The lights are so bright!") and even seem to react to them (wincing and turning away) but might not be having any inner experience at all. No one knows whether there could be such a zombie, but then again, because of the problem of other minds, none of us will ever know for sure that another person is *not* a zombie.

Even the consciousness meter used by anesthesiologists falls short. It certainly does not give the anesthesiologist any special insight into what it is like to be the patient on the operating table; it only predicts whether patients will *say* they were conscious. We simply lack the ability to directly perceive the consciousness of others. In short, *you* are the only thing in the universe you will ever truly know what it is like to be.

The problem of other minds also means there is no way you can tell if another person's experience of anything is at all like yours. Although you know what the colour red looks like to you, for instance, you cannot know whether it looks the same to other people. Maybe they are seeing what you see as blue and just calling it red in a consistent way. If their inner experience "looks" blue, but they say it looks hot and is the colour of a tomato, you will never be able to tell that their experience differs from yours. Of course, most people have come to trust each other in describing their inner lives, reaching the general assumption that other human minds are pretty much like their own. But they do not know this for a fact, and they cannot know it directly.

How do people perceive other minds? Researchers conducting a large online survey asked people to compare the minds of 13 different targets, such as a baby, a chimp, a robot, a man, and a woman, on 18 different mental capacities, such as feeling pain, pleasure, hunger, and consciousness (see **FIGURE 5.1** on the next page) (Gray, Gray, & Wegner, 2007). Respondents who were judging the mental capacity to feel pain, for example, compared pairs of targets: Is a frog or a dog more able to feel pain? Is a baby or a robot more able to feel pain? When the researchers examined all the comparisons on the different mental capacities with the computational technique of factor analysis (see the Intelligence chapter), they found that people judge minds according to two main capacities: the capacity for *experience* (such as the ability to feel pain, pleasure,

> How do people perceive other minds?

Unlike philosophers's zombies, these fictional zombies have the standard zombie look. But how do you know those around you are really conscious the same way that you are?

BECKY ROCKWOOD/GETTY IMAGES

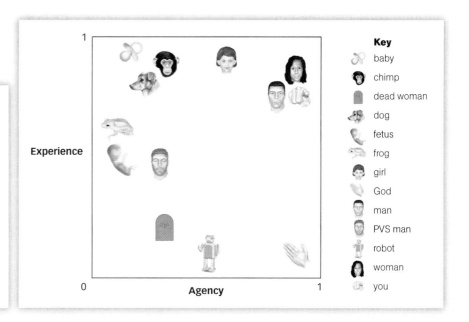

▶ Figure **5.1 Dimensions of Mind Perception** When participants judged the mental capacities of 13 targets, two dimensions of mind perception were discovered (Gray et al., 2007). Participants perceived minds as varying in the capacity for experience (such as abilities to feel pain or pleasure) and in the capacity for agency (such as abilities to plan or exert self-control). They perceived normal adult humans (male, female, or "you," the respondent) to have minds on both dimensions, whereas other targets were perceived to have reduced experience or agency. The man in a persistent vegetative state ("PVS man"), for example, was judged to have only some experience and very little agency.

hunger, consciousness, anger, or fear) and the capacity for *agency* (such as the ability for self-control, planning, memory, or thought). As shown in Figure 5.1, respondents rated some targets as having little experience or agency (the dead woman), others as having experiences but little agency (the baby), and yet others as having both experience and agency (adult humans). Still others were perceived to have agency without experiences (the robot, God). The perception of minds, then, involves more than just whether something has a mind. People appreciate that minds both have experiences and lead us to perform actions.

> **How does the capacity for experience differ from the capacity for agency?**

Ultimately, the problem of other minds is a problem for psychological science. As you will remember from the Methods chapter, the scientific method requires that any observation made by one scientist should, in principle, be available for observation by any other scientist. But if other minds are not observable, how can consciousness be a topic of scientific study? One radical solution is to eliminate consciousness from psychology entirely and follow the other sciences into total objectivity by renouncing the study of *anything* mental. This was the solution offered by behaviourism, and it turned out to have its own shortcomings, as you saw in the Psychology: Evolution of a Science chapter. Despite the problem of other minds, modern psychology has embraced the study of consciousness. The astonishing richness of mental life simply cannot be ignored.

## The Mind–Body Problem

▼ Figure **5.2 Seat of the Soul** Descartes imagined that the seat of the soul—and consciousness—might reside in the pineal gland located in the ventricles of the brain. This original drawing from Descartes (1662) shows the pineal gland (H) nicely situated for a soul, right in the middle of the brain.

Another mystery of consciousness is the **mind–body problem,** *the issue of how the mind is related to the brain and body.* French philosopher and mathematician René Descartes (1596–1650) is famous for proposing, among other things, that the human body is a machine made of physical matter but that the human mind or soul is a separate entity made of a "thinking substance." He suggested that the mind has its effects on the brain and body through the pineal gland, a small structure located near the centre of the brain (see **FIGURE 5.2**). In fact, the pineal gland is not even a nerve structure but is rather an endocrine gland, and so is poorly equipped to serve as a centre of human consciousness. We now know that, far from the tiny connection between mind and brain in the pineal gland that was proposed by Descartes, the mind and brain are connected everywhere to each other. In other words, "the mind is what the brain does" (Minsky, 1986, p. 287).

SCIENCE SOURCE

But Descartes was right in pointing out the difficulty of reconciling the physical body with the mind. Most psychologists assume that mental events are intimately tied to brain events, such that every thought, perception, or feeling is associated with a particular pattern of activation of neurons in the brain (see the Neuroscience and Behaviour chapter). Thinking about a particular person, for instance, occurs with a unique array of neural connections and activations. If the neurons repeat that pattern, then you must be thinking of the same person; conversely, if you think of the person, the brain activity occurs in that pattern.

One telling set of studies, however, suggests that the brain's activities *precede* the activities of the conscious mind. The electrical activity in the brains of volunteers was measured using sensors placed on their scalps as they repeatedly decided when to move a hand (Libet, 1985). Participants were also asked to indicate exactly when they consciously chose to move by reporting the position of a dot moving rapidly around the face of a clock just at the point of the decision (**FIGURE 5.3a**). As a rule, the brain begins to show electrical activity around half a second before a voluntary action (535 milliseconds [ms], to be exact). This makes sense because brain activity certainly seems to be necessary to get an action started.

**mind–body problem**
The issue of how the mind is related to the brain and body.

What this experiment revealed, though, was that the brain also started to show electrical activity before the person's conscious decision to move. As shown in **FIGURE 5.3b**, these studies found that the brain becomes active more than 300 ms before participants report that they are consciously trying to move. The feeling that you are consciously willing your actions, it seems, may be a result rather than a cause of your brain activity. Although your personal intuition is that you *think* of an action and *then* do it, these experiments suggest that your brain is getting started before *either* the thinking or the doing, preparing the way for both thought and action. Quite simply, it may appear to us that our minds are leading our brains and bodies, but the order of events may be the other way around (Haggard & Tsakiris, 2009; Wegner, 2002).

What comes first: brain activity or thinking?

Consciousness has its mysteries, but psychologists like a challenge. Although researchers may not be able to know exactly how consciousness arises from the brain, this does not prevent them from collecting people's reports of conscious experiences and learning how these reports reveal the nature of consciousness.

▲ Figure 5.3 **The Timing of Conscious Will** (*a*) In Benjamin Libet's experiments, the participant was asked to move fingers at will while watching a dot move around the face of a clock to mark the moment at which the action was consciously willed. Meanwhile, EEG sensors timed the onset of brain activation and EMG sensors timed the muscle movement. (*b*) The experiment showed that brain activity (EEG) precedes the willed movement of the finger (EMG), but that the reported time of consciously willing the finger to move follows the brain activity.

## The Nature of Consciousness

How would you describe your own consciousness? Researchers examining people's descriptions suggest that consciousness has four basic properties (intentionality, unity, selectivity, and transience), that it occurs on different levels, and that it includes a range of different contents. Let us examine each of these points in turn.

NORTH CAROLINA MUSEUM OF ART/CORBIS

▲ Figure **5.4** **Bellotto's Dresden and Closeup** (*left*) You may think the people on the bridge in the distance (in the red outline) seem finely detailed in *View of Dresden with the Frauenkirche at Left* by Bernardo Bellotto (1720–1780). However, when you examine the detail closely (*right*), you discover that the people are made of brushstrokes merely *suggesting* people—an arm here, a torso there. Consciousness produces a similar impression of "filling in," as it seems to consist of extreme detail even in areas that are peripheral (Dennett, 1991).

**dichotic listening**
A task in which people wearing headphones hear different messages presented to each ear.

Participants in a dichotic listening experiment hear different messages played to the right and left ears, and may be asked to "shadow" one of the messages by repeating it aloud.

IMAGE SOURCE PLUS/ALAMY

## Four Basic Properties

The first property of consciousness is *intentionality*, the quality of being directed toward an object. Consciousness is always *about* something. Psychologists have tried to measure the relationship between consciousness and its objects, examining the size and duration of the relationship. How long can consciousness be directed toward an object, and how many objects can it take on at one time? Researchers have found that conscious attention is limited. Despite all the lush detail you see in your mind's eye, the kaleidoscope of sights and sounds and feelings and thoughts, the object of your consciousness at any one moment is just a small part of all of this (see **FIGURE 5.4**). To describe how this limitation works, psychologists refer to three other properties of consciousness: unity, selectivity, and transience.

The second basic property of consciousness is *unity*, which is the ability to integrate information from all of the body's senses into one coherent whole. As you read this book, your five senses are taking in a great deal of information. Your eyes are scanning lots of black squiggles on a page (or screen) while also sensing an enormous array of shapes, colours, depths, and textures in your periphery; your hands are gripping a heavy book (or computer); your butt and feet may sense pressure from gravity pulling you against a chair or floor; and you may be listening to music or talking in another room, while smelling the odour of freshly made popcorn (or your roommate's dirty laundry). Although your body is constantly sensing an enormous amount of information from the world around you, your brain—amazingly—integrates all of this information into the experience of one unified consciousness (or two in the case of the split-brain patients described in the Neuroscience and Behaviour chapter).

The third property of consciousness is *selectivity*, the capacity to include some objects but not others. While binding the many sensations around you into a coherent whole, your mind must make decisions about which pieces of information to include, and which to exclude. Inattentional blindness, which you learned about in the Sensation and Perception chapter, is an example of selectivity. Selectivity is also shown through studies of **dichotic listening,** *in which people wearing headphones hear different messages in each ear.* Research participants were instructed to repeat aloud the words they heard in one ear while a different message was presented to the other ear (Cherry, 1953). As a result of focusing on the words they were supposed to repeat, participants noticed little of the second message, often not even realizing that at some point it changed from English to German! So, consciousness *filters out* some information. At the same time, participants did notice when the voice in the unattended ear changed from a man's to a woman's. Participants in another study were especially likely to notice if their own name was spoken into the unattended ear (Moray, 1959). This suggests that the selectivity of consciousness can also work to *tune in* other information. Perhaps you, too, have noticed how abruptly your attention is diverted from whatever conversation you are having when someone else within earshot at a party mentions your name. Selectivity is not only a property of waking consciousness: the mind works this way in other states. People are more sensitive to their own name than others' names, for example, even during sleep (Oswald, Taylor, & Triesman, 1960). This is why, when you are trying to wake someone, it is best to say the person's name.

> **How does your mind know which information to allow into consciousness, and which to filter out?**

The fourth and final basic property of consciousness is *transience,* or the tendency to change. Consciousness wiggles and fidgets like a toddler in the seat behind you on an airplane. The mind wanders not just sometimes, but incessantly, from one "right now" to the next "right now" and then on to the next (Wegner, 1997). William James, whom you met way back in the Psychology: Evolution of a Science chapter, famously described consciousness as a stream: "Consciousness … does not appear to itself chopped up in bits. Such words as 'chain' or 'train' do not describe it. … It is nothing jointed; it flows. A 'river' or a 'stream' are the metaphors by which it is most naturally described" (James, 1890, Vol. 1, p. 239). Books written in the "stream of consciousness" style, such as James Joyce's *Ulysses,* illustrate the whirling, chaotic, and constantly changing flow of consciousness. Here is an excerpt with Molly Bloom speaking:

> I wished I could have picked every morsel of that chicken out of my fingers it was so tasty and browned and as tender as anything only for I did not want to eat everything on my plate those forks and fishslicers were hallmarked silver too I wish I had some I could easily have slipped a couple into my muff when I was playing with them then always hanging out of them for money in a restaurant for the bit you put down your throat we have to be thankful for our mangy cup of tea itself as a great compliment to be noticed the way the world is divided in any case if its going to go on I want at least two other good chemises for one thing and but I do not know what kind of drawers he likes none at all I think did not he say yes and half the girls in Gibraltar never wore them either naked as God made them that Andalusian singing her Manola she did not make much secret of what she hadnt yes and the second pair of silkette stockings is laddered after one days wear I could have brought them back to Lewers this morning and kicked up a row and made that one change them only not to upset myself and run the risk of walking into him and ruining the whole thing and one of those kidfitting corsets Id want advertised cheap in the Gentlewoman with elastic gores on the hips he saved the one I have but thats no good what did they say they give a delightful figure line 11/6 obviating that unsightly broad appearance across the lower back to reduce flesh my belly is a bit too big Ill have to knock off the stout at dinner or am I getting too fond of it... (1922/2013, p. 625).

The stream of consciousness may flow in this way partly because of the limited capacity of the conscious mind. We humans can hold only so much information in mind, after all, so when more information is selected, some of what is currently there must disappear. As a result, our focus of attention keeps changing. The stream of consciousness flows so inevitably that it even changes our perspective when we view a constant object like a Necker cube (see **FIGURE 5.5**).

## Levels of Consciousness

Consciousness can also be understood as having levels, ranging from minimal consciousness to full consciousness to self-consciousness. These levels of consciousness would probably all register as "conscious" on that wakefulness meter for surgery patients you read about at the beginning of the chapter. The levels of consciousness that psychologists distinguish involve different qualities of awareness of the world and of the self.

In its minimal form, consciousness is just a connection between the person and the world. When you sense the sun coming in through the window, for example, you

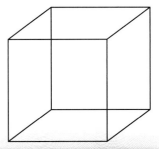

▲ Figure **5.5** **The Necker Cube** This cube has the property of reversible perspective in that you can bring one or the other of its two square faces to the front in your mind's eye. Although it may take a while to reverse the figure at first, once people have learned to do it, they can reverse it regularly, about once every 3 s (Gomez et al., 1995). The stream of consciousness flows even when the target is a constant object.

Full consciousness involves a consciousness of oneself, such as thinking about the act of driving while driving a car. How is this different from self-consciousness?

**minimal consciousness**
A low-level kind of sensory awareness and responsiveness that occurs when the mind inputs sensations and may output behaviour.

**full consciousness**
Consciousness in which you know and are able to report your mental state.

**self-consciousness**
A distinct level of consciousness in which the person's attention is drawn to the self as an object.

Self-consciousness is a curse and a blessing. Looking in a mirror can make people evaluate themselves on deeper attributes such as honesty as well as superficial ones such as appearance.

might turn toward the light. Such **minimal consciousness** is *a low-level kind of sensory awareness and responsiveness that occurs when the mind inputs sensations and may output behaviour* (Armstrong, 1980). This kind of sensory awareness and responsiveness could even happen when someone pokes you during sleep and you turn over. Something seems to register in your mind, at least in the sense that you experience it, but you may not think at all about having had the experience. It could be that animals or, for that matter, even plants can have this minimal level of consciousness. But because of the problem of other minds and the notorious reluctance of animals and plants to talk to us, we cannot know for sure that they *experience* the things that make them respond. At least in the case of humans, we can safely assume that there is something it "feels like" to be them and that when they are awake, they are at least minimally conscious.

Human consciousness is often more than minimal, of course, but what exactly gets added? Consider the glorious feeling of waking up on a spring morning as rays of sun stream across your pillow. It is not just that you are having this experience: Being fully conscious means that you are also *aware* that you are having this experience. The critical ingredient that accompanies **full consciousness** is that you *know and are able to report your mental state.* That is a subtle distinction: Being fully conscious means that you are aware of having a mental state while you are experiencing the mental state itself. When you have a hurt leg and mindlessly rub it, for instance, your pain may be minimally conscious. After all, you seem to be experiencing pain because you have acted and are indeed rubbing your leg. It is only when you realize that it hurts, though, that the pain becomes fully conscious. Have you ever been driving a car and suddenly realized that you do not remember the past 15 minutes of driving? Chances are that you were not unconscious, but instead minimally conscious. When you are completely aware and thinking about your driving, you have moved into the realm of full consciousness. Full consciousness involves not only thinking about things but also thinking about the fact that you are thinking about things (Jaynes, 1976).

> What factor of full consciousness distinguishes it from minimal consciousness?

Full consciousness involves a certain consciousness of oneself; the person notices the self in a particular mental state ("Here I am, reading this sentence."). However, this is not quite the same thing as *self*-consciousness. Sometimes consciousness is entirely flooded with the self ("Not only am I reading this sentence, but I have a blemish on the end of my nose today that makes me feel like guiding a sleigh."). Self-consciousness focuses on the self to the exclusion of almost everything else. William James (1890) and other theorists have suggested that **self-consciousness** is yet another *distinct level of consciousness in which the person's attention is drawn to the self as an object* (Morin, 2006). Most people report experiencing such self-consciousness when they are embarrassed; when they find themselves the focus of attention in a group; when someone focuses a camera on them; or when they are deeply introspective about their thoughts, feelings, or personal qualities.

Self-consciousness brings with it a tendency to evaluate yourself and notice your shortcomings. Looking in a mirror, for example, is all it takes to make people evaluate themselves—thinking not just about their appearance, but also about whether they are good or bad in other ways. People go out of their way to avoid mirrors when they have done something they are ashamed of (Duval & Wicklund, 1972). Self-consciousness can certainly spoil a good mood, so much so that a tendency to be chronically self-conscious is associated with depression (Pyszczynski, Holt, & Greenberg, 1987). However, because it makes people self-critical, the self-consciousness that results when people see their own mirror images can make them briefly more helpful, more cooperative, and less aggressive (Gibbons, 1990). Perhaps everyone would be a bit more civilized if mirrors were held up for them to see themselves as objects of their own scrutiny.

> When do people go out of their way to avoid mirrors?

# Disorders of Consciousness

Improvements in medical intensive care in the last several years means that more patients are surviving severe brain injury caused by an illness or accident. Such brain damage can produce a transient or permanent *disorder of consciousness,* in which the patient is not able to demonstrate either full consciousness or self-consciousness. Doctors and researchers distinguish several different disorders of consciousness, and these can either be transient stages on the road to recovery or more permanent conditions.

Patients in a *coma* look a bit like they are asleep—their eyes are closed and they are unresponsive. This is the typical state right after injury, and usually does not last long. Patients in a coma typically recover full consciousness, or progress into a vegetative state or a state of minimal consciousness within a month or so (Multi-Society Task Force on PVS, 1994).

Patients in a *vegetative state* alternate between eyes-open and eyes-closed states: they have regular periods of time in which they appear to be "awake." Patients may move their limbs and eyes, swallow, smile, cry, grunt, moan, or scream, but— and this is key to the diagnosis—none of these behaviours are *produced reliably in response to external stimulation.* In other words, there is no evidence that patients are aware of themselves or their surroundings, as demonstrated by reliable, purposeful responding to sensory stimulation (such as being touched or hearing their name called). This state may be a temporary condition as patients recover or may be permanent.

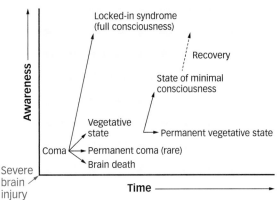

◀ Disorders of consciousness can be transient, as a patient recovers from brain damage, or can be permanent. It can be very difficult to observe when a severely injured patient is recovering awareness. Most measures rely on the patient being able to respond behaviourally, which is not always possible even when the patient is aware.

Patients in a *minimally consciousness state* can respond reliably but somewhat inconsistently to sensory stimulation. Again this condition can be temporary, preceding recovery of full awareness, or may be permanent.

*Locked-in syndrome* is a rare condition in which patients have full awareness, but cannot demonstrate it because they cannot move any voluntary muscles. The French journalist, Jean-Dominique Bauby, wrote *The Diving Bell and the Butterfly* after he suffered a massive stroke that left him with locked-in syndrome. Patients with locked-in syndrome can, like Bauby, sometimes move their eyes voluntarily up and down, and can use this movement to communicate. Some locked-in patients do not have even this minimal control of voluntary muscles. This is not a disorder of consciousness, but can easily be mistaken for one.

How do doctors determine whether a patient is aware? Traditionally, they observe the patient's behaviour and judge whether the patient is repeatedly able to respond to

commands (like "raise your left arm"), or to the sound of his or her name being spoken. However, brain damage can also make it difficult for patients to move their muscles voluntarily in order to produce a behaviour that the doctor can see or hear. In recent years, brain-imaging methods have given researchers and physicians a direct window on to brain activity. (Brain activity is, after all, the wellspring of behaviour—for the left arm to be raised, there first must be a specific pattern of arm-raising activity in the brain.) Brain activity measures can be used to assess disorders of consciousness more accurately (see The Real World: Anyone for Tennis?). We now know that, out of every 100 people diagnosed as being in a vegetative state using traditional bedside assessment, between 10 and 40 will turn out to be conscious to some degree when assessed using these more sensitive measures (Monti et al., 2010), and about a third of patients diagnosed as minimally conscious may be fully conscious (Cruse et al., 2012b).

▼ Coma, vegetative state, and minimally conscious state are all disorders of consciousness that occur after severe brain injury. Locked-in syndrome is not a disorder of consciousness, but can be mistaken for vegetative state because the patient cannot behaviourally demonstrate that they are conscious.

## Disorders of Consciousness

| Diagnosis | Arousal/wakefulness | Awareness | Communication |
|---|---|---|---|
| Coma | Do not open eyes<br>No sleep-awake pattern | No evidence | None |
| Vegetative state | Open eyes<br>Sleep-awake pattern | No evidence | None |
| Minimally conscious state | Open eyes<br>Sleep-wake pattern | Inconsistent but reproducible evidence | Ranges from none to inconsistent, but reproducible |
| Locked-in syndrome | Open eyes<br>Sleep-wake pattern | Fully aware | Consistent, using vertical eye movement |

**Dilbert**

Most animals cannot follow this path to civilization. The typical dog, cat, or bird seems mystified by a mirror, ignoring it or acting as though there is some other critter back there. However, chimpanzees that have spent time with mirrors sometimes behave in ways that suggest they recognize themselves in a mirror. To examine this, researchers painted an odourless red dye over the eyebrow of an anesthetized chimp and then watched when the awakened chimp was presented with a mirror (Gallup, 1977). If the chimp interpreted the mirror image as a representation of some other chimp with an unusual approach to cosmetics, we would expect it just to look at the mirror or perhaps to reach toward it. But the chimp reached toward its *own eye* as it looked into the mirror—not the mirror image—suggesting that it recognized the image as a reflection of itself.

Versions of this experiment have now been repeated with many different animals, and it turns out that, like humans, animals such as chimpanzees and orangutans (Gallup, 1997), possibly dolphins (Reiss & Marino, 2001), and maybe even elephants (Plotnik, de Waal, & Reiss, 2006) and magpies (Prior, Schwartz, & Güntürkün, 2008) recognize their own mirror images. Dogs, cats, crows, monkeys, and gorillas have been tested, too, but do not seem to know they are looking at themselves. Even humans do not have self-recognition right away. Infants do not recognize themselves in mirrors until they have reached about 18 months of age (Lewis & Brooks-Gunn, 1979). The experience of self-consciousness, as measured by self-recognition in mirrors, is limited to a few animals and to humans only after a certain stage of development.

A chimpanzee tried to wipe off the red dye on its eyebrow in the Gallup experiment. This suggests that some animals recognize themselves in the mirror.

## Conscious Contents

What is on your mind? For that matter, what is on everybody's mind? One way to learn what is on people's minds is to ask them, and much research has called on people simply to *think aloud.* A more systematic approach is the *experience-sampling technique,* in which people are asked to report their conscious experiences at particular times. Equipped with electronic beepers or called on cell phones, for example, participants are asked to record their current thoughts when asked at random times throughout the day (Bolger, Davis, & Rafaeli, 2003).

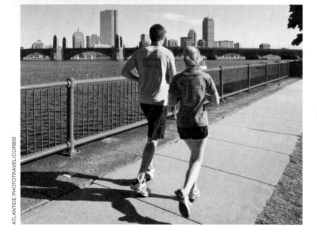

One concern on many students' minds is diet and exercise to keep in shape.

Experience-sampling studies show that consciousness is dominated by the immediate environment—what is seen, felt, heard, tasted, and smelled—all are at the forefront of the mind. Much of consciousness beyond this orientation to the environment turns to the person's *current concerns,* or what the person is thinking about repeatedly (Klinger, 1975). **TABLE 5.1** (on the next page) shows the results of a Minnesota study where 175 undergraduate students were asked to report their current concerns (Goetzman, Hughes, & Klinger, 1994). The researchers sorted the concerns into the categories shown in the table. Keep in mind that these concerns are ones the students did not mind reporting to psychologists; their private preoccupations may have been different and probably far more interesting.

Think for a moment about your own current concerns. What topics have been on your mind the most in the past day or two? Your mental "to do" list may include things you want to get, keep, avoid, work on, remember, and so on (Little, 1993). Items on the list often pop into mind, sometimes even with an emotional punch ("The test in this class is tomorrow!"). People in one study had their skin conductance level (SCL) measured to assess their emotional responses (Nikula, Klinger, & Larson-Gutman, 1993). SCL sensors attached to their fingers indicated when sweat appeared on their skin—a good indication that they were thinking about something distressing. Once in a while, SCL would rise spontaneously, and at these times the researchers quizzed the participants about their conscious thoughts. These emotional moments, compared to those when SCL was normal, often corresponded with a current concern popping into mind. Thoughts that are not emotional all by themselves can still come to mind with an emotional bang when they are topics of current concern.

We discussed thinking about our current concerns before, but what

> **How do researchers study subjective experience?**

is our subjective experience when actually carrying out the events of our daily lives? We are, of course, each engaged in our daily lives, but rarely examine what our moment-by-moment experiences are like, or make cross-experience comparisons. Researchers are now using experience-sampling methods to record the emotions people experience during everyday activities with interesting results. One recent study collected data from over 900 working women by asking them to reflect on the events of the past day and record how they felt while engaging in each activity (Kahneman et al., 2004). Some of the results are as expected. For instance, as shown in **TABLE 5.2**, people score lowest on positive affect when commuting, working, and doing housework, and unfortunately this is how we spend a large part of our day. The women in this study reported having the most positive affect while being intimate with another person, although they only did this for 12 minutes of the day. Some less intuitive findings are the activities that fell in between the two. In survey studies parents often report that they are happiest when spending time with their children but, when asked about actual events of the prior day, being with their children ranked just two ticks above housework and well below other activities like shopping, watching TV, and making more children.

> **Table 5.1**

### What is on Your Mind? University Students' Current Concerns

| Current Concern Category | Example | Frequency of Students Who Mentioned the Concern |
|---|---|---|
| Family | Gain better relations with immediate family | 40% |
| Roommate | Change attitude or behaviour of roommate | 29% |
| Household | Clean room | 52% |
| Friends | Make new friends | 42% |
| Dating | Desire to date a certain person | 24% |
| Sexual intimacy | Abstaining from sex | 16% |
| Health | Diet and exercise | 85% |
| Employment | Get a summer job | 33% |
| Education | Go to graduate school | 43% |
| Social activities | Gain acceptance into a campus organization | 34% |
| Religious | Attend church more | 51% |
| Financial | Pay rent or bills | 8% |
| Government | Change government policy | 14% |

*Source:* Goetzman, E. S., Hughes, T., & Klinger, E. (1994). *Current concerns of college students in a midwestern sample.* University of Minnesota, Morris.

> **Table 5.2**

### How Was Your Day? Women's Ratings of Level of Positive Affect and Amount of Time in Daily Activities

| Activities | Mean Affect Rating | |
|---|---|---|
| | **Positive Affect** | **Mean Hours/Day** |
| Intimate relations | 5.1 | 0.2 |
| Socializing | 4.59 | 2.3 |
| Relaxing | 4.42 | 2.2 |
| Pray/worship/meditate | 4.35 | 0.4 |
| Eating | 4.34 | 2.2 |
| Exercising | 4.31 | 0.2 |
| Watching TV | 4.19 | 2.2 |
| Shopping | 3.95 | 0.4 |
| Preparing food | 3.93 | 1.1 |
| On the phone | 3.92 | 2.5 |
| Napping | 3.87 | 0.9 |
| Taking care of my children | 3.86 | 1.1 |
| Computer/e-mail/Internet | 3.81 | 1.9 |
| Housework | 3.73 | 1.1 |
| Working | 3.62 | 6.9 |
| Commuting | 3.45 | 1.6 |

*Source:* Kahneman, D., Krueger, A. B., Schkade, D. A., Schwartz, N., & Stone, A. A. (2004). A survey method for characterizing daily life experience: The day reconstruction method (Table 1). *Science, 306,* 1776–1780.

**▲ Figure 5.6 The Default Network Activated during Daydreaming** An fMRI scan shows that many areas, known as the default network, are active when the person is not given a specific mental task to perform during the scan (Mason et al., 2007).

**Daydreaming.** Current concerns do not seem all that concerning, however, during *daydreaming,* a state of consciousness in which a seemingly purposeless flow of thoughts comes to mind. When thoughts drift along this way, it may seem as if you are just wasting time. The brain, however, is active even when there is no specific task at hand. This mental work done in daydreaming was examined in an fMRI study of people resting in the scanner (Mason et al., 2007). Usually, people in brain scanning studies do not have time to daydream much because they are kept busy with mental tasks—scans cost money and researchers want to get as much data as possible for their bucks. But when people are *not* busy, they still show a widespread pattern of activation in many areas of the brain—now known as the *default network* (Gusnard & Raichle, 2001). The study by Mason and her colleagues revealed that this network became activated whenever people worked on a mental task that they knew so well that they could daydream while doing it (see **FIGURE 5.6**). The areas of the default network are known to be involved in thinking about social life, about the self, and about the past and future—all the usual haunts of the daydreaming mind (Mitchell, 2006).

> What part of the brain is active during daydreaming?

**Thought Suppression.** The current concerns that populate consciousness can sometimes get the upper hand, transforming daydreams or everyday thoughts into rumination and worry. Thoughts that return again and again, or problem-solving attempts that never seem to succeed, can come to dominate consciousness. When this happens, people may exert **mental control,** *the attempt to change conscious states of mind.* For example, someone troubled by a recurring worry about the future ("What if I can't get a decent job when I graduate?") might choose to try *not* to think about this because it causes too much anxiety and uncertainty. Whenever this thought comes to mind, the person engages in **thought suppression,** the *conscious avoidance of a thought.* This may seem like a perfectly sensible strategy because it eliminates the worry and allows the person to move on to think about something else.

Or does it? The great Russian novelist, Fyodor Dostoyevsky (1863/1988, p. 49), remarked on the difficulty of thought suppression: "Try to pose for yourself this task: not to think of a polar bear, and you will see that the cursed thing will come to mind every minute." Inspired by this observation, Daniel Wegner and his colleagues (1987) gave people this exact task in the laboratory. Participants were asked to try not to think about a white bear for 5 minutes while they recorded all their thoughts aloud into a tape recorder. In addition, they were asked to ring a bell if the thought of a white bear came to mind. On average, they mentioned the white bear or rang the bell (indicating the thought) more than once per minute. Thought suppression simply did not work and instead produced a flurry of returns of the unwanted thought. What is more, when some research participants later were specifically asked to change tasks and deliberately *think* about a white bear, they became oddly preoccupied with it. A graph of their bell rings in **FIGURE 5.7** (on the next page) shows that these participants had the white bear come to mind far more often than did people who had only been asked to think about the bear from the outset, with no prior suppression. This **rebound effect of thought suppression,** *the tendency of a thought to return to consciousness with greater frequency following suppression,* suggests that attempts at mental control may be difficult indeed. The act of trying to suppress a thought may itself cause that thought to return to consciousness in a robust way.

**The Ironic Monitor.** Similar to thought suppression, other attempts to steer consciousness in any direction can result in mental states that are precisely the opposite of those desired. How ironic: Trying to consciously achieve one task may produce precisely the opposite outcome! These ironic effects seem most likely to occur when the person is distracted or under stress. People who are distracted while they are trying to get into a good mood, for example, tend to become sad (Wegner, Erber, &

Go ahead, look away from the book for a minute and try not to think about a white bear.

**mental control**
The attempt to change conscious states of mind.

**thought suppression**
The conscious avoidance of a thought.

**rebound effect of thought suppression**
The tendency of a thought to return to consciousness with greater frequency following suppression.

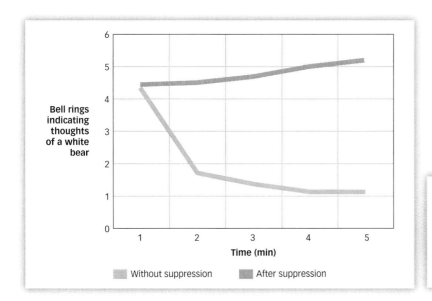

◄ Figure 5.7 **Rebound Effect** Research participants were first asked to try not to think about a white bear, and then they were asked to think about it and to ring a bell whenever it came to mind. Compared to those who were simply asked to think about a bear without prior suppression, those people who *first* suppressed the thought showed a rebound of increased thinking (Wegner et al., 1987).

Zanakos, 1993), and those who are distracted while trying to relax actually become more anxious than those who are not trying to relax (Wegner, Broome, & Blumberg, 1997). Likewise, an attempt not to overshoot a golf putt, undertaken during distraction, often yields the unwanted overshot (Wegner, Ansfield, & Pilloff, 1998). The theory of **ironic processes of mental control** proposes that such *ironic errors occur because the mental process that monitors errors can itself produce them* (Wegner, 1994a, 2009). In the attempt not to think of a white bear, for instance, a small part of the mind is ironically *searching* for the white bear.

This ironic monitoring process is not present in consciousness. After all, trying *not* to think of something would be useless if monitoring the progress of suppression required keeping that target in consciousness. For example, if trying not to think of a white bear meant that you consciously kept repeating to yourself, "No white bear! No white bear!" then you have failed before you have begun: That thought is present in consciousness even as you strive to eliminate it. Rather, the ironic monitor is a process of the mind that works *outside* of consciousness, making us sensitive to all the things we do not want to think, feel, or do so that we can notice and consciously take steps to regain control if these things come back to mind. As this unconscious monitoring whirs along in the background, it unfortunately increases the person's sensitivity to the very thought that is unwanted. Ironic processes are mental functions that are needed for effective mental control—they help in the process of banishing a thought from consciousness—but they can sometimes yield the very failure they seem designed to overcome. Ironic effects of mental control arise from processes that work outside of consciousness, so they remind us that much of the mind's machinery may be hidden from our view, lying outside the fringes of our experience.

**Is consciously avoiding a worrisome thought a sensible strategy?**

**ironic processes of mental control**
Mental processes that can produce ironic errors because monitoring for errors can itself produce them.

## The Unconscious Mind

Many mental processes are unconscious, in the sense that they occur without our experience of them. When we speak, for instance, "We are not really conscious either of the search for words, or of putting the words together into phrases, or of putting the phrases into sentences. … The actual process of thinking … is not conscious at all … only its preparation, its materials, and its end result are consciously perceived" (Jaynes, 1976, p. 41). Just to put the role of consciousness in perspective, think for a moment about the mental processes involved in simple addition. What happens in

There are no conscious steps between hearing an easy problem (what is four plus five?) and thinking of the answer—unless you have to count on your fingers.

**dynamic unconscious**
An active system encompassing a lifetime of hidden memories, the person's deepest instincts and desires, and the person's inner struggle to control these forces.

**repression**
A mental process that removes unacceptable thoughts and memories from consciousness and keeps them in the unconscious.

consciousness between hearing a problem (what is four plus five?) and thinking of the answer (nine)? Probably nothing—the answer just appears in the mind. But this is a piece of calculation that must take at least a bit of thinking. After all, at a very young age you may have had to solve such problems by counting on your fingers. Now that you do not have to do that anymore (please tell me you do not have to do that anymore), the answer seems to pop into your head automatically, by virtue of a process that does not require you to be aware of any underlying steps and, for that matter, does not even *allow* you to be aware of the steps. The answer just suddenly appears.

In the early part of the twentieth century, when structuralist psychologists, such as Edward Titchener, believed that introspection was the best method of research (see the Psychology: Evolution of a Science chapter), research volunteers trained in describing their thoughts tried to discern what happens when a simple problem brings to mind a simple answer (e.g., Watt, 1905). They drew the same blank you probably did. Nothing conscious seems to bridge this gap, but the answer comes from somewhere, and this emptiness points to the unconscious mind. To explore these hidden recesses, we can look at the classical theory of the unconscious introduced by Sigmund Freud and then at the modern cognitive psychology of unconscious mental processes.

### Freudian Unconscious

The true champion of the unconscious mind was Sigmund Freud. As you read in the Psychology: Evolution of a Science chapter, Freud's psychoanalytic theory viewed conscious thought as the surface of a much deeper mind made up of unconscious processes. Far more than just a collection of hidden processes, Freud described a **dynamic unconscious**—*an active system encompassing a lifetime of hidden memories, the person's deepest instincts and desires, and the person's inner struggle to control these forces.* The dynamic unconscious might contain hidden sexual thoughts about one's parents, for example, or destructive urges aimed at a helpless infant—the kinds of thoughts people keep secret from others and may not even acknowledge to themselves. According to Freud's theory, the unconscious is a force to be held in check by **repression,** *a mental process that removes unacceptable thoughts and memories from consciousness and keeps them in the unconscious.* Without repression, a person might think, do, or say every unconscious impulse or animal urge, no matter how selfish or immoral. With repression, these desires are held in the recesses of the dynamic unconscious.

Freud looked for evidence of the unconscious mind in speech errors and lapses of consciousness, or what are commonly called *Freudian slips.* Forgetting the name of someone you dislike, for example, is a slip that seems to have special meaning. Freud believed that errors are not random and instead have some surplus meaning that may appear to have been created by an intelligent unconscious mind, even though the person consciously disavows them. For example, when reporting on the news that members of the United States military had killed Osama bin Laden, several reporters and commentators at Fox News, a conservative American news outlet, independently reported that *Obama* bin Laden was dead. This slip even appeared as a printed announcement on one of its news shows.

Did the Fox News slip mean anything? One experiment revealed that slips of speech can indeed be prompted by a person's pressing concerns (Motley & Baars, 1979). Research participants in one group were told they might receive minor electric shocks, whereas those in another group heard no mention of this. Each person was then asked to read quickly through a

**What do Freudian slips tell us about the unconscious mind?**

After the death of Osama bin Laden, several staff members at the conservative Fox News channel slipped and reported on the death of *Obama* bin Laden.

series of word pairs, including *shad bock*. Those in the group warned about shock more often slipped in pronouncing this pair, blurting out *bad shock*.

Unlike errors created in experiments such as this one, many of the meaningful errors Freud attributed to the dynamic unconscious were not predicted in advance and so seem to depend on clever after-the-fact interpretations. Such interpretations can be wrong. Suggesting a pattern to a series of random events is not the same as scientifically predicting and explaining when and why an event should happen. Anyone can offer a reasonable, compelling explanation for an event after it has already happened, but the true work of science is to offer testable hypotheses that are evaluated based on reliable evidence. Freud's (1901/1938) book, *The Psychopathology of Everyday Life*, suggests not so much that the dynamic unconscious produces errors but that Freud himself was a master at finding meaning in errors that might otherwise have seemed random.

## A Modern View of the Cognitive Unconscious

Modern psychologists share Freud's interest in the impact of unconscious mental processes on consciousness and on behaviour. However, rather than Freud's vision of the unconscious as a teeming menagerie of animal urges and repressed thoughts, the current study of the unconscious mind views it as the factory that builds the products of conscious thought and behaviour (Kihlstrom, 1987; Wilson, 2002). The **cognitive unconscious** includes *all the mental processes that give rise to a person's thoughts, choices, emotions, and behaviour even though they are not experienced by the person.*

One indication of the cognitive unconscious at work is when a person's thoughts or behaviours are changed by exposure to information outside of consciousness. This happens in **subliminal perception**, when *thought or behaviour is influenced by stimuli that a person cannot consciously report perceiving.* Worries about the potential of subliminal influence were first provoked in 1957, when a marketer, James Vicary, claimed he had increased concession sales at a New Jersey theatre by flashing the words "Eat Popcorn" and "Drink Coke" briefly on-screen during movies. It turns out his story was a hoax, and many attempts to increase sales using similar methods have failed. But the very idea of influencing behaviour outside of consciousness created a wave of alarm about insidious "subliminal persuasion" that still concerns people today (Epley, Savitsky, & Kachelski, 1999; Pratkanis, 1992).

Although the story above was a hoax, factors outside our conscious awareness can indeed influence our behaviour. For example, one classic study reported that exposure to information about getting old can make a person walk more slowly. John Bargh and his colleagues had undergraduate students complete a survey that called for them to make sentences with various words (1996). The students were not informed that most of the words were commonly associated with aging (*Florida, grey, wrinkled*), and even afterward they did not report being aware of this trend. In this case, the "aging" idea was not presented subliminally, just not very noticeably. As these research participants left the experiment, they were clocked as they walked down the hall. Compared with those not exposed to the aging-related words, the participants walked more slowly! Just as with subliminal perception, a passing exposure to ideas can influence actions without conscious awareness.

The unconscious mind can be a kind of "mental butler," taking over background tasks that are too tedious, subtle, or bothersome for consciousness to trifle with (Bargh & Chartrand, 1999; Bargh & Morsella, 2008; Bower, 1999). Psychologists have long debated just how smart this mental butler might be. Freud attributed great intelligence to the unconscious, believing that it harbours complex motives and inner conflicts and that it expresses these in an astonishing array of thoughts and emotions, as well as psychological disorders (see the Psychological Disorders chapter). Contemporary

**cognitive unconscious**
All the mental processes that give rise to a person's thoughts, choices, emotions, and behaviour even though they are not experienced by the person.

**subliminal perception**
Thought or behaviour that is influenced by stimuli that a person cannot consciously report perceiving.

Do people in a movie theatre need any subliminal messages to get them to eat popcorn? Probably not. Would subliminal messages make them more likely to eat popcorn? Maybe, but not much.

Choosing a roommate can be like playing the lottery: You win some, you lose some, and then you lose some more.

cognitive psychologists wonder whether the unconscious is so smart, however, and point out that some unconscious processes even seem downright "dumb" (Loftus & Klinger, 1992). For example, the unconscious processes that underlie the perception of subliminal visual stimuli do not seem able to understand the combined meaning of word pairs, although they can understand single words. To the *conscious* mind, for example, a word pair such as *enemy loses* is somewhat positive—it is good to have your enemy lose. However, subliminal presentations of this word pair make people think of negative things, as though the unconscious mind is simply adding together the unpleasantness of the single words *enemy* and *loses* (Greenwald, 1992). Perhaps the mental butler is not all that bright.

In some cases, however, the unconscious mind can make better decisions than the conscious mind. Participants in an experiment were asked to choose which of three hypothetical people with many different qualities they would prefer to have as a roommate (Dijksterhuis, 2004). One candidate was objectively better, with more positive qualities, and participants who were given 4 minutes to make a *conscious decision* tended to choose that one. A second group was asked for an *immediate decision* as soon as the information display was over, and a third group was encouraged to reach an *unconscious decision*. This group was also given 4 minutes after the display ended to give their answer (as the conscious group

**What evidence shows the unconscious mind is a good decision maker?**

# Anyone for Tennis?

THE REAL WORLD

In 1999, Scott Routley was seriously injured in a car accident when he pulled out in front of a Sarnia police cruiser. For 12 years he was considered by doctors to be in a vegetative state: showing periods of apparent eyes-open wakefulness, but without any signs of awareness of himself or his environment and without any apparent ability to communicate. Definitely not (it was thought), in any state to play tennis. This view of Scott changed dramatically when he underwent a series of fMRI scans at the University of Western Ontario.

For many years, Adrian Owen and his colleagues at the University of Western Ontario, working with researchers in Cambridge, UK, and in Liège, Belgium, have been evaluating whether, and how, fMRI can be used to detect signs of consciousness in brain-damaged patients. Traditional bedside measures of awareness rely on the patient being able to make observable movements, which some patients just cannot do, leading to conscious, aware patients being mistaken for vegetative ones (as illustrated in Hot Science: Disorders of Consciousness). First, the researchers used fMRI to show that two mental imagery tasks reliably activate very different brain regions in healthy "control" individuals. The control group was asked to imagine moving their arms as though

swinging a tennis racquet at a ball, which activated motor areas of the brain Then, they were asked to imagine wandering from room to room in their house, and visualizing what they might see in each place, which activated visual and motor areas (Owen et al.,

2006). Next, the researchers demonstrated that some patients who had been diagnosed as vegetative were also able to reliably generate these distinct patterns. Out of 54 diagnosed as vegetative, five were able to reliably generate a tennis-playing pattern of activity

▲ 39-year-old Scott Routley was considered to be in a vegetative state for 12 years following a car crash. However, recently in an experiment conducted by researchers at University of Western Ontario using fMRI, Scott Routley was asked to imagine swinging a tennis racquet at a ball. Brain imaging results showed that the areas of his brain that were activated during this task were the same as those for the control group. This demonstrated that Scott is aware and can answer questions.

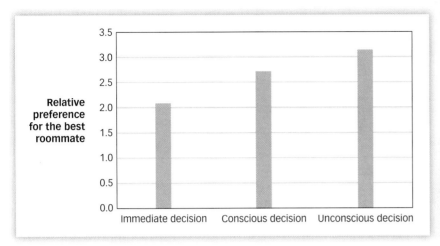

MONTI, M. M., VANHAUDENHUYSE, A., COLEMAN, M. R., BOLY, M., PICKARD, J. D., TSHIBANDA, L., OWEN, A. M., & LAUREYS, S. (2010). WILLFUL MODULATION OF BRAIN ACTIVITY IN DISORDERS OF CONSCIOUSNESS (FIGURE 1), NEW ENGLAND JOURNAL OF MEDICINE, 362, 579–589.

◀ Figure 5.8 **Decisions** People making roommate decisions who had some time for unconscious deliberation chose better roommates than those who thought about the choice consciously or those who made snap decisions (Dijksterhuis, 2004).

had been given), but during this interval their conscious minds were occupied with solving a set of anagrams. As you can see in **FIGURE 5.8,** the unconscious decision group showed a stronger preference for the good roommate than did the immediate decision or conscious decision groups. Unconscious minds seemed *better able* than conscious minds to sort out the complex information and arrive at the best choice. You can sometimes end up more satisfied with decisions you make going with your gut than with the decisions you consciously agonize over.

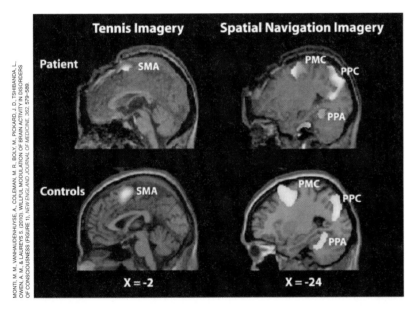

◀ This image shows the distinct patterns of activity in a healthy control and in a brain-damaged patient resulting from two different mental imagery tasks. The patient, previously diagnosed as being in a vegetative state, was able to follow commands to "imagine playing tennis" or "imagine moving around the rooms of your house," and generated the same patterns as the healthy controls. This ability to reliably engage in purposeful mental activity indicates awareness.

when asked to imagine playing tennis, and a spatial-navigation pattern of activity when asked to imagine going from room to room in their house. This is voluntary command following—conceptually equivalent to correctly raising your left or right arm when asked to do so—and is a hallmark of agency, which was identified on page 185 as one of the characteristics of conscious awareness (Monti et al., 2010).

When the researchers used this fMRI method with Scott, he was able to reliably generate the tennis and spatial-navigation patterns of activity on command. This indicated, much to the surprise of his doctors, that Scott was not in a vegetative state after all. The researchers went a step further and used this method to ask Scott simple yes-or-no questions. They did this by instructing Scott to imagine playing tennis if he wished to respond *yes* to a question, and to imagine navigating around his house if he wished to respond *no*. The distinct patterns of brain activity for these two tasks could then be interpreted as meaning *yes* or *no*. The researchers started by asking Scott questions to which they knew the answers, such as whether his father's name was Jim (it was). He correctly answered many such questions, indicating that he was fully conscious. The researchers then did something they had never tried with a patient before: They asked Scott a question that only he could know the answer to "Are you in pain?" Much to everyone's relief, the answering brain activity indicated *no*.

IN SUMMARY

► Consciousness is a mystery of psychology because other people's minds cannot be perceived directly and because the relationship between mind and body is perplexing.

► Consciousness has four basic properties: intentionality, unity, selectivity, and transience. It can also be understood in terms of levels: minimal consciousness, full consciousness, and self-consciousness.

► Conscious contents can include current concerns, daydreams, and unwanted thoughts.

► Unconscious processes are sometimes understood as expressions of the Freudian dynamic unconscious, but they are more commonly viewed as processes of the cognitive unconscious that create our conscious thought and behaviour.

► The cognitive unconscious is at work when subliminal perception and unconscious decision processes influence thought or behaviour without the person's awareness.

# Sleep and Dreaming: Good Night, Mind

What is it like to be asleep? Sometimes it is like nothing at all. Sleep can produce a state of unconsciousness in which the mind and brain apparently turn off the functions that create experience: The theatre in your mind is closed. But this is an oversimplification because the theatre actually seems to reopen during the night for special shows of bizarre cult films—in other words, dreams. Dream consciousness involves a transformation of experience that is so radical it is commonly considered an **altered state of consciousness:** *a form of experience that departs significantly from the normal subjective experience of the world and the mind.* Such altered states can be accompanied by changes in thinking, disturbances in the sense of time, feelings of the loss of control, changes in emotional expression, alterations in body image and sense of self, perceptual distortions, and changes in meaning or significance (Ludwig, 1966). The world of sleep and dreams, the two topics in this section, provides two unique perspectives on consciousness: a view of the mind without consciousness and a view of consciousness in an altered state.

> **Why are dreams considered an altered state of consciousness?**

## Sleep

Consider a typical night. As you begin to fall asleep, the busy, task-oriented thoughts of the waking mind are replaced by wandering thoughts and images and odd juxtapositions, some of them almost dreamlike. This presleep consciousness is called the *hypnagogic state.* On some rare nights you might experience a *hypnic jerk,* a sudden quiver or sensation of dropping, as though missing a step on a staircase. No one is quite sure why these happen. Eventually, your presence of mind goes away entirely. Time and experience stop, you are unconscious, and in fact there seems to be no "you" there to have experiences. But then come dreams, whole vistas of a vivid and surrealistic consciousness you just do not get during the day, a set of experiences that occur with the odd prerequisite that there is nothing "out there" you are actually experiencing. More patches of unconsciousness may occur, with more dreams here and there. And finally, the glimmerings of waking consciousness return again in a foggy and imprecise form as you enter postsleep consciousness (the *hypnopompic state*) and then awake, often with bad hair.

**altered state of consciousness**
A form of experience that departs significantly from the normal subjective experience of the world and the mind.

***Dreamers*, by Albert Joseph Moore (1879/1882)** Although their bodies are in the same room, their minds are probably worlds apart.

## Sleep Cycle

The sequence of events that occurs during a night of sleep is part of one of the major rhythms of human life, the cycle of sleep and waking. This **circadian rhythm** is *a naturally occurring 24-hour cycle*, from the Latin *circa* (about) and *dies* (day). Even people sequestered in underground buildings without clocks ("time-free environments") who are allowed to sleep when they want tend to have a rest–activity cycle of about 25.1 hours (Aschoff, 1965). This slight deviation from 24 hours is not easily explained (Lavie, 2001), but it seems to underlie the tendency many people have to want to stay up a little later each night and wake up a little later each day. We are 25.1-hour people living in a 24-hour world.

The sleep cycle is far more than a simple on–off routine, however, as many bodily and psychological processes ebb and flow in this rhythm. In 1929 researchers made EEG (electroencephalograph) recordings of the human brain for the first time (Berger, 1929) (see the Neuroscience and Behaviour chapter). Before this, many people had offered descriptions of their nighttime experiences, and researchers knew that there are deeper and lighter periods of sleep, as well as dream periods. But no one had been able to measure much of anything about sleep without waking up the sleeper and ruining it. The EEG recordings revealed a regular pattern of changes in electrical activity in the brain accompanying the circadian cycle. While waking, these changes involve alternation between high-frequency activity (*beta waves*) during alertness and lower-frequency activity (*alpha waves*) during relaxation.

The largest changes in EEG occur during sleep. These changes show a regular pattern over the course of the night that allowed sleep researchers to identify five sleep stages (see **FIGURE 5.9** on the next page). In stage 1, the EEG moves to frequency patterns even lower than alpha waves (*theta waves*). In stage 2, these patterns are interrupted by short bursts of activity called *sleep spindles* and *K complexes,* and the sleeper becomes somewhat more difficult to awaken. The deepest stages of sleep are stages 3 and 4, known as slow-wave sleep, in which the EEG patterns show activity called *delta waves.*

> **What do EEG recordings tell us about sleep?**

During stage 5, **REM sleep,** *a stage of sleep characterized by rapid eye movements and a high level of brain activity,* EEG patterns become high-frequency sawtooth waves, similar to beta waves, suggesting that the mind at this time is as active as it is during waking (see Figure 5.9). Using an **electrooculograph (EOG)**—*an instrument that measures eye movements*—during sleep, researchers found that sleepers wakened

**circadian rhythm**
A naturally occurring 24-hour cycle.

**REM sleep**
A stage of sleep characterized by rapid eye movements and a high level of brain activity.

**electrooculograph (EOG)**
An instrument that measures eye movements.

**► Figure 5.9 EEG Patterns during the Stages of Sleep**
The waking brain shows high-frequency beta wave activity, which changes during drowsiness and relaxation to lower-frequency alpha waves. Stage 1 sleep shows lower-frequency theta waves, which are accompanied in stage 2 by irregular patterns called sleep spindles and K complexes. Stages 3 and 4 are marked by the lowest frequencies, delta waves. During REM sleep, EEG patterns return to higher-frequency sawtooth waves that resemble the beta waves of waking.

during REM periods reported having dreams much more often than those wakened during non-REM periods (Aserinsky & Kleitman, 1953). During REM sleep, the pulse quickens, blood pressure rises, and there are telltale signs of sexual arousal. At the same time, measurements of muscle movements indicate that the sleeper is very still, except for a rapid side-to-side movement of the eyes. (Watch someone sleeping and you may be able to see the REMs through their closed eyelids.)

Although many people believe that they do not dream much (if at all), some 80 percent of people awakened during REM sleep report dreams. If you have ever wondered whether dreams actually take place in an instant or whether they take as long to happen as the events they portray might take, the analysis of REM sleep offers an answer. Sleep researchers William Dement and Nathaniel Kleitman (1957) woke volunteers either 5 minutes or 15 minutes after the onset of REM sleep and asked them to judge, on the basis of the events in the remembered dream, how long they had been dreaming. Sleepers in 92 of 111 cases were correct, suggesting that dreaming occurs in "real time." The discovery of REM sleep has offered many insights into dreaming, but not all dreams occur in REM periods. Some dreams are also reported in other sleep stages, but not as many—and the dreams that occur at those times are described as less wild than REM dreams and more like normal thinking.

Putting EEG and REM data together produces a picture of how a typical night's sleep progresses through cycles of sleep stages (see **FIGURE 5.10**). In the first hour of

> **What are the stages in a typical night's sleep?**

the night, you fall all the way from waking to the fourth and deepest stage of sleep, the stage marked by delta waves. These slow waves indicate a general synchronization of neural firing, as though the brain is doing one thing at this time rather than many: the neuronal equivalent of "the wave" moving through the crowd at a stadium as lots of individuals move together in synchrony. You then return to lighter sleep stages, eventually reaching REM and dreamland. Note that although REM sleep is lighter than that of lower stages, it is deep enough that you may be difficult to awaken. You then continue to cycle between REM and slow-wave sleep stages every 90 minutes or so throughout the night. Periods of REM last longer as the night goes on, and lighter sleep stages predominate between these periods, with the deeper slow-wave stages 3 and 4 disappearing halfway through the night. Although you are either unconscious or dream-conscious at the time, your brain and mind cycle through a remarkable array of different states each time you have a night's sleep.

Psychologists learn about what happens when we sleep by collecting EOG, EEG, and other measurements from research volunteers while they sleep in sleep laboratories, like this one.

## Sleep Needs and Deprivation

How much do people sleep? The answer depends on the age of the sleeper (Dement, 1999). Newborns will sleep 6 to 8 times in 24 hours, often totalling more than 16 hours. Their napping cycle gets consolidated into "sleeping through the night," usually sometime between 9 and 18 months, but occasionally even later. The typical 6-year-old child might need 11 or 12 hours of sleep, and the progression to less sleep then continues into adulthood, when the average is about 7 to 7.5 hours per night. With aging, people can get along with even a bit less sleep than that. Over a whole lifetime, we get about 1 hour of sleep for every 2 hours we are awake.

This is a lot of sleeping. Could we tolerate less? Monitored by William Dement, Randy Gardner stayed up for 264 hours and 12 minutes in 1965 for a science project. When 17-year-old Randy finally did go to sleep, he slept only 14 hours and 40 minutes and awakened essentially recovered (Dement, 1978).

Feats like this one suggest that sleep might be expendable. This is the theory behind the classic all-nighter that you may have tried on the way to a rough exam. But it turns out that this theory is mistaken. Robert Stickgold and his colleagues (2000) found that when people learning a difficult perceptual task are kept up all night after

> **What is the relationship between sleep and learning?**

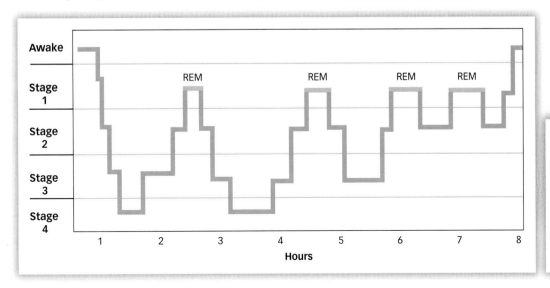

◄ Figure **5.10** **Stages of Sleep during the Night** Over the course of the typical night, sleep cycles into deeper stages early on and then more shallow stages later. REM periods become longer in later cycles, and the deeper slow-wave sleep of stages 3 and 4 disappears halfway through the night.

Sleep following learning is essential for memory consolidation. Sleep during class, on the other hand, not so much.

they have finished practising the task, their learning of the task is wiped out. Even after two nights of catch-up sleep, they show little indication of their initial training on the task. Sleep following learning appears to be essential for memory consolidation (see Hot Science: Sleep on It, p. 233 in the Memory chapter). It is as though memories normally deteriorate unless sleep occurs to help keep them in place. Studying all night may help you cram for the exam, but it will not make the material stick, which pretty much defeats the whole point.

Sleep turns out to be a necessity rather than a luxury in other ways as well. At the extreme, sleep loss can be fatal. When rats are forced to break Randy Gardner's human waking record and stay awake even longer, they have trouble regulating their body temperature and lose weight although they eat much more than normal. Their bodily systems break down and they die, on average, in 21 days (Rechtshaffen et al., 1983). Shakespeare called sleep "nature's soft nurse," and it is clear that even for healthy young humans, a few hours of sleep deprivation each night can have a cumulative detrimental effect: reducing mental acuity and reaction time, increasing irritability and depression, and increasing the risk of accidents and injury (Coren, 1997).

Some studies have deprived people of different sleep stages selectively by waking them whenever certain stages are detected. Studies of REM sleep deprivation indicate that this part of sleep is important psychologically. Memory problems and excessive aggression are observed in both humans and rats after only a few days of being wakened whenever REM activity starts (Ellman et al., 1991). The brain must value something about REM sleep because REM deprivation causes a rebound of more REM sleep the next night (Brunner et al., 1990). Deprivation from slow-wave sleep (in stages 3 and 4), in turn, has more physical effects, with just a few nights of deprivation leaving people feeling, fatigued, and hypersensitive to muscle and bone pain (Lentz et al., 1999).

**Why do we need to sleep?**

It is clearly dangerous to neglect the need for sleep. But why would we have such a need in the first place? All animals appear to sleep, although the amount of sleep required varies quite a bit (see **FIGURE 5.11**). Giraffes sleep less than 2 hours daily, whereas brown bats snooze for almost 20 hours. These variations in sleep needs, and the very existence of a need, are hard to explain. Is the restoration that happens during the unconsciousness of sleep something that simply cannot be achieved during consciousness? Sleep is, after all, potentially costly in the course of evolution. The

▶ Figure 5.11 All animals and insects seem to require sleep, although in differing amounts. Next time you oversleep and someone accuses you of "sleeping like a baby," you might tell them that instead that you were sleeping like a tiger, or a brown bat.

AVERAGE DAILY SLEEP TOTALS

sleeping animal is easy prey, so the habit of sleep would not seem to have developed so widely across species unless it had significant benefits that made up for this vulnerability. Theories of sleep have not yet determined why the brain and body have evolved to need these recurring episodes of unconsciousness.

## Sleep Disorders

In answer to the question, "Did you sleep well?," comedian Stephen Wright said, "No, I made a couple of mistakes." Sleeping well is something everyone would love to do, but unfortunately many people are deeply troubled by sleep disorders. The most common disorders that plague sleep include insomnia, sleep apnea, and somnambulism.

**Insomnia,** *difficulty in falling asleep or staying asleep,* is perhaps the most common sleep disorder. About 30–48 percent of people report symptoms of insomnia, 9–15 percent report insomnia severe enough to lead to daytime complaints, and 6 percent of people meet criteria for a diagnosis of insomnia, which requires persistent and impairing sleep problems (Bootzin & Epstein, 2011; Ohayon, 2002). Unfortunately, insomnia often is a persistent problem and most people with insomnia experience it for at least a year (Morin et al., 2009).

There are many potential causes of insomnia. It can result from lifestyle choices such as working night shifts (self-induced insomnia), or it can occur in response to depression, anxiety, or some other condition (secondary insomnia), or sometimes there are no obvious causal factors (primary insomnia). Regardless of type, insomnia can be exacerbated by worrying about insomnia (Borkevec, 1982). No doubt you have experienced some nights when sleeping was a high priority, such as before a class presentation or an important interview, and you have found that you were unable to fall asleep. The desire to sleep initiates an ironic process of mental control—a heightened sensitivity to signs of sleeplessness—and this sensitivity interferes with sleep. In fact, participants in an experiment who were instructed to go to sleep quickly became hypersensitive and had more difficulty sleeping than those who were not instructed to hurry (Ansfield, Wegner, & Bowser, 1996). The paradoxical solution for insomnia in some cases, then, may be to give up the pursuit of sleep and instead find something else to do.

Not trying so hard to sleep is probably better than another common remedy—the use of sleeping pills. Although sedatives can be useful for brief sleep problems associated with emotional events, their long-term use is not effective. To begin with, most sleeping pills are addictive. People become dependent on the pills to sleep and may need to increase the dose over time to achieve

> **What are some problems caused by sleeping pills?**

the same effect. Even in short-term use, sedatives can interfere with the normal sleep cycle. Although they promote sleep, they can reduce the proportion of time spent in REM and slow-wave sleep (Qureshi & Lee-Chiong, 2004), robbing people of dreams and their deepest sleep stages. As a result, the quality of sleep achieved with pills may not be as high as without, and there may be side effects such as grogginess and irritability during the day. Finally, stopping the use of sleeping pills suddenly can produce insomnia that is worse than before.

**Sleep apnea** is *a disorder in which the person stops breathing for brief periods while asleep.* A person with apnea usually snores because apnea involves an involuntary obstruction of the breathing passage. When episodes of apnea occur for over 10 seconds at a time and recur many times during the night, they may cause many awakenings and sleep loss or insomnia. Apnea occurs most often in middle-age overweight men (Punjabi, 2008) and may go undiagnosed because it is not easy for the sleeper to notice. Bed partners may be the ones who finally get tired of the snoring

**insomnia**
Difficulty in falling asleep or staying asleep.

**sleep apnea**
A disorder in which the person stops breathing for brief periods while asleep.

INSOMNIA JEOPARDY

| WAYS IN WHICH PEOPLE HAVE WRONGED ME | STRANGE NOISES | DISEASES I PROBABLY HAVE | MONEY TROUBLES | WHY DID I SAY/DO THAT? | IDEAS FOR A SCREENPLAY |
|---|---|---|---|---|---|
| $10 | $10 | $10 | $10 | $10 | $10 |
| $20 | $20 | $20 | $20 | $20 | $20 |
| $30 | $30 | $30 | $30 | $30 | $30 |
| $40 | $40 | $40 | $40 | $40 | $40 |
| $50 | $50 | $50 | $50 | $50 | $50 |

**somnambulism (or sleepwalking)**
Occurs when a person arises and walks around while asleep.

**narcolepsy**
A disorder in which sudden sleep attacks occur in the middle of waking activities.

**sleep paralysis**
The experience of waking up unable to move.

**night terrors (or sleep terrors)**
Abrupt awakenings with panic and intense emotional arousal.

and noisy gasping for air when the sleeper's breathing restarts, or the sleeper may eventually seek treatment because of excessive sleepiness during the day. Therapies involving weight loss, drugs, or sleep masks that push air into the nasal passage, or surgery may solve the problem.

**Somnambulism** (or **sleepwalking**), occurs when *a person arises and walks around while asleep.* Sleepwalking is more common in children, peaking between the ages of 4 and 8 years, with 15–40 percent of children experiencing at least one episode (Bhargava, 2011). Sleepwalking tends to happen early in the night, usually in slow-wave sleep, and sleepwalkers may awaken during their walk or return to bed without waking, in which case they will probably not remember the episode in the morning. The sleepwalker's eyes are usually open in a glassy stare. Walking with hands outstretched is uncommon except in cartoons. Sleepwalking is not usually linked to any additional problems and is only problematic in that sleepwalkers sometimes engage in strange or unwise behaviours such as urinating in places other than the toilet and leaving the house while still sleeping. People who walk while they are sleeping do not tend to be very coordinated and can trip over furniture or fall down stairs. After all, they are sleeping. Contrary to popular belief, it is safe to wake sleepwalkers or lead them back to bed (but best to wait until after they finish their business).

There are other sleep disorders that are less common. **Narcolepsy** is *a disorder in which sudden sleep attacks occur in the middle of waking activities.* Narcolepsy involves the intrusion of a dreaming state of sleep (with REM) into waking and is often accompanied by unrelenting excessive sleepiness and uncontrollable sleep attacks lasting from 30 seconds to 30 minutes. This disorder appears to have a genetic basis, as it runs in families, and can be treated effectively with medication. **Sleep paralysis** is *the experience of waking up unable to move* and is sometimes associated with narcolepsy. This eerie experience usually happens as you are awakening from REM sleep but before you have regained motor control. This period typically lasts only a few seconds or minutes and can be accompanied by hypnopompic (when awakening) or hypnagogic (when falling asleep) hallucinations in which dream content may appear to occur in the waking world. A very clever series of recent studies suggests that sleep paralysis accompanied by hypnopompic hallucinations of figures being in one's bedroom seems to explain many perceived instances of alien abductions and recovered memories of sexual abuse (aided by therapists who used hypnosis to help the sleepers [incorrectly] piece it all together) (McNally & Clancy, 2005). **Night terrors** (or **sleep terrors**) are *abrupt awakenings with panic and intense emotional arousal.* These terrors, which occur most often in children and in only about 2 percent of adults (Ohayon, Guilleminault, & Priest, 1999), happen most often in non-REM sleep early in the sleep cycle and do not usually have dream content the sleeper can report.

Is it safe to wake a sleepwalker?

To sum up, there is a lot going on when we close our eyes for the night. Humans follow a pretty regular sleep cycle, going through the five stages of sleep during the night. Disruptions to that cycle, either from sleep deprivation or sleep disorders, can produce negative consequences for waking consciousness. But something else happens during a night's sleep that affects our consciousness, both while asleep and when we wake up.

## Dreams

Pioneering sleep researcher William C. Dement (1959) said, "Dreaming permits each and every one of us to be quietly and safely insane every night of our lives." Indeed, dreams do seem to have a touch of insanity about them. We experience crazy things in dreams, but even more bizarre is the fact that we are the writers, producers, and directors of the crazy things we experience. Just what are these experiences, and how can they be explained?

Sleepwalkers in cartoons have their arms outstretched and eyes closed, but that is just for cartoons. A real-life sleepwalker usually walks normally with eyes open, sometimes with a glassy look.

ESTHALTO/MATTHIEU SPOHN/GETTY IMAGES

## Dream Consciousness

Dreams depart dramatically from reality. You may dream of being naked in public, of falling from a great height, of sleeping through an important appointment, of your teeth being loose and falling out, or of being chased (Holloway, 2001). These things do not happen much in reality unless you are having a very bad life. The quality of consciousness in dreaming is also altered significantly from waking consciousness. There are five major characteristics of dream consciousness that distinguish it from the waking state (Hobson, 1988).

> **What distinguishes dream consciousness from the waking state?**

> We intensely feel *emotion,* whether it is bliss or terror or love or awe.

> Dream *thought* is illogical: The continuities of time, place, and person do not apply. You may find you are in one place and then another, for example, without any travel in between—or people may change identity from one dream scene to the next.

> *Sensation* is fully formed and meaningful; visual sensation is predominant, and you may also deeply experience sound, touch, and movement (although pain is very uncommon).

> Dreaming occurs with *uncritical acceptance,* as though the images and events are perfectly normal rather than bizarre.

> We have *difficulty remembering* the dream after it is over. People often remember dreams only if they are awakened during the dream and even then may lose recall for the dream within just a few minutes of waking. If waking memory were this bad, you could be standing around half-naked in the street much of the time, having forgotten your destination, clothes, and lunch money.

Not all of our dreams are fantastic and surreal, however. Far from the adventures in nighttime insanity storied by Freud, dreams are often ordinary (Domhoff, 2007). We often dream about mundane topics that reflect prior waking experiences or "day residue." Current conscious concerns pop up (Nikles et al., 1998), along with images from the recent past. A dream may even incorporate sensations experienced during sleep, as when sleepers in one study were led to dream of water when drops were sprayed on their faces during REM sleep (Dement & Wolpert, 1958). The day residue does not usually include episodic memories; that is, complete daytime events replayed in the mind. Rather, dreams that reflect the day's experience tend to single out sensory experiences or objects from waking life. Rather than simply being a replay of that event, dreams often consist of "interleaved fragments of experience" from different times and places that our mind weaves together into a single story (Wamsley & Stickgold, 2011). For instance, after a fun day at the beach with your roommates, your dream that night might include cameo appearances by bouncing beach balls or a flock of seagulls. One study had research participants play the computer game Tetris® and found that participants often reported dreaming about the Tetris geometrical figures falling down—even though they seldom reported dreams about being in the experiment or playing the game (Stickgold et al., 2001). Even severely amnesic individuals who could not recall playing the game at all reported Tetris-like images appearing in their dreams (Stickgold et al., 2000). The content of dreams takes snapshots from the day rather than retelling the stories of what you have done or seen. This means that dreams often come without clear plots or story lines, so they may not make a lot of sense.

Dreams often are quite intense, vivid, and illogical. In this scene from the movie *Inception*, the dream sequence shows a cityscape being folded over and over, defying the laws of gravity.

WARNER BROS/THE KOBAL COLLECTION/ART RESOURCE

GOETHE HOUSE AND MUSEUM/SNARK/ART RESOURCE, NY

**The Nightmare, by Henry Fuseli (1790)**
Fuseli depicts not only a mare in this painting but also an incubus—an imp perched on the dreamer's chest that is traditionally associated with especially horrifying nightmares.

Some of the most memorable dreams are nightmares, and these frightening dreams can wake up the dreamer (Levin & Nielsen, 2009). One set of daily dream logs from undergraduates suggested that the average student has about 24 nightmares per year (Wood & Bootzin, 1990), although some people may have them as often as every night. Children have more nightmares than adults, and people who have experienced traumatic events are inclined to have nightmares that relive those events. Following the 1989 earthquake in the San Francisco Bay area, for example, undergraduate students who had experienced the quake reported more nightmares than those who had not and often reported that the dreams were about the quake (Wood et al., 1992). This effect of trauma may not only produce dreams of the traumatic event: When police officers experience "critical incidents" of conflict and danger, they tend to have more nightmares in general (Neylan et al., 2002).

## Dream Theories

Dreams are puzzles that cry out to be solved. How could you not want to make sense out of these experiences? Although dreams may be fantastic and confusing, they are emotionally riveting, filled with vivid images from your own life, and they seem very real. The search for dream meaning goes all the way back to biblical figures, who interpreted dreams and looked for prophecies in them. In the Old Testament, the prophet Daniel (a favourite of two of the authors of this book) curried favour with King Nebuchadnezzar of Babylon by interpreting the king's dream. The question of what dreams mean has been burning since antiquity, mainly because the meaning of dreams is usually far from obvious.

In the first psychological theory of dreams, Freud (1900/1965) proposed that dreams are confusing and obscure because the dynamic unconscious creates them precisely *to be* confusing and obscure. According to Freud's theory, dreams represent wishes, and some of these wishes are so unacceptable, taboo, and anxiety producing that the mind can only express them in disguised form. Freud believed that many of the most unacceptable wishes are sexual. For instance, he would interpret a dream of a train going into a tunnel as symbolic of sexual intercourse. According to Freud, the **manifest content** of a dream, *a dream's apparent topic or superficial meaning*, is a smoke screen for its **latent content**, *a dream's true underlying meaning*. For example, a dream about a tree burning down in the park across the street from where a friend once lived (the manifest content) might represent a camouflaged wish for the death of the friend (the latent content). In this case, wishing for the death of a friend is unacceptable, so it is disguised as a tree on fire. The problem with Freud's approach is that there is an infinite number of potential interpretations of any dream and finding the correct one is a matter of guesswork—and of convincing the dreamer that one interpretation is superior to the others.

Although dreams may not represent elaborately hidden wishes, there is evidence that they do feature the return of suppressed thoughts. Researchers asked volunteers to think of a personal acquaintance and then to spend 5 minutes before going to bed writing down whatever came to mind (Wegner, Wenzlaff, & Kozak, 2004). Some participants were asked to suppress thoughts of this person as they wrote, others were asked to focus on thoughts of the person, and yet others were asked just to write freely about anything. The next morning, participants wrote dream reports. Overall, all participants mentioned dreaming more about the person they had named than about other people. But they most often dreamed of the person they named if they were in the group that had

> **What is the evidence that we dream about our suppressed thoughts?**

**manifest content**
A dream's apparent topic or superficial meaning.

**latent content**
A dream's true underlying meaning.

been assigned to suppress thoughts of the person the night before. This finding suggests that Freud was right to suspect that dreams harbour unwanted thoughts. Perhaps this is why actors dream of forgetting their lines, travellers dream of getting lost, and football players dream of fumbling the ball.

Another key theory of dreaming is the **activation–synthesis model** (Hobson & McCarley, 1977). This theory proposes that *dreams are produced when the brain attempts to make sense of random neural activity that occurs during sleep.* During waking consciousness, the mind is devoted to interpreting lots of information that arrives through the senses. You figure out that the odd noise you are hearing during class is your cell phone vibrating, for example, or you realize that the strange smell in the hall outside your room must be from burned popcorn. In the dream state, the mind does not have access to external sensations, but it keeps on doing what it usually does: interpreting information. Because that information now comes from neural activations that occur without the continuity provided by the perception of reality, the brain's interpretive mechanisms can run free. This might be why, for example, a person in a dream can sometimes change into someone else. There is no actual person being perceived to help the mind keep a stable view. In the mind's effort to perceive and give meaning to brain activation, the person you view in a dream about a grocery store might seem to be a clerk but then change into your favourite teacher when the dream scene moves to your school. The great interest people have in interpreting their dreams the next morning may be an extension of the interpretive activity they have been doing all night.

The Freudian theory and the activation–synthesis theory differ in the significance they place on the meaning of dreams. In Freud's theory, dreams begin with meaning, whereas in the activation–synthesis theory, dreams begin randomly—but meaning can be added as the mind lends interpretations in the process of dreaming. Dream research has not yet sorted out whether one of these theories or yet another might be the best account of the meaning of dreams.

**activation–synthesis model**
The theory that dreams are produced when the brain attempts to make sense of random neural activity that occurs during sleep.

# CULTURE & COMMUNITY

### What Do Dreams Mean to Us around the World?

A recent study (Morewedge & Norton, 2009) assessed how people from three different cultures evaluate their dreams. Participants were asked to rate different theories of dreaming on a scale of 1 (*do not agree at all*) to 7 (*agree completely*). A significant majority of students from the United States, South Korea, and India agreed with the Freudian theory that dreams have meanings. Only small percentages believed the other options, that dreams provide a means to solve problems, promote learning, or are by-products of unrelated brain activity. The accompanying figure illustrates the findings across all three cultural groups. It appears that in many parts of the world, people have an intuition that dreams contain something deep and relevant.

Freud theorized that dreams represent unacceptable wishes that the mind can only express in disguised form. The activation–synthesis model proposes that dreams are produced when the mind attempts to make sense of random neural activity that occurs during sleep. Suppose a man is expecting a visit from his mother-in-law; the night before her arrival, he dreams that a bus is driven through the living room window of his house. How might Freud have interpreted such a dream? How might the activation–synthesis model interpret such a dream?

## The Dreaming Brain

What happens in the brain when we dream? Several studies have made fMRI scans of people's brains during sleep, focusing on the areas of the brain that show changes in activation during REM periods. These studies show that the brain changes that occur during REM sleep correspond clearly with certain alterations of consciousness that occur in dreaming. **FIGURE 5.12** shows some of the patterns of activation and deactivation found in the dreaming brain (Nir & Tononi, 2010; Schwartz & Maquet, 2002).

In dreams there are heights to look down from, dangerous people lurking, the occasional monster, some minor worries, and at least once in a while that major exam you have forgotten about until you walk into class. These themes suggest that the brain areas responsible for fear or emotion somehow work overtime in dreams, and it turns out that this is clearly visible in fMRI scans. The amygdala is involved in responses to threatening or stressful events, and indeed the amygdala is quite active during REM sleep.

The typical dream is also a visual wonderland, with visual events present in almost all dreams. However, there are fewer auditory sensations, even fewer tactile sensations, and almost no smells or tastes. This dream "picture show" does not involve actual perception, of course, just the imagination of visual events. It turns out that the areas of the brain responsible for visual perception are *not* activated during dreaming, whereas the visual association areas in the occipital lobe that are responsible for visual imagery *do* show activation (Braun et al., 1998). Your brain is smart enough to realize that it is not really seeing bizarre images but acts instead as though it is imagining bizarre images.

During REM sleep, the prefrontal cortex shows relatively less arousal than it usually does during waking consciousness. What does this mean for the dreamer? As a rule, the prefrontal areas are associated with planning and executing actions, and often dreams seem to be unplanned and rambling. Perhaps this is why dreams often do not have very sensible story lines— they have been scripted by an author whose ability to plan is inactive.

> **What do fMRIs tell us about why dreams do not have coherent story lines?**

Another odd fact of dreaming is that while the eyes are moving rapidly, the body is otherwise very still. During REM sleep, the motor cortex is activated, but spinal

▶ Figure **5.12** **Brain Activation and Deactivation during REM Sleep** Brain areas shaded red are activated during REM sleep; those shaded blue are deactivated. (*a*) The medial view shows activation of the amygdala, the visual association areas, the motor cortex, and the brain stem and deactivation of the prefrontal cortex. (*b*) The ventral view shows activation of other visual association areas and deactivation of the prefrontal cortex (Schwartz & Maquet, 2002).

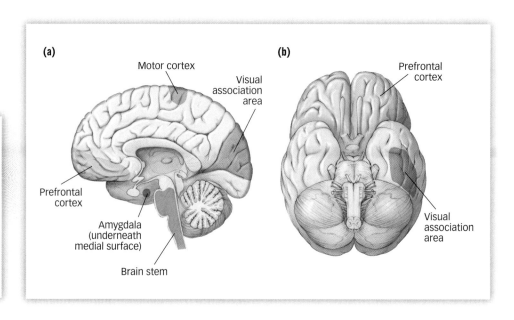

neurons running through the brain stem inhibit the expression of this motor activation (Lai & Siegal, 1999). This turns out to be a useful property of brain activation in

**What purpose does dreaming serve?**

dreaming; otherwise, you might get up and act out every dream! Individuals suffering from one rare sleep disorder, in fact, lose the normal muscular inhibition accompanying REM sleep and so act out their dreams, thrashing around in bed or stalking around the bedroom (Mahowald & Schenck, 2000). However, most people who are moving during sleep are probably not dreaming. The brain specifically inhibits movement during dreams, perhaps to keep us from hurting ourselves.

## IN SUMMARY

▶ Sleeping and dreaming present a view of the mind in an altered state of consciousness.

▶ During a night's sleep, the brain passes in and out of five stages of sleep; most dreaming occurs in the REM sleep stage.

▶ Sleep needs decrease over the life span, but being deprived of sleep and dreams has psychological and physical costs.

▶ Sleep can be disrupted through disorders that include insomnia, sleep apnea, somnambulism, narcolepsy, sleep paralysis, and night terrors.

▶ In dreaming, the dreamer uncritically accepts changes in emotion, thought, and sensation but poorly remembers the dream on awakening.

▶ Theories of dreaming include Freud's psychoanalytic theory and the activation–synthesis model.

▶ fMRI studies of the brain in dreaming reveal activations associated with visual imagery, reductions of other sensations, increased sensitivity to emotions such as fear, lessened capacities for planning, and the prevention of movement.

# Drugs and Consciousness: Artificial Inspiration

The author of the dystopian novel *Brave New World*, Aldous Huxley (1932), once wrote of his experiences with the drug mescaline. *The Doors of Perception* described the intense experience that accompanied his departure from normal consciousness. He described "a world where everything shone with the Inner Light, and was infinite in its significance. The legs, for example, of a chair—how miraculous their tubularity, how supernatural their polished smoothness! I spent several minutes—or was it several centuries?—not merely gazing at those bamboo legs, but actually *being* them" (Huxley, 1954, p. 22).

Being the legs of a chair? This is probably better than being the seat of a chair, but it still sounds like an odd experience. Yet, many people seek out such experiences, often through using drugs. **Psychoactive drugs** are *chemicals that influence consciousness or behaviour by altering the brain's chemical message system*. You read about several such drugs in the Neuroscience and Behaviour chapter when we explored the brain's system of neurotransmitters. And you will read about them in a different light when we turn to their role in the treatment of psychological disorders in the Treatment chapter. Whether these drugs are used for entertainment, for treatment, or for other reasons,

**psychoactive drugs**
Chemicals that influence consciousness or behaviour by altering the brain's chemical message system.

they each exert their influence either by increasing the activity of a neurotransmitter (the agonists) or decreasing its activity (the antagonists).

Some of the most common neurotransmitters are serotonin, dopamine, gamma-aminobutyric acid (GABA), and acetylcholine. Drugs alter the functioning of neurotransmitters by preventing them from bonding to sites on the postsynaptic neuron, by inhibiting their reuptake to the presynaptic neuron, or by enhancing their bonding and transmission. Different drugs can intensify or dull transmission patterns, creating changes in brain electrical activities that mimic natural operations of the brain. For example, a drug such as Valium (benzodiazepine) induces sleep but prevents dreaming and so creates a state similar to slow-wave sleep; that is, what the brain naturally develops several times each night. Other drugs prompt patterns of brain activity that do not occur naturally, however, and their influence on consciousness can be dramatic. Like Huxley experiencing himself becoming the legs of a chair, people using drugs can have experiences unlike any they might find in normal waking consciousness or even in dreams. To understand these altered states, let us explore how people use and abuse drugs, and examine the major categories of psychoactive drugs.

## Drug Use and Abuse

Why do children sometimes spin around until they get dizzy and fall down? There is something strangely attractive about states of consciousness that depart from the norm, and people throughout history have sought out these altered states by dancing, fasting, chanting, meditating, and ingesting a bizarre assortment of chemicals to intoxicate themselves (Tart, 1969). People pursue altered consciousness even when there are costs, from the nausea that accompanies dizziness to the life-wrecking obsession with a drug that can come with addiction. In this regard, the pursuit of altered consciousness can be a fatal attraction.

Often, drug-induced changes in consciousness begin as pleasant and spark an initial attraction. Researchers have measured the attractiveness of psychoactive drugs by seeing how hard laboratory animals will work to get them. In one study researchers allowed rats to administer cocaine to themselves intravenously by pressing a lever (Bozarth & Wise, 1985). Rats given free access to cocaine increased their use over the course of the 30-day study. They not only continued to self-administer at a high rate but also occasionally binged to the point of giving themselves convulsions. They stopped grooming themselves and eating until they lost on average almost a third of their body weight. About 90 percent of the rats died by the end of the study. Rats do show more attraction to sweets such as sugar or saccharine than they do to cocaine (Lenoir et al., 2007), but their interest in cocaine is deadly serious.

Rats are not tiny little humans, of course, so such research is not a firm basis for understanding human responses to cocaine. But these results do make it clear that cocaine is addictive and that the consequences of such addiction can be dire. Studies of self-administration of drugs in laboratory animals show that animals will work to obtain not only cocaine but also alcohol, amphetamines, barbiturates, caffeine, MDMA (Ecstasy), nicotine, opiates (such as morphine and heroin), phencyclidine (PCP), and THC (tetrahydrocannabinol, the active ingredient in marijuana). There are some psychoactive drugs that animals will not work for (such as mescaline or the antipsychotic drug phenothiazine), suggesting that these drugs have less potential for causing addiction (Bozarth, 1987).

People usually do not become addicted to a psychoactive drug the first time they use it. They may experiment a few times, then try again, and eventually find that their tendency to use the drug increases over time due to several factors, such as drug tolerance, physical dependence, and psychological dependence. **Drug tolerance** is

> **What is the allure of altered consciousness?**

Why do kids enjoy spinning around until they get so dizzy that they fall down? Even from a young age, there seems to be something enjoyable about altering states of consciousness.

MATTHEW NOCK

*the tendency for larger drug doses to be required over time to achieve the same effect.* Physicians who prescribe morphine to control pain in their patients are faced with tolerance problems because steadily greater amounts of the drug may be needed to dampen the same pain. With increased tolerance comes the danger of drug overdose; recreational users find they need to use more and more of a drug to produce the same high. But then, if a new batch of heroin or cocaine is more concentrated than usual, the "normal" amount the user takes to achieve the same high can be fatal.

Self-administration of addictive drugs can also be prompted by withdrawal symptoms, which result when drug use is discontinued. Some withdrawal symptoms signal *physical dependence,* when pain, convulsions, hallucinations, or other unpleasant symptoms accompany withdrawal. People who suffer from physical dependence seek to continue drug use to avoid becoming physically ill. A common example is the "caffeine headache" some people complain of when they have not had their daily jolt of java. Other

> **What problems can arise in drug withdrawal?**

withdrawal symptoms result from *psychological dependence,* a strong desire to return to the drug even when physical withdrawal symptoms are gone. Drugs can create an emotional need over time that continues to prey on the mind, particularly in circumstances that are reminders of the drug. Some ex-smokers report longing wistfully for an after-dinner smoke, for example, even years after they have successfully quit the habit.

Drug addiction reveals a human frailty: our inability to look past the immediate consequences of our behaviour to see and appreciate the long-term consequences. Although we would like to think that our behaviour is guided by a rational analysis of future consequences, more typically occasions when we "play first, pay later" lead directly to "let's just play a lot right now." There is something intensely inviting about the prospect of a soon-to-be-had pleasure and something pale, hazy, and distant about the costs this act might bring at some future time. For example, given the choice of receiving $1 today or $2 a week later, most people will take the $1 today. However, if the same choice is to be made for some date a year in the future (when the immediate pleasure of today's windfall is not so strong), people choose to wait and get the $2 (Ainslie, 2001). The immediate satisfaction associated with taking most drugs may outweigh a rational analysis of the later consequences that can result from taking those drugs, such as drug addiction.

The psychological and social problems stemming from drug addiction are major. For many people, drug addiction becomes a way of life, and for some, it is a cause of death. Like the cocaine-addicted rats in the study noted earlier (Bozarth & Wise, 1985), some people become so attached to a drug that their lives are ruled by it. However, this is not always the end of the story. This ending is most well-known because the addict becomes a recurrent, visible social problem, "publicized" through repeated crime and repeated appearances in prisons and treatment programs. But a life of addiction is not the only possible end point of drug use. Stanley Schachter (1982) suggested that the visibility of addiction is misleading and that in fact many people overcome addictions. He found that 64 percent of a sample of people who had a history of cigarette smoking had quit successfully,

BETTMANN/CORBIS

Many soldiers serving in Vietnam became addicted to heroin while there. Robins and colleagues (1980) found that after returning home to the United States, the vast majority left their drug habit behind and were no longer addicted.

**drug tolerance**
The tendency for larger doses of a drug to be required over time to achieve the same effect.

DAVID SIPRESS/THE NEW YORKER COLLECTION/CARTOONBANK.COM

*"Hi, my name is Barry, and I check my E-mail two to three hundred times a day."*

although many had to try again and again to achieve their success. Indeed, large-scale studies conducted in the 1980s, 1990s, and 2000s consistently show that approximately 75 percent of those with substance use disorders overcome their addiction, with the biggest drop in use occurring between ages 20–30 (Heyman, 2009). One classic study of American soldiers who became addicted to heroin while serving in Vietnam during the Vietnam War (1955–1975) found that, 3 years after their return, only 12 percent remained addicted (Robins et al., 1980). The return to the attractions and obligations of normal life, as well as the absence of the familiar places and faces associated with their old drug habit, made it possible for returning soldiers to successfully quit. Although addiction is dangerous, it is not necessarily incurable.

**What are the statistics on overcoming addiction?**

It may not be accurate to view all recreational drug use under the umbrella of "addiction." Many people at this point in the history of Western society, for example, would not call the repeated use of caffeine an addiction, and some do not label the use of alcohol, tobacco, or marijuana in this way. In other times and places, however, each of these has been considered a terrifying addiction worthy of prohibition and public censure. In the early seventeenth century, for example, tobacco use was punishable by death in Germany, by castration in Russia, and by decapitation in China (Corti, 1931). Not a good time to be a smoker. By contrast, cocaine, heroin, marijuana, and amphetamines have each been popular and even recommended as medicines at several points throughout history, each without any stigma of addiction attached (Inciardi, 2001).

Although "addiction" as a concept is familiar to most of us, there is no standard clinical definition of what an addiction actually is. The concept of addiction has been extended to many human pursuits, giving rise to such terms as *sex addict*, *gambling addict*, *workaholic*, and, of course, *chocoholic*. Societies react differently at different times and in different places, with some uses of drugs ignored, other uses encouraged, others simply taxed, and yet others subjected to intense prohibition (see **FIGURE 5.13**). Rather than viewing *all* drug use as a problem, it is important to consider the costs and benefits of such use and to establish ways to help people choose behaviours that are informed by this knowledge (Parrott et al., 2005).

▶ Figure **5.13** **Laws on Cannabis Use around the World** The map shows the various countries around the world and their laws regarding cannabis use as of December 13, 2013.

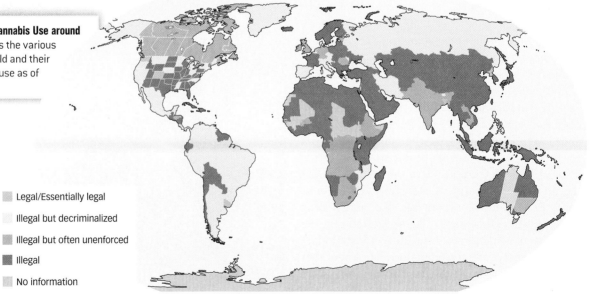

■ Legal/Essentially legal

■ Illegal but decriminalized

■ Illegal but often unenforced

■ Illegal

■ No information

# Types of Psychoactive Drugs

Four in five North Americans use caffeine in some form every day, but not all psychoactive drugs are this familiar. To learn how both the well-known and lesser-known drugs influence the mind, let us consider several broad categories of drugs: depressants, stimulants, narcotics, hallucinogens, and marijuana. **TABLE 5.3** summarizes what is known about the potential dangers of these different types of drugs.

## Depressants

**Depressants** are *substances that reduce the activity of the central nervous system.* The most commonly used depressant is alcohol, and others include barbiturates, benzodiazepines, and toxic inhalants (such as glue or gasoline). Depressants have a sedative or calming effect, tend to induce sleep in high doses, and can arrest breathing in extremely high doses. Depressants can produce both physical and psychological dependence.

**Alcohol.** Alcohol is king of the depressants, with its worldwide use beginning in prehistory, its easy availability in most cultures, and its widespread acceptance as a socially approved substance. Sixty-three percent of Canadians 15 years of age and over report having had a drink in the previous month, and 17 percent report binging on alcohol (over 5 drinks in succession) at least once a month over the previous year. This rate is higher for young adults (aged 20–34): Thirty-two percent of them report binging regularly (Statistics Canada, 2013a).

Alcohol's initial effects, euphoria and reduced anxiety, feel pretty positive. As it is consumed in greater quantities, drunkenness results, bringing slowed reactions, slurred speech, poor judgment, and other reductions in the effectiveness of thought and action. The exact way in which alcohol influences neural mechanisms is still not understood but, like other depressants, alcohol increases activity of the neurotransmitter GABA (De Witte, 1996). As you read in the Neuroscience and Behaviour chapter, GABA normally inhibits the transmission of neural impulses, and so one effect of alcohol is as an inhibitor—a chemical that stops the firing of other neurons. But there are many contradictions. Some people using alcohol become loud and aggressive, others become emotional and weepy, others become sullen, and still others

**depressants**
Substances that reduce the activity of the central nervous system.

> **Table 5.3**

**Dangers of Drugs**

| Drug | Overdose (Can taking too much cause death or injury?) | Physical Dependence (Will stopping use make you sick?) | Psychological Dependence (Will you crave it when you stop using it?) |
|---|---|---|---|
| Depressants | | | |
| Alcohol | X | X | X |
| Benzodiazepines/Barbiturates | X | X | X |
| Toxic inhalants | X | X | X |
| Stimulants | | | |
| Amphetamines | X | X | X |
| MDMA (Ecstasy) | X | | ? |
| Nicotine | X | X | X |
| Cocaine | X | X | X |
| Narcotics (opium, heroin, morphine, methadone, codeine) | X | X | X |
| Hallucinogens (LSD, mescaline, psilocybin, PCP, ketamine) | X | | ? |
| Marijuana | | ? | ? |

**expectancy theory**
The idea that alcohol effects can be produced by people's expectations of how alcohol will influence them in particular situations.

**balanced placebo design**
A study design in which behaviour is observed following the presence or absence of an actual stimulus and also following the presence or absence of a placebo stimulus.

**alcohol myopia**
A condition that results when alcohol hampers attention, leading people to respond in simple ways to complex situations.

Which theory, expectancy theory or alcohol myopia, views a person's response to alcohol as being (at least partially) learned, through a process similar to observational learning?

IMAGE SOURCE/GETTY IMAGES

turn giddy—and the same person can experience each of these effects in different circumstances. How can one drug do this? Two theories have been offered to account for these variable effects: *expectancy theory* and *alcohol myopia.*

> Why do people experience being drunk differently?

**Expectancy theory** suggests that *alcohol effects can be produced by people's expectations of how alcohol will influence them in particular situations* (Marlatt & Rohsenow, 1980). So, for instance, if you have watched friends or family drink at weddings and notice that this often produces hilarity and gregariousness, you could well experience these effects yourself should you drink alcohol on a similarly festive occasion. Seeing people getting drunk and fighting in bars, in turn, might lead to aggression after drinking.

The expectancy theory has been tested in studies that examine the effects of actual alcohol ingestion independent of the *perception* of alcohol ingestion. In experiments using a **balanced placebo design,** *behaviour is observed following the presence or absence of an actual stimulus and also following the presence or absence of a placebo stimulus.* In such a study, participants are given drinks containing alcohol or a substitute liquid, and some people in each group are led to believe they had alcohol and others are led to believe they did not. People told they are drinking alcohol when they are not, for instance, might get a touch of vodka on the plastic lid of a cup to give it the right odour when the drink inside is merely tonic water. These experiments often show that the belief that one has had alcohol can influence behaviour as strongly as the ingestion of alcohol itself (Goldman, Brown, & Christiansen, 1987). You may have seen people at parties getting rowdy after only one beer—perhaps because they expected this effect rather than because the beer actually had this influence.

Another approach to the varied effects of alcohol is the theory of **alcohol myopia,** which proposes that *alcohol hampers attention, leading people to respond in simple ways to complex situations* (Steele & Josephs, 1990). This theory recognizes that life is filled with complicated pushes and pulls, and our behaviour is often a balancing act. Imagine that you are really attracted to someone who is dating your friend. Do you make your feelings known or focus on your friendship? The myopia theory holds that when you drink alcohol, your fine judgment is impaired. It becomes hard to appreciate the subtlety of these different options, and the inappropriate response is to veer full tilt one way or the other. So, alcohol might lead you to make a wild pass at your friend's date or perhaps just cry in your beer over your timidity—depending on which way you happened to tilt in your myopic state.

In one study on the alcohol myopia theory, men (half of whom were drinking alcohol) watched a video showing an unfriendly woman and then were asked how acceptable it would be for a man to act sexually aggressive toward a woman (Johnson, Noel, & Sutter-Hernandez, 2000). The unfriendly woman seemed to remind them that sex was out of the question and, indeed men who were drinking alcohol and had seen this video were no more likely to think sexual advances were acceptable than men who were sober. However, when the same question was asked of a group of men who had seen a video of a *friendly* woman, those who were drinking were more inclined to recommend sexual overtures than those who were not, even when these overtures might be unwanted. Apparently, alcohol makes the complicated decisions involved in relationships seem simple ("Gee, she was so friendly")—and potentially open to serious misjudgments.

Both the expectancy and myopia theories suggest that people using alcohol will often go to extremes (Cooper, 2006). In fact, it seems that drinking is a major contributing factor to social problems that result from extreme behaviour. Drinking while driving is a main cause of auto accidents. For example, out of 2541 traffic fatalities in Canada in 2010, an estimated 1082 (42 percent) were related to alcohol impairment (MADD Canada, 2013). A survey of undergraduate women revealed that alcohol contributes to approximately 76 percent of cases of incapacitated rape (rape after the victim is incapacitated by self-induced intoxication) and 72 percent of drug- or alcohol-facilitated rapes (in which the perpetrator deliberately intoxicates the victim prior to rape) (McCauley et al., 2009).

**Barbiturates, Benzodiazepines, and Toxic Inhalants.** Compared to alcohol, the other depressants are much less popular but are still widely used and abused. Barbiturates such as Seconal or Nembutal are prescribed as sleep aids and as anesthetics before surgery. Benzodiazepines such as Valium and Xanax are also called minor tranquilizers and are prescribed as antianxiety drugs. These drugs are prescribed by physicians to treat anxiety or sleep problems, but they are dangerous when used in combination with alcohol because they can cause respiratory depression. Physical dependence is possible because withdrawal from long-term use can produce severe symptoms (including convulsions), and psychological dependence is common as well. Finally, toxic inhalants are perhaps the most alarming substances in this category (Ridenour & Howard, 2012). These drugs are easily accessible in the vapours of inexpensive household products such as glue, hair spray, nail polish remover, or gasoline. Sniffing or "huffing" vapours from these products can promote temporary effects that resemble drunkenness, but overdoses can be lethal, and continued use holds the potential for permanent neurological damage (Howard et al., 2011). Worryingly, inhalant abuse often affects younger children, who may also abuse other substances, and it is especially common in individuals from minority and marginalized populations.

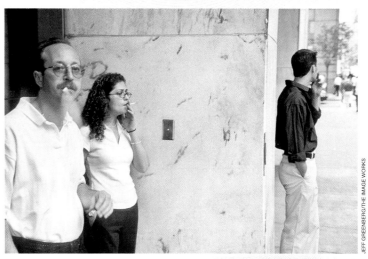

People will often endure significant inconveniences to maintain their addictions.

## Stimulants

**Stimulants** are *substances that excite the central nervous system, heightening arousal and activity levels.* They include caffeine, amphetamines, nicotine, cocaine, modafinil, and Ecstasy, and sometimes have a legitimate pharmaceutical purpose. Amphetamines (also called *speed*), for example, were originally prepared for medicinal uses and as diet drugs; however, amphetamines such as Methedrine and Dexedrine are widely abused, causing insomnia, aggression, and paranoia with long-term use. Stimulants increase

 **Do stimulants create dependency?**

the levels of dopamine and norepinephrine in the brain, thereby inducing higher levels of activity in the brain circuits that depend on these neurotransmitters. As a result, they increase alertness and energy in the user, often producing a euphoric sense of confidence and a kind of agitated motivation to get things done. Stimulants produce physical and psychological dependence, and their withdrawal symptoms involve depressive effects such as fatigue and negative emotions.

Ecstasy (also known as MDMA, "X," or "E"), an amphetamine derivative, is a stimulant but it has added effects somewhat like those of hallucinogens (we will talk about those shortly). Ecstasy is particularly known for making users feel empathic and close to those around them. It is used often as a party drug to enhance the group feeling at dance clubs or raves, but it has unpleasant side effects such as causing jaw clenching and interfering with the regulation of body temperature. The rave culture has popularized pacifiers and juices as remedies for these problems, but users remain highly susceptible to heatstroke and exhaustion. Although Ecstasy is not as likely as some other drugs to cause physical or psychological dependence, it nonetheless can lead to

**stimulants**
Substances that excite the central nervous system, heightening arousal and activity levels.

some dependence. What is more, the impurities sometimes found in street pills are also dangerous (Parrott, 2001). Ecstasy's potentially toxic effect on serotonin neurons in the human brain is under debate, although mounting evidence from animal and human studies suggests that sustained use is associated with damage to serotonergic neurons and potentially associated problems with mood, attention and memory, and impulse control (Kish et al., 2010; Urban et al., 2012).

Cocaine is derived from leaves of the coca plant, which has been cultivated by indigenous peoples of the Andes for millennia and chewed as a medication. Yes, the urban legend is true: Coca-Cola contained cocaine until 1903 and still may use coca leaves (with cocaine removed) as a flavouring—although the company's not telling (Pepsi-Cola never contained cocaine and is probably made from something brown). Sigmund Freud tried cocaine and wrote effusively about it for a while. Cocaine (usually snorted) and crack cocaine (smoked) produce exhilaration and euphoria and are seriously addictive, both for humans and the rats you read about earlier in this chapter. Withdrawal takes the form of an unpleasant crash, and dangerous side effects of cocaine use include both psychological problems such as insomnia, depression, aggression, and paranoia, as well as physical problems such as death from a heart attack or hyperthermia (Marzuk et al., 1998). Although cocaine has enjoyed popularity as a party drug, its extraordinary potential to create dependence and potentially lethal side effects should be taken very seriously.

> **What are some of the dangerous side effects of cocaine use?**

Nicotine is something of a puzzle. This is a drug with almost nothing to recommend it to the newcomer. It usually involves inhaling smoke that does not smell that great, at least at first, and there is not much in the way of a high either—at best, some dizziness or a queasy feeling. So why do people do it? Tobacco use is motivated far more by the unpleasantness of quitting than by the pleasantness of using. The positive effects people report from smoking—relaxation and improved concentration, for example—come chiefly from relief from withdrawal symptoms (Baker, Brandon, & Chassin, 2004). The best approach to nicotine is to never get started.

Smoking tobacco can be very difficult to quit. National Public Radio recently reported one interesting strategy being tried in Japan is filling ashtrays with soap and encouraging people to blow bubbles rather than smoke cigarettes (Craft, 2012).

### Narcotics

Opium, which comes from poppy seeds, and its derivatives heroin, morphine, methadone, and codeine (as well as prescription drugs such as Demerol and Oxycontin), are known as **narcotics** (or **opiates**), *highly addictive drugs derived from opium that relieve pain.* Narcotics induce a feeling of well-being and relaxation that is enjoyable but can also induce stupor and lethargy. The addictive properties of narcotics are powerful, and long-term use produces both tolerance and dependence. Because these drugs are often administered with hypodermic syringes, they also introduce the danger of diseases such as hepatitis and HIV when users share syringes. Unfortunately, these drugs are especially alluring because they mimic the brain's own internal relaxation and well-being system.

> **Why are narcotics especially alluring?**

The brain produces endogenous opioids or endorphins, which are neurotransmitters closely related to opiates. As you learned in the Neuroscience and Behaviour chapter, endorphins play a role in how the brain copes internally with pain and stress. These substances reduce the experience of pain naturally. When you exercise for a while and start to feel your muscles burning, for example, you may also find that there comes a time when the pain eases—sometimes even *during* exercise. Endorphins are secreted in the pituitary gland and other brain sites as a response to injury or exertion, creating a kind of natural remedy (like the "runner's high") that subsequently reduces

**narcotics (or opiates)**
Highly addictive drugs derived from opium that relieve pain.

pain and increases feelings of well-being. When people use narcotics, the brain's endorphin receptors are artificially flooded, however, reducing receptor effectiveness and possibly also depressing the production of endorphins. When external administration of narcotics stops, withdrawal symptoms are likely to occur.

## Hallucinogens

The drugs that produce the most extreme alterations of consciousness are the **hallucinogens,** *drugs that alter sensation and perception, and often cause visual and auditory hallucinations.* These include LSD (lysergic acid diethylamide, or acid), mescaline, psilocybin, PCP (phencyclidine), and ketamine (an animal anesthetic). Some of these drugs are derived from plants (mescaline from peyote cactus, psilocybin or "shrooms" from mushrooms) and have been used by people since ancient times. For example, the ingestion of peyote plays a prominent role in some Native American religious practices. The other hallucinogens are largely synthetic. LSD was first made by chemist Albert Hofman in 1938, leading to a rash of experimentation that influenced popular culture in the 1960s. Timothy Leary, at the time a lecturer in the Department of Psychology at Harvard, championed the use of LSD to "turn on, tune in, and drop out"; the Beatles sang of "*Lucy* in the *Sky* with *Diamonds*" (denying, of course, that this might be a reference to LSD); and the wave of interest led many people to experiment with hallucinogens.

The experiment was not a great success. These drugs produce profound changes in perception. Sensations may seem unusually intense, stationary objects may seem to move or change, patterns or colours may appear, and these perceptions may be

Psychedelic art and music of the 1960s were inspired by some visual and auditory effects of drugs such as LSD.

ANDREW HERYGERS CREATIVE/SUPERSTOCK

**What are the effects of hallucinogens?**

accompanied by exaggerated emotions ranging from blissful transcendence to abject terror. These are the "I have-become-the-legs-of-a-chair!" drugs. But the effects of hallucinogens are dramatic and unpredictable, creating a psychological roller-coaster ride that some people find intriguing and others find deeply disturbing. Hallucinogens are the main class of drugs that animals will not work to self-administer, so it is not surprising that in humans these drugs are unlikely to be addictive. Hallucinogens do not induce significant tolerance or dependence, and overdose deaths are rare. Although hallucinogens still enjoy a marginal popularity with people interested in experimenting with their perceptions, they have been more a cultural trend than a dangerous attraction.

## Marijuana

**Marijuana** (or **cannabis**) *is a plant whose leaves and buds contain a psychoactive drug called tetrahydrocannabinol (THC).* When smoked or eaten, either as is or in concentrated form as *hashish,* this drug produces an intoxication that is mildly hallucinogenic. Users describe the experience as euphoric, with heightened senses of sight and sound and the perception of a rush of ideas. Marijuana affects judgment and short-term memory, and impairs motor skills and coordination—making driving a car or operating heavy equipment a poor choice during its use ("Dude, where's my bulldozer?"). Researchers have found that receptors in the brain that respond to THC (Stephens, 1999) are normally activated by a neurotransmitter called *anandamide* that is naturally produced in the brain (Wiley, 1999). Anandamide is involved in the regulation of mood, memory, appetite, and pain perception and has been found temporarily to stimulate overeating in laboratory animals, much as marijuana does in humans (Williams & Kirkham, 1999). Some chemicals found in dark chocolate also mimic anandamide, although very weakly, perhaps accounting for the well-being some people claim they enjoy after a "dose" of chocolate.

**hallucinogens**
Drugs that alter sensation and perception, and often cause visual and auditory hallucinations.

**marijuana (or cannabis)**
The leaves and buds of the hemp plant, which contain a psychoactive drug called tetrahydrocannabinol (THC).

**gateway drug**
A drug whose use increases the risk of the subsequent use of more harmful drugs.

**hypnosis**
A social interaction in which one person (the hypnotist) makes suggestions that lead to a change in another person's (the subject's) subjective experience of the world.

The addiction potential of marijuana is not strong, as tolerance does not seem to develop, and physical withdrawal symptoms are minimal. Psychological dependence is possible, however, and some people do become chronic users. Marijuana use has been widespread throughout the world for recorded history, both as a medicine for pain and/or nausea and as a recreational drug, but its use remains controversial. Marijuana abuse and dependence have been linked with increased risk of depression, anxiety, and other forms of psychopathology. Many people also are concerned that marijuana (along with alcohol and tobacco) is a **gateway drug,** *a drug whose use increases the risk of the subsequent use of more harmful drugs.* The gateway theory has gained mixed support, with recent studies challenging this theory and suggesting that early-onset drug use in general, regardless of type of drug, increases the risk of later drug problems (Degenhardt et al., 2010).

> **What are the risks of marijuana use?**

### IN SUMMARY

▶ Psychoactive drugs influence consciousness by altering the brain's chemical messaging system and intensifying or dulling the effects of neurotransmitters.

▶ Drug tolerance can result in overdose, and physical and psychological dependence can lead to addiction.

▶ Major types of psychoactive drugs include depressants, stimulants, narcotics, hallucinogens, and marijuana.

▶ The varying effects of alcohol, a depressant, are explained by theories of alcohol expectancy and alcohol myopia.

# Hypnosis: Open to Suggestion

You may have never been hypnotized, but you have probably heard or read about it. Its wonders are often described with an air of amazement, and demonstrations of stage hypnosis make it seem very powerful and mysterious. When you think of hypnosis, you may envision people completely under the power of a hypnotist, who is ordering them to dance like a chicken or perhaps "regress" to early childhood and talk in childlike voices. Many common beliefs about hypnosis are false. **Hypnosis** refers to *a social interaction in which one person (the hypnotist) makes suggestions that lead to a change in another person's (the subject's) subjective experience of the world* (Kirsch et al., 2011). The essence of hypnosis is in leading people to expect that certain things will happen to them that are outside their conscious will (Wegner, 2002).

## Induction and Susceptibility

To induce hypnosis, a hypnotist may ask the person to be hypnotized to sit quietly and focus on some item, such as a spot on the wall (or a swinging pocket watch), and then make suggestions to the person about what effects hypnosis will have (e.g., "your eyelids are slowly closing" or "your arms are getting heavy"). Even without hypnosis, some suggested behaviours might commonly happen just because a person is concentrating on them—just thinking about their eyelids slowly closing, for instance, may make many people shut their eyes briefly or at least blink. In hypnosis, however, suggestions may be made—and followed by people in a susceptible state of mind—for very unusual behaviour that most people would not normally do, such as flapping their arms and making loud clucking sounds

Not everyone is equally hypnotizable. Susceptibility varies greatly. Some highly suggestible people are very easily hypnotized, most people are only moderately influenced, and some people are entirely unaffected by attempts at hypnosis. Susceptibility is not easily predicted by a person's personality traits. A hypnotist will typically test someone's hypnotic susceptibility with a series of suggestions designed to put a person into a more easily influenced state of mind. One of the best indicators of a person's susceptibility is the person's own judgment. So, if you think you might be hypnotizable, you may well be (Hilgard, 1965). People with active, vivid imaginations, or who are easily absorbed in activities such as watching a movie, are also somewhat more prone to be good candidates for hypnosis (Sheehan, 1979; Tellegen & Atkinson, 1974).

> **What makes someone easy to hypnotize?**

## Hypnotic Effects

From watching stage hypnotism, you might think that the major effect of hypnosis is making people do peculiar things. So what do we actually know to be true about hypnosis? There are some impressive demonstrations that suggest real changes occur in those under hypnosis. At the 1849 festivities for Prince Albert of England's birthday, for example, a hypnotized guest was asked to ignore any loud noises and then did not even flinch when a pistol was fired near his face. These days, hypnotists are discouraged from using firearms during stage shows, but they often have volunteers perform other impressive feats. One common claim for superhuman strength under hypnosis involves asking a hypnotized person to become "stiff as a board" and lie unsupported with shoulders on one chair and feet on another while the hypnotist stands on the hypnotized person's body.

Stage hypnotists often perform an induction on the whole audience and then bring some of the more susceptible members on stage for further demonstrations.

Studies have demonstrated that hypnosis can undermine memory, but with important limitations. People susceptible to hypnosis can be led to experience **posthypnotic amnesia,** *the failure to retrieve memories following hypnotic suggestions to forget.* Ernest Hilgard (1986) taught a hypnotized person the populations of some remote cities, for example, and then suggested that the participant forget the study session; the person was quite surprised after the session at being able to give the census figures correctly. Asked how he knew the answers, the individual decided he might have learned them from a TV program. Such amnesia can then be reversed in subsequent hypnosis.

Importantly, research has found that only memories that were lost under hypnosis can be retrieved through hypnosis. The false claim that hypnosis helps people to unearth memories that they are not able to retrieve in normal consciousness seems to have surfaced because hypnotized people often make up memories to satisfy the hypnotist's suggestions. For example, Paul Ingram, a sheriff's deputy accused of sexual abuse by his daughters in the 1980s, was asked by interrogators in session after session to relax and imagine having committed the crimes. He emerged from these sessions having confessed to dozens of horrendous acts of "satanic ritual abuse." These confessions were called into question, however, when independent investigator Richard Ofshe used the same technique to ask Ingram about a crime that Ofshe had simply made up out of thin air, something of which Ingram had never been accused. Ingram produced a three-page handwritten confession, complete with dialogue (Ofshe, 1992). Still, prosecutors in the case accepted Ingram's guilty plea, and he was only released in 2003 after a public outcry and years of work on his defense. After a person

**posthypnotic amnesia**
The failure to retrieve memories following hypnotic suggestions to forget.

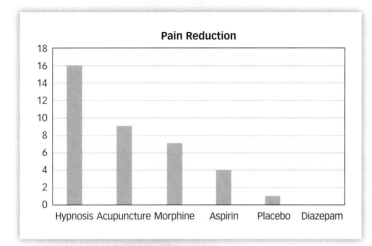

**Pain Reduction**

▲ Figure **5.14 Hypnotic Analgesia** The degree of pain reduction reported by people using different techniques for the treatment of laboratory-induced pain. Hypnosis wins (Stern et al., 1977).

**hypnotic analgesia**
The reduction of pain through hypnosis in people who are susceptible to hypnosis.

| Congruent | Incongruent | Neutral |
|-----------|-------------|---------|
| red | red | desk |
| green | green | chair |
| blue | blue | table |
| yellow | yellow | coat |
| black | black | recipe |

▲ Figure **5.15 Example of Stroop Stimuli** For which list is it easiest to name the colour of the ink that each word is written in? For which list is it hardest?

claims to remember something, even under hypnosis, it is difficult to convince others that the memory was false (Loftus & Ketchum, 1994).

Hypnosis can lead to measurable physical and behavioural changes in the body. One well-established effect is **hypnotic analgesia,** *the reduction of pain through hypnosis in people who are susceptible to hypnosis.* For example, one study (see **FIGURE 5.14**) found that for pain induced in volunteers in the laboratory, hypnosis was more effective than morphine, diazepam (Valium), aspirin, acupuncture, or placebos (Stern et al., 1977). For people who are hypnotically susceptible, hypnosis can be used to control pain in surgeries and dental procedures, in some cases more effectively than any form of anesthesia (Druckman & Bjork, 1994; Kihlstrom, 1985).

> What evidence supports the idea that hypnosis leads to observable changes in the body?

Hypnosis also has been shown to enable people to control mental processes previously believed to be beyond conscious control. For instance, the Stroop task (Stroop, 1935) is a classic psychological test in which a person is asked to name the colour of words on a page (appearing in ink that is red, blue, green, etc.). This is a simple task. However, sometimes the words themselves are the names of colours, but are printed in a different colour of the ink. It turns out that people are significantly slower, and make more errors, when naming ink colours that do not match the content of the word (e.g., when the word "blue" is written in red ink) than if the content is neutral or congruent (e.g., if the word "desk" or "red" is written in red ink) (see **FIGURE 5.15**). This effect is present no matter how hard we try. Amazingly, the effect is completely eliminated when highly suggestible people are hypnotized and told to respond to all words the same way (Raz et al., 2002). Importantly, though, follow-up studies have revealed that hypnotic induction is not required to eliminate the Stroop effect. It turns out that simply suggesting to highly suggestible people that they should respond to all words the same has the same effect as hypnosis (Lifshitz et al., 2013). This suggests that hypnotic effects may be the result of highly suggestible people complying with the suggestions of others.

Nevertheless, people under hypnotic suggestion are not merely telling hypnotists what they want to hear. Instead, they seem to be experiencing what they have been asked to experience. Under hypnotic suggestion, for example, regions of the brain responsible for colour vision are activated in highly hypnotizable people when they are asked to perceive colour, even when they are really shown grey stimuli (Kosslyn et al., 2000). While engaged in the Stroop task, people who can eliminate the Stroop effect under suggestion show decreased activity in the anterior cingulate cortex (ACC), the part of the brain involved in conflict monitoring (**FIGURE 5.16** on the next page) (Raz, Fan, & Posner, 2005), consistent with the lack of conflict perceived between the colour name and ink. Overall, hypnotic suggestion appears to change the subjective perception of those experiencing it, as reflected by changes in their self-report, behaviour, and brain activity.

## IN SUMMARY

▶ Hypnosis is an altered state of consciousness characterized by suggestibility.

▶ Although many claims for hypnosis overstate its effects, hypnosis can create the experience that one's actions are occurring involuntarily, create analgesia, and even change brain activations in ways that suggest that hypnotic experiences are more than imagination.

(a)    (b)

▲ Figure **5.16** **Brain Activity during Hypnosis** (*a*) Researchers found that the anterior cingulate cortex is activated in all people during the Stroop task. The anterior cingulate cortex (shown in the crosshairs) is involved in conflict monitoring. (*b*) However, under hypnosis, highly suggestible people show decreased activation in this brain region compared to less hypnotizable people (Raz et al., 2005).

RAZ ET AL. 2005

# OTHER VOICES

## The Blink of an Eye

On December, 8, 1995, Jean-Dominique Bauby was 43, the chief editor of the French fashion magazine *ELLE*, and the father of two children, Théophile and Céleste. He was sophisticated, well-travelled, and enjoyed his active life. That day, a catastrophic stroke sent him into a coma from which he emerged aware, but totally paralyzed: unable to breathe, eat, or swallow without assistance.

As incapacitated as he was, he was able to write a remarkable memoir, *Le scaphandre et le papillon,* which he "dictated" to an assistant one letter at a time by blinking his left eyelid. The letters of the alphabet, organized in order of frequency, were presented on a screen, his assistant would point to each in turn, and Bauby would blink once, *yes,* at the appropriate letter. In the long hours of solitude at night in his hospital bed, he would compose and memorize the sections of the memoir, to be dictated the next morning. His story was translated into English as *The Diving Bell and the Butterfly.*

In his book Bauby detailed the mundane experiences of every day life—how the morning light looked coming in through the old curtain on the window of his hospital room. He described the items in the room—pictures of his family and friends, drawings made by his children, a little toy cyclist given to him by a friend. He described how he felt: his head felt very heavy, his heels hurt, his chest was congested, his hands hurt, but he could not tell if they were icy cold or burning hot. He felt like he was imprisoned in an old fashioned diving bell.

He was frustrated at no longer being able to communicate fluently (he was a witty and engaging conversationalist before the stroke). Jokes and witticisms that he would normally use fell flat when they were dictated labouriously, one letter at a time. The enforced humourlessness was one of the main limitations of his condition.

He related how one day he was playing hangman with his son (since he could guess letters one at a time). He was suddenly overcome by an intense grief because although his son was physically close, he could not ruffle his hair, hug him close, or even touch him. He called this situation "monstrous … horrible," and startled his son when an involuntary sob escaped him.

Despite the sadness of his situation, he also noted the beauty of memory and imagination: how, like a butterfly, his thoughts could go where they please—to the tip of South America, to King Midas's court, to castles in Spain, to the woman he loved, or to childhood fantasies.

Bauby wrote about the reality of his situation—the horror, the humour, and the infinite possibilities of the human imagination—through one fluttering eyelid. This movement, although minuscule, was his one channel of communication and therefore all-important. How do you think the people around him discovered that he was aware, and that he could communicate by blinking? What would they have had to do to figure that out?

Bauby died of heart failure in late winter of 1997, a few days after the publication of his extraordinary memoir.

Quotations from Bauby, J. (1997). *The diving bell and the butterfly.* London, UK: Fourth Estate.

PHOTO BY PAUL COOPER/REX USA (400359i)

▲ Jean-Dominique Bauby before his stroke.

# Chapter Review

1. Which of the following is NOT a basic property of consciousness?
   a. intentionality
   b. disunity
   c. selectivity
   d. transience

2. Currently, unconscious processes are understood as
   a. a concentrated pattern of thought suppression.
   b. a hidden system of memories, instincts, and desires.
   c. a blank slate.
   d. unexperienced mental processes that give rise to thoughts and behaviour.

3. The __ unconscious is at work when subliminal and unconscious processes influence thought and behaviour.
   a. minimal
   b. repressive
   c. dynamic
   d. cognitive

4. The cycle of sleep and waking is one of the major patterns of human life called
   a. the circadian rhythm.
   b. the sleep stages.
   c. the altered state of consciousness.
   d. subliminal perception.

5. Sleep needs __ over the life span.
   a. decrease
   b. increase
   c. fluctuate
   d. remain the same

6. During dreaming, the dreamer __ changes in emotion, thought, and sensation.
   a. is skeptical of
   b. is completely unconscious of
   c. uncritically accepts
   d. views objectively

7. Which explanation of dreams proposes that they are produced when the mind attempts to make sense of random neural activity that occurs in the brain during sleep?
   a. Freud's psychoanalytic theory
   b. the activation–synthesis model
   c. the cognitive unconscious model
   d. the manifest content framework

8. fMRI studies of the dreaming brain reveal all of the following EXCEPT
   a. increased sensitivity to emotions.
   b. activations associated with visual activity.
   c. increased capacity for planning.
   d. prevention of movement.

9. Psychoactive drugs influence consciousness by altering the effects of
   a. agonists.
   b. neurotransmitters.
   c. amphetamines.
   d. spinal neurons.

10. Tolerance for drugs involves
    a. larger doses being required over time to achieve the same effect.
    b. openness to new experiences.
    c. the initial attraction of drug use.
    d. the lessening of the painful symptoms that accompany withdrawal.

11. Drugs that heighten arousal and activity levels by affecting the central nervous system are
    a. depressants.
    b. stimulants.
    c. narcotics.
    d. hallucinogens.

12. Alcohol expectancy refers to
    a. alcohol's initial effects of euphoria and reduced anxiety.
    b. the widespread acceptance of alcohol as a socially approved substance.
    c. alcohol leading people to respond in simple ways to complex situations.
    d. people's beliefs about how alcohol will influence them in particular situations.

13. Hypnosis has been proven to have
    a. an effect on physical strength.
    b. a positive effect on memory retrieval.
    c. an analgesic effect.
    d. an age-regression effect.

14. Which of the following four individuals is LEAST likely to be a good candidate for hypnosis?
    a. Jake, who spends lots of time watching movies
    b. Ava, who is convinced she is easily hypnotizable
    c. Evan, who has an active, vivid imagination
    d. Isabel, who loves to play sports

## KEY TERMS

activation–synthesis model (p. 203)

alcohol myopia (p. 210)

altered state of consciousness (p. 194)

balanced placebo design (p. 210)

circadian rhythm (p. 195)

cognitive unconscious (p. 191)

coma (p. 185)

consciousness (p. 178)

depressants (p. 209)

dichotic listening (p. 182)

disorder of consciousness (p. 185)

drug tolerance (p. 207)

dynamic unconscious (p. 190)

electrooculograph (EOG) (p. 195)

expectancy theory (p. 210)

full consciousness (p. 184)

gateway drug (p. 214)

hallucinogens (p. 213)

hypnosis (p. 214)

hypnotic analgesia (p. 216)

insomnia (p. 199)

ironic processes of mental control (p. 189)

latent content (p. 202)

locked-in symdrome (p. 185)

manifest content (p. 202)

marijuana (or cannabis) (p. 213)

mental control (p. 188)

mind–body problem (p. 181)

minimal consciousness (p. 184)

narcolepsy (p. 200)

narcotics (or opiates) (p. 212)

night terrors (or sleep terrors) (p. 200)

phenomenology (p. 179)

posthypnotic amnesia (p. 215)

problem of other minds (p. 179)

psychoactive drugs (p. 205)

rebound effect of thought suppression (p. 188)

REM sleep (p. 195)

repression (p. 190)

self-consciousness (p. 184)

sleep apnea (p. 199)

sleep paralysis (p. 200)

somnambulism (or sleepwalking) (p. 200)

stimulants (p. 211)

subliminal perception (p. 191)

thought suppression (p. 188)

vegetative state (p. 185)

## CHANGING MINDS

1. "I had a really weird dream last night," your friend tells you. "I dreamed that I was trying to fly like a bird but I kept flying into clotheslines. I looked it up online, and dreams where you're struggling to fly mean that there is someone in your life who's standing in your way and preventing you from moving forward. I suppose that has to be my boyfriend, so maybe I'd better break up with him." Based on what you have read in this chapter, what would you tell your friend about the reliability of dream interpretation?

2. During an early-morning class, you notice your friend yawning, and you ask if he slept well the night before. "On weekdays, I'm in class all day, and I work the night shift," he says. "So I don't sleep much during the week. But I figure it's okay because I make up for it by sleeping in late on Saturday mornings." Is it realistic for your friend to assume that he can balance regular sleep deprivation with rebound sleep on the weekends?

3. You and a friend are watching the 2010 movie *Inception*, starring Leonardo DiCaprio as a corporate spy. DiCaprio's character is hired by a businessman named Saito to plant an idea in the unconscious mind of a competitor while he sleeps. According to the plan, when the competitor awakens, he will be compelled to act on the idea, to the secret benefit of Saito's company. "It's a cool idea," your friend says, "but it's pure science fiction. There's no such thing as an unconscious mind, and no way that unconscious ideas could influence the way you act when you're conscious." What would you tell your friend? What evidence do we have that the unconscious mind exists and can influence conscious behaviour?

## ANSWERS TO KEY CONCEPT QUIZ

1. b; 2. d; 3. d; 4. a; 5. a; 6. c; 7. b; 8. c; 9. b; 10. a; 11. b; 12. d; 13. c; 14. d

Need more help? Additional resources are located in Launchpad at:
www.worthpublishers.com/launchpad/schacter3ecanadian

6

# Memory

▲ Encoding: Transforming Perceptions into Memories
Semantic Encoding
Visual Imagery Encoding
Organizational Encoding
Encoding of Survival-Related Information

▲ Storage: Maintaining Memories over Time
Sensory Storage
Short-Term Storage and Working Memory
Long-Term Storage
HOT SCIENCE Sleep on It
Memories, Neurons, and Synapses

▲ Retrieval: Bringing Memories to Mind
Retrieval Cues: Reinstating the Past
Consequences of Retrieval
Separating the Components of Retrieval
CULTURE & COMMUNITY Does Culture Affect Childhood Amnesia?

▲ Multiple Forms of Memory: How the Past Returns
Explicit and Implicit Memory
Semantic and Episodic Memory
THE REAL WORLD Is Google Hurting our Memories?

▲ Memory Failures: The Seven Sins of Memory
1. Transience
2. Absentmindedness
3. Blocking
4. Memory Misattribution
5. Suggestibility
6. Bias
7. Persistence
Are the Seven Sins Vices or Virtues?
OTHER VOICES Early Memories

JILL PRICE WAS 12 YEARS OLD when she began to suspect that she possessed an unusually good memory. Studying for a Grade 7 science final on May 30, her mind drifted and she became aware that she could recall vividly everything she had been doing on May 30 of the previous year. A month later, something similar happened: Enjoying vanilla custards at Paradise Cove near Los Angeles, California with her friend Kathy, Jill recalled that they had done the same thing precisely a year earlier. Expecting that Kathy would recall the episode as easily as she did, Jill was surprised when Kathy replied blankly: "We did?"

Remembering specifics of events that occurred a year ago may not seem so extraordinary—you can probably recall what you did for your last birthday, or where you spent last New Year's Day—but can you recall the details of what you did exactly 1 year ago today? Or what you did a week, a month, 6 months, or 6 years before that day? Probably not, but Jill Price can.

As she grew older, Jill's memory flashes became even more frequent. Now in her late 40s, Jill can recall clearly and in great detail what has happened to her *every single day since early 1980* (Price & Davis, 2008). This is not just Jill's subjective impression. Dr. James McGaugh, a well-known memory researcher based at the University of California–Irvine, and his colleagues tested Jill's memory over a period of a few years and came up with some shocking results (Parker, Cahill, & McGaugh, 2006). For example, they asked Jill to recall the dates of each Easter from 1980 to 2003, which is a pretty tough task considering that Easter can fall on any day between March 22 and April 15. Even though she had no idea that she would be asked this question, Jill recalled the correct dates quickly and easily; nobody else the researchers tested came close. When Jill was asked what had happened on particular dates, she was able to accurately report significant events (*August 16, 1977*? "Tuesday, Elvis [Presley] died." *December 21, 1988*? "Lockerbie [Scotland] plane crash"). When asked the dates of particular events that had occurred years earlier (When did the Persian Gulf War start? When did Princess Diana die? When did the Concorde plane crash?), she

Jill Price can accurately remember just about everything that has happened to her during the past 30 years, as confirmed by her diary, but Jill's extraordinary memory is more of a curse than a blessing.

DAN TUFFS/CONTRIBUTOR, GETTY IMAGES

**memory**
The ability to store and retrieve information over time.

**encoding**
The process of transforming what we perceive, think, or feel into an enduring memory.

**storage**
The process of maintaining information in memory over time.

**retrieval**
The process of bringing to mind information that has been previously encoded and stored.

rattled them off without a hitch (Wednesday, January 16, 1991; August 30, 1997; July 25, 2000). The researchers also asked Jill about the details of what she had been doing on various randomly chosen dates, and they checked Jill's recall against her personal diary. Again, Jill answered quickly and accurately: *July 1, 1986?*—"I see it all, that day, that month, that summer. Tuesday. Went with (friend's name) to (restaurant name)." *October 3, 1987?*—"That was a Saturday. Hung out at the apartment all weekend, wearing a sling—hurt my elbow." *April 27, 1994?*—"That was Wednesday. That was easy for me because I knew where I was exactly. I was down in Florida. I was summoned to come down and to say goodbye to my grandmother who they all thought was dying but she ended up living" (Parker et al., 2006, pp. 39–40).

Jill's memory is a gift we would all love to have—right? Not necessarily. Here is what Jill has to say about her ability: "Most have called it a gift but I call it a burden. I run my entire life through my head every day and it drives me crazy!!!" (Parker et al., 2006, p. 35).

Researchers still do not understand all the reasons why Jill Price can remember her past so much more fully than the rest of us, but it turns out that Jill is not alone. Jill's extraordinary memory abilities became widely known after a *60 Minutes* story that featured her and Dr. McGaugh. That story elicited a flurry of inquiries to Dr. McGaugh from other people around the world who thought that they, too, possessed the spectacular memory abilities demonstrated by Jill. Although most of them did not, McGaugh and his colleagues identified 11 other individuals with "highly superior autobiographical memory" abilities that resemble those they had seen in Jill Price (LePort et al., 2012). The researchers discovered differences in the structure of several brain regions known to be involved in memory in the superior autobiographical memory group compared with a control group, suggesting that further study of these unusual individuals might help to understand the nature of memory more generally.

**MEMORY IS** *THE ABILITY TO STORE AND RETRIEVE INFORMATION OVER TIME.* Even though few of us possess the extraordinary memory abilities of Jill Price and the handful of others with highly superior autobiographical memory, each of us has a unique identity that is intricately tied to the things we have thought, felt, done, and experienced. Memories are the residue of those events, the enduring changes that experience makes in our brains and leaves behind when it passes. If an experience passes without leaving a trace, it might just as well not have happened. But as Jill's story suggests, remembering all that has happened is not necessarily a good thing, either—a point we will explore more fully later in the chapter.

The ease with which someone like Jill can instantly remember her past should not blind us from appreciating how complex that act of remembering really is. Because memory is so remarkably complex, it is also remarkably fragile (Schacter, 1996). We all have had the experience of forgetting something we desperately wanted to remember or of remembering something that never really happened. Why does memory serve us so well in some situations and play such cruel tricks on us in other cases? When can we trust our memories and when should we view them skeptically? Is there just one kind of memory, or are there many? These are among the questions that psychologists have asked and answered.

As you have seen in other chapters, the mind's mistakes provide key insights into its fundamental operation, and there is no better illustration of this than in the realm of memory. In this chapter, we will consider the three key functions of memory: **encoding,** *the process of transforming what we perceive, think, or feel into an enduring memory;* **storage,** *the process of maintaining information in memory over time;* and **retrieval,** *the process of bringing to mind information that has been previously encoded and stored.* We will then examine several different kinds of memory and focus on the ways in which errors, distortions, and imperfections can reveal the nature of memory itself.

# Encoding: Transforming Perceptions into Memories

Bubbles P., a professional gambler with no formal education, who spent most of his time shooting craps at local clubs or playing high-stakes poker, had no difficulty rattling off 20 numbers, in either forward or backward order, after just a single glance (Ceci, DeSimone, & Johnson, 1992). Most people can listen to a list of numbers and then repeat them from memory—as long as the list is no more than about seven items long (try it for yourself using **FIGURE 6.1**).

How did Bubbles accomplish his astounding feats of memory? For at least 2000 years, people have thought of memory as a recording device that makes exact copies of information that comes in through our senses, and then stores those copies for later use. This idea is simple and intuitive. It is also completely incorrect. Memories are made by combining information we *already* have in our brains with new information that comes in through our senses. In this way memory is like cooking; starting from a recipe but improvising along the way, we add old information to new information, mix, shake, bake, and out pops a memory. Memories are *constructed,* not recorded, and encoding is the process by which we transform what we perceive, think, or feel into an enduring memory. Let us look at three types of encoding processes—semantic encoding, visual imagery encoding, and organizational encoding—and then consider the possible survival value of encoding for our ancestors.

> **How is making a memory like following a recipe?**

```
        2 8
       6 9 1
      0 4 7 3
     8 7 4 5 4
    9 0 2 4 8 1
   5 7 4 2 2 9 6
  6 4 7 1 9 3 0 4
 3 5 6 7 1 8 4 8 5
1 0 2 8 8 3 4 7 2 9
4 7 2 0 8 2 7 4 2 6 4
7 3 1 0 9 3 4 3 5 1 3 8
```

◀ Figure **6.1** **Digit Memory Test** How many digits can you remember? Start on the first row and cover the rows below it with a piece of paper. Study the numbers in the row for 1 second and then cover that row again. After a couple of seconds, try to repeat the numbers. Then uncover the row to see if you were correct. If so, continue down to the next row, using the same instructions, until you cannot recall all the numbers in a row. The number of digits in the last row you can remember correctly is your digit span. Bubbles P. could remember 20 random numbers, or about five rows deep. How did you do?

## Semantic Encoding

Memories are a combination of old and new information, so the nature of any particular memory depends as much on the old information already in our memories as it does on the new information coming in through our senses. In other words, how we remember something depends on how we think about it at the time. For example, as a professional gambler, Bubbles found numbers unusually meaningful, so when he saw a string of digits, he tended to think about their meanings. He might have thought about how they related to his latest bet at the racetrack or to his winnings after a long night at the poker table. Whereas you might try to memorize the string 22061823 by saying it over and over, Bubbles would think about betting $220 at 6-to-1 odds on horse number 8 to place 2nd in the 3rd race. Indeed, when Bubbles was tested with materials other than numbers—faces, words, objects, or locations—his memory performance was no better than average.

In a seminal experiment, Toronto researchers Fergus Craik and Endel Tulving presented participants with a series of words and asked them to make one of three types of judgments (Craik & Tulving, 1975): *semantic judgments* required the participants to think about the meaning of the words (Is *hat* a type of clothing?); *rhyme judgments* required the participants to think about the sound of the words (Does *hat* rhyme with *cat*?); and *visual judgments* required the participants to think about

> Have you ever wondered why you can remember 20 experiences (your favourite camping trip, your 16th birthday party, your first day at university, etc.) but not 20 digits? One reason is that we often think about the meaning behind our experiences, so we semantically encode them without even trying (Craik & Tulving, 1975).

**semantic encoding**
The process of relating new information in a meaningful way to knowledge that is already stored in memory.

**visual imagery encoding**
The process of storing new information by converting it into mental pictures.

**organizational encoding**
The process of categorizing information according to the relationships among a series of items.

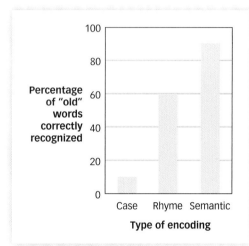

This figure shows the results of the experiment conducted by University of Toronto psychologists Fergus Craik and Endel Tulving (1975). When participants encoded word lists by making a case judgment on each word, they correctly recognized only 15 percent of the words later. In dramatic contrast, when they had to process the meaning of the word, correct performance was over 80 percent. This demonstrates that processing words for meaning leads to better encoding into long-term memory than does processing words for merely structural characteristics.

the appearance of the words (Is *HAT* written uppercase or lowercase?). The type of judgment task influenced how participants thought about each word—what old information they combined with the new—and had a powerful impact on their memories. Those participants who made semantic judgments (i.e., had thought about the meaning of the words) had much better memory for the words than did participants who thought about how the word looked or sounded. The results of these and many other studies have shown that long-term retention is greatly enhanced by **semantic encoding,** *the process of relating new information in a meaningful way to knowledge that is already stored in memory* (Brown & Craik, 2000).

> **Which is most effective, semantic, rhyme, or visual judgment, and why?**

So where does this semantic encoding take place? What is going on in the brain when this type of information processing occurs? Studies reveal that semantic encoding is uniquely associated with increased activity in the lower left part of the frontal lobe and the inner part of the left temporal lobe (**FIGURE 6.2a**) (Demb et al., 1995; Kapur et al., 1994; Wagner et al., 1998). In fact, the amount of activity in each of these two regions during encoding is directly related to whether people later remember an item. The more activity there is in these areas, the more likely the person will remember the information.

## Visual Imagery Encoding

In Athens in 477 BCE, the Greek poet Simonides had just left a banquet when the ceiling collapsed and killed all the people inside. Simonides was able to name every one of the dead simply by visualizing each chair around the banquet table and recalling the person who had been sitting there. Simonides was not the first, but he was among the most proficient, to use **visual imagery encoding,** *the process of storing new information by converting it into mental pictures.*

If you wanted to use Simonides's method to create an enduring memory, you could simply convert the information that you wanted to remember into a visual image and then store it in a familiar location. For instance, if you were going to the grocery store and wanted to remember to buy soft drinks, popcorn, and cheese dip, you could use the rooms in your house as locations and imagine your living room flooded in soft drinks, your bedroom pillows stuffed with popcorn, and your bathtub as a greasy pond of cheese dip. When you arrived at the store, you could then take a mental walk around your house and "look" into each room to remember the items you needed to purchase.

Numerous experiments have shown that visual imagery encoding can substantially improve memory. In one experiment, participants who studied lists of words by creating visual images of them later recalled twice as many items as participants who just mentally repeated the words (Schnorr & Atkinson, 1969). Why does visual imagery encoding work so well? First, visual imagery encoding does some of the same things that semantic

> **How does visual encoding influence memory?**

encoding does: When you create a visual image, you relate incoming information to knowledge already in memory. For example, a visual image of a parked car might help you create a link to your memory of your first kiss.

Second, when you use visual imagery to encode words and other verbal information, you end up with two different mental *placeholders* for the items—a visual one and a verbal one—which gives you more ways to remember them than just a verbal placeholder

Semantic encoding involves relating new information in a meaningful way to facts you already know; visual imagery encoding involves storing new information by converting it into mental pictures. How might you use both kinds of encoding to help store a new fact, such as the date of a friend's birthday that falls on, say, November 24?

RADIUS IMAGES/ALAMY

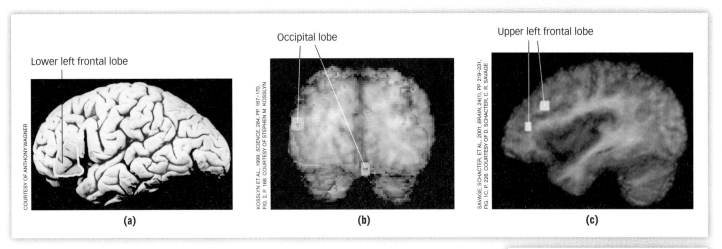

Lower left frontal lobe

Occipital lobe

Upper left frontal lobe

COURTESY OF ANTHONY WAGNER

KOSSLYN ET AL., 1999, *SCIENCE*, 284, PP. 167–170, FIG. 2, P. 168. COURTESY OF STEPHEN M. KOSSLYN

SAVAGE, SCHACTER, ET AL., 2001, *BRAIN*, 241(1), PP. 219–231, FIG. 1C, P. 226. COURTESY OF D. SCHACTER, C. R. SAVAGE

(a)        (b)        (c)

alone (Paivio, 1971, 1986). Visual imagery encoding activates visual processing regions in the occipital lobe (see **FIGURE 6.2b**), which suggests that people actually enlist the visual system when forming memories based on mental images (Kosslyn et al., 1993).

## Organizational Encoding

Have you ever ordered dinner with a group of friends and watched in amazement as your server took the order without writing anything down? To find out how this is done, one researcher spent 3 months working in a restaurant where servers routinely wrote down orders but then left the written order at the customer's table before proceeding to the kitchen and *telling* the cooks what to make (Stevens, 1988). The researcher wired the servers with microphones and asked them to think aloud, that is, to say what they were thinking as they walked around all day doing their jobs. The researcher found that as soon as the server left a customer's table, he or she immediately began *grouping* or *categorizing* the orders into hot drinks, cold drinks, hot foods, and cold foods. The servers grouped the items into a sequence that matched the layout of the kitchen, first placing drink orders, then hot food orders, and finally cold food orders. The servers remembered their orders by relying on **organizational encoding,** *the process of categorizing information according to the relationships among a series of items.*

For example, suppose you had to memorize the words *peach, cow, chair, apple, table, cherry, lion, couch, horse, desk.* The task seems difficult, but if you organize the items into three categories—fruit (*peach, apple, cherry*), animals (*cow, lion, horse*), and furniture (*chair, table, couch, desk*)—the task becomes much easier. Studies have shown that instructing people to sort items into categories like this is an effective way to enhance their subsequent recall of those items

> **Why might mentally organizing the material for an exam enhance your retrieval of that material?**

(Mandler, 1967). Even more complex organizational schemes have been used, such as the hierarchy in **FIGURE 6.3** on the next page (Bower et al., 1969). People can improve their recall of individual items by organizing them into multiple-level categories, all the way from a general category such as *animals*, through intermediate categories such as *birds* and *songbirds,* down to specific examples such as *wren* and *sparrow.*

▲ Figure **6.2** **Brain Activity during Different Types of Judgments** fMRI studies reveal that different parts of the brain are active during different types of judgments: (*a*) during semantic judgments, the lower left frontal lobe is active; (*b*) during visual judgments, the occipital lobe is active; and (*c*) during organizational judgments, the upper left frontal lobe is active.

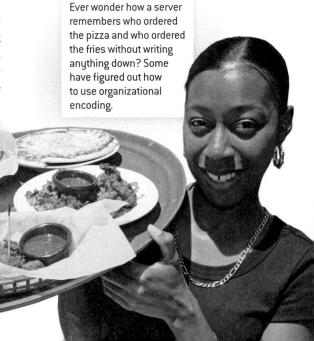

Ever wonder how a server remembers who ordered the pizza and who ordered the fries without writing anything down? Some have figured out how to use organizational encoding.

JEFF GREENBERG/ALAMY

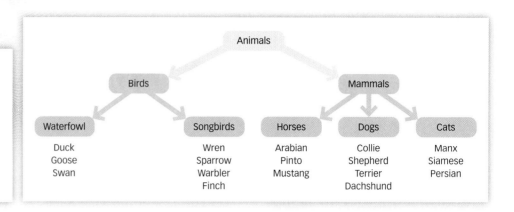

▶ Figure **6.3** **Organizing Words into a Hierarchy** Organizing words into conceptual groups and relating them to one another—such as in this example of a hierarchy—makes it easier to reconstruct the items from memory later (Bower et al., 1969). Keeping track of the 17 items in this example can be facilitated by remembering the hierarchical groupings they fall under.

Just as semantic and visual imagery encoding activates distinct regions of the brain, so, too, does organizational encoding. As you can see in **FIGURE 6.2c** (on the previous page), organizational encoding activates the upper surface of the left frontal lobe (Fletcher, Shallice, & Dolan, 1998; Savage et al., 2001). Different types of encoding strategies appear to rely on different areas of brain activation.

## Encoding of Survival-Related Information

Encoding new information is critical to many aspects of everyday life—prospects for attaining your degree would be pretty slim without this ability—and the survival of our ancestors likely depended on encoding and later remembering such things as the sources of food and water or where a predator appeared (Nairne & Pandeirada, 2008; Sherry & Schacter, 1987).

Recent experiments have addressed these ideas by examining encoding of survival-related information. The experiments were motivated by an evolutionary perspective based on Darwin's principle of natural selection: The features of an organism that help it survive and reproduce are more likely than other features to be passed on to subsequent generations (see the Psychology: Evolution of a Science chapter). Therefore, memory mechanisms that help us to survive and reproduce should be preserved by natural selection, and our memory systems should be built in a way that allows us to remember especially well encoded information that is relevant to our survival.

To test this idea, the researchers gave participants three different encoding tasks (Nairne, Thompson, & Pandeirada, 2007). In the survival-encoding condition, participants were asked to imagine that they were stranded in the grasslands of a foreign land without any survival materials and that over the next few months they would need supplies of food and water and also need to protect themselves from predators. The researchers then showed participants randomly chosen words (e.g., *stone, meadow, chair*) and asked them to rate on a 1 to 5 scale how relevant each item would be to survival in the hypothetical situation. In the moving-encoding condition, a second group of participants was asked to imagine that they were planning to move to a new home in a foreign land, and to rate on a 1 to 5 scale how useful each item might be in helping them to set up a new home. Finally, in the pleasantness-encoding condition, a third group was shown the same words and asked to rate on a 1 to 5 scale the pleasantness of each word.

The findings, displayed in **FIGURE 6.4** (on the next page), show that participants recalled more words after the survival-encoding task than after either the moving or pleasantness tasks. In later studies, the researchers found that survival encoding resulted in higher levels of recall than several other non-survival-encoding tasks involving semantic encoding, imagery encoding, or organizational encoding (Nairne, Pandeirada, & Thompson, 2008). Exactly what about survival encoding produces

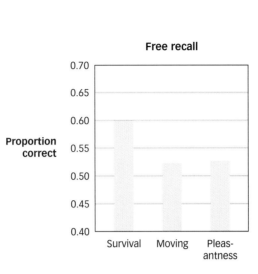

**Free recall**

Proportion correct

◀ Figure **6.4** **Survival Encoding Enhances Later Recall** What does a pouncing cougar that may threaten our survival have to do with recall? People recall more words after survival encoding (Nairne et al., 2007).

such high levels of memory? Survival encoding draws on elements of semantic, visual imagery, and organizational encoding, which may give it an advantage over any one of the other three (Burns, Hwang, & Burns, 2011). Also, survival encoding encourages participants to engage in extensive planning, which in turn benefits memory and may account for much of the benefit of survival encoding. For example, when participants imagine scenarios in which they are stranded in grasslands without food, and encode a series of words with respect to their survival relevance, survival scenarios that *do* involve planning produce superior subsequent memory compared with survival scenarios that do *not* involve planning. Critically, superior recall is also observed for scenarios that *involve planning but not survival*, such as planning a dinner party (Klein, Robertson, & Delton, 2011). Of course, planning for the future is itself critical for our long-term survival, so these findings are still broadly consistent with an evolutionary perspective in which memory is built to support planning and related forms of thinking about the future that enhance our chances of survival (Klein et al., 2011; Schacter, 2012; Suddendorf & Corballis, 2007).

## IN SUMMARY

▶ Encoding is the process of transforming into a lasting memory the information our senses take in. Most instances of spectacular memory performance reflect the skillful use of encoding strategies rather than so-called photographic memory. Memory is influenced by the type of encoding we perform regardless of whether we consciously intend to remember an event or a fact.

▶ Semantic encoding, visual imagery encoding, and organizational encoding all increase memory, but they use different parts of the brain to accomplish that task.

▶ Encoding information with respect to its survival value is a particularly effective method for increasing subsequent recall, perhaps because our memory systems have evolved in a way that allows us to remember especially well information that is relevant to our survival.

**sensory memory**
A type of storage that holds sensory information for a few seconds or less.

**iconic memory**
A fast-decaying store of visual information.

**echoic memory**
A fast-decaying store of auditory information.

# Storage: Maintaining Memories over Time

Encoding is the process of turning perceptions into memories. But one of the hallmarks of a memory is that you can bring it to mind on Tuesday, not on Wednesday, and then bring it to mind again on Thursday. So where are our memories when we are not using them? Clearly, those memories are stored in some form in your brain. As pointed out earlier, *storage is the process of maintaining information in memory over time*. There are three major kinds of memory storage: sensory, short-term, and long-term. As these names suggest, the three kinds of storage are distinguished primarily by the amount of time over which a memory is retained.

## Sensory Storage

**Sensory memory** is *a type of storage that holds sensory information for a few seconds or less*. In a series of classic experiments, research participants were asked to remember rows of letters (Sperling, 1960). In one version of the procedure, participants viewed three rows of four letters each, as shown in **FIGURE 6.5**. The researcher flashed the letters on a screen for just 1/20th of a second. When asked to remember all 12 of the letters they had just seen, participants recalled fewer than half. There were two possible explanations for this: Either people simply could not encode all the letters in such a brief period of time, or they had encoded the letters but forgotten them while trying to recall everything they had seen.

| X | L | W | F |
| J | B | O | V |
| K | C | Z | R |

▲ Figure **6.5** **Iconic Memory Test** When a grid of letters is flashed on screen for only 1/20th of a second, it is difficult to recall individual letters. But if prompted to remember a particular row immediately after the grid is shown, research participants will do so with high accuracy. Sperling used this procedure to demonstrate that although iconic memory stores the whole grid, the information fades away too quickly for a person to recall everything (Sperling, 1960).

To test the two ideas, the researcher relied on a clever trick. Just after the letters disappeared from the screen, a tone sounded that cued the participants to report the letters in a particular row. A *high* tone cued participants to report the contents of the top row, a *medium* tone cued participants to report the contents of the middle row, and a *low* tone cued participants to report the contents of the bottom row. When asked to report only a single row, people recalled almost all of the letters in that row! Because the tone sounded after the letters disappeared from the screen, the researchers concluded that people could have recalled the same number of letters from any of the rows, had they been asked. Participants had no way of knowing which of the three rows would be cued, so the researcher inferred that virtually all the letters had been encoded. In fact, if the tone was substantially delayed, participants could not perform the task because the information had slipped away from their sensory memories. Like the afterimage of a flashlight, the 12 letters flashed on a screen are visual icons, a lingering trace stored in memory for a very short period.

Because we have more than one sense, we have more than one kind of sensory memory. **Iconic memory** is *a fast-decaying store of visual information*. A similar storage area serves as a temporary warehouse for sounds. **Echoic memory** is *a fast-decaying store of auditory information*. When you have difficulty understanding what someone has just said, you probably find yourself replaying the last few words—listening to them echo in your "mind's ear," so to speak. When you do that, you are accessing information that is being held in your echoic memory store. The hallmark of both the iconic and echoic memory stores is that they hold information for a very short time. Iconic memories usually decay in about 1 second or less, and echoic memories usually decay in about 5 seconds (Darwin, Turvey, & Crowder, 1972). These two sensory memory stores are a bit like doughnut shops: The products come in, they sit briefly on the shelf, and then they are discarded. If you want one, you have to grab it fast.

> **How long is information held in iconic and echoic memory before it decays?**

## Short-Term Storage and Working Memory

A second kind of memory storage is **short-term memory,** which *holds nonsensory information for more than a few seconds but less than a minute.* For example, if someone tells you a telephone number, you can usually repeat it back with ease—but only for a few seconds. In one study, research participants were given consonant strings to remember, such as DBX and HLM. After seeing each string, participants were asked to count backward from 100 by 3 for varying amounts of time and were then asked to recall the strings (Peterson & Peterson, 1959). As shown in **FIGURE 6.6**, memory for the consonant strings declined rapidly, from approximately 80 percent after a 3-second delay to less than 20 percent after a 20-second delay. These results suggest that information can be held in the short-term memory store for about 15 to 20 seconds.

What if 15 to 20 seconds is not enough time? What if we need the information for a while longer? We can use a trick that allows us to get around the natural limitations of our short-term memories. **Rehearsal** is *the process of keeping information in short-term memory by mentally repeating it.* If someone gives you a telephone number and you cannot put it immediately into your cell phone or write it down, you say it over and over to yourself until you can. Each time you repeat the number, you are re-entering it into short-term memory, giving it another 15 to 20 seconds of shelf life.

> **Why is it helpful to repeat a telephone number you are trying to remember?**

Short-term memory is limited in how *long* it can hold information, and also limited in how *much* information it can hold. Not only can most people keep approximately seven numbers in short-term memory, but if they put more new numbers in, then old numbers begin to fall out (Miller, 1956). Short-term memory is not limited to numbers, of course. It can also hold about seven letters or seven words—even though those seven words contain many more than seven letters. In fact, short-term memory can hold about seven *meaningful items* at once (Miller, 1956). Therefore, one way to increase storage is to group several letters into a single meaningful item. **Chunking** involves *combining small pieces of information into larger clusters or chunks that are more easily held in short-term memory.* Servers who use organizational encoding (p. 225) to organize customer orders into groups are essentially chunking the information, giving themselves less to remember.

Short-term memory was originally conceived of as a kind of "place" where information is kept for a limited amount of time. More recently, British researchers developed and refined a more dynamic model of a limited-capacity memory system, **working memory,** which refers to *active maintenance of information in short-term storage* (Baddeley & Hitch, 1974). Working memory includes subsystems that store and manipulate visual images or verbal information, as well as a central executive that coordinates the subsystems (Baddeley, 2001). If you wanted to keep the arrangement of pieces on a chessboard in mind as you contemplated your next move, you would be relying on working memory. Working memory includes the visual representation of the positions of the pieces, your mental manipulation of the possible moves, and your awareness of the flow of information into and out of memory, all stored for a limited amount of time. In short, the working memory model acknowledges both the limited nature of this kind of memory storage and the activities that are commonly associated with it.

Research conducted in the context of this model has taught us that working memory plays an important role in many aspects of our cognitive lives. For example, studies

**short-term memory**
A type of storage that holds nonsensory information for more than a few seconds but less than a minute.

**rehearsal**
The process of keeping information in short-term memory by mentally repeating it.

**chunking**
Combining small pieces of information into larger clusters or chunks that are more easily held in short-term memory.

**working memory**
Active maintenance of information in short-term storage.

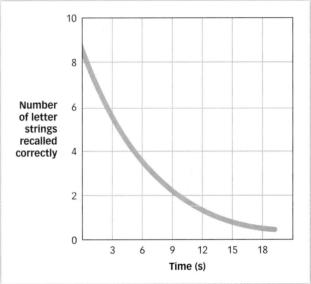

▲ Figure **6.6** **The Decline of Short-Term Memory** A 1959 experiment showed how quickly short-term memory fades without rehearsal. On a test for memory of three-letter strings, research participants were highly accurate when tested a few seconds after exposure to each string, but if the test was delayed another 15 seconds, people barely recalled the strings at all (Peterson & Peterson, 1959).

**long-term memory**
A type of storage that holds information for hours, days, weeks, or years.

of individuals with neurological damage to the verbal subsystem of working memory reveal that, not only do they have problems holding onto strings of digits and letters for a few seconds, they also have difficulty learning novel words. This suggests a link between this part of the working memory system and the ability to learn language (Baddeley, 2001; Gathercole, 2008).

Brain imaging studies indicate that the central executive component of working memory depends on regions within the frontal lobe that are important for controlling and manipulating information on a wide range of cognitive tasks (Baddeley, 2001). Children who score low on working memory tasks have difficulty learning new information and performing well in the classroom (Alloway et al., 2009). Can working memory skills be trained, and can such training enhance cognitive functioning? This question has become a hot research topic over the past few years (Klingberg, 2010; Shipstead, Redick, & Engle, 2012).

In typical studies, participants are first given extensive practice performing working memory tasks that require the maintenance and manipulation of visual or verbal information. They are then tested on new working memory tasks that have not been specifically taught, as well as on other cognitive tasks that tap into capacities such as reasoning, comprehension, or sustained attention. Some encouraging results have been reported. For example, elementary school students trained on several working memory tasks (about 35 minutes/day for at least 20 days over a 5- to 7-week time period) showed improvement on other working memory tasks when compared with untrained low working memory children (Holmes, Gathercole, & Dunning, 2009). These gains were evident even when the children were tested 6 months after training. There was also some evidence of improvement on math tasks. However, working memory training studies typically compare a working memory training group with control groups that do not perform any kind of training, or perform less challenging training tasks than the working memory group performs, so it is not clear whether working memory training in particular is responsible for the effects that are observed (Slagter, 2012). Indeed, a recent study that used a control condition involving active processing (a visual search task) found that working memory training improved performance on the working memory task that was trained, but did not result in improvements on other cognitive tasks (Redick et al., 2013). More research will be needed to determine whether working memory training produces any general improvements in cognitive performance (Shipstead et al., 2012).

## Long-Term Storage

The artist Franco Magnani was born in Pontito, Italy, in 1934. In 1958, he left his village to see the rest of the world and settled in San Francisco, California in the 1960s. Soon after arriving, Magnani began to suffer from a strange illness. Every night he experienced feverish dreams of Pontito, in which he recalled the village in vivid detail. The dreams soon penetrated his waking life in the form of overpowering recollections, and Magnani decided that the only way to rid himself of these images was to capture them on canvas. For the next 20 years, he devoted much of his time to painting, in exquisite detail, his memories of his beloved village. Many years later, photographer Susan Schwartzenberg went to Pontito, armed with a collection of Magnani's paintings, and photographed each scene from the perspective of the paintings. As you can see in the images, the correspondence between the paintings and the photographs was striking (Sacks, 1995; Schacter, 1996).

Even years after leaving home in Pontito, Italy, painter Franco Magnani was able to create a near-perfect reproduction of what he had seen there. Magnani's painting (*left*), based on a memory of a place he had not seen for years, is remarkably similar to the photograph (*right*) Susan Schwartzenberg took of the actual scene.

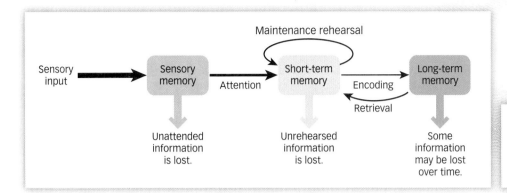

◀ Figure **6.7** **The Flow of Information through the Memory System** Information moves through several stages of memory as it gets encoded, stored, and made available for later retrieval.

Many years intervened between Magnani's visual perception and artistic reconstruction of the village, suggesting that very detailed information can sometimes be stored for a very long time. In contrast to the time-limited sensory memory and short-term memory stores, **long-term memory** is *a type of storage that holds information for hours, days, weeks, or years*. In contrast to both sensory and short-term memory, long-term memory has no known capacity limits (see **FIGURE 6.7**). For example, most people can recall 10 000 to 15 000 words in their native language, tens of thousands of facts (The capital of France is Paris and $3 \times 3 = 9$), and an untold number of personal experiences. Just think of all the song lyrics you can recite by heart, and you will understand that you have a lot of information tucked away in long-term memory!

Amazingly, people can recall items from long-term memory even if they have not thought of them for years. For example, researchers have found that even 50 years after graduation, people can accurately recognize about 90 percent of their high school classmates from yearbook photographs (Bahrick, 2000). The feat is more remarkable when you consider that probably most of this information had not been accessed for years before the experiment.

## The Role of the Hippocampus as Index

Where is long-term memory located in the brain? The clues to answering this question come from individuals who are unable to store long-term memories. Not everyone has the same ability to encode information into long-term memory. In 1953, 27-year-old Henry Molaison suffered from severe epilepsy and was not responding to medication (Scoville & Milner, 1957). In a desperate attempt to stop the seizures, Henry's surgeon removed parts of his temporal lobes, including the hippocampus and some surrounding regions (**FIGURE 6.8**). After the operation, Henry could converse easily,

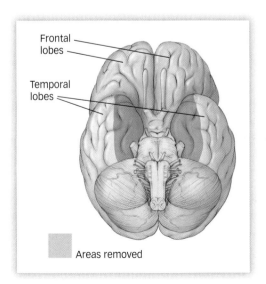

Frontal lobes

Temporal lobes

Areas removed

◀ Figure **6.8** **The Hippocampus Patient** Henry Molaison had his hippocampus and adjacent structures of the medial temporal lobe (indicated by the shaded area) surgically removed to stop his epileptic seizures (*left*). As a result, he could not remember things that happened after the surgery. Henry (*right*), better known to the world as patient H.M., passed away on December 2, 2008, at the age of 82 at a nursing home near Hartford, Connecticut. Henry's catastrophic inability to encode new long-term memories was discovered by Montreal psychologist Brenda Milner in 1953, and Molaison participated in countless memory experiments between that time and his death. In so doing, he made fundamental contributions to our understanding of memory and the brain.

**anterograde amnesia**
The inability to transfer new information from the short-term store into the long-term store.

**retrograde amnesia**
The inability to retrieve information that was acquired before a particular date, usually the date of an injury or surgery.

**consolidation**
The process by which memories become stable in the brain.

use and understand language, and perform well on intelligence tests, but he could not remember anything that happened to him after the operation. Henry could repeat a telephone number with no difficulty, suggesting that his short-term memory store was just fine (Corkin, 2002, 2013; Hilts, 1995; Squire, 2009). But after information left the short-term store, it was gone forever. For example, he would often forget that he had just eaten a meal or fail to recognize the hospital staff who helped him on a daily basis. Studies of Henry and others have shown that the hippocampal region of the brain is critical for putting new information into the long-term store. When this region is damaged, individuals suffer from a condition known as **anterograde amnesia,** which is *the inability to transfer new information from the short-term store into the long-term store.*

Some individuals with amnesia also suffer from **retrograde amnesia,** which is *the inability to retrieve information that was acquired before a particular date, usually the date of an injury or surgery.* The fact that Henry had much worse anterograde than retrograde amnesia suggests that the hippocampal region is not the site of long-term memory. Indeed, research has shown that different aspects of a single memory—its sights, sounds, smells, emotional content—are stored in different places in the cortex (Damasio, 1989; Schacter, 1996; Squire & Kandel, 1999). Some psychologists have argued that the hippocampal region acts as a kind of "index" that links together all of these otherwise separate bits and pieces so that we remember them as one memory (Schacter, 1996; Squire, 1992; Teyler & DiScenna, 1986). Over time, this index may become less necessary.

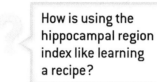

How is using the hippocampal region index like learning a recipe?

Going back to our cooking analogy, you can think of the hippocampal region index like a printed recipe. The first time you make a pie, you need the recipe to help you retrieve all the ingredients and then mix them together in the right amounts. As you bake more and more pies, though, you do not need to rely on the printed recipe anymore. Similarly, although the hippocampal region index is critical when a new memory is first formed, it may become less important as the memory ages. Another possibility is that the hippocampal index remains involved over long periods of time with some memories (highly detailed recollections of personal experiences, the kinds of memories that give us the feeling that we are almost reliving a past experience), but does not stay involved in less detailed, more general memories (Harand et al., 2012; Winocur, Moscovitch, & Bontempi, 2010). In terms of the cooking analogy, you might need to rely on a recipe each time you cook a complex meal with many details, but not when you cook a simpler meal with a less detailed recipe. Scientists are still debating the extent to which the hippocampal region helps us to remember details of our old memories (Bayley, Gold, et al., 2005; Kirwan et al., 2008; Moscovitch et al., 2006; Squire & Wixted, 2011; Winocur et al., 2010), but the notion of the hippocampus as an index explains why people like Henry cannot make new memories and why they can remember old ones.

## Memory Consolidation

The idea that the hippocampus becomes less important over time for maintaining memories is closely related to the concept of **consolidation,** *the process by which memories become stable in the brain* (McGaugh, 2000). Shortly after encoding, memories exist in a fragile state in which they can be easily disrupted; once consolidation has occurred, they are more resistant to disruption. One type of consolidation operates over seconds or minutes. For example, when someone experiences a head injury in a car crash and later cannot recall what happened during the few seconds or minutes before the crash—but can recall other events normally—the head injury probably prevented consolidation of short-term memory into long-term memory. Another type of consolidation occurs over much longer periods of time—days, weeks, months, and years—and likely involves transfer of information from the hippocampus to more permanent storage sites in the cortex. The operation of this longer-term consolidation process is why individuals with retrograde amnesia with hippocampal damage can recall memories from childhood relatively normally, but are impaired when recalling experiences that occurred just a few years prior to the time they became amnesic (Kirwan et al., 2008; Squire & Wixted, 2011).

How does a memory become consolidated? The act of recalling a memory, thinking about it, and talking about it with others probably contributes to consolidation (Moscovitch et al., 2006). And though you may not be aware of it, consolidation gets a boost from something that you do effortlessly every night: sleep. As explained in the Hot Science box, mounting evidence gathered during the past decade indicates that sleep plays an important role in memory consolidation.

# HOT SCIENCE

# Sleep on It

Thinking about pulling an all-nighter before your next big test? Here is a reason to reconsider: Our minds do not simply shut off when we sleep (see the Consciousness chapter), and in fact, sleep may be as important to our memories as wakefulness.

Nearly a century ago, Jenkins and Dallenbach (1924) reported that recall of recently learned information is greater immediately after sleeping than after the same amount of time spent awake. But Jenkins and Dallenbach did not think that sleep played an active role in strengthening or consolidating memory. They argued instead that being asleep passively protects us from encountering information that interferes with our ability to remember. As is explained by retroactive interference (see p. 250), that is a valid argument. However, during the past few years, evidence has accumulated that shows sleep plays an active role in memory consolidation, doing more than simply protecting us from waking interference (Diekelmann & Born, 2010; Ellenbogen, Payne, & Stickgold, 2006). Sleep selectively enhances the consolidation of memories that reflect the meaning or gist of an experience (Payne et al., 2009), as well as emotionally important memories (Payne et al., 2008), suggesting that sleep helps us to remember what is important and to discard what is trivial.

This idea is reinforced by recent evidence which shows that the beneficial effects of sleep on subsequent memory are observed only when people expect to be tested. In one study, Ines Wilhelm and her colleagues (2011) found that after studying a list of word pairs, participants who were informed that their memory would be tested later showed improved recall after sleep compared with an equivalent period of wakefulness. But a separate group that had not been informed of the memory test (and did not suspect it) showed no improvement in recall after sleep compared with wakefulness.

In an additional study (van Dongen et al., 2012), participants studied pictures of either buildings or furniture that were each associated with a particular location on a slide (see below). Soon after, participants received a memory test for the picture–location associations. They were then instructed that they would be retested 14 hours later for either the building pictures or the furniture pictures (the relevant category) and would not be retested on the other type of picture (the irrelevant category). Half of the participants were tested after sleep (initial learning was in the afternoon for these individuals) and half after remaining awake (initial learning was in the morning for these individuals). On the retest, there was less forgetting for the relevant than irrelevant categories in the sleep group, but there was no such difference in the wake group. Furthermore, for participants in the sleep group, the amount of time spent sleeping was correlated with retention of relevant information but not with retention of irrelevant information; those participants who slept longer retained more of the relevant information.

So, when you find yourself nodding off after hours of studying for your exam, the science is on the side of a good night's sleep.

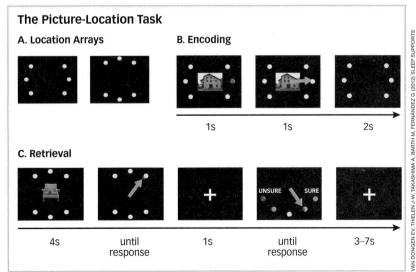

**The Picture-Location Task**

**A. Location Arrays**

**B. Encoding**

1s    1s    2s

**C. Retrieval**

4s    until response    1s    until response    3–7s

UNSURE    SURE

VAN DONGEN EV, THIELEN J-W, TAKASHIMA A, BARTH M, FERNANDEZ G (2012) SLEEP SUPPORTS SELECTIVE 'RETENTION OF ASSOCIATIVE MEMORIES BASED ON RELEVANCE FOR FUTURE UTILIZATION. PLOS ONE 7(8): E43426. DOI:10.1371/JOURNAL.PONE.0043426. © VAN DONGEN ET AL.

**reconsolidation**
Memories can become vulnerable to disruption when they are recalled, requiring them to become consolidated again.

Many researchers have long believed that a fully consolidated memory becomes a permanent fixture in the brain, more difficult to get rid of than a computer virus. But another line of research that has developed rapidly in recent years suggests that things are not so simple. Experiments have shown that even seemingly consolidated *memories can become vulnerable to disruption when they are recalled, thus requiring them to be consolidated again*. This process is called **reconsolidation** (Dudai, 2012; Nader & Hardt, 2009). Evidence for reconsolidation mainly comes from experiments with rats showing that when animals are cued to retrieve a new memory that was acquired a day earlier, giving the animal a drug (or an electrical shock) that prevents initial consolidation will cause forgetting (Nader, Shafe, & LeDoux, 2000; Sara, 2000). Critically, if the animal is not actively retrieving the memory, the same drug (or shock) has no effect when given a day after initial encoding. This finding is surprising because it was once thought that when memories are consolidated, drugs or shock that prevent initial consolidation no longer have any impact. To the contrary, it appears that each time they are retrieved, memories become vulnerable to disruption and have to be reconsolidated.

> When is a consolidated memory vulnerable to disruption?

Might it be possible one day to eliminate painful memories by disrupting reconsolidation? Recent research with traumatized individuals suggests it could be: When a traumatic event was reactivated after administration of a drug that reduces anxiety,

Has seeing too many shark movies left you afraid to swim in the ocean? What evidence is there that someday we might be able to erase painful memories?

PM IMAGES/PHOTODISC/GETTY IMAGES

there was a subsequent reduction in traumatic symptoms (Brunet et al., 2008, 2011). Other research with nontraumatized individuals has shown that something like this happens, without the use of drugs, as a result of reactivating a fear memory (being shocked in the presence of a particular object) a day after the memory was acquired. Adding nonfearful information to the reactivated memory (presenting the object again without shock) a few minutes later—when the memory is vulnerable to reconsolidation—resulted in long-lasting reduction of fear responses to the object, whereas adding nonfearful information to the reactivated memory 6 hours later—when the memory is no longer vulnerable to reconsolidation—did not have a long-lasting effect (Schiller et al., 2010). Related work indicates that disrupting reconsolidation can seemingly eliminate a conditioned fear memory in a part of the brain called the *amygdala*, which we will learn later in this chapter plays a key role in emotional memory (Agren et al., 2012). Reconsolidation thus appears to be a key memory process with many important implications.

## Memories, Neurons, and Synapses

We have already discussed parts of the brain that are related to memory storage, but we have not said much about how or where memories are stored. Research suggests that memory storage depends critically on the *spaces* between neurons. You will recall from the Neuroscience and Behaviour chapter that a *synapse* is the small space between the axon of one neuron and the dendrite of another, and neurons communicate by sending neurotransmitters across these synapses. As it turns out, sending a neurotransmitter across a synapse is not like sending a toy boat across a pond because the act of sending actually *changes* the synapse. Specifically, it strengthens the connection between the two neurons, making it easier for them to transmit to each other the next time. As the famous Canadian neuroscientist Donald Olding Hebb said, "cells that fire together wire together" (Hebb, 1949).

The idea that the connections between neurons are strengthened by their communication, making communication easier the next time, provides the neurological basis for long-term memory, and much of what we know about this comes from the tiny sea slug *Aplysia*. The story of *Aplysia* and memory is closely linked with the work of neuroscientist Eric Kandel, who won the Nobel Prize in 2000 for his work with the creature. When Kandel first became interested in *Aplysia* back in the late 1950s, there were only two researchers in the entire world studying the tiny slug. But *Aplysia* was attractive to Kandel because it is relatively uncomplicated and has an extremely simple nervous system consisting of only 20 000 neurons (compared to roughly 100 billion in the human brain), so Kandel followed his intuition and studied *Aplysia* (Kandel, 2006).

When an experimenter stimulates *Aplysia*'s tail with a mild electric shock, the slug immediately withdraws its gill, and if the experimenter does it again a moment later, *Aplysia* withdraws its gill even more quickly. If the experimenter comes back an hour later and shocks *Aplysia*, the withdrawal of the gill happens as slowly as it did the first time, as if *Aplysia* cannot "remember" what happened an hour earlier (Abel et al., 1995). But if the experimenter shocks *Aplysia* over and over, it does develop an enduring "memory" that can last for days or even weeks. Research suggests that this long-term storage involves the growth of new synaptic connections between neurons (Abel et al., 1995; Kandel, 2006; Squire & Kandel, 1999). So, learning in *Aplysia* is based on changes involving the synapses for both short-term storage (enhanced neurotransmitter release) and long-term storage (growth of new synapses). Any experience that results in memory produces physical changes in the nervous system—even if you are a slug.

If you are something more complex than a slug—say, a chimpanzee or your roommate—a similar process of synaptic strengthening happens in the hippocampus,

> **How does building a memory produce a physical change in the nervous system?**

which we have seen is an area crucial for storing new long-term memories. In the early 1970s, researchers applied a brief electrical stimulus to a neural pathway in a rat's hippocampus (Bliss & Lømo, 1973). They found that the electrical current produced a stronger connection between synapses that lay along the pathway and that the strengthening lasted for hours or even weeks. They called this **long-term potentiation** (more commonly known as **LTP**), *a process whereby communication across the synapse between neurons strengthens the connection, making further communication easier.* Long-term potentiation has a number of properties that indicate to researchers that it plays an important role in long-term memory storage: It occurs in several pathways within the hippocampus; it can be induced rapidly; and it can last for a long time. In fact, drugs that block LTP can turn rats into rodent versions of Henry Molaison: The animals have great difficulty remembering where they have been recently and become easily lost in a maze (Bliss, 1999; Morris et al., 1986).

SPENCER PLATT/NEWSMAKERS/GETTY IMAGES

Nobel Prize–winning neuroscientist Eric Kandel took a risk and studied the tiny sea slug *Aplysia* based in part on a lesson he had learned from his wife regarding their recent marriage, which encouraged him to trust his intuition: "Denise was confident that our marriage would work, so I took a leap of faith and went ahead. I learned from that experience that there are many situations in which one cannot decide on the basis of cold facts alone—because the facts are often insufficient. One ultimately has to trust one's unconscious, one's instincts, one's creative urge. I did this again in choosing *Aplysia*" (Kandel, 2006, p. 149).

**long-term potentiation (LTP)**
A process whereby communication across the synapse between neurons strengthens the connection, making further communication easier.

© DONNA IKENBERRY/ART DIRECTORS & TRIP/ALAMY

By studying the sea slug *Aplysia californica*'s extremely simple nervous system, researchers were able to determine that long-term memory storage depends on the growth of new synaptic connections between neurons.

## IN SUMMARY

► There are several different types of memory storage:

  ► Sensory memory holds information for a second or two.

  ► Short-term or working memory retains information for about 15 to 20 seconds.

  ► Long-term memory stores information anywhere from minutes to years or decades.

► The hippocampus and nearby structures play an important role in long-term memory storage, as shown by the severe amnesia of individuals such as Henry Molaison. The hippocampus is also important for memory consolidation, the process that makes memories increasingly resistant to disruption over time. Sleep contributes importantly to memory consolidation.

► Memory storage depends on changes in synapses, and long-term potentiation (LTP) increases synaptic connections.

# Retrieval: Bringing Memories to Mind

There is something fiendishly frustrating about piggy banks. You can put money in them, you can shake them around to assure yourself that the money is there, but you cannot easily get the money out. If memories were like coins in a piggy bank, stored but inaccessible, what would be the point of saving them in the first place? Retrieval is the process of bringing to mind information that has been previously encoded and stored, and it is perhaps the most important of all memory processes (Roediger, 2000; Schacter, 2001a).

## Retrieval Cues: Reinstating the Past

One of the best ways to retrieve information from *inside* your head is to encounter information *outside* your head that is somehow connected to it. The information outside your head is called a **retrieval cue,** *external information that is associated with stored information and helps bring it to mind.* Retrieval cues can be incredibly effective. How many times have you said something like, "I *know* who played Hermione in the *Harry Potter* movies, but I just cannot remember her name"? Then a friend gives you a hint ("Wasn't she also in *The Bling Ring*?"), which instantly brings the answer to mind ("Emma Watson!").

In one experiment, undergraduates studied lists of words, such as *table, peach, bed, apple, chair, grape,* and *desk* (Tulving & Pearlstone, 1966). Later, the students were asked to write down all the words from the list that they could remember. When they were absolutely sure that they had emptied their memory stores of every last word that was in them, the experimenters again asked the students to remember the words on the list, but this time, the experimenters provided retrieval cues, such as "furniture" or "fruit." The students who were sure that they had done all the remembering they possibly could were suddenly able to remember more words. These results suggest that information is sometimes *available* in memory even when it is momentarily *inaccessible*, and that retrieval cues help us bring inaccessible information to mind.

Hints are one kind of retrieval cue, but they are not the only kind. The **encoding specificity principle** states that *a retrieval cue can serve as an effective reminder when it helps re-create the specific way in which information was initially encoded* (Tulving & Thomson, 1973). External contexts often make powerful retrieval cues (Hockley, 2008). For example, in one study divers learned some words on land and other words

Retrieval cues are hints that help bring stored information to mind. How does this explain the fact that most students prefer multiple-choice exams to fill-in-the-blank exams?

AP PHOTO/POCONO RECORD, ADAM RICH

What is an example of a retrieval cue you have used?

underwater; they recalled the words best when they were tested in the same dry or wet environment in which they had initially learned them because the environment itself served as a retrieval cue (Godden & Baddeley, 1975). Recovering alcoholics often experience a renewed urge to drink when visiting places in which they once drank because those places serve as retrieval cues. There may even be some wisdom to finding a seat in a classroom, sitting in it every day, and then sitting in it again when you take the test because the feel of the chair and the sights you see may help you remember the information you learned while you sat there.

Retrieval cues need not be external contexts—they can also be inner states. **State-dependent retrieval** is *the tendency for information to be better recalled when the person is in the same state during encoding and retrieval*. For example, retrieving information when you are in a sad or happy mood increases the likelihood that you will retrieve sad or happy episodes (Eich, 1995), which is part of the reason it is so hard to "look on the bright side" when you are feeling low. Similarly, you would probably expect a fellow student who studied for an exam while drunk to perform poorly, and you would probably be right—but only if he or she made the mistake of taking the exam while sober! Studies of state-dependent retrieval suggest that if the student studied while drunk, he or she would probably perform poorly the next day, but he or she would perform better if he or she had cereal for breakfast instead of getting drunk (Eich, 1980; Weissenborn, 2000). Why should that be? Because a person's physiological or psychological state at the time of encoding is associated with the information that is encoded. For example, being in a good mood affects patterns of electrical activity in parts of the brain responsible for semantic processing, suggesting that mood has a direct influence on semantic encoding (Kiefer et al., 2007). If the person's state at the time of retrieval matches the person's state at the time of encoding, the state itself serves as a retrieval cue—a bridge that connects the moment at which we experience something to the moment at which we remember it. Retrieval cues can even be thoughts themselves, as when one thought calls to mind another, related thought (Anderson et al., 1976).

The encoding specificity principle makes some unusual predictions. For example, you learned earlier that making semantic judgments about a word (e.g., What does *brain* mean?) usually produces more durable memory for the word than does making rhyme judgments (e.g., What rhymes with *brain*?). So if you were shown a cue card of the word "brain," and your friend was asked to think about what *brain* means while you were asked to think of a word that rhymes with *brain*, we would expect your friend to remember the word better the next day if we simply asked you both, "Hey, what was that word you saw yesterday?" However, if instead of asking that question, we asked you both, "What was that word that rhymed with *train*?" the retrieval cue would match your encoding context better than your friend's, and we would expect you to remember it better than your friend did. Data from memory experiments suggest that this is what happens in real-life situations (Fisher & Craik, 1977). This is a fairly astounding finding. The principle of **transfer-appropriate processing** is *the idea that memory is likely to transfer from one situation to another when the encoding and retrieval contexts of the situations match* (Morris, Bransford, & Franks, 1977; Roediger, Weldon, & Challis, 1989).

## Consequences of Retrieval

Human memory differs substantially from computer memory. Simply retrieving a file from your computer does not have any effect on the likelihood that the file will open again in the future. Not so with human memory. Retrieval does not merely provide a readout of what is in memory, it also changes the state of the memory system in important ways.

**retrieval cue**
External information that is associated with stored information and helps bring it to mind.

**encoding specificity principle**
The idea that a retrieval cue can serve as an effective reminder when it helps re-create the specific way in which information was initially encoded.

**state-dependent retrieval**
The tendency for information to be better recalled when the person is in the same state during encoding and retrieval.

**transfer-appropriate processing**
The idea that memory is likely to transfer from one situation to another when the encoding and retrieval contexts of the situations match.

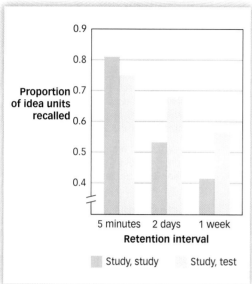

**▲ Figure 6.9** **Memory Testing Benefits Long-Term Retention** With a 5-minute retention interval, the study–study condition results in slightly higher recall. But the results change dramatically with retention intervals of 2 days and 1 week: at these longer delays, the study–test condition yields much higher levels of recall than does the study–study condition (Roediger & Karpicke, 2006).

## Retrieval Can Improve Subsequent Memory

Psychologists have known for some time that the act of retrieval can strengthen a retrieved memory, making it easier to remember that information at a later time (Bjork, 1975). Does this finding surprise you? Probably not. Repeating an item usually improves memory for that item, so the act of retrieval might boost subsequent memory simply because the information is repeated, resulting in the same benefit you would receive from studying the information twice instead of once. Makes sense, right? Wrong. It turns out that retrieving information from memory has different effects than studying it again.

This point was made dramatically in an experiment where participants studied brief stories and then either studied them again or were given a test that required retrieving the stories (Roediger & Karpicke, 2006). Participants were then given a final recall test for the stories either 5 minutes, 2 days, or 1 week later. As shown in **FIGURE 6.9**, at the 5-minute delay, studying the stories twice resulted in slightly higher recall than studying and retrieving them. Critically, the opposite occurred at the 2-day and 1-week delays: Retrieval produced much higher levels of recall than did an extra study exposure. A subsequent experiment using foreign vocabulary items also revealed that retrieval of the items produced a much bigger benefit on a delayed vocabulary test than did further study (Karpicke & Roediger, 2008). These findings have potentially important implications for learning in educational contexts (Karpicke, 2012), which we will explore further in the Learning chapter (p. 265).

> Should students spend more time testing themselves on material (retrieval), or studying it over and over?

## Retrieval Can Impair Subsequent Memory

As much as retrieval can help memory, that is not always the case. **Retrieval-induced forgetting** is *a process by which retrieving an item from long-term memory impairs subsequent recall of related items* (Anderson, 2003; Anderson, Bjork, & Bjork, 1994).

Let us see how a typical experiment on retrieval-induced forgetting works (Anderson et al., 1994). Participants first studied word pairs consisting of a category name and an example from that category (e.g., *fruit–orange, fruit–apple, tree–elm, tree–birch*). Then they practised recalling some of the items from a few of the studied categories by retrieving the target in response to a category cue and the initial letters of the target. As an example, for the fruit category participants would practise recalling *orange* to the cue "fruit or____," but would not practise recalling *apple*. The general idea is that while they are practising recall of *orange*, participants are trying to suppress the competitor *apple*. For other categories (e.g., *trees*), no retrieval practice was given for any of the studied pairs. Later, the participants were given a final test for all the words they initially studied. Not surprisingly, on the final test participants remembered words that they practised (e.g., *orange*) better than words from categories that they did not practise (e.g., *elm*). But what happened on the final test to the items such as *apple*, which were not practised, and which participants presumably had to suppress while they practised recall of related items? Those items were recalled most poorly of all, indicating that retrieving the similar target items (e.g., *orange*) caused subsequent forgetting of the related but suppressed items (e.g., *apple*). In fact, even if you do not successfully retrieve the target, the act of suppressing the competitors while you attempt to retrieve the target still reduces your ability to retrieve the competitors at a later time (Storm et al., 2006).

> How can retrieval-induced forgetting occur during conversations?

Can you think of any examples of how retrieval-induced forgetting could affect memory in everyday life? Here are two. First, retrieval-induced forgetting can occur during conversations: When a speaker selectively talks about some aspects of memories shared with a

**retrieval-induced forgetting**
A process by which retrieving an item from long-term memory impairs subsequent recall of related items.

listener and does not mention related information, both the listener and the speaker later have a harder time remembering the omitted events (Cuc, Koppel, & Hirst, 2007; Hirst & Echterhoff, 2012). This effect occurs even for memories as important as those of the terrorist attacks in the United States on September 11, 2001 (Coman, Manier, & Hirst, 2009). Second, retrieval-induced forgetting can affect eyewitness memory. When witnesses to a staged crime are questioned about some details of the crime scene, their ability to later recall related details that they were not asked about is impaired compared with witnesses who were not questioned at all initially (MacLeod, 2002; Shaw, Bjork, & Handal, 1995). These findings suggest that initial interviews with eyewitnesses should be as complete as possible in order to avoid potential retrieval-induced forgetting of significant details that are not probed during an interview (MacLeod & Saunders, 2008).

## Retrieval Can Change Subsequent Memory

In addition to improving and impairing subsequent memory, the act of retrieval can also change what we remember from an experience. Consider a recent experiment in which participants went on a tour of a museum, where they took some time to view designated exhibits, each of which contained several different stops (St. Jacques & Schacter, 2013). The participants took the tour while wearing a camera that, every 15 seconds, automatically took pictures of what was in front of them. Two days later, participants visited the memory laboratory (in a separate building) for a "reactivation session." After memories of some of the stops were reactivated by looking at photographs of them, participants were asked to rate, on a 1 to 5 scale, how vividly they re-experienced what had happened at each stop. Next, the participants were shown novel photographs of *unvisited* stops within the exhibit, then were asked to judge how closely these novel photographs were related to the photographs of the stops that they had actually seen in that exhibit. Finally, the participants were given a memory test 2 days after the reactivation session.

Participants sometimes incorrectly remembered that the stop shown in the novel photograph had been part of the original tour. Most importantly, participants who tended to make this mistake also tended to have more vivid recollections during the reactivation session. In other words, retrieving and vividly re-experiencing memories of what participants actually did see at the museum led them to incorporate into their memory information that was not part of their original experience. This finding may be related to the phenomenon of reconsolidation that we discussed earlier (p. 234), where reactivating a memory temporarily makes it vulnerable to disruption and change. At the very least, this finding reinforces the idea that retrieving a memory involves far more than a simple readout of information.

As part of a recent experiment, participants wore cameras that took pictures every 15 seconds as they toured a museum.

## Separating the Components of Retrieval

Before leaving the topic of retrieval, let us look at how the process actually works. There is reason to believe that *trying* to recall an incident and *successfully* recalling one

**How is brain activity different when *trying* to recall versus *successfully* recalling?**

are fundamentally different processes that occur in different parts of the brain (Moscovitch, 1994; Schacter, 1996). For example, regions in the left frontal lobe show heightened activity when people *try* to retrieve information that was presented to them earlier (Oztekin, Curtis, & McElree, 2009; Tulving et al., 1994). This activity may reflect the mental effort of struggling to dredge up the past event (Lepage et al., 2000). However, *successfully* remembering a past experience tends to be accompanied by activity in the hippocampal region (see **FIGURE 6.10** on the next page) (Eldridge et al., 2000; Giovanello, Schnyer, & Verfaellie, 2004; Schacter, Alpert, et al., 1996). Furthermore, successful

High recall minus baseline

Low recall minus baseline

Left frontal lobe

Hippocampus

► Figure **6.10** **PET Scans of Successful and Unsuccessful Recall** When people successfully remembered words they saw earlier in an experiment (achieving high levels of recall on a test), the hippocampus showed increased activity. When people tried but failed to recall words they had seen earlier (achieving low levels of recall on a test), the left frontal lobe showed increased activity (Schacter, Alpert, et al., 1996).

recall also activates parts of the brain that play a role in processing the sensory features of an experience. For instance, recall of previously heard sounds is accompanied by activity in the auditory cortex (the upper part of the temporal lobe), whereas recall of previously seen pictures is accompanied by activity in the visual cortex (in the occipital lobe) (Wheeler, Petersen, & Buckner, 2000). Although retrieval may seem like a single process, brain studies suggest that separately identifiable processes are at work.

This sheds some light on the phenomenon we just discussed: retrieval-induced forgetting. Recent fMRI evidence indicates that during memory retrieval, regions within the frontal-lobe that are involved in retrieval effort play a role in suppressing competitors (Benoit & Anderson, 2012; Kuhl et al., 2007; Wimber et al., 2009). When hippocampal activity during retrieval practice signals successful recall of an unwanted competitor, frontal-lobe mechanisms are recruited that help to suppress the competitor. Once the competitor is suppressed, the frontal lobe no longer has to work as hard at controlling retrieval, ultimately making it easier to recall the target

## CULTURE & COMMUNITY

### Does Culture Affect Childhood Amnesia?

You can easily recall many experiences from different times in your life. But you probably have few or no memories from the first few years of your life, which is called *childhood amnesia* or *infantile amnesia*. On average, an individual's first memory dates to about 3 to 3 1/2 years of age (Dudycha & Dudycha, 1933; Waldfogel, 1948), with women reporting slightly earlier first memories (3.07 years of age) than men (3.4 years) (Howes, Siegel, & Brown, 1993). But these estimates are based on individuals from Western (i.e., North American and European) cultures, which emphasize talking about the past. First memories are seen at later ages in Asian cultures that place less emphasis on talking about the past, such as Korea and China (MacDonald, Uesiliana, & Hayne, 2000; Mullen, 1994; Peterson, Wang, & Hou, 2009). A comparison of Canadian and Chinese children showed that first memories of 8-year-old children in both cultures come from younger ages than the first memories of 14-year-old children, suggesting that early memories fade or disappear as children age (Peterson et al., 2009). Critically, the first memories of the 14-year-old Chinese children came from a later age than did the first memories of the 14-year-old Canadians. In fact, the onset of childhood amnesia in the Chinese 14-year-olds was identical to that of North American adults. Culture thus has a significant impact on even our earliest memories.

ZHANG BO/GETTY IMAGES

▲ First memories are seen later in cultures that place less emphasis on talking about the past.

item (Kuhl et al., 2007). In addition, successful suppression of an unwanted memory causes reduced activity in the hippocampus (Anderson et al., 2004). These findings make sense once we understand the specific roles played by particular brain regions in the retrieval process.

---

### IN SUMMARY

▶ Whether we remember a past experience depends on whether retrieval cues are available to trigger recall. Retrieval cues are effective when they are given in the same context as when we encoded an experience. Moods and inner states can serve as retrieval cues.

▶ Retrieving information from memory has consequences for later remembering. Retrieval improves subsequent memory of the retrieved information, as exemplified by the beneficial effect of testing on later recall. However, retrieval can impair subsequent remembering of related information that is not retrieved. It can also change subsequent remembering when novel information is associated with vivid recollections.

▶ Retrieval can be separated into the effort we make while trying to remember what happened in the past and the successful recovery of stored information. Neuroimaging studies suggest that trying to remember activates the left frontal lobe, whereas successful recovery of stored information activates the hippocampus and regions in the brain related to sensory aspects of an experience.

---

# Multiple Forms of Memory: How the Past Returns

In 1977, neurologist Oliver Sacks interviewed a young man named Greg who had a tumour in his brain that wiped out his ability to remember day-to-day events. One thing Greg could remember was his life during the 1960s in New York's Greenwich Village, years before the tumour formed, when Greg's primary occupation seemed to be attending rock concerts by his favourite band, the Grateful Dead. Greg's memories of those Dead concerts stuck with him over the following years, when he was living in a long-term care hospital and being interviewed regularly by Dr. Sacks. In 1991, Dr. Sacks took Greg to a Dead concert at New York's Madison Square Garden, wondering whether such a momentous event might jolt his memory into action. "That was fantastic," Greg told Dr. Sacks as they left the concert. "I will always remember it. I had the time of my life." But when Dr. Sacks saw Greg the next morning and asked him whether he recalled the previous night's Dead concert at the Garden, Greg drew a blank: "No, I have never been to the Garden" (Sacks, 1995, pp. 76–77).

Although Greg was unable to make new memories, some of the new things that happened to him seemed to leave a mark. For example, Greg did not recall learning that his father had died, but he did seem sad and withdrawn for years after hearing the news. Similarly, Henry Molaison could not make new memories after his surgery, but if he played a game in which he had to track a moving target, his performance gradually improved with each round (Milner, 1962). Greg could not consciously remember hearing about his father's death, and Henry could not consciously remember playing the tracking game, but both showed clear signs of having been permanently changed by experiences that they so rapidly forgot. In other words, they *behaved* as though they were remembering things while claiming to remember nothing at all. This suggests that there must be several kinds of memory, some that are accessible to conscious recall, and some that we cannot consciously access (Eichenbaum & Cohen, 2001; Schacter & Tulving, 1994; Schacter, Wagner, & Buckner, 2000; Squire & Kandel, 1999).

## Explicit and Implicit Memory

The fact that people can be changed by past experiences without having any awareness of those experiences suggests that there must be at least two different classes of memory (**FIGURE 6.11**). **Explicit memory** occurs *when people consciously or intentionally retrieve past experiences.* Recalling last summer's vacation, incidents from a novel you just read, or facts you studied for a test all involve explicit memory. Indeed, anytime you start a sentence with "I remember …," you are talking about an explicit memory. **Implicit memory** occurs when *past experiences influence later behaviour and performance, even without an effort to remember them or an awareness of the recollection* (Graf & Schacter, 1985; Schacter, 1987). Implicit memories are not consciously recalled, but their presence is "implied" by our actions. Greg's persistent sadness after his father's death, even though he had no conscious knowledge of the event, is an example of implicit memory. So is Henry Molaison's improved performance on a tracking task that he did not consciously remember doing. So is the ability to ride a bike or tie your shoelaces, ice skate, or play guitar: You may know how to do these things, but you probably cannot describe how to do them. Such knowledge reflects a particular kind of implicit memory called **procedural memory,** which refers to *the gradual acquisition of skills as a result of practice, or "knowing how" to do things.*

> What type of memory is it when you just "know how" to do something?

One of the hallmarks of procedural memory is that the things you remember are automatically translated into actions. Sometimes you can explain how it is done (put one finger on the third fret of the E string, one finger …) and sometimes you cannot (get on the bike and … well, uh … just balance). The fact that people who have amnesia can acquire new procedural memories suggests that the hippocampal structures that are usually damaged in these individuals may be necessary for explicit memory, but they are not needed for implicit procedural memory. In fact, it appears that brain regions outside the hippocampal area (including areas in the motor cortex) are involved in procedural memory. The Learning chapter discusses this evidence further, where you will also see that procedural memory is crucial for learning various kinds of motor, perceptual, and cognitive skills.

Not all implicit memories are procedural or "how to" memories. For example, in one experiment, college students were asked to study a long list of words, including items such as *avocado, mystery, climate, octopus,* and *assassin* (Tulving, Schacter, & Stark, 1982). Later, explicit memory was tested by showing participants some of these words along with new ones they had not seen and asking them which words were on

MARK BLINCH/REUTERS/LANDOV

Ice skaters like Joannie Rochette rely heavily on procedural memory to acquire and use the skills needed to skate at a high level.

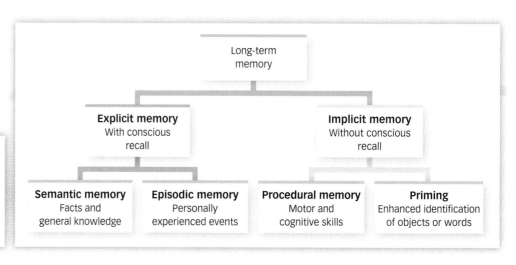

► Figure **6.11** **Multiple Forms of Memory** Explicit and implicit memories are distinct from each other. Thus, a person with amnesia may lose explicit memory, yet display implicit memory for material that she or he cannot consciously recall learning.

Long-term memory

Explicit memory
With conscious recall

Implicit memory
Without conscious recall

Semantic memory
Facts and general knowledge

Episodic memory
Personally experienced events

Procedural memory
Motor and cognitive skills

Priming
Enhanced identification of objects or words

the list. To test implicit memory, participants received word fragments and were asked to come up with a word that fit the fragment. Try the test yourself:

ch – – – – nk     o – t – p – –     – og – y – – –     – l – m – te

You probably had difficulty coming up with the answers for the first and third fragments (*chipmunk, bogeyman*) but had little problem coming up with answers for the second and fourth (*octopus, climate*). Seeing *octopus* and *climate* on the original list made those words more accessible later, during the fill-in-the-blanks test. This is an example of **priming,** which refers to *an enhanced ability to think of a stimulus, such as a word or object, as a result of a recent exposure to the stimulus* (Tulving & Schacter, 1990). Just as priming a pump makes water flow more easily, priming the memory system makes some information more accessible. In the fill-in-the-blanks experiment, people showed priming for studied words even when they failed to consciously remember that they had seen them earlier. This suggests that priming is an example of implicit, not explicit, memory.

> How does priming make memory more efficient?

A truly stunning example of this point comes from a study by Mitchell (2006) in which participants first studied black-and-white line drawings depicting everyday objects. Later, the participants were shown fragmented versions of the drawings that are difficult to identify; some of them depicted objects that had been studied earlier in the experiment, whereas others depicted new objects that had not been studied. Mitchell found that participants correctly identified more fragmented drawings of studied than new objects, and identified more studied objects than did participants in a control group who had never seen the pictures—a clear demonstration of priming (see **FIGURE 6.12**). This is not so interesting in itself—such priming had been demonstrated nearly 40 years earlier (Warrington & Weiskrantz, 1968). But here is the stunning part: The fragmented drawing test was given 17 years after presentation of the study list! By that time, participants had little or no explicit memory of having seen the

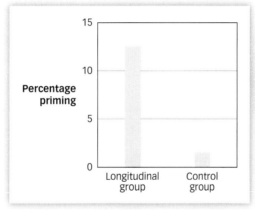

drawings, and some had no recollection that they had ever participated in the experiment! "I am sorry—I really do not remember this experiment at all," said one 36-year-old man who showed a strong priming effect. A 36-year-old woman who showed even more priming stated simply, "Do not remember anything about it" (Mitchell, 2006, p. 929). These observations confirm that priming is an example of implicit memory, and also that priming can persist over very long periods of time.

As such, you would expect amnesic individuals such as Henry Molaison and Greg to show priming. In fact, many experiments have shown that amnesic individuals can show substantial priming effects—often as large as healthy, nonamnesic individuals—even though they have no explicit memory for the items they studied (Warrington & Weiskrantz, 1968). These and other similar results suggest that priming, like procedural memory, does not require the hippocampal structures that are damaged in cases of amnesia (Schacter & Curran, 2000).

If the hippocampal region is not required for procedural memory and priming, what parts of the brain are involved? Experiments have revealed that priming is associated with *reduced* activity in various regions of the cortex that are activated when people perform an unprimed task. For instance, when research participants are shown the word stem *mot___* or *tab___* and are asked to provide the first word that comes to mind, parts of the occipital lobe involved in visual processing and parts of the frontal

**explicit memory**
The act of consciously or intentionally retrieving past experiences.

**implicit memory**
The influence of past experiences on later behaviour and performance, even without an effort to remember them or an awareness of the recollection.

**procedural memory**
The gradual acquisition of skills as a result of practice, or "knowing how" to do things.

**priming**
An enhanced ability to think of a stimulus, such as a word or object, as a result of a recent exposure to the stimulus.

◀ Figure **6.12 Long-Term Priming of Visual Objects** Participants who viewed drawings of common objects, and 17 years later were given a test in which they tried to identify the objects from fragmented drawings (longitudinal group), showed a strong priming effect; by contrast, participants who had not seen the drawings 17 years earlier (control group) showed nonsignificant priming (Mitchell, 2006).

**semantic memory**
A network of associated facts and concepts that make up our general knowledge of the world.

**episodic memory**
The collection of past personal experiences that occurred at a particular time and place.

lobe involved in word retrieval become active. But if people perform the same task after being primed by seeing *motel* and *table,* there is less activity in these same regions (Buckner et al., 1995; Schott et al., 2005). Something similar happens when people see pictures of everyday objects on two different occasions. On the second exposure to a picture, there is less activity in parts of the visual cortex that were activated by seeing the picture initially. Priming seems to make it easier for parts of the cortex that are involved in perceiving a word or object to identify the item after a recent exposure to it (Schacter, Dobbins, & Schnyer, 2004; Wiggs & Martin, 1998). This suggests that the brain saves a bit of processing time after priming (see **FIGURE 6.13**).

Neuroimaging studies also indicate that different brain systems are involved in two distinct forms of priming: *perceptual priming,* which reflects implicit memory for the sensory features of an item (e.g., the visual characteristics of a word or picture), and *conceptual priming,* which reflects implicit memory for the meaning of a word or how you would use an object. Studies using fMRI indicate that perceptual priming depends primarily on regions toward the back of the brain, such as the visual cortex, whereas conceptual priming depends more on regions toward the front of the brain, such as the frontal lobes (Wig, Buckner, & Schacter, 2009). There is also some evidence that perceptual priming is associated primarily with the right cerebral hemisphere, whereas conceptual priming is associated with the left hemisphere (Schacter, Wig, & Stevens, 2007).

## Semantic and Episodic Memory

Consider these two questions: (1) What do we remember at 11 a.m. on November 11 every year? and (2) What is the most moving Remembrance Day service you have ever attended? Most Canadians know the answer to the first question (we commemorate those people who lost their lives in military service) but we all have our own answers to the second. Although both of these questions require you to search your long-term memory and explicitly retrieve information that is stored there, one requires you to dredge up a fact that every Canadian should know and that is not part of your personal autobiography, and one requires you to revisit a particular time and place—or episode—from your personal past. These memories are called *semantic* and *episodic* memories, respectively (Tulving, 1972, 1983, 1998). **Semantic memory** is *a network of associated facts and concepts that make up our general knowledge of the world,* whereas **episodic memory** is *the collection of past personal experiences that occurred at a particular time and place.*

Episodic memory is special because it is the only form of memory that allows us to engage in mental time travel, projecting ourselves into the past and revisiting events

► Figure **6.13** **Primed and Unprimed Processing of Stimuli** Priming is associated with reduced levels of activation in the cortex on a number of different tasks. In each pair of fMRIs, the images on the upper left (A, C) show brain regions in the frontal lobe (A) and occipital/temporal lobe (C) that are active during an unprimed task (in this case, providing a word response to a visual word cue). The images on the lower right within each pair (B, D) show reduced activity in the same regions during the primed version of the same task.

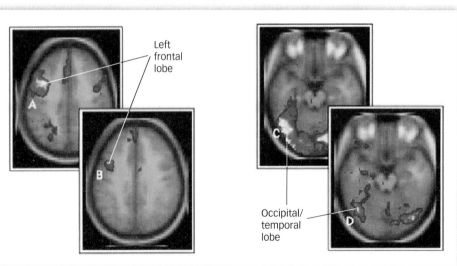

D. L. SCHACTER & R. L. BUCKNER, 1998, PRIMING AND THE BRAIN, *NEURON*, 20, PP. 185–195.

AP PHOTO TOM HANSON/CP

Remembering why we observe Remembrance Day is an example of using our semantic memory.

that have happened to us. This ability allows us to connect our pasts and our presents and construct a cohesive story of our lives. People who have amnesia can usually travel back in time and revisit episodes that occurred before they became amnesic, but they are unable to revisit episodes that happened later. For example, Greg could not travel back to any time after 1969 because that is when he stopped being able to create new episodic memories. But can people with amnesia create new semantic memories?

**What form of memory uses mental time travel?**

Researchers have studied three young adults who suffered damage to the hippocampus during birth as a result of difficult deliveries that interrupted oxygen supply to the brain (Brandt et al., 2009; Vargha-Khadem et al., 1997). Their parents noticed that the children could not recall what happened during a typical day, had to be constantly reminded of appointments, and often became lost and disoriented. In view of their hippocampal damage, you might also expect that each of the three would perform poorly in school and might even be classified as learning challenged. Remarkably, however, all three children learned to read, write, and spell, developed normal vocabularies, and acquired other kinds of semantic knowledge that allowed them to perform well in school. Based on this evidence, researchers have concluded that the hippocampus is not necessary for acquiring new *semantic* memories.

## Episodic Memory and Imagining the Future

We have already seen that episodic memory allows us to travel backward in time, but it turns out that episodic memory also plays a role in allowing to us to travel forward in time. A Canadian amnesic man known by the initials K.C. provided an early clue. K.C. could not recollect any specific episodes from his past, and when asked to imagine a future episode—such as what he might do tomorrow—he reported a complete "blank" (Tulving, 1985). Consistent with this observation, more recent findings from individuals with hippocampal amnesia reveal that some of them have difficulty imagining new experiences, such as sunbathing on a sandy beach (Hassabis et al., 2007), or events that might happen in their everyday lives (Race, Keane, & Verfaellie, 2011). Something similar happens with aging. When asked either to recall episodes that actually occurred in their pasts or imagine new episodes that might occur in their futures, older adults provided fewer details about what happened, or what might happen, than did college students (Addis, Wong, & Schacter, 2008; Schacter, Gaesser, & Addis, 2012). Consistent with these findings, neuroimaging studies reveal that a network of brain regions known to be involved in episodic memory—including the

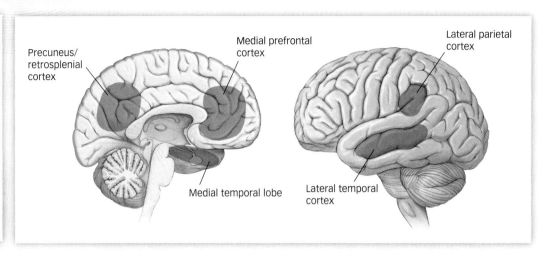

▶ Figure **6.14** **Remembering the Past and Imagining the Future Depend on a Common Network of Brain Regions** A common brain network is activated when people remember episodes that actually occurred in their personal pasts and when they imagine episodes that might occur in their personal futures. This network includes the hippocampus, a part of the medial temporal lobe long known to play an important role in episodic memory (Schacter, Addis, & Buckner, 2008).

hippocampus—shows similarly increased activity when people remember the past and imagine the future (Addis, Wong, & Schacter, 2007; Okuda et al., 2003; Schacter, Addis, et al., 2012; Szpunar, Watson, & McDermott, 2007) (see **FIGURE 6.14**).

Taken together, these observations strongly suggest that we rely heavily on episodic memory to envision our personal futures (Schacter, Addis, & Buckner, 2008; Szpunar, 2010). Episodic memory is well-suited to the task, because it is a flexible system that allows us to recombine elements of past experience in new ways, so that we can mentally try out different versions of what might happen (Schacter, 2012; Schacter & Addis, 2007; Suddendorf & Corballis, 2007). For example, when you imagine having a difficult conversation with a friend that will take place in a couple of days, you can draw on past experiences to envisage different ways in which the conversation might unfold, and hopefully avoid saying things that, based on past experience, are likely to make the situation worse. As we will discuss later, however, this flexibility of episodic memory might also be responsible for some kinds of memory errors (see p. 249).

> **How does episodic memory help us imagine our futures?**

## Social Influences on Remembering: Collaborative Memory

So far we have focused mainly on memory in individuals functioning on their own. But this is an incomplete picture that is missing something important: other people. Remembering serves important social functions. Getting together with friends or family to talk about memories of shared experiences is a familiar and enjoyable activity for most of us. When we post photographs of parties or vacations on social media sites, we are effectively sharing memories with our friends. And we are quick to communicate our memories to others: In a diary study where American college students recorded a memorable event each day for a week, they disclosed 62 percent of these events to others before the end of the day on which the event occurred (Pasupathi, McLean, & Weeks, 2009). Sharing memories with others can strengthen them (Hirst & Echterhoff, 2012), but we have already seen that talking about some aspects of a memory but omitting other related events, can also produce retrieval-induced forgetting (see p. 238) (Coman et al., 2009; Cuc et al., 2007). Psychologists have become increasingly interested in how people remember in groups, which is now referred to as *collaborative memory* (Rajaram, 2011).

In a typical collaborative memory experiment, participants first encode a set of target materials, such as a list of words, on their own (just like in the traditional memory experiments that we have already considered). Things start to get interesting at the time of retrieval, when participants work together in small groups (usually two or three participants) to try to remember the target items. The number of items recalled by this group can then be compared with the number of items recalled by individuals who are trying to recall items on their own, without any help from others. The collaborative group typically recalls more target items than any individual (Hirst & Echterhoff, 2012; Weldon, 2001), suggesting that collaboration benefits memory. That makes a lot of sense and generally fits with our intuitions about what should happen in such a situation (Rajaram, 2011). For example, Tim might recall an item that Emily forgot, and Eric might remember items that neither Tim nor Emily recalled, so the sum total of the group will exceed what any one person can recall.

But things get really interesting when we compare the performance of the collaborative group to the performance of what is called a *nominal group*: the combined recall of several individuals recalling target items on their own. Let us consider a nominal group of three compared with a collaborative group of three. In the nominal group, let us assume that after studying a list of eight words, Tim recalls items 1, 2, and 8, Emily recalls items 1, 4, and 7, and Eric recalls items 1, 5, 6, and 8. Functioning on their own, Tim, Emily, and Eric recalled in combination seven of the eight items that were presented (nobody recalled item 3). The surprising finding now reported by many studies is that the collaborative group typically recalls fewer items than the nominal group; that is, when they remember together, Tim, Emily, and Eric will come up with fewer total items than when they remember on their own (Basden et al., 1997; Hirst & Echterhoff, 2012; Rajaram, 2011; Rajaram & Pereira-Pasarin, 2010; Weldon, 2001). This negative effect of group recall on memory is known as *collaborative inhibition*: the same number of individuals working together recall fewer items than they would on their own.

What is going on here? Most people believe that, based on intuition, working together should increase rather than decrease recall (Rajaram, 2011). Why does it turn out otherwise? One possibility is that in a group, some individuals are prone to "social loafing": They let others do the work and do not pull their own weight. Although social loafing is well known to occur in groups (Karau & Williams, 1993), memory

> **Why does a collaborative group typically recall fewer items than a nominal group?**

researchers have tested this account of collaborative inhibition and rejected it (Barber, Rajaram, & Fox, 2012). A more likely account is that when recalling items together, the retrieval strategies used by individual members of the group disrupt those used by others (Basden et al., 1997; Hirst & Echterhoff, 2012; Rajaram, 2011). For example, suppose that Tim goes first and recalls items in the order that they were presented. This retrieval strategy may be disruptive to Emily, who prefers to recall the last item first and then work backward through the list.

But collaborative recall has other benefits. When individuals recall information together in a group, they are exposed to items recalled by others they may not recall themselves, which improves their memory when they are retested at a later time (Blumen & Rajaram, 2008). And when group members discuss what they have recalled, they can help each other to correct and reduce memory errors (Ross, Blatz, & Schryer, 2008). These observations fit with earlier work showing that couples in close relationships often rely on collaborative remembering (also called *transactive memory*) (Wegner, Erber, & Raymond, 1991), where each member of the couple remembers certain kinds of information that they can share with the other. (Can you rely on your computer for collaborative remembering? See The Real World: Is Google Hurting our Memories?) So, next time you are sharing memories of a past activity with friends, you will be shaping your memories for both better and worse.

Remembering as a collaborative group leads to greater recall than would be achieved by any single member of the group, but less than that produced by a nominal group of individuals remembering on their own.

BLEND IMAGES/ALAMY

THE REAL WORLD

# Is Google Hurting our Memories?

Take some time to try to answer a simple question before returning to reading this box: What country has a national flag that is not rectangular? Now let us discuss what went through your mind as you searched for an answer (the correct one is Nepal). Did you start thinking about the shapes of national flags? Take a mental walk through a map of the world? Or did you think instead about computers—more specifically, about typing the question into Google? There was probably a time not too long ago when most people would have tried to conjure up images of national flags or take a mental world tour, but recent research conducted in the lab of one of your textbook authors indicates that nowadays, most of us think about computers and Google searches when confronted with questions of this kind (Sparrow, Liu, & Wegner, 2011).

Sparrow and her colleagues found that people were slower to name the colour in which a computer word (e.g., Google, Internet, Yahoo) was printed than the colour in which a noncomputer word (e.g., Nike, table, Yoplait) was printed after they were given difficult general knowledge questions (like the one about nonrectangular flags) than after they were given easy questions to which they knew the answers. The slow colour naming to computer words suggests that people were thinking about things related to computers after being given difficult questions, which interfered with their ability to name the colour in which the word was printed. The researchers concluded that we are now so used to searching for information on Google when we do not immediately know the answer to a question that we immediately think of computers, rather than searching our memories. Thinking about computers when faced with a tough question makes sense: We will probably come up with the answer more quickly if we do a Google search than if we think about what different flags look like. But this result also raises troubling questions: Is reliance on computers and the Internet having an adverse effect on human memory? If we

▲ What does your computer remember for you?

rely on Google for answers, are we unknowingly making our memories obsolete?

Sparrow and her colleagues conducted additional experiments aimed at addressing these kinds of questions. In one of them, they found that participants had a harder time remembering bits of trivia ("An ostrich's eye is bigger than its brain") that they typed into a computer when they were told that the computer would save their answers than when they were told that the answers would be erased. But in later experiments, they found that when people saved information to one of several folders on a computer, they were often able to remember where they saved it even when they did not remember the information itself. People seemed to be using the computer in an efficient way to help remember facts, while relying on their own memories to recall where those facts could be found. Sparrow and colleagues suggested that people may be adapting their memories to the demands of new technology, relying on computers in a way that is similar to how we sometimes rely on other people (friends, family members, or colleagues) to remember things that we may not remember ourselves. This is similar to what we discussed as *collaborative memory*, and just as collaborative remembering with other people has both helpful and harmful effects, so does collaborative remembering with our computers.

## IN SUMMARY

▶ Long-term memory consists of several different forms. Explicit memory is the act of consciously or intentionally retrieving past experiences, whereas implicit memory refers to the unconscious influence of past experiences on later behaviour and performance, such as procedural memory and priming. Procedural memory involves the acquisition of skills as a result of practice, and priming is a change in the ability to recognize or identify an object or a word as the result of past exposure to it.

▶ People who have amnesia are able to retain implicit memory, including procedural memory and priming, but they lack explicit memory.

▶ Episodic memory is the collection of personal experiences from a particular time and place; it allows us both to recollect the past and imagine the future. Semantic memory is a networked, general, impersonal knowledge of facts, associations, and concepts.

▶ Collaborative memory refers to remembering in groups. Collaborative remembering can both impair memory (collaborative inhibition) and enhance it by exposing people to new information and helping to correct errors.

# Memory Failures: The Seven Sins of Memory

You probably have not given much thought to breathing today, and the reason is that from the moment you woke up, you have been doing it effortlessly and well. But the moment breathing fails, you are reminded of just how important it is. Memory is like that. Every time we see, think, notice, imagine, or wonder, we are drawing on our ability to use information stored in our brains, but it is not until this ability fails that we become acutely aware of just how much we should treasure it. We have seen in other contexts how an understanding of foibles and errors of human thought and action reveals the normal operation of various behaviours. Such memory errors—the "seven sins" of memory—cast similar illumination on how memory normally operates and how often it operates well (Schacter, 1999, 2001b). We will discuss each of the seven sins in detail below.

## 1. Transience

Wilder Penfield was a famous Canadian neurosurgeon who founded the Montreal Neurological Institute and developed the effective surgical treatment of epilepsy. Before operating on a patient, he would stimulate regions of their brain with electrical probes. This was done while the patient was awake on the operating table (under local anaesthesia). His intent was to identify the regions of the brain responsible for generating the seizures, but in the process he was able to create detailed maps of the function of the human cortex. Stimulation in one area would cause the left hand to twitch. Stimulation in another area would cause the patient to report a tingling in their right leg. Many of the experiences reported by patients after stimulation had the character of amazingly detailed, vivid memories. For example, a patient might hear the voice of a cousin in Africa, or see a man and dog walking along a road near his place in the country. During such experiences, the patient was simultaneously aware of being in the operating room. These "memories" (as they seemed to be) were so detailed that, to Penfield, it seemed as though the cortex must contain a permanent record of all past experience. In fact, only a small minority of his patients reported such experiences, and whether or not they are memories is impossible to know—it now seems very likely that they were not memories at all. In fact, memories can and do degrade with time. The culprit here is **transience:** *forgetting what occurs with the passage of time.*

Transience occurs during the storage phase of memory, after an experience has been encoded and before it is retrieved. You have already seen the workings of transience—rapid forgetting—in sensory storage and short-term storage. Transience also occurs in long-term storage, as was first illustrated in the late 1870s by Hermann Ebbinghaus, a German philosopher who tested his own memory for lists of nonsense syllables at different delays after studying them (Ebbinghaus, 1885/1964). His results are illustrated in the forgetting curve shown in **FIGURE 6.15** on the next page. Ebbinghaus noted a rapid drop-off in retention during the first few tests, followed by a slower rate of forgetting on later tests—a general pattern confirmed by many subsequent memory researchers (Wixted & Ebbensen, 1991). So, for example, when English speakers were tested for memory of Spanish vocabulary acquired during high school or college courses 1 to 50 years previously, there was a rapid drop-off in memory during the first 3 years after the students' last class, followed by tiny losses in later years (Bahrick, 1984, 2000). In all these studies, memories did not fade at a constant rate as time passed; most forgetting happened soon after an event occurred, with increasingly less forgetting as more time passed.

Not only do we forget memories with the passage of time, the quality of our memories also changes. At early time points on the forgetting curve—minutes, hours, and

**transience**
Forgetting what occurs with the passage of time.

Wilder Penfield was, during his lifetime, called "the greatest living Canadian" for his contributions to the surgical treatment of people suffering from neurological disorders including epilepsy, and for his research into the functions of the living brain.

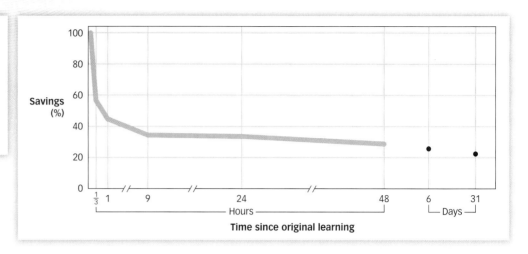

► Figure **6.15** **The Curve of Forgetting**
Hermann Ebbinghaus measured his retention at various delay intervals after he studied lists of nonsense syllables. Retention was measured in percent savings, that is, the percentage of time needed to relearn the list compared to the time needed to learn it initially.

**retroactive interference**
Situations in which information learned later impairs memory for information acquired earlier.

**proactive interference**
Situations in which information learned earlier impairs memory for information acquired later.

**absentmindedness**
A lapse in attention that results in memory failure.

**prospective memory**
Remembering to do things in the future.

As an example of transience, when there is a delay between the hearing and retelling of the story, someone unfamiliar with Native American legends would more likely recount the general gist than the specific details. This image by Charles Livingston Bull is titled, *Hawk made a light by striking the flints together, and set fire to the ball.*

days—memory preserves a relatively detailed record, allowing us to reproduce the past with reasonable if not perfect accuracy. But with the passing of time, we increasingly rely on our general memories for what usually happens and attempt to reconstruct the details by inference and even sheer guesswork. Transience involves a gradual switch from specific to more general memories (Brewer, 1996; Eldridge, Barnard, & Bekerian, 1994; Thompson et al., 1996). In one early study, British research participants read a brief Native American folktale that had odd imagery and unfamiliar plots in it, and then recounted it as best they could after a delay (Bartlett, 1932). The readers made interesting but understandable errors, often eliminating details that did not make sense to them or adding elements to make the story more coherent. As the specifics of the story slipped away, the general meaning of the events stayed in memory but usually with elaborations and embellishments that were consistent with the readers' world view. Because the story was unfamiliar to the readers, they raided their stores of general information and patched together a reasonable recollection of what *probably* happened.

> How might general memories come to distort specific memories?

Yet another way that memories can be distorted is by interference from other memories. For example, if you carry out the same activities at work each day, by the time Friday rolls around, it may be difficult to remember what you did on Monday because later activities blend in with earlier ones. This is an example of **retroactive interference,** *situations in which later learning impairs memory for information acquired earlier* (Postman & Underwood, 1973). **Proactive interference,** in contrast, refers to *situations in which earlier learning impairs memory for information acquired later*. If you use the same parking lot each day at work or at school, you have probably gone out to find your car and then stood there confused by the memories of having parked it on previous days.

## 2. Absentmindedness

The great cellist Yo-Yo Ma put his treasured $2.5 million instrument in the trunk of a taxicab in Manhattan and then rode to his destination. After a 10-minute trip, he paid the driver and left the cab, forgetting his cello. Minutes later, Ma realized what he had done and called the police. Fortunately, they tracked down the taxi and recovered the instrument within hours (Finkelstein, 1999). But how had the celebrated cellist forgotten about something so important that had occurred only 10 minutes earlier? Transience is not a likely culprit. As soon as Mr. Ma realized what he had done with his instrument, he recalled where he had put it. This information had not disappeared from his memory (which is why he was able to tell the police where the cello was). Instead, Yo-Yo Ma was a victim of **absentmindedness**, *a lapse in attention that results in memory failure*.

What makes people absentminded? One common cause is lack of attention. Attention plays a vital role in encoding information into long-term memory. Without proper attention, material is much less likely to be stored properly and recalled later. In studies of divided attention, research participants are given materials to remember, such as a list of words, a story, or a series of pictures. At the same time, they are required to perform an additional task that draws their attention away from the material. For example, in one study, participants listened to lists of 15 words for a later memory test (Craik et al., 1996). They were allowed to pay full attention to some of the lists, but while they heard other lists, they simultaneously viewed a visual display containing four boxes and pressed different keys to indicate where an asterisk was appearing and disappearing. On a later test, participants recalled far fewer words from the list they had heard while their attention was divided.

What happens in the brain when attention is divided? In one study, volunteers tried to learn a list of word pairs while researchers scanned their brains with positron emission tomography (PET) (Shallice et al., 1994). Some people simultaneously performed a task that took little attention (they moved a bar the same way over and over), whereas other people simultaneously performed a task that took a great deal of attention (they moved a bar over and over but in a novel, unpredictable way each time). The researchers observed less activity in the participants' lower left frontal lobe when their attention was divided. As you saw earlier, greater activity in the lower left frontal region during encoding is associated with better memory. Dividing attention, then, prevents the lower left frontal lobe from playing its normal role in semantic encoding, and the result is absentminded forgetting. More recent research using fMRI has shown that divided attention also leads to less hippocampal involvement in encoding (Kensinger, Clarke, & Corkin, 2003; Uncapher & Rugg, 2008). Given the importance of the hippocampus to episodic memory, this finding may help to explain why absentminded forgetting is sometimes so extreme, as when we forget where we put our keys or glasses only moments earlier.

**How is memory affected for someone whose attention is divided?**

Yo-Yo Ma with his $2.5 million cello. The famous cellist lost it when he absentmindedly forgot that he had placed the instrument in a taxicab's trunk minutes earlier.

Another common cause of absentmindedness is forgetting to carry out actions that we planned to do in the future. On any given day, you need to remember the times and places that your classes meet, you need to remember with whom and where you are having lunch, you need to remember which grocery items to pick up for dinner, and you need to remember which page of this book you were on when you fell asleep. In other words, you have to remember to remember, and this is called **prospective memory,** *remembering to do things in the future* (Einstein & McDaniel, 1990, 2005).

Failures of prospective memory are a major source of absentmindedness. Avoiding these problems often requires having a cue available at the moment you need to remember to carry out an action. For example, air traffic controllers must sometimes postpone an action, such as granting a pilot's request to change altitude, but remember to carry out that action a few minutes later when conditions change. In a simulated air traffic control experiment, researchers provided controllers with electronic signals to remind them to carry out a deferred request 1 minute later. The reminders were made available either during the

Talking on a cell phone while driving is a common occurrence of divided attention in everyday life; texting is even worse. This can be dangerous, and an increasing number of provinces have banned the practice.

**blocking**
A failure to retrieve information that is available in memory even though you are trying to produce it.

**memory misattribution**
Assigning a recollection or an idea to the wrong source.

**source memory**
Recall of when, where, and how information was acquired.

**false recognition**
A feeling of familiarity about something that has not been encountered before.

Suppose that, mentally consumed by planning for a psychology test the next day, you place your keys in an unusual spot, and later forget where you put them. Is this more likely to reflect the memory sin of transience, absentmindedness, or blocking?

STILLFX/AGEFOTOSTOCK

1-minute waiting period or at the time the controller needed to act on the deferred request. The controllers' memory for the deferred action improved only when the reminder was available at the time needed for retrieval. Providing the reminder during the waiting period did not help (Vortac, Edwards, & Manning, 1995). An early reminder, then, is no reminder at all.

## 3. Blocking

Have you ever tried to recall the name of a famous actor or a book you have read—and felt that the answer was on the tip of your tongue, rolling around in your head *somewhere* but just out of reach at the moment? This tip-of-the-tongue experience is a classic example of **blocking,** *a failure to retrieve information that is available in memory even though you are trying to produce it.* The sought-after information has been encoded and stored, and a cue is available that would ordinarily trigger recall of it. The information has not faded from memory, and you are not forgetting to retrieve it. Rather, you are experiencing a full-blown retrieval failure, which makes this memory breakdown especially frustrating. It seems absolutely clear that you should be able to produce the information you seek, but the fact of the matter is that you cannot. Researchers have described the tip-of-the-tongue state, in particular, as "a mild torment, something like [being] on the brink of a sneeze" (Brown & McNeill, 1966, p. 326).

Studies have found that when people are in tip-of-the-tongue states, they often know something about the item they cannot recall, such as the meaning of a word (Schwartz, 2002). When experimenters induced tip-of-the-tongue states by playing participants theme songs from 1950s and 1960s television shows and asking for the names of the shows, people who were blocked on *The Munsters* often came up with another comically ghoulish sitcom, *The Addams Family* (Riefer, Kevari, & Kramer, 1995).

Blocking occurs especially often for the names of people and places (Cohen, 1990; Semenza, 2009; Valentine, Brennen, & Brédart, 1996). Why? Because their links to related concepts and knowledge are weaker than for common names. That somebody's last name is Baker does not tell us much about the person, but saying that he *is* a baker does. To illustrate this point, researchers showed people pictures of cartoon and comic strip characters, some with descriptive names that highlight key features of the character (e.g., Grumpy, Snow White, Scrooge) and others with arbitrary names (e.g., Aladdin, Mary Poppins, Pinocchio) (Brédart & Valentine, 1998). Even though the two types of names were equally familiar to participants in the experiment, they blocked less often on the descriptive names than on the arbitrary names.

> Why is Snow White's name easier to remember than Mary Poppins?

Although it is frustrating when it occurs, blocking is a relatively infrequent event for most of us. However, it occurs more often as we grow older, and it is a very common complaint among people in their 60s and 70s (Burke et al., 1991; Schwartz, 2002). Even more striking, some individuals with brain damage live in a nearly perpetual tip-of-the-tongue state (Semenza, 2009). One such individual could recall the names of only 2 of 40 famous people when she saw their photographs, compared to 25 of 40 for healthy volunteers in the control group (Semenza & Zettin, 1989). Yet she could still recall correctly the occupations of 32 of these people—the same number as healthy people could recall. This case and similar ones have given researchers important clues about what parts of the brain are involved in retrieving proper names. Name blocking usually results from damage to parts of the left temporal lobe on the surface of the cortex, most often as a result of a stroke. In fact, studies that show strong activation of regions within the temporal lobe when people recall proper names support this idea (Damasio et al., 1996; Gorno-Tempini et al., 1998).

## 4. Memory Misattribution

**Memory misattribution** errors, which involve *assigning a recollection or an idea to a wrong source*, are some of the primary causes of eyewitness misidentifications. For example, the memory researcher Donald Thomson was accused of rape based on the victim's detailed recollection of his face, but he was eventually cleared when it turned out he had an airtight alibi. At the time of the rape, Thomson was giving a live television interview on the subject of distorted memories! The victim had been watching the show just before she was assaulted and misattributed her memory of Thomson's face to the rapist (Schacter, 1996; Thomson, 1988). Thomson's case, though dramatic, is not an isolated occurrence: Faulty eyewitness memory was a factor in more than 75 percent of the first 310 American cases in which individuals were shown to be innocent by DNA evidence after conviction for crimes they did not commit (Innocence Project, 2012). See **FIGURE 6.16** for another example of memory misattribution.

Part of memory is knowing where our memories came from. This is known as **source memory,** *recall of when, where, and how information was acquired* (Johnson, Hashtroudi, & Lindsay, 1993; Mitchell & Johnson, 2009; Schacter, Harbluk, &

> What can explain a déjà vu experience?

McLachlan, 1984). People sometimes correctly recall a fact they learned earlier or accurately recognize a person or object they have seen before but misattribute the source of this knowledge—just as happened to the rape victim in the Donald Thomson incident (Davies, 1988). Such misattribution could be the cause of déjà vu experiences, where you suddenly feel that you have been in a situation before even though you cannot recall any details. A present situation that is similar to a past experience may trigger a general sense of familiarity that is mistakenly attributed to having been in the exact situation previously (Brown, 2004; Reed, 1988).

Individuals with damage to the frontal lobes are especially prone to memory misattribution errors (Schacter et al., 1984; Shimamura & Squire, 1987). This is probably because the frontal lobes play a significant role in effortful retrieval processes, which are required to dredge up the correct source of a memory. These individuals sometimes produce bizarre misattributions. In 1991, a British photographer in his mid-40s known as M.R. was overcome with feelings of familiarity about people he did not know. He kept asking his wife whether each new passing stranger was "somebody"—a screen actor, television newsperson, or local celebrity. M.R.'s feelings were so intense that he often could not resist approaching strangers and asking whether they were indeed famous celebrities. When given formal tests, M.R. recognized the faces of actual celebrities as accurately as did healthy volunteers in the control group. But M.R. also "recognized" more than 75 percent of unfamiliar faces, whereas healthy volunteers hardly ever did. Neurological exams revealed that M.R. suffered from multiple sclerosis, which had caused damage to his frontal lobes (Ward et al., 1999). Psychologists call the type of memory misattribution made by M.R. **false recognition,** *a feeling of familiarity about something that has not been encountered before.*

The subjective experience for M.R., as in everyday déjà vu experiences, is characterized by a strong sense of familiarity without any recall of associated details. Other individuals with neurological damage exhibit a recently discovered type of memory misattribution called déjà vécu: They feel strongly—but mistakenly—that they have already lived through an experience and remember the details of what happened (Moulin et al., 2005). For example, when watching television, one such individual was certain that he recalled seeing each show before, even when he was watching an

▲ Figure **6.16** **Memory Misattribution** Another common form of memory misattribution is unintentional plagiarism: forgetting the source of an idea and assuming that you have come up with it yourself. In 1971, musician George Harrison had a huge hit worldwide with the song "My Sweet Lord." Due to its similarity with the earlier Chiffons' hit "He's So Fine" (written by Ronnie Mack), Harrison was sued. In 1976 the court found that he had "subconsciously" copied the earlier song, but that the lack of awareness was not a mitigating factor–the court recommended that he pay $1.6 million in damages to the copyright owner of "He's So Fine."

## Table 6.1

### False Recognition

| | |
|---|---|
| Sour | Thread |
| Candy | Pin |
| Sugar | Eye |
| Bitter | Sewing |
| Good | Sharp |
| Taste | Point |
| Tooth | Prick |
| Nice | Thimble |
| Honey | Haystack |
| Soda | Pain |
| Chocolate | Hurt |
| Heart | Injection |
| Cake | Syringe |
| Tart | Cloth |
| Pie | Knitting |

entirely new episode. When he went shopping, he constantly thought it was unnecessary to buy needed items because he remembered having done so already. Although the basis of this strange disorder is not well understood, it probably involves disruption to parts of the temporal lobe that normally generate a subjective feeling of remembering (Moulin et al., 2005).

But we are all vulnerable to memory misattribution. Take the following test and there is a good chance that you will experience false recognition for yourself. First, study the two lists of words presented in **TABLE 6.1** by reading each word for about 1 second. When you are done, return to this paragraph for more instructions, but do not look back at the table! Now try to recognize which of the following words appeared on the list you just studied: *taste, bread, needle, king, sweet, thread.* If you think that *taste* and *thread* were on the lists you studied, you are right. And if you think that *bread* and *king* were not on those lists, you are also right. But if you think that *needle* or *sweet* appeared on the lists, you are dead wrong.

Most people make exactly the same mistake, claiming with confidence that they saw *needle* and *sweet* on the list. This occurs because all the words in the lists are associated with *needle* or *sweet*. Seeing each word in the study list activates related words. Because *needle* and *sweet* are related to all of the associates, they become more activated than other words—so highly activated that only minutes later, people swear that they actually studied the words (Deese, 1959; Gallo, 2006, 2010; Roediger & McDermott, 1995, 2000). In fact, brain scanning studies using PET and fMRI show that many of the same brain regions are active during false recognition and true recognition, including the hippocampus (Cabeza et al., 2001; Schacter, Reiman, et al., 1996) (see **FIGURE 6.17**). Similar results are obtained when people view a series of common objects (e.g., cars, umbrellas) and then are later shown a new object that looks like one they saw earlier: They often falsely recognize the similar new item, and many of the same brain regions become active during this kind of false recognition as during true recognition (Gutchess & Schacter, 2012; Slotnick & Schacter, 2004).

However, false recognition can be reduced (Schacter, Israel, & Racine, 1999). For example, recent evidence shows that when participants are given a choice between an object that they actually saw (e.g., a car) and a visually similar new object (a different car that looks like the one they saw), they almost always choose the car that they actually saw and thus avoid making a false recognition error (Guerin et al., 2012a, 2012b). This finding suggests that false recognition occurs, at least in part, because when presented with a similar new object on its own, participants do not

▼ Figure **6.17** **Hippocampal Activity during True and False Recognition** Many brain regions show similar activation during true and false recognition, including the hippocampus. The figure shows results from an fMRI study of true and false recognition of visual shapes (Slotnick & Schacter, 2004). A plot of the activity level in the strength of the fMRI signal from the hippocampus over time (a) shows that after a few seconds, there is comparable activation for true recognition of previously studied shapes (red line) and false recognition of similar shapes that were not presented (yellow line). Both true and false recognition show increased hippocampal activity compared with correctly classifying unrelated shapes as new (purple line). The brain scan (b) shows a region of the left hippocampus.

recollect specific details about the object they actually studied, but these details need to be retrieved in order to correctly indicate that the similar object is new. Yet this information is available in memory, as shown by the ability of participants to correctly choose between the studied object and the visually similar new object. When people experience a strong sense of familiarity about a person, object, or event but lack specific recollections, a potentially dangerous recipe for memory misattribution is in place, both in the laboratory and also in real-world situations involving eyewitness memory. Understanding this point may be a key to reducing the dangerous consequences of misattribution in eyewitness testimony.

## 5. Suggestibility

On October 4, 1992, an El Al cargo plane crashed into an apartment building in a southern suburb of Amsterdam, killing 39 residents and all 4 members of the airline crew. The disaster dominated news in the Netherlands for days as people viewed footage of the crash scene and read about the catastrophe. Ten months later, Dutch psy-

**How can eyewitnesses be mislead?**

chologists asked a simple question of university students: "Did you see the television film of the moment the plane hit the apartment building?" Fifty-five percent answered yes (Crombag, Wagenaar, & Van Koppen, 1996). All of this might seem perfectly normal except for one key fact: There was no television film of the moment when the plane actually crashed. The researchers had asked a suggestive question that implied that television film of the crash had been shown. Respondents may have viewed television film of the post-crash scene, and they may have read, imagined, or talked about what might have happened when the plane hit the building, but they most definitely did not see it. The suggestive question led participants to misattribute information from these or other sources to a film that did not exist. **Suggestibility** is the *tendency to incorporate misleading information from external sources into personal recollections.*

If misleading details can be implanted in people's memories, is it also possible to suggest entire episodes that never occurred? The answer seems to be yes (Loftus, 1993, 2003). In one study, the research participant, a teenager named Chris, was asked by his older brother, Jim, to try to remember the time Chris had been lost

In 1992, an El Al cargo plane crashed into an apartment building in a suburb of Amsterdam. When Dutch psychologists asked students if they had seen the television film of the plane crashing, a majority said they had. In fact, no such footage exists (Crombag et al., 1996).

in a shopping mall at age 5. He initially recalled nothing, but after several days, Chris produced a detailed recollection of the event. He recalled that he "felt so scared I would never see my family again" and remembered that a kindly old man wearing a flannel shirt found him crying (Loftus, 1993, p. 532). But according to Jim and other family members, Chris was never lost in a shopping mall. Of 24 participants in a larger study on implanted memories, approximately 25 percent falsely remembered being lost as a child in a shopping mall or in a similar public place (Loftus & Pickrell, 1995).

People develop false memories in response to suggestions for some of the same reasons memory misattribution occurs. We do not store all the details of our experiences in memory, making us vulnerable to accepting suggestions about what might have happened or should have happened. In addition, visual imagery plays an important role in constructing false memories (Goff & Roediger, 1998).

**Why can childhood memories be influenced by suggestion?**

**suggestibility**
The tendency to incorporate misleading information from external sources into personal recollections.

Asking people to imagine an event like spilling punch all over the bride's parents at a wedding increases the likelihood that they will develop a false memory of it (Hyman & Pentland, 1996).

Suggestibility played an important role in a controversy that arose during the 1980s and 1990s concerning the accuracy of childhood memories that people recalled during psychotherapy. One highly publicized example involved a woman named Diana Halbrooks (Schacter, 1996). After a few months in psychotherapy, she began recalling disturbing incidents from her childhood, for example, that her mother had tried to kill her and that her father had abused her sexually. Although her parents denied that these events had ever occurred, her therapist encouraged her to believe in the reality of her memories. Eventually Diana Halbrooks stopped therapy and came to realize that the "memories" she had recovered were inaccurate.

How could this happen? A number of the techniques used by psychotherapists to try to pull up forgotten childhood memories are clearly suggestive (Poole et al., 1995). Specifically, research has shown that imagining past events and hypnosis can help create false memories (Garry et al., 1996; Hyman & Pentland, 1996; McConkey, Barnier, & Sheehan, 1998). More recent studies show that memories that people remember spontaneously on their own are corroborated by other people at about the same rate as the memories of individuals who never forgot their abuse, whereas memories recovered in response to suggestive therapeutic techniques are virtually never corroborated by others (McNally & Geraerts, 2009).

## 6. Bias

In 2000, the outcome of a very close race to decide the next American president, between George W. Bush and Al Gore, was decided by the Supreme Court 5 weeks after the election had taken place. The day after the election (when the result was still in doubt), supporters of Bush and Gore were asked to predict how happy they would be after the outcome of the election was determined (Wilson, Meyers, & Gilbert, 2003). These same respondents reported how happy they felt with the outcome on the day after Al Gore conceded. And 4 months later, the participants recalled how happy they had been right after the election was decided.

Bush supporters, who eventually enjoyed a positive result (their candidate took office), were understandably happy the day after the Supreme Court's decision. However, their retrospective accounts *over*estimated how happy they were at the time. Conversely, Gore supporters were not pleased with the outcome. But when polled 4 months after the election was decided, Gore supporters *under*estimated how happy they actually were at the time of the result. In both groups, recollections of happiness were at odds with existing reports of their actual happiness at the time (Wilson et al., 2003).

These results illustrate the problem of **bias**, *the distorting influences of present knowledge, beliefs, and feelings on recollection of previous experiences.* Sometimes what people remember from their pasts says less about what actually happened than about what they think, feel, or believe now. Researchers have also found that our current moods can bias our recall of past experiences (Bower, 1981; Buchanan, 2007; Eich, 1995). So, in addition to helping you recall actual sad memories (as you saw earlier in this chapter), a sad mood can also bias your recollections of experiences that may not have been so

How happy do you think you would be if the candidate you supported won an election? Do you think you would accurately remember your level of happiness if you recalled it several months later? Chances are good that bias in the memory process would alter your recollection of your previous happiness. Indeed, 4 months after they heard the outcome of the 2000 presidential election, supporters of Bush (*left*) overestimated how happy they were, whereas supporters of Gore (*right*) underestimated how happy they were.

sad. *Consistency bias* is the bias to reconstruct the past to fit the present. One researcher asked Americans in 1973 to rate their attitudes toward a variety of controversial social issues, including legalization of marijuana, women's rights, and aid to minorities (Markus, 1986). They were asked to make the same rating again in 1982 and also to indicate what their attitudes had been in 1973. Researchers found that participants' recollections of their 1973 attitudes in 1982 were more closely related to what they believed in 1982 than to what they had actually said in 1973.

> **How does your current outlook colour your memory of a past event?**

Whereas consistency bias exaggerates the similarity between past and present, *change bias* is the tendency to exaggerate differences between what we feel or believe now and what we felt or believed in the past. In other words, *change biases* also occur. For example, most of us would like to believe that our romantic attachments grow stronger over time. In one study, dating couples were asked, once a year for 4 years, to assess the present quality of their relationships and to recall how they felt in past years (Sprecher, 1999). Couples who stayed together for the 4 years recalled that the strength of their love had increased since they last reported on it. Yet their actual ratings at the time did not show any increases in love and attachment. Objectively, the couples did not love each other more today than yesterday. But they did from the subjective perspective of memory.

A special case of change bias is *egocentric bias*, the tendency to exaggerate the change between present and past in order to make ourselves look good in retrospect. For example, students sometimes remember feeling more anxious before taking an exam than they actually reported at the time (Keuler & Safer, 1998), and blood donors sometimes recall being more nervous about giving blood than they actually were (Breckler, 1994). In both cases, change biases colour memory and make people feel that they behaved more bravely or courageously than they actually did. Similarly, when American university students tried to remember high school grades and their memories were checked against actual transcripts, they were highly accurate for grades of A (89 percent correct) and extremely inaccurate for grades of D (29 percent correct) (Bahrick, Hall, & Berger, 1996). The same kind of egocentric bias occurs with memory for college grades: 81 percent of students inflated the actual grade, and this bias was evident even when participants were asked about their grades soon after graduation (Bahrick, Hall, & DaCosta, 2008). People were remembering the past as they wanted it to be rather than the way it was.

## 7. Persistence

The artist Melinda Stickney-Gibson awoke in her apartment to the smell of smoke. She jumped out of bed and saw black plumes rising through cracks in the floor. Raging flames had engulfed the entire building, and there was no chance to escape except by jumping from her third-floor window. Shortly after she crashed to the ground, the building exploded into a brilliant fireball. Although she survived the fire and the fall, Melinda became overwhelmed by memories of the fire. When Melinda sat down in front of a blank canvas to start a new painting, her memories of that awful night intruded. Her paintings, which were previously bright, colourful abstractions, became dark meditations that included only black, orange, and ochre—the colours of the fire (Schacter, 1996).

Melinda Stickney-Gibson's experiences illustrate memory's seventh and most deadly sin, **persistence:** *the intrusive recollection of events that we wish we could forget*. Melinda's experience is far from unique; persistence frequently occurs after disturbing or traumatic incidents, such as the fire that destroyed her home. Although being able to recall memories quickly is

**bias**
The distorting influences of present knowledge, beliefs, and feelings on recollection of previous experiences.

**persistence**
The intrusive recollection of events that we wish we could forget.

The way each member of this happy couple recalls earlier feelings toward the other depends on how each currently views their relationship.

ANDERSEN ROSS/
PHOTOLIBRARY

**flashbulb memories**
Detailed recollections of when and where we heard about shocking events.

usually considered a good thing, in the case of persistence, that ability mutates into an unwelcome burden.

Controlled laboratory studies have revealed that emotional experiences tend to be better remembered than nonemotional ones. For instance, memory for unpleasant pictures, such as mutilated bodies, or pleasant ones, such as attractive men and women, is more accurate than for emotionally neutral pictures, such as household objects (Ochsner, 2000). Emotional arousal seems to focus our attention on the central features of an event. In one experiment, people who viewed an emotionally arousing sequence of slides involving a bloody car accident remembered more of the central themes and fewer peripheral details than people who viewed a nonemotional sequence (Christianson & Loftus, 1987).

Intrusive memories are undesirable consequences of emotional experiences because emotional experiences generally lead to more vivid and enduring recollections than nonemotional experiences do. One line of evidence comes from the study of **flashbulb memories,** which are *detailed recollections of when and where we heard about emotionally intense events* (Brown & Kulik, 1977). For example, most people in North America can recall exactly where they were and how they heard about the

> How does emotional trauma affect memory?

September 11, 2001, terrorist attacks in which passenger aircraft were deliberately flown into the the World Trade Center in New York City—almost as if a mental flashbulb had gone off automatically and recorded the event in long-lasting and vivid detail (Kvavilashvili et al., 2009). Several studies have shown that flashbulb memories are not always entirely accurate, but they are generally better remembered than mundane news events from the same time (Larsen, 1992; Neisser & Harsch, 1992). Enhanced retention of flashbulb memories is partly attributable to the emotional arousal elicited by events such as the 9/11 terrorist attacks, and partly attributable to the fact that we tend to talk and think a lot about these experiences. Recall that semantic encoding enhances memory: When we talk about flashbulb experiences, we elaborate on them and thus further increase the memorability of those aspects of the experience that we discuss (Hirst et al., 2009).

Why do our brains succumb to persistence? A key player in the brain's response to emotional events is a small, almond-shaped structure called the *amygdala*, shown in **FIGURE 6.18** on the next page. The amygdala influences hormonal systems that kick

Some events are so emotionally charged that we form unusually detailed memories of when and where we heard about them. Examples include Paul Henderson's winning goal in the 1972 hockey series Team Canada played against the Soviet Union, and the terrorist attack in the United States on September 11, 2001. These flashbulb memories generally persist much longer than memories for ordinary events.

into high gear when we experience an arousing event; these stress-related hormones, such as adrenaline and cortisol, mobilize the body in the face of threat—and they also enhance memory for the experience. Damage to the amygdala does not result in a general memory deficit. Individuals with amygdala damage, however, do not remember emotional events any better than nonemotional events (Cahill & McGaugh, 1998).

For example, consider what happened when people viewed a series of photographic slides that began with a mother walking her child to school and later included an emotionally arousing event: the child being hit by a car. When tested later, the research participants remembered the arousing event better than the mundane ones. But individuals with amygdala damage remembered the mundane and emotionally arousing events equally well (Cahill & McGaugh, 1998). PET and fMRI scans show that when healthy people view a slide sequence that includes an emotionally arousing event, the level of activity in the amygdala at the time they see it is a good predictor of their subsequent memory for the slide. When there is heightened activity in the amygdala as people watch emotional events, there is a better chance that they will recall those events on a later test (Cahill et al., 1996; Kensinger & Schacter, 2005, 2006). And when people are given a drug that interferes with the amygdala-mediated release of stress hormones, their memory for the emotional sections is no better than their memory for the mundane sections.

In many cases, there are clear benefits to forming strong memories for highly emotional events, particularly those that are life-threatening. In the case of persistence, though, such memories may be too strong—strong enough to interfere with other aspects of daily life.

## Are the Seven Sins Vices or Virtues?

You may have concluded that evolution has burdened us with an extremely inefficient memory system that is so prone to error that it often jeopardizes our well-being. Not so. The seven sins are the price we pay for the many benefits that memory provides, the occasional result of the normally efficient operation of the human memory system (Schacter, 2001b).

Consider transience, for example. It would be great to remember all the details of every incident in your life, no matter how much time had passed. Or would it? Do you remember Jill Price, the woman we described at the beginning of this chapter, who has this ability and said it drives her crazy (see p. 221)?

It is helpful and sometimes important to forget information that is not current, like an old phone number. If we did not gradually forget information over time, our minds

**How are we better off with imperfect memories?** would be cluttered with details that we no longer need (Bjork, 2011; Bjork & Bjork, 1988). Information that is used infrequently is less likely to be needed in the future than information that is used more frequently over the same period (Anderson & Schooler, 1991, 2000). Memory, in essence, makes a bet that when we have not used information recently, we probably will not need it in the future. We win this bet more often than we lose it, making transience an adaptive property of memory. But we are acutely aware of the losses—the frustrations of forgetting—and are never aware of the wins. This is why people are often quick to complain about their memories: The drawbacks of forgetting are painfully evident, but the benefits of forgetting are hidden.

Similarly, absentmindedness and blocking can be frustrating, but they are side effects of our memory's usually successful attempt to sort through incoming information, preserving details that are worthy of attention and recall, and discarding those that are less worthy.

▲ Figure **6.18** **The Amygdala's Influence on Memory** The amygdala, located next to the hippocampus, responds strongly to emotional events. Individuals with amygdala damage are unable to remember emotional events any better than nonemotional ones (Cahill & McGaugh, 1998).

Amygdala          Hippocampus

Memory misattribution and suggestibility both occur because we often fail to recall the details of exactly when and where we saw a face or learned a fact. This is because memory is adapted to retain information that is most likely to be needed in the environment in which it operates. We seldom need to remember all the precise contextual details of every experience. Our memories carefully record such details only when we think they may be needed later, and most of the time we are better off for it. Furthermore, we often use memories to anticipate possible future events. As discussed earlier, memory is flexible, allowing us to recombine elements of past experience in new ways, so that we can mentally try out different versions of what might happen. But this very flexibility—a strength of memory—may sometimes produce misattribution errors in which elements of past experience are miscombined (Schacter & Addis, 2007; Schacter, Guerin, & St. Jacques, 2011). Bias skews our memories so that we depict ourselves in an overly favourable light, but it can produce the benefit of contributing to our overall sense of contentment. Holding positive illusions about ourselves can lead to greater psychological well-being (Taylor, 1989). Although persistence can cause us to be haunted by traumas that we would be better off forgetting, overall, it is probably adaptive to remember threatening or traumatic events that could pose a threat to survival.

Although each of the seven sins can cause trouble in our lives, they have an adaptive side as well. You can think of the seven sins as costs we pay for benefits that allow memory to work as well as it does most of the time.

## IN SUMMARY

► Memory's mistakes can be classified into seven sins.

▸ Transience is reflected by a rapid decline in memory followed by more gradual forgetting. With the passing of time, memory switches from detailed to general. Both decay and interference contribute to transience.

▸ Absentmindedness results from failures of attention, shallow encoding, and the influence of automatic behaviours, and is often associated with forgetting to do things in the future.

▸ Blocking occurs when stored information is temporarily inaccessible, as when information is on the tip of the tongue.

▸ Memory misattribution happens when we experience a sense of familiarity but do not recall, or mistakenly recall, the specifics of when and where an experience occurred. Misattribution can result in eyewitness misidentification or false recognition. Individuals suffering from frontal lobe damage are especially susceptible to false recognition.

▸ Suggestibility gives rise to implanted memories of small details or entire episodes. Suggestive techniques such as hypnosis or visualization can promote vivid recall of suggested events, and therapists' use of suggestive techniques may be responsible for some individuals' false memories of childhood traumas.

▸ Bias reflects the influence of current knowledge, beliefs, and feelings on memory or past experiences. Bias can lead us to make the past consistent with the present, exaggerate changes between past and present, or remember the past in a way that makes us look good.

▸ Persistence reflects the fact that emotional arousal generally leads to enhanced memory, whether we want to remember an experience or not. Persistence is partly attributable to the operation of hormonal systems influenced by the amygdala.

► Although each of the seven sins can cause trouble in our lives, they have an adaptive side as well. You can think of the seven sins as costs we pay for benefits that allow memory to work as well as it does most of the time.

# OTHER VOICES

## Early Memories

**Charles Fernyhough**
is a psychologist at
Durham University
in England, and the
author of several
books, including *The
Baby in the Mirror:
A Child's World from
Birth to Three* (2008).

PHOTO: LANN

n this eloquent passage from his recent book about memory, *Pieces of Light,* psychologist Charles Fernyhough (2012, pp. 1–2) described his attempt to remember the first fish that he ever caught. He comes up with what he thinks may be the answer, but how does he really know?

"Can you remember?"

It starts with a question from my 7-year-old son. We are in the grounds of our rented cottage in the Baixa Alentejo, killing time before we head to the Algarve coast for a boat trip. With his holiday money, Isaac has bought himself a hand-held toy that fires little foam rockets prodigious distances up into the air, and he has lost one of them on the graveled ground behind the swimming pool. As we search, he has been chattering away about how he wants to go fishing with me when we get home from Portugal. I have told him that I used to go fishing, as a child of about his age, with my uncle in the lake in the grounds of my grandparents' house in Essex. Then, out of the blue, he asks the question:

"Can you remember the first fish you ever caught?"

I stand straight and look out at the farmland that slopes away from our hillside vantage point. I have not been fishing in thirty-five years, but my thoughts have occasionally returned to my outings with my uncle. When they do, certain images rise out of the past. I can picture the greenish lake with its little island in the middle, how mysterious and unreachable that weeping willowed outcrop looked to my small-scale imaginings. I can sense my jocular young uncle next to me, his stretches of silence punctuated with kindly teasing. I remember the feel of the crustless bits of white bread soaked in pond water that we used to squidge on to the fish-hooks as bait, and the excitement (for a keen young amateur naturalist) of an afternoon visitation from a stoat, scurrying along by the bullrushes with its black-tipped tail bobbing. I remember the weird, faintly gruesome exercise of extracting the hook from a rudd's mouth and then throwing the muscular sliver back into the lake to restart its perforated life. But I have never thought about the moment of feeling the tug on the line, the thrill that prefigured the landing of a fish. And I have certainly not had the question framed like this, narrowing my remembering down to the first time it ever happened.

"I don't know," I reply. "I *think* so."

What accounts for my uncertainty?

Try to recall your own earliest memory of a specific event from your life: How do you know when your recollection took place? How do you know that what you are remembering is the actual event? What kind of evidence would you require to be convinced that your memory is valid? Can you think of an experiment that might be conducted to provide that evidence?

One way to address this problem is to ask people about memories for events that have clearly definable dates, such as the birth of a younger sibling, the death of a loved one, or a family move. For example, one study found that individuals can recall events surrounding the birth of a sibling that occurred when they were about 2.4 years old (Eacott & Crawley, 1998).

Do you think that firm conclusions can be drawn from these kinds of studies? Can it be that memories of these early events are based on family conversations that took place long after the events occurred? An adult or a child who remembers having ice cream in the hospital as a 3-year-old when his baby sister was born may be recalling what his parents told him after the event (see the Culture & Community box on p. 240). Carefully designed studies may bring us closer to answering the kinds of questions raised by Charles Fernyhough's response to his son's innocent question, but we still have a long way to go before we can provide convincing answers to the mysteries posed by our earliest memories.

Charles Fernyhough, *Pieces of Light: How the New Science of Memory Illuminates the Stories We Tell About Our Pasts.* London: Profile Books Ltd., 2012 / New York: Harper, 2013. Copyright © Charles Fernyhough, 2012. Reprinted by permission of the author, Profile Books Ltd., and HarperCollins Publishers.

# Chapter Review

## KEY CONCEPT QUIZ

**1.** Encoding is the process
   a. by which we transform what we perceive, think, or feel into an enduring memory.
   b. of maintaining information in memory over time.
   c. of bringing to mind information that has been previously stored.
   d. through which we recall information previously learned but forgotten.

**2.** What is the process of relating new information in a meaningful way to knowledge that is already in memory?
   a. spontaneous encoding
   b. organization encoding
   c. semantic encoding
   d. visual imagery encoding

**3.** Our human ancestors depended on the encoding of
   a. organizational information.
   b. reproductive mechanisms.
   c. survival-related information.
   d. pleasantness conditions.

**4.** What kind of memory storage holds information for a second or two?
   a. retrograde memory
   b. working memory
   c. short-term memory
   d. sensory memory

**5.** The process by which memories become stable in the brain is called
   a. consolidation.
   b. long-term memory.
   c. iconic memory.
   d. hippocampal indexing.

**6.** Long-term potentiation occurs through
   a. the interruption of communication between neurons.
   b. the strengthening of synaptic connections.
   c. the reconsolidation of disrupted memories.
   d. sleep.

**7.** The increased likelihood of recalling a sad memory when you are in a sad mood is an illustration of
   a. the encoding specificity principle.
   b. state-dependent retrieval.
   c. transfer-appropriate processing.
   d. memory accessibility.

**8.** Which of the following statements regarding the consequences of memory retrieval is false?
   a. Retrieval-induced forgetting can affect eyewitness memory.
   b. The act of retrieval can strengthen a retrieved memory.
   c. Retrieval can impair subsequent memory.
   d. Retrieval boosts subsequent memory through the repetition of information.

**9.** Neuroimaging studies suggest that *trying* to remember activates the
   a. left frontal lobe.
   b. hippocampal region.
   c. occipital lobe.
   d. upper temporal lobe.

**10.** The act of consciously or intentionally retrieving past experiences is
   a. priming.
   b. procedural memory.
   c. implicit memory.
   d. explicit memory.

**11.** People who have amnesia are able to retain all of the following except
   a. explicit memory.
   b. implicit memory.
   c. procedural memory.
   d. priming.

**12.** Remembering a family reunion that you attended as a child illustrates
   a. semantic memory.
   b. procedural memory.
   c. episodic memory.
   d. perceptual priming.

**13.** The rapid decline in memory, followed by more gradual forgetting, is reflected by
   a. chunking.
   b. blocking.
   c. absentmindedness.
   d. transience.

**14.** Eyewitness misidentification or false recognition is most likely a result of
   a. memory misattribution.
   b. suggestibility.
   c. bias.
   d. retroactive interference.

**15.** The fact that emotional arousal generally leads to enhanced memory is supported by
   a. egocentric bias.
   b. persistence.
   c. proactive interference.
   d. source memory.

## KEY TERMS

absentmindedness (p. 250)
anterograde amnesia (p. 232)
bias (p. 257)
blocking (p. 252)
chunking (p. 229)
consolidation (p. 232)
echoic memory (p. 228)
encoding (p. 222)
encoding specificity principle (p. 237)
episodic memory (p. 244)
explicit memory (p. 243)

false recognition (p. 252)
flashbulb memories (p. 258)
iconic memory (p. 228)
implicit memory (p. 243)
long-term memory (p. 230)
long-term potentiation (LTP) (p. 235)
memory (p. 222)
memory misattribution (p. 252)
organizational encoding (p. 224)
persistence (p. 257)
priming (p. 243)

proactive interference (p. 250)
procedural memory (p. 243)
prospective memory (p. 250)
reconsolidation (p. 234)
rehearsal (p. 229)
retrieval (p. 222)
retrieval-induced forgetting (p. 238)
retrieval cue (p. 237)
retroactive interference (p. 250)
retrograde amnesia (p. 232)
semantic encoding (p. 224)
semantic memory (p. 244)

sensory memory (p. 228)
short-term memory (p. 229)
source memory (p. 252)
state-dependent retrieval (p. 237)
storage (p. 222)
suggestibility (p. 255)
transfer-appropriate processing (p. 237)
transience (p. 249)
visual imagery encoding (p. 224)
working memory (p. 229)

# CHANGING MINDS

1. A friend of yours lost her father to cancer when she was a very young child. "I really wish I remembered him better," she says. "I know all the memories are locked in my head. I am thinking of trying hypnotism to unlock some of those memories." You explain that we do not, in fact, have stored memories of everything that ever happened to us locked in our heads. What examples could you give of ways in which memories can be lost over time?

2. Another friend of yours has a very vivid memory of sitting with his parents in the living room on September 11, 2001, watching live television as the Twin Towers fell in New York City during the terrorist attacks. "I remember my mother was crying," he says, "and that scared me more than the pictures on the TV." Later, he goes home for a visit and discusses the events of 9/11 with his mother—and is stunned when she assures him that he was actually in school on the morning of the attacks and was only sent home at lunchtime, after the towers had fallen. "I don't understand," he tells you afterward. "I think she must be confused, because I have a perfect memory of that morning." Assuming your friend's mother is recalling events correctly, how would you explain to your friend the ways in which his snapshot memory could be wrong? What memory sin might be at fault?

3. You ask one of your psychology classmates if she wants to form a study group to prepare for an upcoming exam. "No offence," she says,

"but I can study the material best by just reading the chapter eight or nine times, and I can do that without a study group." What is wrong with your classmate's study plan? In what ways might the members of a study group help one another learn more effectively?

4. You and a friend go to a party on campus where you meet a lot of new people. After the party, your friend says, "I liked a lot of the people we met, but I'll never remember all their names. Some people just have a good memory, and some don't, and there's nothing I can do about it." What advice could you give your friend to help him remember the names of people he meets at the next party?

5. A friend of yours who is taking a criminal justice class reads about a case in which the conviction of an accused murderer was later overturned, based on DNA evidence. "It's a travesty of justice," she says. "An eyewitness clearly identified the man by picking him out of a lineup and then identified him again in court during the trial. No results from a chemistry lab should count more than eyewitness testimony." What is your friend failing to appreciate about eyewitness testimony? What sin of memory could lead an eyewitness to honestly believe she is identifying the correct man when she is actually making a false identification?

# ANSWERS TO KEY CONCEPT QUIZ

1. a; 2. c; 3. c; 4. d; 5. a; 6. b; 7. b; 8. d; 9. a; 10. d; 11. a; 12. c; 13. d; 14. a; 15. b.

# Learning

# 7

▲ **Classical Conditioning: One Thing Leads to Another**
The Development of Classical Conditioning: Pavlov's Experiments
The Basic Principles of Classical Conditioning
THE REAL WORLD Understanding Drug Overdoses
Conditioned Emotional Responses: The Case of Little Albert
A Deeper Understanding of Classical Conditioning

▲ **Operant Conditioning: Reinforcements from the Environment**
The Development of Operant Conditioning: The Law of Effect
B. F. Skinner: The Role of Reinforcement and Punishment
CULTURE & COMMUNITY Are There Cultural Differences in Reinforcers?
The Basic Principles of Operant Conditioning
A Deeper Understanding of Operant Conditioning
HOT SCIENCE Dopamine and Reward Learning in Parkinson's Disease

▲ **Observational Learning: Look at Me**
Observational Learning in Humans
Observational Learning in Animals
Neural Elements of Observational Learning

▲ **Implicit Learning: Under the Radar**
Cognitive Approaches to Implicit Learning
Implicit and Explicit Learning Use Distinct Neural Pathways

▲ **Learning in the Classroom**
Techniques for Learning
Testing Aids Attention
Control of Learning
OTHER VOICES Online Learning

JENNIFER, A 45-YEAR-OLD MILITARY NURSE, LIVED quietly in a rural area of the United States with her spouse of 21 years and their two children before she served 19 months abroad during the Iraq war. In Iraq, she provided care to soldiers from different countries as well as to Iraqi civilians, prisoners, and militant extremists.

Jennifer served 4 months of her assignment in a prison hospital near Baghdad, where she witnessed many horrifying events. The prison was the target of relentless mortar fire, resulting in numerous deaths and serious casualties, including bloody injuries and loss of limbs. Jennifer worked 12- to 14-hour shifts, trying to avoid incoming fire while tending to some of the most gruesomely wounded cases. She frequently encountered the smell of burnt flesh and the sight of "young, mangled bodies" as part of her daily duties (Feczer & Bjorklund, 2009, p. 285).

This repetitive trauma took a toll on Jennifer, and when she returned to her home, it became evident that she had not left behind her war experiences. Jennifer thought about them repeatedly and they profoundly influenced her reactions to many aspects of everyday life. The sight of blood or the smell of cooking meat made her sick to her stomach, to the point that she had to stop eating meat. The previously innocent sound of a helicopter approaching, which in Iraq signalled that new wounded bodies were about to arrive, now created in Jennifer heightened feelings of fear and anxiety. She regularly awoke from nightmares concerning the most troubling aspects of her Iraq experiences, such as tending to soldiers with multiple amputations. In the words of the authors who described her case, Jennifer was "forever changed" by her Iraq experiences (Feczer & Bjorklund, 2009). And that is one reason why Jennifer's story is a compelling, although disturbing, introduction to the topic of learning.

Much of what happened to Jennifer after she returned to her home reflects the operation of a kind of learning based on association. Sights, sounds, and smells in Iraq had become associated with negative emotions in a way that created an enduring bond, so that encountering similar sights, sounds, and smells at home elicited similarly intense negative feelings.

During the 4 months that she served at a prison hospital near Baghdad during the Iraq war, Jennifer learned to associate the sound of an arriving helicopter with wounded bodies. That learned association had a long-lasting influence on her.

AP PHOTO/JOHN MOORE

How might psychologists use the concept of habituation to explain the fact that today's action movies tend to show much more graphic violence than movies of the 1980s, which in turn tended to show more graphic violence than movies of the 1950s?

**LEARNING IS SHORTHAND FOR A COLLECTION OF DIFFERENT TECHNIQUES,** procedures, and outcomes that produce changes in an organism's behaviour. Learning psychologists have identified and studied as many as 40 different kinds of learning. However, there is a basic principle at the core of all of them. **Learning** involves *the acquisition of new knowledge, skills, or responses from experience that results in a relatively permanent change in the state of the learner.* This definition emphasizes these key ideas:

> Learning is based on experience.
> Learning produces changes in the organism.
> These changes are relatively permanent.

Think about Jennifer's time in Iraq and you will see all of these elements: Experiences such as the association between the sound of an approaching helicopter and the arrival of wounded bodies changed the way Jennifer responded to certain situations in a way that lasted for years.

Learning can also occur in much simpler, nonassociative forms. You are probably familiar with the phenomenon of **habituation,** *a general process in which repeated or prolonged exposure to a stimulus results in a gradual reduction in responding.* If you have ever lived under the flight path of your local airport, near railroad tracks, or by a busy highway, you have probably noticed the deafening roar as a Boeing 737 made its way toward the landing strip, the clatter of a train speeding down the track, or the sound of traffic when you first moved in. After a while, the roar was not quite so deafening anymore and eventually you probably no longer noticed the sounds of the planes, trains, or automobiles in your vicinity. This welcome reduction in responding reflects the operation of habituation.

Habituation occurs even in the simplest organisms. For example, in the Memory chapter you learned about the sea slug *Aplysia*, studied in detail by Nobel Prize winner Eric Kandel (2006). Kandel and his colleagues showed clearly that *Aplysia* exhibits habituation: When lightly touched, the sea slug initially withdraws its gill, but the response gradually weakens after repeated light touches. In addition, *Aplysia* exhibits another simple form of learning known as **sensitization,** which occurs when *presentation of a noxious stimulus leads to an increased response to a later stimulus.* For example, Kandel found that after receiving a strong shock, *Aplysia* showed an increased gill withdrawal response to a light touch. In a similar manner, people whose houses have been broken into may later become hypersensitive to late-night sounds that would not have bothered them previously.

Although these simple kinds of learning are important, in this chapter we will focus on more complex kinds of learning that psychologists have studied intensively. As you will recall from the Psychology: Evolution of a Science chapter, a sizable chunk of psychology's history was devoted to behaviourism, with its insistence on measuring only observable, quantifiable behaviour and its dismissal of mental activity as irrelevant and unknowable. Behaviourism was the major outlook of most psychologists working from the 1930s through the 1950s, the period during which most of the fundamental work on learning theory took place.

You might find the intersection of behaviourism and learning theory a bit surprising. After all, at one level learning seems abstract: Something intangible happens to you, and you think or behave differently thereafter. It seems logical that you would need to explain that transformation in terms of a change in mental outlook. However, most behaviourists argued that learning's "permanent change in experience" could be demonstrated equally well in almost any organism: rats, dogs, pigeons, mice, pigs, or humans. From this perspective, behaviourists viewed learning as a purely behavioural activity requiring no mental activity.

In many ways the behaviourists were right. Much of what we know about how organisms learn comes directly from the behaviourists' observations of behaviours. However, they also overstated their case. There are some important cognitive considerations (i.e., elements of mental activity) that need to be addressed in order to understand the learning process. In the first two sections of this chapter, we will discuss the development and basic principles of two major approaches to learning: classical conditioning and operant conditioning. We will then move on to see that some important kinds of learning occur simply by watching others, and that such observational learning plays an important role in the cultural transmission of behaviour. Next, we will discover that some kinds of learning can occur entirely outside of awareness. Finally, we will discuss learning in a context that should matter a lot to you: the classroom.

# Classical Conditioning: One Thing Leads to Another

American psychologist John B. Watson kick-started the behaviourist movement, arguing that psychologists should "never use the terms *consciousness, mental states, mind, content, introspectively verifiable, imagery,* and the like" (Watson, 1913, p. 166). Watson's firebrand stance was fuelled in large part by the work of a Russian physiologist, Ivan Pavlov (1849–1936).

Pavlov was awarded the Nobel Prize in Physiology in 1904 for his work on the salivation of dogs. Pavlov studied the digestive processes of laboratory animals by surgically implanting test tubes into the cheeks of dogs to measure their salivary responses to different kinds of foods. Serendipitously, his explorations into spit and drool revealed the mechanics of one form of learning, which came to be called classical conditioning. **Classical conditioning** occurs *when a neutral stimulus produces a response after being paired with a stimulus that naturally produces a response.* In his classic experiments, Pavlov showed that dogs learned to salivate to neutral stimuli such as a bell or a tone after that stimulus had been associated with another stimulus that naturally evokes salivation, such as food.

## The Development of Classical Conditioning: Pavlov's Experiments

Pavlov's basic experimental setup involved cradling dogs in a harness to administer the foods and to measure the salivary response, as shown in **FIGURE 7.1**. He noticed that dogs that had previously been in the experiment began to produce a kind of "anticipatory" salivary response as soon as they were put in the harness, before any food was presented. Pavlov and his colleagues regarded these responses as annoyances at first because they interfered with collecting naturally occurring salivary secretions. In reality, the dogs were behaving in line with the four basic elements of classical conditioning:

> When the dogs were initially presented with a plate of food, they began to salivate. No surprise here—placing food in front of most animals will launch the salivary process. Pavlov called the presentation of food an **unconditioned stimulus (US),** *something that reliably produces a naturally occurring reaction in an organism.*

> He called the dogs' salivation an **unconditioned response (UR),** *a reflexive reaction that is reliably produced by an unconditioned stimulus.*

**learning**
The acquisition of new knowledge, skills, or responses from experience that results in a relatively permanent change in the state of the learner.

**habituation**
A general process in which repeated or prolonged exposure to a stimulus results in a gradual reduction in responding.

**sensitization**
A simple form of learning that occurs when presentation of a noxious stimulus leads to an increased response to a later stimulus.

**classical conditioning**
A type of learning that occurs when a neutral stimulus produces a response after being paired with a stimulus that naturally produces a response.

**unconditioned stimulus (US)**
Something that reliably produces a naturally occurring reaction in an organism.

**unconditioned response (UR)**
A reflexive reaction that is reliably produced by an unconditioned stimulus.

▼ Figure **7.1** **Pavlov's Apparatus for Studying Classical Conditioning** Pavlov presented auditory stimuli to the animals using a bell or a tuning fork. Visual stimuli could be presented on the screen.

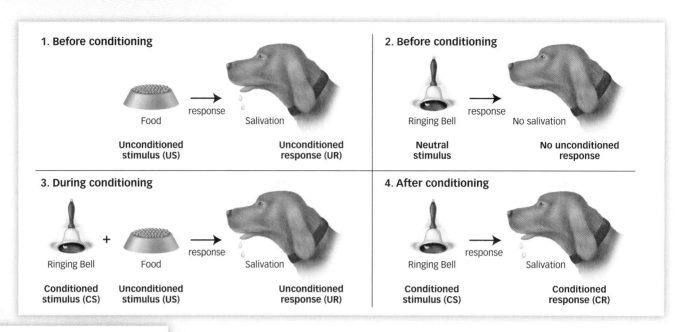

1. Before conditioning

Food → response → Salivation

Unconditioned stimulus (US) → Unconditioned response (UR)

2. Before conditioning

Ringing Bell → response → No salivation

Neutral stimulus → No unconditioned response

3. During conditioning

Ringing Bell + Food → response → Salivation

Conditioned stimulus (CS)   Unconditioned stimulus (US) → Unconditioned response (UR)

4. After conditioning

Ringing Bell → response → Salivation

Conditioned stimulus (CS) → Conditioned response (CR)

▲ Figure 7.2 **The Elements of Classical Conditioning** In classical conditioning, a previously neutral stimulus (such as the sound of a bell) is paired with an unconditioned stimulus (such as the presentation of food). After several trials associating the two, the conditioned stimulus (the sound) alone can produce a conditioned response.

**conditioned stimulus (CS)**
A previously neutral stimulus that produces a reliable response in an organism after being paired with a US.

**conditioned response (CR)**
A reaction that resembles an unconditioned response but is produced by a CS.

**acquisition**
The phase of classical conditioning when the CS and the US are presented together.

**second-order conditioning**
Conditioning where a new, neutral CS is paired with a stimulus that became associated with the US in an earlier procedure.

> Pavlov soon discovered that he could make the dogs salivate to neutral stimuli, things that do not usually make animals salivate such as the ringing of a bell. In various experiments, Pavlov paired the presentation of food with the sound of a bell, the ticking of a metronome, the humming of a tuning fork, or the flash of a light (Pavlov, 1927). Sure enough, he found that the dogs salivated to these sounds and flashes, each of which had become a **conditioned stimulus (CS),** *a previously neutral stimulus that produces a reliable response in an organism after being paired with a US* (see **FIGURE 7.2**).

> Nothing in nature would make a dog salivate to the sound of a bell. However, when the CS (the sound of a bell) is paired over time with the US (the food), the animal will learn to associate food with the sound and eventually the CS alone is sufficient to produce a response, or salivation. This response resembles the UR, but Pavlov called it the **conditioned response (CR),** *a reaction that resembles an unconditioned response but is produced by a CS.* In this example, the dogs' salivation (CR) was eventually prompted by the sound of the bell (CS) alone because the sound of the bell and the food (US) had been associated so often in the past.

Consider your own dog (or cat). Does your dog always know when her dinner is coming, preparing just short of pulling up a chair and tucking a napkin into her collar? It is as though she has one eye on the clock every day, waiting for the dinner hour. Alas, your dog is no clock-watching wonder hound. Instead, the presentation of food (the US) has become associated with a complex CS—your getting up, moving into the kitchen, opening the cabinet, working the can opener—such that the CS alone signals to your dog that food is on the way and therefore initiates the CR of her getting ready to eat.

**Why do some dogs seem to know when it is dinnertime?**

## The Basic Principles of Classical Conditioning

When Pavlov's findings first appeared in the scientific and popular literature (Pavlov, 1923a, 1923b), they produced a flurry of excitement because psychologists now had demonstrable evidence of how conditioning produced learned behaviours. This was the kind of behaviourist psychology John B. Watson was proposing: An organism experiences events or stimuli that are observable and measurable, and changes in that organism can be directly observed and measured. Dogs learned to salivate to the sound of a buzzer, and there was no need to resort to explanations about why it had happened, what the dog wanted, or how the animal thought about the situation. In other words, there was no need to consider the mind in this classical conditioning paradigm, and this appealed to Watson and the behaviourists. Pavlov also appreciated the significance of his discovery and embarked on a systematic investigation of the mechanisms of classical conditioning. Let us take a closer look at some of these principles. (As The Real World box shows, these principles help explain how drug overdoses occur.)

## Acquisition

Remember when you first got your dog? Chances are she did not seem too smart, especially the way she stared at you vacantly as you went into the kitchen, not anticipating that food was on the way. That is because learning through classical conditioning requires some period of association between the CS and US. This period is called **acquisition,** *the phase of classical conditioning when the CS and the US are presented together.* During the initial phase of classical conditioning, typically there is a gradual increase in learning: It starts low, rises rapidly, and then slowly tapers off, as shown on the left side of **FIGURE 7.3.** Pavlov's dogs gradually increased their amount of salivation over several trials of pairing a tone with the presentation of food, and similarly, your dog eventually learned to associate your kitchen preparations with the subsequent appearance of food. After learning has been established, *the CS by itself will reliably elicit the CR.*

## Second-Order Conditioning

After conditioning has been established, a phenomenon called **second-order conditioning** can be demonstrated: *conditioning where a new, neutral CS is paired with a stimulus that became associated with the US in an earlier procedure.* For example, in an early study Pavlov repeatedly paired a new CS, a black square, with the now reliable tone. After a number of training trials, his dogs produced a salivary response to the black square even though the square itself had never been directly associated with the food. Second-order conditioning helps explain why some people desire money to the point that they hoard it and value it even more than the objects it purchases.

"I THINK MOM'S USING THE CAN OPENER."

◀ Figure **7.3 Acquisition, Extinction, and Spontaneous Recovery** In classical conditioning, the CS is originally neutral and produces no specific response. After several trials pairing the CS with the US, the CS alone comes to elicit the salivary response (the CR). Learning tends to take place fairly rapidly and then levels off as stable responding develops. In extinction, the CR diminishes quickly until it no longer occurs. A rest period, however, is typically followed by spontaneous recovery of the CR. In fact, a well-learned CR may show spontaneous recovery after more than one rest period even though there have been no additional learning trials.

Money is initially used to purchase objects that produce gratifying outcomes, such as an expensive car. Although money is not directly associated with the thrill of a drive in a new sports car, it is directly associated with CSs that result in gratifying outcomes (like a sports car, a new smart phone, or a movie channel subscription). Such repeated exposure means that, eventually, money is desirable for its own sake.

## Extinction and Spontaneous Recovery

After Pavlov and his colleagues had explored the process of acquisition extensively, they turned to the next logical question: What would happen if they continued to present the CS (tone) but stopped presenting the US (food)? As shown on the right

**THE REAL WORLD**

# Understanding Drug Overdoses

All too often, police are confronted with a perplexing and tragic problem: the sudden death of addicts from a drug overdose. These deaths are puzzling for at least three reasons: The victims are often experienced drug users; the dose taken is usually not larger than what they usually take; and the deaths tend to occur in unusual settings. Experienced drug users are just that: experienced! So, you would think that the chances of an overdose would be lower than usual.

McMaster neuroscientist Shepard Siegel realized that classical conditioning provides some insight into how these deaths occur. First, when classical conditioning takes place, the CS is more than a simple bell or tone: It also includes the overall *context* within which the conditioning takes place. Indeed, Pavlov's dogs often began to salivate even as they approached the experimental apparatus. Second, many CRs are compensatory reactions to the US. Heroin, for example, slows down a person's breathing rate, so the body responds with a compensatory reaction that speeds up breathing in order to maintain a state of balance or homeostasis, a critically important CR.

These two finer points of classical conditioning help explain the apparent paradox of fatal heroin overdoses in experienced drug users (Siegel, 1984, 2005). When the drug is injected, the entire setting (the drug paraphernalia, the room, the lighting, the addict's usual companions) functions as the CS, and the addict's brain reacts to the heroin by secreting neurotransmitters that counteract its effects. Over time, this protective physiological response becomes

part of the CR, and like all CRs, it occurs in the presence of the CS but prior to the actual administration of the drug. These compensatory physiological reactions are also what make drug abusers take increasingly larger doses to achieve the same effect. Ultimately, these reactions produce *drug tolerance*, discussed in the Consciousness chapter.

These principles of classical conditioning can explain why taking drugs in a new environment can be fatal for a longtime drug user. If an addict injects the usual dose in a setting that is sufficiently novel or where heroin has never been taken before, the CS is now altered, so that the physiological compensatory CR that usually serves a protective function either does not occur or is substantially decreased (Siegel et al., 2000). As a result, the addict's usual dose becomes an overdose and death often results. Intuitively, addicts may stick with the crack houses, opium dens, or "shooting galleries" with which they are familiar for just this reason. Overdose in unfamiliar environments has also been shown experimentally: Rats that have had extensive experience with morphine in one setting

were much more likely to survive dose increases in that same setting than in a novel one (Siegel, 1976; Siegel et al., 2000). This same basic effect occurs with a variety of drugs. For example, university students show less tolerance for the intoxicating effects of alcohol when they consume it in the presence of a novel cue (a peppermint-flavoured drink) than a familiar one (a beer-flavoured drink) (Siegel, 2005).

Understanding these principles has had its benefits. For example, the brain's compensatory response to a drug, when elicited by the familiar contextual cues ordinarily associated with drug taking that constitute the CS, can be experienced by the addict as withdrawal symptoms. In *cue exposure therapies*, an addict is exposed to drug-related cues without being given the usual dose of the drug itself, eventually resulting in extinction of the association between the contextual cues and the effects of the drug. After such treatment, encountering familiar drug-related cues will no longer result in the compensatory response linked to withdrawal symptoms, thereby making it easier for a recovering addict to remain abstinent (Siegel, 2005).

◄ Although publicly funded drug-injection facilities are controversial, they are safe places for addicts to use drugs. In addition to providing clean needles and access to health care, the consistent environment becomes part of the addict's CS. Without such legal sites (like this one in Vancouver), addicts may be pushed to use drugs in new situations when illegal sites are closed down, contributing to fatalities.

CP IMAGES/DARRYL DYCK

side of the first panel in Figure 7.3, behaviour declines abruptly and continues to drop until eventually the dog ceases to salivate to the sound of the tone. This process is called **extinction,** *the gradual elimination of a learned response that occurs when the CS is repeatedly presented without the US.* The term was introduced because the conditioned response is "extinguished" and no longer observed.

> **How does conditioned behaviour change when the unconditioned stimulus is removed?**

Having established that he could produce learning through conditioning and then extinguish it, Pavlov wondered if this elimination of conditioned behaviour was permanent. Is a single session of extinction sufficient to knock out the CR completely, or is there some residual change in the dog's behaviour so that the CR might reappear? To explore this question, Pavlov extinguished the classically conditioned salivation response and then allowed the dogs to have a short rest period. When they were brought back to the lab and presented with the CS again, they displayed **spontaneous recovery,** *the tendency of a learned behaviour to recover from extinction after a rest period.* This phenomenon is shown in the middle panel in Figure 7.3. Notice that this recovery takes place even though there have not been any additional presentations of the CS and US. Some spontaneous recovery of the conditioned response even takes place in what is essentially a second extinction session after another period of rest (see the right-hand panel in Figure 7.3). Clearly, extinction had not completely erased the learning that had been acquired. The ability of the CS to elicit the CR was weakened, but it was not eliminated.

## Generalization and Discrimination

If you get a new can opener, do you think your dog will be stumped, unable to anticipate the presentation of her food? Will a whole new round of conditioning need to be established with this modified CS?

Probably not. It would not be very adaptive for an organism if each little change in the CS–US pairing required an extensive regimen of new learning. Rather, the phenomenon of **generalization** tends to take place: *The CR is elicited even though the stimulus is slightly different from the CS used during acquisition.* This means that the conditioning generalizes to stimuli that are similar to the CS used during the original training. As you might expect, the more the new stimulus changes, the less conditioned responding is observed. If you replaced a manual can opener with an electric can opener, your dog would probably show a much weaker conditioned response (Pearce, 1987; Rescorla, 2006).

> **How can a change in can opener affect a conditioned dog's response?**

When an organism generalizes to a new stimulus, two things are happening. First, by responding to the new stimulus used during generalization testing, the organism demonstrates that it recognizes the similarity between the original CS and the new stimulus. Second, by displaying *diminished* responding to that new stimulus, it also tells us that it notices a difference between the two stimuli. In the second case, the organism shows **discrimination,** *the capacity to distinguish between similar but distinct stimuli.* Generalization and discrimination are two sides of the same coin. The more organisms show one, the less they show the other, and training can modify the balance between the two.

**extinction**
The gradual elimination of a learned response that occurs when the CS is repeatedly presented without the US.

**spontaneous recovery**
The tendency of a learned behaviour to recover from extinction after a rest period.

**generalization**
The CR is elicited even though the stimulus is slightly different from the CS used during acquisition.

**discrimination**
The capacity to distinguish between similar but distinct stimuli.

Your first electric can opener may cause your dog some confusion, but likely only for a little while.

GVICTORIA/SHUTTERSTOCK

## Conditioned Emotional Responses: The Case of Little Albert

Before you conclude that classical conditioning is merely a sophisticated way to train your dog, let us revisit the larger principles of Pavlov's work. Classical conditioning demonstrates that durable, substantial changes in behaviour can be achieved simply by setting up the proper conditions. It was this kind of simplicity that appealed to behaviourists. In fact, Watson and his followers thought that it was possible to develop general explanations of pretty much *any* behaviour of *any* organism based on classical conditioning principles. As a step in that direction, Watson embarked on a controversial study with his research assistant Rosalie Rayner (Watson & Rayner, 1920). To support his contention that even complex behaviours were the result of conditioning, Watson enlisted the assistance of 9-month-old "Little Albert." Albert was a healthy, well-developed child, and, by Watson's assessment, "stolid and unemotional" (Watson & Rayner, 1920, p. 1). Watson wanted to see if such a child could be classically conditioned to experience a strong emotional reaction, namely, fear.

Watson presented Little Albert with a variety of stimuli: a white rat, a dog, a rabbit, various masks, and a burning newspaper. Albert's reactions in most cases were curiosity or indifference, and he showed no fear of any of the items. Watson also established that something *could* make him afraid. While Albert was watching Rayner, Watson unexpectedly struck a large steel bar with a hammer, producing a loud noise. Predictably, this caused Albert to cry, tremble, and be generally displeased.

Watson and Rayner then led Little Albert through the acquisition phase of classical conditioning. Albert was presented with a white rat. As soon as he reached out to touch it, the steel bar was struck. This pairing occurred again and again over several trials. Eventually, the sight of the rat alone caused Albert to recoil in terror, crying and clamouring to get away from it. In this situation, a US (the loud sound) was paired with a CS (the presence of the rat) such that the CS all

> **Why did Albert fear the rat?**

by itself was sufficient to produce the CR (a fearful reaction). Little Albert also showed stimulus generalization. The sight of a white rabbit, a seal-fur coat, and a Santa Claus mask produced the same kinds of fear reactions in the infant.

What was Watson's goal in all this? First, he wanted to show that a relatively complex reaction could be conditioned using Pavlovian techniques. Second, he wanted to show that emotional responses such as fear and anxiety could be produced by classical conditioning and therefore need not be the product of deeper unconscious processes or early life experiences as Freud and his followers had argued (see the Psychology: Evolution of a Science chapter). Instead, Watson proposed that fears could be learned, just like any other behaviour. Third, Watson wanted to confirm that conditioning could be applied to humans as well as to other animals. This study was controversial in its cavalier treatment of a young child, especially given that Watson and Rayner did not follow up with Albert or his mother during the ensuing years (Harris, 1979). Modern ethical guidelines that govern the treatment of research participants ensure that this kind of study could not be conducted today. At the time, however, it was consistent with a behaviourist view of psychology.

The kind of conditioned fear responses that were at work in Little Albert's case were also important in the case of Jennifer, who, as described in the opening story, experienced fear and anxiety when hearing the previously innocent sound of an approaching helicopter as a result of her experiences in Iraq. If Jennifer has learned to associate fear and anxiety with previously neutral stimuli (so that they are now CSs) perhaps an effective treatment would be to help her learn to associate those CSs with safety and comfort? Indeed, a therapy that has proven effective in dealing with such trauma-induced fears is based directly on principles of classical conditioning:

John Watson and Rosalie Rayner show Little Albert an unusual bunny mask. Why does the mere presence of these experimenters not serve as a conditioned stimulus in itself?

What response do you think the manufacturers of Royale bathroom tissue are looking for when they feature kittens on their packaging?

Individuals are repeatedly exposed to conditioned stimuli associated with their trauma in a safe setting in an attempt to extinguish the conditioned fear response (Bouton, 1988; Rothbaum & Schwartz, 2002). However, conditioned emotional responses include much more than just fear and anxiety responses. Advertisers, for example, understand that conditioned emotional responses can include various kinds of positive emotions that they would like potential customers to associate with their products, which may be why attractive women are commonly involved in advertisements for products geared toward young males, including beer and sports cars. Just as money becomes desirable through second-order conditioning (by association with other desirable things) so do advertisers hope that their products become desirable through association with other desirable things. The warm and fuzzy feeling that envelops you when watching playful kittens in a bathroom tissue commercial represents a type of conditioned emotional response.

## A Deeper Understanding of Classical Conditioning

As a form of learning, classical conditioning could be reliably produced: It had a simple set of principles and applications to real-life situations. In short, classical conditioning offered a good deal of utility for psychologists who sought to understand the mechanisms underlying learning, and it continues to do so today.

Since the time of Pavlov, though, classical conditioning has been subjected to deeper scrutiny in order to understand exactly how, when, and why it works. Let us examine three areas that give us a closer look at the mechanisms of classical conditioning: the cognitive, neural, and evolutionary elements.

### The Cognitive Elements of Classical Conditioning

As we have seen, Pavlov's work was a behaviourist's dream come true. In this view, conditioning is something that *happens* to a dog, a rat, or a person, apart from what the organism thinks about the conditioning situation. However, although the dogs salivated when their feeders approached (see Psychology: Evolution of a Science), they did not salivate when Pavlov did. Eventually someone was bound to ask an important question: *Why not?* After all, Pavlov also delivered the food to the dogs, so why did he not become a CS? Indeed, if Watson was present whenever the unpleasant US was sounded, why did Little Albert not come to fear *him*?

Somehow, Pavlov's dogs were sensitive to the fact that Pavlov was not a *reliable* indicator of the arrival of food. Pavlov was linked with the arrival of food, but he was also linked with other activities that had nothing to do with food, including checking on the apparatus, bringing the dog from the kennel to the laboratory, and standing around and talking with his assistants.

Robert Rescorla and Allan Wagner (1972) were the first to theorize that classical conditioning occurs when an animal has learned to set up an *expectation*. The sound of a bell, because of its systematic pairing with food, served to set up this cognitive state for the laboratory dogs; Pavlov, because of the lack of any reliable link with food, did not. In fact, in situations such as this, many responses are actually being conditioned. When the bell sounds, the dogs also wag their tails, make begging sounds, and look toward the food source (Jenkins et al., 1978). In short, what is really happening is something like the situation shown in **FIGURE 7.4.**

▼ Figure **7.4** **Expectation in Classical Conditioning** In the Rescorla–Wagner model of classical conditioning, a CS serves to set up an expectation. The expectation in turn leads to an array of behaviours associated with the presence of the CS.

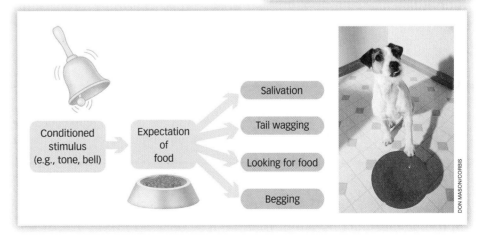

The Rescorla–Wagner model introduced a cognitive component that accounted for a variety of classical conditioning phenomena that were difficult to understand from a simple behaviourist point of view. For example, the model predicted that conditioning would be easier when the CS was an *unfamiliar* event than when it was familiar. The reason is that familiar events, being familiar, already have expectations associated with them, making new conditioning difficult. In short, classical conditioning might appear to be a primitive process, but it is actually quite sophisticated and incorporates a significant cognitive element.

> How does the role of expectation in conditioning challenge behaviourist ideas?

One issue that arises from this cognitive view of classical conditioning concerns the role of consciousness. In the Rescorla–Wagner model, the cognitive elements are not necessarily conscious. Rather, they likely reflect the operation of nonconscious associative mechanisms that do more than just record co-occurrences of events: They link those co-occurrences to prior experiences, generating an expectation. Studies of classical conditioning in humans indicate that conditioning can occur without conscious awareness of the relationship between the CS and US. The exception is when special conditioning procedures are used in which a brief time interval is inserted between the CS and the US. Under these circumstances, consciousness of the relationship between the CS and US appears to be necessary for conditioning to occur (Clark, Manns, & Squire, 2002; Clark & Squire, 1998). However, even the tiny sea slug *Aplysia* exhibits some evidence for this kind of conditioning, and scientists do not believe that *Aplysia* is capable of consciousness. After all, conditioning in *Aplysia* involves just a few neurons, as opposed to millions of neurons and complex brain systems in humans (Bekinschtein et al., 2011). This observation reminds us that even though there are many cross-species similarities in classical conditioning, there are also differences.

## The Neural Elements of Classical Conditioning

Pavlov saw his research as providing insights into how the brain works. After all, he was trained in medicine, not psychology, and was a bit surprised when psychologists became excited by his findings. Recent research has clarified some of what Pavlov hoped to understand about conditioning and the brain.

A series of pioneering experiments conducted across several decades by Richard Thompson and his colleagues focused on classical conditioning of eyeblink responses in the rabbit. In the most basic type of eyeblink conditioning, the CS (a tone) is immediately followed by the US (a puff of air), which elicits a reflexive eyeblink response. After many CS–US pairings, the eyeblink response occurs in response to the CS alone. Thompson and colleagues showed convincingly that the cerebellum is critical for the occurrence of eyeblink conditioning (Thompson, 2005). Studies of people with lesions to the cerebellum supported these findings by demonstrating impaired eyeblink conditioning (Daum et al., 1993). Rounding out the picture, more recent neuroimaging findings in healthy young adults show activation in the cerebellum during the eyeblink conditioning (Cheng et al., 2008). As you learned in the Neuroscience and Behaviour chapter, the cerebellum is part of the hindbrain and plays an important role in motor skills and learning.

In addition to eyeblink conditioning, fear conditioning has been extensively studied. Also in the Neuroscience and Behaviour chapter, you saw that the amygdala plays an important role in the experience of emotion, including fear and anxiety. So, it should come as no surprise that the amygdala, particularly an area known as the *central nucleus*, is also critical for emotional conditioning.

Consider a rat who is conditioned to a series of CS–US pairings where the CS is a tone and the US is a mild electric shock. When rats experience sudden painful stimuli in nature, they show a defensive reaction, known as *freezing*, where they crouch down and sit motionless. In addition, their autonomic nervous systems go to work: Heart rate and blood pressure increase, and various hormones associated with stress are released. When fear conditioning takes place, these two components—one behavioural and one physiological—occur, except that now they are elicited by the CS.

The central nucleus of the amygdala plays a role in producing both of these outcomes through two distinct connections with other parts of the brain. If connections

**What is the role of the amygdala in fear conditioning?**

linking the amygdala to the midbrain are disrupted, the rat does not exhibit the behavioural freezing response. If the connections between the amygdala and the hypothalamus are severed, the autonomic responses associated with fear cease (LeDoux et al., 1988). Hence, the action of the amygdala is an essential element in fear conditioning, and its links with other areas of the brain are responsible for producing specific features of conditioning. The amygdala is involved in fear conditioning in people as well as rats and other animals (Olsson & Phelps, 2007; Phelps & LeDoux, 2005).

## The Evolutionary Elements of Classical Conditioning

In addition to this cognitive component, evolutionary mechanisms also play an important role in classical conditioning. As you learned in the Psychology: Evolution of a Science chapter, evolution and natural selection go hand in hand with adaptiveness: Behaviours that are adaptive allow an organism to survive and thrive in its environment. In the case of classical conditioning, psychologists began to appreciate how this type of learning could have adaptive value. Much research exploring this adaptiveness has focused on conditioned food aversions.

Consider this example: A psychology professor was once on a job interview in Southern California, and his hosts took him to lunch at a Middle Eastern restaurant. Suffering from a case of bad hummus, he was up all night long, and developed a lifelong aversion to hummus.

On the face of it, this looks like a case of classical conditioning. The hummus was the CS, a bacterium or some other source of toxicity was the US, and the resulting nausea was the UR. The UR (the nausea) became linked to the once-neutral CS (the hummus) and became a CR (an aversion to hummus). But there are several peculiar aspects to this case. The psychologist's hosts also ate the hummus, yet none of them reported feeling ill. It is not clear, then, what the US was; it could not have been anything that was actually in the food. Furthermore, the time between the hummus and the distress was several hours; classical conditioning of a CR typically requires that the CS occurs at the same time as the UR (or only very shortly before it). Most baffling, this aversion was cemented with a single acquisition trial. Usually it takes several pairings of a CS and UR to establish learning.

These peculiarities are not so peculiar from an evolutionary perspective. Any species that forages or consumes a variety of foods needs to develop a mechanism by which it can learn to avoid any food that once made it ill. To have adaptive value, this mechanism should have several properties:

> There should be rapid learning that occurs in perhaps one or two trials. If learning takes more trials than this, the animal could die from eating a toxic substance.

> Conditioning should be able to take place over very long intervals, perhaps up to 12–24 hours. Toxic substances often do not cause illness immediately, so the organism would need to form an association between the food and the illness over a longer term.

> The organism should develop the aversion to the smell or taste of the food rather than its ingestion. It is more adaptive to reject a potentially toxic substance based on smell alone than it is to ingest it.

© PAULCOWAN DREAMSTIME.COM

Under certain conditions, people may develop food aversions. This serving of hummus looks inviting and probably tastes delicious, but at least one psychologist avoids it like the plague.

**biological preparedness**
A propensity for learning particular kinds of associations over others.

> Learned aversions should occur more often with novel foods than familiar ones. It is not adaptive for an animal to develop an aversion to everything it has eaten on the particular day it got sick. Our psychologist friend did not develop an aversion to the pop he drank with lunch or the scrambled eggs he had for breakfast that day; however, the sight and smell of hummus do make him uneasy.

John Garcia and his colleagues illustrated the adaptiveness of classical conditioning in a series of studies with rats (Garcia & Koelling, 1966). They used a variety of CSs (visual, auditory, tactile, taste, and smell) and several different USs (injection of a toxic substance, radiation) that caused nausea and vomiting hours later. The researchers found weak or no conditioning when the CS was a visual, auditory, or tactile stimulus, but a strong food aversion developed with stimuli that have a distinct taste and smell.

Indeed, this feature of conditioned taste aversion has been used to deal with an unanticipated side effect of radiation and chemotherapy. Cancer patients who experience nausea from their treatments often develop aversions to foods they ate before the therapy. Broberg and Bernstein (1987) reasoned that a simple technique should minimize the negative consequences of this effect. They gave their patients an unusual food (coconut- or root-beer–flavoured candy) at the end of the last meal before undergoing treatment. Sure enough, the conditioned food aversions that the patients developed were overwhelmingly for one of the unusual flavours and not for any of the other foods in the meal. Other than any root beer or coconut fans among the sample, patients were spared developing aversions to common foods that they were more likely to eat.

> **How has cancer patients' discomfort been eased by our understanding of food aversions?**

Studies such as these suggest that evolution has provided each species with a kind of **biological preparedness,** *a propensity for learning particular kinds of associations over others*, so that some behaviours are relatively easy to condition in some species but not others. For example, the taste and smell stimuli that produce food aversions in rats do not work with most species of birds. Birds depend primarily on visual cues for finding food and are relatively insensitive to taste and smell. However, as you might guess, it is relatively easy to produce a food aversion in birds using an unfamiliar visual stimulus as the CS, such as a brightly coloured food (Wilcoxon, Dragoin, & Kral, 1971). Indeed, most researchers agree that conditioning works best with stimuli that are biologically relevant to the organism (Domjan, 2005).

Rats can be difficult to poison because of learned taste aversions, which are an evolutionarily adaptive element of classical conditioning. Here a worker tries his best in the sewers of Paris.

BOYER/ROGER VIOLLET/GETTY IMAGES

## IN SUMMARY

▶ Classical conditioning can be thought of as an exercise in pairing a neutral stimulus with a meaningful event or stimulus. Ivan Pavlov's initial work paired a neutral tone (a conditioned stimulus) with a meaningful act: the presentation of food to a hungry animal (an unconditioned stimulus). As he and others demonstrated, the pairing of a CS and US during the acquisition phase of classical conditioning eventually allows the CS, all by itself, to elicit a response called a conditioned response (CR).

▶ Classical conditioning was embraced by behaviourists such as John B. Watson, who viewed it as providing a foundation for a model of human behaviour. As a behaviourist, Watson believed that no higher-level functions, such as thinking or awareness, needed to be invoked to understand behaviour.

▶ Later researchers showed, however, the underlying mechanism of classical conditioning turned out to be more complex (and more interesting) than the simple association between a CS and a US. Classical conditioning involves setting up expectations and is sensitive to the degree to which the CS functions as a genuine predictor of the US, indicating that classical conditioning can involve some degree of cognition.

▶ The cerebellum plays an important role in eyeblink conditioning, whereas the amygdala is important for fear conditioning.

▶ The evolutionary aspects of classical conditioning show that each species is biologically predisposed to acquire particular CS–US associations based on its evolutionary history. In short, classical conditioning is not an arbitrary mechanism that merely forms associations. Rather, it is a sophisticated mechanism that evolved precisely because it has adaptive value.

# Operant Conditioning: Reinforcements from the Environment

The study of classical conditioning is the study of behaviours that are already in an organism's repertoire. The animal already *knows how* to salivate, or feel anxious, fearful, or nauseated. Classical conditioning allows these behaviours to be triggered by new stimuli in the environment, but does not change the form of the behaviour. Classical conditioning is all about the stimuli (like CSs and USs) that come before a response and trigger it; it has nothing to say about how stimuli that come *after* a response (such as rewards, and punishments) might exert control over behaviour. So how does an animal learn new behaviours?

We turn now to a different form of learning: **operant conditioning,** *a type of learning in which the consequences of an organism's behaviour determine the likelihood of that behaviour being repeated in the future.* The study of operant conditioning is the exploration of the powerful effects of reward and punishment on behaviour.

## The Development of Operant Conditioning: The Law of Effect

The study of how active behaviour affects the environment began at about the same time as classical conditioning. In fact, Edward L. Thorndike (1874–1949) first examined active behaviours back in the 1890s, before Pavlov published his findings. Thorndike's research focused on *instrumental behaviours*; that is, behaviour that required an organism to *do* something, solve a problem, or otherwise manipulate elements of its environment (Thorndike, 1898). For example, Thorndike completed several experiments using a puzzle box, which was a wooden crate with a door that would open when a concealed lever was moved in the right way (see **FIGURE 7.5**). A hungry cat placed in a puzzle box would try various behaviours to get out—scratching at the door, meowing loudly, sniffing the inside of the box, putting its paw through the openings—but only one behaviour opened the door and led to food: tripping the lever in just the right way. After this happened, Thorndike placed the cat back in the box for another round. Do not get the wrong idea. Thorndike probably *really liked* cats. Far from teasing them, he was after an important behavioural principle.

Fairly quickly, the cats became quite skilled at triggering the lever for their release. Notice what is going on. At first, the cat enacts any number of likely (but ultimately ineffective) behaviours, but only one behaviour leads to freedom and food. Over time, the ineffective behaviours become less and less frequent, and the one instrumental behaviour (going right for the latch) becomes more

▲ Figure 7.5 **Thorndike's Puzzle Box** In Thorndike's original experiments, food was placed just outside the door of the puzzle box, where the cat could see it. If the cat triggered the appropriate lever, it would open the door and let the cat out.

**What is the relationship between behaviour and reward?**

**operant conditioning**
A type of learning in which the consequences of an organism's behaviour determine the likelihood of that behaviour being repeated in the future.

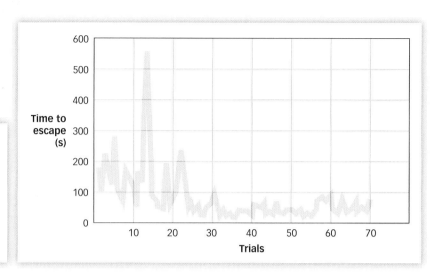

▶ Figure **7.6** **The Law of Effect** Thorndike's cats displayed trial-and-error behaviour when trying to escape from the puzzle box. They made lots of irrelevant movements and actions until, over time, they discovered the solution. Once they figured out what behaviour was instrumental in opening the latch, they stopped all other ineffective behaviours and escaped from the box faster and faster.

**law of effect**
Behaviours that are followed by a "satisfying state of affairs" tend to be repeated and those that produce an "unpleasant state of affairs" are less likely to be repeated.

**operant behaviour**
Behaviour that an organism produces that has some impact on the environment.

B. F. Skinner with one of his many research participants.

frequent (see **FIGURE 7.6**). From these observations, Thorndike developed the **law of effect:** *Behaviours that are followed by a "satisfying state of affairs" tend to be repeated and those that produce an "unpleasant state of affairs" are less likely to be repeated.*

The circumstances that Thorndike used to study learning were very different from those in studies of classical conditioning. Remember that in classical conditioning experiments, the experimenter provides the stimuli (CS and/or US) and then the animal responds. But in Thorndike's work, the behaviour of the animal determined what happened next. If the behaviour was "correct" (i.e., the latch was triggered), the animal was rewarded with food. Incorrect behaviours produced no results and the animal was stuck in the box until it performed the correct behaviour. Although different from classical conditioning, Thorndike's work resonated with most behaviourists at the time: It was still observable, quantifiable, and free from explanations involving the mind (Galef, 1998).

## B. F. Skinner: The Role of Reinforcement and Punishment

Several decades after Thorndike's work, B. F. Skinner (1904–1990) coined the term **operant behaviour** to refer to *behaviour that an organism produces that has some impact on the environment.* In Skinner's system, all of these emitted behaviours "operated" on the environment in some manner, and the environment responded by providing events that either strengthened those behaviours (i.e., they *reinforced* them) or made them less likely to occur (i.e., they *punished* them). Skinner's elegantly simple observation was that most organisms do *not* behave like a dog in a harness, passively waiting to receive food no matter what the circumstances. Rather, most organisms are like cats in a box, actively engaging the environment in which they find themselves to reap rewards (Skinner, 1938, 1953).

In order to study operant behaviour scientifically, Skinner developed a variation on Thorndike's puzzle box. The *operant conditioning chamber,* or *Skinner box,* as it is commonly called (shown in **FIGURE 7.7** on the next page), allows a researcher to study the behaviour of small organisms in a controlled environment.

Skinner's approach to the study of learning focused on *reinforcement* and *punishment.* These terms, which have commonsense connotations, turned out to be rather difficult to define. For example, some people love roller coasters, whereas others find them horrifying; the chance to go on one will be reinforcing for one group but punishing for another. Dogs can be trained with praise and a good belly rub—procedures that are nearly useless for most cats. Skinner settled on a neutral definition that would characterize each term by its effect on behaviour. Therefore, a **reinforcer** is *any stimulus or event that functions to increase the likelihood of the behaviour that led to it*, whereas a **punisher** is *any stimulus or event that functions to decrease the likelihood of the behaviour that led to it.*

Whether a particular stimulus acts as a reinforcer or a punisher depends in part on whether it increases or decreases the likelihood of a behaviour. Presenting food is usually reinforcing and produces an increase in the behaviour that led to it; removing food is often punishing and leads to a decrease in the behaviour. Turning on an electric shock is typically punishing (and decreases the behaviour that led to it); turning it off is rewarding (and increases the behaviour that led to it).

To keep these four possibilities distinct, Skinner used the term *positive* for situations in which a stimulus was presented and *negative* for situations in which it was removed. Consequently, there is both *positive reinforcement* (where a rewarding stimulus is presented) and *negative reinforcement* (where an unpleasant stimulus is removed), as well as *positive punishment* (where an unpleasant stimulus is administered) and *negative punishment* (where a rewarding stimulus is removed). Here the words *positive* and *negative* mean, respectively, something that is *added* or something that is *taken away*, but do not mean "good" or "bad" as they do in everyday speech. As you can see from **TABLE 7.1,** positive and negative reinforcement increase the likelihood of the behaviour; positive and negative punishment decrease the likelihood of the behaviour.

▲ Figure **7.7  Skinner Box**  In a typical Skinner box, or *operant conditioning chamber*, a rat, pigeon, or other suitably sized animal is placed in this environment and observed during learning trials that use operant conditioning principles.

> ▶ Table  **7.1**

### Reinforcement and Punishment

|  | Increases the Likelihood of Behaviour | Decreases the Likelihood of Behaviour |
|---|---|---|
| Stimulus is presented | Positive reinforcement | Positive punishment |
| Stimulus is removed | Negative reinforcement | Negative punishment |

These distinctions can be confusing at first; after all, "negative reinforcement" and "punishment" both sound like they should be "bad" and produce the same type of behaviour. However, negative reinforcement involves something "good": it is the *removal* of something unpleasant, like a shock, and the absence of a shock is indeed pleasant.

> **Why is reinforcement more constructive than punishment in learning desired behaviour?**

Reinforcement is generally more effective than punishment in promoting learning. There are many reasons (Gershoff, 2002), but one reason is this: Punishment signals that an unacceptable behaviour has occurred, but it does not specify what should be done instead. Spanking a young child for starting to run into a busy street certainly stops the behaviour, but it does not promote any kind of learning about the *desired* behaviour such as teaching the child to look both ways before stepping into the street.

## Primary and Secondary Reinforcement and Punishment

Reinforcers and punishers often gain their functions from basic biological mechanisms. A pigeon that pecks at a target in a Skinner box is usually reinforced with food pellets, just as an animal who learns to escape a mild electric shock has avoided

**reinforcer**
Any stimulus or event that functions to increase the likelihood of the behaviour that led to it.

**punisher**
Any stimulus or event that functions to decrease the likelihood of the behaviour that led to it.

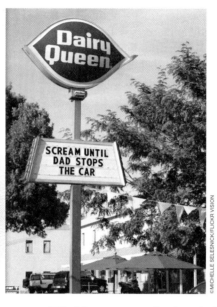

Negative reinforcement involves the removal of something unpleasant from the environment. When Daddy stops the car, he gets a reward: His little monster stops screaming. However, from the perspective of the child, this is positive reinforcement. The child's tantrum results in something positive added to the environment—stopping for a snack.

the punishment of tingly paws. Food, comfort, shelter, or warmth are examples of *primary reinforcers* because they help satisfy biological needs. However, the vast majority of reinforcers or punishers in our daily lives have little to do with biology: Verbal approval, a bronze trophy, or money all serve powerful reinforcing functions, yet none of them taste very good or help keep you warm at night. The point is, we learn to perform a lot of behaviours based on reinforcements that have little or nothing to do with biological satisfaction.

These *secondary reinforcers* derive their effectiveness from their associations with primary reinforcers through classical conditioning. For example, money starts out as a neutral CS that, through its association with primary USs like acquiring food or shelter, takes on a conditioned emotional element. Flashing lights, originally a neutral CS, acquire powerful negative elements through association with a speeding ticket and a fine.

## Immediate versus Delayed Reinforcement and Punishment

A key determinant of the effectiveness of a reinforcer is the amount of time between the occurrence of a behaviour and the reinforcer: The more time that elapses, the less effective the reinforcer (Lattal, 2010; Renner, 1964). This was dramatically illustrated in experiments with hungry rats in which food reinforcers were given at varying times after the rat pressed the lever (Dickinson, Watt, & Griffiths, 1992). Delaying reinforcement by even a few seconds led to a reduction in the number of times the rat subsequently pressed the lever, and extending the delay to a minute rendered the food reinforcer completely ineffective (see **FIGURE 7.8**). The most likely explanation for this effect is that delaying the reinforcer made it difficult for the rats to figure out exactly what behaviour they needed to perform in order to obtain it. In the same way, parents who wish to reinforce their children for playing quietly with a piece of candy should provide the candy while the child is still playing quietly; waiting until later when the child may be engaging in other behaviours—perhaps making a racket with pots and pans—will make it more difficult for the child to link the reinforcer with the behaviour of playing quietly (Powell et al., 2009).

The greater potency of immediate versus delayed reinforcers may help us to appreciate why it can be difficult to engage in behaviours that have long-term benefits. The smoker who desperately wants to quit smoking will be reinforced immediately by the feeling of relaxation that results from lighting up, but may have to wait years to be reinforced with better health that results from quitting; the dieter who sincerely wants to lose weight may easily succumb to the temptation of a chocolate sundae that provides reinforcement now, rather than waiting weeks or months for the reinforcement (looking and feeling better) that would be associated with losing excess weight.

> How does the concept of delayed reinforcement relate to difficulties with quitting smoking?

▼ Figure **7.8** **Delay of Reinforcement** Rats pressed a lever in order to obtain a food reward. Researchers varied the amount of time between the lever press and the delivery of food reinforcement. The number of lever presses declined substantially with longer delays.

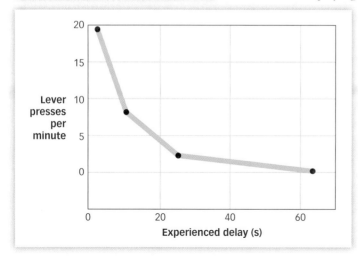

## CULTURE & COMMUNITY

### Are There Cultural Differences in Reinforcers?

Reinforcers play a critical role in operant conditioning, and operant approaches that use positive reinforcement have been applied extensively in everyday settings such as behaviour therapy (see Treatment of Psychological Disorders, pp. 637–639). Surveys designed to assess what kinds of reinforcers are rewarding to individuals have revealed that there can be wide differences among various groups (Dewhurst, & Cautela, 1980; Houlihan et al., 1991).

Recently, 750 high school students from America, Australia, Denmark, Honduras, Korea, Spain, and Tanzania were surveyed in order to evaluate possible cross-cultural differences among reinforcers (Homan et al., 2012). The survey asked students to rate on a 5-point scale how rewarding they found a range of activities, including listening to music, playing various kinds of sports, shopping, reading, spending time with friends, and so on. The American researchers hypothesized that American high school students would differ most strongly from high school students in the third-world countries of Tanzania and Honduras, and that is what they found. The differences between American and Korean students were nearly as large and, somewhat surprisingly, so were the differences between American and Spanish students. There were much smaller differences between Americans and their Australian or Danish counterparts. For example, of the 30 activities evaluated, "Hang with friends" was ranked as the most rewarding activity by American, Australian, and Danish teens. It ranked 5th in Spain, 6th in Honduras, 9th in Korea, and did not make the top-10 list at all for Tanzanian students, who ranked shopping and reading the highest.

These results should be taken with a grain of salt because the researchers did not control for variables other than culture that could influence their results, such as economic status. Nonetheless, they suggest that cultural differences should be considered in the design of programs or interventions that rely on the use of reinforcers to influence the behaviour of individuals who come from different cultures.

Similar considerations apply to punishment: As a general rule, the longer the delay between a behaviour and the administration of punishment, the less effective the punishment will be in suppressing the targeted behaviour (Kamin, 1959; Lerman & Vorndran, 2002). The reduced effectiveness of delayed punishment can be a serious problem in non-laboratory settings, because in everyday life it is often difficult to administer punishment immediately or even soon after a problem behaviour has occurred (Meindl & Casey, 2012). For example, a parent whose child misbehaves at a shopping mall may be unable to punish the child immediately with a time-out because it is impractical in the mall setting. Some problem behaviours, such as cheating, can be difficult to detect immediately and therefore punishment is necessarily delayed. Research in both the laboratory and everyday settings suggests several strategies for increasing the effectiveness of delayed punishment, including increasing the severity of the punishment or attempting to bridge the gap between the behaviour and the punishment with verbal instructions (Meindl & Casey, 2012). The parent in the shopping mall, for example, might tell the misbehaving child exactly when and where a later time-out will occur.

Suppose you are the mayor of a suburban town and you want to institute some new policies to decrease the number of drivers who speed on residential streets. How might you use punishment to decrease the behaviour you dislike (speeding)? How might you use reinforcement to increase the behaviour you desire (safe driving)? Based on the principles of operant conditioning you read about in this section, which approach do you think might be most fruitful?

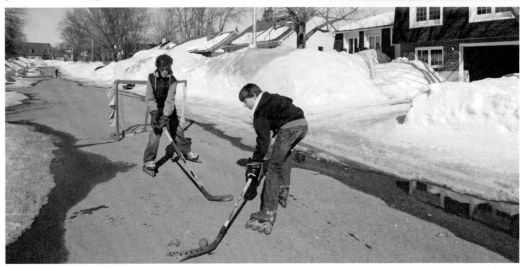

PHILLIPPE RENAULT/HEMIS/ALAMY

# The Basic Principles of Operant Conditioning

After establishing how reinforcement and punishment produced learned behaviour, Skinner and other scientists began to expand the parameters of operant conditioning. This took the form of investigating some phenomena that were well known in classical conditioning (such as discrimination, generalization, and extinction) as well as some practical applications, such as how best to administer reinforcement or how to produce complex learned behaviours in an organism. Let us look at some of these basic principles of operant conditioning.

## Discrimination, Generalization, and the Importance of Context

We all take off our clothes at least once a day, but usually not in public. We scream at rock concerts, but not in libraries. We say, "Please pass the gravy," at the dinner table, but not in a classroom. Although these observations may seem like nothing more than common sense, Thorndike was the first to recognize the underlying message: Learning takes place *in contexts*, not in the free range of any plausible situation. As Skinner rephrased it later, most behaviour is under *stimulus control*, which develops when a particular response only occurs when an appropriate *discriminative stimulus*, a stimulus that indicates that a response will be reinforced, is present. Skinner (1972) discussed this process in terms of a "three-term contingency": In the presence of a *discriminative stimulus* (classmates drinking coffee together in Tim Hortons), a *response* (joking comments about a psychology professor's increasing waistline and receding hairline) produces a *reinforcer* (laughter among classmates). The same response in a different context—the professor's office—would most likely produce a very different outcome.

> **What does it mean to say that learning takes place in contexts?**

Stimulus control, perhaps not surprisingly, shows both discrimination and generalization effects similar to those we saw with classical conditioning. To demonstrate this, researchers used either a painting by the French Impressionist Claude Monet or one of Pablo Picasso's paintings from his Cubist period for the discriminative stimulus (Watanabe, Sakamoto, & Wakita, 1995). Participants in the experiment were only reinforced if they responded when the appropriate painting was presented. After training, the participants discriminated appropriately; those trained with the Monet

In research on stimulus control, participants trained with Picasso paintings, such as the one on the left, responded to other paintings by Picasso or even to paintings by other Cubists. Participants trained with Monet paintings, such as the one on the right, responded to other paintings by Monet or by other French Impressionists. Interestingly, the participants in this study were pigeons.

TATE GALLERY, LONDON/ART RESOURCE, NY

TATE GALLERY, LONDON/ART RESOURCE, NY

painting responded when other paintings by Monet were presented and those trained with a Picasso painting reacted when other Cubist paintings by Picasso were shown. And as you might expect, Monet-trained participants did not react to Picassos and Picasso-trained participants did not respond to Monets. What is more, the research participants showed that they could generalize *across* painters as long as they were from the same artistic tradition. Those trained with Monet responded appropriately when shown paintings by Auguste Renoir (another French Impressionist), and the Picasso-trained participants responded to artwork by Cubist painter Henri Matisse, despite never having seen those paintings before. If these results do not seem particularly startling to you, it might help to know that the research participants were pigeons who were trained to key-peck to these various works of art. Stimulus control, and its ability to foster stimulus discrimination and stimulus generalization, is effective even if the stimulus has no meaning to the respondent.

## Extinction

In classical conditioning, a CR extinguishes when the animal learns that the CS no longer predicts the US. Similarly, an operant behaviour undergoes extinction when the behaviour no longer predicts reward; in other words, when the reinforcements stop. Pigeons cease pecking at a key if food is no longer presented following the behaviour. You would not put more money into a vending machine if it failed to give you its promised chocolate bar or pop. Warm smiles that are are not returned will quickly disappear. On the surface, extinction of operant behaviour looks like that of classical conditioning: The response rate drops off fairly rapidly and, if a rest period is provided, spontaneous recovery is typically seen.

However, there is an important difference. In operant conditioning, the reinforcements only occur when the proper response has been made, and they do not always

**How is the concept of extinction different in operant conditioning versus classical conditioning?**

occur even then. Not every trip into the forest produces nuts for a squirrel, auto salespeople do not sell to everyone who takes a test drive, and researchers run many experiments that do not work out and never get published. Yet these behaviours do not weaken and gradually extinguish. In fact, they typically become stronger and more resilient. Curiously, then, extinction is a bit more complicated in operant conditioning than in classical conditioning because it depends, in part, on how often reinforcement is received. In fact, this principle is an important cornerstone of operant conditioning that we will examine next.

## Schedules of Reinforcement

Skinner was intrigued by the apparent paradox surrounding extinction, and in his autobiography, he described how he began studying it (Skinner, 1979). He was labouriously rolling ground rat meal and water to make food pellets to reinforce the rats in his early experiments. It occurred to him that perhaps he could save time and effort by not giving his rats a pellet for every bar press but instead delivering food on some intermittent schedule. The results of this hunch were dramatic. Not only did the rats continue bar pressing, but they also shifted the rate and pattern of bar pressing depending on the timing and frequency of the presentation of the reinforcers. Unlike classical conditioning, where the sheer *number* of learning trials was important, in operant conditioning the *pattern* with which reinforcements appeared was crucial.

Skinner explored dozens of what came to be known as *schedules of reinforcement* (Ferster & Skinner, 1957) (see **FIGURE 7.9** on the next page). The two most important are *interval schedules*, based on the time intervals between reinforcements, and *ratio schedules*, based on the ratio of responses to reinforcements.

**fixed-interval schedule (FI)**
An operant conditioning principle in which reinforcers are presented at fixed-time periods, provided that the appropriate response is made.

**variable-interval schedule (VI)**
An operant conditioning principle in which behaviour is reinforced based on an average time that has expired since the last reinforcement.

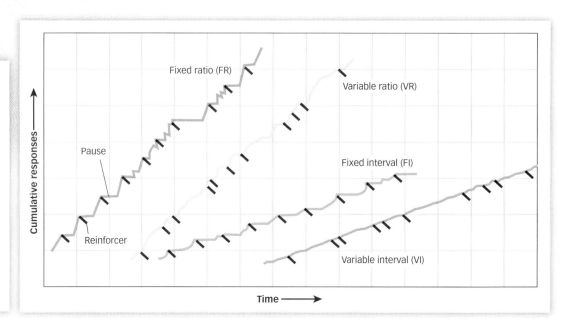

▶ Figure **7.9** **Reinforcement Schedules** Different schedules of reinforcement produce different rates of responding. These lines represent the amount of responding that occurs under each type of reinforcement. The black slash marks indicate when reinforcement was administered. Notice that ratio schedules tend to produce higher rates of responding than do interval schedules, as shown by the steeper lines for fixed-ratio and variable-ratio reinforcement.

**Interval Schedules.** Under a **fixed-interval schedule (FI),** *reinforcers are presented at fixed-time periods, provided that the appropriate response is made.* For example, on a 2-minute fixed-interval schedule, a response will be reinforced, but only after 2 minutes have expired since the last reinforcement. Rats and pigeons in Skinner boxes produce predictable patterns of behaviour under these schedules. They show little responding right after the presentation of the reinforcement, but as the next time interval draws to a close, they show a burst of responding. Many undergraduates behave exactly like this. They do relatively little work until just before the upcoming exam, then engage in a burst of reading and studying.

Under a **variable-interval schedule (VI),** *a behaviour is reinforced based on an average time that has expired since the last reinforcement.* For example, on a 2-minute variable-interval schedule, responses will be reinforced every 2 minutes *on average* but not after each 2-minute period. Variable-interval schedules typically produce steady, consistent responding because the time until the next reinforcement is less predictable. Variable-interval schedules are not encountered that often in real life, although one example might be radio promotional giveaways, such as tickets to rock concerts. The reinforcement—getting the tickets—might average out to once an hour across the span of the broadcasting day, but the presentation of the reinforcement is variable: It might come early in the 10:00 o'clock hour, later in the 11:00 o'clock hour, immediately into the 12:00 o'clock hour, and so on.

Both fixed-interval schedules and variable-interval schedules tend to produce slow, methodical responding because the reinforcements follow a time scale that is independent of how many responses occur. It does not matter if a rat on a fixed-interval schedule presses a bar 1 time during a 2-minute period or 100 times: The reinforcing food pellet will not drop out of the shoot until 2 minutes have elapsed, regardless of the number of responses before that 2 minutes is up.

Students cramming for an exam often show the same kind of behaviour as pigeons being reinforced under a fixed-interval schedule.

How does a radio station use scheduled reinforcements to keep you listening?

Radio station promotions and giveaways often follow a variable-interval schedule of reinforcement.

Ratio Schedules. Under a **fixed-ratio schedule (FR),** *reinforcement is delivered after a specific number of responses have been made.* One schedule might present reinforcement after every fourth response, a different schedule might present reinforcement after every 20 responses; the special case of presenting reinforcement after *each* response is called *continuous reinforcement,* and it is what drove Skinner to investigate these schedules in the first place. Notice that, in each example, the ratio of reinforcements to responses, once set, remains fixed.

There are many situations in which people, sometimes unknowingly, find themselves being reinforced on a fixed-ratio schedule: Book clubs often give you a free book after a set number of regular purchases; pieceworkers get paid after making a fixed

> How do ratio schedules work to keep you spending your money?

number of products; and some credit card companies return to their customers a percentage of the amount charged. When a fixed-ratio schedule is operating, it is possible, in principle, to know exactly when the next reinforcer is due. A laundry pieceworker on a 10-response, fixed-ratio schedule who has just washed and ironed the ninth shirt knows that payment is coming after the next shirt is done.

Under a **variable-ratio schedule (VR),** *the delivery of reinforcement is based on a particular average number of responses.* For example, if a laundry worker was following a 10-response variable-ratio schedule instead of a fixed-ratio schedule, she or he would

These pieceworkers in a textile factory get paid following a fixed-ratio schedule: They receive payment after a number of shirts have been sewn.

still be paid, on average, for every 10 shirts washed and ironed but not for *each* 10th shirt. Slot machines in a modern casino pay off on variable-ratio schedules that are determined by the random number generator that controls the play of the machines. A casino might advertise that they pay off on "every 100 pulls on average," which could be true. However, one player might hit a jackpot after 3 pulls on a slot machine, whereas another player might not hit a jackpot until after 80 pulls. The ratio of responses to reinforcements is variable, which probably helps casinos stay in business.

Slot machines in casinos pay out following a variable-ratio schedule. This helps explain why some gamblers feel incredibly lucky, whereas others (like this chap) cannot believe they can play a machine for so long without winning a thing.

Not surprisingly, variable-ratio schedules produce slightly higher rates of responding than fixed-ratio schedules primarily because the organism never knows when the next reinforcement is going to appear. What is more, the higher the ratio, the higher the response rate tends to be; a 20-response variable-ratio schedule will produce considerably more responding than a 2-response variable-ratio schedule. When schedules of reinforcement provide **intermittent reinforcement,** *when only some of the responses made are followed by reinforcement,* they produce behaviour that is much more resistant to extinction than a continuous reinforcement schedule. One way to think about this effect is to recognize that the more irregular and intermittent a schedule is, the more difficult it becomes for an organism to detect when it has actually been placed on extinction.

For example, if you have just put a dollar into a pop machine that, unbeknownst to you, is broken, no pop comes out. Because you are used to getting your pops on a continuous reinforcement schedule—one dollar produces one pop—this abrupt change in the environment is easily noticed and you are unlikely to put additional money into the machine: You would quickly show extinction. However, if you have put your dollar into a slot machine that, unbeknownst to you, is broken, do you stop after one or two plays? Almost certainly not. If you are a regular slot player, you are used to going for many plays in a row without winning anything, so it is difficult to tell that anything is out of the ordinary. Under conditions of intermittent reinforcement, all organisms will

**fixed-ratio schedule (FR)**
An operant conditioning principle in which reinforcement is delivered after a specific number of responses have been made.

**variable-ratio schedule (VR)**
An operant conditioning principle in which the delivery of reinforcement is based on a particular average number of responses.

**intermittent reinforcement**
An operant conditioning principle in which only some of the responses made are followed by reinforcement.

Imagine you own an insurance company and you want to encourage your salespeople to sell as many policies as possible. You decide to give them bonuses, based on the number of policies sold. How might you set up a system of bonuses using an FR schedule? Using a VR schedule? Which system do you think would encourage your salespeople to work harder, in terms of making more sales?

show considerable resistance to extinction and continue for many trials before they stop responding. This effect has even been observed in infants (Weir et al., 2005).

This relationship between intermittent reinforcement schedules and the robustness of the behaviour they produce is called the **intermittent reinforcement effect,** *the fact that operant behaviours that are maintained under intermittent reinforcement schedules resist extinction better than those maintained under continuous reinforcement.* In one extreme case, Skinner gradually extended a variable-ratio schedule until he managed to get a pigeon to make an astonishing 10 000 pecks at an illuminated key for one food reinforcer! Behaviour maintained under a schedule like this is virtually immune to extinction.

## Shaping through Successive Approximations

Have you ever been to Marineland and wondered how the dolphins learn to jump up in the air, twist around, splash back down, do a somersault, and then jump through a hoop, all in one smooth motion? Well, they do not. Wait—of course they do—you have seen them. It is just that they do not learn to do all those complex aquabatics in *one* smooth motion. Rather, elements of their behaviour are shaped over time until the final product looks like one smooth motion.

Skinner noted that the trial-by-trial experiments of Pavlov and Thorndike were rather artificial. Behaviour rarely occurs in fixed frameworks where a stimulus is presented and then an organism has to engage in some activity or another. We are continuously acting and behaving, and the world around us reacts in response to our actions. Most of our behaviours, then, are the result of **shaping,** *learning that results from the reinforcement of successive steps to a final desired behaviour.* The outcomes of one set of behaviours shape the next set of behaviours, whose outcomes shape the next set of behaviours, and so on.

> How can operant conditioning produce complex behaviours?

Skinner realized the potential power of shaping one day in 1943 when he was working on a wartime project sponsored by General Mills in a lab on the top floor of a flour mill where pigeons frequently visited (Peterson, 2004). In a lighthearted moment, Skinner and his colleagues decided to see whether they could teach the pigeons to "bowl" by swiping with their beaks at a ball that Skinner had placed in a box along with some pins. Nothing worked until Skinner decided to reinforce any response even remotely related to a swipe, such as merely looking at the ball. "The result amazed us," Skinner recalled. "In a few minutes the ball was caroming off the walls of the box as if the pigeon had been a champion squash player" (Skinner, 1958, p. 974). Skinner applied this insight in his later laboratory research. For example, he noted that if you put a rat in a Skinner box and wait for it to press the bar, you could end up waiting

B. F. Skinner shaping a dog named Agnes. In the span of 20 minutes, Skinner was able to use reinforcement of successive approximations to shape Agnes's behaviour. The result was a pretty neat trick: to wander in, stand on hind legs, and jump.

1 Minute      4 Minutes      8 Minutes

a very long time: Bar pressing just is not very common in a rat's natural repertoire of responses. However, it is relatively easy to shape bar pressing. Watch the rat closely: If it turns in the direction of the bar, deliver a food reward. This will reinforce turning toward the bar, making such a movement more likely. Now wait for the rat to take a step toward the bar before delivering food; this will reinforce moving toward the bar. After the rat walks closer to the bar, wait until it touches the bar before presenting the food. Notice that none of these behaviours is the final desired behaviour (reliably pressing the bar). Rather, each behaviour is a *successive approximation* to the final product, or a behaviour that gets incrementally closer to the overall desired behaviour. In the dolphin example—and indeed, in many instances of animal training in which relatively simple animals seem to perform astoundingly complex behaviours—you can think through how each smaller behaviour is reinforced until the overall sequence of behaviour is performed reliably.

## Superstitious Behaviour

Everything we have discussed so far suggests that one of the keys to establishing reliable operant behaviour is the correlation between an organism's response and the occurrence of reinforcement. In the case of continuous reinforcement, when every response is followed by the presentation of a reinforcer, there is a one-to-one, or perfect, correlation. In the case of intermittent reinforcement, the correlation is weaker (i.e., not every response is met with the delivery of reinforcement), but it is not zero. As you read in the Methods in Psychology chapter, however, just because two things are correlated (i.e., they tend to occur together in time and space) does not imply that there is causality (i.e., the presence of one reliably causes the other to occur).

Skinner (1948) designed an experiment that illustrates this distinction. He put several pigeons in Skinner boxes, set the food dispenser to deliver food every 15 seconds, and left the birds to their own devices. Later he returned and found the birds engaging

> **How would a behaviourist explain superstitions?**

in odd, idiosyncratic behaviours, such as pecking aimlessly in a corner or turning in circles. He referred to these behaviours as "superstitious" and offered a behaviourist analysis of their occurrence. The pigeons, he argued, were simply repeating behaviours that had been accidentally reinforced. A pigeon that just happened to have pecked randomly in the corner when the food showed up had connected the delivery of food to that behaviour. Because this pecking behaviour was reinforced by the delivery of food, the pigeon was likely to repeat it. Now pecking in the corner was more likely to occur, and it was more likely to be reinforced 15 seconds later when the food appeared again. For each pigeon, the behaviour reinforced would most likely be whatever the pigeon happened to be doing when the food was first delivered.

**intermittent reinforcement effect**
The fact that operant behaviours that are maintained under intermittent reinforcement schedules resist extinction better than those maintained under continuous reinforcement.

**shaping**
Learning that results from the reinforcement of successive steps to a final desired behaviour.

12 Minutes

16 Minutes

20 Minutes

People believe in many different superstitions and engage in all kinds of superstitious behaviours. Professional athletes and coaches are notoriously superstitious. Patrick Roy was perhaps the greatest goaltender the Montreal Canadiens ever had. During games he would talk to the goal posts, and touch them, expressing his gratitude to them when a puck was deflected. Before games, he would dress in his equipment in a very specific order and then, once on the ice, he would skate backward toward the net before turning around at the last second. Skinner thought superstitions resulted from the unintended reinforcement of inconsequential behaviour.

Edward Chace Tolman advocated a cognitive approach to operant learning and provided evidence that in maze-learning experiments, rats develop a mental picture of the maze, which he called a cognitive map.

Skinner's pigeons acted as though there was a causal relationship between their behaviours and the appearance of food when it was merely an accidental correlation.

Although some researchers questioned Skinner's characterization of these behaviours as superstitious (Staddon & Simmelhag, 1971), later studies have shown that reinforcing adults or children using schedules in which reinforcement is not contingent on their responses can produce seemingly superstitious behaviour. It seems that people, like pigeons, behave as though there is a correlation between their responses and reward when in fact the connection is merely accidental (Bloom et al., 2007; Mellon, 2009; Ono, 1987; Wagner & Morris, 1987). Such findings should not be surprising to sports fans. Baseball players who enjoy several home runs on a day when they happened not to have showered are likely to continue that tradition, laboring under the belief that the accidental correlation between poor personal hygiene and a good day at bat is somehow causal. This "stench causes home runs" hypothesis is just one of many examples of human superstitions (Gilbert et al., 2000; Radford & Radford, 1949).

## A Deeper Understanding of Operant Conditioning

Like classical conditioning, operant conditioning also quickly proved to be a powerful approach to learning. But B. F. Skinner, like Watson before him, was satisfied to observe an organism perform a learned behaviour; he did not look for a deeper explanation of mental processes (Skinner, 1950). In this view, an organism behaved in a certain way as a response to stimuli in the environment, not because there was any wanting, wishing, or willing by the animal in question. However, some research on operant conditioning digs deeper into the underlying mechanisms that produce the familiar outcomes of reinforcement. Like we did earlier in the chapter with classical conditioning, let us examine three elements that expand our view of operant conditioning: the cognitive, neural, and evolutionary elements of operant conditioning.

### The Cognitive Elements of Operant Conditioning

Edward Chace Tolman (1886–1959) was one of the first researchers to question Skinner's strictly behaviourist interpretation of learning, and was the strongest early advocate of a cognitive approach to operant learning. Tolman argued that there was more to learning than just knowing the circumstances in the environment (the properties of the stimulus) and being able to observe a particular outcome (the reinforced response). Instead, Tolman proposed that an animal established a means–ends relationship. That is, the conditioning experience produced knowledge or a belief that, in this particular situation, a specific reward (the end state) will appear if a specific response (the means to that end) is made.

Tolman's means–ends relationship may remind you of the Rescorla–Wagner model of classical conditioning. Rescorla argued that the CS functions by setting up an expectation about the arrival of a US, and "expectations" most certainly involve cognitive processes. In both Rescorla's and Tolman's theories, the stimulus does not directly evoke a response; rather, it establishes an internal cognitive state, which then produces the behaviour. These cognitive theories of learning focus less on the stimulus–response (SR) connection and more on what happens in the organism's mind when faced with the stimulus. During the 1930s and 1940s, Tolman and his students conducted studies that focused on *latent learning* and *cognitive maps*, two phenomena that strongly suggest that simple S–R interpretations of operant learning behaviour are inadequate.

**Latent Learning and Cognitive Maps.** In **latent learning,** *something is learned, but it is not manifested as a behavioural change until sometime in the future.* Latent learning can easily be established in rats and occurs without any obvious reinforcement, a finding that posed a direct challenge to the then-dominant behaviourist position that all learning required some form of reinforcement (Tolman & Honzik, 1930a).

Tolman gave three groups of rats access to a complex maze every day for over 2 weeks. The control group never received any reinforcement for navigating the maze. They were simply allowed to run around until they reached the goal box at the end of the maze. In **FIGURE 7.10** you can see that over the 2 weeks of the study, the control group (in green) got a little better at finding their way through the maze, but not by much. A second group of rats received regular reinforcements; when they reached the goal box, they found a small food reward there. Not surprisingly, these rats showed clear learning, as can be seen in blue in Figure 7.10. A third group was treated exactly like the control group for the first 10 days and then rewarded for the last 7 days. This group's behaviour (in orange) was quite striking. For the first 10 days, they behaved like the rats in the control group. However, during the final 7 days, they behaved a lot like the rats in the second group that had been reinforced every day. Clearly, the rats in this third group had learned a lot about the maze and the location of the goal box during those first 10 days even though they had not received any reinforcements for their behaviour. In other words, they showed evidence of latent learning.

These results suggested to Tolman that beyond simply learning "start here, end here," his rats had developed a sophisticated mental picture of the maze. Tolman called this a **cognitive map,** *a mental representation of the physical features of the environment.* Tolman thought that the rats had developed a mental picture of the maze, along the lines of "make two lefts, then a right, then a quick left at the corner," and he devised several experiments to test that idea (Tolman & Honzik, 1930b; Tolman, Ritchie, & Kalish, 1946).

> **What are cognitive maps and why are they a challenge to behaviourism?**

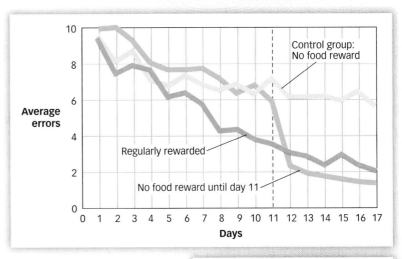

▲ Figure **7.10** **Latent Learning** Rats in a control group that never received any reinforcement (in green) improved at finding their way through the maze over 17 days but not by much. Rats that received regular reinforcements (in blue) showed fairly clear learning; their error rate decreased steadily over time. Rats in the latent learning group (in orange) were treated exactly like the control group rats for the first 10 days and then like the regularly rewarded group for the last 7 days. Their dramatic improvement on day 12 shows that these rats had learned a lot about the maze and the location of the goal box even though they had never received reinforcements. Notice, also, that on the last 7 days, these latent learners actually seem to make *fewer* errors than their regularly rewarded counterparts.

**Further Support for Cognitive Explanations.** One simple experiment provided support for Tolman's theories and wreaked havoc with the noncognitive explanations offered by staunch behaviourists. Tolman trained a group of rats in the maze shown in **FIGURE 7.11a** on the next page. As you can see, rats run down a straightaway, take a left, a right, a long right, and then end up in the goal box at the end of the maze. Because we are looking at it from above, we can see that the rat's position at the end of the maze, relative to the starting point, is "diagonal to the upper right." Of course, all the rat in the maze sees are the next set of walls and turns until it eventually reaches the goal box. Nonetheless, rats learned to navigate this maze without error or hesitation after about four nights. Clever rats. But they were more clever than you think.

After they had mastered the maze, Tolman changed things around a bit and put them in the maze shown in **FIGURE 7.11b.** The goal box was still in the same place relative to the start box. However, many alternative paths now spoked off the main platform, and the main straightaway that the rats had learned to use was blocked. Most behaviourists would predict that the rats in this situation—running down a familiar path only to find it blocked—would show stimulus generalization and pick the next closest path, such as one immediately adjacent to the straightaway. This was not what Tolman observed. When faced with the blocked path, the rats instead ran all the way down the path that led directly to the goal box. The rats had formed a sophisticated cognitive map of their environment and behaved in a way that suggested they were successfully following that map after the conditions had changed. Latent learning and cognitive maps suggest that operant conditioning involves much more than an animal responding to a stimulus. Tolman's experiments strongly suggest that there is a cognitive component, even in rats, to operant learning.

**latent learning**
Something is learned, but it is not manifested as a behavioural change until sometime in the future.

**cognitive map**
A mental representation of the physical features of the environment.

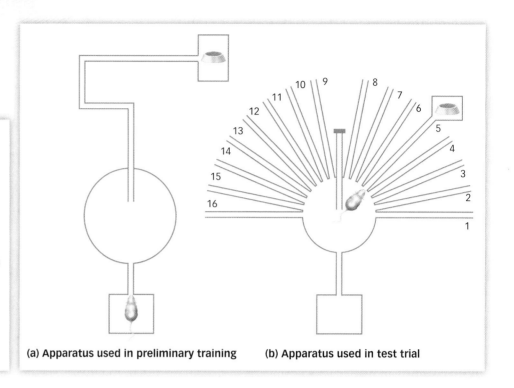

▶ Figure **7.11 Cognitive Maps** (*a*) Rats trained to run from a start box to a goal box in the maze on the left mastered the task quite readily. When those rats were then placed in the maze on the right (*b*), in which the main straightaway had been blocked, they did something unusual. Rather than simply backtrack and try the next closest runway (i.e., those labelled 8 or 9 in the figure), which would be predicted by stimulus generalization, the rats typically chose runway 5, which led most directly to where the goal box had been during their training. The rats had formed a cognitive map of their environment and knew where they needed to end up spatially, compared to where they began.

(a) Apparatus used in preliminary training       (b) Apparatus used in test trial

**Learning to Trust: For Better or Worse.** Cognitive factors also played a key role in an experiment examining learning and brain activity (using fMRI) in people who played a "trust" game with a fictional partner (Delgado, Frank, & Phelps, 2005). On each trial, a participant could either keep a $1 reward or transfer the reward to a partner, who would receive $3. The partner could then either keep the $3 or share half of it with the participant. When playing with a partner who was willing to share the reward, the participant would be better off transferring the money, but when playing with a partner who did not share, the participant would be better off keeping the reward in the first place. Participants in such experiments typically find out who is trustworthy on the basis of trial-and-error learning during the game, transferring more money to partners who reinforce them by sharing.

In the study by Delgado and his colleagues, participants were given detailed descriptions of their partners that either portrayed the partners as trustworthy, neutral, or suspect. Even though during the game itself the sharing behaviour of the three types of partners did not differ—they each reinforced participants to the same extent through sharing—the participants' cognitions about their partners had powerful effects. Participants transferred more money to the trustworthy partner than to the others, essentially ignoring the trial-by-trial feedback that would ordinarily shape their playing behaviour, thus reducing the amount of reward they received. Highlighting the power of the cognitive effect, signals in a part of the brain that ordinarily distinguishes between positive and negative feedback were evident only when participants played with the neutral partner; these feedback signals were absent when participants played with the trustworthy partner and reduced when participants played with the suspect partner.

These kinds of effects might help us to understand otherwise perplexing real-life cases such as that of con artist Bernard Madoff, who in March 2009 pleaded guilty to swindling numerous American investors out of billions of dollars in a highly publicized case that attracted worldwide attention. Madoff had been the chairman of the American stock exchange NASDAQ and seemed to his investors an extremely trustworthy figure with whom one could

**Why might cognitive factors have been a factor in people's trust of Bernie Madoff?**

safely invest money. Those powerful cognitions might have caused investors to miss danger signals that otherwise would have led them to learn about the true nature of Madoff's operation. If so, the result was one of the most expensive failures of learning in modern history.

## The Neural Elements of Operant Conditioning

Soon after psychologists came to appreciate the range and variety of things that could function as reinforcers, they began looking for underlying brain mechanisms that might account for these effects. The first hint of how specific brain structures might contribute to the process of reinforcement came from the discovery of what came to be called *pleasure centres*. McGill researchers James Olds and Peter Milner inserted tiny electrodes into different parts of a rat's brain and allowed the animal to control electric stimulation of its own brain by pressing a bar. They discovered that some brain areas, particularly those in the limbic system (see the Neuroscience and Behaviour chapter), produced what appeared to be intensely positive experiences: The rats would press the bar repeatedly to stimulate these structures. The researchers observed that these rats would ignore food, water, and other life-sustaining necessities for hours on end simply to receive stimulation directly in the brain. They then called these parts of the brain *pleasure centres* (Olds, 1956) (see **FIGURE 7.12**).

Bernard Madoff, shown here leaving a court hearing in March 2009, pleaded guilty to fraud after swindling billions of dollars from investors who trusted him.

In the years since these early studies, researchers have identified a number of structures and pathways in the brain that deliver rewards through stimulation (Wise, 1989, 2005). The neurons in the *medial forebrain bundle*, a pathway that meanders its way from the midbrain through the *hypothalamus* into the *nucleus accumbens*, are the most susceptible to stimulation that produces pleasure. This is not surprising because psychologists have identified this bundle of cells as crucial to behaviours that clearly involve pleasure, such as eating, drinking, and engaging in sexual activity. Second, the neurons all along this pathway and especially those in the nucleus accumbens itself are all *dopaminergic* (i.e., they secrete the neurotransmitter *dopamine*). Remember from the Neuroscience and Behaviour chapter that higher levels of dopamine in the brain are usually associated with positive emotions. During recent years, several competing hypotheses about the precise role of dopamine have emerged, including the idea that dopamine is more closely linked with the expectation of reward than with reward itself (Fiorillo, Newsome, & Schultz, 2008; Schultz, 2006, 2007), or that dopamine is more closely associated with wanting or even craving something rather than simply liking it (Berridge, 2007).

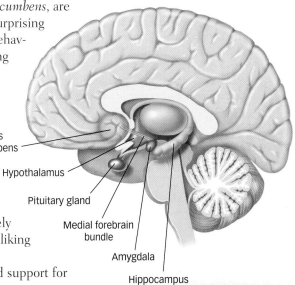

Nucleus accumbens
Hypothalamus
Pituitary gland
Medial forebrain bundle
Amygdala
Hippocampus

▲ Figure **7.12** **Pleasure Centres in the Brain** The nucleus accumbens, medial forebrain bundle, and hypothalamus are all major pleasure centres in the brain.

Whichever view turns out to be correct, researchers have found good support for a reward centre in which dopamine plays a key role. First, as you have just seen, rats will work to stimulate this pathway at the expense of other basic needs (Olds & Fobes,

> How do specific brain structures contribute to the process of reinforcement?

1981). However, if drugs that block the action of dopamine are administered to the rats, they cease pressing the lever for stimulation (Stellar, Kelley, & Corbett, 1983). Second, drugs such as cocaine, amphetamine, and opiates activate these pathways and centres (Moghaddam & Bunney, 1989), but dopamine-blocking drugs dramatically diminish their reinforcing effects (White & Milner, 1992). Third, fMRI studies show activity in the nucleus accumbens in heterosexual men looking at pictures of attractive women (Aharon et al., 2001) and in individuals who believe they are about to receive money (Cooper et al., 2009; Knutson et al., 2001). Finally, rats given primary reinforcers such as food or water, or who are allowed to engage in sexual activity, show increased dopamine secretion in the nucleus accumbens—but only if they are hungry, thirsty, or sexually aroused (Damsma et al., 1992). This last finding is exactly what we might expect given our earlier discussion of the complexities of reinforcement. After all, food tastes a lot better when we are hungry and sexual activity is more pleasurable when we are aroused. These biological structures underlying rewards and reinforcements probably evolved to ensure that species engaged in activities that helped survival and reproduction. (To learn the relationship between dopamine and Parkinson's, see the Hot Science box below.)

# Dopamine and Reward Learning in Parkinson's Disease

Many of us have relatives or friends who have been affected by Parkinson's disease (recall Michael J. Fox), which causes difficulty moving and involves the loss of neurons that use dopamine. As you learned in the Neuroscience and Behaviour chapter, the drug L-dopa is often used to treat Parkinson's disease because it spurs surviving neurons to produce more dopamine. Dopamine also plays a key role in reward-related learning.

Researchers have focused on the role of dopamine in reward-based learning, especially the *expectation* of reward. A key idea is that dopamine plays an important role in *reward prediction error*: the difference between the actual reward received versus the amount of predicted or expected reward. For example, when an animal presses a lever and receives an unexpected food reward, a *positive* prediction error occurs (a better than expected outcome) and the animal learns to press the lever again. By contrast, when an animal expects to receive a reward from pressing a lever but does not receive it, a *negative* prediction error occurs (a worse than expected outcome) and the animal will subsequently be less likely to press the lever again. Reward prediction error can thus serve as a kind of "teaching signal" that helps the animal to learn to behave in a way that maximizes reward.

In pioneering studies linking reward prediction error to dopamine, Wolfram Schultz and his colleagues recorded activity in dopamine neurons located in the reward centres of a monkey's brain. They found that those neurons showed increased activity when the monkey received unexpected juice rewards and decreased activity when the monkey did not receive expected juice rewards. This suggests that dopamine neurons play an important role in generating the reward prediction error (Schultz, 2006, 2007; Schultz, Dayan, & Montague,

1997). Schultz's observations have been backed up by studies using neuroimaging techniques to show that human brain regions involved in reward-related learning also produce reward prediction error signals, and that dopamine is involved in generating those signals (O'Doherty et al., 2003; Pessiglione et al., 2006).

So, how do these findings relate to people with Parkinson's disease? Several studies report that reward-related learning can be impaired in persons with Parkinson's (Dahger & Robbins, 2009). Other studies provide evidence that when individuals with Parkinson's perform reward-related learning tasks, the reward prediction error signal is disrupted (Schonberg et al., 2010). Recent studies have examined the influence of Parkinson's treatment drugs on reward-related learning and the reward prediction error signal. In one study, participants with Parkinson's who were either treated with L-dopa (combined in some participants with drugs that stimulate dopamine receptors) or not, were given a reward-learning task that involved choosing between two computer-animated crab traps; one was much more likely than the other to contain the reward (i.e., a crab) (Rutledge et al., 2009). After each trial, participants were given feedback concerning their choice. Participants on dopaminergic drugs had a higher learning rate than those not on the

drugs. However, there was greater learning for the positive reward prediction error (learning based on positive outcomes) than for the negative reward prediction error (learning based on negative outcomes).

These results may relate to another intriguing feature of Parkinson's disease: Some individuals develop serious problems with compulsive gambling, shopping, and related impulsive behaviours. Such problems seem to be largely the consequence of Parkinson's drugs that stimulate dopamine receptors (Ahlskog, 2011; Weintraub, Papay, & Siderowf, 2013). Voon and her colleagues (2011) studied individuals who developed gambling and shopping problems only after contracting Parkinson's disease and receiving treatment with drugs that stimulate dopamine receptors. Those individuals were scanned with fMRI while they performed a reward-learning task in which they chose between stimuli that had a greater or lesser probability of producing a monetary gain or loss. Their performance was compared to that of individuals with Parkinson's without gambling and shopping problems, either on or off drug treatment. Compared with both of these groups, those who had compulsive gambling and shopping problems showed an increase in the rate of learning from gains. Importantly, they also showed an increased positive reward prediction error signal in the striatum, a subcortical region in the basal ganglia (see Figure 3.16 on p. 98) that is rich in dopamine receptors and has been linked with the reward prediction error. The researchers suggested that these results likely reflected an effect of the drug treatment on individuals who are susceptible to compulsive behaviours.

More studies will be needed to unravel the complex relations among dopamine, reward prediction error, learning, and Parkinson's disease, but the studies to date suggest that such research should have important practical as well as scientific implications.

## The Evolutionary Elements of Operant Conditioning

As you will recall, classical conditioning has an adaptive value that has been fine-tuned by evolution. Not surprisingly, we can also view operant conditioning from an evolutionary perspective. This viewpoint grew out of a set of curious observations from the early days of conditioning experiments. Several behaviourists who were using simple T mazes like the one shown in **FIGURE 7.13** to study learning in rats discovered that if a rat found food in one arm of the maze on the first trial of the day, it typically ran down the *other* arm on the very next trial. A staunch behaviourist would not expect the rats to behave this way. After all, the rats in these experiments were hungry and they had just been reinforced for turning in a particular direction. According to operant conditioning, this should *increase* the likelihood of turning in that same direction, not reduce it. With additional trials the rats eventually learned to go to the arm with the food, but they had to learn to overcome this initial tendency to go the wrong way. How can we explain this?

What was puzzling from a behaviourist perspective makes sense when viewed from an evolutionary perspective. Rats are foragers and, like all foraging species, they have evolved a highly adaptive strategy for survival. They move around in their environment looking for food. If they find it somewhere, they eat it (or store it) and then go look somewhere else for more. If they do not find food, they forage in another part of the environment. So, if the rat just found food in the *right* arm of a T maze, the obvious place to look next time is the *left* arm. The rat knows that there is not more food in the right arm because it just ate the food it found there! Indeed, foraging animals such as rats have well-developed spatial representations that allow them to search their environment efficiently. If given the opportunity to explore a complex environment like the multi-arm maze shown in **FIGURE 7.14,** rats will systematically go from arm to arm collecting food, rarely returning to an arm they have previously visited (Olton & Samuelson, 1976).

**What explains a rat's behaviour in a T maze?**

Two of Skinner's former students, Keller Breland and Marian Breland, were among the first researchers to discover that it was not just rats in T mazes that presented a problem for behaviourists (Breland & Breland, 1961). The Brelands pointed out that psychologists and the organisms they study often seemed to "disagree" on what the organisms should be doing. Their argument was simple: When this kind of dispute develops, the animals are always right, and the psychologists had better rethink their theories.

The Brelands, who made a career out of training animals for commercials and movies, often used pigs because pigs are surprisingly good at learning all sorts of tricks. However, they discovered that it was extremely difficult to teach a pig the simple task of dropping coins in a box. Instead of depositing the coins, the pigs persisted in rooting with

▲ Figure **7.13** **A Simple T Maze** When rats find food in the right arm of a typical T maze, on the next trial, they will often run to the left arm of the maze. This contradicts basic principles of operant conditioning: If the behaviour of running to the right arm is reinforced, it should be more likely to occur again in the future. However, this behaviour is perfectly consistent with a rat's evolutionary preparedness. Like most foraging animals, rats explore their environments in search of food and seldom return to where food has already been found. Quite sensibly, if food has already been found in the right arm of the T maze, the rat will search the left arm next to see if more food is there.

▼ Figure **7.14** **A Complex T Maze** Like many other foraging species, rats placed in a complex T maze such as this one show evidence of their evolutionary preparedness. These rats will systematically travel from arm to arm in search of food, never returning to arms they have already visited.

Start

Start

The misbehaviour of organisms: Pigs are biologically predisposed to root out their food, just as raccoons are predisposed to wash their food. Trying to train either species to behave differently can prove to be an exercise in futility.

them as if they were digging them up in soil, tossing them in the air with their snouts and pushing them around. The Brelands tried to train raccoons at the same task, with different but equally dismal results. The raccoons spent their time rubbing the coins between their paws instead of dropping them in the box.

Having learned the association between the coins and food, the animals began to treat the coins as stand-ins for food. Pigs are biologically predisposed to root out their food, and raccoons have evolved to clean their food by rubbing it with their paws. That is exactly what each species of animal did with the coins.

The Brelands' work shows that all species, including humans, are biologically predisposed to learn some things more readily than others and to respond to stimuli in ways that are consistent with their evolutionary history (Gallistel, 2000). Such adaptive behaviours, however, evolved over extraordinarily long periods and in particular environmental contexts. If those circumstances change, some of the behavioural mechanisms that support learning can lead an organism astray. Raccoons that associated coins with food failed to follow the simple route to obtaining food by dropping the coins in the box; "nature" took over and they wasted time rubbing the coins together. The point is that, although much of every organism's behaviour results from predispositions sharpened by evolutionary mechanisms, these mechanisms sometimes can have ironic consequences.

## IN SUMMARY

▶ Operant conditioning, as developed by B. F. Skinner, is a process by which behaviours are reinforced and therefore become more likely to occur, where complex behaviours are shaped through reinforcement, and where the contingencies between actions and outcomes are critical in determining how an organism's behaviours will be displayed.

▶ Like Watson, Skinner tried to explain behaviour without considering cognitive, neural, or evolutionary mechanisms. However, as with classical conditioning, this approach turned out to be incomplete.

▶ Operant conditioning has clear cognitive components: Organisms behave as though they have expectations about the outcomes of their actions and adjust their actions accordingly. Cognitive influences can sometimes override the trial-by-trial feedback that usually influences learning.

▶ Studies with both animals and people highlight the operation of a neural reward centre that impacts learning.

▶ The associative mechanisms that underlie operant conditioning have their roots in evolutionary biology. Some things are relatively easily learned and others are difficult; the history of the species is usually the best clue as to which will be which.

# Observational Learning: Look at Me

Four-year-old Rodney and his 2-year-old sister Margie had always been told to keep away from the stove, good advice for any child and many an adult. Being a mischievous imp, however, Rodney decided one day to heat up a burner and place his hand over it until the singeing of his flesh led him to recoil, shrieking in pain. Rodney was more scared than hurt, really—and no one hearing this story doubts that he learned something important that day. But little Margie, who stood by watching these events unfold, *also* learned the same lesson. Rodney's story is a behaviourist's textbook example: The administration of punishment led to a learned change in his behaviour. But how can we explain Margie's learning? She received neither punishment nor reinforcement—indeed, she did not even have direct experience with the wicked appliance—yet it is arguable that she is just as likely to keep her hands away from stoves in the future as Rodney is.

Margie's is a case of **observational learning,** in which *learning takes place by watching the actions of others.* Observational learning challenges behaviourism's reinforcement-based explanations of classical and operant conditioning, but there is no doubt that this type of learning produces changes in behaviour. In all societies, appropriate social behaviour is passed on from generation to generation largely through observation (Bandura, 1965). The rituals and behaviours that are a part of our culture are acquired by each new generation, not only through deliberate training of the young, but also through young people observing the patterns of behaviours of their elders and each other (Flynn & Whiten, 2008). Tasks such as using chopsticks or learning to operate a TV's remote control are more easily acquired if we watch these activities being carried out before we try ourselves. Even complex motor tasks, such as performing surgery, are learned in part through extensive observation and imitation of models. And anyone who is about to undergo surgery is grateful for observational learning. Just the thought of a generation of surgeons acquiring their surgical techniques using the trial-and-error techniques studied by Thorndike, or the shaping of successive approximations that captivated Skinner, would make any of us very nervous.

> Why might a younger sibling appear to learn faster than a firstborn?

Observational learning plays an important role in surgical training, as illustrated by the medical students observing famed German surgeon Vincenz Czerny (beard and white gown) perform stomach surgery in 1901 at a San Francisco hospital.

## Observational Learning in Humans

In a series of studies that have become landmarks in psychology, Canadian psychologist Albert Bandura and his colleagues investigated the parameters of observational learning (Bandura, Ross, & Ross, 1961) (for additional discussion of Bandura's work, see the Social Psychology chapter). The researchers escorted individual preschoolers into a play area, where they found a number of desirable toys that 4-year-olds typically like. An adult *model,* someone whose behaviour might serve as a guide for others, was then led into the room and seated in the opposite corner, where there were several other toys, including a Bobo doll, which is a large inflatable plastic toy with a weighted bottom that allows it to bounce back upright when knocked down. The adult played quietly for a bit but then started aggressing toward the Bobo doll, knocking it down,

**observational learning**
A condition in which learning takes place by watching the actions of others.

**diffusion chain**
A process in which individuals initially learn a behaviour by observing another individual perform that behaviour, and then serve as a model from which other individuals learn the behaviour.

jumping on it, hitting it with the mallet, kicking it around the room, and yelling "Pow!" and "Kick him!" When the children who observed these actions were later allowed to play with a variety of toys, including a child-size Bobo doll, they were more than twice as likely to interact with it in an aggressive manner as a group of children who had not observed the aggressive model.

So what? Kids like to break stuff, and after all, Bobo dolls are made to be punched. Although that is true, as **FIGURE 7.15** shows, the degree of imitation that the children showed was startling. In fact, the adult model purposely used novel behaviours such as hitting the doll with a toy mallet or throwing it up in the air so that the researchers could distinguish aggressive acts that were clearly the result of observational learning. The children in these studies also showed that they were sensitive to the consequences of the actions they observed. When they saw the adult models being punished for behaving aggressively, the children showed considerably less aggression. When the children observed a model being rewarded and praised for aggressive behaviour, they displayed an increase in aggression (Bandura, Ross, & Ross, 1963). The observational learning seen in Bandura's studies has implications for social learning and cultural transmission of behaviours, norms, and values (Bandura, 1977, 1994).

> What did the Bobo doll experiment show about children and aggressive behaviour?

Recent research with children has shown that observational learning is well suited to seeding behaviours that can spread widely across a culture through a process called a **diffusion chain,** where *individuals initially learn a behaviour by observing another individual perform that behaviour, and then serve as a model from which other individuals learn the behaviour* (Flynn, 2008; Flynn & Whiten, 2008). Experiments investigating the operation of diffusion chains in preschool-aged children have used a procedure in which a child (B) observes an adult model (A) performing a target act, such as using a novel

▼ Figure **7.15** **Beating Up Bobo** Children who were exposed to an adult model who behaved aggressively toward a Bobo doll were likely to behave aggressively themselves. This behaviour occurred in the absence of any direct reinforcement. Observational learning was responsible for producing the children's behaviours.

tool to obtain a reward. Then, child B serves as a model for another child, C, who watches B perform the target act, followed by child D observing C perform the target act, and so forth. The evidence to date indicates that children can learn how to use a novel tool by observing an adult model use that tool and, more importantly, can then serve as effective models for other children to learn how to use the tool.

Initial studies of diffusion chains showed that behaviours such as novel tool use could be spread accurately across 10 children (Flynn & Whiten, 2008; Horner et al., 2006), and more recent work indicates faithful transmission of tool use across a diffusion chain comprised of 20 children (Hopper et al., 2010). These findings of transmission across multiple "cultural generations" underscore that observational learning is well suited for transmission through a diffusion chain, and is thus a potentially powerful means of influencing our culture.

Observational learning is important in many domains of everyday life. Sports provide a good example. Coaches in just about all sports rely on observational learning when they demonstrate critical techniques and skills to players, and athletes also have numerous opportunities to observe other athletes perform. Studies of varsity and recreational level athletes in both team and individual sports indicate that they all report relying heavily on observational learning to improve their performance of critical skills in their respective sports, with varsity athletes reporting an even greater reliance on observational learning than recreational athletes (Wesch, Law, & Hall, 2007). But can merely observing a skill result in an improvement in performing that skill without actually practising it? A number of studies have shown that observing someone else perform a motor task, ranging from reaching for a target to pressing a sequence of keys, can produce robust learning in the observer. In fact, observational learning sometimes results in just as much learning as practising the task itself (Heyes & Foster, 2002; Mattar & Gribble, 2005; Vinter & Perruchet, 2002).

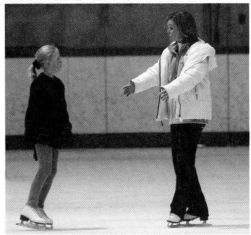

Coaches like former Canadian figure skating champion Josée Chouinard, rely on observational learning when they demonstrate techniques to athletes.

## Observational Learning in Animals

Humans are not the only creatures capable of learning through observing. A wide variety of species learn by observing. In one study, for example, pigeons watched other pigeons get reinforced for either pecking at the feeder or stepping on a bar. When placed in the box later, the pigeons tended to use whatever technique they had observed other pigeons using earlier (Zentall, Sutton, & Sherburne, 1996).

In an interesting series of studies, researchers showed that laboratory-raised rhesus monkeys that had never seen a snake would develop a fear of snakes simply by observing the fear reactions of other monkeys (Cook & Mineka, 1990; Mineka & Cook, 1988). In fact, the fear reactions of these lab-raised monkeys were so authentic and pronounced that they could function as models for still *other* lab-raised monkeys, creating a kind of observational learning "chain." These results also support our earlier discussion of how each species has evolved particular biological predispositions for specific behaviours. Virtually every rhesus monkey raised in the wild has a fear of snakes, which strongly suggests that such a fear is one of this species' predispositions. This research also helps to explain why some phobias that humans suffer from, such as a fear of heights (acrophobia) or enclosed spaces (claustrophobia), are so common, even in people who have never had unpleasant experiences in these contexts (Mineka & Ohman, 2002). The fears may emerge not from specific conditioning experiences but from observing and learning from the reactions of others.

One of the most important questions about observational learning in animals concerns whether monkeys and chimpanzees can learn to use tools by observing tool use in others, which we have already seen can be accomplished by young children. In one of the first controlled studies to examine this issue, chimpanzees observed a model (the experimenter) use a metal bar shaped like a T to pull items of food toward them (Tomasello et al., 1987). Compared with a group that did not observe any tool use,

Monkeys can learn to fear snakes through observational learning if they see another monkey reacting with fear to the sight of a snake. But monkeys cannot be trained to fear flowers through observational learning—no matter how many times they watch another monkey who has been conditioned to fear the same flower. How does the principle of biological preparedness account for this finding?

these chimpanzees showed more learning when later performing the task themselves. However, the researchers noted that the chimpanzees hardly ever used the tool in the exact same way that the model did. So, in a later experiment, they introduced a novel twist (Nagell, Olguin, & Tomasello, 1993). In one condition, a model used a rake in its normal position (with the teeth pointed to the ground) to capture a food reward, which was rather inefficient because the teeth were widely spaced and the food sometimes slipped between them. In a second condition, the model flipped over the rake, so that the teeth were pointed up and the flat edge of the rake touched the ground—a more effective procedure for capturing the food. Both groups who observed tool use performed better when trying to obtain the food themselves than did a control group who did not observe a model use the tool. However, the chimpanzees who observed the more efficient procedure did not use it any more often than did those who observed the less efficient procedure; the two groups performed identically. By contrast, 2-year-old children exposed to the same conditions used the rake in the exact same way that each of the models did in the two observational learning conditions. The chimpanzees seemed only to be learning that the tool could be used to obtain food, whereas the children learned something specific about how to use the tool.

The chimpanzees in these studies had been raised by their mothers in the wild. In a related study, the researchers asked whether chimpanzees who had been raised in environments that also included human contact could learn to imitate the exact actions performed by a model (Tomasello, Savage-Rumbaugh, & Kruger, 1993). The answer was a resounding yes: Chimpanzees raised in a more human-like environment showed more specific observational learning than did those who had been reared by their mothers and performed similarly to human children. This finding led Tomasello and his colleagues (1993) to put forth what they termed the *enculturation hypothesis*:

> **What are the cognitive differences between chimpanzees raised among humans versus raised in the wild?**

Being raised in a human culture has a profound effect on the cognitive abilities of chimpanzees, especially their ability to understand the intentions of others when performing tasks such as using tools, which in turn increases their observational learning capacities. Others have criticized the hypothesis (Bering, 2004), noting that there is relatively little evidence in support of it beyond the results of the study (Tomasello et al., 1993).

However, more recent research has found something similar in capuchin monkeys, who are known for their tool use in the wild, such as employing branches or stone hammers to crack open nuts (Boinski, Quatrone, & Swartz, 2000; Fragaszy et al., 2004) or using stones to dig up buried roots (Moura & Lee, 2004). Fredman and Whiten (2008) studied monkeys who had been reared in the wild by their mothers or by human families in Israel as part of a project to train the monkeys to aid quadriplegics. A model demonstrated two ways of using a screwdriver to gain access to a food reward hidden in a box. Some monkeys observed the model poke through a hole in the centre of the box, whereas others watched him pry open the lid at the rim of the box (see **FIGURE 7.16**). A control group did not observe any use of the tool. Both mother-reared and human-reared monkeys showed evidence of observational learning compared with those in the control group, but the human-reared monkeys carried out the exact action they had observed more often than the mother-reared monkeys.

▼ Figure **7.16** **Observational Learning** Monkeys who had been reared in the wild by their mothers or by human families watched a model either (*left*) poke a screwdriver through a hole in the centre of a box to obtain a food reward or (*right*) pry open the lid. Both groups showed some evidence of observational learning, but the human-reared monkeys were more likely to carry out the exact action they had watched.

Although this evidence implies that there is a cultural influence on the cognitive processes that support observational learning, the researchers noted that the effects on observational learning could be attributed to any number of influences on the human-reared monkeys, including more experience with tools, more attention to a model's behaviour, or as originally suggested by Tomasello and his colleagues (1993), increased sensitivity to the intentions of others. Thus, more work is needed to understand the exact nature of those processes (Bering, 2004; Tomasello & Call, 2004).

## Neural Elements of Observational Learning

Observational learning involves a neural component as well. As you read in the Neuroscience and Behaviour chapter, *mirror neurons* are a type of cell found in the brains of primates (including humans). Mirror neurons fire when an animal performs an action, such as when a monkey reaches for a food item. More importantly, however, mirror neurons also fire when an animal watches someone *else* perform the same specific task (Rizzolatti & Craighero, 2004). Although this "someone else" is usually a fellow member of the same species, some research suggests that mirror neurons in monkeys also fire when they observe humans performing an action (Fogassi et al., 2005). For example, monkeys' mirror neurons fired when they observed humans grasping for a piece of food, either to eat it or to place it in a container.

Mirror neurons, then, may play a critical role in the imitation of behaviour as well as the prediction of future behaviour (Rizzolatti, 2004). Mirror neurons are thought to be represented in specific subregions in the frontal and parietal lobes, and there is evidence that individual subregions respond most strongly to observing certain kinds of actions (see **FIGURE 7.17**). If appropriate neurons fire when another organism is seen performing an action, it could indicate an awareness of intentionality, or that the animal is anticipating a likely course of future actions. Although the exact functions of mirror neurons continue to be debated (Hickok, 2009), both of these elements— rote imitation of well-understood behaviours and an awareness of how behaviour is likely to unfold—contribute to observational learning.

**What do mirror neurons do?**

Studies of observational learning in healthy adults have shown that watching someone else perform a task engages some of the same brain regions that are activated when people actually perform the task themselves. Do you consider yourself a good dancer? Have you ever watched someone who is a good dancer—a friend or maybe a celebrity on *Dancing with the Stars*—in the hopes of improving your own dance floor moves? In a recent fMRI study, participants performed two tasks for several days prior to scanning: practising dance sequences to unfamiliar techno-dance songs, and watching music videos containing other dance sequences accompanied by unfamiliar techno-dance songs (Cross et al., 2009). They were then scanned while viewing videos of sequences that they had previously danced or watched, as well as videos of untrained sequences.

Analysis of the fMRI data revealed that in comparison with the untrained sequences, viewing the previously danced or watched sequences recruited a largely similar brain network, including regions considered to be part of the mirror neuron system and a couple of brain regions that showed more activity for previously danced than watched videos. The results of a surprise dancing test given to participants after the conclusion of scanning showed that performance was better on sequences previously watched than on the untrained sequences, demonstrating significant observational learning, but was best of all on the previously danced sequences (Cross et al., 2009). So, while watching *Dancing with the Stars* might indeed improve your dancing skills, practising on the dance floor should help even more.

▼ Figure **7.17 Mirror Neuron System**
Regions in the frontal lobe (area 44) and parietal lobe (area 40) are thought to be part of the mirror neuron system in humans.

Area 40

Area 44

Observing skilled dancers, such as Bill Nye the Science Guy amd Tyne Stecklein on *Dancing with the Stars,* engages many of the same brain regions as does actual dance practice, and can produce significant learning.

Related evidence indicates that observational learning of some motor skills relies on the motor cortex, which is known to be critical for motor learning. For example, when participants watch another individual engage in a task that involves making a complex reaching movement, significant observational learning occurs (Mattar & Gribble, 2005). To examine whether the observational learning depends on the motor cortex, researchers applied transcranial magnetic stimulation (TMS) to the motor cortex just after participants observed performance of the reaching movement (as you learned in the Neuroscience and Behaviour chapter, TMS results in a temporary disruption in the function of the brain region to which it is applied). Strikingly, applying TMS to the motor cortex greatly reduced the amount of observational learning, whereas applying TMS to a control region outside the motor cortex had no effect on observational learning (Brown, Wilson, & Gribble, 2009).

These findings indicate that some kinds of observational learning are grounded in brain regions that are essential for action. When one organism patterns its actions on another organism's behaviours, learning is speeded up and potentially dangerous errors (think of Margie, who will not burn her hand on the stove) are prevented.

## IN SUMMARY

▶ Observational learning is based on cognitive mechanisms such as attention, perception, memory, or reasoning. But observational learning also has roots in evolutionary biology and for the most basic of reasons: It has survival value. Observational learning is an important process by which species gather information about the world around them.

▶ Observational learning has important social and cultural consequences, as it appears to be well suited for transmission of novel behaviours across individuals. Chimpanzees and monkeys can benefit from observational learning, especially those reared in settings that include humans.

▶ The mirror neuron system becomes active during observational learning, and many of the same brain regions are active during observation and performance of a skill. Observational learning is closely tied to parts of the brain that are involved in action.

# Implicit Learning: Under the Radar

It is safe to assume that people are sensitive to the patterns of events that occur in the world around them. Most people do not stumble through life thoroughly unaware of what is going on. Okay, maybe your roommate does. But people usually are attuned to linguistic, social, emotional, or sensorimotor events in the world around them so much so that they gradually build up internal representations of those patterns that were acquired without explicit awareness. This process is often called **implicit learning,** or *learning that takes place largely independent of awareness of both the process and the products of information acquisition.* Because it occurs without awareness, implicit learning is knowledge that sneaks in "under the radar."

Habituation, which we discussed at the outset of the chapter, is a very simple kind of implicit learning where repeated exposure to a stimulus results in a reduced response. Habituation occurs even in a simple organism such as *Aplysia*, which lacks the brain structures necessary for explicit learning, such as the hippocampus

> How can you learn something without being aware of it?

Ten years ago, no one knew how to type using thumbs; now just about all teenagers do it automatically.

(Eichenbaum, 2008; Squire & Kandel, 1999). In contrast, some forms of learning start out explicitly but become more implicit over time. When you first learned to drive a car, for example, you probably devoted a lot of attention to the many movements and sequences that needed to be carried out simultaneously ("step lightly on the accelerator while you push the turn indicator and look in the rearview mirror while you turn the steering wheel"). That complex interplay of motions is now probably quite effortless and automatic for you. Explicit learning has become implicit over time. These distinctions in learning might remind you of similar distinctions in memory and for good reason. In the Memory chapter, you read about the differences between *implicit* and *explicit* memories. Do implicit and explicit learning mirror implicit and explicit memory? It is not that simple, but it is true that learning and memory are inextricably linked. Learning produces memories, and conversely, the existence of memories implies that knowledge was acquired, that experience was registered and recorded in the brain, or that learning has taken place.

**How are learning and memory linked?**

**implicit learning**
Learning that takes place largely independent of awareness of both the process and the products of information acquisition.

## Cognitive Approaches to Implicit Learning

Interest in implicit learning among psychologists was sparked when researchers began to investigate how children learned language and social conduct (Reber, 1967). Most children, by age 6 or 7, are linguistically sophisticated and fairly social. Yet most children reach this state with very little explicit awareness that they have learned something, and with equally little awareness of what it was they have actually learned. As an example, although children are often given explicit rules of social conduct ("Do not chew with your mouth open"), they learn how to behave in a civilized way through experience. They are probably not aware of when or how they learned a particular course of action and may not even be able to state the general principle underlying their behaviour. Yet most kids have learned not to eat with their feet, to listen when they are spoken to, and not to kick the dog.

To investigate implicit learning in the laboratory, in early studies, research participants were asked to memorize strings of 15 or 20 letters. The letter strings, which at first glance look like nonsense syllables, were actually formed using a complex set of rules called an *artificial grammar* (see **FIGURE 7.18**). Participants were not told anything about the rules, but with experience, they gradually developed a vague, intuitive sense of the "correctness" of particular letter groupings. These letter groups became familiar to the participants and they processed them more rapidly and efficiently than the "incorrect" letter groupings (Reber, 1967, 1996).

Take a look at the letter strings shown in Figure 7.18. The ones on the left are correct and follow the rules of the artificial grammar; the ones on the right all violate the rules. The differences are pretty subtle and, if you have not been through the learning phase of the experiment, both sets look a lot alike. In fact, each nongrammatical string only has a single letter violation. Research participants are asked to classify new letter strings based on whether they follow the rules of the grammar. People turn out to be quite good at this task (usually they get 60 to 70 percent correct), but they are unable to demonstrate much in the way of explicit awareness of the rules and regularities that they are using. The experience is similar to coming across a sentence with a grammatical error. You are immediately aware that something is wrong and you can certainly make the sentence grammatical but, unless you are a trained linguist, you will probably find it difficult to articulate which rules of English grammar were violated or which rules you used to repair the sentence.

**Why are tasks learned implicitly difficult to explain to others?**

| Grammatical Strings | Nongrammatical Strings |
|---|---|
| VXJJ | VXTJJ |
| XXVT | XVTVVJ |
| VJTVXJ | VJTTVTV |
| VJTVTV | VJTXXVJ |
| XXXXVX | XXXVTJJ |

▲ Figure **7.18** **Artificial Grammar and Implicit Learning** These are examples of letter strings formed by an artificial grammar. Research participants are exposed to the rules of the grammar and are later tested on new letter strings. Participants show reliable accuracy at distinguishing the valid, grammatical strings from the invalid, nongrammatical strings even though they usually cannot explicitly state the rule they are following when making such judgments. Using an artificial grammar is one way of studying implicit learning (Reber, 1996).

Other studies of implicit learning have used a *serial reaction time* task (Nissen & Bullemer, 1987). Here research participants are presented with five small boxes on a computer screen. Each box lights up briefly, and when it does, the participant is asked to press the button that is just underneath that box as quickly as possible. Like the artificial grammar task, the sequence of lights appears to be random, but in fact it follows a pattern. Research participants eventually get faster with practice as they learn to anticipate which box is most likely to light up next. But, if asked, they are generally unaware that there is a pattern to the lights.

Implicit learning has some characteristics that distinguish it from explicit learning. For example, when asked to carry out implicit tasks, people differ relatively little from one another, but on explicit tasks (such as conscious problem solving), they show large individual-to-individual differences (Reber, Walkenfeld, & Hernstadt, 1991). Implicit learning also seems to be unrelated to IQ: People with high scores on standard intelligence tests are no better at implicit learning tasks, on average, than those whose scores are more modest (Reber & Allen, 2000). Implicit learning changes little across the life span. Researchers discovered well-developed implicit learning of complex, rule-governed auditory patterns in 8-month-old infants (Saffran, Aslin, & Newport, 1996). Infants heard streams of speech that contained experimenter-defined nonsense words. For example, the infants might hear a sequence such as "pabikudaropitibudo," and then "tibudodaropipabiku," and then "pabikutibudodaropi," and so on.

STEVE SMITH/PURESTOCK

Implicit learning, which is involved in acquiring and retaining the skills needed to ride a bicycle, tends to be less affected by age than explicit learning.

The infants were not given any explicit clues as to which sounds were "words" and which were not, but after several sequences, the infants showed signs that they had learned the novel words *pabiku*, *daropi*, and *tibudo*. The infants learned about the invariants in the sequences—that, for example, the syllables *pabiku* were always heard in order like that, whereas *ku* was sometimes followed by *da* and sometimes by *ti*. Because they heard the invariant sequences (like *pabiku*) over and over again, they became familiar: like words. Infants tend to prefer novel information, and they spent more time listening to novel nonsense words that had not been presented earlier than to the nonsense words such as *pabiku* that had been presented. Remarkably, the infants in this study were as good at learning these sequences as university students. At the other end of the life span, researchers have found that implicit learning abilities extend well into old age and that they decline more slowly than explicit learning abilities (Howard & Howard, 1997).

Implicit learning is remarkably resistant to various disorders that are known to affect explicit learning. A group of patients suffering from various psychoses were so severely impaired that they could not solve simple problems that university students had little difficulty with. Yet those patients were able to solve an artificial grammar learning task about as well as university students (Abrams & Reber, 1988). Other studies have found that profoundly amnesic patients not only show normal implicit memories, but also display virtually normal implicit learning of artificial grammar (Knowlton, Ramus, & Squire, 1992). You learned in the Memory chapter that the profoundly amnesic patient Henry Molaison learned normally on the tracking game that Brenda Milner gave him, even though he had no memory of having performed the task before (Milner, 1962). In contrast, several studies have shown that dyslexic children, who fail to acquire reading skills despite normal intelligence and good educational opportunities, exhibit deficits in implicit learning of artificial grammars (Pavlidou, Williams, & Kelly, 2009) and implicit learning of motor and spatial sequences on the serial reaction time task (Bennett et al., 2008; Orban, Lungu, & Doyon, 2008; Stoodley et al., 2008). These findings suggest that problems with implicit learning play an important role in developmental dyslexia and need to be taken into account when developing remedial programs (Stoodley et al., 2008).

## Implicit and Explicit Learning Use Distinct Neural Pathways

The fact that individuals suffering amnesia show intact implicit learning strongly suggests that the brain structures that underlie implicit learning are distinct from those that underlie explicit learning. As we learned in the Memory chapter, amnesic individuals are characterized by lesions to the hippocampus and nearby structures in the medial temporal lobe; accordingly, these regions are not necessary for implicit learning (Bayley, Frascino, & Squire, 2005). What is more, it appears that distinct regions of the brain may be activated depending on how people approach a task.

For example, in one study, participants saw a series of dot patterns, each of which looked like an array of stars in the night sky (Reber et al., 2003). Actually, all the stimuli were constructed to conform to an underlying prototypical dot pattern. The dots, however, varied so much that it was virtually impossible for a viewer to guess that they all had this common structure. Before the experiment began, half of the participants were told about the existence of the prototype; in other words, they were given instructions that encouraged explicit processing. The others were given standard implicit learning instructions: They were told nothing other than to attend to the dot patterns.

The participants were then scanned as they made decisions about new dot patterns, attempting to categorize them into those that conformed to the prototype and those that did not. Interestingly, both groups performed equally well on this task, correctly classifying about 65 percent of the new dot patterns. However, the brain scans revealed that the two groups were making these decisions using very different parts of their brains (see **FIGURE 7.19**). Participants who were given the explicit instructions showed *increased* brain activity in the prefrontal cortex, parietal cortex, hippocampus, and a variety of other areas known to be associated with the processing of explicit memories. Those given the implicit instructions showed *decreased* brain activation primarily in the occipital region, which is involved in visual processing. This finding suggests that participants recruited distinct brain structures in different ways depending on whether they were approaching the task using explicit or implicit learning.

> What technology shows that implicit and explicit learning are associated with separate structures of the brain?

◄ Figure **7.19** **Implicit and Explicit Learning Activate Different Brain Areas** Research participants were scanned with fMRI while engaged in either implicit or explicit learning about the categorization of dot patterns. The occipital region (in blue) showed decreased brain activity after implicit learning. The areas in yellow, orange, and red showed increased brain activity during explicit learning, including the left temporal lobe (*far left*), right frontal lobe (*second from left and second from right*), and parietal lobe (*second from right and far right*) (Reber et al., 2003).

Other studies have begun to pinpoint the brain regions that are involved in two of the most commonly used implicit learning tasks: artificial grammar learning and sequence learning on the serial reaction time task. Several fMRI studies have shown that Broca's area—which, as you learned in the Neuroscience and Behaviour chapter, plays a key role in language production—is turned on during artificial grammar learning (Forkstam et al., 2006; Petersson, Forkstam, & Ingvar, 2004). Furthermore, activating Broca's area by applying electrical stimulation to the nearby scalp enhances implicit learning of artificial grammar, most likely by facilitating acquisition of grammatical rules (De Vries et al., 2010). In contrast, the motor cortex appears critical for sequence learning on the serial reaction time task. When the motor cortex was temporarily disabled by the application of a recently developed type of TMS that lasts for a long time (so that participants could perform the task without having TMS constantly applied while they are doing so), sequence learning was abolished (Wilkinson et al., 2010).

## IN SUMMARY

▶ Implicit learning is a process that detects, learns, and stores patterns without the application of explicit awareness on the part of the learner.

▶ Simple behaviours such as habituation can reflect implicit learning, but complex behaviours, such as language use or socialization, can also be learned through an implicit process.

▶ Tasks that have been used to document implicit learning include artificial grammar and serial reaction time tasks.

▶ Implicit and explicit learning differ from each other in a number of ways: There are fewer individual differences in implicit than explicit learning; psychotic and amnesic patients with explicit learning problems can exhibit intact implicit learning; and neuroimaging studies indicate that implicit and explicit learning recruit distinct brain structures, sometimes in different ways.

# Learning in the Classroom

In this chapter we have considered several different types of learning from behavioural, cognitive, evolutionary, and neural perspectives. Yet it may seem strange to you that we have not discussed the kind of learning to which you are currently devoting much of your life: learning in educational settings such as the classroom. Way back in the first chapter of this book (Psychology: Evolution of a Science), we reviewed some techniques that we think are useful for studying the material in this course and others (see The Real World: Improving Study Skills, pp. 10–11). But, we did not say much about the actual research that supports these suggestions. During the past several years, psychologists have published a great deal of work specifically focused on enhancing learning in educational settings. Let us consider what some of this research says about learning techniques, and then turn to the equally important topic of exerting control over learning processes.

## Techniques for Learning

Students use a wide variety of study techniques in attempts to increase learning. Popular techniques—ones that you might use yourself—include highlighting and underlining, re-reading, summarizing, and visual imagery mnemonics (Annis & Annis, 1982; Wade, Trathen, & Schraw, 1990). How effective are these and other techniques? A team of psychologists that specialize in learning recently published a comprehensive analysis of research concerning 10 learning techniques that are used to by students

(Dunlosky et al., 2013). They considered the usefulness of each technique across four main variables: learning conditions (e.g., how often and in what context the technique is used), to-be-learned materials (e.g., texts, math problems, concepts), student characteristics (e.g., age and ability level), and outcome measures (e.g., rote retention, comprehension, problem solving). Based on the picture that emerged across these four variables, Dunlosky et al. evaluated the overall usefulness of each technique and classified it as high, moderate, or low utility. **TABLE 7.2** provides a brief description of each of the 10 techniques and the overall utility assessment for each one.

Despite their popularity, highlighting, re-reading, summarizing, and visual imagery mnemonics all received a low utility assessment. That does not mean that these techniques have no value whatsoever for improving learning, but it does indicate that each one has significant limitations and that time could be better spent using other approaches—a reason why none of these techniques appeared in The Real World: Improving Study Skills. The feature did review strategies that roughly correspond to two of the techniques in Table 7.2 that received a moderate utility assessment—elaboration interrogation and self-explanation—and we also discussed some material related to these techniques in the Memory chapter (pp. 242–244). Furthermore, the feature highlighted both of the techniques that received high utility assessments: distributed practice and practice testing. Let us take a deeper look at some of the research that supports the beneficial effects of these two effective techniques, which have been intensively investigated during the past few years.

## Distributed Practice

Cramming for exams (neglecting to study for an extended period of time and then studying intensively just before an exam) (Vacha & McBride, 1993) is a common occurrence in educational life. Surveys of undergraduates across a range of universities indicate that anywhere from about 25 percent to as many as 50 percent of students report relying on cramming as part of their studying technique (McIntyre & Munson, 2008). Though cramming is better than not studying at all, when students cram for an exam, they repeatedly study the to-be-learned information with little or

### Table 7.2

**Rating the Effectiveness of Study Techniques**

| Technique | Description | Utility |
|---|---|---|
| Elaborative interrogation | Generating an explanation for why an explicitly stated fact or concept is true | Moderate |
| Self-explanation | Explaining how new information is related to known information, or explaining steps taken during problem solving | Moderate |
| Summarization | Writing summaries (of various lengths) of to-be-learned texts | Low |
| Highlighting/underlining | Marking potentially important portions of to-be-learned material while reading | Low |
| Keyword mnemonic | Using keywords and mental images of text materials while reading or listening | Low |
| Imagery for text | Attempting to form mental images of text materials while reading or listening | Low |
| Re-reading | Re-reading text material again after an initial reading | Low |
| Practice testing | Self-testing or taking practice tests of to-be-learned material | High |
| Distributed practice | Implementing a schedule of practice that spreads out study activities over time | High |
| Interleaved practice | Implementing a schedule of practice that mixes different kinds of problems, or a schedule of study that mixes different kinds of material, within a single study session | Moderate |

AGEFOTOSTOCK/SUPERSTOCK

Studying well in advance of an exam, so that you can take breaks and distribute study time, will generally produce a better outcome than cramming at the last minute.

no time between repetitions, a procedure known as *massed practice*. Such students are thus denying themselves the benefits of distributed practice, which involves spreading out study activities so that more time intervenes between repetitions of the to-be-learned information (and students who rely on cramming are also inviting some of the health and performance problems we outlined in The Real World: The Perils of Procrastination on p. 4).

The benefits of distributed practice relative to massed practice have been known for a long time; in fact, they were first reported in the classic studies of Ebbinghaus (1885/1964) concerning retention of nonsense syllables (see the Memory chapter). What is most impressive is just how widespread the benefits of distributed practice are: They have been observed for numerous different kinds of materials, including foreign vocabulary, definitions, and face–name pairs, and have been demonstrated not only in undergraduates, but also in children, older adults, and individuals with memory problems due to brain damage (Dunlosky et al., 2013). A review of 254 separate studies involving more than 14 000 participants concluded that, on average, participants retained 47 percent of studied information after distributed practice compared with 37 percent after massed practice (Cepeda et al., 2006).

Despite all the evidence indicating that distributed practice is an effective learning strategy, we still do not fully understand why that is so. One promising idea is that when engaging in massed practice, retrieving recently studied information is relatively easy, whereas during distributed practice, it is more difficult to retrieve information that was studied less recently. More difficult retrievals benefit subsequent learning more than easy retrievals, in line with idea of "desirable difficulties" (Bjork & Bjork, 2011) introduced in The Real World: Improving Study Skills. Whatever the explanation for the effects of distributed practice, there is no denying its benefits for students.

## Practice Testing

Practice testing, like distributed practice, has proven useful across a wide range of materials, including learning of stories, facts, vocabulary, and lectures (Dunlosky et al., 2013; Karpicke, 2012) (see also the LearningCurve system associated with this text, which uses practice testing). As you learned in the Memory chapter, practice testing is effective, in part, because actively retrieving an item from memory on a test improves subsequent retention of that item more than simply studying it again (Roediger & Karpicke, 2006). Yet when asked about their preferred study strategies, students indicated by a wide margin that they prefer re-reading materials to testing themselves (Karpicke, 2012). The benefits of testing tend to be greatest when the test is difficult and requires considerable retrieval effort (Pyc & Rawson, 2009), also consistent with the desirable difficulties hypothesis (Bjork & Bjork, 2011). Not

> **Why does a difficult practice test have the greatest benefit?**

only does testing increase verbatim learning of the exact material that is tested, it also enhances the *transfer* of learning from one situation to another (Carpenter, 2012). For example, if you are given practice tests with short-answer questions, such testing improves later performance on both short-answer and multiple-choice questions more than re-reading (Kang, McDermott, & Roediger, 2007). Testing also improves the ability to draw conclusions from the studied material, which is an important part of learning and often critical to performing well in the classroom (Karpicke & Blunt, 2011).

## Testing Aids Attention

Recent laboratory research by one of your textbook authors highlights yet another benefit of testing: Including brief tests during a lecture can improve learning by reducing the tendency to mind wander (Szpunar, Khan, & Schacter, 2013). How often have you found your mind wandering—thinking about your evening plans, recalling a scene from a movie, or texting a friend—in the midst of a lecture that you know that you ought to be attending to carefully? It has probably happened more than once. Research indicates that students' minds wander frequently during classroom lectures (Bunce, Flens, & Neiles, 2011; Lindquist & McLean, 2011; Wilson & Korn, 2007). Critically, such mind wandering impairs learning of the lecture material (Risko et al., 2012). In the study by Szpunar and his colleagues (2013), participants watched a videotaped statistics lecture that was divided into four segments. All of the participants were told that they might or might not be tested after each segment; they were also encouraged to take notes during the lectures.

> Participants in the *tested* group received brief tests on each segment.

> Participants in the *nontested* group did not receive a test until after the final segment (they worked on arithmetic problems after each of the earlier segments).

> Participants in a *re-read* group were shown, but not tested on, the same material as the tested group after each segment.

At random times during the lectures, participants in all groups were probed about whether they were paying attention to the lecture or mind wandering off to other top-

**How does taking practice tests help focus a wandering mind?**

ics. Participants in the nontested and re-read groups indicated that they were mind wandering in response to about 40 percent of the probes, but the incidence of mind wandering was cut in to half, to about 20 percent, in the tested group. Participants in the tested group took significantly more notes during the lectures, and retained significantly more information from the lecture on a final test than did than participants in the other two groups, who performed similarly. Participants in the tested group were also less anxious about the final test than those in the other groups. These results indicate that part of the value of testing comes from encouraging people to sustain attention to a lecture in a way that discourages task-irrelevant activities such as mind wandering and encourages task-relevant activities such as note taking. Because these benefits of testing were observed in response to a videotaped lecture, they apply most directly to online learning, where taped lectures are the norm (see Other Voices: Online Learning), but there is every reason to believe that the results would apply in live classroom settings as well.

## Control of Learning

It is the night before the final exam in your introductory psychology course. You have put in a lot of time reviewing your course notes and the material in this textbook, and you feel that you have learned most of it pretty well. You are coming down the home stretch with little time left, and you have got to decide whether to devote those precious remaining minutes to studying psychological disorders or social psychology. How do you make that decision? What are its potential consequences? An important part of learning involves assessing how well we know something and how much more time we need to devote to studying it.

Recent research has shown that people's judgments about what they have learned play a critical role in guiding further study and learning (Dunlosky & Thiede, 2013; Metcalfe, 2009). Experimental evidence reveals that these subjective assessments, which psychologists refer to as *judgments of learning* (JOLs), have a causal influence on learning: People typically devote more time to studying items that they judge they have not learned well (Metcalfe & Finn, 2008; Son & Metcalfe, 2000).

The finding that JOLs are causally related to decisions about how much to study a particular item is important because JOLs are sometimes inaccurate (Castel, McCabe, & Roediger, 2007). For example, after reading and re-reading a chapter or article in preparation for a test, the material will likely feel quite familiar, and that feeling may convince you that you have learned the material well enough that you do not need to study it further. However, the feeling of familiarity can be misleading: It may be the result of a low-level process such as perceptual priming (see the Memory chapter) and not the kind of learning that will be required to perform well on an exam (Bjork & Bjork, 2011). Similarly, recent research has shown that students are sometimes overconfident in judging how well they have learned definitions of new terms, and fail to study them effectively (Dunlosky & Rawson, 2012). One way to avoid being fooled by such misleading subjective impressions is to test yourself from time to time when studying for an exam under exam-like conditions, and in the case of learning definitions, carefully compare your answers to the actual definitions.

> In what ways can JOLs be misleading?

So, if you are preparing for the final exam in this course and need to decide whether to devote more time to studying psychological disorders or social psychology, try to exert control over learning by testing yourself on material from the two chapters; you can use the results of those tests to help you decide which chapter requires further work. Heed

# OTHER VOICES

## Online Learning

**Daphne Koller** is a professor of computer science at Stanford University.

PHOTO BY HECTOR GARCIA-MOLINA

Online learning has become a hot topic recently as a result of new online initiatives from a number of leading brick-and-mortar universities. Daphne Koller, a professor of computer science at Stanford University, is one of the founders of the popular online learning platform, Coursera. She wrote the following article several months before the launch of Coursera in April 2012.

Our education system is in a state of crisis. Among developed countries, the United States is 55th in quality rankings of elementary math and science education, 20th in high school completion rate and 27th in the fraction of [university] students receiving undergraduate degrees in science or engineering.

As a society, we can and should invest more money in education. But that is only part of the solution. The high costs of high-quality education put it off limits to large parts of the population, both in the United States and abroad, and threaten the school's place in society as a whole. We need to significantly reduce those costs while at the same time improving quality.

If these goals seem contradictory, let's consider an example from history. In the 19th century, 60 percent of the American work force was in agriculture, and there were frequent food shortages. Today, agriculture accounts for less than 2 percent of the work force, and there are food surpluses.

The key to this transition was the use of technology—from crop rotation strategies to GPS-guided farm machinery—which greatly increased productivity. By contrast, our approach to education has remained largely unchanged since the Renaissance: From [elementary school] through [university], most teaching is done by an instructor lecturing to a room full of students, only some of them paying attention.

How can we improve performance in education, while cutting costs at the same time? In 1984, Benjamin Bloom showed that individual tutoring had a huge advantage over standard lecture environments: The average tutored student performed better than 98 percent of the students in the standard class.

Until now, it has been hard to see how to make individualized education affordable. But I argue that technology may provide a path to this goal.

Consider the success of the Khan Academy, which began when Salman Khan tried to teach math remotely to his young cousins. He recorded short videos with explanations and placed them on the Web, augmenting them with automatically graded exercises. This simple approach was so compelling that by now, more than 700 million videos have been watched by millions of viewers.

At Stanford, we recently placed three computer science courses online, using a similar format. Remarkably, in the first four weeks, 300 000 students registered for these courses, with millions of video views and hundreds of thousands of submitted assignments.

What can we learn from these successes? First, we see that video content is engaging to students—many of whom grew up on YouTube—and easy for instructors to produce.

Second, presenting content in short, bite-size chunks, rather than monolithic hour-long lectures, is better suited to students' attention spans, and provides the flexibility to tailor instruction to individual students. Those with less preparation can dwell longer on background material without feeling uncomfortable about how they might be perceived by classmates or the instructor.

Conversely, students with an aptitude for the topic can move ahead rapidly, avoiding boredom and disengagement. In short, everyone has access to a personalized experience that resembles individual tutoring.

Watching passively is not enough. Engagement through exercises and assessments is a critical component of learning. These exercises are designed not just to evaluate the student's learning, but also, more important, to enhance understanding by prompting recall and placing ideas in context.

the conclusion from researchers (Bjork, Dunlosky, & Kornell, 2013) that becoming a more sophisticated and effective learner requires understanding: (a) key features of learning and memory; (b) effective learning techniques; (c) how to monitor and control one's own learning; and (d) biases that can undermine judgments of learning.

## IN SUMMARY

▶ Research on learning techniques indicates that some popular study methods such as high-lighting, underlining, and re-reading have low utility, whereas other techniques such as practice testing and distributed practice have high utility.

▶ Practice testing improves retention and transfer of learning and can also enhance learning and reduce mind wandering during lectures.

▶ Judgments of learning play a causal role in determining what material to study, but they can be misleading.

Moreover, testing allows students to move ahead when they master a concept, rather than when they have spent a stipulated amount of time staring at the teacher who is explaining it.

For many types of questions, we now have methods to automatically assess students' work, allowing them to practice while receiving instant feedback about their performance. With some effort in technology development, our ability to check answers for many types of questions will get closer and closer to that of human graders.

Of course, these student–computer interactions can leave many gaps. Students need to be able to ask questions and discuss the material. How do we scale the human interaction to tens of thousands of students?

Our Stanford courses provide a forum in which students can vote on questions and answers, allowing the most important questions to be answered quickly—often by another student. In the future, we can adapt Web technology to support even more interactive formats, like real-time group discussions, affordably and at large scale.

More broadly, the online format gives us the ability to identify what works. Until now, many education studies have been based on populations of a few dozen students. Online technology can capture every click: what students watched more than once, where they paused, what mistakes they made. This mass of data is an invaluable resource for understanding the learning process and figuring out which strategies really serve students best.

Some argue that online education cannot teach creative problem-solving and critical-thinking skills. But to practice problem-solving, a student must first master certain concepts. By providing a cost-effective solution for this first step, we can focus precious classroom time on more interactive problem-solving activities that achieve deeper understanding—and foster creativity.

In this format, which we call the flipped classroom, teachers have time to interact with students, motivate them and challenge them. Though attendance in my Stanford class is optional, it is considerably higher than in many standard lecture-based classes. And after the Los Altos school district in Northern California adopted this blended approach, using the Khan Academy, seventh graders in a remedial math class sharply improved their performance, with 41 percent reaching advanced or proficient levels, up from 23 percent.

A 2010 analysis from the Department of Education, based on 45 studies, showed that online learning is as effective as face-to-face learning, and that blended learning is considerably more effective than either.

Online education, then, can serve two goals. For students lucky enough to have access to great teachers, blended learning can mean even better outcomes at the same or lower cost. And for the millions here and abroad who lack access to good, in-person education, online learning can open doors that would otherwise remain closed.

Nelson Mandela said, "Education is the most powerful weapon which you can use to change the world." By using technology in the service of education, we can change the world in our lifetime.

Koller makes a strong positive case for online learning, and the rapid spread of online courses since the publication of this article indicates that others agree with her. Furthermore, Koller's comments about the delivery of information in "bite-sized chunks" and the use of testing are generally consistent with the recent findings of Karl Szpunar and his colleagues (2013) discussed in the main text showing that intermittent testing can reduce mind wandering during online lectures. But online learning is not without its critics. For example, in a *New York Times* op-ed article written some 6 months after Koller's column, when Harvard and MIT announced their own online plans, David Brooks (2012a) raised some important questions: "If a few star professors can lecture to millions, what happens to the rest of the faculty? Will academic standards be as rigorous? What happens to the students who do not have enough intrinsic motivation to stay glued to their laptop hour after hour? How much communication is lost—gesture, mood, eye contact—when you are not actually in a room with a passionate teacher and students?"

What do you see as the major challenges for online learning? How important is face-to-face interaction in your own educational experience? What kind of research would you like to see done to further the effectiveness of online learning?

# Chapter Review

## KEY CONCEPT QUIZ

**1.** In classical conditioning, the learned association between the conditioned and unconditioned stimuli produces
a. a neutral stimulus.
b. a conditioned response.
c. an unconditioned response.
d. another conditioned stimulus.

**2.** What occurs when a conditioned stimulus no longer predicts an unconditioned stimulus?
a. generalization
b. spontaneous recovery
c. extinction
d. acquisition

**3.** What did Watson and Rayner seek to demonstrate about behaviourism through the Little Albert experiment?
a. Conditioning involves a degree of cognition.
b. Classical conditioning has an evolutionary component.
c. Behaviourism alone cannot explain human behaviour.
d. Even sophisticated behaviours such as emotion are subject to classical conditioning.

**4.** Which part of the brain is involved in the classical conditioning of fear?
a. the amygdala
b. the cerebellum
c. the hippocampus
d. the hypothalamus

**5.** After having a bad experience with a particular type of food, people can develop a lifelong aversion to the food. This suggests that conditioning has a(n) ___ aspect.
a. cognitive
b. evolutionary
c. neural
d. behavioural

**6.** Which of the following is NOT an accurate statement concerning operant conditioning?
a. Actions and outcomes are critical to operant conditioning.
b. Operant conditioning involves the reinforcement of behaviour.
c. Complex behaviours cannot be accounted for by operant conditioning.
d. Operant conditioning has associative mechanisms with roots in evolutionary behaviour.

**7.** Which of the following mechanisms have no role in Skinner's approach to behaviour?
a. cognitive
b. neural
c. evolutionary
d. all of the above

**8.** Latent learning provides evidence for a cognitive element in operant conditioning because
a. it occurs without any obvious reinforcement.
b. it requires both positive and negative reinforcement.
c. it points toward the operation of a neural reward centre.
d. it depends on a stimulus–response relationship.

**9.** Activity of neurons in the ___ contributes to the process of reinforcement.
a. hippocampus
b. pituitary gland
c. medial forebrain bundle
d. parietal lobe

**10.** Which of the following mechanisms does NOT help form the basis of observational learning?
a. attention
b. perception
c. punishment
d. memory

**11.** Neural research indicates that observational learning is closely tied to brain areas that are involved in
a. memory.
b. vision.
c. action.
d. emotion.

**12.** What kind of learning takes place largely independent of awareness of both the process and the products of information acquisition?
a. latent learning
b. implicit learning
c. observational learning
d. conscious learning

**13.** The process in which repeated or prolonged exposure to a stimulus results in a gradual reduction in responding is called
a. habituation.
b. explicit learning.
c. serial reaction time.
d. delay conditioning.

**14.** Which of the following statements about implicit learning is inaccurate?
a. Some forms of learning start out explicitly but become more implicit over time.
b. Implicit learning occurs even in the simplest organisms.
c. People with high scores on intelligence tests are more adept at implicit learning tasks.
d. Children learn language and social conduct largely through implicit learning.

**15.** Responding to implicit instructions results in decreased brain activation in which part of the brain?
a. the hippocampus
b. the parietal cortex
c. the prefrontal cortex
d. the occipital region

**16.** Which study strategy has been shown to be the most effective?
a. highlighting text
b. re-reading
c. summarizing
d. taking practice tests

## KEY TERMS

acquisition (p. 268)

biological preparedness (p. 276)

classical conditioning (p. 267)

cognitive map (p. 289)

conditioned response (CR)
(p. 268)

conditioned stimulus (CS) (p. 268)

diffusion chain (p. 296)

discrimination (p. 271)

extinction (p. 271)

fixed-interval schedule (FI) (p. 283)

fixed-ratio schedule (FR) (p. 285)

generalization (p. 271)

habituation (p. 267)

implicit learning (p. 301)

intermittent reinforcement (p. 285)

intermittent reinforcement effect
(p. 287)

latent learning (p. 289)

law of effect (p. 278)

learning (p. 267)

observational learning (p. 295)

operant behaviour (p. 278)

operant conditioning (p. 277)

punisher (p. 279)

reinforcer (p. 279)

second-order conditioning
(p. 268)

sensitization (p. 267)

shaping (p. 287)

spontaneous recovery (p. 271)

unconditioned response (UR)
(p. 267)

unconditioned stimulus (US)
(p. 267)

variable-interval schedule (VI)
(p. 283)

variable-ratio schedule (VR)
(p. 285)

## CHANGING MINDS

1. A friend is taking a class in childhood education. "Back in the old days," she says, "teachers used physical punishment, but of course that's not allowed any more. Now, a good teacher should only use reinforcement. When children behave, teachers should provide positive reinforcement, like praise. When children misbehave, teachers should provide negative reinforcement, like scolding or withholding privileges." What is your friend misunderstanding about reinforcement? Can you give better examples of how negative reinforcement could be productively applied in an elementary school classroom?

2. A friend of your family is trying to train her daughter to make her bed every morning. You suggest she tries positive reinforcement. A month later, the woman reports back to you. "It is not working very well," she says. "Every time she makes her bed, I put a gold star on the calendar, and at the end of the week, if there are seven gold stars, I give Vicky a reward—a piece of licorice. But so far, she's only earned the licorice twice." How could you explain why the desired behaviour—bed-making—might not increase as a result of this reinforcement procedure?

3. While studying for the exam, you ask your study partner to provide a definition of classical conditioning. "In classical conditioning," she says, "there's a stimulus—the CS—that predicts an upcoming event, the US. Usually, it is something bad, like an electric shock, nausea, or a frightening loud noise. The learner makes a response, the CR, in order to prevent the US. Sometimes, the US is good, like food for Pavlov's dogs, and then the learner makes the response in order to earn the US." What is wrong with this definition?

4. One of your classmates announces that he liked the last chapter (on memory) better than the current chapter on learning. "I want to be a psychiatrist," he says, "so I mostly care about human learning. Conditioning might be a really powerful way to train animals to push levers or perform tricks, but it really doesn't have much relevance to how humans learn things." How similar is learning in humans and other animals? What real-world examples can you provide to show that conditioning does occur in humans?

## ANSWERS TO KEY CONCEPT QUIZ

1. b; 2. c; 3. d; 4. a; 5. b; 6. c; 7. d; 8. a; 9. c; 10. c; 11. c; 12. b; 13. a; 14. c; 15. d; 16. d.

# 8

# Emotion and Motivation

▲ **Emotional Experience:**
**The Feeling Machine**
What Is Emotion?
The Emotional Body
The Emotional Brain
The Regulation of Emotion

▲ **Emotional Communication:**
**Msgs w/o Wrds**
Communicative Expression
**HOT SCIENCE** The Body of Evidence
Deceptive Expression
**OTHER VOICES** I Used to Get Invited to
Poker Games…
**CULTURE & COMMUNITY** Is It What You
Say or How You Say It?

▲ **Motivation: Getting Moved**
The Function of Emotion
Instincts and Drives
What the Body Needs
**THE REAL WORLD** Jeet Jet?
What the Mind Wants

EONARDO IS 5 YEARS OLD AND CUTE AS A BUTTON. He can do many of the things that other 5-year-olds can do: solve puzzles, build towers of blocks, and play guessing games with grown-ups. But unlike other 5-year-olds, Leonardo has never been proud of his abilities, angry at his mother, or bored with his lessons. That is because Leonardo has a condition that makes him unable to experience emotions of any kind. He has never felt joy or sorrow, delight or despair, shame, envy, annoyance, excitement, gratitude, or regret. He has never laughed or cried.

Leonardo's condition has had a profound impact on his life. For example, because he does not experience emotions, he is not motivated to do things that bring most children pleasure, such as eating cookies or playing hide-and-seek or watching Saturday morning cartoons. And because he does not feel, he does not have any intuitions about what others are feeling, which can make social interaction a challenge. His mother has spent years teaching him how to make the facial expressions that indicate emotions such as surprise and sadness, and how to detect those facial expressions in others. Leonardo now knows that he should smile when someone says something nice to him and that he should raise his eyebrow once in a while to show interest in what people are saying. Leonardo is a quick learner, and he has gotten so good at this that when strangers interact with him they find it hard to believe that deep down inside he is feeling nothing at all.

So when Leonardo's mother smiles at him, he always smiles back. And yet, she is keenly aware that Leonardo is merely making the faces he was taught to make and that he does not really love her.

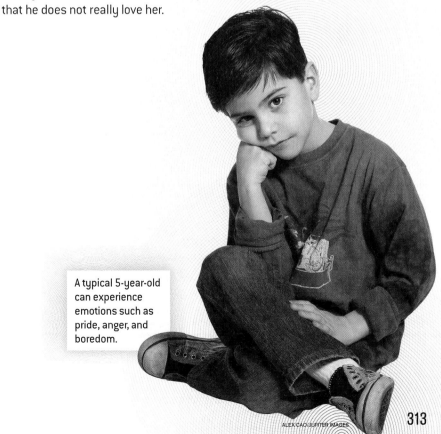

A typical 5-year-old can experience emotions such as pride, anger, and boredom.

ALEX CAO/JUPITER IMAGES

313

Leonardo and his "mom," MIT Professor Cynthia Breazeal.

"I never realized they had feelings."

But that is okay. Although Leonardo cannot return her affection, Dr. Cynthia Breazeal still considers him one of the greatest robots she has ever designed (Breazeal, 2009).

**YES, LEONARDO IS A MACHINE. HE CAN SEE AND HEAR,** he can remember and reason. But despite his adorable smile and knowing wink, he cannot feel a thing, and that makes him infinitely different than us. Our ability to love and to hate, to be amused and annoyed, to feel elated and devastated, is an essential element of our humanity, and a person who could not feel these things would seem a lot like a robot to the rest of us. But what exactly are these things we call emotions and why are they so essential? In this chapter we will explore these questions. We will start by discussing the nature of emotions and seeing how they relate to the states of our bodies and our brains. Next we will see how people express their emotions, and how they use those expressions to communicate with each other. Finally, we will examine the essential role that emotions play in motivation—how they inform us, and how they compel us do everything from making war to making love.

# Emotional Experience: The Feeling Machine

Leonardo does not know what love feels like and there is no way to teach him, because trying to describe the feeling of love to someone who has never experienced it is a bit like trying to describe the colour green to someone who was born blind. We could tell Leonardo what causes the feeling ("It happens whenever I see Marilynn") and we could tell him about its consequences ("I breathe hard and say goofy stuff"), but in the end these descriptions would miss the point because the essential feature of love—like the essential feature of all emotions—is the *experience*. It *feels* like something to love, and what it feels like is love's defining attribute (Heavey, Hurlburt, & Lefforge, 2012).

It is almost impossible not to feel something when you look at this photograph, and it is almost impossible to say exactly what you are feeling.

## What Is Emotion?

How can we study something whose defining attribute defies description? Psychologists have developed a clever technique that capitalizes on the fact that although people cannot always say what an emotional experience feels like ("Love is … um … uh …"), they usually can say how similar one experience is to another ("Love is more like happiness than like anger"). By asking people to rate the similarity of dozens of emotional experiences, psychologists have been able to use a technique known as *multidimensional scaling* to create a map of those experiences. The mathematics behind this technique is complex, but the logic is simple. If you drew up a list of the distances between a half-dozen Canadian cities, handed the list to a friend, and challenged her to turn those distances into a map, your friend would have to draw something like a map of Canada (see **FIGURE 8.1**). Why? Because there is no other map that allows every city to appear at precisely the right distance from every other.

The same technique can be used to generate a map of the emotional landscape. If you listed the similarity of a large number of emotional experiences (assigning smaller distances to those that feel similar and larger distances to those that feel dissimilar) and then challenged a friend to incorporate them into a map, your friend would be forced to draw a map like the one shown in **FIGURE 8.2**. This is the unique map that allows every emotional experience to be precisely the right distance from every other. What good is this map? As it turns out, maps do not just show how close things are to each other: They also reveal the *dimensions* on which those things vary. For example, the map in Figure 8.2 reveals that emotional experiences differ on two dimensions called *valence* (how positive or negative the experience is) and *arousal* (how active or passive the experience is). Research shows that all emotional

> **Why do psychologists use multidimensional scaling?**

|           | St John's | Halifax | Ottawa | Winnipeg | Whitehorse | Victoria |
|-----------|-----------|---------|--------|----------|------------|----------|
| St John's | 0         | 1484    | 2727   | 4802     | 8109       | 7506     |
| Halifax   | 1484      | 0       | 1435   | 3510     | 6814       | 6214     |
| Ottawa    | 2727      | 1435    | 0      | 2146     | 5385       | 4429     |
| Winnipeg  | 4802      | 3510    | 2146   | 0        | 3292       | 2378     |
| Whitehorse| 8109      | 6814    | 5385   | 3292     | 0          | 2484     |
| Victoria  | 7506      | 6214    | 4429   | 2378     | 2484       | 0        |

▲ Figure 8.1 **From Distances to Maps**
Knowing the distances between things—like cities, for example—allows us to draw a map that reveals the dimensions on which they vary.

◀ Figure 8.2 **Two Dimensions of Emotion**
Just as cities can be mapped by their longitude and latitude, emotions can be mapped by their arousal and valence.

**emotion**
A positive or negative experience that is associated with a particular pattern of physiological activity.

**James–Lange theory**
The theory that a stimulus triggers activity in the body, which in turn produces an emotional experience in the brain.

**Cannon–Bard theory**
The theory that a stimulus simultaneously triggers activity in the body and emotional experience in the brain.

**two-factor theory**
The theory that emotions are based on inferences about the causes of physiological arousal.

experiences can be described by their unique coordinates on this two-dimensional map (Russell, 1980; Watson & Tellegen, 1985; Yik, Russell, & Steiger, 2011).

This map of emotional experience suggests that any definition of emotion must include two things: first, the fact that emotional experiences are good or bad; and second, the fact that these experiences have characteristic levels of bodily arousal. With these two facts in mind, we can define **emotion** as *a positive or negative experience that is associated with a particular pattern of physiological activity*. As you are about to see, the first step in understanding emotion involves understanding how the experience part and the physiological activity part of this definition are related.

## The Emotional Body

You probably think that if you walked into your kitchen right now and saw a bear nosing through the cupboards, you would feel fear, your heart would start to pound, and the muscles in your legs would prepare you for running. But in the late nineteenth century, William James suggested that the events that produce an emotion might actually happen in the opposite order: First you see the bear, then your heart starts pounding and your leg muscles contract, and *then* you experience fear, which is nothing more than your experience of your body's response. As James (1884, pp. 189–190) wrote, "Bodily changes follow directly the perception of the exciting fact. … And feeling of the same changes as they occur *is* the emotion." For James, each unique emotional experience was the result of a unique pattern of physiological responses, and he suggested that without all the heart pounding and muscle clenching, there would be no experience of emotion at all. Psychologist Carl Lange suggested something similar at about the same time, so the idea, now known as the **James–Lange theory** of emotion, is that a *stimulus triggers activity in the body, which in turn produces an emotional experience in the brain*. According to this theory, emotional experience is the consequence—not the cause—of our physiological reactions to objects and events in the world.

James's former student, Walter Cannon, did not like this idea very much, and so together with *his* student, Philip Bard, he proposed an alternative. The **Cannon–Bard theory** of emotion is the theory that *a stimulus simultaneously triggers activity in the body and emotional experience in the brain* (Bard, 1934; Cannon, 1929). Cannon claimed that his theory was better than the James–Lange theory for several reasons. First, he noted, emotions happen quickly even though the body often reacts slowly. For example, a blush is a bodily response to embarrassment that takes 15 to 30 seconds to occur, and yet, people feel embarrassed within seconds of noticing that, oh say, their pants have fallen off in public. So how could the blush be the cause of the feeling? Second, people often have difficulty accurately detecting bodily responses, such as changes in their heart rates. If people cannot detect changes in their heart rates, then how can they experience those changes as an emotion? Third, nonemotional stimuli—such as an increase in room temperature—can cause the same bodily response as emotional stimuli do. So why do not people feel afraid when they get a fever? Finally, Cannon noted that there simply were not enough unique patterns of bodily activity to account for all the unique emotional experiences people have. If many different emotional experiences are associated with the same pattern of bodily activity, then how could that pattern of activity be the sole determinant of the emotional experience?

These are all good questions, and about 30 years after Cannon asked them, psychologists Stanley Schachter and Jerome Singer supplied some answers (Schachter & Singer, 1962). James and Lange were right, they claimed, to equate emotion with the perception of

Did Princess Kate make Prince William blush by embarrassing him, or did she embarrass him by making him blush? The experience of embarrassment precedes blushing by up to 30 seconds, so it is unlikely that blushing is the cause of the emotional experience.

ANDREW MILLIGAN–WPA POOL/GETTY IMAGES

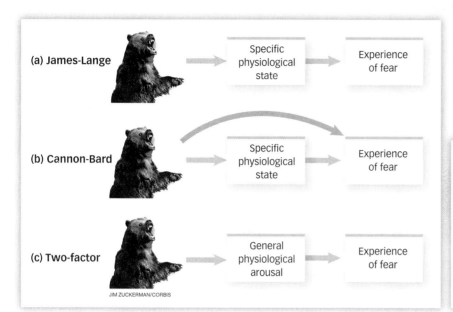

(a) James-Lange → Specific physiological state → Experience of fear

(b) Cannon-Bard → Specific physiological state → Experience of fear

(c) Two-factor → General physiological arousal → Experience of fear

JIM ZUCKERMAN/CORBIS

◄ Figure 8.3 **Classic Theories of Emotion** Classic theories make different claims about the origins of emotion. The James–Lange theory suggests that stimuli trigger specific physiological states, which are then experienced as emotions (a). The Cannon–Bard theory suggests that stimuli trigger both specific physiological states and emotional experiences independently (b). The two-factor theory suggests that stimuli trigger general physiological arousal whose cause the brain interprets, and this interpretation leads to emotional experience (c).

one's bodily reactions. But Cannon and Bard were right, they claimed, to note that there are not nearly enough distinct bodily reactions to account for the wide variety of emotions that human beings can experience. Whereas James and Lange had suggested that different emotions are *different experiences* of *different patterns* of bodily activity, Schachter and Singer claimed that different emotions are merely *different interpretations* of *a single pattern* of bodily activity, which they called "undifferentiated physiological arousal" (see **FIGURE 8.3**).

Schachter and Singer's **two-factor theory** of emotion is the theory that *emotions are based on inferences about the causes of physiological arousal*. When you see a bear in your kitchen, your heart begins to pound. Your brain quickly scans the environment, looking for a reasonable explanation for all that pounding, and notices, of all things, a bear. Having noticed both a bear and a pounding heart, your brain then does what brains do so well: It puts two and two together, makes a logical inference, and interprets your arousal as fear. In other words, when you are physiologically aroused in the presence of something that you think should scare you, you label that arousal as *fear*. But if you have precisely the same bodily response in the presence of something that you think should delight you, then you might label that arousal as *excitement*. According to Schachter and Singer, people have the same physiological reaction to all emotional stimuli, but they interpret that reaction differently on different occasions.

> **How did the two-factor theory of emotion expand on earlier theories?**

How has the two-factor model fared in the last half-century? One of the model's claims has fared very well. For instance, participants in one study (Schachter & Singer, 1962) were injected with epinephrine, which causes physiological arousal, and then exposed to either a goofy or a nasty confederate. Just as the two-factor theory predicted, when the confederate acted goofy, participants concluded that they were feeling *happy*, but when the confederate acted nasty, participants concluded that they were feeling *angry*. Subsequent research has shown that when people are aroused in other ways—say, by having them ride an exercise bike in the laboratory— they subsequently find attractive people more attractive, annoying people more annoying, and funny cartoons funnier, as if they were interpreting their exercise-induced arousal as attraction, annoyance, or amusement

The fact that people can mistake physical arousal for romantic attraction may help explain why so many first dates involve roller coasters. This couple—American reality television personalities Spencer Pratt and Heidi Montag—ended up getting married a few years after this photograph was taken. Since then, they have had some ups and downs.

ANDREW SHAWAF/PACIFICCOASTNEWS/NEWS.COM

(Byrne et al., 1975; Dutton & Aron, 1974; Zillmann, Katcher, & Milavsky, 1972). In fact, these effects occur even when people merely *think* they are aroused—for example, when they hear an audiotape of a rapidly beating heart and are led to believe that the heartbeat they are hearing is their own (Valins, 1966). It appears that the two-factor model is right when it suggests that people make inferences about the causes of their arousal and that those inferences influence their emotional experience (Lindquist & Barrett, 2008).

However, research has not been so kind to the model's claim that all emotional experiences are merely different interpretations of the same bodily state. For example, researchers measured participants' physiological reactions as they experienced six different emotions and found that anger, fear, and sadness each produced a higher heart rate than disgust; that fear and disgust produced higher galvanic skin response (sweating) than did sadness or anger; and that anger produced a larger increase in finger temperature than did fear (Ekman, Levenson, & Friesen, 1983) (see **FIGURE 8.4**). These findings have been replicated across different age groups, professions, genders, and cultures (Levenson, Ekman, & Friesen, 1990; Levenson et al., 1991, 1992). In fact, some physiological responses seem unique to a single emotion. For example, a blush is the result of increased blood volume in the subcutaneous capillaries in the face, neck, and chest, and research suggests that people blush when they feel embarrassment but not when they feel any other emotion (Leary et al., 1992). Similarly, certain patterns of activity in the parasympathetic branch of the autonomic nervous system (which is responsible for slowing and calming rather than speeding and exciting) seem uniquely related to prosocial emotions such as compassion (Oately, Keltner, & Jenkins, 2006).

So which of these duos was right? James and Lange were right when they suggested that patterns of physiological response are not the same for all emotions. But Cannon and Bard were right when they suggested that people are not perfectly sensitive to these patterns of response, which is why people must sometimes make inferences about what they are feeling. Our bodily activity and our mental activity are both the causes and the consequences of our emotional experience. The precise nature of their interplay is not yet fully understood, but as you are about to see, much progress has been made over last few decades by following the trail of emotion from the beating heart to the living brain.

▼ Figure **8.4**  **The Physiology of Emotion** Contrary to the claims of the two-factor theory, different emotions do seem to have different underlying patterns of physiological arousal. Anger, fear, and sadness all produce higher heart rates compared to happiness, surprise, and disgust (*a*). Anger produces a much larger increase in finger temperature than any other emotion (*b*).

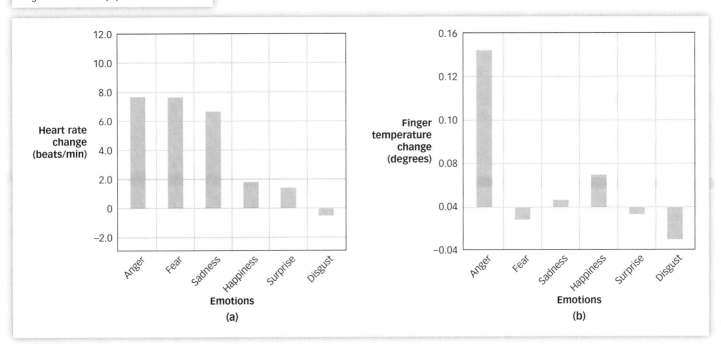

## The Emotional Brain

In the late 1930s, psychologist Heinrich Klüver and physician Paul Bucy made an accidental discovery. A few days after performing brain surgery on a monkey named Aurora, they noticed that she was acting strangely. First, Aurora would eat just about anything and have sex with just about anyone—as though she could no longer distinguish between good and bad food, or between good and bad mates. Second, Aurora seemed absolutely fearless and unflappable, remaining calm when she was handled by experimenters, and even when she was confronted by snakes that would terrify a normal monkey (Klüver & Bucy, 1937, 1939). What had happened to her? As it turned out, during the surgery, Klüver and Bucy had accidentally damaged a structure in Aurora's brain called the *amygdala*. Subsequent studies confirmed that the amygdala plays a special role in producing emotions such as fear. For example, in one study, researchers performed an operation so that information entering a monkey's left eye was transmitted to its amygdala, but information entering the monkey's right eye was not (Downer, 1961). When the monkey was allowed to see a threatening stimulus with only its left eye, it responded with fear and alarm, but when it was allowed to see the threatening stimulus with only its right eye, it was calm and unruffled. Research with humans shows much the same thing. For example, people normally have superior memory for emotionally evocative words such as *death* or *vomit*, but people whose amygdalae are damaged (LaBar & Phelps, 1998) or who take drugs that temporarily impair neurotransmission in the amygdala (van Stegeren et al., 1998) do not (see **FIGURE 8.5**). Interestingly, although people with amygdala damage often do not feel fear when they *see* a threat, they do feel fear when they *experience* a threat, for example, when they suddenly find they cannot breathe (Feinstein et al., 2013).

The tourist and the tiger have something in common: Each has an amygdala that is working at lightning speed to decide whether the other is a threat. Why did nature design the brain to make this particular decision so quickly?

◄ Figure **8.5** **Emotion Recognition and the Amygdala** Facial expressions of emotion were morphed into a continuum that ran from happiness to surprise to fear to sadness to disgust to anger and back to happiness. This sequence was shown to a patient with bilateral amygdala damage and to a control group of 10 people without brain damage. Although the patient's recognition of happiness, sadness, and surprise was generally in line with that of the control group, her recognition of anger, disgust, and fear was impaired (Calder et al., 1996).

What exactly does the amygdala do? Is it some sort of "fear centre"? Not exactly (Cunningham & Brosch, 2012). Before an animal can feel fear, its brain must first decide that there is something to be afraid of. This decision is called an **appraisal,** which is *an evaluation of the emotion-relevant aspects of a stimulus* (Arnold, 1960; Ellsworth & Scherer, 2003; Lazarus, 1984; Roseman, 1984; Roseman & Smith, 2001; Scherer, 1999, 2001). The amygdala is critical to making these appraisals. In essence, the amygdala is an extremely fast and sensitive threat detector (Whalen et al., 1998). Psychologist Joseph LeDoux (2000) mapped the route that information about a stimulus takes through the brain and found that it is transmitted simultaneously along two distinct routes: the "fast pathway," which goes from the thalamus directly to the

**appraisal**
An evaluation of the emotion-relevant aspects of a stimulus.

**▲ Figure 8.6 The Fast and Slow Pathways of Fear** According to Joseph LeDoux (2000), information about a stimulus takes two routes simultaneously: the "fast pathway" (shown in pink), which goes from the thalamus directly to the amygdala, and the "slow pathway" (shown in green), which goes from the thalamus to the cortex and then to the amygdala. Because the amygdala receives information from the thalamus before it receives information from the cortex, people can be afraid of something before they know what it is like Janet Leigh in the famous shower scene in the movie *Psycho.*

**emotion regulation**
The strategies people use to influence their own emotional experience.

**re-appraisal**
Changing one's emotional experience by changing the way one thinks about the emotion-eliciting stimulus.

amygdala, and the "slow pathway," which goes from the thalamus to the cortex and *then* to the amygdala (see **FIGURE 8.6**). This means that while the cortex is slowly using the information to conduct a full-scale investigation of the stimulus's identity and importance ("This seems to be an animal … probably a mammal … perhaps a member of the genus *Ursus* …"), the amygdala has already received the information directly from the thalamus and is making one very fast and very simple decision: "Is this a threat?" If the amygdala's answer to that question is yes, it initiates the neural processes that ultimately produce the bodily reactions and conscious experience that we call fear.

The cortex takes much longer to process this information, but when it finally does, it sends a signal to the amygdala. That signal can tell the amygdala to maintain the state of fear ("We have now analyzed all the data up here and, sure enough, that thing is a bear—and bears bite!") or decrease it ("Relax, it is just some guy in a bear costume"). When experimental subjects are instructed to *experience* emotions such as sadness, fear, and anger, they show increased activity in the amygdala and decreased activity in the cortex (Damasio et al., 2000), but when they are asked to *inhibit* these emotions, they show increased cortical activity and decreased amygdala activity (Ochsner et al., 2002). In a sense, the amygdala presses the emotional gas pedal and the cortex then hits the brakes. That is why both adults with cortical damage and children (whose cortices are not well developed) have difficulty inhibiting their emotions (Stuss & Benson, 1986).

Studies of the brain suggest that emotion is part of a primitive system that prepares us to react rapidly and on the basis of little information to things that are relevant to our survival and well-being. While our new cortex identifies a stimulus, considers what it knows about it, and carefully plans a response, our ancient amygdala does what it has done so well for all those millennia before the cortex evolved: It makes a split-second decision about the significance of the objects and events in our environment and, when necessary, prepares our hearts and our legs to get our butts out of the woods.

> **How do the limbic system and cortex interact to produce emotion?**

## The Regulation of Emotion

You may or may not care about hedgehogs, earwax, or the War of 1812, but if you are human, you almost certainly care about what you are feeling. **Emotion regulation** refers to *the strategies people use to influence their own emotional experience,* and although people occasionally want to experience negative emotions rather than positive emotions (Erber, Wegner, & Therriault, 1996; Michaela et al., 2009; Parrott, 1993; Tamir & Ford, 2012), most of the time people would rather feel good than bad.

Nine out of 10 people report that they attempt to regulate their emotional experience at least once a day (Gross, 1998), and they describe more than a thousand different strategies for doing so (Parkinson & Totterdell, 1999). Some of these are behavioural strategies (e.g., avoiding situations that trigger unwanted emotions) and some are cognitive strategies (e.g., recruiting memories that trigger the desired emotion) (Webb, Miles, & Sheeran, 2012). Research shows that people do not always know which strategies will be most effective. For example, people tend to think that *suppression,* which involves inhibiting the outward signs of an emotion, is an effective strategy. But by and large, it is not (Gross, 2002). Conversely, people tend to think that *affect labelling,* which involves putting one's feelings into words, will have little impact on their emotions, when in fact, it is generally effective in reducing the intensity of emotional states (Lieberman et al., 2011).

One of the best strategies for emotion regulation is **re-appraisal**, which involves *changing one's emotional experience by changing the way one thinks about the* *emotion-eliciting stimulus* (Ochsner et al., 2009). For example, participants in one study who watched a video of a circumcision that was described as a joyous religious ritual had slower heart rates and reported less distress than did participants who watched the same video but

> **How, and how well, does re-appraisal work?**

did not hear the same description (Lazarus & Alfert, 1964). In another study, participants' brains were scanned as they saw photographs that induced negative emotions, such as a photograph of a woman crying during a funeral. Some participants were then asked to re-appraise the picture, for example, by imagining that the woman in the photograph was at a wedding rather than a funeral. The results showed that when participants initially saw the photograph, their amygdalae became active. But as they re-appraised the picture, several key areas of the cortex became active, and moments later, their amygdalae were deactivated (Ochsner et al., 2002). In other words, participants were able to turn down the activity of their own amygdalae simply by thinking about the photograph in a different way.

Re-appraisal is an important skill. Some people are better at it than others (Malooly, Genet, & Siemer, 2013), and the ability to re-appraise is associated with both mental and physical health (Davidson, Putnam, & Larson, 2000; Gross & Munoz, 1995). Indeed, as you will learn in the Stress and Health chapter, therapists often attempt to alleviate depression and distress by teaching people how to re-appraise key events in their lives (Jamieson, Mendes, & Nock, 2013). On the other hand, this ability can allow us to be less compassionate toward those who are suffering (Cameron & Payne, 2011). About 2000 years ago, Roman emperor Marcus Aurelius wrote: "If you are distressed by anything external, the pain is not due to the thing itself, but to your estimate of it; and this you have the power to revoke at any moment." Modern science suggests that the emperor was on to something.

AP PHOTO/RICK BOWMER

Emotion regulation can be difficult. In 2011, the city of Portland, in the American Northwest, flushed 8 million gallons of drinking water simply because a man was seen urinating in this reservoir. Although the miniscule amount of urine posed no health threat, it made people feel disgusted—and the inability to regulate that emotion cost the citizens of Portland nearly $30 000.

## IN SUMMARY

▶ Emotional experiences are difficult to describe, but psychologists have identified their two underlying dimensions: arousal and valence.

▶ Psychologists have spent more than a century trying to understand how emotional experience and physiological activity are related. The James–Lange theory suggests that a stimulus causes a physiological reaction, which leads to an emotional experience; the Cannon–Bard theory suggests that a stimulus causes both an emotional experience and a physiological reaction simultaneously; and Schachter and Singer's two-factor theory suggests that a stimulus causes undifferentiated physiological arousal about which people draw inferences. None of these theories are entirely right, but each has elements that are supported by research.

▶ Emotions are produced by the complex interaction of limbic and cortical structures (see Figure 3.16 on p. 98). Information about a stimulus is sent simultaneously to the amygdala (which makes a quick appraisal of the stimulus's goodness or badness) and the cortex (which does a slower and more comprehensive analysis of the stimulus). In some instances, the amygdala will trigger an emotional experience that the cortex later inhibits.

▶ People care about their emotional experiences and use many strategies to regulate them. Re-appraisal involves changing the way one thinks about an object or event, and is one of the most effective strategies for emotion regulation.

**emotional expression**
An observable sign of an emotional state.

**universality hypothesis**
Emotional expressions have the same meaning for everyone.

# Emotional Communication: Msgs w/o Wrds

Leonardo the robot may not be able to feel, but he sure can smile. And wink. And nod. Indeed, one of the reasons why people who interact with Leonardo find it so hard to think of him as a machine is that Leonardo *expresses* emotions that he does not actually have. An **emotional expression** is *an observable sign of an emotional state*, and while robots can be taught to exhibit them, human beings seem to do it quite naturally.

Leonardo's face is capable of expressing a wide range of emotions (Breazeal, 2003).

Our emotional states express themselves in a wide variety of ways. For example, they change the way we talk—from our intonation and inflection to the loudness and duration of our speech—and research shows that listeners can infer emotional states from vocal cues alone with better-than-chance accuracy (Banse & Scherer, 1996; Frick, 1985). Observers can also estimate emotional states from the direction of a person's gaze, the rhythm of their gait, or even from a brief touch on the arm (Dael, Mortillaro, & Scherer, 2012; Dittrich et al., 1996; Hertenstein et al., 2009; Keltner & Shiota, 2003; Wallbott, 1998). In some sense, we are walking, talking advertisements for what is going on inside us.

> **Why are we "walking, talking advertisements" of our inner states?**

Of course, no part of your body is more exquisitely designed for communicating emotion than your face. Underneath your face lie 43 muscles that are capable of creating more than 10 000 unique configurations, which enable you to convey information about your emotional state with an astonishing degree of subtlety and specificity (Ekman, 1965). Psychologists Paul Ekman and Wallace Friesen (1971) spent years cataloguing the muscle movements of which the human face is capable. They isolated 46 unique movements, which they called *action units*, and they gave each one a number and a name, such as "cheek puffer," "dimpler," and "nasolabial deepener" (which, coincidentally enough, are also the names of heavy metal bands). Research has shown that combinations of these action units are reliably related to specific emotional states (Davidson et al., 1990). For example, when we feel happy, our

On September 19, 1982, Scott Fahlman posted a message to an Internet user's group that read, "I propose the following character sequence for joke markers: :-) Read it sideways." And so the emoticon was born. Fahlman's smile (above right) is a sign of happiness, whereas his emoticon is a symbol.

*zygomatic major* (a muscle that pulls our lip corners up) and our *obicularis oculi* (a muscle that crinkles the outside edges of our eyes) produce a unique facial expression that psychologists describe as "action units 6 and 12" and that the rest of us simply call smiling (Ekman & Friesen, 1982; Frank, Ekman, & Friesen, 1993; Steiner, 1986).

## Communicative Expression

Why are our emotions written all over our faces? In 1872, Charles Darwin published *The Expression of the Emotions in Man and Animals*, in which he speculated about the evolutionary significance of emotional expression. Darwin noticed that human and nonhuman animals share certain facial and postural expressions, and he suggested that these expressions were meant to communicate information about internal states. It is not hard to see how such communications could be useful (Shariff & Tracy, 2011). For example, if a dominant animal can bare its teeth and communicate the message, "I am angry at you," and if a subordinate animal can lower its head and communicate the message, "I am afraid of you," then the two can establish a pecking order without actually spilling any blood. Darwin suggested that emotional expressions are a convenient way for one animal to let another animal know how it is feeling and therefore how it is prepared to act. In this sense, emotional expressions are a bit like the words of a nonverbal language.

According to Charles Darwin (1872/1998), both human and nonhuman animals use facial expressions to communicate information about their internal states.

## The Universality of Expression

Of course, a language only works if everybody speaks the same one, which is why Darwin advanced the **universality hypothesis,** which suggests that *emotional expressions have the same meaning for everyone.* In other words, every human being naturally expresses happiness with a smile, and every human being naturally understands that a smile signifies happiness.

There is some evidence for Darwin's hypothesis. For example, people who have never seen a human face make the same facial expressions as those who have. Congenitally blind people smile when they are happy (Galati, Scherer, & Ricci-Bitt, 1997; Matsumoto & Willingham, 2009), and 2-day-old infants make a disgust face when bitter chemicals are put in their mouths (Steiner, 1973, 1979). In addition, people are fairly accurate when judging the emotional expressions of members of other cultures (Ekman & Friesen, 1971; Elfenbein & Ambady, 2002; Frank & Stennet, 2001; Haidt & Keltner, 1999). Not only do Chileans, Americans, and Japanese all recognize a smile as a sign of happiness and a frown as a sign of sadness, but so do members of preliterate cultures. In the 1950s, researchers took photographs of Westerners expressing anger, disgust, fear, happiness, sadness, and surprise (see **FIGURE 8.7**) and showed them to members of the South Fore, a people who lived a Stone Age existence in the highlands of Papua New Guinea and who at that point had had little contact with the modern world. Researchers asked these participants to match each photograph to a word (such as "happy" or "afraid") and discovered that the South Fore made matches that were essentially the same as those made by Americans. (The one exception to this

> **What evidence suggests that facial expressions are universal?**

▼ Figure **8.7** **Six Basic Emotions** Humans all over the globe generally agree that these six faces are displaying anger, disgust, fear, happiness, sadness, and surprise. What might account for this widespread agreement? (Adapted from Arellano, Varona, & Perales, 2008.)

In 2013, Nobuyuki Tsujii won the prestigious Van Cliburn International Piano competition. Although he was born blind and has never seen a facial expression, winning a million dollar prize immediately gave rise to a million dollar smile.

Is this woman feeling happy or sad? See page 330.

rule was that the Fore had trouble distinguishing expressions of surprise from expressions of fear, perhaps because for people who live in the wild, surprises are rarely pleasant.) Evidence of this sort has convinced many psychologists that facial displays of at least six emotions—*anger, disgust, fear, happiness, sadness,* and *surprise*—are universal. And a few other emotions—*embarrassment, amusement, guilt, shame,* and *pride*—may have universal patterns of facial expression as well (Keltner, 1995; Keltner & Buswell, 1996; Keltner & Haidt, 1999; Keltner & Harker, 1998; Tracy et al., 2013).

But not all psychologists are convinced. For example, recent research (Gendron et al., in press) shows that like the South Fore, members of an isolated tribe called the Himba can match faces to emotion words just as Americans do. But when the Himba are instead asked to match faces that are "feeling the same way" to each other, they produce matches that are quite unlike those produced by their American counterparts. Studies such as these suggest that the universality hypothesis may be stated too strongly. At present, we can say with confidence that there is considerable agreement among all humans about the emotional meaning of many facial expressions, but that this agreement is not perfect.

## The Cause and Effect of Expression

Members of different cultures express many emotions in the same ways, but why? After all, they do not speak the same languages, so why do they smile the same smiles and frown the same frowns? The answer is that words are *symbols,* but facial expressions are *signs.* Symbols are arbitrary designations that have no causal relationship with the things they symbolize. English speakers use the word *cat* to indicate a particular animal, but there is nothing about felines that actually causes this particular sound to pop out of our mouths, and we are not surprised when other human beings make different sounds—such as *popoki* or *gatto*—to indicate the same thing. In contrast, facial expressions are not arbitrary symbols of emotion. They are signs of emotion because signs are *caused* by the things they signify. The feeling of happiness *causes* the contraction of the zygomatic major; thus that contraction is a sign of that feeling in the same way a footprint in the snow is a sign that someone walked there.

Of course, just as a symbol (*bat*) can have more than one meaning (wooden club or flying mammal), so, too, can a sign. Is the man in the photograph at left feeling joy or sorrow? In fact, these two emotions often produce rather similar facial expressions, so how do we tell them apart? Research suggests that one answer is *context.* When someone says, "The centrefielder hit the ball with the bat," the sentence provides a context that tells us that *bat* means "club" and not "mammal." Similarly, the context in which a facial expression occurs often tells us what that expression means (Aviezer et al., 2008; Barrett, Mesquita, & Gendron, 2011; Meeren, van Heijnsbergen, & de Gelder, 2005). It is difficult to tell what the man in the photograph is feeling. But if you turn to page 329 and see the photograph in context, you will have no trouble. Indeed, when you return to this page, you may well wonder how you could *ever* have had any trouble.

Our emotional experiences cause our emotional expressions, but it also works the other way around. The **facial feedback hypothesis** (Adelmann & Zajonc, 1989; Izard, 1971; Tomkins, 1981) suggests that *emotional expressions can cause the emotional experiences they signify.* For instance, people feel happier when they are asked to make the sound of a long *e* or to hold a pencil in their teeth (both of which cause contraction of the zygomatic major) than when they are asked to make the sound of a long *u* or to hold a pencil in their lips (Strack, Martin, & Stepper, 1988;

Why do emotional expressions cause emotional experience?

**facial feedback hypothesis**
Emotional expressions can cause the emotional experiences they signify.

## HOT SCIENCE

# The Body of Evidence

What can you tell from a face? Much less than you realize. Aviezer, Trope, and Todorov (2012) showed participants faces taken from pictures of tennis players who had either just won a point (Faces 2, 3, and 5 in the figure shown here) or lost a point (Faces 1, 4, and 6) and asked them to guess whether the athlete was experiencing a positive or negative emotion. As the leftmost bars of the graph show, participants could not tell. They guessed that the "winning faces" and the "losing faces" were experiencing equal amounts of somewhat negative emotion.

Next, the researchers showed a new group of participants bodies (without faces) taken from pictures of tennis players who had either just won a point (Body 1 in the figure) or lost a point (Body 2), and asked them to make the same judgment. As the middle bars show, participants were quite good at this. Participants guessed that "winning bodies" were experiencing positive emotions and that "losing bodies" were experiencing negative emotions.

Finally, the researchers showed a new group of participants the athletes' bodies *and* faces together. As the rightmost bars show, participants' ratings of the body–face combinations were identical to their ratings of the bodies alone, suggesting that when participants made their guesses, they relied entirely on the athletes' bodies

and not on their faces. And yet, when they were later asked which information they had relied on most, more than half the participants said they had relied on the faces!

It seems that facial expressions of emotion are more ambiguous than most of us realize. When we see people expressing anger, fear, or joy, we are using information from their bodies, their voices, and their physical and social contexts to figure out what they are feeling. Yet, we mistakenly believe that we are getting most of our information from their facial expression.

The moral of the story? Next time you want to know how a losing athlete feels, concentrate more on defeat than deface. (Sorry).

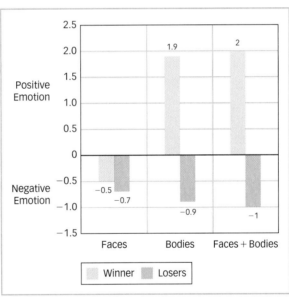

Hillel Aviezer, Yaacov Trope, and Alexander Todorov. Body Cues, Not Facial Expressions, Discriminate Between Intense Positive and Negative Emotions. *Science, 30,* November 2012: Vol. 338, no. 6111, pp. 1225–1229. DOI: 10.1126/science.1224313

Zajonc, 1989) (see **FIGURE 8.8** on the next page). Similarly, when people are instructed to arch their brows they find facts more surprising, and when instructed to wrinkle their noses they find odours less pleasant (Lewis, 2012). These things happen because facial expressions and emotional states become strongly associated with each other over time (remember Pavlov?), and eventually each can bring about the other. These effects are not limited to the face. For example, people feel more assertive when instructed to make a fist (Schubert & Koole, 2009) and rate others as more hostile when instructed to extend their middle fingers (Chandler & Schwarz, 2009).

The fact that emotional expressions can cause the emotional experiences they signify may help explain why people are generally so good at recognizing the emotional expressions of others. Many studies show that people unconsciously mimic other people's body postures and facial expressions (Chartrand & Bargh, 1999; Dimberg,

▲ Figure **8.8** **The Facial Feedback Hypothesis** Research shows that people who hold a pencil with their teeth feel happier than those who hold a pencil with their lips. These two postures cause contraction of the muscles associated with smiling and frowning, respectively.

A popular form of cosmetic surgery is the Botox injection, which paralyzes certain facial muscles. Former *American Idol* and *X Factor* judge Simon Cowell (quoted in Davis, 2008) gets them regularly and says, "Botox is no more unusual than toothpaste. … It works, you do it once a year—who cares?" Well, maybe he should. Some evidence suggests that Botox injections can impair both the experience of emotion (Davis et al., 2010) and the ability to process emotional information (Havas et al., 2010). What phenomenon have you learned about so far that might explain how this could happen?

1982). When we see someone smile (or even when we read about someone smiling), our zygomatic major contracts ever so slightly—as yours almost surely is right now (Foroni & Semin, 2009). (By the way, the tendency to ape the facial expressions of our interaction partners is so natural that, yes, even apes do it [Davila Ross, Menzler, & Zimmermann, 2008].) Because facial expressions can cause the emotions they signify, mimicking another person's facial expression allows us to feel what they are feeling and therefore identify their emotions.

What is the evidence for this? First, people find it difficult to identify other people's emotions when they are unable to make facial expressions of their own, for example, if their facial muscles are paralyzed with Botox (Niedenthal et al., 2005). People also find it difficult to identify other people's emotions when they are unable to *experience* emotions of their own (Hussey & Safford, 2009; Pitcher et al., 2008). For example, people with amygdala damage do not normally feel fear and anger, and are typically poor at recognizing the expressions of those emotions in others (Adolphs, Russell, & Tranel, 1999). On the flip side, people who are naturally quite good at figuring out what others are feeling tend to be natural mimics (Sonnby-Borgstrom, Jonsson, & Svensson, 2003), and their mimicry seems to pay off: Negotiators who mimic the facial expressions of their opponents earn more money than those who do not (Maddux, Mullen, & Galinsky, 2008). In the Consciousness chapter, you learned about mirror neurons: neurons that fire when an animal (or person) executes a particular action, and when the animal sees someone else perform the same action. You may not be surprised to know that mirror neurons are also thought to play a critical role in displaying and in understanding facial expressions of emotion.

## Deceptive Expression

Our emotional expressions can communicate our feelings truthfully—or not. When a friend makes a sarcastic remark about our haircut, we truthfully express our contempt with an arched brow and a reinforcing hand gesture; but when our boss makes the same remark, we swallow hard and fake a pained smile. Our knowledge that it is permissible to show contempt for a peer but not a superior is a **display rule,** which is a *norm for the appropriate expression of emotion* (Ekman, 1972; Ekman & Friesen, 1968). Obeying a display rule requires several techniques:

> *Intensification* involves exaggerating the expression of one's emotion, as when a person pretends to be more surprised by a gift than she really is.

> *De-intensification* involves muting the expression of one's emotion, as when the loser of a contest tries to look less distressed than he really is.

> *Masking* involves expressing one emotion while feeling another, as when a poker player tries to look distressed rather than delighted as she examines a hand with four aces.

> *Neutralizing* involves feeling an emotion but displaying no expression, as when a judge tries not to betray his leanings while lawyers are making their arguments (see **FIGURE 8.9** on the next page).

Although people in different cultures use many of the same techniques, they use them in the service of different display rules. For example, in one study, Japanese and American university students watched an unpleasant video of car accidents and amputations (Ekman, 1972; Friesen, 1972). When the students did not know that the experimenters were observing them, Japanese and American students made similar expressions of disgust, but when they realized

**How does emotional expression differ across cultures?**

that they were being observed, the Japanese students (but not the American students) masked their disgust with pleasant expressions. In many Asian countries it is considered rude to display negative emotions in the presence of a respected person, and so citizens of these countries tend to mask or neutralize their expressions. The fact that different cultures have different display rules may also help explain the fact that people are better at recognizing the facial expressions of people from their own cultures (Elfenbein & Ambady, 2002).

Our attempts to obey our culture's display rules do not always work out so well. Darwin (1899/2007) noted that "those muscles of the face which are least obedient to the will, will sometimes alone betray a slight and passing emotion" (p. 64). Anyone who has ever watched the loser of a beauty pageant congratulate the winner knows that voices, bodies, and faces are "leaky" instruments that often betray a person's emotional state. Even when people smile bravely to mask their disappointment, for example, their faces tend to express small bursts of disappointment that last just 1/5 to 1/25 of a second (Porter & ten Brinke, 2008). These *micro-expressions* happen so quickly that they are almost impossible to detect with the naked eye. Four other features that are more readily observable seem to distinguish between sincere and insincere facial expressions (Ekman, 2003).

◄ Figure **8.9** **Neutralizing** Can you tell what this man is feeling? He sure hopes not. Doyle Brunson is a champion poker player who knows how to keep a "poker face," which is a neutral expression that provides little information about his emotional state.

> *Morphology*: Certain facial muscles tend to resist conscious control, and for a trained observer, these so-called *reliable muscles* are quite revealing. For example, the zygomatic major raises the corners of the mouth, and this happens when people smile spontaneously or when they force themselves to smile. But only a genuine, spontaneous smile engages the obicularis oculi, which crinkles the corners of the eyes (see **FIGURE 8.10**).

> *Symmetry*: Sincere expressions are a bit more symmetrical than insincere expressions. A slightly lop-sided smile is less likely to be genuine than is a perfectly even one.

> *Duration*: Sincere expressions tend to last between 0.5 s and 5 s, and expressions that last for shorter or longer periods are more likely to be insincere.

> *Temporal patterning*: Sincere expressions appear and disappear smoothly over a few seconds, whereas insincere expressions tend to have more abrupt onsets and offsets.

▲ Figure **8.10** **Crinkle Eyes** Which Justin Bieber just won six Billboard music awards? Check out the eyes. Only one Bieber is showing the telltale "corner crinkle" that signifies genuine happiness. The other one might be having second thoughts about the pompadour 'do.

Our emotions do not just leak on our faces: They leak all over the place. Research has shown that many aspects of our verbal and nonverbal behaviour are altered when we tell a lie (DePaulo et al., 2003). For example, liars speak more slowly, take longer to respond to questions, and respond in less detail than do those who are telling the truth. Liars are also less fluent, less engaging, more uncertain, more tense, and less pleasant than truth-tellers. Oddly enough, one of the telltale signs of a liar is that his or her performances tend to be just a bit too good. A liar's speech lacks the little imperfections that are typical of truthful speech, such as superfluous detail ("I noticed that the robber was wearing the same shoes that I saw on sale last week at The Bay and I found myself wondering what he paid for them"), spontaneous correction ("He

**display rule**
A norm for the appropriate expression of emotion.

was six feet tall … well, no, actually more like six-two"), and expressions of self-doubt ("I think he had blue eyes, but I am really not sure").

Given the reliable differences between sincere and insincere expressions, you might think that people would be quite good at telling one from the other. In fact, studies show that people are dreadful at this, and under most circumstances perform barely better than chance (DePaulo, Stone, & Lassiter, 1985; Ekman, 1992; Zuckerman, DePaulo, & Rosenthal, 1981; Zuckerman & Driver, 1985). One reason for this is that people have a strong bias toward believing that others are sincere, which explains why people tend to mistake liars for truth-tellers more often than they mistake truth-tellers for liars (Gilbert, 1991). A second reason is that people do not seem to know what they should attend to and what they should ignore (Vrij et al., 2011). For instance, people think that fast talking is a sign of lying when actually it is not, and that slow talking is not a sign of lying when actually it is. People are bad lie detectors who do not even know how bad they are: The correlation between a person's ability to detect lies and the person's confidence in that ability is essentially zero (DePaulo et al., 1997).

When people cannot do something well (e.g., adding numbers or picking up 10-tonne rocks), they typically turn the job over to machines (see **FIGURE 8.11**). Can machines detect lies better than we can? The answer is yes, but that is not saying very much. The most widely used lie detection machine is the *polygraph*, which measures a variety of physiological responses that are associated with stress, which people often feel when they are afraid of being caught in a lie. A polygraph can detect lies at a rate that is significantly better than chance, but its error rate is still too high to make it a reliable lie detector. For example, let us imagine that 10 of the 10 000 people coming through a particular airport are terrorists and that when hooked up to a polygraph, they all claim to be innocent. A polygraph that was set to *maximum* sensitivity would catch 8 of the 10 terrorists lying, but it would also mistakenly catch 1598 innocent people. A polygraph set to *minimum* sensitivity would mistakenly catch just 39 innocent people, but would only catch 2 of the 10 real terrorists. And these numbers assume that terrorists do not know how to fool a polygraph, which is something that people can, in fact, be trained to do. No wonder the American National Academy of Sciences (2003) warned, "Given its level of accuracy, achieving a high probability of identifying individuals who pose major security risks in a population with a very low

> What is the problem with lie-detecting machines?

For Canadian hockey fans of a certain age, hockey changed forever on August 9, 1988, the day that Edmonton Oiler Wayne "The Great One" Gretzky was traded to the Los Angeles Kings. Gretzky himself was in tears at the press conference announcing the move. Crying is very difficult to control and thus provides reliable information about the intensity of a person's emotions.

▶ Figure **8.11** **Lie Detection Machines** Some researchers hope to replace the polygraph with accurate machines that measure changes in blood flow in the brain and the face. As the top panel shows, some areas of the brain are more active when people tell lies than when they tell the truth (shown in red), and some are more active when people tell the truth than when they tell lies (shown in blue) (Langleben et al., 2005). The bottom panel shows images taken by a thermal camera that detects the heat caused by blood flow to different parts of the face. The images show a person's face before (*left*) and after (*right*) telling a lie (Pavlidis, Eberhardt, & Levine, 2002). Although neither of these new techniques is extremely accurate, that could soon change.

Right side      Left side      Anterior

proportion of such individuals would require setting the test to be so sensitive that hundreds, or even thousands, of innocent individuals would be implicated for every major security violator correctly identified" (p. 6). In short, neither people nor machines are particularly good at lie detection, which is why lying remains such a popular sport.

# OTHER VOICES

## I Used to Get Invited to Poker Games ...

**Stephen Porter** is Professor in Psychology at University of British Columbia (Okanagan). He has published many papers in academic journals on aspects of memory related to law, such as eyewitness testimony and false memories, and on psychopaths and violent behaviour.

PHOTO COURTESY OF DR. STEPHEN PORTER

Stephen Porter received his Bachelor's degree from Acadia University, and his Ph.D. in Forensic Psychology (that area of psychology dealing with the justice system and law) from the University of British Columbia. One of his main areas of research concerns the detection of deception—how to tell if someone is lying to you.

As a registered forensic psychologist, he has been consulted by Canadian courts, has served as an expert witness during trials, and has been consulted by police in unsolved crime investigations. Dr. Porter has worked with law enforcement officials, mental-health workers, judges, and others to sensitize them to the subtle physical cues that accurately indicate deception. The following interview with Dr. Porter is excerpted and edited from the website all-about-body-language.com.

### Why did you choose the detection of lying as a research topic?

Two reasons. First, I have always been fascinated by how people "read" one another and how we unconsciously communicate covert information in our speech, body language, and facial expressions. I have an interest in how this communication "arms race" developed through evolution.

Secondly, before becoming an academic I was a prison psychologist and let's say I was duped once or twice! I decided to embark on a major study of the strategies people use to detect lies and the way in which deception is actually communicated by liar.

### Does a defendant's physical appearance matter to how they are treated by legal professionals and others?

It has an extremely powerful but largely unconscious effect. Part of my deception seminars focuses on the natural biases that we bring to the table in trying to detect lies. In reality, it's not only defendants but anyone we meet for the first time! The brain decides on a stranger's trustworthiness and attractiveness in milliseconds, and this affects the way that we perceive any new information about the person in the near future. This can work in either direction. We find that a nasty person who happens to have a "trustworthy"-looking face can easily win the trust of others and effectively prey on them financially, sexually, or violently. Think Bernie Madoff and his sympathetic-looking "grandfather" face. On the other hand, jurors perceive a defendant who happens to be "untrustworthy" looking as being deceptive on the stand. They then require less evidence to convict and are less willing to exonerate the person when DNA shows someone else did the crime. Research in the U.S. shows that stereotypically Black defendants are more likely (than other Black defendants in similar cases) to be given the death sentence.

### What are 'high-stakes' lies?

"High-stakes" lies are those of extreme consequence both for the liar and the target of the lie. In one's personal life this would include lying to conceal infidelity, for example. I've been interested in lies occurring in the contexts of crime, terrorism, governments, and business or corporations. Unlike everyday white lies, most high-stakes lies are accompanied by powerful emotions—fear, remorse, anger, or even excitement—that must be hidden and/or faked in a convincing way. Consider the would-be terrorist, smiling and chatting politely with airport staff while secretly feeling intense hatred and contempt towards his intended targets, and perhaps fear of discovery and/or death. Or the husband publicly pleading for the safe return of his wife who, in reality, he has murdered. Each of these liars must monitor his/her body language, facial expressions, and stories while dealing with an awareness of the potent consequences of getting caught. And in many cases a failure to spot such lies can lead to catastrophe. Think Prime Minister Neville Chamberlain believing Hitler's face-to-face promise that he would not invade Czechoslovakia. Scout's honour! Our recent international study [cited below] clearly shows the ways in which such deceivers unconsciously betray themselves in their facial expressions and speech to the keen observer.

ten Brinke, L., & Porter, S. (2012). Cry me a river: Identifying the behavioural consequences of extremely high-stakes interpersonal deception. *Law and Human Behavior, 36,* 469–477.

ten Brinke, L., Porter, S., & Baker, A. (2012). Darwin the detective: Observable facial muscle contractions reveal emotional high-stakes lies. *Evolution and Human Behavior, 33,* 411–416.

### Are there differences between laboratory studies of deception and actual police interviewing?

Yes—huge differences in terms of motivation and consequences. We know that higher motivation levels in liars means more behavioural "leakage". Among police officers or other professional lie catchers their own high motivation to catch deceivers can help but in some cases impair detection because "tunnel vision" kicks in. These kinds of dynamics are not captured in laboratory studies. This is why we and others are studying actual police interrogations or lies in other "naturalistic" settings, such as family members pleading to the media for the return of a missing relative.

### How does your knowledge of deception affect your private life?

If I told you I'd have to kill you. Let's just say I used to get invited to poker games.

Stephen Porter and his colleagues have studied deception in terms of evolution. What could be the evolutionary purpose for being able to tell lies convincingly? If we are social animals that depend on our emotions to help us understand the world, when would being able to manipulate other people's emotions work to our advantage? Why are we so good at telling lies and yet so bad at detecting them?

By permission of Craig Baxter from http://www.all_about_body_language. com/steve-porter.html.

## CULTURE & COMMUNITY

### Is It What You Say or How You Say It?

We can learn a lot about people by paying attention both to what they say and to how they say it. But recent evidence (Ishii, Reyes, & Kitayama, 2003) suggests that some cultures place more emphasis on one of these than on the other.

Research participants heard a voice pronouncing pleasant or unpleasant words (such as *pretty* or *complaint*) in either a pleasant or an unpleasant tone of voice. On some trials, they were told to ignore the word and to classify the pleasantness of the voice; on other trials, participants were told to ignore the voice and classify the pleasantness of the word.

Which of these kinds of information was more difficult to ignore? It depended on the participant's nationality. American participants found it relatively easy to ignore the speaker's tone of voice, but relatively difficult to ignore the pleasantness of the word being spoken. Japanese participants, on the other hand, found it relatively easy to ignore the pleasantness of the word, but relatively difficult to ignore the speaker's tone of voice. It seems that, in America, what you say matters more than how you say it, but in Japan, just the opposite is true.

STOCKBYTE/GETTY IMAGES

This bride is crying tears of joy on her wedding day.

When someone is lying, he or she usually wants to conceal that fact from others. Individuals may wish to conceal their internal states in many other situations as well: feelings of disgust caused by food served at a dinner party, anxiety related to asking someone out on a date, or feelings of jealousy when a romantic partner talks enthusiastically about a new friend. Although it may feel like your innermost feelings are on public display at such awkward times, in fact, they are not. For example, public speakers tend to believe that their nervousness is obvious to their audience, and this makes them even more nervous. In fact, studies demonstrate that a speaker's emotional state is not nearly as evident to the audience as the speaker believes (Savitsky & Gilovich, 2003). Reassuring speakers that the audience cannot perceive their nervousness leads to less anxiety and a better performance (Savitsky & Gilovich, 2003).

### IN SUMMARY

► The voice, the body, and the face all communicate information about a person's emotional state.

► Darwin suggested that these emotional expressions are the same for all people and are universally understood, and research suggests that this is generally true.

► Emotions cause expressions, but expressions can also cause emotions.

► Emotional mimicry allows people to experience and hence identify the emotions of others.

► Not all emotional expressions are sincere because people use display rules to help them decide which emotions to express.

► Different cultures have different display rules, but people enact those rules using the same techniques.

► There are reliable differences between sincere and insincere emotional expressions and between truthful and untruthful utterances, but people are generally poor at determining when an expression is sincere or an utterance is truthful. The polygraph can distinguish true from false utterances with better-than-chance accuracy, but its error rate is troublingly high. In general, people are pretty good at concealing their internal states from others when they want to.

# Motivation: Getting Moved

Leonardo is a robot, so he does what he is programmed to do, but nothing more. Because he does not have wants and urges—does not crave friendship or desire chocolate or hate homework—he does not initiate his own behaviour. He can learn, but he cannot yearn, and thus he is not motivated to act in the same way that we are. **Motivation** refers to *the purpose for or psychological cause of an action*, and it is no coincidence that the words *emotion* and *motivation* share a common linguistic root that means "to move." Unlike robots, human beings act because their emotions move them, and emotions do this in two different ways: First, emotions provide people with *information* about the world; and second, emotions are the *objectives* toward which people strive. Let us examine each of these in turn.

## The Function of Emotion

In the old science fiction film *Invasion of the Body Snatchers*, a young couple suspects that most of the people they know have been kidnapped by aliens and replaced with replicas. This sort of bizarre belief is a common story device in bad movies, but it is also the primary symptom of Capgras syndrome (see **FIGURE 8.12**). People who suffer from this syndrome typically believe that one or more of their family members are imposters. As one Capgras sufferer told her doctor, "He looks exactly like my father, but he really is not. He's a nice guy, but he is not my father. ... Maybe my father employed him to take care of me, paid him some money so he could pay my bills" (Hirstein & Ramachandran, 1997, p. 438).

This woman's dad had not been body-snatched, of course, nor had he hired his own stunt double. Rather, this woman sustained damage to the neural connections between her temporal lobe (where faces are identified) and her limbic system (where emotions are generated). As a result, when she saw her father's face, she recognized it, but because this information was not transmitted to her limbic system, she did not feel the warm emotions that her father's face should have produced. Her father "looked right" but did not "feel right," so she concluded that the man before her was an imposter (see Figure 8.12).

People with Capgras syndrome use their emotional experience as information about the world and, as it turns out, so do the rest of us. For example, people report having better lives when they are asked about their lives on a sunny day rather than a rainy day. Why? Because people naturally feel happier on sunny days, and they use their happiness as information about the quality of their lives (Schwarz & Clore, 1983). People who are in good moods believe that they have a higher probability of winning a lottery than do people who are in bad moods. Why? Because people use their moods as information about the likelihood of succeeding at a task (Isen & Patrick, 1983). We all know that satisfying lives and bright futures make us feel good—so when we feel good, we conclude that our lives must be satisfying and our futures must be bright. Because the world influences our emotions, our emotions can provide information about the world (Schwarz, Mannheim, & Clore, 1988). Indeed, recent research suggests that people

**motivation**
The purpose for or psychological cause of an action.

In 1956's *Invasion of the Body Snatchers*, little Jimmy Grimaldi tells the nurse and the doctor that his mother has been replaced by a replica. Their response? Chill him out with drugs and send him home to be eaten by aliens.

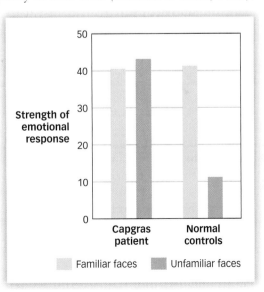

◄ Figure **8.12** **Capgras Syndrome** This graph shows the emotional responses (as measured by skin conductance) of a patient with Capgras syndrome and a group of control participants to a set of familiar and unfamiliar faces. Although the controls have stronger emotional responses to the familiar than to the unfamiliar faces, the Capgras patient has similar emotional responses to both (Hirstein & Ramachandran, 1997).

When we try to make a decision, we often ask how we "feel" about it. If we could not feel, then we would not know which alternative to choose. Without emotions, Rihanna would just stand there until someone gave her a Grammy for Best Hot Pink Stiletto.

who trust their feelings to provide this kind of information tend to make more accurate predictions and better decisions than people who do not (Mikels et al., 2011; Pham, Lee, & Stephen, 2012).

The information we get from our emotions is so useful that we can actually be lost without it. When neurologist Antonio Damasio was asked to examine a patient with an unusual form of brain damage, he asked the patient to choose between two dates for an appointment. It sounds like a simple decision, but for the next half hour, the patient enumerated reasons for and against each of the two possible dates, completely unable to decide in favour of one option or the other (Damasio, 1994). The problem was not any impairment of the patient's ability to think or reason. On the contrary, he could think and reason all too well. What he could not do was feel. The patient's injury had left him unable to experience emotion, so when he entertained one option ("If I come next Tuesday, I will have to cancel my lunch with Fred"), he did not feel any better or any worse than when he entertained another ("If I come next Wednesday, I will have to get up early to catch the bus"). And because he *felt* nothing when he thought about his options, he could not decide which one was best. Studies show that when individuals with this particular form of brain damage are given the opportunity to gamble, they make a lot of reckless bets because they do not feel the twinge of anxiety that tells them they are about to do something stupid. On the other hand, under certain conditions, such individuals make excellent investors, precisely because they are willing to take risks that most of us would not (Shiv et al., 2005).

> **How might emotions help us make decisions?**

If the first function of emotion is to provide us with information about the world, then the second function is to tell us what to do with that information. The **hedonic principle** is *the claim that people are motivated to experience pleasure and avoid pain*, and this claim has a long history. The ancient Greek philosopher Aristotle (350 BCE/1998) argued that the hedonic principle explained everything there was to know about human motivation: "It is for the sake of this that we all do all that we do." We want many things, from peace and prosperity to health and security, but we want them for just one reason, and that is that they make us feel good. "Are these things good for any other reason except that they end in pleasure, and get rid of and avert pain?" asked Plato (380 BCE/1956). "Are you looking to any other standard but pleasure and pain when you call them good?" Plato and Aristotle were suggesting that pleasure is not just good: It is what good *means*.

According to the hedonic principle, then, our emotional experience can be thought of as a gauge that ranges from bad to good, and our primary motivation—perhaps even our *sole* motivation—is to keep the needle on the gauge as close to *good* as possible. Even when we voluntarily do things that tilt the needle in the opposite direction, such as letting the dentist drill our teeth or waking up early for a boring class, we are doing these things because we believe that they will nudge the needle toward *good* in the future and keep it there longer.

## Instincts and Drives

If our primary motivation is to keep the needle on *good*, then which things push the needle in that direction and which things push it away? And where do these things get the power to push our needle around, and exactly how do they do the pushing? The answers to such questions lie in two concepts that have played an unusually important role in the history of psychology: *instincts* and *drives*.

### Instincts

When a newborn baby is given a drop of sugar water, it smiles, and when it is given a cheque for $10 000, it acts like it could not care less. By the time the baby goes to university, these responses pretty much reverse. It seems clear that nature endows us with

**hedonic principle**
The claim that people are motivated to experience pleasure and avoid pain.

certain motivations and that experience endows us with others. William James (1890) called the natural tendency to seek a particular goal an *instinct*, which he defined as "the faculty of acting in such a way as to produce certain ends, without foresight of the ends, and without previous education in the performance" (p. 383). According to James, nature hardwired penguins, parrots, puppies, and people to want certain things without training and to execute the behaviours that produce these things without thinking. He and other psychologists of his time tried to make a list of what those things were.

Unfortunately, they were quite successful, and in just a few decades their list of instincts had grown preposterously long and included some rather exotic entries, such

> **Does an *instinct* explain behaviour, or just name it?**

as "the instinct to be secretive" and "the instinct to grind one's teeth." By 1924, sociologist Luther Bernard counted 5759 instincts and concluded that after three decades of list making, the term seemed to be suffering from "a great variety of usage and the almost universal lack of critical standards" (Bernard, 1924, p. 21). Furthermore, some psychologists began to worry that attributing the tendency for people to befriend each other to an "affiliation instinct" was more of a description than an explanation (Ayres, 1921; Dunlap, 1919; Field, 1921).

By 1930, the concept of instinct had fallen out of fashion. Not only did it fail to explain anything, but it also flew in the face of Western psychology's hot new trend: behaviourism. Behaviourists rejected the concept of instinct on two grounds. First, they believed that behaviour should be explained by the external stimuli that evoke it and not by the hypothetical internal states on which it presumably depends. John Watson (1913) had written that "the time seems to have come when psychology must discard all reference to consciousness" (p. 163), and behaviourists saw instincts as just the sort of unnecessary "mind blather" that Watson forbade. Second, behaviourists wanted nothing to do with the notion of inherited behaviour because they believed that all complex behaviour was learned. Because instincts were inherited tendencies that resided inside the organism, behaviourists considered them doubly repugnant.

All animals are born with instincts. In the annual running of the bulls in Pamplona, Spain, no one has to teach the bulls to chase the runners, and no one has to teach the runners to flee.

## Drives

But within a few decades, some of Watson's younger followers began to realize that the strict prohibition against the mention of internal states made certain phenomena difficult to explain. For example, if all behaviour is a response to an external stimulus, then why does a rat that is sitting still in its cage at 9:00 a.m. start wandering around and looking for food by noon? Nothing in the cage has changed, so why has the rat's behaviour changed? What visible, measurable, external stimulus is the wandering rat responding to? The obvious answer is that the rat is responding to something inside itself, which meant that Watson's young followers (the "new behaviourists" as they called themselves) were forced to look inside the rat to explain its wandering. How could they do that without talking about the "thoughts" and "feelings" that Watson had forbidden them to mention?

They began by noting that bodies are a bit like thermostats. When thermostats detect that the room is too cold, they send signals that initiate corrective actions such

> **In what ways is the human body like a thermostat?**

as turning on a furnace. Similarly, when bodies detect that they are underfed, they send signals that initiate corrective actions such as eating. **Homeostasis** is *the tendency for a system to take action to keep itself in a particular state*, and two of the new behaviourists, Clark Hull and Kenneth Spence, suggested that rats, people, and thermostats are all homeostatic mechanisms. To survive, an organism needs to maintain precise levels of nutrition, warmth, and so on, and when these levels depart from an optimal point, the organism receives a signal to take corrective action. That signal is called a **drive,** which is *an internal state caused by physiological needs*.

**homeostasis**
The tendency for a system to take action to keep itself in a particular state.

**drive**
An internal state caused by physiological needs.

VISIONS OF AMERICA, LLC/ALAMY

Aristotle claimed that water had "gravity" and fire had "levity" and that these properties made them go downward and upward, respectively. It now seems obvious that Aristotle was merely describing the motion of these elements and not really explaining it—much as William James did when he attributed behaviour to instinct. By the way, that is Plato and Aristotle standing together under the arch in Raphael's 1509 masterpiece *The School of Athens*.

According to Hull and Spence, it is not food per se that organisms find rewarding; it is the reduction of the drive for food. Hunger is a drive, a drive is an internal state, and when organisms eat, they are attempting to change their internal state.

Although the words *instinct* and *drive* are no longer widely used in psychology, both concepts have something to teach us. The concept of instinct reminds us that nature endows organisms with a tendency to seek certain things, and the concept of drive reminds us that this seeking is initiated by an internal state. The psychologist William McDougall (1930) called the study of motivation *hormic psychology*, which is a term derived from the Greek word for "urge," and people clearly do have urges—some of which they acquire through experience and some of which they do not—that motivate them to take certain actions. What kinds of urges do we have, and what kinds of actions do we take to satisfy them?

## What the Body Needs

Abraham Maslow (1954) attempted to organize the list of human urges (or, as he called them, *needs*) in a meaningful way (see **FIGURE 8.13**). He noted that some needs (such as the need to eat) must be satisfied before others (such as the need to have friends), and he built a hierarchy of needs that had the most immediate needs at the bottom and the most deferrable needs at the top. Maslow suggested that, as a rule, people are more likely to experience a need when the needs below it are met. So when people are hungry or thirsty or exhausted, they are less likely to seek intellectual fulfillment or moral clarity (see **FIGURE 8.14** on the next page). According to Maslow, the needs that take precedence are typically those we share with other animals. For example, because all animals must survive and reproduce, all animals need to eat and mate. Human beings have these needs as well, but as you are about to see, they are more powerful and more complicated than most of us imagine (Kenrick et al., 2010).

> **Why do some motivations take precedence over others?**

### Survival: The Motivation for Food

Animals convert matter into energy by eating, and they are driven to do this by an internal state called *hunger*. But what is hunger and where does it come from? At every moment, your body is sending signals to your brain about its current energy state. If your body needs energy, it sends a signal to tell your brain to switch hunger on, and if your body has sufficient energy, it sends a different signal to tell your brain to switch hunger off (Gropp et al., 2005). No one knows precisely what these signals are or how they are sent and received, but research has identified a variety of candidates.

For example, *ghrelin* is a hormone that is produced in the stomach and appears to be a signal that tells the brain to switch hunger on (Inui, 2001; Nakazato et al., 2001). When people are injected with ghrelin, they become intensely hungry and eat about 30 percent more than usual (Wren et al., 2001). Interestingly, ghrelin also binds to neurons in the hippocampus and temporarily improves learning and memory (Diano et al., 2006) so that we become just a little bit better at locating food when our bodies need it most. *Leptin* is a chemical secreted by fat cells, and it appears to be a signal that tells the brain to switch hunger off. It seems to do this by making

▼ Figure **8.13** **Maslow's Hierarchy of Needs** Human beings are motivated to satisfy a variety of needs. Psychologist Abraham Maslow thought these needs formed a hierarchy, with physiological needs forming a base and self-actualization needs forming a pinnacle. He suggested that people do not experience higher needs until the needs below them have been met.

Need for self-actualization

Esteem needs

Belongingness and love needs

Safety and security needs

Physiological needs

food less rewarding (Farooqi et al., 2007). People who are born with a leptin deficiency have trouble controlling their appetites (Montague et al., 1997). For example, in 2002, medical researchers reported on the case of a 9-year-old girl

> **What purpose does hunger serve?**

who weighed 90 kg (200 pounds), but after just a few leptin injections, she reduced her food intake by 84 percent and attained normal weight (Farooqi et al., 2002). Some researchers think the idea that chemicals turn hunger on and off is far too simple since animals do not eat indiscriminately; they seem to compensate for macronutrient deficiencies in their diet by selectively consuming food high in that missing nutrient (like protein) (Dibattista & Holder, 1998). This suggests that there may be different hunger signals depending on the nutritional state of the animal (Rozin & Kalat, 1971).

Whether hunger is one signal or many, the primary receiver of these signals is the hypothalamus. Different parts of the hypothalamus receive different signals (see **FIGURE 8.15**). The *lateral hypothalamus* receives orexigenic signals, and when it is destroyed, animals sitting in a cage full of food will starve themselves to death. The *ventromedial hypothalamus* receives anorexigenic signals, and when it is destroyed, animals will gorge themselves to the point of illness and obesity (Miller, 1960; Steinbaum & Miller, 1965). These two structures were once thought to be the "hunger centre" and "satiety centre" of the brain, but it turns out that this view is far too simple (Woods et al., 1998). Hypothalamic structures play an important role in turning hunger on and off, but the precise way in which they execute these functions is complex and poorly understood (Stellar & Stellar, 1985).

## Eating Disorders

Feelings of hunger tell us when to eat and when to stop. But for the estimated 600 000 Canadians with eating disorders, eating is a much more complicated affair (Government of Canada, 2006). For instance, **bulimia nervosa** is *an eating disorder characterized by binge eating followed by purging.* People with bulimia typically ingest large quantities of food in a relatively short period and then take laxatives or induce vomiting to purge the food from their bodies. These people are caught in a cycle: They eat to ease negative emotions such as sadness and anxiety, but then concern about weight gain leads them to experience negative emotions such as guilt and self-loathing, and these emotions then lead them to purge (Sherry & Hall, 2009; cf. Haedt-Matt & Keel, 2011).

**Anorexia nervosa** is *an eating disorder characterized by an intense fear of being fat and severe restriction of food intake.* People with anorexia tend to have a distorted body image that leads them to believe they are fat when they are actually emaciated, and they tend to be high-achieving perfectionists who see their severe control of eating as a triumph of will over impulse. Contrary to what you might expect, people with anorexia have extremely *high* levels of ghrelin in their blood, which suggests that their bodies are trying desperately to switch hunger on but that hunger's call is being suppressed, ignored, or overridden (Ariyasu et al., 2001). Like most eating disorders, anorexia strikes more women than men, and 40 percent of newly identified cases of anorexia are among women 15 to 19 years old.

Anorexia may have both cultural and biological causes (Klump & Culbert, 2007). For example, women with anorexia typically believe that thinness equals beauty, and

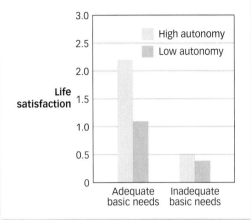

▲ Figure **8.14** **When Do Higher Needs Matter?** Maslow was right. A recent study of 77 000 people in the world's 51 poorest nations (Martin & Hill, 2012) showed that if people have their basic needs met, then autonomy (i.e., freedom to make their own decisions) increases their satisfaction with their lives. But when people do not have their basic needs met, autonomy makes little difference.

Lateral hypothalamus

Ventromedial hypothalamus

◄ Figure **8.15** **Hunger, Satiety, and the Hypothalamus** The hypothalamus comprises many parts. In general, the lateral hypothalamus receives the signals that turn hunger on and the ventromedial hypothalamus receives the signals that turn hunger off.

**bulimia nervosa**
An eating disorder characterized by binge eating followed by purging.

**anorexia nervosa**
An eating disorder characterized by an intense fear of being fat and severe restriction of food intake.

Bar Refaeili is Israel's best known supermodel. In 2012, Israel enacted a law banning models whose body mass index is under 18.5 from appearing in advertisements. So a 172-cm (5' 8") model must weigh at least 54 kg (119 pounds).

it is not hard to understand why. The average woman is 163 cm (5′4″) tall and weighs 69 kg (140 pounds), and so has a Body Mass Index (BMI) of 26.6. The typical fashion model is between 172 cm (5′8″) and 180 cm (5′11″), with a BMI of 16.2, which is considered underweight. Indeed, most university-age women report wanting to be thinner than they are (Rozin, Trachtenberg, & Cohen, 2001), and nearly 1 in 5 reports being *embarrassed* to be seen buying a chocolate bar (Rozin, Bauer, & Catanese, 2003). But anorexia is not just "vanity run amok" (Striegel-Moore & Bulik, 2007). Many researchers believe that there are as-yet-undiscovered biological and/or genetic components to the illness as well. For example, although anorexia primarily affects women, men have a sharply increased risk of becoming anorexic if they have a female twin who has the disorder (Procopio & Marriott, 2007), suggesting that anorexia may have something to do with prenatal exposure to female hormones.

What causes anorexia?

Bulimia and anorexia are problems for many people. But Canada's most pervasive eating-related problem is obesity. Currently, 35 percent of adult Canadians are overweight, and 25 percent are obese (Public Health Agency of Canada, 2011a). To give you a sense for what this means, "overweight" for a person who is 170 cm (5′6″) tall would be 73 kg (161 pounds) or more; and obese would be 87 kg (192 pounds) or more. Rates of obesity across the country vary substantially, but are increasing everywhere (see **FIGURE 8.16**). Rates of unhealthy weight are increasing among children as well. In 1978, only 15 percent of children were overweight or obese—by 2007, 29 percent of adolescents had unhealthy weights (Statistics Canada, 2010). This is a problem that most adolescents do not outgrow: in fact, many continue to gain excess weight (Public Health Agency of Canada, 2009).

**FIGURE 8.17** and **TABLE 8.1** (both on the next page) allow you to compute your BMI, and the odds are that you will not like what you learn. Although BMI is a better predictor of mortality for some people than for others (Romero-Corral et al., 2006; van Dis et al., 2009), most researchers agree that an extremely high BMI is unhealthy. Every year, obesity-related illnesses cost our nation about $4 billion (Eisenberg et al., 2011; Public Health Agency of Canada, 2009) and affected adults appear to die 3 to 7 years earlier than individuals at a healthy weight (Peeters et al., 2003). In addition to these physical risks, obese people tend to be viewed negatively by others, have lower self-esteem, and have a lower quality of life (Hebl & Heatherton, 1997; Kolotkin, Meter, & Williams, 2001). Obese women earn about 7 percent less than their non-obese counterparts (Lempert, 2007), and the stigma of obesity is so powerful that average-weight people are viewed negatively if they even have a relationship with someone who is obese (Hebl & Mannix, 2003). All of this is terribly unfair, of course. As one scientist noted, we need to declare "a war on obesity, not the obese" (Friedman, 2003).

► Figure 8.16 **The Geography of Obesity** The chart shows the proportion of the adult population with a BMI in the obese range, and how this has changed over time. Obesity rates are increasing, and are particularly high in the Atlantic provinces and the North.

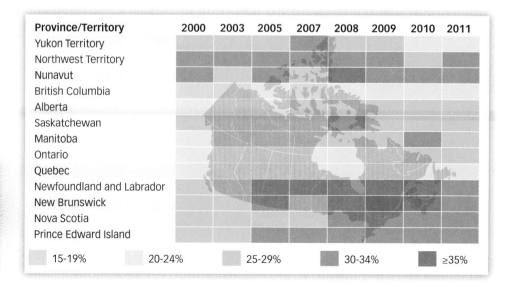

▶ Figure 8.17 **Determining BMI** Find your weight along the vertical axis. Draw a horizontal line from that value. Find your height on the horizontal axis. Draw a vertical line. The point of intersection of the two lines indicates your BMI. Use Table 8.1 to determine your level of health.

### Table 8.1

#### Health Risk Classification According to Body Mass Index (BMI)

| Classification | BMI Category (kg/m²) | Health Problems Risk |
|---|---|---|
| Underweight | < 18.5 | increased |
| Normal weight | 18.5–24.9 | least |
| Overweight | 25.0–29.9 | increased |
| Obese Class I | 30.0–34.9 | high |
| Obese Class II | 35.0–39.9 | very high |
| Obese Class III | ≥ 40.0 | extremely high |

*Source:* Health Canada, 2003. *Canadian Guidelines for Body Weight Classification in Adults.* Ottawa: Minister of Public Works and Government Services Canada.

Obesity has many causes. For example, obesity is highly heritable (Allison et al., 1996) and may have a genetic component, which may explain why a disproportionate amount of the weight gained by Canadians in the past few decades has been gained by those who were already the heaviest (Public Health Agency of Canada, 2011a). Some studies suggest that "obesogenic" toxins in the environment can disrupt the functioning of the endocrine system and predispose people to obesity (Grün & Blumberg, 2006; Newbold et al., 2005), whereas other studies suggest that obesity can be caused by a dearth of "good bacteria" in the gut (Liou et al., 2013). Whatever the cause, obese people are often leptin-resistant (i.e., their brains do not respond to the chemical message that shuts hunger off) and even leptin injections do not seem to help (Friedman & Halaas, 1998; Heymsfield et al., 1999).

Genes, pollutants, and bacteria have all been implicated in the tendency toward obesity. But in most cases the cause of obesity is not such a mystery: We simply eat too much. We eat when we are hungry, of course, but we also eat when we are sad or anxious, or when we are presented with a visually appealing or delicious food, or when everyone else is eating (Herman, Roth, & Polivy, 2003). Sometimes we eat simply because the clock tells us to, which is why people with amnesia will happily eat a second lunch shortly after finishing an unremembered first one (Rozin et al., 1998) (see The Real World: Jeet Jet?). Although all of these factors influence eating in both normal-weight and obese individuals, work by University of Toronto researchers suggests that obese individuals are particularly sensitive to the sensory qualities of food. In other words, obese individuals overeat more when presented with highly palatable (high fat, high sugar) foods than do normal-weight individuals (Herman & Polivy, 2008). Why does this happen? After all, most of us do not breathe ourselves sick or sleep ourselves sick, so why do we eat ourselves sick?

**Why do people overeat?**

Blame the design. Hundreds of thousands of years ago, the main food-related problem facing our ancestors was starvation, and humans evolved two strategies to avoid it. First, we developed a strong attraction to foods that provide large amounts of energy per bite (in other words, foods that are calorically rich), which is why most of us prefer

Times have changed. People today are often astonished to see that advertisements once promised to help young women *gain* weight to become popular.

## THE REAL WORLD

# Jeet Jet?*

n 1923, a reporter for the *New York Times* asked the British mountaineer George Leigh Mallory why he wanted to climb Mount Everest. Mallory replied: "Because it is there."

Apparently, that is also the reason why we eat. Brian Wansink and colleagues (2005) wondered whether the amount of food people eat is influenced by the amount of food they see in front of them. So they invited participants to their laboratory, sat them down in front of a large bowl of tomato soup, and told them to eat as much as they wanted. In one condition of the study, a server came to the table and refilled the participant's bowl whenever it got down to about a quarter full. In another condition, the bowl was not refilled by a server. Rather, unbeknownst to the participants, the bottom of the bowl was connected by a long tube to a large vat of soup, so whenever the participant ate from the bowl it would slowly and almost imperceptibly refill itself.

▲ Researcher Brian Wansink and his bottomless bowl of soup.

What the researchers found was sobering. Participants who unknowingly ate from a "bottomless bowl" consumed a whopping 73 percent more soup than those who ate from normal bowls—and yet, they did not think they had consumed more and they did not report feeling any more full.

It seems that we find it easier to keep track of what we are eating than how much, and this can cause us to overeat even when we are trying our best to do just the opposite. For instance, one study showed that diners at an Italian restaurant often chose to eat butter on their bread rather than dipping it in olive oil because they thought that doing so would reduce the number of calories per slice. And they were right. What they did not realize, however, is that they would unconsciously compensate for this reduction in calories by eating 23 percent more bread during the meal (Wansink & Linder, 2003).

This and other research suggests that one of the best ways to reduce our waists is simply to count our bites.

*"Jeet jet?" is a phrase by Pittsburghers that means "Did you eat yet?"

---

**metabolism**
The rate at which energy is used by the body.

Idris Lewis and his wife both fit into the trousers he used to wear in 2009 when he weighed 165 kg (364 pounds). Unfortunately, dieting rarely works. Most people who lose significant amounts of weight regain most or all of it within a year (Polivy & Herman, 2002).

hamburgers and milkshakes to celery and water. Second, we developed an ability to store excess food energy in the form of fat, which enabled us to eat more than we needed when food was plentiful and then live off our reserves when food was scarce. We are beautifully engineered for a world in which high calorie foods are scarce, and the problem is that we do not live in that world anymore. Instead, we live in a world in which the fatty miracles of modern technology—from chocolate cupcakes to sausage pizzas—are inexpensive and readily available. As two researchers recently wrote, "We evolved on the savannahs of Africa; we now live in Candyland" (Power & Schulkin, 2009). To make matters worse, many of Candyland's foods tend to be high in saturated fat, which has the paradoxical effect of making the brain *less* sensitive to some of the chemical messengers that tell us to stop eating (Benoit et al., 2009).

It is all too easy to overeat and become overweight or obese, and it is all too difficult to reverse course. The human body resists weight loss in two ways. First, when we gain weight, we experience an increase in both the size and the number of fat cells in our bodies (usually in our abdomens if we are male and in our thighs and buttocks if we are female). But when we lose weight, we experience a decrease in the size of our fat cells but no decrease in their number. Once our bodies have added a fat cell, that cell is pretty much there to stay. It may become thinner when we diet, but it is unlikely to die.

Second, our bodies respond to dieting by decreasing our **metabolism,** which is *the rate at which energy is used by the body.* When our bodies sense that we are living through a famine (which is what they conclude when we refuse to feed them), they find more efficient ways to turn food into fat: a great trick for our ancestors but a real nuisance for us. Indeed, when rats are overfed, then put on diets, then overfed again and put on diets again, they gain weight faster and lose it more slowly

**Why is dieting so difficult and ineffective?**

The x-axis is labeled "Estimated year of painting" ranging from 1000 to 2000. The y-axis is labeled "Relative size of main dish" ranging from 0.00 to 10.00.

the second time around, which suggests that with each round of dieting, their bodies become increasingly efficient at converting food to fat (Brownell et al., 1986). The bottom line is that avoiding obesity is easier than overcoming it (Casazza et al., 2013).

And avoiding it is not as difficult as you might think. For instance, just by placing hard-boiled eggs approximately 25 cm away from the more healthful ingredients in a salad bar, researchers reduced the number of eggs that customers ate by about 10 percent (Rozin et al., 2011). Replacing the serving spoons with tongs reduced the amount by about 16 percent. In one study, snacking students ate fewer Pringles when every seventh chip was coloured red, presumably because the colour coding allowed them to keep track of how much they were eating (Geier, Wansink, & Rozin, 2012). In another study, people ate 22 percent less pasta with tomato sauce when they used a white plate instead of a red plate, presumably because the white plate provided a stark contrast that allowed them to see what they were eating (van Ittersum & Wansink, 2012). These and dozens of other studies show that small changes in our environments can prevent big changes in our waistlines.

One reason why obesity rates are rising is that "normal portions" keep getting larger. When researchers analyzed 52 depictions of *The Last Supper* that were painted between the years 1000 and 1800, they found that the average plate size increased by 66 percent (Wansink & Wansink, 2010).

## Reproduction: The Motivation for Sex

Food motivates us because it is essential to our survival. But sex is also essential to our survival (at least to the survival of our DNA), which is why evolution has ensured that a desire for sex is wired deep into the brain of almost every one of us. In some ways, that wiring scheme is simple: Glands secrete hormones that travel through the blood to the brain and stimulate sexual desire. But which hormones, which parts of the brain, and what triggers the launch in the first place?

The hormone dihydroepiandosterone (DHEA) seems to be involved in the initial onset of sexual desire. Both boys and girls begin producing this slow-acting hormone at about the age of 6, which may help explain why boys and girls both experience their initial sexual interest at about the age of 10, despite the fact that boys reach puberty much later than girls. Two other hormones have more gender-specific effects. Both males and females produce testosterone and estrogen, but males produce more of the former and females produce more of the latter. As you will learn in the Development chapter, these two hormones are largely responsible for the physical and psychological changes that characterize puberty. But are they also responsible for the waxing and waning of sexual desire in adults?

*"Come back, young man. He needs a booster shot."*

The red colouration on the female gelada's chest (*left*) indicates that she is in estrus and amenable to sex. The sexual interest of a female human being (*right*) is not limited to a particular time in her monthly cycle.

The answer appears to be yes—as long as those adults are rats. Testosterone increases the sexual desire of male rats by acting on a particular area of the hypothalamus, and estrogen increases the sexual desire of female rats by acting on a different area of the hypothalamus. Lesions to these areas reduce sexual motivation in the respective genders, and when testosterone or estrogen is applied to these areas, sexual motivation increases. In short, testosterone regulates sexual desire in male rats and estrogen regulates both sexual desire and fertility in female rats.

The story for human beings is far more interesting. The females of most mammalian species (e.g., dogs, cats, and rats) have little or no interest in sex except when their estrogen levels are high, which happens when they are ovulating (i.e., when they are "in estrus" or "in heat"). In other words, estrogen regulates both ovulation and sexual interest in these mammals. But female human beings can be interested in sex at any point in their monthly cycles. Although the level of estrogen in a woman's body changes dramatically over the course of her monthly menstrual cycle, studies suggest that sexual desire changes little, if at all. Somewhere in the course of our evolution, it seems, women's sexual interest became independent of their ovulation.

Some theorists have speculated that the advantage of this independence was that it made it more difficult for males to know whether a female was in the fertile phase of her monthly cycle. Male mammals often guard their mates jealously when their mates are ovulating, but go off in search of other females when their mates are not. If a male cannot use his mate's sexual receptivity to tell when she is ovulating, then he has no choice but to stay around and guard her all the time. For females who are trying to keep their mates at home so that they will contribute to the rearing of children, sexual interest that is continuous and independent of fertility may be an excellent strategy.

> **Why do female humans not show clear signs of ovulation?**

If estrogen is not the hormonal basis of women's sex drives, then what is? Two pieces of evidence suggest that the answer is testosterone—the same hormone that drives male sexuality. First, when women are given testosterone, their sex drives increase. Second, men naturally have more testosterone than women do, and they generally have stronger sex drives. Men are more likely than women to think about sex, have sexual fantasies, seek sex and sexual variety (whether positions or partners), masturbate, want sex at an early point in a relationship, sacrifice other things for sex, have permissive attitudes toward sex, and complain about low sex drive in their partners (Baumeister, Cantanese, & Vohs, 2001). All of this suggests that testosterone may be the hormonal basis of sex drive in both men and women.

### Sexual Activity

Men and women may have different levels of sexual drive, but their physiological responses during sex are fairly similar. Prior to the 1960s, data on human sexual behaviour consisted primarily of people's answers to questions about their sex lives (and you may have noticed that this is a topic about which people do not always tell the truth). William Masters and Virginia Johnson changed all that by conducting groundbreaking studies in which they actually measured the physical responses of hundreds of volunteers as they masturbated or had sex in the laboratory (Masters & Johnson, 1966). Their work led to a deeper understanding of the **human sexual response cycle,** which refers to *the stages of physiological arousal during sexual activity* (see **FIGURE 8.18** on the next page). Human sexual response has four phases:

**human sexual response cycle**
The stages of physiological arousal during sexual activity.

> During the *excitement phase*, muscle tension and blood flow increase in and around the sexual organs, heart and respiration rates increase, and blood pressure rises. Both men and women may experience erect nipples and a "sex flush" on the skin of the upper body and face. A man's penis typically becomes erect or partially erect and his testicles draw upward, while a woman's vagina typically becomes lubricated and her clitoris becomes swollen.

> During the *plateau phase*, heart rate and muscle tension increase further. A man's urinary bladder closes to prevent urine from mixing with semen, and muscles at the base of his penis begin a steady rhythmic contraction. A man's Cowper gland may secrete a small amount of lubricating fluid (which, by the way, often contains enough sperm to cause pregnancy). A woman's clitoris may withdraw slightly, and her vagina may become more lubricated. Her outer vagina may swell, and her muscles may tighten and reduce the diameter of the opening of the vagina.

> During the *orgasm phase*, breathing becomes extremely rapid and the pelvic muscles begin a series of rhythmic contractions. Both men and women experience quick cycles of muscle contraction of the anus and lower pelvic muscles, and women often experience uterine and vaginal contractions as well. During this phase, men ejaculate about two to five millilitres of semen (depending on how long it has been since their last orgasm and how long they were aroused prior to ejaculation). Ninety-five percent of heterosexual men and 69 percent of heterosexual women reported having an orgasm during their last sexual encounter (Richters et al., 2006); although roughly 15 percent of women never experience orgasm, less than half experience orgasm from intercourse alone, and roughly half report having "faked" an orgasm at least once (Wiederman, 1997). The frequency with which women have orgasms seems to have a genetic component (Dawood et al., 2005). And it goes without saying that when men and women have orgasms, they typically experience them as intensely pleasurable.

> During the *resolution phase*, muscles relax, blood pressure drops, and the body returns to its resting state. Most men and women experience a *refractory period*, during which further stimulation does not produce excitement. This period may last from minutes to days and is typically longer for men than for women.

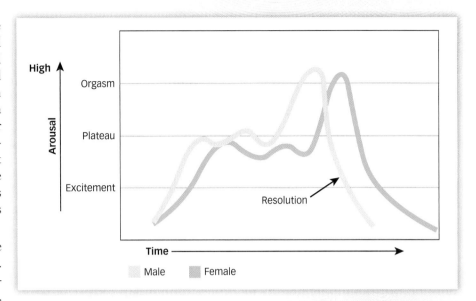

▲ Figure **8.18** **The Human Sexual Response Cycle** The pattern of the sexual response cycle is quite similar for men and for women. Both men and women go through the excitement, plateau, orgasm, and resolution phases, though the timing of their response may differ.

Although sex is typically a prerequisite for reproduction, the vast majority of sexual acts are not meant to produce babies. University students, for example, are rarely aiming to get pregnant, but they do have sex because of *physical attraction* ("The person had beautiful eyes"), as a *means to an end* ("I wanted to be popular"), to increase *emotional connection* ("I wanted to communicate at a deeper level"), and to *alleviate insecurity* ("It was the only way my partner would spend time with me") (Meston & Buss, 2007). Although men are more likely than women to report having sex for purely physical reasons, **TABLE 8.2** (on the next page) shows that men and women do not differ dramatically in their most frequent responses about why they have sex. It is worth noting that not all sex is motivated by reasons like these: About half of university-age women and a quarter of

**Why do people have sex?**

> Table 8.2

**Reasons for Sex**

Top Ten Reasons Why Women and Men Report Having Sex

|  | Women | Men |
|---|---|---|
| 1 | I was attracted to the person. | I was attracted to the person. |
| 2 | I wanted to experience the physical pleasure. | It feels good. |
| 3 | It feels good. | I wanted to experience the physical pleasure. |
| 4 | I wanted to show my affection to the person. | It is fun. |
| 5 | I wanted to express my love for the person. | I wanted to show my affection to the person. |
| 6 | I was sexually aroused and wanted the release. | I was sexually aroused and wanted the release. |
| 7 | I was "horny." | I was "horny." |
| 8 | It is fun. | I wanted to express my love for the person. |
| 9 | I realized I was in love. | I wanted to achieve an orgasm. |
| 10 | I was "in the heat of the moment." | I wanted to please my partner. |

*Source:* Meston & Buss, 2007.

university-age men report having unwanted sexual activity in a dating relationship (O'Sullivan & Allegeier, 1998). We will have much more to say about sexual attraction and relationships in the Social Psychology chapter.

## What the Mind Wants

Survival and reproduction are every animal's first order of business, so it is no surprise that we are strongly motivated by food and sex. But we are motivated by other things too. We crave kisses of both the chocolate and romantic variety, but we also crave friendship and respect, security and certainty, wisdom and meaning, and a whole lot more. Our psychological motivations can be every bit as powerful as our biological motivations, but they differ in two ways.

First, although we share our biological motivations with most other animals, our psychological motivations are relatively unique. Chimps and rabbits and robins and turtles are all motivated to have sex, but only human beings seem motivated to imbue the act with meaning. Second, although our biological motivations are few—food, sex, oxygen, sleep, and a handful of other things—our psychological motivations are virtually limitless. The things we care about feeling and thinking, knowing and believing, having and being are so numerous and varied that no psychologist has ever been able to make a complete list (Hofmann, Vohs, & Baumeister, 2012). Nonetheless, even if you looked at an incomplete list, you would quickly notice that psychological motivations vary on three key dimensions: extrinsic versus intrinsic, conscious versus unconscious, and approach versus avoidance. Let us examine each of these.

### Intrinsic versus Extrinsic

Taking a psychology exam and eating a french fry are different in many ways. One makes you tired and the other makes you chubby, one requires that you move your lips and the other requires that you do not, and so on. But the key difference between these activities is that one is a means to an end and one is an end in itself. An **intrinsic motivation** is *a motivation to take actions that are themselves rewarding.* When we eat a french fry because it tastes good, exercise

Mohamed Bouazizi was a fruit seller. In 2010 he set himself on fire to protest his treatment by the Tunisian government, and his dramatic suicide ignited the revolution that came to be known as "Arab Spring." Clearly, psychological needs—such as the need for justice—can be even more powerful than biological needs.

because it feels good, or listen to music because it sounds good, we are intrinsically motivated. These activities do not *have* a payoff: They *are* a payoff. Conversely, an **extrinsic motivation** is *a motivation to take actions that lead to reward.* When we floss our teeth so we can avoid gum disease (and get dates), when we work hard for money so we can pay our rent (and get dates), and when we take an exam so we can get a university degree (and get money to get dates), we are extrinsically motivated. None of these things directly bring pleasure, but all may lead to pleasure in the long run.

Extrinsic motivation gets a bad rap. Canadians tend to believe that people should "follow their hearts" and "do what they love," and we feel sorry for students who choose courses just to please their parents and for parents who choose jobs just to earn a pile of money. But the fact is that our ability to engage in behaviours that are

> **Why should people delay gratification?**

unrewarding in the present because we believe they will bring greater rewards in the future is one of our species' most significant talents, and no other species can do it quite as well as we can (Gilbert, 2006). In research on the ability to delay gratification (Ayduk et al., 2007; Mischel et al., 2004), people are typically faced with a choice between getting something they want right now (e.g., a scoop of ice cream) or waiting and getting more of what they want later (e.g., two scoops of ice cream). Waiting for ice cream is a lot like taking an exam or flossing: It is not much fun, but you do it because you know you will reap greater rewards in the end. Studies show that 4-year-old children who can delay gratification are judged to be more intelligent and socially competent 10 years later and have higher university admissions test scores when they enter university (Mischel, Shoda, & Rodriguez, 1989). In fact, the ability to delay gratification is a better predictor of a child's grades in school than is the child's IQ (Duckworth & Seligman, 2005). Apparently there is something to be said for extrinsic motivation.

There is a lot to be said for intrinsic motivation too (Patall, Cooper, & Robinson, 2008). People work harder when they are intrinsically motivated, they enjoy what they do more, and they do it more creatively. Both kinds of motivation have advantages, which is why many of us try to build lives in which we are both intrinsically and extrinsically motivated by the same activity—lives in which we are paid the big bucks for doing exactly what we like to do best. Who has not fantasized about becoming an artist or an athlete or Kanye West's personal party planner? Alas, research suggests that it is difficult to get paid for doing what you love and still end up loving what you

> **Why do rewards sometimes backfire?**

do because extrinsic rewards can undermine intrinsic interest (Deci, Koestner, & Ryan, 1999; Henderlong & Lepper, 2002). For example, in one study, university students who were intrinsically interested in a puzzle either were paid to complete it or completed it for free, and those who were paid were less likely to play with the puzzle later on (Deci, 1971). In a similar study, children who enjoyed drawing with Magic Markers were either promised or not promised an award for using them, and those who were promised the award were less likely to use the markers later (Lepper, Greene, & Nisbett, 1973). It appears that under some circumstances people take rewards to indicate that an activity is not inherently pleasurable ("If they had to pay me to do that puzzle, it could not have been a very fun one"); thus rewards can cause people to lose their intrinsic motivation.

Just as rewards can undermine intrinsic motivation, punishments can create it. In one study, children who had no intrinsic interest in playing with a toy suddenly gained an interest when the experimenter threatened to punish them if they touched it (Aronson, 1963). University students who had no intrinsic motivation to cheat on a test were more likely to do so if the experimenter explicitly warned against it (Wilson & Lassiter, 1982). Threats can suggest that a forbidden activity is desirable, and they can also have the paradoxical consequence of promoting the very behaviours they are

**intrinsic motivation**
A motivation to take actions that are themselves rewarding.

**extrinsic motivation**
A motivation to take actions that lead to reward.

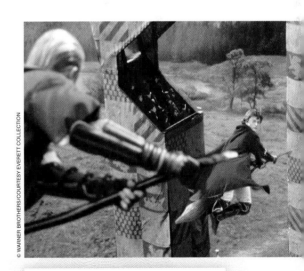

© WARNER BROTHERS/COURTESY EVERETT COLLECTION

In *Harry Potter and the Chamber of Secrets,* the Hogwarts house that wins a quidditch match gets points awarded— these count toward the annual House Cup championship. How do you think that the extrinsic motivation of points awarded to Gryffindor for winning quidditch matches may influence Harry Potter's intrinsic motivation to play the game?

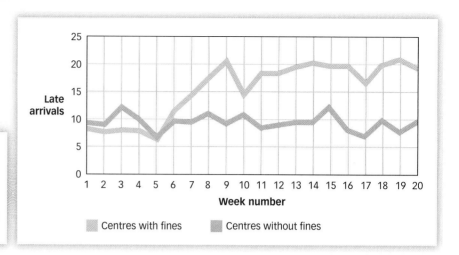

▶ Figure **8.19** **When Threats Backfire**
Threats can cause behaviours that were once intrinsically motivated to become extrinsically motivated. Daycare centres that instituted fines for late-arriving parents saw an increase in the number of parents who arrived late.

meant to discourage. For example, when a group of daycare centres got fed up with parents who arrived late to pick up their children, some of them instituted a financial penalty for tardiness. As **FIGURE 8.19** shows, the financial penalty caused an *increase* in late arrivals (Gneezy & Rustichini, 2000). Why? Because parents are intrinsically motivated to fetch their kids and they generally do their best to be on time. But when the daycare centres imposed a fine for late arrival, the parents became extrinsically motivated to fetch their children—and because the fine was not particularly large, they decided to pay a small financial penalty in order to leave their children in daycare for an extra hour. When threats and rewards change intrinsic motivation into extrinsic motivation, unexpected consequences can follow.

### Conscious versus Unconscious

When prizewinning artists or scientists are asked to explain their achievements, they typically say things like, "I wanted to liberate colour from form" or "I wanted to cure diabetes." They almost never say, "I wanted to exceed my father's accomplishments, thereby proving to my mother that I was worthy of her love." People clearly have **conscious motivations,** which are *motivations of which people are aware,* but they also have **unconscious motivations,** which are *motivations of which people are not aware* (Aarts, Custers, & Marien, 2008; Bargh et al., 2001; Hassin, Bargh, & Zimerman, 2009).

For example, psychologists David McClelland and John Atkinson argued that people vary in their **need for achievement,** which is *the motivation to solve worthwhile problems* (McClelland et al., 1953). They argued that this basic motivation is unconscious and thus must be measured with special techniques such as the Thematic Apperception Test, which presents people with a series of drawings and asks them to tell stories about them. The amount of "achievement-related imagery" in the person's story ostensibly reveals the person's unconscious need for achievement. (You will learn more about these sorts of tests in the Personality chapter.) Although there has been much controversy about the validity and reliability of measures such as these (Lilienfeld, Wood, & Garb, 2000; Tuerlinckx, De Boeck, & Lens, 2002), research shows that a person's responses on this test reliably predict the person's behaviour in certain circumstances. For example, they can predict a child's grades in school (Khalid, 1991). Research also suggests that this motivation can be "primed" in much the same way that thoughts and feelings can be primed. For example, when words such as *achievement* are presented on a computer screen so rapidly that people cannot consciously perceive them, those people will work especially hard to solve a puzzle (Bargh et al., 2001) and will feel especially unhappy if they fail (Chartrand & Kay, 2006).

What determines whether we are conscious of our motivations? Most actions have more than one motivation, and Robin Vallacher and Daniel Wegner (1985, 1987) have

**conscious motivations**
Motivations of which people are aware.

**unconscious motivations**
Motivations of which people are not aware.

**need for achievement**
The motivation to solve worthwhile problems.

suggested that the ease or difficulty of performing the action determines which of these motivations we will be aware of. When actions are easy (e.g., screwing in a light bulb), we are aware of our most *general motivations* (e.g., to be helpful), but when actions are difficult (e.g., wrestling with a light bulb that is stuck in its socket), we are aware of our more specific motivations (e.g., to get the threads aligned). Vallacher and

> **What makes people conscious of their motivations?**

Wegner argued that people are usually aware of the general motivations for their behaviour and only become aware of their more specific motivations when they encounter problems. For example, participants in an experiment drank coffee either from a normal mug or from a mug that had a heavy weight attached to the bottom, which made the mug difficult to manipulate. When asked what they were doing, those who were drinking from the normal mug explained that they were "satisfying needs," whereas those who were drinking from the weighted mug explained that they were "swallowing" (Wegner et al., 1984). The ease with which we can execute an action is one of many factors that determine whether we are or are not conscious of our motivations.

## Approach versus Avoidance

The poet James Thurber (1956) wrote: "All men should strive to learn before they die/ What they are running from, and to, and why." The hedonic principle describes two conceptually distinct motivations: a motivation to "run to" pleasure and a motivation to "run from" pain. The first it what psychologists call an **approach motivation,** which is *a motivation to experience a positive outcome.* The second is an **avoidance motivation,** which is *a motivation not to experience a negative outcome.* Pleasure is not just the lack of pain, and pain is not just the lack of pleasure. They are independent experiences that occur in different parts of the brain (Davidson et al., 1990; Gray, 1990).

Research suggests that, all else being equal, avoidance motivations tend to be more powerful than approach motivations. Most people will turn down a chance to bet on a coin flip that would pay them $10 if it came up heads but would require them to pay $8 if it came up tails, because they believe that the pain of losing $8 will be more intense than the pleasure of winning $10 (Kahneman & Tversky, 1979). Because people expect losses to have more powerful emotional consequences than equal-size gains, they will take more risks to avoid a loss than to achieve a gain. When participants are told that a disease is expected to kill 600 people and are asked to choose between administering Vaccine A, which will save exactly 200 people, or Vaccine B, which has a one-third chance of saving everybody and a two-thirds chance of saving nobody, about three-quarters of them decide to play it safe and select Vaccine A. Yet, when people are given a choice between Vaccine C, which will allow exactly 400 people to die, or Vaccine D which has a one-third chance of allowing no one to die and a two-thirds chance of allowing everyone to die, about three quarters of them decide to take the gamble and select Vaccine D (Tversky & Kahneman, 1981). Now, if you do the math you will quickly see that Vaccine A and Vaccine C are identical, as are Vaccine B and Vaccine D. The descriptions of the identical vaccines are just two ways of saying the same thing. And yet, when vaccines are described in terms of the number of lives lost (as C and D are) instead of the number of lives gained (as A and B are), most people are ready to take a big risk. It is interesting to note that monkeys show the same tendency (Lakshminarayanan, Chen, & Santos, 2011).

On average, avoidance motivation is stronger than approach motivation, but the relative strength of these two tendencies does differ somewhat from person to person. **TABLE 8.3** on the next page shows a series of questions that have been used to measure the relative strength of a person's approach and avoidance tendencies (Carver & White, 1994). Research shows that people who are described by the high-approach items are happier when rewarded than those who are not, and that those

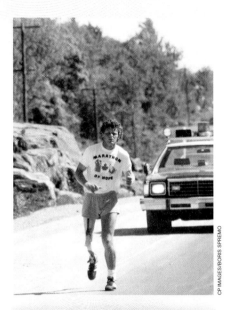

Terry Fox was clearly high on need for achievement. Having lost his right leg to cancer, he intended to fundraise for the disease by running from St John's to Victoria. In 1980 he ran for 143 days and 5373 km, through gale force winds, rainstorms, stress injuries, and fatigue (probably related to recurrent cancer), before he was forced by his illness to stop outside of Thunder Bay. His achievement raised $12 million for cancer research (worth $35 million today). Since then, Terry Fox Runs in schools and communities across the country have raised more than half a billion dollars for cancer research.

**approach motivation**
A motivation to experience a positive outcome.

**avoidance motivation**
A motivation not to experience a negative outcome.

who are described by the high-avoidance items are more anxious when threatened than those who are not (Carver, 2006). Just as some people seem to be more responsive to rewards than to punishments (and vice versa), some people tend to think about their behaviour as attempts to get reward rather than to avoid punishment (and vice versa). People who have a *promotion focus* tend to think in terms of achieving gains whereas people who have a *prevention focus* tend to think in terms of avoiding losses (Higgins, 1997). In one study, participants were given an anagram task. Some were told that they would be paid $4 for the experiment, but they could earn an extra dollar by finding 90 percent or more of all the possible words. Others were told that they would be paid $5 for the experiment, but they could avoid losing a dollar by not missing more than 10 percent of all the possible words. People who had a promotion focus performed better in the first case than in the second, but people who had a prevention focus performed better in the second case than in the first (Shah, Higgins, & Friedman, 1998). Similarly, people with a high need for achievement tend to be somewhat more motivated by their hope for success, whereas people with a low need for achievement tend to be somewhat more motivated by their fear of failure.

> **What is the difference between being motivated to avoid and being motivated to approach?**

> **Table 8.3**

### Scale for Measuring the Behavioural Inhibition System and Behavioural Activation System

To what extent do each of these items describe you? The items in red measure the strength of your avoidance tendency and the items in green measure the strength of your approach tendency.

- Even if something bad is about to happen to me, I rarely experience fear or nervousness. (LOW AVOIDANCE)
- I go out of my way to get things I want. (HIGH APPROACH)
- When I am doing well at something, I love to keep at it. (HIGH APPROACH)
- I am always willing to try something new if I think it will be fun. (HIGH APPROACH)
- When I get something I want, I feel excited and energized. (HIGH APPROACH)
- Criticism or scolding hurts me quite a bit. (HIGH AVOIDANCE)
- When I want something, I usually go all-out to get it. (HIGH APPROACH)
- I will often do things for no other reason than that they might be fun. (HIGH APPROACH)
- If I see a chance to get something I want, I move on it right away. (HIGH APPROACH)
- I feel pretty worried or upset when I think or know somebody is angry at me. (HIGH AVOIDANCE)
- When I see an opportunity for something I like, I get excited right away. (HIGH APPROACH)
- I often act on the spur of the moment. (HIGH APPROACH)
- If I think something unpleasant is going to happen, I usually get pretty "worked up." (HIGH AVOIDANCE)
- When good things happen to me, it affects me strongly. (HIGH APPROACH)
- I feel worried when I think I have done poorly at something important. (HIGH AVOIDANCE)
- I crave excitement and new sensations. (HIGH APPROACH)
- When I go after something, I use a "no holds barred" approach. (HIGH APPROACH)
- I have very few fears compared to my friends. (LOW AVOIDANCE)
- It would excite me to win a contest. (HIGH APPROACH)
- I worry about making mistakes. (HIGH AVOIDANCE)

*Source:* Carver & White, 1994.

And what is probably the biggest thing that people want to avoid? All animals strive to stay alive, but only human beings realize that this striving is ultimately in vain and that death is life's inevitable end. Some psychologists have suggested that the motivation to avoid the anxiety associated with death creates a sense of "existential terror" and that much of our behaviour is merely an attempt to manage it. **Terror management theory** is *a theory about how people respond to knowledge of their own mortality,* and it suggests that—a shared set of beliefs about what is good and right and true (Greenberg, Solomon, & Arndt, 2008; Solomon et al., 2004). These beliefs allow people to see themselves as more than mortal animals because they inhabit a world of meaning in which they can achieve symbolic immortality (e.g., by leaving a great legacy or having children) and perhaps even literal immortality (e.g., by being pious and earning a spot in the afterlife). According to this theory, our cultural worldview is a shield that buffers us against the anxiety that the knowledge of our own mortality creates.

A "credit card surcharge" and a "cash discount" are precisely the same thing. But they sure do not feel that way! RyanAir customers were outraged in 2012 when the airline imposed a 2 percent surcharge on customers who paid with credit cards. Would the airline have been wiser to raise their ticket prices by 2 percent and then offer a 2 percent discount to customers who paid with cash?

Terror management theory gives rise to the *mortality-salience hypothesis*, which is the prediction that people who are reminded of their own mortality will work to reinforce their cultural worldviews. In the last 20 years, this hypothesis has been supported by nearly 400 studies. The results show that when people are reminded of death (often in very subtle ways, such as by flashing the word "death" for just a few milliseconds in a laboratory, or by stopping people on a street corner that happens to be near a graveyard), they are more likely to praise and reward those who share their cultural worldviews, derogate and punish those who do not, value their spouses and defend their countries, feel disgusted by "animalistic" behaviours such as breastfeeding, and so on. All of these responses are presumably ways of shoring up one's cultural worldview and thereby defending against the anxiety that reminders of one's own mortality naturally elicit.

> **How do people deal with knowledge of death?**

## IN SUMMARY

▶ Emotions motivate us indirectly by providing information about the world, but they also motivate us directly.

▶ The hedonic principle suggests that people approach pleasure and avoid pain, and that this basic motivation underlies all others. All organisms are born with some motivations and acquire others through experience.

▶ When the body experiences a deficit, we experience a drive to remedy it. Biological motivations generally take precedence over psychological motivations. An example of a biological motivation is hunger, which is the result of a complex system of physiological processes, and problems with this system can lead to eating disorders and obesity, both of which are difficult to overcome. Another example of a biological motivation is sexual interest. Men and women experience roughly the same sequence of physiological events during sex, they engage in sex for most of the same reasons, and both have sex drives that are regulated by testosterone.

▶ People have many psychological motivations that vary on three key dimensions. Intrinsic motivations can be undermined by extrinsic rewards and punishments. People tend to be conscious of their more general motivations unless difficulty with the production of action forces them to become conscious of more specific motivations that are typically unconscious. Avoidance motivations are generally more powerful than approach motivations, although this is truer for some people than for others.

**terror management theory**
A theory about how people respond to knowledge of their own mortality.

# Chapter Review

## KEY CONCEPT QUIZ

1. Emotions can be described by their location on the two dimensions of
   a. motivation and scaling.
   b. arousal and valence.
   c. stimulus and reaction.
   d. pain and pleasure.

2. Which theorists claimed that that a stimulus simultaneously causes both an emotional experience and a physiological reaction?
   a. Cannon and Bard
   b. James and Lange
   c. Schacter and Singer
   d. Klüver and Bucy

3. Which brain structure is most directly involved in the rapid appraisal of whether a stimulus is good or bad?
   a. the cortex
   b. the hypothalamus
   c. the amygdala
   d. the thalamus

4. Through _____, we change an emotional experience by changing the meaning of the emotion-eliciting stimulus.
   a. deactivation
   b. appraisal
   c. valence
   d. re-appraisal

5. Which of the following does NOT provide any support for the universality hypothesis?
   a. Congenitally blind people make the facial expressions associated with the basic emotions.
   b. Infants only days old react to bitter tastes with expressions of disgust.
   c. Robots have been engineered to exhibit emotional expressions.
   d. Researchers have discovered that isolated people living a Stone Age existence with little contact with the outside world recognize the emotional expressions of Westerners.

6. _____ is the idea that emotional expressions can cause emotional experiences.
   a. A display rule
   b. Expressional deception
   c. The universality hypothesis
   d. The facial feedback hypothesis

7. Two friends have asked you to help them settle a disagreement. You hear each side of the story and have an emotional response to one viewpoint, but you do not express it. This is an example of which display rule?
   a. de-intensification
   b. masking
   c. neutralizing
   d. intensification

8. Which of the following does NOT distinguish sincere from insincere expressions?
   a. temporal patterning
   b. duration
   c. symmetry
   d. levity

9. Which of the following statements is inaccurate?
   a. Certain facial muscles are reliably engaged by sincere facial expressions.
   b. Even when people smile bravely to mask disappointment, their faces tend to express small bursts of disappointment.
   c. Studies show that human lie detection ability is extremely good.
   d. Polygraph machines detect lies at a rate better than chance, but their error rate is still quite high.

10. The hedonic principle states that
    a. emotions provide people with information.
    b. people are motivated to experience pleasure and avoid pain.
    c. people use their moods as information about the likelihood of succeeding at a task.
    d. motivations are acquired solely through experience.

11. According to the early psychologists, an unlearned tendency to seek a particular goal is called
    a. an instinct.
    b. a drive.
    c. a motivation.
    d. a corrective action.

12. According to Maslow, our most basic needs are
    a. self-actualization and self-esteem.
    b. biological.
    c. unimportant until other needs are met.
    d. belongingness and love.

13. Which of the following is NOT a dimension on which psychological motivations vary?
    a. intrinsic—extrinsic
    b. conscious—unconscious
    c. avoid—approach
    d. appraisal—re-appraisal

14. Which of the following statements is true?
    a. Men and women engage in sex for many of the same reasons.
    b. Boys and girls experience initial sexual interest at different ages.
    c. The sequence of physiological arousal for men and women differs dramatically.
    d. The human male sex drive is regulated by testosterone while the human female sex drive is regulated by estrogen.

15. Which of the following activities is most likely the result of extrinsic motivation?
    a. completing a crossword puzzle
    b. pursuing a career as a musician
    c. having ice cream for dessert
    d. flossing one's teeth

## KEY TERMS

anorexia nervosa (p. 335)
appraisal (p. 319)
approach motivation (p. 345)
avoidance motivation (p. 345)
bulimia nervosa (p. 335)
Cannon–Bard theory (p. 316)
conscious motivation (p. 344)

display rule (p. 327)
drive (p. 333)
emotion (p. 316)
emotional expression (p. 322)
emotion regulation (p. 320)
extrinsic motivation (p. 343)
facial feedback hypothesis (p. 324)

hedonic principle (p. 332)
homeostasis (p. 333)
human sexual response cycle
   (p. 340)
intrinsic motivation (p. 343)
James–Lange theory (p. 316)
metabolism (p. 338)

motivation (p. 331)
need for achievement (p. 344)
re-appraisal (p. 320)
terror management theory (p. 347)
two-factor theory (p. 316)
unconscious motivation (p. 344)
universality hypothesis (p. 322)

## CHANGING MINDS

1. A friend is nearing graduation and has received a couple of job offers. "I went on the first interview," she says, "and I really liked the company, but I know you shouldn't go with your first impressions on difficult decisions. You should be completely rational and not let your emotions get in the way." Are emotions always barriers to rational decision making? In what ways can emotions help guide our decisions?

2. While watching television, you and a friend hear about a celebrity who punched a fan in a restaurant. "I just lost it," the celebrity said. "I saw what I was doing, but I just couldn't control myself." According to the television report, the celebrity was sentenced to anger management classes. "I'm not excusing the violence," your friend says, "but I'm not sure anger management classes are any use either. You can't control your emotions; you just feel them." What example could you give your friend of ways in which we can attempt to control our emotions?

3. One of your friends has just been dumped by her boyfriend, and she is devastated. She has spent days in her room, crying and refusing to go out. You and your roommate decide to keep a close eye on her during this tough time. "Negative emotions are so destructive," your

roommate says. "We would all be better off without them." What would you tell your roommate? In what ways are negative emotions critical for our survival and success?

4. A friend is majoring in education. He says: "Today we discussed ways to help disadvantaged kids at school. In particular, the idea of giving cash rewards to high-school students who passed their classes or did well on standardized tests was really popular. But that's bribing kids to get good grades, and as soon as you stop paying them, they'll stop studying." Your friend is assuming that extrinsic motivation undermines intrinsic motivation. In what ways is the picture more complicated?

5. One of your friends is a gym rat who spends all his free time working out and is very proud of his ripped abdominal muscles. His roommate, though, is very overweight. "I keep telling him to diet and exercise," your friend says, "but he never loses any weight. If he just had a little more willpower, he could succeed." What would you tell your friend? When an individual has difficulty losing weight, what factors may contribute to this difficulty?

## ANSWERS TO KEY CONCEPT QUIZ

1. b; 2. a; 3. c; 4. d; 5. c; 6. d; 7. c; 8. a; 9. c; 10. b; 11. a; 12. b; 13. d;
14. a; 15. d.

Need more help? Additional resources are located in Launchpad at:
*www.worthpublishers.com/launchpad/schacter3ecanadian*

# 9

# Language and Thought

▲ Language and Communication:
From Rules to Meaning
The Complex Structure of Human Language
Language Development
Theories of Language Development

▲ Language Development and the Brain
Broca's Area and Wernicke's Area of the
Brain
Involvement of the Right Cerebral
Hemisphere
Bilingualism and the Brain
OTHER VOICES Canada's Future Has to Be
Bilingual
Can Other Species Learn Human Language?

▲ Language and Thought:
How Are They Related?
Language and Colour Processing
Language and the Concept of Time

▲ Concepts and Categories:
How We Think
Psychological Theories of Concepts and
Categories
Concepts, Categories, and the Brain

▲ Decision Making:
Rational and Otherwise
The Rational Ideal
The Irrational Reality
CULTURE & COMMUNITY Does Culture
Influence Optimism Bias?
Why Do We Make Decision-Making Errors?
Decision Making and the Brain

▲ Problem Solving: Working It Out
Means–Ends Analysis
Analogical Problem Solving
Creativity and Insight
HOT SCIENCE Sudden Insight and the Brain

▲ Transforming Information:
How We Reach Conclusions
Practical, Theoretical, and Syllogistic
Reasoning
THE REAL WORLD From Zippers to Political
Extremism: An Illusion of Understanding
Reasoning and the Brain

AN ENGLISH BOY NAMED CHRISTOPHER SHOWED an amazing talent for languages. By the age of 6, he had learned French from his sister's schoolbooks; he acquired Greek from a textbook in only 3 months. His talent was so prodigious that grown-up Christopher could converse fluently in 16 languages. When tested on English–French translations, he scored as well as a native French speaker. Presented with a made-up language, he figured out the complex rules easily, even though advanced language students found them virtually impossible to decipher (Smith & Tsimpli, 1995).

If you have concluded that Christopher is extremely smart, perhaps even a genius, you are wrong. His scores on standard intelligence tests are far below normal. He fails simple cognitive tests that 4-year-old children pass with ease, and he cannot even learn the rules for simple games like tic-tac-toe. Despite his dazzling talent, Christopher lives in a halfway house because he does not have the cognitive capacity to make decisions, reason, or solve problems in a way that would allow him to live independently.

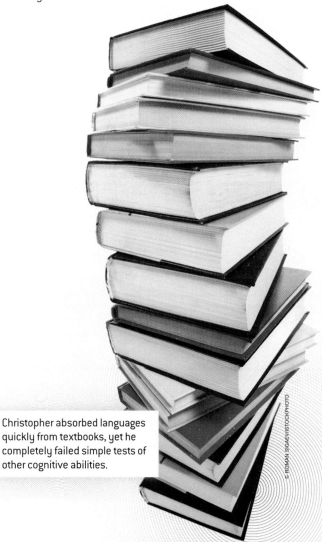

Christopher absorbed languages quickly from textbooks, yet he completely failed simple tests of other cognitive abilities.

**language**
A system for communicating with others using signals that are combined according to rules of grammar and convey meaning.

**grammar**
A set of rules that specify how the units of language can be combined to produce meaningful messages.

CHRISTOPHER'S STRENGTHS AND WEAKNESSES OFFER COMPELLING EVIDENCE that cognition is composed of distinct abilities. People who learn languages with lightning speed are not necessarily gifted at decision making or problem solving. People who excel at reasoning may have no special ability to master languages. In this chapter, you will learn about five key higher cognitive functions: acquiring and using language, forming concepts and categories, making decisions, solving problems, and reasoning. We excel at these functions compared with other animals, and they help define who we are as a species. We will learn about each of these abilities by examining evidence that reveals their unique psychological characteristics, and we will learn about their distinct neural underpinnings by considering individuals with brain lesions as well as neuroimaging studies. But despite clear differences among them, these five cognitive abilities share something important in common: They are critical to our functioning in just about all aspects of our everyday existence—including work, school, and personal relationships—and as we have already seen with Christopher, impairment of these cognitive abilities can result in major and lasting disruptions to our lives.

# Language and Communication: From Rules to Meaning

Most social species have systems of communication that allow them to transmit messages to each other. Honeybees communicate the location of food sources by means of a "waggle dance" that indicates both the direction and distance of the food source from the hive (Kirchner & Towne, 1994; Von Frisch, 1974). Vervet monkeys have three different warning calls that uniquely signal the presence of their main predators: a leopard, an eagle, and a snake (Cheney & Seyfarth, 1990). A leopard call provokes them to climb higher into a tree; an eagle call makes them look up into the sky. Each different warning call conveys a particular meaning and functions like a word in a simple language.

**Language** is *a system for communicating with others using signals that are combined according to rules of grammar and convey meaning.* **Grammar** is *a set of rules that specify how the units of language can be combined to produce meaningful messages.* Language allows individuals to exchange information about the world, coordinate group action, and form strong social bonds.

Human language may have evolved from signalling systems used by other species. However, three striking differences distinguish human language from vervet monkey yelps, for example. First, the complex structure of human language distinguishes it from simpler signalling systems. Most humans can express a wide range of ideas and concepts as well as generate an essentially infinite number of novel sentences. Second, humans use words to refer to intangible things, such as *unicorn* or *democracy.* These words could not have originated as simple alarm calls. Third, we use language to name, categorize, and describe things to ourselves when we think, which influences how knowledge is organized in our brains. It is doubtful that honeybees consciously think, "I will fly north today to find more honey so the queen will be impressed!"

In this section, we will examine the elements of human language that contribute to its complex structure, the ease with which we acquire language despite this complexity, and how both biological and environmental

**What are the distinctions between human language and animal communication?**

Honeybees communicate with each other about the location of food by doing a waggle dance that indicates the direction and distance of food from the hive.

MEDIA BAKERY

influences shape language acquisition and use. We will also look at startling disorders that reveal how language is organized in the brain and at researchers' attempts to teach apes human language. Finally, we will consider the long-standing puzzle of how language and thought are related.

## The Complex Structure of Human Language

Compared with other forms of communication, human language is a relatively recent evolutionary phenomenon, emerging as a spoken system no more than 1 to 3 million years ago and as a written system as little as 6000 years ago. There are approximately 4000 human languages, which linguists have grouped into about 50 language families (Nadasdy, 1995). Despite their differences, all of these languages share a basic structure involving a set of sounds and rules for combining those sounds to produce meanings.

**What do all languages have in common?**

### Basic Characteristics

*The smallest units of sound that are recognizable as speech rather than as random noise* are **phonemes.** These building blocks of spoken language differ in how they are produced. For example, when you say *ba,* your vocal cords start to vibrate as soon as you begin the sound, but when you say *pa,* there is a 60-millisecond lag between the time you start the *p* sound and the time your vocal cords start to vibrate. *B* and *p* are classified as separate phonemes in English because they differ in the way they are produced by the human speaker.

Every language has **phonological rules** that *indicate how phonemes can be combined to produce speech sounds.* For example, the initial sound *ts* is acceptable in German but not in English. Typically, people learn these phonological rules without instruction, and if the rules are violated, the resulting speech sounds so odd that we describe it as speaking with an accent.

Phonemes are combined to make **morphemes,** *the smallest meaningful units of language* (see **FIGURE 9.1**). For example, your brain recognizes the *p* sound you make at the beginning of *pat* as a speech *sound,* but it carries no particular meaning. The morpheme *pat,* on the other hand, is recognized as an element of speech that carries meaning.

All languages have grammar rules that generally fall into two categories: rules of morphology and rules of syntax. **Morphological rules** *indicate how morphemes can be combined to form words.* Two classes of morphemes—content morphemes and

**phoneme**
The smallest unit of sound that is recognizable as speech rather than as random noise.

**phonological rules**
A set of rules that indicate how phonemes can be combined to produce speech sounds.

**morphemes**
The smallest meaningful units of language.

**morphological rules**
A set of rules that indicate how morphemes can be combined to form words.

▼ Figure **9.1** **Units of Language** A sentence—the largest unit of language—can be broken down into progressively smaller units: phrases, morphemes, and phonemes. In all languages, phonemes and morphemes form words, which can be combined into phrases and ultimately into sentences.

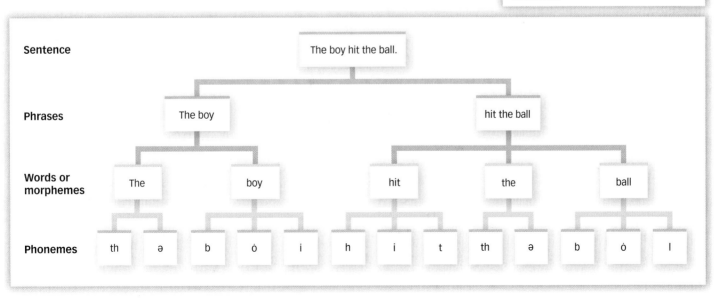

**syntactical rules**
A set of rules that indicate how words can be combined to form phrases and sentences.

**deep structure**
The meaning of a sentence.

**surface structure**
How a sentence is worded.

function morphemes—can be distinguished. *Content morphemes* refer to things and events (e.g., *cat, dog, take*) or are affixes that, when added to a base word, change its meaning or part of speech. Examples of affixes that are content morphemes include *re-*, as in *replay* and *redo*, since *re-* changes the meaning of the base word (e.g., play, do). Similarly, adding the affix *-able*, as in *playable* and *doable*, changes the meaning of the base word (changing them from verbs to adjectives). *Function morphemes* serve grammatical functions, such as tying sentences together (*and, or, but*) or indicating time (*when*). Function morphemes also include affixes that indicate the grammatical role of a base word, such as those required for plurals and for verb agreement. For example, the *-s* on the end of *cats* and the *-ed* or *-ing* on the end of *walked* or *walking* are function morphemes. It is the function morphemes that make human language grammatically complex enough to permit us to express abstract ideas rather than simply to point verbally to real objects in the here and now.

Content and function morphemes can be combined and recombined to form an infinite number of new sentences, which are governed by syntax. **Syntactical rules** *indicate how words can be combined to form phrases and sentences.* A simple syntactical rule in English is that every sentence must contain one or more nouns, which may be combined with adjectives or articles to create noun phrases (see **FIGURE 9.2**). A sentence also must contain one or more verbs, which may be combined with adverbs or articles to create verb phrases. So, the utterance "dogs bark" is a full sentence, but "the big grey dog over by the building" is not.

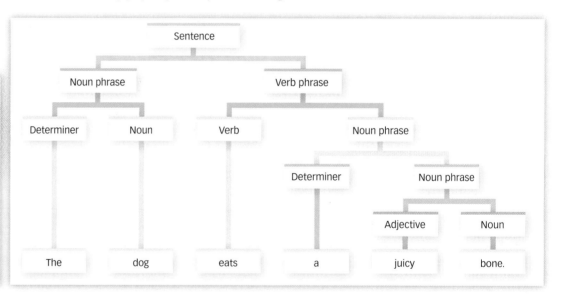

▶ Figure **9.2 Syntactical Rules** Syntactical rules indicate how words can be combined to form sentences. Every sentence must contain one or more nouns, which may be combined with adjectives or articles to create a noun phrase. A sentence also must contain one or more verbs, which may be combined with noun phrases, adverbs, or articles to create a verb phrase.

## Meaning: Deep Structure versus Surface Structure

Sounds and rules are critical ingredients of human language that allow us to convey meaning. A sentence can be constructed in a way that obeys syntactical and other rules, yet be entirely lacking in meaning or *semantics*, as in the famous example provided by linguist Noam Chomsky (1957, p. 15), "Colourless green ideas sleep furiously." Though we would not be breaking any grammatical rules by uttering such a sentence, we could expect to elicit head scratches and strange looks from any nearby listeners. Language usually conveys meaning quite well, but everyday experience shows us that misunderstandings can occur. These errors sometimes result from differences between the deep structure of sentences and their surface structure (Chomsky, 1957). **Deep structure** refers to *the meaning of a sentence*. **Surface structure** refers to *how a sentence is worded*. "The dog chased the cat" and "The cat was chased by the dog" mean the same thing (they have the same deep structure) even though on the surface their structures are different.

To generate a sentence, you begin with a deep structure (the meaning of the sentence) and create a surface structure (the particular words) to convey that meaning. When you comprehend a sentence, you do the reverse, processing the surface structure in order to extract the deep structure. After the deep structure is extracted, the surface structure is usually forgotten (Jarvella, 1970, 1971). In one study, researchers played tape-recorded stories to volunteers and then asked them to pick the sentences they had heard (Sachs, 1967). Participants frequently confused sentences they heard with sentences that had the same deep structure but a different surface structure. For example, if they heard the sentence "He struck John on the shoulder," they often mistakenly claimed they had heard "John was struck on the shoulder by him." In contrast, they rarely misidentified "John struck him on the shoulder" because this sentence has a different deep structure from the original sentence.

> **Is the meaning or wording of a sentence typically more memorable?**

Why are we able to communicate effectively when we quickly forget the surface structure of sentences? Why might this be an evolutionary benefit?

## Language Development

Language is a complex cognitive skill, yet we can carry on complex conversations with playmates and family before we begin school. Three characteristics of language development are worth bearing in mind. First, children learn language at an astonishingly rapid rate. The average 1-year-old has a vocabulary of 10 words. This tiny vocabulary expands to over *10 000* words in the next 4 years, requiring the child to learn, on average, about 6 or 7 new words *every day*. Second, children make few errors while learning to speak and, as we will see shortly, the errors they do make usually result from applying, but overgeneralizing, grammatical rules they have learned. This is an extraordinary feat. There are over 3 *million* ways to rearrange the words in any 10-word sentence, but only a few of these arrangements will be both grammatically correct and meaningful (Bickerton, 1990). Third, children's *passive mastery* of language develops faster than their *active mastery*. At every stage of language development, children understand language better than they speak.

### Distinguishing Speech Sounds

At birth, infants can distinguish among all of the contrasting sounds that occur in all human languages. Within the first 6 months of life, they lose this ability, and, like their parents, can only distinguish among the contrasting sounds in the language they hear being spoken around them. For example, two distinct sounds in English are the *l* sound and the *r* sound, as in *lead* and *read*. These sounds are not distinguished in Japanese; instead, the *l* and *r* sounds fall within the same phoneme. Japanese adults cannot hear the difference between these two sounds, but American adults can distinguish between them easily—and so can Japanese infants under 6 months or so of age.

> **What language ability do infants have that adults do not?**

In one study of 1 to 4-month-old infants, researchers constructed a tape of a voice saying "la-la-la" or "ra-ra-ra" repeatedly (Eimas et al., 1971). They rigged a pacifier so that whenever an infant sucked on it, a tape player that broadcast the *la-la* tape was activated. When the *la-la* sound began playing in response to their sucking, the infants were delighted and kept sucking on the pacifier to keep the *la-la* sound playing. After a while, they began to lose interest, and sucking frequency declined to about half of its initial rate. At this point, the experimenters switched the tape so that *ra-ra* was repeatedly broadcast. The Japanese infants began sucking again with vigour, indicating that they could hear the difference between the old, boring *la* sound and the new, interesting *ra* sound.

In this videotaped test, the infant watches an animated toy animal while a single speech sound is repeated. After a few repetitions, the sound changes and then the display changes, and then they both change again. If the infant switches her attention when the sound changes, she is anticipating the new display, which demonstrates that she can discriminate between the sounds.

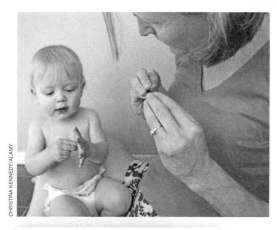

Deaf infants who learn sign language from their parents start babbling with their hands around the same time that hearing infants babble vocally.

Infants can distinguish among speech sounds, but they cannot produce them reliably, relying mostly on cooing (i.e., simple vowel-like sounds, such as *ah-ah*), cries, laughs, and other vocalizations to communicate. Between the ages of about 4 and 6 months, they begin to babble speech sounds. Babbling involves combinations of vowels and consonants that sound like real syllables but are meaningless. Regardless of the language they hear spoken, all infants go through the same babbling sequence. For example, *d* and *t* appear in infant babbling before *m* and *n*. Even deaf infants babble sounds they have never heard, and they do so in the same order as hearing infants do (Ollers & Eilers, 1988). This is evidence that infants are not simply imitating the sounds they hear and suggests that babbling is a natural part of the language development process. Recent research has shown that babbling serves as a signal that the infant is in a state of focused attention and ready to learn (Goldstein et al., 2010). Deaf infants do not babble as much, however, and their babbling is delayed relative to hearing infants (11 months rather than 6 months).

In order for vocal babbling to continue, however, infants must be able to hear themselves. In fact, delayed babbling or the cessation of babbling merits testing for possible hearing difficulties. Babbling problems can lead to speech impairments, but they do not necessarily prevent language acquisition. Deaf infants whose parents communicate using American Sign Language (ASL) begin to babble with their hands at the same age that hearing children begin to babble vocally—between 4 and 6 months (Petitto & Marentette, 1991). Their babbling consists of sign language syllables that are the fundamental components of ASL.

## Language Milestones

At about 10 to 12 months of age, infants begin to utter (or sign) their first words. By 18 months, they can say about 50 words and can understand several times more than that. Toddlers generally learn nouns before verbs, and the nouns they learn first are names for everyday, concrete objects (e.g., chair, table, milk) (see **TABLE 9.1** on the next page). At about this time, their vocabularies undergo explosive growth. By the time the average child begins school, a vocabulary of 10 000 words is not unusual. By fifth grade, the average child knows the meanings of 40 000 words. By university, the average student's vocabulary is about 200 000 words. **Fast mapping,** in which *children map a word onto an underlying concept after only a single exposure*, enables them to learn at this rapid pace (Kan & Kohnert, 2008; Mervis & Bertrand, 1994). This astonishingly easy process contrasts dramatically with the effort required later to learn other concepts and skills, such as arithmetic or writing.

Around 24 months, children begin to form two-word sentences, such as "more milk" or "throw ball." Such sentences are referred to as **telegraphic speech** because

**Language Milestones**

| Average Age | Language Milestones |
|---|---|
| 0–4 months | Can tell the difference between speech sounds (phonemes) that are not distinguished in their native language. Cooing, especially in response to speech. |
| 4–6 months | Babbles consonants. |
| 6–10 months | Understands some words and simple requests. Can no longer reliably distinguish sounds that are not in their native language. |
| 10–12 months | Begins to use single words. |
| 12–18 months | Vocabulary of 30 to 50 words (simple nouns, adjectives, and verbs). |
| 18–24 months | Two-word phrases ordered according to syntactic rules. Vocabulary of 50 to 200 words. Understands rules. |
| 24–36 months | Vocabulary of about 1000 words. Production of phrases and incomplete sentences. |
| 36–60 months | Vocabulary grows to more than 10 000 words; production of full sentences; mastery of grammatical morphemes (such as -ed for past tense) and function words (such as the, and, but). Can form questions and negations. |

they are *devoid of function morphemes and consist mostly of content words*. Yet despite the absence of function words, such as prepositions or articles, these two-word sentences tend to be grammatical; the words are ordered in a manner consistent with the syntactical rules of the language children are learning to speak. So, for example, toddlers will say "throw ball" rather than "ball throw" when they want you to throw the ball to them, and "more milk" rather than "milk more" when they want you to give them more milk. With these seemingly primitive expressions, 2-year-olds show that they have already acquired an appreciation of the syntactical rules of the language they are learning.

**In what way do 2-year-olds show a basic understanding of language rules?**

## The Emergence of Grammatical Rules

Evidence of the ease with which children acquire grammatical rules comes from some interesting errors that children make while forming sentences. If you listen to average 2- or 3-year-old children speaking, you may notice that they use the correct past-tense versions of common verbs, as in the expressions "I ran" and "you ate." By the age of 4 or 5, the same children will be using incorrect forms of these verbs, saying such things as "I runned" or "you eated," forms most children are unlikely to have ever heard (Prasada & Pinker, 1993). The reason is that very young children memorize the particular sounds (i.e., words) that express what they want to communicate. But as children acquire the grammatical rules of their language, they tend to *overgeneralize*. For example, if a child overgeneralizes the rule that past tense is indicated by *-ed*, then *run* becomes *runned* or even *ranned* instead of *ran*.

**Why is it unlikely that children are using imitation to pick up language?**

These errors show that language acquisition is not simply a matter of imitating adult speech. Instead, children acquire grammatical rules by listening to the speech around them and using the rules to create verbal forms they have never heard. They manage this without explicit awareness of the grammatical rules they have learned. In fact, few children or adults can articulate these rules of their native language, yet the speech they produce obeys these rules.

By about 3 years of age, children begin to generate complete simple sentences that include function words (e.g., "Give me *the* ball" and "That belongs *to* me"). The

**fast mapping**
The fact that children can map a word onto an underlying concept after only a single exposure.

**telegraphic speech**
Speech that is devoid of function morphemes and consists mostly of content words.

sentences increase in complexity over the next 2 years. By 4 to 5 years of age, many aspects of the language acquisition process are complete. As children continue to mature, their language skills become more refined, with added appreciation of subtler communicative uses of language, such as humour, sarcasm, or irony.

## Language Development and Cognitive Development

Language development typically unfolds as a sequence of steps in which one milestone is achieved before moving on to the next. Nearly all infants begin with one-word utterances before moving on to telegraphic speech and then to simple sentences that include function morphemes. It is hard to find solid evidence of infants launching immediately into speaking in sentences—even though you may occasionally hear reports of such feats from proud parents, including possibly your own! This orderly progression could result from general cognitive development that is unrelated to experience with a specific language (Shore, 1986; Wexler, 1999). For example, perhaps infants begin with one- and then two-word utterances because their short-term memories are so limited that initially they can only hold in mind a word or two; additional cognitive development might be necessary before they have the capacity to put together a simple sentence. By contrast, the orderly progression might depend on experience with a specific language, reflecting a child's emerging knowledge of that language (Bates & Goodman, 1997; Gillette et al., 1999).

These two possibilities are difficult to tease apart, but recent research has begun to do so using a novel strategy: examining the acquisition of English by internationally adopted children who did not know any English prior to adoption (Snedeker, Geren, & Shafto, 2007, 2012). According to government statistics, there were just over 8600 international adoptions to the United States in 2012 (U.S. Department of State, 2013). Although most of those adoptees are infants or toddlers, a significant proportion is composed of preschoolers. Studying the acquisition of English in such an older population provides a unique opportunity to explore the relationship between language development and cognitive development. If the orderly sequence of milestones that characterizes the acquisition of English by infants is a by-product of general cognitive development, then different patterns should be observed in older internationally adopted children, who are more advanced cognitively than infants. However, if the milestones of language development are critically dependent on experience with a specific language—English—then language learning in older adopted children should show the same orderly progression as seen in infants.

> **Why are studies of internationally adopted children especially useful?**

Snedeker and her colleagues (2007) examined preschoolers ranging from 2½ to 5½ years old, 3 to 18 months after they were adopted from China. They did so by mailing materials to parents, who periodically recorded language samples in their homes and also completed questionnaires concerning specific features of language observed in their children. These data were compared to similar data obtained from monolingual infants. The main result was clear-cut: Language acquisition in preschool-aged adopted children showed the same orderly progression of milestones that characterizes infants. These children began with one-word utterances before moving on to simple word combinations. Furthermore, their vocabulary, just like that of infants, was initially dominated by nouns and they produced few function morphemes.

These results indicate that some of the key milestones of language development depend on experience with English. However, the adopted children did add new words to their vocabularies more quickly than infants did, perhaps reflecting an influence of general cognitive development. Overall, though, the main message from this study is that observed shifts in early language development reflect specific characteristics of language learning rather than general

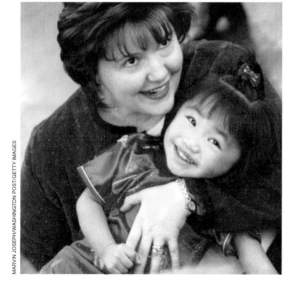

Chinese preschoolers who are adopted by English-speaking parents progress through the same sequence of linguistic milestones as do infants born into English-speaking families, suggesting that these milestones reflect experience with English rather than general cognitive development.

MARVIN JOSEPH/WASHINGTON POST/GETTY IMAGES

limitations of cognitive development. A later study provided additional support for this general conclusion, but also produced new evidence for a role of cognitive development in specific aspects of language (Snedeker et al., 2012). For example, adopted preschoolers acquire words that refer to the past or the future, such as *tomorrow*, *yesterday*, *before*, or *after*, much more quickly than do infants, perhaps reflecting that infants have difficulty representing these abstract concepts and therefore take longer to learn the words than more cognitively sophisticated preschoolers.

## Theories of Language Development

We know a good deal about how language develops, but what underlies the process? The language acquisition process has been the subject of considerable controversy and (at times) angry exchanges among scientists coming from three different approaches: behaviourist, nativist, and interactionist.

### Behaviourist Explanations

According to B. F. Skinner's behaviourist explanation of language learning, we learn to talk in the same way we learn any other skill: through reinforcement, shaping, extinction, and the other basic principles of operant conditioning that you learned about in the Learning chapter (Skinner, 1957). As infants mature, they begin to vocalize. Those vocalizations that are not reinforced gradually diminish, and those that are reinforced remain in the developing child's repertoire. So, for example, when an infant gurgles "prah," most parents are pretty indifferent. However, a sound that even remotely resembles "da-da" is likely to be reinforced with smiles, whoops, and cackles of "Goooood baaaaaby!" by doting parents. Maturing children also imitate the speech patterns they hear. Then parents or other adults shape those speech patterns by reinforcing those that are grammatical and ignoring or punishing those that are ungrammatical. "I no want milk" is likely to be squelched by parental clucks and titters, whereas "No milk for me, thanks" will probably be reinforced.

> To a behaviourist, why will an infant repeat "da-da" and not "prah"?

The behavioural explanation is attractive because it offers a simple account of language development, but the theory cannot account for many fundamental characteristics of language development (Chomsky, 1986; Pinker, 1994; Pinker & Bloom, 1990).

> First, parents do not spend much time teaching their children to speak grammatically. In one well-documented study, researchers found that parents typically respond more to the truth content of their children's statements than to the grammar (Brown & Hanlon, 1970). So, for example, when a child expresses a sentiment such as "Nobody like me," his or her mother will respond with something like "Why do you think that?" or "I like you!" rather than "Now, listen carefully and repeat after me: Nobody likes me."

> Second, children generate many more grammatical sentences than they ever hear. This shows that children do not just imitate; they learn the rules for generating sentences. You will recall that the same deep structure can generate a multitude of surface structures. It is highly unlikely that each of those separate surface structures was heard, reinforced, and learned by the developing child; it is much more likely that children simply acquire the ability to generate grammatical sentences.

> Third, as you read earlier in this chapter, the errors children make when learning to speak tend to be overgeneralizations of grammatical rules. The behaviourist explanation would not predict these overgeneralizations if children were learning through trial and error or simply imitating what they hear. That is, it would be difficult to overgeneralize if language development consisted solely of reinforced individual sentences or phrases.

## Nativist Explanations

The study of language and cognition underwent an enormous change in the 1950s, when linguist Noam Chomsky (1957, 1959) published a blistering reply to the behaviourist approach. According to Chomsky, language-learning capacities are built into the brain, which is specialized to acquire language rapidly through simple exposure to speech. Chomsky and others have argued that humans have a particular ability for language that is separate from general intelligence. This **nativist theory** holds that *language development is best explained as an innate, biological capacity.* According to Chomsky, the human brain is equipped with a **language acquisition device (LAD),** *a collection of processes that facilitate language learning.* Language processes naturally emerge as the infant matures, provided the infant receives adequate input to maintain the acquisition process.

Christopher's story is consistent with the nativist view of language development: His genius for language acquisition, despite his low overall intelligence, indicates that language capacity can be distinct from other mental capacities. Other individuals show the opposite pattern: People with normal or nearly normal intelligence can find certain aspects of human language difficult or impossible to learn. This condition is known as **genetic dysphasia,** *a syndrome characterized by an inability to learn the grammatical structure of language despite having otherwise normal intelligence.* Genetic dysphasia tends to run in families, and a single dominant gene has been implicated in its transmission (Gontier, 2008; Gopnik, 1990a, 1990b; Vargha-Khadem et al., 2005). Consider some sentences generated by children with the disorder:

*She remembered when she hurts herself the other day.*

*Carol is cry in the church.*

Notice that the ideas these children are trying to communicate are intelligent. Their problems with grammatical rules persist even if they receive special language training. When asked to describe what she did over the weekend, one child wrote, "On Saturday I watch TV." Her teacher corrected the sentence to "On Saturday, I watch*ed* TV," drawing attention to the *-ed* rule for describing past events. The following week, the child was asked to write another account of what she did over the weekend. She wrote, "On Saturday I wash myself and I watched TV and I went to bed." Notice that although she had memorized the past-tense forms *watched* and *went,* she could not generalize the rule to form the past tense of another word (*washed*).

As predicted by the nativist view, studies of people with genetic dysphasia suggest that normal children learn the grammatical rules of human language with ease in part because they are "wired" to do so. This biological predisposition to acquire language explains why newborn infants can make contrasts among phonemes that occur in all human languages—even phonemes they have never heard spoken. If we learned language through imitation, as behaviourists theorized, infants would only distinguish the phonemes they would actually heard. The nativist theory also explains why deaf infants babble speech sounds they have never heard and why the pattern of language development is similar in children throughout the world. These characteristics of language development are just what would be expected if our biological heritage provided us with the broad mechanics of human language.

> **How would a nativist explain why deaf infants babble?**

Also consistent with the nativist view is evidence that language can be acquired only during a restricted period of development, as has been observed with songbirds. If young songbirds are prevented from hearing adult birds sing during a particular period in their early lives, they do not learn to sing. A similar mechanism seems to affect human language learning, as illustrated by the tragic case of Genie (Curtiss, 1977). At the age of 20 months, Genie was tied to a chair by her parents and kept in virtual isolation. Her father forbade Genie's mother and brother to speak to her, and he himself

"GOT IDEA. TALK BETTER. COMBINE WORDS. MAKE SENTENCES."

© SIDNEY HARRIS

**nativist theory**
The view that language development is best explained as an innate, biological capacity.

**language acquisition device (LAD)**
A collection of processes that facilitate language learning.

**genetic dysphasia**
A syndrome characterized by an inability to learn the grammatical structure of language despite having otherwise normal intelligence.

only growled and barked at her. She remained in this brutal state until the age of 13. Genie's life improved substantially and she received years of language instruction, but it was too late. Her language skills remained extremely primitive. She developed a basic vocabulary and could communicate her ideas, but she could not grasp the grammatical rules of English.

Similar cases have been reported, with a common theme: Once puberty is reached, acquiring language becomes extremely difficult (Brown, 1958). Data from studies of language acquisition in immigrants support this conclusion. In one American study, researchers found that the proficiency with which immigrants spoke English depended not on how long they would lived in the United States, but on their age at immigration (Johnson & Newport, 1989). Those who arrived as children were the most proficient, whereas those who immigrated after puberty, showed a significant decline in proficiency regardless of the number of years in their new country. More recent work using fMRI shows that acquiring a second language early in childhood (between 1 and 5 years of age) results in very different representation of that language in the brain than does acquiring that language much later (after 9 years of age) (Bloch et al., 2009).

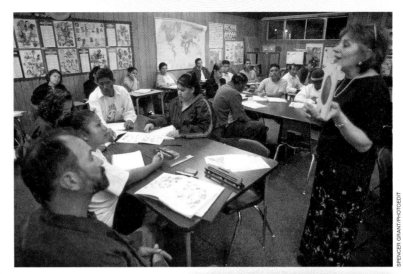

Immigrants who learn English as a second language are more proficient if they start to learn English before puberty rather than after.

## Interactionist Explanations

Nativist theories are often criticized because they do not explain *how* language develops; they merely explain why. A complete theory of language acquisition requires an explanation of the processes by which the innate, biological capacity for language combines with environmental experience. The interactionist approach is that although infants are born with an innate ability to acquire language, social interactions play a crucial role in language. Interactionists point out that parents tailor their verbal interactions with children in ways that simplify the language acquisition process: They speak slowly, enunciate clearly, and use simpler sentences than they do when speaking with adults (Bruner, 1983; Farrar, 1990).

**How does the interactionist theory of language acquisition differ from behaviourist and nativist theories?**

Further evidence of the interaction of biology and experience comes from a fascinating study of deaf children's creation of a new language (Senghas, Kita, & Ozyurek, 2004). Prior to about 1980, deaf children in Nicaragua stayed at home and usually had little contact with other deaf individuals. In 1981, some deaf children began to attend a new vocational school. At first, the school did not teach a formal sign language, and none of the children had learned to sign at home, but the children gradually began to communicate using hand signals that they invented.

Over the past 30 years, their sign language has developed considerably (Pyers et al., 2010), and researchers have studied this new language for the telltale characteristics of languages that have evolved over much longer periods. For instance, mature languages typically break down experience into separate components. When we describe something in motion, such as a rock rolling down a hill, our language separates the type of movement (rolling) and the direction of movement (down). If we simply made a gesture, however, we would use a single continuous downward movement to indicate this motion. This is exactly what the first children to develop the Nicaraguan sign

How does the evolution of the Nicaraguan deaf children's sign language support the interactionist explanation of language development?

**aphasia**
Difficulty in producing or comprehending language.

language did. But younger groups of children, who have developed the sign language further, use separate signs to describe the direction and the type of movement—a defining characteristic of mature languages. That the younger children did not merely copy the signs from the older users suggests that a predisposition exists to use language to dissect our experiences. Thus, their acts of creation nicely illustrate the interplay of nativism (the predisposition to use language) and experience (growing up in an insulated deaf culture).

---

## IN SUMMARY

▶ Human language is characterized by a complex organization—from phonemes to morphemes to phrases and finally to sentences.

▶ Each of these levels of human language is constructed and understood according to grammatical rules that are acquired early in development, even without being taught explicitly. Instead, children appear to be biologically predisposed to process language in ways that allow them to extract these grammatical rules from the language they hear.

---

# Language Development and the Brain

As the brain matures, specialization of specific neurological structures takes place, and this allows language to develop (Kuhl, 2010; Kuhl & Rivera-Gaxiola, 2008). Where, then, are the language centres of the brain?

## Broca's Area and Wernicke's Area of the Brain

In early infancy, language processing is distributed across many areas of the brain. But language processing gradually becomes more and more concentrated in two areas, Broca's area and Wernicke's area, sometimes referred to as the language centres of the brain. As the brain matures, these areas become increasingly specialized for language, so much so that damage to them results in a serious condition called **aphasia,** *difficulty in producing or comprehending language.*

> **How does language processing change in the brain as the child matures?**

*Broca's area* is located in the left frontal cortex and is involved in the production of the sequential patterns in vocal and sign languages (see **FIGURE 9.3**). As you saw in the Psychology: Evolution of a Science chapter, Broca's area is named after French physician Paul Broca, who first reported on speech problems resulting from damage to a specific area of the left frontal cortex (Broca, 1861, 1863). Individuals with this damage, resulting in *Broca's aphasia,* understand language relatively well, although they have increasing comprehension difficulty as grammatical structures get more complex. But their real struggle is with speech production. Typically, they speak in short, staccato phrases that consist mostly of content morphemes (e.g., *cat, dog*). Function morphemes (e.g., *and, but*) are usually missing and grammatical structure is impaired. A person with the condition might say something like "Ah, Monday, uh, Casey park. Two, uh, friends, and, uh, 30 minutes."

*Wernicke's area,* located in the left temporal cortex, is involved in language comprehension (whether spoken or signed). German neurologist Carl Wernicke first described the area that bears his name after observing speech difficulty in patients who had sustained damage to the left posterior temporal cortex (Wernicke, 1874). Individuals with *Wernicke's aphasia* differ from those with Broca's aphasia in two ways: They can produce grammatical speech, but it tends to be meaningless, and they have considerable difficulty comprehending language. A person suffering from Wernicke's

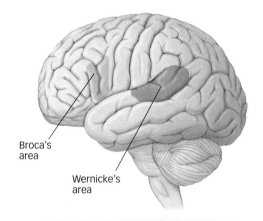

Broca's area

Wernicke's area

▲ Figure 9.3 **Broca's and Wernicke's Areas**
Neuroscientists study people with brain damage in order to better understand how the brain normally operates. When Broca's area is damaged, people have a hard time producing sentences. When Wernicke's area is damaged, people can produce sentences, but they tend to be meaningless.

aphasia might say something like, "Feel very well. In other words, I used to be able to work cigarettes. I do not know how. Things I could not hear from are here."

In normal language processing, Wernicke's area is highly active when we make judgments about word meaning, and damage to this area impairs comprehension of spoken and signed language, although the ability to identify nonlanguage sounds is unimpaired. For example, Japanese can be written using symbols that, like the English alphabet, represent speech sounds, or by using pictographs that, like Chinese pictographs, represent ideas. Japanese persons who suffer from Wernicke's aphasia encounter difficulties in writing and understanding the symbols that represent speech sounds but not pictographs (Sasanuma, 1975).

## Involvement of the Right Cerebral Hemisphere

As important as Broca's and Wernicke's areas are for language, they are not the entire story. Three kinds of evidence indicate that the right cerebral hemisphere also contributes to language processing, especially to language comprehension (Jung-Beeman, 2005). First, when words are presented to the right hemisphere of healthy participants using divided visual field techniques (see the Neuroscience chapter), the right hemisphere shows some capacity for processing meaning. Second, individuals with damage to the right hemisphere sometimes have subtle problems with language comprehension. Third, and most directly related to language development, some children who have had their entire left hemispheres removed during adolescence as a treatment for epilepsy can recover many of their language abilities.

## Bilingualism and the Brain

Around the world, most people grow up speaking more than one language. Bilingualism (or multilingualism) is the norm, rather than the exception. In Canada, over 200 languages are represented, and more than a third of the population speaks more than one language fluently (Statistics Canada, 2012a). (See the Other Voices box for an opinion on the state of bilingualism in Canada.) What is the effect of such rich language development on the brain?

Early studies of bilingual children seemed to suggest that bilingualism slows or interferes with normal cognitive development. When compared with monolingual children, bilingual children performed more slowly when processing language, and their IQ scores were lower. A re-examination of these studies, however, revealed several crucial flaws. First, the tests were given in English even when that was not the child's primary language. Second, the bilingual participants were often first- or second-generation immigrants whose parents were not proficient in English. Finally, the bilingual children came from lower socioeconomic backgrounds than the monolingual children (Andrews, 1982).

Later studies controlled for these factors, revealing a very different picture of bilingual children's cognitive skills. The available evidence concerning language acquisition indicates that bilingual and monolingual children do not differ significantly in the course and rate of many aspects of their language development (Nicoladis & Genesee, 1997). In fact, middle-class children who are fluent in two languages have been found to score higher than monolingual children on several measures of cognitive functioning, including executive control capacities such as the ability to prioritize information and flexibly focus attention (Bialystok, 1999, 2009; Bialystok, Craik, & Luk, 2012). The idea here is that bilingual individuals benefit from exerting executive control in their daily lives when they attempt to suppress the language that they do not want to use. Recent evidence indicates that bilingualism also has benefits much later in life: Bilingual individuals tend to have a later onset of Alzheimer's disease than monolingual individuals, perhaps reflecting that during their lives they

THINKSTOCK

Wernicke's aphasia spares the ability of Japanese individuals to understand pictographs like this one despite their problems understanding speech sounds.

have built up a greater amount of back-up cognitive ability or "cognitive reserve" (Schweizer et al., 2012). These findings are consistent with research showing that learning a second language produces lasting changes in the brain (Mechelli et al., 2004; Stein et al., 2009). For example, the grey matter in a part of the left parietal lobe that is involved in language is denser in bilingual than in monolingual individuals, and the increased density is most pronounced in those who are most proficient in using their second language (see **FIGURE 9.4** on the next page) (Mechelli et al., 2004).

# OTHER VOICES

## Canada's Future Has to Be Bilingual

Canada is a country composed of many different ethnic groups. Multiculturalism is a feature of Canada of which many Canadians are proud. Language is an important part of multiculturalism. Bilingualism when relating to French and English is an important but sometimes contentious subject in Canada as Robert Rothon, the executive director of Canadian Parents for French (in Montreal) can tell you. In 2012, Robert Rothon wrote the following article in *The Montreal Gazette* to help people understand the most recent statistics on language and to provide a more positive perspective on the issue.

Late last month, Statistics Canada began releasing data on language from the 2011 federal census. Many commentators, particularly in Quebec, interpreted the results negatively, both in terms of trends within Quebec and across all of Canada as far as bilingual and French speakers are concerned.

However, Canadian Parents for French, a pan-Canadian organization that promotes French-second-language (FSL) education, has analyzed the data and sees a more encouraging demographic picture.

First of all, it is not true that the percentage of French-English bilingual speakers is declining. There was, in fact, a small rise from 2006 to 2011 as well as a corresponding decline in the percentage of unilingual English and French speakers in Canada. This decline in proportional terms, however, is due to the rising numbers of immigrants whose mother tongue is not an official-language of Canada. Put another way, fewer Canadians are unilingual than before.

In Quebec, close to 98 percent of the population speaks French or English, and of this group, a significant number speak both languages.

In addition, the number of people who identify their mother tongue as both English and French has been increasing since 2006.

The census also provided information linking Canada's linguistic landscape to its labour force. Here, CPF would like to underline the fact that official-language bilinguals, regardless of mother tongue, have an employment rate higher than the national average, and an unemployment rate under the national average. This is true in Quebec as well as in Canada as a whole.

All of this points to the increasing presence and value of official-language bilingualism. It is clear that individual bilingualism is an asset on the job market—for the bilingual Quebecer in particular.

Some of the francophone organizations working on behalf of French first-language instruction believe that an increase in English second-language instruction would increase bilingualism and lead to the inevitable erosion of the strength of French in Quebec and Canada, through a form of "soft" assimilation. The reality is different. In Quebec, bilingual speakers are a great asset to the province; a large percentage of official-language bilinguals have long embraced, or are currently adopting, French-language culture.

Nationally, official-language bilingualism is helping to increase the French-speaking population of Canada.

French is far from disappearing from Canada.

Currently, no language is on track to outnumber French as Canada's second most widely spoken language. Punjabi comes in at a distant third, with not quite 500,000 speakers, in contrast to the 21 percent of Canadians who can speak French.

Many parents who don't speak one of Canada's two official languages are trying to enrol their children in French-second-language programs outside Quebec, and it is only a lack of school-board capacity to meet this demand that is limiting enrolment growth. Despite this limitation, school boards are doing their best. Both British Columbia and Alberta have sustained growth in French-second-language programs for over the past decade. Ontario saw a 6.9 percent increase in enrolment in French immersion between 2009 and 2010. Across the country, there was a 10 percent increase in enrolment in French-second-language programs between 2009 and 2011.

In Quebec, Montreal is an excellent example of how official-language bilingualism is positively shaping the nation. According to the census, the large majority of immigrants settling in Montreal know French, and more than half of the immigrant population speaks both French and English.

A strong case can be made that Montreal is the city that attracts the best and brightest of official-language bilinguals: anglophones and allophones who want to learn and improve their French, and francophones who are not threatened by English and who appreciate non-francophones who are trying to learn French.

With the release of the 2011 census, it is easy to see how linguistic duality is linked—both in Quebec and in Canada as a whole. English–French bilingualism is on the rise, as is the number of allophones who speak either one or both official languages. This is something that Canadians, as citizens of one of the relatively few countries with more than one official language, should be proud to see.

Are you convinced by Rothon's arguments? If not, why? And if so, how far do you think that the educational system should go in promoting multilingual education? What about the possible impact of devoting more time in early grades to teaching languages rather than other subjects? What kinds of research would you want to see done to evaluate the effects of early instruction in second- or third-languages?

Robert Rothon and Shaunpal Jandu, "Opinion: Happily, Canadian bilingualism on the rise," *Montreal Gazette*, November 21, 2012. By permission of Robert Rothon, Executive Director, Canadian Parents for French.

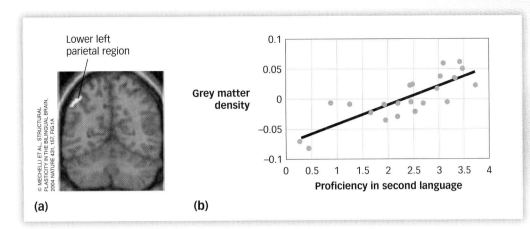

(a) (b)

© MECHELLI ET AL., STRUCTURAL PLASTICITY IN THE BILINGUAL BRAIN, 2004 NATURE 431, 157, FIG.1.A

◄ Figure **9.4 Bilingualism Alters Brain Structure** Learning a second language early in life increases the density of grey matter in the brain. (*a*) A view of the lower left parietal region, which has denser grey matter in bilingual relative to monolingual individuals. (*b*) As proficiency in a second language increases, so does the density of grey matter in the lower parietal region. People who acquired a second language earlier in life were also found to have denser grey matter in this region. Interestingly, this area corresponds to the same area that is activated during verbal fluency tasks (Mechelli et al., 2004).

Some studies have revealed disadvantages, however. Bilingual children tend to have a smaller vocabulary in each language than their monolingual peers (Portocarrero, Burright, & Donovick, 2007); they also process language more slowly than monolingual children and can sometimes take longer to formulate sentences (Bialystok, 2009; Taylor & Lambert, 1990). Thus, learning a second language produces a number of benefits along with some costs.

## Can Other Species Learn Human Language?

The human vocal tract and the extremely nimble human hand are better suited to human language than are the throats and paws of other species. Nonetheless, attempts have been made to teach nonhuman animals, particularly apes, to communicate using human language.

Early attempts to teach apes to speak failed dismally because their vocal tracts cannot accommodate the sounds used in human languages (Hayes & Hayes, 1951). Later attempts to teach apes human language have met with more success, including teaching them to use American Sign Language and computer-monitored keyboards that display geometric symbols that represent words. Allen and Beatrix Gardner were the first to use ASL with apes (Gardner & Gardner, 1969). The Gardners worked with a young female chimpanzee named Washoe as though she were a deaf child, signing to her regularly, rewarding her correct efforts at signing, and assisting her acquisition of signs by manipulating her hands in a process referred to as *molding*. In 4 years, Washoe learned approximately 160 words and could construct simple sentences, such as "More fruit." She also formed novel word constructions such as "water bird" for "duck." After a fight with a rhesus monkey, she signed, "Dirty monkey!" This constituted a creative use of the term because she had only been taught the use of *dirty* to refer to soiled objects.

Other chimpanzees were immersed in ASL in a similar fashion, and Washoe and her companions were soon signing to each other, creating a learning environment conducive to language acquisition. One of Washoe's cohorts, a chimpanzee named Lucy, learned to sign "drink fruit" for watermelon. When Washoe's second infant died, her caretakers arranged for her to adopt an infant chimpanzee named Loulis.

In a few months, young Loulis, who was not exposed to human signers, learned 68 signs simply by watching Washoe communicate with the other chimpanzees. People who have observed these interactions and are themselves fluent in ASL report little difficulty in following the conversations (Fouts & Bodamer, 1987). One such observer, a *New York Times* reporter who spent some time with Washoe, reported, "Suddenly I realized I was conversing with a member of another species in my native tongue."

Other researchers have taught bonobo chimpanzees to communicate using a geometric keyboard system (Savage-Rumbaugh, Shanker, & Taylor, 1998). Their star

©FRIENDS OF WASHOE, CHIMPANZEE & HUMAN COMMUNICATION INSTITUTE, CENTRAL WASHINGTON UNIVERSITY

Allen and Beatrix Gardner used sign language to teach the female chimpanzee Washoe about 160 words. Washoe could also construct simple sentences and combine words in novel ways.

Kanzi, a young male chimpanzee, learned hundreds of words and word combinations through a keyboard system as he watched researchers try to teach his mother.

pupil, Kanzi, learned the keyboard system by watching researchers try to teach his mother. Like Loulis, young Kanzi picked up the language relatively easily (his mother never did learn the system), suggesting that like humans, birds, and other species, apes experience a critical period for acquiring communicative systems.

Kanzi has learned hundreds of words and has combined them to form thousands of word combinations. Also like human children, his passive mastery of language appears to exceed his ability to produce language. In one study, researchers tested 9-year-old Kanzi's understanding of 660 spoken sentences. The grammatically complex sentences asked him to perform simple actions, such as "Go get the balloon that's in the microwave" and "Pour the Perrier into the Coke." Some sentences were also potentially misleading, such as "Get the pine needles that are in the refrigerator," when there were pine needles in clear view on the floor. Impressively, Kanzi correctly carried out 72 percent of the 660 requests (Savage-Rumbaugh & Lewin, 1996).

These results indicate that apes can acquire sizable vocabularies, string words together to form short sentences, and process sentences that are grammatically complex. Their skills are especially impressive because human language is hardly their normal means of communication. Research with apes also suggests that the neurological "wiring" that allows us to learn language overlaps to some degree with theirs (and perhaps with other species').

> **What do studies of apes and language teach us about humans and language?**

Equally informative are the limitations apes exhibit when learning, comprehending, and using human language. The first limitation is the size of the vocabularies they acquire. As mentioned, Washoe's and Kanzi's vocabularies number in the hundreds, but an average 4-year-old human child has a vocabulary of approximately 10 000 words. The second limitation is the type of words they can master, primarily names for concrete objects and simple actions. Apes (and several other species) have the ability to map arbitrary sounds or symbols onto objects and actions, but learning, say, the meaning of the word *economics* would be difficult for Washoe or Kanzi. In other words, apes can learn signs for concepts they understand, but their conceptual repertoire is smaller and simpler than that of humans.

"He says he wants a lawyer."

The third and perhaps most important limitation is the complexity of grammar that apes can use and comprehend. Apes can string signs together, but their constructions rarely exceed three or four words, and when they do, they are rarely grammatical. Comparing the grammatical structures produced by apes with those produced by human children highlights the complexity of human language as well as the ease and speed with which we generate and comprehend it.

## IN SUMMARY

▶ Our abilities to produce and comprehend language depend on distinct regions of the brain, with Broca's area critical for language production and Wernicke's area critical for comprehension.

▶ Bilingual and monolingual children show similar rates of language development. However, some bilingual children show greater executive control capacities, such as the ability to prioritize information and flexibly focus attention, and they tend to have a later onset of Alzheimer's disease.

▶ Nonhuman primates can learn new vocabulary and construct simple sentences, but there are significant limitations on the size of their vocabularies and the grammatical complexity they can handle.

# Language and Thought: How Are They Related?

Language is such a dominant feature of our mental world that it is tempting to equate language with thought. Some theorists have even argued that language is simply a means of expressing thought. The **linguistic relativity hypothesis** maintains that *language shapes the nature of thought*. This idea was championed by Benjamin Whorf (1956), an engineer who studied language in his spare time and was especially interested in Native American languages. The most frequently cited example of linguistic relativity comes from the Inuit in Canada. Their language has many different terms for frozen white flakes of precipitation, for which we use the word *snow*. Whorf believed that because they have so many terms for snow, the Inuit perceive and think about snow differently than do English speakers.

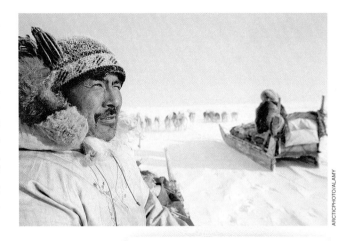

The Inuit in Canada use many different terms for snow, leading Benjamin Whorf (1956) to propose that they think about snow differently than do English speakers.

## Language and Colour Processing

Whorf has been criticized for the anecdotal nature of his observations (Pinker, 1994), and some controlled research has cast doubt on Whorf's hypothesis. Eleanor Rosch (1973) studied the Dani, an isolated agricultural tribe living in New Guinea. They have only two terms for colours that roughly refer to "dark" and "light." If Whorf's hypothesis were correct, you would expect the Dani to have problems perceiving and learning different shades of colour. But in Rosch's experiments, they learned shades of colour just as well as people who have many more colour terms in their first language. However, more recent evidence shows that language may indeed influence colour processing (Roberson et al., 2004). Researchers compared English children with African children from a cattle-herding tribe in Namibia known as the Himba. The English have 11 basic colour terms, but the Himba, who are largely isolated from the outside world, have only five. For example, they use the term *serandu* to refer to what English speakers would call red, pink, or orange.

> **How does language influence our understanding of colour?**

**linguistic relativity hypothesis**
The proposal that language shapes the nature of thought.

Researchers showed a series of coloured tiles to each child and then asked the child to choose that colour from an array of 22 different colours. The youngest children, both English and Himba, who knew few or no colour names, tended to confuse similar colours. But as the children grew and acquired more names for colours, their choices increasingly reflected the colour terms they had learned. English children made fewer errors matching tiles that had English colour names; Himba children made fewer errors for tiles with colour names in Himba. These results reveal that language can indeed influence how children think about colours.

Similar effects have been observed in adults. Consider the 20 blue rectangles shown in **FIGURE 9.5**, which you will easily see change gradually from lightest blue on the left to darkest blue on the right. What you might not know is that in Russian, there are different words for light blue (*goluboy*) and dark blue (*siniy*). Researchers investigated whether Russian speakers would respond differently to patches of blue when they fell into different linguistic categories rather than into the same linguistic category (Winawer et al., 2007). Both Russian and English speakers on average classified rectangles 1 to 8 as light blue and

▼ Figure **9.5** **Language Affects How We Think About Colour** Unlike English, the Russian language has different words for light blue and dark blue. Russian speakers asked to pick which of the two bottom squares matched the colour of the single square above responded more quickly when one of the bottom squares was called *goluboy* (light blue) and the other was called *siniy* (dark blue) than when both were referred to by the same name. English speakers took about the same amount of time.

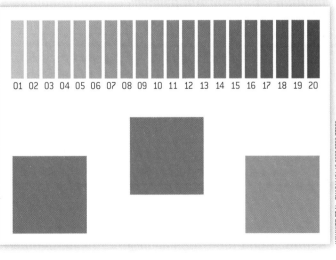

01 02 03 04 05 06 07 08 09 10 11 12 13 14 15 16 17 18 19 20

WINAWER ET AL., PNAS V 104-19 2007 7780-7785? 2007 NATIONAL ACADEMY OF SCIENCES, USA

9 to 20 as dark blue, but only Russian speakers use different words to refer to the two classes of blue. In the experimental task, participants were shown three blue squares, as in the lower part of Figure 9.5, and were asked to pick which of the two bottom squares matched the colours of the top square. Russian speakers responded more quickly when one of the bottom squares was *goluboy* and the other was *siniy* than when both bottom squares were *goluboy* or both were *siniy*, whereas English speakers took about the same amount of time to respond in the two conditions (Winawer et al., 2007). As with children, language can affect how adults think about colours.

## Language and the Concept of Time

In another study exploring the relationship between language and thought, researchers looked at the way people think about time. In English, we often use spatial terms: We look *forward* to a promising future or move a meeting *back* to fit our schedule (Casasanto & Boroditsky, 2008). We also use these terms to describe horizontal spatial relations, such as taking three steps *forward* or two steps *back* (Boroditsky, 2001). In contrast, speakers of Mandarin (Chinese) often describe time using terms that refer to a vertical spatial dimension: Earlier events are referred to as *up*, and later events as *down*. To test the effect of this difference, researchers showed English speakers and Mandarin speakers either a horizontal or vertical display of objects and then asked them to make a judgment involving

> How does a horizontal concept of time contrast with a vertical concept of time?

time, such as whether March comes before April (Boroditsky, 2001). English speakers were faster to make the time judgments after seeing a horizontal display, whereas for Mandarin speakers the opposite was true. When English speakers learned to use Mandarin spatial terms, their time judgments were also faster after seeing the vertical display! This result nicely shows another way in which language can influence thought.

Bear in mind, though, that either thought or language ability can be severely impaired while the capacity for the other is spared, as illustrated by the dramatic case of Christopher that you read earlier in this chapter—and as we will see again in the next section. These kinds of observations have led some researchers to suggest that Whorf was only "half right" in his claims about the effect of language on thought (Regier & Kay, 2009). Consistent with this idea, others suggest that it is overly simplistic to talk in general terms about whether language influences thought, and that researchers need to be more specific about the exact ways in which language influences thought. For example, Wolff and Holmes (2011) rejected the idea that language entirely determines thought. But they also pointed out that there is considerable evidence that language can influence thought both by highlighting specific properties of concepts and by allowing us to formulate verbal rules that help to solve problems. Thus, recent research has started to clarify the ways in which the linguistic relativity hypothesis is right and the ways in which it is wrong.

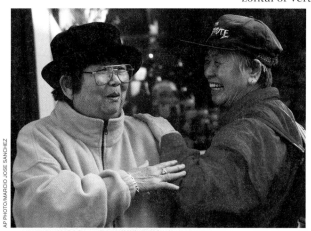

Westerners talk about moving a meeting *forward* or *back* a few days, a horizontal concept of time. Speakers of Mandarin talk about the same meeting as moving *up* or *down,* a vertical concept of time.

## IN SUMMARY

▶ The linguistic relativity hypothesis maintains that language shapes the nature of thought.

▶ Recent studies on colour processing and time judgments point to an influence of language on thought. However, it is also clear that language and thought are to some extent separate.

# Concepts and Categories: How We Think

In October 2000, a 69-year old man known by the initials J.B. went for a neuro-logical assessment because he was having difficulty understanding the meaning of words, even though he still performed well on many other perceptual and cognitive tasks. In 2002, as his problems worsened, he began participating in a research project concerned with the role of language in naming, recognizing, and classifying colours (Haslam et al., 2007). As the researchers observed J.B. over the next 15 months, they documented that his colour language deteriorated dramatically; he had great difficulty naming colours and could not even match objects with their typical colours (e.g., strawberry and red, banana and yellow). Yet even as his language deteriorated, J.B. could still classify colours normally, sorting colour patches into groups of green, yellow, red, and blue in the exact same manner that healthy participants did. J.B. retained an intact concept of colours despite the decline of his language ability—a finding that suggests that we need to look at factors in addition to language in order to understand concepts (Haslam et al., 2007).

**Concept** refers to a *mental representation that groups or categorizes shared features of related objects, events, or other stimuli*. A concept is an abstract representation, description, or definition that serves to desig-nate a class or category of things. The brain organizes our concepts about the world, classifying them into categories based on shared simi-larities. Our category for *dog* may be something like "small, four-footed animal with fur that wags its tail and barks." Our category for *bird* may be something like "small, winged, beaked creature that flies." We form these categories in large part by noticing similarities among objects and events that we experience in everyday life. For example, your concept of a chair might include such features as sturdiness, relative flatness, and an object that you can sit on. That set of attributes defines a category of objects in the world—desk chairs, recliner chairs, flat rocks, bar stools, and so on—that can all be described in that way.

Concepts are fundamental to our ability to think and make sense of the world. We will first compare various theories that explain the formation of concepts and then consider studies that link the formation and organization of concepts to the brain. As with other aspects of cognition, we can gain insight into how concepts are organized by looking at some instances in which they are rather disorganized. We will encounter some unusual disorders that help us understand how concepts are organized in the brain.

**Why are concepts useful to us?**

**concept**
A mental representation that groups or categorizes shared features of related objects, events, or other stimuli.

*"Attention everyone! I'd like to introduce the newest member of our family."*

There is family resemblance between family members despite the fact that there is no defining feature that they all have in common. Instead, there are shared common features. Someone who also shares some of those features may be categorized as belonging to the family.

## Psychological Theories of Concepts and Categories

Early psychological theories described concepts as rules that specify the necessary and sufficient conditions for membership in a particular cat-egory. A *necessary condition* is something that must be true of the object in order for it to belong to the category. For example, suppose you were trying to determine whether an unfamiliar animal was a dog. It is nec-essary that the creature be a mammal; otherwise it does not belong to the category *dog* because all dogs are mammals. A *sufficient condition* is something that, if it is true of the object, proves that it belongs to the category. Suppose someone told you that the creature was a German shepherd and you know that a German shepherd is a type of dog. *German shepherd* is a sufficient condition for membership in the category *dog*.

▲ Figure **9.6** **Family Resemblance Theory** The family resemblance here is unmistakable, even though no two Smith brothers share all the family features. The prototype is brother 9. He has it all: brown hair, large ears, large nose, mustache, and glasses.

**family resemblance theory**
Members of a category have features that appear to be characteristic of category members but may not be possessed by every member.

**prototype**
The "best" or "most typical" member of a category.

▶ Figure **9.7** **Critical Features of a Category** We tend to think of a generic bird as possessing a number of critical features, but not every bird possesses all of those features. In North America, a wren is a better example of a bird than a penguin or an ostrich.

Most natural categories, however, cannot be so easily defined in terms of this classical approach of necessary and sufficient conditions. For example, what is your definition of *dog*? Can you come up with a rule of "dogship" that includes all dogs and excludes all non-dogs? Most people cannot, but they still use the term *dog* intelligently, easily classifying animals as dogs or non-dogs. Three theories seek to explain how people perform these acts of categorization.

## Family Resemblance Theory

Eleanor Rosch put aside necessity and sufficiency to develop a theory of concepts based on family resemblance. The **family resemblance theory** states that *members of a category have features that appear to be characteristic of category members but may not be possessed by every member* (Rosch, 1973, 1975; Rosch & Mervis, 1975; Wittgenstein, 1953/1999). For example, you and your brother may have your mother's eyes, although you and your sister may have your father's high cheekbones. There is a strong family resemblance between you, your parents, and your siblings despite the fact that there is no necessarily defining feature that you all have in common. Similarly, many members of the *bird* category have feathers and wings, so these are the characteristic features. Anything that has these features is likely to be classified as a bird because of this "family resemblance" to other members of the *bird* category. **FIGURE 9.6** illustrates family resemblance theory.

## Prototype Theory

Building on the idea of family resemblance, Rosch also proposed that psychological categories (those that we form naturally) are best described as organized around a **prototype,** the "best" or "most typical" member of a category. A prototype possesses most (or all) of the most characteristic features of the category. For North Americans, the prototype of the *bird* category would be something like a wren: a small animal with feathers and wings that flies through the air, lays eggs, and migrates (see **FIGURE 9.7**). If you lived in Antarctica, your prototype of a bird might be a penguin: a small animal that has flippers, swims, and lays eggs. According to *prototype theory,* if your prototypical bird is a robin, then a canary would be considered a better example of a bird than would an ostrich because a canary has more features in common with a robin than an ostrich does. People make category judgments by comparing new instances to the category's prototype. This contrasts with the classical approach to concepts in which something either is or is not an example of a concept (i.e., it either does or does not belong in the category *dog* or *bird*).

| Properties | Generic bird | Wren | Blue heron | Golden eagle | Domestic goose | Penguin |
|---|---|---|---|---|---|---|
| Flies regularly | ✔ | ✔ | ✔ | ✔ | | |
| Sings | ✔ | ✔ | ✔ | | | |
| Lays eggs | ✔ | ✔ | | ✔ | ✔ | ✔ |
| Is small | ✔ | ✔ | | | | |
| Nests in trees | ✔ | ✔ | | | | |

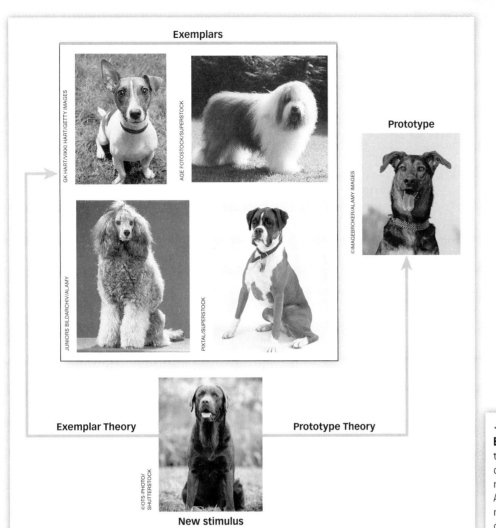

Exemplars

Prototype

Exemplar Theory

Prototype Theory

New stimulus

◄ Figure 9.8 **Prototype Theory and Exemplar Theory** According to prototype theory, we classify new objects by comparing them to the "prototype" (or most typical) member of a category. According to exemplar theory, we classify new objects by comparing them to all category members.

## Exemplar Theory

In contrast to prototype theory, **exemplar theory** holds that *we make category judgments by comparing a new instance with stored memories for other instances of the category* (Medin & Schaffer, 1978). Imagine that you are out walking in the woods, and from the corner of your eye you spot a four-legged animal that might be a wolf or a coyote but that reminds you of your cousin's German shepherd. You figure it must be a dog and continue to enjoy your walk rather than fleeing in a panic. You probably categorized this new animal as a dog because it bore a striking resemblance to other dogs you have encountered; in other words, it was a good example (or an *exemplar*) of the category *dog*. Exemplar theory does a better job than prototype theory in accounting for certain aspects of categorization, especially in that we recall not only what a *prototypical* dog looks like but also what *specific* dogs look like. **FIGURE 9.8** illustrates the difference between prototype theory and exemplar theory.

## Concepts, Categories, and the Brain

Studies that have attempted to link concepts and categories to the brain have helped to make sense of the theories we just considered. For example, in one set of studies (Marsolek, 1995), participants classified prototypes faster when the stimuli were presented to the right visual field, meaning that the left hemisphere received the input first (see the Neuroscience chapter for a discussion of how the two hemispheres

**exemplar theory**
A theory of categorization that argues that we make category judgments by comparing a new instance with stored memories for other instances of the category.

*"Don't panic. It's only a prototype."*

of the brain receive input from the outside world). In contrast, participants classified previously seen exemplars faster when images were presented to the left visual field (meaning that the right hemisphere received the input first). These results suggest a role for both exemplars and prototypes: The left hemisphere is primarily involved in forming prototypes and the right hemisphere is mainly active in recognizing exemplars.

More recently, researchers using neuroimaging techniques have also concluded that we use both prototypes and exemplars when forming concepts and categories. The visual cortex is involved in forming prototypes, whereas the prefrontal cortex and basal ganglia are involved in learning exemplars (Ashby & Ell, 2001; Ashby & O'Brien, 2005). This evidence suggests that exemplar-based learning involves analysis and decision making (prefrontal cortex), whereas prototype formation is a more holistic process involving image processing (visual cortex).

> **How do prototypes and exemplars relate to each other?**

Some of the most striking evidence linking concepts and categories with the brain originated in a pioneering study conducted over 30 years ago. Two neuropsychologists (Warrington & McCarthy, 1983) described a man with brain damage who could not recognize a variety of human-made objects or retrieve any information about them, but his knowledge of living things and foods was perfectly normal. In the following year, neuropsychologists (Warrington & Shallice, 1984) reported on four individuals with brain damage who exhibited the reverse pattern: They could recognize information about human-made objects, but their ability to recognize information about living things and foods was severely impaired. Over 100 similar cases have since been reported (Martin & Caramazza, 2003). These unusual cases became the basis for a syndrome called **category-specific deficit,** *an inability to recognize objects that belong to a particular category, although the ability to recognize objects outside the category is undisturbed.*

Category-specific deficits like these have been observed even when the brain trauma that produces them occurs shortly after birth. Two researchers reported the case of Adam, a 16-year-old boy who suffered a stroke a day after he was born (Farah & Rabinowitz, 2003). Adam has severe difficulty recognizing faces and other biological objects. When shown a picture of a cherry, he identified it as "a Chinese yo-yo." When shown a picture of a mouse, he identified it as an owl. He made errors like these on 79 percent of the animal pictures and 54 percent of the plant pictures he was shown. In contrast, he made errors only 15 percent of the time when identifying pictures of nonliving things, such as spatulas, brooms, and cigars. What is so important about this case? The fact that 16-year-old Adam exhibited category-specific deficits despite suffering a stroke when he was only 1 day old strongly suggests that the brain is "prewired" to organize perceptual and sensory inputs into broad-based categories, such as living and nonliving things.

The type of category-specific deficit suffered depends on where the brain is damaged. Deficits usually result when an individual suffers a stroke or other trauma to areas in the left hemisphere of the cerebral cortex (Mahon & Caramazza, 2009). Damage to the front part of the left temporal lobe results in difficulty identifying humans; damage to the lower left temporal lobe results in difficulty identifying animals; and damage to the region where the temporal lobe meets the occipital and parietal lobes impairs the ability to retrieve names of tools (Damasio et al., 1996). Similarly, when healthy people undertake the same task, imaging studies have demonstrated that the same regions of the brain are more active during naming of tools than animals and vice versa, as shown in **FIGURE 9.9** (Martin, 2007; Martin & Chao, 2001).

**category-specific deficit**
A neurological syndrome that is characterized by an inability to recognize objects that belong to a particular category, although the ability to recognize objects outside the category is undisturbed.

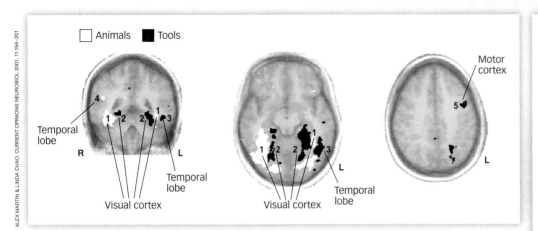

ALEX MARTIN & LINDA CHAO, CURRENT OPINIONS NEUROBIOL 2001, 11:194–201

◀ Figure **9.9** **Brain Areas Involved in Category-Specific Processing** Participants were asked to silently name pictures of animals and tools while they were scanned with fMRI. Areas in white, including parts of the visual cortex and temporal lobe, labelled (1, 4), showed greater activity when participants named animals. Areas in black, including other parts of the visual cortex and temporal lobe (2, 3) and a region of the motor cortex (5), showed greater activity when participants named tools. Note that the images are left/right reversed.

How do particular brain regions develop category preferences for objects such as tools or animals? One possibility is that these preferences develop from the specific visual experiences that individuals have during the course of their lives. An alternative possibility is suggested by the study of Adam that we just considered: The brain may be prewired such that particular regions respond more strongly to some categories than others. A recent study tested these ideas by examining the activity of category-preferential regions in adults who have been blind since birth (Mahon et al., 2009). While in the fMRI scanner, blind and sighted individuals each heard a series of words,

**What is the role of vision in category-specific organization?**

including some words that referred to animals and others that referred to tools. For each word, participants made a judgment about the size of the corresponding object. The critical finding was that category-preferential regions showed highly similar patterns of activity in the blind and sighted individuals. In both groups, for example, regions in the visual cortex and temporal lobe responded to animals and tools in much the same manner as shown in Figure 9.9.

These results provide compelling evidence that category-specific organization of visual regions does not depend on an individual's visual experience. The category-specific organization could conceivably have arisen from interactions with objects that blind individuals have had involving senses other than vision, such as touch (Peelen & Kastner, 2009). However, when combined with the observations of Adam, the simplest explanation may be that category-specific brain organization is innately determined (Bedny & Saxe, 2012; Mahon et al., 2009).

## IN SUMMARY

▶ We organize knowledge about objects, events, or other stimuli by creating concepts, prototypes, and exemplars.

▶ We acquire concepts using three theories: family resemblance theory, which states that items in the same category share certain features, if not all; prototype theory, which uses the most typical member of a category to assess new items; and exemplar theory, which states that we compare new items with stored memories of other members of the category.

▶ Neuroimaging studies have shown that prototypes and exemplars are processed in different parts of the brain.

▶ Studies of people with cognitive and visual deficits have shown that the brain organizes concepts into distinct categories, such as living things and human-made things, and also suggest that visual experience is not necessary for the development of such categories.

# Decision Making: Rational and Otherwise

We use categories and concepts to guide the hundreds of decisions and judgments we make during the course of an average day. Some decisions are easy (what to wear, what to eat for breakfast, and whether to walk, ride a bicycle, or drive to class) and some are more difficult (which car to buy, which apartment to rent, who to hang out with on Friday night, and even which job to take after graduation). Some decisions are made based on sound judgments. Others are not.

## The Rational Ideal

Economists contend that if we are rational and are free to make our own decisions, we will behave as predicted by **rational choice theory**: *We make decisions by determining how likely something is to happen, judging the value of the outcome, and then multiplying the two* (Edwards, 1955). This means that our judgments will vary depending on the value we assign to the possible outcomes. Suppose, for example, you were asked to choose between a 10 percent chance of gaining $500 and a 20 percent chance of gaining $2000. The rational person would choose the second alternative because the expected payoff is $400 ($2000 × 20%), whereas the first offers an expected gain of only $50 ($500 × 10%). Selecting the option with the highest expected value seems so straightforward that many economists accept the basic ideas in rational choice theory. But how well does this theory describe decision making in our everyday lives? In many cases, the answer is not very well.

## The Irrational Reality

Is the ability to classify new events and objects into categories always a useful skill? Alas, no. These strengths of human decision making can turn into weaknesses when certain tasks inadvertently activate these skills. In other words, the same principles that allow cognition to occur easily and accurately can pop up to bedevil our decision making.

### Judging Frequencies and Probabilities

Consider the following list of words:

> *block table block pen telephone block disk glass table block telephone block watch table candy*

You probably noticed that the words *block* and *table* occurred more frequently than the other words did. In fact, studies have shown that people are quite good at estimating *frequency,* or simply the number of times something will happen. This skill matters quite a bit when it comes to decision making. In contrast, we perform poorly on tasks that require us to think in terms of *probabilities,* or the likelihood that something will happen.

Even with probabilities, however, performance varies depending on how the problem is described. In one experiment, 100 physicians were asked to predict the incidence of breast cancer among women whose mammogram screening tests showed possible evidence of breast cancer. The physicians were told to take into consideration the rarity of breast cancer (1 percent of the population at the time the study was done) and radiologists' record in diagnosing the condition (correctly recognized only 79 percent of the time and falsely diagnosed almost 10 percent of the time). Of the 100 physicians, 95 estimated the probability that cancer was present to be about 75 percent! The correct answer was 8 percent. The physicians apparently experienced difficulty taking so much information into account when making their decision (Eddy, 1982). Similar dismal results have been reported with a number of medical screening tests (Hoffrage & Gigerenzer, 1996; Windeler & Kobberling, 1986).

> **Why is a better decision more likely when considering frequency, versus likelihood, that something will happen?**

People do not always make rational choices. When a lottery jackpot is larger than usual, more people will buy lottery tickets, thinking that they might well win big. However, more people buying lottery tickets reduces the likelihood of any one person winning the lottery. Ironically, people have a better chance at winning a lottery with a relatively small jackpot.

© BRITISH RETAIL PHOTOGRAPHY/ALAMY

**rational choice theory**
The classical view that we make decisions by determining how likely something is to happen, judging the value of the outcome, and then multiplying the two.

However, dramatically different results were obtained when the study was repeated using *frequency* information instead of *probability* information. Stating the problem as "10 out of every 1000 women actually have breast cancer" instead of "1 percent of women actually have breast cancer" led 46 percent of the physicians to derive the right answer, compared to only 8 percent who came up with the right answer when the problem was presented using probabilities (Hoffrage & Gigerenzer, 1998). This finding suggests, at a minimum, that when seeking advice (even from a highly skilled decision maker), make sure your problem is described using frequencies rather than probabilities.

## Availability Bias

Take a look at the list of names in **FIGURE 9.10.** Now look away from the book and estimate the number of male names and female names in the figure. Did you notice that some of the women on the list are famous and none of the men are? Was your estimate off because you thought the list contained more women's than men's names (Tversky & Kahneman, 1973, 1974)? The reverse would have been true if you had looked at a list with the names of famous men and unknown women because people typically fall prey to **availability bias:** *Items that are more readily available in memory are judged as having occurred more frequently.*

| | |
|---|---|
| Jennifer Aniston | Robert Kingston |
| Judy Smith | Gilbert Chapman |
| Frank Carson | Gwyneth Paltrow |
| Alice Munro | Martin Mitchell |
| Daniel Hunt | Thomas Hughes |
| Henry Vaughan | Michael Drayton |
| Agatha Christie | Julia Roberts |
| Arthur Hutchinson | Adrienne Clarkson |
| Jennifer Lopez | Jack Lindsay |
| Allan Nevins | Richard Gilder |
| Jane Austen | George Nathan |
| Joseph Litton | Britney Spears |

▲ Figure **9.10 Availability Bias** Looking at this list of names, estimate the number of women's and men's names.

The availability bias affects our estimates because memory strength and frequency of occurrence are directly related. Frequently occurring items are remembered more easily than *infrequently* occurring items, so you naturally conclude that items for which you have better memory must also have been more frequent. Unfortunately, better memory in this case was not due to greater *frequency,* but to greater *familiarity.*

**How are memory strength and frequency of occurrence related?**

Shortcuts such as the availability bias are sometimes referred to as **heuristics,** *fast and efficient strategies that may facilitate decision making but do not guarantee that a solution will be reached.* Heuristics are mental shortcuts, or "rules of thumb," that are often—but not always—effective when approaching a problem (Swinkels, 2003). In contrast, an **algorithm** is *a well-defined sequence of procedures or rules that guarantees a solution to a problem.* Consider, for example, two approaches to constructing a PowerPoint presentation involving features you rarely use, such as inserting movies and complex animations: (1) You try to remember what you did the last time you tried to do a similar presentation; (2) You follow a set of step-by-step directions that you wrote down the last time you did something similar, which tells you exactly how to insert movies and build complex animations.

The first procedure is an intelligent heuristic that may be successful, but you could continue searching your memory until you finally run out of time or patience. The second strategy is a series of well-defined steps that, if properly executed, will guarantee a solution.

## The Conjunction Fallacy

The availability bias illustrates a potential source of error in human cognition. Unfortunately, it is not the only one. Consider the following description:

> Linda is 31 years old, single, outspoken, and very bright. In university, she majored in philosophy. As a student, she was deeply concerned with issues of discrimination and social justice and also participated in antinuclear demonstrations.
>
> Which state of affairs is more probable?
>
> a. Linda is a bank teller.
> b. Linda is a bank teller and is active in the feminist movement.

In one study, 89 percent of participants rated option (b) as more probable than option (a) (Tversky & Kahneman, 1983), although that is logically impossible. Let us

**availability bias**
Items that are more readily available in memory are judged as having occurred more frequently.

**heuristic**
A fast and efficient strategy that may facilitate decision making but does not guarantee that a solution will be reached.

**algorithm**
A well-defined sequence of procedures or rules that guarantees a solution to a problem.

say there is a 20 percent chance that Linda is a bank teller; after all, there are plenty of occupations she might hold. Independently, let us say there is also a 20 percent chance that she is active in the feminist movement; she probably has lots of interests. The joint probability that *both* things are true simultaneously is the product of their separate probabilities. In other words, the 20 percent chance that she is a teller multiplied by the 20 percent chance that she is in the feminist movement produces a 4 percent chance that both things are true at the same time ($0.20 \times 0.20 = 0.04$, or 4%). The combined probability of events is always less than the independent probability of each event; therefore, it is always *more* probable that any one state of affairs is true than is a set of events simultaneously.

This is called the **conjunction fallacy** because *people think that two events are more likely to occur together than either individual event.* The fallacy is that with more and more pieces of information, people think there is a higher probability that all are true. Actually, the probability diminishes rapidly. Based on her description, do you think Linda also voted for the Liberal candidate in the last election? Do you think she also writes poetry? Do you think she has also signed her name to fair-housing petitions? With each additional bit of information, you probably think you are getting a better and better description of Linda, but as you can see in **FIGURE 9.11**, the likelihood of all those events being true *at the same time* is very small.

> **How can more information sometimes lead people to wrong conclusions?**

### Representativeness Heuristic

Think about the following situation:

A panel of psychologists wrote 100 descriptions based on interviews with engineers and lawyers. THE DESCRIPTIONS CAME FROM 70 ENGINEERS AND 30 LAWYERS. You will be shown a random selection of these descriptions. Read each and then pause and decide if it is more likely that the person is an engineer or a lawyer. Note your decision and read on.

1. Jack enjoys reading books on social and political issues. During the interview, he displayed particular skill at argument.

2. Tom is a loner who enjoys working on mathematical puzzles during his spare time. During the interview, his speech remained fairly abstract and his emotions were well controlled.

3. Harry is a bright man and an avid racquetball player. During the interview, he asked many insightful questions and was very well spoken.

Research participants were shown a series of descriptions like these and asked after each one to judge the likelihood that the person described was a lawyer or an engineer (Kahneman & Tversky, 1973). Remember, of the descriptions, 70 were engineers and 30 were lawyers. If participants took this proportion into consideration, their judgments should have reflected the fact that there were more than twice as many engineers as lawyers. But researchers found that people did not use this information and based their judgments solely on how closely the description matched their concepts of lawyers and engineers. So, the majority of participants thought descriptions such as 1 were more likely to be lawyers, those like 2 were more likely to be engineers, and those like 3 could be either.

Consider participants' judgments about Harry. His description does not sound like a lawyer's or an engineer's, so most people said he was *equally likely* to hold either occupation. But the pool contains more than twice as many engineers as lawyers, so it is far *more* likely that Harry is an engineer. People seem to ignore information about *base rate*, or the existing

> **What can cause people to ignore the *base rate* of an event?**

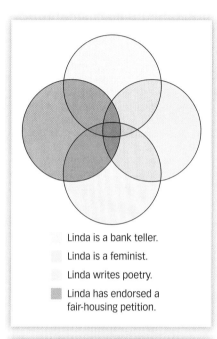

▲ Figure **9.11 The Conjunction Fallacy** People often think that with each additional bit of information, the probability that all the facts are simultaneously true of a person increases. In fact, the probability decreases dramatically. Notice how the intersection of all these possibilities is much smaller than the area of any one possibility alone.

Linda is a bank teller.
Linda is a feminist.
Linda writes poetry.
Linda has endorsed a fair-housing petition.

**conjunction fallacy**
When people think that two events are more likely to occur together than either individual event.

probability of an event, basing their judgments on similarities to categories. Researchers call this the **representativeness heuristic:** *making a probability judgment by comparing an object or event to a prototype of the object or event* (Kahneman & Tversky, 1973). Thus, the probability judgments were skewed toward the participants' prototypes of lawyer and engineer. The greater the similarity, the more likely they were judged to be members of that category despite the existence of much more useful base rates.

Heuristics such as availability, representativeness, or the conjunction fallacy highlight both the strengths and weaknesses of the way we think. We are very good at forming categories based on prototypes and making classification judgments on the basis of similarity to prototypes. Judging probabilities is not our strong suit. As we saw earlier in this chapter, the human brain easily processes frequency information, and decision-making performance can usually be improved if probability problems are reframed using frequencies.

## Framing Effects

You have seen that, according to rational choice theory, our judgments will vary depending on the value we place aon the expected outcome. So how effective are we at assigning value to our choices? Studies show that **framing effects,** which occur when *people give different answers to the same problem depending on how the problem is phrased (or framed)*, can influence the assignment of value.

For example, if people are told that a particular drug has a 70 percent effectiveness rate, they are usually pretty impressed: 70 percent of the time the drug cures what ails

> Is a 70% success rate better than a 30% failure rate?

you sounds like a good deal. Tell them instead that a drug has a 30 percent failure rate—30 percent of the time it does no good—and they typically perceive it as risky, potentially harmful, and something to be avoided. Notice that the information is the same: A 70 percent effectiveness rate means that 30 percent of the time, it is ineffective. The way the information is framed, however, leads to substantially different conclusions (Tversky & Kahneman, 1981).

One of the most striking framing effects is the **sunk-cost fallacy,** which occurs when *people make decisions about a current situation based on what they have previously invested in the situation*. Imagine waiting in line for 3 hours, paying $100 for a ticket to the Warped Tour to see your favourite bands, and waking on the day of the outdoor concert to find that it is bitterly cold and rainy. If you go, you will feel miserable. But you go anyway, reasoning that the $100 you paid for the ticket and the time you spent in line will have been wasted if you stay home.

Notice that you have two choices: (1) Spend $100 and stay comfortably at home or (2) spend $100 and endure many uncomfortable hours in the rain. The $100 is gone in either case: It is a sunk cost, irretrievable at the moment of your decision. But the way you framed the problem created a problem: Because you invested time and money, you feel obligated to follow through, even though it is something you no longer want. If you can turn off this feeling and ask whether you would rather spend $100 to be comfortable or spend it to be miserable, the smart choice is clear: Stay home and listen to the podcast!

The Concorde supersonic jet owed its marginal commercial life (1976–2003) to the sunk-cost fallacy. The development of this aircraft was jointly funded by the governments of the United Kingdom and France. It was beautiful, and as safe as any other passenger jet, but it was very expensive and a convincing business case for a faster-than-sound aircraft was never made. Few orders came in, and it was clear early on that the Concorde would never be profitable. Although several attempts were made to kill the program, France and the United Kingdom kept investing, since they had already invested billions of dollars.

sidebar

**representativeness heuristic**
A mental shortcut that involves making a probability judgment by comparing an object or event to a prototype of the object or event.

**framing effects**
When people give different answers to the same problem depending on how the problem is phrased (or framed).

**sunk-cost fallacy**
A framing effect in which people make decisions about a current situation based on what they have previously invested in the situation.

ROGER HOLDEN/GETTY IMAGES

The Concorde was in development for several years, and its advanced technology meant that costs spiralled. It was a very expensive aircraft to buy, fly, and maintain, and it carried relatively few passengers. It also had very high fuel consumption, which in the 1970s (after the 1973 oil crisis) was not popular with airlines. All in all, it was clear to everyone that there would be very little or no market for the aircraft once it was developed. So why did the United Kingdom and France continue to invest in it?

# CULTURE & COMMUNITY

## Does Culture Influence Optimism Bias?

In addition to heuristics and biases described in this chapter, human decision making often reflects the effects of *optimism bias*: People believe that they are more likely to experience positive events and less likely to experience negative events in the future, compared with other people (Sharot, 2011; Weinstein, 1980). Several studies have found that optimism bias is greater in North Americans than in individuals from Asian cultures such as Japan (Heine & Lehman, 1995; Klein & Helweg-Larsen, 2002). One recent study examined optimism bias concerning the risk of natural disasters and terrorist attacks in American, Japanese, and Argentinean mental health workers who had received training in responding to such events (Gierlach, Blesher, & Beutler, 2010). Evidence for optimism bias was evident to some degree in all three samples: Participants in each country judged that they were at lower risk of experiencing a disaster than others in their country. However, optimism bias was strongest in the American sample. This bias was most clearly evident in responses across cultures to questions regarding vulnerability to terrorist attacks. Despite America's recent experience with terrorist attacks, Americans judged themselves to be at lower risk of a terrorist attack than did Japanese or Argentineans.

Findings such as these may ultimately be helpful in attempting to understand *why* the optimism bias occurs. Although many possibilities have been suggested (Sharot, 2011), researchers have not yet come up with a theory that explains all the relevant evidence. Focusing on cultural similarities and differences in optimism bias may help to achieve that goal, although we should not be unrealistically optimistic that we will achieve it any time soon!

# Why Do We Make Decision-Making Errors?

As you have seen, everyday decision making seems riddled with errors and short-comings. Our decisions vary wildly depending on how a problem is presented (e.g., frequencies versus probabilities or framed in terms of losses rather than savings), and we seem to be prone to fallacies, such as the sunk-cost fallacy or the conjunction fallacy. Psychologists have developed several explanations for why everyday decision making suffers from these failings. We will review two of the most influential theories: prospect theory and the frequency format hypothesis.

## Prospect Theory

According to a totally rational model of inference, people should make decisions that maximize value; in other words, they should seek to increase what psychologists and economists call *expected utility*. We face decisions like this every day. If you are making a decision that involves money and money is what you value, then you should choose the outcome that is likely to bring you the most money. When deciding which of two apartments to rent, you would compare the monthly expenses for each and choose the one that leaves more money in your pocket.

As you have seen, however, people often make decisions that are inconsistent with this simple principle. The question is, why? To explain these effects, Amos Tversky and Daniel Kahneman (1992) developed **prospect theory:** *People choose to take on risk when evaluating potential losses and avoid risks when evaluating potential gains.* These decision processes take place in two phases.

> **Why will most people take more risks to avoid losses than to make gains?**

> First, people simplify available information.
> So, in a task like choosing an apartment, they tend to ignore a lot of potentially useful information because apartments differ in so many ways (the closeness of restaurants, the presence of a swimming pool, the colour of the carpet, and

**prospect theory**
People choose to take on risk when evaluating potential losses and avoid risks when evaluating potential gains.

so forth). Comparing each apartment on each factor is simply too much work; focusing only on differences that matter is more efficient.

> In the second phase, people choose the prospect that they believe offers the best value. This value is personal and may differ from an objective measure of "best value." For example, you might choose the apartment with higher rent because you can walk to eight great bars and restaurants.

Prospect theory makes other assumptions that account for people's choice patterns. One assumption, called the *certainty effect*, suggests that when making decisions, people give greater weight to outcomes that are a sure thing. When deciding between playing a lottery with an 80 percent chance of winning $4000 or receiving $3000 outright, most people choose the $3000, even though the expected value of the first choice is $200 more ($4000 × 80 percent = $3200)! Apparently, people weigh certainty much more heavily than expected payoffs when making choices.

Prospect theory also assumes that in evaluating choices, people compare them to a reference point. For example, suppose you are still torn between two apartments. The $400 monthly rent for apartment A is discounted $10 if you pay before the fifth of the month. A $10 surcharge is tacked onto the $390 per month rent for apartment B if you pay after the fifth of the month. Although the apartments are objectively identical in terms of cost, different reference points may make apartment A seem psychologically more appealing than apartment B.

Prospect theory also assumes that people are more willing to take risks to avoid losses than to achieve gains. Given a choice between a definite $300 rebate on your first month's rent or spinning a wheel that offers an 80 percent chance of getting a $400 rebate, you will most likely choose the lower sure payoff over the higher potential payoff ($400 × 80% = $320). However, given a choice between a sure fine of $300 for damaging an apartment or spinning a wheel that has an 80 percent chance of a $400 fine, most people will choose the higher potential loss over the sure loss. This asymmetry in risk preferences shows that we are willing to take on risk if we think it will ward off a loss, but we are risk-averse if we expect to lose some benefits.

**Stephen Harper**

**Justin Trudeau**

**Elizabeth May**

**frequency format hypothesis**
The proposal that our minds evolved to notice how frequently things occur, not how likely they are to occur.

According to rational choice theory, people evaluate all options when making a decision and choose the alternative with the greatest benefit to them. However, psychological research shows us that this is not always the case. How might some political candidates use the conjunction fallacy, framing effects, or prospect theory to influence voters' evaluations of their opponents or their opponents' views?

## Frequency Format Hypothesis

According to the **frequency format hypothesis,** *our minds evolved to notice how frequently things occur, not how likely they are to occur* (Gigerenzer, 1996; Gigerenzer & Hoffrage, 1995). Thus, we interpret, process, and manipulate information about frequency with comparative ease because that is the way quantitative information usually occurs in natural circumstances. For example, the 20 men, 15 women, 5 dogs, 13 cars, and 2 bicycle accidents you encountered on the way to class came in the form of frequencies, not probabilities or percentages.

**Why are we better at estimating frequencies than probabilities?**

Probabilities and percentages are, evolutionarily speaking, recent developments, emerging in the mid-seventeenth century (Hacking, 1975). Millennia passed before humans developed these cultural notions, and years of schooling are needed to use them competently as everyday cognitive tools. Thus, our susceptibility to errors when dealing with probabilities is not surprising.

In contrast, people can track frequencies virtually effortlessly and flawlessly (Hasher & Zacks, 1984). We are also remarkably good at recognizing how often two events occur together (Mandel & Lehman, 1998; Spellman, 1996; Waldmann, 2000). Infants as young as 6 months of age can tell the difference between displays that differ in the number of items present (Starkey, Spelke, & Gelman, 1983, 1990). Frequency monitoring is a basic biological capacity rather than a skill learned through formal instruction. According to the frequency format hypothesis, presenting statistical information in frequency format rather than probability format results in improved performance because it capitalizes on our evolutionary strengths (Gigerenzer & Hoffrage, 1995; Hertwig & Gigerenzer, 1999).

## Decision Making and the Brain

A man identified as Elliot (whom you met briefly in the Psychology: Evolution of a Science chapter) was a successful businessman, husband, and father prior to developing a brain tumour. After surgery, his intellectual abilities seemed intact, but he was unable to differentiate between important and unimportant activities and would spend hours at mundane tasks. He lost his job and got involved in several risky financial ventures that bankrupted him. He had no difficulty discussing what had happened, but his descriptions were so detached and dispassionate that it seemed as though his abstract intellectual functions had become dissociated from his social and emotional abilities.

Research confirms that this interpretation of Elliot's downfall is right on track. In one study, researchers looked at how healthy volunteers differed from people with prefrontal lobe damage on a gambling task that involves risky decision making (Bechara et al., 1994, 1997). Four decks of cards were placed face down, and participants were required to make 100 selections of cards that specified an amount of play money they could win or lose. Two of the decks usually provided large payoffs or large losses, whereas the other two provided smaller payoffs and losses. While playing the game, the participants' galvanic skin responses (GSRs) were recorded to measure heightened emotional reactions.

The performance of players with prefrontal lobe damage mirrored Elliot's real-life problems: They selected cards equally from the riskier and the safer decks, leading most to eventually go bankrupt. At first, the healthy volunteers also selected from each deck equally, but they gradually shifted to choosing primarily from the safer decks. This difference in strategy occurred even though both groups showed strong emotional reactions to big gains and losses, as measured by their comparable GSR scores. The two groups differed in one important way. As the game progressed, the healthy participants began to show anticipatory emotional reactions when they even *considered* choosing a card from the risky deck. Their GSR scores jumped dramatically even before they were able to say that some decks were riskier than others (Bechara et al., 1997). The participants with prefrontal damage did not show these anticipatory feelings when they were thinking about selecting a card from the risky deck. Apparently, their emotional reactions did not guide their thinking, so they continued to make risky decisions, as shown in **FIGURE 9.12** (on the next page).

Further studies of the participants with prefrontal damage suggest that their risky decision making grows out of insensitivity to the future consequences of their behaviour (Naqvi, Shiv, & Bechara, 2006). Unable to think beyond immediate consequences,

> **What is the relationship of the prefrontal cortex to risky behaviour?**

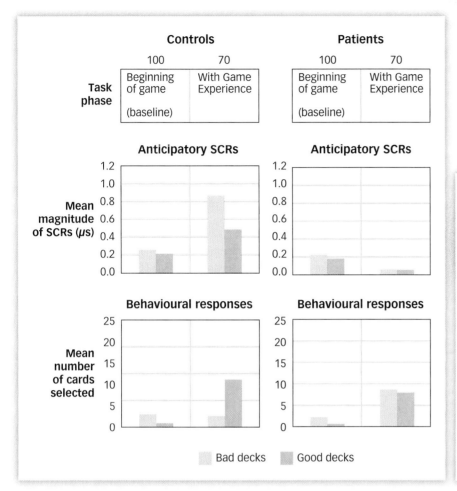

◄ Figure **9.12** **The Neuroscience of Risky Decision Making** In a study of risky decision making, researchers compared healthy controls' choices to those made by people with damage to the prefrontal cortex. Participants played a game in which they selected a card from one of four decks. Two of the decks were made up of riskier cards, that is, cards that provided large payoffs or large losses. The other two contained safer cards—those with much smaller payoffs and losses. At the beginning of the game, both groups chose cards from the two decks with equal frequency. Over the course of the game, the healthy controls avoided the bad decks and showed large emotional responses (SCRs, or skin conductance responses) when they even considered choosing a card from a risky deck. Participants with prefrontal brain damage, on the other hand, continued to choose cards from the two decks with equal frequency and showed no evidence of emotional learning and eventually went bankrupt.

[From Bechara et al., 1997.]

they could not shift their choices in response to a rising rate of losses or a declining rate of rewards (Bechara, Tranel, & Damasio, 2000). Interestingly, substance-dependent individuals, such as alcoholics and cocaine addicts, act the same way. Most perform as poorly on the gambling task as do individuals with prefrontal damage (Bechara et al., 2001). More recent work has extended these impairments on the gambling task across cultures to Chinese adolescents with binge-drinking problems (Johnson, Xiao, et al., 2008). These findings have potentially important implications for such everyday issues as road safety. A recent study focused on people who had been convicted of driving while impaired with alcohol (DWI). Offenders who performed poorly on the gambling task were much more likely to commit repeated DWI offenses than those who performed well on the gambling task (Bouchard, Brown, & Nadeau, 2012). Related recent work has documented gambling task impairments in binge eaters, another group in which there is an insensitivity to the future consequences of behaviour (Danner et al. 2012).

Neuroimaging studies of healthy individuals have provided evidence that fits well with the earlier studies of individuals with damage to the prefrontal cortex: When performing the gambling task, an area in the prefrontal cortex is activated when participants need to make risky decisions as compared to safe decisions. Indeed, the activated region is in the part of the prefrontal cortex that is typically damaged in participants who perform poorly on the gambling task, and greater activation in this region is correlated with better task performance in healthy individuals (Fukui et al., 2005; Lawrence et al., 2009). Taken together, the neuroimaging and lesion studies show clearly that aspects of risky decision making depend critically on the contributions of the prefrontal cortex.

IN SUMMARY

▶ Human decision making often departs from a completely rational process, and the mistakes that accompany this departure tell us a lot about how the human mind works.

▶ The values we place on outcomes weigh so heavily in our judgments that they sometimes overshadow objective evidence. When people are asked to make probability judgments, they will turn the problem into something they know how to solve, such as judging memory strength, judging similarity to prototypes, or estimating frequencies. This can lead to errors of judgment.

▶ When a problem fits their mental algorithms, people show considerable skill at making appropriate judgments. In making a judgment about the probability of an event, performance can vary dramatically.

▶ Because we feel that avoiding losses is more important than achieving gains, framing effects can affect our choices. Emotional information also strongly influences our decision making, even when we are not aware of it. Although this influence can lead us astray, it often is crucial for making decisions in everyday life.

▶ The prefrontal cortex plays an important role in decision making, and patients with prefrontal damage make more risky decisions than do non-brain-damaged indiviuals.

# Problem Solving: Working It Out

You have a problem when you find yourself in a place where you do not want to be. In such circumstances, you try to find a way to change the situation so that you end up in a situation you *do* want. Let us say that it is the night before a test, and you are trying to study but just cannot settle down and focus on the material. This is a situation you do not want. So, you try to think of ways to help yourself focus. You might begin with the material that most interests you, or provide yourself with rewards, such as a music break or a trip to the refrigerator. If these activities enable you to get down to work, your problem is solved.

Two major types of problems complicate our daily lives. The first and most frequent is the *ill-defined problem,* one that does not have a clear goal or well-defined solution paths. Your study block is an ill-defined problem: Your goal is not clearly defined (i.e., somehow get focused), and the solution path for achieving the goal is even less clear (i.e., there are many ways to gain focus). Most everyday problems (being a better person, finding that special someone, achieving success) are ill defined. In contrast, a *well-defined problem* is one with clearly specified goals and clearly defined solution paths. Examples include following a clear set of directions to get to school, solving simple algebra problems, or playing a game of chess.

## Means–Ends Analysis

In 1945, German psychologist Karl Duncker reported some important studies of the problem-solving process. He presented people with ill-defined problems and asked them to "think aloud" while solving them (Duncker, 1945). Based on what people said about how they solve problems, Duncker described problem solving in terms of **means–ends analysis**, *a process of searching for the means or steps to reduce the differences between the current situation and the desired goal.* This process usually took the following steps:

1. Analyze the goal state (i.e., the desired outcome you want to attain).
2. Analyze the current state (i.e., your starting point, or the current situation).

Even though it may not be easy to put together this Lego model, having instructions for assembly makes it a well-defined problem.

CORBIS COLLECTION/ALAMY

3. List the differences between the current state and the goal state.
4. Reduce the list of differences by
   - Direct means (a procedure that solves the problem without intermediate steps).
   - Generating a subgoal (an intermediate step on the way to solving the problem).
   - Finding a similar problem that has a known solution.

Consider, for example, one of Duncker's problems:

> A patient has an inoperable tumour in his abdomen. The tumour is inoperable because it is surrounded by healthy but fragile tissue that would be severely damaged during surgery. How can the patient be saved?

The *goal state* is a patient without the tumour and with undamaged surrounding tissue. The *current state* is a patient with an inoperable tumour surrounded by fragile tissue. The *difference* between these two states is the tumour. A *direct-means solution* would be to destroy the tumour with X-rays, but the required X-ray dose would destroy the fragile surrounding tissue and possibly kill the patient. A *subgoal* would be to modify the X-ray machine to deliver a weaker dose. After this subgoal is achieved, a direct-means solution could be to deliver the weaker dose to the patient's abdomen. But this solution will not work either: The weaker dose would not damage the healthy tissue but also would not kill the tumour. So, what to do? Find a similar problem that has a known solution. Let us see how this can be done.

## Analogical Problem Solving

When we engage in **analogical problem solving,** we attempt to *solve a problem by finding a similar problem with a known solution and applying that solution to the current problem.* Consider the following story:

> An island surrounded by bridges is the site of an enemy fortress. The massive fortification is so strongly defended that only a very large army could overtake it. Unfortunately, the bridges would collapse under the weight of such a huge force. So, a clever general divides the army into several smaller units and sends the units over different bridges, timing the crossings so that the many streams of soldiers converge on the fortress at the same time and the fortress is taken.

Does this story suggest a solution to the tumour problem? It should. Removing a tumour and attacking a fortress are very different problems, but the two problems are analogous because they share a common structure: The *goal state* is a conquered fortress with undamaged surrounding bridges. The *current state* is an occupied fortress surrounded by fragile bridges. The *difference* between the two states is the occupying enemy. The *solution* is to divide the required force into smaller units that are light enough to spare the fragile bridges and send them down the bridges simultaneously so that they converge on the fortress. The combined units will form an army strong enough to take the fortress (see **FIGURE 9.13**).

This analogous problem of the island fortress suggests the following direct-means solution to the tumour problem:

> Surround the patient with X-ray machines and simultaneously send weaker doses that converge on the tumour. The combined strength of the weaker X-ray doses will be sufficient to destroy the tumour, but the individual doses will be weak enough to spare the surrounding healthy tissue.

Did this solution occur to you after reading the fortress story? In studies that have used the tumour problem, only 10 percent of participants spontaneously generated the correct solution. This percentage rose to 30 percent if participants read the island fortress problem or other analogous story. However, the success climbed dramatically

**means–ends analysis**
A process of searching for the means or steps to reduce differences between the current situation and the desired goal.

**analogical problem solving**
Solving a problem by finding a similar problem with a known solution and applying that solution to the current problem.

▼ Figure 9.13 **Analogical Problem Solving**
Just as smaller, lighter battalions can reach the fortress without damaging the bridges, many small X-ray doses can destroy the tumour without harming the delicate surrounding tissue. In both cases, the additive strength achieves the objective.

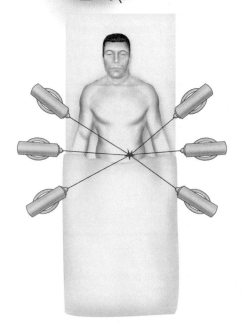

to 75 percent among participants who had a chance to read more than one analogous problem or were given a deliberate hint to use the solution to the fortress story (Gick & Holyoak, 1980).

Why was the fortress problem so ineffective by itself? Problem solving is strongly affected by superficial similarities between problems, and the relationship between the tumour and fortress problems lies deep in their structure (Catrambone, 2002).

> Why are analogies useful in problem solving?

## Creativity and Insight

Analogical problem solving shows us that successfully solving a problem often depends on learning the principles underlying a particular type of problem and also that solving lots of problems improves our ability to recognize certain problem types and generate effective solutions. Some problem solving, however, seems to involve brilliant flashes of insight and creative solutions that have never before been tried. Creative and insightful solutions often rely on restructuring a problem so that it turns into a problem you already know how to solve (Cummins, 2012).

### Genius and Insight

Consider the exceptional mind of the mathematician Friedrich Gauss (1777–1855). One day, Gauss's elementary schoolteacher asked the class to add up the numbers 1 through 10. While his classmates laboriously worked their sums, Gauss had a flash of insight that caused the answer to occur to him immediately. Gauss imagined the numbers 1 through 10 as weights lined up on a balance beam, as shown in **FIGURE 9.14**. Starting at the left, each "weight" increases by 1. In order for the beam to balance, each weight on the left must be paired with a weight on the right. You can see this by starting at the middle and noticing that $5 + 6 = 11$, then moving outward, $4 + 7 = 11$, $3 + 8 = 11$, and so on. This produces five number pairs that add up to 11. Now the problem is easy. Multiply. Gauss's genius lay in restructuring the problem in a way that allowed him to notice a very simple and elegant solution to an otherwise tedious task—a procedure, by the way, that generalizes to series of any length.

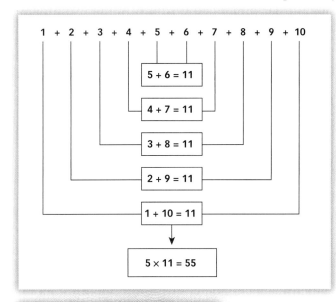

▲ Figure **9.14 Genius and Insight** Young Friedrich Gauss imagined the scheme shown here and quickly reduced a laborious addition problem to an easy multiplication task. Gauss's early insight led him to realize later an intriguing truth: This simple solution generalizes to number series of any length.

(From Wertheimer, 1945/1982.)

According to Gestalt psychologists, insights such as these reflect a spontaneous restructuring of a problem. A sudden flash of insight contrasts with incremental problem-solving procedures in which one gradually gets closer and closer to a solution. Early researchers studying insight found that people were more likely to solve a non-insight problem if they felt they were gradually getting "warmer" (incrementally closer to the solution). But whether someone felt warm did not predict the likelihood of their solving an insight problem (Metcalfe & Wiebe, 1987). The solution for an insight problem seemed to appear out of the blue, regardless of what the participant felt.

> What is the role of the unconscious in flashes of insight?

Later research, however, suggests that sudden insightful solutions may actually result from unconscious incremental processes (Bowers et al., 1990). In one study, research participants were shown paired, three-word series like those in **FIGURE 9.15** (on the next page) and asked to find a fourth word that was associated with the three words in each series. However, only one series in each pair had a common associate. Solvable series were termed *coherent,* whereas those with no solution were called *incoherent.*

**functional fixedness**
The tendency to perceive the functions of objects as fixed.

Even if participants could not find a solution, they could reliably decide, more than by chance alone, which of the pairs was coherent. However, if insightful solutions actually occur in a sudden, all-or-nothing manner, their performance should have been no better than chance. Thus, the findings suggest that even insightful problem solving is an incremental process—one that occurs outside of conscious awareness. The process works something like this: The pattern of clues that constitute a problem unconsciously activates relevant information in memory. Activation then spreads through the memory network, recruiting additional relevant information (Bowers et al., 1990). When sufficient information has been activated, it crosses the threshold of awareness and we experience a sudden flash of insight into the problem's solution.

Finding a connection between the words *strawberry* and *traffic* might take some time, even for someone motivated to figure out how they are related. But if the word *strawberry* activates *jam* in long-term memory (see the Memory chapter) and the activation spreads from *strawberry* to *traffic,* the solution to the puzzle may suddenly spring into awareness without the thinker knowing how it got there. What would seem like a sudden insight would really result from an incremental process that consists of activation spreading through memory, adding new information as more knowledge is activated. Nonetheless, studies of brain activity during problem solving reveal striking differences between problems solved by sudden insight and those solved by using more deliberate strategies (see the Hot Science box).

## Functional Fixedness

If insight is a simple incremental process, why is not its occurrence more frequent? In the research discussed previously, participants produced insightful solutions only 25 percent of the time. Insight is rare because problem solving (like decision making) suffers from framing effects. In problem solving, framing tends to limit the types of solutions that occur to us. **Functional fixedness**—*the tendency to perceive the functions of objects as fixed*—is a process that constricts our thinking. Look at **FIGURES 9.16** and **9.17** and see if you can solve the problems before reading on. In

| Coherent | Incoherent |
|----------|------------|
| Playing  | Still      |
| Credit   | Pages      |
| Report   | Music      |
| Blank    | Light      |
| White    | Folk       |
| Lines    | Head       |
| Ticket   | Town       |
| Shop     | Root       |
| Broker   | Car        |
| Magic    | House      |
| Plush    | Lion       |
| Floor    | Butter     |
| Base     | Swan       |
| Snow     | Army       |
| Dance    | Mask       |
| Gold     | Noise      |
| Stool    | Foam       |
| Tender   | Shade      |

Solutions:
card, paper, pawn, carpet, ball, bar

◀ Figure **9.15 Insightful Solutions Are Really Incremental** Participants were asked to find a fourth word that was associated with the other three words in each series. Even if they could not find a solution, they could reliably choose which series of three words were solvable and which were not. Try to solve these.

[From Bowers et al., 1990.]

▲ Figure **9.16 Functional Fixedness and the Candle Problem** How can you use these objects—a box of matches, thumbtacks, and a candle—to mount the candle on the wall so that it illuminates the room? Give this problem some thought before you check the answer in Figure 9.19 on page 387.

◀ Figure **9.17 Functional Fixedness and the String Problem** The strings hung from hooks on either side of the ceiling are long enough to be tied together, but they are positioned too far apart to reach one while holding on to the other. Using the tools shown on the table, how can you accomplish the task? Compare your answer to that in Figure 9.20 on page 387.

▲ Figure **9.18** **The Nine-Dot Problem**
Connect all nine dots with four straight lines without lifting your pencil from the paper. Compare your answer to those in Figure 9.21 on page 388.

Figure 9.16, your task is to illuminate a dark room using the following objects: some thumbtacks, a box of matches, and a candle. In Figure 9.17, you need to tie the two strings together, but they are too far apart to reach one while holding on to the other. Using the items on the table, you are expected to reach the string that is too far away to grasp.

Difficulty solving these problems derives from our tendency to think of the objects only in terms of their normal, typical, or "fixed" functions. We do not think to use the matchbox for a candleholder because boxes typically hold matches, not candles. Similarly, using the hammer as a pendulum weight does not spring to mind because hammers are typically used to pound things. Did functional fixedness prevent you from solving these problems? (The solutions are shown in **FIGURES 9.19** and **9.20**.)

Sometimes framing limits our ability to generate a solution. Before reading on, look at **FIGURE 9.18**. Without lifting your pencil from the page, try to connect all nine dots with only four straight lines. To solve this problem, you must allow the lines you draw to extend outside the imaginary box that surrounds the dots (see **FIGURE 9.21**). This constraint does not reside in the problem but in the mind of the problem solver (Kershaw & Ohlsson, 2004). Despite the apparent sudden flash of insight that seems to yield a solution to problems of this type, research indicates that the thought processes people use when solving even this type of insight problem are best described as an incremental, means–ends analysis (MacGregor, Ormerod, & Chronicle, 2001).

HOT SCIENCE

# Sudden Insight and the Brain

The "aha!" moment that accompanies a sudden flash of insight is a compelling experience, one that highlights that solving a problem based on insight *feels* radically different from solving it through step-by-step analysis or trial and error. This difference in subjective experience suggests that something different is going on in the brain when we solve a problem using insight instead of analytic strategies (Kounios & Beeman, 2009).

To examine brain activity associated with insight, researchers used a procedure called *compound remote associates* that is similar in some respects to the three-word problems displayed in Figure 9.15. Each compound remote associates problem consists of three words, such as *crab*, *pine*, and *sauce*. Sometimes people solve these problems with a flash of insight: The solution word (*apple!*) suddenly pops into their minds, seemingly out of nowhere. Other times, people solve the problem by using analytic strategies that involve trying out different alternatives generating a compound word for *crab* and then assessing whether they fit *pine* and *sauce*. *Crabgrass*, works, but grass does not work with *pine* and *sauce*. *Crabapple?* Problem solved.

Participants are instructed to press a button the moment a solution comes to mind, then describe whether they arrived at the solution via insight or through an analytic strategy. In an initial study, researchers used the electroencephalograph (EEG) (see the Neuroscience chapter) to measure brain electrical activity as participants attempted to solve the problems. What they observed was striking: Beginning about one-third of a second before participants came up with a solution, there was a sudden and dramatic burst of high-frequency electrical activity (40 cycles per second or gamma band) for problems solved via insight as compared with problems solved via analytic strategies (Jung-Beeman et al., 2004). This activity was centred over the front part of the right temporal lobe, slightly above the right ear. The researchers then performed a similar study using fMRI to measure brain activity, and found that this right temporal area was the only region in the entire brain that showed greater activity for insight solutions compared with solutions based on analytic strategies.

The great French scientist Louis Pasteur once stated: "Chance favors only the prepared mind." Inspired by this observation, researchers asked whether brain activity occurring just before presentation of a problem influenced whether that problem was solved via insight or analytic strategies

(Kounios et al., 2006). It did. In the moments before a problem was solved with an insight solution, there was increased activity deep in the frontal lobes, in a part of the brain known as the anterior cingulate, which controls cognitive processes such as the ability to switch attention from one thing to another. The researchers suggested that this increased activity in the anterior cingulate allowed participants to attend to and detect associations that were only weakly activated, perhaps at a subconscious level, and that facilitate sudden insight.

A related study with the compound remote associates task revealed that when people were in a positive mood, they solved more problems with insight than people who were in a less positive mood (Subramaniam et al., 2009). Moreover, as shown in the figure, positive mood was associated with heightened activity in the anterior cingulate during the moments before a problem was presented—suggesting that being in a positive mood helps to prepare the brain for sudden insight by "turning on" the anterior cingulate and thereby increasing one's ability to detect associations that aid problem solution. This link between positive mood and insight might help explain a striking recent finding: Moderate levels of alcohol intoxication resulted in enhanced performance on the

▲ Figure 9.19 **The Solution to the Candle Problem** What makes this problem difficult is that the usual function of the box (to hold matches) interferes with recognizing that it can be tacked to the wall to serve as a candleholder.

▲ Figure 9.20 **The Solution to the String Problem** The usual function of the hammer (to pound things) interferes with recognizing that it can also serve as a weighted pendulum to swing the string into the person's grasp.

remote associates task, and also produced a stronger feeling that problem solutions are the result of sudden insight (Jarosz, Colflesh, & Wiley, 2012). Alternatively, the beneficial effects of alcohol could be attributable to a reduction in controlled, focused processing, which frees up the ability to generate distant associations.

Brain activity prior to problem solving provides clues about which individuals are more likely to rely on insight over analytic strategies to solve compound remote associates (Kounios et al., 2008). Using EEG to measure resting brain activity, researchers found that insight problem solvers showed more resting activity in the right cerebral hemisphere than did analytic problem solvers, which is consistent with other research linking creativity with right-hemisphere activity (Folley & Park, 2005; Howard-Jones et al., 2005).

The results of these studies suggest that the familiar image of a light bulb going off in your head when you experience an "aha!" moment is on the mark: Those moments are indeed accompanied by something like an electrical power surge in the brain, and are preceded by specific types of electrical activity patterns. It seems likely that future research will tell us much more about how to turn on the mental light bulb and keep it burning bright.

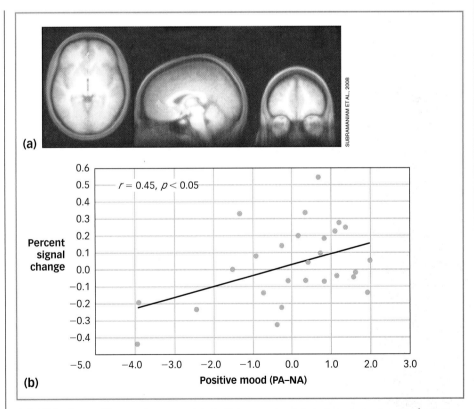

▲ (a) Being in a positive mood was associated with increased activity in the anterior cingulate (yellow area) in the moments before people solved a problem via sudden insight. (b) Positive mood (Positive Affect–Negative Affect) is associated with heightened activity in the anterior cingulate, suggesting an increase in one's ability to create associations needed for problem solving.

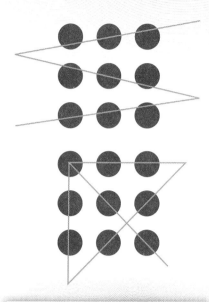

▲ Figure 9.21 **Two Solutions to the Nine-Dot Problem** Solving this problem requires "thinking outside the box," that is, going outside the imaginary box implied by the dot arrangement. The limiting box is not really there; it is imposed by the problem solver's perceptual set.

**IN SUMMARY**

▶ Like concept formation and decision making, problem solving is a process in which new inputs (in this case, problems) are interpreted in terms of old knowledge. Problems may be ill defined or well defined, leading to less or more obvious solutions.

▶ The solutions we generate depend as much on the organization of our knowledge as they do on the objective characteristics of the problems. Means—ends analysis and analogical problem solving offer pathways to effective solutions, although we often frame things in terms of what we already know and already understand.

▶ Sometimes, as in the case of functional fixedness, that knowledge can restrict our problem-solving processes, making it difficult to find solutions that should be easy to find.

# Transforming Information: How We Reach Conclusions

**Reasoning** is *a mental activity that consists of organizing information or beliefs into a series of steps in order to reach conclusions.* Not surprisingly, sometimes our reasoning seems sensible and straightforward, and other times it seems a little off. Consider some reasons offered by people who filed actual insurance accident claims (www.swapmeetdave.com):

> "I left for work this morning at 7:00 a.m. as usual when I collided straight into a bus. The bus was 5 minutes early."

> "Coming home, I drove into the wrong house and collided with a tree I don't have."

> "My car was legally parked as it backed into another vehicle."

> "The indirect cause of the accident was a little guy in a small car with a big mouth."

> "Windshield broke. Cause unknown. Probably voodoo."

When people like these hapless drivers argue with you in a way that seems inconsistent or poorly thought out, you may accuse them of being "illogical." Logic is a system of rules that specifies which conclusions follow from a set of statements. To put it another way, if you know that a given set of statements is true, logic will tell you which other statements *must* also be true. If the statement "Jack and Jill went up the hill" is true, then according to the rules of logic, the statement "Jill went up the hill" must also be true. To accept the truth of the first statement while denying the truth of the second statement would be a contradiction. Logic is a tool for evaluating reasoning, but it should not be confused with the process of reasoning itself. Equating logic and reasoning would be like equating carpenter's tools (logic) with building a house (reasoning).

## Practical, Theoretical, and Syllogistic Reasoning

Earlier in the chapter, we discussed decision making, which often depends on reasoning with probabilities. Practical reasoning and theoretical reasoning also allow us to make decisions (Walton, 1990). **Practical reasoning** is *figuring out what to do, or reasoning directed toward action.* Means—ends analysis is one kind of practical reasoning. An example is figuring out how to get to a concert across town if you do not have a car. In contrast, **theoretical reasoning** (also called *discursive reasoning*)

**reasoning**
A mental activity that consists of organizing information or beliefs into a series of steps in order to reach conclusions.

**practical reasoning**
Figuring out what to do, or reasoning directed toward action.

**theoretical reasoning (or discursive reasoning)** Reasoning directed toward arriving at a belief.

is *reasoning directed toward arriving at a belief.* We use theoretical reasoning when we try to determine which beliefs follow logically from other beliefs.

Suppose you asked your friend Bruce to take you to a concert, and he said that his car was not working. You would undoubtedly find another way to get to the concert. If you then spied him driving into the concert parking lot, you might reason: "Bruce told me his car was not working. He just drove into the parking lot. If his car was not working, he could not drive it here. So, either he suddenly fixed it, or he was lying to me. If he was lying to me, he's not much of a friend." Notice the absence of an action-oriented goal. Theoretical reasoning is just a series of inferences concluding in a belief—in this case, about your so-called friend's unfriendliness!

If you concluded from these examples that we are equally adept at both types of reasoning, experimental evidence suggests you are wrong. People generally find figuring out what to do easier than deciding which beliefs follow logically from other beliefs. In cross-cultural studies, this tendency to respond practically when theoretical reasoning is sought has been demonstrated in individuals without schooling. Consider, for example, this dialogue between a Nigerian rice farmer, a member of the preliterate Kpelle people, and an American researcher (Scribner, 1975, p. 155):

Experimenter: All Kpelle men are rice farmers. Mr. Smith (this is a Western name) is not a rice farmer. Is he a Kpelle man?

Farmer: I do not know the man in person. I have not laid eyes on the man himself.

Experimenter: Just think about the statement.

Farmer: If I know him in person, I can answer that question, but since I do not know him in person, I cannot answer that question.

Experimenter: Try and answer from your Kpelle sense.

Farmer: If you know a person, if a question comes up about him, you are able to answer. But if you do not know a person, if a question comes up about him, it is hard for you to answer it.

As this excerpt shows, the farmer does not seem to understand that the problem can be resolved with theoretical reasoning. Instead, he is concerned with retrieving and verifying facts, a strategy that does not work for this type of task.

A very different picture emerges when members of preliterate cultures are given tasks that require practical reasoning. One well-known study of rural Kenyans illustrates a typical result (Harkness, Edwards, & Super, 1981). The problem describes a dilemma in which a boy must decide whether to obey his father and give the family some of the money he has earned, even though his father previously promised that the boy could keep it all. After hearing the dilemma, the participants were asked what the boy should do. Here is a typical response from a villager:

A child has to give you what you ask for just in the same way as when he asks for anything you give it to him. Why then should he be selfish with what he has? A parent loves his child and maybe the son refused without knowing the need of helping his father. ... By showing respect to one another, friendship between us is assured, and as a result this will increase the prosperity of our family.

This preliterate individual had little difficulty understanding this practical problem.

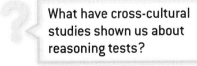
**What have cross-cultural studies shown us about reasoning tests?**

His response is intelligent, insightful, and well reasoned. A principal finding from this kind of cross-cultural research is that the appearance of competency on reasoning tests depends more on whether the task makes sense to participants than on their problem-solving ability.

Educated individuals in industrial societies are prone to similar failures in reasoning, as illustrated by **belief bias:** *People's judgments about whether to accept*

**belief bias**
People's judgments about whether to accept conclusions depend more on how believable the conclusions are than on whether the arguments are logically valid.

**syllogistic reasoning**
Determining whether a conclusion follows from two statements that are assumed to be true.

*conclusions depend more on how believable the conclusions are than on whether the arguments are logically valid* (Evans, Barston, & Pollard, 1983) (see also The Real World box). For example, **syllogistic reasoning** assesses *whether a conclusion follows from two statements that are assumed to be true*. Consider the two following syllogisms, evaluate the argument, and ask yourself whether or not the conclusions must be true if the statements are true:

### Syllogism 1

Statement 1: No cigarettes are inexpensive.

Statement 2: Some addictive things are inexpensive.

Conclusion: Some addictive things are not cigarettes.

## THE REAL WORLD

# From Zippers to Political Extremism: An Illusion of Understanding

Zippers are extremely helpful objects and we have all used them more times than we could possibly recall. Most of us also think that we have a pretty good understanding of how a zipper works—at least until we are asked to provide a step-by-step explanation. In experiments by Rozenblit and Keil (2002), participants initially rated the depth of their understanding of various everyday objects (e.g., zippers, flush toilets, sewing machines) or procedures (e.g., how to make chocolate cookies from scratch), tried to provide detailed, step-by-step explanations, viewed expert descriptions and diagrams, and then re-rated their depth of understanding. The second set of ratings was significantly lower than the first. Attempting to explain the workings of the objects and procedures, and then seeing the much more detailed expert description, led participants to realize that they had greatly overestimated the depth of their understanding, which Rozenblit and Keil referred to as *the illusion of explanatory depth*. Additional experiments revealed that the illusion of explanatory depth can occur as a consequence of attempting to generate detailed explanations even when expert descriptions are not subsequently provided.

Recent research suggests that the illusion of explanatory depth applies to a very different domain of everyday life: political extremism. Many pressing issues of our times, such as climate change and national security, share two features: They involve complex policies and tend to generate extreme views at either end of

the political spectrum. Fernbach and his colleagues (2013) asked whether polarized views occur because people think that they understand the relevant policies in greater depth than they actually do. To investigate this hypothesis, the researchers asked American participants to rate their positions regarding six contemporary American political policies (sanctions on Iran for its nuclear program, raising the retirement age for social security, single-payer health care system, cap-and-trade system for carbon emissions, national flat tax, and merit-based pay for teachers) on a 7-point scale ranging from *strongly against* to *strongly in favour*. Next, the participants rated their understanding of each of the six policies on the 7-point scale used previously by Rozenblit and Keil (2002). Participants were then asked to generate detailed explanations of two of the six policies, followed in each case by a second set of ratings concerning their positions and their level of understanding of all the policies.

Fernbach and his colleagues (2013) found that after attempting to generate detailed explanations, participants

provided lower ratings of understanding and less extreme positions concerning all six policies than they had previously. Furthermore, those participants who exhibited the largest decreases in their pre- versus post-explanation understanding ratings also exhibited the greatest moderation of their positions as a result of explaining them. Were these changes simply a result of thinking more deeply about the policies, or were they specifically attributable to generating explanations? To address this issue, the researchers conducted an additional experiment in which some participants provided explanations of policies, whereas others listed reasons why they held their positions. Once again, generating explanations led to lower understanding ratings and less extreme positions. However, no such changes were observed in participants who listed reasons why they held their views. A final experiment showed that after generating explanations, participants indicated that they would be less likely to make donations to relevant advocate groups, reflecting moderation of their positions.

The overall pattern of results supports the idea that extreme political views are enabled, at least in part, by an illusion of explanatory depth: Once people realize that they do not understand the relevant policy issues in as much depth as they had thought, their views moderate. There probably are not too many psychological phenomena that are well-illustrated by both political policies and the workings of zippers, but the illusion of explanatory depth is one of them.

## Syllogism 2

Statement 1: No addictive things are inexpensive.

Statement 2: Some cigarettes are inexpensive.

Conclusion: Some cigarettes are not addictive.

If you are like most people, you probably concluded that the reasoning is valid in Syllogism 1 but flawed in Syllogism 2. Indeed, researchers found that nearly 100 percent of participants accepted the first conclusion as valid, but fewer than half accepted the second (Evans, Barston, & Pollard, 1983). But notice that the syllogisms are in exactly the same form. This form of syllogism is valid, so both conclusions are valid. Evidently, the believability of the conclusions influences people's judgments.

## Reasoning and the Brain

Research using fMRI provides novel insights into belief biases on reasoning tasks. In *belief-laden* trials, participants were scanned while they reasoned about syllogisms that could be influenced by knowledge affecting the believability of the conclusions. In *belief-neutral* trials, syllogisms contained obscure terms whose meanings were unknown to participants, as in the following example:

## Syllogism 3

Statement 1: No codes are highly complex.

Statement 2: Some quipu are highly complex.

Conclusion: No quipu are codes.

Belief-neutral reasoning activated different brain regions than did belief-laden reasoning (as shown in **FIGURE 9.22**). Activity in a part of the left temporal lobe involved in retrieving and selecting facts from long-term memory increased during belief-laden reasoning. In contrast, that part of the brain showed little activity and parts of the parietal lobe involved in mathematical reasoning and spatial representation showed greater activity during belief-neutral reasoning (Goel & Dolan, 2003). This evidence suggests that participants took different approaches to the two types of reasoning tasks, relying on previously encoded memories in belief-laden reasoning and on more abstract thought processes in belief-neutral reasoning. These findings fit with other results from neuroimaging studies indicating that there is no single reasoning centre in the brain; different types of reasoning tasks call on distinct processes that are associated with different brain regions (Goel, 2007).

(a) Belief-neutral reasoning

(b) Belief-laden reasoning

COURTESY VINOD GOEL

Upper parietal lobe

Front left temporal lobe

◀ Figure 9.22 **Active Brain Regions in Reasoning** These images from an fMRI study show that different types of reasoning activate different brain regions. (*a*) Areas within the parietal lobe were especially active during logical reasoning that is not influenced by prior beliefs (belief-neutral reasoning), whereas (*b*) an area within the left temporal lobe showed enhanced activity during reasoning that was influenced by prior beliefs (belief-laden reasoning). This suggests that people approach each type of reasoning problem in a different way.

## IN SUMMARY

▶ The success of human reasoning depends on the content of the argument or scenario under consideration. People seem to excel at practical reasoning while stumbling when theoretical reasoning requires evaluation of the truth of a set of arguments.

▶ Belief bias describes a distortion of judgments about conclusions of arguments, causing people to focus on the believability of the conclusions rather than on the logical connections between the premises.

▶ Neuroimaging provides evidence that different brain regions are associated with different types of reasoning.

▶ We can see here and elsewhere in the chapter that some of the same strategies that earlier helped us to understand perception, memory, and learning—carefully examining errors and trying to integrate information about the brain into our psychological analyses—are equally helpful in understanding language and thought.

# Chapter Review

## KEY CONCEPT QUIZ

1. The combining of words to form phrases and sentences is governed by
   a. phonological rules.
   b. morphological rules.
   c. structural rules.
   d. syntactical rules.

2. Which of the following statements about language development is inaccurate?
   a. Language acquisition is largely a matter of children imitating adult speech.
   b. Deep structure refers to the meaning of a sentence, while surface structure refers to how it is constructed.
   c. By the time the average child begins school, a vocabulary of 10 000 words is not unusual.
   d. Children's passive mastery of language develops faster than their active mastery.

3. Language development as an innate, biological capacity is explained by
   a. fast mapping.
   b. behaviourism.
   c. nativist theory.
   d. interactionist explanations.

4. A collection of processes that facilitate language learning is referred to as
   a. phonological rules.
   b. dysphasia.
   c. a language acquisition device.
   d. grammatical generalizations.

5. Damage to the brain region called Broca's area results in
   a. failure to comprehend language.
   b. difficulty in producing grammatical speech.
   c. the reintroduction of infant babbling.
   d. difficulties in writing.

6. The linguistic relativity hypothesis maintains that
   a. language and thought are separate cognitive phenomena.
   b. words have different meanings to different cultures.
   c. human language is too complex for nonhuman animals to acquire.
   d. language shapes the nature of thought.

7. The "most typical" member of a category is a(n)
   a. prototype.
   b. exemplar.
   c. concept.
   d. definition.

8. Which theory of how we form concepts is based on our judgment of features that appear to be characteristic of category members but may not be possessed by every member?
   a. prototype theory
   b. family resemblance theory
   c. exemplar theory
   d. heuristic theory

9. The inability to recognize objects that belong to a particular category, although the ability to recognize objects outside the category is undisturbed is called
   a. category-preferential organization.
   b. cognitive–visual deficit.
   c. a category-specific deficit.
   d. aphasia.

**10.** Making use of which of the following would most likely lead to a solution to a problem?
   a. rational choice theory
   b. probability
   c. a heuristic
   d. an algorithm

**11.** People give different answers to the same problem depending on how the problem is phrased because of
   a. the availability bias.
   b. the conjunction fallacy.
   c. the representativeness heuristic.
   d. framing effects.

**12.** The view that people choose to take on risk when evaluating potential losses and avoid risks when evaluating potential gains describes
   a. expected utility.
   b. the frequency format hypothesis.
   c. prospect theory.
   d. the sunk-cost fallacy.

**13.** People with damage to the prefrontal cortex are prone to
   a. heightened anticipatory emotional reactions.
   b. risky decision making.
   c. galvanic skin response.
   d. extreme sensitivity to behavioural consequences.

**14.** Miranda decides on a goal, analyzes her current situation, lists the differences between her current situation and her goal, then settles on strategies to reduce those differences. Miranda is engaging in
   a. means–ends analysis.
   b. analogical problem solving.
   c. capitalizing on insight.
   d. functional fixedness.

**15.** What kind of reasoning is aimed at deciding on a course of action?
   a. theoretical
   b. belief
   c. syllogistic
   d. practical

## KEY TERMS

algorithm (p. 375)

analogical problem solving (p. 383)

aphasia (p. 362)

availability bias (p. 375)

belief bias (p. 390)

category-specific deficit (p. 372)

concept (p. 369)

conjunction fallacy (p. 376)

deep structure (p. 354)

exemplar theory (p. 371)

family resemblance theory (p. 370)

fast mapping (p. 357)

framing effects (p. 377)

frequency format hypothesis (p. 379)

functional fixedness (p. 384)

genetic dysphasia (p. 360)

grammar (p. 352)

heuristic (p. 375)

language (p. 352)

language acquisition device (LAD) (p. 360)

linguistic relativity hypothesis (p. 367)

means–ends analysis (p. 383)

morphemes (p. 353)

morphological rules (p. 353)

nativist theory (p. 360)

phoneme (p. 353)

phonological rules (p. 353)

practical reasoning (p. 388)

prospect theory (p. 378)

prototype (p. 370)

rational choice theory (p. 374)

reasoning (p. 388)

representativeness heuristic (p. 377)

sunk-cost fallacy (p. 377)

surface structure (p. 354)

syllogistic reasoning (p. 390)

syntactical rules (p. 354)

telegraphic speech (p. 357)

theoretical reasoning (or discursive reasoning) (p. 388)

## CHANGING MINDS

**1.** You mention to a friend that you have just learned that the primary language we learn can shape the way that we think. Your friend says that people are people everywhere, and that this cannot be true. What evidence could you describe to support your point?

**2.** In September, 2011, *Wired* magazine ran an article discussing the fourth-down decisions of National Football League coaches. On fourth down, a coach can choose to play aggressively and go for a first down (or even a touchdown), or the coach can settle for a punt or a field goal, which are safer options but result in fewer points than a touchdown. Statistically, the riskier play results in greater point gain, on average, than playing it safe. But in reality, coaches choose the safer plays over 90 percent of the time. Reading this article, one of your friends is incredulous. "Coaches aren't stupid, and they want to win," he says. "Why would they always make the wrong decision?" Your friend is assuming that humans are rational decision makers. In what ways is your friend wrong? What might be causing the irrational decision making by football coaches?

## ANSWERS TO KEY CONCEPT QUIZ

1. d; 2. a; 3. c; 4. c; 5. b; 6. d; 7. a; 8. b; 9. c; 10. d; 11. d; 12. c; 13. b; 14. a; 15. d.

Need more help? Additional resources are located in Launchpad at:
*www.worthpublishers.com/launchpad/schacter3ecanadian*

# Intelligence

▲ **How Can Intelligence Be Measured?**
The Intelligence Quotient
The Intelligence Test
**THE REAL WORLD** Look Smart

▲ **What Is Intelligence?**
A Hierarchy of Abilities
The Middle-Level Abilities

▲ **Where Does Intelligence Come From?**
Genetic Influences on Intelligence
Environmental Influences on Intelligence
**HOT SCIENCE** Dumb and Dumber?
Genes and Environments

▲ **Who Is Most Intelligent?**
Individual Differences in Intelligence
Group Differences in Intelligence
Improving Intelligence
**OTHER VOICES** How Science Can Build a Better You

WHEN ANNE MCGARRAH DIED AT THE age of 57, she had lived more years than she could count. That is because Anne could not count at all. Like most people with Williams syndrome, she could not add 3 and 7, could not make change for a dollar, and could not distinguish right from left. Her disability was so severe that she was unable to care for herself or hold a full-time job. So what did she do with her time?

I love to read. Biographies, fiction, novels, different articles in newspapers, articles in magazines, just about anything. I just read a book about a young girl— she was born in Scotland—and her family who lived on a farm. … I love listening to music. I like a little bit of Beethoven, but I specifically like Mozart and Chopin and Bach. I like the way they develop their music—it is very light, it is very airy, and it is very cheerful music. I find Beethoven depressing. (Finn, 1991, p. 54)

Although people with Williams syndrome are often unable to tie their own shoes or make their own beds, they typically have gifts for music and language. Williams syndrome is caused by the absence of 20 genes on chromosome 7. No one knows why this tiny genetic glitch so profoundly impairs people's general cognitive abilities, yet leaves them with a few special talents.

People with Williams syndrome have a distinct "elfin" facial appearance and diminished cognitive abilities, but they often have unusual gifts for music and language.

**intelligence**
The ability to direct one's thinking, adapt to one's circumstances, and learn from one's experiences.

WAS ANNE MCGARRAH INTELLIGENT? IT SEEMS ODD TO SAY that someone is intelligent when she cannot do simple addition. But it seems equally odd to say that someone is unintelligent when she can articulate the difference between baroque counterpoint and nineteenth-century romanticism. In a world of Albert Einsteins and Homer Simpsons, we would have no trouble distinguishing the geniuses from the dullards. But ours is a world of people like Anne McGarrah and people like us: people who are sometimes brilliant, often bright, usually competent, and occasionally dimmer than broccoli. So, what exactly *is* intelligence? About 20 years ago, 52 scientific experts came together to answer this very question, and they concluded that **intelligence** is *the ability to direct one's thinking, adapt to one's circumstances, and learn from one's experiences* (Gottfredson, 1997). As you will see, that definition captures much of what scientists and laypeople mean when they use that term.

For more than a century, psychologists have been asking four questions about intelligence: *How* can it be measured? *What* exactly is it? *Where* does it come from? *Who* has it and who does not? As you will see, intelligence is a set of abilities that can be measured quite accurately, it is the product of both genes and experience, and it is something that some people and some groups have more of than others.

## How Can Intelligence Be Measured?

In the 1920s, psychologist Henry Goddard administered intelligence tests to Europeans arriving at Ellis Island, the main immigration gateway to the United States, and concluded that the overwhelming majority of Jews, Hungarians, Italians, and Russians were "feebleminded." Goddard also used his tests to identify feebleminded American families (who, he claimed, were largely responsible for the nation's social problems) and suggested that the government should segregate them in isolated colonies and "take away from these people the power of procreation" (Goddard, 1913, p. 107). The United States subsequently passed laws restricting the immigration of people from Southern and Eastern Europe, and 27 states passed laws requiring the sterilization of "mental defectives." Although Canada did not exclude immigrants to the same degree as the United States, sterilization laws were also passed in British Columbia and Alberta in the 1920s. In Alberta, an amendment in 1937 allowed for the sterilization of "mental defectives" without their consent, and this law stayed on the books until 1972. Over 2800 procedures were performed in total, including 50 in the last year of the law.

From Goddard's day to our own, intelligence tests have been used to rationalize prejudice and discrimination against people of different races, religions, and nationalities. Although intelligence testing has achieved many notable successes, its history is marred by more than its share of fraud and disgrace (Chorover, 1980; Lewontin, Rose, & Kamin, 1984). The fact that intelligence tests have occasionally been used to further detestable ends is especially ironic because, as you are about to see, such tests were originally developed for the most noble of purposes: to help underprivileged children succeed in school.

When immigrants arrived in the United States by boat in the 1920s, they were given intelligence tests, which supposedly revealed whether they were "feebleminded."

©BETTMANN/CORBIS

# The Intelligence Quotient

At the end of the nineteenth century, France instituted a sweeping set of education reforms that made a primary school education available to children of every social

**Why were intelligence tests originally developed?**

class, and suddenly French classrooms were filled with a diverse mix of children who differed dramatically in their readiness to learn. The French government called on Alfred Binet and Theodore Simon to create a test that would allow educators to develop remedial programs for those children who lagged behind their peers (Siegler, 1992). "Before these children could be educated," Binet (1909) wrote, "they had to be selected. How could this be done?"

Binet and Simon worried that if teachers were allowed to do the selecting, then the remedial classrooms would be filled with poor children, and that if parents were allowed to do the selecting, then the remedial classrooms would be empty. So they set out to develop an objective test that would provide an unbiased measure of a child's ability. They began, sensibly enough, by looking for tasks that the best students in a class could perform and that the worst students could not—in other words, tasks that could distinguish the best and worst students and thus predict a future child's success in school. The tasks they tried included solving logic problems, remembering words, copying pictures, distinguishing edible and inedible foods, making rhymes, and answering questions such as, "When anyone has offended you and asks you to excuse him, what ought you to do?" Binet and Simon settled on 30 of these tasks and assembled them into a test that they claimed could measure a child's "natural intelligence." What did they mean by that phrase?

Alfred Binet (1857–1911) (*left*) and Theodore Simon (1872–1961) (*right*) developed the first intelligence test to identify children who needed remedial education.

> We here separate natural intelligence and instruction … by disregarding, insofar as possible, the degree of instruction which the subject possesses. … We give him nothing to read, nothing to write, and submit him to no test in which he might succeed by means of rote learning. In fact, we do not even notice his inability to read if a case occurs. It is simply the level of his natural intelligence that is taken into account. (Binet, 1909)

Binet and Simon designed their test to measure a child's *aptitude* for learning independent of the child's prior educational *achievement,* and it was in this sense that they called theirs a test of natural intelligence. They suggested that teachers could use their test to estimate a particular child's "mental level" simply by computing the average test score of many children in different age groups and then finding the age group whose average test score was most like that of the particular child's. For example, a child who was 10 years old but whose score was about the same as the score of the average 8-year-old was considered to have the mental level of an 8-year-old and thus to need remedial education.

German psychologist William Stern (1914) suggested that this mental level could be

**How do the two kinds of intelligence quotients differ?**

thought of as a child's *mental age* and that the best way to determine whether a child was developing normally was to examine the ratio of the child's mental age to the child's physical age. American psychologist Lewis Terman (1916) formalized this

**ratio IQ**
A statistic obtained by dividing a person's mental age by the person's physical age and then multiplying the quotient by 100 (see *deviation IQ*).

**deviation IQ**
A statistic obtained by dividing a person's test score by the average test score of people in the same age group and then multiplying the quotient by 100 (see *ratio IQ*).

In 2012, 4-year old Heidi Hankins became one of the youngest people ever admitted to Mensa, an organization for people with unusually high IQs. Heidi's IQ is 159—about the same as Albert Einstein's.

comparison by developing a statistic called *the intelligence quotient* or *IQ score*. There are two ways to compute an IQ score, each of which has a unique problem.

> **Ratio IQ** *is a statistic obtained by dividing a person's mental age by the person's physical age and then multiplying the quotient by 100.* According to this formula, a 10-year-old child whose test score was about the same as the average 10-year-old child's test score would have a ratio IQ of 100 because $(10/10) \times 100 = 100$. But a 10-year-old child whose test score was about the same as the average 8-year-old child's test score would have a ratio IQ of 80 because $(8/10) \times 100 = 80$. So what is the problem? Well, a 7-year-old who performs like the average 14-year-old has a ratio IQ of 200, and that high score seems reasonable because a 7-year-old who can do algebra is obviously pretty smart. But a 20-year-old who performs like the average 40-year-old will also have a ratio IQ of 200, and that does not seem very reasonable at all.

> **Deviation IQ** is a *statistic obtained by dividing a person's test score by the average test score of people in the same age group and then multiplying the quotient by 100.* According to this formula, a person who scored the same as the average person his or her age would have a deviation IQ of 100. The deviation IQ overcomes the problem with the ratio IQ inasmuch as a 20-year-old who scores like the average 40-year-old is not mistakenly labelled a genius. Alas, the deviation IQ has a different problem: It does not allow us to compare people of different ages. A 5-year-old and a 65-year-old might both have a deviation IQ of 100 because they both scored the same as their average peer, but that does not mean that the 5-year-old and 65-year-old are equally intelligent. Which one is smarter? We cannot tell by comparing deviation IQs.

Each of the methods for computing IQ has a problem—but luckily, each has a different problem so they can be used in combination. Psychologists typically compute ratio IQ when testing children and compute deviation IQ when testing adults.

## The Intelligence Test

Most modern intelligence tests have their roots in the test developed more than a century ago by Binet and Simon. For instance, the *Stanford–Binet Intelligence Scale* is based on Binet and Simon's original test and was initially updated by Lewis Terman and his colleagues at Stanford University. Probably the most widely used modern intelligence test is the *Wechsler Adult Intelligence Scale* (WAIS), named after its originator, psychologist David Wechsler. Like Binet and Simon's original test, it measures intelligence by asking respondents to answer questions and solve problems. Respondents are required to see similarities and differences between ideas and objects, to draw inferences from evidence, to work out and apply rules, to remember and manipulate material, to construct shapes, to articulate the meaning of words, to recall general knowledge, to explain practical actions in everyday life, to use numbers, to attend to details, and so forth. In the spirit of Binet and Simon's early test, none of the tests require writing words. Some sample problems from the WAIS are shown in **TABLE 10.1** (on the next page).

These sample problems may look to you like fun and games (perhaps minus the fun part), but decades of research show that a person's performance on tests like the WAIS predict a wide variety of important life outcomes (Deary, Batty, & Gale, 2008; Deary, Batty, Pattie, & Gale, 2008; Der, Batty, & Deary, 2009; Gottfredson & Deary, 2004; Leon et al., 2009; Richards et al., 2009; Rushton & Templer, 2009; Whalley & Deary, 2001). For example, intelligence test scores are excellent predictors of income. One study compared siblings who had significantly different IQs and found that the less intelligent sibling earned roughly half of what the more intelligent sibling earned over the course of their lifetimes (Murray, 2002) (see **FIGURE 10.1** on the next page).

> Table 10.1

### The Tests and Core Subtests of the Wechsler Adult Intelligence Scale IV (WAIS-IV)

| Test | Core Subtest | Questions and Tasks |
|---|---|---|
| Verbal Comprehension Test | Vocabulary | The test taker is asked to tell the examiner what certain words mean. For example: *chair* (easy), *hesitant* (medium), and *presumptuous* (hard). |
| | Similarities | The test taker is asked what 19 pairs of words have in common. For example: In what way are an apple and a pear alike? In what way are a painting and a symphony alike? |
| | Information | The test taker is asked several general knowledge questions. These cover people, places, and events. For example: How many days are in a week? What is the capital of France? Name three oceans. Who wrote *The Inferno*? |
| Perceptual Reasoning Test | Block Design | The test taker is shown 2-D patterns made up of red and white squares and triangles and is asked to reproduce these patterns using cubes with red and white faces. |
| | Matrix Reasoning | The test taker is asked to add a missing element to a pattern so that it progresses logically. For example: Which of the four symbols at the bottom goes in the empty cell of the table? |
| | Visual Puzzles | The test taker is asked to complete visual puzzles like this one: "Which three of these pictures go together to make this puzzle?" |
| Working Memory Test | Digit Span | The test taker is asked to repeat a sequence of numbers. Sequences run from two to nine numbers in length. In the second part of this test, the sequences must be repeated in reversed order. An easy example is to repeat 3-7-4. A harder one is 3-9-1-7-4-5-3-9. |
| | Arithmetic | The test taker is asked to solve arithmetic problems, progressing from easy to difficult ones. |
| Processing Speed Test | Symbol Search | The test taker is asked to indicate whether one of a pair of abstract symbols is contained in a list of abstract symbols. There are many of these lists, and the test taker does as many as he or she can in 2 min. |
| | Coding | The test taker is asked to write down the number that corresponds to a code for a given symbol (e.g., a cross, a circle, and an upside-down T) and does as many as he or she can in 90 s. |

▼ Figure 10.1 **Income and Intelligence among Siblings** This graph shows the average annual salary of a person who has an IQ of 90 to 109 (shown in pink) and of his or her siblings who have higher or lower IQs (shown in blue).

One reason for this is that intelligent people have a variety of traits that promote economic success. For example, they are more patient, they are better at calculating risk, and they are better at predicting how other people will act and how they should respond (Burks et al., 2009). But the main reason why intelligent people earn much more money than their less intelligent counterparts (or siblings!) is that they get more education (Deary et al., 2005; Nyborg & Jensen, 2001). In fact, a person's IQ is a better predictor of the amount of education he or

**What important life outcomes do intelligence test scores predict?**

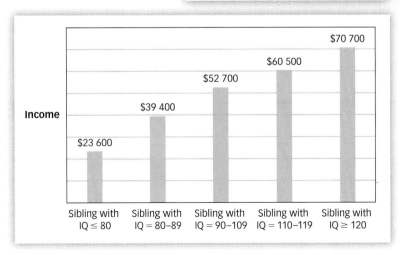

she will receive than is the person's social class (Deary, 2012; Deary et al., 2005). Intelligent people spend more time in school and perform better when they are there: The correlation between IQ and academic performance is roughly $r = 0.50$ across a wide range of people and situations. This continues after school ends. Intelligent people perform so much better at their jobs (Hunter & Hunter, 1984) that one pair of researchers concluded that "for hiring employees without previous experience in the job, the most valid measure of future performance and learning is general mental ability" (Schmidt & Hunter, 1998, p. 262) (see The Real World box).

Intelligent people are not just wealthier, they are healthier as well. Researchers who have followed millions of people over decades have found a strong correlation between intelligence and both health and longevity. Intelligent people are less likely to smoke, and are more likely to exercise and eat well (Batty et al., 2007; Weiser et al., 2010). Not surprisingly, they also live longer. In fact, every 15 point increase in a young person's IQ is associated with a 24 percent decrease in his or her ultimate risk of death from a wide variety of causes, including cardiovascular disease, suicide, homicide, and accidents (Calvin et al., 2010). Health and wealth are related, of course, and some data suggest that intelligence promotes longevity by allowing people to succeed in school, which allows them to get better jobs, which allows them to earn more money, which allows them to avoid illnesses such as cardiovascular disease (Deary, Weiss, & Batty, 2011). However it happens, the bottom line is clear: Intelligence matters. In case you are now seriously considering ways to change your IQ (see the Other Voices feature at the end of this chapter), remember that intelligence is only one of many factors that predict important life outcomes. For example, you learned in the Emotion

**THE REAL WORLD**

# Look Smart

Your interview is in 30 minutes. You have checked your hair twice, eaten your weight in breath mints, combed your résumé for typos, and rehearsed your answers to all the standard questions. Now you have to dazzle them with your intelligence whether you have got it or not. Because intelligence is one of the most valued of all human traits, we are often in the business of trying to make others think we are smart regardless of whether that is true. So we make clever jokes and drop the names of some of the longer books we have read in the hope that prospective employers, prospective dates, prospective customers, and prospective in-laws will be appropriately impressed.

But are we doing the right things, and if so, are we getting the credit we deserve? Research shows that ordinary people are, in fact, reasonably good judges of other people's intelligence (Borkenau & Liebler, 1995). For example, observers can look at a pair of photographs and reliably determine which of the two people in them is smarter (Zebrowitz et al., 2002). When observers watch 1-minute videotapes of different people engaged in social interactions, they can accurately estimate which

person has the highest IQ—even if they see the videos without sound (Murphy, Hall, & Colvin, 2003).

People base their judgments of intelligence on a wide range of cues, from physical features (being tall and attractive) to dress (being well groomed and wearing glasses) to behaviour (walking and talking quickly). And yet, none of these cues

AP PHOTO/TIM JOHNSON

is actually a reliable indicator of a person's intelligence. The reason why people are such good judges of intelligence is that in addition to all these useless cues, they also take into account one very useful cue: eye gaze. As it turns out, intelligent people hold the gaze of their conversation partners both when they are speaking and when they are listening, and observers know this, which is what enables them to estimate a person's intelligence accurately, despite their mythical beliefs about the informational value of spectacles and neckties (Murphy et al., 2003). All of this is especially true when the observers are women (who tend to be better judges of intelligence) and the people being observed are men (whose intelligence tends to be easier to judge).

The bottom line? Breath mints are fine and a little gel on the cowlick certainly cannot hurt, but when you get to the interview, do not forget to stare.

◀ Wahad Mehood is interviewing for a job as a petroleum engineer with EPC Global. Studies show that when a job candidate holds an interviewer's gaze, the interviewer is more likely to consider the candidate to be intelligent. And the interviewer is right!

and Motivation chapter that the ability to delay gratification is a powerful predictor of academic, health, and financial outcomes (Mischel et al., 2004; Duckworth & Seligman, 2005). Recent research suggests that psychological well-being (happiness) is another very important predictor (De Neve & Oswald, 2012).

## IN SUMMARY

▶ Intelligence is a mental ability that enables people to direct their thinking, adapt to their circumstances, and learn from their experiences.

▶ Intelligence tests produce a score known as an intelligence quotient or IQ. Ratio IQ is the ratio of a person's mental to physical age and deviation IQ is the deviation of a person's test score from the average score of his or her peers.

▶ Intelligence test scores predict a variety of important life outcomes, such as scholastic performance, job performance, health, and wealth. Other important predictors include psychological well-being and the ability to delay gratification.

# What Is Intelligence?

Hayley Wickenheiser is generally considered the finest female hockey player in the world. Originally from Shaunavon, Saskatchewan, she was a member of the Canadian women's national ice hockey team in the Winter Olympics in 1998, 2002, 2006, 2010, and 2014, winning one silver and four gold medals. Wickenheiser is the all-time leading scorer in the women's tournament at the Olympics, and was twice voted tournament Most Valuable Player (2002 and 2006). She is also one of the first two women to be featured as a playable character in a professional sports league video game: the EA sports game "NHL 13." But Hayley's athletic prowess does not end at hockey—she plays softball too. In 1994, when she was 16, she was named All-Canadian Shortstop and Top Batter at the Canadian Midget Nationals, and represented Canada at the 2000 Summer Olympic games in Sydney, Australia where she had the team's highest batting average.

Hockey and softball are very different sports, rely on different sets of skills, and Hayley herself would probably say that, if she were to choose, she is better at hockey. However, Hayley Wickenheiser's brilliance on the hockey rink and on the softball field suggests that, to some extent, these different sports might draw on a common factor of *athleticism*. But how can we measure athleticism directly? If we measure it using hockey, Hayley comes out on top. If we measure it using softball, she is fantastic, but probably not the best. The science of intelligence has grappled with a similar issue for more than a hundred years. As we have seen, intelligence scores predict important outcomes from academic success to longevity. But like athleticism, it is hard to measure directly; it can only be indirectly assessed through various tests.

## A Hierarchy of Abilities

Charles Spearman was a student of Wilhelm Wundt (who founded the first experimental psychology laboratory), and he set out to address this very issue. Spearman invented a technique known as **factor analysis,** which is *a statistical technique that explains a large number of correlations in terms of a small number of underlying factors.* (We will get into a bit more detail about this in the next section.) Although Spearman's technique was complex, his reasoning was simple: If there really is a single, general ability called *intelligence* that enables people to perform a variety of intelligent

Intelligence is highly correlated with income. Ken Jennings has won more money on television game shows than any other human being—over three million dollars. He was defeated just twice on *Jeopardy:* in 2004 by Nancy Zerg, and in 2011 by an IBM computer named Watson. (In response to being beaten by a machine Jennings graciously said, "I for one welcome our new computer overlords.")

Hayley Wickenheiser is an extraordinary hockey player and a very good softball player. So is she or is she not a great athlete?

**factor analysis**
A statistical technique that explains a large number of correlations in terms of a small number of underlying factors.

**two-factor theory of intelligence**
A theory that suggests that every task requires a combination of a general ability (g) and skills that are specific to the task (s).

Dr. Jennifer Richeson received a so-called genius award from the MacArthur Foundation for her research in social psychology. Spearman's notion of general ability suggests that because she is *really* good at science, then she is probably at least *pretty* good at many other things, such as dancing. And in fact, she is!

behaviours, then those who have this ability should do well at just about everything and those who lack it should do well at just about nothing. In other words, if intelligence is a single, general ability, then there should be a very strong, positive correlation between people's performances on all kinds of tests.

To find out if there was, Spearman (1904) measured how well school-age children could discriminate small differences in colour, auditory pitch, and weight. He then correlated these scores with the children's grades in different academic subjects as well as with their teachers' estimates of their intellectual ability. His research revealed two things. First, it revealed that most of these measures were indeed positively correlated: Children who scored high on one measure (e.g., distinguishing the musical note C-sharp from D) tended to score high on the other measures (e.g., solving algebraic equations). Some psychologists have called this finding "the most replicated result in all of psychology" (Deary, 2000, p. 6), and in fact, even *mice* show a strong positive correlation between performances on different kinds of cognitive tests (Matzel et al., 2003). Second, Spearman's research revealed that although different measures were positively correlated, they were not perfectly correlated: The child who had the very highest score on one measure did not necessarily have the very highest score on *every* measure. Spearman combined these two facts into a **two-factor theory of intelligence,** which suggested that *every task requires a combination of a general ability (g) and skills that are specific to the task (s).*

As sensible as Spearman's conclusions were, not everyone agreed with them. Louis Thurstone (1938) noticed that, although scores on most tests were indeed positively correlated, scores on one kind of verbal test were more highly correlated with scores on another kind of verbal test than they were with scores on perceptual tests. Thurstone took this "clustering of correlations" to mean that there was actually no such thing as *g* and that there were, instead, a few stable and independent mental abilities such as perceptual ability, verbal ability, and numerical ability, which he called the *primary mental abilities.* These primary mental abilities were neither general like *g* (e.g., a person might have strong verbal abilities and weak numerical abilities), nor specific like *s* (e.g., a person who had strong verbal abilities tended both to speak and read well). In essence, Thurstone argued that just as we have games called *hockey* and *softball* but no game called *athletics*, so we have abilities such as verbal ability and perceptual ability but no general ability called intelligence. **TABLE 10.2** shows the primary mental abilities that Thurstone identified.

The debate among Spearman, Thurstone, and other mathematical giants was quite technical, and it raged for half a century as psychologists debated the existence of *g*. But in the 1980s, a new mathematical technique called *confirmatory factor analysis* brought the debate to a quiet close by revealing that Spearman and Thurstone had

> **Table 10.2**

**Thurstone's Primary Mental Abilities**

| Primary Mental Ability | Description |
| --- | --- |
| Word Fluency | Ability to solve anagrams and to find rhymes, etc. |
| Verbal Comprehension | Ability to understand words and sentences |
| Numerical Ability | Ability to make mental and other numerical computations |
| Spatial Visualization | Ability to visualize a complex shape in various orientations |
| Associative Memory | Ability to recall verbal material, learn pairs of unrelated words, etc. |
| Perceptual Speed | Ability to detect visual details quickly |
| Reasoning | Ability to induce a general rule from a few instances |

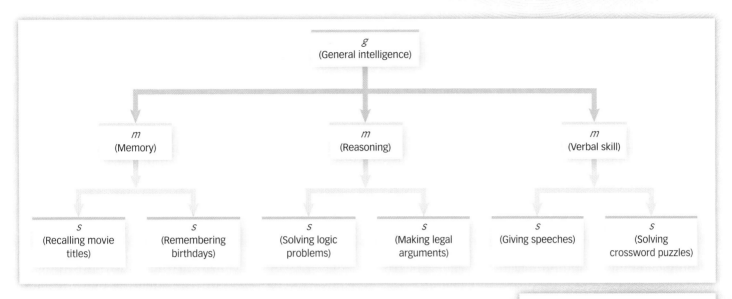

▲ Figure **10.2** **A Three-Level Hierarchy**
Most intelligence test data are best described by a three-level hierarchy with general intelligence (g) at the top, specific abilities (s) at the bottom, and a small number of middle-level abilities (m) (sometimes called group factors) in the middle.

each been right in his own way. Specifically, this new technique showed that the correlations between scores on different mental ability tests are best described by a three-level hierarchy (see **FIGURE 10.2**) with a *general factor* (like Spearman's g) at the top, *specific factors* (like Spearman's s) at the bottom, and a set of factors called *group factors* (like Thurstone's *primary mental abilities*) in the middle (Gustafsson, 1984). A re-analysis of massive amounts of data collected over 60 years from more than 130 000 healthy adults, schoolchildren, infants, college students, people with learning disabilities, and people with mental and physical illnesses has shown that almost every study done over the past half-century results in a three-level hierarchy of this kind (Carroll, 1993). This hierarchy suggests that people have a very general ability called intelligence, which is made up of a small set of middle-level abilities, which are made up of a large set of specific abilities that are unique to particular tasks. Although this resolution to a hundred years of disagreement is not particularly exciting, it appears to have the compensatory benefit of being true.

> How was the debate between Spearman and Thurstone resolved?

## The Middle-Level Abilities

Hayley Wickenheiser is perhaps a better hockey than softball player, but she plays both sports much better than most people can. Her specific abilities allow her to be more successful at one sport than another, but her general ability allows her to outperform 99.9 percent of the world's population on both the rink and the field. It is easy to see that Haley has both specific abilities (scoring) and a general ability (athleticism), but it is not so easy to say precisely what her middle-level abilities are. Should we draw a distinction between speed and power, between guile and patience, or between the ability to work with a team or perform as an individual? Should we describe her athleticism as a function of 3 middle-level abilities or 4? or 6? or 92?

Similar questions arise when we consider intelligence. Most psychologists agree that there are very specific mental abilities as well as a very general mental ability and that one of the important challenges is to describe the middle-level abilities that lie between them. Some psychologists have taken a *data-based approach* to this problem by starting with people's responses on intelligence tests and then looking to see what kinds of independent clusters these responses form. Other psychologists have taken a *theory-based approach* to this problem by starting with a broad survey of human

**fluid intelligence**
The ability to see abstract relationships and draw logical inferences.

**crystallized intelligence**
The ability to retain and use knowledge that was acquired through experience.

abilities and then looking to see which of these abilities intelligence tests measure—or fail to measure. These approaches have led to rather different suggestions about the best way to describe the middle-level abilities that constitute intelligence.

### The Data-Based Approach

One way to determine the nature of the middle-level abilities is to start with the data and go where they lead us. Just as Spearman and Thurstone did, we could compute the correlations among the performances of a large number of people on a large number of tests and then see how those correlations cluster. For example, imagine that we tested how quickly and well a large group of people could (a) balance teacups, (b) understand Shakespeare, (c) swat flies, and (d) sum the whole numbers between 1 and 1000. Now imagine that we computed the correlation among scores on each of these tests and observed a pattern of correlations like the one shown in **FIGURE 10.3a**. What would this pattern tell us?

This pattern suggests that a person who can swat flies well can also balance teacups well and that a person who can understand Shakespeare well can also sum numbers well, but that a person who can swat flies well and balance teacups well may or may not be able to sum numbers or understand Shakespeare well. From this pattern, we could conclude that there are two middle-level abilities (shown in **FIGURE 10.3b**), which we might call *physical coordination* (the ability that allows people to swat flies and balance teacups) and *academic skill* (the ability that allows people to understand Shakespeare and sum numbers). This pattern suggests that different specific abilities such as fly swatting and teacup balancing are made possible by a single middle-level ability called physical coordination, and that this middle-level ability is unrelated to the other middle-level ability, academic skill, which enables people to sum numbers and understand Shakespeare. As this example reveals, simply by examining the pattern of correlations between different tests, we can divine the nature and number of the middle-level abilities.

In the real world, of course, there are more than four tests. So what kinds of patterns do we observe when we calculate the correlations among the tests of mental ability that psychologists actually use? This is precisely what psychologist John Carroll (1993) set out to discover in his landmark analysis of intelligence test scores from

> How do patterns of correlation reveal the middle-level abilities?

▼ Figure **10.3** **Patterns of Correlation Can Reveal Middle-Level Abilities**. The pattern of correlations shown in (*a*) suggests that these four specific abilities can be thought of as instances of the two middle-level abilities, as shown in (*b*) physical coordination and academic skill.

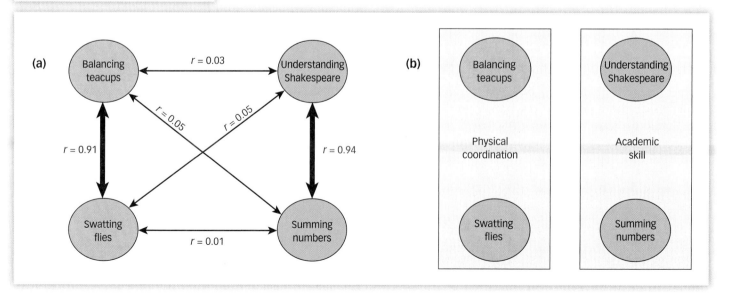

nearly 500 studies conducted over a half century. Carroll found that the pattern of correlations among these tests suggested the existence of eight independent middle-level abilities: *memory and learning, visual perception, auditory perception, retrieval ability, cognitive speediness, processing speed, crystallized intelligence,* and *fluid intelligence.*

Although most of the abilities on this list are self-explanatory, the last two are not. **Fluid intelligence** is *the ability to see abstract relationships and draw logical inferences;* **crystallized intelligence** is *the ability to retain and use knowledge that was acquired through experience* (Horn & Cattell, 1966). If we think of the brain as an information-processing device, then crystallized intelligence refers to the "information" part and fluid intelligence refers to the "processing" part (Salthouse, 2000). Whereas crystallized intelligence is generally assessed by tests of vocabulary, factual information, and so on, fluid intelligence is generally assessed by tests that pose novel, abstract problems that must be solved under time pressure, such as Raven's Progressive Matrices Test (shown in **FIGURE 10.4**). The distinction between these two kinds of intelligence is not just conceptual; it is neural. Tests of fluid intelligence and crystallized intelligence seem to activate different regions of the brain, which may explain why impairment of one kind of intelligence does not necessitate impairment of the other. For example, autism and Alzheimer's dementia both impair crystallized intelligence, but leave fluid intelligence virtually intact, whereas damage to the prefrontal cortex (whether through accident, normal aging, or other form of dementia) does the opposite (Blair, 2006).

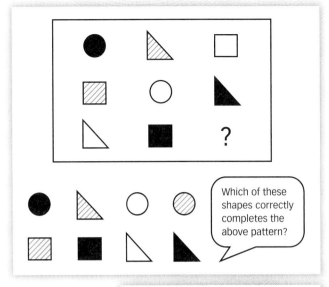

Which of these shapes correctly completes the above pattern?

▲ Figure **10.4 Raven's Progressive Matrices Test** This item from Raven's Progressive Matrices Test measures nonverbal reasoning abilities and is unlikely to be culturally biased.

## The Theory-Based Approach

The data-based approach attempts to discover the middle-level abilities by analyzing people's responses to questions on intelligence tests. The good thing about this approach is that its conclusions are based on hard evidence. But the bad thing about

> **What are the advantages of a theory-based approach to intelligence?**

this approach is that it is incapable of discovering any middle-level ability that the intelligence tests it uses did not already measure (Stanovich, 2009). For example, no intelligence test asks people to find three new uses for an origami fish or to answer the question, "What is the question you thought you would be asked but were not?" As a result, the scores from these tests may be incapable of revealing the middle-level abilities such as imagination or creativity. Are there middle-level abilities to which the data-based approach is blind?

Psychologist Robert Sternberg (1999) has argued that, in fact, there are three kinds of intelligence, only one of which is measured by standard intelligence tests. *Analytic intelligence* is the ability to identify and define problems and to find strategies for solving them; *practical intelligence* is the ability to apply and implement these solutions in everyday settings; and *creative intelligence* is the ability to generate solutions that other people do not. According to Sternberg, standard intelligence tests typically confront people with clearly defined problems that have one right answer and then supply all the information needed to solve them. These kinds of problems measure analytic intelligence. But everyday life confronts people with situations in which they must formulate the *problem,* find the information needed to solve it, and then choose among multiple acceptable solutions. These situations require practical and creative intelligence. Some studies suggest that these different kinds of intelligence are independent. For example, workers at milk-processing plants develop complex strategies for efficiently combining partially filled cases of milk, and not only do they outperform highly educated white-collar workers, but their performance is also unrelated to their

Alzheimer's and related diseases that cause dementia affect half a million Canadians. Canadian actor James Doohan, best known as "Scotty" of the *Star Trek* television series and movies, was diagnosed with Alzheimer's disease in 2004. He died in 2005 from complications due to this and other diseases. Although Alzheimer's impairs crystallized intelligence, it leaves fluid intelligence relatively intact (Matsuda & Saito, 1998).

*"I don't have to be smart, because someday I'll just hire lots of smart people to work for me."*

scores on intelligence tests, suggesting that practical and analytic intelligence are not the same thing (Scribner, 1984). Sternberg has argued that tests of practical intelligence are better than tests of analytic intelligence at predicting a person's job performance, though such claims have been criticized (Brody, 2003; Gottfredson, 2003).

Of course, not all of the problems that intelligence enables us to solve are analytical, practical, or creative. For instance, how do you tell a friend that she talks too much without hurting her feelings? How do you cheer yourself up after failing a test? How do you know whether you are feeling anxious or angry? Psychologists John Mayer and Peter Salovey define **emotional intelligence** as *the ability to reason about emotions and to use emotions to enhance reasoning* (Mayer, Roberts, & Barsade, 2008; Salovey & Grewal, 2005). Emotionally intelligent people know what kinds of emotions a particular event will trigger, they can identify, describe, and manage their emotions, they know how to use their emotions to improve their decisions, and they can identify other people's emotions from facial expressions and tones of voice. Furthermore, they do all this quite easily, which is why emotionally intelligent people show *less* neural activity when solving emotional problems than emotionally unintelligent people do (Jausovec & Jausovec, 2005; Jausovec, Jausovec, & Gerlic, 2001). These skills are also quite important for social relationships. Emotionally intelligent people have better social skills and more friends (Eisenberg et al., 2000; Mestre et al., 2006; Schultz, Izard, & Bear, 2004), they are judged to be more competent in their interactions (Brackett et al., 2006), and they have better romantic relationships (Brackett, Warner, & Bosco, 2005) and workplace relationships (Elfenbein et al., 2007; Lopes et al., 2006). Given all this, it is not surprising that emotionally intelligent people tend to be happier (Brackett & Mayer, 2003; Brackett et al., 2006) and more satisfied with their lives (Ciarrochi, Chan, & Caputi, 2000; Mayer, Caruso, & Salovey, 1999). In contrast, **alexithymia** is *a low emotional intelligence whereby a person has difficulty identifying and describing their own emotions, and in appreciating the emotional states of others*. Recent research from University of British Columbia (Holder, Love, & Timoney, 2014) indicates that 18.5 percent of undergraduates score high on measures of alexithymia, and that higher levels of alexithymia are associated with depression, low levels of life satisfaction, and poorer quality romantic relationships.

> What skills are particularly strong in emotionally intelligent people?

The data-based approach is also blind to middle-level abilities that are valued in cultures where intelligence tests are not common. For instance, Westerners regard people as intelligent when they speak quickly and often, but Africans regard people as intelligent when they are deliberate and quiet (Irvine, 1978). The Confucian tradition emphasizes the ability to behave properly, the Taoist tradition emphasizes humility and self-knowledge, and the Buddhist tradition emphasizes determination and mental effort (Yang & Sternberg, 1997). Unlike Western societies, many African and Asian societies conceive of intelligence as including social responsibility and cooperativeness (Azuma & Kashiwagi, 1987; Serpell, 1974; White & Kirkpatrick, 1985), and the word for *intelligence* in Zimbabwe, *ngware*, means to be wise in social relationships. Definitions of intelligence may even differ within a culture: Californians of Latino ancestry are more likely to equate intelligence with social competence, whereas Californians of Asian ancestry are more likely to equate it with

> How does the concept of intelligence differ across cultures?

---

**1.**

**2.**

Tom felt worried when he thought about all the work he needed to do. He believed he could handle it—if only he had the time. When his supervisor brought him an additional project, he felt _____. (Select the best choice.)

| Emotion | Select one: |
|---|---|
| a. Happy | ○ |
| b. Angry | ○ |
| c. Fearful | ○ |
| d. Sad | ○ |

| Emotion | Select one: |
|---|---|
| a. Frustrated and anxious | ○ |
| b. Content and calm | ○ |
| c. Ashamed and accepting | ○ |
| d. Sad and guilty | ○ |

Two items from a test of emotional intelligence. Item 1 measures the accuracy with which a person can read emotional expressions (*left*). Item 2 measures the ability to predict emotional responses to external events (*right*). The correct answer to both questions is A. [From Mayer, Roberts, & Barsade, 2008.]

**emotional intelligence**
The ability to reason about emotions and to use emotions to enhance reasoning.

**alexithymia**
A low emotional intelligence whereby a person has difficulty identifying and describing their own emotions, and in appreciating the emotional states of others.

cognitive skill (Okagaki & Sternberg, 1993). Some researchers take all this to mean that different cultures have radically different conceptualizations of intelligence, but others are convinced that what appear to be differences in the conceptualization of intelligence are really just differences in language. They argue that every culture values the ability to solve important problems and that what really distinguishes cultures is the *kinds* of problems that are considered to be important.

## IN SUMMARY

▶ People who score well on one test of mental ability *usually* score well on others, which suggests that there is a property called *g* (general intelligence).

▶ People who score well on one test of mental ability do not *always* score well on others, which suggests that there are properties called *s* (specific abilities).

▶ Research reveals that between *g* and *s* are several middle-level abilities (*m*).

▶ The data-based approach suggests that there are eight middle-level abilities.

▶ The theory-based approach suggests that there may be middle-level abilities that standard intelligence tests do not measure, such as practical, creative, and emotional intelligence. Non-Western cultures may include measures of social responsibility and cooperation in their definitions of intelligence.

Africans tend to think of intelligent people as deliberate and quiet. *Thought is hallowed in the lean oil of solitude*, wrote Nigerian poet Wole Soyinka, who spent nearly 2 years in solitary confinement for his radical writing. A decade later he won the Nobel Prize in Literature.

# Where Does Intelligence Come From?

No one is born knowing calculus and no one has to be taught how to blink. Some things are learned, others are not. But almost all of the really *interesting* things about people are a joint product of the innate characteristics with which their genes have endowed them and of the experiences they have in the world. Intelligence is one of those really interesting things that is influenced both by nature and by nurture. Let us start with nature.

## Genetic Influences on Intelligence

The notion that intelligence is "in the blood" has been with us for a long time. For example, in *The Republic*, the philosopher Plato suggested that some people are born to rule, others to be soldiers, and others to be tradesmen. But it was not until late in the nineteenth century that this suggestion became the subject of scientific inquiry. Sir Francis Galton was a half cousin of Charles Darwin, and his contributions to science ranged from meteorology to fingerprinting. Late in life, Galton (1869) became interested in the origins of intelligence. He did careful genealogical studies of eminent families and collected measurements from over 12 000 people that ranged from head size to the ability to discriminate tones. As the title of his book *Hereditary Genius* suggests, he concluded that intelligence was inherited. Was he right?

Sir Francis Galton (1822–1911) studied the physical and psychological traits that appeared to run in families. In his book *Hereditary Genius,* he concluded that intelligence was largely inherited.

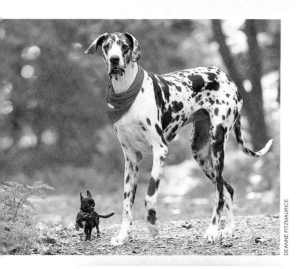

Small genetic differences can make a big difference. A single gene on chromosome 15 determines whether a dog will be too small for your pocket or too large for your garage.

**fraternal twins (or dizygotic twins)**
Twins who develop from two different eggs that were fertilized by two different sperm (see *identical twins*).

**identical twins (or monozygotic twins)**
Twins who develop from the splitting of a single egg that was fertilized by a single sperm (see *fraternal twins*).

**heritability coefficient**
A statistic (commonly denoted as $h^2$) that describes the proportion of the difference among people in a given population that can be explained by differences in their genes.

## Studying Relatives

The fact that intelligence appears to "run in families" is not very good evidence of this genetic influence. After all, brothers and sisters share genes, but they share many other things as well. They typically grow up in the same house, go to the same schools, read many of the same books, and have many of the same friends. Members of a family may have similar levels of intelligence because they share genes, environments, or both. To separate the influence of genes and environments, we need to examine the intelligence test scores of people who share genes but not environments (e.g., biological siblings who are separated at birth and raised by different families), people who share environments but not genes (e.g., adopted siblings who are raised together), and people who share both (e.g., biological siblings who are raised together).

> Why are the intelligence test scores of relatives so similar?

There are several kinds of siblings with different degrees of genetic relatedness. When siblings have the same biological parents but different birthdays, they share on average 50 percent of their genes. **Fraternal twins** (or **dizygotic twins**) *develop from two different eggs that were fertilized by two different sperm*, and although they happen to have the same birthday, they are merely siblings who shared a womb and they, too, share on average 50 percent of their genes. **Identical twins** (or **monozygotic twins**) *develop from the splitting of a single egg that was fertilized by a single sperm*, and unlike other siblings, they are genetic copies of each other, sharing nearly 100 percent of their genes. (Occasional mutations can affect one twin and not the other, so similarity is less than 100 percent.)

These different degrees of genetic relatedness allow psychologists to estimate the influence that genes have on intelligence. Studies show that the IQs of identical twins are strongly correlated when the twins are raised in the same household ($r = 0.86$), but they are also strongly correlated when the twins are separated at birth and raised in different households ($r = 0.78$). In fact, as you will notice from **TABLE 10.3** (on the next page), identical twins who are raised apart have more similar IQs than do fraternal twins who are raised together.

What this means is that people who share all their genes have similar IQs regardless of whether they share their environments. Indeed, the correlation between the intelligence test scores of identical twins who have never met is about the same as the correlation between the intelligence test scores of a single person who has taken the test twice! By comparison, the intelligence test scores of unrelated people raised in the same household (e.g., two siblings, one or both of whom were adopted) are correlated only modestly, about $r = 0.26$ (Bouchard & McGue, 2003). These patterns of correlation suggest that genes play an important role in determining intelligence. This should not surprise us. Intelligence is, in part, a function of how the brain works, and

These photographs were made by blending the face of a 32-year old woman with the face of her mother (*left*) and the face of her father (*right*). Because physical appearance is highly heritable, the resemblance between family members can often be quite striking. The photographs were taken from the "Genetic Portraits" series by Quebec artist Ulric Collette.

Table 10.3

**Intelligence Test Correlations between People with Different Relationships**

| Relationship | Shared Home? | Shared Genes (%) | Correlation between Intelligence Test Scores (r) |
|---|---|---|---|
| **Twins** Identical twins (n = 4672) | yes | 100 | 0.86 |
| Identical twins (n = 93) | no | 100 | 0.78 |
| Fraternal twins (n = 5533) | yes | 50 | 0.60 |
| **Parents and Children** Parent–biological child (n = 8433) | yes | 50 | 0.42 |
| Parent–biological child (n = 720) | no | 50 | 0.24 |
| Nonbiological parent–adopted child (n = 1491) | yes | 0 | 0.19 |
| **Siblings** Biological siblings (2 parents in common) (n = 26 473) | yes | 50 | 0.47 |
| Nonbiological siblings (no parents in common) (n = 714) | yes | 0 | 0.32 |
| Biological siblings (2 parents in common) (n = 203) | no | 50 | 0.24 |

*Source:* Plomin et al., 2001, p. 168.

given that brains are designed by genes, it would be quite remarkable if genes *did not* play a role in determining a person's intelligence. Indeed, a mere 20 genes on a single chromosome are all that separates you from a person with Williams syndrome. Clearly, genes influence intelligence.

## Heritability

But exactly how powerful is that influence? The **heritability coefficient** (commonly denoted as $h^2$) is *a statistic that describes the proportion of the difference among people in a given population that can be explained by differences in their genes.* When the data from numerous studies of children and adults are analyzed together, the heritability of intelligence is roughly 0.5, which is to say that about 50 percent of the difference between people's intelligence test scores is due to genetic differences between them (Plomin & Spinath, 2004; Plomin et al., 2013; cf. Chabris et al., 2012).

This fact may tempt you to conclude that half your intelligence is due to your genes and half is due to your experiences, but that is not right. To understand why, consider the rectangles in **FIGURE 10.5**. These rectangles clearly differ in size, and if you were asked to say what percentage of that difference was due to differences in the rectangles' heights and what percentage was due to differences in the rectangles' widths, you would correctly say that 100 percent of the difference in their sizes was due to differences in their widths and 0 percent was due to differences in their heights (which are, after all, identical). Good answer. Now, if you were asked to say how much of rectangle A's size was due to its height and how much was due to its width, you would correctly say, "That's a silly question." It is a silly question because a rectangle's size is a product of *both* its height and its width and it cannot be "due" to one more or less than the other.

Tamara Rabi and Adriana Scott were 20 years old when they met in a McDonald's parking lot near New York City. "I am just standing there looking at her," Adriana recalled. "It was a shock. I saw me" (Gootman, 2003). The two soon discovered that they were twins who had been separated at birth and adopted by different families.

◄ Figure 10.5 **How to Ask a Silly Question** These four rectangles differ in size. How much of the difference in their sizes is due to differences in their widths and how much is due to differences in their heights? Answer: 100 percent and 0 percent, respectively. Now, how much of rectangle A's size is due to width and how much is due to height? Answer: That is a silly question.

A     B     C     D

Research shows that intelligence is more heritable in wealthy neighbourhoods than in poor ones.

Similarly, if you measured the intelligence of all the people at a hockey game and were then asked to say what percentage of the difference in their intelligences was due to differences in their genes and what percentage was due to differences in their experiences, you could reasonably guess that about 50 percent of the difference was due to each of these factors. That is what the heritability coefficient of 0.5 suggests. But if you were next asked to say how much of the intelligence of the annoying guy with the bad haircut in Row 17, Seat 4 was due to his genes and how much was due to his experiences, you could only reply, "That's a silly question." It is a silly question because the intelligence of a particular person is a joint product of both genes and experience—just like the size of a particular rectangle is a joint product of both its height and width—and cannot be "due" to one of these things more than another.

The heritability coefficient tells us why people in a particular group differ from one another; thus its value can change depending on the particular group of people we measure. For example, the heritability of intelligence among wealthy children is about 0.72 and among poor children about 0.10 (Turkheimer et al., 2003). How can that be? Well, if we assume that wealthy children have fairly similar environments—that is, if they all have nice homes with books, plenty of free time, ample nutrition, and so on—then all the differences in their intelligence must be due to the one and only factor that distinguishes them from each other, namely, their genes. Conversely, if we assume that poor children have fairly different environments—that is, some have books and free time and ample nutrition while others have little or none of these—then the difference in their intelligences may be due to either of the factors that distinguish them, namely, their genes and their environments (Tucker-Drob et al., 2010). The value of the heritability coefficient also depends on the age of the people being measured and is typically larger among adults than among children (see **FIGURE 10.6**), which suggests that the environments of any pair of 65-year-olds tend to be more similar than the environments of any pair of 3-year-olds. In short, when people have identical experiences, then the difference in their intelligences must be due to the difference in their genes, and when people have identical genes, then the difference in their intelligences must be due to the difference in their experiences. It may seem paradoxical, but in a science-fictional world of perfect clones, the heritability of intelligence (and of everything else) would be zero.

> Why is $h^2$ higher among wealthy people than among poor people?

Does this imply that in a science-fictional world of individuals who lived in exactly the same kinds of houses and received exactly the same kinds of meals, educations, parental care, and so on, the heritability coefficient would be 1.00? Not likely. Two unrelated people who live in the same household will have *some* but not *all* of their experiences in common. The **shared environment** refers to *those environmental factors that are experienced by all relevant members of a household.* For example, siblings raised in the same household have about the same level of affluence, the same number and type of books, the same diet, and so on. The **nonshared environment** refers to *those environmental factors that are not experienced by all relevant members of a household.* Siblings raised in the same household

▼ Figure **10.6** **Age and Heritability of Intelligence** The heritability of intelligence generally increases with the age of the sample measured.

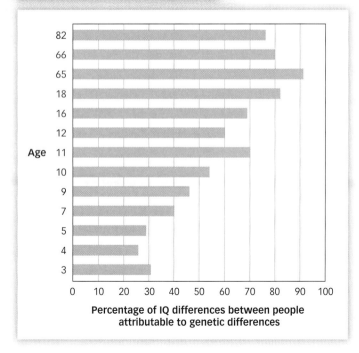

Age

Percentage of IQ differences between people attributable to genetic differences

First-born children tend to be more intelligent than their later-born siblings. But when a first-born child dies in infancy and the second-born child becomes the oldest child in the family, that second-born child ends up being just as intelligent as the average first-born child (Kristensen & Bjerkedal, 2007). This suggests that first-borns are smarter than their siblings because they experience a different family environment. Rob Ford (*left*) is the youngest of four children, and Doug Ford (*right*) is the eldest (and, perhaps, the smartest).

may have very different friends and teachers and may contract different illnesses. This may be why the correlation between the IQ scores of siblings is greater when they are close in age (Sundet, Eriksen, & Tambs, 2008). Being raised in the same household is only a rough measure of the similarity of two people's experiences (Turkheimer & Waldron, 2000); thus, studies of twins may overestimate the influence of genes and underestimate the influence of experiences (Nisbett, 2009). As psychologist Eric Turkheimer (2000, p. 162) noted,

> The appropriate conclusion [to draw from twin studies] is not so much that the family environment does not matter for development, but rather that the part of the family environment that is shared by siblings does not matter. What does matter is the individual environments of children, their peers, and the aspects of their parenting that they do not share.

## Environmental Influences on Intelligence

Canadians believe that every individual should have an equal chance to succeed in life, and one of the reasons why we bristle when we hear about genetic influences on intelligence is that we mistakenly believe that our genes are our destinies—that

**In what ways is intelligence like height?**

"genetic" is a synonym for "unchangeable" (Pinker, 2003). In fact, traits that are strongly influenced by genes may also be strongly influenced by the environment. Height is a heritable trait, which is why tall parents tend to have tall children; and yet, the average height of boys in what is now South Korea has increased by more than 18 cm (7 inches) in the last 50 years simply because of changes in nutrition (Nisbett, 2009). In 1848, 25 percent of all Dutch men were rejected by the military because they were less than 157 cm (5′ 2″) tall, but today the average Dutch man is over 183 cm (6′) tall (Max, 2006). Genes may explain why two people who have the same diet differ in height—that is, why Chang-sun is taller than Kwan-ho and why Thijs is taller than Daan—but they do not dictate how tall any of these boys will actually grow up to be.

Is intelligence like height in this regard? Alfred Binet (1909) thought so:

> A few modern philosophers … assert that an individual's intelligence is a fixed quantity that cannot be increased. We must protest and react against this brutal pessimism. … With practice, training, and above all method, we manage to increase our attention, our memory, our judgment, and literally to become more intelligent than we were before.

It turns out that Binet was right. As **FIGURE 10.7** on the next page shows, intelligence changes over time (Owens, 1966; Schaie, 1996, 2005; Schwartzman, Gold, & Andres,

At 213 cm (7′) Pieter Gijselaar is taller than most of his friends—but not *that* much taller. The Dutch government recently adjusted building codes so that doors must now be 230 cm (7′ 6.5″) high.

**shared environment**
Those environmental factors that are experienced by all relevant members of a household (see *nonshared environment*).

**nonshared environment**
Those environmental factors that are not experienced by all relevant members of a household (see *shared environment*).

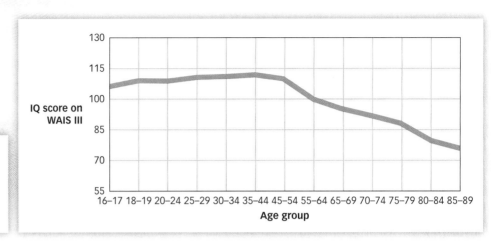

▶ Figure **10.7 Absolute Intelligence Changes Over Time** For most people, intelligence increases between adolescence and middle age and then declines thereafter.

[Data from Kaufman, 2001.]

1987). For most people, intelligence increases between adolescence and middle age and then declines thereafter. The sharpest decline occurs in old age (Kaufman, 2001; Salthouse, 1996a, 2000; Schaie, 2005), and may be due to a general slowing of the brain's processing speed (Salthouse, 1996b; Zimprich & Martin, 2002). Age-related declines are more evident in some domains than in others. For example, on tests that measure vocabulary, general information, and verbal reasoning, people show only small changes from the ages of 18 to 70, and some scores may even increase, but on tests that are timed, have abstract material, involve making new memories, or require reasoning about spatial relationships, most people show marked declines in performance after middle age (Avolio & Waldman, 1994; Lindenberger & Baltes, 1997; Rabbitt et al., 2004; Salthouse, 2001). In general, older people do well on tests of crystallized intelligence and perform more poorly on tests of fluid intelligence.

Not only does intelligence change over the life span, but it also changes over generations. The *Flynn effect* refers to the accidental discovery by James Flynn that the average IQ score is 30 points higher than it was about a century ago (Dickens & Flynn, 2001; Flynn, 2012; cf. Lynn, 2013). The average person today has an IQ greater than 95 percent of the people who were living in 1900! Why is each generation scoring higher than the one before it? Some researchers give the credit to improved nutrition, schooling, and parenting (Lynn, 2009; Neisser, 1998), and some suggest that the least intelligent people are being left out of the mating game (Mingroni, 2007). But most (and that includes Flynn himself) believe that the industrial and technological revo-

Khatijah (*front row, second from right*), who is 105 years old, sits with five generations of her family. The Flynn Effect suggests that intelligence is increasing across generations.

lutions have changed the nature of daily living such that people now spend more and more time solving precisely the kinds of abstract problems that intelligence tests include—and as we all know, practice makes perfect (Flynn, 2012). In other words, you are likely to score higher on an IQ test than your grandparents did because your daily life is more like an IQ test than theirs was!

Now, here is a fact that is almost sure to confuse you: Although intelligence changes over the lifetime, there is a strong correlation between an individual's performance on intelligence tests that are taken at two different times (Deary, 2000; Deary et al., 2004; Deary, Batty, & Gale, 2008; Deary, Batty, Pattie, & Gale, 2008). **TABLE 10.4** (on the next page) shows the results of several studies that demonstrate this fact. How can that be? If intelligence changes over time, then why is there such a strong correlation between tests taken in childhood and tests taken in old age? The answer is that intelligence does change over time, but it changes in much the same way for everyone. The large correlations between tests administered at different times merely tell us that the people who got the best (or worst) scores when the test was administered the first time also tended to get the best (or worst) scores when it was administered the second time. You already know that the same thing happens with height. People get taller as they go from childhood to adulthood, and yet, the tallest child is likely to be among the tallest adults. Like height, a person's absolute level of intelligence changes over time, but his or her level of intelligence *relative to others* stays about the same.

The fact that intelligence changes over the life span and across generations shows that it is not "a fixed quantity that cannot be increased." Our genes may determine the *range* in which our IQ is likely to fall, but our experiences determine the exact *point* in that range at which it does fall (Hunt, 2011) (see **FIGURE 10.8**). Two of the most powerful experiential factors are economics and education.

> Table 10.4

### The Correlation Between Scores on Intelligence Tests Taken Over Time

| Study | Mean Initial Age (years) | Mean Follow-up Age (years) | Correlation (r) |
| --- | --- | --- | --- |
| 1 | 2 | 9 | 0.56 |
| 2 | 14 | 42 | 0.68 |
| 3 | 19 | 61 | 0.78 |
| 4 | 25 | 65 | 0.78 |
| 5 | 30 | 43 | 0.64–0.79 |
| 6 | 50 | 70 | 0.90 |

*Source:* Adapted from Deary, 2000.

## Economics

Maybe money cannot buy love, but it sure appears to buy intelligence. One of the best predictors of a person's intelligence is the income, education, and occupations of the parents by whom he or she was raised—what scientists call *socioeconomic status* (SES). Studies suggest that being raised in a high-SES family rather than a low-SES family is worth between 12 and 18 IQ points (Nisbett, 2009; van IJzendoorn, Juffer, & Klein Poelhuis, 2005). For example, one study compared pairs of siblings who were born to low-SES parents. In each case, one of the siblings was raised by his or her low-SES parents and the other was adopted and raised by a high-SES family. On average, the child who had been raised by high-SES parents had an IQ that was 14 points higher than his or her sibling (Schiff et al., 1978). Although these siblings had similar genes, they ended up with dramatically different IQs simply because one was raised by wealthier parents.

Exactly how does SES influence intelligence? One way is by influencing the brain itself. Low-SES children have poorer nutrition and, in some places, medical care; they experience greater daily stress; and they are more

**Why are wealthier people more intelligent?**

likely to be exposed to environmental toxins such as air pollution and lead—all of which can impair brain development (Chen, Cohen, & Miller, 2010; Evans, 2004; Hackman & Farah, 2008). The fact that low SES can impair a child's brain development may explain why children who experience poverty in early childhood are less intelligent than those who experience poverty in middle or late childhood (Duncan et al., 1998).

SES affects the brain, and it also affects the environment in which that brain lives and learns. Intellectual stimulation increases intelligence (Nelson et al., 2007), and research shows that high-SES parents are more likely to provide it (Nisbett, 2009). For instance, high-SES parents are more likely to read to their children and to connect what they are reading to the outside world ("Billy has a rubber ducky. Who do you know who has a rubber ducky?") (Heath, 1983; Lareau, 2003). When high-SES parents talk to their children, they tend to ask stimulating questions ("Do you think a ducky likes to eat grass?"), whereas low-SES parents tend to give instructions ("Please put your ducky away") (Hart & Risley, 1995). By the age of 3, the average high-SES child has heard 30 million different words, while the average low-SES child has heard only 10 million different words, and as a result, the high-SES child knows 50 percent more words than his or her low-SES counterpart. These differences in the intellectual richness of the home environment may explain why children from low-SES families

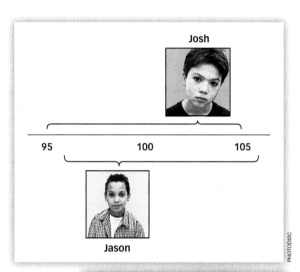

▲ Figure 10.8 **Genes and Environment** Genes may establish the range in which a person's intelligence *may* fall, but environment determines the point in that range at which the person's intelligence *will* fall. Although Jason's genes give him a better chance to be smart than Josh's genes do, differences in their diets could easily cause Josh to have a higher IQ than Jason.

PHOTODISC

# Dumb and Dumber?

For most of human history, the smartest people had the most children, and our species reaped the benefits. But in the middle of the nineteenth century, this effect began to reverse and the smartest people began having fewer children, a trend that scientists call *dysgenic fertility*. That trend continues today.

But wait. If the smartest people are having the fewest children, and if IQ is largely heritable, then why—as James Flynn showed—is IQ rising over generations?

Some researchers suspect that two things are happening at once: Our inherited intelligence is going down over generations, but our acquired intelligence is going up! In other words, we were all born with a *slightly* less capable brain than our parents had, but this small effect is masked because we were born into a world that *greatly* boosted our intelligence with everything from nutrition to video games! How can we tell whether this hypothesis is right?

Francis Galton was the first to suggest that reaction time (the speed with which a person can respond to a stimulus) is a basic indicator of mental ability, and his suggestion has been confirmed

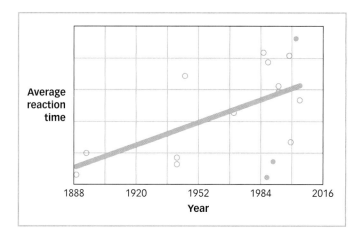

by modern research (Deary, Der, & Ford, 2001). Recently, a group of researchers (Woodley, te Nijenhuis, & Murphy, 2013) went back and analyzed all available data on human reaction time collected between 1884 and 2004 (including data collected by Galton himself) and what they found was striking: The average reaction time has gotten slower since the Victorian era! The figure above shows the average reaction time of people in different studies conducted in different years.

Does this mean that we are innately less clever and that this fact is being obscured by the big IQ boost we get from our environments? Maybe, but maybe not. There are problems with using old data that were collected under unknown circumstances, and the participants in older studies were probably not representative of the entire population. Nonetheless, the finding is provocative because it suggests that modern life may be an even more powerful cognitive enhancer than we realize.

show a decrease in intelligence during the summer when school is not in session, whereas children from high-SES families do not (Burkham et al., 2004; Cooper et al., 1996). Clearly, poverty is the enemy of intelligence (Evans & Kim, 2012). The relationship between SES and intelligence is not one way. Not only does SES influence intelligence, but intelligence influences SES: via education.

## Education

Alfred Binet believed that if poverty was intelligence's enemy, then education was its friend. And he was right about that too. The correlation between the amount of formal education a person receives and his or her intelligence is quite large, somewhere in the range of $r = 0.55 - 0.90$ (Ceci, 1991; Neisser et al., 1996). One reason why this correlation is so large is that smart people tend to stay in school, but the other reason is that school makes people smarter (Ceci & Williams, 1997). When schooling is delayed because of war, political strife, or the simple lack of qualified teachers, children show a measurable decline in intelligence (Nisbett, 2009). Indeed, in places where children born in the first 9 months of a calendar year typically start school an entire year earlier than those born in the last 3 months of the same year, people with late birthdays tend to have lower intelligence test scores than people with early birthdays (Baltes & Reinert, 1969).

Does this mean that anyone can become a genius just by showing up for class? Unfortunately not. Although education reliably increases intelligence, its impact is small, and some studies suggest that it tends to enhance test-taking ability more than general cognitive ability and that its effects vanish within a few years (Perkins & Grotzer, 1997). In other words, education seems to produce increases in intelligence that are smaller, narrower, and shorter-lived than we would like. That might mean that education just cannot change intelligence all that much, or it might mean that education is potentially very powerful, but that modern schools are not very good at providing it. Researchers lean toward the latter conclusion. Although most experiments in education have failed to produce substantial intellectual gains for students, a few have been quite successful (Nisbett, 2009), which shows that education *can* substantially increase intelligence even if it does not *usually* do so. No one knows just how big the impact of an optimal education could be, but it seems clear that our current educational system is less than optimal.

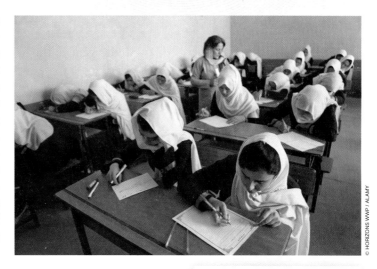

Education increases intelligence. But not everyone is in favour of that. In Afghanistan, for example, some members of the Taliban attack young girls with acid, guns, and poison to keep them from attending school.

## Genes and Environments

Both genes and environment influence intelligence. But that should not lead you to think of genes and environments as two separate ingredients that are somehow blended together like flour and sugar in a recipe for IQ. The fact is that genes and environments interact in complex ways that make the distinction between them a bit murky.

For example, imagine a gene that made people enjoy the smell of library dust or that made them unusually sensitive to the glare produced by television sets. People who had such a gene might well read more books and thus end up being smarter. Would their increased intelligence be due to their genes or to their environments? Well, if they had not had those genes, then they would not have gone to the library, but if they had not gone to the library, then they would not have gotten smarter. The fact is that genes can exert some of their most powerful influences not by changing the structure of a person's brain, but by changing the person's environment (Dickens & Flynn, 2001; Nisbett, 2009; Plomin et al., 2001). A gene that made someone sociable might lead her to have good relationships with peers, which might lead her to stay in school longer, which might lead her to become smarter. Would we call such a gene a "sociability gene" or an "intelligence gene" (Posthuma & de Geus, 2006)? Would we attribute that person's intelligence to her genes or to the environment that her genes enabled her to create? As these questions suggest, genes and environments are not independent influences on intelligence, and the clear difference between nature and nurture is not as clear as it might first appear.

> **How might genes exert their influence on intelligence?**

Roundworms that have a gene called NPR-1 dislike low-oxygen environments, which just so happens to be where the bacteria hang out. As a result, these roundworms get fewer infections. Is NPR-1 a health gene?

## IN SUMMARY

▶ Both genes and environments influence intelligence.

▶ The heritability coefficient ($h^2$) tells us what portion of the difference among people in a given population is attributable to differences in their genes.

▶ Relative intelligence is generally stable over time, but absolute intelligence changes.

▶ Socioeconomic status (SES) has a powerful influence on intelligence, and education has a moderate influence.

# Who Is Most Intelligent?

If everyone in the world were equally intelligent, we probably would not even have a word for it. What makes intelligence such an interesting and important topic is that some individuals—and some groups of individuals—have more of it than others.

## Individual Differences in Intelligence

The average IQ is 100, and the vast majority of us—about 70 percent in fact—have IQs between 85 and 115 (see **FIGURE 10.9**). The people who score well above this large middle range are said to be *intellectually gifted*, and the people who score well below it are said to be *intellectually disabled*. The people who live at opposite ends of this continuum have one thing in common: They are more likely to be male than female. Although males and females have the same average IQ, the distribution of males' IQ scores is more variable than the distribution of females' IQ scores, which means that there are more males than females at both the very top and the very bottom of the IQ range (Hedges & Nowell, 1995; Lakin, 2013; Wai, Putallaz, & Makel, 2012). Some of this difference is surely due to the different ways in which boys and girls are socialized. Whether some of this difference is also due to innate biological differences between males and females remains a hotly debated issue in psychology (Ceci, Williams, & Barnett, 2009; Nisbett et al., 2012; Spelke, 2005).

▶ Figure **10.9** **The Normal Curve of Intelligence** Deviation IQ scores produce a normal curve. This graph shows the percentage of people who score in each range of IQ. Note that about 70 percent (68 percent to be exact) of the population have an IQ that falls in the yellow shaded region around 100.

The artist Vincent van Gogh was the iconic "tortured genius." But data suggest that it is low intelligence, and not high intelligence, that is most strongly associated with mental illness.

Those of us who occupy the large middle of the intelligence spectrum often embrace a number of myths about those who live at the extremes. For example, movies typically portray the "tortured genius" as a person (usually a male person) who is brilliant, creative, misunderstood, despondent, and more than a little bit weird. Although some psychologists do think there is a link between creative genius and certain forms of psychopathology (Gale et al., 2012; Jamison, 1993; cf. Schlesinger, 2012), for the most part Hollywood has the relationship between intelligence and mental illness backwards: People with very high intelligence are *less* prone to mental illness than are people with very low intelligence (Dekker & Koot, 2003; Didden et al., 2012; Walker et al., 2002). Indeed, a 15 point *decrease* in IQ at age 20 is associated with a 50 percent *increase* in the risk of later hospitalization for schizophrenia, mood disorder, and alcohol-related disorders (Gale et al., 2010) as well as for personality disorders (Moran et al., 2009). Just as intelligence seems to buffer people against physical illness, it seems to buffer people against mental illness as well.

Another staple of Hollywood's vivid imagination is the "maladjusted child braniac." In fact, research suggests that very high IQ children are about as well-adjusted as their peers, and any special social or emotional problems they have seem to stem largely from a lack of appropriate scholastic opportunities (Garland & Zigler, 1999; Neihart, 1999). Being intellectually gifted does not necessarily make a child's life worse, but it also does not necessarily make it better. For instance, profoundly gifted children are no more likely than moderately intelligent children to become major contributors to the fields in which they work (Richert, 1997; Terman & Oden, 1959). No one knows why the gifts of childhood do not always ripen into the fruits of adulthood: Perhaps there is a natural limit on how much intelligence can improve one's outcomes, or perhaps the educational system fails to help gifted children make the best use of their talents (Robinson & Clinkenbeard, 1998; Winner, 2000).

It is worth noting that gifted children are rarely gifted in all departments, but instead have gifts in a single domain such as mathematics, language, or music. More than 95 percent of gifted children show a sharp disparity between their mathematical and verbal abilities (Achter, Lubinski, & Benbow, 1996). Because gifted children tend to be "single-gifted," they also tend to be single-minded, displaying a "rage to master" the domain in which they excel. As one expert noted, "one cannot tear these children away from activities in their area of giftedness, whether they involve an instrument, a computer, a sketch pad, or a math book. These children … can focus so intently on work in this domain that they lose sense of the outside world" (Winner, 2000, p. 162). Indeed, some research suggests that the one thing that most clearly distinguishes gifted children from their less gifted peers is the sheer amount of time they spend engaged in their domain of excellence (Ericsson & Charness, 1999). A large part of nature's gift may be the capacity for passionate devotion to a single activity (Mayer et al., 1989; cf. Hambrick et al., 2013).

> **What one thing most clearly distinguishes gifted children?**

On the other end of the intelligence spectrum are people with intellectual disabilities, which can range from mild ($50 < IQ < 69$) to moderate ($35 < IQ < 49$) to severe ($20 < IQ < 34$) to profound ($IQ < 20$). About 70 percent of people with IQs in this range are male. Two of the most common causes of intellectual disability are *Down syndrome* (caused by the presence of a third copy of chromosome 21) and *fetal alcohol syndrome* (caused by a mother's alcohol use during pregnancy). These intellectual disabilities are quite general, and people who have them typically show impaired performance on most or all cognitive tasks. Perhaps the greatest myth about the intellectually disabled is that they are unhappy. A recent survey of people with Down syndrome (Skotko, Levine, & Goldstein, 2011) revealed that more than 96 percent are happy with their lives, like who they are, and like how they look. People with intellectual disabilities face many challenges, and being misunderstood is one of the most difficult.

Dustin Bean has Down Syndrome, but that did not prevent him from earning a black belt in Kung Fu (or from showing off several precision moves to Bruce Lee's widow).

## Group Differences in Intelligence

In the early 1900s, Stanford professor Lewis Terman improved on Binet and Simon's work and produced the intelligence test now known as the Stanford–Binet Intelligence Scale. Among the things his test revealed was that whites performed better than non-whites. "Are the inferior races really inferior, or are they merely unfortunate in their lack of opportunity to learn?" he asked, and then answered unequivocally: "Their dullness seems to be racial, or at least inherent in the family stocks from which they come." He went on to suggest that "children of this group should be segregated into separate classes … [because] they cannot master abstractions but they can often be made into efficient workers" (Terman, 1916, pp. 91–92).

A century later, these sentences make most of us cringe. Terman appeared to be making three claims: First, that intelligence is influenced by genes; second, that members of some racial groups score better than others on intelligence tests; and third, that the difference in scores is due to a difference in genes. Virtually all modern

Research suggests that men tend to outperform women in abstract mathematical and scientific domains and women tend to outperform men on production and comprehension of complex prose. Sonya Kovalevskaya (1850–1891), who was regarded as one of the greatest mathematicians of her time, wrote: "It seems to me that the poet must see what others do not see, must look deeper than others look. And the mathematician must do the same thing. As for myself, all my life I have been unable to decide for which I had the greater inclination, mathematics or literature" (Kovalevskaya, 1978, p. 35).

scientists agree that Terman's first two claims are true: Intelligence *is* influenced by genes and some groups *do* perform better than others on intelligence tests. However, Terman's third claim—that differences in genes are the *reason* why some groups outperform others—is not a fact. Indeed, it is a provocative conjecture that has been the subject of both passionate and acrimonious debate. What does science have to tell us about it?

Before answering that question we should be clear about one thing: Between-group differences in intelligence are not inherently troubling. No one is troubled by the possibility that Nobel laureates are on average more intelligent than shoe salesmen, and that includes the shoe salesmen. On the other hand, most of us *are* troubled by the possibility that people of one gender, race, or nationality may be more intelligent than people of another because intelligence is a valuable commodity and it does not seem fair for a few groups to corner the market by accidents of birth or geography.

But fair or not, they do. Asians routinely outscore Caucasians, who routinely outscore Latinos, who routinely outscore blacks (Neisser et al., 1996; Rushton, 1995). Women routinely outscore men on tests that require rapid access to and use of semantic information, production and comprehension of complex prose, fine motor skills, and perceptual speed of verbal intelligence, and men routinely outscore women on tests that require transformations in visual or spatial memory, certain motor skills, spatiotemporal responding, and fluid reasoning in abstract mathematical and scientific domains (Halpern, 1997; Halpern et al., 2007). Indeed, group differences in performance on intelligence tests "are among the most thoroughly documented findings in psychology" (Suzuki & Valencia, 1997, p. 1104). Although the average difference between groups is considerably less than the average difference within groups, so that there is a huge amount of overlap between the groups, Terman was right when he noted that some groups perform better than others on intelligence tests. The question is why?

## Tests and Test Takers

One possibility is that there is something wrong with the tests. In fact, there is now little doubt that the earliest intelligence tests asked questions whose answers were more likely to be known by members of one group (usually white Western Europeans) than by members of another. For example, when Binet and Simon asked students, "When anyone has offended you and asks you to excuse him, what ought you to do?," they were looking for answers such as "accept the apology graciously." Answers such as "demand three goats" would have been counted as wrong. But intelligence tests have come a long way in a century, and one would have to look hard to find questions on a modern intelligence test that have the same blatant cultural bias that Binet and Simon's test did (Suzuki & Valencia, 1997). Moreover, group differences emerge even on those portions of intelligence tests that measure nonverbal skills, such as Raven's Progressive Matrices Test (see Figure 10.4). It would be difficult to argue that the large differences between the average scores of different groups is due entirely—or even largely—to a cultural bias in IQ tests.

Of course, even when test *questions* are unbiased, testing *situations* may not be. For example, studies show that African American students perform more poorly on tests if they are asked to report their race at the top of the answer sheet, because doing so causes them to feel anxious about confirming racial stereotypes (Steele & Aronson, 1995) and anxiety naturally interferes with test performance (Reeve, Heggestad, & Lievens, 2009). European American students do not show the same effect when asked to report their race. When Asian American women are reminded of their gender, they perform unusually poorly on tests of mathematical skill, presumably because they are aware of stereotypes suggesting

> **How can the testing situation affect a person's performance on an IQ test?**

*"I don't know anything about the bell curve, but I say heredity is everything."*

that women cannot do mathematics. But when the same women are instead reminded of their ethnicity, they perform unusually *well* on such tests, presumably because they are aware of stereotypes suggesting that Asians are especially good at mathematics (Shih, Pittinsky, & Ambady, 1999). Indeed, when women read an essay suggesting that mathematical ability is strongly influenced by genes, they perform more poorly on subsequent mathematics tests (Dar-Nimrod & Heine, 2006). Findings such as these remind us that the situation in which intelligence tests are administered can affect members of different groups differently and may cause group differences in performance that do not reflect group differences in actual intelligence.

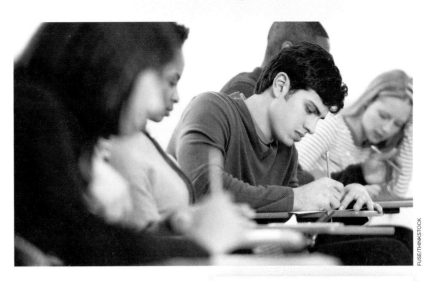

Writing entrance exams such as the Medical College Admission Test (MCAT) can cause a lot of stress. When people are anxious about the possibility of confirming a racial or gender stereotype, their test performance can suffer.

## Environments and Genes

Biases in the testing situation may explain some of the between-group differences in intelligence test scores, but probably not all. If we assume that some of these differences reflect real differences in the abilities that intelligence tests are meant to measure, then what accounts for these ability differences?

There is broad agreement among scientists that environment plays a major role. For example, African American children have lower birth weights, poorer diets, higher rates of chronic illness, poorer medical care, attend worse schools, and are three times

> **How can environmental factors help explain between-group differences in intelligence?**

more likely than European American children to live in single-parent households (Acevedo-Garcia et al., 2007; National Center for Health Statistics, 2004). Given the vast differences between the SES of European Americans and African Americans, it is not very surprising that African Americans score on average 10 points lower on IQ tests than do European Americans. Do genes play any role in this difference? So far, scientists have not found a single fact that requires such a conclusion, but they have found several facts that make such a conclusion difficult to accept. For example, the average African American has about 20 percent European genes, but those who have more are no smarter than those who have fewer, which is not what we would expect if European genes made people smart (Loehlin, 1973; Scarr et al., 1977). Similarly, African American children and mixed-race children have different amounts of European genes, and yet, when they are adopted into middle-class families, their IQs do not differ (Moore, 1986). These facts do not rule out the possibility that between-group differences in intelligence are caused by genetic differences, but they do make that possibility unlikely.

What would it take to prove that behavioural and psychological differences between groups have a genetic origin? It would take the kind of evidence that scientists often find when they study the *physical* differences between groups. For example, people who have hepatitis C are often given a prescription for antiviral drugs, and European Americans typically benefit more from this treatment than African Americans do. Although physicians once thought this was because European Americans were more likely to *take* the medicine they were given, scientists have recently discovered a gene that makes people unresponsive to these antiviral drugs—and guess what? African Americans are much more likely than European Americans to have that gene (Ge et al., 2009). This kind of clear-cut evidence of genetic differences between groups is exactly what is lacking in the debate on the causes of between-group differences in intelligence. As one researcher recently noted, "No individual genetic variants are conclusively related to intelligence or its change with age in healthy individuals" (Deary, 2012, p. 463). This may mean that intelligence is influenced by many very tiny genetic effects rather than by a few major "intelligence genes" (Davies et al., 2011). Until researchers can locate such genes, and until they can show that those genes are more prevalent in one group than another, most psychologists are unlikely to be persuaded by genetic explanations of between-group differences in intelligence. Indeed, some experts, such as psychologist Richard Nisbett, believe the debate is all but over: "Genes account for none of the difference in IQ between blacks and whites; measurable environmental factors plausibly account for all of it" (Nisbett, 2009, p. 118).

## Improving Intelligence

Intelligence can be improved—by money, for example, and by education. But most people cannot just snap their fingers and become wealthier, and education takes time. Is there anything that average parents can do to raise their child's IQ? Researchers recently analyzed the data from all the high-quality scientific studies on this question that have been performed over the last few decades (Protzko, Aronson, & Blair, 2013), and they found that four things reliably raise a child's intelligence. First, supplementing the diets of pregnant women and neonates with long-chain polyunsaturated fatty acids (a substance found in breast milk) raises children's IQ by about 4 points. Second, enrolling low-SES infants in early educational interventions raises their IQ by about 6 points (though surprisingly, enrolling them at a younger age seems to be no better than enrolling them at an older age). Third, reading to children in an interactive manner raises their IQ by about 6 points (and in this case, the earlier the parent starts reading the better). Fourth and finally, sending children to preschool raises their IQ by about 6 points. Clearly, there are some things that parents can do to make their kids smarter.

Perhaps all this will be simpler in the future. *Cognitive enhancers* are drugs that produce improvements in the psychological processes that underlie intelligent behaviour. For example, stimulants such as Ritalin (methylphenidate) and Adderall (mixed amphetamine salts) can enhance cognitive performance (Elliott et al., 1997; Halliday et al., 1994; McKetin et al., 1999), which is why there has been an increase in their use by healthy students over the past few years. Surveys suggest that almost 7 percent of students in American universities have used prescription stimulants for cognitive enhancement, and that on some campuses the number is as high as 25 percent (McCabe et al., 2005). Across Canadian university campuses, the percentages range from 1 to 33 percent (Ainsworth-Vincze, 2009). These drugs improve people's ability to focus attention and manipulate information in working memory, and improve flexibly control responses (Sahakian & Morein-Zamir, 2007). Cognitive performance can also be enhanced by a class of drugs called ampakines (Ingvar et al., 1997). Modafinil is one such drug, and it has been shown to improve short-term memory and planning abilities in healthy, young volunteers (Turner et al., 2003).

We should of course be worried about the abuse of these drugs. Nonetheless, the distinction between enhancing cognition by taking drugs and enhancing it by other means is not cut and dried. As one distinguished group of scientists (Greely et al., 2008, p. 703) recently concluded, "Drugs may seem distinctive among enhancements in that they bring about their effects by altering brain function, but in reality so does any intervention that enhances cognition. Recent research has identified beneficial neural changes engendered by exercise, nutrition and sleep, as well as instruction and reading." In other words, if both drugs and exercise enhance cognition by altering the way the brain

Millionaire Robert Graham opened the Repository for Germinal Choice in 1980 to collect sperm from Nobel laureates and mathematical prodigies and allow healthy young women to be inseminated with it. His so-called "genius factory" produced more than 200 children but closed after his death in 1999.

ERIC MYER PHOTOGRAPHY INC.

functions, then what exactly is the difference between them? Other scientists believe this question will soon be moot because cognitive enhancement will be achieved

> **How might your children enhance their intelligence?**

not by altering the brain's chemistry in university, but by altering its basic structure at birth. By manipulating the genes that guide hippocampal development, scientists have created a strain of "smart mice" that have extraordinary memory and learning abilities, leading the researchers to conclude that "genetic enhancement of mental and cognitive attributes such as intelligence and memory in mammals is feasible" (Tang et al., 1999, p. 64). Although no one has yet developed a safe and powerful "smart pill" or "smart gene therapy," many experts believe that this will happen in the next few years (Farah et al., 2004; Rose, 2002; Turner & Sahakian, 2006). When it does, we will need a whole lot of wisdom to know how to handle it.

## OTHER VOICES

# How Science Can Build a Better You

**David Ewing Duncan** is an award-winning author and journalist whose most recent book is *When I'm 164: The new science of radical life extension, and what happens if it succeeds.*

CHRIS HARDY PHOTOGRAPHY

Intelligence is a highly prized commodity that buys people a lot of the good things in life. It can be increased by a solid education and a healthy diet, and everyone's in favour of those things. But it can also be increased by drugs—and there is little doubt that in the near future it will be increased by other even more powerful technologies. Is this a bad idea or a moral imperative? How will we decide who gets to use these technologies and who gets left behind? Author David Ewing Duncan thinks that these are critically important questions that we must answer now—*before* the "Age of Enhancement" begins. The following is an abridged version of his article that appeared in *The New York Times.*

... Over the last couple of years during talks and lectures, I have asked thousands of people a hypothetical question that goes like this: "If I could offer you a pill that allowed your child to increase his or her memory by 25 percent, would you give it to them?"

The show of hands in this informal poll has been overwhelming, with 80 percent or more voting no.

Then I asked a follow-up question. "What if this pill was safe and increased your kid's grades from a B average to an A average?" People tittered nervously, looked around to see how others were voting as nearly half said yes. (Many did not vote at all.)

"And what if all of the other kids are taking the pill?" I asked. The tittering stopped and nearly everyone voted yes.

No pill now exists that can boost memory by 25 percent. Yet neuroscientists tell me that pharmaceutical companies are testing compounds in early stage human trials that may enable patients with dementia and other memory-stealing diseases to have better recall. No one knows if these will work to improve healthy people, but it is possible that one will work in the future.

More intriguing is the notion that a supermemory or attention pill might be used someday by those with critical jobs like pilots, surgeons, police officers—or the chief executive of the United States. In fact, we may demand that they use them, said the bioethicist Thomas H. Murray. "It might actually be immoral for a surgeon not to take a drug that was

safe and steadied his hand," said Mr. Murray, the former president of the Hastings Center, a bioethics research group. "That would be like using a scalpel that was not sterile." ...

For years, scientists have been manipulating genes in animals to make improvements in neural performance, strength and agility, among other augmentations. Directly altering human DNA using "gene therapy" in humans remains dangerous and fraught with ethical challenges. But it may be possible to develop drugs that alter enzymes and other proteins associated with genes for, say, speed and endurance or dopamine levels in the brain connected to improved neural performance.

Synthetic biologists contend that re-engineering cells and DNA may one day allow us to eliminate diseases; a few believe we will be able to build tailor-made people. Others are convinced that stem cells might one day be used to grow fresh brain, heart or liver cells to augment or improve cells in these and other organs.

Not all enhancements are high-tech or invasive. Neuroscientists are seeing boosts from neuro-feedback and video games designed to teach and develop cognition and from meditation and improvements in diet, exercise and sleep. "We may see a convergence of several of these technologies," said the neurologist Adam Gazzaley of the University of California at San Francisco. He is developing brain-boosting games with developers and engineers who once worked for Lucas Arts, founded by the "Star Wars" director George Lucas. ...

Ethical challenges for the coming Age of Enhancement include, besides basic safety questions, the issue of who would get the enhancements, how much they would cost, and who would gain an advantage over others by using them. In a society that is already seeing a widening gap between the very rich and the rest of us, the question of a democracy of equals could face a critical test if the well-off also could afford a physical, genetic or bionic advantage. It also may challenge what it means to be human.

Still, the enhancements are coming, and they will be hard to resist. The real issue is what we do with them once they become irresistible.

## IN SUMMARY

▶ Some groups outscore others on intelligence tests because (a) testing situations impair the performance of some groups more than others, and (b) some groups live in less healthful and stimulating environments.

▶ There is no compelling evidence to suggest that between-group differences in intelligence are due to genetic differences.

▶ The distinction between genetic and environmental influences on intelligence can be murky. For example, genes can influence an organism's behaviour by determining which environments it is drawn to.

▶ Intelligence is correlated with mental health, and gifted children are as well-adjusted as their peers.

▶ Human intelligence can be temporarily increased by cognitive enhancers such as Ritalin and Adderall, and nonhuman intelligence has been permanently increased by genetic manipulation.

# Chapter Review

## KEY CONCEPT QUIZ

1. Which of the following abilities is not an accepted feature of intelligence?
   a. the ability to direct one's thinking
   b. the ability to adapt to one's circumstances
   c. the ability to care for oneself
   d. the ability to learn from one's experiences

2. Intelligence tests
   a. were first developed to help children who lagged behind their peers.
   b. were developed to measure aptitude rather than educational achievement.
   c. have been used for detestable ends.
   d. all of the above.

3. Intelligence tests have been shown to be predictors of
   a. academic performance.
   b. mental health.
   c. physical health.
   d. all of the above.

4. People who score well on one test of mental ability usually score well on others, suggesting that
   a. tests of mental ability are perfectly correlated.
   b. intelligence cannot be measured meaningfully.
   c. there is a general ability called intelligence.
   d. intelligence is genetic.

5. The two-factor theory suggests that intelligence is a combination of general ability and
   a. factor analysis.
   b. specific abilities.
   c. primary mental abilities.
   d. creative intelligence.

6. Most scientists now believe that intelligence is best described
   a. as a set of group factors.
   b. by a two-factor framework.
   c. as a single, general ability.
   d. by a three-level hierarchy.

7. Standard intelligence tests typically measure
   a. analytic intelligence.
   b. practical intelligence.
   c. creative intelligence.
   d. all of the above.

8. Intelligence is influenced by
   a. genes alone.
   b. genes and environment.
   c. environment alone.
   d. neither genes nor environment.

9. The heritability coefficient is a statistic that describes how much of the difference among people in a given population can be explained by
   a. the nature of the specific test.
   b. differences in their environment.
   c. differences in their genes.
   d. their age at the time of testing.

10. Intelligence changes
    a. over the life span and across generations.
    b. over the life span but not across generations.
    c. across generations but not over the life span.
    d. neither across generations nor over the life span.

11. A person's socioeconomic status (SES) has a(n) ____ effect on intelligence.
   a. powerful
   b. negligible
   c. unsubstantiated
   d. unknown

12. Which of the following statements is false?
   a. Modern intelligence tests have a very strong cultural bias.
   b. Testing situations can impair the performance of some groups more than others.
   c. Test performance can suffer if the test taker is concerned about confirming a racial or gender stereotype.
   d. Some ethnic groups perform better than others on intelligence tests.

13. On which of the following does broad agreement exist among scientists?
   a. Differences in the intelligence test scores of different ethnic groups are clearly due to genetic differences between those groups.
   b. Differences in the intelligence test scores of different ethnic groups are caused in part by factors such as low birth weight and poor diet that are more prevalent in some groups than in others.
   c. Differences in the intelligence test scores of different ethnic groups always reflect real differences in intelligence.
   d. Genes that are strongly associated with intelligence have been found to be more prevalent in some ethnic groups than in others.

14. Gifted children tend to
   a. be equally gifted in several domains.
   b. be gifted in a single domain.
   c. lose their special talent in adulthood.
   d. change the focus of their interests relatively quickly.

## KEY TERMS

alexithymia (p. 406)

crystallized intelligence (p. 404)

deviation IQ (p. 398)

emotional intelligence (p. 406)

factor analysis (p. 401)

fluid intelligence (p. 404)

fraternal twins (or dizygotic twins) (p. 408)

heritability coefficient (p. 408)

identical twins (or monozygotic twins) (p. 408)

intelligence (p. 396)

nonshared environment (p. 411)

ratio IQ (p. 398)

shared environment (p. 411)

two-factor theory of intelligence (p. 402)

## CHANGING MINDS

1. In biology class, the topic turns to genetics. The professor describes the "Doogie" mouse, named after a 1990s television show starring Neil Patrick Harris as a child genius named Doogie Howser. Doogie mice have a genetic manipulation that makes them smarter than other, genetically normal mice. Your classmate turns to you. "I knew it," she said. "There's a 'smart gene' after all—some people have it, and some people don't, and that's why some people are intelligent and some people aren't." What would you tell her about the role genetics play in intelligence? What other factors, besides genes, play an important role in determining an individual's intelligence?

2. One of your friends tells you about his sister. "We're very competitive," he says. "But she's smarter. We both took IQ tests when we were kids, and she scored 104 but I only scored 102." What would you tell your friend about the relationship between IQ scores and intelligence? What do IQ scores really measure?

3. A speaker visiting your university notes that there are still gender differences in academia; for example, in mathematics departments across the country, women make up only about 26 percent of assistant professors and 10 percent of full professors. One of your classmates notes that the statistic is not surprising: "Girls don't do as well as boys at mathematics," he says. "So it's not surprising that fewer girls choose mathematics-related careers." Based on what you have read in the text about group differences in intelligence, why might women perform more poorly then men on tests of mathematics or science, even if the groups actually have similar ability?

4. One of your female cousins has a young son, and she is very proud of the boy's accomplishments. "He's very smart," she says. "I know this because he has a great memory: He gets 100 percent on all his vocabulary tests." What kind of skills do vocabulary tests measure? Although these skills are important for intelligence, what other abilities contribute to an individual's overall intelligence?

## ANSWERS TO KEY CONCEPT QUIZ

1. c; 2. d; 3. d; 4. c; 5. b; 6. d; 7. a; 8. b; 9. c; 10. a; 11. a; 12. a; 13. b; 14. b.

# 11

# Development

▲ **Prenatality: A Womb with a View**
Prenatal Development
Prenatal Environment
**OTHER VOICES** Men, Who Needs Them?

▲ **Infancy and Childhood: Becoming a Person**
Perceptual and Motor Development
Cognitive Development
**HOT SCIENCE** A Statistician in the Crib
**THE REAL WORLD** Walk This Way
Social Development
Moral Development

▲ **Adolescence: Minding the Gap**
The Protraction of Adolescence
Sexuality
Parents and Peers

▲ **Adulthood: Change We Cannot Believe In**
Changing Abilities
**HOT SCIENCE** The End of History Illusion
Changing Goals
Changing Roles
**OTHER VOICES** You Are Going to Die

HIS MOTHER CALLED HIM ADI AND showered him with affection, but his father was not so kind. As his sister later recalled, "Adi challenged my father to extreme harshness and got his sound thrashing every day. … How often on the other hand did my mother caress him and try to obtain with her kindness where the father could not succeed with harshness." Although his father wanted him to become a civil servant, Adi's true love was art, and his mother quietly encouraged that gentler interest. Adi was just 18 years old when his mother was diagnosed with terminal cancer, and he was heartbroken when she died.

But Adi had little time for grieving. As he later wrote, "Poverty and hard reality compelled me to make a quick decision. I w as faced with the problem of somehow making my own living." Adi resolved to make that living as an artist. He applied to art school but he was flatly rejected. Motherless and penniless, Adi wandered the city streets for 5 long years, sleeping on park benches, living in homeless shelters, and eating in soup kitchens, while trying desperately to sell his sketches and watercolours.

In just 10 years, Adi had achieved the fame he desired, and more. Today his paintings are sought by collectors, who pay significant sums to acquire them. The largest collection of Adi's work is owned by the United States government, which keeps the pieces locked in a room in Washington, DC. The curator of the collection, Marylou Gjernes, once remarked, "I often looked at them and wondered, 'What if? What if he had been accepted into art school? Would World War II have happened?'" The curator's question makes sense because while the artist's mother called him Adi, the rest of us know him as Adolf Hitler.

Adi painted in many styles, including the precise and well-structured watercolour shown here. In 2013, one of his paintings sold at auction for $40 000.

INTERFOTO/ALAMY

MAKSYM BONDACHUK/SHUTTERSTOCK

**WHY IS IT SO DIFFICULT TO IMAGINE THE GREATEST MASS MURDERER** of the twentieth century as a gentle child who loved to draw, as a compassionate adolescent who cared for his ailing mother, or as a dedicated young adult who endured cold and hunger for the sake of art? After all, *you* did not begin as the person you are today, and odds are that you are not yet in finished form. From birth to infancy, from childhood to adolescence, from young adulthood to old age, human beings change over time. Their development includes both dramatic transformations and striking consistencies in the way they look, think, feel, and act. **Developmental psychology** is *the study of continuity and change across the life span,* and in the last century, developmental psychologists have discovered some truly amazing things about this metamorphosis.

COURTESY OF DANIEL GILBERT

From infancy to childhood to adolescence to adulthood, people exhibit both continuity and change.

Let us start where *you* started. We will first examine the 9-month period between conception and birth and see how prenatal events set the stage for everything to come. Then we will examine childhood, during which children must learn how to think about the world and their relationship to it, to understand and bond with others, and to tell the difference between right and wrong. Next, we will examine a relatively new invention called adolescence, which is the stage at which children become both independent and sexual. Finally, we will examine adulthood, the stage at which people typically leave their parents, find mates, and have children.

SIDNEY HARRIS/THE NEW YORKER COLLECTION/CARTOONBANK.COM

**developmental psychology**
The study of continuity and change across the life span.

**zygote**
A fertilized egg that contains chromosomes from both an egg and a sperm.

**germinal stage**
The 2-week period of prenatal development that begins at conception.

**embryonic stage**
The period of prenatal development that lasts from the second week until about the eighth week.

## Prenatality: A Womb with a View

You probably calculate your age by counting your birthdays. But the fact is that on the day you were born, you were already 9 months old. The *prenatal stage* of development ends with birth and begins 9 months earlier when about 200 million sperm make the journey from a woman's vagina, through her uterus, and on to her fallopian tubes. That journey is a perilous one. Many of the sperm have defects that prevent them from swimming vigorously enough to make any progress, and others get stuck in the spermatazoidal equivalent of a traffic jam in which too many sperm are headed in the same direction at the same time. Of those that do manage to make their way through the uterus, many will take a wrong turn and end up in the fallopian tube that does not contain an egg. In fact, a mere 200 or so of the original 200 million sperm will manage to find the correct fallopian tube and get close enough to an egg to release digestive enzymes that erode the egg's protective outer layer. The moment the first sperm manages to penetrate the egg's coating, the egg will release a chemical that seals the coating and keeps all the other sperm from entering. After triumphing over 199 999 999 of its closest friends, this single successful sperm will shed its tail and fertilize the egg. About 12 hours later, the egg will merge with the nuclei of the sperm, and the prenatal development of a unique human being will begin.

## Prenatal Development

A **zygote** is *a fertilized egg that contains chromosomes from both an egg and a sperm.* From the first moment of its existence, a zygote has one thing in common with the person it will someday become: sex. Each human sperm and each human egg contain 23 *chromosomes*. One of these chromosomes (the twenty-third) comes in two varieties known as X and Y. An egg always has an X chromosome, but a sperm can have either an X or a Y chromosome. If the egg is fertilized by a sperm that has a Y chromosome, then the zygote is male (XY), and if it is fertilized by a sperm that has an X chromosome, then the zygote is female (XX).

The **germinal stage** is *the 2-week period of prenatal development that begins at conception.* During this stage, the one-celled zygote divides into two cells that then divide into four cells that then divide into eight cells, and so on. By the time an infant is born, its body contains trillions of cells, each of which came from the original zygote, and each of which contains exactly one set of 23 chromosomes from the sperm and one set of 23 chromosomes from the egg.

> **What are the three prenatal stages?**

During the germinal stage, the zygote migrates back down the fallopian tube and implants itself in the wall of the uterus. This too is a difficult journey, and about half of the zygotes do not complete it, either because they are defective or because they implant themselves in an inhospitable part of the uterus. Male zygotes are especially unlikely to complete this journey and no one understands why (though several comedians have suggested that it is because male zygotes are especially unwilling to stop and ask for directions).

If the zygote successfully implants itself in the uterine wall, it earns the right to be called an *embryo* and a new stage of development begins. The **embryonic stage** is *a period of prenatal development that lasts from the second week until about the eighth week* (see **FIGURE 11.1**). During this stage, the embryo continues to divide and its cells begin to differentiate. Merely 2.5 cm long, the embryo already has a beating heart and other body parts, such as arms and legs. Embryos that have XY chromosomes begin to produce a hormone called testosterone, which masculinizes their reproductive organs.

At about 9 weeks, the embryo gets a new name: *fetus*. The **fetal stage** is *a period of prenatal development that lasts from the ninth week until birth.* The fetus has a skeleton

This electron micrograph shows several human sperm, one of which is fertilizing an egg. Contrary to what many people think, fertilization does not happen right away. It typically happens 1 to 2 days after intercourse, but can happen as long as 5 days later.

EYE OF SCIENCE/SCIENCE SOURCE

CLAUDE EDELMANN/SCIENCE SOURCE

BIOPHOTO ASSOCIATES/SCIENCE SOURCE

JAMES STEVENSON/SCIENCE SOURCE

◄ Figure **11.1** Human beings undergo amazing development in the 9 months of prenatal development. These images show an embryo at 30 days (about the size of a poppy seed), an embryo at 8 to 9 weeks (about the size of an olive), and a fetus at 5 months (about the size of a pomegranate).

and muscles that make it capable of movement. It develops a layer of insulating fat beneath its skin, and its digestive and respiratory systems mature. The cells that will ultimately become the brain divide very quickly around the third and fourth week after conception, and this process is more or less complete by 24 weeks. During the fetal stage, brain cells begin to generate axons and dendrites (which permit communication with other brain cells). They also begin to undergo a process (described in the Neuroscience and Behaviour chapter) known as **myelination,** which is *the formation of a fatty sheath around the axons of a neuron.* Just as plastic sheathing insulates a wire, myelin insulates a brain cell and prevents the leakage of neural signals that travel along the axon. This process starts during the fetal stage but does not end for years; the myelination of the cortex, for example, continues into adulthood.

Although the brain undergoes rapid and complex growth during the fetal period, at birth it is nowhere near its adult size. Whereas a newborn chimpanzee's brain is nearly 60 percent of its adult size, a newborn human's brain is only 25 percent of its adult size, which is to say that 75 percent of a human's brain development occurs outside the womb. Why are humans born with such underdeveloped brains?

First, adult humans have huge heads. If a newborn human's head were 60 percent of its adult size—like a newborn chimp's head is—then that human would never be newborn because it could never pass through its mother's birth canal. Second, one of our species' greatest talents is its ability to adapt to a wide range of novel environments that differ in climate, social structure, and so on. Rather than arriving in the world with a fully developed brain that may or may not meet the requirements of its environment, human beings arrive with brains that do much of their developing *within* the very environments in which they ultimately must function. The fact that our underdeveloped brains are specifically shaped by the unique social and physical environment into which we are born is one of the main reasons why we are so adaptable.

> **Why are human beings born with underdeveloped brains?**

## Prenatal Environment

The womb is an environment that has a powerful impact on development (Coe & Lubach, 2008; Glynn & Sandman, 2011; Wadhwa, Sandman, & Garite, 2001). For example, the *placenta* is the organ that physically links the bloodstreams of the mother and the embryo or fetus and permits the exchange of certain chemicals. That is why the foods a woman eats during pregnancy can affect her unborn child. The children of mothers who receive insufficient nutrition during pregnancy often have physical problems (Stein et al., 1975) and psychological problems, most notably an increased risk of schizophrenia and antisocial personality disorder (Neugebauer, Hoek, & Susser, 1999; Susser, Brown, & Matte, 1999). The foods a woman eats during pregnancy can also shape her child's food preferences: Studies show that infants tend to like the foods and spices that their mothers ate while they were in utero (Mennella, Johnson, & Beauchamp, 1995).

> **How does the uterine environment affect the unborn child?**

But it is not just food that affects the fetus. Almost anything a woman eats, drinks, inhales, injects, sniffs, snorts, or rubs on her skin can pass through the placenta. *Agents that impair prenatal development* are called **teratogens,** which literally means "monster makers." Teratogens include environmental poisons such as lead in the water, paint dust in the air, or mercury in fish, but the most common teratogens can be purchased at your local liquor or convenience store. **Fetal alcohol spectrum disorder (FASD)** is *a developmental disorder that stems from heavy alcohol use by the mother during pregnancy.* It is called a "spectrum disorder" because it manifests in different levels

KAREN HUNT/CORBIS

This chimp and boy share a deep interest in dirt, bugs, and leaves. But one big difference between them is that the chimp was born with a nearly adult-sized brain, whereas the boy was born with a brain that will ultimately quadruple in size.

**fetal stage**
The period of prenatal development that lasts from the ninth week until birth.

**myelination**
The formation of a fatty sheath around the axons of a neuron.

**teratogens**
Agents that impair prenatal development, such as drugs and viruses.

**fetal alcohol spectrum disorder (FASD)**
A developmental disorder that stems from heavy alcohol use by the mother during pregnancy.

## OTHER VOICES

# Men, Who Needs Them?

**Greg Hampikian** is a professor of biology and criminal justice at Boise State University and the director of the Idaho Innocence Project.

PHOTO COURTESY OF GREG HAMPIKIAN

As several of the authors of this book are men, they are very much in favour of their continued existence. But in this only-slightly-tongue-in-cheek essay, biologist Greg Hampikian (2012) does a nice job of explaining just how biologically unimportant men are to the perpetuation of our species.

… With expanding reproductive choices, we can expect to see more women choose to reproduce without men entirely. Fortunately, the data for children raised by only females is encouraging. As the Princeton sociologist Sara S. McLanahan has shown, poverty is what hurts children, not the number or gender of parents.

That's good, since women are both necessary and sufficient for reproduction, and men are neither. From the production of the first cell (egg) to the development of the fetus and the birth and breast-feeding of the child, fathers can be absent. They can be at work, at home, in prison or at war, living or dead.

Think about your own history. Your life as an egg actually started in your mother's developing ovary, before she was born; you were wrapped in your mother's fetal body as it developed within your grandmother.

After the two of you left Grandma's womb, you enjoyed the protection of your mother's prepubescent ovary. Then, sometime between 12 and 50 years after the two of you left your grandmother, you burst forth and were sucked by her fimbriae into the fallopian tube. You glided along the oviduct, surviving happily on the stored nutrients and genetic messages that Mom packed for you.

Then, at some point, your father spent a few minutes close by, but then left. A little while later, you encountered some very odd tiny cells that he had shed. They did not merge with you, or give you any cell membranes or nutrients—just an infinitesimally small packet of DNA, less than one-millionth of your mass.

Over the next nine months, you stole minerals from your mother's bones and oxygen from her blood, and you received all your nutrition, energy and immune protection from her. By the time you were born your mother had contributed six to eight pounds of your weight. Then as a parting gift, she swathed you in billions of bacteria from her birth canal and groin that continue to protect your skin, digestive system and general health. In contrast, your father's 3.3 picograms of DNA comes out to less than one pound of male contribution since the beginning of Homo sapiens 107 billion babies ago.

And while birth seems like a separation, for us mammals it is just a new form of attachment to our female parent. If your mother breast-fed you, as our species has done for nearly our entire existence, then you suckled from her all your water, protein, sugar, fats and even immune protection. She sampled your diseases by holding you close and kissing you, just as your father might have done; but unlike your father, she responded to your infections by making antibodies that she passed to you in breast milk.

I don't dismiss the years I put in as a doting father, or my year at home as a house husband with two young kids. And I credit my own father as the more influential parent in my life. Fathers are of great benefit. But that is a far cry from "necessary and sufficient" for reproduction.

If a woman wants to have a baby without a man, she just needs to secure sperm (fresh or frozen) from a donor (living or dead). The only technology the self-impregnating woman needs is a straw or turkey baster, and the basic technique hasn't changed much since Talmudic scholars debated the religious implications of insemination without sex in the fifth century. If all the men on earth died tonight, the species could continue on frozen sperm. If the women disappear, it's extinction.

Ultimately the question is, does "mankind" really need men? With human cloning technology just around the corner and enough frozen sperm in the world to already populate many generations, perhaps we should perform a cost–benefit analysis.

It's true that men have traditionally been the breadwinners. But women have been a majority of college graduates since the 1980s, and their numbers are growing. It is also true that men have, on average, a bit more muscle mass than women. But in the age of ubiquitous weapons, the one with the better firepower (and knowledge of the law) triumphs.

Meanwhile women live longer, are healthier and are far less likely to commit a violent offense. If men were cars, who would buy the model that doesn't last as long, is given to lethal incidents and ends up impounded more often?

Recently, the geneticist J. Craig Venter showed that the entire genetic material of an organism can be synthesized by a machine and then put into what he called an "artificial cell." This was actually a bit of press-release hyperbole: Mr. Venter started with a fully functional cell, then swapped out its DNA. In doing so, he unwittingly demonstrated that the female component of sexual reproduction, the egg cell, cannot be manufactured, but the male can.

When I explained this to a female colleague and asked her if she thought that there was yet anything irreplaceable about men, she answered, "They're entertaining."

Gentlemen, let's hope that's enough.

of severity that depend on many factors such as the amount the mother drinks, how often she drinks, and whether periods of heavy drinking coincided with critical periods of development in the embryo and fetus. Children with FASD have a variety of brain abnormalities and cognitive deficits (Carmichael Olson et al., 1997; Streissguth et al., 1999). The prevalence of FASD is estimated to be approximately 9.1 per 1000 live births, based on American data from Seattle, Washington (Sampson et al., 1994). However, prevalence varies dramatically across communities—some Canadian First

This child has some of the telltale facial features associated with FASD: short eye openings, a flat midface, a flat ridge under the nose, a thin upper lip, and an underdeveloped jaw.

Nations communities have much higher estimated prevalence (between 25 and 101 per 1000) (Square, 1997; Asante & Nelms-Maztke, 1985). Canada has a strong international reputation in the field of FASD research, and Canadian researchers are currently investigating the abnormal development of the brain in FASD, prevention of FASD in Aboriginal communities, and interventions that may help to prevent or reduce the impact of disabilities associated with prenatal alcohol exposure.

Tobacco is the other common teratogen, and there is no debate about its effects. About 20 percent of American mothers admit to smoking during pregnancy (Substance Abuse and Mental Health Services Administration, 2005). The half-million infants to which they annually give birth are smaller (Horta et al., 1997) and more likely to have perceptual and attentional problems in childhood (Espy et al., 2011; Fried & Watkinson, 2000). Even secondhand smoke can lead to reduced birth weight and deficits in attention and learning (Makin, Fried, & Watkinson, 1991; Windham, Eaton, & Hopkins, 1999). The embryo is more vulnerable to teratogens than is the fetus, but structures such as the central nervous system remain vulnerable throughout the entire prenatal period. Approximately 10 percent of women in Canada smoke during pregnancy (Al-Sahab, Saqib, Hauser, & Tamim, 2010), and 11 percent are exposed to second-hand smoke during pregnancy (Crane et al., 2011). Both maternal smoking and second-hand smoke have been associated with a higher risk of stillbirth and infant death before the first birthday, as well as lower birth weight (birth weight is a general indicator of the health and maturity of the baby), and a smaller head circumference (Crane et al., 2011).

The prenatal environment is rich with chemicals, and it is also rich with information. Unlike an automobile, which operates only after it has been fully assembled, the human brain is operating while it is being built, and research shows that the developing fetus can sense stimulation and learn from it. Wombs are dark because only the brightest light can filter through the mother's abdomen, but they are not quiet. The fetus can hear its mother's heartbeat, the gastrointestinal sounds associated with her digestion, and her voice. How do we know? Newborns will suck a nipple more vigorously when they hear the sound of their mother's voice than when they hear the voice of a female stranger (Querleu et al., 1984), demonstrating that they are more familiar with the former. Similarly, newborns whose mothers read aloud from *The Cat in the Hat* during their pregnancies react as though the story is familiar (DeCasper & Spence, 1986). Newborns who are presented with words from two languages prefer hearing their mother's native language—unless their mother is bilingual, in which case they are just as happy to hear both languages (Byers-Heinlein, Burns, & Werker, 2010). What newborns hear even influences the sounds they make at birth: French newborns cry with a rising melody and German newborns with a falling melody, mimicking the cadence of their mother's native tongue (Mampe et al., 2009). Clearly, the fetus is listening.

**What can a fetus hear?**

## IN SUMMARY

▶ Developmental psychologists study continuity and change across the life span.

▶ The prenatal stage of development begins when a sperm fertilizes an egg, producing a zygote. The zygote, which contains chromosomes from both the egg and the sperm, develops into an embryo at 2 weeks and then into a fetus at 8 weeks.

▶ The fetal environment has important physical and psychological influences on the fetus. In addition to the food a pregnant woman eats, teratogens, or agents that impair fetal development, can affect the fetus. Some of the most common teratogens are alcohol and tobacco.

▶ Although the fetus cannot see much in the womb, it can hear sounds and become familiar with those it hears often, such as its mother's voice.

# Infancy and Childhood: Becoming a Person

Newborns may appear to be capable of little more than squalling and squirming, but in the last decade, researchers have discovered that they are much more sophisticated than they appear. **Infancy** is *the stage of development that begins at birth and lasts between 18 and 24 months* and, as you will see, a lot more happens during this stage than meets the untrained eye.

## Perceptual and Motor Development

New parents like to stand around the crib and make goofy faces at the baby because they think the baby will be amused. In fact, newborns have a rather limited range of vision. The level of detail that a newborn can see at a distance of 6.1 m (20 feet) is roughly equivalent to the level of detail that an adult can see at 183 m (600 feet)

> **What do newborns see?**

(Banks & Salapatek, 1983), which is to say that they are missing out on a lot of the cribside shenanigans. On the other hand, when stimuli are 20 to 50 cm (8 to 12 inches) away (about the distance between a nursing infant's eyes and its mother's face), newborns are visually quite responsive. How do we know what newborns are seeing? In one study, newborns were shown a circle with diagonal stripes over and over again. The infants stared a lot at first, and then less and less on each subsequent presentation. Recall from the Learning chapter that *habituation* is the tendency for organisms to respond less intensely to a stimulus as the frequency of exposure to that stimulus increases, and infants habituate just like the rest of us do. So what happened when the researchers rotated the circle 90°? The newborns once again stared intently, indicating that they had noticed the change in the circle's orientation (Slater, Morison, & Somers, 1988).

Newborns are especially attentive to social stimuli. For example, newborns in one study were shown a circle, a circle with scrambled facial features, or a circle with a regular face. When the circle was moved across their fields of vision, the newborns tracked the circle by moving their heads and eyes—but they tracked the circle with the regular face longer than they tracked the others (Johnson et al., 1991). Newborns do more than simply track social stimuli. Researchers in one study stood close to some newborns while sticking out their tongues and stood close to other newborns while pursing their lips. Newborns in the first group stuck out their own tongues more often than those in the second group did, and newborns in the second group pursed their lips more often than those in the first group did (Meltzoff & Moore, 1977). Indeed, newborns have been shown to mimic facial expressions in their very first *hour* of life (Reissland, 1988) and to mimic speech sounds as early as 12 weeks (Kuhl & Meltzoff, 1996).

Although infants can use their eyes right away, they must spend considerably more time learning how to use their other parts. **Motor development** is *the emergence of the ability to execute physical actions* such as reaching,

> **Why are infants born with reflexes?**

grasping, crawling, and walking. Infants are born with a small set of **reflexes,** which are *specific patterns of motor response that are triggered by specific patterns of sensory stimulation.* For example, the *rooting reflex* is the tendency for infants to move their mouths toward any object that touches their cheek, and the *sucking reflex* is the tendency to suck any object that enters their mouths. These two reflexes allow newborns to find their mother's nipple and begin feeding—a behaviour so vitally important that nature took no chances and hardwired it into every one of us. Interestingly, these and other reflexes that are present at birth seem to disappear in the first few months as infants learn to execute more sophisticated motor behaviour.

Infants mimic the facial expressions of adults—and vice versa, of course!

**infancy**
The stage of development that begins at birth and lasts between 18 and 24 months.

**motor development**
The emergence of the ability to execute physical action.

**reflexes**
Specific patterns of motor response that are triggered by specific patterns of sensory stimulation.

**cephalocaudal rule**
The "top-to-bottom" rule that describes the tendency for motor skills to emerge in sequence from the head to the feet.

**proximodistal rule**
The "inside-to-outside" rule that describes the tendency for motor skills to emerge in sequence from the centre to the periphery.

Motor skills develop through practice. In just 1 hour in a playroom, the average 12- to 19-month-old infant takes 2368 steps, travels 0.6 km, and falls 17 times (Adolph et al., 2012).

If reflexes disappear as more voluntary motor behaviour develops, does this mean that the reflexes interfere with voluntary motor behaviour (McGraw, 1943)? A simple study by McGill University researcher Phil Zelazo and his colleagues demonstrates that this is not the case (Zelazo, 1972, 1976; Zelazo, Zelazo, & Kolb, 1972). In fact, in at least one instance, an early "disappearing" reflex (the "stepping reflex" in which young babies reflexively "step" on a solid surface) appeared to facilitate later motor development. The researchers elicited the stepping reflex every day in a group of young infants. Not only did the stepping reflex not disappear along the "normal" developmental trajectory in these infants, but they developed voluntary walking earlier than untrained infants. The researchers concluded that the involuntary walking reflex could be transformed into voluntary walking (Zelazo, 1983).

The development of these more sophisticated behaviours tends to obey two general rules. The first is the **cephalocaudal rule** (or the "top-to-bottom" rule), which describes *the tendency for motor skills to emerge in sequence from the head to the feet.* Infants tend to gain control over their heads first, their arms and trunks next, and their legs last. A young infant who is placed on her stomach may lift her head and her chest by using her arms for support, but she typically has little control over her legs. The second rule is the **proximodistal rule** (or the "inside-to-outside" rule), which describes *the tendency for motor skills to emerge in sequence from the centre to the periphery.* Infants learn to control their trunks before their elbows and knees, which they learn to control before their hands and feet (see **FIGURE 11.2**).

> **In what order do infants learn to use parts of their bodies?**

Motor skills generally emerge in an orderly sequence but not on a strict timetable. Rather, the timing of these skills is influenced by many factors, such as the infant's incentive for reaching, body weight, muscular development, and general level of activity. In one study, infants who had visually stimulating mobiles hanging above their cribs began reaching for objects 6 weeks earlier than infants who did not (White & Held, 1966). Furthermore, different infants seem to acquire the same skill in different ways. By closely following the development of four infants, one study examined

► Figure **11.2 Motor Development**
Infants learn to control their bodies from head to feet and from centre to periphery. These skills do not emerge on a strict timetable, but they do emerge in a strict sequence.

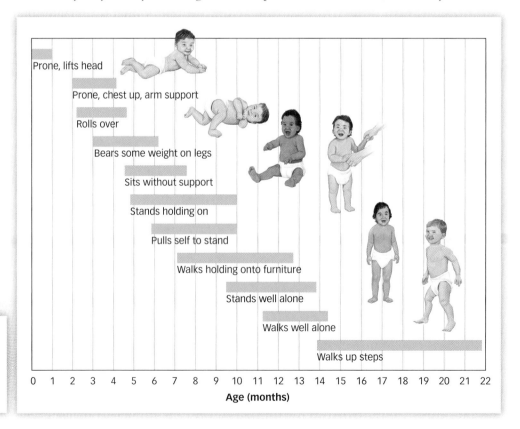

how children learn to reach (Thelen et al., 1993). Two of the infants were especially energetic and initially produced large circular movements of both arms. To reach accurately, these infants had to learn to dampen these large circular movements by holding their arms rigid at the elbow and swiping at an object. The other two infants were less energetic and did not produce large, circular movements. Thus, their first step in learning to reach involved learning to lift their arms against the force of gravity and extend them forward. Detailed observations such as these suggest that, although most infants learn how to reach, different infants learn in different ways (Adolph & Avoilio, 2000).

## Cognitive Development

Infants can hear and see and move their bodies. But can they think? In the first half of the twentieth century, a Swiss biologist named Jean Piaget became interested in this question. He noticed that when confronted with difficult problems (Does the big glass have more liquid in it than the small glass? Can Billy see what you see?), children of the same age made roughly the same mistakes. And as they aged, they stopped making these mistakes at about the same time. This led Piaget to suggest that children move through discrete stages of **cognitive development,** which is *the emergence of the ability to think and understand.* Between infancy and adulthood, children must come to understand three important things: (a) how the physical world works, (b) how their minds represent the world, and (c) how other minds represent the world. Let us see how children accomplish these three essential tasks.

> **What are the three essential tasks of cognitive development?**

### Discovering the World

Piaget (1954) suggested that cognitive development occurs in four stages: the *sensorimotor* stage, the *pre-operational* stage, the *concrete operational* stage, and the *formal operational* stage (see **TABLE 11.1**). The **sensorimotor stage** is *the stage of cognitive development that begins at birth and lasts through infancy.* As the word *sensorimotor* suggests, infants at this stage are mainly busy using their ability to *sense* and their ability to *move* to acquire information about the world. By actively exploring their environments with their eyes, mouths, and fingers, infants begin to construct **schemas,** which are *theories about the way the world works.* For example, an infant sitting in a highchair might notice that every time he or she drops something, it falls to the floor. A bit later, the infant notices that a fistful of food does not make a sound when dropped, but when the spoon is dropped, it clatters. These consistent observations can lead to predictions ("When I drop this, I will hear a sound"), just like any other theory.

**cognitive development**
The emergence of the ability to think and understand.

**sensorimotor stage**
A stage of cognitive development that begins at birth and lasts through infancy in which infants acquire information about the world by sensing it and moving around within it.

**schemas**
Theories about the way the world works.

Jean Piaget (1896–1980) was the father of modern developmental psychology, as well as the last man to look good in a beret.

During the sensorimotor stage, infants explore with their hands and mouths, learning important lessons about the physical world such as, "If you whack Jell-O hard enough, you can actually wear it."

> **Table 11.1**

### Piaget's Four Stages of Cognitive Development

| Stage | Characteristic |
|---|---|
| Sensorimotor (Birth–2 years) | Infant experiences world through movement and senses, develops schemas, begins to act intentionally, and shows evidence of understanding object permanence. |
| Pre-operational (2–6 years) | Child acquires motor skills but does not understand conservation of physical properties. Child begins this stage by thinking egocentrically but ends with a basic understanding of other minds. |
| Concrete operational (6–11 years) | Child can think logically about physical objects and events and understands conservation of physical properties. |
| Formal operational (11 years and up) | Child can think logically about abstract propositions and hypotheticals. |

**assimilation**
The process by which infants apply their schemas in novel situations.

**accommodation**
The process by which infants revise their schemas in light of new information.

**object permanence**
The belief that objects continue to exist even when they are not visible.

As every scientist knows, the key advantage of having a theory is that one can use it to predict and control what will happen in novel situations. If an infant learns that tugging at a stuffed animal causes the toy to come closer, then that observation is incorporated into the infant's theory about how physical objects behave, and the infant can later use that theory when he or she wants a different object to come closer, such as a rattle or a ball.

> **What happens at the sensorimotor stage?**

Piaget called this **assimilation,** which happens when *infants apply their schemas in novel situations.* Of course, if the infant tugs the tail of the family cat, the cat is likely to sprint in the opposite direction. Infants' theories about the world ("Things come closer if I pull them") are occasionally disconfirmed, and so infants must occasionally adjust their schemas in light of their new experiences ("Aha! Only *inanimate* things come closer when I pull them"). Piaget called this **accommodation,** which happens when *infants revise their schemas in light of new information.*

What kinds of schemas do infants develop, apply, and adjust? Piaget suggested that infants lack some very basic understandings about the physical world and therefore must acquire them through experience. For example, when you put your shoes in the closet, you know that they exist even after you close the closet door, and you would be rather surprised if you opened the door a moment later and found the closet empty. But accord-

> **When do children acquire a theory of object permanence?**

ing to Piaget, this would not surprise an infant because infants do not have a theory of **object permanence,** which is *the belief that objects exist even when they are not visible.* Piaget noted that in the first few months of life, infants act as though objects stop existing the moment they are out of sight. For instance, he observed that a 2-month-old infant will track a moving object with her eyes, but once the object leaves her visual field, she will not search for it. Put the shoes in the closet and—poof!—they are gone!

Was Piaget right? As a general rule, when infants demonstrate an ability, then they definitely have it, but when they fail to demonstrate an ability, they may lack the ability *or* the test may not be sensitive enough to reveal it. Modern research shows that when other tests are used, infants can demonstrate their sense of object permanence much earlier than Piaget realized (Shinskey & Munakata, 2005). For instance, in one study, infants were shown a miniature drawbridge that flipped up and down (see **FIGURE 11.3**). Once the infants got used to this, they watched as a box was placed behind the drawbridge—in its path but out of their sight. Some infants then saw a *possible* event: The drawbridge began to flip and then suddenly stopped, as if

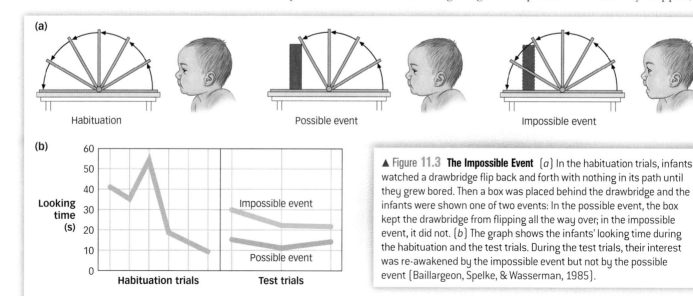

(a) Habituation    Possible event    Impossible event

(b) Looking time (s)

Habituation trials    Test trials

Impossible event
Possible event

▲ Figure **11.3** **The Impossible Event** [*a*] In the habituation trials, infants watched a drawbridge flip back and forth with nothing in its path until they grew bored. Then a box was placed behind the drawbridge and the infants were shown one of two events: In the possible event, the box kept the drawbridge from flipping all the way over; in the impossible event, it did not. [*b*] The graph shows the infants' looking time during the habituation and the test trials. During the test trials, their interest was re-awakened by the impossible event but not by the possible event (Baillargeon, Spelke, & Wasserman, 1985).

impeded by the box that the infants could not see. Other infants saw an *impossible* event: The drawbridge began to flip and then continued, as if unimpeded by the box. What did infants do? Four-month-old infants stared longer at the impossible event than at the possible event, suggesting that they were puzzled by it (Baillargeon, Spelke, & Wasserman, 1985). The only thing that could have made it puzzling, of course, was the fact that the unseen box was not stopping the progress of the drawbridge (Fantz, 1964).

Studies such as these suggest that infants do indeed have some understanding of object permanence by the time they are just 4 months old. For example, what do infants see when they look at the line labelled A in **FIGURE 11.4**? Adults see a continuous blue line that is being obstructed by the solid orange block in front of it. Do infants see line A as continuous and obstructed, or do they see it as two blue objects on either side of an orange object? Studies show that when infants are allowed to become familiar with line A, they are subsequently more surprised by line C than by line B, despite the fact that line C actually *looks* more like line A than does line B (Kellman & Spelke, 1983). This suggests that infants see line A as a continuous line. Infants clearly do not think of the world only in terms of its visible parts, and at a very early age they seem to "know" that objects continue to exist even when they are out of sight (Wang & Baillargeon, 2008).

Piaget (1927/1977, p. 199) wrote: "The child's first year of life is unfortunately still an abyss of mysteries for the psychologist. If only we could know what is going on in a baby's mind while observing him in action, we could certainly understand everything there is to psychology." Although the mystery of the infant mind is still far from solved, it is no longer an abyss. Research has taught us a great deal about what infants do and do not know, and the general conclusion is that they know much more than Piaget (or their parents) ever suspected (Gopnik, 2012).

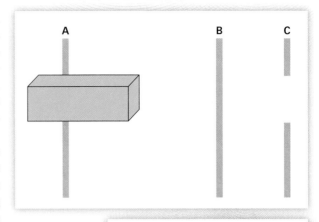

▲ Figure 11.4 **Object Permanence**
Do infants see line A as continuous or broken? Infants who are shown line A are subsequently more interested when they are shown line C than line B. This indicates that they consider C more novel than B, which suggests that the infants saw line A as continuous and not broken (Kellman & Spelke, 1983).

## A Statistician in the Crib

HOT SCIENCE

A magician asks you to shuffle a deck of cards and then name your favourite. He then dons a blindfold, reaches out his hand, and pulls your favourite card from the deck. You are astonished—and the reason you are astonished is that you know that when a magician reaches into a deck of 52 cards, the odds that he will pick your favourite by sheer chance alone are rather small.

Would that trick astonish an infant? That is pretty hard to imagine. After all, to appreciate the trick, one has to understand a basic rule of statistics, namely, that random samples look roughly like the populations from which they are drawn. But recent research (Denison, Reed, & Xu, 2013) suggests that infants as young as 24 weeks understand just that.

In one study, researchers showed infants two boxes: one had mostly pink balls and just a few yellows; the other had mostly yellow balls with a few pinks. The infants then watched as an experimenter closed her eyes and reached into the mostly pink box, pulled out some balls, and deposited them in a little container in front of the infant. Sometimes she deposited four pinks and a yellow, and sometimes she deposited four yellows and a pink. What did the infants do?

When the experimenter pulled mainly pink balls from a mainly pink box, the infants glanced and then looked away. But when she pulled mainly yellow balls from a mainly pink box, they stared like bystanders at a train wreck. The fact that infants looked longer at the improbable sample than at the probable sample suggests that they found the former more astonishing; in other words, they had some basic understanding of how random sampling works.

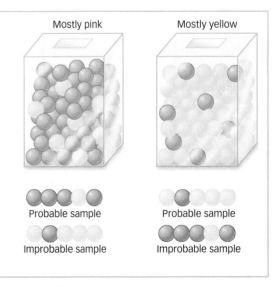

This study—like so many in developmental psychology—teaches us that infants know a lot more than anyone could guess from casual observation of their behaviour.

**childhood**
The stage of development that begins at about 18 to 24 months and lasts until about 11 to 14 years.

**pre-operational stage**
The stage of cognitive development that begins at about 2 years and ends at about 6 years, during which children develop a preliminary understanding of the physical world.

**concrete operational stage**
The stage of cognitive development that begins at about 6 years and ends at about 11 years, during which children learn how various actions or "operations" can affect or transform "concrete" objects.

**conservation**
The notion that the quantitative properties of an object are invariant despite changes in the object's appearance.

When pre-operational children are shown two equal-size glasses filled with equal amounts of liquid, they correctly say that neither glass "has more." But when the contents of one glass are poured into a taller, thinner glass, they incorrectly say that the taller glass now "has more." Concrete operational children do not make this mistake because they recognize that operations such as pouring change the appearance of the liquid but not its actual volume.

## Discovering the Mind

The long period following infancy is called **childhood,** which is *the period that begins at about 18 to 24 months and lasts until about 11 to 14 years.* According to Piaget, children enter childhood at one stage of cognitive development and leave at another. They enter in the **pre-operational stage,** which is *the stage of cognitive development that begins at about 2 years and ends at about 6 years, during which children develop a preliminary understanding of the physical world.* They exit at the **concrete operational stage,** which is *the stage of cognitive development that begins at about 6 years and ends at about 11 years, during which children learn how actions or "operations" can transform the "concrete" objects of the physical world.*

The difference between these stages is nicely illustrated by one of Piaget's clever experiments in which he showed children a row of cups and asked them to place an egg in each. Pre-operational children were able to do this, and afterward they readily agreed that there were just as many eggs as there were cups. Then Piaget removed the eggs and spread them out in a long line that extended beyond the row of cups. Pre-operational children incorrectly claimed that there were now more eggs than cups, pointing out that the row of eggs was longer than the row of cups and hence there must be more of them. Concrete operational children, on the other hand, correctly reported that the number of eggs did not change when they were spread out in a longer line. They understood that *quantity* is a property of a set of concrete objects that does not change when an operation such as *spreading out* alters the set's appearance (Piaget, 1954). Piaget called the child's insight **conservation,** which is *the notion that the quantitative properties of an object are invariant despite changes in the object's appearance.*

> What distinguishes the pre-operational and concrete operational stages?

Why do pre-operational children not seem to grasp the notion of conservation? Piaget suggested that children have several tendencies that explain this mistake. For instance, *centration* is the tendency to focus on just one property of an object to the exclusion of all others. Whereas adults can consider several properties at once, children focus on the length of the line of eggs without simultaneously considering the amount of space between each egg. Piaget also suggested that children fail to think about *reversibility.* That is, they do not consider the fact that the operation that made the line of eggs longer could be reversed: The eggs could be repositioned more closely together, and the line would become shorter. Both of these tendencies make it difficult for the pre-operational child to recognize that a *longer line of eggs* does not necessarily mean *more eggs.*

But there is an even deeper reason why pre-operational children do not fully grasp the notion of conservation: They do not fully grasp the fact that they have *minds* and that these minds contain *mental representations* of the world! As adults, we naturally distinguish between the subjective and the objective, between appearances and realities, between things in the mind and things in the world. We realize that things are not always as they seem: A wagon can *be* red but *look* grey at dusk, and a highway can *be* dry but *look* wet in the heat. We make a distinction between the way things *are* and the way we *see* them. Visual illusions delight us precisely because we know that they look like *this* but are really like *that.* Pre-operational children do not make this distinction. When something *looks* grey or wet, they assume it *is* grey or wet.

As children move from the pre-operational to the concrete operational stage, they have a major epiphany that will stay with them for the rest of their lives: The way the world *appears* is not necessarily the way the world really *is.* They realize that their minds represent—and hence can misrepresent—the objects in the world, and this enables them to solve problems that require them to ignore an object's subjective appearance (cf. Deák, 2006). For instance, concrete operational children can understand that when a ball of clay is rolled, stretched, or flattened, it is still the same amount of clay despite the fact that it looks larger in one form than in another. They can understand that when water is poured from a short, wide beaker into a tall, thin cylinder, it is still the same amount of water despite the fact that the water level in the cylinder is higher. They can understand that when a sponge is painted grey to look like a rock, it is still a sponge despite its appearance. Once children can make a distinction between objects and their mental representations of those objects, they begin to understand that certain operations—such as squishing, pouring, and spreading out—can change what an object *looks* like without changing what the object *is* like.

Once children are at the concrete operational stage, they can readily solve physical problems involving egg-spreading and clay-squishing. They learn to solve non-physical problems with equal ease at the **formal operational stage,** which is *the final stage of cognitive development that begins around the age of 11, during which children learn to reason about abstract concepts.* Childhood ends when formal operations begin.

> **What is the essential feature of the formal operational stage?**

People who move on to this stage (and Piaget believed that some people never did) are able to reason systematically about abstract concepts such as *liberty* and *love* and about hypotheticals and counterfactuals—about events that have not yet happened, and about events that might have happened but did not. There are no concrete objects in the world to which words such as *liberating* or *loving* refer, and yet people at the formal operational stage can think and reason about such concepts in the same way that a concrete operational child can think and reason about squishing and folding. The ability to generate, consider, reason about, or mentally "operate on" abstract objects, is the hallmark of formal operations.

## Discovering Other Minds

As children develop, they discover their own minds, but they also discover the minds of others. Because pre-operational children do not fully grasp the fact that they have minds that mentally represent objects, they also do not fully grasp the fact that other people have minds that may mentally represent the same objects in different ways. As such, pre-operational children generally expect others to see the world as they do. When 3-year-old children are asked what a person on the opposite side of a table is seeing, they typically claim that the other person sees what they see. **Egocentrism** is *the failure to understand that the world appears differently to different people.* Egocentrism is a hallmark of the pre-operational stage and it reveals itself in a variety of interesting ways.

**Perceptions and Beliefs.** Just as 3-year-old children do not realize that other people do not see what they see, they also do not realize that other people do not know what they know. This fact has been demonstrated in hundreds of studies using *the false-belief task* (Wimmer & Perner, 1983). In the standard version of this task, children

> **What does the false-belief task show?**

see a puppet named Maxi deposit some chocolate in a cupboard and then leave the room. A second puppet arrives a moment later, finds the chocolate, and moves it to a different cupboard. The children are then asked where Maxi will look for the chocolate when he returns: in the first cupboard where he initially put it, or in the second cupboard where the children know it currently is. Most 5-year-olds realize that Maxi will search the first cupboard because Maxi did not see what the children saw, namely, that the chocolate was moved. But 3-year-olds typically claim that Maxi will look in the second cupboard. Why? Because that is where *the children* know the chocolate to be—and what they know, everyone knows! Children are able to do the false-belief task somewhere between the ages of 4 to 6 (Callaghan et al., 2005), and children in some cultures are able to do it it earlier than children in others (Liu et al., 2008).

**formal operational stage**
The final stage of cognitive development that begins around the age of 11, during which children learn to reason about abstract concepts.

**egocentrism**
The failure to understand that the world appears differently to different people.

People who reach the formal operational stage can reason about abstract concepts such as freedom and justice. These protesters are taking part in a demonstration in Toronto, calling for justice in the the shooting death of a youth by local police.

When young children are told to hide, they sometimes cover their eyes. Because they cannot see you, they assume that you cannot see them (Russell, Gee, & Bullard, 2012).

Some researchers believe that the false-belief task, like Piaget's test for object permanence, does not allow very young children to demonstrate their true abilities, and several recent studies have shown that much younger children can indeed do modified versions of the false-belief task (Baillargeon, Scott, & He, 2010; Onishi & Baillargeon, 2005; Rubio-Fernandez & Geurts, 2012; Senju et al., 2011; Southgate, Senju, & Csibra, 2007). But it is not clear that very young children do these tasks the same way as older children do, namely, by truly understanding that other people can have beliefs that differ from their own (Apperly & Butterfill, 2009; Low & Watts, 2013). Whatever very young children are doing, their performances are impressive, and it seems clear that children begin to understand the nature of other minds much earlier than Piaget suspected.

Just as egocentrism affects children's understandings of others' minds, so does it affect their understanding of their own minds. In a classic study, University of Toronto researchers showed young children a box of Smarties and then opened it, revealing that it contained pencils instead of candy. Then the researchers closed the box and asked, "When I first showed you the box all closed up like this, what did you think was inside?" Although most 5-year-olds said Smarties, most 3-year-olds said pencils (Gopnik & Astington, 1988). For the 3-year-old child, a past self is like another person, and so the past self must have known what the child now knows.

**Desires and Emotions.** Different people have different perceptions and beliefs. They also have different desires and emotions. Do children understand that these aspects of other people's mental lives may also differ from their own? Surprisingly, even very young children who do not yet fully understand that others have different perceptions or beliefs do seem to understand that other people have different desires. For

> **Do children understand emotions better than beliefs?**

example, a 2-year-old who likes dogs can understand that other children do not like dogs, and can correctly predict that other children will avoid dogs that the child herself would approach. When 18-month-old toddlers see an adult express disgust while eating a food that the toddlers enjoy, they hand the adult a different food, as if they understand that different people have different tastes (Repacholi & Gopnik, 1997). Interestingly, young children understand other people's desires best when their own desires have already been fulfilled and are not competing for their attention (Atance, Bélanger, & Meltzoff, 2010).

In contrast, children take a much longer time to understand that other people may have emotional reactions unlike their own. When 5-year-olds hear a story in which Little Red Riding Hood knocks on her grandmother's door, unaware that a wolf is inside waiting to devour her, they realize that Little Red Riding Hood does not know what they know; nonetheless, they expect Little Red Riding Hood to feel what they feel, namely, fear (Bradmetz & Schneider, 2004; DeRosnay et al., 2004; Harris et al., 1989). When asked where Maxi will look for the chocolate that was moved while Maxi was out of the room, they correctly say that Maxi will look in the original location, but they incorrectly say that Maxi feels sad. It is only at about 6 years of age that children come to understand that because they and others have different knowledge, they and others may also experience different emotions in the same situation.

**Theory of Mind.** Clearly, children have a whole lot to learn about how the mind works—and most of them eventually do. The vast majority of children ultimately come to understand that they and others have minds and that these minds represent

*"You're five. How could you possibly understand the problems of a five-and-a-half-year-old?"*

the world in different ways. Once children understand these things, they are said to have acquired a **theory of mind,** which is *the understanding that human behaviour is guided by mental representations.*

theory of mind
The understanding that human behaviour is guided by mental representations.

Most of us eventually acquire a theory of mind, but two groups of people are somewhat slower to do so. Children with *autism* (a disorder we will cover in more depth in the Psychological Disorders chapter) typically have difficulty communicating with other people and making friends, and some psychologists have suggested that this is because they have trouble acquiring a theory of mind (Frith, 2003). Although children with autism are typically normal on most intellectual dimensions—and sometimes far better than normal—they have difficulty understanding the inner lives of other people (Dawson et al., 2007).

> **Which children have special difficulty acquiring a theory of mind?**

They do not seem to understand that other people can have false beliefs (Baron-Cohen, Leslie, & Frith, 1985; Senju et al., 2009), and they have special trouble understanding belief-based emotions such as embarrassment and shame (Baron-Cohen, 1991; Heerey, Keltner, & Capps, 2003). Interestingly, until children acquire a theory of mind they are generally not susceptible to the phenomenon of "contagious yawning" (Platek et al., 2003), and in fact, people with autism are also less likely to "catch a yawn" (Senju et al., 2007).

The second group of children who lag behind their peers in acquiring a theory of mind is a subset of deaf children: those with parents who cannot communicate with them (either because the child has not received a cochlear implant, or because the parents do not know sign language). These children are slow to learn to communicate because they do not have ready access to any form of conventional language, and this restriction seems to slow the development of their understanding of other minds. Like children with autism, they display difficulties in understanding false beliefs even at 5 or 6 years of age (DeVilliers, 2005; Peterson & Siegal, 1999). Learning a language, either spoken or signed, seems to help children acquire a theory of mind (Pyers & Senghas, 2009).

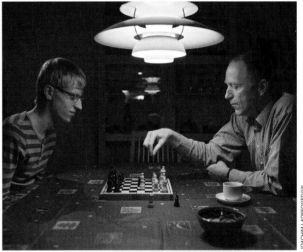

People with autism often have an unusual ability to concentrate on small details, words, and numbers for extended periods of time. Thorkil Sonne (*right*) started a company called Specialisterne.com, which places people with autism—like his son Lars (*left*)—at jobs that they can do better than more "neurotypical" people can.

The age at which children acquire a theory of mind appears to be influenced by a variety of other factors, such as the number of siblings the child has, the frequency with which the child engages in pretend play, whether the child has an imaginary companion, and the socioeconomic status of the child's family. But of all the factors researchers have studied, language seems to be the most important (Astington & Baird, 2005). Children's language skills are an excellent predictor of how well they perform on false-belief tasks (Happé, 1995). The way that caregivers talk to children is also a good predictor of how well children do these tasks. Perhaps not surprisingly, children whose caregivers frequently talk about thoughts and feelings tend to be good at understanding beliefs and belief-based emotions. Some psychologists speculate that children benefit from hearing psychological words such as *want, think, know,* and *sad;* others suggest that children benefit from the grammatically complex sentences that typically contain these psychological words; and some believe that caregivers who use psychological words are also more effective in getting children to reflect on mental states. Whatever the explanation, it is clear that language—and especially language about thoughts and feelings—is an important tool for helping children make sense of their own and others' minds (Harris, de Rosnay, & Pons, 2005).

**Piaget Remixed.** Cognitive development is an amazing and complex journey, and Piaget's ideas about it were nothing short of groundbreaking. Few psychologists have had such a profound impact on the field. Many of these ideas have held up quite well, but in the last few decades, psychologists have discovered two general ways

Development is not the step-like progression that Piaget imagined. Children who are transitioning between stages may act more mature one day and less mature the next.

in which Piaget got it wrong. First, Piaget thought that children graduated from one stage to another in the same way that they graduated from kindergarten to first grade: a child is in kindergarten *or* first grade, he or she is never in both, and there is an exact moment of transition to which everyone with a clock or a calendar can point. Modern psychologists see development as more fluid and continuous: a less step-like progression than Piaget believed. Children who are transitioning between stages may perform more mature behaviours one day and less mature behaviours the next. Cognitive development is more like the change of seasons than it is like graduation.

The second thing about which Piaget was mistaken was the ages at which these transitions occur. By and large, they happen *earlier* than he realized (Gopnik, 2012). For example, Piaget suggested that infants had no sense of object permanence because they did not actively search for objects that were moved out of their sight. But when researchers use experimental procedures that allow infants to "show what they know," even 4-month-olds display a sense of object permanence. Piaget suggested that it takes many years until children can overcome their egocentrism enough to realize that others do not know what they know, but new experimental procedures have detected some evidence of this understanding in 13-month-old infants (Baillargeon et al., 2010). Every year, clever researchers find new ways of testing infants and children, and every year, textbook authors must lower the age at which cognitive milestones are achieved.

> What did Piaget get wrong?

## Discovering Our Cultures

Piaget saw the child as a lone scientist who made observations, developed theories, and then revised those theories in light of new observations. And yet, most scientists do not start from scratch. Rather, they receive training from more experienced scientists and they inherit the theories and methods of their disciplines. According to Russian psychologist Lev Vygotsky, children do much the same thing. Vygotsky was born in 1896, the same year as Piaget, but unlike Piaget, he believed that cognitive development was largely the result of the child's interaction with members of his or her own culture rather than his or her interaction with concrete objects. Vygotsky noted that cultural tools, such as language and counting systems, exert a strong influence on cognitive development (Vygotsky, 1978).

Children are not lone explorers who discover the world for themselves but members of families, communities, and societies that teach them much of what they need to know.

For example, in English, the numbers beyond 20 are named by a decade (twenty) that is followed by a digit (one) and their names follow a logical pattern (twenty-one, twenty-two, twenty-three, etc.). In Chinese, Japanese, and Korean, the numbers from 11 to 19 are similarly constructed (ten-one, ten-two, ten-three…). But in English, the names of the numbers between 11 and 19 either reverse the order of the decade and the digit (sixteen, seventeen) or are entirely arbitrary (eleven, twelve). The difference in the regularity of these two systems makes a big difference to the children who must learn them. It is obvious to a Chinese-speaking child that 12—which is called "ten-two"—can be decomposed into 10 and 2, but it is not so obvious to an English-speaking child, who calls the number "twelve" (see **FIGURE 11.5** on the next page). In one study, children from many countries were asked to hand an experimenter a certain number of bricks. Some of the bricks were single, and some were glued together in strips of 10. When Asian children were asked to hand the experimenter 26 bricks, they tended to hand over two strips of 10 plus six singles. Non-Asian children tended to use the clumsier strategy of counting out 26 single bricks (Miura et al., 1994). Results such as these suggest that the regularity of the counting system that children inherit can

> How does culture affect cognitive development?

promote or discourage their discovery of the fact that two-digit numbers can be decomposed (Gordon, 2004; Imbo & LeFevre, 2009).

Of course, if you have ever tried to train a pet snake, you already know that not all species are well prepared to learn from others. Human beings are the champions in this regard, because we have three skills that make us nature's most exceptional students (Meltzoff et al., 2009; Striano & Reid, 2006).

> If an adult turns her head to the left, young infants (3 months) and older infants (9 months) will look to the left. But if the adult first closes her eyes and then looks to the left, the young infant will look to the left but the older infant will not (Brooks & Meltzoff, 2002). This suggests that older infants are not following the adult's head movements, but rather, they are following her gaze: They are trying to see what they think she is seeing. If older infants can hear but not see an adult, they will use auditory cues to determine which way the adult must be looking and will then look in that direction (Rossano, Carpenter, & Tomasello, 2012). The ability to focus on what another person is focused on is known as *joint attention* and it is a prerequisite for learning what others have to teach (see **FIGURE 11.6**).

> Infants are natural mimics who often do what they see adults do (Jones, 2007). But very early on, infants begin to mimic adults' *intentions* rather than their actions per se. When an 18-month-old sees an adult's hand slip as the adult tries to pull the lid off a jar, the infant will not copy the slip, but will instead perform the *intended* action by removing the lid (Meltzoff, 1995, 2007). The tendency to do what an adult does—or what an adult meant to do—is known as *imitation*. By the age of 3, children begin to copy adults so precisely that they will even copy parts of actions that they know to be pointless, a phenomenon called *overimitation* (Lyons, Young, & Keil, 2007; Simpson & Riggs, 2011).

> An infant who approaches a new toy will often stop and look back at his or her mother, examining her face for cues about whether mom thinks the toy is or is not dangerous. The ability to use another person's reactions as information about how we should think about the world is known as *social referencing* (Kim, Walden, & Knieps, 2010; Walden & Ogan, 1988). (You will learn a lot more about how adults continue to use this skill when we discuss *informational influence* in the Social Psychology chapter.)

Joint attention ("I see what you see"), imitation ("I do what you do"), and social referencing ("I think what you think") are the three basic abilities that allow infants to learn from other members of their species.

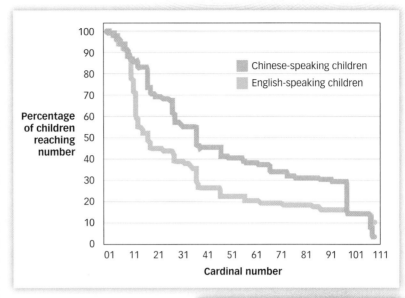

▲ Figure **11.5** **Twelve or Ten-Two?** The arbitrary English "twelve" versus the logical Chinese "ten-two" may put children learning counting in English at a disadvantage. As this graph shows, the percentage of English-speaking children who can count through the cardinal numbers drops off suddenly when they hit the number 11, whereas the percentage of Chinese-speaking children shows a more gradual decline (Miller, Smith, & Zhu, 1995).

▼ Figure **11.6** **Joint Attention** Joint attention allows children to learn from others. When a 12-month-old infant interacts with an adult (a) who then looks at an object (b), the infant will typically look at the same object (c)—but only when the adult's eyes are open (Meltzoff et al., 2009).

(a)

(b)

(c)

A.N. MELTZOFF, P.K. KUHL, T.J. SENJOWSKI, & J. MOVELLAN. "FOUNDATIONS FOR A NEW SCIENCE OF LEARNING". PUBLISHED IN SCIENCE, 2009, VOL. 325, JULY 17, PP. 284–288.

# Walk This Way

Parents often complain that their children will not take their advice. But research shows that even 18-month-old infants know when to listen to their parents—and when to ignore them.

Researchers (Tamis-LeMonda et al., 2008) built an inclined plane whose steepness could be adjusted (as shown in the photograph below), put some infants at the top and their moms at the bottom, and then watched to see whether the infants would attempt to walk down the plane and toward their mothers. Sometimes the plane was adjusted so that it was clearly flat and safe, sometimes it was adjusted so that it was clearly steep and risky, and sometimes it was adjusted somewhere between these two extremes. Mothers were instructed either to encourage their infants to walk down the plane or to discourage them from doing so.

So what did the infants do? Did they trust their mothers or did they trust their eyes? As you can see in the figure below, when the inclined plane was clearly safe or clearly risky, infants ignored their mothers. They typically trotted down the flat plane even when mom advised against it and refused to try the risky plane even when mom said it was okay. But when the plane was somewhere between safe and risky, the infants tended to follow mom's advice.

These data show that infants use social information in a very sophisticated way. When their senses provide unambiguous information about the world, they ignore what people tell them. But when their senses leave them unsure about what to do, they readily accept parental advice. It appears that from the moment children start to walk, they know when to listen to their parents and when to shake their heads, roll their eyes, and do what they darn well please.

COURTESY OF KAREN ADOLPH

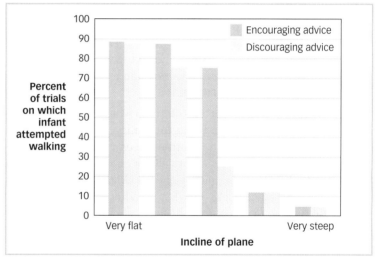

## Social Development

Unlike baby turtles, baby humans cannot survive without their caregivers. But what exactly do caregivers provide? Some obvious answers are warmth, safety, and food, and those obvious answers are right. But caregivers also provide something that is far less obvious but every bit as essential to an infant's development.

During World War II, psychologists studied infants who were living in orphanages while awaiting adoption. Although these children were warm, safe, and well fed, many were developmentally impaired, both physically and psychologically, and nearly 40 percent died before they could be adopted (Spitz, 1949). A few years later, psychologist Harry Harlow (1958; Harlow & Harlow, 1965) discovered that infant rhesus monkeys that were warm, safe, and well fed, but were not allowed any social contact for the first 6 months of their lives, developed a variety of behavioural abnormalities. They compulsively rocked back and forth while biting themselves, and if they were introduced to other monkeys, they avoided them entirely. These socially isolated monkeys turned out to be incapable of communicating with or learning from others of their kind, and when the females matured and became mothers, they ignored, rejected, and sometimes even attacked their own infants. Harlow also discovered that when socially isolated monkeys were put in a cage with two "artificial mothers"—one

Harlow's monkeys preferred the comfort and warmth of a soft cloth mother (*left*) to the wire mother (*right*) even when the wire mother was associated with food.

that was made of wire and dispensed food and one that was made of cloth and dispensed no food—they spent most of their time clinging to the soft cloth mother despite the fact that the wire mother was the source of their nourishment. Clearly, infants of all these species require something more from their caregivers than mere sustenance. But what?

## Becoming Attached

When Konrad Lorenz was a child he became the proud owner of a duck, and he quickly noticed something very interesting. Several decades later, the thing he had noticed helped him win the Nobel Prize. As he explained in his acceptance speech, "From a neighbour, I got a one-day-old duckling and found, to my intense joy, that it transferred its following response to my person." Ducklings normally follow their mother everywhere she goes, and what Lorenz discovered as a child (and then proved scientifically as an adult) is that new hatchlings will faithfully follow the first moving object to which they are exposed. If that object is a human being or a tennis ball, then the hatchling will ignore its mother and follow that object instead. Lorenz theorized that nature designed birds so that the first moving object they saw was *imprinted* on their brains as "the thing I must always stay near" (Lorenz, 1952).

Psychiatrist John Bowlby was fascinated by Lorenz's work, as well as by Harlow's studies of rhesus monkeys reared in isolation and the work on children reared in orphanages, and he sought to understand how human infants form attachments to their caregivers (Bowlby, 1969, 1973, 1980). Bowlby began by noting that from the moment they are born, ducks waddle after their mothers and monkeys cling to their mothers' furry chests because the newborns of both species must stay close to their caregivers to survive. Human infants, he suggested, have a similar need, but they are much less physically developed than ducks or monkeys and therefore can neither waddle nor cling. What they can do is smile and cry. Because they do not have webbed feet or furry hands that allow them to stay close to their caregivers, they use what they do have to keep their caregivers close to them. When an infant cries, gurgles, coos, makes eye contact, or smiles, most adults reflexively move toward the infant, and Bowlby suggested that this is *why* infants have been designed to emit these signals.

According to Bowlby, infants initially send these signals to anyone within visual or auditory range. For the first 6 months or so, they keep a "mental tally" of who responds most often and most promptly to their signals, and soon they begin to target the best and fastest responder, also known as the *primary caregiver*. This person quickly becomes the emotional centre of the infant's universe. Infants feel secure in

Like hatchlings, human infants need to stay close to their mothers to survive. Unlike hatchlings, human infants know how to get their mothers to come to them rather than the other way around.

**How does an infant identify the primary caregiver?**

Children are naturally social creatures who readily develop relationships with caregivers and peers. Toddlers who spend time with a responsive robot will begin to treat it like a classmate instead of like a toy (Tanaka, Cicourel, & Movellan, 2007).

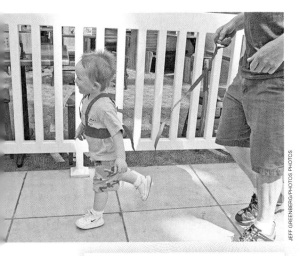

It does not take a psychologist to see that this child is securely attached.

**attachment**
The emotional bond that forms between newborns and their primary caregivers.

**Strange Situation**
A behavioural test used to determine a child's attachment style.

the primary caregiver's presence and will happily crawl around, exploring their environments with their eyes, ears, fingers, and mouths. But if their primary caregiver gets too far away, infants begin to feel insecure, and they take action to decrease the distance between themselves and their primary caregiver, perhaps by crawling toward their caregiver or perhaps by crying until their caregiver moves toward them. Bowlby believed that all of this happens because evolution has equipped human infants with a social reflex that is every bit as basic as the physical reflexes that cause them to suck and to grasp. Bowlby called this social reflex **attachment:** *the emotional bond that forms between newborns and their primary caregivers.*

Attachment theory emphasizes the importance of the emotional bond with a primary caregiver for a child's emotional development. And yet, more than 60 percent of primary caregivers with children under 3 years of age in Canada work outside the home. What are the effects of day care on attachment? As you might expect, this has been a hot research topic for a few decades. In the 1980s, many studies examined the effects of day care on the development of babies. They focused on day care centres attached to universities, and no developmental differences were found between children in day care and those cared for at home. In fact, for children from disadvantaged backgrounds, day care seems to have been beneficial. Subsequent work indicated that the uniformly high quality of the day cares included in these early studies was key to the observed outcomes. In all centres, staff were carefully selected, trained, and stayed for several years; there were low infant to caregiver ratios; communication between parents and caregivers was good; and the programs were age-appropriate and well designed.

Does day care that is not of such high quality affect the development of infants? Research in this area is difficult to conduct, since in general more affluent, educated parents put their children in high-quality day cares, which poorer, less educated people cannot afford. Any differences observed between types of day care may be due to the different backgrounds of the children. But the consensus emerging from many studies, in a variety of countries is that, in general, the quality of day care is of paramount importance. If a child is in high-quality day care, an infant's attachment to his or her parents is not affected. In general, greater prevalence of insecure attachment is only observed if care is of poor quality, is used for many hours a week, and then only if the primary caregiver is low in sensitivity and responsiveness to his or her infant.

Bowlby's work was completed at a time (1930s to 1950s) and in a place (Great Britain) in which fathers worked, and mothers stayed home and looked after the children. Some of his views (like the idea that a baby forms a unique and special bond with a single primary caregiver) are probably the result of his time and place. Different situations, such as when the mother is not the primary caregiver, or when multiple adult caregivers are involved, have been accommodated into the attachment framework. What is undisputed in Bowlby's contribution is the great importance of attachment to the normal emotional development of children.

Infants who are deprived of the opportunity to become attached experience a variety of negative consequences (Gillespie & Nemeroff, 2007; O'Connor & Rutter, 2000; Rutter, O'Connor, & the English and Romanian Adoptees Study Team, 2004). But even when attachment does happen, it can happen more or less successfully (Ainsworth et al., 1978). Psychologist Mary Ainsworth developed a way to measure this: **Strange Situation** is *a behavioural test used to determine a child's attachment style.* The test involves bringing a child and his or her primary caregiver (usually the child's mother) to a laboratory room and then staging a series of episodes, including ones in which the primary caregiver briefly leaves the room and then returns, while psychologists monitor the infant's reaction. Research shows that those reactions tend to fall into one of four patterns known as *attachment styles.*

**How is attachment assessed?**

> About 60 percent of American infants have a *secure* attachment style. When the caregiver leaves, the infant may or may not be distressed. When she returns, nondistressed infants will acknowledge her with a glance or greeting, and distressed infants will go to her and are calmed by her presence.

> About 20 percent of American infants have an *avoidant* attachment style. When the caregiver leaves, the infant will not be distressed, and when she returns the infant will not acknowledge her.

> About 15 percent of American infants have an *ambivalent* attachment style. When the caregiver leaves the infant will be distressed, and when she returns the infant will rebuff her, refusing any attempt at calming while arching his or her back and squirming to get away.

> About 5 percent or fewer American infants have a *disorganized* attachment style. These infants show no consistent pattern of response to their caregiver's leaving and returning.

Research has shown that a child's behaviour in the Strange Situation in the laboratory correlates fairly well with his or her behaviour at home (Solomon & George, 1999) (see **FIGURE 11.7**). Nonetheless, it is not unusual for a child's attachment style to change over time (Lamb, Sternberg, & Prodromidis, 1992). And although some aspects of attachment styles appear to be stable across cultures—secure attachment is the most common style all over the world (van IJzendoorn & Kroonenberg, 1988)—other aspects of attachment styles vary across cultures. For example, German children (whose parents tend to foster independence) are more likely to have avoidant than ambivalent attachment styles, whereas Japanese children (whose mothers typically stay home and do not leave them in the care of others) are more likely to have ambivalent than avoidant attachment styles (Takahashi, 1986).

## Where Do Attachment Styles Come From?

A child's attachment style is determined in part by the child's biology. Different children are born with different **temperaments,** or *characteristic patterns of emotional reactivity* (Thomas & Chess, 1977). Whether measured by parents' reports or by physiological indices such as heart rate or cerebral blood flow, very young children vary in their tendency toward fearfulness, irritability, activity, positive affect, and other emotional traits (Rothbart & Bates, 1998). These differences are unusually stable over time. For example, infants who react fearfully to novel stimuli—such as sudden movements, loud sounds, or unfamiliar people—tend to be more subdued, less social, and less positive at 4 years old (Kagan, 1997). These temperamental differences among infants appear to result from innate biological differences (Baker et al., 2013). For example, 10 to 15 percent of infants have a highly reactive limbic system (which, you may recall from the Neuroscience and Behaviour chapter, is a collection of brain regions including the amygdala that play an important role in emotional reaction). These infants thrash and cry when shown a new toy or a new person, and they become children who tend to avoid novel people, objects, and situations, and then adults who are quiet, cautious, and shy (Schwartz et al., 2003).

The infant's biologically based temperament plays a role in determining his or her attachment style, but for the most part, attachment style is determined by the infant's social interactions with his or her caregiver. Studies have shown that mothers of securely attached infants tend to be especially sensitive to signs of their child's emotional state, especially good at detecting their infant's "request" for reassurance, and especially responsive to that request (Ainsworth et al., 1978; De Wolff & van IJzendoorn, 1997). Mothers of infants with an ambivalent attachment style tend to respond inconsistently, only sometimes attending to their infants when they show signs of distress. Mothers of

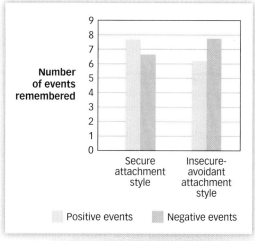

▲ Figure **11.7** **Attachment Style and Memory** We often remember best those events that fit with our view of the world. Researchers assessed 1-year-old children's attachment styles with the Strange Situation task. Two years later, the same group of children were shown a puppet show in which some happy events (e.g., the puppet got a present) or unhappy events (e.g., the puppet spilled his juice) occurred. Securely attached children later remembered more of the happy events than the unhappy ones, but insecurely attached children showed the opposite pattern (Belsky, Spritz, & Crnic, 1996).

**temperaments**
Characteristic patterns of emotional reactivity.

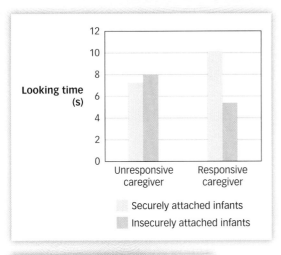

▲ Figure **11.8** **Working Models** Do infants really have internal working models? It appears they do. Psychologists know that infants stare longer when they see something they do not expect, and securely attached infants stare longer at a cartoon of a mother ignoring rather than comforting her child, whereas insecurely attached infants do just the opposite (Johnson, Dweck, & Chen, 2007).

**internal working model of relationships**
A set of beliefs about the self, the primary caregiver, and the relationship between them.

▼ Figure **11.9** **Parents' Attachment Styles** Attachment is an interaction between two people, and both of them—the primary caregiver and the child—play a role in determining the nature of the child's working model. Studies show that securely attached infants tend to have parents who themselves have secure working models of attachment (van IJzendoorn, 1995). Why might that be?

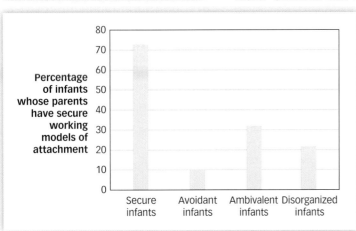

infants with an avoidant attachment style are typically indifferent to their child's need for reassurance and may even reject their attempts at physical closeness (Isabelle, 1993). As a result of all this, infants develop an **internal working model of relationships,** which is *a set of beliefs about the self, the primary caregiver, and the relationship between them* (Bretherton & Munholland, 1999). Infants with different attachment styles appear to have different working models of relationships (see **FIGURE 11.8**). Specifically, infants with a secure attachment style act as though they are *certain that their primary caregiver will respond* when they feel insecure; infants with an avoidant attachment style act as though they are *certain that their primary caregiver will not respond*; and infants with an ambivalent attachment style act as though they are *uncertain about whether their primary caregiver will respond*. Infants with a disorganized attachment style seem to be confused about their caregivers, which has led some psychologists to speculate that this style primarily characterizes children who have been abused (Carolson, 1998; Cicchetti & Toth, 1998).

If the caregiver's responsiveness determines (in large part) the child's working model, and if the child's working model determines (in large part) the child's attachment style, then what determines the caregiver's responsiveness (see **FIGURE 11.9**)? Differences in how caregivers respond are probably due (in large part) to differences in their ability to read their infant's emotional states. Caregivers who are highly sensitive to these signs are almost twice as likely to have a securely attached child as are mothers who are less sensitive (van IJzendoorn & Sagi, 1999). Mothers who think of their infants as unique individuals with emotional lives and not just as creatures with urgent physical needs are more likely to have infants who are securely attached (Meins, 2003; Meins et al., 2001). Although such data are merely correlational, there is reason to suspect that a mother's sensitivity and responsiveness are a *cause* of the infant's attachment style. For instance, researchers studied a group of young mothers whose infants were particularly irritable or difficult. When the infants were about 6 months old, half the mothers were randomly chosen to participate in a training program designed to sensitize them to their infants' emotional signals and to encourage them to be more responsive. The results showed that when the children were 18 months, 24 months, and 3 years old, those whose mothers had received the training were considerably more likely to have a secure attachment style than were those whose mothers did not receive the training (van den Boom, 1994, 1995).

> How do caregivers influence an infant's attachment style?

## Do Attachment Styles Matter?

Does an infant's attachment style have any influence on his or her subsequent development? Children who were securely attached as infants do better than children who were not securely attached on a wide variety of measures, from their psychological well-being (Madigan et al., 2013) to their academic achievement (Jacobson & Hoffman, 1997) to the quality of their relationships (McElwain, Booth-LaForce, & Wu, 2011; Schneider, Atkinson, & Tardif, 2001; Simpson, Collins, & Salvatore, 2011; Steele et al., 1999; Vondra et al., 2001).

For example, in one study that tracked people from infancy to adulthood, researchers found that 1-year-old infants who displayed insecure attachment during the Strange Situation experienced more negative emotions when trying to resolve major relationship conflicts with their romantic partners at age 21 (Simpson et al., 2007). And 1-year-old infants who displayed secure attachment styles in the Strange Situation task went on to become adults who rebounded more quickly from conflicts with their romantic partners (Salvatore et al., 2011). Some psychologists have suggested that people apply the working models they developed as infants to their later relationships with teachers, friends, and lovers: In other words, attachment style causes infants to become more or less successful adults (Sroufe, Egeland, & Kruetzer, 1990). But other psychologists argue that an infant's attachment style is correlated with subsequent outcomes only because both of these are caused by the same environment: In other words, sensitive and responsive caregivers cause both the infant's attachment style and his or her later adult outcomes (Lamb et al., 1985).

Does spending time in day care impair the attachment process? A massive long-term study showed that attachment style is strongly influenced by maternal sensitivity and responsiveness, but not by the quality, amount, stability, or type of day care (Friedman & Boyle, 2008).

## Moral Development

From the moment of birth, human beings can make one distinction quickly and well, and that is the distinction between pleasure and pain. Before their bottoms hit their very first diapers, infants can tell when something feels good or bad, and can demonstrate to anyone within earshot that they strongly prefer the former. Over the next few years, they begin to notice that their pleasures ("Throwing food is fun") are often someone else's pains ("Throwing food makes Mom mad"), which is a bit of a problem because infants need these other people to survive. So they start to learn how to balance their needs and the needs of those around them, and they do this in part by developing a distinction between *right* and *wrong*.

### Knowing What is Right

How do children think about right and wrong? Piaget had something to say about this too. He spent time playing games with children and

> **According to Piaget, what three shifts characterize moral development?**

quizzing them about how they came to know the rules of these games and what they thought should happen to children who broke those rules. By listening carefully to what children said, Piaget concluded that the child's moral thinking develops in three important ways (Piaget, 1932/1965).

According to Piaget, young children do not realize that moral rules can vary across persons and cultures. For instance, most North Americans think it is immoral to eat a dog, but most Vietnamese disagree.

> First, Piaget noticed that children's moral thinking tends to shift *from realism to relativism*. Very young children regard moral rules as real, inviolable truths about the world. For the young child, right and wrong are like day and night: They exist in the world and do not depend on what people think or say. That is why young children generally do not think that a bad action (such as hitting someone) can ever be good, even if everyone agreed to allow it. As they mature, children begin to realize that some moral rules (e.g., wives should obey their husbands) are inventions and not discoveries and that people can therefore agree to adopt them, change them, or abandon them entirely.

> Second, Piaget noticed that children's moral thinking tends to shift *from prescriptions to principles*. Young children think of moral rules as guidelines for specific actions in specific situations ("Each child can play with the tablet computer for 5 minutes and must then pass it to the child sitting to their left"). As they mature, children come to see that rules are expressions of more general principles, such as fairness and equity, which means that specific rules can be abandoned or modified when they fail to uphold the general principle ("If Jason missed his turn with the tablet computer, then he should get two turns now").

> Third and finally, Piaget noticed that children's moral thinking tends to shift from *outcomes* to *intentions*. For the young child, an unintentional action that causes great harm ("Josh accidentally broke Dad's tablet computer") seems

**preconventional stage**
A stage of moral development in which the morality of an action is primarily determined by its consequences for the actor.

**conventional stage**
A stage of moral development in which the morality of an action is primarily determined by the extent to which it conforms to social rules.

**postconventional stage**
A stage of moral development in which the morality of an action is determined by a set of general principles that reflect core values.

"more wrong" than an intentional action that causes slight harm ("Josh got mad and broke Dad's pencil") because young children tend to judge the morality of an action by its outcome rather than by the actor's intentions. As they mature, children begin to see that the morality of an action is critically dependent on the actor's state of mind.

Piaget's observations about the development of moral thinking have generally held up quite well, although he once again seemed to overestimate the ages at which some of these transitions take place. For example, research shows that children as young as 3 years old do sometimes consider people's intentions when judging the morality of their actions (Yuill & Perner, 1988). Psychologist Lawrence Kohlberg used Piaget's insights to produce a detailed theory of the development of moral reasoning (Kohlberg, 1963, 1986). According to Kohlberg, moral reasoning proceeds through three basic stages. Kohlberg (1958) based his theory on people's responses to a series of dilemmas such as this one:

A woman was near death from a special kind of cancer. There was one drug that the doctors thought might save her. It was a form of radium that a druggist in the same town had recently discovered. The drug was expensive to make, but the druggist was charging ten times what the drug cost him to make. He paid $200 for the radium and charged $2000 for a small dose of the drug. The sick woman's husband, Heinz, went to everyone he knew to borrow the money, but he could only get together about $1000, which is half of what it cost. He told the druggist that his wife was dying and asked him to sell it cheaper or let him pay later. But the druggist said: "No, I discovered the drug and I am going to make money from it." So Heinz got desperate and broke into the man's store to steal the drug for his wife. Should the husband have done that?

On the basis of their responses, Kohlberg concluded that most children are at the **preconventional stage,** which is *a stage of moral development in which the morality of an action is primarily determined by its consequences for the actor.* Immoral actions are simply those for which one is punished, and the appropriate resolution to any moral dilemma is to choose the behaviour with the least likelihood of punishment. For example, children at this stage often base their moral judgment of Heinz on the relative costs of one decision ("It would be bad if he got blamed for his wife's death") and another ("It would be bad if he went to jail for stealing").

> What are Kohlberg's three stages of moral development?

Kohlberg argued that children are preconventional, but somewhere around adolescence they move to the **conventional stage**, which is *a stage of moral development in which the morality of an action is primarily determined by the extent to which it conforms to social rules.* People at this stage believe that everyone should uphold the generally accepted norms of their cultures, obey the laws of society, and fulfill their civic duties and familial obligations. They argue that Heinz must weigh the dishonour he will bring upon himself and his family by stealing (i.e., breaking a law) against the guilt he will feel if he allows his wife to die (i.e., failing to fulfill a duty). People at this stage are concerned not just about spankings and prison sentences but also about the approval of others. Immoral actions are those for which one is condemned.

Finally, Kohlberg believed that in adulthood, some adults (but not all) move to the **postconventional stage,** which is *a stage of moral development in which the morality of an action is determined by a set of general principles that reflect core values,* such as the right of freedom, equality, and diversity. When a behaviour violates these principles, it is immoral, and if a law requires these principles to be violated, then it should be disobeyed. For a person who has reached the postconventional stage, a woman's life is always more important than a shopkeeper's profits and so stealing the drug is not only a moral behaviour, it is a moral obligation.

"You've been circling three days, and your prey won't die—what's your position, ethically speaking?"

Research supports Kohlberg's general claim that moral reasoning shifts from an emphasis on punishment to an emphasis on social rules and finally to an emphasis on ethical principles (Walker, 1988). But research also suggests that these stages are not quite as discrete as Kohlberg thought. For instance, a single person may use preconventional, conventional, and postconventional thinking in different circumstances, which suggests that the developing person does not "reach a stage" so much as he "acquires a skill" that he may or may not use on a particular occasion.

> What was Kohlberg right about and wrong about?

The use of the male pronoun here is intentional. Because Kohlberg developed his theory by studying a sample of American boys, some critics have suggested that it does not describe the development of moral thinking in girls (Gilligan, 1982) or in non-Westerners (Simpson, 1974). The first of these criticisms has received little scientific support (Jaffee & Hyde, 2000; Turiel, 1998), but the second has. For example, some non-Western societies value obedience and community over liberty and individuality; thus, the moral reasoning of people in those societies may *appear* to reflect a conventional devotion to social norms when it *actually* reflects a postconventional consideration of ethical principles. Other critics have noted that, although a child's level of moral reasoning is positively correlated with his or her moral behaviour (Blasi, 1980), the correlation is not strong, and this is particularly true when the moral behaviour involves doing a good deed rather than refraining from doing a bad deed (Haidt, 2001; Thoma et al., 1999). These critics suggest that how people reason about morality may be interesting in and of itself, but does not tell us very much about how people will behave in their everyday lives. But if moral reasoning does not determine moral behaviour, then what does?

During World War II, many Albanian Muslims shielded their Jewish neighbours from the Nazis. Baba Haxhi Dede Reshatbardhi (pictured) was one of those who saved so many Jewish lives.

## Feeling What is Right

Research on moral reasoning suggests that people are like judges in a court of law, using rational analysis—sometimes simple and sometimes sophisticated—to distinguish between right and wrong. But moral dilemmas do not just make us think; they also make us *feel*. Consider this one:

> You are standing on a bridge. Below you can see a runaway trolley hurtling down the track toward five people who will be killed if it remains on its present course. You are sure that you can save these people by flipping a lever that will switch the trolley onto a different track, where it will kill just one person instead of five. Is it morally permissible to divert the trolley and prevent five deaths at the cost of one?

Now consider a slightly different version of this problem:

> You and a large man are standing on a bridge. Below you can see a runaway trolley hurtling down the track toward five people who will be killed if it remains on its present course. You are sure that you can save these people by pushing the large man onto the track, where his body will be caught up in the trolley's wheels and stop it before it kills the five people. Is it morally permissible to push the large man and prevent five deaths at the cost of one?

These scenarios are illustrated in **FIGURE 11.10** (on the next page). If you are like most people, you concluded that is morally permissible to pull a switch but not to push a man (Greene et al., 2001). In both cases you had to decide whether to sacrifice one human life in order to save five, and in one case you said yes and in another you said no. How can moral reasoning yield such inconsistent conclusions? It cannot, and the odds are that you did not reach these conclusions by moral reasoning at all. Rather, you simply had a strong negative emotional reaction to the thought of pushing another human being into the path of an oncoming trolley and watching him get killed by it, and that reaction instantly led you to conclude that pushing him was wrong. Sure, you may have come up with a few good arguments to support this conclusion ("What if he turned around and hurt?" or "I would hate to get blood on my new shoes"), but those arguments probably followed rather than preceded your conclusion (Greene, 2013).

(a)                                                                                      (b)

▲ Figure **11.10 The Trolley Problem** Why does it seem permissible to trade one life for five lives by pulling a switch but not by pushing a man from a bridge? Research suggests that the scenario shown in (b) elicits a more negative emotional response than does the scenario shown in (a), and this emotional response may be the basis for our moral intuitions.

The way people respond to cases such as these has convinced some psychologists that moral judgments are the consequences—and not the causes—of emotional reactions (Haidt, 2001). According to this *moral intuitionist* perspective, we have evolved to react emotionally to a small family of events that are particularly relevant to reproduction and survival, and we have developed the distinction between right and wrong as a way of labelling and explaining these emotional reactions (Hamlin, Wynn, & Bloom, 2007). For instance, most of us think that incest disgusts us because it is wrong, but another possibility is that we consider it wrong because it disgusts us. Incest is a poor method for producing genetically viable offspring, and so nature may have selected for people who are disgusted by it. Our reasoning about the immorality of incest may be the *consequence* of that disgust and not its *cause*.

> Do moral judgments come before or after emotional reactions?

Some research supports the moral intuitionist perspective. For example, in one study, people who had brain damage that prevented them from experiencing normal emotions treated the two situations shown in Figure 11.10 identically, choosing in both cases to sacrifice one life to save five (Koenigs et al., 2007). In another study (Wheatley & Haidt, 2005), participants were hypnotized and told that whenever they heard the word *take,* they would experience "a brief pang of disgust … a sickening feeling in your stomach." After they came out of the hypnotic state, the participants were asked to rate the morality of several actions. Sometimes the description of the action contained the word *take* ("How immoral is it for a police officer to *take* a bribe?") and sometimes it did not ("How immoral is it for a police officer to *accept* a bribe?"). Participants rated the action as less moral when it contained the word *take,* suggesting that their negative feelings were causing—rather than being caused by—their moral reasoning.

All of this suggests that we consider it immoral to push someone onto the tracks simply because the idea of watching someone suffer makes us feel bad (Greene et al., 2001). In fact, research has shown that watching someone suffer activates the very same brain regions that are activated when we suffer ourselves (Carr et al., 2003) (see the discussion of mirror neurons in the Neuroscience and Behaviour chapter). In one study, women received a shock or watched their romantic partners receive a shock on different parts of their bodies. The regions of the women's brains that processed information about the location of the shock were activated only when the women experienced the shock themselves, but the regions that processed emotional information were activated

> What happens when we see others suffer?

whether the women received the shock or observed it (Singer et al., 2004). Similarly, the emotion-relevant brain regions that are activated when a person smells a foul odour are also activated when the person sees someone else smelling the foul odour (Wicker et al., 2003). Studies such as these suggest that our brains respond to other people's *expressions* of suffering by creating within us the *experience* of suffering, and this mechanism may have evolved because it allows us to know instantly what others are feeling (de Waal, 2012). The fact that we can actually *feel* another person's suffering may explain why even a small child who is incapable of sophisticated moral reasoning still considers it wrong when someone hurts someone else, especially when the person being hurt is similar to the child (Hamlin et al., 2013).

This may also explain why our aversion to watching others suffer begins so early in childhood (Warneken & Tomasello, 2009). When adults pretend to hit their thumbs with a hammer, even very young children seem alarmed and will attempt to comfort them (Zahn-Waxler et al., 1992). Indeed, even very young children distinguish between actions that are wrong because they violate a social rule and actions that are wrong because they cause suffering. When asked whether it would be okay to leave toys on the floor in a school that allowed such behaviour, young children tend to say it would. But when asked whether it would be okay to hit another child in a school that allowed such behaviour, young children tend to say it would not (Smetana, 1981; Smetana & Braeges, 1990). Young children say that hitting is wrong even when an adult instructs someone to do it (Laupa & Turiel, 1986). It appears that from a very early age, other people's suffering can become our suffering, and this leads us to conclude that the actions that caused the suffering are immoral.

CREASOURCE/CORBIS

Most people are upset by the suffering of others, and research suggests that even young children have this response, which may be the basis of their emerging morality.

## IN SUMMARY

▶ Infants have a limited range of vision, but they can see and remember objects that appear within it. They learn to control their bodies from the top down and from the centre out.

▶ Infants slowly develop theories about how the world works. Piaget believed that these theories developed through four stages, in which children learn basic facts about the world, such as the fact that objects continue to exist even when they are out of sight, and the fact that objects have enduring properties that are not changed by superficial transformations. Children also learn that their minds represent objects; hence objects may not be as they appear, and others may not see them as the child does.

▶ Cognitive development also comes about through social interactions in which children are given tools for understanding that have been developed over millennia by members of their culture.

▶ At a very early age, human beings develop strong emotional ties to their primary caregivers. The quality of these ties is determined both by the caregiver's behaviour and the child's temperament.

▶ People get along with each other by learning and obeying moral principles.

▶ Children's reasoning about right and wrong is initially based on an action's consequences, but as they mature, children begin to consider the actor's intentions as well as the extent to which the action obeys abstract moral principles.

▶ Moral judgments may be caused by our emotional reactions to the suffering of others.

**adolescence**
The period of development that begins with the onset of sexual maturity (about 11 to 14 years of age) and lasts until the beginning of adulthood (about 18 to 21 years of age).

**puberty**
The bodily changes associated with sexual maturity.

**primary sex characteristics**
Bodily structures that are directly involved in reproduction.

**secondary sex characteristics**
Bodily structures that change dramatically with sexual maturity but that are not directly involved in reproduction.

# Adolescence: Minding the Gap

Between childhood and adulthood is an extended developmental stage that may not qualify for a "hood" of its own, but that is clearly distinct from the stages that come before and after. **Adolescence** is *the period of development that begins with the onset of sexual maturity (about 11 to 14 years of age) and lasts until the beginning of adulthood (about 18 to 21 years of age).* Unlike the transition from embryo to fetus or from infant to child, this transition is sudden and clearly marked. In just 3 or 4 years, the average adolescent gains about 18 kg and grows about 20 cm. For girls, all this growing starts at about the age of 10 and ends when they reach their full heights at about the age of 15.5. For boys it starts at about the age of 12 and ends at about the age of 17.5.

The beginnings of this growth spurt signals the onset of **puberty**, which refers to *the bodily changes associated with sexual maturity.* These changes involve **primary sex characteristics,** which are *bodily structures that are directly involved in reproduction,* for example, the onset of menstruation in girls and the enlargement of the testes, scrotum, and penis and the emergence of the capacity for ejaculation in boys. They also involve **secondary sex characteristics,** which are *bodily structures that change dramatically with sexual maturity but that are not directly involved in reproduction,* for example, the enlargement of the breasts and the widening of the hips in girls and the appearance of facial hair, pubic hair, underarm hair, and the lowering of the voice in both genders. This pattern of changes is caused by increased production of estrogen in girls and testosterone in boys.

Just as the body changes during adolescence, so too does the brain. For example, there is a marked increase in the growth rate of tissue connecting different regions of the brain just before puberty (Thompson et al., 2000). The Czech–Canadian researcher Tomáš Paus and his colleagues have demonstrated that the connections between two regions essential for language function—Broca's area and Wernicke's area in the left hemisphere—become stronger and denser between the ages of 4 and 17 (Paus et al., 1999). These connections presumably allow brain areas to share information faster and more efficiently (see **FIGURE 11.11** on the next page).

> **How does the brain change at puberty?**

But the most important neural changes occur in the prefrontal cortex, the part of the brain associated with the ability to regulate emotions, and to control attention and behaviour. An infant's brain forms many more new synapses than it actually needs,

Adolescents are often described as gawky because different parts of their faces and bodies mature at different rates. But as politician Justin Trudeau can attest, the gawkiness generally clears up.

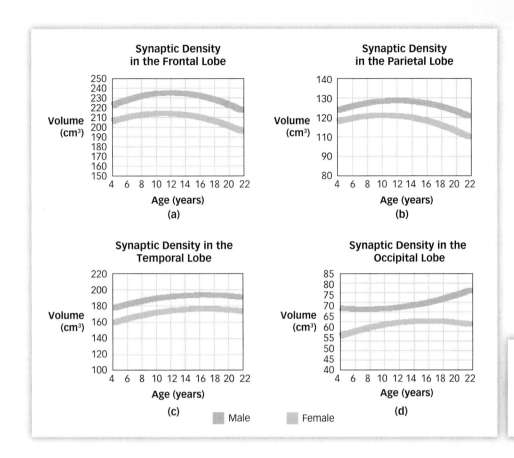

◄ Figure **11.11** **Your Brain and Puberty**
The development of neurons peaks in the frontal and parietal lobes at about age 12 (*a, b*), in the temporal lobe at about age 16 (*c*), and continues to increase in the occipital lobe through age 20 (*d*).

and by the time children are 2 years old they have about 15 000 synapses per neuron, which is roughly twice as many as the average adult (Huttenlocher, 1979). This early period of *synaptic proliferation* is followed by a period of *synaptic pruning* in which the connections that are not frequently used are eliminated. This is a clever system that allows the brain's wiring to be determined in part by its experience in the world. Scientists used to think that this process ended early in life, but recent evidence suggests that the prefrontal cortex undergoes a second wave of synaptic proliferation just before puberty, and a second round of synaptic pruning during adolescence (Giedd et al., 1999). During this period, the prefrontal cortex also seems to be forming faster, more efficient connections with the rest of the brain (Paus, 2005). Clearly, the adolescent brain is a work in progress.

## The Protraction of Adolescence

The age at which puberty begins varies across individuals (e.g., people tend to reach puberty at about the same age as their same-sexed parent did) and across cultures (e.g., African American girls tend to reach puberty before European American girls do). It also varies across generations (Malina, Bouchard, & Beunen, 1988). For example, in Scandinavia, the United Kingdom, and the United States, the age of first menstruation was between 16 and 17 years in the nineteenth century but was approximately 13 years in 1960. A more recent study found that the average age of breast development for Danish girls has decreased by an entire year since 1992 alone (Aksglaede et al., 2009). The average age at which American boys begin puberty has now fallen to between 9 and10 years old (Herman-Giddens et al., 2012). Why so much earlier now than just a few decades ago? Puberty is

**How has the onset of puberty changed over the last century?**

About 60 percent of preindustrial societies do not even have a word for adolescence (Schlegel & Barry, 1991). When a Krobo female menstruates for the first time, older women take her into seclusion for 2 weeks and teach her about sex, birth control, and marriage. Afterward, a public ceremony called the durbar is held, and the young female who that morning was regarded as a child is thereafter regarded as an adult.

▼ Figure 11.12 **How Do Peers Affect Decision Making?** Adolescents make better decisions when no one is around! Participants in one study played a video driving game with or without their peers in the room. The presence of peers greatly increased the number of risks taken and crashes experienced by adolescents, but had little or no effect on adults (Gardner & Steinberg, 2005).

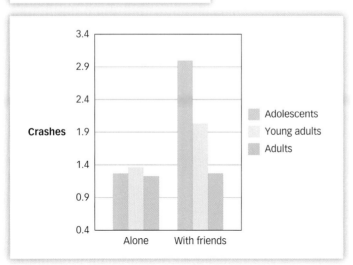

accelerated by body fat (Kim & Smith, 1998), and the decrease in the age of the onset is largely due to improved diet and health (Ellis & Garber, 2000). But puberty in girls can also be hastened by exposure to environmental toxins that mimic estrogen (Buck Louis et al., 2008) or by stressful family situations (Belsky, 2012).

The increasingly early onset of puberty has important psychological consequences. Just two centuries ago, the gap between childhood and adulthood was relatively brief because people became physically mature at roughly the same time that they were ready to accept adult roles in society, and these roles did not normally require them to have extensive schooling. But in modern societies, people typically spend 3 to 10 years in school after they reach puberty. Thus, while the age at which people become physically adult has decreased, the age at which they are prepared or allowed to take on adult responsibilities has increased, and so the period between childhood and adulthood has become *protracted*. What are the consequences of a protracted adolescence?

Adolescence is often characterized as a time of internal turmoil and external recklessness, and some psychologists have speculated that the protraction of adolescence is in part to blame for its sorry reputation (Moffitt, 1993). According to these theorists, adolescents are adults who have temporarily been denied a place in adult society, mostly through the school system and through restrictions on the types of work that adolescents in Western countries like Canada and the United States are permitted to do (Epstein, 2007a). American teenagers are subjected to 10 times as many restrictions as adults, and twice as many restrictions as American Marines on active duty or incarcerated felons (Epstein, 2007a). As such, they feel especially compelled to do things to protest these restrictions and demonstrate their adulthood, such as smoking, drinking, using drugs, having sex, and committing crimes. In a sense, adolescents are people who are forced to live in a strange gap between two worlds, and the pathologies of adolescence are partly a result of this predicament. As one researcher noted, "Trapped in the frivolous world of peer culture, they learn virtually everything they know from one another rather than from the people they are about to become. Isolated from adults and wrongly treated like children, it is no wonder that some teens behave, by adult standards, recklessly or irresponsibly" (Epstein, 2007b).

But the storm and stress of adolescence is by no means inevitable (Steinberg & Morris, 2001). Research suggests that the "moody adolescent" who is a victim of "raging hormones" is largely a myth. Adolescents are no moodier than children (Buchanan, Eccles, & Becker, 1992), and fluctuations in their hormone levels have only a tiny impact on their moods (Brooks-Gunn, Graber, & Paikoff, 1994). Although they can be more impulsive and susceptible to peer influence than adults (see **FIGURE 11.12**), they are just as capable of making wise decisions based on good information (Steinberg, 2007). It is true that the majority of adolescents dabble in misbehaviour, but they do not actually major in it. For example, more than 60 percent of 15 to 17 year olds in Canada report having used alcohol in the last year (Canadian Public Health Association, n.d.), but few develop drinking problems or allow alcohol to impair their academic success or personal relationships (Hughs, Power, & Francis, 1992; Johnston, Bachman, & O'Malley, 1997). Most adolescent experiments have no long-term consequences, and the vast majority of adolescents who try drugs or break the law end up becoming sober, law-abiding adults (Steinberg, 1999). In short, the hijinks of adolescence are typically minor and temporary, and in some cultures they barely occur at all (Epstein, 2007b). Adolescence is not a terribly troubled time for most people, and most adolescents "age out" of any troubles they get themselves into (Sampson & Laub, 1995).

> **Are adolescent problems inevitable?**

These students are unlikely to become reckless adults (*left*). However, this rule only applies to those who live: The young driver of this car (*right*) crashed into a tree and died at the scene. Alcohol may have been a factor.

## Sexuality

Puberty can be a difficult time, but it is especially difficult for girls who reach it earlier than their peers. These girls are more likely to experience a range of negative consequences, from distress and depression to delinquency and disease (Mendle, Turkheimer, & Emery, 2007) (see **FIGURE 11.13**). This happens for several reasons (Ge & Natsuaki, 2009). First, early bloomers do not have as much time as their peers do

> **What makes adolescence especially difficult?**

to develop the skills necessary to cope with adolescence (Petersen & Grockett, 1985), but because they look so mature, people expect them to act like adults. In other words, early puberty creates unrealistic expectations and demands that the adolescent may have trouble fulfilling. Second, early blooming girls draw the attention of older men, who may lead them into a variety of unhealthy activities (Ge, Conger, & Elder, 1996). Some research suggests that for girls, the *timing* of puberty has a greater influence on emotional and behavioural problems than does the occurrence of puberty itself (Buchanan et al., 1992). The timing of puberty does not have such consistent effects on boys: Some studies suggest that early maturing boys do better than their peers, some show they do worse, and some show that there is no difference at all (Ge, Conger, & Elder, 2001). Interestingly, recent research suggests that for boys, *tempo*, the speed with which they transition from the first to the last stages of puberty, may be a better predictor of negative outcomes than is timing (Mendle et al., 2010).

For some adolescents, puberty is additionally complicated by the fact that they are attracted to members of the same sex. Most gay men report having become aware of their sexual orientation between the ages of 6 and 18, and most lesbians report having become aware between the ages of 11 and 26 (Calzo et al., 2011). Not only does their sexual orientation make gay adolescents different from the vast majority of their peers (a mere 2 percent of Canadian adults identify themselves as lesbian, gay, or bisexual) (Statistics Canada, 2004), but it can also subject them to disapproval from family, friends, and community. In a recent survey (Pew Research Center Global Attitudes Project, 2013), almost 1 in 5 Canadians said that homosexuality is a way of life that should not be accepted by society, and Canada is much more accepting of homosexuality than are many other nations (see **FIGURE 11.14** on the next page). In some countries, gay citizens are imprisoned or sentenced to death.

▼ Figure **11.13** **Early Puberty** Early puberty is a source of psychological distress for girls (Ge, Conger, & Elder, 1996).

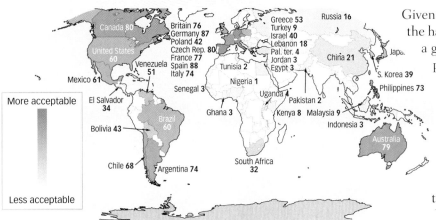

BY PERMISSION OF PEW GLOBAL ATTITUDES PROJECT.

▲ Figure **11.14** **Polling Trends** The 2013 Pew Research Center Global Attitudes Project, a survey of adults' attitudes in 39 countries, revealed huge variability from region to region in the percentage of people who said that homosexuality should be accepted by society.

Jane Clementi's 18-year-old son Tyler committed suicide in 2010 after a college roommate videotaped him kissing another man. She later said, "I think some people think that sexual orientation can be changed or prayed over. But I know sexual orientation is not up for negotiation. I don't think my children need to be changed. I think that what needed changing is attitudes, or myself, or maybe some other people I know" (quoted in Zernike, 2012).

Given so much social disapproval, it is little wonder that the happiness and well-being of homosexual adolescents is a great concern to mental-health professionals. Several provincial legislatures have enacted anti-bullying laws in the last decade, aimed at reducing and ending bullying against students. For example, the *Ontario Accepting Schools Act* is aimed at reducing gender-based violence and acts of homophobia in primary and secondary schools, and allows students at any school in the province to set up clubs called "Gay Straight Alliances." The hope that this will promote tolerance of all people, regardless of sexual orientation.

What determines whether a person's sexuality is primarily oriented toward the same or the opposite sex? For a long time, psychologists believed that a person's sexual orientation depended primarily on his or her upbringing. For example, psychoanalytic theorists claimed that boys who grow up with a domineering mother and a submissive father are less likely to identify with their father and are therefore more likely to become homosexual. Okay. Nice theory. But the *fact* is that scientific research has failed to identify *any* aspect of parenting that has a significant impact on a child's ultimate sexual orientation (Bell, Weinberg, & Hammersmith, 1981). Perhaps the most telling fact is that children raised by homosexual couples and children raised by heterosexual couples are equally likely to become heterosexual adults (Patterson, 1995). There is also little support for the idea that a person's early sexual encounters have a lasting impact on his or her sexual orientation (Bohan, 1996).

> Is sexual orientation a matter of nature or nurture?

So what *does* determine a person's sexual orientation? There is now considerable evidence to suggest that biology plays the major role. Not only do gay people have a larger proportion of gay siblings than do heterosexuals (Bailey et al., 1999), but the identical twin of a gay man (with whom he shares 100 percent of his genes) has a 50 percent chance of being gay, whereas the fraternal twin or non-twin brother of a gay man (with whom he shares 50 percent of his genes) has only a 15 percent chance (Bailey & Pillard, 1991; Gladue, 1994). A similar pattern has emerged in studies of lesbians (Bailey et al., 1993). Some evidence suggests that the fetal environment may play a role in determining sexual orientation and that high levels of androgens in the womb may predispose a person—whether male or female—later to develop a sexual preference for women (Ellis & Ames, 1987; Meyer-Bahlberg et al., 1995). Perhaps this is why the brains of gay people tend to look like the brains of straight people of the opposite sex (Savic & Lindstrom, 2008). For example, the brain's two hemispheres tend to be unequally sized among straight men and lesbians (both of whom are attracted to women), but equally sized among straight women and gay men (both of whom are attracted to men).

Of course, genes and prenatal biology cannot be the sole determinant of a person's sexual orientation because many homosexual men and women have identical twins who shared both their fetal environment and their genes, and who are nonetheless heterosexual. There must be other factors and, at present, we just do not know what they are. But one thing we do know is that regardless of what leads people to have a particular sexual orientation, there is no evidence that it can be changed by so-called conversion therapy (American Psychological Association, 2009). It is also worth noting that about 1 percent of people claim to have no sexual orientation of any kind and have never experienced sexual attraction to either gender (Bogaert, 2004). The science of sexual orientation is still young and fraught with conflicting findings, but one thing that seems abundantly clear is that sexual orientation is *not* simply a matter of choice.

In 2005, 43% of Canadian teens aged 15 to 19 reported having had sexual intercourse at least once, with no difference between men and women (Rotermann, 2008). Interestingly, the rate at which young Canadian women engage in sex is dropping. In 1996/1997, 51% of young women aged 15 to 19 reported having sexual intercourse at least once, compared to 43% in 2005. The proportion of adolescents reporting experience with sexual intercourse was higher among 18 to 19 year olds (approximately 67%) than among 15 to 17 year olds (approximately 33%) and was higher in Quebec (58%) than in the other Canadian provinces (see **TABLE 11.2**). **FIGURE 11.15** shows the general trends in sexual activity among male and female teens from 1996 to 2005.

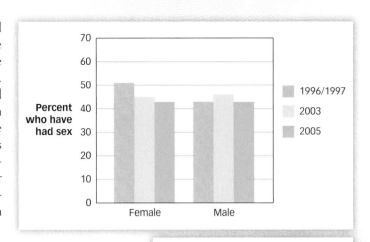

▲ Figure **11.15** **Teenage Sex** The percentage of Canadian teenagers who have had sex has been declining in recent years (Rotermann, 2008).

### Table 11.2

**Trends in Sexual Activity across Provinces and Territories**

|  | 1996/1997 (%) | 2003 (%) | 2005 (%) |
|---|---|---|---|
| **Age Group** | | | |
| 15 to 17 | 32 | 30 | 29 |
| 18 to 19 | 70 | 68 | 65 |
| **Province** | | | |
| Newfoundland and Labrador | 46 | 54 | 49 |
| Prince Edward Island | 37 | 52 | 35 |
| Nova Scotia | 31 | 49 | 49 |
| New Brunswick | 43 | 52 | 43 |
| Quebec | 59 | 62 | 58 |
| Ontario | 41 | 40 | 37 |
| Manitoba | 39 | 43 | 39 |
| Saskatchewan | 54 | 39 | 43 |
| Alberta | 44 | 39 | 39 |
| British Columbia | 47 | 37 | 40 |

The human papilloma virus is a sexually transmitted disease that can lead to cervical cancer. Luckily, there is a vaccine that can prevent it. Studies show that young women who have been vaccinated do not have sex earlier than those who have not been vaccinated (Bednarczyk et al., 2012).

The best scientific evidence suggests that sex education leads teens to delay having sex for the first time,

**Why do many adolescents make unwise choices about sex?**

increases the likelihood they will use birth control when they do have sex, and lowers the likelihood that they will get pregnant or catch a sexually transmitted disease (Mueller, Gavin, & Kulkarni, 2008; Satcher, 2001). Although young people between the ages of 15 to 24 years have among the highest rates of sexually transmitted infections, condom use is increasing: in 2003, 62% of sexually active people aged 15 to 24 reported than they had used condoms the last time they had intercourse. This proportion increased to 68% in 2009–2010 (Rotermann, 2012).

HORIZONS WWP/ALAMY

## Parents and Peers

"Who am I?" is a question asked by amnesiacs and adolescents, who tend to ask it for different reasons. Children's views of themselves and their world are tightly tied to the views of their parents, but puberty creates a new set of needs that begins to snip away at those bonds by orienting adolescents toward peers rather than parents. Psychologist Erik Erikson (1959) characterized each stage of life by the major task confronting the individual at that stage. His *stages of psychosocial development* (shown in **TABLE 11.3**) borrow from the work of Sigmund Freud, and suggest that the major task of adolescence is the development of an adult identity. Whereas children define themselves almost entirely in terms of their relationships with parents and siblings, adolescence marks a shift in emphasis from family relations to peer relations.

Two things can make this shift difficult. First, children cannot choose their parents, but adolescents can choose their peers. As such, adolescents have the power to shape themselves by joining groups that will lead them to develop new values, attitudes, beliefs, and perspectives. In a sense, the adolescent has the opportunity to invent the adult he or she will soon become, and the responsibility this opportunity entails can be overwhelming. Second, as adolescents strive for greater autonomy, their parents naturally rebel. For instance, parents and adolescents tend to disagree about the age at which certain adult behaviours—such as staying out late or having sex—are permissible, and you do not need a scientist to tell you which position each party in this conflict tends to hold (Holmbeck & O'Donnell, 1991). Because adolescents and parents often have different ideas about who should control the adolescent's behaviour, their relationships become more conflictive and less close, and their interactions become briefer and less frequent (Larson & Richards, 1991). Even so, adolescents and their parents

> How do family and peer relationships change during adolescence?

*"You're free-range when I say you're free-range."*

---

▶ **Table 11.3**

**Erikson's Stages of Psychosocial Development**

According to Erikson, at each "stage" of development a "key event" creates a challenge or "crisis" that a person can resolve positively or negatively.

| Ages | Stage | Key Event | Crisis | Positive Resolution |
|---|---|---|---|---|
| **1.** Birth to 12–18 months | Oral–sensory | Feeding | Trust vs. mistrust | Child develops a belief that the environment can be counted on to meet his or her basic physiological and social needs. |
| **2.** 18 months to 3 years | Muscular–anal | Toilet training | Autonomy vs. shame/doubt | Child learns what he or she can control and develops a sense of free will and corresponding sense of regret and sorrow for inappropriate use of self-control. |
| **3.** 3–6 years | Locomotor | Independence | Initiative vs. guilt | Child learns to begin action, to explore, to imagine, and to feel remorse for actions. |
| **4.** 6–12 years | Latency | School | Industry vs. inferiority | Child learns to do things well or correctly in comparison to a standard or to others. |
| **5.** 12–18 years | Adolescence | Peer relationships | Identity vs. role confusion | Adolescent develops a sense of self in relationship to others and to own internal thoughts and desires. |
| **6.** 19–40 years | Young adulthood | Love relationships | Intimacy vs. isolation | Person develops the ability to give and receive love; begins to make long-term commitment to relationships. |
| **7.** 40–65 years | Middle adulthood | Parenting | Generativity vs. stagnation | Person develops interest in guiding the development of the next generation. |
| **8.** 65 to death | Maturity | Reflection on and acceptance of one's life | Ego integrity vs. despair | Person develops a sense of acceptance of life as it was lived and the importance of the people and relationships that the individual developed over the life span. |

have surprisingly few conflicts (Chung, Flook, & Fuligni, 2009), and when they do argue it tends to be over minor issues, such as dress and language (which may explain why teenagers argue more with their mothers, who are typically in charge of such issues, than with their fathers) (Caspi et al., 1993).

Adolescents pull away from their parents, but more importantly, they move toward their peers. Studies show that across a wide variety of cultures, historical epochs, and even species, peer relations evolve in a similar way (Dunphy, 1963; Weisfeld, 1999). Young adolescents initially form groups or "cliques" with same-sexed peers, many of whom were friends during childhood (Brown, Mory, & Kinney, 1994). Next, male cliques and female cliques begin to meet in public places, such as town squares or shopping malls, and they begin to interact—

Adolescents form same-sex cliques that meet opposite-sex cliques in public places. Eventually, these people will form mixed-sex cliques, pair off into romantic relationships, get married, have children, and then worry about then when they do all the same things.

but only in groups and only in public. After a few years, the older members of these same-sex cliques peel off and form smaller, mixed-sex cliques, which may assemble in private as well as in public, but usually assemble as a group. Finally, couples (typically a male and a female) peel off from the small, mixed-sex clique and begin romantic relationships.

Studies show that throughout adolescence, people spend increasing amounts of time with opposite-sex peers while maintaining the amount of time they spend with same-sex peers (Richards et al., 1998), and they accomplish this by spending less time with their parents (Larson & Richards, 1991). Although peers exert considerable influence on the adolescent's beliefs and behaviours, this influence generally occurs because adolescents respect, admire, and like their peers and not because their peers pressure them (Susman et al., 1994). In fact, as they age, adolescents show an increasing tendency to resist peer pressure (Steinberg & Monahan, 2007). Acceptance by peers is of tremendous importance to adolescents, and those who are rejected by their peers tend to be withdrawn, lonely, and depressed (Pope & Bierman, 1999). Fortunately for those of us who were seventh-grade nerds, individuals who are unpopular in early adolescence can become popular in later adolescence as their peers become less rigid and more tolerant (Kinney, 1993).

## IN SUMMARY

▶ Adolescence is a stage of development that is distinct from those stages that come before and after it. It begins with a growth spurt and with puberty, the onset of sexual maturity of the human body. Puberty is occurring earlier than ever before, and the entrance of young people into adult society is occurring later.

▶ During this "in-between stage," adolescents are somewhat more prone to do things that are risky or illegal, but they rarely inflict serious or enduring harm on themselves or others.

▶ During adolescence, sexual interest intensifies and, in some cultures, sexual activity begins. Sexual activity typically follows a script, many aspects of which are standard across cultures. Although most people are attracted to members of the opposite sex, some are not, and research suggests that biology plays a key role in determining a person's sexual orientation.

▶ As adolescents seek to develop their adult identities, they seek increasing autonomy from their parents and become more peer-oriented, forming single-sex cliques, followed by mixed-sex cliques, and finally pairing off as couples.

**adulthood**
The stage of development that begins around 18 to 21 years and ends at death.

# Adulthood: Change We Cannot Believe In

It takes fewer than 7000 days for a single-celled zygote to become a registered voter. **Adulthood** is *the stage of development that begins around 18 to 21 years and ends at death.* Because physical change slows from a gallop to a crawl, many of us think of adulthood as the destination to which the process of development finally delivers us, and that once we have arrived, our journey is pretty much complete. Nothing could be further from the truth because a whole host of physical, cognitive, and emotional changes take place between our first legal beer and our last legal breath.

## Changing Abilities

The early 20s are the peak years for health, stamina, vigour, and prowess, and because our psychology is so closely tied to our biology, these are also the years during which most of our cognitive abilities are at their sharpest. At this very moment you probably see farther, hear better, remember more, and weigh less than you ever will again. Enjoy it while you can. Your physical peak will last for just a few dozen months more—and then, somewhere between the ages of 26 and 30, you will begin the slow and steady decline that will not end until you do. Just 10 or 15 years after puberty, your body will begin to break down. Your muscles will be replaced by fat, your skin will become less elastic, your hair will thin and your bones will weaken, your sensory abilities will

## HOT SCIENCE

# The End of History Illusion

"I have finally arrived." That is the feeling that many young adults have when they look back at the fast-paced changes of childhood and adolescence, and look forward to the relatively smooth sailing of adulthood. But recent research suggests that this feeling of having arrived is actually an illusion—and one that people succumb to throughout their entire lives.

In a recent study (Quoidbach, Gilbert, & Wilson, 2013), researchers asked thousands of people to recall how much their personalities had changed in the last 10 years, or to predict how much their personalities

would change in the next 10 years. They then compared the "looking back" memories of people who were a particular age with the "looking forward" predictions of people who were 10 years younger. So, for example, they compared how much 18-year-olds thought their personalities *would change* with how much 28-year-olds remembered their personalities *had changed,* and they did this for people from 18 to 68 years old.

As the graph shows, people who were looking back at a particular decade of life saw much more change than people who were looking forward to it—and this was true of every decade between 18 and 68!

The researchers found precisely the same pattern when they asked people to remember and predict changes in their basic values and preferences. They called this phenomenon the *end of history illusion.*

Adulthood, it seems, is a period of life that is characterized by unanticipated change, or "change we cannot believe in." Although both teenagers and their grandparents seem to think that the pace of personal change has slowed to a crawl and that they have finally become the people they will forever be, the data suggest that it simply is not so. Change slows but never stops, and its pace is faster than we expect.

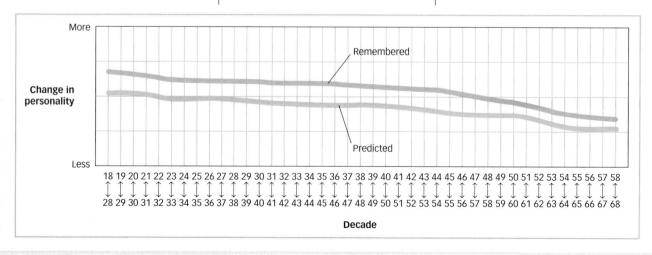

become less acute, and your brain cells will die at an accelerated rate. If you are a woman, your ovaries will stop producing eggs and you will become infertile. If you are a man, your erections will be softer and fewer and farther between. Other than being more resistant to colds and less sensitive to pain, your elderly body just will not work as well as your youthful body does. But it is better than the alternative! In Canada today, 84% of males and 90% of females will reach age 65 and older. What is this stage of life like, cognitively and emotionally?

As these physical changes accumulate, they begin to have measurable psychological consequences (Salthouse, 2006) (see **FIGURE 11.16**). For instance, as your brain ages, your prefrontal cortex and its associated subcortical connections will deteriorate more quickly than the other areas of your brain (Raz, 2000), and you will experience a noticeable decline on cognitive tasks that require effort, initiative, or strategy. Your memory will worsen, though not all kinds will worsen at the same rate. You will experience a greater decline in working memory (the ability to hold information "in mind") than in long-term memory (the ability to retrieve information), a greater decline in episodic memory (the ability to remember particular past events) than in semantic memory (the ability to remember general information such as the meanings of words), a greater decline in retrieval accuracy than recognition accuracy, a greater decline in … um … something else that we cannot remember just now.

> **What physical and psychological changes are associated with adulthood?**

But it is not all bad news. Even though your cognitive machinery will get rustier, research suggests that you will partially compensate by using it much more skillfully (Bäckman & Dixon, 1992; Salthouse, 1987). Older chess players *remember* chess positions much more poorly than younger players do, but they *play* just as well because they learn to search the board more efficiently (Charness, 1981). Older typists *react* more slowly than younger typists do, but they *type* just as quickly and accurately as because they are better at anticipating the next word in spoken or written text (Salthouse, 1984). There is a good reason that most CEOs, prime ministers, presidents, and other decision makers are over 25. Older airline pilots are considerably worse than younger pilots when it comes to keeping a list of words in short-term memory, but this age difference disappears when those words are the heading commands that pilots receive from the control tower every day (Morrow et al., 1994). All of this suggests that older adults are compensating for the age-related declines they experience in memory and attention (Park & McDonough, 2013).

> **How do adults compensate for their declining abilities?**

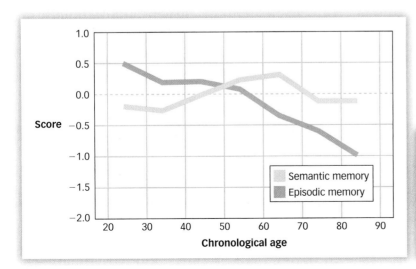

◀ Figure **11.16 Cognitive Decline** After the age of 20, people show gradual but steady declines on some measures of cognitive performance but not others (Salthouse, 2006). For example, the ability to recall past events (episodic memory) declines as we age, but the ability to recall the meanings of words (semantic memory) does not.

One week before his 58th birthday, commercial pilot Chesley Sullenberger made a perfect emergency landing in a river and saved the lives of everyone on board. None of the passengers wished they had a younger pilot.

How do they do that? As you know from the Neuroscience and Behaviour chapter, young brains are highly differentiated, that is, they have different parts that do different things. We now know that as the brain ages it becomes *de-differentiated* (Lindenberger & Baltes, 1994). For example, regions of the visual cortex that specialize in face and scene perception in younger people are much less specialized in older people (Grady et al., 1992; Park et al., 2004). It appears that the brain is like a group of specialists that work independently when they are young and able, but that pull together as a team when each of the specialists get older and slower (Park & McDonough, 2013). For example, when young adults try to keep verbal information in working memory, the left prefrontal cortex is more strongly activated than the right, and when young adults try to keep spatial information in working memory, the right prefrontal cortex is more strongly activated than the left (Smith & Jonides, 1997). But this *bilateral asymmetry* pretty much disappears in older adults, which suggests that the older brain is compensating for the declining abilities of each individual neural structure by calling on its other neural structures to help out (Cabeza, 2002) (see **FIGURE 11.17**). The physical machinery breaks down as time passes, and one of the ways in which the brain rises to that challenge is by changing its division of labour.

▶ Figure **11.17** **Bilaterality in Older and Younger Brains** Across a variety of tasks, older adult brains show bilateral activation and young adult brains show unilateral activation. One explanation for this is that older brains compensate for the declining abilities of one neural structure by calling on other neural structures for help (Cabeza, 2002).

## Changing Goals

One reason why Grandpa cannot find his car keys is that his prefrontal cortex does not work as well as it used to. But another reason is that the location of car keys just is not the sort of thing that grandpas want to spend their precious time memorizing

**How do informational goals change in adulthood?**

(Haase, Heckhausen, & Wrosch, 2013). According to *socioemotional selectivity theory* (Carstensen & Turk-Charles, 1994), younger adults are largely oriented toward the acquisition of information that will be useful to them in the future (e.g., reading reviews), whereas older adults are generally oriented toward information that brings emotional satisfaction in the present (e.g., reading novels). Because young people have such long futures, they invest their time attending to, thinking about, and remembering potentially useful information that can serve them well tomorrow. Because older people have much shorter futures, they spend their time attending to, thinking about, and remembering positive information that serves them well today (see **FIGURE 11.18**).

For example, older people perform *much* more poorly than younger people when they are asked to remember a series of unpleasant faces, but only *slightly* more poorly when they are asked to remember a series of pleasant faces (Mather & Carstensen, 2003). Whereas younger adults show equal amounts of amygdala activation when they see very pleasant or very unpleasant pictures, older adults show much more activation when they see very pleasant than very unpleasant pictures, suggesting

◀ Figure **11.18** **Memory for Pictures** Memory generally declines with age, but the ability to remember negative information—such as unpleasant pictures—declines much more quickly than the ability to remember positive information (Carstensen et al., 2000).

**Is late adulthood a happy or unhappy time for most people?**

that older adults just are not attending to information that does not make them happy (Mather et al., 2004). Indeed, compared to younger adults, older adults are generally better at sustaining positive emotions and curtailing negative ones (Isaacowitz, 2012; Isaacowitz & Blanchard-Fields, 2012; Lawton et al., 1992; Mather & Carstensen, 2005). They also experience fewer negative emotions (Carstensen et al., 2000; Charles, Reynolds, & Gatz, 2001; Mroczek & Spiro, 2005; Schilling, Wahl, & Wiegering, 2013), and are more accepting of them when they do (Shallcross et al., 2013). Given all this, you should not be surprised to learn that late adulthood is consistently reported to be one of the happiest and most satisfying periods of life (see **FIGURE 11.19** on the next page). You *should not* be surprised, but then you probably are because young adults vastly overestimate the problems of aging (Pew Research Center for People & the Press, 2009) (see **FIGURE 11.20** on the next page).

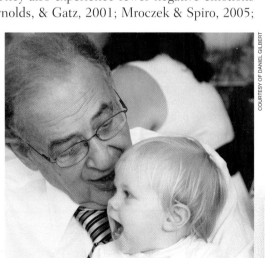

COURTESY OF DANIEL GILBERT

As people age, they prefer to spend time with family and a few close friends rather than large circles of acquaintances.

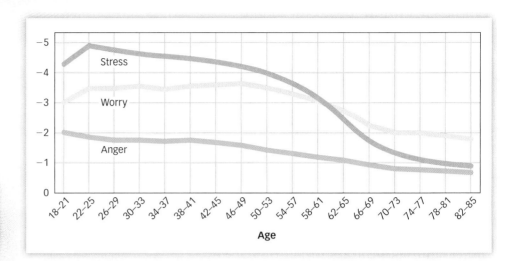

▶ Figure **11.19** **Emotions and Age** Older adults experience much lower levels of stress, worry, and anger than younger adults do (Stone et al., 2010).

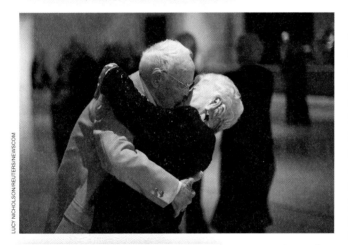

Getting old is not as bad as people think, and it even holds a few nice surprises. For example, one study of women aged 40 to 100 showed that the oldest women were nearly twice as likely as the youngest ones to report being "very satisfied" with their sex lives (Trompeter, Bettencourt, & Barrett-Connor, 2012).

Because having a short future orients people toward emotionally satisfying rather than intellectually profitable experiences, older adults become more selective about their interaction partners, choosing to spend time with family and a few close friends rather than with a large circle of acquaintances. One study monitored a group of people from the 1930s to the 1990s and found that their rate of interaction with acquaintances declined from early to middle adulthood, but their rate of interaction with spouses, parents, and siblings remained stable or increased (Carstensen, 1992). A study of older adults who ranged in age from 69 to 104 found that the oldest adults had fewer peripheral social partners than the younger adults did, but they had just as many emotionally close partners whom they identified as members of their "inner circle" (Lang & Carstensen, 1994). "Let's go meet some new people" is not something that most 60-year-olds tend to say, but "Let's go hang out with some old friends" is. It is sad but instructive to note that many of these same cognitive and emotional changes can be observed among younger people who have discovered that their futures will be short because of a terminal illness (Carstensen & Fredrickson, 1998).

▶ Figure **11.20** **It is Better Than You Think** Research shows that young adults overestimate the problems of old age (Pew Research Center for People & the Press, 2009).

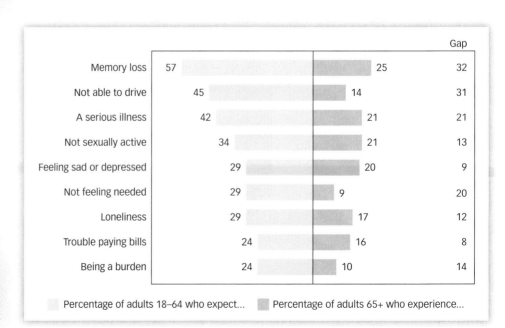

|  | | | Gap |
|---|---|---|---|
| Memory loss | 57 | 25 | 32 |
| Not able to drive | 45 | 14 | 31 |
| A serious illness | 42 | 21 | 21 |
| Not sexually active | 34 | 21 | 13 |
| Feeling sad or depressed | 29 | 20 | 9 |
| Not feeling needed | 29 | 9 | 20 |
| Loneliness | 29 | 17 | 12 |
| Trouble paying bills | 24 | 16 | 8 |
| Being a burden | 24 | 10 | 14 |

 Percentage of adults 18–64 who expect...      Percentage of adults 65+ who experience...

## Changing Roles

The psychological separation from parents that begins in adolescence usually becomes a physical separation in adulthood. In virtually all human societies, young adults leave home, get married, and have children of their own. Being in a committed long-term relationship and parenthood are two of the most significant aspects of adult life. Census statistics suggest that if you are right now of university-age, Canadian, then you are likely to get married at around the age of 30, have approximately 1.7 children, and consider both your partner and your children to be your greatest sources of joy. Indeed, a whopping 93 percent of (American) mothers say that their children are a source of happiness all or most of the time (Pew Research Center for People & the Press, 1997).

But do marriage and children really make us happy? Research shows that married people live longer (see **FIGURE 11.21**), have more frequent sex (and enjoy that sex more), and earn several times as much money as unmarried people do (Waite, 1995). Given these differences, it is no surprise that married people report being happier than unmarried people—whether those unmarried people are single, widowed, divorced, or cohabiting (Johnson & Wu, 2002). That is why many researchers consider marriage one of the best investments individuals can make in their own happiness. But other researchers suggest that married people may be happier because happy people may be more likely to get married, and that marriage may be the consequence—and not the cause—of happiness (Lucas et al., 2003). The general consensus among scientists seems to be that both of these positions have merit: Even before marriage, people who end up married tend to be happier than those who never marry, but marriage does seem to confer further benefits.

> **What does research say about marriage, children, and happiness?**

Children are another story. In general, research suggests that children do not increase their parents' happiness, and may even decrease it (DiTella, MacCulloch, & Oswald, 2003; Simon, 2008; Senior, 2014). For example, parents typically report lower marital satisfaction than do nonparents—and the more children they have, the less satisfaction they report (Twenge, Campbell, & Foster, 2003). Studies of marital satisfaction at different points in the life span reveal an interesting pattern of peaks and valleys: Marital satisfaction starts out high, plummets at about the time that the children are in diapers,

Does marriage make people happy or do happy people tend to get married?

▼ Figure **11.21** **Til Death Do Us Part** Married people live longer than unmarried people, and this is true of both men and women. But while widowed men die as young as never-married and divorced men do (*a*), widowed women live longer than never-married or divorced women do (*b*). In other words, the loss of a wife is always bad, but the loss of a husband is only bad if you let him live! (Lillard & Waite, 1995)

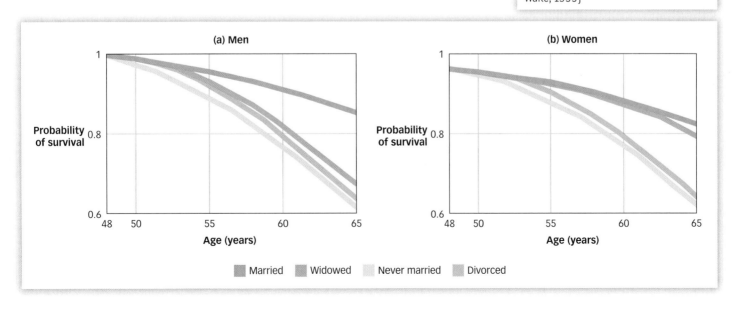

(a) Men — Probability of survival / Age (years)

(b) Women — Probability of survival / Age (years)

Married   Widowed   Never married   Divorced

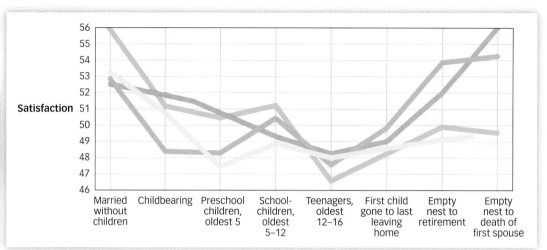

▶ Figure **11.22 Marital Satisfaction over the Life Span** This graph shows the results of four independent studies of marital satisfaction among men and women. All four studies suggest that marital satisfaction is highest before children are born and after they leave home (Walker, 1977).

begins to recover, plummets again when the children are in adolescence, and returns to its premarital levels only when children leave home (see **FIGURE 11.22**). Although the proportion of stay-at-home fathers has nearly doubled in the last 20 years (from 7% to 13%) (Statistics Canada, 2012b), and the proportion of fathers assuming the role of primary caregiver for some period of time in infancy has increased ten-fold since 2000, mothers still generally do more child care than fathers. It is therefore not surprising that the negative impact of parenthood is stronger for women than for men. Women with young children are especially likely to experience role conflicts ("How am I supposed to manage being a full-time lawyer and a full-time mother?") and restrictions of freedom ("I never get to play tennis anymore"). A study that measured the moment-to-moment happiness of American women as they went about their daily activities found that women were less happy when taking care of their children than when eating, exercising, shopping, napping, or watching television—and only slightly happier than when they were doing housework (Kahneman et al., 2004). The relationship between children and happiness seems to change after children leave home: a survey of 200 000 older people in 86 countries has shown that, independent of sex, income, or partnership status, parents of adult children are happier the more children they have (Margolis & Myrskylä, 2011).

Does all of this mean that children cause unhappiness or happiness? Not necessarily. Because researchers cannot randomly assign people to be parents or nonparents, studies of the effects of parenthood are necessarily correlational. What does seem clear is that raising children is a challenging job that most people find especially rewarding when they are not in the middle of doing it.

## IN SUMMARY

▶ Older adults show declines in working memory, episodic memory, and retrieval tasks, but they often develop strategies to compensate.

▶ Gradual physical decline begins early in adulthood and has clear psychological consequences, some of which are offset by increases in skill and expertise.

▶ Older people are more oriented toward emotionally satisfying information, which influences their basic cognitive performance, the size and structure of their social networks, and their general happiness.

▶ For most people, adulthood means leaving home, living with a committed long-term partner, and having children. People with a long-term partner are typically happier, but children and the responsibilities that parenthood entails present a significant challenge, for the first few years of a child's life, at least.

## OTHER VOICES

# You Are Going to Die

**Tim Kreider** is an essayist and cartoonist whose newest book is *We Learn Nothing*.

Human development begins at conception and ends at death. Most of us would rather think about the conception part. Getting old seems scary and depressing, and one of the reasons why we send elderly people to retirement homes may be that we are afraid to watch our loved ones decline. The essayist Tim Kreider (2013) thinks this is a terrible loss—not for older people, but for younger ones.

My sister and I recently toured the retirement community where my mother has announced she will be moving. I have been in some bleak clinical facilities for the elderly where not one person was compos mentis and I had to politely suppress the urge to flee, but this was nothing like that. It was a very cushy modern complex housed in what used to be a seminary, with individual condominiums with big kitchens and sun rooms, equipped with fancy restaurants, grills and snack bars, a fitness centre, a concert hall, a library, an art room, a couple of beauty salons, a bank and an ornate chapel of Italian marble. You could walk from any building in the complex to another without ever going outside, through underground corridors and glass-enclosed walkways through the woods. Mom described it as "like a college dorm, except the boys aren't as good-looking." Nonetheless I spent much of my day trying not to cry.

At all times of major life crisis, friends and family will crowd around and press upon you the false emotions appropriate to the occasion. "That's so great!" everyone said of my mother's decision to move to an assisted-living facility. "It's really impressive that she decided to do that herself." They cited their own stories of 90-year-old parents grimly clinging to drafty dilapidated houses, refusing to move until forced out by strokes or broken hips. "You should be really relieved and grateful." "She'll be much happier there." The overbearing unanimity of this chorus suggests to me that its real purpose is less to reassure than to suppress, to deny the most obvious and natural emotion that attends this occasion, which is sadness.

My sadness is purely selfish, I know. My friends are right; this was all Mom's idea, she's looking forward to it, and she really will be happier there. But it also means losing the farm my father bought in 1976, where my sister and I grew up, where Dad died in 1991. We're losing our old phone number, the one we have had since the Ford administration, a number I know as well as my own middle name. However infrequently I go there, it is the place on earth that feels like home to me, the place I'll always have to go back to in case adulthood falls through. I hadn't realized, until I was forcibly divested of it, that I'd been harbouring the idea that someday, when this whole crazy adventure was over, I would at some point be nine again, sitting around the dinner table with Mom and Dad and my sister. And beneath it all, even at age 45, there is the irrational, little-kid fear: Who's going to take care of me? I remember my mother telling me that when her own mother died, when Mom was in her 40s, her first thought was: *I'm an orphan*.

Plenty of people before me have lamented the way that we in industrialized countries regard our elderly as unproductive workers or obsolete products, and lock them away in institutions instead of taking them into our own homes out of devotion and duty. Most of these critiques are directed at the indifference and cruelty thus displayed to the elderly; what I wonder about is what it's doing to the rest of us.

Segregating the old and the sick enables a fantasy, as baseless as the fantasy of capitalism's endless expansion, of youth and health as eternal, in which old age can seem to be an inexplicably bad lifestyle choice, like eating junk food or buying a minivan, that you can avoid if you're well-educated or hip enough. So that when through absolutely no fault of your own your eyesight begins to blur and you can no longer eat whatever you want without consequence and the hangovers start lasting for days, you feel somehow ripped off, lied to. Aging feels grotesquely unfair. As if there ought to be someone to sue.

We don't see old or infirm people much in movies or on TV. We love explosive gory death onscreen, but we're not so enamored of the creeping, gray, incontinent kind. Aging and death are embarrassing medical conditions, like hemorrhoids or eczema, best kept out of sight. Survivors of serious illness or injuries have written that, once they were sick or disabled, they found themselves confined to a different world, a world of sick people, invisible to the rest of us. Denis Johnson writes in his novel *Jesus' Son:* "You and I don't know about these diseases until we get them, in which case we also will be put out of sight."

My own father died at home, in what was once my childhood bedroom. He was, in this respect at least, a lucky man. Almost everyone dies in a hospital now, even though absolutely nobody wants to, because by the time we're dying all the decisions have been taken out of our hands by the well, and the well are without mercy. Of course we hospitalize the sick and the old for some good reasons (better care, pain relief), but I think we also segregate the elderly from the rest of society because we're afraid of them, as if age might be contagious. Which, it turns out, it is.

… You are older at this moment than you've ever been before, and it is the youngest you're ever going to get. The mortality rate is holding at a scandalous 100 percent. Pretending death can be indefinitely evaded with hot yoga or a gluten-free diet or antioxidants or just by refusing to look is craven denial. "Facing it, always facing it, that's the way to get through," Conrad wrote in *Typhoon.* "Face it." He was talking about more than storms. The sheltered prince Siddartha Gautama was supposedly set on the path to becoming the Buddha when he was out riding and happened to see an old man, a sick man and a dead man. Today he'd be spared the discomfiture, and the enlightenment, unless he were riding mass transit.

Just yesterday my mother sent me a poem she first read in college—Langston Hughes's "Mother to Son." She said she could still remember where she was, in her dorm room at Goshen College, when she came across it in her American Lit book. The title notwithstanding, it does not make for Hallmark-card copy. *Life for me ain't been no crystal stair.* It tells us that this life is not a story or an adventure or a journey of spiritual self-discovery; it's a slog. And it orders us to keep going, don't you dare give up, no matter what. Because I'm your mother, that's why.

Do you agree with Kreider: Do we do a disservice to the young when we segregate the old?

# Chapter Review

1. The sequence of prenatal development is
   a. fetus, embryo, zygote.
   b. zygote, embryo, fetus.
   c. embryo, zygote, fetus.
   d. zygote, fetus, embryo.

2. Learning begins
   a. in the womb.
   b. at birth.
   c. in the newborn stage.
   d. in infancy.

3. The proximodistal rule states that
   a. motor skills emerge in sequence from the centre to the periphery.
   b. motor skills emerge in sequence from the top to the bottom.
   c. motor skills such as rooting are hardwired by nature.
   d. simple motor skills disappear as more sophisticated motor skills emerge.

4. Motor skills, such as reaching, are
   a. acquired in an orderly sequence and on a strict timetable.
   b. acquired on a strict timetable, but not in an orderly sequence.
   c. influenced by the infant's incentive.
   d. acquired by the same method by all infants.

5. Piaget believed that infants construct _____, which are theories about the way the world works.
   a. assimilations
   b. accommodations
   c. schemas
   d. habituations

6. Once children understand that human behaviour is guided by mental representations, they are said to have acquired
   a. joint attention.
   b. a theory of mind.
   c. formal operational ability.
   d. egocentrism.

7. When infants in a new situation examine their mother's face for cues about what to do, they are demonstrating an ability known as
   a. joint attention.
   b. social referencing.
   c. imitation.
   d. all of the above.

8. The capacity for attachment may be innate, but the quality of attachment is influenced by
   a. the child's temperament.
   b. the primary caregiver's ability to read their child's emotional state.
   c. the interaction between the child and the primary caregiver.
   d. all of the above.

9. A child's attachment style is
   a. assessed by a behavioural test known as Strange Situation.
   b. most commonly a secure attachment style, except across cultures.
   c. generally different in the home than it appears in the laboratory.
   d. unchangeable over time.

10. According to Kohlberg, each stage in the development of moral reasoning is characterized by a specific focus. What is the correct sequence of these stages?
   a. focus on consequences, focus on ethical principles, focus on social rules
   b. focus on ethical principles, focus on social rules, focus on consequences
   c. focus on consequences, focus on social rules, focus on ethical principles
   d. focus on social rules, focus on consequences, focus on ethical principles

11. Evidence indicates that Canadian adolescents are
   a. moodier than children.
   b. victims of raging hormones.
   c. likely to develop drinking problems.
   d. living in a protracted gap between childhood and adulthood.

12. Scientific evidence suggests that _____ play(s) a key role in determining a person's sexual orientation.
   a. personal choices
   b. parenting styles
   c. sibling relationships
   d. biology

13. Adolescents place the greatest emphasis on relationships with
   a. peers.
   b. parents.
   c. siblings.
   d. nonparental authority figures.

14. The peak years for health, stamina, vigour, and prowess are
   a. childhood.
   b. the early teens.
   c. the early 20s.
   d. the early 30s.

15. Data suggest that, for most people, the last decades of life are
   a. characterized by an increase in negative emotions.
   b. spent attending to the most useful information.
   c. extremely satisfying.
   d. a time during which they begin to interact with a much wider circle of people.

## KEY TERMS

accommodation (p. 434)

adolescence (p. 452)

adulthood (p. 460)

assimilation (p. 434)

attachment (p. 444)

cephalocaudal rule (p. 432)

childhood (p. 436)

cognitive development (p. 433)

concrete operational stage (p. 436)

conservation (p. 436)

conventional stage (p. 448)

developmental psychology (p. 426)

egocentrism (p. 437)

embryonic stage (p. 426)

fetal alcohol spectrum disorder
 (FASD) (p. 428)

fetal stage (p. 426)

formal operational stage (p. 437)

germinal stage (p. 426)

infancy (p. 431)

internal working model of
 relationships (p. 446)

motor development (p. 431)

myelination (p. 428)

object permanence (p. 434)

postconventional stage (p. 448)

preconventional stage (p. 448)

pre-operational stage (p. 436)

primary sex characteristics (p. 452)

proximodistal rule (p. 432)

puberty (p. 452)

reflexes (p. 431)

schemas (p. 433)

secondary sex characteristics
 (p. 452)

sensorimotor stage (p. 433)

Strange Situation (p. 444)

temperaments (p. 445)

teratogens (p. 428)

theory of mind (p. 439)

zygote (p. 426)

## CHANGING MINDS

1. One of your friends recently got married and she and her husband are planning to have children. You mention to your friend that once this happens she will have to stop drinking. She scoffs. "They make it sound as though a pregnant woman who drinks alcohol is murdering her baby. Look, my mom drank wine every weekend when she was pregnant with me and I'm just fine." What is your friend failing to understand about the effects of alcohol on prenatal development? What other teratogens might you tell her about?

2. You are at the grocery store when you spot a crying child in a stroller. The mother picks up the child and cuddles him until he stops crying. A grocery clerk is standing next to you, stocking the shelves. He leans over and says, "Now, that's bad parenting. If you pick up and cuddle a child every time the child cries, you're reinforcing the behaviour, and the result will be a very spoiled child." Do you agree? What do studies

of attachment tell us about the effects of picking up and holding children when they cry?

3. You and your roommate are watching a movie in which a young man tells his parents that he is gay. The parents react badly and decide that they should send him to a "camp" where he can learn to change his sexual orientation. Your roommate turns to you: "Do you know anything about this? Can people really be changed from gay to straight?" Based on what you have read in this text, what would you tell your friend about the factors determining sexual orientation?

4. One of your cousins has just turned 30 and, to his horror, he has discovered a grey hair. "This is the end," he says. "Soon I'll start losing my eyesight, growing new chins, and forgetting how to use a cell phone. Aging is just one long, slow, agonizing decline." What could you tell your cousin to cheer him up? Does everything in life get worse with aging?

## ANSWERS TO KEY CONCEPT QUIZ

1. b; 2. a; 3. a; 4. c; 5. c; 6. b; 7. b; 8. d; 9. a; 10. c; 11. d; 12. d; 13. a; 14. c; 15. c.

Need more help? Additional resources are located in Launchpad at:
*www.worthpublishers.com/launchpad/schacter3ecanadian*

# Personality

▲ **Personality: What It Is and How It Is Measured**
Describing and Explaining Personality
Measuring Personality

▲ **The Trait Approach: Identifying Patterns of Behaviour**
Traits as Behavioural Dispositions and Motives
The Search for Core Traits
**HOT SCIENCE** Personality on the Surface
Traits as Biological Building Blocks
**THE REAL WORLD** Are There "Male" and "Female" Personalities?

▲ **The Psychodynamic Approach: Forces That Lie beneath Awareness**
The Structure of the Mind: Id, Ego, and Superego
Psychosexual Stages and the Development of Personality

▲ **The Humanistic–Existential Approach: Personality as Choice**
Human Needs and Self-Actualization
Personality as Existence

▲ **The Social–Cognitive Approach: Personalities in Situations**
Consistency of Personality across Situations
Personal Constructs
**CULTURE & COMMUNITY** Does Your Personality Change According to the Language You Are Speaking, or Who You Are Speaking With?
Personal Goals and Expectancies

▲ **The Self: Personality in the Mirror**
Self-Concept
Self-Esteem
**OTHER VOICES** Does the Study of Personality Lack … Personality?

GROWING UP, STEFANI JOANNE ANGELINA GERMANOTTA seemed to have personality. As a child, she was said to have shown up at the occasional family gathering naked. As the pop star now known as Lady Gaga, she continues the tradition of being different. Her first albums, *The Fame* and *The Fame Monster,* and the fact that she calls her fans "Little Monsters" and herself the "Mother Monster," hinted she might have issues. But she, like most of us, is not one-dimensional. Yes, her style is eccentric and seems silly to many (we are looking at you, raw meat dress), but she also is a serious supporter of humanitarian and personal causes, including equality for people who are gay, bisexual, lesbian, or transgendered (as in her song "Born This Way"). Lady Gaga is one of a kind. She has personality in an important sense—she has qualities that make her psychologically different from other people.

Singer Lady Gaga in her meat dress at the MTV Video Music Awards, September 2010.

PRESS ASSOCIATION VIA AP IMAGES

471

**personality**
An individual's characteristic style of behaving, thinking, and feeling.

Don Cherry

Angela Merkel

Miley Cyrus

How would you describe each of these personalities?

Chris Hadfield

**THE FORCES THAT CREATE ANY ONE PERSONALITY ARE ALWAYS** something of a mystery. Your personality is different from anyone else's and expresses itself pretty consistently across settings—at home, in the classroom, and elsewhere. But how and why do people differ psychologically? By studying many unique individuals, psychologists seek to gather enough information to answer these central questions of personality psychology scientifically.

**Personality** is *an individual's characteristic style of behaving, thinking, and feeling.* Whether Lady Gaga's quirks are real or merely for publicity, they are certainly hers and they show her distinct personality. In this chapter, we will explore personality, first by looking at what it is and how it is measured, and then by focusing on each of four main approaches to understanding personality: trait–biological, psychodynamic, humanistic–existential, and social–cognitive. Psychologists have personalities, too (well, *most* of them), so their different approaches, even to the topic of personality, should not be that surprising. At the end of the chapter, we discuss the psychology of self to see how our views of what we are like can shape and define our personality.

# Personality: What It Is and How It Is Measured

If someone said, "You have no personality," how would you feel? Like a cookie-cutter person, a boring, greyish lump who should go out and get a personality as soon as possible? As a rule, people do not usually strive for a personality—one seems to develop naturally as we travel through life. As psychologists have tried to understand the process of personality development, they have pondered questions of description (*how* do people differ?), explanation (*why* do people differ?), and the more quantitative question of measurement (how can personality be *assessed*?).

## Describing and Explaining Personality

As the first biologists earnestly attempted to classify all plants and animals (whether lichens or ants or fossilized lions), personality psychologists began by labelling and describing different personalities. And just as biology came of age with Darwin's theory of evolution, which *explained* how differences among species arose, the maturing study of personality also has developed explanations of the basis for psychological differences among people.

Most personality psychologists focus on specific, psychologically meaningful individual differences, characteristics such as honesty, anxiousness, or moodiness. Still, personality is often in the eye of the beholder. When one person describes another as "a conceited jerk," for example, you may wonder whether you have just learned more about the describer or the person being described. Interestingly, studies that ask acquaintances to describe each other find a high degree of similarity among any one individual's descriptions of many different people ("Jason thinks that Carlos is considerate, Renata is kind, and Jean Paul is nice to others"). In contrast, resemblance is quite low when many people describe one person ("Carlos thinks Jason is smart, Renata thinks he is competitive, and Jean Paul thinks he has a good sense of humour") (Dornbusch et al., 1965).

> **What does it mean to say that personality is in the eye of the beholder?**

What leads Lady Gaga to all of her entertaining extremes? In general, explanations of personality differences are concerned with (1) *prior events* that can shape an individual's personality or (2) *anticipated events* that might motivate the person to reveal particular personality characteristics. In a biological prior event, Stefani Germanotta received genes from her parents that may have led her to develop into the sort of person who loves putting on a display (not to mention putting on raw meat) and stirring up controversy. Researchers interested in events that happen prior to our behaviour study our genes, brains, and other aspects of our biological makeup, and also delve into our subconscious and into our circumstances and interpersonal surroundings. The consideration of *anticipated events* emphasizes the person's own, subjective perspective and often seems intimate and personal in its reflection of the person's inner life (hopes, fears, and aspirations).

Of course, our understanding of how the baby named Stefani Germanotta grew into the adult Lady Gaga (or the life of any person) also depends on insights into the interaction between the prior and anticipated events: We need to know how her history may have shaped her motivations.

## Measuring Personality

Of all the things psychologists have set out to measure, personality may be one of the toughest. How do you capture the uniqueness of a person? What aspects of people's personalities are important to know about, and how should we quantify them? The general personality measures can be classified broadly into personality inventories and projective techniques.

### Personality Inventories

To learn about an individual's personality, you could follow the person around and, clipboard in hand, record every single thing the person does, says, thinks, and feels (including how long this goes on before the person calls the police). Some observations might involve your own impressions (Day 5: seems to be getting irritable); others would involve objectively observable events that anyone could verify (Day 7: grabbed my pencil and broke it in half, then bit my hand).

Psychologists have figured out ways to obtain objective data on personality without driving their subjects to violence. The most popular technique is **self-report,** *a method in which people provide subjective information about their own thoughts, feelings, or behaviours, typically via questionnaire or interview.* In most self-report measures, respondents are asked to circle a number on a scale indicating the degree to which they endorse that item as being self-descriptive (e.g., reporting on a scale of 0–5 to what extent they believe they are a "worrier") or to indicate whether an item is true or false in describing them. For each respondent, the researcher then combines his or her answers to get a general sense of the individual's personality with respect to a particular domain. **TABLE 12.1** shows the 10 items from a self-report test of different personality traits (Gosling, Rentfrow, & Swann, 2003). In this case, the respondent is asked to indicate whether each personality trait applies to him or her. To score the measure you simply add up the two items for each of the five traits listed at the bottom of the table.

How is a self-report scale created? The usual strategy is to collect sets of self-descriptive statements that indicate different degrees of a personality characteristic. To measure friendliness, for example, you could ask people to rate their agreement with statements ranging from "I am somewhat friendly" to "I am very outgoing," and even to "I love being around people every minute of the day." Adding up the number of statements the person endorses that indicate friendliness (and subtracting endorsements of those that indicate unfriendliness) yields a measure of the person's self-reported friendliness. Scales based on the content of self-reports have been devised to assess a whole range of personality characteristics, all the way from general tendencies such as overall happiness (Lyubomirsky, 2008; Lyubomirsky & Lepper, 1999)

**self-report**
A method in which people provide subjective information about their own thoughts, feelings, or behaviours, typically via questionnaire or interview.

> **Table 12.1**

**Ten-Item Personality Inventory (TIPI)**

Here are a number of personality traits that may or may not apply to you. Please write a number next to each statement to indicate the extent to which *you agree or disagree with that statement*. You should rate the extent to which the pair of traits applies to you, even if one characteristic applies more strongly than the other.

1 = Disagree strongly
2 = Disagree moderately
3 = Disagree a little
4 = Neither agree nor disagree
5 = Agree a little
6 = Agree moderately
7 = Agree strongly

**I see myself as:**

1. \_\_\_\_ Extraverted, enthusiastic
2. \_\_\_\_ Critical, quarrelsome
3. \_\_\_\_ Dependable, self-disciplined
4. \_\_\_\_ Anxious, easily upset
5. \_\_\_\_ Open to new experiences, complex
6. \_\_\_\_ Reserved, quiet
7. \_\_\_\_ Sympathetic, warm
8. \_\_\_\_ Disorganized, careless
9. \_\_\_\_ Calm, emotionally stable
10. \_\_\_\_ Conventional, uncreative

TIPI scale scoring (R = reverse-scored items): Extraversion (1, 6R); Agreeableness (2R, 7); Conscientiousness (3, 8R); Emotional Stability (4R, 9); Openness to Experience (5, 10R).

*Source:* Gosling, Rentfrow, & Swann, 2003.

**Minnesota Multiphasic Personality Inventory (MMPI)**
A well-researched, clinical questionnaire used to assess personality and psychological problems.

to specific ones such as responding rapidly to insults (Swann & Rentfrow, 2001) or complaining about poor service (Lerman, 2006).

One of the most commonly used personality tests is the **Minnesota Multiphasic Personality Inventory (MMPI),** *a well-researched, clinical questionnaire used to assess personality and psychological problems.* The MMPI was developed in 1939 and has been revised several times over the years, leading up to the current version, the MMPI–2–RF (restructured form) (Ben-Porath & Tellegen, 2008). The MMPI–2–RF consists of 338 self-descriptive statements to which the respondent answers "true," "false," or "cannot say." The MMPI–2–RF measures a wide range of psychological constructs: clinical problems (e.g., antisocial behaviour, thought dysfunction), somatic problems (e.g., head pain, cognitive complaints), internalizing problems (e.g., anxiety, self-doubt), externalizing problems (e.g., aggression, substance abuse), and interpersonal problems (e.g., family problems, avoidance). The MMPI–2–RF also includes *validity scales* that assess a person's attitudes toward test taking and any tendency to try to distort the results by faking answers.

Personality inventories ask people to report what traits they possess; however, many psychologists believe that people do not always know what is in their mind. Can we rely on people to accurately report on their personality?

JEFF GREENBERG/GETTY IMAGES

Personality inventories such as the MMPI–2–RF are easy to administer: All that is needed is the test and a pencil (or a computer-based version). The respondent's scores are then calculated and compared with the average ratings of thousands of other test takers. Because no human interpretation of the responses is needed (i.e., "true" means true, "false" means false, etc.), any potential biases of the person giving the test are minimized. Of course, an accurate measurement of personality will only occur if people provide accurate responses. Although self-report test results are easy to obtain, critics of this approach highlight several limitations. One problem is that many people have a tendency to respond in a socially desirable way, such that they underreport things that are unflattering or embarrassing. Perhaps even more problematic is that there

> **What are some limitations of personality inventories?**

are many things we do not know about ourselves and so are unable to report! Studies show that people often are inaccurate in their self-report about what they have experienced in the past, what factors are motivating their behaviours in the present, or how they will feel or behave in the future (Wilson, 2009).

## Projective Techniques

A second, somewhat controversial, class of tools for evaluating personality designed to circumvent the limitations of self-report mentioned above, is **projective tests,** which are *tests designed to reveal inner aspects of individuals' personalities by analysis of their responses to a standard series of ambiguous stimuli.* The developers of projective tests assume that people will project personality factors that are below awareness—wishes, concerns, impulses, and ways of seeing the world—onto the ambiguous stimuli and will not censor these responses. Probably best-known is the **Rorschach Inkblot Test,** *a projective technique in which respondents' inner thoughts and feelings are believed to be revealed by analysis of their responses to a set of unstructured inkblots.* An example inkblot is shown in **FIGURE 12.1.** Responses are scored according to complicated systems (derived in part from research with people with psychological disorders) that classify what people see (Exner, 1993; Rapaport, 1946). For example, most people who look at Figure 12.1 report seeing birds or people. Someone who reports seeing something very unusual (e.g., "I see two purple tigers eating a velvet cheeseburger") may be experiencing thoughts and feelings that are very different from those of most other people.

▼ Figure **12.1** **Sample Rorschach Inkblot** Test takers are shown a card such as this sample and asked, "What might this be?" What they perceive, where they see it, and why it looks that way are assumed to reflect unconscious aspects of their personality.

SPENCER GRANT/PHOTOEDIT

The **Thematic Apperception Test (TAT)** is *a projective technique in which respondents' underlying motives, concerns, and the way they see the social world are believed to be revealed through analysis of the stories they make up about ambiguous pictures of people.* To get a sense of the test, look at **FIGURE 12.2.** The test administrator shows the respondent the card and asks him or her to tell a story about the picture, asking questions such as: Who are those people? What is happening? What led them to this moment? What will happen next? Different people tell very different stories about the image. In creating the stories, the respondent is thought to identify with the main characters and to project his or her view of others and the world onto the other details in the drawing. Thus, any details that are not obviously drawn from the picture are believed to be projected onto the story from the respondent's own desires and internal conflicts.

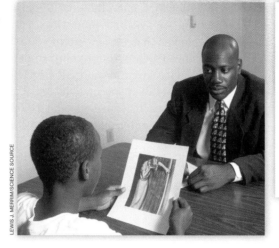

◀ Figure 12.2 **Sample TAT Card**
Test takers are shown cards with ambiguous scenes such as this sample and are asked to tell a story about what is happening in the picture. The main themes of the story, the thoughts and feelings of the characters, and how the story develops and resolves are considered useful indices of unconscious aspects of an individual's personality (Murray, 1943).

Many of the TAT drawings tend to elicit a consistent set of themes, such as successes and failures, competition and jealousy, conflict with parents and siblings, feelings about intimate relationships, aggression, and sexuality. For instance, one card that shows an older man standing over a child lying in bed tends to elicit themes regarding relationships that respondents have with an older man in their life, such as a relationship with a father, teacher, boss, or therapist. The interviewer might be interested in learning whether respondents see the person lying down as a male or female, and whether they report that the man standing is trying to help or harm the person lying down. Consider a story proposed by a young man in response to this card: "The boy lying down had a hard day at school. He worked so hard studying for his exam that when he came home after taking the test he fell asleep with his clothes on. No matter how hard the boy tries, he can never make his father happy. The father is sick and tired of the son not doing well in school and so he is going to kill him. He suffocates the boy and the boy dies." The test administrator might interpret this response as indicating that the respondent perceives that his father has high expectations that are not being met, and perhaps that the father is disappointed and angry with the young man.

The value of projective tests is debated by psychologists. Although they continue to be widely used by practising clinicians, critics argue that tests such as the Rorschach and the TAT are open to the biases of the examiner. A TAT story like the one above may *seem* revealing; however, the examiner must always add an interpretation (Was this about the respondent's actual father, about his own concerns about his academic failures, or about trying to be funny or provocative?), and that interpretation could well be the scorer's *own* projection into the mind of the test taker. Thus, despite the rich picture of a personality and the insights into an individual's motives that these tests appear to offer, projective tests should be understood primarily as a way in which a psychologist can get to know someone personally and intuitively (McClelland et al., 1953). When measured by rigorous scientific criteria, projective tests such as the TAT and the Rorschach have not been found to be reliable or valid in predicting behaviour (Lilienfeld, Lynn, & Lohr, 2003).

**What might limit the validity of the information obtained from projective tests?**

Newer personality measurement methods are moving beyond both self-report inventories and projective tests (Robins, Fraley, & Krueger, 2007). High-tech methods such as wireless communication, real-time computer analysis, and automated behaviour

**projective tests**
Tests designed to reveal inner aspects of individuals' personalities by analysis of their responses to a standard series of ambiguous stimuli.

**Rorschach Inkblot Test**
A projective technique in which respondents' inner thoughts and feelings are believed to be revealed by analysis of their responses to a set of unstructured inkblots.

**Thematic Apperception Test (TAT)**
A projective technique in which respondents' underlying motives, concerns, and the way they see the social world are believed to be revealed through analysis of the stories they make up about ambiguous pictures of people.

The EAR (electronically activated recorder) sampled conversations of hundreds of participants and found that women and men are equally talkative (Mehl et al., 2009).

identification open the door to personality measurements that are leaps beyond following the person around with a clipboard—and can lead to surprising findings. The stereotype that women are more talkative than men, for example, was challenged by findings when 396 university students in the United States and Mexico each spent several days wearing an EAR (electronically activated recorder) that captured random snippets of their speech (Mehl et al., 2009). The result? Women and men were *equally* talkative, each averaging about 16 000 words per day. The advanced measurement of how people differ (and how they do not) is a key step in understanding personality.

## IN SUMMARY

▶ In psychology, personality refers to a person's characteristic style of behaving, thinking, and feeling.

▶ Personality psychologists attempt to find the best ways to describe personality, to explain how personalities come about, and to measure personality.

▶ Two general classes of personality tests are personality inventories, such as the MMPI–2–RF, and projective techniques, such as the Rorschach Inkblot Test and the TAT. Newer high-tech methods are proving to be even more effective.

# The Trait Approach: Identifying Patterns of Behaviour

Imagine writing a story about the people you know. To capture their special qualities, you might describe their traits: Meaghan is *friendly, aggressive,* and *domineering;* Amin is *flaky, humorous,* and *superficial.* With a dictionary and a free afternoon, you might even be able to describe William as *perspicacious, flagitious,* and *callipygian.* The trait approach to personality uses such trait terms to characterize differences among individuals. In attempting to create manageable and meaningful sets of descriptors, trait theorists face two significant challenges: narrowing down the almost infinite set of adjectives and answering the more basic question of why people have particular traits and whether they arise from biological or hereditary foundations.

## Traits as Behavioural Dispositions and Motives

One way to think about personality is as a combination of traits. This was the approach of Gordon Allport (1937), one of the first trait theorists, who believed people could be described in terms of traits just as an object could be described in terms of its properties. He saw a **trait** as *a relatively stable disposition to behave in a particular and consistent way.* For example, a person who keeps his books organized alphabetically in bookshelves, hangs his clothing neatly in the closet, knows the schedule for the local bus, keeps a clear agenda in a daily planner, and lists birthdays of friends and family in his calendar can be said to have the trait of *orderliness.* This trait consistently manifests itself in a variety of settings.

The orderliness trait *describes* a person but does not *explain* his or her behaviour. Why does the person behave in this way? There are two basic ways in which a trait might serve as an explanation: The trait may be a pre-existing disposition of the person that causes the person's behaviour, or it may be a motivation that guides the person's behaviour. Allport saw traits as pre-existing dispositions, causes of behaviour that reliably trigger the behaviour. The person's

**How might traits explain behaviour?**

**trait**
A relatively stable disposition to behave in a particular and consistent way.

orderliness, for example, is an inner property of the person that will cause the person to straighten things up and be tidy in a wide array of situations. Other personality theorists, such as Henry Murray (the creator of the TAT), suggested instead that traits reflect motives. Just as a hunger motive might explain someone's many trips to the snack bar, a need for orderliness might explain the neat closet, organized calendar, and familiarity with the bus schedule (Murray & Kluckhohn, 1953). Researchers examining traits as causes have used personality inventories to measure them, whereas those examining traits as motives have more often used projective tests.

Researchers have described and measured hundreds of different personality traits over the past several decades. Back in the 1940s, in the wake of World War II, psychologists were very interested in right-wing *authoritarianism,* or the tendency toward political conservatism, obedience to authority, and conformity. At that time, researchers were trying to understand what had made people support the rise of Nazi Germany and Fascism (Adorno et al., 1950). Although research on the personality traits that lead to authoritarianism continues (Perry & Sibley, 2012), the topic became less focal for researchers once World War II receded into history. Examples of other traits that have come into vogue over the years include cognitive complexity, defensiveness, sensation seeking, and optimism. As with television shows and hairstyles, fashions in trait dimensions come and go over time.

By many accounts, Bashar al-Assad is a despotic ruler who imprisons, tortures, and kills those who oppose him. Why would anyone want to follow such a dictator? The study of the authoritarian personality was inspired by the idea that some people might follow most anyone because their personalities make them adhere to hierarchies of authority, submitting to those above them and dominating those below them.

## The Search for Core Traits

Picking a fashionable trait and studying it in depth does not get us very far in the search for the core of human character: the basic set of traits that defines how humans differ from one another. People may differ strongly in their choice of Coke versus Pepsi, or dogs versus cats, but are these differences important? How have researchers tried to discover the core personality traits?

### Classification Using Language

The study of core traits began with an exploration of how personality is represented in the store of wisdom we call *language.* Generation after generation, people have described people with words, so early psychologists proposed that core traits could be discerned by finding the main themes in all the adjectives used to describe personality. In one such analysis, a painstaking count of relevant words in a dictionary of English resulted in a list of over 18 000 potential traits (Allport & Odbert, 1936)! Attempts to narrow down the list to a more manageable set depend on the idea that traits might be related in a hierarchical pattern (see **FIGURE 12.3** on the next page), with more general or abstract traits at higher levels than more specific or concrete traits. Perhaps the more abstract traits represent the core of personality.

To identify this core, researchers have used the computational procedure called *factor analysis,* described in the Intelligence chapter, which sorts trait terms or self-descriptions into a small number of underlying dimensions, or *factors,* based on how people use the traits to rate themselves. In a typical study using factor analysis, hundreds of people rate themselves on hundreds of adjectives, indicating how accurately each one describes their personality. The researcher then conducts calculations to determine similarities in the raters' usage, for example, whether people who describe themselves as *ambitious* also describe themselves as *active* but not *laid-back* or *contented.* Factor analysis can also reveal which adjectives are unrelated. For example, if people who describe themselves as *ambitious* are neither more nor less likely to describe themselves as *creative* or *innovative,* the factor analysis would reveal that *ambitiousness* and *creativity/innovativeness* represent different

How do psychologists identify the core personality traits?

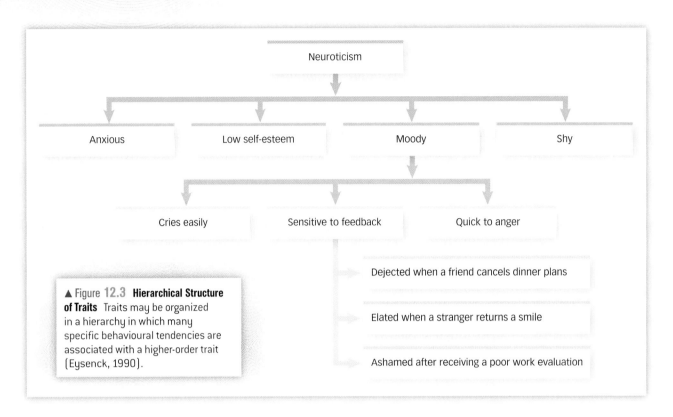

▲ Figure 12.3 **Hierarchical Structure of Traits** Traits may be organized in a hierarchy in which many specific behavioural tendencies are associated with a higher-order trait (Eysenck, 1990).

factors. Each factor is typically presented as a continuum, ranging from one extreme trait (such as *ambitious*) to its opposite (in this case, *laid-back*).

Different factor analysis techniques have yielded different views of personality structure. Cattell (1950) proposed a 16-factor theory of personality (way less than 18 000, but still a lot), whereas others have proposed theories with far fewer basic dimensions (John, Naumann, & Soto, 2008). Later, Hans Eysenck (1967) simplified things nicely with a model of personality with only two major traits (although he later expanded it to three). Eysenck's two-factor analysis identified one dimension that distinguished people who are sociable and active (extraverts) from those who are more introspective and quiet (introverts). His analysis also identified a second dimension ranging from the tendency to be very neurotic or emotionally unstable to the tendency to be more emotionally stable. He believed that many behavioural tendencies could be understood in terms of their relation to the core traits of Extraversion and Neuroticism. The third factor he proposed was Psychoticism, which refers to the extent to which a person is impulsive or hostile. (Notably, the term "psychotic" nowadays refers to an abnormal mental state marked by detachment from reality. This is discussed further in the Psychological Disorders chapter.)

## The Big Five Dimensions of Personality

Today most researchers agree that personality is best captured by 5 factors rather than 2, 3, 16, or 18 000 (John & Srivastava, 1999; McCrae & Costa, 1999). The **Big Five,** as they are affectionately called, are *the traits of the five-factor personality model: openness to experience, conscientiousness, extraversion, agreeableness, and neuroticism* (see **TABLE 12.2**). (Remember them by the initials O.C.E.A.N.) The five-factor model, which overlaps with the pioneering work of Cattell and Eysenck, is now widely preferred for several reasons. First, modern factor analysis techniques confirm that this set

▶ Table 12.2

### The Big Five Factor Model

| | High on trait | Low on trait |
|---|---|---|
| Openness to experience | imaginative . . . . . . . . . down-to-earth<br>variety . . . . . . . . . . . . . . . . . routine<br>independent . . . . . . . . . . conforming | |
| Conscientiousness | organized . . . . . . . . . . . disorganized<br>careful . . . . . . . . . . . . . . . . . careless<br>self-disciplined . . . . . . . . weak-willed | |
| Extraversion | social . . . . . . . . . . . . . . . . . retiring<br>fun loving . . . . . . . . . . . . . . . . sober<br>affectionate . . . . . . . . . . . . reserved | |
| Agreeableness | softhearted . . . . . . . . . . . . ruthless<br>trusting . . . . . . . . . . . . . suspicious<br>helpful . . . . . . . . . . . . uncooperative | |
| Neuroticism | worried . . . . . . . . . . . . . . . . . . calm<br>insecure . . . . . . . . . . . . . . . . secure<br>self-pitying . . . . . . . . . . self-satisfied | |

*Source:* McCrae & Costa, 1990, 1999.

of five factors strikes the right balance between accounting for as much variation in personality as possible while avoiding overlapping traits. Second, in a large number of studies using different kinds of data (people's descriptions of their own personalities, other people's descriptions of their personalities, interviewer checklists, and behavioural observation) the same five factors have emerged. Third, and perhaps most important, the basic five-factor structure seems to show up across a wide range of participants, including children, adults in other cultures, and even among those who use other languages, suggesting that the Big Five may be universal (John & Srivastava, 1999).

**What are the strengths of the five-factor model?**

In fact, the Big Five dimensions are so universal that they show up even when people are asked to evaluate the traits of complete strangers (Passini & Norman, 1966). This finding suggests that these dimensions of personality might reside in the eye of the beholder: categories that people use to evaluate others regardless of how well they know them. However, it is not all perception. The reality of these traits has been clearly established in research showing that self-reports on the Big Five are associated with predictable patterns of behaviour and social outcomes. People identified as high in extraversion, for example, tend to choose to spend time with lots of other people and are more likely than introverts to look people in the eye. People high in conscientiousness generally perform well at work and tend to live longer. People low in conscientiousness and low in agreeableness are more likely than average to be juvenile delinquents (John & Srivastava, 1999). It turns out that the Big Five personality traits also predict people's online behaviour on social networking sites like Facebook (see the Hot Science box).

**Big Five**
The traits of the five-factor model: openness to experience, conscientiousness, extraversion, agreeableness, and neuroticism.

## HOT SCIENCE

# Personality on the Surface

When you judge someone as friend or foe, interesting or boring, worth hiring or firing, how do you do it? It is nice to think that your impressions of personality are based on solid foundations—something deep. You would not judge personality based on something as shallow as someone's looks, would you? You would not form an impression of them from looking at what pops up on Google images or on their Facebook page, would you? These things may seem to be flimsy bases for understanding personality, but it turns out that some valid personality judgments can be made from exactly such superficial cues. And in certain cases, such judgments are remarkably accurate.

It turns out that you can get some accurate information about a book by judging its cover. Recent studies have shown that extraverts smile more than others and appear more stylish and healthy (Naumann et al., 2009), and people high in openness to experience are more likely to have tattoos and other body modifications (Nathanson, Paulhus, & Williams, 2006). Findings like these suggest that people can manipulate their surface identities to try to make desired impressions on others, and that surface signs of personality might therefore be false or misleading. However, one recent study of people's Facebook pages, which are clearly surface expressions of personality intended for others to see, found that the personalities people project online are more highly related to their real personalities than to the personalities they describe as their ideals (Back et al., 2010). The signs of personality that appear on the surface may be more than skin deep.

Going one step further, it turns out that people's Facebook activity is significantly associated with their self-reported personality traits. For instance, people high on extraversion report having more Facebook friends as well as making more status updates and comments. Posting updates and comments also is higher in Facebook users with elevated self-esteem. People high on agreeableness make more comments on their friends' posts, whereas those high on sensation seeking and openness to experience report playing a lot of games. And as you might have guessed, people high on narcissism post lots of comments, especially about their ideal self, as well as lots of pictures of themselves (Seidman, 2013; Wang et al., 2012).

▲ They say you cannot judge a book by its cover, but some new research suggests you can judge a person by their Facebook page.

AP PHOTO/PABLO MARTINEZ MONSIVAIS

Interestingly, research on the Big Five has shown that people's personalities tend to remain fairly stable throughout their lifetime: Scores at one time in life correlate strongly with scores at later dates, even decades later (Caspi, Roberts, & Shiner, 2005). William James offered the opinion that "in most of us, by the age of thirty, the character has set like plaster, and will never soften again" (James, 1890, p. 121), but this turns out to be too strong a view. Some variability is typical in childhood, and though there is less in adolescence, some personality change can even occur in adulthood for some people (Srivistava et al., 2003).

## Traits as Biological Building Blocks

Can we explain *why* a person has a stable set of personality traits? Many trait theorists have argued that unchangeable brain and biological processes produce the remarkable stability of traits over the life span. Allport viewed traits as characteristics of the brain that influence the way people respond to their environment. And, as you will see, Eysenck searched for a connection between his trait dimensions and specific individual differences in the workings of the brain.

Brain damage certainly can produce personality change, as the classic case of Phineas Gage so vividly demonstrates (see the Neuroscience and Behaviour chapter). You may recall that after the blasting accident that blew a steel rod through his frontal lobes, Gage showed a dramatic loss of social appropriateness and conscientiousness (Damasio, 1994). In fact, when someone experiences a profound change in personality, testing often reveals the presence of brain pathologies such as stroke, brain tumour, or changes consistent with dementia (Feinberg, 2001). The administration of antidepressant medication and other pharmaceutical treatments that change brain chemistry can also trigger personality changes, making people, for example, somewhat more extraverted and less neurotic (Bagby et al., 1999; Knutson et al., 1998).

### Genes, Traits, and Personality

Some of the most compelling evidence for the importance of biological factors in personality comes from the domain of behavioural genetics. Like researchers studying genetic influences on intelligence (see the Intelligence chapter), personality psychologists have looked at correlations between the traits in monozygotic, or identical, twins, who share the same genes, and dizygotic, or fraternal, twins, who on average share only half of their genes. The evidence has been generally consistent: In one review of studies involving over 24 000 twin pairs, for example, identical twins proved markedly more similar to each other in personality than did fraternal twins (Loehlin, 1992).

> **What do studies of twins tell us about personality?**

Simply put, the more genes you have in common with someone, the more similar your personalities are likely to be. Genes seem to influence most personality traits, and current estimates place the average genetic component of personality in the range of 0.40 to 0.60. These heritability coefficients, as you learned in the Intelligence chapter, indicate that roughly half the variability among individuals results from genetic factors (Bouchard & Loehlin, 2001). Of course, genetic factors do not account for everything and the remaining half of the variability in personality remains to be explained by differences in life experiences and other factors (see also The Real World box). Studies of twins suggest that the extent to which the Big Five traits derive from genetic differences ranges from 0.35 to 0.49 (see **TABLE 12.3**).

As in the study of intelligence, potential confounding factors must be ruled out to ensure that effects are truly due to genetics and not to environmental experiences. Are identical twins treated more similarly, and do they have a greater *shared environment* than fraternal twins? As children, were they dressed in the same snappy outfits and placed on the same soccer teams, and could this somehow have produced similarities

**Table 12.3**

**Heritability Estimates for the Big Five Personality Traits**

| Trait Dimension | Heritability |
| --- | --- |
| Openness | 0.45 |
| Conscientiousness | 0.38 |
| Extraversion | 0.49 |
| Agreeableness | 0.35 |
| Neuroticism | 0.41 |

*Source:* Loehlin, 1992.

**THE REAL WORLD**

# Are There "Male" and "Female" Personalities?

Do you think there is a typical female personality or a typical male personality? Researchers have found some reliable differences between men and women with respect to their self-reported traits, attitudes, and behaviours. Some of these findings conform to North American stereotypes of masculine and feminine. For example, researchers have found women to be more verbally expressive, more sensitive to nonverbal cues, and more nurturing than are men. Males are more physically aggressive than females, but females engage in more relational aggression (e.g., using relationships to harm someone, such as intentionally excluding them from a social group) than do males, even from a very young age (Crick & Grotpeter, 1995). Other gender differences include males having more assertiveness, slightly higher self-esteem, a more casual approach to sex, and greater sensation seeking than females. On the Big Five, studies across dozens of cultures around the world show that women are higher on neuroticism, extraversion, agreeableness, and conscientiousness; in terms of openness, women report greater openness to feelings and men greater openness to ideas (Costa, Terracciano, & McCrae, 2001; Schmitt et al., 2008). On a variety of other personality characteristics, including helpfulness, men and women on average show no reliable differences. Overall, men and women seem to be far more similar in personality than they are different (Hyde, 2005).

Although the gender differences in personality are quite small, they tend to get a lot of attention. There is debate about the origins of gender differences in personality, which often involves contrasting an evolutionary biological perspective with a social–cognitive perspective known as *social role theory*. The evolutionary perspective holds that men and women have evolved different personality characteristics, in part because their reproductive success depends on different behaviours. For instance, aggressiveness in men may have an adaptive value in intimidating sexual rivals; women who are agreeable and nurturing may have evolved to protect and ensure the survival of their offspring (Campbell, 1999) as well as to secure a reliable mate and provider (Buss, 1989).

◀ Cultures differ in their appreciation of male and female characteristics, but the Hindu deity Ardhanarishwara represents the value of combining both parts of human nature. Male on one side and female on the other, this god is symbolic of the dual nature of the sacred. The only real problem with such side-by-side androgyny comes in finding clothes that fit.

GIFT OF JEAN AND FRANCIS MARSHALL/BERKELEY ART MUSEUM/PACIFIC FILM ARCHIVE

According to social role theory, personality characteristics and behavioural differences between men and women result from cultural standards and expectations that assign them: socially permissible jobs, activities, and family positions (Eagly & Wood, 1999). Because of their physical size and their freedom from childbearing, men historically took roles of greater power—roles that in post-industrial society do not necessarily require physical strength. These differences then snowball, with men generally taking roles that require assertiveness and aggression (e.g., executive, school principal, surgeon) and women pursuing roles that emphasize greater supportiveness and nurturance (e.g., nurse, day care worker, teacher).

Regardless of the source of gender differences in personality, the degree to which people identify personally with masculine and feminine stereotypes may tell us about important personality differences between individuals. Sandra Bem (1974) designed a scale (the Bem Sex Role Inventory) that assesses the degree of identification with stereotypically masculine and feminine traits. Bem suggested that psychologically *androgynous* people (those who adopt the best of both worlds and identify with positive feminine traits such as kindness and positive masculine traits such as assertiveness) might be better adjusted than people who identify strongly with only one sex role.

An interesting wrinkle to this whole story is that although personality traits are fairly stable, they do shift a bit over time. In general, people become more conscientious in their 20s (got to keep that job!), and more agreeable in their 30s (got to keep those friends!). Neuroticism decreases with age, but only among women (Srivastava et al., 2003). So enjoy the personality you have now, because it may be changing soon.

### Bem Sex Role Inventory Sample Items

Respondents taking the Bem Sex Role Inventory rate themselves on each of the items without seeing the gender categorization. Then the scale is scored for masculinity (use of stereotypically masculine items), femininity (use of stereotypically feminine items), and androgyny (the tendency to use both the stereotypically masculine and feminine adjectives to describe oneself) (Bem, 1974).

| Masculine items | Feminine items |
|---|---|
| Self-reliant | Yielding |
| Defends own beliefs | Affectionate |
| Independent | Flatterable |
| Assertive | Sympathetic |
| Forceful | Sensitive to the needs of others |

in their personalities? Studies of identical twins reared far apart in adoptive families—an experience that pretty much eliminates the potential effect of shared environmental factors—suggest that shared environments have little impact: Reared-apart identical twins end up just as similar in personality as those who grow up together (McGue & Bouchard, 1998; Tellegen et al., 1988).

Indeed, one provocative, related finding is that such shared environmental factors as parental divorce or parenting style may have little direct impact on personality (Plomin & Caspi, 1999). According to these researchers, simply growing up in the same family does not make people very similar. In fact, when two siblings are similar, this is thought to be primarily due to genetic similarities.

Researchers also have assessed specific behavioural and attitude similarities in twins, and the evidence for heritability in these studies is often striking. One study that examined 3000 pairs of identical and fraternal twins found evidence for the genetic transmission of conservative views regarding topics such as socialism, church authority, the death penalty, and mixed-race marriage (Martin et al., 1986). It is very unlikely that a specific gene is directly responsible for a complex psychological outcome like beliefs about social or political issues. Rather, a set of genes (or, more likely, many sets of genes interacting) may produce specific characteristics or tendencies to think in a conservative versus liberal manner. One recent study examined the DNA of 13 000 people and measured the extent to which they reported conservative versus liberal attitudes and found associations between conservatism–liberalism and chromosomal regions linked to mental flexibility, or the extent to which a person changes his or her thinking in response to shifts in the environment, which could be one of the factors influencing our views on social and political issues (Hatemi et al., 2011). Current research by psychological scientists is aimed at better understanding how variations in our genetic code may contribute to the development of personality.

KANAI, R., FEILDEN, T., FIRTH, C. & REES, G. (2011). POLITICAL ORIENTATIONS ARE CORRELATED WITH BRAIN STRUCTURES IN YOUNG ADULTS. *CURRENT BIOLOGY,* 21(8), PP. 677–680. FIGURE 1.

Both genetics and environment influence the structure of the brain. British scientists have recently discovered that even in young adults (mean age 23.5) political orientation is related to differences in brain structure. Participants indicated their political orientation on a four-point scale from 1 (liberal) to 4 (conservative). Greater liberalism was associated with increased grey matter volume in a region near the front of the brain called the anterior cingulate cortex (*a*), whereas greater conservatism was associated with a greater volume in the right amygdala (*b*) (Kanai et al., 2011). These differences in brain structure probably reflect the emotional and cognitive traits of individuals, which are reflected in their inclinations towards one political orientation or the other. For example, conservatism is associated with a psychological need to avoid uncertainty (need for order, intolerance of ambiguity and lack of openness to experience) and to manage threats (anxiety around death and perception of the world as a dangerous place) (Jost et al., 2007).

## Do Animals Have Personalities?

Another source of evidence for the biological basis of human personality comes from the study of nonhuman animals. Any dog owner, zookeeper, or cattle farmer can tell you that individual animals have characteristic patterns of behaviour. One Missouri woman who reportedly enjoyed raising chickens in her suburban home said that "the best part" was "knowing them as individuals" (Tucker, 2003). As far as we know, this pet owner did not give her feathered companions a personality test, though researcher Sam Gosling (1998) used this approach in a study of a group of spotted hyenas. Well, not exactly. He recruited four human observers to use personality scales to rate the different hyenas in the group. When he examined ratings on the scales, he found five dimensions; three closely resembled the Big Five traits of neuroticism (i.e., fearfulness, emotional reactivity), openness to experience (i.e., curiosity), and agreeableness (i.e., absence of aggression).

In similar studies of guppies and octopi, individual differences in traits resembling extraversion and neuroticism were reliably observed (Gosling & John, 1999). In each study, researchers identified particular behaviours that they felt reflected each trait based on their observation of the animals' normal repertoire of activities. Octopi, for example, seldom get invited to parties, so they cannot be assessed for their socializing tendencies ("He was all hands!"), but they do vary in terms of whether they prefer to eat in the safety of their den or are willing to venture out at feeding time, and so a behaviour that corresponds to extraversion can reasonably be assessed (Gosling & John, 1999). Because different observers seem to agree on where an animal falls on a given dimension, the findings do not simply reflect a particular observer's imagination or tendency to *anthropomorphize* (i.e., to attribute human characteristics to nonhuman animals). Such findings of cross-species commonality in behavioural styles help support the idea that there are biological mechanisms that underlie personality traits shared by many species.

> **Why study animal behavioural styles?**

From an evolutionary perspective, differences in personality reflect alternative adaptations that species—human and nonhuman—have evolved to deal with the challenges of survival and reproduction. For example, if you were to hang around a bar for an evening or two, you would soon see that humans have evolved more than one way to attract and keep a mate. People who are extraverted would probably show off to attract attention, whereas you would be likely to see people high in agreeableness displaying affection and nurturance (Buss, 1996). Both approaches might work well to attract mates and reproduce successfully—depending on the environment. Through this process of natural selection, those characteristics that have proved successful in our evolutionary struggle for survival have been passed on to future generations.

How would you rate this honey badger? Is it antagonistic or agreeable? Neurotic or emotionally stable? Researchers have found that even animals appear to have personalities. Or should they be called "animalities"?

## Traits in the Brain

What neurophysiological mechanisms might influence the development of personality traits? Much of the thinking on this topic has focused on the extraversion–introversion dimension. In his personality model, Eysenck (1967) speculated that extraversion and introversion might arise from individual differences in cortical arousal. Eysenck suggested that extraverts pursue stimulation because their *reticular formation* (the part of the brain that regulates arousal or alertness, as described in the Neuroscience and Behaviour chapter) is not easily stimulated. To achieve greater cortical arousal and feel fully alert, Eysenck argued, extraverts seek out social interaction, parties, and other activities to achieve mental stimulation. In contrast, introverts may prefer reading or quiet activities because their cortex is very easily stimulated to a point higher than optimal alertness.

> **What neurological differences explain why extraverts pursue more stimulation than introverts?**

Behavioural and physiological research generally supports Eysenck's view. When introverts and extraverts are presented with a range of intense stimuli, introverts respond more strongly, including salivating more when a drop of lemon juice is placed on their tongues and reacting more negatively to electric shocks or loud noises (Bartol & Costello, 1976; Stelmack, 1990). This reactivity has an impact on the ability to concentrate: Extraverts tend to perform well at tasks that are done in a noisy, arousing context (such as bartending or teaching), whereas introverts are better at tasks that require concentration in tranquil contexts (such as the work of a librarian or nighttime security guard) (Geen, 1984; Lieberman & Rosenthal, 2001; Matthews & Gilliland, 1999).

In a refined version of Eysenck's ideas about arousability, Jeffrey Gray (1970) proposed that the dimensions of extraversion–introversion and neuroticism reflect two basic brain systems. The *behavioural activation system* (*BAS*), essentially a "go" system, activates approach behaviour in response to the anticipation of reward. The extravert has a highly reactive BAS and will actively engage the environment, seeking social reinforcement and be on the go. The *behavioural inhibition system* (*BIS*), a "stop" system, inhibits behaviour in response to stimuli signalling punishment. The anxious person, in turn, has a highly reactive BIS and will focus on negative outcomes and be on the lookout for stop signs. Because these two systems operate independently, it is possible for someone to be both a go and a stop person (simultaneously activated and inhibited), caught in a constant conflict between these two traits. Studies of brain electrical activity (EEG) and functional brain imaging (fMRI) suggest that individual differences in activation and inhibition arise through the operation of distinct brain systems underlying these

Extraverts pursue stimulation in the form of people, loud noise, and bright colours. Introverts tend to prefer softer, quieter settings. Pop quiz: Nicki Minaj—introvert or extrovert?

**psychodynamic approach**
An approach that regards personality as formed by needs, strivings, and desires largely operating outside of awareness—motives that can also produce emotional disorders.

tendencies (DeYoung & Gray, 2009). Even more recently, studies have suggested that the core personality traits described above may arise from individual differences in the volume of the different brain regions associated with each trait. For instance, self-reported neuroticism is correlated with the volume of brain regions involved in sensitivity to threat; agreeableness with areas associated with processing information about the mental states of other people; conscientiousness with regions involved in self-regulation; and extraversion with areas associated with processing information about reward (DeYoung et al., 2010). Research aimed at understanding how the structure and activity of our brains can contribute to the formation of our personality traits is still in its early stages, but represents a growing area of the field that many believe holds great promise for helping us better understand how we each develop into the unique people that we are.

## IN SUMMARY

▶ The trait approach tries to identify personality dimensions that can be used to characterize an individual's behaviour. Researchers have attempted to boil down the potentially huge array of things people do, think, and feel into some core personality dimensions.

▶ Many personality psychologists currently focus on the Big Five personality factors: openness to experience, conscientiousness, extraversion, agreeableness, and neuroticism.

▶ To address the question of why traits arise, trait theorists often adopt a biological perspective, examining links between personality and brain functioning.

TIME LIFE PICTURES/MANSELL/TIME LIFE PICTURES/GETTY IMAGES

Sigmund Freud was the first psychology theorist to be honoured with his own bobble-head doll. Let us hope he is not the last.

# The Psychodynamic Approach: Forces That Lie beneath Awareness

Rather than trying to understand personality in terms of broad theories for describing individual differences, Freud looked for personality in the details: the meanings and insights revealed by careful analysis of the tiniest blemishes in a person's thought and behaviour. Working with patients who came to him with disorders that did not seem to have any physical basis, he began by interpreting the origins of their everyday mistakes and memory lapses, errors that have come to be called *Freudian slips*.

Freud used the term *psychoanalysis* to refer to both his theory of personality and his method of treating patients. Freud's ideas were the first of many theories building on his basic idea that personality is a mystery to the person who "owns" it because we cannot know our own deepest motives. The theories of Freud and his followers (discussed in the Treatment chapter) are referred to as the **psychodynamic approach,** *an approach that regards personality as formed by needs, strivings, and desires largely operating outside of awareness—motives that can also produce emotional disorders.* The real engines of personality, in this view, are forces of which we are largely unaware.

THE PHOTO WORKS

Psychologists call this construct the **dynamic unconscious,** *an active system encompassing a lifetime of hidden memories, the person's deepest instincts and desires, and the person's inner struggle to control those forces.* The power of the unconscious is believed to come from its early origins—experiences that shaped the mind before a person could even put thoughts and feelings into words—and from its contents, which are embarrassing, unspeakable, and even frightening because they operate without any control by consciousness. Imagine having violent competitive feelings toward your father ("I wish I could beat the old man at something, or just beat him up") or a death wish toward a sibling ("It would be so great if my punk sister fell down the stairs"). Whew! Impulses like that are assumed to remain in the unconscious because such powerful forces would be too much for consciousness to bear. This battle, psychodynamic psychologists believe, goes on beneath the surface in an ongoing struggle among parts of the mind.

## The Structure of the Mind: Id, Ego, and Superego

To explain the emotional difficulties that beset his patients, Freud proposed that the mind consists of three independent, interacting, and often conflicting systems: the id, the superego, and the ego.

The most basic system, the **id,** is *the part of the mind containing the drives present at birth; it is the source of our bodily needs, wants, desires, and impulses, particularly our sexual and aggressive drives.* The id operates according to the *pleasure principle,* the psychic force that motivates the tendency to seek immediate gratification of any impulse. If governed by the id alone, you would never be able to tolerate the buildup of hunger while waiting to be served at a restaurant but would simply grab food from tables nearby.

Opposite the id is the **superego,** *the mental system that reflects the internalization of cultural rules, mainly learned as parents exercise their authority.* The superego consists of a set of guidelines, internal standards, and other codes of conduct that regulate and control our behaviours, thoughts, and fantasies. It acts as a kind of conscience, punishing us when it finds we are doing or thinking something wrong (by producing guilt or other painful feelings) and rewarding us (with feelings of pride or self-congratulation) for living up to ideal standards.

The final system of the mind, according to psychoanalytic theory, is the **ego,** *the component of personality, developed through contact with the external world, that enables us to deal with life's practical demands.* The ego operates according to the *reality principle,* the regulating mechanism that enables the individual to delay gratifying immediate needs and function effectively in the real world. It is the mediator between the id and the superego. The ego helps you resist the impulse to snatch others' food and also finds the restaurant and pays the cheque.

Freud believed that the relative strength of the interactions among the three systems of mind (i.e., which system is usually dominant) determines an individual's basic personality structure. Together the id force of personal needs, the superego force of pressures to quell those needs, and the ego force of reality's demands create constant internal conflict. He believed that the dynamics among the id, superego, and ego are largely governed by *anxiety,* an unpleasant feeling that arises when unwanted thoughts or feelings occur, such as when the id seeks a gratification that the ego thinks will lead to real-world dangers or that the superego sees as leading to punishment. When the ego receives an "alert signal" in the form of anxiety, it launches into a defensive position in an attempt to ward off the anxiety. According to Freud, it does so using

> **According to Freud, how is personality shaped by the interaction of the id, superego, and ego?**

---

**dynamic unconscious**
An active system encompassing a lifetime of hidden memories, the person's deepest instincts and desires, and the person's inner struggle to control those forces.

**id**
The part of the mind containing the drives present at birth; it is the source of our bodily needs, wants, desires, and impulses, particularly our sexual and aggressive drives.

**superego**
The mental system that reflects the internalization of cultural rules, mainly learned as parents exercise their authority.

**ego**
The component of personality, developed through contact with the external world, that enables us to deal with life's practical demands.

**defence mechanisms**
Unconscious coping mechanisms that reduce anxiety generated by threats from unacceptable impulses.

"I'm sorry, I'm not speaking to anyone tonight. My defense mechanisms seem to be out of order."

one of several different **defence mechanisms,** *unconscious coping mechanisms that reduce anxiety generated by threats from unacceptable impulses* (see **TABLE 12.4**). Psychodynamically oriented psychologists believe that defence mechanisms help us overcome anxiety and engage effectively with the outside world and that our characteristic style of defence becomes our signature in dealing with the world—and an essential aspect of our personality.

▶ **Table 12.4**

### Defence Mechanisms

Repression is the first defence the ego tries, but if it is inadequate, then other defence mechanisms may come into play.

| Defence Mechanism | Description | Example |
|---|---|---|
| Repression | Removing painful experiences and unacceptable impulses from the conscious mind: "motivated forgetting." | Not lashing out physically in anger; putting a bad experience out of your mind. |
| Rationalization | Supplying a reasonable sounding explanation for unacceptable feelings and behaviour to conceal (mostly from oneself) one's underlying motives or feelings. | Dropping calculus "allegedly" because of poor ventilation in the classroom. |
| Reaction formation | Unconsciously replacing threatening inner wishes and fantasies with an exaggerated version of their opposite. | Being rude to someone you are attracted to. |
| Projection | Attributing one's own threatening feelings, motives, or impulses to another person or group. | Judging others as being dishonest because you believe that you are dishonest. |
| Regression | Reverting to an immature behaviour or earlier stage of development, a time when things felt more secure, to deal with internal conflict and perceived threat. | Using baby talk, even though able to use appropriate speech, in response to distress. |
| Displacement | Shifting unacceptable wishes or drives to a neutral or less threatening alternative. | Slamming a door; yelling at someone other than the person you are mad at. |
| Identification | Dealing with feelings of threat and anxiety by unconsciously taking on the characteristics of another person who seems more powerful or better able to cope. | A bullied child becoming a bully. |
| Sublimation | Channelling unacceptable sexual or aggressive drives into socially acceptable and culturally enhancing activities. | Diverting anger to the football or rugby field, or other contact sport. |

## Psychosexual Stages and the Development of Personality

Freud also proposed that a person's basic personality is formed before 6 years of age during a series of sensitive periods, or life stages, when experiences influence all that will follow. Freud called these periods **psychosexual stages,** *distinct early life stages through which personality is formed as children experience sexual pleasures from specific body areas and caregivers redirect or interfere with those pleasures.* He argued that as a result of adult interference with pleasure-seeking energies, the child experiences conflict. At each stage, a different bodily region, or *erotogenic* zone, dominates the child's subjective experience (e.g., during the oral stage, pleasure centres on the mouth). Each region represents a battleground between the child's id impulses and the adult external world.

Problems and conflicts encountered at any psychosexual stage, Freud believed, will influence personality in adulthood. Conflict resulting from a person's being deprived or, paradoxically, overindulged at a given stage could result in **fixation,** *a phenomenon in which a person's pleasure-seeking drives become psychologically stuck, or arrested, at a particular psychosexual stage.* Freud described particular personality traits as being derived from fixations at the different psychosexual stages. Here is how he explained each stage and the effects of fixation at each stage.

> In the first year and a half of life, the infant is in the **oral stage,** *the first psychosexual stage, in which experience centres on the pleasures and frustrations associated with the mouth, sucking, and being fed.* Infants who are deprived of pleasurable feeding or indulgently overfed are believed to have a personality style in which they are focused on issues related to fullness and emptiness and what they can "take in" from others.

> Between 2 and 3 years of age, the child moves on to the **anal stage,** *the second psychosexual stage, in which experience is dominated by the pleasures and frustrations associated with the anus, retention and expulsion of feces and urine, and toilet training.* Individuals who have had difficulty negotiating this conflict are believed to develop a rigid personality and remain preoccupied with issues of control.

> Between the ages of 3 and 5 years, the child is in the **phallic stage,** *the third psychosexual stage, in which experience is dominated by the pleasure, conflict, and frustration associated with the phallic–genital region as well as coping with powerful incestuous feelings of love, hate, jealousy, and conflict.* According to Freud, children in the phallic stage experience the **Oedipus conflict,** *a developmental experience in which a child's conflicting feelings toward the opposite-sex parent are (usually) resolved by identifying with the same-sex parent.*

> A more relaxed period in which children are no longer struggling with the power of their sexual and aggressive drives occurs between the ages of 5 and 13, as children experience the **latency stage,** *the fourth psychosexual stage, in which the primary focus is on the further development of intellectual, creative, interpersonal, and athletic skills.* Because Freud believed that the most significant aspects of personality development occur before

MARTHA HOLMES/TIME LIFE PICTURES/GETTY IMAGES

One of the id's desires is to make a fine mess (a desire that is often frustrated early in life, perhaps during the anal stage). Famous American painter Jackson Pollock found a way to make extraordinarily fine messes—behaviour that at some level all of us envy.

**psychosexual stages**
Distinct early life stages through which personality is formed as children experience sexual pleasures from specific body areas and caregivers redirect or interfere with those pleasures.

**fixation**
A phenomenon in which a person's pleasure-seeking drives become psychologically stuck, or arrested, at a particular psychosexual stage.

**oral stage**
The first psychosexual stage, in which experience centres on the pleasures and frustrations associated with the mouth, sucking, and being fed.

**anal stage**
The second psychosexual stage, in which experience is dominated by the pleasures and frustrations associated with the anus, retention and expulsion of feces and urine, and toilet training.

**phallic stage**
The third psychosexual stage, in which experience is dominated by the pleasure, conflict, and frustration associated with the phallic–genital region as well as coping with powerful incestuous feelings of love, hate, jealousy, and conflict.

**Oedipus conflict**
A developmental experience in which a child's conflicting feelings toward the opposite-sex parent are (usually) resolved by identifying with the same-sex parent.

**latency stage**
The fourth psychosexual stage, in which the primary focus is on the further development of intellectual, creative, interpersonal, and athletic skills.

**genital stage**
The fifth and final psychosexual stage, the time for the coming together of the mature adult personality with a capacity to love, work, and relate to others in a mutually satisfying and reciprocal manner.

**self-actualizing tendency**
The human motive toward realizing our inner potential.

the age of 6 years, psychodynamic psychologists do not speak of fixation at the latency period. Simply making it to the latency period relatively undisturbed by conflicts of the earlier stages is a sign of healthy personality development.

> At puberty and thereafter, the fifth and final stage of personality development occurs. The **genital stage** is *the time for the coming together of the mature adult personality with a capacity to love, work, and relate to others in a mutually satisfying and reciprocal manner.* Freud believed that people who are fixated in a prior stage fail to develop healthy adult sexuality and a well-adjusted adult personality.

What should we make of all this? On the one hand, the psychoanalytic theory of psychosexual stages offers an intriguing picture of early family relationships and the extent to which they allow the child to satisfy basic needs and wishes. On the other hand, critics argue that psychodynamic explanations lack any real evidence and tend to focus on provocative after-the-fact interpretation rather than testable prediction. The psychosexual stage theory offers a compelling set of story plots for interpreting lives once they have unfolded, but has not generated clear-cut predictions supported by research.

> **Why do critics say Freud's psychosexual stages are more interpretation than explanation?**

## IN SUMMARY

▶ Freud believed that the personality results from forces that are largely unconscious, shaped by the interplay among id, superego, and ego.

▶ Defence mechanisms are methods the mind may use to reduce anxiety generated from unacceptable impulses.

▶ Freud also believed that the developing person passes through a series of psychosexual stages and that failing to progress beyond one of the stages results in fixation, which is associated with corresponding personality traits.

# The Humanistic–Existential Approach: Personality as Choice

In the 1950s and 1960s, psychologists began to try to understand personality from a viewpoint quite different from trait theory's biological determinism and Freud's focus on unconscious drives from unresolved childhood experiences. These new humanistic and existential theorists turned attention to how humans make *healthy choices* that create their personalities. *Humanistic psychologists* emphasized a positive, optimistic view of human nature that highlights people's inherent goodness and their potential for personal growth. *Existentialist psychologists* focused on the individual as a responsible agent who is free to create and live his or her life while negotiating the issue of meaning and the reality of death. The *humanistic–existential approach* integrates these insights with a focus on how a personality can become optimal.

## Human Needs and Self-Actualization

Humanists see the **self-actualizing tendency,** *the human motive toward realizing our inner potential,* as a major factor in personality. The pursuit of knowledge, the expression of one's creativity, the quest for spiritual enlightenment, and the desire

Decades of research have shown that growing up in a distressed neighbourhood is associated with worse educational, occupational, and health outcomes. Humanistic psychologists would suggest that people in such settings must struggle to meet their basic daily needs and so do not have opportunities for self-actualization.

to give to society all are examples of self-actualization. As you saw in the Emotion and Motivation chapter, the noted humanistic theorist Abraham Maslow (1943) proposed a *hierarchy of needs,* a model of essential human needs arranged according to their priority, in which basic physiological and safety needs must be satisfied before a person can afford to focus on higher-level psychological needs. Only when these basic needs are satisfied can one pursue higher needs, culminating in *self-actualization*: the need to be good, to be fully alive, and to find meaning in life.

**What is it to be self-actualized?**

Humanist psychologists explain individual personality differences as arising from the various ways that the environment facilitates—or blocks—attempts to satisfy psychological needs. For example, someone with the inherent potential to be a great scientist, artist, parent, or teacher might never realize these talents if his or her energies and resources are instead directed toward meeting basic needs of security, belongingness, and the like. Research indicates that when people shape their lives around goals that do not match their true nature and capabilities, they are less likely to be happy than those whose lives and goals do match (Ryan & Deci, 2000).

It feels great to be doing exactly what you are capable of doing. Mihaly Csikszentmihalyi (1990) found that engagement in tasks that exactly match one's abilities creates a mental state of energized focus that he called *flow* (see **FIGURE 12.4**). Tasks that are below our abilities cause boredom, those that are too challenging cause anxiety, and those that are "just right" lead to the experience of flow. If you know how to play the piano, for example, and are playing a Chopin prelude that you know well enough that it just matches your abilities, you are likely to experience this optimal state. People report being happier at these times than at any other times. Humanists believe that such peak experiences, or states of flow, reflect the realization of one's human potential and represent the height of personality development.

## Personality as Existence

Existentialists agree with humanists about many of the features of personality but focus on challenges to the human condition that are more profound than the lack of a nurturing environment. Rollo May (1983) and Victor Frankl (2000), for example, argued that specific aspects of the human condition, such as awareness of our own existence and the ability to make choices about how to behave, have a double-edged quality: They bring an extraordinary richness and dignity to human life, but they also force us to confront realities that are difficult to face, such as the prospect of our own death. The **existential approach** is *a school of thought that regards personality as governed by an individual's ongoing choices and decisions in the context of the realities of life and death.*

According to the existential perspective, the difficulties we face in finding meaning in life and in accepting the responsibility of making free choices provoke a type of anxiety existentialists call *angst* (the anxiety of fully being). The human ability to consider limitless numbers of goals and actions is exhilarating, but it can also open the door to profound questions such as: Why am I here? What is the meaning of my life?

**What is angst, and how is it created?**

Thinking about the meaning of existence also can evoke an awareness of the inevitability of death. What, then, should we do with each moment? What is the purpose of living if life as we know it will end one day, perhaps even today? Alternatively, does life have more meaning given that it is so temporary? Existential theorists do not

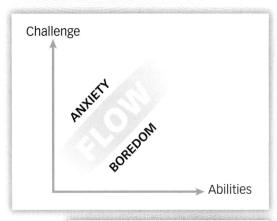

▲ Figure **12.4 Flow Experience** It feels good to do things that challenge your abilities but that do not challenge them too much. Csikszentmihalyi (1990) described this feeling between boredom and anxiety as the "flow experience."

Calgary piano prodigy Jan Lisiecki probably experiences flow when playing Chopin.

**existential approach**
A school of thought that regards personality as governed by an individual's ongoing choices and decisions in the context of the realities of life and death.

**social–cognitive approach**
An approach that views personality in terms of how the person thinks about the situations encountered in daily life and behaves in response to them.

suggest that people consider these profound existential issues on a day-to-day and moment-to-moment basis. Rather than ruminate about death and meaning, people typically pursue superficial answers that help them deal with the angst and dread they experience, and the defences they construct form the basis of their personalities (Binswanger, 1958; May, 1983). Some people organize their lives around obtaining material possessions; others may immerse themselves in drugs or addictive behaviours such as compulsive web browsing, video gaming, or television watching in order to numb the mind to existential realities.

For existentialists, a healthier solution is to face the issues head-on and learn to accept and tolerate the pain of existence. Indeed, being fully human means confronting existential realities rather than denying them or embracing comforting illusions. This requires the courage to accept the inherent anxiety and the dread of nonbeing that is part of being alive. Such courage may be bolstered by developing supportive relationships with others who can supply unconditional positive regard. There is something about being loved that helps take away the angst.

## IN SUMMARY

► The humanistic–existential approach to personality grew out of philosophical traditions that are at odds with most of the assumptions of the trait and psychoanalytic approaches.

► Humanists see personality as directed by an inherent striving toward self-actualization and development of our unique human potentials.

► Existentialists focus on angst and the defensive response people often have to questions about the meaning of life and the inevitability of death.

# The Social–Cognitive Approach: Personalities in Situations

What is it like to be a person? The **social–cognitive approach** *views personality in terms of how the person thinks about the situations encountered in daily life and behaves in response to them.* Bringing together insights from social psychology, cognitive psychology, and learning theory, this approach emphasizes how the person experiences and interprets situations (Bandura, 1986; Mischel & Shoda, 1999; Ross & Nisbett, 1991; Wegner & Gilbert, 2000).

Researchers in social cognition believe that both the current situation and learning history are key determinants of behaviour, and focus on how people *perceive* their environments. People think about their goals, the consequences of their behaviour, and how they might achieve certain things in different situations (Lewin, 1951). The social–cognitive approach looks at how personality and situation interact to cause behaviour, how personality contributes to the way people construct situations in their own minds, and how people's goals and expectancies influence their responses to situations.

> Do researchers in social cognition think that personality arises from past experiences or from the current environment?

*"He's not very exciting in social situations, but on the net he's a wildman!"*

MICK STEVENS ©THE NEW YORKER COLLECTION WWW.CARTOONBANK.COM

## Consistency of Personality across Situations

Although social—cognitive psychologists attribute behaviour both to the individual's personality and to his or her situation, situation can often trump personality. For example, a person would have to be pretty strange to act exactly the same way at a memorial service and at a keg party. In their belief that the strong push and pull of situations can influence almost everyone, social—cognitive psychologists are somewhat at odds with the basic assumptions of classic personality psychology; that is, that personality characteristics (such as traits, needs, unconscious drives) cause people to behave in the same way across situations and over time. At the core of the social—cognitive approach is a natural puzzle, the **person—situation controversy,** which focuses on *the question of whether behaviour is caused more by personality or by situational factors.*

This controversy began in earnest when Walter Mischel (1968) argued that measured personality traits often do a poor job of predicting individuals' behaviour. Mischel reviewed decades of research that compared scores on standard personality tests with actual behaviour, looking at evidence from studies asking questions such as "Does a person with a high score on a test of introversion actually spend more time alone than someone with a low score?" Mischel's disturbing conclusion: The average correlation between trait and behaviour is only about 0.30. This is certainly better than zero (i.e., no relation at all) but not very good when you remember that a perfect prediction is represented by a correlation of 1.0.

Mischel also noted that knowing how a person will behave in one situation is not particularly helpful in predicting the person's behaviour in another situation. For example, in classic studies, Hugh Hartshorne and Mark May (1928) assessed children's honesty by examining their willingness to cheat on a test and found that such dishonesty was not consistent from one situation to another. The assessment of a child's trait of honesty in a cheating situation was of almost no use in predicting whether the child would act honestly in a different situation, such as when given the opportunity to steal money. Mischel proposed that measured traits do not predict behaviours very well because behaviours are determined more by situational factors than personality theorists were willing to acknowledge.

Is there no personality, then? Do we all just do what situations require? The person—situation controversy has inspired many studies in the years since Mischel's critique, and

**Does personality or the current situation predict a person's behaviour?**

it turns out that information about both personality and situation are necessary to predict behaviour accurately (Fleeson, 2004; Mischel, 2004). Some situations are particularly powerful, leading most everyone to behave similarly regardless of personality (Cooper & Withey, 2009). At a funeral, almost everyone looks sombre, and during an earthquake, almost everyone shakes. But in more moderate situations, personality can come forward to influence behaviour (Funder, 2001). Among the children in Hartshorne and May's (1928) studies, cheating versus not cheating on a test was actually a fairly good predictor of cheating on a test later—as long as the situation was similar. Personality consistency, then, appears to be a matter of when and where a certain kind of behaviour tends to be shown (see the Culture & Community box on the next page). Social—cognitive theorists believe these patterns of personality consistency arise from the way different people interpret situations and from the ways different people pursue goals within situations.

## Personal Constructs

How can we understand differences in the way situations are interpreted? Recall our notion of personality often existing in the eye of the beholder. Situations may exist in the eye of the beholder as well. One person's gold mine may be another person's

Is a student who cheats on a test more likely than others to steal candy or lie to his grandmother? Social—cognitive research indicates that behaviour in one situation does not necessarily predict behaviour in a different situation.

**person—situation controversy**
The question of whether behaviour is caused more by personality or by situational factors.

# CULTURE & COMMUNITY

### Does Your Personality Change According to Which Language You Are Speaking, or Who You are Speaking With?

The personalities of people from different cultures can often diverge. For instance, Cantonese–English bilingual speakers in Hong Kong exhibited rather different personality traits depending on whether they were speaking Cantonese or English, and whether they were speaking with a Chinese or Caucasian interviewer (Chen & Bond, 2010). The British colonial history of Hong Kong has strongly influenced its political structure, educational institutions, and culture, and this is evident in the fact that many ethnic Chinese undergraduate students in Hong Kong are fluently bilingual.

Such students were interviewed in four conditions: talking with a Caucasian interviewer in English, with the same interviewer in Cantonese, with a Chinese interviewer in English, and with that interviewer in Cantonese. Two different Caucasian and two different Chinese interviewers were used to control for interviewer effects, and all interviews were conducted from scripts (counterbalanced across conditions). In all the interviews, participants answered general information questions about themselves, their hobbies, and their social activities. All interviewers wore the same clothing and were trained to standardize their language and nonverbal behaviours. The four interviews with each participant were recorded (only the participant, not interviewer, was visible). The videos were observed by two Cantonese–English people (who were not participants in the experiment and did not know the purpose of the experiment). After each video, each observer judged the participant's extraversion, openness to experience, and assertiveness (e.g., "Did the participant seem extraverted?") on a six-point scale, ranging from 1 (*strongly disagree*) to 6 (*strongly agree*).

Observers ratings depended both on the language in which people were speaking and on the ethnicity of the interviewer. Participants

were rated as substantially less extraverted, open to experience, and assertive when the participants were speaking with a Chinese interviewer in Cantonese than when they were speaking with a Caucasian interviewer in either language. When participants spoke with a Chinese interviewer in English, ratings were somewhat lower than when speaking with a Caucasian interviewer, but still higher than when speaking Cantonese with a Chinese interviewer. These results suggest that bilinguals, when they interact with people from different cultures, exhibit personality traits that correspond to their perceptions of "typical" personality in those cultures.

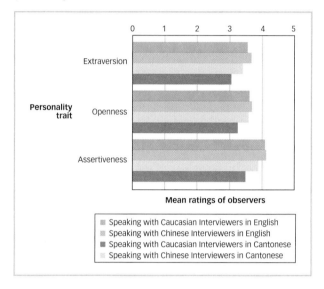

**Mean ratings of observers**

■ Speaking with Caucasian Interviewers in English
■ Speaking with Chinese Interviewers in English
■ Speaking with Caucasian Interviewers in Cantonese
■ Speaking with Chinese Interviewers in Cantonese

**personal constructs**
Dimensions people use in making sense of their experiences.

Are two of these people taller and one shorter? Are two bareheaded while one wears a hood? Or are two the daughters and one the mom? George Kelly held that the personal constructs we use to distinguish among people in our lives are basic elements of our own personalities.

useless hole in the ground. George Kelly (1955) long ago realized that these differences in perspective could be used to understand the *perceiver's* personality. He suggested that people view the social world from differing perspectives and that these different views arise through the application of **personal constructs,** *dimensions people use in making sense of their experiences.* Consider, for example, different individuals' personal constructs of a clown: One person may see him as a source of fun, another as a tragic figure, and yet another as so frightening that McDonald's must be avoided at all costs.

**Why does everyone not love clowns?**

Kelly assessed personal constructs about social relationships by asking people to (1) list the people in their life, (2) consider three of the people and state a way in which two of them are similar to each other and different from the third, and (3) repeat this for other triads of people to produce a list of the dimensions used to classify friends and family. One respondent might focus on the degree to which people (self included) are lazy or hardworking, for example; someone else might attend to the degree to which people are sociable or unfriendly.

Kelly proposed that different personal constructs (*construals*) are the key to personality differences; that is, different construals lead people to engage in different behaviours. Taking a long break from work for a leisurely lunch might seem lazy to you. To your friend, the break might seem an ideal opportunity to catch up with friends and she or he may wonder why you always choose to eat at your desk. Social–cognitive theory explains different responses to situations with the idea that people experience and interpret the world in different ways.

# Personal Goals and Expectancies

Social–cognitive theories also recognize that a person's unique perspective on situations is reflected in his or her personal goals, which are often conscious. In fact, people can usually tell you their goals, whether they are to find a date for this weekend, get a good grade in psychology, establish a fulfilling career, or just get this darn bag of chips open. These goals often reflect the tasks that are appropriate to the person's situation and, in a larger sense, fit the person's role and stage of life (Cantor, 1990; Klinger, 1977; Little, 1983; Vallacher & Wegner, 1985). For instance, common goals for adolescents include being popular, achieving greater independence from parents and family, and getting into a good university. Common goals for adults include developing a meaningful career, finding a mate, securing financial stability, and starting a family.

People translate goals into behaviour in part through **outcome expectancies,** *a person's assumptions about the likely consequences of a future behaviour.* Just as a laboratory rat learns that pressing a bar releases a food pellet, we learn that "if I am friendly toward people, they will be friendly in return," and "if I ask people to pull my finger, they will withdraw from me." So we learn to perform behaviours that we expect will have the outcome of moving us closer to our goals. Outcome expectancies are learned through direct experience, both bitter and sweet, and through merely observing other people's actions and their consequences.

Outcome expectancies combine with a person's goals to produce the person's characteristic style of behaviour. An individual with the goal of making friends and the expectancy that being kind will produce warmth in return is likely to behave very differently from an individual whose goal is to achieve fame at any cost and who believes that shameless self-promotion is the route to fame. We do not all want the same things from life, clearly, and our personalities largely reflect the goals we pursue and the expectancies we have about the best ways to pursue them.

People differ in their generalized expectancy for achieving goals. Some people seem to feel that they are fully in control of what happens to them in life, whereas others feel that the world doles out rewards and punishments to them irrespective of their actions. Julian Rotter (1966) developed a questionnaire (see **TABLE 12.5**) to measure *a person's tendency to perceive the control of rewards as internal to the self or external in the environment,* a disposition he called **locus of control.** People whose answers suggest that they believe they control their own destiny are said to have an *internal* locus of control, whereas those who believe that outcomes are random, determined by luck, or controlled by other people are described as having an *external* locus of control. These beliefs translate into individual differences in emotion and behaviour. For example, people with an internal locus of control tend to be less anxious, achieve more, and cope better with stress than do people with an external orientation (Lefcourt, 1982). To get a sense of your standing on this trait dimension, choose one of the options for each of the sample items from the locus-of-control scale in Table 12.5.

> **What is the advantage of an internal locus of control?**

Some days you feel like a puppet on a string. If you have an external locus of control, you may feel that way most days.

**outcome expectancies**
A person's assumptions about the likely consequences of a future behaviour.

**locus of control**
A person's tendency to perceive the control of rewards as internal to the self or external in the environment.

| Table 12.5 |
| --- |

### Rotter's Locus-of-Control Scale

For each pair of items, choose the option that most closely reflects your personal belief. Then check the answer key below to see if you have more of an internal or external locus of control.

1. a. Many of the unhappy things in people's lives are partly due to bad luck.
   b. People's misfortunes result from the mistakes they make.

2. a. I have often found that what is going to happen will happen.
   b. Trusting to fate has never turned out as well for me as making a decision to take a definite course of action.

3. a. Becoming a success is a matter of hard work; luck has little or nothing to do with it.
   b. Getting a good job depends mainly on being in the right place at the right time.

4. a. When I make plans, I am almost certain that I can make them work.
   b. It is not always wise to plan too far ahead because many things turn out to be a matter of good or bad fortune anyhow.

*Source:* Rotter, 1966.

**Answers:** A more internal locus of control would be reflected in choosing options 1b, 2b, 3a, and 4a.

▶ The social–cognitive approach focuses on personality as arising from individuals' behaviour in situations. Situations mean different things to different people, as suggested by Kelly's personal construct theory.

▶ According to social–cognitive personality theorists, the same person may behave differently in different situations but should behave consistently in similar situations.

▶ People translate their goals into behaviour through outcome expectancies, their assumptions about the likely consequences of future behaviours.

# The Self: Personality in the Mirror

Imagine that you wake up tomorrow morning, drag yourself into the bathroom, look into the mirror, and do not recognize the face looking back at you. This was the plight of a patient studied by neurologist Todd Feinberg (2001). The woman, married for 30 years and the mother of two grown children, one day began to respond to her mirror image as if it were a different person. She talked to and challenged the person in the mirror. When there was no response, she tried to attack it as if it were an intruder. Her husband, shaken by this bizarre behaviour, brought her to the neurologist, who was gradually able to convince her that the image in the mirror was in fact herself.

Most of us are pretty familiar with the face that looks back at us from every mirror. We develop the ability to recognize ourselves in mirrors by 18 months of age (as discussed in the Consciousness chapter), and we share this skill with chimpanzees

What do these self-portraits of Frida Kahlo, Vincent van Gogh, Pablo Picasso, Salvador Dalí, Wanda Wulz, and Jean-Michel Basquiat reveal about each artist's self-concept?

KAHLO • © ALBRIGHT-KNOX ART GALLERY/CORBIS

VAN GOGH • © DEAGOSTINI/SUPERSTOCK

PICASSO • © PAINTING/ALAMY

DALI • BY PERMISSION OF THE SALVADOR DALI ESTATE. © PHILIPPE HALSMAN/MAGNUM

WULZ • ALINARI/ART RESOURCE, NY

BASQUIAT • BANQUE D'IMAGES, ADAGP/ART RESOURCE, NY

and other apes that have been raised in the presence of mirrors. Self-recognition in mirrors signals our amazing capacity for reflexive thinking, for directing attention to our own thoughts, feelings, and actions—an ability that enables us to construct ideas about our own personality. Unlike a cow, which will never know that it has a poor sense of humour, or a cat, which will never know that it is awfully friendly, humans have rich and detailed self-knowledge.

Admittedly, none of us know all there is to know about our own personality. In fact, sometimes others may know us better than we know ourselves (Vazire & Mehl, 2008). But we do have enough self-knowledge to respond reliably to personality inventories and report on our traits and behaviours. These observations draw on what we think about ourselves (our *self-concept*) and on how we feel about ourselves (our *self-esteem*). Self-concept and self-esteem are critically important facets of personality, not just because they reveal how people see their own personalities, but because they also guide how people think others will see them.

**self-concept**
A person's explicit knowledge of his or her own behaviours, traits, and other personal characteristics.

## Self-Concept

In his renowned psychology textbook, William James (1890) included a theory of self in which he pointed to the self's two facets, the *I* and the *Me*. The *I* is the self that thinks, experiences, and acts in the world; it is the self as a *knower*. The *Me* is the self that is an object in the world; it is the self that is *known*. The *I* is much like consciousness, then, a perspective on all of experience (see the Consciousness chapter), but the *Me* is less mysterious: It is just a concept of a person.

> **Explain the difference between *I* and *Me*.**

If asked to describe your *Me*, you might mention your physical characteristics (male or female, tall or short, dark-skinned or light), your activities (listening to hip-hop, alternative rock, jazz, or classical music), your personality traits (extraverted or introverted, agreeable or independent), or your social roles (student, son or daughter, member of a hiking club, krumper). These features make up the **self-concept**, *a person's explicit knowledge of his or her own behaviours, traits, and other personal characteristics.* A person's self-concept is an organized body of knowledge that develops from social experiences and has a profound effect on a person's behaviour throughout life.

### Self-Concept Organization

Almost everyone has a place for memorabilia, a drawer or box somewhere that holds all those sentimental keepsakes—photographs, yearbooks, cards and letters, maybe that scrap of the old security blanket—all memories of "life as *Me*." Perhaps you have wanted to organize these things sometime but have never gotten around to it. Fortunately, the knowledge of ourselves that we store in our *autobiographical memory* seems to be organized naturally in two ways: as narratives about episodes in our lives and in terms of traits (as would be suggested by the distinction between episodic and semantic memory discussed in the Memory chapter).

The aspect of the self-concept that is a *self-narrative* (a story that we tell about ourselves) can be brief or very lengthy. Your life story could start with your birth and upbringing, describe a series of defining moments, and end where you are today. You could select specific events and experiences, goals and life tasks, and memories of places and

> **What is your life story as you see it— your self-narrative?**

A key aspect of our personality involves our self-narrative, or the story we tell about ourselves. In the award-winning movie *Forrest Gump*, the title character shared his self-narrative with the other characters and the movie audience through a voice-over that runs through out the film. What would you include in the self-narrative of your life?

PARAMOUNT/THE KOBAL COLLECTION/ART RESOURCE

Does the doctor think she is an ordinary person just doing her job or does she think she is a saviour? Think about your own self-narrative (what you have done) and self-concept (how you view yourself). Are there areas that do not match up? Are there things that you have done, good or bad, that are not part of your self-concept? How might you explain that?

people that have influenced you. Self-narrative organizes the highlights (and low blows) of your life into a story in which you are the leading character and binds them together into your self-concept (McAdams, 1993; McLean, 2008). Psychodynamic and humanistic–existential psychologists suggest that people's self-narratives reflect their fantasies and thoughts about core motives and approaches to existence.

Self-concept is also organized in a more abstract way, in terms of personality traits. Just as you can judge an object on its attributes (Is this apple green?), you are able to judge yourself on any number of traits—whether you are considerate or smart or lazy or active or, for that matter, green—and do so quite reliably, making the same rating on multiple occasions. Hazel Markus (1977) observed that each person finds certain unique personality traits particularly important for conceptualizing the self. One person might define herself as independent, for example, whereas another might not care much about her level of independence but instead emphasize her sense of style. Markus called the traits people use to define themselves *self-schemas,* emphasizing that they draw information about the self into a coherent scheme. Markus asked people to indicate whether they had a trait by pressing response buttons labelled *me* or *not me*. She found that participants' judgment reaction times were faster for self-schemas than for other traits. It is as though some facets of the self-concept have almost a knee-jerk quality—letting us tell quickly who we are and who we are not.

Medial prefrontal cortex

▶ Figure 12.5 **Self-Concept in the Brain** fMRI scans reveal that the medial prefrontal cortex (MPFC) is activated (shown here in red and yellow) when people make judgments of whether they possess certain personality traits compared to judging whether the traits apply to someone else.

(From Kelley et al., 2002.)

Research also shows that the traits people use to judge the self tend to stick in memory. When people make judgments of themselves on traits, they later recall the traits better than when they judge other people on the same traits (Rogers, Kuiper, & Kirker, 1977). For example, answering a question such as "Are you generous?"—no matter what your answer—is likely to enhance your memory for the trait *generous*. In studies of this effect of *self-relevance* on memory, researchers using brain imaging technologies have found that the simple activity of making judgments about the trait self-concept is accompanied by activation of the medial prefrontal cortex (MPFC), a brain area involved in understanding people (Mitchell, Heatherton, & Macrae, 2002). This activation is stronger, however, when people are judging their own standing on traits (see **FIGURE 12.5**) than when they are judging the standing of someone else (Kelley et al., 2002). Such stronger activation, then, is linked with better memory for the traits being judged (Macrae et al., 2004). Studies have not been entirely conclusive about which brain areas are most involved in the processing of self-information (Morin, 2002), but they do show that memory for traits is strengthened when the MPFC is activated during self-judgments.

How do our behaviour self-narratives and trait self-concepts compare? These two methods of self-conceptualization do not always match up. You may think of yourself

> **Why do traits not always reflect knowledge of behaviour?**

as an honest person, for example, but also recall that time you nabbed a handful of change from your parents' dresser and conveniently forgot to replace it. The traits we use to describe ourselves are generalizations, and not every episode in our life stories may fit. In fact, research suggests that the stores of knowledge about our behaviours and traits are not very

well integrated (Kihlstrom, Beer, & Klein, 2002). In people who develop amnesia, for example, memory for behaviours can be lost even though the trait self-concept remains stable (Klein, 2004). People can have a pretty strong sense of who they are even though they may not remember a single example of when they acted that way.

## Causes and Effects of Self-Concept

How do self-concepts arise, and how do they affect us? In some sense, you learn something about yourself every day. Although we can gain self-knowledge in private moments of insight, we more often arrive at our self-concepts through interacting with others. Young children in particular receive plenty of feedback from their parents, teachers, siblings, and friends about their characteristics, and this helps them to form an idea of who they are. Even adults would find it difficult to hold a view of the self as "kind" or "smart" if no one else ever shared this impression. The sense of self, then, is largely developed and maintained in relationships with others.

Over the course of a lifetime, however, we become less and less impressed with what others have to say about us. Social theorist George Herbert Mead (1934) observed that all the things people have said about us accumulate after a while into what we see as a kind of consensus held by the "generalized other." We typically adopt this general view of ourselves and hold on to it stubbornly. As a result, the person who says you are a jerk may upset you momentarily, but you bounce back, secure in the knowledge that you actually are not a jerk. And just as we might argue vehemently with someone who tried to tell us a refrigerator is a pair of underpants, we are likely to defend our self-concept against anyone whose view of us departs from our own.

Because it is so stable, a major effect of the self-concept is to promote consistency in behaviour across situations (Lecky, 1945). As existential theorists emphasize, people derive a comforting sense of familiarity and stability from knowing who they are. We

> **How does self-concept influence behaviour?**

tend to engage in what William Swann (1983, 2012) called **self-verification,** *the tendency to seek evidence to confirm the self-concept,* and we find it disconcerting if someone sees us quite differently from the way we see ourselves. In one study, Swann

(1983) gave people who considered themselves submissive feedback that they seemed very dominant and forceful. Rather than accepting this discrepant information, they went out of their way to act in an extremely submissive manner. Our tendency to project into the world our concept of the self contributes to personality coherence. This talent for self-reflection enables the personality to become self-sustaining.

*"I don't want to be defined by who I am."*

**self-verification**
The tendency to seek evidence to confirm the self-concept.

**self-esteem**
The extent to which an individual likes, values, and accepts the self.

# Self-Esteem

When you think about yourself, do you feel good and worthy? Do you like yourself, or do you feel bad and have negative, self-critical thoughts? **Self-esteem** is *the extent to which an individual likes, values, and accepts the self.* Thousands of studies have examined differences between people with high self-esteem (who generally like themselves) and those with relatively low self-esteem (who are less keen on, and may actively dislike, themselves). Researchers who study self-esteem typically ask participants to fill out a self-esteem questionnaire, such as one shown in **TABLE 12.6** (Rosenberg, 1965). This widely used measure of self-esteem asks people to evaluate themselves in terms of each statement. People who strongly agree with the positive statements about themselves and strongly disagree with the negative statements are considered to have high self-esteem.

Although some personality psychologists have argued that self-esteem determines virtually everything about a person's life (from the tendency to engage in criminal activity and violence to professional success), evidence has accumulated that the benefits of high self-esteem are less striking and all-encompassing but still significant. In general, compared with people with low self-esteem, those with high self-esteem tend to live happier and healthier lives, cope better with stress, and be more likely to persist at difficult tasks. In contrast, individuals with low self-esteem are more likely, for example, to perceive rejection in ambiguous feedback from others and develop eating disorders than those with high self-esteem (Baumeister et al., 2003). How does this aspect of personality develop, and why does everyone—whether high or low in self-esteem—seem to *want* high self-esteem?

## Sources of Self-Esteem

Some psychologists contend that high self-esteem arises primarily from being accepted and valued by significant others (Brown, 1993). Other psychologists focus on the influence of specific self-evaluations: judgments about one's value or competence in specific domains such as appearance, athletics, or scholastics.

### Table 12.6

**Rosenberg Self-Esteem Scale**

Consider each statement and circle SA for strongly agree, A for agree, D for disagree, and SD for strongly disagree.

| | | | | |
|---|---|---|---|---|
| 1. On the whole, I am satisfied with myself. | SA | A | D | SD |
| 2. At times, I think I am no good at all. | SA | A | D | SD |
| 3. I feel that I have a number of good qualities. | SA | A | D | SD |
| 4. I am able to do things as well as most other people. | SA | A | D | SD |
| 5. I feel I do not have much to be proud of. | SA | A | D | SD |
| 6. I certainly feel useless at times. | SA | A | D | SD |
| 7. I feel that I am a person of worth, at least on an equal plane with others. | SA | A | D | SD |
| 8. I wish I could have more respect for myself. | SA | A | D | SD |
| 9. All in all, I am inclined to feel that I am a failure. | SA | A | D | SD |
| 10. I take a positive attitude toward myself. | SA | A | D | SD |

*Source:* Rosenberg, 1965.

**Scoring:** For items 1, 3, 4, 7, and 10, SA = 3, A = 2, D = 1, SD = 0; for items 2, 5, 6, 8, and 9, the scoring is reversed, with SA = 0, A = 1, D = 2, SD = 3. The higher the total score, the higher one's self-esteem.

An important factor is whom people choose for comparison. For example, James (1890) noted that an accomplished athlete who is the second best in the world should feel pretty proud, but this athlete might not if the standard of comparison involves

> **How do comparisons with others affect self-esteem?**

being best in the world. In fact, athletes in the 1992 Olympics who had won silver medals looked less happy during the medal ceremony than those who had won bronze medals (Medvec, Madey, & Gilovich, 1995). If the actual self is seen as falling short of the ideal self (the person that they would like to be) people tend to feel sad or dejected; when they become aware that the actual self is inconsistent with the self they have a duty to be, they are likely to feel anxious or agitated (Higgins, 1987).

Unconscious perspectives we take on feedback can also affect our sense of self-worth. In one study, researchers looked at the effect of an authority figure's disapproval on self-esteem. They examined the self-esteem of young, Catholic, female undergraduates who had read an article from *Cosmopolitan*, which described a woman's sexual dream (in PG-13 language), and who had either seen a photograph of a disapproving-looking pope or a photograph of an unfamiliar disapproving person. The photographs were shown subliminally, that is, in such brief flashes that the women could not consciously recognize whom they had seen. In self-ratings made afterward, the women in the disapproving-pope group showed a marked reduction in self-esteem compared with the other women: They rated themselves as less competent, more anxious, and less moral. In the words of the researchers, self-esteem can be influenced when an important authority figure is "watching you from the back of your mind" (Baldwin, Carrell, & Lopez, 1989, p. 435).

Self-esteem is also affected by what kinds of domains we consider most important in our self-concept. One person's self-worth might be entirely contingent on, for example, how well she does in school, whereas another's self-worth might be based on her physical attractiveness (Crocker & Wolfe, 2001; Pelham, 1985). The first person's self-esteem might receive a big boost when she gets an A on an exam, but much less of a boost when she is complimented on her new hairstyle, and this effect might be exactly reversed in the second person.

This is silver medallist Svetlana Tsarukaeva of Russia, gold medallist Maiya Maneza of Kazakhstan, and bronze medallist Christine Girard of Canada following the 63 kg group A weightlifting event at the 2012 Summer Olympics in London, UK. Notice that the silver medallist does not look as happy as the gold and bronze winners.

## The Desire for Self-Esteem

What is so great about self-esteem? Why do people want to see themselves in a positive light and avoid seeing themselves negatively? The key theories on the benefits of self-esteem focus on status, belonging, and security.

Does self-esteem feel good because it reflects our degree of social dominance or status? People with high self-esteem seem to carry themselves in a way that is similar to high-status animals of other social species. Dominant male gorillas, for example, appear confident and comfortable and not anxious or withdrawn. Perhaps high

> **How might self-esteem have played a role in evolution?**

self-esteem in humans reflects high social status or suggests that the person is worthy of respect, and this perception triggers natural affective responses (Barkow, 1980; Maslow, 1937).

Could the desire for self-esteem come from a basic need to belong or be related to others? Evolutionary theory holds that early humans who managed to survive to pass on their genes were those able to maintain good relations with others rather than being cast out to fend for themselves. Clearly, belonging to groups is

**self-serving bias**
People's tendency to take credit for their successes but downplay responsibility for their failures.

*Survivor, The Bachelor, Big Brother:* Why are shows in which everyone is fighting to remain a part of the group so popular today? Is it because they play on evolutionary desire to belong? (Or do people just like to see other people get kicked out of the club?)

adaptive, as is knowing whether you are accepted. Thus, self-esteem could be a kind of "sociometer," an inner gauge of how much a person feels included by others at any given moment (Leary & Baumeister, 2000). According to evolutionary theory, then, we seek higher self-esteem because we have evolved to seek out belongingness in our families, work groups, and culture, and higher self-esteem indicates that we are being accepted.

The idea that self-esteem is a matter of security is consistent with the existential and psychodynamic approaches to personality. The studies of mortality salience discussed in the Emotion and Motivation chapter suggest that the source of distress underlying negative self-esteem is ultimately the fear of death (Solomon, Greenberg, & Pyszczynski, 1991). In this view, humans find it anxiety provoking, in fact terrifying, to contemplate their own mortality, and so they try to defend against this awareness by immersing themselves in activities (such as earning money or dressing up to appear attractive) that their culture defines as meaningful and valuable. The desire for self-esteem may stem from a need to find value in ourselves as a way of escaping the anxiety associated with recognizing our mortality. The higher our self-esteem, the less anxious we feel with the knowledge that someday we will no longer exist.

Whatever the reason that low self-esteem feels so bad and high self-esteem feels so good, people are generally motivated to see themselves positively. In fact, we often process information in a biased manner in order to feel good about the self. Research on the **self-serving bias** shows that *people tend to take credit for their successes but downplay responsibility for their failures.* You may have noticed this tendency in yourself, particularly in terms of the attributions you make about exams when you get a good grade (I studied really intensely, and I am good at that subject) or a bad grade (The test was ridiculously tricky and the professor is unfair).

On the whole, most people satisfy the desire for high self-esteem and maintain a reasonably positive view of self by engaging in the self-serving bias (Miller & Ross, 1975; Shepperd, Malone, & Sweeny, 2008). In fact, if people are asked to rate themselves across a range of characteristics, they tend to see themselves as better than the average person in most domains (Alicke et al., 1995). For example, 90 percent of drivers describe their driving skills as better than average, and 86 percent of workers rate their performance on the job as above average. Even

*"I suffer from accurate self-esteem."*

among university professors, 94 percent feel they are above average in teaching ability compared with other professors (Cross, 1977). These kinds of judgments simply cannot be accurate, statistically speaking, because the average of a group of people has to be the average, not better than average! This particular error may be adaptive,

> **What is the relationship between self-serving bias and depression?**

however. People who do not engage in this self-serving bias to boost their self-esteem tend to be more at risk for depression, anxiety, and related health problems (Taylor & Brown, 1988).

On the other hand, a few people take positive self-esteem to the extreme. Unfortunately, seeing yourself as way, way better than average (a trait called **narcissism,** *a grandiose view of the self combined with a tendency to seek admiration from and exploit others*) brings some costs. In fact, at its extreme, narcissism is considered a personality disorder (see the Psychological Disorders chapter). Research has documented disadvantages of an overinflated view of self, most of which arise from the need to defend that grandiose view at all costs. For example, when highly narcissistic adolescents were given reason to be ashamed of their performance on a task, their aggressiveness increased in the form of willingness to deliver loud blasts of noise to punish their opponent in a laboratory game (Thomaes et al., 2008).

## Implicit Egotism

What is your favourite letter of the alphabet? About 30 percent of people answer by picking what just happens to be the first letter of their first name. Could this choice indicate that some people think so highly of themselves that they base judgments of seemingly unrelated topics on how much it reminds them of themselves?

This *name-letter effect* was discovered some years ago (Nuttin, 1985), but more recently researchers have gone on to discover how broad the egotistic bias in preferences can be. Brett Pelham and his colleagues have found subtle yet systematic biases toward this effect when people choose their home cities, streets, and even occupations

> **Do people choose homes and occupations based in part on their own names?**

(Pelham, Mirenberg, & Jones, 2002). When the researchers examined the rolls of people moving into several southern American states, for example, they found people named George were more likely than those with other names to move to Georgia. The same was true for Florences (Florida), Kenneths (Kentucky), and

Louises (Louisiana). You can guess where the Virginias tended to relocate. People whose last name is Street seem biased toward addresses ending in *street,* whereas Lanes like lanes. The name effect seems to work for occupations as well: Slightly more people named Dennis and Denise chose dentistry and Lauras and Lawrences chose law compared with other occupations. Although the biases are small, they are consistent across many tests of the hypothesis.

These biases have been called expressions of *implicit egotism* because people are not typically aware that they are influenced by the wonderful sound of their own names (Pelham, Carvallo, & Jones, 2005). When Regina moves to Regina, she is not likely to volunteer that she did so because it matched her name. Yet people who show this egotistic bias in one way also tend to show it in others: People who strongly prefer their own name letter also are likely to pick their birth date as their favourite number (Koole, Dijksterhuis, & van Knippenberg, 2001). And people who like their name letter were also found to evaluate themselves positively on self-ratings of personality traits. This was especially true when the self-ratings were made in response to instructions to work *quickly.* The people who preferred their name letter made snap judgments of themselves that leaned in a positive direction, suggesting that their special self-appreciation was an automatic response.

**narcissism**
A trait that reflects a grandiose view of the self combined with a tendency to seek admiration from and exploit others.

©MAXSTOCK/ALAMY IMAGES

If you were trying to light up a room with a letter, would your first choice also be your initial?

At some level, of course, a bit of egotism is probably good for us. It is sad to meet someone who hates her own name or whose snap judgment of self is "I am worthless." Yet in another sense, implicit egotism is a curiously subtle error: a tendency to make biased judgments of what we will do and where we will go in life just because we happen to have a certain name. Yes, the bias is only a small one. But your authors wonder: Could we have found better people to work with had we not fallen prey to this bias in our choice of colleagues? The first three authors (Dan, Dan, and Dan) thought they were breaking this cycle by adding a non-Dan author, only to realize that Matt was being added shortly after he decided to move his family (including children Matthew and Maya) to Massachusetts.

The self is the part of personality that the person knows and can report about. Some of the personality measures we have seen in this chapter (such as personality inventories based on self-reports) are really no different from measures of self-concept. Both depend on the person's perceptions and memories of the self's behaviour and traits. But personality runs deeper than this as well. The unconscious forces identified in psychodynamic approaches provide themes for behaviour and sources of mental disorder that are not accessible for self-report. The humanistic and existential approaches remind us of the profound concerns we humans face and the difficulties we may have in understanding all the forces that shape our self-views. Finally, in emphasizing how personality shapes our perceptions of social life, the social–cognitive approach brings the self back to centre stage. The self, after all, is the hub of each person's social world.

## IN SUMMARY

▶ The self-concept is a person's knowledge of self, including both specific self-narratives and more abstract personality traits or self-schemas.

▶ People's self-concept develops through social feedback, and people often act to try to confirm these views through a process of self-verification.

▶ Self-esteem is a person's evaluation of self; it is derived from being accepted by others, as well as by how we evaluate ourselves by comparison to others. Theories proposed to explain why we seek positive self-esteem suggest that we do so to achieve perceptions of status, or belonging, or of being symbolically protected against mortality.

▶ People strive for positive self-views through self-serving biases and implicit egotism.

# OTHER VOICES

## Does the Study of Personality Lack ... Personality?

**David Brooks** is a columnist for the *New York Times*, a commentator on *CNN*, and the author of several popular books on behavioural science.

PHOTO: ©JOSH HANER/ COURTESY OF THE NEW YORK TIMES

As described in this chapter, some of the field's older ideas about personality (such as those in the sections on psychodynamic and humanistic–existential approaches) are very intriguing but lacking in evidence, and so are not widely studied these days. Instead, personality researchers today are aiming to understand what aspects of our personalities are passed through which genes, and how the Big Five might map onto brain structure and functioning. The old approaches lacked evidence, but is something lacking in the newer approaches to studying personality? David Brooks seems to think so.

... In the twentieth century, psychoanalysts were a big deal. There were a number of best-selling authors spinning theories about the psyche, which had a large impact on how people saw the world and themselves. This includes not only Freud and Jung, but also people like Erick Erikson, Erich Fromm, Carl Rogers, Viktor Frankl and Philip Rieff. Today we are more into cognition and the brain. Over the years, attention has shifted from the soul to the personality to decision-making. Preoccupations have migrated from salvation to psychic security to success.

When it comes to treating mental illness, I guess I am glad we have made this shift. I put more faith in medications and cognitive therapies than in Freudian or Jungian analysis. But something has been lost as well as gained. We are less adept at talking about personalities and neuroses than we were when psychoanalysts held center stage.

For example, in the middle of the twentieth century, a woman named Karen Horney (pronounced HOR-nigh) crafted a series of influential theories about personality. Like many authors of these intellectually ambitious theories, she was raised in Europe and migrated to the United States before World War II. More than most of her male counterparts, Horney felt that people were driven by anxiety and the desire for security. People who have been seriously damaged, she argued, tend to react in one of three ways. ...

Some people respond to their wounds by moving against others. These domineering types seek to establish security by conquering and outperforming other people. They deny their own weaknesses. They are rarely plagued by self-doubt. They fear dependence and helplessness. They use their children and spouses as tools to win prestige for themselves. ...

Other people respond to anxiety by moving toward others. These dependent types try to win people's affections by being compliant. They avoid conflict. They become absorbed by their relationships, surrendering their individual opinions. They regard everyone else as essentially good, even people who have been cruel. ...

Other people move away from others. These detached types try to isolate themselves and adopt an onlooker's attitude toward life. As Terry D. Cooper summarizes the category in his book, *Sin, Pride and Self-Acceptance,* "To guarantee peace, it is necessary to leave the battleground of interpersonal relationships, where there is constant threat of being captured." ...

The domineering person believes that, if he wins life's battles, nothing can hurt him. The dependent person believes that, if he shuns private gain and conforms to the wishes of others, then the world will treat him nicely. The detached person believes that, if he asks nothing of the world, the world will ask nothing of him. These are ideal types, obviously, conceptual categories. They join a profusion of personality types that were churned out by various writers in the mid-twentieth century: the inner directed, the outer directed, the Organization Man, the anal retentive, the narcissist, the outsider.

The books that explained these theories were good bad books. The good bad book (I am deriving the category from a phrase from Orwell) makes sweeping claims, and lumps people into big groups. Sometimes these claims are not really defensible intellectually. But they are thought-provoking and useful. They provide categories and handles the rest of us can use to understand the people around us, seeing where the category fits and thinking more precisely about where it does not.

We are probably poorer now that people like Horney have sunk to near oblivion—less adept at analyzing personality. We probably have less practice analyzing personalities. ...

Is David Brooks right? The study of personality has been away from big picture explanations like those of Freud, Maslow, and Frankl, which attempt to explain why we behave the way we do with one overarching theory, and toward efforts to break down personality into smaller constructs and understand how nature and nurture produce these core traits. But have we actually gotten worse at understanding personality? On balance, should interesting theories that make intriguing assumptions about people's personalities, but have no data to support their accuracy, be retained simply because they tell a more interesting story? If you are reading this book, you represent the future of psychology. How can we better understand and measure human personality? What are the most important future steps?

# Chapter Review

## KEY CONCEPT QUIZ

1. From a psychological perspective, personality refers to
   a. a person's characteristic style of behaving, thinking, and feeling.
   b. physiological predispositions that manifest themselves psychologically.
   c. past events that have shaped a person's current behaviour.
   d. choices people make in response to cultural norms.

2. Projective techniques to assess personality involve
   a. personal inventories.
   b. self-reporting.
   c. responses to ambiguous stimuli.
   d. actuarial methodology.

3. A relatively stable disposition to behave in a particular and consistent way is a
   a. motive.
   b. goal.
   c. trait.
   d. reflex.

4. Which of the following is NOT one of the Big Five personality factors?
   a. conscientiousness
   b. agreeableness
   c. neuroticism
   d. orderliness

5. Compelling evidence for the importance of biological factors in personality is best seen in studies of
   a. parenting styles.
   b. identical twins reared apart.
   c. brain damage.
   d. factor analysis.

6. If you were hungry, which of Freud's systems of the mind would impel you to start grabbing food off people's plates upon entering a restaurant?
   a. the id
   b. the reality principle
   c. the ego
   d. the pleasure principle

7. After performing poorly on an exam, you drop a class, saying that you and the professor are just a poor match. According to Freud, what defence mechanism are you employing?
   a. regression
   b. rationalization
   c. projection
   d. reaction formation

8. According to Freud, a person who is preoccupied with his or her possessions, money, issues of submission and rebellion, and concerns about cleanliness versus messiness is fixated at which psychosexual stage?
   a. the oral stage
   b. the anal stage
   c. the latency stage
   d. the genital stage

9. Humanists see personality as directed toward the goal of
   a. existentialism.
   b. self-actualization.
   c. healthy adult sexuality.
   d. sublimation.

10. According to the existential perspective, the difficulties we face in finding meaning in life and in accepting the responsibility for making free choices provoke a type of anxiety called
    a. angst.
    b. flow.
    c. the self-actualizing tendency.
    d. mortality salience.

11. Which of the following is NOT an emphasis of the social–cognitive approach?
    a. how personality and situation interact to cause behaviour
    b. how personality contributes to the way people construct situations in their own minds
    c. how people's goals and expectancies influence their responses to situations
    d. how people confront realities rather than embrace comforting illusions

12. According to social–cognitive theorists, _____ are the dimensions people use in making sense of their experiences.
    a. personal constructs
    b. outcome expectancies
    c. loci of control
    d. personal goals

13. What we think about ourselves is referred to as our _____ and how we feel about ourselves is referred to as our _____.
    a. self-narrative; self-verification
    b. self-concept; self-esteem
    c. self-concept; self-verification
    d. self-esteem; self-concept

14. What is the focus of the key theories on the benefits of self-esteem?
    a. status
    b. belonging
    c. security
    d. all of the above

15. When people take credit for their successes but downplay responsibility for their failures, they are exhibiting
    a. narcissism.
    b. implicit egoism.
    c. the self-serving bias.
    d. the name-letter effect.

# KEY TERMS

anal stage (p. 487)
Big Five (p. 479)
defence mechanisms (p. 486)
dynamic unconscious (p. 485)
ego (p. 485)
existential approach (p. 489)
fixation (p. 487)
genital stage (p. 488)
id (p. 485)

latency stage (p. 487)
locus of control (p. 493)
Minnesota Multiphasic Personality
    Inventory (MMPI) (p. 474)
narcissism (p. 501)
Oedipus conflict (p. 487)
oral stage (p. 487)
outcome expectancies (p. 493)
person–situation controversy
    (p. 491)

personal constructs (p. 492)
personality (p. 472)
phallic stage (p. 487)
projective tests (p. 475)
psychodynamic approach (p. 484)
psychosexual stages (p. 487)
Rorschach Inkblot Test (p. 475)
self-actualizing tendency (p. 488)
self-concept (p. 495)

self-esteem (p. 498)
self-report (p. 473)
self-serving bias (p. 500)
self-verification (p. 497)
social–cognitive approach (p. 490)
superego (p. 485)
Thematic Apperception Test (TAT)
    (p. 475)
trait (p. 476)

# CHANGING MINDS

1. A prominent political candidate makes a Freudian slip on live television, calling his mother "petty"; he corrects himself quickly and says
he meant to say "pretty." The next day the video has gone viral, and
the morning talk shows discuss the possibility that the candidate has
an unresolved Oedipal conflict; if so, he is stuck in the phallic stage
and is likely a relatively unstable person preoccupied with issues of
seduction, power, and authority (which may be why he is a politician).
Your roommate knows you are taking a psychology class and asks for
your opinion: "Can we really tell that a person is sexually repressed,
and maybe in love with his own mother, just because he stumbled over
a single word?" How would you reply? How widely are Freud's ideas
about personality accepted by modern psychologists?

2. While reading a magazine, you come across an article on the
nature–nurture controversy in personality. The magazine describes
several adoption studies in which adopted children (who share no
genes with each other, but grow up in the same household) are no
more like each other than complete strangers. This suggests that
family environment—and the influence of parental behaviour—on
personality is very weak. You show the article to a friend, who has
trouble believing the results: "I always thought parents who don't show
affection produce kids who have trouble forming lasting relationships."

How would you explain to your friend the relationship between nature,
nurture, and personality?

3. One of your friends has found an online site that offers personality
testing. He takes the test and reports that the results prove he is an
"intuitive" rather than a "sensing" personality, who likes to look at
the big picture rather than focusing on tangible here-and-now experiences. "This explains a lot," he says, "like why I have trouble remembering details like other people's birthdays, and why it's hard for me
to finish projects before the deadline." Aside from warning your friend
about the dangers of self-diagnosis via Internet quizzes, what would
you tell him about the relationship between personality types and
behaviour? How well do scores on personality tests predict a person's
actual behaviour?

4. One of your friends tells you that her boyfriend cheated on her, so she
will never date him or anyone who has ever been unfaithful because
"once a cheat, always a cheat." She goes on to explain that personality
and character are stable over time, so people will always make the
same decisions and repeat the same mistakes over time. What do we
know about the interaction between personality and situations that
might confirm or deny her statements?

# ANSWERS TO KEY CONCEPT QUIZ

1. a; 2. c; 3. c; 4. d; 5. b; 6. a; 7. b; 8. b; 9. b; 10. a; 11. d; 12. a; 13. b;
14. d; 15. c.

# 13

# Social Psychology

▲ Social Behaviour:
Interacting with People
Survival: The Struggle for Resources
HOT SCIENCE Mouse Over
Reproduction: The Quest for Immortality
THE REAL WORLD Making the Move
Breaking Up: When the Costs Outweigh
the Benefits

▲ Social Influence: Controlling People
The Hedonic Motive:
Pleasure Is Better Than Pain
CULTURE & COMMUNITY Free Parking
The Approval Motive: Acceptance
Is Better Than Rejection
OTHER VOICES 91% of All Students Read
This Box and Love It
The Accuracy Motive:
Right Is Better Than Wrong

▲ Social Cognition:
Understanding People
HOT SCIENCE The Wedding Planner
Stereotyping: Drawing Inferences
from Categories
Attribution: Drawing Inferences
from Actions

TERRY, ROBERT, AND JOHN HAVE SOMETHING IN COMMON: They have all been tortured. Terry was an British hostage negotiator working in Lebanon when he was kidnapped by Hezbollah guerrillas; Robert was a semi-pro boxer living in Louisiana when he was arrested and sent to prison; and John was an American naval aviator when he was shot down and captured by the North Vietnamese during the Vietnam War. All three men experienced a variety of tortures, and all agree about which was the worst.

Terry: I soon realized that if I was to survive it was essential to maintain a strong inner life … because the threat of dissolving into madness was ever present.

Robert: It was a nightmare. I saw men so desperate that they ripped prison doors apart, starved and mutilated themselves … it takes every scrap of humanity to stay focused and sane.

John: It's an awful thing. It crushes your spirit and weakens your resistance more effectively than any other form of mistreatment.

The cruel technique that these three men are describing has nothing to do with electric shock or waterboarding. It does not require wax, rope, or razor blades. It is a remarkably simple technique that has been used for thousands of years to break the body and destroy the mind. It is called solitary confinement. Terry Waite spent 4 years in a cell by himself, Robert King spent 29, and John McCain spent 2.

When we think of torture, we usually think of techniques designed to cause pain by depriving people of something they desperately need, such as oxygen, water, food, or sleep. But the need for social interaction is every bit as vital. Studies of prisoners show that extensive periods of isolation can induce symptoms of psychosis (Grassian, 2006), and even in smaller doses, social isolation takes a toll. Ordinary people who are socially isolated are more likely to become depressed, to become ill, and to die prematurely. In fact, social isolation is as bad for your health as being obese or smoking (Cacioppo & Patrick, 2008; House, Landis, & Umberson, 1988).

Terry Waite, Robert King, and John McCain each spent years in isolation and described it as the worst form of torture.

SAMIR HUSSEIN/GETTY IMAGES

© ANN HARKNESS

© BROOKS KRAFT/CORBIS

**social psychology**
The study of the causes and consequences of sociality.

**aggression**
Behaviour with the purpose of harming another.

**WHAT KIND OF ANIMAL GETS SICK OR GOES CRAZY WHEN LEFT ALONE?** Our kind. Human beings are the most social species on the planet and everything about us—from the structure of our brains to the structure of our societies—is influenced by that fact. **Social psychology** is *the study of the causes and consequences of sociality.* We will start our tour of this field by examining *social behaviour* (how people interact with each other) and see how social behaviour solves problems that every living creature faces. Next we will examine *social influence* (how people change each other) and see that people have three basic motivations that make them responsive to the actions of others. Finally, we will examine *social cognition* (how people think about each other) and see how people use information to make judgments about others.

# Social Behaviour: Interacting with People

Centipedes are not social. Neither are snails or brown bears. In fact, most animals are loners who prefer solitude to company. So why not us?

All animals must survive and reproduce, and being social is one strategy for accomplishing these two important goals. When it comes to finding food or fending off enemies, herds and packs and flocks can often do what individuals cannot, and that is why over millions of years many different species have found it useful to become social. But of the thousands and thousands of social species on our planet, only four have become *ultrasocial*, which means that they form societies in which large numbers of individuals divide labour and cooperate for mutual benefit. Those four species are the hymenoptera (i.e., ants, bees, and wasps), the termites, the naked mole rats, and us (Haidt, 2006). Even in this fine company we distinguish ourselves, because only we form societies of genetically *un*related individuals. Indeed, some scientists believe that the complexity of living in large social groups is the primary reason why nature endowed us with such big brains (Sallet et al., 2011; Shultz & Dunbar, 2010; Smith et al., 2010). If 10 000 years ago you had rounded up all the mammals on Earth and placed them on a gigantic bathroom scale, human beings would have accounted for about 0.01 percent of the total mass, but today we would account for 98 percent. We are the heavyweight champions of survival and reproduction because we are deeply social, and as you are about to see, much of our social behaviour revolves around these two basic goals.

Human beings are the only animals that build large-scale social networks of unrelated individuals. According to Facebook, Lady Gaga has about 60 million friends, virtually none of whom share her genes.

ERIKA GOLDRING/FILMMAGIC/GETTY IMAGES

## Survival: The Struggle for Resources

Animals have a problem: survival. To survive, animals must find resources such as food, water, and shelter. The problem is that these resources are necessarily scarce, because if they were not, then the population would increase until they were. Animals often solve this problem by hurting or helping each other. *Hurting* and *helping* are antonyms and you might expect them to have little in common, but as you will see, these disparate behaviours are actually two solutions to the same problem (Hawley, 2002).

### Aggression

The simplest way to solve the problem of scarce resources is to take those resources and then kick the stuffing out of anyone who tries to stop you. **Aggression** is *behaviour with the purpose of harming another* (Anderson & Bushman, 2002; Bushman

& Huesmann, 2010), and it is a strategy used by just about every animal on the planet. Aggression is used by animals as a way of getting the resources they need. The **frustration–aggression hypothesis** suggests that *animals aggress when their desires are frustrated* (Dollard et al., 1939). The chimp wants the banana (*desire*) but the pelican is about to take it (*frustration*), so the chimp threatens the pelican with its fist (*aggression*). The robber wants the money (*desire*) but the teller has it all locked up (*frustration*), so the robber threatens the teller with a gun (*aggression*).

The frustration–aggression hypothesis is right as far as it goes, but many scientists think it does not go far enough. They argue that the *cause* of aggressive behaviour is negative affect (more commonly known as *feeling bad*) and that a frustrated desire is just one of many things that might induce negative affect (Berkowitz, 1990). If animals aggress when they feel bad, then *anything* that makes them feel bad should increase aggression—and evidence suggests that it does. Laboratory rats that are given painful electric shocks will attack anything in their cage, including other animals, stuffed dolls, or even tennis balls (Kruk et al., 2004). People who are made to put their hands in ice water or to sit in a very hot room are more likely to blast others with noise weapons or make others eat hot chili in subsequent experiments (Anderson, 1989; Anderson, Bushman, & Groom, 1997). The idea that aggression is a response to negative affect may even explain why so many acts of aggression—from violent crime to athletic brawls—are more likely to occur on hot days when people are feeling irritated and uncomfortable (see **FIGURE 13.1**). It is worth noting that not every kind of negative affect gives rise to aggression; for example, when people feel disgusted they actually become less likely to aggress (Pond et al., 2012).

Of course, not everyone aggresses every time they feel bad. So who does and why? Research suggests that both biology and culture play important roles in determining if and when people will aggress.

**Biology and Aggression.** If you wanted to know whether someone was likely to engage in aggression and you could ask them just one question, it should be "Are you male or female?" (Wrangham & Peterson, 1997). Crimes such as assault, battery, and murder are almost exclusively perpetrated by men—and especially by young men—who are responsible for about 90 percent of the murders and 80 percent of the violent crimes in Canada (Boyce & Cotter, 2013). Although most societies encourage males to be more aggressive than females (more on that shortly), male aggressiveness is not merely the product of socialization. Studies show that aggression is strongly correlated

**frustration–aggression hypothesis**
A principle stating that animals aggress when their goals are thwarted.

▼ Figure **13.1** **Hot and Bothered**
Professional pitchers have awfully good aim, so when they hit batters with the baseball, it is safe to assume that it was not an accident. Data from nearly 60 000 major league baseball games shows that, as the temperature on the field increases, so does the likelihood that a pitcher will hit a batter. This effect becomes even stronger when members of the pitcher's own team have been hit by pitches, suggesting that the pitcher is seeking revenge (Larrick et al., 2011).

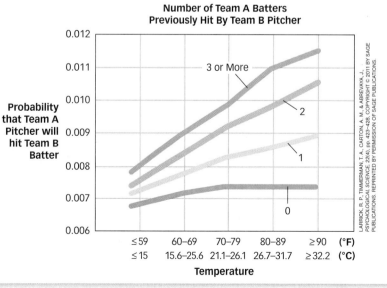

Number of Team A Batters
Previously Hit By Team B Pitcher

Probability that Team A Pitcher will hit Team B Batter

3 or More

2

1

0

| | ≤59 | 60–69 | 70–79 | 80–89 | ≥90 | (°F) |
| | ≤15 | 15.6–25.6 | 21.1–26.1 | 26.7–31.7 | ≥32.2 | (°C) |

Temperature

LARRICK, R. P., TIMMERMAN, T. A., CARTON, A. M. & ABREVAYA, J. PSYCHOLOGICAL SCIENCE, 22(4), pp. 423–428. COPYRIGHT © 2011 BY SAGE PUBLICATIONS. REPRINTED BY PERMISSION OF SAGE PUBLICATIONS.

with the presence of a hormone called *testosterone*, which is typically higher in men than in women, in younger men than in older men, and in violent criminals than in nonviolent criminals (Dabbs et al., 1995).

Testosterone does not directly cause aggression, but rather, seems to make people feel powerful and confident in their ability to prevail (Eisenegger et al., 2010; Eisenegger, Haushofer, & Fehr, 2011). Male chimpanzees with high testosterone tend to stand tall and hold their chins high (Muller & Wrangham, 2004), and human beings with high testosterone walk more purposefully, focus more directly on the people they are talking to, and speak in a more forward and independent manner (Dabbs et al., 2001). Testosterone also makes people more sensitive to provocation (Ronay & Galinsky, 2011) and less sensitive to signs of retaliation. Participants in one experiment watched a face as its expression changed from neutral to threatening and were asked to respond as soon as the expression became threatening (see **FIGURE 13.2**). Participants who were given a small dose of testosterone before the experiment were slower to recognize the threatening expression (van Honk & Schutter, 2007). Failing to recognize that the person you are criticizing is getting angry is a good way to end up in a fight.

VAN HONK ET AL., 2007

Testosterone (51%)

Placebo (43%)

0        50        100

**Percentage morph change**

▲ Figure **13.2 I Spy Threat** Subjects who were given testosterone needed to see a more threatening expression before they were able to recognize it as such (van Honk & Schutter, 2007).

One of the most reliable ways to elicit aggression in males is to challenge their status or dominance. Indeed, three quarters of all murders can be classified as "status competitions" or "contests to save face" (Daly & Wilson, 1988). Contrary to popular wisdom, it is not men with *low* self-esteem but men with unrealistically *high* self-esteem who are most prone to aggression, because such men are especially likely to perceive others' actions as a challenge to their inflated sense of their own status (Baumeister, Smart, & Boden, 1996). Men seem especially sensitive to these challenges when they are competing for the attention of women (Ainsworth & Maner, 2012).

Although women can be just as aggressive as men, their aggression tends to be more premeditated than impulsive and more likely to be focused on attaining or protecting a resource than on attaining or protecting their status. Women are *much* less likely than men to aggress without provocation or to aggress in ways that cause physical injury, but they are only *slightly* less likely than men to aggress when provoked or to aggress in ways that cause psychological injury (Bettencourt & Miller, 1996; Eagly & Steffen, 1986). Indeed, women may even be *more* likely than men to aggress by causing social harm, for example, by ostracizing others (Benenson et al., 2011) or by spreading malicious rumours about them (Crick & Grotpeter, 1995).

Under what circumstances do women aggress?

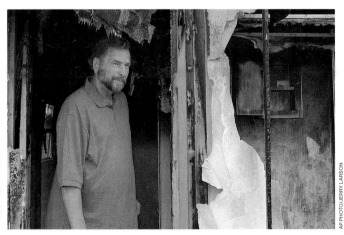

Men often aggress in response to status threats. In 2005, John Anderson (*right*) called Russell Tavares (*left*) a "nerd" on a social networking site. So Tavares got in his car, drove 2100 km, and burned down Anderson's trailer. "I didn't think anybody was stupid enough to try to kill anybody over an Internet fight," said Anderson. Tavares was later sentenced to 7 years in prison.

AP PHOTO/MCLENNAN COUNTY SHERIFF'S DEPARTMENT

AP PHOTO/JERRY LARSON

**Culture and Aggression.** William James (1911, p. 272) wrote that "our ancestors have bred pugnacity into our bone and marrow and thousands of years of peace will not breed it out of us." Was he right? Although aggression is clearly part of our evolutionary heritage, that does not mean it is inevitable. Indeed, the number of wars and the rate of murder have decreased by orders of magnitude in the last century alone. As psychologist Steven Pinker (2007) noted,

> We have been getting kinder and gentler. Cruelty as entertainment, human sacrifice to indulge superstition, slavery as a labor-saving device, conquest as the mission statement of government, genocide as a means of acquiring real estate, torture and mutilation as routine punishment, the death penalty for misdemeanors and differences of opinion, assassination as the mechanism of political succession, rape as the spoils of war, pogroms as outlets for frustration, homicide as the major form of conflict resolution—all were unexceptionable features of life for most of human history. But, today, they are rare to nonexistent in the West, far less common elsewhere than they used to be, concealed when they do occur, and widely condemned when they are brought to light.

Just as aggression varies with time, so too does it vary with geography (see **FIGURE 13.3**). For example, violent crime in the United States is more prevalent in the South, where men are taught to react aggressively when they feel their status has been

> What evidence suggests that culture can influence aggression?

challenged (Brown, Osterman, & Barnes, 2009; Nisbett & Cohen, 1996). In one set of experiments, researchers insulted American volunteers from Northern and Southern states and found that Southerners were more likely to experience a surge of testosterone and to feel that their status had been diminished by the insult (Cohen et al., 1996). When a large man walked directly toward them as they were leaving the experiment, insulted Southerners got "right up in his face" before giving way, whereas Northerners just stepped aside. Of course, in the control condition in which participants were *not* insulted, Southerners stepped aside *before* Northerners did, which is to say that when they are not being insulted, Southerners are *more* polite than Northerners.

Variation over time and geography shows that culture can play an important role in determining whether our innate capacity for aggression will result in aggressive

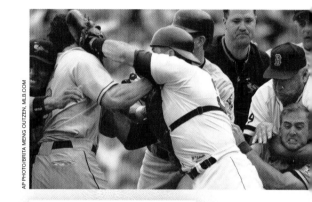

AP PHOTO/BRITA MENG OUTZEN, MLB.COM

Pitchers born in Southern states of America are 40 percent more likely than those born in Northern states to hit batters with their pitches (Timmerman, 2007).

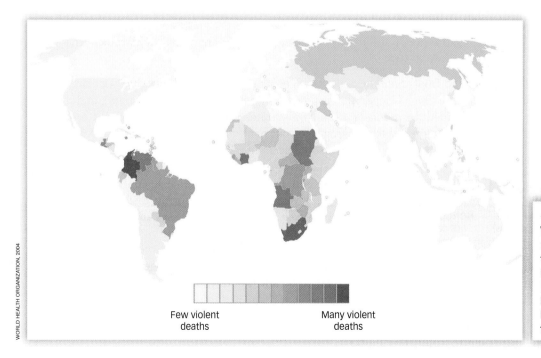

WORLD HEALTH ORGANIZATION, 2004

Few violent deaths        Many violent deaths

◀ Figure **13.3** **The Geography of Violence** When it comes to violence, culture matters a lot. Interestingly, one factor that distinguishes between more and less violent nations is gender equality (Caprioli, 2003; Melander, 2005). The better a nation's women are treated, the lower that nation's likelihood of going to war.

Culture has a strong influence on violence. In war-torn countries like Iraq, where murder, unfortunately, is a possible part of everyday life, young boys stage a mock execution. In India, a teenager who is a member of the Jain religion wears a mask at all times so that she will not harm insects or microbes by inhaling them.

behaviour (Leung & Cohen, 2011). People learn by example, which is why some researchers believe that watching violent television shows and playing violent video games can make people more aggressive (Anderson et al., 2010) and less cooperative (Sheese & Graziano, 2005; cf. Ferguson, 2010). But cultures can provide good examples as well as bad ones (Fry, 2012). In the mid-1980s, an unusual disease killed the most aggressive males in a particular troop of wild baboons in Kenya, leaving only the least aggressive males. A decade later, researchers discovered that a new "pacifist culture" had emerged among the descendants of the peaceful males. This new generation of male baboons was less aggressive, more likely to affiliate with females, and more tolerant of low-ranking males (Sapolsky & Share, 2004). If baboons can learn to get along, then surely people can too.

## Cooperation

Aggression is one way to solve the problem of scarce resources, but it is not the most inventive way, because when individuals work together they can often each get more resources than any could get alone. **Cooperation** is *behaviour by two or more individuals that leads to mutual benefit* (Deutsch, 1949; Pruitt, 1998), and it is one of our species' greatest achievements—right up there with language, fire, and the electric guitar (Axelrod, 1984; Axelrod & Hamilton, 1981; Nowak, 2006). Every roadway and supermarket, every iPod and cell phone, every ballet and surgery is the result of cooperation, and it is difficult to think of an important human achievement that could have occurred without it.

**Risk and Trust.** So if the benefits of cooperation are clear, then why do we not cooperate all the time? Cooperation is potentially beneficial, but it is also *risky*, and a simple game called *the prisoner's dilemma* illustrates why. Imagine that you and your friend have been arrested for hacking into your bank's mainframe computer and directing a few million dollars to your personal accounts. You are now being interrogated separately. The detectives tell you that if you and your friend both confess, you will each get 10 years in prison for felony theft, and if you both refuse to confess, you will each get 1 year in prison for, oh say, disturbing the peace. However, if one of you confesses and the other does not, then the one who confesses will go free and the one who does not confess will be put away for 30 years. What should you do? If you study **FIGURE 13.4,** you will see that you and your friend would be wise to cooperate. If you trust your friend and refuse to confess, and if your friend trusts you and refuses to confess, then you will both get a light sentence. But look what happens if you trust your

▼ Figure **13.4 The Prisoner's Dilemma Game** The prisoner's dilemma game illustrates the benefits and costs of cooperation. Players A and B receive benefits whose size depends on whether they independently decide to cooperate. Mutual cooperation leads to a relatively moderate benefit to both players, but if only one player cooperates, then the cooperator gets no benefit and the noncooperator gets a large benefit.

|  | COOPERATION (B does not confess) | NONCOOPERATION (B confesses) |
|---|---|---|
| **COOPERATION (A does not confess)** | A gets 1 year B gets 1 year | A gets 30 years B gets 0 years |
| **NONCOOPERATION (A confesses)** | A gets 0 years B gets 30 years | A gets 10 years B gets 10 years |

friend and then your friend double-crosses you: Your friend gets to go home and wash his car while you spend the next three decades making his license plates.

The prisoner's dilemma is more than a game. It mirrors the potential costs and benefits of cooperation in everyday life. For example, if everyone pays his or her taxes, then the tax rate stays low and everyone enjoys the benefits of sturdy bridges and first-rate museums. If no one pays taxes, then the bridges fall down and the museums shut their doors. There is clearly a *moderate* benefit to everyone if everyone pays taxes, but there is a *huge* benefit to the few noncooperators who do not pay taxes while everyone else does because they get to use the bridges and enjoy the museums for free. This dilemma makes it difficult for people to decide whether to pay taxes and risk being chumps or to cheat and risk having the bridges collapse and the museums shut down. If you are like most people, you would be perfectly willing to cooperate in this sort of dilemma but you worry that others will not do the same.

> **What makes cooperation risky?**

Life is a strategic game, and we value those who play it honourably and despise those who do not. When people are asked what single trait they most want those around them to have, the answer is *trustworthiness* (Cottrell, Neuberg, & Li, 2007), and when those around us fail to demonstrate that quality we react bitterly. For example, the *ultimatum game* requires one player (the divider) to divide a monetary prize into two parts and offer one of the parts to a second player (the decider), who can either accept or reject the offer. If the decider rejects the offer, then both players get nothing and the game is over. Studies show that deciders typically reject offers that they consider unfair because they would rather get nothing than get cheated (Fehr & Gaechter, 2002; Thaler, 1988). In other words, people will *pay* to punish someone who has treated them unfairly. Nonhumans also seem to dislike unfair treatment. In one study, monkeys were willing to work for a slice of cucumber until they saw the experimenter give another monkey a more delicious food for doing less work (Brosnan & de Waal, 2003). At that point the first set of monkeys went on strike and refused to participate further.

**Groups and Favouritism.** Cooperation requires that we take a risk by benefitting those who have not yet benefitted us and then *trusting* them to do the same. But whom can we trust?

A **group** is *a collection of people who have something in common that distinguishes them from others.* Every one of us is a member of many groups—from families and teams to religions and nations. Although these groups are quite different, they have one thing in common, which is that the people in them tend to be especially nice to each other. **Prejudice** is *a positive or negative evaluation of another person based on his or her group membership,* and **discrimination** is *a positive or negative behaviour toward another person based on his or her group membership*

> **What is the difference between prejudice and discrimination?**

(Dovidio & Gaertner, 2010). One of the defining characteristics of groups is that members are positively prejudiced toward fellow members and tend to discriminate in their favour (DiDonato, Ullrich, & Krueger, 2011). The tendency to favour one's own group is evolutionarily ancient (Fu et al., 2012; Mahajan et al., 2011), arises early in development (Dunham, Chen, & Banaji, 2013), and is easily elicited (Efferson, Lalive, & Fehr, 2008). Even when people are randomly assigned to be members of meaningless groups such as "Group 1" or "Group 2," they still give preferential treatment to members of their own group (Hodson & Sorrentino, 2001; Locksley, Ortiz, & Hepburn, 1980). It appears that simply knowing that "I am one of *us* and not one of *them*" is sufficient to produce prejudice and discrimination (Tajfel et al., 1971).

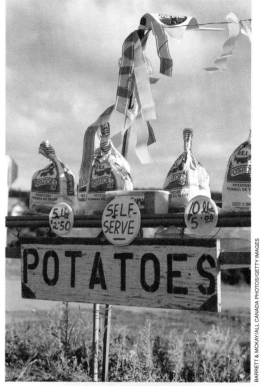

BARRETT & MCKAY/ALL CANADA PHOTOS/GETTY IMAGES

Prince Edward Island is known for the variety of potatoes it produces. You will see many potato stands along the roads in PEI. Payment of goods is by the honour system, where buyers leave their money in a cash box. If just a few people cheated, it would not affect the potato prices, but if too many cheated, then the prices would have to rise. How would you decide whether to pay or to cheat?

**cooperation**
Behaviour by two or more individuals that leads to mutual benefit.

**group**
A collection of people who have something in common that distinguishes them from others.

**prejudice**
A positive or negative evaluation of another person based on his or her group membership.

**discrimination**
Positive or negative behaviour toward another person based on his or her group membership.

**common knowledge effect**
The tendency for group discussions to focus on information that all members share.

**group polarization**
The tendency for groups to make decisions that are more extreme than any member would have made alone.

**groupthink**
The tendency for groups to reach consensus in order to facilitate interpersonal harmony.

**deindividuation**
A phenomenon that occurs when immersion in a group causes people to become less aware of their individual values.

**diffusion of responsibility**
The tendency for individuals to feel diminished responsibility for their actions when they are surrounded by others who are acting the same way.

**social loafing**
The tendency for people to expend less effort when in a group than when alone.

Because group members can be relied on to favour each other, group membership makes cooperation less risky.

But if groups have benefits, they also have costs. For example, when groups try to make decisions, they rarely do better than the best member would have done alone—and they quite often do worse (Minson & Mueller, 2012). One reason is that groups do not fully capitalize on the expertise of their members (Hackman & Katz, 2010). For instance, groups (such as a school board) often give too little weight to the opinions of members who are experts (the professor) and too much weight to the opinions of members who happen to be high in status (the mayor) or especially talkative (the mayor). Groups are also susceptible to the **common knowledge effect**, which is *the tendency for group discussions to focus on information that all members share* (Gigone & Hastie, 1993). The problem with this is that the information everyone shares (the size of the gymnasium) is often relatively unimportant, whereas the truly important information (how a school in a different district solved its budget crisis) is known to just a few. In addition, group discussion often acts as an "amplifier" of initial opinions. **Group polarization** is *the tendency for groups to make decisions that are more extreme than any member would have made alone* (Myers & Lamm, 1975). A group whose members come to the table with moderate opinions ("We should probably just renovate the auditorium") can end up making an extreme decision ("We are going to build a new high school!") simply because, in the course of discussion, each member was exposed to many different arguments in favour of a single position (Isenberg, 1986). Finally, members of groups care about how other members feel and are sometimes reluctant to "rock the boat" even when it needs a good rocking. **Groupthink** is *the tendency for groups to reach consensus in order to facilitate interpersonal harmony* (Janis, 1982). Harmony is important (especially if the group is a choir), but studies show that groups often sacrifice the goodness of their decisions in order to achieve it (Turner & Pratkanis, 1998). For all of these reasons, groups underperform individuals in a wide variety of tasks.

> **What are the costs of groups?**

The costs of groups go beyond bad decisions because people in groups sometimes do terrible things that none of their members would do alone (Yzerbyt & Demoulin, 2010). Lynching, rioting, gang-raping—why do we behave so badly when we assemble in groups?

One reason is **deindividuation,** which occurs *when immersion in a group causes people to become less concerned with their personal values.* We may want to grab the Rolex from the jeweller's window or plant a kiss on the attractive stranger in the library, but we sometimes do not do these things because they conflict with our personal values. Research shows that people are most likely to consider their personal values when their attention is focused on themselves (Wicklund, 1975), and being assembled in groups draws our attention to others and *away* from ourselves. As a result, we are less likely to consider our own personal values and instead adopt the group's values (Postmes & Spears, 1998).

A second reason why groups behave badly is **diffusion of responsibility,** which refers to *the tendency for individuals to feel diminished responsibility for their actions when they are surrounded by others who are acting the same way.* Diffusion of responsibility is the main culprit behind something you have probably observed many times—a phenomenon known as **social loafing** which refers to *the tendency for people to expend less effort when in a group than alone.* For example, individuals in large groups are less likely than individuals in small groups to clap loudly after a performance

*"Hey, we're sheep. Everything seems like a good idea."*

When are people most and least likely to cheat? Researchers posted a picture above the coffee pot in an office that had an "honour system," and found that people were less likely to cheat when the picture showed eyes than when it showed flowers (Bateson, Nettle, & Roberts, 2006). Other researchers paid people to sit alone in a room and complete puzzles for cash, and found that people were less likely to cheat when the lights was bright than when the lights were low (Zhong, Bohns, & Gino, 2010). Can you explain these two results with a single principle?

(Latané, Williams, & Harkins, 1979), exert effort in a team sport (Williams et al., 1989), leave good tips at restaurants (Freeman et al., 1975), donate money to charity (Wiesenthal, Austrom, & Silverman, 1983), and even say hello to passersby (Jones & Foshay, 1984). But the diffusion of responsibility has much more pernicious effects. For example, studies of **bystander intervention**—which is *the act of helping strangers in an emergency situation*—reveal that people are less likely to help an innocent person in distress when there are many other bystanders present, simply because they assume that one of the other bystanders is more responsible than they are (Darley & Latané, 1968; Latané & Nida, 1981). If you saw a fellow student cheat on an exam, you would probably feel more responsible for reporting the incident if you were taking the test in a group of 3 than in a group of 3000 (see **FIGURE 13.5**).

If groups make bad decisions and foster bad behaviour, then might we be better off without them? Probably not. One of the best predictors of a person's general well-being is the quality and extent of their group memberships (Myers & Diener, 1995). People who are excluded from groups are typically anxious, lonely, depressed, and at increased risk for illness and premature death (Cacioppo & Patrick, 2008; Cohen, 1988; Leary, 1990). Belonging is not just a source of psychological and physical well-being but also a source of identity (Ellemers, 2012; Leary, 2010; Tajfel & Turner, 1986), which is why people typically describe themselves by listing the groups of which they are members ("I am a Canadian architect"). Groups may cause us to misjudge and misbehave, but they are also the key to our happiness and well-being. Can't live with 'em, can't live without 'em.

**bystander intervention**
The act of helping strangers in an emergency situation.

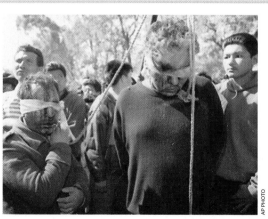

◀ Figure **13.5** **Mob Size and Level of Atrocity** Groups are capable of horrible things. These two men were rescued by police just as residents of their town prepared to lynch them for stealing a car. Because larger groups provide more opportunity for deindividuation and diffusion of responsibility, their atrocities become more horrible as the ratio of mob members to victims becomes larger (Leader, Mullen, & Abrams, 2007).

# HOT SCIENCE

# Mouse Over

How much would you pay to save a life? The answer may depend on whether the decision is yours alone. Genetics laboratories that breed mice for experiments often end up with surplus mice. Because it is so expensive to house and feed these mice for their entire life spans, surplus mice are typically killed. Researchers at the University of Bonn decided to see how much people would pay to keep just one surplus mouse alive (Falk & Szech, 2013). They offered participants 10 euros (about $15) to participate in their study. After participants accepted, they showed them a picture of a mouse that was destined to be killed and told them that if they would give back the 10 euros, it would be used to support the mouse for the rest of its natural life. The majority of participants—54 percent to be exact—offered to give back their payment in order to save the mouse's life.

But when the researchers put the mouse's fate in the hands of *two* participants, the results changed dramatically. In a second condition of the study, the participants negotiated about what would happen to the mouse. Specifically, the participants were told that if they could agree on a way to split 20 euros, then they would each receive the amount they agreed to and the mouse would die. If they could not agree on a way to split the money, then they would each

TETRA IMAGES/ALAMY

receive nothing and the mouse would be allowed to live out its natural life. If a participant wanted the mouse to live, then all he or she had to do was to refuse to come to an agreement about how to split the money. So what did these participants do? This time the majority of participants—72 percent to be exact—came to an agreement with their partner and sent the mouse to its demise.

Why did this happen? When people make joint decisions, each feels diminished responsibility for it. Participants in the first condition were faced with a moral dilemma: *Do I take the money, which I am tempted to do, or save the mouse, which I suppose is the right thing to do?* No matter what they decided, the decision was theirs. But participants in the second condition made their decision together, and thus probably found it easier to give in to temptation because they had someone else with whom to share the blame.

## Altruism

Cooperation solves the problem of scarce resources. But is that the only reason we cooperate with others? Are not we ever just … well, *nice?* **Altruism** is *behaviour that benefits another without benefitting oneself,* and for centuries, scientists and philosophers have argued about whether people are ever truly altruistic. That might seem like an odd argument to have. After all, people give their blood to the injured, their food to the homeless, and their arms to the elderly. We volunteer, we tithe, we donate. People do nice things all the time! Is not that evidence of altruism?

Well, not exactly. Behaviours that appear to be altruistic often have hidden benefits for those who do them. Consider some simple examples in the realm of animal behaviour. Birds and squirrels make alarm calls when they see a predator, which puts them at increased risk of being eaten but allows their fellow birds and squirrels to escape. Ants and bees spend their lives caring for the offspring of the queen rather than bearing offspring of

> Are human beings ever truly altruistic?

their own. Although these behaviours appear to be altruistic, they actually are not because the helpers are *genetically related* to the helpees. The squirrels most likely to make alarm calls are those most closely related to the other squirrels in the den (Maynard-Smith, 1965), and although honeybees do raise the queen's offspring, an odd genetic quirk causes honeybees to be more closely related to those offspring than they would be to their own. Any animal that promotes the survival of its relatives is actually promoting the survival of its own genes (Hamilton, 1964). **Kin selection** is *the process by which evolution selects for individuals who cooperate with their relatives,* and cooperating with related individuals is not really altruistic. Cooperating with unrelated individuals is not necessarily altruistic either. Male baboons will risk injury to help an unrelated male baboon win a fight, and monkeys will spend time grooming unrelated monkeys when they could be doing something else, but as it turns out, the

**altruism**
Behaviour that benefits another without benefitting oneself.

**kin selection**
The process by which evolution selects for individuals who cooperate with their relatives.

Ground squirrels put themselves in danger when they warn others about predators, but those they warn share their genes, so the behaviour is not truly altruistic. In contrast, Christine Karg-Palerio donated her kidney anonymously to someone she would never even meet. "If I had a spare, I would do it again," she said.

animals that give favours tend to get favours in return. **Reciprocal altruism** is *behaviour that benefits another with the expectation that those benefits will be returned in the future,* and despite the second word in this term, it is not actually altruistic (Trivers, 1972). Indeed, reciprocal altruism is merely cooperation extended over time.

The behaviour of nonhuman animals provides little if any evidence of genuine altruism (cf. Bartal, Decety, & Mason, 2011). So what about us? Are we any different? Like other animals, we tend to help our kin more than strangers (Burnstein, Crandall, & Kitayama, 1994; Komter, 2010) and we tend to expect those we help to help us in return (Burger et al., 2009). But unlike other animals, we *do* sometimes provide benefits to complete strangers who have no chance of repaying us (Batson, 2002; Warneken & Tomasello, 2009). We hold the door for people who share precisely none of our genes and tip waiters in restaurants to which we will never return. And we do more than that. As the World Trade Center burned on the morning of September 11, 2001, civilians in sailboats headed *toward* the destruction rather than away from it, initiating the largest waterborne evacuation in American history. As one observer remarked, "If you are out on the water in a pleasure craft and you see those buildings on fire, in a strictly rational sense you should head to New Jersey. Instead, people went into potential danger and rescued strangers. That's social" (Dreifus, 2003). Human beings can be truly altruistic, and some studies suggest that they are actually more altruistic than they realize (Miller & Ratner, 1998).

## Reproduction: The Quest for Immortality

All animals must survive and reproduce. Social behaviour is useful for survival, but it is an absolute prerequisite for reproduction, which does not happen until people get very, very social. The first step on the road to reproduction is finding someone who wants to travel that road with us. How do we do that?

### Selectivity

With the exception of a few well-known rock stars, people do not mate randomly.

**Why are women choosier than men?**

Rather, they *select* their sexual partners, and as anyone who has lived on earth for more than 7 full minutes knows, women tend to be more selective than men (Feingold, 1992a; Fiore et al., 2010). When researchers asked an attractive person to approach strangers on a college campus and ask, "Would you go out with me?" they found that roughly half of the men and half of the women agreed to the request for a date. On the other

**reciprocal altruism**
Behaviour that benefits another with the expectation that those benefits will be returned in the future.

CREATAS IMAGES/
PICTUREQUEST

If men could become pregnant, how might their behaviour change? Among sea horses, it is the male that carries the young and, not coincidentally, males are more selective than are females.

hand, when the attractive person said to strangers, "Would you go to bed with me?" the researchers found that *none* of the women and *three quarters* of the men agreed to the request for sex (Clark & Hatfield, 1989). There are many reasons why a woman in this situation might turn down a sexual offer (Conley, 2011), but research suggests that women tend to be choosier than men in most other situations as well (Buss & Schmitt, 1993; Schmitt et al., 2012).

One reason for this is biology. Men produce billions of sperm in their lifetimes, their ability to conceive a child tomorrow is not inhibited by having conceived one today, and conception has no significant physical costs. On the other hand, women produce a small number of eggs in their lifetimes, conception eliminates their ability to conceive for at least 9 more months, and pregnancy produces physical changes that increase their nutritional requirements and put them at risk of illness and death. Therefore, if a man mates with a woman who does do not produce healthy offspring or who will not do her part to raise them, he has lost nothing but 10 minutes and a teaspoon of bodily fluid. But if a woman makes the same mistake, she has lost a precious egg, borne the costs of pregnancy, risked her life in childbirth, and missed at least 9 months of other reproductive opportunities. Clearly, our basic biology makes sex a riskier proposition for women than for men.

DR. PAUL ZAHL/
SCIENCE SOURCE

But if basic biology pushes women to be choosier then men, culture and experience can push every bit as hard (Petersen & Hyde, 2010; Zentner, & Mitura, 2012). For example, women may be choosier than men simply because they are approached more often (Conley et al., 2011) or because the reputational costs of promiscuity are higher (Eagly & Wood, 1999; Kasser & Sharma, 1999). Indeed, when sex becomes expensive for men (e.g., when they are choosing a long-term mate rather than a short-term date), they can be every bit as choosey as women (Kenrick et al., 1990). In fact, relatively minor changes in the courtship ritual can actually cause men to be *choosier* than women (see The Real World box). The point is that biology makes sex a riskier proposition for women than for men, but cultures can exaggerate, equalize, or even reverse those risks. The higher the risk, the more selective people of both genders tend to be.

## Attraction

For most of us, there is a very small number of people with whom we are willing to have sex, an even smaller number of people with whom we are willing to have children, and a staggeringly large number of people with whom we are unwilling to have either. So when we meet someone new, how do we decide which of these categories they belong in? Many things go into choosing a date, a lover, or a partner for life, but perhaps none is more important than the simple feeling we call *attraction* (Berscheid & Reis, 1998). Research suggests that this feeling is caused by a range of factors that can be roughly divided into three kinds: the situational, the physical, and the psychological.

**Situational Factors.** One of the best predictors of any kind of interpersonal relationship is the physical proximity of the people involved (Nahemow & Lawton, 1975). In one study, students who had been randomly assigned to university housing almost a year earlier were asked to name their three closest friends, and nearly half named their next-door neighbour (Festinger, Schachter, & Back, 1950). We tend to think that we select our romantic partners on the basis of their personalities, appearances, and so on—and we do—but we only get to select from the pool of people we have met, and the likelihood of meeting a potential partner naturally increases with proximity. Before you ever start ruling out potential mates, geography has already ruled out 99.999 percent of the world's population for you. Proximity not only provides the opportunity for

# THE REAL WORLD

# Making the Move

When it comes to selecting romantic partners, women tend to be choosier than men, and most scientists think that has a lot to do with differences in their reproductive biology. But psychologists Eli Finkel and Paul Eastwick (2009) thought that it might also have something to do with the nature of the courtship dance itself.

When it comes to approaching a potential romantic partner, the person with the most interest should be most inclined to "make the first move." Of course, in most cultures, men are *expected* to make the first move. Could it be that making the first move *causes* men to think that they have more interest than women do and causes women to think they have less? In other words, could the rule about first moves be one of the *reasons* why women are choosier?

To find out, the researchers teamed up with a local speed dating service and created two kinds of speed dating events. In the traditional event, the women stayed in their seats and the men moved around the room, stopping to spend a few minutes chatting with each woman. In the nontraditional event, the men stayed in their seats and the women moved around the room, stopping to spend a few minutes chatting with each man. When the event was over, the researchers asked

each man and woman privately to indicate whether they wanted to exchange phone numbers with any of the potential partners they would met.

The results were striking (see the accompanying figure). When men made the move (as they traditionally do), women were the choosier gender. That is, men wanted to get a lot more phone numbers than women wanted to give. But when women made the move, men were the choosier gender, and women asked for more numbers than men were willing to hand over. Apparently, approaching someone makes us eager and being approached makes us cautious. One reason why women are so often the choosier gender may simply be that, in most cultures, men are expected to make the first move.

GREG GILBERT KRT/NEWSCOM

attraction, it also provides the motivation: People work especially hard to like those with whom they expect to have interaction (Darley & Berscheid, 1967). When you are assigned a roommate or an office mate, you know that your day-to-day existence will be a whole lot easier if you like them than if you do not, and so you go out of your way to notice their good qualities and ignore their bad ones.

Proximity provides something else as well. Every time we encounter a person, that person becomes a bit more familiar to us, and people generally prefer familiar to novel stimuli. The **mere exposure effect** is *the tendency for liking to increase with the frequency of exposure* (Bornstein, 1989; Zajonc, 1968). For instance, in some experiments, geometric shapes, faces, or alphabetical characters were flashed on a computer screen so quickly that participants were unaware of having seen them. Participants were then shown some of the "old" stimuli that had been flashed across the screen as well as some "new" stimuli that had not. Although they could not reliably say which stimuli were old and which were new, they did tend to *like* the old stimuli better than the new ones (Monahan, Murphy, & Zajonc, 2000). The fact that mere exposure leads to liking may explain why university students who were randomly assigned to seats during a brief psychology experiment were likely to be friends with the person they sat next to a full year later (Back, Schmukle, & Egloff, 2008). There

> **Why does proximity influence attraction?**

**mere exposure effect**
The tendency for liking to increase with the frequency of exposure.

"I am a beast, I am an animal, I am that monster in the mirror." Like it or not, the mirror is the place where Usher most often sees himself. As a result, he probably prefers pictures of himself that are printed in reverse (*above left*), whereas his fans probably prefer pictures of him that are not (*above right*). One consequence of the mere exposure effect is that people tend to like the photographic images with which they are most familiar (Mita, Dermer, & Knight, 1977).

are some circumstances under which "familiarity breeds contempt" (Norton, Frost, & Ariely, 2007), but for the most part familiarity seems to breed liking (Reis et al., 2011).

Attraction can be the result of geographical accidents that put people in the same place at the same time, but some places and times are clearly better than others. In one study, Canadian researchers Donald Dutton and Arthur Aron observed men as they crossed the Capilano Bridge (in Vancouver) as it was swaying. An attractive female researcher approached the men, either when they were in the middle of the bridge or after they had finished crossing it, and asked them to complete a survey. After they did so, she gave each man her telephone number and offered to explain her project in greater detail if he called. Results showed that the men were more likely to call the woman when they had met her in the middle of the swaying bridge (Dutton & Aron, 1974). Why? You may recall from the Emotion and Motivation chapter that people can misinterpret physiological arousal as a sign of attraction (Byrne et al., 1975; Schachter & Singer, 1962). The men were presumably more aroused when they were in the middle of a swaying bridge, and some of those men mistook their arousal for attraction.

**Physical Factors.** Once people are in the same place at the same time, they can begin to learn about each other's personal qualities, and in most cases, the first quality they learn about is the other person's appearance. You probably knew that appearance influences attraction, but this influence may be stronger than you thought. In one study, researchers arranged a dance for first-year university students and randomly assigned each student to an opposite-sex partner. Midway through the dance, the students confidentially reported how much they liked their partner, how attractive they thought their partner was, and how much they would like to see their partner again. The researchers measured many of the students' attributes—from their attitudes to their personalities—and they found that the partner's physical appearance was the *only* attribute that influenced the students' feelings of attraction (Walster et al., 1966). Field studies confirm this finding. For instance, one study found that a man's height and a woman's weight were among the best predictors of how many responses a personal advertisement received (Lynn & Shurgot, 1984), and another study found that physical attractiveness was the *only* factor that predicted the online dating choices of both women and men (Green, Buchanan, & Heuer, 1984). Superficiality, thy name is human!

When people are in arousing situations together, they may become attracted. Ben Bostic and Laura Zych were strangers when their US Airways flight crash-landed in the Hudson River, New York, in 2009. Now they are a couple.

▲ Figure **13.6** **Height Matters** NFL quarterback Tom Brady is 6'4" (193 cm) and his wife, supermodel Gisele Bunchen, is 5'10" (178 cm). Research shows that tall people earn $789 more per inch per year. The graph shows the average hourly wage of adult white men in the United States classified by height (Mankiw & Weinzierl, 2010).

Beauty gets us more than dates (Etcoff, 1999; Langlois et al., 2000). Beautiful people have more sex, more friends, and more fun than the rest of us do (Curran & Lippold, 1975), and they even earn about 10 percent more money over the course of their lives (see **FIGURE 13.6**) (Hamermesh & Biddle, 1994). We tend to think that beautiful people also have superior personal qualities (Dion, Berscheid, & Walster, 1972; Eagly et al., 1991), and in some cases they do. For instance, because beautiful people have more friends and more opportunities for social interaction, they tend to have better social skills than less beautiful people (Feingold, 1992b). Appearance is so powerful that it even influences how mothers treat their own children: Mothers are more affectionate and playful when their children are attractive than unattractive (Langlois et al., 1995). Indeed, the only real disadvantage of being beautiful is that it can sometimes cause others to feel threatened (Agthe, Spörrle, & Maner, 2010). It is interesting to note that men and women are equally influenced by the appearance of their potential partners (Eastwick et al., 2011), but men are more willing to admit it (Feingold, 1990).

> **Why is physical appearance so important?**

So yes, it pays to be beautiful. But what exactly constitutes beauty? The answer to that question varies across cultures. In Canada, for example, most women want to be slender, but in Mauritania, young girls are forced to drink up to 19 L of high-fat milk every day so that they will someday be obese enough to attract a husband. As one Mauritanian woman noted, "Men want women to be fat, and so they are fat. Women want men to be skinny, and so they are skinny" (LaFraniere, 2007). In Canada, most men want to be tall, but in Ghana, most men are short and consider height a curse. "To be a tall person can be quite embarrassing," said one particularly altitudinous Ghanaian man. "When you are standing in a crowd, the short people start to jeer at you," said another (French, 1997).

Beauty may vary across cultures, but it is not entirely in the eye of the beholder. Different cultures have different standards of beauty, but those standards have a lot in common (Cunningham et al., 1995). For example, people in all cultures seem to have similar preferences about the ideal body, face, and age of their romantic partners.

> *Body shape.* Male bodies are considered most attractive when they approximate an inverted triangle (i.e., broad shoulders with a narrow waist and hips), and female bodies are considered most attractive when they approximate an hourglass (i.e., broad shoulders and hips with a narrow waist). In fact, the most attractive female body across many cultures seems to be the "perfect hourglass" in which the waist is precisely 70 percent the size of the hips (Singh, 1993).

Standards of beauty can vary across cultures. Mauritanian women long to be obese (*left*). Ghanian men are grateful to be short (*right*).

Culture may determine whether men prefer women who are heavy or thin, but in all cultures men seem to prefer this particular waist-to-hip ratio.

> *Symmetry.* People in all cultures seem to prefer faces and bodies that are *bilaterally symmetrical*—that is, faces and bodies whose left half is a mirror image of the right half (Perilloux, Webster, & Gaulin, 2010; Perrett et al., 1999).

> *Age.* Characteristics such as large eyes, high eyebrows, and a small chin make people look immature or "baby-faced" (Berry & McArthur, 1985). As a general rule, female faces are considered more attractive when they have immature features, and male faces are considered more attractive when they have mature features (Cunningham, Barbee, & Pike, 1990; Zebrowitz & Montepare, 1992). Women prefer older men and men prefer younger women in every human culture ever studied (Buss, 1989).

But why? Is there any rhyme or reason to this list of scenic attractions? Some psychologists think so. They suggest that nature has designed us to be attracted to people who (a) have good genes and (b) will be good parents (Gallup & Frederick, 2010; Neuberg, Kenrick, & Schaller, 2010). The features we all find attractive happen to be reliable indicators of these things. For example:

> *Body shape.* Testosterone causes male bodies to become "inverted triangles" just as estrogen causes female bodies to become "hourglasses." Men who are high in testosterone tend to be socially dominant and therefore have more resources to devote to their offspring, whereas women who are high in estrogen tend to be especially fertile and potentially have more offspring to make use of those resources. In other words, body shape is an indicator of male dominance and female fertility. In fact, women who have the perfect hourglass figure do tend to bear healthier children than do women with other waist-to-hip ratios (Singh, 1993).

**What kind of information does physical appearance convey?**

> *Symmetry.* Symmetry is a sign of genetic health (Jones et al., 2001; Thornhill & Gangestad, 1993), which may explain why people are so good at detecting it. Indeed, women can distinguish between symmetrical and asymmetrical men *by smell,* and their preference for symmetrical men is especially pronounced when they are ovulating (Thornhill & Gangestad, 1999).

> *Age.* Younger women are generally more fertile than older women, whereas older men generally have more resources than younger men. Thus, a youthful appearance is a signal of a woman's ability to bear children, just as a mature appearance is a signal of a man's ability to raise them.

(a)  (b)  (c)  (d)

If the feeling we call *attraction* is simply nature's way of telling us that we are in the presence of a person who has good genes and a propensity to be a good parent, then it is not any wonder that people in different cultures appreciate so many of the same features in the opposite sex. Of course, appreciation is one thing and action is another, and studies show that while everyone may *desire* the most beautiful person in the room, most people tend to approach, date, and marry someone who is about as attractive as they are (Berscheid et al., 1971; Lee et al., 2008).

**Psychological Factors.** If attraction is all about big biceps and high cheekbones, then why do not we just skip the small talk and pick our mates from photographs? Because for human beings, attraction is about much more than that. Physical appearance is assessed easily and early (Lenton & Francesconi, 2010), and it determines who draws our attention and quickens our pulse. But once people begin interacting they quickly move beyond appearances (Cramer, Schaefer, & Reid, 1996; Regan, 1998). People's *inner* qualities—their personalities, points of view, attitudes, beliefs, values, ambitions, and abilities—play an important role in determining their sustained interest in each other, and there is not much mystery about the kinds of inner qualities that most people find attractive. For example, intelligence, sense of humour, sensitivity, and ambition seem to be high on just about everybody's list, whereas "experienced serial killer" does not seem to make anyone's list (Daniel et al., 1985).

How much wit and wisdom do we want our mate to have? Research suggests that people are most attracted to those who are similar (Byrne, Ervin, & Lamberth, 1970; Byrne & Nelson, 1965; Hatfield & Rapson, 1992; Neimeyer & Mitchell, 1988). We marry people with similar levels of education, religious backgrounds, ethnicities, socioeconomic statuses, and personalities (Botwin, Buss, & Shackelford, 1997; Buss, 1985; Caspi & Herbener, 1990). We are even attracted to those who use pronouns the same way we do (Ireland et al., 2010). In fact, of all the variables psychologists have ever studied, *gender* appears to be the only one for which the majority of people have a consistent preference for dissimilarity.

Why is similarity so attractive? First, it is easy to interact with people who are similar to us because we can instantly agree on a wide range of issues, such as what to eat,

**Why is similarity such a powerful determinant of attraction?**

where to live, how to raise children, and how to spend our money. Second, when someone shares our attitudes and beliefs, we feel more confident that those attitudes and beliefs are correct (Byrne & Clore, 1970). Indeed, research shows that when a person's attitudes or beliefs are challenged, they become even more attracted to similar others (Greenberg et al., 1990; Hirschberger, Florian, & Mikulincer, 2002). Third, if we like people who share our attitudes and beliefs, then we can reasonably expect them to like us for the same reason, and *being liked* is a

Straight women find men sexiest when their faces are displaying pride (a) and least sexy when they are displaying happiness (b); straight men find women least sexy when their faces are displaying pride (c) and sexiest when they are displaying happiness (d) (Tracy & Beall, 2011).

Similarity is a very strong source of attraction.

**passionate love**
An experience involving feelings of euphoria, intimacy, and intense sexual attraction.

**companionate love**
An experience involving affection, trust, and concern for a partner's well-being.

**social exchange**
The hypothesis that people remain in relationships only as long as they perceive a favourable ratio of costs to benefits.

**comparison level**
The outcome people feel they should receive, in terms of rewards and costs, from their relationship.

**comparison level for alternatives**
The availability, and the cost–benefit ratio, of an alternative outcome.

**equity**
A state of affairs in which the cost–benefit ratios of two partners are roughly equal.

Humans and birds have something in common: Their offspring are utterly helpless at birth and require a lot of parental care. As a result, both people and birds have enduring relationships. And both seem to sing about it.

powerful source of attraction (Aronson & Worchel, 1966; Backman & Secord, 1959; Condon & Crano, 1988). Although we tend to like people who like us, it is worth noting that we *especially* like people who like us and who *do not* like anyone else (Eastwick et al., 2007).

Our desire for similarity goes beyond attitudes and beliefs and extends to abilities as well. For example, we may admire extraordinary skill in athletes and actors, but when it comes to friends and lovers, extraordinary people can threaten our self-esteem and make us feel a bit nervous about our own competence (Tesser, 1991). As such, we are generally attracted to competent people who—like us—have small pockets of incompetence. Why? It seems that people who are annoyingly perfect are perfectly annoying. Having a flaw or two "humanizes" people and makes them seem more accessible—and more similar to us (Aronson, Willerman, & Floyd, 1966).

## Relationships

Once we have selected and attracted a mate, we are ready to reproduce. (Note: It is perfectly fine to pause for dinner.) Human reproduction ordinarily happens in the context of committed, long-term relationships (Clark & Lemay, 2010). Only a few animals have such relationships, so why are we among them?

One answer is that we are born half-baked. Because human beings have large heads to house their large brains, a fully developed human infant could not pass through the mother's birth canal. So human infants are *born before they are fully developed*. That means they need a lot more care than one parent can provide. If human infants were like tadpoles—ready at birth to swim, find food, and escape predators—then their parents might not need to form and maintain relationships. But human infants are remarkably helpless creatures that require years of intense care before they can fend for themselves, and that is one reason why human adults tend to do their reproducing in the context of committed, long-term relationships. (By the way, some baby birds also require more food than one adult caretaker can provide, and the adults of those species also tend to form long-term relationships.)

> **Why do people form long-term romantic relationships?**

**Love and Commitment.** In most cultures, adults settle into committed, long-term relationships in which they live together, and often have children. (While such relationships have traditionally been celebrated with marriage, rates of marriage are declining in Canada, although rates of enduring relationships are not.) But when asked, people do not say that they got together to solve the big-headed baby problem; they say that they did it for love. The fact that people marry for love seems so obvious that you may be surprised to learn that it only became obvious in the past century or so (Brehm, 1992; Fisher, 1993; Hunt, 1959). Ancient Greeks and Romans married, but they considered love a form of madness (Heine, 2010). Twelfth-century Europeans married but thought of love as a game to be played by knights and ladies of the court (who happened to be married and not to the knights). Throughout history, marriage has traditionally served a variety of economic (and decidedly unromantic) functions—ranging from cementing agreements between clans to paying back debts—and in many cultures, that is how it is still regarded. In fact, it was not until the seventeenth century that Westerners started to think that love might be a *reason* to get married.

But what exactly is love? Psychologists distinguish between two basic kinds: **passionate love,** which is *an experience involving feelings of euphoria, intimacy, and intense sexual attraction,* and **companionate love,** which is *an experience involving affection, trust, and concern for a partner's well-being* (Acevedo & Aron, 2009; Hatfield, 1988; Rubin, 1973; Sternberg, 1986). The ideal romantic relationship gives rise to both types of love, but the speeds, trajectories, and durations of the two experiences are markedly different (see **FIGURE 13.7** on the next page). Passionate love is what brings people together: It has a rapid onset, reaches its peak quickly, and begins to diminish within just a few months (Aron et al., 2005). Companionate love is what keeps people together: It takes some time to get started, grows slowly, and need never stop growing (Gonzaga et al., 2001).

## Breaking up: When the Costs Outweigh the Benefits

Recent Statistics Canada data indicate that for every two couples who get married, one couple gets divorced. But why? Although feelings of love, happiness, and satisfaction may lead us to a committed, long-term relationship, the lack of those feelings does not seem to lead us to break-up.

> **How do people weigh the costs and benefits of their relationships?**

Marital satisfaction is only weakly correlated with marital stability (Karney & Bradbury, 1995), suggesting that relationships break up or remain intact for reasons other than the satisfaction of those involved (Drigotas & Rusbult, 1992; Rusbult & Van Lange, 2003). Relationships offer both benefits (love, sex, and financial security) and costs (responsibility, conflict, loss of freedom). **Social exchange** is *the hypothesis that people remain in relationships only as long as they perceive a favourable ratio of costs to benefits* (Homans, 1961; Thibaut & Kelley, 1959). For example, a relationship that provides an acceptable level of benefits at a reasonable cost will probably be maintained, and one that does not will not. Research suggests that this hypothesis is generally true, but there are three important caveats:

> The acceptableness of any cost–benefit ratio depends on the alternatives. A person's **comparison level** refers to *the outcome people feel they should receive, in terms of rewards and costs, from their relationship*. The **comparison level for alternatives** refers to *the availability, and the cost–benefit ratio, of an alternative outcome* (Rusbult et al., 1991; Thibaut & Kelley, 1959). If people feel that the cost–benefit ratio of being alone, or of an available alternative, outweighs the costs and benefits of the current relationship, they will not be as committed and their current relationship is more likely to break up (Felmlee, Sprecher, & Bassin, 1990). This caveat may help to explain why celebrities seem to trade partners so often; readily available attractive alternative partners may be an "occupational hazard" of being a celebrity.

> People may want their cost–benefit ratios to be high, but they also want them to be roughly the same as their partner's. Studies show that people care about **equity,** which is *a state of affairs in which the cost–benefit ratios of two partners are roughly equal* (Bolton & Ockenfels, 2000; Messick & Cook, 1983; Walster, Walster, & Berscheid, 1978). For example, spouses are more distressed when their respective cost–benefit ratios are *different* than when their cost–benefit ratios are *unfavourable*, and this is true even when their cost–benefit ratio is *more* favourable than their partner's (Schafer & Keith, 1980). Indeed, people who give too much are sometimes disliked just as much as those who give too little (Parks & Stone, 2010).

> Relationships can be thought of as investments into which people pour resources such as time, money, and affection, and research suggests that once people have poured resources into a relationship, they are willing to settle for less favourable cost–benefit ratios (Kelley, 1983; Rusbult, 1983). This is one of the reasons why people are much more likely to end new marriages

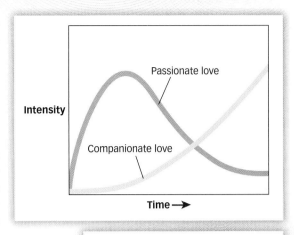

▲ Figure **13.7 Passionate and Companionate Love**  Companionate and passionate love have different time courses and trajectories. Passionate love begins to cool within just a few months, but companionate love can grow slowly but steadily over years.

*"This next one goes out to all those who have ever been in love, then become engaged, gotten married, participated in the tragic deterioration of a relationship, suffered the pains and agonies of a bitter divorce, subjected themselves to the fruitless search for a new partner, and ultimately resigned themselves to remaining single in a world full of irresponsible jerks, noncommittal weirdos, and neurotic misfits."*

**social influence**
The ability to control another person's behaviour.

than old ones (Bramlett & Mosher, 2002; Cherlin, 1992). McGill researcher John Lydon and his colleagues have found that the degree to which a romantic relationship has been incorporated into people's self-identity (has become part of how they see themselves) predicts how strongly people will protect the relationship. Threats to the relationship become threats to the self, and are treated accordingly (Linardatos & Lydon, 2011).

## IN SUMMARY

▶ Survival and reproduction require scarce resources, and aggression and cooperation are two ways to get them.

▶ Aggression often results from negative affect, which can be caused by almost anything—from being insulted to being hot. The likelihood that a person will aggress when they feel negative affect is determined both by biological factors (such as testosterone level) and cultural factors (such as geography).

▶ Cooperation is beneficial but risky, and one strategy for reducing its risks is to form groups whose members are biased in favour of each other. Unfortunately, groups often decide and behave badly.

▶ Although behaviours that appear to be altruistic often have hidden benefits for the person who does them, there is little doubt that human beings can behave altruistically.

▶ Both biology and culture tend to make the costs of reproduction higher for women than for men, which is one reason why women tend to be choosier when selecting potential mates.

▶ Attraction is determined by situational factors (such as proximity), physical factors (such as symmetry), and psychological factors (such as similarity).

▶ Human reproduction usually occurs within the context of a long-term relationship. People weigh the costs and benefits of their relationships and tend to dissolve them when they think they can or should do better, when they and their partners have very different cost–benefit ratios, or when they have little invested in the relationship.

# Social Influence: Controlling People

Those of us who grew up watching cartoons on Saturday mornings have usually thought a bit about which of the standard superpowers we would most like to have. Super strength and super speed have obvious benefits, invisibility and X-ray vision could be interesting as well as lucrative, and there is a lot to be said for flying. But when it comes right down to it, the ability to control other people would probably be the most useful. After all, who needs to lift a tractor or catch a bad guy if someone else can be convinced to do it? The things we want from life—gourmet food, interesting jobs, big houses, fancy cars—can be given to us by others, and the things we want most—loving families, loyal friends, admiring children, appreciative employers—cannot be had in any other way.

**Social influence** is *the ability to control another person's behaviour* (Cialdini & Goldstein, 2004). But how does it work? If you want someone to give you their time, money, allegiance, or affection, you would be wise to consider first what it is *they* want. People have three basic motivations that make them susceptible to social influence (Bargh, Gollwitzer, & Oettingen, 2010; Fiske, 2010). First, people are motivated to experience pleasure and to avoid experiencing pain (the *hedonic motive*). Second,

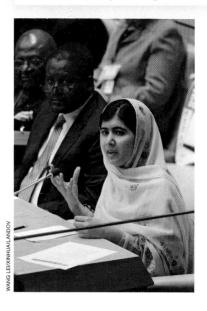

Malala Yousafzai, a 15-year-old Pakistani girl who stood up for women's rights despite being hunted by the Taliban, was named one of the world's 100 most influential people by *Time* magazine.

people are motivated to be accepted and to avoid being rejected (the *approval motive*). Third, people are motivated to believe what is right and to avoid believing what is wrong (the *accuracy motive*). As you will see, most social influence attempts appeal to one or more of these motives.

## The Hedonic Motive: Pleasure Is Better Than Pain

If there is an animal that prefers pain to pleasure it must be very good at hiding because no one has ever seen it. Pleasure seeking is the most basic of all motives, and social influence often involves creating situations in which others can achieve more pleasure by doing what we want them to do than by doing something else. Parents, teachers, governments, and businesses influence our behaviour by offering rewards and threatening punishments (see **FIGURE 13.8**). There is nothing mysterious about how these influence attempts work, and

> **How effective are rewards and punishments?**

they are often quite effective. When the Republic of Singapore warned its citizens that anyone caught chewing gum in public would face a year in prison and a $5500 fine, the rest of the world was outraged; but when the outrage subsided, it was hard to ignore the fact that gum chewing in Singapore had fallen to an all-time low. A good caning gets your attention every time.

You will recall from the Memory chapter that even a sea slug will repeat behaviours that are followed by rewards and avoid behaviours that are followed by punishments. Although the same is generally true of human beings, there are some instances in which rewards and punishments can backfire. For example, children in one study were allowed to play with coloured markers and then some were given a "Good Player Award." When the children were given markers the next day, those who had received an award were less likely to play with them than were those who had not received an award (Lepper, Greene, & Nisbett, 1973). Why? Because children who had received an award the first day came to think of drawing as something one does to receive rewards, and if no one was going to give them an award, then why the heck should they do it (Deci, Koestner, & Ryan, 1999)? Similarly, rewards and punishments can

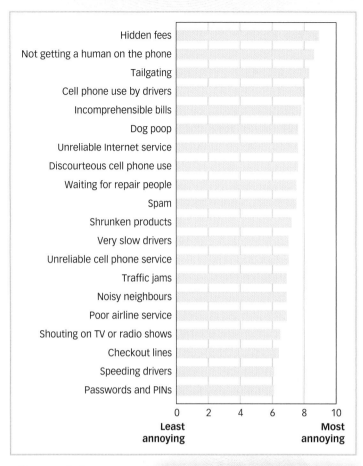

| | |
|---|---|
| Hidden fees | |
| Not getting a human on the phone | |
| Tailgating | |
| Cell phone use by drivers | |
| Incomprehensible bills | |
| Dog poop | |
| Unreliable Internet service | |
| Discourteous cell phone use | |
| Waiting for repair people | |
| Spam | |
| Shrunken products | |
| Very slow drivers | |
| Unreliable cell phone service | |
| Traffic jams | |
| Noisy neighbours | |
| Poor airline service | |
| Shouting on TV or radio shows | |
| Checkout lines | |
| Speeding drivers | |
| Passwords and PINs | |

0   2   4   6   8   10
**Least annoying**      **Most annoying**

Other people are the source of most rewards—and, it appears, most punishments, too. In a 2010 survey that asked Americans to identify the things that annoyed them most, 19 of the top 20 annoyances were caused by other people. The remaining annoyance was caused by other people's dogs.

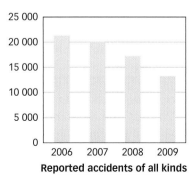

25 000
20 000
15 000
10 000
5 000
0
2006   2007   2008   2009
**Reported accidents of all kinds among drivers under 18 in Massachusetts**

◄ Figure **13.8 The Cost of Speeding** The penalty for speeding in Massachusetts used to be a modest fine. In 2006, the legislature changed the law so that drivers under 18 who are caught speeding now lose their licenses for 90 days—and to get them back they have to pay $500, attend 8 hours of training classes, and retake the state's driving exam. Guess what? Deaths among drivers under 18 fell by 38 percent in just 3 years. In other words, more than 8000 young lives were saved by appealing to the hedonic motive.

http://www.boston.com/news/local/massachusetts/articles/2010/04/18/steep_drop_in_teen_driver_fatalities/

# CULTURE & COMMUNITY

## Free Parking

People do not like to be manipulated, and they get upset when someone threatens their freedom to do as they wish. Is this a uniquely Western reaction? To find out, psychologist Eva Jonas and her colleagues asked American university students one of two favours and then measured how irritated they felt (Jonas et al., 2009). In one case, they asked students if they would give up their right to park on campus for a week ("Would you mind if I used your parking card so I can participate in a research project in this building?"). In the other case, they asked students if they would give up *everyone's* right to park on campus for a week ("Would you mind if we closed the entire parking lot for a tennis tournament?"). How did students react to these requests?

It depended on their culture. As the figure shows, European American students were more irritated by a request that limited their freedom than by a request that limited everyone's freedom ("If nobody can park, that's inconvenient. But if everybody except *me* can park, that's unfair!"). But Latino and Asian American students had precisely the opposite reactions ("The needs of the requestor outweigh the needs of one student, but they do not outweigh the needs of all students"). It appears that people do indeed value freedom—but not necessarily their own.

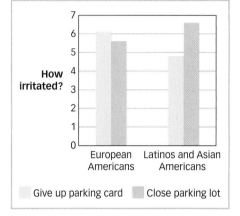

How irritated?

European Americans — Latinos and Asian Americans

▢ Give up parking card  ▮ Close parking lot

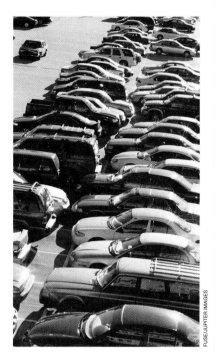

FUSE/JUPITER IMAGES

backfire simply because people do not like being manipulated with them. Researchers placed signs in two restrooms on a university campus: "Please do not write on these walls" and "Do not write on these walls under any circumstances." Two weeks later, the walls in the second restroom had more graffiti on the walls, presumably because students did not appreciate the threatening tone of the second sign and wrote on the walls just to prove that they could (Pennebaker & Sanders, 1976).

## The Approval Motive: Acceptance Is Better Than Rejection

Other people stand between us and starvation, predation, loneliness, and all the other things that make getting shipwrecked such an unpopular pastime. We depend on others for safety, sustenance, and solidarity, and so we are powerfully motivated to have others like us, accept us, and approve of us (Baumeister & Leary, 1995; Leary, 2010). Like the hedonic motive, this motive leaves us vulnerable to social influence.

### Normative Influence

Consider the many things you know about elevators. When you get on an elevator you are supposed to face forward and not talk to the person next to you even if you were talking to that person before you got on the elevator unless you are the only two people on the elevator in which case it is okay to talk and face sideways but still not backward. Although no one ever taught you this rule, you probably picked it up somewhere along the way. The unwritten rules that govern social behaviour are called **norms,** which are *customary standards for behaviour that are widely shared by members of a culture* (Cialdini, 2013; Miller & Prentice, 1996). We learn norms with exceptional ease and we obey them with exceptional fidelity because we know that if we do not, others will

> **How are we influenced by other people's behaviour?**

**norms**
Customary standards for behaviour that are widely shared by members of a culture.

**norm of reciprocity**
The unwritten rule that people should benefit those who have benefitted them.

**normative influence**
A phenomenon that occurs when another person's behaviour provides information about what is appropriate.

**door-in-the-face technique**
An influence strategy that involves getting someone to deny an initial request.

**conformity**
The tendency to do what others do simply because others are doing it.

not approve of us. For example, every human culture has a **norm of reciprocity,** which is *the unwritten rule that people should benefit those who have benefitted them* (Gouldner, 1960). When a friend buys you lunch, you return the favour; and if you do not, your friend gets miffed. Indeed, the norm of reciprocity is so strong that when researchers randomly pulled the names of strangers from a telephone directory and sent them all Christmas cards, they received Christmas cards back from most (Kunz & Woolcott, 1976).

Norms are a powerful weapon in the game of social influence. **Normative influence** occurs when *another person's behaviour provides information about what is appropriate* (see **FIGURE 13.9**). For example, waiters know all about the norm of reciprocity, which is why they often give customers a piece of candy along with the bill. Studies show that customers who receive a candy feel obligated to do "a little extra" for the waiter who did "a little extra" for them (Strohmetz et al., 2002). Indeed, people will sometimes refuse small gifts precisely because they do not want to feel indebted to the gift giver (Shen, Wan, & Wyer, 2011).

The norm of reciprocity involves swapping, but the thing being swapped does not have to be a favour. The **door-in-the-face technique** is *an influence strategy that involves getting someone to deny an initial request.* Here is how it works: You ask someone for something more valuable than you really want, you wait for that person to refuse (to "slam the door in your face"), and then you ask the person for what you really want. For example, when researchers asked university students to volunteer to supervise adolescents who were going on a field trip, only 17 percent of the students agreed. But when the researchers first asked students to commit to spending 2 hours per week for 2 years working at a youth detention centre (to which every one of the students said no) and *then* asked them to supervise a field trip, 50 percent of the students agreed (Cialdini et al., 1975). Why? The norm of reciprocity! The researchers began by asking for a large favour, which the student refused. Then the researchers made a concession by asking for a smaller favour. Because the researchers made a concession, the norm of reciprocity demanded that the student make one too—and half of them did!

## Conformity

People can influence us by invoking familiar norms, such as the norm of reciprocity. But if you have ever found yourself sneaking a peek at the diner next to you, hoping to

> **Why do we do what we see other people doing?**

discover whether the little fork is supposed to be used for the shrimp or the salad, then you know that other people can influence us by defining *new* norms in ambiguous, confusing, or novel situations. **Conformity** is *the tendency to do what others do simply because others are doing it,* and it results in part from normative influence.

In a classic study, psychologist Solomon Asch had participants sit in a room with seven other people who appeared to be ordinary participants, but who were actually trained actors (Asch, 1951, 1956). An experimenter explained that the participants would be shown cards with three printed lines and that his or her job was simply to say which of the three lines matched a "standard line" that was printed on another card (see **FIGURE 13.10** on the next page). The experimenter held up a card and then

**On average, your risk of becoming obese increases by ...**

. . . **57%** if someone you consider a friend becomes obese.

. . . **171%** if a very close friend becomes obese.

. . . **100%** if you are a man and your male friend becomes obese.

. . . **38%** if you are a woman and your female friend becomes obese.

. . . **37%** if your spouse becomes obese.

. . . **40%** if one of your siblings becomes obese.

. . . **67%** if you are a woman and your sister becomes obese.

. . . **44%** if you are a man and your brother becomes obese.

©FRANCIS DEAN/DEAN PICTURES/THE IMAGE WORKS

▲ Figure **13.9** **The Perils of Connection** Other people's behaviour defines what is "normal," which is one of the reasons why obesity "spreads" through social networks (Christakis & Fowler, 2007).

*Source:* Analysis of 12 067 participants in the Framingham Heart Study from 1971 to 2003 James Abundis/Globe Staff

Have you ever wondered which big spender left the bill as a tip? In fact, the bills are often put there by the very people you are tipping because they know that the presence of notes will suggest to you that others are leaving big tips and that it would be socially appropriate for you to do the same. By the way, the customary gratuity for someone who writes a textbook for you is 15 percent. But most students spend more.

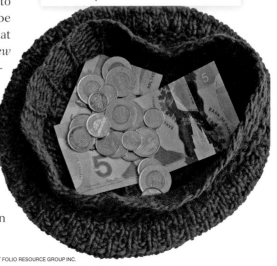

FIRST FOLIO RESOURCE GROUP INC.

The perplexed research participant (*centre*), flanked by confederates (who are "in" on the experiment), is on the verge of conformity in one of Solomon Asch's line-judging experiments.

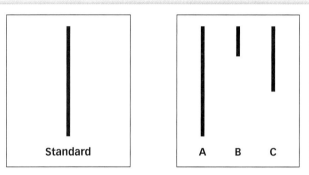

▲ Figure **13.10** **Asch's Conformity Study** If you were asked which of the lines on the right (A, B, or C) matches the standard line on the left, what would you say? Research on conformity suggests that your answer would depend, in part, on how other people in the room answered the same question.

asked each person to answer in turn. The real participant was among the last to be called on. Everything went well on the first two trials, but then on the third trial something really strange happened: the actors all began giving the same wrong answer! What did the real participants do? Seventy-five percent of them conformed and announced the wrong answer on at least one trial. Subsequent research has shown that these participants did not actually misperceive the length of the lines, but were instead succumbing to normative influence (Asch, 1955; Nemeth & Chiles, 1988). Giving the wrong answer was apparently "the right thing to do" and so participants did it.

The behaviour of others can tell us what is proper, appropriate, expected, and accepted (in other words, it can define a norm) and once a norm is defined, we feel obliged to honour it. When a Holiday Inn in Tempe, Arizona, left a variety of different "message cards" in guests' bathrooms in the hopes of convincing those guests to reuse their towels rather than laundering them every day, it discovered that the single most effective message was the one that simply read: "Seventy five percent of our guests use their towels more than once" (Cialdini, 2005). When the electricity provider in Sacramento, California randomly selected 35 000 customers and sent them electric bills showing how their energy consumption compared to that of their neighbours (see **FIGURE 13.11**), consumption fell by 2 percent (Kaufman, 2009). Clearly, normative influence can be a force for good.

## Obedience

Other people's behaviour can provide information about norms, but in most situations there are a few people whom we all recognize as having special authority both to define the norms and to enforce them. The guy who works at the movie theatre may be some high school fanboy with a bad haircut and a 10:00 p.m. curfew, but in the context of the theatre, he is the authority. So when he asks you to put away your cell

▶ Figure **13.11** **Normative Influence at Home** In 2008, the Sacramento Municipal Utility District (the electricity provider in Sacramento, California) randomly selected 35 000 of its customers and sent them electric bills like the one shown here. The bill did not just show how much electricity the customer had used; it also showed how much electricity was used by neighbours who lived in similar-sized homes. When the utility crunched the numbers, they discovered that customers who had received this "compare with the neighbours" bill had reduced their electricity consumption by 2 percent compared to customers who had received a traditional bill (Kaufman, 2009). Clearly, normative influence can be a force for good.

# OTHER VOICES

## 91% of All Students Read This Box and Love It

**Tina Rosenberg** is an editorial writer for the *New York Times*. Her 1995 book *The Haunted Land: Facing Europe's Ghosts After Communism* won both the Pulitzer Prize and the National Book Award.

PHOTO: NOAH GREENBERG PHOTOGRAPHY

Binge drinking is a problem on university campuses across North America (Wechsler & Nelson, 2001). About half of all students report doing it, and those who do are much more likely to miss classes, get behind in their school work, drive drunk, and have unprotected sex. So what to do?

Universities have tried a number of remedies—from education to abstinence—and none of them has worked particularly well. But lately, some schools have taken a new approach called "social norming." Although this approach is surprisingly effective, it is also controversial. Tina Rosenberg's most recent book is *Join the Club: How Peer Pressure Can Transform the World*. In the following essay, she describes both the technique and the controversy.

... Like most universities, Northern Illinois University in DeKalb has a problem with heavy drinking. In the 1980s, the school was trying to cut down on student use of alcohol with the usual strategies. One campaign warned teenagers of the consequences of heavy drinking. "It was the 'don't run with a sharp stick you will poke your eye out' theory of behaviour change," said Michael Haines, who was the coordinator of the school's Health Enhancement Services. When that did not work, Haines tried combining the scare approach with information on how to be well: "It's O.K. to drink if you don't drink too much—but if you do, bad things will happen to you."

That one failed, too. In 1989, 45 percent of students surveyed said they drank more than five drinks at parties. This percentage was slightly higher than when the campaigns began. And students thought heavy drinking was even more common; they believed that 69 percent of their peers drank that much at parties.

But by then Haines had something new to try. In 1987 he had attended a conference on alcohol in higher education sponsored by the United States Department of Education. There Wes Perkins, a professor of sociology at Hobart and William Smith Colleges, and Alan Berkowitz, a psychologist in the school's counseling centre, presented a paper that they had just published on how student drinking is affected by peers. "There are decades of research on peer influence—that's nothing new," Perkins said at the meeting. What was new was their survey showing that when students were asked how much their peers drank, they grossly overestimated the amount. If the students were responding to peer pressure, the researchers said, it was coming from imaginary peers.

The "aha!" conclusion Perkins and Berkowitz drew was this: maybe students' drinking behaviour could be changed by just telling them the truth. ...

Haines surveyed students at Northern Illinois University and found that they also had a distorted view of how much their peers drink. He decided to try a new campaign, with the theme "most students drink moderately." The centrepiece of the campaign was a series of ads in the *Northern Star*, the campus newspaper, with pictures of students and the caption "two thirds of Northern Illinois University students (72%) drink 5 or fewer drinks when they 'party'."

Haines's staff also made posters with campus drinking facts and told students that if they had those posters on the wall when an inspector came around, they would earn $5. (35 percent of the students did have them posted when inspected.) Later they made buttons for students in the fraternity and sorority system—these students drank more heavily—that said "Most of Us," and offered another $5 for being caught wearing one. The buttons were deliberately cryptic, to start a conversation.

After the first year of the social norming campaign, the perception of heavy drinking had fallen from 69 to 61 percent. Actual heavy drinking fell from 45 to 38 percent. The campaign went on for a decade, and at the end of it NIU students believed that 33 percent of their fellow students were episodic heavy drinkers, and only 25 percent really were—a decline in heavy drinking of 44 percent. ...

Why isn't this idea more widely used? One reason is that it can be controversial. Telling [university] students "most of you drink moderately" is very different than saying "don't drink." (It's so different, in fact, that the National Social Norms Institute, with headquarters at the University of Virginia, gets its money from Anheuser Busch—a decision that has undercut support for the idea of social norming.) The approach angers people who lobby for a strong, unmuddied message of disapproval—even though, of course, disapproval does not reduce bad behavior, and social norming does.

Social norming is a powerful but controversial tool for changing behaviour. When we tell students about drinking on campus, should we tell them what is true (even if that truth is a bit ugly) or should we tell them what is best (even if they are unlikely to do it)?

and stop texting in the middle of the movie, you do as you are told. **Obedience** is *the tendency to do what powerful people tell us to do.*

Why do we obey powerful people? Although powerful people are often capable of rewarding and punishing us, research shows that much of their influence is *normative* (Tyler, 1990). Psychologist Stanley Milgram (1963) demonstrated this in one of psychology's most infamous experiments. The participants in this experiment met a middle-aged man who was introduced as another participant, but who was actually a trained actor. An

**Why do we do what others tell us to do?**

**obedience**
The tendency to do what powerful people tell us to do.

▶ Figure **13.12 Milgram's Obedience Studies** The learner (*left*) is being hooked up to the shock generator (*right*) that was used in Stanley Milgram's obedience studies.

In 1971, psychologist Philip Zimbardo built a mock prison in the basement of the Stanford Psychology Department and invited two dozen students to play the roles of either a prisoner or a guard. After 6 days he was forced to halt his observational study because many of the guards had become so abusive toward the prisoners that he feared for their safety (Haney, Banks, & Zimbardo, 1973).

experimenter in a lab coat explained that the participant would play the role of *teacher* and the actor would play the role of *learner*. The teacher and learner would sit in different rooms, the teacher would read words to the learner over a microphone, and the learner would then repeat the words back to the teacher. If the learner made a mistake, the teacher would press a button that delivered an electric shock to the learner (see **FIGURE 13.12**). The shock-generating machine (which was totally fake) offered 30 levels of shock, ranging from 15 V (labelled *slight shock*) to 450 V (labelled *Danger: severe shock*).

After the learner was strapped into his chair, the experiment began. When the learner made his first mistake, the participant dutifully delivered a 15-V shock. As the learner made more mistakes, he received more shocks. When the participant delivered the 75-V shock, the learner cried out in pain. At 150 V, the learner screamed, "Get me out of here. I told you I have heart trouble … I refuse to go on. Let me out!" With every shock, the learner's screams became more agonized as he pleaded pitifully for his freedom. Then, after receiving the 330-V shock, the learner stopped responding altogether. Participants were naturally upset by all this and typically asked the experimenter to stop, but the experimenter simply replied, "You have no choice; you must go on." The experimenter never threatened the participant with punishment of any kind. Rather, he just stood there with his clipboard in hand and calmly instructed the participant to continue. So what did the participants do? Eighty percent of the participants continued to shock the learner even after he screamed, complained, pleaded, and then fell silent. And 62 percent went all the way, delivering the highest possible voltage. Although Milgram's study was conducted nearly half a century ago, a recent replication revealed about the same rate of obedience (Burger, 2009).

Were these people psychopathic sadists? Would normal people electrocute a stranger just because some guy in a lab coat told them to? The answer, it seems, is *yes*—as long as *normal* means being sensitive to social norms. The participants in this experiment knew that hurting others is *often* wrong but not *always* wrong: Doctors give painful injections, and teachers give painful exams. There are many situations in which it is permissible—and even desirable—to cause someone to suffer in the service of a higher goal. The experimenter's calm demeanour and persistent instruction suggested that he, and not the participant, knew what was appropriate in this particular situation, and so the participant did as ordered. Subsequent research confirmed that participants' obedience was due to normative pressure. When the experimenter's authority to define the norm was undermined (e.g., when a second experimenter appeared to disagree with the first or when the instructions were given by a person who was not wearing a lab coat), participants rarely obeyed the instructions. Other factors influenced obedience. For example, obedience dropped dramatically if the experimenter was not physically present, but gave orders remotely (by telephone or voice recording). Obedience also dropped if the participant was in the same room as the learner, so the participant could see as well as hear him—but the obedience rate was still 40 percent. In another condition, the learner received a shock only when his hand rested on a metal shockplate.

At the 150-V level, the learner demanded to be let free, and refused to put his hand on the shockplate. The experimenter then ordered the naive participant to force the learner's hand onto the plate. Even in this condition, 30 percent of participants obeyed (Milgram, 1974; Miller, 1986).

## The Accuracy Motive: Right Is Better Than Wrong

When you are hungry, you open the refrigerator and grab an apple because you know that apples (a) taste good and (b) are in the refrigerator. This action, like most actions, relies on both an **attitude,** which is *an enduring positive or negative evaluation of an object or event,* and a **belief,** which is *an enduring piece of knowledge about an object or event.* In a sense, our attitudes tell us what we should do (*eat an apple*) and our beliefs tell us how to do it (*start by opening the fridge*). If our attitudes or beliefs are inaccurate—that is, if we cannot tell good from bad or true from false—then our actions are likely to be fruitless. Because we rely so much on our attitudes and beliefs, it is not surprising that we are motivated to have the right ones, and that motivation leaves us vulnerable to social influence.

### Informational Influence

If everyone in the mall suddenly ran screaming for the exit, you would probably join them—not because you were afraid that they would disapprove of you if you did not—but because their behaviour would suggest to you that there was something

> How do informational and normative influences differ?

worth running from. **Informational influence** occurs when *another person's behaviour provides information about what is true.* You can observe the power of informational influence yourself just by standing in the middle of the sidewalk, tilting back your head, and staring at the top of a tall building. Research shows that within just a few minutes, other people will stop and stare too (Milgram, Bickman, & Berkowitz, 1969). Why? They will assume that if you are looking, then there must be something worth looking at.

You are the constant target of informational influence. When a salesperson tells you that "most people buy the iPad with extra memory," she is artfully suggesting that you should take other people's behaviour as information about the product. Advertisements that refer to soft drinks as "popular" or books as "best sellers" are reminding you that other people are buying these particular drinks and books, which suggests that they know something you do not and that you would be wise to follow their example.

Situation comedies provide laugh tracks because the producers know that when you hear other people laughing, you will mindlessly assume that something must be funny (Fein, Goethals, & Kugler, 2007; Nosanchuk & Lightstone, 1974). Bars and nightclubs make people stand in line even when there is plenty of room inside because they know that passersby will see the line and assume that the club is worth

**attitude**
An enduring positive or negative evaluation of an object or event.

**belief**
An enduring piece of knowledge about an object or event.

**informational influence**
A phenomenon that occurs when another person's behaviour provides information about what is true.

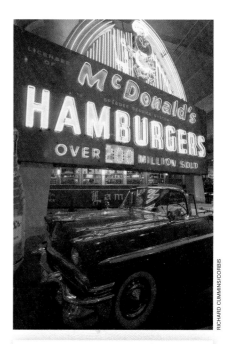

RICHARD CUMMINS/CORBIS

Is McDonald's trying to keep track of sales from the parking lot? Probably not. Rather, they want you to know that other people are buying their hamburgers, which suggests that they are worth buying.

BRIAN GABLE/THE GLOBE AND MAIL/CP IMAGES

Media sources often broadcast the results of polls conducted during elections. Such polls provide information about how well the parties are doing in a campaign. But does that information affect voting behaviour? Research suggests that voters are susceptible to a "bandwagon effect": they will be more likely to vote for a candidate if a poll tells them (accurately or inaccurately) that that candidate is favoured by the electorate (Mehrabian, 1998; Morwitz & Pluzinski, 1996). Although the effect is small, it could significantly influence the results of a closely contested election. Is this a good or bad form of informational influence?

**persuasion**
A phenomenon that occurs when a person's attitudes or beliefs are influenced by a communication from another person.

**systematic persuasion**
The process by which attitudes or beliefs are changed by appeals to reason.

**heuristic persuasion**
The process by which attitudes or beliefs are changed by appeals to habit or emotion.

Why do advertisers hire celebrities to endorse shoes but not cars? Cars are relatively expensive, so people are motivated to process information about them and are therefore persuaded by facts about quality and price. Shoes are relatively inexpensive, so people are not motivated to process information about them and are therefore persuaded by celebrity endorsements.

waiting for. In short, the world is full of objects and events that we know little about, and we can often cure our ignorance by paying attention to the way in which others are acting toward them. Alas, the very thing that makes us open to information leaves us open to manipulation as well.

## Persuasion

When the next federal election rolls around, two things will happen. First, the candidates will say that they intend to win your vote by making arguments that focus on the issues. Second, the candidates will then avoid arguments, ignore issues, and attempt to win your vote with a variety of cheap tricks and emotional appeals. What the candidates promise to do and what they actually do reflect two basic forms of **persuasion,** which occurs when *a person's attitudes or beliefs are influenced by a communication from another person* (Albarracín & Vargas, 2010; Petty & Wegener, 1998). The candidates will promise to persuade you by demonstrating that their positions on the issues are the most practical, intelligent, fair, and beneficial. Having made that promise, they will then devote most of their financial resources to persuading you by other means: for example, by dressing nicely and smiling a lot, by flipping burgers at barbeques and wearing cardigans, by repeatedly "dissing" the other parties' candidates, and so on. In other words, the candidates will promise to engage in **systematic persuasion,** which refers to *the process by which attitudes or beliefs are changed by appeals to reason,* but they will spend most of their time and money engaged in **heuristic persuasion,** which refers to *the process by which attitudes or beliefs are changed by appeals to habit or emotion* (Chaiken, 1980; Petty & Cacioppo, 1986).

How do these two forms of persuasion work? *Systematic persuasion* appeals to logic and reason, and assumes that people will be more persuaded when evidence and arguments are strong rather than weak. *Heuristic persuasion* appeals to habit and emotion, and assumes that rather than weighing evidence and analyzing arguments, people will often use *heuristics* (simple shortcuts or "rules of thumb") to help them decide whether to believe a communication (see the Language and Thought chapter). Which form of persuasion will be more effective depends on whether the person is willing and able to weigh evidence and analyze arguments.

In one study, university students heard a speech that contained either strong or weak arguments in favour of instituting comprehensive exams at their school (Petty, Cacioppo, & Goldman, 1981). Some

> **When is it more effective to appeal to reason or to emotion?**

students were told that the speaker was a university professor, and others were told that the speaker was a high school student—a bit of information that could be used as a shortcut to decide whether to believe the speech. Some students were told that their university was considering implementing these exams right away, whereas others were told that their university was considering implementing these exams in 10 years—a bit of information that made students feel motivated or unmotivated to analyze the evidence. As **FIGURE 13.13** (on the next page) shows, when students were motivated to analyze the evidence, they were systematically persuaded—that is, their attitudes and beliefs were influenced by the strength of the arguments but not by the status of the speaker. But when students were

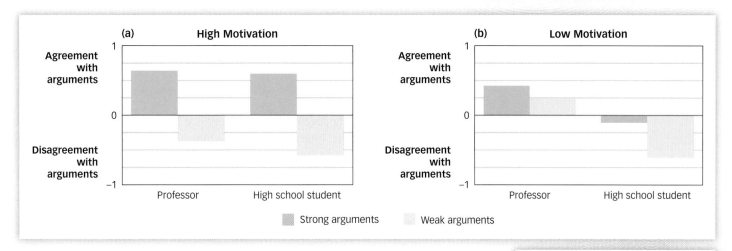

**(a) High Motivation**

Agreement with arguments

Disagreement with arguments

Professor    High school student

**(b) Low Motivation**

Agreement with arguments

Disagreement with arguments

Professor    High school student

Strong arguments        Weak arguments

not motivated to analyze the evidence, they were heuristically persuaded—that is, their attitudes and beliefs were influenced by the status of the speaker but not by the strength of the arguments.

## Consistency

If a friend told you that rabbits had just staged a coup in Antarctica and were halting all carrot exports, you probably would not turn on CBC. You would know right away that your friend was joking (or stupid) because the statement is logically inconsistent with other things that you know are true, for example, that rabbits do not foment revolution and that Antarctica does not export carrots. People evaluate the accuracy of new beliefs by assessing their *consistency* with old beliefs, and although this is not a fool-proof method for determining whether something is true, it provides a pretty good approximation. We are motivated to be accurate, and because consistency is a rough measure of accuracy, we are motivated to be consistent as well (Cialdini, Trost, & Newsom, 1995).

> Why do we care about being consistent?

That motivation leaves us vulnerable to social influence. For example, the **foot-in-the-door technique** involves *making a small request and then following it with a larger request* (Burger, 1999; Freedman & Fraser, 1966). In one study (Pliner et al., 1974), the experimenter went to a Toronto neighbourhood and knocked on doors asking for donations for the Cancer Society. Residents in about one third of the houses in the neighbourhood were simply asked whether they would donate, and 46 percent said they would. The average donation among those who gave money was 58 cents (this was 1974!). The evening before the donation drive, another experimenter canvassed other houses in the neighbourhood, asking residents whether they would be willing to wear a daffodil pin the next day to help publicize the fundraising drive. All residents complied with this request. The next evening, when asked to donate to the Cancer Society, almost twice the proportion of these people (77 percent) said they would, and those people donated an average that was nearly twice as high (92 cents) as in the other group. Why would residents be more likely to grant two requests than one?

Just imagine how the homeowners in the second group felt. They had already agreed to wear a pin publicizing the Cancer Society funding drive, and yet they knew they did not want to donate much money. As they wrestled with this inconsistency, they probably began to experience a feeling called **cognitive dissonance,** which is *an unpleasant state that arises when a person recognizes the inconsistency of his or her actions, attitudes, or beliefs* (Festinger, 1957). When people experience cognitive dissonance they naturally try to alleviate it, and one way to alleviate cognitive dissonance

▲ Figure **13.13** **Systematic and Heuristic Persuasion** (*a*) *Systematic persuasion.* When students were motivated to analyze arguments because they would be personally affected by them, their attitudes were influenced by the strength of the arguments (strong arguments were more persuasive than weak arguments), but not by the status of the communicator (the professor was not more persuasive than the high school student). (*b*) *Heuristic persuasion.* When students were not motivated to analyze arguments because they would not be personally affected by them, their attitudes were influenced by the status of the communicator (the professor was more persuasive than the high school student), but not by the strength of the arguments (strong arguments were no more persuasive than weak arguments) (Petty, Cacioppo, & Goldman, 1981).

**foot-in-the-door technique**
A technique that involves making a small request and following it with a larger request.

**cognitive dissonance**
An unpleasant state that arises when a person recognizes the inconsistency of his or her actions, attitudes, or beliefs.

is to restore consistency among one's actions, attitudes, and beliefs (Aronson, 1969; Cooper & Fazio, 1984). Donating generously to the Cancer Society accomplished that. Recent research shows that this phenomenon can be used to good effect: Hotel guests who were asked at check-in to commit to being a "Friend of the Earth" were 25 percent more likely to re-use their towels during their stay (Baca-Motes et al., 2013).

The fact that we can alleviate cognitive dissonance by changing our actions, attitudes, or beliefs has some interesting implications. For instance, in one study, female university students applied to join a weekly discussion on "the psychology of sex." Women in the control group were allowed to join the discussion, but women in the experimental group were allowed to join the discussion only after first passing an embarrassing test that involved reading pornographic fiction to a strange man. Although the carefully staged discussion was as dull as possible, women in the experimental group found it more interesting than did women in the control group (Aronson & Mills, 1958). Why? Women in the experimental group knew that they had paid a steep price to join the group ("I read all that porn out loud!"), but that belief was inconsistent with the belief that the discussion was worthless. As such, the women experienced cognitive dissonance, which they alleviated by changing their beliefs about the value of the discussion (see the top half of **FIGURE 13.14**). We normally think that people pay for things because they value them, but as this study shows, people sometimes value things because they have paid for them—with money, time, attention, blood, sweat, or tears. It is little wonder that some fraternities use hazing to breed loyalty, that some religions require their adherents to make large personal or monetary sacrifices, that some gourmet restaurants charge outrageous amounts to keep their patrons coming back, or that some men and women play hard to get to maintain their suitors' interest.

We are motivated to be consistent, but there are inevitably times when we just cannot, for example, when we tell a friend that her new hairstyle is "daring" when it actually resembles a wet skunk after an unfortunate encounter with a snowblower. Why do not we experience cognitive dissonance under such circumstances and come to believe our own lies? Because while telling a friend that her hairstyle is daring is inconsistent with the belief that her hairstyle is hideous, it is perfectly consistent with the belief that one should be nice to one's friends. When small inconsistencies are *justified* by large consistencies, cognitive dissonance is reduced.

> **What happens when we are inconsistent?**

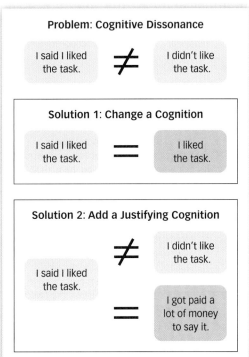

**Problem: Cognitive Dissonance**

I said I liked the task.  ≠  I didn't like the task.

**Solution 1: Change a Cognition**

I said I liked the task.  =  I liked the task.

**Solution 2: Add a Justifying Cognition**

I said I liked the task.  ≠  I didn't like the task.

=  I got paid a lot of money to say it.

▲ Figure **13.14 Alleviating Cognitive Dissonance** Suffering for something of little value can cause cognitive dissonance. One way to alleviate that dissonance is to change your belief about the value of the thing you suffered for.

University of Toronto engineering students engage in one of the many rituals associated with Frosh Week.

For example, participants in one study were asked to perform a dull task that involved turning knobs one way, then the other way, and then back again. After the participants were sufficiently bored, the experimenter explained that he desperately needed a few more people to volunteer for the study, and he asked the participants to go into the hallway, find another person, and tell that person that the knob-turning task was great fun. The experimenter offered some participants $1 to tell this lie, and he offered other participants $20. All participants agreed to tell the lie, and after they did so, they were asked to report their true enjoyment of the knob-turning task. The results showed that participants liked the task *more* when they were paid $1 than $20 to lie about it (Festinger & Carlsmith, 1959). Why? Because the belief *this knob-turning task is dull* was inconsistent with the belief *I recommended the task to that person in the hallway,* but the latter belief was perfectly consistent with the belief that *$20 is a lot of money.* For some participants, the large payment justified the lie, so only those people who received the small payment experienced cognitive dissonance. As such, only the participants who received $1 felt the need to restore consistency by changing their beliefs about the enjoyableness of the task (see the bottom half of Figure 13.14).

**social cognition**
The processes by which people come to understand others.

## IN SUMMARY

▶ People are motivated to experience pleasure and avoid pain (the hedonic motive), and thus can be influenced by rewards and punishments, although these can sometimes backfire.

▶ People are motivated to attain the approval of others (the approval motive), and thus can be influenced by social norms, such as the norm of reciprocity. People often look to the behaviour of others to determine what is normative, and they often end up conforming or obeying, sometimes with disastrous results.

▶ People are motivated to know what is true (the accuracy motive), and thus can be influenced by other people's behaviours and communications. This motivation also causes them to seek consistency among their attitudes, beliefs, and actions.

# Social Cognition: Understanding People

Michael Bublé is sexy and talented. Whether or not you agree with that sentence, it almost certainly activated your medial prefrontal cortex, which is an area of your brain that is activated when you think about the attributes of other people but not about the attributes of inanimate objects such as houses or tools (Mitchell, Heatherton, & Macrae, 2002). Although most of your brain shows diminished activity when you are at rest, this area remains active all the time (Buckner, Andrews-Hanna, & Schacter, 2008). Why does your brain have a specific area that is dedicated to processing information about just *one* of the millions of objects you might encounter, and why is this area constantly switched on?

Of the millions of objects you might encounter, other human beings are the single most important. **Social cognition** is *the processes by which people come to understand others,* and your brain is doing it all day long. Whether you know it or not, your brain is constantly making inferences about others people's thoughts and feelings, beliefs and desires, abilities and aspirations, intentions, needs, and characters. It bases these inferences on two kinds of information: the categories to which people belong, and the things they do and say.

Thinking about singer Michael Bublé activates your medial prefrontal cortex. *Especially if it's a beautiful day. And even if he just hasn't met you yet.*

PIER MARCO TACCA/GETTY IMAGES

# The Wedding Planner

The human brain has nearly tripled in size in just 2 million years. The *social brain hypothesis* (Shultz & Dunbar, 2010) suggests that this happened primarily so that people could manage the everyday complexities of living in large social groups. What are those complexities?

Well, just think of what you would need to know in order to seat people at a wedding. Does Uncle Jacob like Grandma Nora, does Grandma Nora hate Cousin Caleb, and if so, does Uncle Jacob hate Cousin Caleb too? With a guest list of just 150 people there are more than 10 000 of these dyadic relationships to consider—and yet, people who cannot balance a chequebook or solve a Sudoku somehow manage to do tasks like this one all the time. Are people social savants?

In a recent study (Mason et al., 2010), researchers sought to answer this question by directly comparing people's abilities to solve social and nonsocial problems. The nonsocial problem involved drawing inferences about metals. Participants were told that there were two basic groups of metals, and that metals in the same group "attracted" each other, whereas

metals in different groups "repelled" each other. Then, over a series of trials, participants were told about the relationships between particular metals and were asked to draw inferences about the missing relationship. For example, participants were told that *gold* and *tin* were both repelled by *platinum*, and they were then asked to infer the relationship between *gold* and *tin*. (The correct answer is "They are attracted to each other.")

The experimenters also gave participants a social version of this problem. Participants were told about two groups of people. People who were in the same group were said to be attracted to each other, whereas people who were in different groups were said to be repelled by each other. Then, over a series of trials, participants learned about the relationships between particular people—for example, they learned that *Goldie* and *Tim* were both repelled by *Patrick*—and were then asked to infer the missing relationship between *Goldie* and *Tim*. (The correct answer is "They are attracted to each other.")

Although the social and nonsocial tasks were logically identical, results showed that participants were considerably faster *and* more accurate when drawing inferences about people than about metals. When the researchers replicated the study inside an MRI machine, they discovered that both tasks activated brain areas known to play a role in deductive reasoning, but that only the social task activated brain regions known to play a role in understanding other minds.

It appears that our ability to think about people outshines our ability to think about most everything else, which is good news for the social brain hypothesis—as well as for wedding planners far and wide.

## Stereotyping: Drawing Inferences from Categories

You will recall from the Language and Thought chapter that categorization is the process by which people identify a stimulus as a member of a class of related stimuli. Once we have identified a novel stimulus as a member of a category ("That's a textbook"), we can then use our knowledge of the category to make educated guesses about the properties of the novel stimulus ("It is probably expensive") and act accordingly ("I think I will borrow it from the library").

What we do with textbooks we also do with people. No, not the borrowing part. The educated guessing part. **Stereotyping** is *the process by which people draw inferences about others based on their knowledge of the categories to which others belong.* The moment we categorize a person as an adult, a male, a baseball player, and a Russian, we can use our knowledge of those categories to make some educated guesses about him, for example, that he shaves his face but not his legs, that he understands the infield fly rule, and that he knows more about Vladimir Putin than we do. When we offer children candy instead of cigarettes or ask gas station attendants for directions instead of financial advice, we are making inferences about people whom we have never met before based solely on their category membership. As these examples suggest, stereotyping is a very helpful process (Allport, 1954). And yet, ever since the word was coined by the journalist Walter Lippmann in 1936, it has had a distasteful connotation. Why? Because stereotyping

Stereotypes can be inaccurate. This man does not fit most people's stereotype of a police officer or a Sikh, but he is both.

**How are stereotypes useful?**

is a helpful process that can often produce harmful results, and it does so because stereotypes tend to have four properties: They are inaccurate, overused, self-perpetuating, and automatic.

## Stereotypes Can Be Inaccurate

The inferences we draw about individuals are only as accurate as our stereotypes about the categories to which they belong. Although there was no evidence to indicate that Jews were especially materialistic or that African Americans were especially lazy, American university students held such beliefs for most of the last century (Gilbert, 1951; Karlins, Coffman, & Walters, 1969; Katz & Braly, 1933). They were not born holding these beliefs, so how did they acquire them? There are only two ways to acquire a belief about anything: to see for yourself or to take somebody else's word for it. In fact, most of what we know about the members of human categories is hearsay—stuff we picked up from hearing other people talk. Many of the people who believe stereotypes about Jews or African Americans have never actually met a member of either group, and their beliefs are a result of listening too closely to what others told them. In the process of inheriting the wisdom of our culture, it is inevitable that we also will inherit its ignorance too.

But even direct observation can produce inaccurate stereotypes. For example, research participants in one study were shown a long series of positive and negative behaviours and were told that each behaviour had been performed by a member of one of two groups: Group A or Group B (see **FIGURE 13.15**). The behaviours were carefully arranged so that each group behaved negatively exactly one third of the time. However, there were more positive than negative behaviours in the series, and there were more members of Group A than of Group B. As such, negative behaviours were rarer than positive behaviours, and Group B members were rarer than Group A members. After seeing the behaviours, participants correctly reported that Group A had behaved negatively one third of the time. However, they incorrectly reported that Group B had behaved negatively more than *half* the time (Hamilton & Gifford, 1976).

Why did this happen? Bad behaviour was rare and being a member of Group B was rare. Thus, participants were especially likely to notice when the two co-occurred ("Aha! There's one of those unusual Group B people doing an unusually awful thing again"). These findings help explain why members of majority groups tend to overestimate the number of crimes (which are relatively rare events) committed by members of minority groups (who are relatively rare people, hence the word *m-i-n-o-r-i-t-y*). The point here is that even when we directly observe people, we can end up with inaccurate beliefs about the groups to which they belong.

## Stereotypes Can Be Overused

Because all thumbtacks are pretty much alike, our stereotypes about thumbtacks (small, cheap, painful when chewed) are quite useful. We will rarely be mistaken if we generalize from one thumbtack to another. But human categories are so variable that our stereotypes may offer only

**stereotyping**
The process by which people draw inferences about others based on their knowledge of the categories to which others belong.

|  | Good acts | Bad acts |
|---|---|---|
| Group A | ● ● ● ● ● <br> ● ● ● ● ● <br> ● ● ● ● ● <br> ● ● ● ● ● | ● ● <br> ● ● <br> ● ● <br> ● ● |
| Group B | ● ● <br> ● ● <br> ● ● | ● <br> ● <br> ● |

◀ Figure **13.15** **Seeing Correlations That Are not Really There** Both Group A and Group B each perform two-thirds good acts and one-third bad acts. However, Group B and bad acts are both rare, leading people to notice and remember their co-occurrence, which leads them to perceive a correlation between group membership and behaviour that is not really there.

> **Why might we have inaccurate beliefs about groups even after directly observing them?**

*"Great—now I'm gonna be suspicious of every poodle I meet."*

FARLEY KATZ/THE NEW YORKER COLLECTION WWW.CARTOONBANK.COM

the vaguest of clues about the individuals who populate those categories. You probably believe that men have greater upper body strength than women do, and this belief is right *on average*. But the upper body strength of individuals *within* each of these categories is so varied that you cannot easily predict how much weight a particular person can lift simply by knowing that person's gender. The inherent variability of human categories makes stereotypes much less useful than they seem.

Alas, we do not always recognize this because the mere act of categorizing a stimulus tends to warp our perceptions of that category's variability. For instance, participants in some studies were shown a series of lines of different lengths (see **FIGURE 13.16**) (McGarty & Turner, 1992; Tajfel & Wilkes, 1963). For one group of participants, the longest lines were labelled *Group A* and the shortest lines were labelled *Group B,* as they are on the right side of Figure 13.16. For the second group of participants, the lines were shown without these category labels, as they are on the left side of Figure 13.16. Interestingly, those participants who saw the category labels *overestimated* the similarity of the lines that shared a label and *underestimated* the similarity of lines that did not.

> How does categorization warp perception?

You have probably experienced this phenomenon yourself. For instance, we all identify colours as members of categories such as *blue* or *green,* and this leads us to overestimate the similarity of colours that share a category label and to underestimate the similarity of colours that do not. That is why we see discrete *bands* of colour when we look at rainbows, which are actually a smooth chromatic continuum (see **FIGURE 13.17**). When two cities are in the same country (London and Ottawa) people tend to underestimate their distance, but when two cities are in different countries (London and Cincinnati) they tend to overestimate their distance (Burris & Branscombe, 2005). Indeed, people believe that they are more likely to feel an earthquake that happens 370 km away when the earthquake happens in their province rather than a neighbouring province (Mishra & Mishra, 2010).

What is true of colours and cities is true of people as well. The mere act of categorizing people as blacks or whites, Jews or Gentiles, artists or accountants, can cause us to underestimate the variability within those categories ("All artists are wacky") and to overestimate the variability between them ("Artists are much wackier than accountants"). When we underestimate the variability of a human category, we overestimate how useful our stereotypes can be (Park & Hastie, 1987; Rubin, & Badea, 2012).

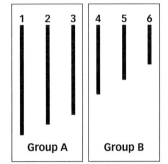

▲ Figure **13.16** **How Categorization Warps Perception** People who see the lines on the right tend to *overestimate the similarity* of lines 1 and 3 and *underestimate the similarity* of lines 3 and 4. Simply labelling lines 1–3 *Group A* and lines 4–6 *Group B* causes the lines within a group to seem more similar to each other than they really are, and the lines in different groups to seem more different from each other than they really are.

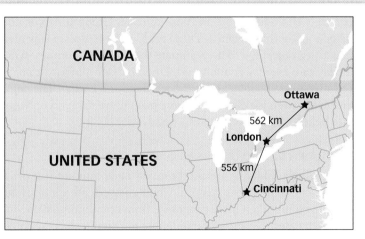

▶ Figure **13.17** **Perceiving Categories** Categorization can influence how we see colours and estimate distances.

## Stereotypes Can Be Self-Perpetuating

When we meet a truck driver who likes ballet more than football or a senior citizen who likes Drake more than Bach, why do not we simply

**In what way is a stereotype like a virus?**

abandon our stereotypes of these groups? The answer is that stereotypes tend to be self-perpetuating. Like viruses and parasites, once they take up residence inside us, they resist even our most concerted efforts to eradicate them. Here are three reasons why:

> When people know that observers have a negative stereotype about them, they may experience **stereotype threat**, which is *the fear of confirming the negative beliefs that others may hold* (Aronson & Steele, 2004; Schmader, Johns, & Forbes, 2008; Walton & Spencer, 2009). Ironically, this fear may cause them to behave in ways that confirm the very stereotype that threatened them. In one study (Steele & Aronson, 1995), African American and white students took a test, and half the students in each group were asked to list their race at the top of the exam. When students were not asked to list their race they performed at their academic level, but when students were asked to list their race, African American students became anxious about confirming a negative stereotype of their group, which caused them to perform well below their academic level (see **FIGURE 13.18**). Stereotypes perpetuate themselves in part by causing the stereotyped individual to behave in ways that confirm the stereotype.

> Even when people do *not* confirm stereotypes, observers often think they have. **Perceptual confirmation** is *the tendency for people to see what they expect to see* and this tendency helps perpetuate stereotypes. In one study, participants listened to a radio broadcast of a university basketball game and were asked to evaluate the performance of one of the players. Although all participants heard the same prerecorded game, some were led to believe that the player was African American and others were led to believe that the player was white. Participants' stereotypes led them to expect different performances from athletes of different ethnic origins—and the participants perceived just what they expected. Those who believed the player was African American thought he had demonstrated greater athletic ability but less intelligence than did those who thought he was white (Stone, Perry, & Darley, 1997). Stereotypes perpetuate themselves in part by biasing our perception of individuals, leading us to believe that those individuals have confirmed our stereotypes even when they have not (Fiske, 1998).

> So what happens when people clearly *disconfirm* our stereotypes? **Subtyping** is *the tendency for people who receive disconfirming evidence to modify their stereotypes rather than abandon them* (Weber & Crocker, 1983). For example, most of us think of people who work in public relations as sociable. In one study, participants learned about a PR agent who was *slightly* unsociable, and the results showed that their stereotypes about PR agents shifted a bit to accommodate this new information. So far, so good. But when participants learned about a PR agent who was *extremely* unsociable, their stereotypes did not change at all (Kunda & Oleson, 1997). Instead, they decided that extremely unsociable PR agent was "an exception to the rule," which allowed them to keep their stereotypes intact. Subtyping is a powerful method for preserving our stereotypes in the face of contradictory evidence.

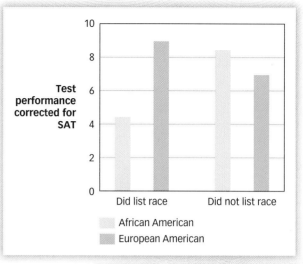

▲ Figure **13.18** **Stereotype Threat** When asked to indicate their race before taking an exam, African American students performed below their academic level (as determined by their SAT scores).

**stereotype threat**
The fear of confirming the negative beliefs that others may hold.

**perceptual confirmation**
The tendency for people to see what they expect to see.

**subtyping**
The tendency for people who receive disconfirming evidence to modify their stereotypes rather than abandon them.

Many of us think that nuns are traditional and proper. Does this photograph of Sister Rosa Elena nailing Sister Amanda de Jesús with a snowball change your stereotype, or are you tempted to subtype them instead?

BRIAN PLONKA/THE SPOKESMAN REVIEW

## Stereotyping Can Be Automatic

If we recognize that stereotypes are inaccurate and self-perpetuating (as you now do), then why do not we just make a firm resolution to stop using them? The answer is that stereotyping happens *unconsciously* (which means that we do not always know we are doing it) and *automatically* (which means that we often cannot avoid doing it even when we try) (Banaji & Heiphetz, 2010; Greenwald, McGhee, & Schwartz, 1998; Greenwald & Nosek, 2001).

Research using the Implicit Association Test shows that 70 percent of white Americans find it easier to associate white faces with positive stimuli such as "peace," and black faces with negative concepts such as "bomb," than the other way around. Surprisingly, 40 percent of African Americans show this same pattern.

For example, in one study, participants played a video game in which photographs of black or white men holding either guns or cameras were flashed on the screen for less than 1 second each. Participants earned money by shooting men with guns and lost money by shooting men with cameras. The results showed that participants made two kinds of mistakes: They tended to shoot black men holding cameras and tended not to shoot white men holding guns (Correll et al., 2002). Although the photographs appeared on the screen so quickly that participants did not have enough time to consciously consider their stereotypes, those stereotypes worked unconsciously, causing them to mistake a camera for a gun when it was in the hands of a black man and a gun for a camera when it was in the hands of a white man. Sadly, black participants were just as likely to make this pattern of errors as were white participants. Why did this happen?

Stereotypes comprise all the information about human categories that we have absorbed over the years from friends and uncles, books and blogs, jokes and movies and late-night television. When we see black men holding guns in rap videos, our minds associate these two things, and although we realize that we are watching art and not real life, the association is made and remembered. Later, we cannot *decide* not to be influenced by that association any more than we can *decide* not to be influenced by our second-grade teacher or the smell of french fries.

**Can we decide not to stereotype?**

In fact, some research suggests that trying not to use our stereotypes can make matters worse instead of better. Participants in one study were shown a photograph of a tough-looking male "skinhead" and were asked to write an essay describing a typical day in his life. Some of the participants were told that they should not allow their stereotypes about skinheads to influence their essays, and others were given no such instructions. Next, the experimenter brought each participant to a room with eight empty chairs. The first chair had a jacket draped over it, and the experimenter explained that it belonged to a skinhead, who had gone to use the restroom. Where did participants choose to sit? Participants who had earlier been told not to use their stereotypes sat farther away from the jacket than did participants who had been given no instructions (Macrae et al., 1994). As you know from reading the Consciousness chapter, thought suppression is ironic business that often causes us to do the very thing we were trying to avoid doing (Wegner et al., 1987).

Although stereotyping is unconscious and automatic, it is not inevitable (Blair, 2002; Kawakami et al., 2000; Milne & Grafman, 2001; Rudman, Ashmore, & Gary,

In 2007, Reuters news photographer Namir Noor-Eldeen was shot to death in Iraq by American soldiers in a helicopter who mistook his camera for a weapon. Would they have made the same mistake if Noor-Eldeen had been blonde or female?

2001). For instance, police officers who receive special training before playing the camera or gun video game described earlier do not show the same biases that ordinary people do (Correll et al., 2007). Like ordinary people, they take a few milliseconds longer to decide not to shoot a black man than a white man, indicating that their stereotypes are unconsciously and automatically influencing their thinking. But unlike ordinary people, they do not actually *shoot* black men more often than white men, indicating that they have learned how to keep those stereotypes from influencing their behaviour. Other studies show that even simple games and exercises can reduce the automatic influence of stereotypes (Phills et al., 2011; Todd et al., 2011).

## Attribution: Drawing Inferences from Actions

In 1963, Dr. Martin Luther King Jr. gave a speech in which he described his vision for America: "I have a dream that my four children will one day live in a nation where they will not be judged by the colour of their skin but by the content of their character." Research on stereotyping demonstrates that Dr. King's concerns are still well justified; we judge others by the colour of their skin—as well as by their gender, nationality, religion, age, and occupation—and in so doing, we sometimes make mistakes. But are we any better at judging people if we could somehow turn off our stereotypes and treat each person as an individual?

Not necessarily. Treating a person as an individual means judging them by their own words and deeds. This is more difficult than it sounds because the relationship

> When does a person's behaviour tell us something about them?

between what a person *is* and what a person *says or does* is not always straightforward. An honest person may lie to save a friend from embarrassment, and a dishonest person may tell the truth to bolster her credibility. Happy people have some weepy moments, polite people can be rude in traffic, and people who despise us can be flattering when they need a favour. In short, people's behaviour sometimes tells us about the kinds of people they are, but sometimes it simply tells us about the kinds of situations they happen to be in.

To understand people, we need to know not only *what* they did but also *why* they did it. Is the batter who hit the home run a talented slugger, or was the wind blowing in just the right direction at just the right time? Is the politician who gave the pro-life speech really opposed to abortion, or was she just trying to win the conservative vote? When we answer questions such as these, we are making **attributions,** which are *inferences about the causes of people's behaviours* (Epley & Waytz, 2010; Gilbert, 1998). We make *situational attributions* when we decide that a person's behaviour was caused by some temporary aspect of the situation in which it happened ("He was lucky that the wind carried the ball into the stands"), and we make *dispositional attributions* when we decide that a person's behaviour was caused by a relatively enduring tendency to think, feel, or act in a particular way ("He's got a great eye and a powerful swing").

How do we know whether to make a dispositional or a situational attribution? According to the *covariation model* (Kelley, 1967), we must consider the consistency, consensuality, and distinctiveness of the action. For example, why is the man in the photograph in **FIGURE 13.19** (on the next page) wearing a watermelon helmet? Does he have a goofy personality (*dispositional attribution*) or is he just a regular guy who is on his way to a Saskatchewan football game (*situational attribution*)? According to the covariation model, you can answer this question by asking whether his behaviour is *consistent* (does he usually wear this hat?), *consensual* (are other people wearing this hat?), and *distinctive* (does he do other goofy things?). If it turns out that he wears this hat every day (*high consistency*), and if today no one else is wearing a melon hat (*low consensus*),

attribution
An inference about the cause of a person's behaviour.

*"For God's sake, think! Why is he being so nice to you?"*

S. GROSS

SAM GROSS/THE NEW YORKER COLLECTION/CARTOONBANK.COM

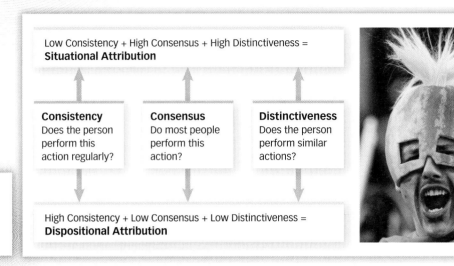

Low Consistency + High Consensus + High Distinctiveness =
**Situational Attribution**

**Consistency**
Does the person perform this action regularly?

**Consensus**
Do most people perform this action?

**Distinctiveness**
Does the person perform similar actions?

High Consistency + Low Consensus + Low Distinctiveness =
**Dispositional Attribution**

▶ Figure **13.19** **The Covariation Model of Attribution** The covariation model tells us whether to make a dispositional or situational attribution for a person's action.

**correspondence bias**
The tendency to make a dispositional attribution even when we should instead make a situational attribution.

Are people who steal "bad people"? What should we make of the fact that groceries, including infant formula, are among the most shoplifted items, and that shoplifting of groceries increases when unemployment is high? Research on the correspondence bias suggests that it is easy to blame people's outcomes on their dispositions, such as stupidity and criminality, and difficult to consider the ways in which they might be victims of their situations.

and if he tends to do other goofy things, such as wear clown shoes and say "honk, honk" to passersby (*low distinctiveness*), then you should probably make a dispositional attribution ("He's a certified goofball"). On the other hand, if he rarely wears this hat (*low consistency*), if today lots of other people are wearing watermelons (*high consensus*), and if he does not tend to do other goofy things (*high distinctiveness*), then you should probably make a situational attribution ("He's a Roughriders fan on game day"). As Figure 13.19 shows, patterns of consistency, consensus, and distinctiveness provide useful information about the cause of a person's behaviour.

As sensible as this seems, research suggests that people do not always use this information as they should. The **correspondence bias** is *the tendency to make a dispositional attribution when we should instead make a situational attribution* (Gilbert & Malone, 1995; Jones & Harris, 1967; Ross, 1977). This bias is so common and so basic that it is often called the *fundamental attribution error*. For example, volunteers in one experiment played a trivia game in which one participant acted as the quizmaster and made up a list of unusual questions, another participant acted as the contestant and tried to answer those questions, and a third participant acted as the observer and simply watched the game. The quizmasters tended to ask tricky questions based on their own idiosyncratic knowledge, and contestants were generally unable to answer them. After watching the game, the observers were asked to decide how knowledgeable the quizmaster and the contestant were. Although the quizmasters had asked good questions and the contestants had given bad answers, it should have been clear to the observers that all this asking and answering was a product of the roles they had been assigned to play and that the contestant would have asked equally good questions and the quizmaster would have given equally bad answers had their roles been reversed. And yet observers tended to rate the quizmaster as more knowledgeable than the contestant (Ross, Amabile, & Steinmetz, 1977) and were more likely to choose the quizmaster as their own partner in an upcoming game (Quattrone, 1982). Even when we know that a successful athlete had a home field advantage or that a successful entrepreneur had family connections, we tend to attribute their success to talent and tenacity.

What causes the correspondence bias? First, the situational causes of behaviour are often invisible (Ichheiser, 1949). For example, professors tend to assume that fawning students really do admire them in spite of the strong incentive for students to kiss up to those who control their grades. The problem is that professors can literally *see* students laughing at witless jokes and applauding after boring lectures, but they cannot *see* "control over grades." Situations are not as tangible or visible as behaviours,

> **Why do we tend to make dispositional attributions?**

Kiefer Sutherland (son of Canadian actor Donald Sutherland) and Carrie Fisher (daughter of famous entertainers Debbie Reynolds and Eddie Fisher) were both successful actors. Was their success due to the content of their characters, or to the opportunities that came with their family names?

so it is all too easy to ignore them (Taylor & Fiske, 1978). Second, situational attributions tend to be more complex than dispositional attributions and require more time and attention. When participants in one study were asked to make attributions while performing a mentally taxing task (namely, keeping a seven-digit number in mind), they had no difficulty making dispositional attributions, but they found it quite difficult to make situational attributions (Gilbert, Pelham, & Krull, 1988; Winter & Uleman, 1984). In short, information about situations is hard to get and hard to use, so we tend to believe that other peoples' actions are caused by their dispositions even when there is a perfectly reasonable situational explanation.

The correspondence bias is stronger in some cultures than others (Choi, Nisbett, & Norenzayan, 1999), among some people than others (D'Agostino & Fincher-Kiefer, 1992; Li et al., 2012), and under some circumstances than others. For example, we seem to be more prone to correspondence bias when judging other people's behaviour than when judging our own. The **actor–observer effect** is *the tendency to make situational attributions for our own behaviours while making dispositional attributions for the identical behaviour of others* (Jones & Nisbett, 1972). When university students are asked to explain why they and their friends chose their majors, they tend to explain their own choices in terms of situations ("I chose economics because my parents told me I have to support myself as soon as I am done with university") and their friends' choices in terms of dispositions ("Leah chose economics because she's materialistic") (Nisbett et al., 1973). The actor–observer effect occurs because people typically have more information about the situations that caused their own behaviour than about the situations that caused other people's behaviour. We can remember getting the please-major-in-something-practical lecture from our parents, but we were not at Leah's house to see her get the same lecture. As observers, we are naturally focused on another person's behaviour, but as actors, we are quite literally focused on the situations in which our behaviour occurs. Indeed, when people are shown videotapes of their conversations that allow them to see themselves from their partner's point of view, they tend to make dispositional attributions for their own behaviour and situational attributions for their partner's (Storms, 1973; Taylor & Fiske, 1975).

## IN SUMMARY

► People make inferences about others based on the categories to which they belong (stereotyping). This method can lead them to misjudge others because stereotypes can be inaccurate, overused, self-perpetuating, unconscious, and automatic.

► People make inferences about others based on their behaviours. This method can lead them to misjudge others because people tend to attribute actions to dispositions even when they should attribute them to situations.

**actor–observer effect**
The tendency to make situational attributions for our own behaviours while making dispositional attributions for the identical behaviour of others.

# Chapter Review

## KEY CONCEPT QUIZ

1. _____ describes the use of force to acquire scarce resources.
   a. Aggression
   b. Frustration
   c. Goal setting
   d. Sociality

2. Someone who hacks into your computer, steals your personal information, and uses it to purchase goods and services in your name is acting on the principle of
   a. aggression.
   b. social cognition.
   c. negative affect.
   d. frustration–aggression.

3. Why are acts of aggression—from violent crime to athletic brawls—more likely to occur on hot days when people are feeling irritated and uncomfortable?
   a. frustration
   b. negative affect
   c. resource scarcity
   d. biology and culture interaction

4. What is the single best predictor of aggression?
   a. temperament
   b. age
   c. gender
   d. status

5. The prisoner's dilemma game illustrates
   a. the hypothesis-confirming bias.
   b. the diffusion of responsibility.
   c. group polarization.
   d. the benefits and costs of cooperation.

6. Which of the following is NOT a downside of being in a group?
   a. Groups are positively prejudiced toward other members and tend to discriminate in their favour.
   b. Groups often show prejudice and discrimination toward nonmembers.
   c. Groups sometimes make poor decisions.
   d. Groups may take extreme actions an individual member would not take alone.

7. Which of the following BEST describes reciprocal altruism?
   a. people becoming less concerned with personal values through immersion in a group
   b. anxiety, loneliness, and depression being caused by exclusion from a group
   c. cooperation extended over long periods of time
   d. the evolutionary process by which individuals cooperate with their relatives

8. Which of the following is NOT an explanation for increased selectivity by women in choosing a mate?
   a. Sex is potentially more costly for women than for men.
   b. Communal styles of child-rearing argue for increased selectivity.
   c. The reputational costs of sex are historically much higher for women than for men.
   d. Pregnancy increases women's nutritional requirements and puts them at risk of illness and death.

9. In terms of attraction, which of the following is a situational factor?
   a. proximity
   b. similarity
   c. appearance
   d. personality

10. The hypothesis that people remain in relationships only as long as they perceive a favourable ratio of costs to benefits is referred to as
    a. companionate love.
    b. the exposure effect.
    c. social exchange.
    d. equity.

11. The _____ motive describes how people are motivated to experience pleasure and to avoid experiencing pain.
    a. emotional
    b. accuracy
    c. approval
    d. hedonic

12. The tendency to do what authorities tell us to do is known as
    a. persuasion.
    b. obedience.
    c. conformity.
    d. the actor–observer effect.

13. What is the process by which people come to understand others?
    a. dispositional attribution
    b. the accuracy motive
    c. social cognition
    d. cognitive dissonance

14. The tendency to make a dispositional attribution even when a person's behaviour was caused by the situation is referred to as
    a. comparison levelling.
    b. stereotyping.
    c. covariation.
    d. correspondence bias.

# KEY TERMS

actor–observer effect (p. 545)
aggression (p. 508)
altruism (p. 516)
attitude (p. 533)
attribution (p. 543)
belief (p. 533)
bystander intervention (p. 515)
cognitive dissonance (p. 535)
common knowledge effect (p. 514)
companionate love (p. 524)
comparison level (p. 524)
comparison level for alternatives (p. 524)

conformity (p. 528)
cooperation (p. 513)
correspondence bias (p. 544)
deindividuation (p. 514)
diffusion of responsibility (p. 514)
discrimination (p. 513)
door-in-the-face technique (p. 528)
equity (p. 524)
foot-in-the-door technique (p. 535)
frustration–aggression hypothesis (p. 509)
group (p. 513)
group polarization (p. 514)

groupthink (p. 514)
heuristic persuasion (p. 534)
informational influence (p. 533)
kin selection (p. 516)
mere exposure effect (p. 519)
normative influence (p. 528)
norm of reciprocity (p. 528)
norms (p. 528)
obedience (p. 531)
passionate love (p. 524)
perceptual confirmation (p. 541)
persuasion (p. 534)

prejudice (p. 513)
reciprocal altruism (p. 517)
social cognition (p. 537)
social exchange (p. 524)
social influence (p. 526)
social loafing (p. 514)
social psychology (p. 508)
stereotype threat (p. 541)
stereotyping (p. 539)
subtyping (p. 541)
systematic persuasion (p. 534)

# CHANGING MINDS

1. One of the MPPs from your province is supporting legislaiton that would impose heavy fines on aggressive drivers who run red lights. One of your classmates thinks this is a good idea. "The textbook taught us a lot about punishment and reward. It's simple. If we punish aggressive driving, its frequency will decline." Is your classmate right? Might the new law backfire? Might another policy be more effective in promoting safe driving?

2. One of your friends is outgoing, funny, and a star athlete on the women's lacrosse team. She has started to date a man who is introverted and prefers playing computer games to attending parties. You tease her about the contrast in personalities, and she replies, "Well, opposites attract." Is she right?

3. In a late 2013 article in the *Toronto Star,* Donna Yawching (who is black) recounts the following story: After parking curbside in downtown Toronto, she was approached by a (white) woman who owned the car in front. The woman asked Yawchingto move her car back so that she could get out more easily. Yawching replied "Oh, I just wanted to leave enough space for someone else to park." After checking to make sure that the woman had not been squeezed in on either side, she added "You can get out easily," and hurried off. When she returned to the car, she found a note on the windshield: "Thanks bitch. You really further your stereotype." Your friend reads this story and says "That's terrible, but surely it's an isolated incident. Sure, there are still a few racist people out there, but if you do surveys and ask people what they think about people of other races, they say they're fine with them." What would you tell your friend?

4. One of your friends has a very unique fashion sense and always wears clothes that are just a little bit different from what everyone else is wearing, for example, a neon orange track suit with a battered fedora. Most of the time, you appreciate your friend for his quirky personality. One day he tells you that he chooses his clothes carefully to make a fashion statement. "Most people follow the crowd," he announces. "I don't. I'm an individual, and I make my own choices, without influence from anyone else." Could he be right? What examples might you provide for or against your friend's claim?

5. A classmate is shaken after learning about the Milgram (1963) study, in which participants were willing to obey orders to administer painful electric shocks to another person, even after he begged them to stop. Worse, the Burger (2009) study shows that it was not just participants "back then" who were capable of this behaviour: Modern participants do the same thing. "Some people are just sheep!" she says. "I know that you and I wouldn't behave like that." Is she right? What evidence would you give her to support or oppose her claim?

6. When your family gathers for a summer barbeque, your cousin Wendy brings her fiancée, Amanda. It is the first time Amanda has met the whole family, and she seems nervous. She talks too much, laughs too loud, and rubs everyone the wrong way. Later, when you are alone with your mother, she rolls her eyes. "It's hard to imagine Wendy wanting to spend the rest of her life married to someone that annoying." You decide to be more generous, because you think your mother might have fallen prey to the correspondence bias. How could you change your mother's mind?

# ANSWERS TO KEY CONCEPT QUIZ

1. a; 2. d; 3. b; 4. c; 5. d; 6. a; 7. c; 8. b; 9. a; 10. c; 11 d; 12. b; 13. c; 14. d.

Need more help? Additional resources are located in Launchpad at:
*www.worthpublishers.com/launchpad/schacter3ecanadian*

# 14

# Stress and Health

▲ **Sources of Stress: What Gets to You**
Stressful Events
Chronic Stressors
**HOT SCIENCE** Can Discrimination Cause Stress and Illness?
Perceived Control over Stressful Events

▲ **Stress Reactions: All Shook Up**
Physical Reactions
Psychological Reactions

▲ **Stress Management: Dealing with It**
Mind Management
Body Management
Situation Management
**CULTURE & COMMUNITY** Oh Canada, Our (New) Home and (Non-)Native Land...

▲ **The Psychology of Illness: Mind over Matter**
Psychological Effects of Illness
Recognizing Illness and Seeking Treatment
**THE REAL WORLD** This is Your Brain on Placebos
Somatic Symptom Disorders
On Being a Patient
Patient–Practitioner Interaction

▲ **The Psychology of Health: Feeling Good**
Personality and Health
Health-Promoting Behaviours and Self-Regulation
**OTHER VOICES** False Hopes and Overwhelming Urges

"HAVE A KNIFE TO YOUR NECK. Don't make a sound. Get out of bed and come with me or I will kill you and your family." These are the words that awoke 14-year-old Elizabeth Smart in the middle of the night of June 5, 2002 while sleeping in her bedroom next to her 9-year-old sister Mary Katherine. Fearing for her life, and that of her family, she kept quiet and left with her abductor. Her little sister, terrified, hid in her bedroom for several hours before waking the girls' parents, who awoke to their daughter saying: "She's gone. Elizabeth is gone." Elizabeth was kidnapped by Brian David Mitchell, a man Elizabeth's parents had hired previously to do some roof work on their home. Mitchell broke into the family's home in Salt Lake City, Utah, through an open window, abducted Elizabeth, and he and his wife Wanda Ileen Barzee held her in captivity for 9 months, during which time Mitchell repeatedly raped her and threatened to kill her and her entire family. Mitchell, Barzee, and Smart were spotted walking down the street by a couple who recognized them from a recent airing of the television show *America's Most Wanted* and called the police. Mitchell and Barzee were apprehended and Elizabeth was returned to her family.

Elizabeth suffered unimaginable circumstances for a prolonged period of time in what can be thought of as one of the most stressful situations possible, especially for a 14-year-old girl. So what became of Elizabeth? Fortunately, she is now safe and sound, happily married, and working as an activist and commentator for ABC News. She endured life-threatening stressors for months, and those experiences undoubtedly affected her in ways that will last her entire lifetime. At the same time, hers is a story of resilience. Despite the very difficult hand she was dealt, she appears to have bounced back and to be leading a happy, productive, and rewarding life. Hers is a story of both stress and health.

This smiling young face is that of Elizabeth Smart, who, between the times of these two photographs, was kidnapped, raped, and tortured for nearly a year. Stressful life events often affect us in ways that cannot be seen from the outside. Fortunately, there are things that we can do in response to even the most stressful of life events that can get us smiling again.

**stressors**
Specific events or chronic pressures that place demands on a person or threaten the person's well-being.

**stress**
The physical and psychological response to internal or external stressors.

**health psychology**
The subfield of psychology concerned with the ways psychological factors influence the causes and treatment of physical illness and the maintenance of health.

FORTUNATELY, VERY FEW OF US WILL EVER HAVE TO ENDURE THE type of stress that Elizabeth Smart lived through. But life can present a welter of frights, bothers, and looming disasters that can be quite difficult to manage. A reckless driver may nearly run you over; you may be discriminated against, threatened, or intimidated in some way; or a fire may leave you out on the street. Life has its **stressors**, *specific events or chronic pressures that place demands on a person or threaten the person's well-being*. Although such stressors rarely involve threats of death, they do have both immediate and cumulative effects that can influence health.

In this chapter, we will look at what psychologists and physicians have learned about the kinds of life events that produce **stress**, *the physical and psychological response to internal or external stressors;* typical responses to such stressors; and ways to manage stress. Stress has such a profound influence on health that we consider stress and health together in this chapter. And because sickness and health are not merely features of the physical body, we then consider the more general topic of **health psychology**, which is *the subfield of psychology concerned with the ways psychological factors influence the causes and treatment of physical illness and the maintenance of health*. You will see how perceptions of illness can affect its course and how health-promoting behaviours can improve the quality of people's lives.

# Sources of Stress: What Gets to You

First of all, what are the sources of stress? A natural catastrophe, such as a hurricane, earthquake, or volcanic eruption, is an obvious source. But, for most of us, stressors are personal events that affect the comfortable pattern of our lives and little annoyances that bug us day after day. Let us look at the life events that can cause stress, chronic sources of stress, and the relationship between lack of perceived control and the impact of stressors.

## Stressful Events

People often seem to get sick after major life events. In pioneering work, Thomas Holmes and Richard Rahe (1967) followed up on this observation, proposing that major life changes cause stress and that increased stress causes illness. To test their idea, they asked people to rate the magnitude of readjustment required by each of many events found to be associated with the onset of illness (Rahe et al., 1964). The resulting list of life events is remarkably predictive: Simply adding up the stress ratings of each life change experienced is a significant indicator of a person's likelihood of future illness (Miller, 1996). Someone who becomes divorced, loses a job, and has a friend die all in the same year, for example, is more likely to get sick than someone who escapes the year with only a divorce.

A version of this list adapted for the life events of university (college) students (and sporting the snappy acronym CUSS, for College Undergraduate Stress Scale) is shown in **TABLE 14.1**. To assess your stressful events, check off any events that have happened to you in the past year and sum your point total. In a large sample of students in an introductory psychology class, the average was 1247 points, ranging from 182 to 2571 (Renner & Mackin, 1998).

Looking at the list, you may wonder why positive events are included. Stressful life events are unpleasant, right? Why would getting married be stressful? Weddings are supposed to be fun, right? Research has shown that

> **Where are you on the stress scale?**

Weddings are positive events, but they also can be stressful due to the often overwhelming amount of planning and decision making involved (and occasionally because of the difficulties managing the interactions of friends and family).

PHOTODISC/DIGITAL VISION/GETTY IMAGES

Table 14.1

**College Undergraduate Stress Scale**

| Event | Stress Rating | Event | Stress Rating |
|---|---|---|---|
| Being raped | 100 | Lack of sleep | 69 |
| Finding out that you are HIV positive | 100 | Change in housing situation (hassles, moves) | 69 |
| Being accused of rape | 98 | Competing or performing in public | 69 |
| Death of a close friend | 97 | Getting in a physical fight | 66 |
| Death of a close family member | 96 | Difficulties with a roommate | 66 |
| Contracting a sexually transmitted disease (other than AIDS) | 94 | Job changes (applying, new job, work hassles) | 65 |
| Concerns about being pregnant | 91 | Declaring a major or concerns about future plans | 65 |
| Finals week | 90 | A class you hate | 62 |
| Concerns about your partner being pregnant | 90 | Drinking or use of drugs | 61 |
| Oversleeping for an exam | 89 | Confrontations with professors | 60 |
| Flunking a class | 89 | Starting a new semester | 58 |
| Having a boyfriend or girlfriend cheat on you | 85 | Going on a first date | 57 |
| Ending a steady dating relationship | 85 | Registration | 55 |
| Serious illness in a close friend or family member | 85 | Maintaining a steady dating relationship | 55 |
| Financial difficulties | 84 | Commuting to campus or work or both | 54 |
| Writing a major (essay) | 83 | Peer pressures | 53 |
| Being caught cheating on a test | 83 | Being away from home for the first time | 53 |
| Drunk driving | 82 | Getting sick | 52 |
| Sense of overload in school or work | 82 | Concerns about your appearance | 52 |
| Two exams in one day | 80 | Getting straight A's | 51 |
| Cheating on your boyfriend or girlfriend | 77 | A difficult class that you love | 48 |
| Getting married | 76 | Making new friends; getting along with friends | 47 |
| Negative consequences of drinking or drug use | 75 | Fraternity or sorority rush | 47 |
| Depression or crisis in your best friend | 73 | Falling asleep in class | 40 |
| Difficulties with parents | 73 | Attending an athletic event | 20 |
| Talking in front of class | 72 | | |

*Source:* Renner & Mackin (1998).
*Note:* To compute your personal life change score, sum the stress ratings for all events that have happened to you in the last year.

compared with negative events, positive events produce less psychological distress and fewer physical symptoms (McFarlane et al., 1980), and that happiness can sometimes even counteract the effects of negative events (Fredrickson, 2000). However, positive events often require readjustment and preparedness that many people find extremely stressful (e.g., Brown & McGill, 1989), so these events are included in computing life-change scores.

## Chronic Stressors

Life would be simpler if an occasional stressful event such as a wedding or a lost job were the only pressures we faced. At least each event would be limited in scope, with a beginning, a middle, and, ideally, an end. But unfortunately, life brings with it continued exposure to **chronic stressors,** *sources of stress that occur continuously or repeatedly.* Strained relationships, discrimination, bullying, overwork, money troubles—small stressors that may be easy to ignore if they happen only occasionally—can accumulate to produce distress and illness. People who report being affected by daily hassles

**chronic stressors**
Sources of stress that occur continuously or repeatedly.

SHUTTERSTOCK

City life can be fun, but the higher levels of noise, crowding, and violence can also be sources of chronic stress.

also report more psychological symptoms (LaPierre et al., 2012) and physical symptoms (Piazza et al., 2013), and these effects often have a greater and longer-lasting impact than major life events.

Many chronic stressors are linked to social relationships. For instance, as described in the Social Psychology chapter, people often form different social groups based on race, culture, interests, popularity, and so on. Being outside the in-group can be stressful. Being actively targeted by members of the in-group can be even more stressful, especially if this happens repeatedly over time (see the Hot Science box). Chronic stressors also can be linked to particular environments. For example, features of city life—noise, traffic, crowding, pollution,

> **What are some examples of environmental factors that cause chronic stress?**

and even the threat of violence—provide particularly insistent sources of chronic stress (Evans, 2006). Rural areas have their own chronic stressors, of course, especially isolation and lack of access to amenities such as health care. The realization that chronic stressors are linked to environments has spawned the subfield of *environmental psychology*, the scientific study of environmental effects on behaviour and health.

In one study of the influence of noise on children, environmental psychologists looked at the impact of attending schools under the flight path to Heathrow Airport in London, England. Did the noise of more than 1250 jets flying overhead each day have an influence beyond making kids yell to be heard? Compared with children from matched control schools in low-noise areas, children going to school in the flight path reported higher levels of noise annoyance and showed poorer reading comprehension (Haines et al., 2001). Next time you fly into an airport, please try to do so more quietly for the children.

## HOT SCIENCE

# Can Discrimination Cause Stress and Illness?

Have you ever been discriminated against because of your race, gender, sexual orientation, or some other characteristic? If so, then you know that this can be a pretty stressful experience. Discrimination that occurs repeatedly over time can be an especially powerful stressor for anyone. But what exactly does it *do* to people?

Recent research has shown that there are a number of ways that discrimination can lead to elevated stress and negative health outcomes. People from socially disadvantaged groups who experience higher levels of stress as a result of discrimination engage more frequently in maladaptive behaviours (e.g., drinking, smoking and overeating) in efforts to cope with stress. They also can experience difficulties in their interactions with healthcare professionals (e.g., clinician biases, patient suspiciousness about treatment) (Major, Mendes, & Dovidio, 2013). Taken together, these factors may help to explain why members of

socially disadvantaged groups have significantly higher rates of health problems than do members of socially advantaged groups (Penner et al., 2010).

New studies are revealing how discrimination can literally "get under the skin" to cause negative health outcomes. One recent study by Jeremy Jamieson and his colleagues (Jamieson, Koslov, et al., 2013) exposed black and white participants to social rejection by either a person of the same race or a different race to test whether there is something particularly harmful about discrimination, versus social rejection in general. To test this, they had research participants deliver a speech to two confederates in different rooms via a video chat program, after which the confederates provided negative feedback about the participant's speech. The confederates were not seen by the participant, but were represented by computer avatars that either matched the participant's race or did not. Interestingly, although the nature

of the rejection was the same in all cases, participants responded very differently if the people rejecting them were from a different race than the same race. Specifically, whereas being rejected by people from their own race was associated with greater displays of shame and physiological changes associated with an avoidance state (increased cortisol), being rejected by members of a different race was associated with displays of anger, greater vigilance for danger, physiological changes associated with an approach state (i.e., higher cardiac output and lower vascular resistance), and higher risk taking.

Studies like this one help to explain some of the health disparities that currently exist across different social groups. The results suggest that discrimination can lead to physiological, cognitive, and behavioural changes that in the short term prepare a person for action, but in the long-term could lead to negative health outcomes.

## Perceived Control over Stressful Events

What do catastrophes, stressful life changes, and daily hassles have in common? Right off the bat, of course, their threat to the person or the status quo is easy to see. Stressors challenge you to *do something*—to take some action to eliminate or overcome the stressor.

Paradoxically, events are most stressful when there is *nothing to do*—no way to deal with the challenge. Expecting that you will have control over what happens to you is associated with effectiveness in dealing with stress. Researchers David Glass and Jerome Singer (1972), in classic studies of *perceived control*, looked at the aftereffects of loud noise on people who could or could not control it. Participants were asked to solve puzzles and proofread in a quiet room or in a room filled with loud noise. Glass and Singer found that bursts of such noise hurt people's performance on the tasks

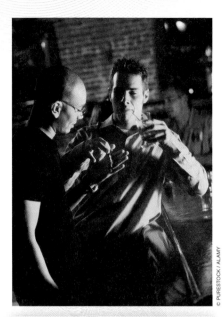

Some stressful life events, like those associated with drunk driving, are within our power to control. We gain control when we give away the keys to a designated driver.

**What makes events most stressful?**

after the noise was over. However, this dramatic decline in performance was prevented among participants who were told during the noise period that they could stop the noise just by pushing a button. They did not actually take this option, but access to the "panic button" shielded them from the detrimental effects of the noise. A similar study in monkeys reached very similar conclusions—one group of monkeys was taught to press a lever to turn off a loud noise, whereas individuals in the "yoked group" were exposed to the identical amount of noise but could not turn it off. These yoked monkeys had higher levels of cortisol (a stress hormone), and were more aggressive than monkeys who could control the noise. Interestingly, when control was removed from the first group, their cortisol and aggression levels were even higher than those in the yoked group (Hanson, Larson, & Snowdon, 1976)! This tells us that perceived control is very important for understanding how we respond to stress.

Subsequent studies have found that a lack of perceived control underlies other response to stressors as well. The stressful effects of crowding, for example, appear to stem from the feeling that you cannot control getting away from the crowded conditions (Evans & Stecker, 2004). Being jammed into a crowded dormitory room may be easier to handle, after all, the moment you realize you could take a walk and get away from it all.

### IN SUMMARY

▶ Stressors are events and threats that place specific demands on a person or threaten the person's well-being.

▶ Sources of stress include major life events (even happy ones), catastrophic events, and chronic hassles, some of which can be traced to a particular environment.

▶ Events are most stressful when we perceive that there is no way to control or deal with the challenge.

## Stress Reactions: All Shook Up

It was a regular Tuesday morning in New York City. University students were sitting in their morning classes. People were arriving at work and the streets were beginning to fill with shoppers and tourists. Then, at 8:46 a.m., American Airlines Flight 11 crashed into the North Tower of the World Trade Center. People watched in horror. How could this have happened? This seemed like a terrible accident. Then at 9:03 a.m., United Airlines Flight 175 crashed into the South Tower of the World Trade Center. There were then reports of a plane crashing into the Pentagon. And

The threat of death or injury, such as that experienced by many in New York City at the time of the 9/11 attacks, can cause significant and lasting physical and psychological stress reactions.

▼ Figure 14.1 **HPA Axis** Just a few seconds after a fearful stimulus is perceived, the hypothalamus activates the pituitary gland to release adrenocorticotropic hormone (ACTH). ACTH then travels through the bloodstream to activate the adrenal glands to release catecholamines and cortisol, which energize the fight-or-flight response.

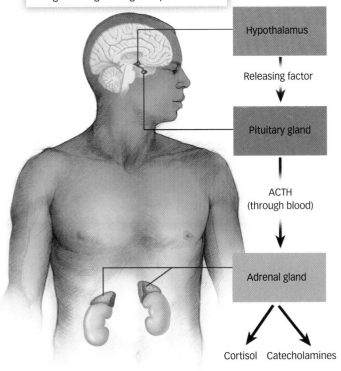

another somewhere in Pennsylvania. The terrorist attacks on the World Trade Center on September 11, 2001, were an enormous stressor that had a lasting impact on many people, physically and psychologically. People living close to the World Trade Center (within 2.4 km) during 9/11 were found to have less grey matter in the amygdala, hippocampus, insula, anterior cingulate, and medial prefrontal cortex relative to those living more than 322 km away during the attacks, suggesting that the stress associated with the attacks may have reduced the size of these parts of the brain that play an important role in emotion, memory, and decision making (Ganzel et al., 2008). Brain measurements were taken more than 3 years after 9/11: This tells us that the event had long-term consequences on brain structure. Children who watched more television coverage of 9/11 had greater symptoms of post-traumatic stress disorder than children who watched less coverage (Otto et al., 2007). People around the United States who had a stronger acute stress response to the events of 9/11 had a 53 percent increased incidence of heart problems over the next 3 years (Holman et al., 2008). Stress can produce changes in every system of the body and mind, stimulating both physical reactions and psychological reactions. Let us consider each in turn.

## Physical Reactions

Walter Cannon (1929) coined a phrase to describe the body's response to any threatening stimulus: the **fight-or-flight response,** *an emotional and physiological reaction to an emergency that increases readiness for action.* The mind asks, "Should I stay and battle this somehow, or should I run like mad?" And the body prepares to react. If you are a cat at this time, your hair stands on end. If you are a human, your hair stands on end, too, but not as visibly. Cannon recognized this common response across species and suspected that it might be the body's first mobilization to any threat.

Research conducted since Cannon's discovery has revealed what is happening in the brain and body during this reaction. Brain activation in response to threat occurs in the hypothalamus, stimulating the nearby pituitary gland, which in turn releases a hormone known as ACTH (short for adrenocorticotropic hormone). ACTH travels through the bloodstream and stimulates the adrenal glands atop the kidneys (see **FIGURE 14.1**). In this cascading response of the HPA (hypothalamic–pituitary–adrenocortical) axis, the adrenal glands are stimulated to release hormones, including the *catecholamines* (epinephrine and norepinephrine), which increase sympathetic nervous system activation (and therefore increase heart rate, blood pressure, and respiration rate) and decrease parasympathetic activation (see the Neuroscience and Behaviour chapter). The increased respiration and blood pressure make more oxygen available to the muscles to energize attack or to initiate escape. The adrenal glands also release *cortisol*, a hormone that increases the concentration of glucose in the blood to make fuel available to the muscles. Everything is prepared for a full-tilt response to the threat.

> **How does the body react to a fight-or-flight situation?**

### General Adaptation Syndrome

What might have happened if the terrorist attacks of 9/11 were spaced out over a period of days or weeks? Starting in the 1930s, Hans Selye, a Canadian scientist working at Université de Montréal, undertook a variety of experiments that looked at the physiological consequences of severe threats to well-being. He subjected rats to heat, cold, infection, trauma, hemorrhage, and other prolonged stressors, making few friends among the rats or their sympathizers, but learning a lot about stress. His stressed-out rats developed physiological responses that included an enlarged adrenal cortex, shrinking of the lymph glands, and ulceration of the stomach. Noting that many different kinds of stressors caused similar patterns of physiological change, he called the reaction the **general adaptation syndrome (GAS)**, which he defined as a *three-stage physiological stress response that appears regardless of the stressor that is encountered*. The GAS is *nonspecific*; that is, the response does not vary, no matter what the source of the repeated stress.

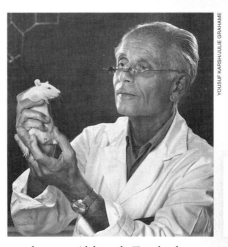

This is Hans Selye with a rat. Given all the stress Selye put rats under, this one looks surprisingly calm.

**What are the three phases of GAS?**

None of this is very good news. Although Friedrich Nietzsche once said, "What does not kill me makes me stronger," Selye found that severe stress takes a toll on the body. He saw the GAS as occurring in three phases (see **FIGURE 14.2**):

> First comes the *alarm phase*, in which the body rapidly mobilizes its resources to respond to the threat. Energy is required, and the body calls on its stored fat and muscle. The alarm phase is equivalent to Cannon's fight-or-flight response.

> Next, in the *resistance phase*, the body adapts to its high state of arousal as it tries to cope with the stressor. Continuing to draw on resources of fat and muscle, it shuts down unnecessary processes: digestion, growth, and sex drive stall; menstruation stops; production of testosterone and sperm decreases. The body is being taxed to generate resistance, and all the fun stuff is put on hold.

> If the GAS continues long enough, the *exhaustion phase* sets in. The body's resistance collapses. Many of the resistance-phase defenses create gradual damage as they operate, leading to costs for the body that can include susceptibility to infection, tumour growth, aging, irreversible organ damage, or death.

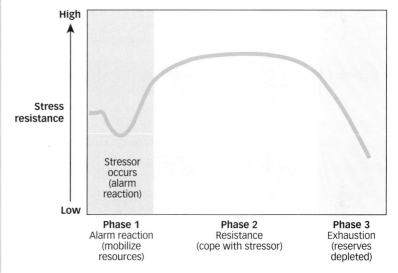

▲ Figure **14.2** **Selye's Three Phases of Stress Response** In Selye's theory, resistance to stress builds over time, but then can only last so long before exhaustion sets in.

## Stress Effects on Health and Aging

Right now, you are (we hope!) enjoying years of healthy living. Unfortunately, as people age, the body slowly begins to break down (just ask any of the authors of this book). Interestingly, recent research has revealed that stress significantly accelerates the aging process. Elizabeth Smart's parents noted that, upon being reunited with her after 9 months of separation, they almost did not recognize her because she appeared to have aged so much (Smart, Smart, & Morton, 2003). Theirs is an extreme example; you can see examples of the effects of stress on aging around you in everyday life. People exposed to chronic stress, whether due to their relationships, job, or something else, experience actual wear and tear on their bodies and increased aging. Take a look at the pictures of the past three Canadian prime ministers before and after their terms

**fight-or-flight response**
An emotional and physiological reaction to an emergency that increases readiness for action.

**general adaptation syndrome (GAS)**
A three-stage physiological stress response that appears regardless of the stressor that is encountered.

**Jean Chrétien**     **Paul Martin**     **Stephen Harper**

Chronic stress can actually speed the aging process. Just look at how much each of our last three prime ministers aged while in office. University can be stressful too, but hopefully not so much so that you have white hair by graduation.

**telomeres**
Caps at the end of each chromosome that protect the ends of chromosomes and prevent them from sticking to each other.

**telomerase**
An enzyme that rebuilds telomeres at the tips of chromosomes.

as prime minister (arguably, one of the most stressful jobs in the world). As you can see, they appear to have aged much more than the 4 to 10 years that passed between their first and second photographs. How exactly can stressors in the environment increase the aging process?

Understanding this process requires knowing a little bit about how aging occurs. The cells in our bodies are constantly dividing, and as part of this process, our chromosomes are repeatedly copied so that our genetic information is carried into the new cells. This process is facilitated by the presence of **telomeres,** *caps at the ends of each chromosome that protect the ends of chromosomes and prevent them from sticking to each other.* They are kind of like the tape at the end of your shoelaces that keeps them from being frayed and not working as efficiently. Each time a cell divides, the telomeres become slightly shorter. If they become too short, cells can no longer divide and this can lead to the development of tumours and a range of diseases. Fortunately, our bodies fix this problem by producing a substance called **telomerase,** *an enzyme that rebuilds telomeres at the tips of chromosomes.* As cells repeatedly divide over the course of our lives, telomerase does its best to re-cap our chromosomes with telomeres. Ultimately, in the end, telomerase cannot keep up telomere production at a sufficient pace, and over time cells lose their ability to divide, causing aging and in the end, cell death. The recent discovery of the function of telomeres and telomerase and their relation to aging and disease by Elizabeth Blackburn and colleagues has been one of the most exciting advances in science in the past several decades.

> What is telomerase and what does it do for us?

Interestingly, social stressors can play an important role in this process. People exposed to chronic stress have shorter telomere length and lower telomerase activity (Epel et al., 2004). Laboratory studies suggest that cortisol can reduce the activity of

Dr. Elizabeth Blackburn (*right*) was awarded a Nobel Prize in 2009 for her groundbreaking discoveries on the functions of telomeres (shown here in yellow) and telomerase (*left*).

telomerase, which in turn leads to shortened telomeres, which has downstream negative effects in the form of accelerated aging and increased risk of a wide range of diseases including cancer, cardiovascular disease, diabetes, and depression (Blackburn & Epel, 2012). This sounds dire, but there are things that you can do to combat this process and potentially live a healthier and longer life! Activities like exercise and meditation seem to prevent chronic stress from shortening telomere length, providing a potential explanation of how these activities may convey health benefits such as longer life and lower risk of disease (Epel et al., 2009; Puterman et al., 2010).

## Stress Effects on the Immune Response

The **immune system** is *a complex response system that protects the body from bacteria, viruses, and other foreign substances.* The system includes white blood cells, such as **lymphocytes** (including T cells and B cells), *that produce antibodies that fight infection.* The immune system is remarkably responsive to psychological influences. *Psychoneuroimmunology* is the study of how the immune system responds to psychological variables, such as the presence of stressors. Stressors can cause hormones known as *glucocorticoids* to flood the brain (described in the Neuroscience and Behaviour chapter), wearing down the immune system and making it less able to fight invaders (Webster Marketon & Glaser, 2008).

> **How does stress affect the immune system?**

For example, in one study, medical student volunteers agreed to receive small wounds to the roof of the mouth. Researchers observed that these wounds healed more slowly during exam periods than during summer vacation (Marucha, Kiecolt-Glaser, & Favagehi, 1998). In another study, a set of selfless, healthy volunteers permitted researchers to swab the common cold virus in their noses (Cohen et al., 1998). You might think that a direct application of the virus would be like exposure to a massive full-facial sneeze and that all the participants would catch colds. The researchers observed, though, that some people got colds and others did not—and stress helped account for the difference. Volunteers who had experienced chronic stressors (lasting a month or longer) were especially likely to suffer colds. In particular, participants who had lost a job or who were going through extended interpersonal problems with family or friends were most susceptible to the virus. Brief stressful life events (those lasting less than a month) had no impact. So if you are fighting with your friends or family, best to get it over with quickly; it is better for your health.

The effect of stress on immune response may help to explain why social status is related to health. Studies of British civil servants beginning in the 1960s found that mortality varied precisely with civil service grade: the higher the classification, the lower the death rate, regardless of cause (Marmot et al., 1991). One explanation is that people in lower-status jobs more often engage in unhealthy behaviour such as smoking and drinking alcohol, and there is evidence of this. But there is also evidence that the stress of living life at the bottom levels of society increases risk of infections by weakening the immune system. People who perceive themselves as low in social status are more prone to suffer from respiratory infections, for example, than those who do not bear this social burden—and the same holds true for low-status male monkeys (Cohen, 1999).

## Stress and Cardiovascular Health

The heart and circulatory system are also sensitive to stress. For example, for several days after Iraq's 1991 missile attack on Israel, heart attack rates went up markedly among citizens in Tel Aviv (Meisel et al., 1991). The full story of how stress affects the cardiovascular system starts earlier than the occurrence of a heart attack: Chronic stress creates changes in the body that increase later vulnerability.

**immune system**
A complex response system that protects the body from bacteria, viruses, and other foreign substances.

**lymphocytes**
White blood cells (including T cells and B cells) that produce antibodies that fight infection.

The main cause of coronary heart disease is *atherosclerosis,* a gradual narrowing of the arteries that occurs as fatty deposits, or plaque, build up on the inner walls of the arteries. Narrowed arteries result in a reduced blood supply and, eventually, when an artery is blocked by a blood clot or detached plaque, in a heart attack. Although smoking, a sedentary lifestyle, and a diet high in fat and cholesterol can cause coronary heart disease, chronic stress also is a major contributor (Krantz & McCeney, 2002). As a result of stress-activated arousal of the sympathetic nervous system, blood pressure goes up and stays up, and this gradually damages the blood vessels. The damaged vessels accumulate plaque, and the more plaque, the greater the likelihood of coronary heart disease. For example, a large study of Finnish men age 42 to 60 found that those who exhibited elevated blood pressure in response to stress and who reported that their work environment was especially stressful showed progressive atherosclerosis of a major artery in the neck during the 4-year study (Everson et al., 1997).

> **How does chronic stress increase the chance of a heart attack?**

In the 1950s, cardiologists Meyer Friedman and Ray Rosenman (1974) conducted a revolutionary study that demonstrated a link between work-related stress and coronary heart disease. They interviewed and tested 3000 healthy middle-aged men and then tracked their subsequent cardiovascular health. Based on their research, Friedman and Rosenman developed the concept of the **Type A behaviour pattern,** which is characterized by *a tendency toward easily aroused hostility, impatience, a sense of time urgency, and competitive achievement strivings.* They compared Type A individuals to those with a less driven behaviour pattern (sometimes called *Type B*). The Type A men were identified not only by their answers to questions in the interview (agreeing that they walk and talk fast, work late, set goals for themselves, work hard to win, and easily get frustrated and angry at others), but also by the pushy and impatient way in which they answered the questions. They watched the clock, barked back answers, and interrupted the interviewer, at some points even slapping him with a fish. Okay, the part about the fish is wrong, but you get the idea: These people were intense. The researchers found that of the 258 men who had heart attacks in the 9 years following the interview, over two thirds had been classified as Type A and only one third had been classified as Type B.

A later study of stress and anger tracked medical students for up to 48 years to see how their behaviour while they were young related to their later susceptibility to coronary problems (Chang et al., 2002). Students who responded to stress with anger and hostility were found to be three times more likely to later develop premature heart disease and six times more likely to have an early heart attack than were students who did not respond with anger. Hostility, particularly in men, predicts heart disease better than any other major causal factor, such as smoking, high caloric intake, or even high levels of LDL cholesterol (Niaura et al., 2002) (see also **FIGURE 14.3**). Stress affects the cardiovascular system to some degree in everyone, but is particularly harmful in those people who respond to stressful events with hostility.

> **What causal factor most predicts heart attacks?**

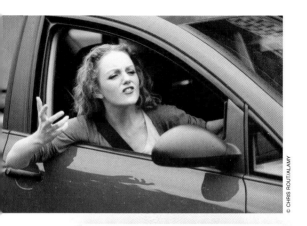
Anywhere in the world, road rage starts to make sense when you believe that all the other drivers on the road are trying to kill you.

▼ Figure **14.3** **Hostility and Coronary Heart Disease** Of 2280 men studied over the course of 3 years, 45 suffered coronary heart disease (CHD) incidents, such as heart attack. Many more of these incidents occurred in the group who had initially scored above the 80th percentile in hostility (Niaura et al., 2002).

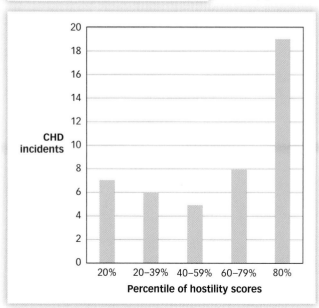

## Psychological Reactions

The body's response to stress is intertwined with responses of the mind. Perhaps the first thing the mind does is try to sort things out—to interpret whether an event is threatening or not—and if it is, whether something can be done about it.

## Stress Interpretation

The interpretation of a stimulus as stressful or not is called *primary appraisal* (Lazarus & Folkman, 1984). Primary appraisal allows you to realize that a small dark spot on your shirt is a stressor (spider!) or that a 113-km/h drop from a great height in a small car full of screaming people may not be (roller coaster!). In a demonstration of the importance of interpretation, researchers used a gruesome film of a subincision (a kind of genital surgery that is part of some tribal initiation rites) to severely stress volunteer participants (Speisman et al., 1964). Self-reports and participants' autonomic arousal (heart rate and skin conductance level) were the measures of stress. Before viewing the film, one group heard an introduction that downplayed the pain and emphasized the coming-of-age aspect of the initiation. This interpretation markedly reduced the film viewers' stress compared with another group whose viewing was preceded by a lecture accentuating the pain and trauma.

Changing your perception of a stressful situation from a "threat" to a "challenge" can actually modify your body's response to the situation and lead to better performance. This approach worked for Eminem's character (B. Rabbit) in the movie *8 Mile*, and it can work for you too.

The next step in interpretation is *secondary appraisal*, determining whether the stressor is something you can handle or not; that is, whether you have control over the event (Lazarus & Folkman, 1984). Interestingly, the body responds differently depending on whether the stressor is perceived as a *threat* (a stressor you believe you might *not* be able to overcome) or a *challenge* (a stressor you feel fairly confident you can control) (Blascovich & Tomaka, 1996). The same midterm exam is seen as a challenge if you are well prepared, but a threat if you did not study. Fortunately, interpretations of stressors can change them from threats to challenges. One recent study (Jamieson et al., 2010) showed that instructing students to reframe their anxiety about an upcoming exam as arousal that will help them on the test actually boosted their sympathetic arousal (signalling a challenge orientation) and improved test performance. Remember this technique next time you are feeling anxious about a test: Increased arousal can improve your performance!

> **What is the difference between a threat and a challenge?**

Although both threats and challenges raise heart rate, threats increase vascular reactivity (such as constriction of the blood vessels, which can lead to high blood pressure). In one study, researchers found that even interactions as innocuous as conversations can produce threat or challenge responses depending on the race of the conversation partner. Asked to talk with another, unfamiliar student, white students showed a challenge reaction when the student was white and a threat reaction when the student was African American (Mendes et al., 2002). Similar threat responses were found when white students interacted with an unexpected partner, such as an Asian student who had an accent characteristic of the American South (Mendes et al., 2007). It is as if social unfamiliarity creates the same kind of stress as lack of preparedness for an exam. Interestingly, having previously interacted with members of an unfamiliar group tempers the threat reaction (Blascovich et al., 2001).

## Burnout

Did you ever take a class from an instructor who had lost interest in the job? The syndrome is easy to spot: The teacher looks distant and blank, almost robotic, giving predictable and humdrum lessons each day, as if it does not matter whether anyone is listening. Now imagine *being* this instructor. You decided to teach because you wanted to shape young minds. You worked hard, and for a while things were great. But one day, you looked up to see a room full of miserable students who were bored and did not care about anything you had to say. They updated their Facebook pages while you talked and started shuffling papers and putting things away long before the end of class. You are happy at work only when you are not in class. When people feel this way, especially about their jobs or careers, they are suffering from **burnout,** *a state of physical,*

**Type A behaviour pattern**
The tendency toward easily aroused hostility, impatience, a sense of time urgency, and competitive achievement strivings.

**burnout**
A state of physical, emotional, and mental exhaustion created by long-term involvement in an emotionally demanding situation and accompanied by lowered performance and motivation.

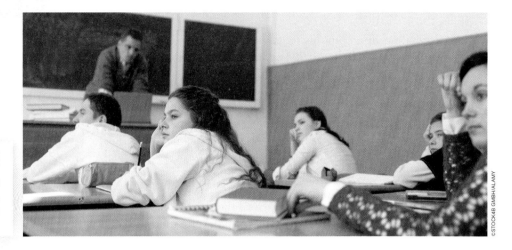

©STOCK4B GMBH/ALMY

Is there anything worse than taking a horribly boring class? How about being the teacher of that class? What techniques could be used to help people in helping professions (teachers, doctors, nurses, etc.) to prevent burnout from stress?

*emotional, and mental exhaustion created by long-term involvement in an emotionally demanding situation and accompanied by lowered performance and motivation.*

Burnout is a particular problem in the helping professions (Maslach, Schaufeli, & Leiter, 2001). Teachers, nurses, clergy, doctors, dentists, psychologists, social workers, police officers, and others who repeatedly encounter emotional turmoil on the job may only be able to work productively for a limited time. Eventually, many succumb to symptoms of burnout: overwhelming exhaustion, a deep cynicism and detachment from the job, and a sense of ineffectiveness and lack of accomplishment (Maslach, 2003). Their unhappiness can even spread to others; people with burnout tend to become disgruntled employees who revel in their coworkers' failures and ignore their coworkers' successes (Brenninkmeijer, Vanyperen, & Buunk, 2001).

> **Why is burnout a problem especially in the helping professions?**

What causes burnout? One theory suggests that the culprit is using your job to give meaning to your life (Pines, 1993). If you define yourself only by your career and gauge your self-worth by success at work, you risk having nothing left when work fails. For example, a teacher in danger of burnout might do well to invest time in family, hobbies, or other self-expressions. Others argue that some emotionally stressful jobs lead to burnout no matter how they are approached, and active efforts to overcome the stress before burnout occurs are important. The stress management techniques discussed in the next section may be lifesavers for people in such jobs.

## IN SUMMARY

▶ The body responds to stress with an initial fight-or-flight reaction, which activates the hypothalamic–pituitary–adrenocortical (HPA) axis and prepares the body to face the threat or run away from it.

▶ The general adaptation syndrome (GAS) outlines three phases of stress response that occur regardless of the type of stressor: alarm, resistance, and exhaustion.

▶ Chronic stress can wear down the immune system, causing susceptibility to infection, aging, tumour growth, organ damage, and death.

▶ Response to stress varies, depending on whether it is interpreted as something that can be overcome or not.

▶ The psychological response to stress can, if prolonged, lead to burnout.

# Stress Management: Dealing with It

Most university students (92 percent) say they occasionally feel overwhelmed by the tasks they face, and over a third say they have dropped courses or received low grades in response to severe stress (Duenwald, 2002). No doubt you are among the lucky 8 percent who are entirely cool and report no stress. But just in case you are not, you may be interested in our exploration of stress management techniques: ways to counteract psychological and physical stress reactions directly by managing your mind and body, and ways to sidestep stress by managing your situation.

## Mind Management

Stressful events are magnified in the mind. If you fear public speaking, for example, just the thought of an upcoming presentation to a group can create anxiety. And if you do break down during a presentation (going blank, for example, or blurting out something embarrassing), intrusive memories of this stressful event could echo in your mind afterward. A significant part of stress management, then, is control of the mind.

### Repressive Coping

Controlling your thoughts is not easy, but some people do seem to be able to banish unpleasant thoughts from the mind. This style of dealing with stress, called **repressive coping**, is characterized by *avoiding situations or thoughts that are reminders of a stressor and maintaining an artificially positive viewpoint.* Everyone has some problems, of course, but repressors are good at deliberately ignoring them (Barnier, Levin, & Maher, 2004). So, for example, when repressors suffer a heart attack, they are less likely than other people to report intrusive thoughts of their heart problems in the days and weeks that follow (Ginzburg, Solomon, & Bleich, 2002).

Like Elizabeth Smart, who for years after her rescue focused in interviews on what was happening in her life now, rather than repeatedly discussing her past in captivity, people often rearrange their lives in order to avoid stressful situations. Many victims of rape, for example, not only avoid the place where the rape occurred, but may move away from their home or neighborhood (Ellis, 1983). Anticipating and attempting to avoid reminders of the traumatic experience, they become wary of strangers, especially men who resemble the assailant, and they check doors, locks, and windows more frequently than before. It may make sense to try to avoid stressful thoughts and situations if you are the kind of person who is good at putting unpleasant thoughts and emotions out of mind (Coifman et al., 2007). For some people, however, the avoidance of unpleasant thoughts and situations is so difficult that it can turn into a grim preoccupation (Parker & McNally, 2008; Wegner & Zanakos, 1994). For those who cannot avoid negative emotions effectively, it may be better to come to grips with them. This is the basic idea of rational coping.

> When is it useful to avoid stressful thoughts and when is avoidance a problem?

### Rational Coping

**Rational coping** involves *facing the stressor and working to overcome it.* This strategy is the opposite of repressive coping and so may seem to be the most unpleasant and

**repressive coping**
Avoiding situations or thoughts that are reminders of a stressor and maintaining an artificially positive viewpoint.

**rational coping**
Facing a stressor and working to overcome it.

Some people are good at deliberately ignoring negative events or thoughts after they occur, and their functioning may be improved as a result. However, those who are not as good at repressing this negative information may do better trying rational coping.

JUSTIN SULLIVAN/GETTY IMAGES

**reframing**
Finding a new or creative way to think about a stressor that reduces its threat.

**stress inoculation training (SIT)**
A reframing technique that helps people to cope with stressful situations by developing positive ways to think about the situation.

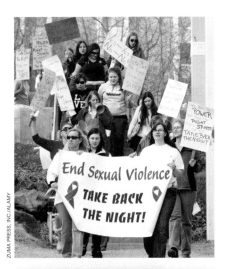

Extremely stressful events, such as rape, are not only acute stressors but often have lasting psychological consequences. Fortunately, there are effective techniques for learning to cope with such events that can lead to improved psychological health.

Writing about your deepest thoughts and feelings has been shown to have a range of beneficial health effects. Just make sure you keep your journal in a safe place.

unnerving thing you could do when faced with stress. It requires approaching, rather than avoiding, a stressor in order to lessen its longer-term negative impact (Hayes, Strosahl, & Wilson, 1999). Rational coping is a three-step process: *acceptance,* coming to realize that the stressor exists and cannot be wished away; *exposure,* attending to the stressor, thinking about it, and even seeking it out; and *understanding,* working to find the meaning of the stressor in your life.

> **What are the three steps in rational coping?**

When the trauma is particularly intense, rational coping may be difficult to undertake. In rape trauma, for example, even accepting that the rape happened takes time and effort; the initial impulse is to deny the event and try to live as though it had never occurred. Psychological treatment may help during the exposure step by helping victims to confront and think about what happened. Using a technique called *prolonged exposure,* rape survivors relive the traumatic event in their imagination by recording a verbal account of the event and then listening to the recording daily. In one study, rape survivors were instructed to seek out objectively safe situations that caused them anxiety or that they had avoided. This sounds like bitter medicine indeed, but it is remarkably effective, producing significant reductions in anxiety and symptoms of post-traumatic stress disorder compared to no therapy and compared to other therapies that promote more gradual and subtle forms of exposure (Foa et al., 1999).

The third element of rational coping involves coming to an understanding of the meaning of the stressful events. A trauma victim may wonder again and again: Why me? How did it happen? Why? Survivors of incest frequently voice the desire to make sense of their trauma (Silver, Boon, & Stones, 1983), a process that is difficult, even impossible, during bouts of suppression and avoidance.

## Reframing

Changing the way you think is another way to cope with stressful thoughts. **Reframing** involves *finding a new or creative way to think about a stressor that reduces its threat.* If you experience anxiety at the thought of public speaking, for example, you might reframe by shifting from thinking of an audience as evaluating you to thinking of yourself as evaluating them, and this might make speech giving easier.

Reframing can be an effective way to prepare for a moderately stressful situation, but if something like public speaking is so stressful that you cannot bear to think about it until you absolutely must, the technique may not be usable. **Stress inoculation training (SIT)** is *a reframing technique that helps people to cope with stressful situations by developing positive ways to think about the situation.* For example, in one study, people who had difficulty controlling their anger were trained to rehearse and reframe their thoughts with phrases like these: "Just roll with the punches, do not get bent out of shape," "You do not need to prove yourself," "I am not going to let him get to me," "It is really a shame he has to act like this," and "I will just let him make a fool of himself." Anger-prone people who practised these thoughts were less likely to become physiologically aroused in response to laboratory-based provocations, both imaginary and real. Subsequent research on SIT has revealed that it can be useful, too, for helping people who have suffered prior traumatic events to become more comfortable living with those events (Foa & Meadows, 1997).

Reframing can take place spontaneously if people are given the opportunity to spend time thinking and writing about stressful events. In an important series of studies, Jamie Pennebaker (1989) found that the physical health of university students improved after they spent a few hours writing about their deepest thoughts and feelings.

> **How has writing about stressful events been shown to be helpful?**

Compared with students who had written about something else, members of the self-disclosure group were less likely in subsequent months to visit the student health centre; they also used less aspirin and achieved better grades (Pennebaker & Chung, 2007). In fact, engaging in such expressive writing was found to improve immune function (Pennebaker, Kiecolt-Glaser, & Glaser, 1988), whereas suppressing emotional topics weakened it (Petrie, Booth, & Pennebaker, 1998). The positive effect of self-disclosing writing may reflect its usefulness in reframing trauma and reducing stress.

## Body Management

Stress can express itself as tension in your neck muscles, back pain, a knot in your stomach, sweaty hands, or the harried face you glimpse in the mirror. Because stress so often manifests itself through bodily symptoms, bodily techniques such as meditation, relaxation therapy, biofeedback, and aerobic exercise are useful in its management.

### Meditation

**meditation**
The practice of intentional contemplation.

**Meditation** is *the practice of intentional contemplation.* Techniques of meditation are associated with a variety of religious traditions and are also practised outside religious contexts. The techniques vary widely. Some forms of meditation call for attempts to clear the mind of thought, others involve focusing on a single thought (e.g., thinking about a candle flame), and still others involve concentration on breathing or on a *mantra* (a repetitive sound such as *om*). At a minimum, the techniques have in common a period of quiet.

Time spent meditating can be restful and revitalizing. Beyond these immediate benefits, many people also meditate in an effort to experience deeper or transformed consciousness. Whatever the reason, meditation does appear to have positive psychological effects (Hölzel et al., 2011). Many believe it does so, in part, by improving control over attention. The focus of many forms of meditation, such as mindfulness meditation, is on teaching ourselves how to remain focused on, and accepting of, our immediate experience. Interestingly, experienced meditators show deactivation in the default mode network (which is associated with mind wandering; see Figure 5.6 in the Consciousness chapter) during meditation relative to non-meditators (Brewer et al., 2011). Even short-term meditation training administered to university undergraduates has been shown to improve the connectivity between parts of the brain involved in conflict monitoring and cognitive and emotional control, and to do so via increased myelination (perhaps due to increased neuron firing) and other axonal changes (see the Neuroscience and Behaviour chapter) (Tang et al., 2012). Taken together, these findings suggest that meditators may be better able to regulate their thoughts and emotions, which may translate to a better ability to manage interpersonal relations, anxiety, and a range of other activities that require conscious effort (Sedlmeier et al., 2012).

> **What are some positive outcomes of meditation?**

### Relaxation

Imagine for a moment that you are scratching your chin. Do not actually do it; just think about it and notice that your body participates by moving ever so slightly, tensing and relaxing in the sequence of the imagined action. Edmund Jacobson (1932) discovered these effects with *electromyography* (EMG), a technique used to measure the subtle activity of muscles. A person asked to imagine rowing a boat or plucking a flower from a bush would produce slight levels of tension in the muscles involved in performing the act. Jacobson also found that thoughts of relaxing the muscles sometimes reduced EMG readings when people did not even report feeling tense. Our bodies respond to all the things we think about doing every day. These thoughts create muscle tension even when we think we are doing nothing at all.

Meditation is the practice of intentional contemplation, and it can also temporarily influence brain activity and enhance the sense of well-being.

Aung San Suu Kyi, the leader of the Burmese (Myanmar) opposition party who was awarded the Nobel Peace Prize in 1991, endured house arrest from 1989 until 2010. She has said that daily meditation helped her through this difficult time by improving her mood, awareness, and clarity.

**relaxation therapy**
A technique for reducing tension by consciously relaxing muscles of the body.

**relaxation response**
A condition of reduced muscle tension, cortical activity, heart rate, breathing rate, and blood pressure.

**biofeedback**
The use of an external monitoring device to obtain information about a bodily function and possibly gain control over that function.

These observations led Jacobson to develop **relaxation therapy,** *a technique for reducing tension by consciously relaxing muscles of the body.* A person in relaxation therapy may be asked to relax specific muscle groups one at a time or to imagine warmth flowing through the body or to think about a relaxing situation. This activity draws on a **relaxation response,** *a condition of reduced muscle tension, cortical activity, heart rate, breathing rate, and blood pressure* (Benson, 1990). Basically, as soon as you get in a comfortable position, quiet down, and focus on something repetitive or soothing that holds your attention, you relax.

Relaxing on a regular basis can reduce symptoms of stress (Carlson & Hoyle, 1993) and even reduce blood levels of cortisol, the biochemical marker of the stress response (McKinney et al., 1997). For example, in individuals who are suffering from tension headache, relaxation reduces the tension that causes the headache; in individuals with cancer, relaxation makes it easier to cope with stressful treatments for the disease; in individuals with stress-related cardiovascular problems, relaxation can reduce the high blood pressure that puts the heart at risk (Mandle et al., 1996).

### Biofeedback

Would not it be nice if, instead of having to learn to relax, you could just flip a switch and relax as fast as possible? **Biofeedback,** *the use of an external monitoring device to obtain information about a bodily function and possibly gain control over that function,* was developed with this goal of high-tech relaxation in mind. You might not be aware right now of whether your fingers are warm or cold, for example, but with an electronic thermometer displayed before you, the ability to sense your temperature might allow you (with a bit of practice) to make your hands warmer or cooler at will (e.g., Roberts & McGrady, 1996).

Biofeedback can help people control physiological functions they are not likely to become aware of in other ways. For example, you probably have no idea right now what brain-wave patterns you are producing. In the late 1950s, Joe Kamiya (1969), a psychologist using the electroencephalograph (also called the EEG and discussed in the Neuroscience and Behaviour chapter), initiated a brain-wave biofeedback revolution when he found that people could change their brain waves from alert beta patterns to relaxed alpha patterns and back again when they were permitted to monitor their own EEG readings.

**How does biofeedback work?**

Recent studies suggest that EEG biofeedback (or neurofeedback) is moderately successful in treating brain-wave abnormalities in disorders such as epilepsy (Yucha & Gilbert, 2004), and in teaching people to down-regulate activity in regions of the brain involved in the strong emotional responses seen in some forms of psychopathology (Hamilton et al., 2010). Often, however, the use of biofeedback to produce relaxation in the brain turns out to be a bit of technological overkill and may not be much more effective than simply having the person stretch out in a hammock and hum a happy tune. Although biofeedback is not a magic bullet that gives people control over stress-induced health troubles, it has proven to be a useful technique for things like increasing relaxation and decreasing chronic pain (Palermo et al., 2011). People who do not benefit from relaxation therapy may find that biofeedback provides a useful alternative.

Biofeedback gives people access to visual or audio feedback showing levels of psychophysiological functions such as heart rate, breathing, brain electrical activity, or skin temperature that they would otherwise be unable to sense directly.

### Aerobic Exercise

A jogger nicely decked out in a neon running suit bounces in place at the crosswalk and then springs away when the signal changes. It is tempting to assume that this jogger is the picture of psychological health: happy, unstressed, and even downright exuberant. As it turns out, the stereotype is true: Studies indicate that *aerobic exercise* (exercise that increases heart rate and oxygen intake for a sustained period) is associated with psychological well-being (Hassmen, Koivula, & Uutela, 2000). But does exercise *cause* psychological well-being, or does psychological well-being cause people to exercise? Perhaps general happiness is what inspires the jogger's bounce. Or could some unknown third factor (neon pants?) cause both the need to exercise and the sense of well-being? As we have mentioned many times, correlation does not always imply causation.

To try to tease apart causal factors, researchers have randomly assigned people to aerobic exercise activities and no-exercise comparison groups and have found that exercise actually does promote stress relief and happiness. One recent meta-analysis (a quantitative review of existing studies) compiled data from 90 studies including

> **What are the benefits of exercise?**

over 10 000 people with chronic illness who were randomly assigned either to an exercise or a no-exercise condition, and found that people assigned to the aerobic exercise condition experienced a significant reduction in depressive symptoms (Herring et al., 2010). Other recent meta-analyses have come to similar conclusions, showing, for instance, that exercise is as effective as the most effective psychological interventions for depression (Rimer et al., 2012), and that exercise even shows positive physical and mental health benefits for individuals with schizophrenia (Gorczynski & Faulkner, 2011). Pretty good effects for a simple, timeless intervention with no side effects!

The reasons for these positive effects are unclear. Researchers have suggested that the effects result from increases in the body's production of neurotransmitters such as serotonin, which can have a positive effect on mood (as discussed in the Neuroscience and Behaviour chapter) or from increases in the production of endorphins (the endogenous opioids discussed in the Neuroscience and Behaviour, and Consciousness chapters) (Jacobs, 1994).

Beyond boosting positive mood, exercise also stands to keep you healthy into the future. Current Canadian government recommendations suggest that 150 minutes a week of exercise, in bouts of 10 minutes or longer, will improve fitness and strength and lead to feeling better (Public Health Agency of Canada, 2011b). Perhaps the simplest thing you can do to improve your happiness and health, then, is to participate regularly in an aerobic activity. Pick something you find fun: Sign up for a dance class, get into a regular basketball game, or start paddling a canoe—just not all at once.

## Situation Management

After you have tried to manage stress by managing your mind and managing your body, what is left to manage? Look around and you will notice a whole world out there. Perhaps that could be managed as well. Situation management involves changing your life situation as a way of reducing the impact of stress on your mind and body. Ways to manage your situation can include seeking out social support, religious or spiritual practice, and finding a place for humour in your life.

### Social Support

The wisdom of the National Safety Council's first rule—"Always swim with a buddy"— is obvious when you are in water over your head, but people often do not realize that the same principle applies whenever danger threatens. Other people can offer help in times of stress. **Social support** is *aid gained through interacting with others*. One of the more self-defeating things you can do in life is fail to connect to people in this way. Just failing to have a life-partner, for example, is bad for your health. Single individuals have an elevated risk of mortality from cardiovascular disease, cancer, pneumonia and influenza, chronic obstructive pulmonary disease, and liver disease and cirrhosis (Johnson, Backlund, et al., 2000). More generally, good ongoing relationships with friends and family and participation in social activities and religious groups can be as healthy for you as exercising and avoiding smoking (Umberson et al., 2006). Social support is helpful on many levels:

AP PHOTO/MATT DUNHAM

Exercise is helpful for the reduction of stress, unless, like John Stibbard, your exercise involves carrying the Olympic torch on a wobbly Capilano Suspension Bridge (in Vancouver) over a 70-m gorge.

**social support**
The aid gained through interacting with others.

> An intimate partner can help you remember to get your exercise and follow your doctor's orders, and together you will probably follow a more healthy diet than you would all alone with your snacks.

> Talking about problems with friends and family can offer many of the benefits of professional psychotherapy, usually without the hourly fees.

> Sharing tasks and helping each other when times get tough can reduce the amount of work and worry in each other's lives.

The helpfulness of strong social bonds, though, transcends mere convenience. Lonely people are more likely than others to be stressed and depressed (Baumeister & Leary, 1995), and they can be more susceptible to illness because of lower-than-normal levels of immune functioning (Kiecolt-Glaser et al., 1984). Many first-year university students experience something of a crisis of social support. No matter how outgoing and popular they were in high school, newcomers typically find the task of developing satisfying new social relationships quite daunting. New friendships can seem shallow, connections with teachers may be perfunctory and even threatening, and social groups that are encountered can seem like islands of lost souls ("Hey, we are forming a club to investigate the lack of clubs on campus—want to join?"). Not surprisingly, research shows that students reporting the greatest feelings of isolation also show reduced immune responses to flu vaccinations (Pressman et al., 2005). Time spent getting to know people in new social situations can be an investment in your own health.

# CULTURE & COMMUNITY

## Oh Canada, Our (New) Home and (Non-)Native Land...

According to the 2006 Canadian census, immigrants accounted for 24 percent of the Canadian population and over one million immigrants arrived in Canada between 2001 and 2006 (Milan, 2011). Three quarters of these immigrants are from Asia, with China and India being the major source countries. Of course, this means that many immigrants have neither English nor French as their mother tongue. Do they find immigration stressful? To some extent, they must: Immigration generally involves leaving friends, extended family, and everything that is familiar behind. The language and culture is also alien, and immigrants often arrive without a guaranteed source of income. Given potential trouble with communication, lack of knowledge of local customs, decreases in social support, and financial uncertainty that accompany immigration, one might expect a higher rate of mental illness amongst new immigrants to Canada.

In fact, the opposite appears to be true: Immigrants are more likely to be in better health than Canadian-born individuals (Newbold, 2009) and report *less* psychological distress, including less depression (Bergeron et al., 2009). This has been attributed to the screening process operating for immigration into Canada and to the self-selection of those who are in good health being most able and willing to immigrate (Laroche, 2000).

Unfortunately, this rosy picture fades quickly—within 10 years of arriving in the country, health, including mental health, deteriorates in immigrants

so that it is indistinguishable from the non-immigrant average. What causes these declines in health over time, and what can help? One protective factor seems to be social support: Immigrants do particularly well when they settle in communities of immigrants with similar backgrounds (Stafford, Newbold, & Ross, 2011). This, in turn, suggests that the reason why health declines in immigrants may have to do with stress caused by financial uncertainty, a lack of social support, and communication difficulties.

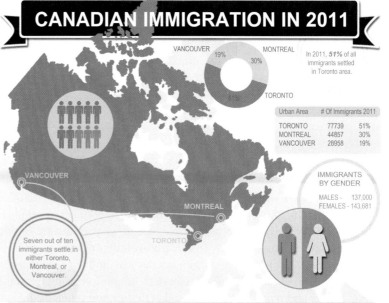

CANADAFAQ.CA INFOGRAPHIC BY PERMISSION OF ART BRANCH INC.
HTTP://WWW.CANADAFAQ.CA/CANADIAN-IMMIGRATION-FACTS.PHP

The value of social support in protecting against stress may be very different for women and men: Whereas women seek support under stress, men are less likely to do so. The fight-or-flight response to stress may be largely a male reaction, according to research on sex differences by Shelley Taylor (2002). Taylor suggested that the female response to stress is to *tend-and-befriend* by taking care of people and bringing them together. Like men, women respond to stressors with sympathetic nervous system arousal and the release of epinephrine and norepineph-

> **Why is the hormone oxytocin a health advantage for women?**

rine; but unlike men, they also release *oxytocin*, a hormone secreted by the pituitary gland in pregnant and nursing mothers. In the presence of estrogen, oxytocin triggers social responses: a tendency to seek out social contacts, nurture others, and create and maintain cooperative groups. After a hard day at work, a man may come home frustrated and worried about his job and end up drinking a beer and fuming alone. A woman under the same type of stress may instead play with her kids or talk to friends on the phone. The tend-and-befriend response to stress may help to explain why women are healthier and have a longer life span than do men. The typical male response amplifies the unhealthy effects of stress, whereas the female response takes a lesser toll on her mind and body and provides social support for the people around her as well.

Women are more likely than men to respond to stress with a *tend-and-befriend* style in which they seek out social contact and cooperative relationships. The commonality of this response style may partly explain the success of the television show *Sex in the City*, in which four young women helped one another through many difficult times (the fabulous outfits did not hurt either).

## Religious Experiences

National polls indicate that about 72 percent of Canadians believe in a god, and many who do, pray at least once per day. Many who believe in a higher power believe that their faith will be rewarded in an afterlife—and it turns out that there may be some benefits here on Earth as well. An enormous body of research has examined the associations between *religiosity* (affiliation with or engagement in the practices of a particular religion) and *spirituality* (having a belief in and engagement with some higher power, not necessarily linked to any particular religion), and positive health outcomes. The helpful effects of religiosity and spirituality have been observed in a wide range of areas including lower rates of heart disease, decreases in chronic pain, and improved psychological health (Seybold & Hill, 2001).

Why do people who endorse religiosity or spirituality have better mental and physical health? Is it divine intervention? Several testable ideas have been proposed. Engagement in religious or spiritual practices, such as attendance at weekly religious services, may lead to the development of a stronger and more extensive social network,

> **Why are religiosity and spirituality associated with health benefits?**

which has well-known health benefits. Those who are religious or spiritual also may fare better psychologically and physically as a result of following the healthy recommendations offered in many religious or spiritual teachings. That is, they may be more likely to follow dietary restrictions, restrain from the use of drugs or alcohol, and endorse a more hopeful and optimistic perspective of daily life events, all of which can lead to more positive health outcomes (Seeman, Dubin, & Seeman, 2003; Seybold & Hill, 2001). On balance, many claims made by some religious groups have not been supported, such as the beneficial effects of intercessory prayer (see **FIGURE 14.4**). Psychologists are actively testing the effectiveness of various religious and spiritual practices with the goal of better understanding how they might help to explain, and improve, the human condition.

▼ Figure **14.4 Pray for me?** To test whether praying for people in their time of need actually helped them, researchers randomly assigned 1802 patients about to undergo cardiac bypass surgery to one of three conditions: those told that they may be prayed for and were; those told that they may be prayed for and were not; and those told that they definitely would be prayed for and were. Unfortunately, there were no differences in the presence of complications between those who were or were not prayed for. To make matters worse, those who knew they would be prayed for and were, experienced significantly more complications than the other two groups (Benson et al., 2006).

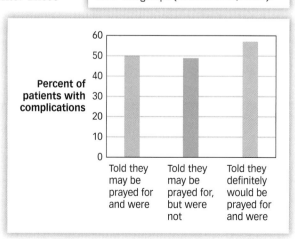

Percent of patients with complications

| Told they may be prayed for and were | Told they may be prayed for, but were not | Told they definitely would be prayed for and were |

When Andrew Mason, CEO of the Internet company Groupon, left his position, his resignation letter read: "After four and a half intense and wonderful years as CEO of Groupon, I have decided that I would like to spend more time with my family. Just kidding—I was fired today." He went on to add, "I am so lucky to have had the opportunity to take the company this far with all of you. I will now take some time to decompress (FYI I am looking for a good fat camp to lose my Groupon 40, if anyone has a suggestion), and then maybe I will figure out how to channel this experience into something productive." This seems like a textbook case of using humour to mitigate stress, which is why we put it, um, you know where.

## Humour

It would be nice to laugh at your troubles and move on. Most of us recognize that humour can diffuse unpleasant situations and bad feelings, and it makes sense that bringing some fun into your life could help to reduce stress. The extreme point of view on this topic is staked out in self-help books with titles such as *Health, Healing, and the Amuse System* and *How Serious Is This? Seeing Humor in Daily Stress.* Is laughter truly the best medicine? Should we close down the hospitals and send in the clowns?

> How does humour mitigate stress?

There is a kernel of truth to the theory that humour can help us cope with stress. For example, humour can reduce sensitivity to pain and distress, as researchers found when they subjected volunteers to an overinflated blood pressure cuff. Participants were more tolerant of the pain during a laughter-inducing comedy audiotape than during a neutral tape or instructed relaxation (Cogan et al., 1987).

Humour can also reduce the time needed to calm down after a stressful event. For example, men viewing a highly stressful film about three industrial accidents were asked to narrate the film aloud, either by describing the events seriously or by making their commentary as funny as possible. Although men in both groups reported feeling tense while watching the film and showed increased levels of sympathetic nervous arousal (increased heart rate and skin conductance, decreased skin temperature), those looking for humour in the experience bounced back to normal arousal levels more quickly than did those in the serious story group (Newman & Stone, 1996).

If laughter and fun can alleviate stress quickly in the short term, do the effects accumulate to improve health and longevity? Sadly, the evidence suggests not (Provine, 2000). A study titled *Do Comics Have the Last Laugh?* tracked the longevity of comedians in comparison to other entertainers and nonentertainers (Rotton, 1992). It was found that the comedians died younger—perhaps after too many nights on stage thinking, *I am dying out here.*

### IN SUMMARY

▶ The management of stress involves strategies for influencing the mind, the body, and the situation.

▶ People try to manage their minds by trying to suppress stressful thoughts or avoid the situations that produce them, by rationally coping with the stressor, and by reframing.

▶ Body management strategies involve attempting to reduce stress symptoms through meditation, relaxation, biofeedback, and aerobic exercise.

▶ Overcoming stress by managing your situation can involve seeking out social support, engaging in religious experiences, or attempting to find humour in stressful events.

# The Psychology of Illness: Mind over Matter

One of the mind's main influences on the body's health and illness is the mind's sensitivity to bodily symptoms. Noticing what is wrong with the body can be helpful when it motivates a search for treatment, but sensitivity can also lead to further problems when it snowballs into a preoccupation with illness that in itself can cause harm.

## Psychological Effects of Illness

Why does it feel so bad to be sick? You notice scratchiness in your throat or the start of sniffles, and you think you might be coming down with something. And in just a few short hours, you are achy all over, energy gone, no appetite, feverish, feeling dull and listless. You are sick. The question is, why does it have to be like this? Why could it not feel good? As long as you are going to have to stay at home and miss out on things anyway, could sickness not be less of a pain?

Sickness makes you miserable for good reason. Misery is part of the *sickness response,* a coordinated, adaptive set of reactions to illness organized by the brain (Hart, 1988; Watkins & Maier, 2005). Feeling sick keeps you home, where you will spread germs to fewer people. More importantly, the sickness response makes you withdraw from activity and lie still, conserving the energy for fighting illness that you would normally expend on other behaviour. Appetite loss is similarly helpful: The energy spent on digestion is conserved. Thus, the behavioural changes that accompany illness are not random side effects; they help the body fight disease. These responses become prolonged and exaggerated with aging—subtle signs that we are losing the fight (Barrientos et al., 2009).

> **What is the benefit of the sickness response?**

How does the brain know it should do this? The immune response to an infection begins with the activation of white blood cells that "eat" microbes and also release *cytokines,* proteins that circulate through the body and communicate among the other white blood cells, and also communicate the sickness response to the brain (Maier & Watkins, 1998). Administration of cytokines to an animal can artificially create the sickness response, and administration of drugs that oppose the action of cytokines can block the sickness response even during an ongoing infection. Cytokines do not enter the brain, but they activate the vagus nerve that runs from the intestines, stomach, and chest to the brain and induce the "I am infected" message (Goehler et al., 2000). Perhaps this is why we often feel sickness in the "gut," a gnawing discomfort in the very centre of the body.

Interestingly, the sickness response can be prompted without any infection at all, merely by the introduction of stress. The stressful presence of a predator's odour, for instance, can produce the sickness response of lethargy in an animal, along with symptoms of infection such as fever and increased white blood cell count (Maier & Watkins, 2000). In humans, the connection between sickness response, immune reaction, and stress is illustrated in depression, a condition in which all the sickness machinery runs at full speed. So, in addition to fatigue and malaise, depressed people show signs characteristic of infection, including high levels of cytokines circulating in the blood (Maes, 1995). Just as illness can make you feel a bit depressed, severe depression seems to recruit the brain's sickness response and make you feel ill (Watkins & Maier, 2005).

## Recognizing Illness and Seeking Treatment

You probably were not thinking about your breathing a minute ago, but now that you are reading this sentence, you notice it. Sometimes we are very attentive to our bodies. At other times, the body seems to be on "automatic," running along unnoticed until specific symptoms announce themselves or are pointed out by an annoying textbook writer.

Directing attention toward the body or away from it can influence the symptoms we perceive. When people are bored, for example, they have more attention available to direct toward their bodies, so they focus more on their physical symptoms.

If you have been reading this very exciting textbook, there is no chance you have been yawning. However, seeing this guy yawning may cause your brain to initiate a yawn response as well.

Pennebaker (1980) audiotaped classrooms and found that people are more likely to cough when someone else has just coughed, but that such psychological contagion is much more likely at boring points in a lecture. Interestingly, coughing is not something people do on purpose (as Pennebaker found when he recorded clusters of coughs among sleeping firefighters). Thus, awareness and occurrence of physical symptoms can be influenced by psychological factors beyond our control.

People differ substantially in the degree to which they attend to and report bodily symptoms. People who report many physical symptoms tend to be negative in other ways as well, describing themselves as anxious, depressed, and under stress (Watson & Pennebaker, 1989). Do people with many symptom complaints truly have a lot of problems or are they just high-volume complainers? To answer this question, researchers used fMRI brain scans to compare the severity of reported sensation of pain with the degree of activation in brain areas usually associated with pain experience. Volunteers underwent several applications of a thermal stimulus (43.3–48.9°C) to the leg, and, as you might expect, some of the participants found it more painful than did others. Scans during the painful events revealed that the anterior cingulate cortex, somatosensory cortex, and prefrontal cortex (areas known to respond to painful body stimulation) were particularly active in those participants who reported higher levels of pain experience (see **FIGURE 14.5**), suggesting that people can report accurately on the extent to which they experience pain (Coghill, McHaffie, & Yen, 2003) (see The Real World box).

> What is the relationship between pain and activity in the brain?

In contrast to complainers, there are those who underreport symptoms and pain or ignore or deny the possibility that they are sick. Insensitivity to symptoms comes with costs: It can delay the search for treatment, sometimes with serious repercussions. Of 2404 patients in one study who had been treated for a heart attack, 40 percent had delayed going to the hospital for over 6 hours from the time they first noticed suspicious symptoms (Gurwitz et al., 1997). Severe chest pain or a history of prior heart surgery did send people to the hospital in a hurry. Those with more subtle symptoms often waited around for hours, however, not calling an ambulance or their doctor,

| 0 | 1 | 2 | 3 | 4 | 5 |
| No Hurt | Hurts Little Bit | Hurts Little More | Hurts Even More | Hurts Whole Lot | Hurts Worst |

How much does it hurt? Pain is a psychological state that can be difficult to measure. One way to put a number on a pain is to have people judge with reference to the external expression of the internal state.

▶ Figure 14.5 **The Brain in Pain** fMRI scans of brain activation in high- (*left*) and low-pain-sensitive (*right*) individuals during painful stimulation. The anterior cingulate cortex and primary somatosensory areas show greater activation in high-pain-sensitive individuals. Levels of activation are highest in yellow and red, then light blue and dark blue (Coghill, McHaffie, & Yen, 2003).

Primary somatosensory areas

Anterior cingulate cortex

Primary somatosensory areas

Anterior cingulate cortex

**High Pain Sensitivity**

**Low Pain Sensitivity**

just hoping the problem would go away, which is not a good idea because many of the treatments that can reduce the damage of a heart attack are most useful when provided early. When it comes to your own health, protecting your mind from distress through the denial of illness can result in exposing your body to great danger.

**THE REAL WORLD**

# This Is Your Brain on Placebos

There is something miraculous about adhesive bandages. Your standard household toddler typically *requires* one for any injury at all, expecting and often achieving immediate relief. It is not unusual to find a child who reports that aches or pains are "cured" if an adhesive bandage has been applied by a helpful adult. Of course, the adhesive bandage is not *really* helping the pain—or is it?

Physicians and psychologists have long puzzled over the *placebo effect*, a clinically significant psychological or physiological response to a therapeutically inert substance or procedure. The classic placebo is the sugar pill, but adhesive bandages, injections, heating pads, neck rubs, homeopathic remedies, and kind words can have placebo effects (Diederich & Goetz, 2008). Even sham brain surgery can be more effective than no treatment at all (McRae et al., 2004). The effect is most marked, however, when the patient knows that a treatment is taking place (Stewart-Williams, 2004). This is also true of active treatments: A morphine injection works much better if you know you are getting it (Benedetti, Maggi, & Lopiano, 2003). Knowledge effects can be remarkably specific, mirroring in detail what patients believe about the nature of medicine, for example, that two pills work better than one and an injection works better than just a pill (de Craen et al., 1999).

How do placebos operate? Do people being treated for pain really feel the pain but distort their report of the experience to make it fit their beliefs about treatment? Or does the placebo actually reduce the pain a patient experiences? Howard Fields and Jon Levine (1984) discovered that placebos trigger the release of endorphins (or *endogenous opioids*), painkilling chemicals similar to morphine that are produced by the brain (see the Consciousness chapter). In their experiments, they found that an injection of naloxone, an opioid-blocking drug, typically reduces the benefit both of an opioid such as morphine and a placebo injection, suggesting that the placebo has its painkilling effects because it triggers the release of endorphins.

▲ Can an adhesive bandage cure all of your aches and pains? Many children, like this little guy, report immediate pain relief following application of a bandage to whatever spot is hurting them. Although most adults know that adhesive bandages do not treat pain, the placebo effect remains powerful throughout the life span.

In another advance in the study of these effects, placebos were found to lower the activation of specific brain areas associated with pain. One set of fMRI studies examined brain activation as volunteers were exposed to electric shock or heat (Wager et al., 2004). In preparation for some exposures to these painful stimuli, a placebo cream was applied to the skin, and the participant was told it was an analgesic that would reduce the pain. Other participants merely experienced the pain. As you can see in the figure below, the fMRI scans showed decreased activation during placebo analgesia in the *thalamus, anterior cingulate cortex,* and *insula,* pain-sensitive brain regions that were activated during untreated pain. These findings suggest that placebos are not leading people to misreport their pain experience, but rather are reducing brain activity in areas that are normally active during pain experience.

Such findings do not mean that next time your stomach aches, you can break out an adhesive bandage and heal yourself. Part of the placebo effect is dependent on the conscious expectation that the placebo will work, and it could be a challenge to make yourself believe you will feel better when you do not. Part of the placebo effect is unconscious, though, a tendency to feel better that is learned through classical conditioning. When you have been healed in the past by a particular doctor or form of treatment, or in a certain setting, unconscious learning mechanisms may lead to improvement if you simply encounter a similar doctor, treatment, or setting again, even if you do not consciously expect to improve (Benedetti, Pollo, et al., 2003). There is something comforting about returning to things that have given you comfort in the past.

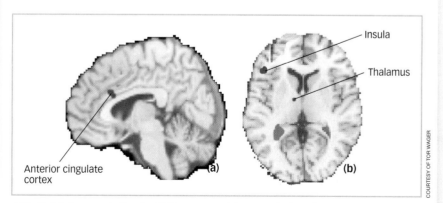

▲ **The Brain's Response to Placebo** fMRI scans reveal that some brain regions normally activated when individuals report pain in response to shocks are deactivated when those individuals are given a placebo analgesic during the shock. These regions include (*a*) the anterior cingulate cortex and (*b*) the insula and thalamus (Wager et al., 2004).

**psychosomatic illness**
An interaction between mind and body that can produce illness.

**somatic symptom disorders**
The set of psychological disorders in which a person with at least one bodily symptom displays significant health-related anxiety, expresses disproportionate concerns about their symptoms, and devotes excessive time and energy to their symptoms or health concerns.

**sick role**
A socially recognized set of rights and obligations linked with illness.

## Somatic Symptom Disorders

The flip side of denial is excessive sensitivity to illness, and it turns out that sensitivity also has its perils. Indeed, hypersensitivity to symptoms or to the possibility of illness underlies a variety of psychological problems and can also undermine physical health. Psychologists studying **psychosomatic illness,** *an interaction between mind and body that can produce illness,* explore ways in which mind (*psyche*) can influence body (*soma*) and vice versa. The study of mind–body interactions focuses on psychological disorders called **somatic symptom disorders,** in which *a person with at least one bodily symptom displays significant health-related anxiety, expresses disproportionate concerns about their symptoms, and devotes excessive time and energy to their symptoms or health concerns.* These are disorders like those that will be discussed in the Psychological Disorders chapter, but their association with symptoms in the body makes them relevant to this chapter's concern with stress and health. Disorders focused on

> How can hypersensitivity to symptoms undermine health?

concerns about physical illness used to be called *somatoform disorders* and included categories like hypochondriasis. Somatoform disorders were those in which people experienced unexplained medical symptoms believed to be generated by a person's mind. However, the focus on psychosomatic illness has shifted from concerns about mentally generated physical symptoms, to excessive psychological concerns about explainable medical symptoms, with the idea that the latter are serious and could benefit from psychological intervention. Some believe this shift in focus is problematic and will lead psychologists and psychiatrists to label normal concern about one's health as a psychological disorder. The interesting and somewhat complicated question of what should be considered a psychological disorder and what should not is something we tackle more directly in the Psychological Disorders chapter.

## On Being a Patient

Getting sick is more than a change in physical state: It can involve a transformation of identity. This change can be particularly profound with a serious illness: A kind of cloud settles over you, a feeling that you are now different, and this transformation can influence everything you feel and do in this new world of illness. You even take on a new role in life, a **sick role:** *a socially recognized set of rights and obligations linked with illness* (Parsons, 1975). The sick person is absolved of responsibility for many everyday obligations and enjoys exemption from normal activities. For example, in addition to skipping school and homework and staying on the couch all day, a sick child can watch TV and avoid eating anything unpleasant at dinner. At the extreme, the sick person can get away with being rude, lazy, demanding, and picky. In return for these exemptions, the sick role also incurs obligations. The properly "sick" individual cannot appear to enjoy the illness or reveal signs of wanting to be sick and must also take care to pursue treatment to end this "undesirable" condition. Parsons observed that illness has psychological, social, and even moral components. You may recall times when you have felt the conflict between sickness and health as though it were a moral decision: Should you drag yourself out of bed and try to make it to the chemistry exam or just slump back under the covers and wallow in your "pain"?

Some people feign medical or psychological symptoms to achieve something they want, a type of behaviour called *malingering.* Because many symptoms of illness cannot be faked (even facial expressions of pain are difficult to simulate) (Williams, 2002), malingering is possible only with a restricted number of illnesses. Faking illness is suspected when the secondary gains of illness, such as the ability to rest, to be freed from performing unpleasant

> What benefits might come from being ill?

Have you ever ridden on public transportation sitting next to a person with a hacking cough? We are bombarded by advertisements for medicines designed to suppress symptoms of illness so we can keep going. Is staying home with a cold socially acceptable or considered malingering? How does this jibe with the concept of the *sick role*?

tasks, or to be helped by others, outweigh the costs. Such gains can be very subtle, as when a child stays in bed because of the comfort provided by an otherwise distant parent, or they can be obvious, as when insurance benefits turn out to be a cash award for Best Actor. Some behaviours that may lead to illness may not be under the patient's control; for example, self-starvation may be part of an uncontrollable eating disorder (see the Emotion and Motivation chapter). For this reason, malingering can be difficult to diagnose and treat (Feldman, 2004).

©DAN ATKIN/ALAMY

## Patient–Practitioner Interaction

Medical care usually occurs through a strange interaction. On one side is a patient, often miserable, who expects to be questioned and examined and possibly prodded, pained, or given bad news. On the other side is a health care provider, who comes in knowing nothing about what brings the patient into the examination room, but hopes to quickly obtain information from the patient by asking lots of extremely personal questions (and examining extremely personal parts of the body); identify the problem and potential solution; help in some way; and achieve all of this as efficiently as possible because more patients are waiting. It seems less like a time for healing than an occasion for major awkwardness. One of the keys to an effective medical care interaction is physician empathy (Spiro et al., 1994). To offer successful treatment, the clinician must simultaneously understand the

Doctor and patient have two modes of interaction, the technical and the interpersonal. Medical training with robot patients may help doctors learn the technical side of health care, but it is likely to do little to improve the interpersonal side.

**Why is it important that a physician be empathic?**

patient's physical state *and* psychological state. Physicians often err on the side of failing to acknowledge patients' emotions, focusing instead on technical issues of the case (Suchman et al., 1997). This is particularly unfortunate because a substantial percentage of patients who seek medical care do so for treatment of psychological and emotional problems (Taylor, 1986). As the Greek physician Hippocrates wrote in the fourth century BCE: "Some patients, though conscious that their condition is perilous, recover their health simply through their contentment with the goodness of the physician." The best physician treats the patient's mind as well as the patient's body.

Another important part of the medical care interaction is motivating the patient to follow the prescribed regimen of care (Miller & Rollnick, 2012). When researchers check compliance by counting the pills remaining in a patient's bottle after a prescription has been underway, they find that patients often do an astonishingly poor job of following doctors' orders (see **FIGURE 14.6**). Compliance deteriorates when the treatment must be *frequent,* as when eyedrops for glaucoma are required every few hours, or *inconvenient* or *painful,* such as drawing blood or performing injections in managing diabetes. Finally, compliance decreases *as the number of treatments increases.* This is a worrisome problem, especially for older patients, who may have difficulty remembering when to take which pill. Failures in medical care may stem from the failure of health care providers to recognize the psychological challenges that are involved in self-care. Helping people to follow doctors' orders involves psychology, not medicine, and is an essential part of promoting health.

▼ Figure **14.6** **Antacid Intake** A scatterplot of antacid intake measured by bottle count plotted against patient's stated intake for 116 patients. When the actual and stated intakes are the same, the point lies on the diagonal line; when stated intake is greater than actual, the point lies above the line. Most patients exaggerated their intake (Roth & Caron, 1978).

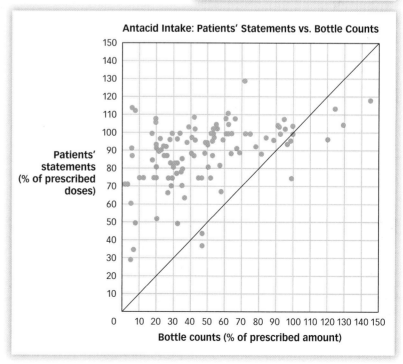

**Antacid Intake: Patients' Statements vs. Bottle Counts**

Patients' statements (% of prescribed doses) vs. Bottle counts (% of prescribed amount)

"Whoa — *way* too much information."

ALEX GREGORY/THE NEW YORKER COLLECTION/WWW.CARTOONBANK.COM

## IN SUMMARY

▶ The psychology of illness concerns how sensitivity to the body leads people to recognize illness and seek treatment.

▶ Somatic symptom disorders can stem from excessive sensitivity to physical problems.

▶ The sick role is a set of rights and obligations linked with illness; some people fake illness in order to accrue those rights.

▶ Successful health care providers interact with their patients to understand both the physical state and the psychological state.

# The Psychology of Health: Feeling Good

Two kinds of psychological factors influence personal health: health-relevant personality traits and health behaviour. Personality can influence health through relatively enduring traits that make some people particularly susceptible to health problems or stress while sparing or protecting others. The Type A behaviour pattern is an example. Because personality is not typically something we choose ("I would like a bit of that sense of humour and extraversion over there, please, but hold the whininess"), this source of health can be outside personal control. In contrast, engaging in positive health behaviours is something anyone can do, at least in principle.

## Personality and Health

Different health problems seem to plague different social groups. For example, South Asian Canadians, even those of healthy weight, are more likely to die from a heart attack earlier than the general population, and First Nations people are more susceptible to diabetes than are Asians or Europeans. Beyond these general social categories, personality turns out to be a factor in Canadians' wellness, with individual differences in optimism and hardiness being important influences (Heart & Stroke Foundation, 2010).

### Optimism

Pollyanna is one of literature's most famous optimists. Eleanor H. Porter's 1913 novel portrayed Pollyanna as a girl who greeted life with boundless good cheer, even when she was orphaned and sent to live with her cruel aunt. Her response to a sunny day was to remark on the good weather, of course, but her response to a gloomy day was to point out how lucky it is that not every day is gloomy! Her crotchety Aunt Polly had exactly the opposite attitude, somehow managing to turn every happy moment into an opportunity for strict correction. A person's level of optimism or pessimism tends to be fairly stable over time, and research comparing the personalities of twins reared together versus those reared apart suggests that this stability arises because these traits are moderately heritable (Plomin et al., 1992). Perhaps Pollyanna and Aunt Polly were each "born that way."

An optimist who believes that "in uncertain times, I usually expect the best" is likely to be healthier than a pessimist who believes that "if something can go wrong for me, it will." One recent review of dozens of studies including tens of thousands of participants concluded that of all of the measures of psychological well-being examined, optimism is the one that most strongly

Adrianne Haslet was approximately 1.2 m away from one of the bombs that exploded at the Boston Marathon in 2013. Although the explosion caused her to lose her left foot, Adrianne vowed that she will continue her career as a dancer—and will run the Boston Marathon in 2014. She is an optimist, and optimism can lead to positive health outcomes.

DONNA SVENNEVIK/ABC VIA GETTY IMAGES

predicted a positive outcome for cardiovascular health (Boehm & Kubzansky, 2012). Importantly, the association between optimism and cardiovascular health remains even after statistically controlling for traditional risk factors for heart disease including depression and anxiety, suggesting that it is not just the absence of psychopathology, but the presence of positive expectancies for the future, that predict positive health outcomes. Does just having positive thoughts about the future make it so? Unfortunately not.

Rather than improving physical health directly, optimism seems to aid in the maintenance of *psychological* health in the face of physical health problems. When sick, optimists are more likely than pessimists to maintain positive emotions, avoid negative emotions such as anxiety and depression, stick to medical regimens their caregivers have prescribed, and keep up their relationships with others. Among women who have surgery for breast cancer, for example, optimists are less likely to experience distress and fatigue after treatment than are pessimists, largely because they keep up social contacts and recreational activities during their treatment (Carver, Lehman, & Antoni, 2003). Optimism also seems to aid in the maintenance of physical health. For instance, optimism appears to be associated with cardiovascular health because optimistic people tend to engage in healthier behaviours like eating a balanced diet and exercising, which in turn leads to a healthier lipid profile (i.e., higher levels of high-density lipoprotein cholesterol that help to prevent buildup in your arteries, and lower triglycerides, which are the chemical form of fat storage in the body), which decreases the risk of heart disease (Boehm et al., 2013). So being optimistic is a positive asset, but it takes more than just hope to obtain positive health benefits.

> **Who is healthier, the optimist or the pessimist? Why?**

The benefits of optimism raise an important question: If the traits of optimism and pessimism are stable over time—even resistant to change—can pessimists ever hope to gain any of the advantages of optimism (Heatherton & Weinberger, 1994)? Research has shown that even die-hard pessimists can be trained to become significantly more optimistic and that this training can improve their psychosocial health outcomes. For example, pessimistic breast cancer patients who received 10 weeks of training in stress management techniques became more optimistic and were less likely than those who received only relaxation exercises to suffer distress and fatigue during their cancer treatments (Antoni et al., 2001).

## Hardiness

Some people seem to be thick-skinned, somehow able to take stress or abuse that could be devastating to others. Are there personality traits that contribute to such resilience and offer protection from stress-induced illness? To identify such traits, Suzanne Kobasa (1979) studied a group of stress-resistant business executives. These individuals reported high levels of stressful life events but had histories of relatively few illnesses compared with a similar group who succumbed to stress by getting sick. The stress-resistant group (Kobasa labelled them *hardy*) shared several traits, all conveniently beginning with the letter C. They showed a sense of *commitment,* an ability to become involved in life's tasks and encounters rather than just dabbling. They exhibited a belief in *control,* the expectation that their actions and words have a causal influence over their lives and environment. And they were willing to accept *challenge,* undertaking change and accepting opportunities for growth.

Can just anyone develop hardiness? Researchers have attempted to teach hardiness with some success. In one such attempt, participants

Sometimes hardiness tips over the edge into foolhardiness. Members of BC's Polar Bear Swim Club take that plunge every New Year's Day.

attended 10 weekly hardiness-training sessions, in which they were encouraged to examine their stresses, develop action plans for dealing with them, explore their bodily reactions to stress, and find ways to compensate for unchangeable situations without falling into self-pity. Compared with control groups (who engaged in relaxation and meditation training or in group discussions about stress), the hardiness-training group reported greater reductions in their perceived personal stress as well as fewer symptoms of illness (Maddi, Kahn, & Maddi, 1998). Hardiness training can have similar positive effects in university students, for some even boosting their GPA (Maddi et al., 2009).

## Health-Promoting Behaviours and Self-Regulation

Even without changing our personalities at all, we can do certain things to be healthy. The importance of healthy eating, safe sex, and giving up smoking are common knowledge. But we do not seem to be acting on the basis of this knowledge. Currently 59.9 percent of Canadian men and 45.0 percent of Canadian women are overweight or obese (Statistics Canada, 2013b). The prevalence of unsafe sex is difficult to estimate, but currently in Canada it is estimated that of every 100 sexually active people, 30 will be found to have a sexually transmitted bacterial infection (chlamydia, gonorrhea, or syphilis). This rate is rising quickly (Public Health Agency of Canada, 2010). Another 71 300 people live with human immunodeficiency virus/acquired immune deficiency syndrome (HIV/AIDS), 25 percent of whom are unaware of their infection, which is usually contracted through unprotected sex with an infected partner (Public Health Agency of Canada, 2012). And despite endless warnings, 16 percent of Canadians still smoke cigarettes (Health Canada, 2013). What is going on?

### Self-Regulation

Doing what is good for you is not necessarily easy. Mark Twain once remarked, "The only way to keep your health is to eat what you do not want, drink what you do not like, and do what you would rather not."

Engaging in health-promoting behaviours involves **self-regulation,** *the exercise of voluntary control over the self to bring the self into line with preferred standards.* When you decide on a salad rather than a cheeseburger, for instance, you control your impulse and behave in a way that will help to make you the kind of person you would prefer to be—a healthy one. Self-regulation often involves putting off immediate gratification for longer-term gains.

> **Why is it difficult to achieve and maintain self-control?**

Self-regulation requires a kind of inner strength or willpower. One theory suggests that self-control is a kind of strength that can be fatigued (Baumeister, Heatherton, & Tice, 1995; Baumeister, Vohs, & Tice, 2007). In other words, trying to exercise control in one area may exhaust self-control, leaving behaviour in other areas unregulated. To test this theory, researchers seated hungry volunteers near a batch of fresh, hot, chocolate chip cookies. They asked some participants to leave the cookies alone but help themselves to a healthy snack of radishes, whereas others were allowed to indulge. When later challenged with an impossibly difficult figure-tracing task, the self-control group was more likely than the self-indulgent group to abandon the difficult task—behaviour interpreted as evidence that they had depleted their pool of self-control (Baumeister et al., 1998). The take-home message from this experiment is that to control behaviour successfully, we need to choose our battles, exercising self-control mainly on the personal weaknesses that are most harmful to health.

JEAN SANDER/FEATUREPICS

Nobody ever said self-control was easy. Probably the only reason you are able to keep yourself from eating this cookie is that it is just a picture of a cookie. Really. Do not eat it.

**self-regulation**
The exercise of voluntary control over the self to bring the self into line with preferred standards.

Sometimes, though, self-regulation is less a matter of brute force than of strategy. Martial artists claim that anyone can easily overcome a large attacker with the use of the right moves, and overcoming our own unhealthy impulses may also be a matter of finesse. Let us look carefully at healthy approaches to some key challenges for self-regulation—eating, safe sex, and smoking—to learn what "smart moves" can aid us in our struggles.

## Eating Wisely

In many Western cultures, the weight of the average citizen is increasing at an alarming rate. One explanation is based on our evolutionary history: In order to ensure their survival, our ancestors found it useful to eat well in times of plenty to store calories for leaner times. In postindustrial societies in the twenty-first century, however, there are no leaner times, and people cannot burn all of the calories they consume (Pinel, Assanand, & Lehman, 2000). But why, then, is obesity not endemic throughout the Western world? Why are people in France leaner on average than North Americans, even though their foods are high in fat? One reason has to do with the fact that activity level in France is greater. Research by Paul Rozin and his colleagues also finds that portion sizes in France are significantly smaller than in the United States, but at the same time, people in France take longer to finish their smaller meals. At a McDonald's in France, diners take an average of 22 minutes to consume a meal, whereas in the United States, they take under 15 minutes (Rozin, Kabnick, et al., 2003). The fact that people in France are eating less food more slowly, may lead them to be more conscious of what they are eating. This, ironically, probably leads to lower french fry consumption.

One of the reasons that people in France are leaner than people in the United States is because the average French diner spends 22 minutes to consume a fast-food meal, whereas the average American diner spends only 15 minutes. How could the length of the average meal influence an individual's body weight?

Short of moving to France, what can you do? Studies indicate that dieting does not always work because the process of conscious self-regulation can be easily undermined by stress, leading people who are trying to control themselves to lose control by overindulging in the very behaviour they had been trying to overcome. This may remind you of a general principle discussed in the Consciousness chapter: Trying hard not to do something can often directly produce the unwanted behaviour (Wegner, 1994a, 1994b).

The restraint problem may be inherent in the very act of self-control (Polivy & Herman, 1992). Rather than dieting, then, heading toward normal weight should

> **Why is exercise a more effective weight-loss choice than dieting?**

involve a new emphasis on exercise and nutrition (Prochaska & Sallis, 2004). In emphasizing what is good to eat, the person can freely think about food rather than trying to suppress thoughts about it. A focus on increasing activity rather than reducing food intake, in turn, gives people another positive and active goal to pursue. Self-regulation is more effective when it focuses on what to do rather than on what *not* to do (Molden, Lee, & Higgins, 2009; Wegner & Wenzlaff, 1996).

## Avoiding Sexual Risks

People put themselves at risk when they have unprotected vaginal, oral, or anal intercourse. Sexually active adolescents and adults are usually aware of such risks, not to mention the risk of unwanted pregnancy, and yet many behave in risky ways nonetheless. Why does awareness not translate into avoidance? Risk takers harbour an *illusion of unique invulnerability,* a systematic bias toward believing that they are less likely to fall victim to the problem than are others (Perloff & Fetzer, 1986). For example, a study of sexually active female university students found that respondents judged their own likelihood of getting pregnant in the next year as less than 10 percent, but estimated the average for other women at the university to be 27 percent (Burger & Burns, 1988). Paradoxically, this illusion was even stronger among women in the sample who reported using inadequate or no contraceptive techniques. The tendency to think "It will not happen to me" may be most pronounced when it probably will.

Unprotected sex often is the impulsive result of last-minute emotions. When thought is further blurred by alcohol or recreational drugs, people often fail to use the latex condoms that can reduce their exposure to the risks of pregnancy, HIV, and many other STDs. Like other forms of self-regulation, the avoidance of sexual risk requires the kind of planning that can be easily undone by circumstances that hamper the ability to think ahead. One approach to reducing sexual risk taking, then, is simply finding ways to help people plan ahead. Sex education programs offer adolescents just such a chance by encouraging them, at a time when they have not had much sexual experience, to think about what they might do when they need to make decisions. Although sex education is sometimes criticized as increasing adolescents' awareness of and interest in sex, the research evidence is clear: Sex education reduces the likelihood that adolescents will engage in unprotected sexual activity and benefits their health (American Psychological Association, 2005). The same holds true for adults.

> **Why does planning ahead reduce sexual risk taking?**

## Not Smoking

One in two smokers dies prematurely from smoking-related diseases such as lung cancer, heart disease, emphysema, and cancer of the mouth and throat. Lung cancer alone kills more people than any other form of cancer, and smoking causes 80 percent of lung cancers. Although the overall rate of smoking in Canada is declining, new smokers abound, and many cannot seem to stop. University students are puffing away along with everyone else, with 10 to 18 percent of university students currently smoking (Health Canada, 2013). In the face of all the devastating health consequences, why do people not quit?

Nicotine, the active ingredient in cigarettes, is addictive, so smoking is difficult to stop once the habit is established (as discussed in the Consciousness chapter). As in other forms of self-regulation, the resolve to quit smoking is fragile and seems to break down under stress. And for some time after quitting, ex-smokers remain sensitive to cues in the environment: Eating or drinking, a bad mood, anxiety, or just seeing someone else smoking is enough to make them want a cigarette (Shiffman et al., 1996). The good news is that the urge decreases and people become less likely to relapse the longer they have been away from nicotine.

Psychological programs and techniques to help people kick the habit include nicotine replacement systems such as gum and skin patches, counselling programs, and hypnosis, but these programs are not always successful. Trying again and again in different ways is apparently the best approach (Schachter, 1982). After all, to quit smoking forever, you only need to quit one more time than you start up. But like the self-regulation of eating and sexuality, the self-regulation of smoking can require effort and thought. The ancient Greeks blamed self-control problems on *akrasia* (weakness of will). Modern psychology focuses less on blaming a person's character for poor self-regulation and points instead toward the difficulty of the task. Keeping healthy by behaving in healthy ways is one of the great challenges of life.

> **To quit smoking forever, how many times do you need to quit?**

GREGORY

*"Boy, I'm going to pay for this tomorrow at yoga class."*

▶ The connection between mind and body can be revealed through the influences of personality and self-regulation of behaviour on health.

▶ The personality traits of optimism and hardiness are associated with reduced risk for illnesses, perhaps because people with these traits can fend off stress.

▶ The self-regulation of behaviours such as eating, sexuality, and smoking is difficult for many people because self-regulation is easily disrupted by stress; strategies for maintaining self-control can pay off with significant improvements in health and quality of life.

# OTHER VOICES

## False Hopes and Overwhelming Urges

By Lisa Willemse

Leading research into eating disorders suggests that overcoming obesity is not merely about addressing weight through an improvement in energy balanc—sometimes the real struggle is in the mind.

Much has been studied and written on the physical and dietary contributors to obesity in recent years. As a result, health practitioners are better equipped to make informed recommendations on portion sizes, food choices and exercise regimens. But we now recognize that obesity is a multifaceted issue, and that dietary approaches alone often ignore the powerful behavioural, cognitive and emotional factors in play.

Few researchers understand this concept better than Dr. Janet Polivy. A professor of psychology at the University of Toronto, Dr. Polivy has been unraveling the complicated psychology behind eating and weight disorders for more than 30 years. Her studies have led to some important findings, among them the False Hope Syndrome and the 'What-the-Hell Effect.'

The False Hope Syndrome emerged from a series of studies looking at why diets and weight loss gimmicks do not work for the majority of patients.

"When most of us approach a diet or weight loss program, our expectations tend to be optimistic, particularly about changing things about ourselves, such as our appearance and body weight," Dr. Polivy explains. "We want to believe the promise diet programs make to us; that it will be fast, easy, effective, and that we will keep the weight off for the long term. But we also want to believe the implicit promises—that if we follow the quick diet we'll get a better job, find our soul mate, have more friends."

Such promises, promoted by books, product packaging and the media, raise expectations falsely and contradict the research evidence, which has conclusively found that weight loss is not easy, fast or permanent.

"There is no magic diet," says Dr. Polivy. "These unrealistic expectations about changing aspects of oneself contribute to the failure of the effort, and the failure often results in lowered self-esteem and self-image."

Dr. Polivy identified the 'What-the-Hell Effect' through a study which looked at eating patterns of dieters and non-dieters. The study, which forced some participants to radically over-exceed their daily caloric intake before being invited to eat ice cream, found that, while most non-dieters declined or ate very little ice cream, dieters tended to eat more ice cream because they had already blown their diet for the day.

The 'What-the-Hell Effect' is a chronic dieter's cue to abandon dietary efforts in the face of overwhelming temptation, and is more common when the dieter is in social events where others are eating food the dieter considers "banned" or eating in quantities larger than the diet allows. "This is much more of a danger if you have been denying yourself for longer periods of time or keeping away from certain foods," says Dr. Polivy. "If everyone else is eating what you want, then it is much harder to refuse. You feel deprived and hard done by—once you feel deprived you are more susceptible to temptation."

Fighting the urge to toss aside a diet, even for a few hours, is particularly challenging in today's society, because we are bombarded with food cues. "Everywhere we look it's all around us, pushing our desires to eat more and reminding us of what we're missing," notes Dr. Polivy.

For obese patients who may be struggling with feelings of inadequacy, failure and low self esteem, these temptations can be too hard to overcome and can be followed by feelings of failure and guilt. Greater understanding and communication about these urges can go a long way in helping patients overcome them, she says.

### DIET'S MENTAL CHALLENGES

Dr. Janet Polivy's research has identified many psychological contributors to obesity, among them:

**False Hope Syndrome**—Dieters place unrealistic expectations about changing aspects of oneself, based on false promises of fast, easy and long-term results conveyed by many diets. These contribute to failure, leading to lowered self-esteem and self-image for the dieter.

**What-The-Hell Effect**—A reaction to overwhelming food stimulus among chronic dieters which causes them to abandon their diet, especially in situations where the dieter has less control over food choices and/or sees others overeating. Feelings of deprivation and hardship exacerbate the urge to eat, and once the diet is broken, a "what-the-hell" attitude leads to binging and further feelings of guilt and failure.

Adapted with permission from CONDUIT magazine, the official publication of the Canadian Obesity Network (www.obesitynetwork.ca). (c) 2009

# Chapter Review

1. What kinds of stressors are you likely to be exposed to if you live in a dense urban area with considerable traffic, noise, and pollution?
   a. cultural stressors
   b. intermittent stressors
   c. chronic stressors
   d. positive stressors

2. In an experiment, two groups are subject to distractions while attempting to complete a task. Group A is told they can quiet the distractions by pushing a button. This information is withheld from Group B. Why will Group A's performance at the task likely be better than Group B's?
   a. Group B is working in a different environment.
   b. Group A has perceived control over a source of performance-impeding stress.
   c. Group B is less distracted than Group A.
   d. The distractions affecting Group B are now chronic.

3. The brain activation that occurs in response to a threat begins in the
   a. pituitary gland.
   c. adrenal gland.
   b. hypothalamus.
   d. corpus callosum.

4. According to the general adaptation syndrome, during the __ phase, the body adapts to its high state of arousal as it tries to cope with a stressor.
   a. exhaustion
   b. alarm
   c. resistance
   d. energy

5. Which of the following statements is most accurate regarding the physiological response to stress?
   a. Type A behaviour patterns have psychological but not physiological ramifications.
   b. The link between work-related stress and coronary heart disease is unfounded.
   c. Stressors can cause hormones to flood the brain, strengthening the immune system.
   d. The immune system is remarkably responsive to psychological influences.

6. Meditation is an altered state of consciousness that occurs
   a. frequently in times of stress.
   b. through hypnosis.
   c. naturally or through special practices.
   d. as a result of dreamlike brain activity.

7. Engaging in aerobic exercise is a way of managing stress by managing the
   a. environment
   b. body.
   c. situation.
   d. intake of air.

8. Finding a new or creative way to think about a stressor that reduces its threat is called
   a. stress inoculation.
   b. repressive coping.
   c. reframing.
   d. rational coping.

9. The positive health outcomes associated with religiosity and spirituality are believed to be the result of all of the following except
   a. enhanced social support.
   b. engagement in healthier behaviour.
   c. endorsement of hope and optimism.
   d. intercessory prayer.

10. Faking an illness is a violation of
    a. malingering.
    b. somatoform disorder.
    c. the sick role.
    d. the Type B pattern of behaviour.

11. Which of the following describes a successful health care provider?
    a. displays empathy
    b. pays attention to both the physical and psychological state of the patient
    c. uses psychology to promote patient compliance
    d. all of the above

12. When sick, optimists are more likely than pessimists to
    a. maintain positive emotions.
    b. become depressed.
    c. ignore their caregiver's advice.
    d. avoid contact with others.

13. Which of the following is NOT a trait associated with hardiness?
    a. a sense of commitment
    b. an aversion to criticism
    c. a belief in control
    d. a willingness to accept challenge

14. Stress __ the self-regulation of behaviours such as eating and smoking.
    a. strengthens
    c. disrupts
    b. has no effect on
    d. normalizes

## KEY TERMS

biofeedback (p. 564)

burnout (p. 559)

chronic stressor (p. 551)

fight-or-flight response (p. 555)

general adaptation syndrome (GAS) (p. 555)

health psychology (p. 550)

immune system (p. 557)

lymphocytes (p. 557)

meditation (p. 563)

psychosomatic illness (p. 572)

rational coping (p. 561)

reframing (p. 562)

relaxation response (p. 564)

relaxation therapy (p. 564)

repressive coping (p. 561)

self-regulation (p. 576)

sick role (p. 572)

social support (p. 566)

somatic symptom disorders (p. 572)

stress (p. 550)

stress inoculation training (SIT) (p. 562)

stressors (p. 550)

telomerase (p. 556)

telomeres (p. 556)

Type A behaviour pattern (p. 559)

## CHANGING MINDS

1. In 2002, researchers compared severe acne in university students during a relatively stress-free period and during a highly stressful exam period. After adjusting for other variables such as changes in sleep or diet, the researchers concluded that increased acne severity was strongly correlated with increased levels of stress. Learning about the study, your roommate is surprised. "Acne is a skin disease," your roommate says. "I don't see how it could have anything to do with your mental state." How would you weigh in on the role of stress in medical diseases? What other examples could you give of ways in which stress can affect health?

2. A friend of yours, who is taking a heavy course load, confides that he is feeling overwhelmed. "I can't take the stress," he says. "Sometimes I daydream of living on an island somewhere, where I can just lie in the sun and have no stress at all." What would you tell your friend about stress? Is all stress bad? What would a life with no stress really be like?

3. One of your classmates spent the summer interning in a neurologist's office. "One of the most fascinating things," she says, "was the patients with psychosomatic illness. Some had seizures or partial paralysis of an arm, and there were no neurological causes—so it was all psychosomatic. The neurologist tried to refer these patients to psychiatrists, but a lot of the patients thought he was accusing them of faking their symptoms, and were very insulted." What would you tell your friend about psychosomatic illness? Could a disease that is "all in the head" really produce symptoms such as seizures or partial paralysis, or are these patients definitely faking their symptoms?

## ANSWERS TO KEY CONCEPT QUIZ

1. c; 2. b; 3. b; 4. c; 5. d; 6. c; 7. b; 8. c; 9. d; 10. c; 11. d; 12. a; 13. b; 14. c.

# 15

# Psychological Disorders

▲ Defining Mental Disorders:
   What Is Abnormal?
   Conceptualizing Mental Disorders
   Classifying Mental Disorders
   Causation of Disorders
   CULTURE & COMMUNITY What do Mental
      Disorders Look Like in Different Parts of
      the World?
   A New Approach to Understanding Mental
      Disorders: RDoC
   THE REAL WORLD How Are Mental Disorders
      Defined and Diagnosed?
   Dangers of Labelling

▲ Anxiety Disorders: When Fears Take Over
   Phobic Disorders
   Panic Disorder
   Generalized Anxiety Disorder

▲ Obsessive-Compulsive Disorder: Trapped
   in a Loop

▲ Post-traumatic Stress Disorder:
   Troubles after a Trauma

▲ Depressive and Bipolar Disorders:
   At the Mercy of Emotions
   Depressive Disorders
   Bipolar Disorder

▲ Schizophrenia and Other Psychotic
   Disorders: Losing the Grasp on Reality
   Symptoms and Types of Schizophrenia
   Biological Factors
   Psychological Factors
   OTHER VOICES Successful and
      Schizophrenic

▲ Disorders of Childhood and Adolescence:
   Difficulties during Development
   Autism Spectrum Disorder
   HOT SCIENCE Optimal Outcome in Autism
      Spectrum Disorder
   Attention-Deficit/Hyperactivity Disorder
   Conduct Disorder

▲ Personality Disorders: Going to Extremes
   Types of Personality Disorders
   Antisocial Personality Disorder

▲ Self-Harm Behaviours: When the Mind
   Turns against Itself
   Suicidal Behaviour
   Non-suicidal Self-Injury

VIRGINIA WOOLF LEFT HER WALKING STICK on the bank of the river, put a large stone in the pocket of her coat, and made her way into the water. Her body was found 3 weeks later. She had written to her husband: "Dearest, I feel certain I am going mad again. … And I shan't recover this time. I begin to hear voices, and I can't concentrate. So I am doing what seems the best thing to do" (Dally, 1999, p. 182). Thus, near Rodmell, Sussex, England, on March 28, 1941, life ended for the prolific novelist and essayist, central figure of the avant-garde literary salon known as the Bloomsbury Group, influential feminist—and unfortunate victim of lifelong "breakdowns," with swings in mood between severe depression and unbridled mania.

The condition afflicting Woolf is now known as bipolar disorder. At one extreme were her episodes of depression: She was sullen and despondent; her creativity came to a halt; and sometimes she was bedridden for months by her illness. These periods alternated with mania, when, as her husband, Leonard, recounted, "She talked almost without stopping for 2 or 3 days, paying no attention to anyone in the room or anything said to her." Her language "became completely incoherent, a mere jumble of dissociated words." At the height of her spells, birds spoke to her in Greek, her dead mother reappeared and scolded her, and voices commanded her to "do wild things." She refused to eat, wrote pages of nonsense, and launched tirades of abuse at her husband and her companions (Dally, 1999, p. 240).

Between these phases, Woolf somehow managed a brilliant literary life. Her Victorian family had seen no reason for a woman to attend university, but the absence of schooling did not prevent her from becoming the extraordinary intellectual figure celebrated in the title of Edward Albee's (1962) play, *Who's Afraid of Virginia Woolf?* All told, she wrote nine novels, a play, five volumes of essays, and more than 14 volumes of diaries and letters. Her novels broke away from traditions of strict plot and setting to explore the inner lives and musings of her characters, and

English novelist and critic, Virginia Woolf (1882–1941), in 1937. Her lifelong affliction with bipolar disorder ended in suicide, but the manic phases of her illness helped to fuel her prolific writing.

©THE PRINT COLLECTOR/ALAMY

583

her observations revealed a keen appreciation of her own experience of psychological disorder. In a letter to a friend, she remarked, "As an experience, madness is terrific … and not to be sniffed at, and in its lava I still find most of the things I write about" (Dally, 1999, p. 240). The price that Woolf paid for her genius, of course, was a dear one, and her husband and companions shared the burden of dealing with her disorder and her death. Disorders of the mind can create immense pain.

**IN THIS CHAPTER, WE FIRST CONSIDER THE QUESTION: WHAT IS ABNORMAL?** Virginia Woolf's bouts of depression and mania and her eventual suicide certainly are abnormal in the sense that most people do not have these experiences, but at times she led a perfectly normal life. The enormously complicated human mind can produce behaviours, thoughts, and emotions that change radically from moment to moment. How do psychologists decide when a person's thoughts, emotions, and behaviours are "disordered?" We will first examine the key factors that must be weighed in making such a decision. We will then focus on several major forms of *mental disorder*: depressive and bipolar disorders; anxiety, obsessive-compulsive, and trauma-related disorders; schizophrenia; disorders that begin in childhood and adolescence; and self-harm behaviours. As we view each type of disorder, we will examine how they manifest and what is known about their prevalence and causes.

The disorders examined in this chapter represent a tragic loss of human potential. The contentment, peace, and love that people could be enjoying are crowded out by pain and suffering when the mind goes awry to create disorders. A scientific approach to mental disorders that views them through a model that considers the biological, psychological, and social factors that combine to cause disorders (appropriately called the *biopsychosocial model*) is beginning to sort out their symptoms and causes. As we see in the next chapter, this approach already offers treatments for some disorders that are remarkably effective, and for other disorders, it offers hope that pain and suffering can be alleviated in the future.

# Defining Mental Disorders: What Is Abnormal?

The concept of a mental disorder is one of those things that seems simple at first glance, but turns out to be very complex and quite tricky (similar to clearly defining "consciousness," "stress," or "personality"). Any extreme variation in your thoughts, feelings, or behaviours is not a mental disorder. For instance, severe anxiety before a test, sadness after the loss of a loved one, or a night of excessive alcohol consumption—although unpleasant—is not necessarily pathological. Similarly, a persistent pattern of deviating from the norm does not qualify a person for a mental disorder. If it did, we would diagnose mental disorders in the most creative and visionary people—anyone whose ideas deviate from those around them.

So what *is* a mental disorder? Perhaps surprisingly, there is not universal agreement on a precise definition of the term "mental disorder." However, there is general agreement that a **mental disorder** can be defined as *a persistent disturbance or dysfunction in behaviour, thoughts, or emotions that causes significant distress or impairment* (Stein et al., 2010; Wakefield, 2007). One way to think about mental disorders is as dysfunctions or deficits in the normal human psychological processes you have learned about throughout this textbook. People with mental disorders have problems with their perception, memory, learning, emotion, motivation, thinking, and social processes. You might ask: But this is still a broad definition, so what kinds of disturbances "count" as mental disorders? How long must they last to be considered

**mental disorder**
A persistent disturbance or dysfunction in behaviour, thoughts, or emotions that causes significant distress or impairment.

Although mental disorders represent deviations from normal behaviour, all deviations from the norm are not disordered. Indeed, people thinking differently about the world, and behaving in ways that deviated from the norm, have brought remarkable advances, such as Mickey Mouse, iPhones, and racial equality.

"persistent?" And how much distress or impairment is required? These are all hotly debated questions in the field. They have been for many years, and likely will be for years to come (as discussed in more detail later).

## Conceptualizing Mental Disorders

Historically speaking, there are reports of people acting strangely or reporting bizarre thoughts or emotions since ancient times. Until fairly recently, such difficulties were conceptualized as the result of religious or supernatural forces. In some cultures, psychopathology is still interpreted as possession by spirits or demons, as enchantment by a witch or shaman, or as God's punishment for wrongdoing. In many societies, including our own, people with psychological disorders have been feared and ridiculed, and often treated as criminals: punished, imprisoned, or put to death for their "crime" of deviating from the normal.

According to the theory of physiognomy, mental disorders could be diagnosed from facial features. This fanciful theory is now considered superstition but was popular from antiquity until the early twentieth century.

Over the past 200 years, these ways of looking at psychological abnormalities have largely been replaced in most parts of the world by a **medical model,** in which *abnormal psychological experiences are conceptualized as illnesses that, like physical illnesses, have biological and environmental causes, defined symptoms, and possible cures.* Conceptualizing abnormal thoughts and behaviours as illness suggests that a first step is to determine the nature of the problem through *diagnosis.*

**What is the first step in helping someone with a psychological disorder?**

In diagnosis, clinicians seek to determine the nature of a person's mental disorder by assessing *signs* (objectively observed indicators of a disorder) and *symptoms* (subjectively reported behaviours, thoughts, and emotions) that suggest an underlying illness. So, for example, just as a self-reported fever, sniffles, and cough are symptoms of a cold, Virginia Woolf's extreme moods, alternating between despondency and wild euphoria, can be seen as

**medical model**
Abnormal psychological experiences are conceptualized as illnesses that, like physical illnesses, have biological and environmental causes, defined symptoms, and possible cures.

SIMONE BECCHETTI/GETTY IMAGES

Extreme shyness or social anxiety disorder? What are some of the criticisms of the medical model?

symptoms of her bipolar disorder. It is important to note the differences among three related general medical and classification terms:

> A *disorder* refers to a common set of signs and symptoms;

> A *disease* is a known pathological process affecting the body; and

> A *diagnosis* is a determination as to whether a disorder or disease is present (Kraemer, Shrout, & Rubio-Stipec, 2007).

Importantly, knowing that a disorder is present (i.e., diagnosed) does not necessarily mean that we know the underlying disease process in the body that gives rise to the signs and symptoms of the disorder.

Viewing mental disorders as medical problems reminds us that people who are suffering deserve care and treatment, not condemnation. Nevertheless, there are some criticisms of the medical model. Some psychologists argue that it is inappropriate to use clients' subjective self-report, rather than physical tests of pathology (as in other areas of medical diagnostics), to determine underlying illness. Others argue that the model often "medicalizes" or "pathologizes" normal human behaviour. For instance, extreme sadness can be considered to be an illness called *major depressive disorder*; extreme shyness can be diagnosed as an illness called *social anxiety disorder*; and trouble concentrating in school is called *attention-deficit/hyperactivity disorder*. Although there are some valid concerns about the current method of defining and classifying mental disorders, it inarguably is a huge advance over older alternatives, such as viewing mental disorders as the work of witchcraft or as punishment for sin. Moreover, psychologists keep these concerns in mind as they work to improve the diagnostic procedures.

## Classifying Mental Disorders

So how is the medical model used to classify the wide range of abnormal behaviours that occur among humans? Psychologists, psychiatrists (physicians concerned with the study and treatment of mental disorders) and most other people working in the area of mental disorders use a standardized system for classifying mental disorders. There are currently two established systems for classifying mental disorders: The International Classification of Diseases (ICD-10) produced by the World Health

Organization, and the ***Diagnostic and Statistical Manual of Mental Disorders (DSM)*** produced by the American Psychiatric Association (APA). Since the *DSM* tends to be the classification used most widely in North America, it is the one we shall focus on. The *DSM* is *a classification system that describes the features used to diagnose each recognized mental disorder and indicates how the disorder can be distinguished from other, similar problems.* Each disorder is named and classified as a distinct illness. The initial version of the *DSM*, published in 1952, and its revision, *DSM–II*, published in 1968, provided a common language for talking about disorders. This was a major advance in the study of mental disorders; however, the diagnostic criteria listed in these early volumes were quite vague and based on thin theoretical assumptions. For instance, people who were extremely depressed or anxious for long periods of time might be given the general diagnosis of "neurosis reaction."

The next two editions of the *DSM* (*DSM–III*, published in 1980 and *DSM–IV*, published in 1994) moved from vague descriptions of disorders to very detailed lists of symptoms (or *diagnostic criteria*) that had to be present in order for a disorder to be diagnosed. For instance, in addition to being extremely sad or depressed (for at least 2 weeks), a person must have at least five of nine agreed upon symptoms of depression (e.g., diminished interest in normally enjoyable activities, significant weight loss or gain, significantly increased or decreased sleep, loss of energy, feelings of worthlessness or guilt, trouble concentrating). The use of these detailed lists of symptoms for each of more than 200 disorders listed led to a dramatic increase in the reliability, or consistency, in diagnosing mental disorders. Two clinicians interviewing the same individual were now much more likely to agree on what mental disorders were present, greatly increasing the credibility of the diagnostic process (and the fields of psychiatry and clinical psychology).

> **How has the *DSM* changed over time?**

In May, 2013, the American Psychiatric Association released an updated manual: *DSM–5*. The *DSM–5* describes 22 major categories containing more than 200 different mental disorders (see **TABLE 15.1**). Along with the disorders listed in these 22 categories, the *DSM–5* describes conditions that may be included as formal disorders, but that, for now, require additional research. In addition, there is a section devoted to cultural considerations in diagnosing mental disorders. Why the switch from Roman to Arabic numerals? The hope is that with more rapid advances in our understanding of mental disorders, rather than wait another 20 years to update the *DSM*, we can make revisions as we learn more (*DSM–5.1, 5.2, 5.3*, and so on).

Each of the 22 chapters in the main body of the *DSM–5* lists the specific criteria that must be met in order for a person to be diagnosed with each disorder. Approximately 1 in 5 Canadians will personally experience a mental disorder in their lifetime (Canadian Mental Health Association, n.d. 1). And, most of those with a mental disorder (greater than 80 percent) report **comorbidity,** which refers to *the co-occurrence of two or more disorders in a single individual* (Gadermann et al., 2012).

## Causation of Disorders

The medical model of mental disorder suggests that knowing a person's diagnosis is useful because any given category of mental illness is likely to have a distinctive cause. In other words, just as different viruses, bacteria, or genetic abnormalities cause different physical illnesses, so a specifiable pattern of causes (or *etiology*) may exist for different psychological disorders. The medical model also suggests that each category of mental disorder is likely to have a common *prognosis,* a typical course over time and susceptibility to treatment and cure. Unfortunately, this basic medical model is usually an oversimplification; it is rarely useful to focus on a *single cause* that is *internal* to the person and that suggests a *single cure.*

*Diagnostic and Statistical Manual of Mental Disorders (DSM)*
A classification system that describes the features used to diagnose each recognized mental disorder and indicates how the disorder can be distinguished from other, similar problems.

**comorbidity**
The co-occurrence of two or more disorders in a single individual.

> Table 15.1

## Main *DSM–5* Categories of Mental Disorders

1. **Neurodevelopmental Disorders:** These are conditions that begin early in development and cause significant impairments in functioning, such as intellectual disability (formerly called "mental retardation"), autism spectrum disorder, and attention-deficit/hyperactivity disorder.

2. **Schizophrenia Spectrum and Other Psychotic Disorders:** This is a group of disorders characterized by major disturbances in perception, thought, language, emotion, and behaviour.

3. **Bipolar and Related Disorders:** These disorders include major fluctuations in mood—from mania to depression—and also can include psychotic experiences, which is why they are placed between the psychotic and depressive disorders in *DSM–5*.

4. **Depressive Disorders:** These are conditions characterized by extreme and persistent periods of depressed mood.

5. **Anxiety Disorders:** These are disorders characterized by excessive fear and anxiety that are extreme enough to impair a person's functioning, such as panic disorder, generalized anxiety disorder, and specific phobia.

6. **Obsessive-Compulsive and Related Disorders:** These are conditions characterized by the presence of obsessive thinking followed by compulsive behaviour in response to that thinking.

7. **Trauma- and Stressor-Related Disorders:** These are disorders that develop in response to a traumatic event, such as post-traumatic stress disorder.

8. **Dissociative Disorders:** These are conditions characterized by disruptions or discontinuity in consciousness, memory, or identity, such as dissociative identity disorder (formerly called "multiple personality disorder").

9. **Somatic Symptom and Related Disorders:** These are conditions in which a person experiences bodily symptoms (e.g., pain, fatigue) associated with significant distress or impairment.

10. **Feeding and Eating Disorders:** These are problems with eating that impair health or functioning, such as anorexia nervosa and bulimia nervosa.

11. **Elimination Disorders:** These involve inappropriate elimination of urine or feces (e.g., bed-wetting).

12. **Sleep–Wake Disorders:** These are problems with the sleep–wake cycle, such as insomnia, narcolepsy, and sleep apnea.

13. **Sexual Dysfunctions:** These are problems related to unsatisfactory sexual activity, such as erectile disorder and premature ejaculation.

14. **Gender Dysphoria:** This is a single disorder characterized by incongruence between a person's experienced/expressed gender and assigned gender.

15. **Disruptive, Impulse-Control, and Conduct Disorders:** These are conditions involving problems controlling emotions and behaviours, such as conduct disorder, intermittent explosive disorder, and kleptomania.

16. **Substance-Related and Addictive Disorders:** This collection of disorders involves persistent use of substances or some other behaviour (e.g., gambling) despite the fact that it leads to significant problems.

17. **Neurocognitive Disorders:** These are disorders of thinking caused by conditions such as Alzheimer's disease or traumatic brain injury.

18. **Personality Disorders:** These are enduring patterns of thinking, feeling, and behaving that lead to significant life problems.

19. **Paraphilic Disorders:** These are conditions characterized by inappropriate sexual activity, such as pedophilic disorder.

20. **Other Mental Disorders:** This is a residual category for conditions that do not fit into one of the above categories but are associated with significant distress or impairment, such as an unspecified mental disorder due to a medical condition.

21. **Medication-Induced Movement Disorders and Other Adverse Effects of Medication:** These are problems with physical movement (e.g., tremors, rigidity) that are caused by medication.

22. **Other Conditions that May be the Focus of Clinical Attention:** These include problems related to abuse, neglect, relationship, and other problems.

*Source:* From *DSM–5* (American Psychiatric Association, 2013).

# CULTURE & COMMUNITY

## What do Mental Disorders Look Like in Different Parts of the World?

Are the mental disorders that are seen in North America also experienced by people in other parts of the world? In an effort to better understand the *epidemiology* (the study of the distribution and causes of health and disease) of mental disorders, Ronald Kessler and colleagues launched the World Health Organization World Mental Health Surveys, a large-scale study in which people from nearly two dozen countries around the world were assessed for the presence of mental disorders (Kessler & Üstün, 2008). The results of this study reveal that the major mental disorders seen in the United States (Canada was not included in the survey) appear similarly in countries and cultures all around the world. For instance, depression, anxiety, attention-deficit/hyperactivity disorder, and substance abuse are

seen all over the globe. They are reported at different rates in different countries (people in the United States reported the highest rates of mental disorders), but anxiety and depression are always the most common, followed by impulse-control and substance use disorders (Kessler et al., 2007).

Although all countries appear to have the common mental disorders described above, it is clear that cultural context can influence how mental disorders are experienced, described, assessed, and treated. To address this issue, the *DSM–5* includes a cultural formulation section that contains a Cultural Formulation Interview (CFI). The CFI includes 16 questions that the clinician asks a client during a mental health assessment in order to help the clinician understand how the client's culture might influence the experience, expression, and explanation of their mental disorder.

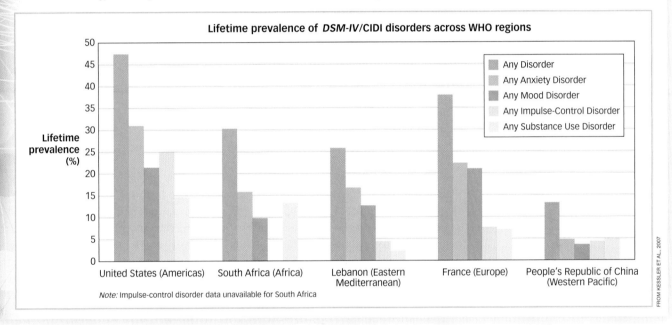

Lifetime prevalence of *DSM-IV*/CIDI disorders across WHO regions

*Note:* Impulse-control disorder data unavailable for South Africa

FROM KESSLER ET AL., 2007

To understand what factors might cause mental disorders, most psychologists take an integrated **biopsychosocial perspective** that *explains mental disorders as the result of interactions among biological, psychological, and social factors.* On the biological side, the focus is on genetic and epigenetic influences (see Figure 3.23 in the Neuroscience and Behaviour chapter), biochemical imbalances, and abnormalities in brain structure and function. The psychological perspective focuses on maladaptive learning and coping, cognitive biases, dysfunctional attitudes, and interpersonal problems. Social factors include poor socialization, stressful life experiences, and cultural and social inequities. The complexity of causation suggests that different individuals can experience a similar psychological disorder (e.g., depression) for different reasons. A person might fall into depression as a result of biological causes (e.g., genetics, hormones), psychological causes (e.g., faulty beliefs, hopelessness, poor strategies for coping with loss), environmental causes (e.g., stress or loneliness), or more likely as a result of some combination of these factors. And, of course, multiple causes mean there may not be one single cure.

The observation that most disorders have both internal (biological and psychological) *and* external (environmental) causes has given rise to a theory known as the

**Why does assessment require looking at a number of factors?**

**biopsychosocial perspective**
Explains mental disorders as the result of interactions among biological, psychological, and social factors.

Mental disorders can be caused by biological, psychological, and environmental factors. The diathesis–stress model suggests that a person may be predisposed for a psychological disorder that remains unexpressed until triggered by stress. Suppose that two identical twins (with the same genetic profile) grow up in the same household (sharing the same parents, the same basic diet, the same access to television, and so on). As a teenager, one twin but not the other develops a mental disorder such as schizophrenia. How could this be?

**diathesis–stress model, **which suggests that *a person may be predisposed for a psychological disorder that remains unexpressed until triggered by stress.* The diathesis is the internal predisposition and the stress is the external trigger. For example, most people were able to cope with their strong emotional reactions to the terrorist attack of September 11, 2001. However, for some who had a predisposition to negative emotions, the horror of the events may have overwhelmed their ability to cope, thereby precipitating a psychological disorder. Although diatheses can be inherited, it is important to remember that heritability is not destiny. A person who inherits a diathesis may never encounter the precipitating stress, whereas someone with little genetic propensity to a disorder may come to suffer from it given the right pattern of stress. The tendency to oversimplify mental disorders by attributing them to single, internal causes is nowhere more evident than in the interpretation of the role of the brain in psychological disorders. Brain scans of people with and without disorders can give rise to an unusually strong impression that psychological problems are internal and permanent, inevitable, and even untreatable. Brain influences and processes are fundamentally important for knowing the full story of psychological disorders, but are not the only chapter in that story.

> What are the limitations of using brain scans for diagnosing mental disorders?

## A New Approach to Understanding Mental Disorders: RDoC

Although the *DSM* provides a useful framework for classifying disorders, there has been a growing concern over the fact that the findings from scientific research on the biopsychosocial factors that appear to cause psychopathology do not map neatly onto individual *DSM* diagnoses. Succinctly characterizing the current state of affairs, Thomas R. Insel, Director of the American National Institute of Mental Health (NIMH; the primary funder of research on mental disorders in the United States), noted that although many people describe the *DSM* as a bible, it is more accurate to think of it like a dictionary that provides labels and current definitions: "People think that everything has to match *DSM* criteria, but you know what? Biology never read that book" (Insel, quoted in Belluck & Carey, 2013, p. A13). In order to better understand what actually causes mental disorders, researchers at the NIMH have proposed a new framework for thinking about mental disorders focused not on the currently defined *DSM* categories of disorders, but on the more basic biological, cognitive, and behavioural constructs that are believed to be the building blocks of mental disorders. This new system is called the **Research Domain Criteria Project (RDoC),** *a new initiative that aims to guide the classification and understanding of mental disorders by revealing the basic processes that give rise to them.* The RDoC is not intended to immediately replace the *DSM*, but to inform future revisions to it in the coming years (see The Real World box).

Using the RDoC, researchers study the causes of abnormal functioning by focusing on biological factors from genes to cells to brain circuits; psychological domains, such as learning, attention, memory; and various social processes and behaviour (see **TABLE 15.2** for a list of domains). The hope is that the RDoC approach will lead to more progress in understanding the underlying causes of mental disorders than does a focus on the traditional labels, and will also reveal links between disorders that were not previously suspected. The long-term goal is to better understand what abnormalities cause different disorders, and to classify disorders based on those underlying causes, rather than on observed symptoms. This approach would bring the study of mental disorders in line with the study of other medical disorders. For example, if

**diathesis–stress model**
Suggests that a person may be predisposed for a psychological disorder that remains unexpressed until triggered by stress.

**Research Domain Criteria Project (RDoC)**
A new initiative that aims to guide the classification and understanding of mental disorders by revealing the basic processes that give rise to them.

> **Table 15.2**

### Draft Research Domain Criteria (RDoC) Matrix

| Domain/Construct | Units of Analysis | | | | | | | |
|---|---|---|---|---|---|---|---|---|
| | Genes | Molecules | Cells | Circuits | Physiology | Behaviour | Self-reports | Paradigms |
| **Negative Valence Systems** | | | | | | | | |
| Acute threat ("fear") | | | | | | | | |
| Potential threat ("anxiety") | | | | | | | | |
| Sustained threat | | | | | | | | |
| Loss | | | | | | | | |
| Frustrative non-reward | | | | | | | | |
| **Positive Valence Systems** | | | | | | | | |
| Approach motivation | | | | | | | | |
| Initial responsiveness to reward | | | | | | | | |
| Sustained responsiveness to reward | | | | | | | | |
| Reward learning | | | | | | | | |
| Habit | | | | | | | | |
| **Cognitive Systems** | | | | | | | | |
| Attention | | | | | | | | |
| Perception | | | | | | | | |
| Working memory | | | | | | | | |
| Declarative memory | | | | | | | | |
| Language behaviour | | | | | | | | |
| Cognitive (effortful) control | | | | | | | | |
| **Systems for Social Processes** | | | | | | | | |
| Affiliation and attachment | | | | | | | | |
| Social communication | | | | | | | | |
| Perception and understanding of self | | | | | | | | |
| Perception and understanding of others | | | | | | | | |
| **Arousal and Regulatory Systems** | | | | | | | | |
| Arousal | | | | | | | | |
| Circadian rhythms | | | | | | | | |
| Sleep and wakefulness | | | | | | | | |

you are experiencing chest pain, severe headaches, fatigue, and difficulty breathing, it is unlikely that you are experiencing four separate disorders (*chest pain disorder, headache disorder,* etc.). Instead, we now know that these are all symptoms of an underlying disease process called hypertension. The RDoC approach similarly aims to shift the focus away from classifying based on surface symptoms and toward an understanding of the processes that give rise to disordered behaviour. For instance, rather than studying cocaine addiction as a distinct disorder, from an RDoC perspective researchers might try to understand what causes abnormalities in "responsiveness to reward," a factor seen in those with excessive cocaine use as well as those with other addictive behaviours. Indeed, recent research has shown that variations in a gene (*DRD2*) that codes for dopamine receptors are associated with abnormalities in connectivity between parts of the frontal lobe and the striatum (described in the Neuroscience and Behaviour chapter). This lack of connectivity is, in turn, related to the impulsiveness and responsiveness to rewards associated with a range of addictive behaviour disorders (Buckholtz & Meyer-Lindenberg, 2012). This may help explain

# How Are Mental Disorders Defined and Diagnosed?

Who decides what goes in the *DSM*? How are these decisions made? In psychology and psychiatry, as in the early days of most areas of the study of human health and behaviour, these decisions currently are made by consensus among leaders in the research field. These leaders meet repeatedly over several years to make decisions about which disorders should be included in the new revision of the *DSM*, and how they should be defined. Over the years, these decisions have been based on descriptive research reporting on which clinical symptoms tend to cluster together. Everyone agrees that we need a system for classifying and defining mental disorders; however, as the currently available body of knowledge about mental disorders grows,

the field is moving beyond simple descriptive diagnostic categories toward ones based on underlying biopsychosocial processes (i.e., the Research Domain Criteria Project). Future decisions about how mental disorders are defined will likely continue to be reached by consensus among leaders in the field, but will be driven more directly by research on the underlying causes of these disorders.

Who decides whether someone has a diagnosis? And how are these decisions made? Over the years, researchers have developed structured clinical interviews that convert the lists of symptoms included in the *DSM* into sets of interview questions through which the clinician (psychologist, psychiatrist, social worker) makes a determination about whether or not a given

person meets criteria for each disorder (Nock et al., 2007). For instance, according to *DSM–5*, a person must have at least five of the nine symptoms of major depressive disorder in order to meet criteria for this disorder. Structured clinical interviews typically include nine questions about depression (one per symptom), and if the person reports that they have at least five of these symptoms, the clinician may conclude that this person is suffering from major depression. Right now diagnoses are determined primarily by client self-report of symptoms. With increasing attention to the underlying causes of mental disorders, many hope that in the future we will have biological and behavioural tests to help us make decisions about who has a mental illness and who does not.

why some people seem to be vulnerable to different kinds of addiction and have trouble inhibiting their reward-seeking behaviour. Importantly, understanding what processes cause problems like addiction will help us to develop more effective treatments, a topic we address in more detail in the next chapter.

You might have noticed that the list of domains in Table 15.2 looks like a slightly more detailed version of the table of contents for this textbook! The RDoC approach has an overall emphasis on neuroscience (Chapter 3), and specific focuses on abnormalities in emotional and motivational systems (Chapters 8), cognitive systems such as memory (Chapter 6), learning (Chapter 7), language and cognition (Chapter 9), social processes (Chapter 13), and stress and arousal (Chapter 14). From the RDoC perspective, mental disorders can be thought of as the result of abnormalities or dysfunctions in normal psychological processes. By learning about many of these processes in this textbook, you will likely have a good understanding of new definitions of mental disorders as they are developed in the years ahead.

The new Research Domain Criteria are trying to help us better understand why people seem to have "addictive personalities" in which they have trouble limiting their engagement in pleasurable experiences.

## Dangers of Labelling

An important complication in the diagnosis and classification of psychological disorders is the effect of labelling. Psychiatric labels can have negative consequences because many carry the baggage of negative stereotypes and stigma, such as the idea that mental disorder is a sign of personal weakness or the idea that psychiatric patients are dangerous. The stigma associated with mental disorders may explain why most people with diagnosable psychological disorders (approximately 60 percent) do not seek treatment (Kessler, Demler, et al., 2005; Wang, Berglund, et al., 2005).

Unfortunately, educating people about mental disorders does not dispel the stigma borne by those with these conditions (Phelan et al., 1997). In fact, expectations created by psychiatric labels can sometimes even compromise the judgment of mental health professionals (Garb, 1998; Langer & Abelson, 1974; Temerlin & Trousdale, 1969). In a classic demonstration of this phenomenon, psychologist David Rosenhan and six associates reported to different mental hospitals complaining of "hearing voices," a

**Why might someone avoid seeking help for a mental illness?**

symptom sometimes found in people with schizophrenia. Each was admitted to a hospital, and each promptly reported that the symptom had ceased. Even so, hospital staff were reluctant to identify these people as normal: It took an average of 19 days for these "patients" to secure their release, and even then they were released with the diagnosis of "schizophrenia in remission" (Rosenhan, 1973). Apparently, once hospital staff had labelled these patients as having a psychological disease, the label stuck.

These effects of labelling are particularly disturbing in light of evidence that the hospitalization of people with mental disorders is seldom necessary. One set of studies followed the lives of patients who were thought to be too dangerous to release and therefore had been kept in the back wards of institutions for years. Their release resulted in no harm to the community (Harding et al., 1987), and further studies have shown that those with a mental disorder are no more likely to be violent than those without a disorder (Elbogen & Johnson, 2009; Monahan, 1992).

Labelling may even affect how labelled individuals view themselves; persons given such a label may come to view themselves not just as mentally disordered, but as hopeless or worthless. Such a view may cause them to develop an attitude of defeat and, as a result, to fail to work toward their own recovery. As one small step toward counteracting such consequences, clinicians have adopted the important practice of applying labels to the disorder and not to the person with the disorder. For example, an individual might be described as "a person with schizophrenia," not as "a schizophrenic." You will notice that we follow this convention in the textbook.

Although we label mental disorders, we should not apply those labels to people. For instance, rather than saying someone "is ADHD," we would say that the person currently meets diagnostic criteria for ADHD.

## IN SUMMARY

▶ The *DSM–5* is a classification system that defines a mental disorder as occurring when the person experiences disturbances of thought, emotion, or behaviour that produce distress or impairment and that arise from internal sources.

▶ According to the biopsychosocial model, mental disorders arise from an interaction of biological, psychological, and social factors, often thought of as a combination of a diathesis (internal predisposition) and stress (environmental life event).

▶ The RDoC is a new classification system that focuses on biological, cognitive, and behavioural aspects of mental disorders.

# Anxiety Disorders: When Fears Take Over

"Okay, time for a pop quiz that will be half your grade for this class." If your instructor had actually said that, you would probably have experienced a wave of anxiety and dread. Your reaction would be appropriate and—no matter how intense the feeling—would not be a sign that you have a mental disorder. In fact, situation-related anxiety is normal and adaptive: in this case, perhaps by reminding you to keep up with your textbook assignments so you are prepared for pop quizzes. When anxiety arises that is out of proportion to real threats and challenges, however, it is maladaptive: It can take hold of people's lives, stealing their peace of mind and undermining their ability to function normally. Pathological anxiety is expressed as an **anxiety disorder,** *the class of mental disorder in which anxiety is the predominant feature.* People commonly experience more than one type of anxiety disorder at a given time, and there is significant *comorbidity* between anxiety and depression (Beesdo et al., 2010; Brown & Barlow, 2002). Among the anxiety disorders recognized in the *DSM–5* are phobic disorders, panic disorder, and generalized anxiety disorder.

**When is anxiety harmful, and when is it helpful?**

**anxiety disorder**
The class of mental disorder in which anxiety is the predominant feature.

**phobic disorders**
Disorders characterized by marked, persistent, and excessive fear and avoidance of specific objects, activities, or situations.

**specific phobia**
A disorder that involves an irrational fear of a particular object or situation that markedly interferes with an individual's ability to function.

**social phobia**
A disorder that involves an irrational fear of being publicly humiliated or embarrassed.

**preparedness theory**
The idea that people are instinctively predisposed toward certain fears.

## Phobic Disorders

Consider Mary, a 47-year-old mother of three, who sought treatment for *claustrophobia*—an intense fear of enclosed spaces. She traced her fear to childhood, when her older siblings would scare her by locking her in closets and confining her under blankets. Her own children grown, she wanted to find a job but could not because of a terror of elevators and other confined places that, she felt, shackled her to her home (Carson, Butcher, & Mineka, 2000). Many people feel a little anxious in enclosed spaces, but Mary's fears were abnormal and dysfunctional because they were disproportionate to any actual risk and impaired her ability to carry out a normal life. The *DSM–5* describes **phobic disorders** as characterized by *marked, persistent, and excessive fear and avoidance of specific objects, activities, or situations.* An individual with a phobic disorder recognizes that the fear is irrational but cannot prevent it from interfering with everyday functioning.

A **specific phobia** is *an irrational fear of a particular object or situation that markedly interferes with an individual's ability to function.* Specific phobias fall into five categories: (1) animals (e.g., dogs, cats, rats, snakes, spiders); (2) natural environments (e.g., heights, darkness, water, storms); (3) situations (e.g., bridges, elevators, tunnels, enclosed places); (4) blood, injections, and injury; and (5) other phobias, including choking or vomiting; and in children, loud noises or costumed characters. Approximately 12 percent of people will develop a specific phobia during their lives (AnxietyBC, n.d.; Kessler, Berglund, et al., 2005), with rates slightly higher among women than men (Kessler et al., 2012).

**Social phobia** involves *an irrational fear of being publicly humiliated or embarrassed.* Social phobia can be restricted to situations such as public speaking, eating in public, or urinating in a public bathroom or generalized to a variety of social situations that involve being observed or interacting with unfamiliar people. Individuals with social phobia try to avoid situations where unfamiliar people might evaluate them, and they experience intense anxiety and distress when public exposure is unavoidable. Social phobia can develop in childhood, but it typically emerges between early adolescence and early adulthood (Kessler, Berglund, et al., 2005). Many people experience social phobia: about 12 percent of men and 14 percent of women qualify for a diagnosis at some time in their lives (Kessler et al., 2012).

Why are phobias so common? The high rates of both specific and social phobias suggest a predisposition to be fearful of certain objects and situations. Indeed, most of the situations and objects of people's phobias could pose a real threat, for example, falling from a high place or being attacked by a vicious dog or a poisonous snake or a spider. Social situations have their own dangers. A roomful of strangers may not attack or bite, but they could form impressions that affect your prospects for friends, jobs, or marriage. And of course, in some very rare cases, they could attack or bite.

Observations such as these are the basis for the **preparedness theory** of phobias, which maintains that *people are instinctively predisposed toward certain fears.* The preparedness theory, proposed by Martin E. P. Seligman (1971), is supported by research showing that both humans and monkeys can quickly be conditioned to have a fear response for stimuli such as snakes and spiders, but not for neutral stimuli such as flowers or toy rabbits (Cook & Mineka, 1989; Öhman, Dimberg, & Öst, 1985). Similarly, research on

The preparedness theory explains why most merry-go-rounds carry children on beautiful horses. This mom might have some trouble getting her daughter to ride on a big spider or snake.

COURTESY OF DANIEL WEGNER

facial expressions has shown that people are more easily conditioned to fear facial expressions of anger than other types of expressions (Öhman, 1996; Woody & Nosen,

**Why might we be predisposed to certain phobias?**

2008). Phobias are particularly likely to form for objects that evolution has predisposed us to avoid. This idea is also supported by studies of the heritability of phobias. Family studies of specific phobias indicate greater concordance rates for identical than for fraternal twins (Kendler, Myers, & Prescott, 2002; O'Laughlin & Malle, 2002). Other studies have found that over 30 percent of first-degree relatives (parents, siblings, or children) of individuals with specific phobias also have a phobia (Fryer et al., 1990).

Temperament may also play a role in vulnerability to phobias. Researchers have found that infants who display excessive shyness and inhibition are at an increased risk for developing a phobic behaviour later in life (Morris, 2001; Stein, Chavira, & Jang, 2001). Neurobiological factors may also play a role. Abnormalities in the neurotransmitters serotonin and dopamine are more common in individuals who report phobias than they are among people who do not (Stein, 1998). In addition, individuals with phobias sometimes show abnormally high levels of activity in the amygdala, an area of the brain linked with the development of emotional associations (discussed in the Emotion and Motivation chapter and in Stein et al., 2001). Interestingly, although people with social phobia report feeling much more distressed than those without social phobia during tasks involving social evaluation (such as giving a speech), they are actually no more physiologically aroused than others (Jamieson, Nock, & Mendes, 2013). This suggests that social phobia may be due to a person's subjective experience of the situation, rather than an abnormal physiological stress response to such situations.

This evidence does not rule out the influence of environments and upbringing on the development of phobic overreactions. As learning theorist John Watson (1924) demonstrated many years ago, phobias can be classically conditioned (see the discussion of Little Albert and the white rat in the Learning chapter). Similarly, the discomfort of a dog bite could create a conditioned association between dogs and pain, resulting in an irrational fear of all dogs. The idea that phobias are learned from emotional experiences with feared objects, however, is not a complete explanation for the occurrence of phobias. Most studies find that people with phobias are no more likely than people without phobias to recall personal experiences with the feared object that could have provided the basis for classical conditioning (Craske, 1999; McNally & Steketee, 1985). Moreover, many people are bitten by dogs, but few develop phobias. Despite its shortcomings, however, the idea that this is a matter of learning provides a useful model for therapy (as you will see in the Treatment chapter).

## Panic Disorder

If you suddenly found yourself in danger of death (That lion is headed straight for us!), a wave of panic might wash over you. People who suffer panic attacks are frequently overwhelmed by such intense fears and by powerful physical symptoms of anxiety, but in the complete absence of actual danger. Wesley, a 20-year-old university student began having panic attacks with increasing frequency, often two or three times a day, when he finally sought help at a clinic. The attacks began with a sudden wave of "intense, terrifying fear" that seemed to come out of nowhere, often accompanied by dizziness, a tightening of the chest, and the thought that he was going to pass out or possibly die. Wesley's attacks had started a few years earlier and occurred intermittently ever since. Wesley decided to come in for treatment because he had begun to avoid buses, trains, and public places for fear that he would have an attack like this and not be able to escape.

THINKSTOCK

Phobias are anxiety disorders that involve excessive and persistent fear of a specific object, activity, or situation. Some phobias may be learned through classical conditioning, in which a conditioned stimulus (CS) that is paired with an anxiety-evoking unconditioned stimulus (US) itself comes to elicit a conditioned fear response (CR). Suppose your friend has a phobia of dogs that is so intense that he is afraid to go outside in case one of his neighbours' dogs barks at him. Using the principles of classical conditioning you learned in the Learning chapter, how might you help him overcome his fear?

**panic disorder**
A disorder characterized by the sudden occurrence of multiple psychological and physiological symptoms that contribute to a feeling of stark terror.

**agoraphobia**
A specific phobia involving a fear of public places.

In panic disorder with agoraphobia, the fear of having a panic attack in public may prevent the person from going outside.

Wesley's condition, called **panic disorder,** is characterized by *the sudden occurrence of multiple psychological and physiological symptoms that contribute to a feeling of stark terror.* The acute symptoms of a panic attack typically last only a few minutes and include shortness of breath, heart palpitations, sweating, dizziness, depersonalization (a feeling of being detached from one's body) or derealization (a feeling that the external world is strange or unreal), and a fear that one is going crazy or about to die. Not surprisingly, panic attacks often send people rushing to emergency rooms or their physicians' offices for what they believe are heart attacks. Unfortunately, because many of the symptoms mimic various medical disorders, a correct diagnosis may take years in spite of costly medical tests that produce normal results (Katon, 1994). According to the *DSM–5* diagnostic criteria, a person has panic disorder only if they experience recurrent unexpected attacks and report significant anxiety about having another attack.

A common complication of panic disorder is **agoraphobia,** *a specific phobia involving a fear of public places.* Many people with agoraphobia, including Wesley, are not frightened of public places in themselves; instead, they are afraid of having a panic attack in a public place or around strangers who might view them with disdain or fail to help them. In severe cases, people who have panic disorder with agoraphobia are unable to leave home, sometimes for years.

> **What is it about public places that many people with agoraphobia fear?**

Panic attacks are fairly common: Up to a third of Canadian adults may have a panic attack each year (Canadian Mental Health Association [BC Division], 2009; Statistics Canada, 2013c) typically during a period of intense stress (Telch, Lucas, & Nelson, 1989). An occasional episode is not sufficient for a diagnosis of panic disorder: The individual also has to experience significant dread and anxiety about having another attack. When this criterion is applied, approximately 37 in 100 people will have diagnosable panic disorder sometime in their lives (Statistics Canada, 2013c). Women are twice as likely as men to develop panic disorder (Statistics Canada, 2013c). Family studies suggest some hereditary component to panic disorder, with 30 to 40 percent of the variance in liability for developing panic disorder attributed to genetic influence (Hettema, Neale, & Kendler, 2001).

In an effort to understand the role that physiological arousal plays in panic attacks, researchers have compared the responses of experimental participants with and without panic disorder to *sodium lactate,* a chemical that produces rapid, shallow breathing and heart palpitations. Those with panic disorder were found to be acutely sensitive to the drug; within a few minutes after administration, 60 to 90 percent experienced a panic attack. Participants without the disorder rarely responded to the drug with a panic attack (Liebowitz et al., 1985).

The difference in responses to the chemical may be due to differing interpretations of physiological signs of anxiety; that is, people who experience panic attacks may be hypersensitive to physiological signs of anxiety, which they interpret as having disastrous consequences for their well-being. Supporting this cognitive explanation is research showing that people who are high in anxiety sensitivity (i.e., they believe that bodily arousal and other symptoms of anxiety can have dire consequences) have an elevated risk for experiencing panic attacks (Olatunji & Wolitzky-Taylor, 2009). Thus, panic attacks may be conceptualized as a "fear of fear" itself.

## Generalized Anxiety Disorder

Gina, a 24-year-old woman, began to experience debilitating anxiety during her first year of graduate school for clinical psychology. At first she worried about whether she was sufficiently completing all of her assignments, then she worried about whether her clients were improving or if she was actually making them worse. Soon her concerns spread to focus on her health (Did she have an undiagnosed medical problem?) as well as that of her boyfriend (He smokes cigarettes … perhaps he is currently giving himself cancer?). She worried incessantly for a year and ultimately took time off from school to get treatment for her worries, extreme agitation, fatigue, and feelings of sadness and depression.

Gina's symptoms are typical of **generalized anxiety disorder (GAD)**—called *generalized* because the unrelenting worries are not focused on any particular threat; they are, in fact, often exaggerated and irrational. GAD is *chronic excessive worry accompanied by three or more of the following symptoms: restlessness, fatigue, concentration problems, irritability, muscle tension, and sleep disturbance.* In people suffering from GAD, the uncontrollable worrying produces a sense of loss of control that can so erode self-confidence that simple decisions seem fraught with dire consequences. For example, Gina struggled to make everyday decisions as basic as which vegetables to buy at the market and how to prepare her dinner.

Approximately 1 in 20 people in Canada suffer from GAD at some time in their lives (Canadian Psychological Association, 2012a; Kessler, Berglund, et al., 2005),

**What factors contribute to GAD?**

with women experiencing GAD at higher rates (8 percent) than men (5 percent) (Kessler et al., 2012). Research suggests that both biological and psychological factors contribute to the risk of GAD. Family studies indicate a mild to modest level of heritability (Norrholm & Ressler, 2009). Although identical twin studies of GAD are rare, some evidence suggests that compared with fraternal twins, identical twins have modestly higher *concordance rates* (the percentage of pairs that share the characteristic) (Hettema et al., 2001). Moreover, teasing out environmental versus personality influences on concordance rates is quite difficult.

Biological explanations of GAD suggest that neurotransmitter imbalances may play a role in the disorder. The precise nature of this imbalance is not clear. *Benzodiazepines* (a class of sedative drugs discussed in the Treatment chapter; e.g., Valium, Librium) that appear to stimulate the neurotransmitter *gamma-aminobutyric acid (GABA)* can sometimes reduce the symptoms of GAD, suggesting a potential role for this neurotransmitter in the occurrence of GAD. However, other drugs that do not directly affect GABA levels (e.g., buspirone and antidepressants such as Prozac) can also be helpful in the treatment of GAD (Gobert et al., 1999; Michelson et al., 1999; Roy-Byrne & Cowley, 1998). To complicate matters, these different prescription drugs do not help all individuals and, in some cases, can produce serious side effects and dependency.

Psychological explanations focus on anxiety-provoking situations in explaining high levels of GAD. The condition is especially prevalent among people who have low incomes, are living in large cities, and/or are in environments rendered unpredictable by political and economic strife. The relatively high rates of GAD among women may also be related to stress because women are more likely than men to live in poverty, experience discrimination, or be subjected to sexual or physical abuse (Koss, 1990; Strickland, 1991). Research shows that unpredictable traumatic experiences in childhood increase the risk of developing GAD, and this evidence also supports the idea that stressful experiences play a role (Torgensen, 1986). Risk of GAD also increases following the experience of a loss or situation associated with future perceived danger (Kendler et al., 2003), such as loss of a home due to foreclosure (McLaughlin et al., 2012). Still, many people who might be expected to develop GAD do not, supporting the diathesis–stress notion that personal vulnerability must also be a key factor in this disorder.

**generalized anxiety disorder (GAD)**
A disorder characterized by chronic excessive worry accompanied by three or more of the following symptoms: restlessness, fatigue, concentration problems, irritability, muscle tension, and sleep disturbance.

The experience of major stressful life events, such as losing a job or home, can lead to generalized anxiety disorder, a condition characterized by chronic, excessive worry.

STURTI/GETTY IMAGES

# Obsessive-Compulsive Disorder: Trapped in a Loop

You may have had the experience of having an irresistible urge to go back to check whether you actually locked the door or turned off the oven, even when you are pretty sure that you did. Or you may have been unable to resist engaging in some superstitious behaviour, such as wearing your lucky shirt on a date or to a sporting event. In some people, such thoughts and actions spiral out of control and become a serious problem.

Karen, a 34-year-old with four children, sought treatment after several months of experiencing intrusive, repetitive thoughts in which she imagined that one or more of her children was having a serious accident. In addition, an extensive series of protective counting rituals hampered her daily routine. For example, when grocery shopping, Karen had the feeling that if she selected the first item (say, a box of cereal) on a shelf, something terrible would happen to her oldest child. If she selected the second item, some unknown disaster would befall her second child, and so on for the four children. The children's ages were also important. The sixth item in a row, for example, was associated with her youngest child, who was 6 years old.

Karen's preoccupation with numbers extended to other activities, most notably, the pattern in which she smoked cigarettes and drank coffee. If she had one cigarette, she felt that she had to smoke at least four in a row or one of her children would be harmed in some way. If she drank one cup of coffee, she felt compelled to drink four more to protect her children from harm. She acknowledged that her counting rituals were irrational, but she became extremely anxious when she tried to stop (Oltmanns, Neale, & Davison, 1991).

Karen's symptoms are typical of **obsessive-compulsive disorder (OCD),** in which *repetitive, intrusive thoughts (obsessions) and ritualistic behaviours (compulsions) designed to fend off those thoughts interfere significantly with an individual's functioning.* Anxiety plays a role in this disorder because the obsessive thoughts typically produce anxiety, and the compulsive behaviours are performed to reduce it. In OCD, these obsessions and compulsions are intense, frequent, and experienced as irrational and excessive. Attempts to cope with the obsessive thoughts by trying to suppress or ignore them are of little or no benefit. In fact (as discussed in the Consciousness chapter), thought suppression can backfire, increasing the frequency and intensity of the obsessive thoughts (Wegner, 1989; Wenzlaff & Wegner, 2000). Despite anxiety's role, in *DSM–5* OCD is classified separately from anxiety disorders because the disorder is believed

> **How effective is willful effort at curing OCD?**

**obsessive-compulsive disorder (OCD)**
A disorder in which repetitive, intrusive thoughts (obsessions) and ritualistic behaviours (compulsions) designed to fend off those thoughts interfere significantly with an individual's functioning.

to have a distinct cause and to be maintained via different neural circuitry in the brain than the anxiety disorders.

Although about 1 in 4 people in Canada report experiencing obsessions or compulsions at some point in their lives (Ruscio et al., 2010), only 1 in 50 will develop actual OCD (Canadian Psychological Association, 2012b; Kessler, Berglund, et al., 2005). Similar to anxiety disorders, rates of OCD are higher among women than men (Kessler et al., 2012). Among those with OCD, the most common obsessions and compulsions involve checking (79 percent), ordering (57 percent), moral concerns (43 percent), and contamination (26 percent) (Ruscio et al., 2010). Although compulsive behaviour is always excessive, it can vary considerably in intensity and frequency. For example, fear of contamination may lead to 15 minutes of hand washing in some individuals, whereas others may need to spend hours with disinfectants and extremely hot water, scrubbing their hands until they bleed.

The obsessions that plague individuals with OCD typically derive from concerns that could pose a real threat (such as contamination or disease), which supports preparedness theory. Thinking repeatedly about whether we have left a stove burner on when we leave the house makes sense, after all, if we want to return to a house that is not "well done." The concept of preparedness places OCD in the same evolutionary context as phobias (Szechtman & Woody, 2006). However, as with phobias, we need to consider other factors to explain why fears that may have served an evolutionary purpose can become so distorted and maladaptive.

Family studies indicate a moderate genetic heritability for OCD: Identical twins show a higher concordance than do fraternal twins. Relatives of individuals with OCD may not have the disorder themselves, but they are at greater risk for other types of anxiety disorders than are members of the general public (Billet, Richter, & Kennedy, 1998). Researchers have not determined the biological mechanisms that may contribute to OCD (Friedlander & Desrocher, 2006), but one hypothesis implicates heightened neural activity in the caudate nucleus of the brain, a portion of the basal ganglia (discussed in the Neuroscience and Behaviour chapter) known to be involved in the initiation of intentional actions (Rappoport, 1990). Drugs that increase the activity of the neurotransmitter serotonin in the brain can inhibit the activity of the caudate nucleus and relieve some of the symptoms of OCD (Hansen et al., 2002). However, this finding does not indicate that overactivity of the caudate nucleus is the cause of OCD. It could also be an effect of the disorder: People with OCD often respond favourably to psychotherapy and show a corresponding reduction in activity in the caudate nucleus (Baxter et al., 1992).

Canadian Howie Mandel is a successful comedian, but his struggle with OCD is no laughing matter. Like approximately 2 percent of people in Canada, Mandel struggles with extreme fears of being contaminated by germs and engages in repeated checking and cleaning behaviours that often interfere with his daily life. He has spoken publicly about his struggles with OCD and about the importance of seeking effective treatment for this condition.

## IN SUMMARY

▶ People with obsessive-compulsive disorder experience recurring, anxiety-provoking thoughts that compel them to engage in ritualistic, irrational behaviours.

# Post-traumatic Stress Disorder: Troubles after a Trauma

Psychological reactions to stress can lead to stress disorders. For example, a person who lives through a terrifying and uncontrollable experience may develop **post-traumatic stress disorder (PTSD)**, a disorder characterized by *chronic physiological arousal, recurrent unwanted thoughts or images of the trauma, and avoidance of things that call the traumatic event to mind.*

Psychological scars left by traumatic events are nowhere more apparent than in war. Many soldiers returning from combat experience symptoms of PTSD, including

**post-traumatic stress disorder (PTSD)**
A disorder characterized by chronic physiological arousal, recurrent unwanted thoughts or images of the trauma, and avoidance of things that call the traumatic event to mind.

The South West Asia Service Medal was introduced in 2002 to recognize Canadian military personnel serving in Afghanistan.

flashbacks of battle, exaggerated anxiety and startle reactions, and even medical conditions that do not arise from physical damage (e.g., paralysis or chronic fatigue). Most of these symptoms are normal, appropriate responses to horrifying events, and for most people, the symptoms subside with time. In PTSD, the symptoms can last much longer. It is estimated that approximately 1 in 20 Canadian soldiers returning from Afghanistan met the criteria for PTSD. This rate is probably too low since there is stigma in the Canadian military about seeking help for symptoms (Howell, 2011). The observed rates of PTSD are even higher in non-Western and developing countries (Keane, Marshall, & Taft, 2006). The effects of PTSD are now recognized not only among the victims, witnesses, and perpetrators of war, but also among ordinary people who are traumatized by terrible events in civilian life. At some time over the course of their lives, about 1 in 10 Canadians are estimated to suffer from PTSD (Canadian Mental Health Association, n.d. 2; Kessler, Berglund, et al., 2005).

Not everyone who is exposed to a traumatic event develops PTSD, suggesting that people differ in their degree of sensitivity to trauma. Research using brain imaging techniques to examine brain structure and function has identified important neural correlates of PTSD. Specifically, those with PTSD show heightened activity in the amygdala (a region associated with the evaluation of threatening information and fear conditioning), decreased activity in the medial prefrontal cortex (a region important in the extinction of fear conditioning), and a smaller sized hippocampus (the part of the brain most linked with memory, as described in the Neuroscience and Behaviour, and Memory chapters) (Shin, Rauch, & Pitman, 2006). Of course, an important question is whether people whose brains have these characteristics are at greater risk for PTSD if traumatized, or if these are the consequences of trauma in some people. For instance, does reduced hippocampal volume reflect a pre-existing condition that makes the brain sensitive to stress, or does the traumatic stress itself somehow kill nerve cells? One important study suggests that although a group of combat veterans with PTSD showed reduced hippocampal volume, so did the identical (monozygotic) twins of those men (see **FIGURE 15.1**), even though the twins had never had any combat exposure or developed PTSD (Gilbertson et al., 2002). This suggests that the veterans' reduced hippocampal volumes were not caused by the combat exposure; instead, both these veterans and their twin brothers might have had a smaller hippocampus to begin with, a pre-existing condition that made them susceptible to developing PTSD when they were later exposed to trauma.

> **What structure in the brain might be an indicator for susceptibility to PTSD?**

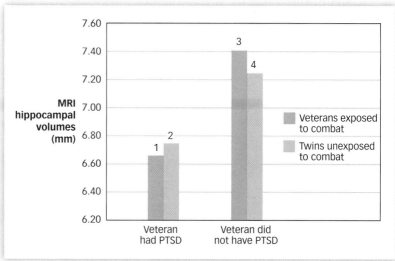

▶ Figure **15.1** **Hippocampal Volumes of War Veterans and Their Identical Twins** Average hippocampal volumes for four groups of participants: (1) combat-exposed veterans who developed PTSD; (2) their combat-unexposed twins with no PTSD themselves; (3) combat-exposed veterans who never developed PTSD; and (4) their unexposed twins, also with no PTSD. Smaller hippocampal volumes were found both for the combat-exposed veterans with PTSD (Group 1) and their twins who had not been exposed to combat (Group 2) in comparison to veterans without PTSD (Group 3) and their twins (Group 4). This pattern of findings suggests that an inherited smaller hippocampus may make some people sensitive to conditions that cause PTSD (Gilbertson et al., 2002).

## IN SUMMARY

▶ Terrifying, life-threatening events, such as combat experience or rape, can lead to the development of post-traumatic stress disorder (PTSD) in which a person experiences chronic physiological arousal, unwanted thoughts or images of the event, and avoidance of things that remind the person of the event.

# Depressive and Bipolar Disorders: At the Mercy of Emotions

You are probably in a mood right now. Maybe you are happy that it is almost time to get a snack or saddened by something you heard from a friend—or you may feel good or bad without having a clue why. As you learned in the Emotion and Motivation chapter, moods are relatively long-lasting, nonspecific emotional states—and *nonspecific* means we often may have no idea what has caused a mood. Changing moods lend variety to our experiences, like different-coloured lights shining on the stage as we play out our lives. However, for people like Virginia Woolf and others with mood disorders, moods can become so intense that they are pulled or pushed into life-threatening actions. **Mood disorders** are *mental disorders that have mood disturbance as their predominant feature* and take two main forms: *depression* (also called *unipolar depression*) and *bipolar disorder* (so named because people go from one end of the emotional pole [extreme depression] to the other [extreme mania]).

## Depressive Disorders

Everyone feels sad, pessimistic, and unmotivated from time to time. But for most people these periods are relatively short-lived and mild. Depression is much more than typical sadness. The experience of Mark, a 34-year-old man who visited his primary care physician complaining of chronic fatigue, is fairly typical. During the visit, he mentioned difficulties falling asleep and staying asleep that left him chronically tired, so much so that he feared maybe he had some kind of medical problem. He complained that over the past 6 months, he no longer had the energy to exercise and had gained 4.5 kg. He also lost all interest in going out with his friends or even talking to other people. Nothing he normally enjoyed, even sexual activity, gave him pleasure anymore; he had trouble concentrating and was forgetful, irritable, impatient, and frustrated. Mark's change in mood and behaviour, and the sense of hopelessness and weariness he felt goes far beyond normal sadness. Instead, depressive disorders are dysfunctional, chronic, and fall outside the range of socially or culturally expected responses.

**What is the difference between depression and sadness?**

**Major depressive disorder** (or **unipolar depression**), which we refer to here simply as "depression," is characterized by *a severely depressed mood and/or inability to experience pleasure that lasts 2 or more weeks and is accompanied by feelings of worthlessness, lethargy, and sleep and appetite disturbance.* In a related condition called **dysthymia,** *the same cognitive and bodily problems as in depression are present, but they are less severe and last longer, persisting for at least 2 years.* When both types co-occur, the resulting condition is called **double depression,** defined as a

**mood disorders**
Mental disorders that have mood disturbance as their predominant feature.

**major depressive disorder (or unipolar depression)**
A disorder characterized by a severely depressed mood and/or inability to experience pleasure that lasts 2 or more weeks and is accompanied by feelings of worthlessness, lethargy, and sleep and appetite disturbance.

**dysthymia**
The same cognitive and bodily problems as in depression are present, but they are less severe and last longer, persisting for at least 2 years.

**double depression**
A moderately depressed mood that persists for at least 2 years and is punctuated by periods of major depression.

*The Blue Devils:* George Cruikshank (1792–1878) portrayed a depressed man tormented by demons offering him methods of suicide, appearing as bill collectors, and making a funeral procession.

BRIDGEMAN ART LIBRARY

Seasonal affective disorder is not merely having the blues because of the weather. It appears to be due to reduced exposure to light in the winter months.

Postpartum depression can strike women out of the blue, often causing new mothers to feel extreme sadness, guilt, and disconnection, and even to experience serious thoughts of suicide. Actress Brooke Shields wrote about her experience with postpartum depression in a popular book on this condition.

*moderately depressed mood that persists for at least 2 years and is punctuated by periods of major depression.*

Some people experience *recurrent depressive episodes in a seasonal pattern,* commonly known as **seasonal affective disorder (SAD)**. In most cases, the episodes begin in fall or winter and remit in spring, and this pattern is due to reduced levels of light over the colder seasons (Westrin & Lam, 2007). Nevertheless, recurrent summer depressive episodes have been reported. A winter-related pattern of depression appears to be more prevalent in higher latitudes.

Approximately 1 in 12 Canadians will experience major depression at some point in their lives (Kessler et al., 2012; Public Health Agency of Canada, 2002a). On average, major depression lasts about 12 weeks (Eaton et al., 2008). However, without treatment, approximately 80 percent of individuals will experience at least one recurrence of the disorder (Judd, 1997; Mueller et al., 1999). Compared with people who have a single episode, individuals with recurrent depression have more severe symptoms, higher rates of depression in their families, more suicide attempts, and higher rates of divorce (Merikangas, Wicki, & Angst, 1994).

Similar to anxiety disorders, the rate of depression is much higher in women (22 percent) than in men (14 percent) (Kessler et al., 2012). Socioeconomic standing has been invoked as an explanation for women's heightened risk: Their incomes are lower than those of men, and poverty could cause depression. Sex differences in hormones are another possibility: Estrogen, androgen, and progesterone influence depression; some women experience *postpartum depression* (depression following childbirth) due to changing hormone balances. It is also possible that the higher rate of depression in women reflects greater willingness by women to face their depression and seek out help, leading to higher rates of diagnosis (Nolen-Hoeksema, 2008). Women have a tendency to accept, disclose, and ruminate on their negative emotions, whereas men are more likely to deny negative emotions and engage in self-distraction such as work and drinking alcohol.

> Why do more women than men experience depression?

## Biological Factors

Heritability estimates for major depression typically range from 33 to 45 percent (Plomin et al., 1997; Wallace, Schnieder, & McGuffin, 2002). However, like most types of mental disorders, heritability rates vary as a function of severity. For example, a relatively large study of twins found that the concordance rates for severe major depression (defined as three or more episodes) were quite high, with a rate of 59 percent for identical twins and 30 percent for fraternal twins (Bertelsen, Harvald, & Hauge, 1977). In contrast, concordance rates for less severe major depression (defined as fewer than three episodes) fell to 33 percent for identical twins and 14 percent for fraternal twins. Heritability rates for dysthymia are low and inconsistent (Plomin et al., 1997). This makes depression about as heritable as complex medical conditions, like type 2 diabetes and asthma.

Beginning in the 1950s, researchers noticed that drugs that increased levels of the neurotransmitters norepinephrine and serotonin could sometimes reduce depression. This observation suggested that depression might be caused by an absolute or relative depletion of these neurotransmitters and sparked a revolution in the pharmacological treatment of depression (Schildkraut, 1965), leading to the development and widespread use of such popular prescription drugs as Prozac and Zoloft, which increase the availability of serotonin in the brain. Further research has shown, however, that reduced levels of these neurotransmitters cannot be the whole story regarding the causes of depression. For example, some studies have found *increases* in norepinephrine activity among depressed individuals (Thase & Howland, 1995). Moreover, even though the antidepressant medications change neurochemical transmission in less than a day, they typically take at least 2 weeks to relieve depressive symptoms and are not effective in decreasing depressive symptoms in many cases. A biochemical model of depression has yet to be developed that accounts for all the evidence.

Newer biological models of depression have tried to understand depression using a diathesis–stress framework. For instance, Avshalom Caspi and his colleagues (2003) found that stressful life events are much more likely to lead to depression among those with a certain genetic trait (vulnerability) related to the activity of the neurotransmitter serotonin: a finding showing that nature and nurture interact to influence brain structure, function, and chemistry in depression (see **FIGURE 15.2**).

Recent research also has begun to tell us what parts of the brain show abnormalities in depression. For instance, some important findings came out of a recent meta-analysis (which is a quantitative synthesis of the results of many individual studies) of 24 brain imaging studies. Results showed that when viewing negative stimuli (words or images), people suffering from depression showed both increased activity in regions of the brain associated with processing emotional information and decreased activity in areas associated with cognitive control (see **FIGURE 15.3**) (Hamilton et al., 2012). Of course, this is not the whole picture and these findings do not explain all of the symptoms seen in depression, why and when depression comes and goes, or how treatment works. Given that depression does not arise due to a single gene or brain region, but likely from the interactions of different biological systems that each give rise to the different psychological traits seen in depression, it will likely be many years before we fully understand the biological causes of this disorder (Krishnan & Nestler, 2008).

**seasonal affective disorder (SAD)** Recurrent depressive episodes in a seasonal pattern.

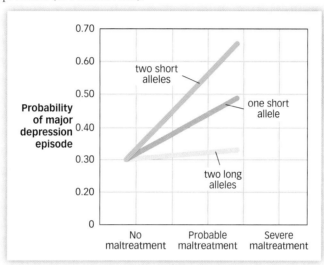

◄ Figure **15.2** **Gene × Environment Interactions in Depression** Stressful life experiences are much more likely to lead to later depression among those with one short, and especially two short, alleles of the serotonin transporter gene. Those with two long alleles (long alleles are associated with more efficient serotonergic functioning) showed no increased risk of depression, even among those who experienced severe maltreatment.

| | Structure | Activity in depression |
|---|---|---|
| A | Amygdala | Increased |
| B | Dorsal ACC | Increased |
| C | Insula and superior temporal gyrus | Increased |
| D | DLPFC | Decreased |
| E | Caudate body | Decreased |

◄ Figure **15.3** **Brain and Depression** When presented with negative information, people with depression show increased activation in regions of the brain associated with emotional processing such as the amygdala, insula, and dorsal anterior cingulate cortex (ACC); and decreased activity in regions associated with cognitive control such as the dorsal striatum and dorsolateral prefrontal cortex (DLPFC) (Hamilton et al., 2012).

The cognitive model of depression is based on approaches to thinking used by the Greek Stoic philosophers nearly 2000 years ago. Epictetus's famous quote: "Men are disturbed not by things, but by the principles and notions which they form concerning things" is commonly cited by cognitive theorists as a guiding principle of the cognitive model of depression.

## Psychological Factors

If optimists see the world through rose-coloured glasses, people who suffer with depression tend to view the world through dark grey lenses. Their negative cognitive style is remarkably consistent and, some argue, begins in childhood with experiences that create a pattern of negative self thoughts (Blatt & Homann, 1992; Gibb, Alloy, & Tierney, 2001). One of the first theorists to emphasize the role of thought in depression, Aaron T. Beck (1967), noted that his depressed patients distorted perceptions of their experiences and embraced dysfunctional attitudes that promoted and maintained negative mood states. His observations led him to develop a *cognitive model of depression*, which states that biases in how information is attended to, processed, and remembered lead to and maintain depression.

Elaborating on this initial idea, researchers proposed a theory of depression that emphasizes the role of people's negative inferences about the causes of their experiences (Abramson, Seligman, & Teasdale, 1978). **Helplessness theory,** which is a part of the cognitive model of depression, maintains that *individuals who are prone to depression automatically attribute negative experiences to causes that are internal (i.e., their own fault), stable (i.e., unlikely to change), and global (i.e., widespread).* For example, a student at risk for depression might view a bad grade on a mathematics test as a sign of low intelligence (internal) that will never change (stable) and that will lead to failure in all his or her future endeavours (global). In contrast, a student without this tendency might have the opposite response, attributing the grade to something external (poor teaching), unstable (a missed study session), and/or specific (boring subject).

> **What is helplessness theory?**

The relationship between one's perceptions and depression has been further developed and supported over the past several decades. The update to Beck's cognitive model suggests that due to a combination of a genetic vulnerability and negative early life events, people with depression have developed a negative *schema* (described in the Development chapter). This negative schema is characterized by biases in

> - interpretations of information (a tendency to interpret neutral information negatively—seeing the world through grey glass);
> - attention (trouble disengaging from negative information);
> - memory (better recall of negative information) (Gotlib & Joormann, 2010).

For example, a student at risk for depression who got a bad grade on a test might interpret a well-intentioned comment from the teacher ("Good job on the test") negatively ("She's being sarcastic!"); have trouble forgetting about both the test score and the perceived negative comment; and have better memory about this test in the future ("Sure, I did well on my English exam, but don't forget about that bad math test last month"). The presence of these biases may help to explain the internal, stable, and global attributions seen in depression. In addition, recent research suggests that some of the differences in brain structure and function seen in those with depression can help to explain some of these cognitive biases. For instance, people with depression show abnormalities in parts of the brain involved in attention and memory, especially when presented with negative information (Disner et al., 2011). Although we do not fully understand the causes of depression, pieces of the puzzle are being discovered and put together as you read this.

**helplessness theory**
The idea that individuals who are prone to depression automatically attribute negative experiences to causes that are internal (i.e., their own fault), stable (i.e., unlikely to change), and global (i.e., widespread).

## Bipolar Disorder

If depression is distressing and painful, would the opposite extreme be better? Not for Virginia Woolf or for Julie, a 20-year-old second-year American university student. When first seen by a clinician, Julie had gone 5 days without sleep and, like Woolf, was extremely active and expressing bizarre thoughts and ideas. She proclaimed to friends that she did not menstruate because she was "of a third sex, a gender above the two human sexes." She claimed to be a "superwoman," capable of avoiding human sexuality and yet still able to give birth. Preoccupied with the politics of global disarmament, she felt that she had switched souls with a Congressman from her state, had tapped into his thoughts and memories, and could save the world from nuclear destruction. She began to campaign for an elected position in the United States government (even though no elections were scheduled at that time). Worried that she would forget some of her thoughts, she had been leaving hundreds of notes about her ideas and activities everywhere, including on the walls and furniture of her dormitory room (Vitkus, 1999).

In addition to her manic episodes, Julie (like Woolf) had a history of depression. The diagnostic label for this constellation of symptoms is **bipolar disorder,** *a condition characterized by cycles of abnormal, persistent high mood (mania) and low mood (depression).* In about two thirds of people with bipolar disorder, manic episodes immediately precede or immediately follow depressive episodes (Whybrow, 1997). The depressive phase of bipolar disorder is often clinically indistinguishable from major depression (Johnson, Cuellar, & Miller, 2009). In the manic phase, which must last at least 1 week to meet *DSM* requirements, mood can be elevated, expansive, or irritable.

Mania is not simply being very happy. People experiencing a manic episode may fail to sleep for several days, purchase four cars in one day, and have thoughts racing through their mind so fast that they are literally unable to form a coherent sentence.

> **Why is bipolar disorder sometimes misdiagnosed as schizophrenia?**

Other prominent symptoms include grandiosity, decreased need for sleep, talkativeness, racing thoughts, distractibility, and reckless behaviour (such as compulsive gambling, sexual indiscretions, and unrestrained spending sprees). Psychotic features such as hallucinations (erroneous perceptions) and delusions (erroneous beliefs) may be present, so the disorder can be misdiagnosed as schizophrenia (described in a later section).

Here's how Kay Redfield Jamison (1995, p. 67) described her own experience with bipolar disorder in *An Unquiet Mind: A Memoir of Moods and Madness.*

> There is a particular kind of pain, elation, loneliness, and terror involved in this kind of madness. When you are high it is tremendous. The ideas and feelings are fast and frequent like shooting stars, and you follow them until you find better and brighter ones. … But, somewhere, this changes. The fast ideas are far too fast, and there are far too many; overwhelming confusion replaces clarity. Memory goes. Humour and absorption on friends' faces are replaced by fear and concern. Everything previously moving with the grain is now against—you are irritable, angry, frightened, uncontrollable, and enmeshed totally in the blackest caves of the mind. You never knew those caves were there. It will never end, for madness carves its own reality.

The lifetime risk for bipolar disorder is about 1 in 40 and does not differ between men and women (Kessler et al., 2012). Bipolar disorder is typically a recurrent condition, with approximately 90 percent of afflicted people suffering from several episodes over a lifetime (Coryell et al., 1995). About 10 percent of people with bipolar disorder have *rapid cycling bipolar disorder,* characterized by at least four mood episodes (either manic or depressive) every year, and this form of the disorder is particularly difficult to treat (Post et al., 2008). Rapid cycling is more common in women than in men and is sometimes precipitated by taking certain kinds of antidepressant drugs (Liebenluft, 1996; Whybrow, 1997). Unfortunately, bipolar disorder tends to be persistent. In one study, 24 percent of the participants had relapsed within 6 months of recovery from an episode, and 77 percent had at least one new episode within 4 years of recovery (Coryell et al., 1995).

Some have suggested that people with psychotic and mood (especially bipolar) disorders have higher creativity and intellectual ability (Andreasen, 2011). In bipolar disorder, the suggestion goes, before the mania becomes too pronounced, the energy,

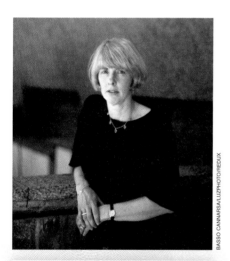

Psychologist Kay Redfield Jamison has written several best-selling books about her own struggles with bipolar disorder.

**bipolar disorder**
A condition characterized by cycles of abnormal, persistent high mood (mania) and low mood (depression).

grandiosity, and ambition that it supplies may help people achieve great things. In addition to Virginia Woolf, notable individuals thought to have had the disorder include Isaac Newton, Vincent van Gogh, Abraham Lincoln, Ernest Hemingway, Winston Churchill, and Theodore Roosevelt.

### Biological Factors

Among the various mental disorders, bipolar disorder has one of the highest rates of heritability, with concordance from 40 to 70 percent for identical twins and 10 percent for fraternal twins (Craddock & Jones, 1999). Like most other disorders, it is likely that bipolar disorder is *polygenic,* arising from the interaction of multiple genes that combine to create the symptoms observed in those with this disorder; however, these have been difficult to identify. Adding to the complexity, there also is evidence of *pleiotropic effects,* in which one gene influences one's susceptibility to multiple disorders. For instance, one recent study revealed a shared genetic vulnerability for bipolar disorder and schizophrenia. The genes linked to both disorders are associated with compromised abilities both in filtering unnecessary information and recognition memory, as well as problems with dopamine and serotonin transmission—factors present in both types of disorders (Huang et al., 2010). A follow-up study examining more than 60 000 people revealed that common genetic risk factors are associated with bipolar disorder and schizophrenia, as well as major depression, autism spectrum disorder, and attention-deficit/hyperactivity disorder. These disorders share overlapping symptoms such as problems with mood regulation, cognitive impairments, and social withdrawal (Cross-Disorder Group of the Psychiatric Genomics Consortium, 2013). Findings like these are exciting because they help us begin to understand why we see similar symptoms in people with what we previously thought were unrelated disorders. Although some genetic links have been made, we currently lack an understanding of how different biological factors work together to create the symptoms observed in bipolar and other disorders.

> What findings offer exciting new evidence of why symptoms of different disorders seem to overlap?

There is growing evidence that the epigenetic changes you learned about in the Neuroscience and Behaviour chapter can help to explain how it is that genetic risk factors influence the development of bipolar and related disorders. Remember how rat pups whose moms spent less time licking and grooming them experienced epigenetic changes (decreased DNA methylation) that led to a poorer stress response? As you might expect, these same kinds of epigenetic effects seem to help explain who develops symptoms of mental disorders and who does not. For instance, studies examining monozygotic twin pairs (identical twins who share 100 percent of their DNA) in which one develops bipolar disorder or schizophrenia and one does not, reveal significant epigenetic differences between the two, with decreased methylation at genetic locations known to be important in brain development and the occurrence of bipolar disorders and schizophrenia (Dempster et al., 2011; Labrie, Pai, & Petronis, 2012).

### Psychological Factors

Stressful life experiences often precede manic and depressive episodes (Johnson, Cuellar, et al., 2008). One study found that severely stressed individuals took an average of 3 times longer to recover from an episode than did individuals not affected by stress (Johnson & Miller, 1997). The stress–disorder relationship is not simple, however: High levels of stress have less impact on people with extraverted personalities than on those with more introverted personalities (Swednsen et al., 1995). Personality characteristics such as neuroticism and conscientiousness have also been found to predict

> How does stress relate to manic-depressive episodes?

increases in bipolar symptoms over time (Lozano & Johnson, 2001). Finally, people living with family members high on **expressed emotion,** which in this context is *a measure of how much hostility, criticism, and emotional overinvolvement are used when speaking about a family member with a mental disorder*, are more likely to relapse than people with supportive families (Miklowitz & Johnson, 2006). This is true not just of those with bipolar disorder: Expressed emotion is associated with higher rates of relapse across a wide range of mental disorders (Hooley, 2007).

**expressed emotion**
A measure of how much hostility, criticism, and emotional overinvolvement are used when speaking about a family member with a mental disorder.

**schizophrenia**
A disorder characterized by the profound disruption of basic psychological processes; a distorted perception of reality; altered or blunted emotion; and disturbances in thought, motivation, and behaviour.

## IN SUMMARY

▶ Mood disorders are mental disorders in which a disturbance in mood is the predominant feature.

▶ Major depression (or unipolar depression) is characterized by a severely depressed mood and/or inability to experience pleasure lasting at least 2 weeks; symptoms include excessive self-criticism, guilt, difficulty concentrating, sleep and appetite disturbances, lethargy, and possibly suicidal thoughts or attempts at suicide. Dysthymia, a related disorder, involves less severe symptoms that persist for at least 2 years.

▶ Bipolar disorder is an unstable emotional condition involving extreme mood swings of depression and mania. The manic phase is characterized by periods of abnormally and persistently elevated, expansive, or irritable mood, lasting at least 1 week.

# Schizophrenia and Other Psychotic Disorders: Losing the Grasp on Reality

Margaret, a 39-year-old mother, believed that God was punishing her for marrying a man she did not love and bringing two children into the world. As her punishment, God had made her and her children immortal so that they would have to suffer in their unhappy home life forever—a realization that came to her one evening when she was washing dishes and saw a fork lying across a knife in the shape of a cross. Margaret found further support for her belief in two pieces of evidence: First, a local television station was rerunning old episodes of *The Honeymooners,* a 1950s situation comedy in which the main characters often argue and shout at each other. She saw this as a sign from God that her own marital conflict would go on forever. Second, she believed (falsely) that the pupils of her children's eyes were fixed in size and would neither dilate nor constrict—a sign of their immortality. At home, she would lock herself in her room for hours and sometimes days. The week before her diagnosis, she kept her 7-year-old son home from school so that he could join her and his 4-year-old sister in reading aloud from the Bible (Oltmanns et al., 1991). Margaret was suffering from the most well-known and widely studied psychotic disorder: schizophrenia. Schizophrenia is one of the most mystifying and devastating of all the mental disorders.

## Symptoms and Types of Schizophrenia

**Schizophrenia** is a psychotic disorder (*psychosis* is a break from reality) characterized by *the profound disruption of basic psychological processes; a distorted perception of reality; altered or blunted emotion; and disturbances in thought, motivation, and behaviour.* Traditionally, schizophrenia was regarded primarily as a disturbance of thought and perception, in which the sense of reality becomes severely distorted and confused. However, this condition is now

What is schizophrenia?

Those suffering from schizophrenia often experience hallucinations and delusions, unable to determine what is real and what has been created by their own mind. The experience of John Nash, a Nobel Prize–winning economist, with schizophrenia was depicted in the book and movie *A Beautiful Mind.*.

**positive symptoms**
Thoughts and behaviours present in schizophrenia but not seen in those without the disorder, such as delusions and hallucinations.

**hallucination**
A false perceptual experience that has a compelling sense of being real despite the absence of external stimulation.

**delusion**
A patently false belief system, often bizarre and grandiose, that is maintained in spite of its irrationality.

**disorganized speech**
A severe disruption of verbal communication in which ideas shift rapidly and incoherently among unrelated topics.

**grossly disorganized behaviour**
Behaviour that is inappropriate for the situation or ineffective in attaining goals, often with specific motor disturbances.

understood to take different forms affecting a wide range of functions. According to the *DSM–5*, schizophrenia is diagnosed when two or more symptoms emerge during a continuous period of at least 1 month with signs of the disorder persisting for at least 6 months. The symptoms of schizophrenia are often separated into *positive, negative,* and *cognitive symptoms.*

**Positive symptoms** of schizophrenia include *thoughts and behaviours not seen in those without the disorder,* such as

> **Hallucinations** are *false perceptual experiences that have a compelling sense of being real despite the absence of external stimulation.* The perceptual disturbances associated with schizophrenia can include hearing, seeing, smelling, or having a tactile sensation of things that are not there. Schizophrenic hallucinations are often auditory (e.g., hearing voices that no one else can hear). Among people with schizophrenia, some 65 percent report hearing voices repeatedly (Frith & Fletcher, 1995). British psychiatrist Henry Maudsley (1886) long ago proposed that these voices are in fact produced in the mind of the person with schizophrenia, and recent research substantiates his idea. In one PET imaging study, auditory hallucinations were accompanied by activation in Broca's area (as discussed in the Neuroscience and Behaviour chapter), the part of the brain associated with the production of language (McGuire, Shah, & Murray, 1993). Unfortunately, the voices heard in schizophrenia seldom sound like the self or like a kindly uncle offering advice. They command, scold, suggest bizarre actions, or offer snide comments. One individual reported a voice saying, "He's getting up now. He's going to wash. It's about time" (Frith & Fletcher, 1995).

> **Delusions** are *patently false beliefs, often bizarre and grandiose, that are maintained in spite of their irrationality.* For example, an individual with schizophrenia may believe that he or she is Jesus Christ, Napoleon, Joan of Arc, or some other well-known person. Such delusions of identity have helped foster the misconception that schizophrenia involves multiple personalities. However, adopted identities in schizophrenia do not alternate, exhibit amnesia for one another, or otherwise "split." Delusions of persecution are also common. Some individuals believe that the CIA, demons, extraterrestrials, or other malevolent forces are conspiring to harm them or control their minds, which may represent an attempt to make sense of the tormenting delusions (Roberts, 1991). People with schizophrenia have little or no insight into their disordered perceptual and thought processes (Karow et al., 2007). Without understanding that they have lost control of their own minds, they may develop unusual beliefs and theories that attribute control to external agents.

> **Disorganized speech** is *a severe disruption of verbal communication in which ideas shift rapidly and incoherently among unrelated topics.* The abnormal speech patterns in schizophrenia reflect difficulties in organizing thoughts and focusing attention. Responses to questions are often irrelevant, ideas are loosely associated, and words are used in peculiar ways. For example, asked by her doctor, "Can you tell me the name of this place?" one patient with schizophrenia responded, "I have not been a drinker for 16 years. I am taking a mental rest after a 'carter' assignment of 'quill.' You know, a 'penwrap.' I had contracts with Warner Brothers Studios and Eugene broke phonograph records but Mike protested. I have been with the police department for 35 years. I am made of flesh and blood—see, Doctor" [pulling up her dress] (Carson et al., 2000, p. 474).

> **Grossly disorganized behaviour** is *behaviour that is inappropriate for the situation or ineffective in attaining goals, often with specific motor disturbances.* A individual might exhibit constant childlike silliness, improper sexual behaviour (such as masturbating in public), disheveled appearance, or loud shouting or swearing. Specific motor disturbances might include strange movements,

rigid posturing, odd mannerisms, bizarre grimacing, or hyperactivity. **Catatonic behaviour** is *a marked decrease in all movement or an increase in muscular rigidity and overactivity.* Individuals with *catatonia* may actively resist movement (when someone is trying to move them) or become completely unresponsive and unaware of their surroundings in a *catatonic stupor.* In addition, individuals receiving drug therapy may exhibit motor symptoms (such as rigidity or spasm) as a side effect of the medication. Indeed, the *DSM–5* includes a diagnostic category labelled *medication-induced movement disorders* that identifies motor disturbances arising from the use of medications of the sort commonly used to treat schizophrenia.

**Negative symptoms** are *deficits or disruptions to normal emotions and behaviours.* They include *emotional and social withdrawal; apathy; poverty of speech; and other indications of the absence or insufficiency of normal behaviour, motivation, and emotion.* These symptoms refer to things missing in people with schizophrenia. Negative symptoms may rob people of emotion, for example, leaving them with flat, deadpan responses, their interest in people or events may be undermined, or their capacity to focus attention may be impaired.

**Cognitive symptoms** are *deficits in cognitive abilities, specifically in executive functioning, attention, and working memory.* These are the most difficult symptoms to notice because they are much less bizarre and public than the positive and negative symptoms. However, these cognitive deficits often play a large role in terms of preventing people with schizophrenia from achieving a high level of functioning, such as maintaining friendships and holding down a job (Green et al., 2000).

Schizophrenia occurs in about 1 percent of the population (Jablensky, 1997) and is slightly more common in men than in women (McGrath et al., 2008). Early versions of the *DSM* suggested that schizophrenia might have a very early onset—in the form of infantile autism—but more recent studies suggest that these disorders are distinct and that schizophrenia rarely develops before early adolescence (Rapoport et al., 2009). The first episode typically occurs in late adolescence or early adulthood (Gottesman, 1991). Despite its relatively low frequency, schizophrenia is the primary diagnosis for nearly 40 percent of all admissions to American state and county mental hospitals; it is the second most frequent diagnosis for inpatient psychiatric admission at other institutions (Rosenstein, Milazzo-Sayre, & Manderscheid, 1990). The disproportionate rate of hospitalization for schizophrenia is a testament to the devastation it causes in people's lives.

This person with schizophrenia is suffering from a symptom called catatonic behaviour, in which he may assume an unusual posture and fail to move for hours.

## Biological Factors

In 1899, when German psychiatrist Emil Kraepelin first described the syndrome we now know as schizophrenia, he remarked that the disorder was so severe that it suggested "organic," or biological, origins. Over the years, accumulating evidence for the role of biology in schizophrenia has come from studies of genetic factors, biochemical factors, and neuroanatomy.

### Genetic Factors

Family studies indicate that the closer a person's genetic relatedness to a person with schizophrenia, the greater the likelihood of developing the disorder (Gottesman, 1991). As shown in **FIGURE 15.4** (on the next page), concordance rates increase dramatically with biological relatedness. The rates are estimates and vary considerably from study to study, but almost every study finds the average concordance rates higher for identical twins (48 percent) than for fraternal twins (17 percent), which suggests a genetic component for the disorder (Torrey et al., 1994).

**What is the role of genetics in schizophrenia?**

**catatonic behaviour**
A marked decrease in all movement or an increase in muscular rigidity and overactivity.

**negative symptoms**
Deficits or disruptions to normal emotions and behaviours (e.g., emotional and social withdrawal; apathy; poverty of speech; and other indications of the absence or insufficiency of normal behaviour, motivation, and emotion).

**cognitive symptoms**
Deficits in cognitive abilities, specifically executive functioning, attention, and working memory.

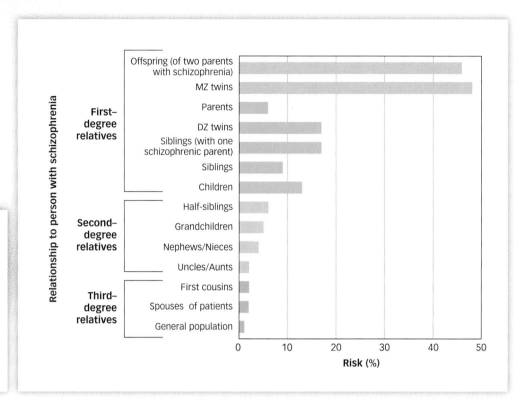

▶ Figure **15.4** **Average Risk of Developing Schizophrenia** The risk of schizophrenia among biological relatives is greater for those with greater degrees of relatedness. An identical (MZ) twin of a twin with schizophrenia has a 48 percent risk of developing schizophrenia, for example, and offspring of two parents with schizophrenia have a 46 percent risk of developing the disorder.

(Adapted from Gottesman, 1991.)

Although genetics clearly have a strong predisposing role in schizophrenia, considerable evidence suggests that environmental factors, such as the prenatal and perinatal environments, also affect concordance rates (Jurewicz, Owen, & O'Donovan, 2001; Thaker, 2002; Torrey et al., 1994). For example, because approximately 70 percent of identical twins share the same prenatal blood supply, toxins in the mother's blood could contribute to the high concordance rate. More recent studies (discussed in the earlier section on bipolar disorder) are contributing to a better understanding of how environmental stressors can trigger epigenetic changes that increase susceptibility to this disorder.

## Biochemical Factors

During the 1950s, major tranquilizers were discovered that could reduce the symptoms of schizophrenia by lowering levels of the neurotransmitter dopamine. The effectiveness of many drugs in alleviating schizophrenic symptoms is related to the drugs' capacity to reduce dopamine's role in neurotransmission in certain brain tracts. This finding suggested the **dopamine hypothesis,** *the idea that schizophrenia involves an excess of dopamine activity.* The hypothesis has been invoked to explain why amphetamines, which increase dopamine levels, often exacerbate symptoms of schizophrenia (Iverson, 2006).

If only things were so simple. Considerable evidence suggests that this hypothesis is inadequate (Moncrieff, 2009). For example, many individuals with schizophrenia do not respond favourably to dopamine-blocking drugs (e.g., major tranquilizers), and those who do seldom show a complete remission of symptoms. Moreover, the drugs block dopamine receptors very rapidly, yet individuals with schizophrenia typically do not show a beneficial response for weeks. Finally, research has implicated other neurotransmitters in schizophrenia, suggesting that the disorder may involve a complex interaction among a host of different biochemicals (Risman et al., 2008; Sawa & Snyder, 2002). In sum, the precise role of neurotransmitters in schizophrenia has yet to be determined.

**dopamine hypothesis**
The idea that schizophrenia involves an excess of dopamine activity.

## Neuroanatomy

When neuroimaging techniques became available, researchers immediately started looking for distinctive anatomical features of the brain in individuals with schizophrenia. The earliest observations revealed enlargement of the *ventricles,* hollow areas filled with cerebrospinal fluid, lying deep within the core of the brain (see **FIGURE 15.5**) (Johnstone et al., 1976). In some individuals (primarily those with chronic, negative symptoms), the ventricles were abnormally enlarged, suggesting a loss of brain tissue mass that could arise from an anomaly in prenatal development (Arnold et al., 1998; Heaton et al., 1994).

FROM KUNUGI ET AL. (2003)

**(a)** Twin with schizophrenia  **(b)** Twin without schizophrenia

◀ Figure 15.5 **Enlarged Ventricles in Schizophrenia** These MRI scans of monozygotic twins reveal that (*a*) the twin affected by schizophrenia shows enlarged ventricles (all the central white space) as compared to (*b*) the unaffected twin (Kunugi et al., 2003).

Understanding the significance of this brain abnormality for schizophrenia is complicated by several factors, however. First, such enlarged ventricles are found in only a minority of cases of schizophrenia. Second, some individuals who do not have schizophrenia also show evidence of enlarged ventricles. Finally, this type of brain abnormality can be caused by the long-term use of some types of antipsychotic medications commonly prescribed in schizophrenia (Breggin, 1990; Gur et al., 1998).

**How are the brains of people with schizophrenia different from those without this disorder?**

Neuroimaging studies provide evidence of a variety of brain abnormalities in schizophrenia. Paul Thompson and his colleagues (2001) examined changes in the brains of adolescents whose MRI scans could be traced sequentially from the onset of schizophrenia. By morphing the images onto a standardized brain, the researchers were able to detect progressive tissue loss beginning in the parietal lobe and eventually encompassing much of the brain (see **FIGURE 15.6**). All adolescents lose some grey matter over time in a kind of normal "pruning" of the brain, but in the case of those developing schizophrenia, the loss was dramatic enough to seem pathological. A variety of specific brain changes found in other studies suggests a clear relationship between biological changes in the brain and the progression of schizophrenia (Shenton et al., 2001).

## Psychological Factors

With all these potential biological contributors to schizophrenia, you might think there would be few psychological or social causes of the disorder. However, several studies do suggest that the family environment plays a role in the development of and recovery from the condition. One large-scale study compared the risk of schizophrenia

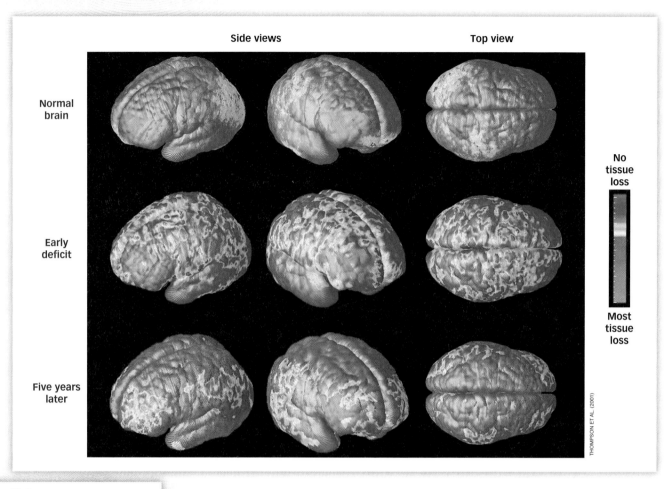

Side views     Top view

Normal brain

Early deficit

Five years later

No tissue loss

Most tissue loss

THOMPSON ET AL. (2001)

▲ Figure 15.6 **Brain Tissue Loss in Adolescent Schizophrenia** MRI scan composites reveal brain tissue loss in adolescents diagnosed with schizophrenia. Normal brains show minimal loss due to "pruning" (*top*) Early-deficit scans reveal loss in the parietal areas (*middle*); individuals at this stage may experience symptoms such as hallucinations or bizarre thoughts. Scans 5 years later reveal extensive tissue loss over much of the cortex (*bottom*); individuals at this stage are likely to suffer from delusions, disorganized speech and behaviour, and negative symptoms such as social withdrawal (Thompson et al., 2001).

in children adopted into healthy families and those adopted into severely disturbed families (Tienari et al., 2004). (Disturbed families were defined as those with extreme conflict, lack of communication, or chaotic relationships.) Among children whose biological mothers had schizophrenia, the disturbed environment increased the likelihood of developing schizophrenia—an outcome that was not found among children who were also reared in disturbed families but whose biological mothers did *not* have schizophrenia. This finding provides support for the diathesis–stress model described earlier.

## IN SUMMARY

▶ Schizophrenia is a severe psychological disorder involving hallucinations, disorganized thoughts and behaviour, and emotional and social withdrawal.

▶ Schizophrenia affects only 1 percent of the population, but it accounts for a disproportionate share of psychiatric hospitalizations.

▶ The first drugs that reduced the availability of dopamine sometimes reduced the symptoms of schizophrenia, suggesting that the disorder involved an excess of dopamine activity, but recent research suggests that schizophrenia may involve a complex interaction among a variety of neurotransmitters.

▶ Risks for developing schizophrenia include genetic factors, biochemical factors (perhaps a complex interaction among many neurotransmitters), brain abnormalities, and a stressful home environment.

# OTHER VOICES

## Successful and Schizophrenic

**Elyn R. Saks** is a law professor at the University of Southern California and the author of the memoir *The Center Cannot Hold: My Journey Through Madness.*

PHOTO BY MIKEL HEALEY, COURTESY ELYN R. SAKS

This chapter describes what we know about the characteristics and causes of mental disorders, and the next chapter describes how these disorders are commonly treated. For some of the more severe disorders, such as schizophrenia, the picture does not look good. People diagnosed with schizophrenia are often informed that it is a lifelong condition, and although current treatments show some effectiveness in decreasing the delusional thinking and hallucinations often present in those with schizophrenia, people with this disorder are often unable to hold down a full-time job, maintain healthy relationships, and achieve a high quality of life.

Elyn Saks is one such person who received a diagnosis of schizophrenia and was informed of this prognosis. She described what happened next in a longer version of the following article that appeared in the *New York Times* (2013).

Thirty years ago, I was given a diagnosis of schizophrenia. My prognosis was "grave": I would never live independently, hold a job, find a loving partner, get married. My home would be a board-and-care facility, my days spent watching TV in a day room with other people debilitated by mental illness. ...

Then I made a decision. I would write the narrative of my life. Today I am a chaired professor at the University of Southern California Gould School of Law. I have an adjunct appointment in the department of psychiatry at the medical school of the University of California, San Diego. The MacArthur Foundation gave me a genius grant.

Although I fought my diagnosis for many years, I came to accept that I have schizophrenia and will be in treatment the rest of my life. What I refused to accept was my prognosis.

Conventional psychiatric thinking and its diagnostic categories say that people like me do not exist. Either I do not have schizophrenia (please tell that to the delusions crowding my mind), or I could not have accomplished what I have (please tell that to U.S.C.'s committee on faculty affairs). But I do, and I have. And I have undertaken research with colleagues at U.S.C. and U.C.L.A. to show that I am not alone. There are others with schizophrenia and such active symptoms as delusions and hallucinations who have significant academic and professional achievements.

Over the last few years, my colleagues ... and I have gathered 20 research subjects with high-functioning schizophrenia in Los Angeles. They suffered from symptoms like mild delusions or hallucinatory behaviour. Their average age was 40. Half were male, half female, and more than half were minorities. All had high school diplomas, and a majority either had or were working toward college or graduate degrees. They were graduate students, managers, technicians and professionals, including a doctor, lawyer, psychologist and chief executive of a nonprofit group. At the same time, most were unmarried and childless, which is consistent with their diagnoses. ... More than three-quarters had been hospitalized between two and five times because of their illness, while three had never been admitted.

How had these people with schizophrenia managed to succeed in their studies and at such high-level jobs? We learned that, in addition to medication and therapy, all the participants had developed techniques to keep their schizophrenia at bay. For some, these techniques were cognitive. An educator with a master's degree said he had learned to face his hallucinations and ask, "What's the evidence for that? Or is it just a perception problem?" Another participant said, "I hear derogatory voices all the time. ... You just gotta blow them off." ...

Other techniques that our participants cited included controlling sensory inputs. For some, this meant keeping their living space simple (bare walls, no TV, only quiet music), while for others, it meant distracting music. "I will listen to loud music if I do not want to hear things," said a participant who is a certified nurse's assistant. Still others mentioned exercise, a healthy diet, avoiding alcohol and getting enough sleep. ...

One of the most frequently mentioned techniques that helped our research participants manage their symptoms was work. "Work has been an important part of who I am," said an educator in our group. "When you become useful to an organization and feel respected in that organization, there's a certain value in belonging there." This person works on the weekends too because of "the distraction factor." In other words, by engaging in work, the crazy stuff often recedes to the sidelines. ...

THAT is why it is so distressing when doctors tell their patients not to expect or pursue fulfilling careers. Far too often, the conventional psychiatric approach to mental illness is to see clusters of symptoms that characterize people. Accordingly, many psychiatrists hold the view that treating symptoms with medication is treating mental illness. But this fails to take into account individuals' strengths and capabilities, leading mental health professionals to underestimate what their patients can hope to achieve in the world. ... A recent *New York Times Magazine* article described a new company that hires high-functioning adults with autism, taking advantage of their unusual memory skills and attention to detail. ...

An approach that looks for individual strengths, in addition to considering symptoms, could help dispel the pessimism surrounding mental illness. Finding "the wellness within the illness," as one person with schizophrenia said, should be a therapeutic goal. Doctors should urge their patients to develop relationships and engage in meaningful work. They should encourage patients to find their own repertory of techniques to manage their symptoms and aim for a quality of life as they define it. And they should provide patients with the resources—therapy, medication and support—to make these things happen.

Elyn Saks's story is amazing and inspiring. It also is quite unusual. How should we incorporate stories like hers and the people in the research study she described? Are these people outliers—simply a carefully selected collection of people who had unusually favourable outcomes (given the large size of Los Angeles, it is reasonable to think one could amass a small sample of such cases)? Or has Professor Saks touched on an important limitation to the way in which the field currently conceptualizes, classifies, and treats mental disorders? Do we focus too much on what is wrong and on how professionalized health care can treat the pathology and not enough on what inherent strengths people have that can help them overcome their challenges, function at a high level, and achieve a high quality of life? These are all questions that are testable with the methods of psychological science, and the answers may help to improve the lives of many people.

# Disorders of Childhood and Adolescence: Difficulties during Development

All of the disorders described above can have their onset during childhood, adolescence, or adulthood. Some often begin early in life (lots of adolescents develop anxiety disorders or depression), and in fact half of all disorders begin by age 14, and three-quarters by age 24 (Kessler, Berglund, et al., 2005), which means if you are 24 years or older, you are almost out of the woods. However, other disorders tend not to begin until early adulthood, such as bipolar disorder and schizophrenia (we did say "almost"). Some disorders *always*, by definition, begin in childhood or adolescence, and if they do not, you are never going to have them. These include autism spectrum disorder, attention-deficit/hyperactivity disorder, conduct disorder, intellectual disability (formerly called *mental retardation*), learning disorders, communication disorders, and motor skill disorders, in addition to many others. The first three are among the most common and well known, so we will review them briefly here.

## Autism Spectrum Disorder

Marco is a 4-year-old only child. His parents have become worried because, although his mother stays home with him all day and tries to play with him and talk with him, he still has not spoken a single word and he shows little interest in trying. He spends much of his time playing with his toy trains, which seem to be the thing he enjoys most in life. He often sits for hours staring at spinning train wheels or pushing a single train back and forth, seeming completely in his own world, uninterested in playing with anyone else. Marco's parents have become concerned about Marco's apparent inability to speak, disinterest in others, and development of some peculiar mannerisms, such as flapping his arms repeatedly for no apparent reason.

**Autism spectrum disorder (ASD)** is *a condition beginning in early childhood in which a person shows persistent communication deficits as well as restricted and repetitive patterns of behaviours, interests, or activities.* In DSM–5, ASD now subsumes multiple disorders that were considered separate in *DSM–IV*: autistic disorder, Asperger's disorder, childhood disintegrative disorder, and pervasive developmental disorder not otherwise specified (i.e., these disorders are no longer recognized in the *DSM*).

The true rate of ASD is difficult to pinpoint, especially given the recent change in diagnostic definition. Estimates from the 1960s indicated that autism was a rare diagnosis, occurring in 4 per 10 000 children. Estimates have been creeping up over time and now stand at approximately 10 to 20 per 10 000 children. If one considers the full range of disorders that now fall under the ASD umbrella in the *DSM–5*, the rate is 60 per 10 000 children (NEDSAC, 2012; Newschaffer et al., 2007). It is unclear whether this increased rate is due to increased awareness and recognition of ASD, better screening and diagnostic tools, or to some other factor. Boys have higher rates of ASD than girls by a ratio of about 4:1.

Early theories of autism described it as "childhood schizophrenia," but it is now understood to be separate from schizophrenia, which is rarely diagnosed in children, emerging mainly in adolescence or young adulthood (Kessler & Wang, 2008). ASD is currently viewed as a heterogeneous set of traits that cluster together in some families (heritability estimates for ASD are as high as 90 percent), leaving some children with just a few mild ASD traits and others with a more severe form of the disorder (Geschwind, 2009). Interestingly, some people with ASD have unique strengths, such as remarkable abilities to perceive or remember details, or to master symbol systems such as mathematics or music (Happé & Vital, 2009).

One current model suggested that ASD can be understood as an impaired capacity for *empathizing,* knowing the mental states of others, combined with a superior ability

> **What is the relationship between ASD and empathy?**

**autism spectrum disorder (ASD)**
A condition beginning in early childhood in which a person shows persistent communication deficits as well as restricted and repetitive patterns of behaviours, interests, or activities.

for *systematizing*, understanding the rules that organize the structure and function of objects (Baron-Cohen & Belmonte, 2005). Consistent with this model, brain imaging studies show that people with autism have comparatively decreased activity in regions associated with understanding the minds of others and greater activation in regions related to basic object perception (Sigman, Spence & Wang, 2006).

Although many people with ASD experience impairments throughout their lives that prevent them from having relationships and holding down a job, many go on to very successful careers. The renowned behavioural scientist and author Temple Grandin (2006) has written of her personal experience with autism. She was diagnosed with autism at age 3, started learning to talk late, and then suffered teasing for odd habits and "nerdy" behaviour. Fortunately, she developed ways to cope and found a niche through her special talent—the ability to understand animal behaviour (Sacks, 1996). She is now a Professor of Animal Science at Colorado State University; a celebrated author of books such as *Animals in Translation*; a designer of animal handling systems used widely in ranching, farming, and zoos; and the central character in a movie (starring Claire Danes) based on her life. Temple Grandin's story lets us know that there are happy endings. Overall, those diagnosed with ASD as children have highly variable trajectories, with some achieving normal or better-than-normal functioning and others struggling with profound disorder. Autism is a childhood disorder that in adulthood can turn out many ways (see the Hot Science box).

Temple Grandin, Professor of Animal Sciences at Colorado State University, is living proof that people with autism spectrum disorder are able to have very successful professional careers.

# Optimal Outcome in Autism Spectrum Disorder

**HOT SCIENCE**

What comes to mind when you think of the word *autism*? What kind of person do you imagine? If an adult, what do you imagine that they do for a living? Can they hold a job? Can they care for themselves? Autism spectrum disorder (ASD) is considered by many to be a lifelong condition in which those affected will forever experience significant difficulties and disability in their interpersonal, education, and occupational functioning. Several recent studies are helping to change this outlook.

Deborah Fein and colleagues (2013) recently described a sample of people who were diagnosed with autism as children, but who no longer met criteria for ASD. How could this be? For years, researchers have noticed that some portion of children diagnosed with autism later fail to meet diagnostic criteria. One recent review suggested that 3 to 25 percent of children ultimately lose their ASD diagnosis over time (Helt et al., 2008). There are several potential explanations for this. The most obvious is that some portion of children diagnosed with ASD are misdiagnosed and do not really have this disorder. Perhaps they are overly shy, or quiet, or develop speech later than other children, and this is misinterpreted as ASD. Another possibility is that children who lose their ASD diagnosis had a milder form of the disorder and/or were identified and treated earlier. There is some support for this idea, as predictors of

▲ Autism was once viewed as a condition with lifelong impairments, including an inability to achieve the educational milestone that these typical students are celebrating. New research suggests that early intervention can help many of those in whom ASD is diagnosed to achieve normal levels of functioning.

recovery from ASD include high IQ, stronger language abilities, and earlier age of identification and treatment (Helt et al., 2008).

The possibility of effectively treating ASD was initially raised in an important study by Ivar Lovaas in 1987. Lovaas assigned 19 children with autism to an intensive behavioural intervention in which they received over 40 hours per week of one-on-one behaviour therapy for 2 years, and 40 children to control conditions in which they received fewer than 10 hours per week of treatment. Amazingly, follow-up of the treated children revealed that 47 percent of those in the intensive behaviour therapy condition obtained a normal level of intellectual and

educational functioning—passing through a normal first grade class—compared to only 2 percent of those in the control conditions.

Extending this earlier work, Geraldine Dawson and colleagues (2010) are testing a program called the Early Start Denver Model (ESDM), an intensive behavioural intervention (20 hours per week for 2 years) similarly designed to improve outcomes among those with ASD. Using a randomized, controlled trials, Dawson and colleagues found that toddlers with ASD who received ESDM, compared to those receiving standard community treatment, showed significant improvements in IQ (a 17-point rise!), language, adaptive and social functioning, and ASD diagnosis. Interestingly, children in the ESDM showed normalized brain activity after treatment (i.e., greater brain activation when viewing faces), which was in turn associated with improved social behaviour; those in the control condition showed the opposite pattern (Dawson et al., 2012).

How effective are intensive behavioural interventions like those described here? Fein and colleagues' (2013) data suggest that some people diagnosed with ASD can achieve optimal outcomes, meaning they do not differ from typically developing people in IQ, language, communication, or socialization—the key deficit areas that characterize ASD. This is currently a very hot area of research, and one that could have implications for those in whom ASD is diagnosed.

**attention-deficit/hyperactivity disorder (ADHD)**
A persistent pattern of severe problems with inattention and/or hyperactivity or impulsiveness that cause significant impairments in functioning.

# Attention-Deficit/Hyperactivity Disorder

Chances are you have had the experience of being distracted during a lecture or while reading one of your *other* textbooks. We all have trouble focusing from time to time. Far beyond normal distraction, **attention-deficit/hyperactivity disorder (ADHD),** is *a persistent pattern of severe problems with inattention and/or hyperactivity or impulsiveness that cause significant impairments in functioning.* This is quite different than occasional mind wandering or bursts of activity. Meeting criteria for ADHD requires having multiple symptoms of inattention (e.g., persistent problems with sustained attention, organization, memory, following instructions), hyperactivity–impulsiveness (e.g., persistent difficulties with remaining still, waiting for a turn, not interrupting others), or both. Most children experience some of these behaviours at some point, but to meet criteria for ADHD, a child has to have many of these behaviours for at least 6 months in at least two settings (e.g., home and school) to the point where they impair the child's ability to perform at school or get along at home.

> **What are the criteria for an ADHD diagnosis?**

Approximately 10 percent of boys and 4 percent of girls meet criteria for ADHD (Polanczyk et al., 2007). The *DSM–5* requires that symptoms of ADHD be present before the age of 12 in order to meet criteria for this disorder. As you can imagine, children and adolescents with ADHD often struggle in the classroom. One recent study of 500 people with ADHD found that about half had a C average or lower, and about one-third were in special classes (Biederman et al., 2006). For a long time ADHD was thought of as a disorder that affects only children and adolescents and that people "age out" of the disorder. However, we now know that in many instances this disorder persists into adulthood. The same symptoms are used to diagnose both children and adults (e.g., children with ADHD may struggle with attention and concentration in the classroom, whereas adults may experience the same problems in meetings). Approximately 4 percent of adults meet criteria for ADHD, and adults with this disorder are more likely to be male, divorced, and unemployed—and most did not receive any treatment for their ADHD (Kessler, Adler, et al., 2006). Unfortunately, most people still think of this as a disorder of childhood and do not realize that adults can suffer from ADHD as well, which could be why so few adults with ADHD receive treatment, and why the disorder often wreaks havoc on job performance and relationships.

Because ADHD, like most disorders, is defined by the presence of a wide range of symptoms, it is unlikely that it emerges from one single cause or dysfunction. The exact cause of ADHD is not known, but there are some promising leads. Genetic studies suggest that there is a strong biological influence and estimate that the heritability of ADHD is 76 percent (Faraone et al., 2005). Brain imaging studies suggest that those with ADHD have smaller brain volumes (Castellanos et al., 2002) as well as structural and functional abnormalities in frontosubcortical networks associated with attention and behavioural inhibition (Makris et al., 2009). The good news is that current drug treatments for ADHD are effective and appear to decrease the risk of later psychological and academic problems (Biederman et al., 2009).

# Conduct Disorder

Michael is an 8-year-old boy whose mother brought him into a local clinic because his behaviour had been getting progressively out of control and his parents and teachers were no longer able to control him. Although Michael's two older brothers and little sisters got along perfectly fine at home and at school, Michael had always gotten into trouble. At home he routinely bullied his siblings, threw glasses and dishes at family members, and on numerous occasions punched and kicked his parents. Outside of the house, Michael had been getting into trouble for stealing from the local store, yelling at his teacher, and spitting at the principal of his school. The last straw came when Michael's parents found him trying to set fire to his bedspread one night. They tried punishing him by taking away his toys, restricting his privileges, and trying to encourage him with a sticker chart, but nothing seemed to change his behaviour.

**Conduct disorder** is a condition in which a child or adolescent engages in a *persistent pattern of deviant behaviour involving aggression to people or animals,*

> **Why is it difficult to pin down the causes of conduct disorder?**

*destruction of property, deceitfulness or theft, or serious rule violations.* Approximately 9 percent of people in the United States report a lifetime history of conduct disorder (12 percent of boys and 7 percent of girls) (Nock et al., 2006). Statistics for Canada are not available, but the rate is probably similar. The rate of 1 in 11 children may seem a bit high, but approximately 40 percent of those with conduct disorder have, on average, only 3 symptoms that cluster into one of three areas: rule breaking, theft/deceit, or aggression toward others. The other 60 percent have more symptoms, on average 6 to 8 of the 15 defined symptoms, with problems in many more areas and a much higher risk of having other mental disorders later in life (Nock et al., 2006).

Meeting criteria for conduct disorder requires having any 3 of the 15 symptoms of conduct disorder. This means there are approximately 32 000 different combinations of symptoms that could lead to a diagnosis, which makes those with conduct disorder a pretty diverse group. This diversity makes it difficult to pin down the causes of conduct disorder. One thing that seems clear is that a wide range of genetic, biological, and environmental factors interact to produce this disorder. Indeed, risk factors for conduct disorder include maternal smoking during pregnancy, exposure to abuse and family violence during childhood, affiliation with deviant peer groups, and the presence of deficits in executive functioning (e.g., decision making, impulsiveness) (Boden et al., 2010; Burke et al., 2002). Researchers currently are attempting to better understand the pathways through which inherited genetic factors interact with environmental stressors (e.g., childhood adversities) to create characteristics in brain structure and function (e.g., reduced activity in brain regions associated with planning and decision making) that interact with environmental factors (e.g., affiliation with deviant peers) to lead to the behaviours that are characteristic of conduct disorder. Not surprisingly, conduct disorder tends to co-occur with other disorders characterized by problems with decision making and impulsiveness, such as ADHD, substance use disorders, and antisocial personality disorder, which is described in more detail in the next section.

**conduct disorder**
A persistent pattern of deviant behaviour involving aggression to people or animals, destruction of property, deceitfulness or theft, or serious rule violations.

Psychologists are attempting to identify the causes of conduct disorder with the hopes of being able to decrease the harmful behaviours, like bullying, that often accompany it.

## IN SUMMARY

▶ Some mental disorders always begin during childhood or adolescence, and in some cases (ASD, ADHD) persist into adulthood.

▶ ASD emerges in early childhood and is a condition in which a person has persistent communication deficits as well as restricted and repetitive patterns of behaviour, interests, or activities.

▶ ADHD begins by age 12 and involves a persistent pattern of severe problems with inattention and/or hyperactivity or impulsiveness that cause significant impairments in functioning.

▶ Conduct disorder begins in childhood or adolescence and involves a persistent pattern of deviant behaviour involving aggression to people or animals, destruction of property, deceitfulness or theft, or serious rule violations.

**personality disorders**
Enduring patterns of thinking, feeling, or relating to others or controlling impulses that deviate from cultural expectations and cause distress or impaired functioning.

# Personality Disorders: Going to Extremes

Think for a minute about high school acquaintances whose personalities made them stand out—not necessarily in a good way. Was there an odd person who did not seem to make sense, wore strange outfits, sometimes would not respond in conversation—or would respond by bringing up weird things like astrology or mind reading? Or perhaps a drama queen, someone whose theatrics and exaggerated emotions turned everything into a big deal? And do not forget the neat freak, the perfectionist obsessed with control, who had the perfectly organized locker, precisely arranged hair, and sweater with zero lint balls. One way to describe such people is to say they simply have *personalities*, the unique patterns of traits we explored in the Personality chapter. But sometimes personality traits can become so rigid and confining that they blend into mental disorders. **Personality disorders** are *enduring patterns of thinking, feeling, or relating to others or controlling impulses that deviate from cultural expectations and cause distress or impaired functioning.* Personality disorders begin in adolescence or early adulthood and are relatively stable over time. Let us look at the types of personality disorders and then take a closer look at one that sometimes lands people in jail: antisocial personality disorder.

## Types of Personality Disorders

The *DSM–5* lists 10 specific personality disorders (see **TABLE 15.3**). They fall into three clusters: (a) *odd/eccentric*, (b) *dramatic/erratic*, and (c) *anxious/inhibited*. The strange high school person, for example, could have *schizotypal personality disorder* (odd/eccentric cluster); the drama queen could have *histrionic personality disorder*

GETTY IMAGES/IMAGE SOURCE

Ever browse a copy of *Architectural Digest* and wonder who would live in one of those perfect homes? A person with obsessive-compulsive personality disorder might fit right in. This personality disorder (characterized by excessive perfectionism) should not be mistaken, by the way, for obsessive-compulsive disorder—the anxiety disorder in which the person suffers from repeated unwanted thoughts or actions.

(dramatic/erratic cluster); the neat freak could have *obsessive-compulsive personality disorder* (anxious/inhibited cluster). In fact, browsing through the list may awaken other high school memories. Do not rush to judgment, however. Most of those kids were probably quite healthy and fell far short of qualifying for a diagnosis; after all, high school can be a rocky time for everyone, which is why personality disorders are not diagnosed in children or adolescents. The *DSM–5* even notes that early personality problems often do not persist into adulthood. Still, the array of personality disorders suggests that there are multiple ways an individual's gift of a unique personality could become a problem.

Personality disorders have been a bit controversial for several reasons. First, critics question whether having a problematic personality is really a disorder. Canadian data are lacking, but estimates of the prevalence of personality disorders in the population range from about 1 in 16 to about 1 in 11 (Public Health Agency of Canada, 2002b), which makes it pretty common. Perhaps it might be better just to admit that a lot of people are difficult and leave it at that. Another question is whether personality problems correspond to "disorders" in that there are distinct *types* or whether such problems might be better understood as extreme values on trait *dimensions* such as the Big Five traits discussed in the Personality chapter (Trull & Durrett, 2005). In *DSM–IV*, personality disorders

> Table 15.3

### Clusters of Personality Disorders

| Cluster | Personality Disorder | Characteristics |
|---------|---------------------|-----------------|
| A. Odd/Eccentric | Paranoid | Distrust in others, suspicion that people have sinister motives. Apt to challenge the loyalties of friends and read hostile intentions into others' actions. Prone to anger and aggressive outbursts but otherwise emotionally cold. Often jealous, guarded, secretive, overly serious. |
| | Schizoid | Extreme introversion and withdrawal from relationships. Prefers to be alone, little interest in others. Humourless, distant, often absorbed with own thoughts and feelings, a daydreamer. Fearful of closeness, with poor social skills, often seen as a "loner." |
| | Schizotypal | Peculiar or eccentric manners of speaking or dressing. Strange beliefs. "Magical thinking" such as belief in ESP or telepathy. Difficulty forming relationships. May react oddly in conversation, not respond, or talk to self. Speech elaborate or difficult to follow. (Possibly a mild form of schizophrenia.) |
| B. Dramatic/Erratic | Antisocial | Impoverished moral sense or "conscience." History of deception, crime, legal problems, impulsive and aggressive or violent behaviour. Little emotional empathy or remorse for hurting others. Manipulative, careless, callous. At high risk for substance abuse and alcoholism. |
| | Borderline | Unstable moods and intense, stormy personal relationships. Frequent mood changes and anger, unpredictable impulses. Self-mutilation or suicidal threats or gestures to get attention or manipulate others. Self-image fluctuation and a tendency to see others as "all good" or "all bad." |
| | Histrionic | Constant attention seeking. Grandiose language, provocative dress, exaggerated illnesses, all to gain attention. Believes that everyone loves them. Emotional, lively, overly dramatic, enthusiastic, and excessively flirtatious. Shallow and labile true emotions. "Onstage." |
| | Narcissistic | Inflated sense of self-importance, absorbed by fantasies of self and success. Exaggerates own achievement, assumes others will recognize they are superior. Good first impressions but poor longer-term relationships. Exploitative of others. |
| C. Anxious/Inhibited | Avoidant | Socially anxious and uncomfortable unless they are confident of being liked. In contrast with schizoid person, yearns for social contact. Fears criticism and worries about being embarrassed in front of others. Avoids social situations due to fear of rejection. |
| | Dependent | Submissive, dependent, requiring excessive approval, reassurance, and advice. Clings to people and fears losing them. Lacking self-confidence. Uncomfortable when alone. May be devastated by end of close relationship or suicidal if breakup is threatened. |
| | Obsessive-compulsive | Conscientious, orderly, perfectionist. Excessive need to do everything "right." Inflexibly high standards and caution can interfere with their productivity. Fear of errors can make them strict and controlling. Poor expression of emotions. (*Not* the same as obsessive-compulsive disorder.) |

*Source:* From *DSM–5* (American Psychiatric Association, 2013).

appeared as a separate type of disorder from all of the other disorders described above (specifically, those major disorders were all in a category called *Axis I* and personality disorders were in *Axis II*. However, in *DSM–5* personality disorders have earned equal footing as full-fledged disorders. One of the most well studied of all the personality disorders is antisocial personality disorder.

## Antisocial Personality Disorder

Henri Desiré Landru began using personal advertisements to attract a woman "interested in matrimony" in Paris in 1914, and he succeeded in seducing 10 of them. He bilked them of their savings, poisoned them, and cremated them in his stove, also disposing of a boy and two dogs along the way. He recorded his murders in a notebook and maintained a marriage and a mistress all the while. The gruesome actions of serial

Henri Desiré Landru (1869–1922) was a serial killer who met widows through advertisements he placed in newspapers' lonely hearts columns. After obtaining enough information to embezzle money from them, he murdered 10 women and the son of one of the women. He was executed for serial murder in 1922.

killers such as Landru leave us frightened and wondering; however, bullies, compulsive liars, and even drivers who regularly speed through a school zone share the same shocking blindness to human pain. The *DSM–5* includes the category of **antisocial personality disorder (APD)** and defines it as *a pervasive pattern of disregard for and violation of the rights of others that begins in childhood or early adolescence and continues into adulthood.*

Adults with an APD diagnosis typically have a history of *conduct disorder* before the age of 15. In adulthood, a diagnosis of APD is given to individuals who show 3 or more of a set of 7 diagnostic signs: illegal behaviour, deception, impulsivity, physical aggression, recklessness, irresponsibility, and a lack of remorse for wrongdoing. About 3.6 percent of the general population has APD, and the rate of occurrence in men is 3 times the rate in women (Grant et al., 2004).

The terms *sociopath* and *psychopath* describe people with APD who are especially coldhearted, manipulative, and ruthless—yet may be glib and charming (Cleckley, 1976; Hare, 1998). Although psychologists usually try to explain the development of abnormal behaviour as a product of childhood experiences or difficult life circumstances, those who work with APD seem less forgiving, often noting the sheer dangerousness of people with this disorder. Many people with APD do commit crimes, and many are caught because of the frequency and flagrancy of their infractions. Among 22 790 prisoners in one study, 47 percent of the men and 21 percent of the women were diagnosed with APD (Fazel & Danesh, 2002). Statistics such as these support the notion of a "criminal personality."

Both the early onset of conduct problems and the lack of success in treatment suggest that career criminality often has an internal cause (Lykken, 1995). Evidence of brain abnormalities in people with APD is also accumulating (Blair, Peschardt, & Mitchell, 2005). One line of investigation has looked at sensitivity to fear in psychopaths and individuals who show no such psychopathology. For example, criminal psychopaths who are shown negative emotional words such as *hate* or *corpse* exhibit less activity in the amygdala and hippocampus than do noncriminals (Kiehl et al., 2001). The two brain areas are involved in the process of fear conditioning (Patrick, Cuthbert, & Lang, 1994), so their relative inactivity in such studies suggests that psychopaths are less sensitive to fear than are other people. Violent psychopaths can target their aggression toward the self as well as others, often behaving in reckless ways that lead to violent ends. It might seem peaceful to go through life "without fear," but perhaps fear is useful in keeping people from the extremes of antisocial behaviour.

**What are some of the factors that contribute to APD?**

## IN SUMMARY

▶ Personality disorders are enduring patterns of thinking, feeling, relating to others, or controlling impulses that cause distress or impaired functioning.

▶ They include three clusters: odd/eccentric, dramatic/erratic, and anxious/inhibited.

▶ Antisocial personality disorder is associated with a lack of moral emotions and behaviour; people with antisocial personality disorder can be manipulative, dangerous, and reckless, often hurting others and sometimes hurting themselves.

**antisocial personality disorder (APD)** A pervasive pattern of disregard for and violation of the rights of others that begins in childhood or early adolescence and continues into adulthood.

# Self-Harm Behaviours: When the Mind Turns against Itself

We all have an innate drive to keep ourselves alive. We eat when we are hungry, get out of the way of fast-moving vehicles, and go to school so we can earn a living to keep ourselves, and our families, alive (see the discussion of evolutionary psychology in the Psychology: Evolution of a Science chapter). One of the most extreme manifestations of abnormal human behaviour is when a person acts in direct opposition to this drive for self-preservation and engages in intentionally self-destructive behaviour. Accounts of people intentionally harming themselves date back to the beginning of recorded history. However, it is only over the past several decades that we have begun to gain an understanding of why people purposely do things to hurt themselves. *DSM–5* includes two self-destructive behaviours in its Section III (disorders in need of further study): suicide behaviour disorder and non-suicidal self-injury disorder.

PIOTR POWIETRZYNSKI/GETTY IMAGES

We all have an innate desire to keep ourselves alive. So why do some people purposely do things to harm themselves?

## Suicidal Behaviour

Tim, a 35-year-old accountant, had by all appearances been living a pretty happy, successful life. He was married to his high school sweetheart and had two young children. Over the past several years, though, his workload had increased and he started to experience severe job-related stress. At around the same time, he and his wife began to experience some financial problems, and his alcohol consumption increased, all of which put significant strain on the family and began to affect his work. Tim's co-workers noted that he had become pretty angry and agitated lately—even yelling at co-workers on a few occasions. One evening Tim and his wife got into a heated argument about the family's finances and Tim's excessive alcohol use; Tim went into the bathroom and swallowed a bottle full of prescription medicine in an effort to end his life. He was taken to the hospital and kept there to be treated for suicidal behaviour.

**Suicide,** which refers to *intentional self-inflicted death*, is the second most common cause of death for people aged 15 to 34 in Canada, claiming 18 out of every 100 000 males, and 5 out of every 100 000 females aged 10 and older (Statistics Canada, 2014). There are large demographic differences in the suicide rate: For instance, in Canada, 75 percent of suicides occur among men, and immigrants are only about half as likely as those born in Canada to commit suicide (Malenfant, 2004). Rates of suicide in Canadian Aboriginal populations are much higher: 56 out of 100 000 for males, and almost 12 out of 100 000 for females (Society, the Individual, and Medicine [SIM], 2013). Unfortunately, we currently do not have a good understanding of why these enormous sociodemographic differences exist.

Nonfatal **suicide attempt,** in which a person engages in *potentially harmful behaviour with some intention of dying*, occurs much more frequently than suicide deaths. Across a range of countries, approximately 9 percent of adults report that they have seriously considered suicide at some point in their lives, 5 percent have made a plan to kill themselves, and 5 percent have actually made a suicide attempt

**suicide**
Intentional self-inflicted death.

**suicide attempt**
When a person engages in potentially harmful behaviour with some intention of dying.

(Nock et al., 2008). As these numbers suggest, only one third of those who think about suicide actually go on to make a suicide attempt. Although many more men than women die by suicide, women experience suicidal thoughts and (nonfatal) suicide attempts at significantly higher rates than do men (Nock et al., 2008). Moreover, the rates of suicidal thoughts and attempts increase dramatically during adolescence and young adulthood. A recent study of a representative sample of approximately 10 000 adolescents in the United States revealed that suicidal thoughts and behaviours are virtually nonexistent before age 10, but then increase dramatically from age 12 to 18 years (see **FIGURE 15.7**) before leveling off during early adulthood (Nock et al., 2013).

The numbers are staggering, but *why* do people try to kill themselves? The short answer is: We do not yet know, and it is complicated. When interviewed in the hospital following their suicide attempt, most people who have tried to kill themselves report that they did so in order to escape from an intolerable state of mind or impossible situation (Boergers, Spirito, & Donaldson, 1998). Consistent with this explanation, research has documented that the risk of suicidal behaviour is significantly increased if a person experiences factors that can create severely distressing states such as the presence of multiple mental disorders (more than 90 percent of people who die by suicide have at least one mental disorder); the experience of significant negative life events during childhood and adulthood (e.g., physical and sexual assault); and the presence of severe medical problems (Nock, Borges, & Ono, 2012). The search is ongoing for a more comprehensive understanding of how and why some people respond to negative life events with suicidal thoughts and behaviours, as well as on methods of better predicting and preventing these devastating outcomes.

> What are some of the factors that contribute to suicidal behaviour?

## Non-suicidal Self-Injury

Louisa, an 18-year-old university student, secretly cuts her lower waist and upper thighs about once per week, typically when she is in the midst of feeling intense anger and hatred, either toward herself or someone else. She has always had a bit of a "hot streak" as she calls it, but it was not until she turned 14 that she started to use

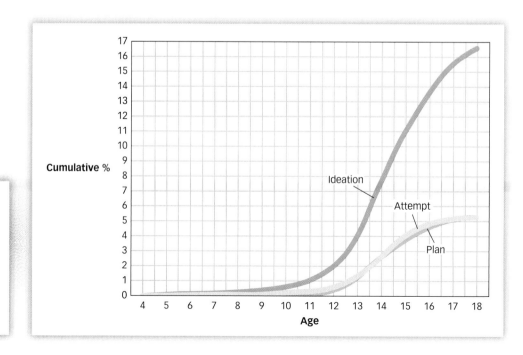

▶ Figure 15.7 **Age of Onset of Suicidal Behaviour During Adolescence** A recent survey of adolescents in the United States shows that although suicidal thoughts and behaviours are quite rare among children (the rate was 0.0 for ages 1 to 4), they increase dramatically starting at age 12 and continuing to climb throughout adolescence.

(Adapted from Nock et al., 2013.)

self-injury as a way to calm herself down. Louisa says that she actually feels a little ashamed after each episode of cutting, but she does not know how else to calm down when she gets really upset and so she has no plans of stopping this behaviour.

Louisa is engaging in a behaviour called **non-suicidal self-injury (NSSI),** the *direct, deliberate destruction of body tissue in the absence of any intent to die*. NSSI has been reported since the beginning of recorded history; however, it is a behaviour that appears to be on the rise over the past few decades. Recent studies suggest that as many as 15 to 20 percent of adolescents and 3 to 6 percent of adults report engaging in NSSI at some point in their lifetime (Klonsky, 2011; Muehlenkamp et al., 2012). The rates appear to be even between males and females, and for people of different races and ethnicities. Like suicidal behaviour, NSSI is virtually absent during childhood, increases dramatically during adolescence, and then appears to decrease across adulthood.

In some parts of the world, cutting or scarification of the skin is socially accepted, and in some cases encouraged as a rite of passage (Favazza, 2011). In parts of the world where self-cutting is not socially encouraged, why would a person purposely hurt him- or herself if not to die? Recent studies suggest that people who engage in self-injury have very strong emotional and physiological responses to negative events, that they perceive this response as intolerable, and that NSSI serves to diminish the intensity of

**What is known so far about why people engage in self-injury?**

this response (Nock, 2009). There also is some evidence that in many instances, people engage in self-injury as a means to communicate distress or elicit help from others (Nock, 2010). Although we are beginning to get an understanding of why some people engage in NSSI, there are many aspects of this behaviour that we do not yet understand, and the study of NSSI is an increasingly active area of research.

Unfortunately, like suicidal behaviour, our understanding of the genetic and neurobiological influences on NSSI is limited, and there currently are no effective medications for these problems. There also is very limited evidence for behavioural interventions or prevention programs (Mann et al., 2005). So, whereas suicidal behaviour and NSSI are some of the most disturbing and dangerous mental disorders, they also, unfortunately, are among the most perplexing. The field has made significant strides in our understanding of these behaviour problems in recent years, but there is a long way to go before we are able to predict and prevent them accurately and effectively.

**non-suicidal self-injury (NSSI)** Direct, deliberate destruction of body tissue in the absence of any intent to die.

JEAN-MICHEL CLAJOT/AURORA PHOTOS

Although in Canada self-injury is considered to be pathological, in some parts of the world scarification of the skin is viewed as a rite of passage into adulthood and a symbol of one's tribe, as in the case of this young man from the Republic of Benin in West Africa.

## IN SUMMARY

▶ Suicide is among the leading causes of death. Most people who die by suicide have a mental disorder, and suicide attempts are most often motivated by an attempt to escape intolerable mental states or situations.

▶ NSSI, like suicidal behaviour, increases dramatically during adolescence, but for many is a persistent problem throughout adulthood. Although NSSI is performed without suicidal intent, like suicidal behaviour, it is most often motivated by an attempt to escape from painful mental states.

# Chapter Review

KEY CONCEPT QUIZ

1. The conception of psychological disorders as diseases that have symptoms and possible cures is referred to as
   a. the medical model.
   b. physiognomy.
   c. the root syndrome framework.
   d. a diagnostic system.

2. The *DSM–5* is best described as a
   a. medical model.
   b. classification system.
   c. set of theoretical assumptions.
   d. collection of physiological definitions.

3. Comorbidity of disorders refers to
   a. symptoms stemming from internal dysfunction.
   b. the relative risk of death arising from a disorder.
   c. the co-occurrence of two or more disorders in a single individual.
   d. the existence of disorders on a continuum from normal to abnormal.

4. Irrational worries and fears that undermine one's ability to function normally are an indication of
   a. a genetic abnormality.
   b. dysthymia.
   c. diathesis.
   d. an anxiety disorder.

5. A(n) ___ disorder involves anxiety tied to a specific object or situation.
   a. generalized anxiety
   b. environmental
   c. panic
   d. phobic

6. Agoraphobia often develops as a result of
   a. preparedness theory.
   b. obsessive-compulsive disorder.
   c. panic disorder.
   d. social phobia.

7. Kelly's fear of germs leads her to wash her hands repeatedly throughout the day, often for a half hour or more, under extremely hot water. From which disorder does Kelly suffer?
   a. panic attacks
   b. obsessive-compulsive disorder
   c. phobia
   d. generalized anxiety disorder

8. Major depression is characterized by a severely depressed mood that lasts at least
   a. 2 weeks.
   b. 1 week.
   c. 1 month.
   d. 6 months.

9. Extreme moods swings between __ characterize bipolar disorder.
   a. depression and mania
   b. stress and lethargy
   c. anxiety and arousal
   d. obsessions and compulsions

10. Schizophrenia is characterized by which of the following?
    a. hallucinations
    b. disorganized thoughts and behaviour
    c. emotional and social withdrawal
    d. all of the above

11. Bipolar disorder is sometimes misdiagnosed as schizophrenia because both disorders may have _____ in common.
    a. periods of mania and depression
    b. recurrent unwanted thoughts or images of trauma
    c. lack of emotions
    d. hallucinations and delusions

12. Autism spectrum disorder (ASD) is characterized by which of the following?
    a. communication deficits and restricted, repetitive behaviour
    b. hallucinations and delusions
    c. suicidal thoughts
    d. all of the above

13. Attention-deficit/hyperactivity disorder (ADHD)
    a. must begin before the age of 7.
    b. never persists into adulthood.
    c. sometimes persists into adulthood.
    d. affects only boys.

14. In Canada, those at highest risk for suicide are
    a. men.
    b. Aboriginal people.
    c. those with a mental disorder.
    d. all of the above

15. Non-suicidal self-injury occurs among __ percent of adolescents.
    a. 1 to 2
    b. 3 to 5
    c. 15 to 20
    d. 50

## KEY TERMS

agoraphobia (p. 596)

antisocial personality disorder (APD) (p. 620)

anxiety disorder (p. 593)

attention-deficit/hyperactivity disorder (ADHD) (p. 616)

autism spectrum disorder (ASD) (p. 614)

biopsychosocial perspective (p. 589)

bipolar disorder (p. 605)

catatonic behaviour (p. 609)

cognitive symptoms (p. 609)

comorbidity (p. 587)

conduct disorder (p. 617)

delusion (p. 608)

*Diagnostic and Statistical Manual of Mental Disorders (DSM)* (p. 587)

diathesis–stress model (p. 590)

disorganized speech (p. 608)

dopamine hypothesis (p. 610)

double depression (p. 601)

dysthymia (p. 601)

expressed emotion (p. 607)

generalized anxiety disorder (GAD) (p. 597)

grossly disorganized behaviour (p. 608)

hallucination (p. 608)

helplessness theory (p. 604)

major depressive disorder (or unipolar depression) (p. 601)

medical model (p. 585)

mental disorder (p. 584)

mood disorders (p. 601)

negative symptoms (p. 609)

non-suicidal self-injury (NSSI) (p. 623)

obsessive-compulsive disorder (OCD) (p. 598)

panic disorder (p. 596)

personality disorders (p. 618)

phobic disorders (p. 594)

positive symptoms (p. 608)

post-traumatic stress disorder (PTSD) (p. 599)

preparedness theory (p. 594)

Research Domain Criteria Project (RDoC) (p. 590)

schizophrenia (p. 607)

seasonal affective disorder (SAD) (p. 603)

social phobia (p. 594)

specific phobia (p. 594)

suicide (p. 621)

suicide attempt (p. 621)

## CHANGING MINDS

1. You catch a television interview with a celebrity who describes his difficult childhood, living with a mother who suffered from major depression. "Sometimes my mother stayed in her bed for days, not even getting up to eat," he says. "At the time, the family hushed it up. My parents were immigrants, and they came from a culture where it was considered shameful to have mental problems. You're supposed to have enough strength of will to overcome your problems, without help from anyone else. So my mother never got treatment." How might the idea of a medical model of psychiatric disorders have helped the celebrity's mother and her family in the decision whether to seek treatment?

2. You are studying for your upcoming psychology exam when your roommate breezes in, saying: "I was just at the gym and I ran into Sue. She's totally schizophrenic: nice one minute, mean the next." You cannot resist the opportunity to set the record straight. What psychiatric disorder is your roommate (incorrectly) attributing to Sue? How is this different from schizophrenia?

3. A friend of yours has a family member who is experiencing severe mental problems, including delusions and loss of motivation. "We went to one psychiatrist," she says, "and got a diagnosis of schizophrenia. We went for a second opinion, and the other doctor said it was probably bipolar disorder. They're both good doctors, and they're both using the same *DSM*—how can they come up with different diagnoses?"

4. After reading the chapter, one of your classmates turns to you with a sigh of relief. "I finally figured it out. I have a deadbeat brother, who always gets himself into trouble and then blames other people for his problems. Even when he gets a ticket for speeding, he never thinks it's his fault—the police were picking on him, or his passengers were urging him to go too fast. I always thought he was just a loser, but now I realize he has a personality disorder!" Do you agree with your classmate's diagnosis of his brother? How would you caution your classmate about the dangers of self-diagnosis, or diagnosis of friends and family?

## ANSWERS TO KEY CONCEPT QUIZ

1. a; 2. b; 3. c; 4. d; 5. d; 6. c; 7. b; 8. a; 9. a; 10. d; 11. d; 12. a; 13. c; 14. d; 15. c.

# Treatment of Psychological Disorders

▲ Treatment: Getting Help to Those Who Need It
Why Many People Fail to Seek Treatment
THE REAL WORLD Types of Psychotherapists
Approaches to Treatment
CULTURE & COMMUNITY Treatment of Psychological Disorders around the World

▲ Psychological Treatments: Healing the Mind through Interaction
Psychodynamic Therapy
Humanistic and Existential Therapies
Behavioural and Cognitive Therapies
HOT SCIENCE "Rebooting" Psychological Treatment
Group Treatments: Healing Multiple Minds at the Same Time

▲ Medical and Biological Treatments: Healing the Mind by Physically Altering the Brain
Antipsychotic Medications
THE REAL WORLD Treating Severe Mental Disorders
Anti-anxiety Medications
Antidepressants and Mood Stabilizers
Herbal and Natural Products
Combining Medication and Psychotherapy
OTHER VOICES Diagnosis: Human
Biological Treatments beyond Medication

▲ Treatment Effectiveness: For Better or for Worse
Treatment Illusions
Treatment Studies
Which Treatments Work?

TODAY WE'RE GOING TO BE TOUCHING a dead mouse I saw in the alley outside my office building," Dr. Jenkins said. "OK, let's do it, I'm ready," Christine responded. The pair walked down to the alley and spent the next 50 minutes touching, then stroking, the dead mouse. They then went back upstairs to plan out what other disgusting things Christine was going to touch over the next 7 days before coming back for her next therapy session. Yes, this is all part of the psychological treatment of Christine's obsessive-compulsive disorder (OCD). It is an approach called *exposure and response prevention* (ERP), in which people are gradually exposed to the content of their obsessions and prevented from engaging in their compulsions. Christine's obsession is that she is going to be contaminated by germs and die of cancer; her compulsive behaviour involves several hours per day of washing her body and scrubbing everything around her with alcohol wipes. After dozens and dozens of exposures, without performing the behaviours that they believe have been keeping them safe, people eventually learn that their obsessive thoughts are not accurate and that they do not have to act out their compulsions. ERP can be a very scary treatment, but it has proven amazingly effective at decreasing obsessions and compulsions and helping people with OCD return to a high level of daily functioning. OCD was widely considered untreatable until the development of ERP, which is now considered to be the most effective way to treat OCD (Foa, 2010). ERP is just one of many approaches currently being used to help people to overcome the mental disorders you learned about in the last chapter.

Exposure-based treatments, in which people learn to face the source of their fear and anxiety, have proven to be an effective way to treat anxiety disorders.

KEITH BINNS/GETTY IMAGES

**THERE ARE MANY DIFFERENT WAYS TO TREAT PSYCHOLOGICAL DISORDERS AND TO** change the thoughts, behaviours, and emotions associated with them. Treatments requiring a person to touch dead animals are not commonplace, but the variety and ingenuity of some of our current treatments are remarkable. In this chapter, we will explore the most common approaches to psychological treatment. We will examine why people need to seek psychological help in the first place, and then explore how psychotherapy for individuals is built on the major theories of the causes and cures of disorders, including psychoanalytic, humanistic, existential, behavioural, and cognitive theories. We also will look into biological approaches to treatment that focus on directly modifying brain structure and function. We will discuss whether treatment works, as well as how we know that treatment works. We will also look to the future by exploring some exciting new directions in the assessment and treatment of disorders using innovative technologies.

## Treatment: Getting Help to Those Who Need It

Estimates suggest that about 1 in every 5 people in Canada suffer from some type of mental disorder at some point in their lifetime (Canadian Mental Health Association, n.d. 1; Kessler, Berglund, et al., 2005). The personal costs of these disorders involve anguish to the sufferers as well as interference in their ability to carry on the activities of daily life. Think about Christine from the example above. If she did not (or could not) seek treatment, she would continue to be crippled by her OCD, which was causing major problems in her life. She had to quit her job at the local coffee shop because she was no longer able to touch money or anything else that had been touched by other people without washing it first. Her relationship with her boyfriend was in trouble because he was growing tired of her constant reassurance seeking regarding cleanliness (hers and his). All of these problems were in turn increasing her anxiety and depression, making her obsessions even stronger. She desperately wanted and needed some way to break out of this vicious cycle. She needed an effective treatment.

The personal and social burdens associated with mental disorders are also enormous. Mental disorders typically have earlier ages of onset than physical disorders and are associated with significant impairments in the form of an inability to carry out daily activities, such as days out of school or work or problems in family and personal relationships. Impairments associated with mental disorders are as severe, and in many cases more severe, than those associated with physical disorders such as cancer, chronic pain, and heart disease (Ormel et al., 2008). For instance, a person with severe depression may be unable to hold down a job or even get organized enough to collect a disability cheque, and people with many disorders stop getting along with family, caring for their children, or trying to help.

> **What are some of the personal, social, and financial costs of mental illness?**

There are financial costs too. In any given week, at least half a million employed people in Canada are unable to work due to mental health problems, and the economic burden for all mental illness is estimated to be $51 billion per year (Centre for Addiction and Mental Health, 2013; Lim et al., 2008; Smetanin et al., 2011). In addition to the personal benefits of treatment, then, society also stands to benefit from the effective treatment of psychological disorders.

Do all people with a mental disorder receive treatment? Not by a long shot. Only about 40 percent of Canadians with mental disorders present themselves for diagnosis and treatment (Lesage et al., 2006). Of those who do seek care, nearly 1 in 3 report that their needs are unmet or only partially met; this is a particular problem for children and youth (Statistics Canada, 2013d). Treatment rates are even lower elsewhere around the world, especially in low-income or developing countries (Wang et al., 2007). Treatment rates are higher for those with more severe mental disorders. However, it is clear that most people with a mental disorder do not receive treatment, and among those who do, the average delay from onset until treatment is first received is over a decade (Wang et al., 2004)!

## Why Many People Fail to Seek Treatment

A physical symptom such as a toothache would send most people to the dentist—a trip that usually results in a successful treatment. The clear source of pain and the

> **What are the obstacles to treatment for the mentally ill?**

obvious solution make for a quick and effective response. In contrast, the path from a mental disorder to a successful treatment is often far less clear and many people are less familiar with when they should seek treatment for a mental disorder or where they should go. In the case of mental disorders, people may fail to get treatment for a number of reasons. Here are three of the most often reported:

1. *People may not realize that they have a mental disorder that could be effectively treated.* Approximately 45 percent of those with a mental disorder who do not seek treatment report that they did not do so because they did not think that they needed to be treated (Mojtabai et al., 2011). Mental disorders are often not taken nearly as seriously as physical illness, perhaps because the origin of mental illness is "hidden" and usually cannot be diagnosed by a blood test or X-ray. Moreover, although most people know what a toothache is and that it can be successfully treated, far fewer people know when they have a mental disorder and what treatments might be available.

2. *There may be barriers to treatment, such as beliefs and circumstances that keep people from getting help.* Individuals may believe that they should be able to handle things themselves. In fact, this is the primary reason that people with a mental disorder give for not seeking treatment (72.6 percent) and for dropping out of treatment prematurely (42.2 percent) (Mojtabai et al., 2011). Other attitudinal barriers for not seeking treatment include believing that the problem was not that severe (16.9 percent of nontreatment seekers), the belief that treatment would be ineffective (16.4 percent), and perceived stigma from others (9.1 percent).

3. *Structural barriers prevent people from physically getting to treatment.* Like finding a good lawyer or plumber, finding the right psychologist can be more difficult than simply flipping through the telephone directory or searching online. This confusion is understandable given the plethora of different types of treatments available (see The Real World box: Types of Psychotherapists). Once you find the therapist for you, you may encounter structural barriers related to not being able to afford treatment (15.3 percent of nontreatment seekers), lack of clinician availability (12.8 percent), inconvenience of attending treatment (9.8 percent), and trouble finding transportation to the clinic (5.7 percent) (Mojtabai et al., 2011).

When your tooth hurts, you go to a dentist. But how do you know when to see a psychologist?

ALLISON LEACH/GETTY IMAGES

**THE REAL WORLD**

# Types of Psychotherapists

What do you do if you are ready to seek the help of a mental health professional? To whom do you turn? Therapists have widely varying backgrounds and training, and this affects the kinds of services they offer. Before you choose a therapist, it is useful to have an understanding of a therapist's background, training, and areas of expertise. There are several major "flavours."

- **Psychologist** A psychologist who practises psychotherapy generally holds a doctorate with specialization in clinical psychology (a Ph.D. or Psy.D.). This degree takes about 5 to 8 years to complete after the bachelor's degree and includes extensive training in therapy, the assessment of psychological disorders, and research. In a few provinces (e.g., Alberta and Saskatchewan) individuals can become chartered psychologists with a master's degree. The psychologist will sometimes have a specialty, such as working with adolescents or helping people overcome sleep disorders, and will usually conduct therapy that involves talking. Psychologists must be licensed by the province or territory, and most jurisdictions require candidates to complete about 2 to 5 years of supervised practical training and a competency exam. If you look for a *psychologist* in the telephone directory or through a clinic, you will usually find someone with this background.

- **Psychiatrist** A psychiatrist is a medical doctor who has completed an M.D. with specialized training in assessing and treating mental disorders. Psychiatrists can prescribe medications, and some also practise psychotherapy. General practice physicians can also prescribe

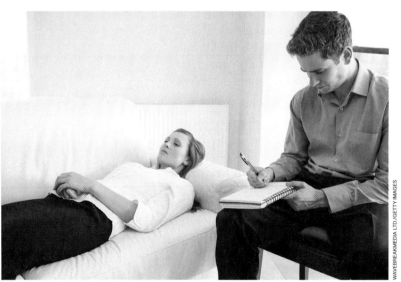

medications for mental disorders and often are the first to see people with such disorders because people consult them for a wide range of health problems. However, general practice physicians do not typically receive much training in the diagnosis or treatment of mental disorders, and they do not practise psychotherapy.

- **Social worker** Social workers have a master's degree in social work and have training in working with people in dire life situations such as poverty, homelessness, or family conflict. Clinical or psychiatric social workers also receive special training to help people in these situations who have mental disorders. Social workers often work in government

Even when people seek and find help, they sometimes do not receive the most effective treatments, which further complicates things. For starters, most of the treatment of mental disorders is not provided by mental health specialists, but by general medical practitioners (Wang et al., 2007). And even when people make it to a mental health specialist, they do not always receive the most effective treatment possible. In fact, only a small percentage of those with a mental disorder (less than 40 percent) receive what would be considered minimally adequate treatment, and only 15.3 percent of those with serious mental illness receive treatment that is considered minimally adequate. Clearly, before choosing or prescribing a therapy, we need to know what kinds of treatments are available and understand which treatments are best for particular disorders.

or private social service agencies and may also work in hospitals or have a private practice.

- **Counsellor** Counsellors have a wide range of training. To be a counselling psychologist, for example, requires a doctorate and practical training—the title uses that key term *psychologist* and is regulated by provincial and territorial laws. But jurisdictions vary in how they define *counsellor* or *counselling therapist*. In some cases, a counsellor must have a master's degree and extensive training in therapy, whereas in others, a counsellor may have minimal training or relevant education.

Some people offer therapy under made-up terms that sound professional—"mind/body healing therapist," for example, or "marital adjustment adviser." Often these terms are simply invented to mislead clients and avoid provincial and territorial regulatory bodies such as the College of Psychologists of BC, and the "therapist" may have no training or expertise at all. And, of course, there are a few people who claim to be licensed practitioners who are not: Louise Wightman, who had once worked as stripper "Princess Cheyenne," was convicted of fraud in 2007 after conducting psychotherapy as a psychologist with dozens of clients. She claimed she did not know the Ph.D. degree she had purchased over the Internet was bogus (Associated Press, 2007). People who offer therapy may be well-meaning and even helpful, but they could do harm too. To be safe, it is important to shop wisely for a therapist whose training and credentials reflect expertise and inspire confidence.

BSIP/UIG/GETTY IMAGES

How should you shop? One way is to start with people you know: your general practice physician, a school psychologist, or a trusted friend or family member who might know of a good therapist. Or you can visit your university clinic or hospital or check the website of your provincial or territorial regulatory body (such as the Ontario College of Psychologists), or the Canadian Register of Health Service Providers in Psychology (CRHSPP); these organizations provide contact details for licensed mental health care providers. When you do contact someone, he or she will often be able to provide you with further advice about who would be just the right kind of therapist to consult.

Before you agree to see a therapist for treatment, you should ask questions such as those below to evaluate whether the therapist's style or background is a good match for your problem:

- What type of therapy do you practise?
- What types of problems do you usually treat?
- For how long do you usually see people in therapy?
- Will our work involve "talking" therapy, medications, or both?
- How effective is this type of therapy for the type of problem I am having?
- What are your fees for therapy, and will health insurance cover them?

Not only will the therapist's answers to these questions tell you about his or her background and experience, but they will also tell you about his or her approach to treating clients. You can then make an informed decision about the type of service you need.

Although you should consider what type of therapist would best fit your needs, the therapist's personality and approach can sometimes be as important as his or her background or training. You should seek out someone who is willing and open to answer questions, who has a clear understanding about the type of problem leading you to seek therapy, and who shows general respect and empathy for you. A therapist is someone you are entrusting with your mental health, and you should only enter into such a relationship when you and the therapist have good rapport.

## Approaches to Treatment

Treatments can be divided broadly into two kinds: (a) psychological treatment, in which people interact with a clinician in order to use the environment to change their brain and behaviour; and (b) biological treatment, in which the brain is treated directly with drugs, surgery or some other direct intervention. In some cases, both psychological *and* biological treatments are used. Christine's OCD, for example, might be treated not only with the ERP but also with medication that decreases her obsessive thoughts and compulsive urges. For many years, psychological treatment was the main form of intervention for psychological disorders because few biological options were available. There have always been folk remedies that propose to have a biological basis—such

Early mental health workers used water dowsing, or "hydrotherapy," for psychological disorders. Here a patient at the Pennsylvania Hospital for the Insane gets a cold "douche bath" (Haskell, 1869). Such treatments were given in the forlorn hope that something might work, but often they were simply torture.

COURTESY UNIVERSITY OF MICHIGAN'S MAKING OF AMERICA HTTP://MOA.UMDL.UMICH.EDU

as hydrotherapy (pouring cold water on those with mental disorders), trephination (drilling holes in the skull to let the evil spirits escape), and bloodletting (the removal of blood from the body)—used to try to cure psychological disorders (Note: Do not try these at home. Turns out they do not work.) As we learn more about the biology and chemistry of the brain, approaches to mental health that begin with the brain are becoming increasingly widespread. As you will see later in the chapter, many effective treatments combine both psychological and biological interventions.

# CULTURE & COMMUNITY

## Treatment of Psychological Disorders around the World

Barriers that keep people from receiving treatment for mental disorders exist all around the world. However, they are greater in some places than in others. One recent study examined what percentage of people with a mental disorder in 17 different countries around the world (not including Canada) received treatment for their disorder in the past year (Wang et al., 2007). Several different findings are interesting to note. First, people with a severe mental disorder are much more likely to be treated. This makes sense. For instance, if your disorder is so severe that it prevents you from going to school or work you will probably seek treatment, but if it does not really interfere with your daily life you may not go for help. Second, people living in high-income countries (as defined by the World Bank) are much more likely to get treatment than those in middle- or low-income countries. This makes sense too. The more resources a country has, the more able it is to make psychological treatments available to its people. Third, most people with a mental disorder do not receive any treatment. This is true even in the countries with the highest income. Even in Canada, a high-income country with free health care, only 1 in 3 adults who experience a mental health problem—and only 1 in 4 children—report that they have sought and received treatment and services (Mental Health Commission of Canada, n.d.). This means that although we have a better understanding of mental disorders than we ever had before (as described in the last chapter), and we have better treatments than ever before (as described in this chapter), we still have to do a much better job removing the barriers that prevent those with mental disorders from getting help.

**Percent of people with a mental disorder who receive treatment**

Legend:
- Serious
- Moderate
- Mild

Y-axis: Percent in treatment (0 to 100)
X-axis: Countries — Nigeria; China, Colombia, S. Africa, Ukraine; Lebanon, Mexico; Belgium, France, Israel, Germany, Italy, Japan, Netherlands, New Zealand, Spain, USA

Income groupings: Low income | Low middle income | High middle income | High income

**psychotherapy**
An interaction between a socially
sanctioned clinician and someone
suffering from a psychological problem,
with the goal of providing support or relief
from the problem.

## IN SUMMARY

▶ Mental illness is often misunderstood, and because of this, it too often goes untreated.

▶ Untreated mental illness can be extremely costly, affecting an individual's ability to function and also causing social and financial burdens.

▶ Many people who suffer from mental illness do not get the help they need; they may be unaware that they have a problem, they may be uninterested in getting help for their problem, or they may face structural barriers to getting treatment.

▶ Treatments include psychotherapy, which focuses on the mind, and medical and biological methods, which focus on the brain and body.

# Psychological Treatments: Healing the Mind through Interaction

Psychological therapy, or **psychotherapy,** *is an interaction between a socially sanctioned clinician and someone suffering from a psychological problem, with the goal of providing support or relief from the problem.* Currently over 500 different forms of psychotherapy exist. Although there are similarities among all the psychotherapies, each approach is unique in its goals, aims, and methods. A survey of 538 psychologists registered with provincial regulatory bodies asked them to describe their theoretical orientation (Hunsley, Ronson, & Cohen, 2013) (see **FIGURE 16.1**). Many of the practising psychologists endorsed more than one orientation, reflecting the fact that they tended to apply an appropriate theoretical perspective suited to the problem at hand, rather than adhering to a single theoretical perspective for all clients and all types of problems. As Figure 16.1 shows, most of the practitioners relied on five orientations in their work. Cognitive–behavioural was the most popular, reflecting the wealth of research studies that demonstrate the efficacy of this approach for a wide range of disorders (Hunsley et al., 2013; Task Force of Empirically Supported Treatments, 1998). Interpersonal therapy is a proven treatment for depression (Markowitz, 1999). It draws on both the cognitive and behavioural orientation and psychodynamic orientation, and is discussed in the psychodynamic theory section. Family systems therapy is a form of group therapy, used to treat issues involving both children and their parents (such as behavioural disorders that may be exacerbated by ineffective parenting). In this chapter, we will examine psychodynamic therapy, humanistic and existential therapy, cognitive behavioural therapy, and group therapy in turn.

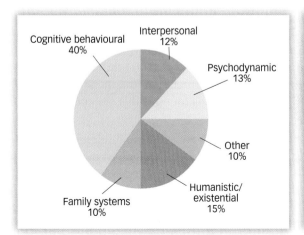

◀ Figure **16.1** **Dominant therapy orientations of Canadian clinical psychologists in 2009/2010.** This chart shows the percentage of practitioners (out of the 538 who returned survey information) who chose each theoretical orientation as one to which they subscribed (Hunsley et al., 2013). The results of a large number of studies conducted over the last 30 years demonstrate the efficacy of cognitive behavioural therapy over other forms of therapy for a wide range of mood, anxiety, substance-abuse, personality, and psychotic disorders, and there is a strong emphasis on evidence-based treatment in Canadian clinical psychology training programs (Hunsley et al., 2013; Task Force of Empirically Supported Treatments, 1998). It is not surprising, therefore, that a cognitive and behavioural orientation is the most popular orientation.

**psychodynamic psychotherapies**
Therapies that explore childhood events and encourage individuals to use this understanding to develop insight into their psychological problems.

**resistance**
A reluctance to cooperate with treatment for fear of confronting unpleasant unconscious material.

In traditional psychoanalysis, the client lies on a couch, with the therapist sitting behind, out of the client's view.

# Psychodynamic Therapy

Psychodynamic psychotherapy has its roots in Freud's psychoanalytically oriented theory of personality. **Psychodynamic psychotherapies** *explore childhood events and encourage individuals to use this understanding to develop insight into their psychological problems.* Psychoanalysis was the first psychodynamic therapy to develop, but it has largely been replaced by modern psychodynamic therapies, such as interpersonal psychotherapy.

## Psychoanalysis

As you saw in the Personality chapter, *psychoanalysis* assumes that people are born with aggressive and sexual urges that are repressed during childhood development through the use of defense mechanisms. Psychoanalysts encourage their clients to bring these repressed conflicts into consciousness so that the clients can understand them and reduce their unwanted influences. Psychoanalysts focus a great deal on early childhood events because they believe that urges and conflicts were likely to be repressed during this time.

Traditional psychoanalysis involves four or five sessions per week over an average of 3 to 6 years (Ursano & Silberman, 2003). During a session, the client reclines on a couch, facing away from the analyst, and is asked to express whatever thoughts and feelings come to mind. Occasionally, the therapist may comment on some of the information presented by the client, but does not express his or her values and judgments. The stereotypic image you might have of psychological therapy—a person lying on a couch talking to a person sitting in a chair—springs from this approach.

## What Happens in Psychoanalysis

The goal of psychoanalysis is for the client to understand the unconscious in a process Freud called *developing insight*. A psychoanalyst can use several key techniques to help the client develop insight, including the following.

**Free Association.** In free association, the client reports every thought that enters the mind, without censorship or filtering. This strategy allows the stream of consciousness to flow unimpeded. If the client stops, the therapist prompts further associations ("And what does that make you think of?"). The therapist may then look for themes that recur during therapy sessions.

**Dream Analysis.** Psychoanalysis may treat dreams as metaphors that symbolize unconscious conflicts or wishes and that contain disguised clues that the therapist can help the client understand. A psychoanalytic therapy session might begin with an invitation for the client to recount a dream, after which the client might be asked to participate in the interpretation by freely associating to the dream.

**Interpretation.** This is the process by which the therapist deciphers the meaning (e.g., unconscious impulses or fantasies) underlying what the client says and does. Interpretation is used throughout therapy, during free association and dream analysis, as well as in other aspects of the treatment. During the process of interpretation, the therapist suggests possible meanings to the client, looking for signs that the correct meaning has been discovered.

**Analysis of Resistance.** In the process of "trying on" different interpretations of the client's thoughts and actions, the therapist may suggest an interpretation that the client finds particularly unacceptable. **Resistance** *is a reluctance to cooperate with treatment for fear of confronting unpleasant*

*"Before we begin, I'd like to say a few words about the concept of 'defence mechanisms'."*

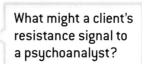

What might a client's resistance signal to a psychoanalyst?

*unconscious material.* For example, the therapist might suggest that the client's problem with obsessive health worries could be traced to a childhood rivalry with her mother for her father's love and attention. The client could find the suggestion insulting and resist the interpretation. The therapist might interpret this resistance as a signal not that the interpretation is wrong but instead that the interpretation is on the right track. If a client always shifts the topic of discussion away from a particular idea, it might signal to the therapist that this is indeed an issue the client could be directed to confront in order to develop insight.

Through the course of meeting so frequently over such a long period of time, the client and psychoanalyst often develop a close relationship. Freud noticed this relationship developing in his analyses and was at first troubled by it: Clients would develop an unusually strong attachment to him, almost as though they were viewing him as a parent or a lover, and he worried that this could interfere with achieving the goal of insight. Over time, however, he came to believe that the development and resolution of this relationship was a key process of psychoanalysis. **Transference** occurs *when the analyst begins to assume a major significance in the client's life and the client reacts to the analyst based on unconscious childhood fantasies.* Successful psychoanalysis involves analyzing the transference so that the client understands this reaction and why it occurs.

## Beyond Psychoanalysis

Although Freud's insights and techniques are fundamental, modern psychodynamic treatments differ from classic psychoanalysis in both their content and procedures. One of the most widely used psychodynamic treatments is **interpersonal psychotherapy (IPT)**, *a form of psychotherapy that focuses on helping clients improve*

> In what common ways do modern psychodynamic theories differ from Freudian analysis?

*current relationships* (Weissman, Markowitz, & Klerman, 2000). In terms of content, rather than using free association, therapists using IPT talk to clients about their interpersonal behaviours and feelings. They pay particular attention to the client's grief (an exaggerated reaction to the loss of a loved one), role disputes (conflicts with a significant other), role transitions (changes in life status, such as starting a new job, getting married, or retiring), or interpersonal deficits (lack of the necessary skills to start or maintain a relationship). The treatment focuses on interpersonal functioning with the assumption that, as interpersonal relations improve, symptoms will subside.

Modern psychodynamic psychotherapies such as IPT also differ from classical psychoanalysis in the procedures used. For starters, in modern psychodynamic therapy the therapist and client typically sit face-to-face. In addition, therapy is less intensive, with meetings often occurring only once a week and therapy lasting months rather than years. In contrast to classical psychoanalysis, modern psychodynamic therapists are more likely to see relief from symptoms as a reasonable goal for therapy (in addition to the goal of facilitating insight), and they are more likely to offer support or advice in addition to interpretation (Barber et al., 2013). Therapists are also now less likely to interpret a client's statements as a sign of unconscious sexual or aggressive impulses. However, other concepts, such as transference and fostering insight into unconscious processes, remain features of most psychodynamic therapies. Freud's couch casts a long shadow.

Although psychodynamic therapy has been around for a long time and continues to be widely practised, there is relatively little evidence for its effectiveness. Comparisons to other forms of treatment such as cognitive behaviour therapy (described later) suggest that psychodynamic therapy is somewhat less effective (Watzke et al., 2012). Moreover, there is some evidence that

**transference**
An event that occurs in psychoanalysis when the analyst begins to assume a major significance in the client's life and the client reacts to the analyst based on unconscious childhood fantasies.

**interpersonal psychotherapy (IPT)**
A form of psychotherapy that focuses on helping clients improve current relationships.

In the movie *Good Will Hunting,* the lead character, played by actor Matt Damon, forms a strong bond with his therapist, played by Robin Williams. As in psychodynamic therapy, the therapist uses their relationship to help break down the patient's defence mechanisms and resolve an inner conflict. The amazing bond that was formed between therapist and patient, and the life-changing treatment delivered is the stuff of therapists' dreams (and Hollywood scripts).

MIRAMAX/THE KOBAL COLLECTION

some of the aspects of psychodynamic therapy long believed to be effective may actually be harmful. For instance, research suggests that the more a therapist makes interpretations about perceived transference in the client, the worse the therapeutic alliance and the worse the clinical outcome (Henry et al., 1994). Despite findings like these, there is some evidence that long-term psychodynamic psychotherapy (lasting at least a year) is more effective than short-term psychotherapy (Leichsenring & Rabung, 2008). Psychodynamic therapy is not as widely used as it once was, but many psychologists still use it in practice, and many people say that they find it helpful.

## Humanistic and Existential Therapies

Humanistic and existential therapies emerged in the middle of the twentieth century, in part as a reaction to the negative views that psychoanalysis holds about human nature. Humanistic and existential therapies assume that human nature is generally positive, and they emphasize the natural tendency of each individual to strive for personal improvement. Humanistic and existential therapies share the assumption that psychological problems stem from feelings of alienation and loneliness, and that those feelings can be traced to failures to reach one's potential (in the humanistic approach) or from failures to find meaning in life (in the existential approach). Although interest in these approaches peaked in the 1960s and 1970s, some therapists continue to use these approaches today. Two well-known types are person-centred therapy (a humanistic approach) and gestalt therapy (an existential approach).

> How does a humanistic view of human nature differ from a psychodynamic view?

### Person-Centred Therapy

**Person-centred therapy** (or **client-centred therapy**) *assumes that all individuals have a tendency toward growth and that this growth can be facilitated by acceptance and genuine reactions from the therapist.* American psychologist Carl Rogers (1902–1987) developed person-centred therapy in the 1940s and 1950s (Rogers, 1951). Person-centred therapy assumes that each person is qualified to determine his or her own goals for therapy, such as feeling more confident or making a career decision, and even the frequency and length of therapy. In this type of nondirective treatment, the therapist tends not to provide advice or suggestions about what the client should be doing, but instead paraphrases the client's words, mirroring the client's thoughts and sentiments (e.g., "I think I hear you saying …"). Person-centred therapists believe that with adequate support, the client will recognize the right things to do.

Rogers encouraged person-centred therapists to demonstrate three basic qualities: congruence, empathy, and unconditional positive regard. Congruence refers to openness and honesty in the therapeutic relationship and ensuring that the therapist communicates the same message at all levels. For example, the same message must be communicated in the therapist's words, the therapist's facial expression, and the therapist's body language. Saying "I think your concerns are valid" while smirking would simply not do. Empathy refers to the continuous process of trying to understand the client by getting inside his or her way of thinking, feeling, and understanding the world. Interestingly, research has shown that the more empathic a client says their clinician is being, the more similarity there is between the client's and therapist's level of physiological arousal in that moment (Marci et al., 2007). This suggests that therapists who are being empathic may really be feeling some of what their clients are feeling. Seeing the world from the client's perspective enables the therapist to better appreciate the client's apprehensions, worries, or fears. Finally, the therapist must treat the client with unconditional positive regard by providing a nonjudgmental, warm, and accepting environment in which the client can feel safe expressing his or her thoughts and feelings.

**person-centred therapy (or client-centred therapy)**
Assumes that all individuals have a tendency toward growth and that this growth can be facilitated by acceptance and genuine reactions from the therapist.

The goal is not to uncover repressed conflicts, as in psychodynamic therapy, but instead to try to understand the client's experience and reflect that experience back to the client in a supportive way, encouraging the client's natural tendency toward growth. This style of therapy is reminiscent of psychoanalysis in its way of encouraging the client toward the free expression of thoughts and feelings.

### Gestalt Therapy

Gestalt therapy was founded by Frederick "Fritz" Perls (1893–1970) and his colleagues in the 1940s and 1950s (Perls, Hefferkine, & Goodman, 1951). **Gestalt therapy** *has the goal of helping the client become aware of his or her thoughts, behaviours, experiences, and feelings and to "own" or take responsibility for them.* Gestalt therapists are encouraged to be enthusiastic and warm toward their clients, an approach they share with person-centred therapists. To help facilitate the client's awareness, gestalt therapists also reflect back to the client their impressions of the client.

As part of gestalt therapy, clients may be encouraged to imagine that another person is sitting across from them in a chair. The client then moves from chair to chair, role-playing what he or she would say to the imagined person and how that person would answer.

Gestalt therapy emphasizes the experiences and behaviours that are occurring at that particular moment in the therapy session. For example, if a client is talking about something stressful that occurred during the previous week, the therapist might shift the attention to the client's current experience by asking, "How do you feel as you describe what happened to you?" This technique is known as focusing. Clients are also encouraged to put their feelings into action. One way to do this is the empty chair technique, in which the client imagines that another person (e.g., a spouse, a parent, a co-worker) is in an empty chair, sitting directly across from the client. The client then moves from chair to chair, alternating from role-playing what he or she would say to the other person and how he or she imagines the other person would respond. Gestalt techniques originated as a form of psychotherapy but are now often used in counselling or "life coaching" to help people prepare for new job or family situations (Grant, 2008).

## Behavioural and Cognitive Therapies

Unlike the talk therapies described above, behavioural and cognitive treatments emphasize actively changing a person's current thoughts and behaviours as a way to decrease or eliminate their psychopathology. In the evolution of psychological treatments, clients started out lying down in psychoanalysis, then sitting in psychodynamic and related approaches, but are often standing and engaging in behaviour-change homework assignments in their everyday life in behavioural and cognitive therapies.

### Behaviour Therapy

Whereas Freud developed psychoanalysis as an offshoot of hypnosis and other techniques used by other clinicians before him, behaviour therapy was developed based on laboratory findings from earlier behavioural psychologists. As you read in the Psychology: Evolution of a Science chapter, behaviourists rejected theories that were based on "invisible" mental properties that were difficult to test and impossible to observe directly. Behaviourists found psychoanalytic ideas particularly hard to test: How do you know whether a person has an unconscious conflict or whether insight has occurred? Behavioural principles, in contrast, focused solely on behaviours that could be observed (e.g., avoidance of a feared object, such as refusing to get on an airplane). **Behaviour therapy** assumes that *disordered behaviour is learned and that symptom relief is achieved through changing overt maladaptive behaviours into more constructive behaviours.* A variety of

> **What primary problem did behaviourists have with psychoanalytic ideas?**

**gestalt therapy**
Has the goal of helping the client become aware of his or her thoughts, behaviours, experiences, and feelings and to "own" or take responsibility for them.

**behaviour therapy**
A type of therapy that assumes that disordered behaviour is learned and that symptom relief is achieved through changing overt maladaptive behaviours into more constructive behaviours.

A behavioural psychologist might treat a temper tantrum using time-out from reinforcement, which is based on the behavioural principle of operant conditioning and ensures that a child will not be rewarded for her undesired behaviour.

MATTHEW NOCK

behaviour therapy techniques have been developed for many disorders, based on the learning principles you encountered in the Learning chapter, including operant conditioning procedures (which focus on reinforcement and punishment) and classical conditioning procedures (which focus on extinction). Here are three examples of behaviour therapy techniques in action:

**Eliminating Unwanted Behaviours.** How would you change a 3-year-old boy's habit of throwing tantrums at the grocery store? A behaviour therapist might investigate what happens immediately before and after the tantrum: Did the child get candy to "shut him up?" The study of operant conditioning shows that behaviour can be influenced by its *consequences* (the reinforcing or punishing events that follow). Adjusting these might help change the behaviour. Making the consequences less reinforcing (no candy!) and more punishing (a period of time-out facing the wall in the grocery store while the parent watches from nearby rather than providing a rush of attention) could eliminate the problem behaviour.

**Promoting Desired Behaviours.** Candy and time-out can have a strong influence on child behaviour, but they work less well with adults. How might you get an individual with schizophrenia to engage in activities of daily living? How would you get a cocaine addict to stop using drugs? A behaviour therapy technique that has proven to be quite effective in such cases is the **token economy,** which involves *giving clients "tokens" for desired behaviours, which they can later trade for rewards.* For instance, in the case of cocaine dependence, the desired behaviour is not using cocaine. Programs that reward non-use (verified by urine samples) with vouchers that can be exchanged for rewards such as money, bus passes, clothes, and so on, have shown an ability to significantly reduce cocaine use and associated psychological problems (Petry, Alessi, & Rash, 2013). Similar systems are used to promote desired behaviours in classrooms, the workplace, and commercial advertising (e.g., airline and credit card rewards programs).

**token economy**
A form of behaviour therapy in which clients are given "tokens" for desired behaviours, which they can later trade for rewards.

**exposure therapy**
An approach to treatment that involves confronting an emotion-arousing stimulus directly and repeatedly, ultimately leading to a decrease in the emotional response.

▶ Table 16.1

### Exposure Hierarchy for Social Phobia

| Item | Fear (0–100) |
|---|---|
| 1. Have a party and invite everyone from work | 99 |
| 2. Go to a holiday party for 1 hour without drinking | 90 |
| 3. Invite Cindy to have dinner and see a movie | 85 |
| 4. Go for a job interview | 80 |
| 5. Ask boss for a day off work | 65 |
| 6. Ask questions in a meeting at work | 65 |
| 7. Eat lunch with co-workers | 60 |
| 8. Talk to a stranger on the bus | 50 |
| 9. Talk to cousin on the telephone for 10 minutes | 40 |
| 10. Ask for directions at the gas station | 35 |

*Source:* Ellis (1991).

**Reducing Unwanted Emotional Responses.** One of the most powerful ways to reduce fear is by gradual exposure to the feared object or situation. **Exposure therapy** involves *confronting an emotion-arousing stimulus directly and repeatedly, ultimately leading to a decrease in the emotional response.* This technique depends on the processes of habituation and response extinction. For example, in Christine's case her clinician gradually exposed her to the content of her obsessions (dirt and germs), which became less and less distressing with repeated exposure.

> How might exposure therapy help treat a phobia or fear of a specific object?

Similarly, for clients who are afraid of social interaction and unable to function at school or work, a behavioural treatment might involve exposure first to imagined situations in which they talk briefly with one person, then a bit longer talk to a medium-sized group, and finally, giving a speech to a large group. It is now known that *in vivo* (live) exposure is more effective than imaginary exposure (Choy, Fyer, & Lipsitz, 2007). In other words, if a person fears social situations, it is better for that person to practise social interaction than merely to imagine it. Behavioural therapists use an exposure hierarchy to expose the client gradually to the feared object or situation. Easier situations are practised first and, as fear decreases, the client progresses to more difficult or frightening situations (see **TABLE 16.1**).

Exposure therapy can also help people overcome unwanted emotional and behavioural responses through *exposure and response prevention*. Persons with OCD, for example, might have recurrent thoughts that their hands are dirty and need washing. Washing stops the uncomfortable feelings of contamination only briefly, though, and they wash again and again in search of relief. In exposure with response prevention, they might be asked in therapy to get their hands dirty on purpose (first by touching a coin picked up from the ground, then by touching a public toilet, and later by touching a dead mouse) and leave them dirty for hours. They may need to do this only a few times to break the cycle and be freed from the obsessive ritual (Foa et al., 2007).

An exposure therapy client with obsessive-compulsive disorder who fears contamination in public restrooms might be given "homework" to visit three such restrooms in a week, touch the toilets, and then *not* wash up.

## Cognitive Therapy

Whereas behaviour therapy focuses primarily on changing a person's behaviour, **cognitive therapy,** as the name suggests, focuses on *helping a client identify and correct any distorted thinking about self, others, or the world* (Beck, 2005). For example, behaviourists might explain a phobia as the outcome of a classical conditioning experience such as being bitten by a dog, where the dog bite leads to the development of a dog phobia through the association of the dog with the experience of pain. Cognitive theorists might instead emphasize the *interpretation* of the event. It might not be the event itself that caused the fear, but rather the individual's beliefs and assumptions about the event and the feared stimulus. In the case of a dog bite, cognitive theorists might focus on a person's new or strengthened belief that dogs are dangerous to explain the fear.

Cognitive therapies use a principal technique called **cognitive restructuring,** which *involves teaching clients to question the automatic beliefs, assumptions, and predic-*

**cognitive therapy**
Focuses on helping a client identify and correct any distorted thinking about self, others, or the world.

**cognitive restructuring**
A therapeutic approach that teaches clients to question the automatic beliefs, assumptions, and predictions that often lead to negative emotions and to replace negative thinking with more realistic and positive beliefs.

> **How might a client restructure a negative self-image into a positive one?**

*tions that often lead to negative emotions and to replace negative thinking with more realistic and positive beliefs.* Specifically, clients are taught to examine the evidence for and against a particular belief or to be more accepting of outcomes that may be undesirable yet still manageable. For example, a depressed client may believe that she is stupid and will never pass her university courses—all on the basis of one poor grade. In this situation, the therapist would work with the client to examine the validity of this belief. The therapist would consider relevant evidence such as grades on previous exams, performance on other coursework, and examples of intelligence outside school. It may be that the client has never failed a course before and has achieved good grades in this particular course in the past. In this case, the therapist would encourage the client to consider all this information in determining whether she is truly "stupid." **TABLE 16.2** shows a variety of potentially irrational ideas that serve to unleash unwanted emotions such as anger, depression, or anxiety.

> **Table 16.2**
>
> ### Common Irrational Beliefs and the Emotional Responses They Can Cause
>
> | Belief | Emotional Response |
> |---|---|
> | I have to get this done immediately. | Anxiety, stress |
> | I must be perfect. | |
> | Something terrible will happen. | |
> | Everyone is watching me. | Embarrassment, social anxiety |
> | I will not be able to make friends. | |
> | People know something is wrong with me. | |
> | I am a loser and will always be a loser. | Sadness, depression |
> | Nobody will ever love me. | |
> | She did that to me on purpose. | Anger, irritability |
> | He is evil and should be punished. | |
> | Things ought to be different. | |
>
> *Source:* Ellis (1991).

Cognitive therapist Aaron Beck's approach to psychotherapy helps people change maladaptive thinking patterns using a direct and rational approach.

Any of these irrational beliefs might bedevil a person with serious emotional problems if left unchallenged and are potential targets for cognitive restructuring. In therapy sessions, the cognitive therapist will help the client to identify evidence that supports, and fails to support, each negative thought in order to help the client generate more balanced thoughts that accurately reflect the true state of affairs. In other words, the clinician tries to remove the dark lens through which the client views the world, not with the goal of replacing it with rose-coloured glasses, but instead with clear glass. Here is a brief sample transcript of what part of a cognitive therapy session might sound like.

**Clinician:** Last week I asked you to keep a thought record of situations that made you feel very depressed, at least one per day, and the automatic thoughts that popped into your mind. Were you able to do that?

**Client:** Yes.

**Clinician:** Great. Did you bring it in with you today?

**Client:** Yes, here it is.

**Clinician:** Wonderful, I am glad you were able to complete this assignment. Let's take a look at this together. What's the first situation that you recorded?

**Client:** Well … I went out on Friday night with my friends, which I thought would be fun and help me to feel better. But I was feeling kind of down about things and I ended up not really talking to anyone, which led me to just sit in the corner and drink all night, which caused me to get so drunk that I passed out at the party. I woke up the next day feeling embarrassed and more depressed than ever.

**Clinician:** OK, sounds like a tough situation. So the situation is you had too much to drink and passed out. The resulting emotion you had was depression. How intense was your feeling of depression on a scale of 0 to 100?

**Client:** 90.

**Clinician:** OK, and what thoughts automatically popped into your head?

**Client:** I can't control myself. I'll never be able to control myself. My friends think I'm a loser and will never want to hang out with me again.

**Clinician:** OK, and which of these thoughts led you to feel most depressed?

**Client:** That my friends think I'm a loser and won't want to hang out with me anymore.

**Clinician:** Alright, so let's focus on that one for a minute. What evidence can you think of that supports this thought?

**Client:** Well … um … I got really drunk and so they *have* to think I'm a loser. I mean, who does that?

**Clinician:** OK, write that down on your thought record in this column here. Anything else? Is there any other evidence you can think of that supports those thoughts?

**Client:** No.

**Clinician:** All right. Now let's take a moment to think about whether there is any evidence that does not support those thoughts. Did anything happen that suggests that your friends don't think you are a loser or that they do want to keep hanging out with you?

**Client:** Well … apparently some kids were making fun of me when I was passed out and my friends stopped them. And they also brought me home safely and then called the next day and joked about what happened and my one friend Tommy said something like "we've all been there" and that he wants to hang out again this weekend.

**Clinician:** OK, great, write that down in this next column. This is very interesting. So on one hand, you feel depressed and have thoughts that you are a loser and your friends do not like you. But on the other hand, you have some pretty real-world evidence that even though you drank too much, they were still there for you and they do in fact want to hang out with you again, yes?

Client:     Yeah, I guess you're right if you put it that way. I didn't think about it like that.

Clinician:  So now if we were going to replace your first thoughts, which don't seem to have a lot of real-world evidence, with a more balanced thought based on the evidence, what would that new thought be?

Client:     Probably something like, my friends probably weren't happy about the fact that I got so drunk because then they had to take care of me, but they are my friends and were there for me and want to keep hanging out with me.

Clinician:  Excellent job. I think that sounds just right based on the evidence, write that down in the next column. And how much do you believe in this new thought on a scale of 0 to 100?

Client:     I think it is actually pretty accurate, so I would say 95.

Clinician:  And thinking about this new more balanced thought rather than your first one, how would you rate your depression?

Client:     Much lower than before. Probably a 40. I'm still not happy that I got so drunk, but less depressed about my friends.

In addition to cognitive restructuring techniques, which try to change a person's thoughts to be more balanced or accurate, some forms of cognitive therapy also include techniques for coping with unwanted thoughts and feelings, techniques that resemble meditation (see the Consciousness chapter). Clients may be encouraged to attend to their troubling thoughts or emotions or be given meditative techniques that allow them to gain a new focus (Hofmann & Asmundson, 2008). One such technique, called **mindfulness meditation,** *teaches an individual to be fully present in each moment; to be aware of his or her thoughts, feelings, and sensations; and to detect symptoms before they become a problem.* Researchers have found mindfulness meditation to be helpful for preventing relapse in depression. In one study, people recovering from depression were about half as likely to relapse during a 60-week assessment period if they received mindfulness meditation-based cognitive therapy than if they received treatment as usual (Teasdale, Segal, & Williams, 2000).

## Cognitive Behavioural Therapy

Historically, cognitive and behavioural therapies were considered distinct systems of therapy, and some people continue to follow this distinction, using solely behavioural *or* cognitive techniques. Today, the extent to which therapists use cognitive versus behavioural techniques depends on the individual therapist as well as the type of problem being treated. Most therapists working with anxiety and depression use *a blend of cognitive and behavioural therapeutic strategies,* often referred to

> **Why do most therapists use a blend of cognitive and behavioural strategies?**

as **cognitive behavioural therapy** (**CBT**). In a way, this technique acknowledges that there may be behaviours that people cannot control through rational thought, but also that there are ways of helping people think more rationally when thought does play a role. In contrast to traditional behaviour therapy and cognitive therapy, CBT is *problem focused,* meaning that it is undertaken for specific problems (e.g., reducing the frequency of panic attacks or returning to work after a bout of depression), and *action oriented,* meaning that the therapist tries to assist the client in selecting specific strategies to help address those problems. The client is expected to *do* things, such as engage in exposure exercises, practise behaviour change skills or use a diary to monitor relevant symptoms (e.g., the severity of depressed mood, panic attack symptoms). This is in contrast to psychodynamic or other therapies where goals may not be explicitly discussed or agreed on and the client's only necessary action is to attend the therapy session.

**mindfulness meditation**
Teaches an individual to be fully present in each moment; to be aware of his or her thoughts, feelings, and sensations; and to detect symptoms before they become a problem.

**cognitive behavioural therapy (CBT)**
A blend of cognitive and behavioural therapeutic strategies.

How might the use of behaviour-change homework improve the effectiveness of behaviour therapy?

©BONNIE KAMIN/PHOTOEDIT

CBT also contrasts with psychodynamic approaches in its assumptions about what the client can know. CBT is *transparent* in that nothing is withheld from the client. By the end of the course of therapy, most clients have a very good understanding of the treatment they have received as well as the specific techniques that are used to make the desired changes. For example, clients with OCD who fear contamination would feel confident in knowing how to confront feared situations such as public washrooms and why confronting this situation is helpful.

Cognitive behavioural therapies have been found to be effective for a number of disorders (Butler et al., 2006) (see the Hot Science box). Substantial effects of CBT have been found for unipolar depression, generalized anxiety disorder, panic disorder, social phobia, post-traumatic stress disorder, and childhood depressive and anxiety disorders. CBT has moderate but less substantial effects for marital distress, anger, somatic disorders, and chronic pain.

## HOT SCIENCE

# "Rebooting" Psychological Treatment

Modern psychotherapy has advanced far beyond the days of Freud and his free-associating patients. We now have more sophisticated treatments that have been developed based on recent advances in psychological science and supported in experimental studies showing that they actually do decrease peoples' psychological suffering. However, psychological treatment is still pretty primitive in many ways. It usually involves a patient meeting once per week with a clinician who attempts to talk them out of their psychological disorder—just as it did in the earliest days of psychological treatment. In a recent paper, Alan Kazdin (and his student Stacey Blase) called for a "rebooting" of psychotherapy research and practice (Kazdin & Blase, 2011). What is needed, they argue, is a portfolio of treatment delivery approaches that take advantage of recent advances in technology.

Although most psychologists providing treatment to those with psychological disorders still use traditional psychotherapy, researchers are developing and testing new methods of assessing and treating disorders that make creative use of new technologies. One of the most exciting recent advances in psychological treatment involves computerized training programs. For example, research suggests that biases in the ways that people process information cause psychological disorders. Cognitive bias modification (CBM) is a computerized intervention that focuses on eliminating these biases (MacLeod & Mathews, 2012). Specifically, people with social anxiety show selective attention for threatening information (e.g., when shown several faces they have an automatic tendency to look at the angrier one). In one form of CBM for social anxiety, the patient completes a computerized training program in which he or she is repeatedly shown pairs of faces, one angry and one neutral, that flash on the screen very quickly (for 500 ms) after which the letter "E" or "F" appears behind one of them and the patient's task is to indicate whether the letter is an "E" or "F." In CBM, the "E" or "F" always, or nearly always, appears behind the neutral face, which over time teaches the person to ignore the angry face and attend to the neutral face, thus reducing their tendency to attend to threatening faces. The training is intended to generalize beyond faces to reduce attention to threatening stimuli in general. In a recent placebo-controlled trial, Sharon Eldar and her colleagues (2012) found that four sessions of CBM led to significant reductions in

symptoms of various anxiety disorders in a sample of anxious children. CBM has been tested for the treatment of a range of different psychological disorders (Beard, Sawyer & Hofmann, 2012) and represents an exciting new direction in treatment development. However, it is important to note that in CBM, as with many novel treatments, several non-replications followed the initial successful trials (e.g., Enock & McNally, 2013), suggesting that the jury is still out regarding the effectiveness of this new type of treatment.

In addition to new forms of treatment that can be administered in clinics, advances in technology are allowing psychologists to bring the clinic into people's everyday life. Psychologists are now using computers, cellular phones, and wearable bio-sensors to measure patients' experiences in the real world in real-time, and also to administer interventions well beyond the clinic walls (e.g., using text messages to remind patients not to smoke or to practise the skills they learned during their last therapy session). The development of 'mobile health' or 'mHealth' interventions has been extremely exciting; however, one recent review found that more than half of interventions that used mobile technologies fail to show any benefit (Kaplan & Stone, 2013). So although the development of portable technological devices has opened up lots of new opportunities for intervention, it is important that psychologists carefully evaluate which can help improve health outcomes, and which are simply fancier ways of providing ineffective treatment.

COURTESY PHILIP M. ENOCK

## Group Treatments: Healing Multiple Minds at the Same Time

It is natural to think of psychopathology as an illness that affects only the individual. A particular person "is depressed," for example, or "has anxiety." Yet each person lives

> **When is group therapy the best option?**

in a world of other people, and interactions with others may intensify and even create disorders. A depressed person may be lonely after moving away from friends and loved ones, or an anxious person could be worried about pressures from parents. These ideas suggest that people might be able to recover from disorders in the same way they got into them—not just as an individual effort, but through social processes.

### Couples and Family Therapy

When a couple is "having problems," neither individual may be suffering from any psychopathology. Rather, it may be the relationship itself that is disordered. *Couples therapy* is when a married, co-habiting, or dating couple is seen together in therapy to work on problems usually arising within the relationship. A traditional use of couples therapy might involve a couple seeking help because they are unhappy with their relationship. In this scenario, both members of the couple are expected to attend therapy sessions and the problem is seen as arising from their interaction rather than from the problems of one half of the couple. Treatment strategies would target changes in *both* parties, focusing on ways to break their repetitive dysfunctional pattern.

What do you do when your relationship is in trouble? One option is couples therapy. In the romantic comedy, *Couples Retreat*, this couple is interacting with a therapist, trying to determine the problem in their relationship. Notice how only one partner is talking... this might be the problem.

There are cases when therapy with even larger groups is warranted. An individual may be having a problem—say, an adolescent is abusing alcohol—but the source of the problem is the individual's relationships with family members; perhaps the mother is herself an alcoholic who subtly encourages the adolescent to drink and the father travels and neglects the family. In this case, it could be useful for the therapist to work with the whole group at once in *family therapy*—psychotherapy involving members of a family. Family therapy can be particularly effective when adolescent children are having problems (Masten, 2004).

In family therapy, the "client" is the entire family. Family therapists believe that problem behaviours exhibited by a particular family member are the result of a dysfunctional family. For example, an adolescent girl suffering from bulimia might be treated in therapy with her mother, father, and older brother. The therapist would work to understand how the family members relate to one another, how the family is organized, and how it changes over time. In discussions with the family, the therapist might discover that the parents' excessive enthusiasm about her brother's athletic career led the girl to try to gain their approval by controlling her weight to become "beautiful." Both couples and family therapy involve more than one person attending therapy together, and the problems and solutions are seen as arising from the *interaction* of these individuals rather than simply from any one individual.

Families enter therapy for many reasons, sometimes to help particular members and other times because there are problems in one or more of the relationships in the family.

### Group Therapy

Taking these ideas one step further, if individuals (or families) can benefit from talking with a psychotherapist, perhaps they can also benefit from talking with other clients who are talking with the therapist. This is **group therapy,** *a technique in which multiple participants (who often do not know one another at the outset) work on their*

**group therapy**
A technique in which multiple participants (who often do not know one another at the outset) work on their individual problems in a group atmosphere.

*individual problems in a group atmosphere*. The therapist in group therapy serves more as a discussion leader than as a personal therapist, conducting the sessions both by talking with individuals and by encouraging them to talk with one another. Group therapy is often used for people who have a common problem, such as substance abuse, but it can also be used for those with differing problems.

Why do people choose group therapy? One advantage is that attending a group with others who have similar problems shows clients that they are not alone in their suffering. In addition, group members model appropriate behaviours for one another and share their insights about how to deal with their problems. Group therapy is often just as effective as individual therapy (e.g., Jonsson & Hougaard, 2008). So, from a societal perspective, group therapy is much more efficient.

> **What are the pros and cons of a group therapy approach?**

Group therapy also has disadvantages. It may be difficult to assemble a group of individuals who have similar needs. This is particularly an issue with CBT, which tends to focus on specific problems such as depression or panic disorder. Group therapy may become a problem if one or more members undermine the treatment of other group members. This can occur if some group members dominate the discussions, threaten other group members, or make others in the group uncomfortable (e.g., attempting to date other members). Finally, clients in group therapy get less attention than they might in individual psychotherapy.

## Self-Help and Support Groups

An important offshoot of group therapy is the concept of *self-help groups* and *support groups*, which are discussion groups that focus on a particular disorder or difficult life experience and are often run by peers who have themselves struggled with the same issues. The most famous self-help and support groups are Alcoholics Anonymous (AA), Gamblers Anonymous, and Al-Anon (a program for the family and friends of those with alcohol problems). Other self-help groups offer support to cancer survivors or to parents of children with autism or to people with mood disorders, eating disorders, and substance abuse problems. In fact, self-help and support groups exist for just about every psychological disorder. In addition to being cost-effective, self-help and support groups allow people to realize that they are not the only ones with a

> **What are the pros and cons of self-help support groups?**

Self-help groups are a cost-effective, time-effective, and treatment-effective solution for dealing with some types of psychological problems. Many people like self-help groups, but are they effective? How could you test this?"

©RICHARD T. NOWITZ/CORBIS

particular problem and give them the opportunity to offer guidance and support to each other based on personal experiences of success.

In some cases, though, self-help and support groups can do more harm than good. Some members may be disruptive or aggressive or encourage one another to engage in behaviours that are countertherapeutic (e.g., avoiding feared situations or using alcohol to cope). People with moderate problems may be exposed to others with severe problems and may become oversensitized to symptoms they might not otherwise have found disturbing. Because self-help and support groups are usually not led by trained therapists, mechanisms to evaluate these groups or to ensure their quality are rarely in place.

AA has 185 000 group meetings that occur around the world (Mack, Franklin, & Frances, 2003). Members are encouraged to follow "12 steps" to reach the goal of lifelong abstinence from all drinking, and the steps include believing in a higher power, practising prayer and meditation, and making amends for harm to others. Most members attend group meetings several times per week, and between meetings they receive additional support from their "sponsor." A few studies examining the effectiveness of AA have been conducted, and it appears that individuals who participate tend to overcome problem drinking with greater success than those who do not participate in AA (Fiorentine, 1999; Morgenstern et al., 1997). However, several tenets of the AA philosophy are not supported by the research. We know that the general AA program is useful, but questions about which parts of this program are most helpful have yet to be studied.

Considered together, the many social approaches to psychotherapy reveal how important interpersonal relationships are for each of us. It may not always be clear how psychotherapy works, whether one approach is better than another, or what particular theory should be used to understand how problems have developed. What is clear, however, is that social interactions between people—both in individual therapy and in all the different forms of therapy in groups—can be useful in treating psychological disorders.

## IN SUMMARY

▶ Psychodynamic therapies, including psychoanalysis, emphasize helping clients gain insight into their unconscious conflicts. Traditional psychoanalysis involves 4 to 5 sessions per week of treatment with a client lying on a couch free-associating, whereas modern psychodynamic therapies involve one session per week with face-to-face interactions in which therapists help clients solve interpersonal problems.

▶ Humanistic approaches (e.g., person-centred therapy) and existential approaches (e.g., gestalt therapy) focus on helping people to develop a sense of personal worth.

▶ Behaviour therapy applies learning principles to specific behaviour problems.

▶ Cognitive therapy is focused on helping people to change the way they think about events in their lives, and teaching them to challenge irrational thoughts.

▶ Cognitive behaviour therapy (CBT), which merges cognitive and behavioural approaches, has been shown to be effective for treating a wide range of psychological disorders.

▶ Group therapies target couples, families, or groups of clients brought together for the purpose of working together to solve their problems.

▶ Self-help and support groups, such as AA, are common in Canada and around the world but are not well studied.

This is a trephined skull from a Stone Age burial site (about 5900–6200 BCE) in the Alsace region of France. Two holes were drilled in the skull and the individual survived, as shown by the regrowth of bone covering the holes (from Alt et al., 1997). Do not try this at home.

SSPL/GETTY IMAGES

# Medical and Biological Treatments: Healing the Mind by Physically Altering the Brain

Ever since someone discovered that a whack to the head can affect the mind, people have suspected that direct brain interventions might hold the keys to a cure for psychological disorders. Archaeological evidence, for example, indicates that the occasional human thousands of years ago was "treated" for some malady by the practice of *trephining* (drilling a hole in the skull), perhaps in the belief that this would release evil spirits that were affecting the mind (Alt et al., 1997). Surgery for psychological disorders is a last resort nowadays, and treatments that focus on the brain usually involve interventions that are less dramatic. The use of drugs to influence the brain was also discovered in prehistory (alcohol, for example, has been around for a long time). Since then, drug treatments have grown in variety, effectiveness, and popularity and they are now the most common medical approach in treating psychological disorders (see **FIGURE 16.2**).

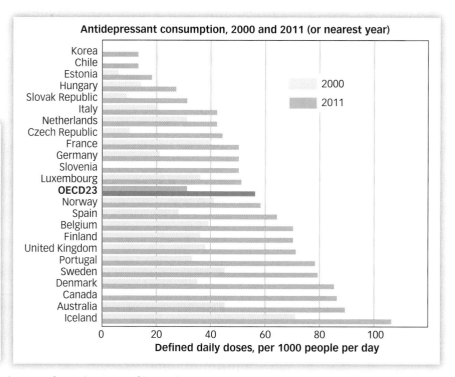

**Antidepressant consumption, 2000 and 2011 (or nearest year)**

Defined daily doses, per 1000 people per day

► Figure **16.2** **Antidepressant Use** The popularity of psychiatric medications has skyrocketed in recent years. A recent report from the Organisation for Economic Co-operation and Development (OECD) reveals that antidepressant use among Canadians is among the highest in the world (the red "OECD23" bars give the average of the 23 countries in the graph). Although prior data was not available for a few countries including Canada, the OECD survey revealed that antidepressant consumption has increased dramatically since 2000 in every other country surveyed, doubling in Australia for example, and increasing four times in the Czech Republic. In Iceland, 30 percent of women over the age of 65 are now being treated with an antidepressant (OECD, 2013).

## Antipsychotic Medications

The story of drug treatments for severe psychological disorders starts in the 1950s, with chlorpromazine (brand name Thorazine), which was originally developed as a sedative, but when administered to people with schizophrenia, often left them euphoric and docile, although they had formerly been agitated and incorrigible (Barondes, 2003). Chlorpromazine was the first in a series of **antipsychotic drugs,** which *treat schizophrenia and related psychotic disorders,* and completely changed the way schizophrenia was managed. Other related medications, such as thioridazine (Mellaril) and haloperidol (Haldol), followed. Before the introduction of antipsychotic drugs, people with schizophrenia often exhibited bizarre symptoms and were sometimes so disruptive and difficult to manage that the only way to protect them (and other people) was to keep them in hospitals for people with mental disorders, which were initially called *asylums* but now are referred to as *psychiatric hospitals* (see The Real World box: Treating Severe Mental Disorders). In the period following the introduction of these drugs, the number of people in psychiatric hospitals decreased by more than

**antipsychotic drugs**
Medications that are used to treat schizophrenia and related psychotic disorders.

# Treating Severe Mental Disorders

Society has never quite known what to do with people who have severe mental disorders. For much of recorded history, mentally ill people have been victims of maltreatment, languishing as paupers in the streets or, worse, suffering inhumane conditions in prisons. One exception was the medieval Islamic world, in which care and kindness were shown to the insane in hospitals. At his hospital in Cairo, the Egyptian ruler Ahmad ibn Tulun (835 CE–884 CE) even introduced music therapy! But these medieval Islamic hospitals were too few to serve the population that depended upon them, a pattern we see recapitulated today, when there are too few resources to adequately treat all who need care.

In medieval Europe, madness was seen as a local problem, with families and local communities assuming responsibility for care. Only a small proportion of the insane (generally those deemed violent or dangerous) were housed institutionally—sometimes in monasteries, or in towers ("fools towers") or in buildings attached to hospitals. The Priory of St Mary of Bethlehem, which later became known as the Bethlem Royal Hospital (more notoriously known as Bedlam), opened in 1247, and 150 years later housed only six insane men.

By 1700, more asylums for the insane were being created. The creation of asylums encouraged humane treatment but did not guarantee it. The Bethlem Royal Hospital was a charity, and charged visitors to view the inmates as a way of financing the institution. One visitor to this human zoo in 1753 remarked, "To my great surprise, I found at least a hundred people, who, having paid their two pence apiece, were suffered,

unattended, to run rioting up and down the wards, making sport and diversion of the miserable inhabitants" (Hitchcock, 2005).

The Enlightenment period in the late eighteenth and early nineteenth century saw a change in how people with mental illness were thought about, and how they were treated. The Enlightenment, closely tied to the Scientific Revolution, was a time when reason and science were seen as ways to reform society, and it became more common to consider mental disorders like other forms of illness that could be treated and cured. Enlightenment figures like Benjamin Rush in the United States and Philippe Pinel in France (both physicians), and William Tuke in Britain established hospitals and asylums in which the insane were not confined, where they received humane treatment, engaged in activities that might now be considered occupational therapy, and from where they could potentially be reintegrated into society.

The eighteenth century asylums were mostly private, but public charitably funded asylums began to spring up about the middle of the 1800s, both in Britain and in North America. By 1900, the number of people with mental illness housed in institutions in France, Britain, the United States, and Canada could be measured in the hundreds of thousands. The age of institutionalization had begun. Despite the early reforms of Pinel, Rush, and others, these institutions were often under-resourced and overcrowded, and became notorious for poor living conditions, lack of hygiene, and ill-treatment of patients. Furthermore, before the advent of drug treatments in the twentieth century, there often was no "treatment" at all for severe disorders and the focus of the asylum was instead merely on

custody (Jones, 1972). These weaknesses of the asylum movement eventually led to another revolution in mental health treatment—the deinstitutionalization movement. The first alternatives involving the integration of patients into the community were hesitantly implemented in the 1920s and 1930s, although asylum numbers continued to increase into the 1950s. The public distaste for psychiatric institutions (asylums) dovetailed with increasing governmental reluctance to bear the cost of funding such institutions, and with the promise held by new drugs that helped people to manage their disorders and live outside hospitals. Deinstitutionalization as public policy was adopted by various Western countries in the 1950s and 1960s, although the pace of reforms varied from country to country. Patients were trained to shop, cook, take public transportation, and otherwise deal with living outside the hospital. They were returned to their families or placed in foster homes or group apartments. Treatment of all but the most untreatable patients was managed through community mental health centres: support units to provide emergency inpatient care as needed but mainly supplying outpatient treatment and assistance in community living (Levine, 1981). The change was astonishingly fast: In Canada, in only 15 years between 1960 and 1975, the number of beds in provincial psychiatric hospitals dropped from 50 000 to only 15 000 (Wasylenki, 2001).

Has this experiment worked? On one hand, treatment for some severe disorders has improved since deinstitutionalization began. The basic drugs that helped people to manage their lives outside mental hospitals have been refined and improved. In addition, the conditions and treatments available in psychiatric hospitals have improved immensely. Contrary to what you may see in the movies, psychiatric units and hospitals look just like other medical floors in general hospitals. However, the provision of community services did not fully compensate for deinstitutionalization. This has led to difficulties in providing adequate care at the community level. People with severe mental illness too often end up on the streets, where they remain homeless, poor, and vulnerable to danger. Treatment for those with serious mental illness has improved over the past 100 or so years, but we clearly still have a long way to go.

▲ What does a modern psychiatric hospital look like? In Hollywood movies, such as this scene from *One Flew Over the Cuckoo's Nest,* they typically are dirty, scary, painted in a drab grey or green colour, and it is always night time. In the real world, they look just like other hospital units in terms of cleanliness, scariness, paint scheme, and the experience of both day and night.

**psychopharmacology**
The study of drug effects on psychological states and symptoms.

two thirds. Antipsychotic drugs made possible the deinstitutionalization of hundreds of thousands of people and gave a major boost to the field of **psychopharmacology,** *the study of drug effects on psychological states and symptoms.*

Antipsychotic medications are believed to block dopamine receptors in parts of the brain such as the mesolimbic area, an area between the tegmentum (in the midbrain) and various subcortical structures (see the Neuroscience and Behaviour chapter). The medication reduces dopamine activity in these areas. The effectiveness of schizophrenia medications led to the dopamine hypothesis (described in the Psychological Disorders chapter), suggesting that schizophrenia may be caused by excess dopamine in the synapse. Research has indeed found that dopamine overactivity in the mesolimbic area of the brain is related to the more bizarre positive symptoms of schizophrenia, such as hallucinations and delusions (Marangell et al., 2003).

> **What do antipsychotic drugs do?**

Although antipsychotic drugs work well for positive symptoms, it turns out that negative symptoms of schizophrenia, such as emotional numbing and social withdrawal, may be related to dopamine *under*activity in the mesocortical areas of the brain (connections between parts of the tegmentum and the cortex). This may help explain why antipsychotic medications do not relieve negative symptoms well. Instead of a medication that blocks dopamine receptors, negative symptoms require a medication that *increases* the amount of dopamine available at the synapse. This is a good example of how medical treatments can have broad psychological effects but not target specific psychological symptoms.

After the introduction of antipsychotic medications, there was little change in the available treatments for schizophrenia for more than a quarter of a century. However, in the 1990s, a new class of antipsychotic drugs was introduced. These newer drugs, which include clozapine (Clozaril), risperidone (Risperidal), and olanzepine (Zyprexa), have become known as *atypical* antipsychotics (the older drugs are now often referred to as *conventional* or *typical* antipsychotics). Unlike the older antipsychotic medications, these newer drugs appear to affect both the dopamine and serotonin systems, blocking both types of receptors. The ability to block serotonin receptors appears to be a useful addition because enhanced serotonin activity in the brain has been implicated in some of the core difficulties in schizophrenia, such as cognitive and perceptual disruptions, as well

> **What are the advantages of the newer, atypical antipsychotic medications?**

as mood disturbances. This may explain why atypical antipsychotics work at least as well as older drugs for the positive symptoms of schizophrenia and also work fairly well for the negative symptoms (Bradford, Stroup, & Lieberman, 2002).

Like most medications, antipsychotic drugs have side effects. The side effects can be sufficiently unpleasant that some people "go off their meds," preferring their symptoms to the drug. One side effect that often occurs with long-term use is *tardive dyskinesia,* a condition of involuntary movements of the face, mouth, and extremities. In fact, people often need to take another medication to treat the unwanted side effects of the conventional antipsychotic drugs. Side effects of the newer medications tend to be different and sometimes milder than those of the older antipsychotics. For that reason, the atypical antipsychotics are now usually the front-line treatments for schizophrenia (Meltzer, 2013).

*"The drug has, however, proved more effective than traditional psychoanalysis."*

PAUL NOTH/THE NEW YORKER COLLECTION/CARTOONBANK.COM

## Anti-anxiety Medications

**Anti-anxiety medications** are *drugs that help reduce a person's experience of fear or anxiety.* The most commonly used antianxiety medications are the benzodiazepines, a

> **What are some reasons for caution when prescribing anti-anxiety medications?**

type of tranquilizer that works by facilitating the action of the neurotransmitter gamma-aminobutyric acid (GABA). As you read in the Neuroscience and Behaviour chapter, GABA inhibits certain neurons in the brain. This inhibitory action can produce a calming effect for the person. Commonly prescribed benzodiazepines include diazepam (Valium), lorazepam (Ativan), and alprazolam (Xanax). The benzodiazepines typically take effect in a matter of minutes and are effective for reducing symptoms of anxiety disorders (Roy-Byrne & Cowley, 2002).

Nonetheless, these days doctors are relatively cautious when prescribing benzodiazepines. One concern is that these drugs have the potential for abuse. They are often associated with the development of *drug tolerance,* which is the need for higher dosages over time to achieve the same effects following long-term use (see the Consciousness chapter). Furthermore, after people become tolerant of the drug, they risk significant withdrawal symptoms when it is discontinued. Some withdrawal symptoms include increased heart rate, shakiness, insomnia, agitation, and anxiety—the very symptoms the drug was taken to eliminate! Therefore, people who take benzodiazepines for extended periods may have difficulty coming off these drugs and should discontinue their medications gradually to minimize withdrawal symptoms (Schatzberg, Cole, & DeBattista, 2003). Another consideration when prescribing benzodiazepines is their side effects. The most common side effect is drowsiness, although benzodiazepines can also have negative effects on coordination and memory. And, benzodiazapines combined with alcohol can depress respiration, potentially causing accidental death.

When anxiety leads to insomnia, drugs known as hypnotics may be useful as sleep aids. One such drug, zolpidem (Ambien), is in wide use and is often effective, but with some reports of sleepwalking, sleep-eating, and even sleep-driving (Hughes, 2007). Another alternative for anxiety is buspirone (Buspar), which has been shown to reduce anxiety among individuals who suffer from generalized anxiety disorder (Roy-Byrne & Cowley, 2002).

## Antidepressants and Mood Stabilizers

**Antidepressants** are *a class of drugs that help lift people's moods.* They were first introduced in the 1950s, when iproniazid, a drug that was used to treat tuberculosis, was found to elevate mood (Selikoff, Robitzek, & Ornstein, 1952). Iproniazid is a *monoamine oxidase inhibitor (MAOI),* a medication that prevents the enzyme monoamine oxidase from breaking down neurotransmitters such as norepinephrine, serotonin, and dopamine. However, despite their effectiveness, MAOIs are rarely prescribed anymore. MAOI side effects such as dizziness and loss of sexual interest are often difficult to tolerate, and these drugs interact with many different medications, including over-the-counter cold medicines. They also can cause dangerous increases in blood pressure when taken with foods that contain tyramine, a natural substance formed from the breakdown of protein in certain cheeses, beans, aged meats, soy products, and draft beer.

A second category of antidepressants is the tricyclic antidepressants, which were also introduced in the 1950s. These include drugs such as imipramine (Tofranil) and amitriptyline (Elavil). These medications block the reuptake of norepinephrine

**anti-anxiety medications**
Drugs that help reduce a person's experience of fear or anxiety.

**antidepressants**
A class of drugs that help lift people's moods.

If you watch American television you have seen advertisements for prescription drugs. Does this direct-to-consumer advertising really work? Sure does! One recent study sent people acting as patients to physicians' offices asking for specific drugs and found that patient requests had a huge impact on doctors' behaviour: Those asking about specific drugs were much more likely to receive a prescription than those who did not make a request (Kravitz et al., 2005).

and serotonin, thereby increasing the amount of neurotransmitter in the synaptic space between neurons. The most common side effects of tricyclic antidepressants include dry mouth, constipation, difficulty urinating, blurred vision, and racing heart (Marangell et al., 2003). Although these drugs are still prescribed, they are used much less frequently than they were in the past because of these side effects.

Among the most commonly used antidepressants today are the *selective serotonin reuptake inhibitors,* or SSRIs, which include drugs such as fluoxetine (Prozac), citalopram (Celexa), and paroxetine (Paxil). The SSRIs work by blocking the reuptake of serotonin in the brain, which makes more serotonin available in the synaptic space between neurons. The greater availability of serotonin in the synapse gives the neuron a better chance of "recognizing" and using this neurotransmitter in sending the desired signal. The SSRIs were developed based on

> What are the most common antidepressants used today? How do they work?

hypotheses that low levels of serotonin are a causal factor in depression. Supporting this hypothesis, SSRIs are effective for depression, as well as for a wide range of other problems. SSRIs are called *selective* because, unlike the tricyclic antidepressants, which work on the serotonin and norepinephrine systems, SSRIs work more specifically on the serotonin system (see **FIGURE 16.3**).

Finally, antidepressants such as Effexor (venlafaxine) and Wellbutrin (ibupropion) offer other alternatives. Effexor is an example of a serotonin and norepinephrine reuptake inhibitor (SNRI); whereas SSRIs act only upon serotonin, SNRIs act on both serotonin and norepinephrine. Wellbutrin, in contrast, is a norepinephrine and dopamine reuptake inhibitor. These and other newly developed antidepressants appear to have fewer (or at least different) side effects than the tricyclic antidepressants and MAOIs.

Most antidepressants can take up to a month before they start to have an effect on mood. Besides relieving symptoms of depression, almost all of the antidepressants effectively treat anxiety disorders, and many of them can resolve other problems, such

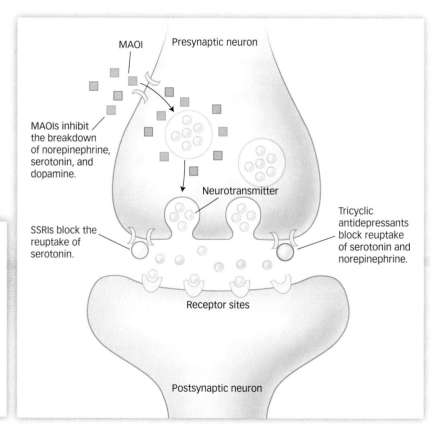

▶ Figure **16.3** **Antidepressant Drug Actions** Antidepressant drugs, such as MAOIs, SSRIs, and tricyclic antidepressants, act on neurotransmitters such as serotonin, dopamine, and norepinephrine by inhibiting their breakdown and blocking reuptake. These actions make more of the neurotransmitter available for release and leave more of the neurotransmitter in the synaptic gap to activate the receptor sites on the postsynaptic neuron. These drugs relieve depression and often alleviate anxiety and other disorders.

as eating disorders. In fact, several companies that manufacture SSRIs have marketed their drugs as treatments for anxiety disorders rather than for their antidepressant effects. Although antidepressants can be effective in treating major depression, they are not recommended for treating bipolar disorder, which is characterized by manic or

**Why are antidepressants not prescribed for bipolar disorder?**

hypomanic episodes (see the Psychological Disorders chapter). Antidepressants are not prescribed because, in the process of lifting one's mood, they might actually trigger a manic episode in a person with bipolar disorder. Instead, bipolar disorder is treated with *mood stabilizers,* which are medications used to suppress swings between mania and depression. Commonly used mood stabilizers include lithium and valproate. Even in unipolar depression, lithium is sometimes effective when combined with traditional antidepressants in people who do not respond to antidepressants alone.

Lithium has been associated with possible long-term kidney and thyroid problems, so people taking lithium must monitor their blood levels of lithium on a regular basis. Furthermore, lithium has a precise range in which it is useful for each person, another reason it should be closely monitored with blood tests. Valproate, in contrast, does not require such careful blood monitoring. Although valproate may have side effects, it is currently the most commonly prescribed drug in the United States for bipolar disorder (Schatzberg et al., 2003). In sum, although the antidepressants are effective for a wide variety of problems, mood stabilizers may be required when a person's symptoms include extreme swings between highs and lows, such as experienced with bipolar disorder.

## Herbal and Natural Products

In a survey of more than 18 000 Canadians 45 years old and over, approximately 15 percent reported using alternative "medications" such as herbal medicines, megavitamins, homeopathic remedies, or naturopathic remedies to treat anxiety and depression (Crabb

**Why are herbal remedies used? Are they actually effective?**

& Hunsley, 2011). Major reasons people use these products are that they are easily available over the counter, are less expensive, and are perceived as "natural" alternatives to synthetic or manmade "drugs." Are herbal and natural products effective in treating mental health problems, or are they just "snake oil?"

The answer to this question is not simple. Currently, herbal products are not considered medications by regulatory agencies like Health Canada, so they are exempt from rigorous research to establish their safety and effectiveness. Instead, herbal products are classified as nutritional supplements and regulated in the same way as food. There is little scientific information about herbal products, including possible interactions with other medications, possible tolerance and withdrawal symptoms, side effects, appropriate dosages, how they work, or even *whether* they work—and the purity of these products often varies from brand to brand (Jordan, Cunningham, & Marles, 2010).

There is research support for the effectiveness of some herbal and natural products, but the evidence is not overwhelming (Lake, 2009). Products such as inositol (a bran derivative), kava (an herb related to black pepper), omega-3 fatty acid (a fish oil), and SAM-e (an amino acid derivative) are sold as health foods and are described as having positive psychological effects of various kinds, but the evidence is mixed. For example, in the case of St. John's wort (a wort, it turns out, is an herb), some studies have shown it has an advantage over a placebo condition (e.g., Lecrubier et al., 2002) for the treatment of depression, whereas others show no advantage (e.g., Hypericum Depression Trial Study Group, 2002). Omega-3 fatty

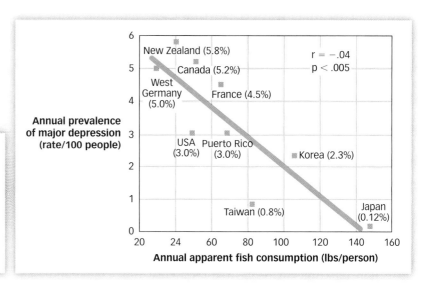

► Figure **16.4** **Omega-3 Fatty Acids and Depression** Recent studies have shown that consumption of omega-3 fatty acids is associated with a wide range of positive mental health outcomes. For instance, Joe Hibbeln (1998) showed that countries that consume more fish (a main dietary source of omega-3s) have significantly lower rates of depression.

acids have been linked with lower rates of depression and suicide, and several treatment studies have repeatedly shown that omega-3s are superior to placebo at decreasing depression (see **FIGURE 16.4**) (Lewis et al., 2011; Parker, Gibson, et al., 2006). Overall, although herbal medications and treatments are worthy of continued research, these products should be closely monitored and used judiciously until more is known about their safety and effectiveness.

## Combining Medication and Psychotherapy

Given that psychological treatments and medications have both shown an ability to treat mental disorders effectively, some natural next questions are: Which is more effective? Is the combination of psychological and medicinal treatments better than either by itself? Many studies have compared psychological treatments, medication, and combinations of these approaches for addressing psychological disorders. The results of these studies often depend on the particular problem being considered. For example, in the cases of schizophrenia and bipolar disorder, researchers have found that medication is more effective than psychological treatment and so is considered a necessary part of treatment; recent studies have tended to examine whether adding psychotherapeutic treatments such as social skills training or cognitive behavioural treatment can be helpful (they can). In the case of mood and anxiety disorders, medication and psychological treatments are equally effective. One study compared cognitive behaviour therapy, imipramine (the antidepressant also known as Tofranil), and the combination of these treatments (CBT plus imipramine) with a placebo (administration of an inert medication) for the treatment of panic disorder (Barlow et al., 2000). After 12 weeks of treatment, either CBT alone or imipramine alone was found to be superior to a placebo. For the CBT plus imipramine condition, the response rate also exceeded the rate for the placebo, but was not significantly better than that for either CBT or imipramine alone. In other words, either treatment was better than nothing, but the combination of treatments was not significantly more effective than one or the other (see **FIGURE 16.5**). More is not always better.

▼ Figure **16.5** **The Effectiveness of Medication and Psychotherapy for Panic Disorder** One study of CBT and medication (imipramine) for panic disorder found that the effects of CBT, medication, and treatment that combined CBT and medication were not significantly different over the short term, though all three were superior to the placebo condition (Barlow et al., 2000).

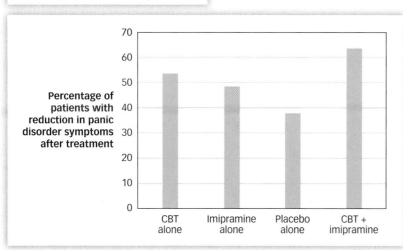

# OTHER VOICES

## Diagnosis: Human

**Ted Gup** is an author and fellow of the Edmond J. Safra Center for Ethics at Harvard University.

PHOTO: SUSAN SYMONES/ INFINITY PORTRAIT DESIGN

Should more people receive psychological treatment or medications? Or should fewer? On one hand, data indicate that most people with a mental disorder do not receive treatment and that untreated mental disorders are an enormous source of pain and suffering. On the other hand, some argue that we have become too quick to label normal human behaviour as "disordered" and too willing to medicate any behaviour, thought, or feeling that makes us uncomfortable. Ted Gup is one of these people. The following is a version of his op-ed piece that appeared in *The New York Times* on April 3, 2013, under the headline "Diagnosis: Human."

The news that 11 percent of school-age children now receive a diagnosis of attention deficit hyperactivity disorder—some 6.4 million—gave me a chill. My son David was one of those who received that diagnosis.

In his case, he was in the first grade. Indeed, there were psychiatrists who prescribed medication for him even before they met him. One psychiatrist said he would not even see him until he was medicated. For a year I refused to fill the prescription at the pharmacy. Finally, I relented. And so David went on Ritalin, then Adderall, and other drugs that were said to be helpful in combating the condition.

In another age, David might have been called "rambunctious." His battery was a little too large for his body. And so he would leap over the couch, spring to reach the ceiling and show an exuberance for life that came in brilliant microbursts.

As a 21-year-old college senior, he was found on the floor of his room, dead from a fatal mix of alcohol and drugs. The date was Oct. 18, 2011. No one made him take the heroin and alcohol, and yet I cannot help but hold myself and others to account. I had unknowingly colluded with a system that devalues talking therapy and rushes to medicate, inadvertently sending a message that self-medication, too, is perfectly acceptable.

My son was no angel (though he was to us) and he was known to trade in Adderall, to create a submarket in the drug among his classmates who were themselves all too eager to get their hands on it. What he did cannot be excused, but it should be understood. What he did was to create a market that perfectly mirrored the society in which he grew up, a culture where Big Pharma itself prospers from the off-label uses of drugs, often not tested in children and not approved for the many uses to which they are put.

And so a generation of students, raised in an environment that encourages medication, are emulating the professionals by using drugs in the classroom as performance enhancers. And we wonder why it is that they use drugs with such abandon. As all parents learn—at times to their chagrin—our children go to school not only in the classroom but also at home, and the culture they construct for themselves as teenagers and young adults is but a tiny village imitating that to which they were introduced as children.

The issue of permissive drug use and over-diagnosis goes well beyond hyperactivity. In May, the American Psychiatric Association will publish its *DSM–5,* the *Diagnostic and Statistical Manual of Mental Disorders.* It is called the bible of the profession. Its latest iteration, like those before, is not merely a window on the profession but on the culture it serves, both reflecting and shaping societal norms. (For instance, until the 1970s, it categorized homosexuality as a mental illness.)

One of the new, more controversial provisions expands depression to include some forms of grief. On its face it makes sense. The grieving often display all the common indicators of depression—loss of interest in life, loss of appetite, irregular sleep patterns, low functionality, etc. But as others have observed, those same symptoms are the very hallmarks of grief itself.

Ours is an age in which the airwaves and media are one large drug emporium that claims to fix everything from sleep to sex. I fear that being human is itself fast becoming a condition. It is as if we are trying to contain grief, and the absolute pain of a loss like mine. We have become increasingly disassociated and estranged from the patterns of life and death, uncomfortable with the messiness of our own humanity, aging and, ultimately, mortality.

Challenge and hardship have become pathologized and monetized. Instead of enhancing our coping skills, we undermine them and seek shortcuts where there are none, eroding the resilience upon which each of us, at some point in our lives, must rely. Diagnosing grief as a part of depression runs the very real risk of delegitimizing that which is most human—the bonds of our love and attachment to one another. The new entry in the *DSM* cannot tame grief by giving it a name or a subsection, nor render it less frightening or more manageable.

The *DSM* would do well to recognize that a broken heart is not a medical condition, and that medication is ill-suited to repair some tears. Time does not heal all wounds, closure is a fiction, and so too is the notion that God never asks of us more than we can bear. Enduring the unbearable is sometimes exactly what life asks of us.

But there is a sweetness even to the intensity of this pain I feel. It is the thing that holds me still to my son. And yes, there is a balm even in the pain. I shall let it go when it is time, without reference to the *DSM*, and without the aid of a pill.

Have we gone too far in labelling and treatment of mental disorders? Or have we not gone far enough? How can we make sure that we are not medicating normal behaviour, while at the same time ensuring that we provide help to those who are suffering with a true mental disorder?

▲ Figure 16.6 **The Effects of Medication and Therapy in the Brain** PET scans of individuals with social phobia showed similar reductions in activations of the amygdala–hippocampus after they received treatment with CBT (*left*) and with citalopram (*right*), an SSRI.

From Furmark et al., 2002.

Given that both therapy and medications are effective, one question is whether they work through similar mechanisms. A study of people with social phobia examined patterns of cerebral blood flow following treatment using either citalopram (an SSRI) or CBT (Furmark et al., 2002). Participants in both groups were alerted to the possibility that they would soon have to speak in public. In both groups, those who responded to treatment showed similar reductions in activation in the amygdala, hippocampus, and neighbouring cortical areas during this challenge (see **FIGURE 16.6**). The amygdala, located next to the hippocampus (see Figure 6.18) plays a significant role in memory for emotional information. These findings suggest that both therapy and medication affect the brain in regions associated with a reaction to threat. Although it might seem that events that influence the brain should be physical—after all, the brain is a physical object—it is important to keep in mind that environmental learning experiences, such as psychological treatment, produce similar influences on the brain.

**Do therapy and medications work through similar mechanisms?**

One complication in combining medication and psychotherapy is that these treatments are often provided by different people. Psychiatrists are trained in the administration of medication in medical school (and they may also provide psychological treatment), whereas psychologists provide psychological treatment but not medication. This means that the coordination of treatment often requires cooperation between psychologists and psychiatrists.

The question of whether psychologists should be licensed to prescribe medications has been a source of debate among psychologists and physicians (Fox et al., 2009). Opponents argue that psychologists do not have the medical training to understand how medications interact with other drugs. Proponents of prescription privileges argue that patient safety would not be compromised as long as rigorous training procedures were established. This issue remains a focus of debate, and at present, the coordination of medication and psychological treatment usually involves a team effort of psychiatry and psychology.

## Biological Treatments beyond Medication

Medication can be an effective biological treatment, but for some people medications do not work or side effects are intolerable. If this group of people does not respond to psychotherapy either, what other options do they have to achieve symptom relief? Some additional avenues of help are available, but some are risky or poorly understood.

One commonly used biological treatment for severe mental disorders is **electroconvulsive therapy (ECT)**, sometimes referred to as *shock therapy*, which is *a treatment that involves inducing a brief seizure by delivering an electrical shock to the brain*. The shock is applied to the person's scalp for less than a second. ECT is primarily used to treat severe depression that has not responded to antidepressant medications, although it may also be useful for treating bipolar disorder (Khalid et al., 2008; Poon et al., 2012). Patients are pretreated with muscle relaxants and are under general anesthetic, so they are not conscious of the procedure. The main side effect of ECT is impaired short-term memory, which usually improves over the first month or two after the end of treatment. In addition,

**Where do people turn if psychological treatment and medication are unsuccessful?**

Electroconvulsive therapy (ECT) can be an effective treatment for severe depression. To reduce the side effects, it is administered under general anesthesia.

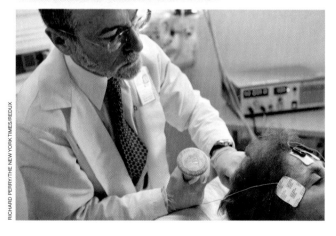

patients undergoing this procedure sometimes report headaches and muscle aches afterward (Marangell et al., 2003). Despite these side effects, the treatment can be effective: ECT is more effective than simulated ECT, placebo, and antidepressant drugs such as tricyclics and MAOIs (Pagnin et al., 2008).

Another biological approach that does not involve medication is **transcranial magnetic stimulation (TMS)**, *a treatment that involves placing a powerful pulsed magnet over a person's scalp, which alters neuronal activity in the brain*. As a treatment for depression, the magnet is placed just above the right or left eyebrow in an effort to stimulate the right or left prefrontal cortex (areas of the brain implicated in depression). TMS is an exciting development because it is noninvasive and has fewer side effects than ECT (see the Neuroscience and Behaviour chapter). Side effects are minimal; they include mild headache and a small risk of seizure, but TMS has no impact on memory or concentration. TMS may be particularly useful in treating depression that is unresponsive to medication (Avery et al., 2009). In fact, a study comparing TMS to ECT found that both procedures were effective, with no significant differences between them (Janicak et al., 2002). Other studies have found that TMS can also be used to treat auditory hallucinations in schizophrenia (Aleman, Sommer, & Kahn, 2007).

**Phototherapy,** *a therapy that involves repeated exposure to bright light,* may be helpful to people who have a seasonal pattern to their depression. This could include people suffering with seasonal affective disorder (SAD) (see the Psychological Disorders chapter), or those who experience depression only in the winter months due to the lack of sunlight. Typically, people are exposed to bright light in the morning, using a lamp designed for this purpose. Phototherapy has not been as well researched as psychological treatment or medication, but the handful of studies available suggest it is approximately as effective as antidepressant medication in the treatment of SAD (Thaler et al., 2011).

In very rare cases, **psychosurgery,** *the surgical destruction of specific brain areas,* may be used to treat psychological disorders. Psychosurgery has a controversial history, beginning in the 1930s with the invention of the lobotomy by Portuguese physician Egas Moniz (1874–1955). After discovering that certain surgical procedures on animal brains calmed behaviour, Moniz began to use similar techniques on violent or agitated human patients. Lobotomies involved inserting an instrument into the brain through the patient's eye socket or through holes drilled in the side of the head. The objective was to sever connections between the frontal lobes and inner brain structures such as the thalamus, known to be involved in emotion. Although some lobotomies produced highly successful results and Moniz received the 1949 Nobel Prize for his work, significant side effects such as extreme lethargy or childlike impulsiveness detracted from these benefits. Lobotomy was used widely for years, leaving many people devastated by these permanent side effects, and because of this there is an ongoing movement challenging the awarding of the Nobel Prize to Moniz. The development of antipsychotic drugs in the 1950s provided a safer way to treat violent individuals and brought the practice of lobotomy to an end (Swayze, 1995).

Psychosurgery is rarely used these days and is reserved only for extremely severe cases for which no other interventions have been effective and the symptoms of the disorder are intolerable to the patient. For instance, psychosurgery is sometimes used in severe cases of OCD in which the person is completely unable to function in their daily life and psychological treatment and medication are not effective. In contrast to the earlier days of lobotomy in which broad regions of brain tissue were destroyed, modern psychosurgery involves a very precise destruction of brain tissue in order to disrupt the brain circuits known to be involved in the generation of obsessions and compulsions. This increased precision has produced better results. For example, people suffering from OCD who fail to respond to treatment (including several trials of medications and cognitive behavioural treatment) may benefit from

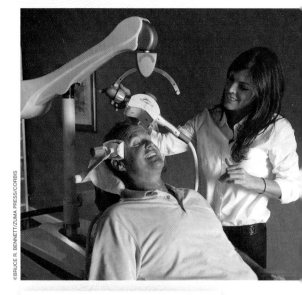

Transcranial magnetic stimulation (TMS) is an exciting new technique that allows researchers and clinicians to change brain activity using a magnetic wand—no surgery is required.

©BRUCE R. BENNETT/ZUMA PRESS/CORBIS

**electroconvulsive therapy (ECT)**
A treatment that involves inducing a brief seizure by delivering an electrical shock to the brain.

**transcranial magnetic stimulation (TMS)**
A treatment that involves placing a powerful pulsed magnet over a person's scalp, which alters neuronal activity in the brain.

**phototherapy**
A therapy that involves repeated exposure to bright light.

**psychosurgery**
Surgical destruction of specific brain areas.

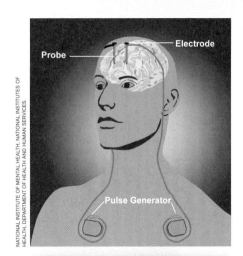

Deep brain stimulation involves the insertion of battery-powered electrodes that deliver electrical pulses to specific areas of the brain believed to be causing a person's mental disorder.

specific surgical procedures called *cingulotomy* and *anterior capsulotomy*. Cingulotomy involves destroying part of the corpus callosum (see Figure 3.18) and cingulate gyrus (the ridge just above the corpus collosum). Anterior capsulotomy involves creating small lesions to disrupt the pathway between the caudate nucleus and putamen. Because of the relatively small number of cases of psychosurgery, there are not as many studies of these techniques as there are for other treatments; however, available studies have shown that psychosurgery typically leads to substantial improvements in both the short and long term for people with severe OCD (Csigó et al., 2010; van Vliet et al., 2013).

A final approach, called *deep brain stimulation* (DBS), combines the use of psychosurgery with the use of electrical currents (as in ECT and TMS). In DBS, a treatment pioneered only recently, a small, battery-powered device is implanted in the body to deliver electrical stimulation to specific areas of the brain known to be involved in the disorder being targeted. This technique has been successful for OCD treatment (Abelson et al., 2009) and can provide benefits for people with a variety of neurologic conditions. The tremor that accompanies Parkinson's disease has proven to be treatable in this way (Perlmutter & Mink, 2006), as have some cases of severe depression that are otherwise untreatable (Mayberg et al., 2005). The early view of psychosurgery as a treatment of last resort is being replaced by a cautious hope that newer, focused treatments that target brain circuits known to be functioning abnormally in those with certain mental disorders can have beneficial effects (Ressler & Mayberg, 2007).

## IN SUMMARY

► Medications have been developed to treat many psychological disorders, including anti-psychotic medications (used to treat schizophrenia and psychotic disorders), anti-anxiety medications (used to treat anxiety disorders), and antidepressants (used to treat depression and related disorders).

► Medications are often combined with psychotherapy.

► Other biomedical treatments include electroconvulsive therapy (ECT), transcranial magnetic stimulation (TMS), and psychosurgery—this last used in extreme cases, when other methods of treatment have been exhausted.

## Treatment Effectiveness: For Better or for Worse

Think back to Christine and the dead mouse at the beginning of the chapter. What if, instead of exposure and response prevention, Christine had been assigned psychoanalysis or psychosurgery? Could these alternatives have been just as effective (and justified) for treating her OCD? Through this chapter, we have explored various psychological and biological treatments that may help people with psychological disorders. But do these treatments actually work, and which ones work better than the others?

As you learned in the Methods in Psychology chapter, pinning down a specific cause for an effect can be a difficult detective exercise. The detection is made even more difficult because people may approach treatment evaluation very unscientifically, often by simply noticing an improvement (or no improvement, or even a worsening of symptoms) and reaching a conclusion based on that sole observation. Determination of a treatment's effectiveness can be misdirected by illusions that can only be overcome by careful, scientific evaluation.

## Treatment Illusions

Imagine you are sick and the doctor says, "Take a pill." You follow the doctor's orders, and you get better. To what do you attribute your improvement? If you are like most

> **What are three kinds of treatment illusions?**

people, you reach the conclusion that the pill cured you. That is one possible explanation, but there are at least three others: Maybe you would have gotten better anyway; maybe the pill was not the active ingredient in your cure; or maybe after you are better, you mistakenly remember having been more ill than you really were. These possibilities point to three potential illusions of treatment: illusions produced by natural improvement, by placebo effects, and by reconstructive memory.

### Natural Improvement

*Natural improvement* is the tendency of symptoms to return to their mean or average level. The illusion in this case happens when you conclude mistakenly that a treatment has made you better when you would have gotten better anyway. People typically turn to therapy or medication when their symptoms are at their worst. When this is the case, the client's symptoms will often improve regardless of whether there was any treatment at all; when you are at rock bottom, there is nowhere to move but up. In most cases, for example, depression that becomes severe enough to make individuals candidates for treatment will tend to lift in several months *no matter what they do*. A person who enters therapy for depression may develop an illusion that the therapy works because the therapy coincides with the typical course of the illness and the person's natural return to health. How can we know if change was caused by the treatment or by natural improvement? As discussed in the Methods in Psychology chapter, we could do an experiment in which we assign half of the people who are depressed to receive treatment and the other half to receive no treatment, and then monitor them over time to see if the ones who got treatment actually show greater improvement. This is precisely how researchers test out different interventions, as described in more detail below.

### Placebo Effects

Recovery could be produced by *nonspecific treatment effects* that are not related to the specific mechanisms by which treatment is supposed to be working. For example, the

> **What is the placebo effect?**

doctor prescribing the medication might simply be a pleasant and hopeful individual who gives the client a sense of hope or optimism that things will improve. Client and doctor alike might attribute the client's improvement to the effects of medication on the brain, whereas the true active ingredient was the warm relationship with the doctor or an improved outlook on life.

Simply knowing that you are getting a treatment can be a nonspecific treatment effect. These instances include the positive influences that can be produced by a **placebo,** *an inert substance or procedure that has been applied with the expectation that a healing response will be produced.* For example, if you take a sugar pill that does not contain any painkiller for a headache thinking it is Tylenol or aspirin, this pill is a placebo. Placebos can have profound effects in the case of psychological treatments. Research shows that a large percentage of individuals with anxiety, depression, and other emotional and medical problems experience significant improvement after a placebo treatment.

One recent study compared the decrease in symptoms of depression seen in 718 patients randomly assigned to receive either antidepressant medication or pill placebo (Fournier et al., 2010). Participants receiving medication showed a dramatic decrease in symptoms over the course of treatment. However, so did those taking placebo.

**placebo**
An inert substance or procedure that has been applied with the expectation that a healing response will be produced.

*"If this doesn't help you don't worry, it's a placebo."*

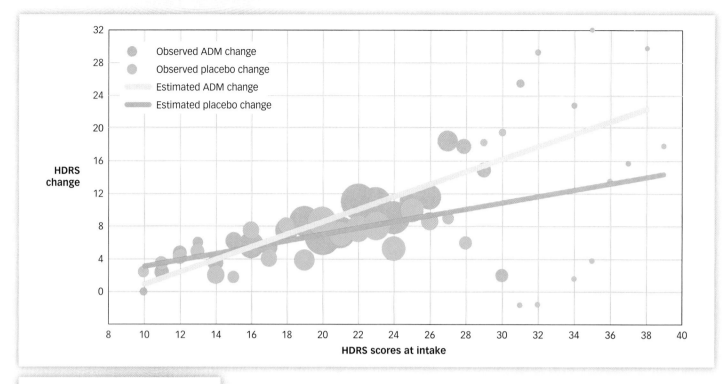

▲ Figure **16.7** **Antidepressants versus Placebos for Depression** A total of 713 depressed individuals from six different studies were given pills to treat their depression. Half were randomly assigned to receive an antidepressant medication (ADM) and half to receive a pill placebo. Importantly, the participants did not know if they were taking an antidepressant or simply a placebo. For those with mild or moderate depression, as measured by the Hamilton Depression Rating Scale (HDRS), antidepressants did not work any better than placebo. However, those with severe depression showed much greater improvement on antidepressants than on placebo. The circle size represents the number of people with data at each point.

[From Fournier et al., 2010.]

Closer examination of the data revealed that for those with mild or moderate depression, placebo is just as effective as antidepressant medication at decreasing a person's symptoms, and it is only in instances of severe depression that antidepressants seem to work better than placebo (see **FIGURE 16.7**).

## Reconstructive Memory

A third treatment illusion can come about when the client's motivation to get well causes errors in *reconstructive memory* for the original symptoms. You might think that you have improved because of a treatment when in fact you are simply misremembering: mistakenly believing that your symptoms before treatment were worse than they actually were. This tendency was first observed in research examining the effectiveness of a study skills class (Conway & Ross, 1984). Some students who wanted to take the class were enrolled, but others were randomly assigned to a waiting list until the class could be offered again. When their study abilities were measured afterward, those students who took the class were no better at studying than their wait-listed counterparts. However, those who took the class *said* that they had improved. How could this be? Those participants recalled their study skills before the class as being worse than they actually had been. This motivated reconstruction of the past was dubbed by Conway and Ross (1984), "Getting What You Want by Revising What You Had." A client who forms a strong expectation of success in therapy might conclude later that even a useless treatment had worked wonders by recalling past symptoms and troubles as worse than they were and thereby making the treatment seem effective.

## Treatment Studies

How can we make sure that we are using treatments that actually work and not wasting time with procedures that may be useless or even harmful? Research psychologists use the approaches covered in the Methods in Psychology chapter to create experiments that test whether treatments are effective for the different mental disorders described in the previous chapter.

*Treatment outcome studies* are designed to evaluate whether a particular treatment works, often in relation to some other treatment or a control condition. For example, to study the outcome of treatment for depression, researchers might compare the self-reported symptoms of two groups of people who were initially depressed: those who received treatment for 6 weeks and a control group that had also been selected for the study but were assigned to a waiting list for later treatment and were simply tested 6 weeks after their selection. The outcome study could determine whether this treatment had any benefit.

Researchers use a range of methods to ensure that any observed effects are not due to the treatment illusions described earlier. For example, the treatment illusions caused by natural improvement and reconstructive memory happen when people compare their symptoms before treatment to their symptoms after treatment. To avoid this, a treatment (or experimental) group and a control group need to be randomly assigned to each condition and then compared at the end of treatment. That way, natural improvement or motivated reconstructive memory cannot cause illusions of effective treatment.

But what should happen to the control group during the treatment? If they simply stay home waiting until they can get treatment later (a wait-list control group), they will

> **Why is a double-blind experiment so important in assessing treatment effectiveness?**

not receive the placebo effects. So, ideally, a treatment should be assessed in a *double-blind experiment*, a study in which both the participant and the researcher/therapist are uninformed about which treatment the participant is receiving. In the case of drug studies, this is not hard to arrange because active drugs and placebos can be made to look alike to both the participants and the researchers during the study. Keeping both participants and researchers "in the dark" is much harder in the study of psychological treatments; in fact, in most cases it is not possible. Both the participant and the therapist can easily notice the differences in treatments such as psychoanalysis and behaviour therapy, for example, so there is no way to keep the beliefs and expectations of both participant and therapist completely out of the picture in evaluating psychotherapy effectiveness. Nevertheless, by comparing treatments either to no treatment or to other active interventions (such as other psychological treatments or medications), researchers can determine which treatments work, and which are most effective for different disorders.

## Which Treatments Work?

The German-born British psychologist Hans Eysenck (1916–1997) reviewed the relatively few studies of psychotherapy effectiveness available in 1957 and raised a furor among therapists by concluding that psychotherapy—particularly psychoanalysis—not only was ineffective but seemed to *impede* recovery (Eysenck, 1957). Much larger numbers of studies have been examined statistically since then, and they support a more optimistic conclusion: The typical psychotherapy client is better off than three quarters of untreated individuals (Seligman, 1995; Smith, Glass, & Miller, 1980). Although critiques of psychotherapy continue to point out weaknesses in how clients are tested, diagnosed, and treated (Baker, McFall, & Shoham, 2009; Dawes, 1994), strong evidence generally supports the effectiveness of many treatments (Nathan & Gorman, 2007), including psychodynamic therapy (Shedler, 2010). The key question then becomes: Which treatments are effective for which problems (Hunsley & Di Giulio, 2002)?

One of the most enduring debates in clinical psychology concerns how the various psychotherapies compare to one another. Some psychologists have argued for years that evidence supports the conclusion that most psychotherapies work about equally well. In this view, common factors shared by all forms of psychotherapy, such as contact with and empathy from a professional, contribute to change (Luborsky et al., 2002; Luborsky & Singer, 1975). In contrast, others have argued that there are important differences among therapies and that certain treatments are more effective than others, especially for treating particular types of problems (Beutler, 2002; Hunsley & Di Giulio, 2002). How can we make sense of these differing perspectives?

**Table 16.3**

**Selected List of Specific Psychological Treatments Compared to Medication or Other Treatments**

| Disorder | Treatment | Results |
|---|---|---|
| Depression | CBT | PT = meds;<br>PT + meds > either alone |
| Panic disorder | CBT | PT > meds at follow-up;<br>PT = meds at end of treatment;<br>both > placebo |
| Post-traumatic stress disorder | CBT | PT > present-centred therapy |
| Tourette's disorder | Habit reversal training | PT > supportive therapy |
| Insomnia | CBT | PT > medication or placebo |
| Depression and physical health in Alzheimer's patients | Exercise and behavioural management | PT > routine medical care |
| Gulf War veterans' illnesses | CBT and exercise | PT > Usual care or alternative treatments |

*Note:* CBT = cognitive behavioural therapy; PT = psychological treatment; meds = medication.
*Source:* Barlow et al. (2013).

In 1995, the American Psychological Association (APA) published one of the first attempts to define criteria for determining whether a particular type of psychotherapy is effective for a particular problem (Task Force on Promotion and Dissemination of Psychological Procedures, 1995). The Canadian Psychological Association (CPA) followed, generally endorsing the APA guidelines, and elaborating upon them in a Canadian context (Task Force on Empirically Supported Treatments, 1998). The official criteria for empirically validated treatments in the APA report defined two levels of empirical support: *well-established treatments,* those with a high level of support (e.g., evidence from several randomized controlled trials), and *probably efficacious treatments,* those with preliminary support. After these criteria were established, a list of empirically supported treatments was published by the APA (Chambless et al., 1998; Woody & Sanderson, 1998). A recent review of such treatments highlighted several specific psychological treatments that have been shown to work as well as, or even better than, other available treatments, including medication (Barlow et al., 2013). **TABLE 16.3** lists several of these treatments.

> **How do psychologists know which treatments work and which might be harmful?**

Some have questioned whether treatments shown to work in well-controlled studies conducted at university clinics will work in the real world. For instance, some have noted that most treatment studies reported in the literature do not have large numbers of participants who are of ethnic minority status, and so it is unclear if these treatments will work with ethnically and culturally diverse groups. One recent, comprehensive review of all available data suggests that although there are gaps in the literature, where there are data available, results suggest that current evidence-based psychological treatments work as well with ethnic minority clients as with white clients (Miranda et al., 2005).

Even trickier than the question of establishing whether a treatment works is whether a psychotherapy or medication might actually do harm. The dangers of drug treatment should be clear to anyone who has read an American magazine advertisement for a drug and studied the fine print with its list of side effects, potential drug interactions, and complications. Many drugs used for psychological treatment may be addictive, creating long-term dependency with serious withdrawal symptoms. The strongest critics of drug treatment claim that drugs do no more than trade one unwanted symptom for another: depression for sexual disinterest, anxiety for intoxication, or agitation for lethargy and dulled emotion (e.g., see Breggin, 2000).

The dangers of psychotherapy are more subtle, but one is clear enough in some cases that there is actually a name for it. **Iatrogenic illness** is *a disorder or symptom that occurs as a result of a medical or psychotherapeutic treatment itself* (e.g., Boisvert & Faust, 2002). Such an illness might arise, for example, when a psychotherapist becomes convinced that a client has a disorder that in fact the client does not have. As a result, the therapist works to

> **How might psychotherapy cause harm?**

help the client accept that diagnosis and participate in psychotherapy to treat that disorder. Being treated for a disorder can, under certain conditions, make a person show signs of that very disorder—and so an iatrogenic illness is born.

There are cases of clients who have been influenced through hypnosis and repeated suggestions in therapy to believe that they have dissociative identity disorder (even

MARY KATE DENNY/PHOTOEDIT

Treatments that are shown to be effective in research studies (which often include only a small percentage of ethnic minority patients) have been found to work equally well with people of different ethnicities (Miranda et al., 2005).

**iatrogenic illness**
A disorder or symptom that occurs as a result of a medical or psychotherapeutic treatment itself.

coming to express multiple personalities) or to believe that they were subjected to traumatic events as a child and "recover" memories of such events when investigation reveals no evidence for these problems prior to therapy (Acocella, 1999; McNally, 2003; Ofshe & Watters, 1994). There are people who have entered therapy with a vague sense that something odd has happened to them and who emerge after hypnosis or other imagination-enhancing techniques with the conviction that their therapist's theory was right: They were abducted by space aliens (Clancy, 2005). Needless to say, a therapy that leads clients to develop such bizarre beliefs is doing more harm than good.

Just as psychologists have created lists of treatments that work, they also have begun to establish lists of treatments that *harm*. The purpose of doing so is to inform other researchers, clinicians, and the public which treatments they should avoid. Many are under the impression that although every psychological treatment may not be effective, some treatment is better than no treatment. However, it turns out that a number of interventions intended to help alleviate people's symptoms actually make them worse! Did your high school have a DARE (Drug Abuse and Resistance Education) program? Have you heard of *Scared Straight,* and boot-camp programs for young offenders? They all sound like they might work, but careful scientific experiments have determined that people who participate in these interventions are actually worse off after doing so (see **TABLE 16.4**) (Lilienfeld, 2007; Ontario Ministry of Children and Youth Services, 2010)!

To regulate the potentially powerful influence of therapies, psychologists hold themselves to a set of ethical standards for the treatment of people with mental disorders (American Psychological Association, 2002; Canadian Psychological Association, 2000). Adherence to these standards is required for membership in the American and Canadian Psychological Associations, and provincial and territorial regulatory bodies also monitor adherence to ethical principles in therapy. These ethical standards in Canada are based on four principles: (1) respect for the dignity of persons, which includes protecting the welfare of vulnerable people and seeking fairness in treatment and avoiding biases; (2) responsible caring, which includes striving to benefit clients and taking care to do no harm; (3) integrity in relationships, by promoting accuracy, honesty, and truthfulness; and (4) responsibility to society, with means that when psychological knowledge is used in the development of social policies, it will only be used for beneficial purposes (i.e., those that reflect the first three principles). When people suffering from mental disorders come to psychologists for help, adhering to these guidelines is the least that psychologists can do. Ideally, in the hope of relieving this suffering, they can do much more.

**Table 16.4**

**Some Psychological Treatments that Cause Harm**

| Type of Treatment | Potential Harm | Source of Evidence |
|---|---|---|
| CISD | Increased risk of PTSD | RCTs |
| Scared Straight | Worsening of conduct problems | RCTs |
| Boot-camp interventions for conduct problems | Worsening of conduct problems | Meta-analysis (review of studies) |
| DARE programs | Increased use of alcohol and drugs | RCTs |

*Note:* CISD = critical-incident stress debriefing; PTSD = post-traumatic stress disorder; RCTs = randomized controlled trials
*Source:* Lilienfeld (2007).

## IN SUMMARY

▶ Observing improvement during treatment does not necessarily mean that the treatment was effective; it might instead reflect natural improvement, nonspecific treatment effects (e.g., the placebo effect), and reconstructive memory processes.

▶ Treatment studies focus on both treatment outcomes and processes, using scientific research methods such as double-blind techniques and placebo controls.

▶ Treatments for psychological disorders are generally more effective than no treatment at all, but some are more effective than others for certain disorders, and both medication and psychotherapy have dangers that ethical practitioners must consider carefully.

# Chapter Review

1. Which of the following is NOT a reason why people fail to get treatment for mental illness?
   a. People may not realize that their disorder needs to be treated.
   b. Levels of impairment for people with mental illness are comparable to or higher than those of people with chronic medical illnesses.
   c. There may be barriers to treatment, such as beliefs and circumstances that keep people from getting help.
   d. Even people who acknowledge they have a problem may not know where to look for services.

2. The different psychodynamic therapies all share an emphasis on
   a. the influence of the collective unconscious.
   b. the importance of taking responsibility for psychological problems.
   c. combining behavioural and cognitive approaches.
   d. developing insight into the unconscious sources of psychological disorders.

3. Which psychoanalytic technique involves the client reporting every thought that enters his or her mind, without censorship or filtering?
   a. transference
   b. free association
   c. interpretation
   d. resistance analysis

4. Which type of therapy would likely work best for someone with an irrational fear of heights?
   a. psychodynamic
   b. gestalt
   c. behavioural
   d. humanistic

5. Mindfulness meditation is part of which kind of therapy?
   a. interpersonal
   b. humanistic
   c. psychodynamic
   d. cognitive

6. Which type of therapy emphasizes action on the part of the client, as well as complete transparency as to the specifics of the treatment?
   a. cognitive behavioural
   b. humanistic
   c. existential
   d. group

7. Examining the failure to reach one's potential reflects the _____ approach, whereas examining one's failure to find meaning in life reflects the _____ approach.
   a. cognitive; behavioural
   b. humanistic; existential
   c. psychodynamic; cognitive behavioural
   d. existential; humanistic

8. Self-help groups are an important offshoot of
   a. cognitive behavioural therapy.
   b. support groups.
   c. person-centred therapy.
   d. group therapy.

9. Antipsychotic drugs were developed to treat
   a. depression.
   b. schizophrenia.
   c. anxiety.
   d. mood disorders.

10. Atypical antipsychotic drugs
    a. act on different neurotransmitters depending on the individual.
    b. affect only the dopamine system.
    c. affect only the serotonin system.
    d. act on both the dopamine and serotonin systems.

11. Which of the following statements is NOT accurate regarding antidepressants?
    a. Current antidepressants act on combinations of different neurotransmitter systems.
    b. Antidepressants have had significantly positive results in the treatment of bipolar disorder.
    c. Antidepressants are also prescribed to treat anxiety.
    d. Most antidepressants can take up to a month before they start to have an effect on mood.

12. What do electroconvulsive therapy, transcranial magnetic stimulation, and phototherapy all have in common?
    a. They incorporate herbal remedies in their treatment regimens.
    b. They may result in the surgical destruction of certain brain areas.
    c. They are considered biological treatments beyond medication.
    d. They are typically used in conjunction with psychotherapy.

13. Antidepressant medications have the strongest effects for people with _____ depression.
    a. no
    b. mild
    c. moderate
    d. severe

14. Current studies indicate that the typical psychotherapy client is better off than _____ of untreated individuals.
    a. one half
    b. the same number
    c. one fourth
    d. three fourths

## KEY TERMS

anti-anxiety medications (p. 649)

antidepressants (p. 649)

antipsychotic drugs (p. 646)

behaviour therapy (p. 637)

cognitive behavioural therapy (CBT) (p. 641)

cognitive restructuring (p. 639)

cognitive therapy (p. 639)

electroconvulsive therapy (ECT) (p. 655)

exposure therapy (p. 638)

gestalt therapy (p. 637)

group therapy (p. 643)

iatrogenic illness (p. 660)

interpersonal psychotherapy (IPT) (p. 635)

mindfulness meditation (p. 641)

person-centred therapy (or client-centred therapy) (p. 636)

phototherapy (p. 655)

placebo (p. 657)

psychodynamic psychotherapies (p. 634)

psychopharmacology (p. 648)

psychosurgery (p. 655)

psychotherapy (p. 633)

resistance (p. 634)

token economy (p. 638)

transcranial magnetic stimulation (TMS) (p. 655)

transference (p. 635)

## CHANGING MINDS

**1.** One of your friends recently lost a close family member in a tragic car accident, and he is devastated. He is not been attending classes, and when you check up on him, you learn that he is not sleeping well or eating regularly. You want to help him but feel a little out of your depth, so you suggest he visit the campus counselling centre and talk to a therapist. "Only crazy people go to therapy," he says. What could you tell your friend to dispel his assumption?

**2.** While you are talking to your bereaved friend, his roommate comes in. The roommate agrees with your suggestion about therapy but takes it further. "I'll give you the name of my therapist. He helped me quit smoking—he'll be able to cure your depression in no time." Why is it dangerous to assume that a good therapist can cure anyone and anything?

**3.** In the Methods in Psychology chapter you read about Louise Hay, whose best-selling book, *You Can Heal Your Life,* promotes a kind of psychotherapy: teaching readers how to change their thoughts and thereby improve not only their inner lives but also their physical health. The chapter quotes Hay as saying that scientific evidence is unnecessary to validate her claims. Is there a scientific basis for the major types of psychotherapy described in this chapter? How is scientific experimentation used to assess their effectiveness?

**4.** In June 2009, pop icon Michael Jackson died after receiving a fatal dose of the anesthetic propofol, which is sometimes used off-label as an anti-anxiety drug; autopsy confirmed that his body contained a cocktail of prescription drugs, including the benzodiazepines lorazepam, and diazepam. (Jackson's cardiologist, Dr. Conrad Murray, was later convicted of involuntary manslaughter for administering the fatal dose.) Other celebrities whose deaths have been attributed to medications commonly prescribed for anxiety and depression include Heath Ledger in 2008 and Amy Winehouse in 2011. "These drugs are dangerous," your roommate notes. "People who have psychological problems should seek out talk therapy for their problems and stay away from the medications, even if they're prescribed by a responsible doctor." You agree that medications can be dangerous if misused, but how would you justify the use of drug treatment for serious mental disorders?

## ANSWERS TO KEY CONCEPT QUIZ

1. b; 2. d; 3. b; 4. c; 5. d; 6. a; 7. b; 8. d; 9. b; 10. d; 11. b; 12. c; 13. d; 14. d.

Need more help? Additional resources are located in Launchpad at:
www.worthpublishers.com/launchpad/schacter3ecanadian

# Glossary

**absentmindedness** A lapse in attention that results in memory failure. (p. 250)

**absolute threshold** The minimal intensity needed to just barely detect a stimulus in 50 percent of the trials. (p. 132)

**accommodation** The process by which infants revise their schemas in light of new information. (p. 434)

**accommodation** The process by which the eye maintains a clear image on the retina. (p. 137)

**acetylcholine (ACh)** A neurotransmitter involved in a number of functions, including voluntary motor control. (p. 88)

**acquisition** The phase of classical conditioning when the CS and the US are presented together. (p. 268)

**action potential** An electric signal that is conducted along a neuron's axon to a synapse. (p. 86)

**activation–synthesis model** The theory that dreams are produced when the brain attempts to make sense of random neural activity that occurs during sleep. (p. 203)

**actor–observer effect** The tendency to make situational attributions for our own behaviours while making dispositional attributions for the identical behaviour of others. (p. 545)

**adolescence** The period of development that begins with the onset of sexual maturity (about 11 to 14 years of age) and lasts until the beginning of adulthood (about 18 to 21 years of age). (p. 452)

**adulthood** The stage of development that begins around 18 to 21 years and ends at death. (p. 460)

**aggression** Behaviour with the purpose of harming another. (p. 508)

**agonists** Drugs that increase the action of a neurotransmitter. (p. 88)

**agoraphobia** A specific phobia involving a fear of public places. (p. 596)

**alcohol myopia** A condition that results when alcohol hampers attention, leading people to respond in simple ways to complex situations. (p. 210)

**alexithymia** A low emotional intelligence whereby a person has difficulty identifying and describing their own emotions, and in appreciating the emotional states of others. (p. 406)

**algorithm** A well-defined sequence of procedures or rules that guarantees a solution to a problem. (p. 375)

**altered state of consciousness** A form of experience that departs significantly from the normal subjective experience of the world and the mind. (p. 194)

**altruism** Behaviour that benefits another without benefitting oneself. (p. 516)

**amygdala** A part of the limbic system that plays a central role in many emotional processes, particularly the formation of emotional memories. (p. 99)

**analogical problem solving** Solving a problem by finding a similar problem with a known solution and applying that solution to the current problem. (p. 383)

**anal stage** The second psychosexual stage, in which experience is dominated by the pleasures and frustrations associated with the anus, retention and expulsion of feces and urine, and toilet training. (p. 487)

**anorexia nervosa** An eating disorder characterized by an intense fear of being fat and severe restriction of food intake. (p. 335)

**antagonists** Drugs that block the function of a neurotransmitter. (p. 88)

**anterograde amnesia** The inability to transfer new information from the short-term store into the long-term store. (p. 232)

**anti-anxiety medications** Drugs that help reduce a person's experience of fear or anxiety. (p. 649)

**antidepressants** A class of drugs that help lift people's moods. (p. 649)

**antipsychotic drugs** Medications that are used to treat schizophrenia and related psychotic disorders. (p. 646)

**antisocial personality disorder (APD)** A pervasive pattern of disregard for and violation of the rights of others that begins in childhood or early adolescence and continues into adulthood. (p. 620)

**anxiety disorder** The class of mental disorder in which anxiety is the predominant feature. (p. 593)

**aphasia** Difficulty in producing or comprehending language. (p. 362)

**apparent motion** The perception of movement as a result of alternating signals appearing in rapid succession in different locations. (p. 154)

**appraisal** An evaluation of the emotion-relevant aspects of a stimulus. (p. 319)

**approach motivation** A motivation to experience a positive outcome. (p. 345)

**area A1** A portion of the temporal lobe that contains the primary auditory cortex. (p. 160)

**area V1** The part of the occipital lobe that contains the primary visual cortex. (p. 141)

**assimilation** The process by which infants apply their schemas in novel situations. (p. 434)

**association areas** Areas of the cerebral cortex that are composed of neurons that help provide sense and meaning to information registered in the cortex. (p. 102)

**attachment** The emotional bond that forms between newborns and their primary caregivers. (p. 444)

**attention-deficit/hyperactivity disorder (ADHD)** A persistent pattern of severe problems with inattention and/or hyperactivity or impulsiveness that cause significant impairments in functioning. (p. 616)

**attitude** An enduring positive or negative evaluation of an object or event. (p. 533)

**attribution** An inference about the cause of a person's behaviour. (p. 543)

**autism spectrum disorder (ASD)** A condition beginning in early childhood in which a person shows persistent communication deficits as well as restricted and repetitive patterns of behaviours, interests, or activities. (p. 614)

**autonomic nervous system (ANS)** A set of nerves that carries involuntary and automatic commands that control blood vessels, body organs, and glands. (p. 93)

**availability bias** Items that are more readily available in memory are judged as having occurred more frequently. (p. 375)

**avoidance motivation** A motivation not to experience a negative outcome. (p. 345)

**axon** The part of a neuron that carries information to other neurons, muscles, or glands. (p. 82)

**balanced placebo design** A study design in which behaviour is observed following the presence or absence of an actual stimulus and also following the presence or absence of a placebo stimulus. (p. 210)

**basal ganglia** A set of subcortical structures that directs intentional movements. (p. 100)

**basilar membrane** A structure in the inner ear that undulates when vibrations from the ossicles reach the cochlear fluid. (p. 159)

**behaviour** Observable actions of human beings and nonhuman animals. (p. 3)

**behaviour therapy** A type of therapy that assumes that disordered behaviour is learned and that symptom relief is achieved through changing overt maladaptive behaviours into more constructive behaviours. (p. 637)

**behavioural neuroscience** An approach to psychology that links psychological processes to activities in the nervous system and other bodily processes. (p. 24)

**behaviourism** An approach that advocates that psychologists restrict themselves to the scientific study of objectively observable behaviour. (p. 16)

**belief** An enduring piece of knowledge about an object or event. (p. 533)

**belief bias** People's judgments about whether to accept conclusions depend more on how believable the conclusions are than on whether the arguments are logically valid. (p. 390)

**bias** The distorting influences of present knowledge, beliefs, and feelings on recollection of previous experiences. (p. 257)

**Big Five** The traits of the five-factor model: openness to experience, conscientiousness, extraversion, agreeableness, and neuroticism. (p. 479)

**binding problem** How features are linked together so that we see unified objects in our visual world rather than free-floating or mis-combined features. (p. 144)

**binocular disparity** The difference in the retinal images of the two eyes that provides information about depth. (p. 152)

**biofeedback** The use of an external monitoring device to obtain information about a bodily function and possibly gain control over that function. (p. 564)

**biological preparedness** A propensity for learning particular kinds of associations over others. (p. 276)

**biopsychosocial perspective** Explains mental disorders as the result of interactions among biological, psychological, and social factors. (p. 589)

**bipolar disorder** A condition characterized by cycles of abnormal, persistent high mood (mania) and low mood (depression). (p. 605)

**blind spot** A location in the visual field that produces no sensation on the retina. (p. 139)

**blocking** A failure to retrieve information that is available in memory even though you are trying to produce it. (p. 252)

**bulimia nervosa** An eating disorder characterized by binge eating followed by purging. (p. 335)

**burnout** A state of physical, emotional, and mental exhaustion created by long-term involvement in an emotionally demanding situation and accompanied by lowered performance and motivation. (p. 559)

**bystander intervention** The act of helping strangers in an emergency situation. (p. 515)

**Cannon–Bard theory** The theory that a stimulus simultaneously triggers activity in the body and emotional experience in the brain. (p. 316)

**case method** A procedure for gathering scientific information by studying a single individual. (p. 64)

**catatonic behaviour** A marked decrease in all movement or an increase in muscular rigidity and overactivity. (p. 609)

**category-specific deficit** A neurological syndrome that is characterized by an inability to recognize objects that belong to a particular category, although the ability to recognize objects outside the category is undisturbed. (p. 372)

**cell body (or soma)** The part of a neuron that coordinates information-processing tasks and keeps the cell alive. (p. 81)

**central nervous system (CNS)** The part of the nervous system that is composed of the brain and spinal cord. (p. 92)

**cephalocaudal rule** The "top-to-bottom" rule that describes the tendency for motor skills to emerge in sequence from the head to the feet. (p. 432)

**cerebellum** A large structure of the hindbrain that controls fine motor skills. (p. 97)

**cerebral cortex** The outermost layer of the brain, visible to the naked eye and divided into two hemispheres. (p. 97)

**change blindness** When people fail to detect changes to the visual details of a scene. (p. 154)

**childhood** The stage of development that begins at about 18 to 24 months and lasts until about 11 to 14 years. (p. 435)

**chromosomes** Strands of DNA wound around each other in a double-helix configuration. (p. 108)

**chronic stressors** Sources of stress that occur continuously or repeatedly. (p. 551)

**chunking** Combining small pieces of information into larger clusters or chunks that are more easily held in short-term memory. (p. 229)

**circadian rhythm** A naturally occurring 24-hour cycle. (p. 195)

**classical conditioning** A type of learning that occurs when a neutral stimulus produces a response after being paired with a stimulus that naturally produces a response. (p. 267)

**cochlea** A fluid-filled tube that is the organ of auditory transduction. (p. 159)

**cognitive behavioural therapy (CBT)** A blend of cognitive and behavioural therapeutic strategies. (p. 641)

**cognitive development** The emergence of the ability to think and understand. (p. 433)

**cognitive dissonance** An unpleasant state that arises when a person recognizes the inconsistency of his or her actions, attitudes, or beliefs. (p. 535)

**cognitive map** A mental representation of the physical features of the environment. (p. 289)

**cognitive neuroscience** The field of study that attempts to understand the links between cognitive processes and brain activity. (p. 25)

**cognitive psychology** The scientific study of mental processes, including perception, thought, memory, and reasoning. (p. 23)

**cognitive restructuring** A therapeutic approach that teaches clients to question the automatic beliefs, assumptions, and predictions that often lead to negative emotions and to replace negative thinking with more realistic and positive beliefs. (p. 639)

**cognitive symptoms** Deficits in cognitive abilities, specifically executive functioning, attention, and working memory. (p. 609)

**cognitive therapy** Focuses on helping a client identify and correct any distorted thinking about self, others, or the world. (p. 639)

**cognitive unconscious** All the mental processes that give rise to a person's thoughts, choices, emotions, and behaviour even though they are not experienced by the person. (p. 191)

**colour-opponent system** Pairs of visual neurons that work in opposition. (p. 141)

**common knowledge effect** The tendency for group discussions to focus on information that all members share. (p. 514)

**comorbidity** The co-occurrence of two or more disorders in a single individual. (p. 587)

**companionate love** An experience involving affection, trust, and concern for a partner's well-being. (p. 524)

**comparison level** The outcome people believe they should receive, in terms of rewards and costs, from their relationship. (p. 524)

**comparison level for alternatives** The availability, and the cost–benefit ratio, of an alternative outcome. (p. 524)

**concept** A mental representation that groups or categorizes shared features of related objects, events, or other stimuli. (p. 369)

**concrete operational stage** The stage of cognitive development that begins at about 6 years and ends at about 11 years, during which children learn how various actions or "operations" can affect or transform "concrete" objects. (p. 436)

**conditioned response (CR)** A reaction that resembles an unconditioned response but is produced by a CS. (p. 268)

**conditioned stimulus (CS)** A previously neutral stimulus that produces a reliable response in an organism after being paired with a US. (p. 268)

**conduct disorder** A persistent pattern of deviant behaviour involving aggression to people or animals, destruction of property, deceitfulness or theft, or serious rule violations. (p. 617)

**cones** Photoreceptors that detect colour, operate under normal daylight conditions, and allow us to focus on fine detail. (p. 139)

**conformity** The tendency to do what others do simply because others are doing it. (p. 528)

**conjunction fallacy** When people think that two events are more likely to occur together than either individual event. (p. 376)

**conscious motivations** Motivations of which people are aware. (p. 344)

**consciousness** A person's subjective experience of the world and the mind. (pp. 8, 178)

**conservation** The notion that the quantitative properties of an object are invariant despite changes in the object's appearance. (p. 436)

**consolidation** The process by which memories become stable in the brain. (p. 232)

**control group** The group of people who are not exposed to the particular manipulation, as compared to the experimental group, in an experiment. (p. 58)

**conventional stage** A stage of moral development in which the morality of an action is primarily determined by the extent to which it conforms to social rules. (p. 448)

**cooperation** Behaviour by two or more individuals that leads to mutual benefit. (p. 512)

**corpus callosum** A thick band of nerve fibres that connects large areas of the cerebral cortex on each side of the brain and supports communication of information across the hemispheres. (p. 100)

**correlation** Two variables are said to "covary" or "be correlated" when variations in the value of one variable are synchronized with variations in the value of the other. (p. 52)

**correlation coefficient** A mathematical measure of both the direction and strength of a correlation, which is symbolized by the letter *r*. (p. 53)

**correspondence bias** The tendency to make a dispositional attribution even when we should instead make a situational attribution. (p. 544)

**crystallized intelligence** The ability to retain and use knowledge that was acquired through experience. (p. 404)

**cultural psychology** The study of how cultures reflect and shape the psychological processes of their members. (p. 28)

**debriefing** A verbal description of the true nature and purpose of a study. (p. 71)

**deep structure** The meaning of a sentence. (p. 354)

**defence mechanisms** Unconscious coping mechanisms that reduce anxiety generated by threats from unacceptable impulses. (p. 486)

**deindividuation** A phenomenon that occurs when immersion in a group causes people to become less aware of their individual values. (p. 514)

**delusion** A patently false belief system, often bizarre and grandiose, that is maintained in spite of its irrationality. (p. 608)

**demand characteristics** Those aspects of an observational setting that cause people to behave as they think someone else wants or expects. (p. 44)

**dendrite** The part of a neuron that receives information from other neurons and relays it to the cell body. (p. 81)

**dependent variable** The variable that is measured in a study. (p. 58)

**depressants** Substances that reduce the activity of the central nervous system. (p. 209)

**developmental psychology** The study of continuity and change across the life span. (p. 426)

**deviation IQ** A statistic obtained by dividing a person's test score by the average test score of people in the same age group and then multiplying the quotient by 100 (see *ratio IQ*). (p. 398)

***Diagnostic and Statistical Manual of Mental Disorders (DSM)*** A classification system that describes the features used to diagnose each recognized mental disorder and indicates how the disorder can be distinguished from other, similar problems. (p. 587)

**diathesis–stress model** Suggests that a person may be predisposed for a psychological disorder that remains unexpressed until triggered by stress. (p. 590)

**dichotic listening** A task in which people wearing headphones hear different messages presented to each ear. (p. 182)

**diffusion chain** A process in which individuals initially learn a behaviour by observing another individual perform that behaviour, and then serve as a model from which other individuals learn the behaviour. (p. 296)

**diffusion of responsibility** The tendency for individuals to feel diminished responsibility for their actions when they are surrounded by others who are acting the same way. (p. 514)

**discrimination** The capacity to distinguish between similar but distinct stimuli. (p. 271)

**discrimination** Positive or negative behaviour toward another person based on his or her group membership. (p. 513)

**disorganized speech** A severe disruption of verbal communication in which ideas shift rapidly and incoherently among unrelated topics. (p. 608)

**display rule** A norm for the appropriate expression of emotion. (p. 327)

**DNA methylation** Adding a methyl group to DNA. (p. 110)

**door-in-the-face technique** An influence strategy that involves getting someone to deny an initial request (p. 528)

**dopamine** A neurotransmitter that regulates motor behaviour, motivation, pleasure, and emotional arousal. (p. 88)

**dopamine hypothesis** The idea that schizophrenia involves an excess of dopamine activity. (p. 610)

**double-blind** An observation whose true purpose is hidden from both the observer and the person being observed. (p. 47)

**double depression** A moderately depressed mood that persists for at least 2 years and is punctuated by periods of major depression. (p. 601)

**drive** An internal state caused by physiological needs. (p. 333)

**drug tolerance** The tendency for larger doses of a drug to be required over time to achieve the same effect. (p. 207)

**dynamic unconscious** An active system encompassing a lifetime of hidden memories, the person's deepest instincts and desires, and the person's inner struggle to control these forces. (pp. 190, 485)

**dysthymia** The same cognitive and bodily problems as in depression are present, but they are less severe and last longer, persisting for at least 2 years. (p. 601)

**echoic memory** A fast-decaying store of auditory information. (p. 228)

**ego** The component of personality, developed through contact with the external world, that enables us to deal with life's practical demands. (p. 485)

**egocentrism** The failure to understand that the world appears differently to different people. (p. 437)

**electroconvulsive therapy (ECT)** A treatment that involves inducing a brief seizure by delivering an electrical shock to the brain. (p. 655)

**electroencephalograph (EEG)** A device used to record electrical activity in the brain. (p. 119)

**electrooculograph (EOG)** An instrument that measures eye movements. (p. 195)

**embryonic stage** The period of prenatal development that lasts from the second week until about the eighth week. (p. 426)

**emotion** A positive or negative experience that is associated with a particular pattern of physiological activity. (p. 316)

**emotional expression** An observable sign of an emotional state. (p. 322)

**emotional intelligence** The ability to reason about emotions and to use emotions to enhance reasoning. (p. 406)

**emotion regulation** The strategies people use to influence their own emotional experience. (p. 320)

**empirical method** A set of rules and techniques for observation. (p. 42)

**empiricism** The belief that accurate knowledge can be acquired through observation. (p. 40)

**encoding** The process of transforming what we perceive, think, or feel into an enduring memory. (p. 222)

**encoding specificity principle** The idea that a retrieval cue can serve as an effective reminder when it helps re-create the specific way in which information was initially encoded. (p. 237)

**endorphins** Chemicals that act within the pain pathways and emotion centres of the brain. (p. 88)

**epigenetic marks** Chemical modifications to DNA that can turn genes on or off. (p. 110)

**epigenetics** Environmental influences that determine whether or not genes are expressed, or the degree to which they are expressed, without altering the basic DNA sequences that constitute the genes themselves. (p. 110)

**episodic memory** The collection of past personal experiences that occurred at a particular time and place. (p. 244)

**equity** A state of affairs in which the cost–benefit ratios of two partners are roughly equal. (p. 524)

**evolutionary psychology** A psychological approach that explains mind and behaviour in terms of the adaptive value of abilities that are preserved over time by natural selection. (p. 25)

**exemplar theory** A theory of categorization that argues that we make category judgments by comparing a new instance with stored memories for other instances of the category. (p. 371)

**existential approach** A school of thought that regards personality as governed by an individual's ongoing choices and decisions in the context of the realities of life and death. (p. 489)

**expectancy theory** The idea that alcohol effects can be produced by people's expectations of how alcohol will influence them in particular situations. (p. 210)

**experiment** A technique for establishing the causal relationship between variables. (p. 56)

**experimental group** The group of people who are exposed to a particular manipulation, as compared to the control group, in an experiment. (p. 58)

**explicit memory** The act of consciously or intentionally retrieving past experiences. (p. 243)

**exposure therapy** An approach to treatment that involves confronting an emotion-arousing stimulus directly and repeatedly, ultimately leading to a decrease in the emotional response. (p. 638)

**expressed emotion** A measure of how much hostility, criticism, and emotional over-involvement are used when speaking about a family member with a mental disorder. (p. 607)

**external validity** An attribute of an experiment in which variables have been defined in a normal, typical, or realistic way. (p. 62)

**extinction** The gradual elimination of a learned response that occurs when the CS is repeatedly presented without the US. (p. 271)

**extrinsic motivation** A motivation to take actions that lead to reward. (p. 343)

**facial feedback hypothesis** Emotional expressions can cause the emotional experiences they signify. (p. 324)

**factor analysis** A statistical technique that explains a large number of correlations in terms of a small number of underlying factors. (p. 401)

**false recognition** A feeling of familiarity about something that has not been encountered before. (p. 252)

**family resemblance theory** Members of a category have features that appear to be characteristic of category members but may not be possessed by every member. (p. 370)

**fast mapping** The fact that children can map a word onto an underlying concept after only a single exposure. (p. 357)

**feature-integration theory** The idea that focused attention is not required to detect the individual features that comprise a stimulus, but is required to bind those individual features together. (p. 145)

**fetal alcohol spectrum disorder (FASD)** A developmental disorder that stems from heavy alcohol use by the mother during pregnancy. (p. 428)

**fetal stage** The period of prenatal development that lasts from the ninth week until birth. (p. 428)

**fight-or-flight response** An emotional and physiological reaction to an emergency that increases readiness for action. (p. 555)

**fixation** A phenomenon in which a person's pleasure-seeking drives become psychologically stuck, or arrested, at a particular psychosexual stage. (p. 487)

**fixed-interval schedule (FI)** An operant conditioning principle in which reinforcers are presented at fixed-time periods, provided that the appropriate response is made. (p. 283)

**fixed-ratio schedule (FR)** An operant conditioning principle in which reinforcement is delivered after a specific number of responses have been made. (p. 285)

**flashbulb memories** Detailed recollections of when and where we heard about shocking events. (p. 258)

**fluid intelligence** The ability to see abstract relationships and draw logical inferences. (p. 404)

**foot-in-the-door technique** A technique that involves making a small request and following it with a larger request. (p. 535)

**formal operational stage** The final stage of cognitive development that begins around the age of 11, during which children learn to reason about abstract concepts. (p. 437)

**fovea** An area of the retina where vision is the clearest and there are no rods at all. (p. 139)

**framing effects** When people give different answers to the same problem depending on how the problem is phrased (or framed). (p. 377)

**fraternal twins (or dizygotic twins)** Twins who develop from two different eggs that were fertilized by two different sperm (see *identical twins*). (p. 408)

**frequency distribution** A graphical representation of measurements arranged by the number of times each measurement was made. (p. 48)

**frequency format hypothesis** The proposal that our minds evolved to notice how frequently things occur, not how likely they are to occur. (p. 379)

**frontal lobe** A region of the cerebral cortex that has specialized areas for movement, abstract thinking, planning, memory, and judgment. (p. 102)

**frustration–aggression hypothesis** A principle stating that animals aggress when their goals are thwarted. (p. 509)

**full consciousness** Consciousness in which you know and are able to report your mental state. (p. 184)

**functional fixedness** The tendency to perceive the functions of objects as fixed. (p. 384)

**functionalism** The study of the purpose mental processes serve in enabling people to adapt to their environment. (p. 11)

**GABA (gamma-aminobutyric acid)** The primary inhibitory neurotransmitter in the brain. (p. 88)

**gate-control theory of pain** A theory of pain perception based on the idea that signals arriving from pain receptors in the body can be stopped, or gated, by interneurons in the spinal cord via feedback from two directions. (p. 166)

**gateway drug** A drug whose use increases the risk of the subsequent use of more harmful drugs. (p. 214)

**gene** The major unit of hereditary transmission. (p. 108)

**general adaptation syndrome (GAS)** A three-stage physiological stress response that appears regardless of the stressor that is encountered. (p. 555)

**generalization** The CR is elicited even though the CS is slightly different from the CS used during acquisition. (p. 271)

**generalized anxiety disorder (GAD)** A disorder characterized by chronic excessive worry accompanied by three or more of the following symptoms: restlessness, fatigue, concentration problems, irritability, muscle tension, and sleep disturbance. (p. 597)

**genetic dysphasia** A syndrome characterized by an inability to learn the grammatical structure of language despite having otherwise normal intelligence. (p. 360)

**genital stage** The fifth and final psychosexual stage, the time for the coming together of the mature adult personality with a capacity to love, work, and relate to others in a mutually satisfying and reciprocal manner. (p. 488)

**germinal stage** The 2-week period of prenatal development that begins at conception. (p. 426)

**Gestalt psychology** A psychological approach that emphasizes that we often perceive the whole rather than the sum of the parts. (p. 21)

**gestalt therapy** Has the goal of helping the client become aware of his or her thoughts, behaviours, experiences, and feelings and to "own" or take responsibility for them. (p. 637)

**glial cells** Support cells found in the nervous system. (p. 82)

**glutamate** The major excitatory neurotransmitter in the brain. (p. 88)

**grammar** A set of rules that specify how the units of language can be combined to produce meaningful messages. (p. 352)

**grossly disorganized behaviour** Behaviour that is inappropriate for the situation or ineffective in attaining goals, often with specific motor disturbances. (p. 608)

**group** A collection of people who have something in common that distinguishes them from others. (p. 513)

**group polarization** The tendency for groups to make decisions that are more extreme than any member would have made alone. (p. 514)

**group therapy** A technique in which multiple participants (who often do not know one another at the outset) work on their individual problems in a group atmosphere. (p. 643)

**groupthink** The tendency for groups to reach consensus in order to facilitate interpersonal harmony. (p. 514)

**habituation** A general process in which repeated or prolonged exposure to a stimulus results in a gradual reduction in responding. (p. 266)

**hair cells** Specialized auditory receptor neurons embedded in the basilar membrane. (p. 159)

**hallucination** A false perceptual experience that has a compelling sense of being real despite the absence of external stimulation. (p. 608)

**hallucinogens** Drugs that alter sensation and perception, and often cause visual and auditory hallucinations. (p. 213)

**haptic perception** The active exploration of the environment by touching and grasping objects with our hands. (p. 164)

**health psychology** The subfield of psychology concerned with ways psychological factors influence the causes and treatment of physical illness and the maintenance of health. (p. 550)

**hedonic principle** The claim that people are motivated to experience pleasure and avoid pain. (p. 332)

**helplessness theory** The idea that individuals who are prone to depression automatically attribute negative experiences to causes that are internal (i.e., their own fault), stable (i.e., unlikely to change), and global (i.e., widespread). (p. 604)

**heritability** A measure of the variability of behavioural traits among individuals that can be accounted for by genetic factors. (p. 111)

**heritability coefficient** A statistic (commonly denoted as $h^2$) that describes the proportion of the difference among people in a given population that can be explained by differences in their genes. (p. 409)

**heuristic** A fast and efficient strategy that may facilitate decision making but does not guarantee that a solution will be reached. (p. 375)

**heuristic persuasion** The process by which attitudes or beliefs are changed by appeals to habit or emotion. (p. 534)

**hindbrain** An area of the brain that coordinates information coming into and out of the spinal cord. (p. 97)

**hippocampus** A structure critical for creating new memories and integrating them into a network of knowledge so that they can be stored indefinitely in other parts of the cerebral cortex. (p. 99)

**histone modification** Adding chemical modifications to proteins called histones that are involved in packaging DNA. (p. 110)

**homeostasis** The tendency for a system to take action to keep itself in a particular state. (p. 333)

**humanistic psychology** An approach to understanding human nature that emphasizes the positive potential of human beings. (p. 15)

**human sexual response cycle** The stages of physiological arousal during sexual activity. (p. 340)

**hypnosis** A social interaction in which one person (the hypnotist) makes suggestions that lead to a change in another person's (the subject's) subjective experience of the world. (p. 214)

**hypnotic analgesia** The reduction of pain through hypnosis in people who are susceptible to hypnosis. (p. 216)

**hypothalamus** A subcortical structure that regulates body temperature, hunger, thirst, and sexual behaviour. (p. 98)

**hypothesis** A falsifiable prediction made by a theory. (p. 40)

**hysteria** A temporary loss of cognitive or motor functions, usually as a result of emotionally upsetting experiences. (p. 13)

**iatrogenic illness** A disorder or symptom that occurs as a result of a medical or psychotherapeutic treatment itself. (p. 660)

**iconic memory** A fast-decaying store of visual information. (p. 228)

**id** The part of the mind containing the drives present at birth; it is the source of our bodily needs, wants, desires, and impulses, particularly our sexual and aggressive drives. (p. 485)

**identical twins (or monozygotic twins)** Twins who develop from the splitting of a single egg that was fertilized by a single sperm (see *fraternal twins*). (p. 408)

**illusions** Errors of perception, memory, or judgment in which subjective experience differs from objective reality. (p. 21)

**illusory conjunction** A perceptual mistake where features from multiple objects are incorrectly combined. (p. 145)

**immune system** A complex response system that protects the body from bacteria, viruses, and other foreign substances. (p. 557)

**implicit learning** Learning that takes place largely independent of awareness of both the process and the products of information acquisition. (p. 301)

**implicit memory** The influence of past experiences on later behaviour and performance, even without an effort to remember them or an awareness of the recollection. (p. 243)

**inattentional blindness** A failure to perceive objects that are not the focus of attention. (p. 154)

**independent variable** The variable that is manipulated in an experiment. (p. 58)

**infancy** The stage of development that begins at birth and lasts between 18 and 24 months. (p. 431)

**informational influence** A phenomenon that occurs when another person's behaviour provides information about what is true. (p. 533)

**informed consent** A written agreement to participate in a study made by an adult who has been informed of all the risks that participation may entail. (p. 71)

**insomnia** Difficulty in falling asleep or staying asleep. (p. 199)

**instrument** Anything that can detect the condition to which an operational definition refers. (p. 44)

**intelligence** The ability to direct one's thinking, adapt to one's circumstances, and learn from one's experiences. (p. 396)

**intermittent reinforcement** An operant conditioning principle in which only some of the responses made are followed by reinforcement. (p. 285)

**intermittent reinforcement effect** The fact that operant behaviours that are maintained under intermittent reinforcement schedules resist extinction better than those maintained under continuous reinforcement. (p. 287)

**internal validity** An attribute of an experiment that allows it to establish causal relationships. (p. 62)

**internal working model of relationships** A set of beliefs about the self, the primary caregiver, and the relationship between them. (p. 446)

**interneurons** Neurons that connect sensory neurons, motor neurons, or other interneurons. (p. 83)

**interpersonal psychotherapy (IPT)** A form of psychotherapy that focuses on helping clients improve current relationships. (p. 635)

**intrinsic motivation** A motivation to take actions that are themselves rewarding. (p. 343)

**introspection** The subjective observation of one's own experience. (p. 8)

**ironic processes of mental control** Mental processes that can produce ironic errors because monitoring for errors can itself produce them. (p. 189)

**James–Lange theory** The theory that a stimulus triggers activity in the body, which in turn produces an emotional experience in the brain. (p. 316)

**just noticeable difference (JND)** The minimal change in a stimulus that can just barely be detected. (p. 132)

**kin selection** The process by which evolution selects for individuals who cooperate with their relatives. (p. 516)

**language** A system for communicating with others using signals that are combined according to rules of grammar and convey meaning. (p. 352)

**language acquisition device (LAD)** A collection of processes that facilitate language learning. (p. 360)

**latency stage** The fourth psychosexual stage, in which the primary focus is on the further development of intellectual, creative, interpersonal, and athletic skills. (p. 487)

**latent content** A dream's true underlying meaning. (p. 202)

**latent learning** Something is learned, but it is not manifested as a behavioural change until sometime in the future. (p. 289)

**law of effect** Behaviours that are followed by a "satisfying state of affairs" tend to be repeated and those that produce an "unpleasant state of affairs" are less likely to be repeated. (p. 278)

**learning** The acquisition of new knowledge, skills, or responses from experience that results in a relatively permanent change in the state of the learner. (p. 266)

**limbic system** A group of forebrain structures including the hypothalamus, the hippocampus, and the amygdala, which are involved in motivation, emotion, learning, and memory. (p. 99)

**linguistic relativity hypothesis** The proposal that language shapes the nature of thought. (p. 367)

**locus of control** A person's tendency to perceive the control of rewards as internal to the self or external in the environment. (p. 493)

**long-term memory** A type of storage that holds information for hours, days, weeks, or years. (p. 230)

**long-term potentiation (LTP)** A process whereby communication across the synapse between neurons strengthens the connection, making further communication easier. (p. 235)

**loudness** A sound's intensity. (p. 158)

**lymphocytes** White blood cells (including T cells and B cells) that produce antibodies that fight infection. (p. 557)

**major depressive disorder (or unipolar depression)** A disorder characterized by a severely depressed mood and/or inability to experience pleasure that lasts 2 or more weeks and is accompanied by feelings of worthlessness, lethargy, and sleep and appetite disturbance. (p. 601)

**manifest content** A dream's apparent topic or superficial meaning. (p. 202)

**manipulation** Changing a variable in order to determine its causal power. (p. 58)

**marijuana (or cannabis)** The leaves and buds of the hemp plant, which contain a psychoactive drug called tetrahydrocannabinol (THC). (p. 211)

**matched pairs technique** A technique whereby each participant is identical to one other participant in terms of a third variable. (p. 56)

**matched samples technique** A technique whereby the participants in two groups are identical in terms of a third variable. (p. 55)

**mean** The average value of all the measurements. (p. 49)

**means–ends analysis** A process of searching for the means or steps to reduce differences between the current situation and the desired goal. (p. 383)

**median** The value that is in the middle, that is, greater than or equal to half the measurements and less than or equal to half the measurements. (p. 49)

**medical model** Abnormal psychological experiences are conceptualized as illnesses that, like physical illnesses, have biological and environmental causes, defined symptoms, and possible cures. (p. 585)

**meditation** The practice of intentional contemplation. (p. 563)

**medulla** An extension of the spinal cord into the skull that coordinates heart rate, circulation, and respiration. (p. 97)

**memory** The ability to store and retrieve information over time. (p. 222)

**memory misattribution** Assigning a recollection or an idea to the wrong source. (p. 252)

**mental control** The attempt to change conscious states of mind. (p. 188)

**mental disorder** A persistent disturbance or dysfunction in behaviour, thoughts, or emotions that causes significant distress or impairment. (p. 584)

**mere exposure effect** The tendency for liking to increase with the frequency of exposure. (p. 519)

**metabolism** The rate at which energy is used by the body. (p. 338)

**mind** The private inner experience of perceptions, thoughts, memories, and feelings. (p. 3)

**mind–body problem** The issue of how the mind is related to the brain and the body. (p. 181)

**mindfulness meditation** Teaches an individual to be fully present in each moment; to be aware of his or her thoughts, feelings, and sensations; and to detect symptoms before they become a problem. (p. 641)

**minimal consciousness** A low-level kind of sensory awareness and responsiveness that occurs when the mind inputs sensations and may output behaviour. (p. 184)

**Minnesota Multiphasic Personality Inventory (MMPI)** A well-researched, clinical questionnaire used to assess personality and psychological problems. (p. 474)

**mirror neurons** Neurons that are active when an animal performs a behaviour, such as reaching for or manipulating an object, and are also activated when another animal observes that animal performing the same behaviour. (p. 103)

**mode** The value of the most frequently observed measurement. (p. 49)

**monocular depth cues** Aspects of a scene that yield information about depth when viewed with only one eye. (p. 150)

**mood disorders** Mental disorders that have mood disturbance as their predominant feature. (p. 601)

**morphemes** The smallest meaningful units of language. (p. 353)

**morphological rules** A set of rules that indicate how morphemes can be combined to form words. (p. 353)

**motivation** The purpose for or psychological cause of an action. (p. 331)

**motor development** The emergence of the ability to execute physical action. (p. 431)

**motor neurons** Neurons that carry signals from the spinal cord to the muscles to produce movement. (p. 82)

**myelination** The formation of a fatty sheath around the axons of a neuron. (p. 428)

**myelin sheath** An insulating layer of fatty material. (p. 82)

**narcissism** A trait that reflects a grandiose view of the self combined with a tendency to seek admiration from and exploit others. (p. 501)

**narcolepsy** A disorder in which sudden sleep attacks occur in the middle of waking activities. (p. 200)

**narcotics (or opiates)** Highly addictive drugs derived from opium that relieve pain. (p. 212)

**nativism** The philosophical view that certain kinds of knowledge are innate or inborn. (p. 6)

**nativist theory** The view that language development is best explained as an innate, biological capacity. (p. 360)

**natural correlation** A correlation observed in the world around us. (p. 55)

**naturalistic observation** A technique for gathering scientific information by unobtrusively observing people in their natural environments. (p. 44)

**natural selection** Charles Darwin's theory that the features of an organism that help it survive and reproduce are more likely than other features to be passed on to subsequent generations. (p. 11)

**need for achievement** The motivation to solve worthwhile problems. (p. 344)

**negative symptoms** Deficits or disruptions to normal emotions and behaviours (e.g., emotional and social withdrawal; apathy; poverty of speech; and other indications of the absence or insufficiency of normal behaviour, motivation, and emotion). (p. 609)

**nervous system** An interacting network of neurons that conveys electrochemical information throughout the body. (p. 92)

**neurons** Cells in the nervous system that communicate with one another to perform information-processing tasks. (p. 80)

**neurotransmitters** Chemicals that transmit information across the synapse to a receiving neuron's dendrites. (p. 86)

**night terrors (or sleep terrors)** Abrupt awakenings with panic and intense emotional arousal. (p. 200)

**nonshared environment** Those environmental factors that are not experienced by all relevant members of a household (see *shared environment*). (p. 411)

**non-suicidal self-injury (NSSI)** Direct, deliberate destruction of body tissue in the absence of any intent to die. (p. 623)

**norepinephrine** A neurotransmitter that is particularly involved in states of vigilance, or heightened awareness of dangers in the environment. (p. 88)

**normal distribution** A mathematically defined distribution in which the frequency of measurements is highest in the middle and decreases symmetrically in both directions. (p. 48)

**normative influence** A phenomenon that occurs when another person's behaviour provides information about what is appropriate. (p. 528)

**norm of reciprocity** The unwritten rule that people should benefit those who have benefitted them. (p. 528)

**norms** Customary standards for behaviour that are widely shared by members of a culture. (p. 528)

**obedience** The tendency to do what powerful people tell us to do. (p. 531)

**object permanence** The belief that objects continue to exist even when they are not visible. (p. 434)

**observational learning** A condition in which learning takes place by watching the actions of others. (p. 295)

**obsessive-compulsive disorder (OCD)** A disorder in which repetitive, intrusive thoughts (obsessions) and ritualistic behaviours (compulsions) designed to fend off those thoughts interfere significantly with an individual's functioning. (p. 598)

**occipital lobe** A region of the cerebral cortex that processes visual information. (p. 100)

**Oedipus conflict** A developmental experience in which a child's conflicting feelings toward the opposite-sex parent are (usually) resolved by identifying with the same-sex parent. (p. 487)

**olfactory bulb** A brain structure located above the nasal cavity beneath the frontal lobes. (p. 169)

**olfactory receptor neurons (ORNs)** Receptor cells that initiate the sense of smell. (p. 168)

**operant behaviour** Behaviour that an organism produces that has some impact on the environment. (p. 278)

**operant conditioning** A type of learning in which the consequences of an organism's behaviour determine whether it will be repeated in the future. (p. 277)

**operational definition** A description of a property in concrete, measurable terms. (p. 44)

**oral stage** The first psychosexual stage, in which experience centres on the pleasures and frustrations associated with the mouth, sucking, and being fed. (p. 487)

**organizational encoding** The process of categorizing information according to the relationships among a series of items. (p. 224)

**outcome expectancies** A person's assumptions about the likely consequences of a future behaviour. (p. 493)

**panic disorder** A disorder characterized by the sudden occurrence of multiple psychological and physiological symptoms that contribute to a feeling of stark terror. (p. 596)

**parasympathetic nervous system** A set of nerves that helps the body return to a normal resting state. (p. 94)

**parietal lobe** A region of the cerebral cortex whose functions include processing information about touch. (p. 101)

**passionate love** An experience involving feelings of euphoria, intimacy, and intense sexual attraction. (p. 524)

**perception** The organization, identification, and interpretation of a sensation in order to form a mental representation. (p. 131)

**perceptual confirmation** The tendency for people to see what they expect to see. (p. 541)

**perceptual constancy** A perceptual principle stating that even as aspects of sensory signals change, perception remains consistent. (p. 147)

**peripheral nervous system (PNS)** The part of the nervous system that connects the central nervous system to the body's organs and muscles. (p. 92)

**persistence** The intrusive recollection of events that we wish we could forget. (p. 257)

**personal constructs** Dimensions people use in making sense of their experiences. (p. 492)

**personality** An individual's characteristic style of behaving, thinking, and feeling. (p. 472)

**personality disorders** Enduring patterns of thinking, feeling, or relating to others or controlling impulses that deviate from cultural expectations and cause distress or impaired functioning. (p. 618)

**person-centred therapy (or client-centred therapy)** Assumes that all individuals have a tendency toward growth and that this growth can be facilitated by acceptance and genuine reactions from the therapist. (p. 636)

**person–situation controversy** The question of whether behaviour is caused more by personality or by situational factors. (p. 491)

**persuasion** A phenomenon that occurs when a person's attitudes or beliefs are influenced by a communication from another person. (p. 534)

**phallic stage** The third psychosexual stage, in which experience is dominated by the pleasure, conflict, and frustration associated with the phallic-genital region as well as coping with powerful incestuous feelings of love, hate, jealousy, and conflict. (p. 487)

**phenomenology** How things seem to the conscious person. (p. 179)

**pheromones** Biochemical odorants emitted by other members of its species that can affect an animal's behaviour or physiology. (p. 171)

**philosophical empiricism** The view that all knowledge is acquired through experience. (p. 6)

**phobic disorders** Disorders characterized by marked, persistent, and excessive fear and avoidance of specific objects, activities, or situations. (p. 594)

**phoneme** The smallest unit of sound that is recognizable as speech rather than as random noise. (p. 353)

**phonological rules** A set of rules that indicate how phonemes can be combined to produce speech sounds. (p. 353)

**phototherapy** A therapy that involves repeated exposure to bright light. (p. 655)

**phrenology** A now defunct theory that specific mental abilities and characteristics, ranging from memory to the capacity for happiness, are localized in specific regions of the brain. (p. 6)

**physiology** The study of biological processes, especially in the human body. (p. 7)

**pitch** How high or low or somewhere in between, a sound is. (p. 158)

**pituitary gland** The "master gland" of the body's hormone-producing system, which releases hormones that direct the functions of many other glands in the body. (p. 99)

**placebo** An inert substance or procedure that has been applied with the expectation that a healing response will be produced. (p. 657)

**place code** The process by which different frequencies stimulate neural signals at specific places along the basilar membrane. (p. 161)

**pons** A brain structure that relays information from the cerebellum to the rest of the brain. (p. 97)

**population** A complete collection of participants who might possibly be measured. (p. 63)

**positive symptoms** Thoughts and behaviours present in schizophrenia but not seen in those without the disorder, such as delusions and hallucinations. (p. 608)

**postconventional stage** A stage of moral development in which the morality of an action is determined by a set of general principles that reflect core values. (p. 448)

**posthypnotic amnesia** The failure to retrieve memories following hypnotic suggestions to forget. (p. 215)

**post-traumatic stress disorder (PTSD)** A disorder characterized by chronic physiological arousal, recurrent unwanted thoughts or images of the trauma, and avoidance of things that call the traumatic event to mind. (p. 599)

**power** An instrument's ability to detect small magnitudes of the property. (p. 44)

**practical reasoning** Figuring out what to do, or reasoning directed toward action. (p. 388)

**preconventional stage** A stage of moral development in which the morality of an action is primarily determined by its consequences for the actor. (p. 448)

**prejudice** A positive or negative evaluation of another person based on his or her group membership. (p. 513)

**pre-operational stage** The stage of cognitive development that begins at about 2 years and ends at about 6 years, during which children develop a preliminary understanding of the physical world. (p. 436)

**preparedness theory** The idea that people are instinctively predisposed toward certain fears. (p. 594)

**primary sex characteristics** Bodily structures that are directly involved in reproduction. (p. 452)

**priming** An enhanced ability to think of a stimulus, such as a word or object, as a result of a recent exposure to the stimulus. (p. 243)

**proactive interference** Situations in which information learned earlier impairs memory for information acquired later. (p. 250)

**problem of other minds** The fundamental difficulty we have in perceiving the consciousness of others. (p. 179)

**procedural memory** The gradual acquisition of skills as a result of practice, or "knowing how" to do things. (p. 243)

**projective tests** Tests designed to reveal inner aspects of individuals' personalities by analysis of their responses to a standard series of ambiguous stimuli. (p. 475)

**prospective memory** Remembering to do things in the future. (p. 250)

**prospect theory** People choose to take on risk when evaluating potential losses and avoid risks when evaluating potential gains. (p. 378)

**prototype** The "best" or "most typical" member of a category. (p. 370)

**proximodistal rule** The "inside-to-outside" rule that describes the tendency for motor skills to emerge in sequence from the centre to the periphery. (p. 432)

**psychoactive drugs** Chemicals that influence consciousness or behaviour by altering the brain's chemical message system. (p. 205)

**psychoanalysis** A therapeutic approach that focuses on bringing unconscious material into conscious awareness to better understand psychological disorders. (p. 14)

**psychoanalytic theory** An approach that emphasizes the importance of unconscious mental processes in shaping feelings, thoughts, and behaviour. (p. 13)

**psychodynamic approach** An approach that regards personality as formed by needs, strivings, and desires largely operating outside of awareness—motives that also can produce emotional disorders. (p. 484)

**psychodynamic psychotherapies** Therapies that explore childhood events and encourage individuals to use this understanding to develop insight into their psychological problems. (p. 634)

**psychology** The scientific study of mind and behaviour. (p. 3)

**psychopharmacology** The study of drug effects on psychological states and symptoms. (p. 648)

**psychophysics** Methods that measure the strength of a stimulus and the observer's sensitivity to that stimulus. (p. 132)

**psychosexual stages** Distinct early life stages through which personality is formed as children experience sexual pleasures from specific body areas and caregivers redirect or interfere with those pleasures. (p. 487)

**psychosomatic illness** An interaction between mind and body that can produce illness. (p. 572)

**psychosurgery** Surgical destruction of specific brain areas. (p. 655)

**psychotherapy** An interaction between a socially sanctioned clinician and someone suffering from a psychological problem, with the goal of providing support or relief from the problem. (p. 633)

**puberty** The bodily changes associated with sexual maturity. (p. 452)

**punisher** Any stimulus or event that functions to decrease the likelihood of the behaviour that led to it. (p. 279)

**random assignment** A procedure that lets chance assign people to the experimental or control group. (p. 61)

**random sampling** A technique for choosing participants that ensures that every member of a population has an equal chance of being included in the sample. (p. 64)

**range** The value of the largest measurement in a frequency distribution minus the value of the smallest measurement. (p. 51)

**ratio IQ** A statistic obtained by dividing a person's mental age by the person's physical age and then multiplying the quotient by 100 (see *deviation IQ*). (p. 398)

**rational choice theory** The classical view that we make decisions by determining how likely something is to happen, judging the value of the outcome, and then multiplying the two. (p. 374)

**rational coping** Facing a stressor and working to overcome it. (p. 561)

**reaction time** The amount of time taken to respond to a specific stimulus. (p. 8)

**re-appraisal** Changing one's emotional experience by changing the way one thinks about the emotion-eliciting stimulus. (p. 320)

**reasoning** A mental activity that consists of organizing information or beliefs into a series of steps in order to reach conclusions. (p. 388)

**rebound effect of thought suppression** The tendency of a thought to return to consciousness with greater frequency following suppression. (p. 188)

**receptors** Parts of the cell membrane that receive the neurotransmitter and initiate or prevent a new electric signal. (p. 86)

**reciprocal altruism** Behaviour that benefits another with the expectation that those benefits will be returned in the future. (p. 517)

**reconsolidation** Memories can become vulnerable to disruption when they are recalled, requiring them to become consolidated again. (p. 234)

**referred pain** Feeling of pain when sensory information from internal and external areas converges on the same nerve cells in the spinal cord. (p. 166)

**reflexes** Specific patterns of motor response that are triggered by specific patterns of sensory stimulation. (p. 431)

**refractory period** The time following an action potential during which a new action potential cannot be initiated. (p. 86)

**reframing** Finding a new or creative way to think about a stressor that reduces its threat. (p. 562)

**rehearsal** The process of keeping information in short-term memory by mentally repeating it. (p. 229)

**reinforcement** The consequences of a behaviour determine whether it will be more or less likely to occur again. (p. 19)

**reinforcer** Any stimulus or event that functions to increase the likelihood of the behaviour that led to it. (p. 279)

**relaxation response** A condition of reduced muscle tension, cortical activity, heart rate, breathing rate, and blood pressure. (p. 564)

**relaxation therapy** A technique for reducing tension by consciously relaxing muscles of the body. (p. 564)

**reliability** The tendency for an instrument to produce the same measurement whenever it is used to measure the same thing. (p. 44)

**REM sleep** A stage of sleep characterized by rapid eye movements and a high level of brain activity. (p. 195)

**representativeness heuristic** A mental shortcut that involves making a probability judgment by comparing an object or event to a prototype of the object or event. (p. 377)

**repression** A mental process that removes unacceptable thoughts and memories from consciousness and keeps them in the unconscious. (p. 190)

**repressive coping** Avoiding situations or thoughts that are reminders of a stressor and maintaining an artificially positive viewpoint. (p. 561)

**Research Domain Criteria Project (RDoC)** A new initiative that aims to guide the classification and understanding of mental disorders by revealing the basic processes that give rise to them. (p. 590)

**resistance** A reluctance to cooperate with treatment for fear of confronting unpleasant unconscious material. (p. 634)

**response** An action or physiological change elicited by a stimulus. (p. 18)

**resting potential** The difference in electric charge when the cell is at rest. (p. 85)

**reticular formation** A brain structure that regulates sleep, wakefulness, and levels of arousal. (p. 97)

**retina** Light-sensitive tissue lining the back of the eyeball. (p. 137)

**retrieval** The process of bringing to mind information that has been previously encoded and stored. (p. 222)

**retrieval cue** External information that is associated with stored information and helps bring it to mind. (p. 237)

**retrieval-induced forgetting** A process by which retrieving an item from long-term memory impairs subsequent recall of related items. (p. 238)

**retroactive interference** Situations in which information learned later impairs memory for information acquired earlier. (p. 250)

**retrograde amnesia** The inability to retrieve information that was acquired before a particular date, usually the date of an injury or surgery. (p. 232)

**rods** Photoreceptors that become active under low-light conditions for night vision. (p. 139)

**Rorschach Inkblot Test** A projective technique in which respondents' inner thoughts and feelings are believed to be revealed by analysis of their responses to a set of unstructured inkblots. (p. 475)

**sample** A partial collection of people drawn from a population. (p. 64)

**schemas** Theories about the way the world works. (p. 433)

**schizophrenia** A disorder characterized by the profound disruption of basic psychological processes; a distorted perception of reality; altered or blunted emotion; and disturbances in thought, motivation, and behaviour. (p. 607)

**scientific method** A procedure for finding truth by using empirical evidence. (p. 40)

**seasonal affective disorder (SAD)** Recurrent depressive episodes in a seasonal pattern. (p. 603)

**secondary sex characteristics** Bodily structures that change dramatically with sexual maturity but that are not directly involved in reproduction. (p. 452)

**second-order conditioning** Conditioning where a new, neutral CS is paired with a stimulus that became associated with the US in an earlier procedure. (p. 268)

**self-actualizing tendency** The human motive toward realizing our inner potential. (p. 488)

**self-concept** A person's explicit knowledge of his or her own behaviours, traits, and other personal characteristics. (p. 495)

**self-consciousness** A distinct level of consciousness in which the person's attention is drawn to the self as an object. (p. 184)

**self-esteem** The extent to which an individual likes, values, and accepts the self. (p. 498)

**self-regulation** The exercise of voluntary control over the self to bring the self into line with preferred standards. (p. 576)

**self-report** A method in which people provide subjective information about their own thoughts, feelings, or behaviours, typically via questionnaire or interview. (p. 473)

**self-selection** A problem that occurs when anything about a person determines whether he or she will be included in the experimental or control group. (p. 58)

**self-serving bias** People's tendency to take credit for their successes but downplay responsibility for their failures. (p. 500)

**self-verification** The tendency to seek evidence to confirm the self-concept. (p. 497)

**semantic encoding** The process of relating new information in a meaningful way to knowledge that is already in memory. (p. 224)

**semantic memory** A network of associated facts and concepts that make up our general knowledge of the world. (p. 244)

**sensation** Simple stimulation of a sense organ. (p. 131)

**sensitization** A simple form of learning that occurs when presentation of a stimulus leads to an increased response to a later stimulus. (p. 266)

**sensorimotor stage** A stage of cognitive development that begins at birth and lasts through infancy in which infants acquire information about the world by sensing it and moving around within it. (p. 433)

**sensory adaptation** Sensitivity to prolonged stimulation tends to decline over time as an organism adapts to current conditions. (p. 135)

**sensory memory** A type of storage that holds sensory information for a few seconds or less. (p. 228)

**sensory neurons** Neurons that receive information from the external world and convey this information to the brain. (p. 82)

**serotonin** A neurotransmitter that is involved in the regulation of sleep and wakefulness, eating, and aggressive behaviour. (p. 88)

**shaping** Learning that results from the reinforcement of successive steps to a final desired behaviour. (p. 287)

**shared environment** Those environmental factors that are experienced by all relevant members of a household (see *nonshared environment*). (p. 411)

**short-term memory** A type of storage that holds nonsensory information for more than a few seconds but less than a minute. (p. 229)

**sick role** A socially recognized set of rights and obligations linked with illness. (p. 572)

**signal detection theory** The response to a stimulus depends both on a person's sensitivity to the stimulus in the presence of noise and on a person's response criterion. (p. 133)

**sleep apnea** A disorder in which the person stops breathing for brief periods while asleep. (p. 199)

**sleep paralysis** The experience of waking up unable to move. (p. 200)

**social cognition** The processes by which people come to understand others. (p. 537)

**social-cognitive approach** An approach that views personality in terms of how the person thinks about the situations encountered in daily life and behaves in response to them. (p. 490)

**social exchange** The hypothesis that people remain in relationships only as long as they perceive a favourable ratio of costs to benefits. (p. 524)

**social influence** The ability to control another person's behaviour (p. 526)

**social loafing** The tendency for people to expend less effort when in a group than when alone. (p. 514)

**social phobia** A disorder that involves an irrational fear of being publicly humiliated or embarrassed. (p. 594)

**social psychology** The study of the causes and consequences of sociality. (pp. 27, 508)

**social support** The aid gained through interacting with others. (p. 566)

**somatic nervous system** A set of nerves that conveys information between voluntary muscles and the central nervous system. (p. 92)

**somatic symptom disorders** The set of psychological disorders in which a person with at least one bodily symptom displays significant health-related anxiety, expresses disproportionate concerns about their symptoms, and devotes excessive time and energy to their symptoms or health concerns. (p. 572)

**somnambulism (or sleepwalking)** Occurs when a person arises and walks around while asleep. (p. 200)

**source memory** Recall of when, where, and how information was acquired. (p. 252)

**specific phobia** A disorder that involves an irrational fear of a particular object or situation that markedly interferes with an individual's ability to function. (p. 594)

**spinal reflexes** Simple pathways in the nervous system that rapidly generate muscle contractions. (p. 94)

**spontaneous recovery** The tendency of a learned behaviour to recover from extinction after a rest period. (p. 271)

**standard deviation** A statistic that describes the average difference between the measurements in a frequency distribution and the mean of that distribution. (p. 51)

**state-dependent retrieval** The tendency for information to be better recalled when the person is in the same state during encoding and retrieval. (p. 237)

**stereotype threat** The fear of confirming the negative beliefs that others may hold. (p. 541)

**stereotyping** The process by which people draw inferences about others based on their knowledge of the categories to which others belong. (p. 539)

**stimulants** Substances that excite the central nervous system, heightening arousal and activity levels. (p. 211)

**stimulus** Sensory input from the environment. (p. 8)

**storage** The process of maintaining information in memory over time. (p. 222)

**Strange Situation** A behavioural test used to determine a child's attachment style. (p. 444)

**stress** The physical and psychological response to internal or external stressors. (p. 550)

**stress inoculation training (SIT)** A reframing technique that helps people to cope with stressful situations by developing positive ways to think about the situation. (p. 562)

**stressors** Specific events or chronic pressures that place demands on a person or threaten the person's well-being. (p. 550)

**structuralism** The analysis of the basic elements that constitute the mind. (p. 8)

**subcortical structures** Areas of the forebrain housed under the cerebral cortex near the very centre of the brain. (p. 97)

**subliminal perception** Thought or behaviour that is influenced by stimuli that a person cannot consciously report perceiving. (p. 191)

**subtyping** The tendency for people who receive disconfirming evidence to modify their stereotypes rather than abandon them. (p. 541)

**suggestibility** The tendency to incorporate misleading information from external sources into personal recollections. (p. 255)

**suicide** Intentional self-inflicted death. (p. 621)

**suicide attempt** When a person engages in potentially harmful behaviour with some intention of dying. (p. 621)

**sunk-cost fallacy** A framing effect in which people make decisions about a current situation based on what they have previously invested in the situation. (p. 377)

**superego** The mental system that reflects the internalization of cultural rules, mainly learned as parents exercise their authority. (p. 485)

**surface structure** How a sentence is worded. (p. 354)

**syllogistic reasoning** Determining whether a conclusion follows from two statements that are assumed to be true. (p. 390)

**sympathetic nervous system** A set of nerves that prepares the body for action in challenging or threatening situations. (p. 93)

**synapse** The junction or region between the axon of one neuron and the dendrites or cell body of another. (p. 82)

**syntactical rules** A set of rules that indicate how words can be combined to form phrases and sentences. (p. 354)

**systematic persuasion** The process by which attitudes or beliefs are changed by appeals to reason. (p. 534)

**taste buds** The organ of taste transduction. (p. 171)

**tectum** A part of the midbrain that orients an organism in the environment. (p. 97)

**tegmentum** A part of the midbrain that is involved in movement and arousal. (p. 97)

**telegraphic speech** Speech that is devoid of function morphemes and consists mostly of content words. (p. 357)

**telomerase** An enzyme that rebuilds telomeres at the tips of chromosomes. (p. 556)

**telomeres** Caps at the end of each chromosome that protect the ends of chromosomes and prevent them from sticking to each other. (p. 556)

**temperaments** Characteristic patterns of emotional reactivity. (p. 445)

**template** A mental representation that can be directly compared to a viewed shape in the retinal image. (p. 148)

**temporal code** The cochlea registers relatively low frequencies (up to about 5000 Hz) via the firing rate of action potentials entering the auditory nerve. (p. 160)

**temporal lobe** A region of the cerebral cortex responsible for hearing and language. (p. 102)

**teratogens** Agents that impair prenatal development, such as drugs and viruses. (p. 428)

**terminal buttons** Knoblike structures that branch out from an axon. (p. 86)

**terror management theory** A theory about how people respond to knowledge of their own mortality. (p. 347)

**thalamus** A subcortical structure that relays and filters information from the senses and transmits the information to the cerebral cortex. (p. 98)

**Thematic Apperception Test (TAT)** A projective technique in which respondents' underlying motives, concerns, and the way they see the social world are believed to be revealed through analysis of the stories they make up about ambiguous pictures of people. (p. 475)

**theoretical reasoning (or discursive reasoning)** Reasoning directed toward arriving at a belief. (p. 388)

**theory** A hypothetical explanation of a natural phenomenon. (p. 40)

**theory of mind** The understanding that human behaviour is guided by mental representations. (p. 439)

**third-variable correlation** Two variables are correlated only because each is causally related to a third variable. (p. 55)

**third-variable problem** The fact that a causal relationship between two variables cannot be inferred from the naturally occurring correlation between them because of the ever-present possibility of third-variable correlation. (p. 56)

**thought suppression** The conscious avoidance of a thought. (p. 188)

**timbre** A listener's experience of sound quality or resonance. (p. 158)

**token economy** A form of behaviour therapy in which clients are given "tokens" for desired behaviours, which they can later trade for rewards. (p. 638)

**trait** A relatively stable disposition to behave in a particular and consistent way. (p. 476)

**transcranial magnetic stimulation (TMS)** A treatment that involves placing a powerful pulsed magnet over a person's scalp, which alters neuronal activity in the brain. (p. 655)

**transduction** What takes place when sensors in the body convert physical signals from the environment into encoded neural signals sent to the central nervous system. (p. 131)

**transfer-appropriate processing** The idea that memory is likely to transfer from one situation to another when the encoding and retrieval contexts of the situations match. (p. 237)

**transference** An event that occurs in psychoanalysis when the analyst begins to assume a major significance in the client's life and the client reacts to the analyst based on unconscious childhood fantasies. (p. 635)

**transience** Forgetting what occurs with the passage of time. (p. 249)

**two-factor theory** The theory that emotions are based on inferences about the causes of physiological arousal. (p. 316)

**two-factor theory of intelligence** A theory that suggests that every task requires a combination of a general ability (*g*) and skills that are specific to the task (*s*). (p. 402)

**Type A behaviour pattern** The tendency toward easily aroused hostility, impatience, a sense of time urgency, and competitive achievement strivings. (p. 559)

**unconditioned response (UR)** A reflexive reaction that is reliably produced by an unconditioned stimulus. (p. 267)

**unconditioned stimulus (US)** Something that reliably produces a naturally occurring reaction in an organism. (p. 267)

**unconscious** The part of the mind that operates outside of conscious awareness but influences conscious thoughts, feelings, and actions. (p. 13)

**unconscious motivations** Motivations of which people are not aware. (p. 344)

**universality hypothesis** Emotional expressions have the same meaning for everyone. (p. 322)

**validity** The goodness with which a concrete event defines a property. (p. 44)

**variable** A property whose value can vary across individuals or over time. (p. 52)

**variable-interval schedule (VI)** An operant conditioning principle in which behaviour is reinforced based on an average time that has expired since the last reinforcement. (p. 283)

**variable-ratio schedule (VR)** An operant conditioning principle in which the delivery of reinforcement is based on a particular average number of responses. (p. 285)

**vestibular system** The three fluid-filled semicircular canals and adjacent organs located next to the cochlea in each inner ear. (p. 167)

**visual acuity** The ability to see fine detail. (p. 135)

**visual form agnosia** The inability to recognize objects by sight. (p. 142)

**visual imagery encoding** The process of storing new information by converting it into mental pictures. (p. 224)

**Weber's law** The just noticeable difference of a stimulus is a constant proportion despite variations in intensity. (p. 133)

**working memory** Active maintenance of information in short-term storage. (p. 229)

**zygote** A fertilized egg that contains chromosomes from both an egg and a sperm. (p. 426)

# References

**Aarts, H., Custers, R., & Marien, H.** (2008). Preparing and motivating behavior outside of awareness. *Science, 319,* 1639.

**Abel, T., Alberini, C., Ghirardi, M., Huang, Y.-Y., Nguyen, P., & Kandel, E. R.** (1995). Steps toward a molecular definition of memory consolidation. In D. L. Schacter (Ed.), *Memory distortion: How minds, brains and societies reconstruct the past* (pp. 298–328). Cambridge, MA: Harvard University Press.

**Abelson, J., Curtis, G., Sagher, O., Albucher, R., Harrigan, M., Taylor, S., ... Giordani, B.** (2009). Deep brain stimulation for refractory obsessive-compulsive disorder. *Biological Psychiatry, 57,* 510–516.

**Abrams, M., & Reber, A. S.** (1988). Implicit learning: Robustness in the face of psychiatric disorders. *Journal of Psycholinguistic Research, 17,* 425–439.

**Abramson, L. Y., Seligman, M. E. P., & Teasdale, J. D.** (1978). Learned helplessness in humans: Critique and reformulation. *Journal of Abnormal Psychology, 87,* 49–74.

**Acevedo, B. P., & Aron, A.** (2009). Does a long-term relationship kill romantic love? *Review of General Psychology, 13,* 59–65.

**Acevedo-Garcia, D., McArdle, N., Osypuk, T. L., Lefkowitz, B., & Krimgold, B. K.** (2007). *Children left behind: How metropolitan areas are failing America's children.* Boston: Harvard School of Public Health.

**Achter, J. A., Lubinski, D., & Benbow, C. P.** (1996). Multipotentiality among the intellectually gifted: "It was never there and already it's vanishing." *Journal of Counseling Psychology, 43,* 65–76.

**Acocella, J.** (1999). *Creating hysteria: Women and multiple personality disorder.* San Francisco: Jossey-Bass.

**Addis, D. R., Wong, A. T., & Schacter, D. L.** (2007). Remembering the past and imagining the future: Common and distinct neural substrates during event construction and elaboration. *Neuropsychologia, 45,* 1363–1377.

**Addis, D. R., Wong, A. T., & Schacter, D. L.** (2008). Age-related changes in the episodic simulation of future events. *Psychological Science, 19,* 33–41.

**Adelmann, P. K., & Zajonc, R. B.** (1989). Facial efference and the experience of emotion. *Annual Review of Psychology, 40,* 249–280.

**Adolph, K. E., & Avoilio, A. M.** (2000). Walking infants adapt locomotion to changing body dimensions. *Journal of Experimental Psychology: Human Perception and Performance, 26,* 1148–1166.

**Adolph, K. E., Cole, W. G., Komati, M., Garciaguirre, J. S., Badaly, D., Lingeman, J. M., ... Sotsky, R. B.** (2012). How do you learn to walk? Thousands of steps and dozens of falls per day. *Psychological Science, 23*(11), 1387–1394. doi:10.1177/0956797612446346

**Adolphs, R., Russell, J. A., & Tranel, D.** (1999). A role for the human amygdala in recognizing emotional arousal from unpleasant stimuli. *Psychological Science, 10,* 167–171.

**Adolphs, R., Tranel, D., Damasio, H., & Damasio, A. R.** (1995). Fear and the human amygdala. *The Journal of Neuroscience, 15,* 5879–5891.

**Adorno, T. W., Frenkel-Brunswik, E., Levinson, D. J., & Sanford, R. N.** (1950). *The authoritarian personality.* New York: Harper & Row.

**Aggleton, J. (Ed.).** (1992). *The amygdala: Neurobiological aspects of emotion, memory and mental dysfunction.* New York: Wiley-Liss.

**Agin, D.** (2007). *Junk science: An overdue indictment of government, industry, and faith groups that twist science for their own gain.* New York: Macmillan.

**Agren, T., Engman, J., Frick, A., Björkstrand, J., Larsson, E. M., Furmark, T., & Fredrikson, M.** (2012). Disruption of reconsolidation erases a fear memory trace in the human amygdala. *Science, 337,* 1550–1552.

**Agthe, M., Spörrle, M., & Maner, J. K.** (2010). Don't hate me because I'm beautiful: Anti-attractiveness bias in organizational evaluation and decision making. *Journal of Experimental Psychology, 46*(6), 1151–1154. doi:10.1016/j.jesp.2010.05.007

**Aharon, I., Etcoff, N., Ariely, D., Chabris, C. F., O'Conner, E., & Breiter, H. C.** (2001). Beautiful faces have variable reward value: fMRI and behavioral evidence. *Neuron, 32,* 537–551.

**Ahlskog, J. E.** (2011). Pathological behaviors provoked by dopamine agonist therapy of Parkinson's disease. *Physiology & Behavior, 104,* 168–172.

**Ainslie, G.** (2001). *Breakdown of will.* New York: Cambridge University Press.

**Ainsworth, M. D. S., Blehar, M. C., Waters, E., & Wall, S.** (1978). *Patterns of attachment: A psychological study of the strange situation.* Hillsdale, NJ: Erlbaum.

**Ainsworth, S. E., & Maner, J. K.** (2012). Sex begets violence: Mating motives, social dominance, and physical aggression in men. *Journal of Personality and Social Psychology, 103*(5), 819–829. doi: 10.1037/a0029428

**Ainsworth-Vincze, C.** (2009, March 9). Brain candy: Can Ritalin turn you into an A student? *Maclean's.* Retrieved from http://oncampus.macleans.ca/education/2009/03/09/brain-candy-can-ritalin-turn-you-into-an-a-student/

**Aksglaede, L., Sorensen, K., Petersen, J. H., Skakkebaek, N. E., & Juul, A.** (2009). Recent decline in age at breast development: The Copenhagen puberty study. *Pediatrics, 123*(5), e932–e939.

**Alasaari, J. S., Lagus, M., Ollila, H. M., Toivola, A., Kivimaki, M., Vahterra, J., ... Paunio, T.** (2012). Environmental stress affects DNA methylation of a CpG rich promoter region of serotonin transporter gene in a nurse cohort. *PLoS One, 7,* e45813. doi:10.1371/journal.pone.0045813

**Albarracín, D., & Vargas, P.** (2010). Attitudes and persuasion: From biology to social responses to persuasive intent. In S. T. Fiske, D. T. Gilbert, & G. Lindzey (Eds.), *The handbook of social psychology* (5th ed., Vol. 1, pp. 389–422). New York: Wiley.

**Albee, E.** (1962). *Who's afraid of Virginia Woolf?* New York: Atheneum.

**Aleman, A., Sommer, I. E., & Kahn, R. S.** (2007). Efficacy of slow repetitive transcranial magnetic stimulation in the treatment of resistant auditory hallucinations in schizophrenia: A meta-analysis. *Journal of Clinical Psychiatry, 68,* 416–421.

**Alicke, M. D., Klotz, M. L., Breitenbecher, D. L., Yurak, T. J., & Vredenburg, D. S.** (1995). Personal contact, individuation, and the better-than-average effect. *Journal of Personality and Social Psychology, 68,* 804–824.

**Allen, P., Larøi, F., McGuire, P.K., & Aleman, A.** (2008). The hallucinating brain: A review of structural and functional neuroimaging studies of hallucinations. *Neuroscience and Biobehavioral Reviews, 32,* 175–191.

**Allison, D. B., Kaprio, J., Korkeila, M., Koskenvuo, M., Neale, M. C., & Hayakawa, K.** (1996). The heritability of body mass index among an international sample of monozygotic twins reared apart. *International Journal of Obesity, 20*(6), 501–506.

**Alloway, T. P., Gathercole, S. E., Kirkwood, H., & Elliott, J.** (2009). The cognitive and behavioral characteristics of children with low working memory. *Child Development, 80,* 606–621.

**Allport, G. W.** (1937). *Personality: A psychological interpretation.* New York: Holt.

**Allport, G. W.** (1954). *The nature of prejudice.* Cambridge, MA: Addison-Wesley.

**Allport, G. W., & Odbert, H. S.** (1936). Trait-names: A psycholexical study. *Psychological Monographs, 47,* 592.

**Al-Sahab, B., Saqib, M., Hauser, G., & Tamim, H.** (2010). Prevalence of smoking during pregnancy and associated risk factors among Canadian women: A national survey. *BioMed Central Pregnancy Childbirth, 10*(24), 1–9.

**Alt, K. W., Jeunesse, C., Buitrago-Téllez, C. H., Wächter, R., Boës, E., & Pichler, S. L.** (1997). Evidence for stone age cranial surgery. *Nature, 387,* 360.

**Alvarez, L. W.** (1965). A pseudo experience in parapsychology. *Science, 148,* 1541.

**American Academy of Pediatrics.** (2000, July 26). *The impact of entertainment violence on children.* Joint statement issued at a meeting of the Congressional Public Health Summit. Retrieved from http://www.aap.org/advocacy/releases/jstmtevc.htm

**American Psychiatric Association.** (2013). *Diagnostic and statistical manual of mental disorders* (5th ed.). Washington, DC: Author.

**American Psychological Association.** (2002). *Ethical principles of psychologists and code of conduct.* Washington, DC: Author. Retrieved from apa.org/code/ethics/index.aspx [includes 2010 amendments].

**American Psychological Association.** (2005). *Resolution in favor of empirically supported sex education and HIV prevention programs for adolescents.* Washington, DC: Author.

**American Psychological Association.** (2009). *Report of the American Psychological Association task force on appropriate therapeutic responses to sexual orientation.* Washington, DC: Author.

**Anand, S., & Hotson, J.** (2002). Transcranial magnetic stimulation: Neurophysiological applications and safety. *Brain and Cognition, 50,* 366–386.

**Anderson, C. A.** (1989). Temperature and aggression: Ubiquitous effects of heat on occurrence of human violence. *Psychological Bulletin, 106,* 74–96.

**Anderson, C. A., Berkowitz, L., Donnerstein, E., Huesmann, L. R., Johnson, J. D., Linz, D., … Wartella, E.** (2003). The influence of media violence on youth. *Psychological Science in the Public Interest, 4,* 81–110.

**Anderson, C. A., & Bushman, B. J.** (2001). Effects of violent video games on aggressive behavior, aggressive cognition, aggressive affect, physiological arousal, and prosocial behavior: A metaanalytic review of the scientific literature. *Psychological Science, 12*(5), 353–359.

**Anderson, C. A., & Bushman, B. J.** (2002). Human aggression. *Annual Review of Psychology, 53,* 27–51.

**Anderson, C. A., Bushman, B. J., & Groom, R. W.** (1997). Hot years and serious and deadly assault: Empirical tests of the heat hypothesis. *Journal of Personality and Social Psychology, 73,* 1213–1223.

**Anderson, C. A., Shibuya, A., Ihori, N., Swing, E. L., Bushman, B. J., Sakamoto, A., … Saleem, M.** (2010). Violent video game effects on aggression, empathy, and prosocial behavior in Eastern and Western countries: A meta-analytic review. *Psychological Bulletin, 136*(2), 151–173. doi: 10.1037/a0018251

**Anderson, J. R., & Schooler, L. J.** (1991). Reflections of the environment in memory. *Psychological Science, 2,* 396–408.

**Anderson, J. R., & Schooler, L. J.** (2000). The adaptive nature of memory. In E. Tulving & F. I. M. Craik (Eds.), *Handbook of memory* (pp. 557–570). New York: Oxford University Press.

**Anderson, M. C.** (2003). Rethinking interference theory: Executive control and the mechanisms of forgetting. *Journal of Memory and Language, 49,* 415–445.

**Anderson, M. C., Bjork, R. A., & Bjork, E. L.** (1994). Remembering can cause forgetting: Retrieval dynamics in long-term memory. *Journal of Experimental Psychology: Learning, Memory, and Cognition, 20,* 1063–1087.

**Anderson, M. C., Ochsner, K. N., Kuhl, B., Cooper, J., Robertson, E., Gabrieli, S. W., … Gabrieli, J. D. E.** (2004). Neural systems underlying the suppression of unwanted memories. *Science, 303,* 232–235.

**Anderson, R. C., Pichert, J. W., Goetz, E. T., Schallert, D. L., Stevens, K. V., & Trollip, S. R.** (1976). Instantiation of general terms. *Journal of Verbal Learning and Verbal Behavior, 15,* 667–679.

**Andreasen, N. C.** (2011). A journey into chaos: Creativity and the unconscious. *Mens Sana Monographs, 9,* 42–53.

**Andrewes, D.** (2001). *Neuropsychology: From theory to practice.* Hove, England: Psychology Press.

**Andrews, I.** (1982). Bilinguals out of focus: A critical discussion. *International Review of Applied Linguistics in Language Teaching, 20,* 297–305.

**Andrews-Hanna, J. R.** (2012). The brain's default network and its adaptive role in internal mentation. *Neuroscientist, 18,* 251–270.

**Annis, L. F., & Annis, D. B.** (1982). A normative study of students' reported preferred study techniques. *Literacy Research and Instruction, 21,* 201–207.

**Ansfield, M., Wegner, D. M., & Bowser, R.** (1996). Ironic effects of sleep urgency. *Behavior Research and Therapy, 34,* 523–531.

**Ansuini, C. G., Fiddler-Woite, J., & Woite, R. S.** (1996). The source, accuracy, and impact of initial sexuality information on lifetime wellness. *Adolescence, 31,* 283–289.

**Antoni, M. H., Lehman, J. M., Klibourn, K. M., Boyers, A. E., Culver, J. L., Alferi, S. M., … Carver, C. S.** (2001). Cognitive-behavioral stress management intervention decreases the prevalence of depression and enhances benefit finding among women under treatment for early-stage breast cancer. *Health Psychology, 20,* 20–32.

**AnxietyBC.** (n.d.) *Specific phobia.* Retrieved from http://www.anxietybc.com/resources/specific.php

**Apicella, C. L., Feinberg, D. R., & Marlowe, F. W.** (2007). Voice pitch predicts reproductive success in male hunter-gatherers. *Biology Letters, 3*(6), 682–684. doi:10.1098/rsbl.2007.0410

**Apperly, I. A., & Butterfill, S. A.** (2009). Do humans have two systems to track beliefs and belief-like states? *Psychological Review, 116,* 953–970.

**Arellano, D., Varona, J., & Perales, F.** (2008). Generation and visualization of emotional states in virtual characters. *Computer Animation and Virtual Worlds, 19*(3–4), 259–270.

**Aristotle.** (1998). *The Nichomachean ethics* (D. W. Ross, Trans.). Oxford, England: Oxford University Press. (Original work circa 350 BCE)

**Ariyasu, H., Takaya, K., Tagami, T., Ogawa, Y., Hosoda, K., Akamizu, T., ... Hosoda, H.** (2001). Stomach is a major source of circulating ghrelin, and feeding state determines plasma ghrelin-like immunoreactivity levels in humans. *Journal of Clinical Endocrinology and Metabolism, 86,* 4753–4758.

**Armstrong, D. M.** (1980). *The nature of mind.* Ithaca, NY: Cornell University Press.

**Arnold, M. B. (Ed.).** (1960). *Emotion and personality: Psychological aspects* (Vol. 1). New York: Columbia University Press.

**Arnold, S. E., Trojanowski, J. Q., Gur, R. E., Blackwell, P., Han, L., & Choi, C.** (1998). Absence of neurodegeneration and neural injury in the cerebral cortex in a sample of elderly patients with schizophrenia. *Archives of General Psychiatry, 55,* 225–232.

**Aron, A., Fisher, H., Mashek, D., Strong, G., Li, H., & Brown, L.** (2005). Reward, motivation, and emotion systems associated with early-stage intense romantic love. *Journal of Neurophysiology, 93,* 327–337.

**Aronson, E.** (1963). Effect of the severity of threat on the devaluation of forbidden behavior. *Journal of Abnormal and Social Psychology, 66,* 584–588.

**Aronson, E.** (1969). The theory of cognitive dissonance: A current perspective. In L. Berkowitz (Ed.), *Advances in experimental social psychology* (Vol. 4, pp. 1–34). New York: Academic Press.

**Aronson, E., & Mills, J.** (1958). The effect of severity of initiation on liking for a group. *Journal of Abnormal and Social Psychology, 59,* 177–181.

**Aronson, E., Willerman, B., & Floyd, J.** (1966). The effect of a pratfall on increasing interpersonal attractiveness. *Psychonomic Science, 4,* 227–228.

**Aronson, E., & Worchel, P.** (1966). Similarity versus liking as determinants of interpersonal attractiveness. *Psychonomic Science, 5,* 157–158.

**Aronson, J., & Steele, C. M.** (2004). Stereotypes and the fragility of academic competence, motivation, and self-concept. In A. J. Elliot & C. S. Dweck (Eds.), *Handbook of competence and motivation* (pp. 436–456). New York: Guilford Press.

**Asante, K. O., & Nelms-Maztke, J.** (1985). *Report on the survey of children with chronic handicaps and fetal alcohol syndrome in the Yukon and Northwest British Columbia.* Whitehorse, YT: Council for Yukon Indians.

**Asch, S. E.** (1946). Forming impressions of personality. *Journal of Abnormal and Social Psychology, 41,* 258–290.

**Asch, S. E.** (1951). Effects of group pressure on the modification and distortion of judgments. In H. Guetzkow (Ed.), *Groups, leadership, and men* (pp. 177–190). Pittsburgh, PA: Carnegie Press.

**Asch, S. E.** (1955). Opinions and social pressure. *Scientific American, 193,* 31–35.

**Asch, S. E.** (1956). Studies of independence and conformity: 1. A minority of one against a unanimous majority. *Psychological Monographs: General and Applied, 70,* 1–70.

**Aschoff, J.** (1965). Circadian rhythms in man. *Science, 148,* 1427–1432.

**Aserinsky, E., & Kleitman, N.** (1953). Regularly occurring periods of eye motility, and concomitant phenomena, during sleep. *Science, 118,* 273–274.

**Ashby, F. G., & Ell, S. W.** (2001). The neurobiology of human category learning. *Trends in Cognitive Sciences, 5,* 204–210.

**Ashby, F. G., & O'Brien, J. B.** (2005). Category learning and multiple memory systems. *Trends in Cognitive Sciences, 9,* 83–89.

**Ashcraft, M. H.** (1998). *Fundamentals of cognition.* New York: Longman.

**Associated Press.** (2007). Former stripper guilty of posing as psychologist. *Boston Herald.* Retrieved from http://www.bostonherald.com

**Astington, J. W., & Baird, J.** (2005). *Why language matters for theory of mind.* Oxford, England: Oxford University Press.

**Atance, C. M., Bélanger, M., & Meltzoff, A. N.** (2010). Preschoolers' understanding of others' desires: Fulfilling mine enhances my understanding of yours. *Developmental Psychology, 46*(6), 1505–1513. doi:10.1037/a0020374

**Avery, D., Holtzheimer, P., III, Fawaz, W., Russo, J., Naumeier, J., Dunner, D., ... Roy-Byrne, P.** (2009). A controlled study of repetitive transcranial magnetic stimulation in medication-resistant major depression. *Biological Psychiatry, 59,* 187–194.

**Aviezer, H., Hassin, R. R., Ryan, J., Grady, C., Susskind, J., Anderson, A., ... Bentin, S.** (2008). Angry, disgusted, or afraid? Studies on the malleability of emotion perception. *Psychological Science, 19,* 724–732.

**Aviezer, H., Trope, Y., & Todorov, A.** (2012). Body cues, not facial expressions, discriminate between intense positive and negative emotions. *Science, 338,* 1225–1229.

**Avolio, B. J., & Waldman, D. A.** (1994). Variations in cognitive, perceptual, and psychomotor abilities across the working life span: Examining the effects of race, sex, experience, education, and occupational type. *Psychology and Aging, 9,* 430–442.

**Axelrod, R.** (1984). *The evolution of cooperation.* New York: Basic Books.

**Axelrod, R., & Hamilton, W. D.** (1981). The evolution of cooperation. *Science, 211,* 1390–1396.

**Ayduk, O., Shoda, Y., Cervone, D., & Downey, G.** (2007). Delay of gratification in children: Contributions to social–personality psychology. In G. Downey, Y. Shoda, & C. Cervone (Eds.), *Persons in context: Building a science of the individual* (pp. 97–109). New York: Guilford Press.

**Ayres, C. E.** (1921). Instinct and capacity. 1. The instinct of belief-in-instincts. *Journal of Philosophy, 18,* 561–565.

**Azuma, H., & Kashiwagi, K.** (1987). Descriptors for an intelligent person: A Japanese study. *Japanese Psychological Research, 29,* 17–26.

**Baars, B. J.** (1986). *The cognitive revolution in psychology.* New York: Guilford Press.

**Baca-Motes, K., Brown, A., Gneezy, A., Keenan, E. A., & Nelson, L. D.** (2013). Commitment and behavior change: Evidence from the field. *Journal of Consumer Research, 39*(5), 1070–1084. doi:10.1086/667226

**Back, M. D., Schmukle, S. C., & Egloff, B.** (2008). Becoming friends by chance. *Psychological Science, 19,* 439–440.

**Back, M. D., Stopfer, J. M., Vazire, S., Gaddis, S., Schmukle, S. C., Egloff, B., & Gosling, S.** (2010). Facebook profiles reflect actual personality not self-idealization. *Psychological Science, 21,* 372–374.

**Backman, C. W., & Secord, P. F.** (1959). The effect of perceived liking on interpersonal attraction. *Human Relations, 12,* 379–384.

**Bäckman, L., Almkvist, O., Andersson, J., Nordberg, A., Winblad, B., Reineck, R., & Långström, B.** (1997). Brain activation in young and older adults during implicit and explicit retrieval. *Journal of Cognitive Neuroscience, 9,* 378–391.

**Bäckman, L., & Dixon, R. A.** (1992). Psychological compensation: A theoretical framework. *Psychological Bulletin, 112,* 259–283.

**Baddeley, A. D.** (2001). Is working memory still working? *American Psychologist, 56,* 851–864.

**Baddeley, A. D., & Hitch, G. J.** (1974). Working memory. In S. Dornic (Ed.), *Attention and performance* (Vol. 6, pp. 647–667). Hillsdale, NJ: Erlbaum.

**Bagby, R. M., Levitan, R. D., Kennedy, S. H., Levitt, A. J., & Joffe, R. T.** (1999). Selective alteration of personality in response to noradrenergic and serotonergic antidepressant medication in depressed sample: Evidence of non-specificity. *Psychiatry Research, 86,* 211–216.

**Bahrick, H. P.** (1984). Semantic memory content in permastore: 50 years of memory for Spanish learned in school. *Journal of Experimental Psychology: General, 113,* 1–29.

**Bahrick, H. P.** (2000). Long-term maintenance of knowledge. In E. Tulving & F. I. M. Craik (Eds.), *The Oxford handbook of memory* (pp. 347–362). New York: Oxford University Press.

**Bahrick, H. P., Hall, L. K., & Berger, S. A.** (1996). Accuracy and distortion in memory for high school grades. *Psychological Science, 7,* 265–271.

**Bahrick, H. P., Hall, L. K., & DaCosta, L. A.** (2008). Fifty years of college grades: Accuracy and distortions. *Emotion, 8,* 13–22.

**Bailey, J. M., & Pillard, R. C.** (1991). A genetic study of male sexual orientation. *Archives of General Psychiatry, 48,* 1089–1096.

**Bailey, J. M., Pillard, R. C., Dawood, K., Miller, M. B., Farrer, L. A., Trivedi, S., ... Murphy, R. L.** (1999). A family history study of male sexual orientation using three independent samples. *Behavior Genetics, 29,* 79–86.

**Bailey, J. M., Pillard, R. C., Neale, M. C., & Agyes, Y.** (1993). Heritable factors influence sexual orientation in women. *Archives of General Psychiatry, 50,* 217–223.

**Baillargeon, R., Scott, R. M., & He, Z.** (2010). False-belief understanding in infants. *Trends in Cognitive Sciences, 14*(3), 110–118.

**Baillargeon, R., Spelke, E. S., & Wasserman, S.** (1985). Object permanence in 5-month-old infants. *Cognition, 20,* 191–208.

**Baker, E., Shelton, K. H., Baibazarova, E., Hay, D. F., & van Goozen, S. H. M.** (2013). Low skin conductance activity in infancy predicts aggression in toddlers 2 years later. *Psychological Science, 24*(6), 1051–1056. doi:10.1177/0956797612465198

**Baker, T. B., Brandon, T. H., & Chassin, L.** (2004). Motivational influences on cigarette smoking. *Annual Review of Psychology, 55,* 463–491.

**Baker, T. B., McFall, R. M., & Shoham, V.** (2009). Current status and future prospects of clinical psychology: Toward a scientifically principled approach to mental and behavioral health care. *Psychological Science in the Public Interest, 9,* 67–103.

**Baldwin, M. W., Carrell, S. E., & Lopez, D. F.** (1989). Priming relationship schemas: My advisor and the pope are watching me from the back of my mind. *Journal of Experimental Social Psychology, 26,* 435–454.

**Baler, R. D., & Volkow, N. D.** (2006). Drug addiction: The neurobiology of disrupted self-control. *Trends in Molecular Medicine, 12,* 559–566.

**Baltes, P. B., & Reinert, G.** (1969). Cohort effects in cognitive development of children as revealed by cross-sectional sequences. *Developmental Psychology, 1,* 169–177.

**Banaji, M. R., & Heiphetz, L.** (2010). Attitudes. In S. T. Fiske, D. T. Gilbert, & G. Lindzey (Eds.), *The handbook of social psychology* (5th ed., Vol. 1, pp. 348–388). New York: Wiley.

**Bandura, A.** (1965). Influence of models' reinforcement contingencies on the acquisition of imitative responses. *Journal of Social and Personality Psychology, 1,* 589–595.

**Bandura, A.** (1977). *Social learning theory.* Englewood Cliffs, NJ: Prentice Hall.

**Bandura, A.** (1986). *Social foundations of thought and action: A social cognitive theory.* Englewood Cliffs, NJ: Prentice Hall.

**Bandura, A.** (1994). Social cognitive theory of mass communication. In J. Bryant & D. Zillmann (Eds.), *Media effects: Advances in theory and research* (pp. 61–90). Hillsdale, NJ: Erlbaum.

**Bandura, A., Ross, D., & Ross, S.** (1961). Transmission of aggression through imitation of adult models. *Journal of Abnormal and Social Psychology, 63,* 575–582.

**Bandura, A., Ross, D., & Ross, S.** (1963). Vicarious reinforcement and imitative learning. *Journal of Abnormal and Social Psychology, 67,* 601–607.

**Banks, M. S., & Salapatek, P.** (1983). Infant visual perception. In M. Haith & J. Campos (Eds.), *Handbook of child psychology: Biology and infancy* (pp. 435–572). New York: Wiley.

**Banse, R., & Scherer, K. R.** (1996). Acoustic profiles in vocal emotion expression. *Journal of Personality and Social Psychology, 70,* 614–636.

**Barber, J. P., Muran, J. C., McCarthy, K. S., & Keefe, J. R.** (2013). Research on dynamic therapies. In M. Lambert (Ed.), *Bergin and Garfield's handbook of psychotherapy and behavior change* (6th ed., pp. 443–494). Hoboken, NJ: Wiley.

**Barber, S. J., Rajaram, S., & Fox, E. B.** (2012). Learning and remembering with others: The key role of retrieval in shaping group recall and collective memory. *Social Cognition, 30,* 121–132.

**Bard, P.** (1934). On emotional experience after decortication with some remarks on theoretical views. *Psychological Review, 41,* 309–329.

**Bargh, J. A., & Chartrand, T. L.** (1999). The unbearable automaticity of being. *American Psychologist, 54,* 462–479.

**Bargh, J. A., Chen, M., & Burrows, L.** (1996). The automaticity of social behavior: Direct effects of trait concept and stereotype activation on action. *Journal of Personality and Social Psychology, 71,* 230–244.

**Bargh, J. A., Gollwitzer, P. M., Lee-Chai, A., Barndollar, K., & Trötschel, R.** (2001). The automated will: Nonconscious activation and pursuit of behavioral goals. *Journal of Personality and Social Psychology, 81,* 1014–1027.

**Bargh, J. A., Gollwitzer, P. M., & Oettingen, G.** (2010). Motivation. In S. T. Fiske, D. T. Gilbert, & G. Lindzey (Eds.), *The handbook of social psychology* (5th ed., Vol. 1, pp. 263–311). New York: Wiley.

**Bargh, J. A., & Morsella, E.** (2008). The unconscious mind. *Perspectives on Psychological Science, 3,* 73–89.

**Barker, A. T., Jalinous, R., & Freeston, I. L.** (1985). Noninvasive magnetic stimulation of the human motor cortex. *Lancet, 2,* 1106–1107.

**Barkow, J.** (1980). Prestige and self-esteem: A biosocial interpretation. In D. R. Omark, F. F. Stayer, & D. G. Freedman (Eds.), *Dominance relations* (pp. 319–322). New York: Garland.

**Barlow, D. H., Bullis, J. R., Comer, J. S., & Ametaj, A. A.** (2013). Evidence-based psychological treatments: An update and a way forward. *Annual Review of Clinical Psychology, 9,* 1–27.

**Barlow, D. H., Gorman, J. M., Shear, M. K., & Woods, S. W.** (2000). Cognitive-behavioral therapy, imipramine, or their combination for panic disorder: A randomized controlled trial. *Journal of the American Medical Association, 283*(19), 2529–2536.

**Barnier, A. J., Levin, K., & Maher, A.** (2004). Suppressing thoughts of past events: Are repressive copers good suppressors? *Cognition and Emotion, 18,* 457–477.

**Baron-Cohen, S.** (1991). Do people with autism understand what causes emotion? *Child Development, 62,* 385–395.

**Baron-Cohen, S., & Belmonte, M. K.** (2005). Autism: A window onto the development of the social and analytic brain. *Annual Review of Neuroscience, 28,* 109–126.

**Baron-Cohen, S., Leslie, A., & Frith, U.** (1985). Does the autistic child have a "theory of mind"? *Cognition, 21,* 37–46.

**Barondes, S.** (2003). *Better than Prozac.* New York: Oxford University Press.

**Barrett, L. F., Mesquita, B., & Gendron, M.** (2011). Context in emotion perception. *Current Directions in Psychological Science, 20*(5), 286–290. doi:10.1177/0963721411422522

**Barrientos, R. M., Watkins, L. R., Rudy, J. W., & Maier, S. F.** (2009). Characterization of the sickness response in young and aging rats following *E. coli* infection. *Brain, Behavior, and Immunity, 23,* 450–454.

**Bartal, I. B.-A., Decety, J., & Mason, P.** (2011). Empathy and pro-social behavior in rats. *Science, 334*(6061), 1427–1430.

**Bartlett, F. C.** (1932). *Remembering: A study in experimental and social psychology.* Cambridge, England: Cambridge University Press.

**Bartol, C. R., & Costello, N.** (1976). Extraversion as a function of temporal duration of electric shock: An exploratory study. *Perceptual and Motor Skills, 42,* 1174.

**Bartoshuk, L. M.** (2000). Comparing sensory experiences across individuals: Recent psychophysical advances illuminate genetic variation in taste perception. *Chemical Senses, 25,* 447–460.

**Bartoshuk, L. M., & Beauchamp, G. K.** (1994). Chemical senses. *Annual Review of Psychology, 45,* 419–445.

**Basden, B. H., Basden, D. R., Bryner, S., & Thomas, R. L.** (1997). A comparison of group and individual remembering: Does collaboration disrupt retrieval strategies? *Journal of Experimental Psychology: Learning, Memory, and Cognition, 23,* 1176–1191.

**Bates, E., & Goodman, J. C.** (1997). On the inseparability of grammar and the lexicon: Evidence from acquisition, aphasia, and real-time processing. *Language and Cognitive Processes, 12,* 507–584.

**Bateson, M., Nettle, D., & Roberts, G.** (2006). Cues of being watched enhance cooperation in a real-world setting. *Biology Letters, 2*(3), 412–414.

**Batson, C. D.** (2002). Addressing the altruism question experimentally. In S. G. Post & L. G. Underwood (Eds.), *Altruism & altruistic love: Science, philosophy, & religion in dialogue* (pp. 89–105). London: Oxford University Press.

**Batty, G. D., Deary, I. J., Schoon, I., & Gale, C. R.** (2007). Mental ability across childhood in relation to risk factors for premature mortality in adult life: The 1970 British Cohort Study. *Journal of Epidemiology & Community Health, 61*(11), 997–1003. doi:10.1136/jech.2006.054494

**Bauby, J.** (1997). *The diving bell and the butterfly.* London: Fourth Estate.

**Baumeister, R. F., Bratslavsky, E., Muraven, M., & Tice, D. M.** (1998). Ego depletion: Is the active self a limited resource? *Journal of Personality and Social Psychology, 74,* 1252–1265.

**Baumeister, R. F., Campbell, J. D., Krueger, J. I., & Vohs, K. D.** (2003). Does high self-esteem cause better performance, interpersonal success, happiness, or healthier lifestyles? *Psychological Science in the Public Interest, 4,* 1–44.

**Baumeister, R. F., Cantanese, K. R., & Vohs, K. D.** (2001). Is there a gender difference in strength of sex drive? Theoretical views, conceptual distinctions, and a review of relevant evidence. *Personality and Social Psychology Review, 5,* 242–273.

**Baumeister, R. F., Heatherton, T. F., & Tice, D. M.** (1995). *Losing control.* San Diego, CA: Academic Press.

**Baumeister, R. F., & Leary, M. R.** (1995). The need to belong: Desire for interpersonal attachments as a fundamental human motivation. *Psychological Bulletin, 117,* 497–529.

**Baumeister, R. F., Smart, L., & Boden, J. M.** (1996). Relation of threatened egotism to violence and aggression: The dark side of high self-esteem. *Psychological Review, 103,* 5–33.

**Baumeister, R. F., Vohs, K. D., & Tice, D. M.** (2007). The strength model of self-control. *Current Directions in Psychological Science, 16,* 351–355.

**Baxter, L. R., Schwartz, J. M., Bergman, K. S., Szuba, M. P., Guze, B. H., Mazziotta, J. C., Alazraki, A., ... Munford, P.** (1992). Caudate glucose metabolic rate changes with both drug behavior therapy for obsessive-compulsive disorder. *Archives of General Psychiatry, 49,* 681–689.

**Bayley, P. J., Frascino, J. C., & Squire, L. R.** (2005). Robust habit learning in the absence of awareness and independent of the medial temporal lobe. *Nature, 436,* 550–553.

**Bayley, P. J., Gold, J. J., Hopkins, R. O., & Squire, L. R.** (2005). The neuroanatomy of remote memory. *Neuron, 46,* 799–810.

**Beard, C., Sawyer, A. T., & Hoffmann, S. G.** (2012). Efficacy of attention bias modification using threat and appetitive stimuli: A meta-analytic review. *Behavior Therapy, 43,* 724–740.

**Bechara, A., Damasio, A. R., Damasio, H., & Anderson, S. W.** (1994). Insensitivity to future consequences following damage to human prefrontal cortex. *Cognition, 50,* 7–15.

**Bechara, A., Damasio, H., Tranel, D., & Damasio, A. R.** (1997). Deciding advantageously before knowing the advantageous strategy. *Science, 275,* 1293–1295.

**Bechara, A., Dolan, S., Denburg, N., Hindes, A., & Anderson, S. W.** (2001). Decision-making deficits, linked to a dysfunctional ventromedial prefrontal cortex, revealed in alcohol and stimulant abusers. *Neuropsychologia, 39,* 376–389.

**Bechara, A., Tranel, D., & Damasio, H.** (2000). Characterization of the decision-making deficit of patients with ventromedial prefrontal cortex lesions. *Brain, 123,* 2189–2202.

**Beck, A. T.** (1967). *Depression: Causes and treatment.* Philadelphia: University of Pennsylvania Press.

**Beck, A. T.** (2005). The current state of cognitive therapy: A 40-year retrospective. *Archives of General Psychiatry, 62,* 953–959.

**Beckers, G., & Zeki, S.** (1995). The consequences of inactivating areas V1 and V5 on visual motion perception. *Brain, 118,* 49–60.

**Bednarczyk, R. A., Davis, R., Ault, K., Orenstein, W., & Omer, S. B.** (2012). Sexual activity-related outcomes after human papillomavirus vaccination of 11- to 12-year-olds. *Pediatrics, 130*(5), 798–805. Doi:10.1542/peds.2912-1516

**Bedny, M., & Saxe, R.** (2012). Insights into the origins of knowledge from the cognitive neuroscience of blindness. *Cognitive Neuropsychology, 29,* 56–84.

**Beek, M. R., Levin, D. T., & Angelone, B.** (2007). Change blindness blindness: Beliefs about the roles of intention and scene complexity in change detection. *Consciousness and Cognition, 16,* 31–51.

**Beesdo, K., Pine, D. S., Lieb, R., & Wittchen, H. U.** (2010). Incidence and risk patterns of anxiety and depressive disorders and categorization of generalized anxiety disorder. *Archives of General Psychiatry, 67,* 47–57.

**Békésy, G. von.** (1960). *Experiments in hearing.* New York: McGraw-Hill.

**Bekinschtein, T. A., Peeters, M., Shalom, D., & Sigman, M.** (2011). Sea slugs, subliminal pictures, and vegetative state patients:

Boundaries of consciousness in classical conditioning. *Frontiers in Psychology, 2,* article 337. doi:10.3389/fpsyg.2011.00337

**Bell, A. P., Weinberg, M. S., & Hammersmith, S. K.** (1981). *Sexual preference: Its development in men and women.* Bloomington: Indiana University Press.

**Belluck, P., & Carey, B.** (2013, May 7). Psychiatry's guide is out of touch with science, experts say. *New York Times,* p. A13. Retrieved from http://www.nytimes.com/2013/05/07/psychiatrys-new-guide-falls-short-experts-say.html

**Belsky, J.** (2012). The development of human reproductive strategies: Progress and prospects. *Current Directions in Psychological Science, 21*(5), 310–316. doi:10.1177/0963721412453588

**Belsky, J., Spritz, B., & Crnic, K.** (1996). Infant attachment security and affective-cognitive information processing at age 3. *Psychological Science, 7,* 111–114.

**Bem, S. L.** (1974). The measure of psychological androgyny. *Journal of Consulting and Clinical Psychology, 42,* 155–162.

**Benedetti, F., Maggi, G., & Lopiano, L.** (2003). Open versus hidden medical treatment: The patient's knowledge about a therapy affects the therapy outcome. *Prevention & Treatment, 6,* Article 1. Retrieved June 23, 2003, from http://content.apa.org/psycarticles/2003-07872-001

**Benedetti, F., Pollo, A., Lopiano, L., Lanotte, M., Vighetti, S., & Rainero, I.** (2003). Conscious expectation and unconscious conditioning in analgesic, motor, and hormonal placebo/nocebo responses. *The Journal of Neuroscience, 23,* 4315–4323.

**Benenson, J. F., Markovits, H., Thompson, M. E., & Wrangham, R. W.** (2011). Under threat of social exclusion, females exclude more than males. *Psychological Science, 22*(4), 538–544. doi: 10.1177/0956797611402511

**Bennett, I. J., Romano, J. C., Howard, J. H., & Howard, D. V.** (2008). Two forms of implicit learning in young adults with dyslexia. *Annals of the New York Academy of Sciences, 1145,* 184–198.

**Benoit, R. G., & Anderson, M. C.** (2012). Opposing mechanisms support the voluntary forgetting of unwanted memories. *Neuron, 76,* 450–460.

**Benoit, S. C., Kemp, C. J., Elias, C. F., Abplanalp, W., Herman, J. P., Migrenne, S., … Clegg, D. J.** (2009). Palmitic acid mediates hypothalamic insulin resistance by altering pkc-theta subcellular localization in rodents. *The Journal of Clinical Investigation, 119*(9), 2577–2589.

**Ben-Porath, Y. S., & Tellegen, A.** (2008). *Minnesota Multiphasic Personality Inventory–2–Restructured Form: Manual for administration, scoring, and interpretation.* Minneapolis: University of Minnesota Press.

**Benson, H. (Ed.).** (1990). *The relaxation response.* New York: Harper Torch.

**Benson, H., Dusek, J. A., Sherwood, J. B., Lam, P., Bethea, C. F., Carpenter, W., … Hibberd, P. L.** (2006). Study of the therapeutic effects of intercessory prayer (STEP) in cardiac bypass patients: A multicenter randomized trial of uncertainty and certainty of receiving intercessory prayer. *American Heart Journal, 151,* 934–942.

**Berger, H.** (1929). Über das Elektrenkephalogramm des Menschen [Electroencephalogram of man]. *Archiv für Psychiatrie und Nervenkrankheiten, 87,* 527–570.

**Bergeron, P., Auger, N., & Hamel, D.** (2009). Weight, general health and mental health: Status of diverse subgroups of immigrants in Canada. *Canadian Journal of Public Health, 100*(3), 215–220.

**Berglund, H., Lindstrom, P., & Savic, I.** (2006). Brain response to putative pheromones in lesbian women. *Proceedings of the National Academy of Sciences, USA, 103,* 8269–8274.

**Bering, J.** (2004). A critical review of the "enculturation hypothesis": The effects of human rearing on great ape social cognition. *Animal Cognition, 7,* 201–212.

**Berkowitz, L.** (1990). On the formation and regulation of anger and aggression: A cognitive-neoassociationistic analysis. *American Psychologist, 45,* 494–503.

**Bernard, L. L.** (1924). *Instinct: A study in social psychology.* New York: Holt.

**Bernat, J. L.** (2009). Ethical issues in the treatment of severe brain injury: The impact of new technologies. *Annals of the New York Academy of Sciences, 1157,* 117–130.

**Berridge, K. C.** (2007). The debate over dopamine's role in reward: The case for incentive salience. *Psychopharmacology, 191,* 391–431.

**Berry, D. S., & McArthur, L. Z.** (1985). Some components and consequences of a babyface. *Journal of Personality and Social Psychology, 48,* 312–323.

**Berry, J. W., Poortinga, Y. H., Segall, M. H., & Dasen, P. R.** (1992). *Cross-cultural psychology: Research and applications.* New York: Cambridge University Press.

**Berscheid, E., Dion, K., Walster, E., & Walster, G. W.** (1971). Physical attractiveness and dating choice: A test of the matching hypothesis. *Journal of Experimental Social Psychology, 7*(2), 173–189.

**Berscheid, E., & Reis, H. T.** (1998). Interpersonal attraction and close relationships. In D. T. Gilbert, S. T. Fiske, & G. Lindzey (Eds.), *The handbook of social psychology* (4th ed., Vol. 2, pp. 193–281). New York: McGraw-Hill.

**Bertelsen, B., Harvald, B., & Hauge, M.** (1977). A Danish twin study of manic-depressive disorders. *British Journal of Psychiatry, 130,* 330–351.

**Bertenthal, B. I., Rose, J. L., & Bai, D. L.** (1997). Perception–action coupling in the development of visual control of posture. *Journal of Experimental Psychology: Human Perception & Performance, 23,* 1631–1643.

**Berthoud, H.-R., & Morrison, C.** (2008). The brain, appetite, and obesity. *Annual Review of Psychology, 59,* 55–92.

**Best, J. B.** (1992). *Cognitive psychology* (3rd ed.). New York: West Publishing.

**Bettencourt, B., A., & Miller, N.** (1996). Gender differences in aggression as a function of provocation: A meta-analysis. *Psychological Bulletin, 119,* 422–447.

**Beutler, L. E.** (2002). The dodo bird is extinct. *Clinical Psychology: Science and Practice, 9,* 30–34.

**Bhargava, S.** (2011). Diagnosis and management of common sleep problems in children. *Pediatrics in Review, 32,* 91.

**Bialystok, E.** (1999). Cognitive complexity and attentional control in the bilingual mind. *Child Development, 70,* 636–644.

**Bialystok, E.** (2009). Bilingualism: The good, the bad, and the indifference. *Bilingualism: Language and Cognitive Processes, 12,* 3–11.

**Bialystok, E., Craik, F. I. M., & Luk, G.** (2012). Bilingualism: Consequences for mind and brain. *Trends in Cognitive Sciences, 16,* 240–250.

**Bickerton, D.** (1990). *Language and species.* Chicago: University of Chicago Press.

**Biederman, I.** (1987). Recognition-by-components: A theory of human image understanding. *Psychological Review, 94,* 115–147.

**Biederman, J., Faraone, S. V., Spencer, T. J., Mick, E., Monuteaux, M. C., & Aleardi, M.** (2006). Functional impairments in adults with self-reports of diagnosed ADHD: A controlled study of 1001 adults in the community. *Journal of Clinical Psychiatry, 67,* 524–540.

**Biederman, J., Monuteaux, M. C., Spencer, T., Wilens, T. E., & Faraone, S. V.** (2009). Do stimulants protect against psychiatric disorders in youth with ADHD? A 10-year follow-up study. *Pediatrics, 124,* 71–78.

**Billet, E., Richter, J., & Kennedy, J.** (1998). Genetics of obsessive-compulsive disorder. In R. Swinson, M. Anthony, S. Rachman, & M. Richter (Eds.), *Obsessive-compulsive disorder: Theory, research, and treatment* (pp. 181–206). New York: Guilford Press.

**Binet, A.** (1909). *Les idées modernes sur les enfants* [Modern ideas about children]. Paris: Flammarion.

**Binswanger, L.** (1958). The existential analysis school of thought. In R. May (Ed.), *Existence: A new dimension in psychiatry and psychology* (pp. 191–213). New York: Basic Books.

**Bjork, D. W.** (1983). *The compromised scientist: William James in the development of American psychology.* New York: Columbia University Press.

**Bjork, D. W.** (1993). *B. F. Skinner: A life.* New York: Basic Books.

**Bjork, E. L., & Bjork, R. A.** (2011). Making things hard on yourself, but in a good way: Creating desirable difficulties to enhance learning. In M. A. Gernsbacher, R. W. Pewe, L. M. Hough, & J. R. Pomerantz (Eds.), *Psychology and the real world: Essays illustrating fundamental contributions to society* (pp. 56–64). New York: Worth Publishers.

**Bjork, R. A.** (1975). Retrieval as a memory modifier: An interpretation of negative recency and related phenomena. In R. L. Solso (Ed.), *Information processing and cognition: The Loyola symposium* (pp. 123–144). Hillsdale, NJ: Erlbaum.

**Bjork, R. A.** (2011). On the symbiosis of remembering, forgetting, and learning. In A. S. Benjamin (Ed.), *Successful remembering and successful forgetting: A festschrift in honor of Robert A. Bjork* (pp. 1–22). London: Psychology Press.

**Bjork, R. A., & Bjork, E. L.** (1988). On the adaptive aspects of retrieval failure in autobiographical memory. In M. M. Gruneberg, P. E. Morris, & R. N. Sykes (Eds.), *Practical aspects of memory: Current research and issues* (pp. 283–288). Chichester, England: Wiley.

**Bjork, R. A., Dunlosky, J., & Kornell, N.** (2013). Self-regulated learning: Beliefs, techniques, and illusions. *Annual Review of Psychology, 64,* 417–444.

**Blackburn, E. H., & Epel, E. S.** (2012). Too toxic to ignore. *Nature, 490,* 169–171.

**Blair, C.** (2006). How similar are fluid cognition and general intelligence? A developmental neuroscience perspective on fluid cognition as an aspect of human cognitive ability. *Behavioral and Brain Sciences, 29*(2), 109–125 (article),125–160 (discussion). doi:10.1017/S0140525X06009034

**Blair, I. V.** (2002). The malleability of automatic stereotypes and prejudice. *Personality and Social Psychology Review, 6,* 242–261.

**Blair, J., Peschardt, K., & Mitchell, D. R.** (2005). *Psychopath: Emotion and the brain.* Oxford, England: Blackwell.

**Blascovich, J., Mendes, W. B., Hunter, S. B., Lickel, B., & Kowai-Bell, N.** (2001). Perceiver threat in social interactions with stigmatized others. *Journal of Personality and Social Psychology, 80,* 253–267.

**Blascovich, J., & Tomaka, J.** (1996). The biopsychosocial model of arousal regulation. In M. P. Zanna (Ed.), *Advances in experimental social psychology* (Vol. 28, pp. 1–51). San Diego, CA: Academic Press.

**Blasi, A.** (1980). Bridging moral cognition and moral action: A critical review of the literature. *Psychological Bulletin, 88,* 1–45.

**Blatt, S. J., & Homann, E.** (1992). Parent–child interaction in the etiology of dependent and self-critical depression. *Clinical Psychology Review, 12,* 47–91.

**Blesch, A., & Tuszynski, M. H.** (2009). Spinal cord injury: Plasticity, regeneration and the challenge of translational drug development. *Trends in Neurosciences, 32,* 41–47.

**Bliss, T. V. P.** (1999). Young receptors make smart mice. *Nature, 401,* 25–27.

**Bliss, T. V. P., & Lømo, W. T.** (1973). Long-lasting potentiation of synaptic transmission in the dentate area of the anesthetized rabbit following stimulation of the perforant path. *Journal of Physiology, 232,* 331–356.

**Bloch, C., Kaiser, A., Kuenzli, E., Zappatore, D., Haller, S., Franceschini, R., … Nitsch, C.** (2009). The age of second language acquisition determines the variability in activation elicited by narration in three languages in Broca's and Wernicke's area. *Neuropsychologia, 47,* 625–633.

**Bloom, C. M., Venard, J., Harden, M., & Seetharaman, S.** (2007). Non-contingent positive and negative reinforcement schedules of superstitious behaviors. *Behavioural Process, 75,* 8–13.

**Blumen, H. M., & Rajaram, S.** (2008). Influence of re-exposure and retrieval disruption during group collaboration on later individual recall. *Memory, 16,* 231–244.

**Boden, J. M., Fergusson, D. M., & Horwood, L. J.** (2010). Risk factors for conduct disorder and oppositional/defiant disorder: Evidence from a New Zealand birth cohort. *Journal of the American Academy of Child and Adolescent Psychiatry, 49,* 1125–1133.

**Boecker, H., Sprenger, T., Spilker, M. E., Henriksen, G., Koppenhoefer, M., Wagner, K. J., …Tolle, T. R.** (2008). The runner's high: Opioidergic mechanisms in the human brain. *Cerebral Cortex, 18,* 2523–2531.

**Boehm, J. K., & Kubzansky, L. D.** (2012). The heart's content: The association between positive psychological well-being and cardiovascular health. *Psychological Bulletin, 138,* 655–691.

**Boehm, J. K., Williams, D. R., Rimm, E. B., Ryff, C., & Kubzansky, L. D.** (2013). Relation between optimism and lipids in midlife. *American Journal of Cardiology, 111,* 1425–1431.

**Boergers, J., Spirito, A., & Donaldson, D.** (1998). Reasons for adolescent suicide attempts: Associations with psychological functioning. *Journal of the American Academy of Child and Adolescent Psychiatry, 37,* 1287–1293.

**Bogaert, A. F.** (2004). Asexuality: Its prevalence and associated factors in a national probability sample. *The Journal of Sex Research, 41,* 279–287.

**Bohan, J. S.** (1996). *Psychology and sexual orientation: Coming to terms.* New York: Routledge.

**Boinski, S., Quatrone, R. P., & Swartz, H.** (2000). Substrate and tool use by brown capuchins in Suriname: Ecological contexts and cognitive bases. *American Anthropologist, 102,* 741–761.

**Boisvert, C. M., & Faust, D.** (2002). Iatrogenic symptoms in psychotherapy: A theoretical exploration of the potential impact of labels, language, and belief systems. *American Journal of Psychotherapy, 56,* 244–259.

**Bolger, N., Davis, A., & Rafaeli, E.** (2003). Diary methods: Capturing life as it is lived. *Annual Review of Psychology, 54,* 579–616.

**Bolton, G. E., & Ockenfels, A.** (2000). ERC: A theory of equity, reciprocity, and competition. *American Economic Review, 90,* 166–193.

**Boomsma, D., Busjahn, A., & Peltonen, L.** (2002). Classical twin studies and beyond. *Nature Reviews Genetics, 3,* 872–882.

**Bootzin, R. R., & Epstein, D. R.** (2011). Understanding and treating insomnia. *Annual Review of Clinical Psychology, 7,* 435–458.

**Borghol, N., Suderman, M., McArdle, W., Racine, A., Hallett, M., Pembrey, M., … Szyf, M.** (2012). Associations with early-life socioeconomic position in adult DNA methylation. *International Journal of Epidemiology, 41,* 62–74.

**Borkenau, P., & Liebler, A.** (1995). Observable attributes as manifestations and cues of personality and intelligence. *Journal of Personality, 63,* 1–25.

**Borkevec, T. D.** (1982). Insomnia. *Journal of Consulting and Clinical Psychology, 50,* 880–895.

**Born, R. T., & Bradley, D. C.** (2005). Structure and function of visual area MT. *Annual Review of Neuroscience, 28,* 157–189.

**Börner, K., Klavans, R., Patek, M., Zoss, A. M., Biberstine, J. R., Light, R. P., Larivière, V., & Boyack, K. W.** (2012). Design and update of a classification system: The UCSD map of science. *PLoS ONE, 7,* e39464.

**Bornstein, R. F.** (1989). Exposure and affect: Overview and metaanalysis of research, 1968–1987. *Psychological Bulletin, 106,* 265–289.

**Boroditsky, L.** (2001). Does language shape thought? Mandarin and English speakers' conceptions of time. *Cognitive Psychology, 43,* 1–22.

**Botwin, M. D., Buss, D. M., & Shackelford, T. K.** (1997). Personality and mate preferences: Five factors in mate selection and marital satisfaction. *Journal of Personality, 65,* 107–136.

**Bouchard, T. J., & Loehlin, J. C.** (2001). Genes, evolution, and personality. *Behavioral Genetics, 31,* 243–273.

**Bouchard, S. M., Brown, T. G., & Nadeau, L.** (2012). Decision making capacities and affective reward anticipation in DWI recidivists compared to non-offenders: A preliminary study. *Accident Analysis and Prevention, 45,* 580–587.

**Bouchard, T. J., & McGue, M.** (2003). Genetic and environmental influences on human psychological differences. *Journal of Neurobiology, 54,* 4–45.

**Bouton, M. E.** (1988). Context and ambiguity in the extinction of emotional learning: Implications for exposure therapy. *Behaviour Research and Therapy, 26,* 137–149.

**Bower, B.** (1999, October 30). The mental butler did it—research suggests that subconscious affects behavior more than thought. *Science News, 156,* 208–282.

**Bower, G. H.** (1981). Mood and memory. *American Psychologist, 36,* 129–148.

**Bower, G. H., Clark, M. C., Lesgold, A. M., & Winzenz, D.** (1969). Hierarchical retrieval schemes in recall of categorical word lists. *Journal of Verbal Learning and Verbal Behavior, 8,* 323–343.

**Bowers, K. S., Regehr, G., Balthazard, C., & Parker, D.** (1990). Intuition in the context of discovery. *Cognitive Psychology, 22,* 72–110.

**Bowlby, J.** (1969). *Attachment and loss: Vol. 1. Attachment.* New York: Basic Books.

**Bowlby, J.** (1973). *Attachment and loss: Vol. 2. Separation.* New York: Basic Books.

**Bowlby, J.** (1980). *Attachment and loss: Vol. 3. Loss: Sadness and depression.* New York: Basic Books.

**Boyack, K. W., Klavans, R., & Börner, K.** (2005). Mapping the backbone of science. *Scientometrics, 64,* 351–374.

**Boyce, J., & Cotter, A.** (2013). *Homicide in Canada, 2012.* Juristat article. Ottawa: Statistics Canada, Canadian Centre for Justice Statistics.

**Boyd, R.** (2008, February 7). Do people use only 10 percent of their brains? *Scientific American.* Retrieved from http://www.scientificamerican.com/article.cfm?id=people-only-use-10-percent-of-brain&page=2

**Bozarth, M. A. (Ed.).** (1987). *Methods of assessing the reinforcing properties of abused drugs.* New York: Springer-Verlag.

**Bozarth, M. A., & Wise, R. A.** (1985). Toxicity associated with longterm intravenous heroin and cocaine self-administration in the rat. *Journal of the American Medical Association, 254,* 81–83.

**Brackett, M. A., & Mayer, J. D.** (2003). Convergent, discriminant, and incremental validity of competing measures of emotional intelligence. *Personality and Social Psychology Bulletin, 29,* 1147.

**Brackett, M. A., Rivers, S. E., Shiffman, S., Lerner, N., & Salovey, P.** (2006). Relating emotional abilities to social functioning: A comparison of self-report and performance measures of emotional intelligence. *Journal of Personality and Social Psychology, 91,* 780.

**Brackett, M. A., Warner, R. M., & Bosco, J.** (2005). Emotional intelligence and relationship quality among couples. *Personal Relationships, 12*(2), 197–212.

**Bradford, D., Stroup, S., & Lieberman, J.** (2002). Pharmacological treatments for schizophrenia. In P. E. Nathan & J. M. Gorman (Eds.), *A guide to treatments that work* (2nd ed., pp. 169–199). New York: Oxford University Press.

**Bradmetz, J., & Schneider, R.** (2004). The role of the counterfactually satisfied desire in the lag between false-belief and false-emotion attributions in children aged 4–7. *British Journal of Developmental Psychology, 22,* 185–196.

**Braet, W., & Humphreys, G. W.** (2009). The role of reentrant processes in feature binding: Evidence from neuropsychology and TMS on late onset illusory conjunctions. *Visual Cognition, 17,* 25–47.

**Bramlett, M. D., & Mosher, W. D.** (2002). *Cohabitation, marriage, divorce, and remarriage in the United States* (Vital and Health Statistics Series 23, No. 22). Hyattsville, MD: National Center for Health Statistics.

**Brandt, K. R., Gardiner, J. M., Vargha-Khadem, F., Baddeley, A. D., & Mishkin, M.** (2009). Impairment of recollection but not familiarity in a case of developmental amnesia. *Neurocase, 15,* 60–65.

**Braun, A. R., Balkin, T. J., Wesensten, N. J., Gwadry, F., Carson, R. E., Varga, M., … Herskovitch, P.** (1998). Dissociated pattern of activity in visual cortices and their projections during rapid eye movement sleep. *Science, 279,* 91–95.

**Breazeal, C.** (2009). Role of expressive behaviour for robots that learn from people. *Philosophical Transactions of the Royal Society (B), 364,* 3527–3538.

**Breckler, S. J.** (1994). Memory for the experiment of donating blood: Just how bad was it? *Basic and Applied Social Psychology, 15,* 467–488.

**Brédart, S., & Valentine, T.** (1998). Descriptiveness and proper name retrieval. *Memory, 6,* 199–206.

**Bredy, T. W., Wu, H., Crego, C., Zellhoefer, J., Sun, Y. E., & Barad, M.** (2007). Histone modifications around individual BDNF gene promoters in prefrontal cortex are associated with extinction of conditioned fear. *Learning and Memory, 14,* 268–276.

**Breggin, P. R.** (1990). Brain damage, dementia, and persistent cognitive dysfunction associated with neuroleptic drugs: Evidence, etiology, implications. *Journal of Mind and Behavior, 11,* 425–463.

**Breggin, P. R.** (2000). *Reclaiming our children.* Cambridge, MA: Perseus Books.

**Brehm, S. S.** (1992). *Intimate relationships* (2nd ed.). New York: McGraw-Hill.

**Breivik, H., Collett, B., Ventafridda, V., Cohen, R., & Gallacher, D.** (2006). Survey of chronic pain in Europe: Prevalence, impact on daily life, and treatment. *European Journal of Pain, 10,* 287–333.

**Breland, K., & Breland, M.** (1961). The misbehavior of organisms. *American Psychologist, 16,* 681–684.

**Brennan, P. A., & Zufall, F.** (2006). Pheromonal communication in vertebrates. *Nature, 444,* 308–315.

**Brenninkmeijer, V., Vanyperen, N. W., & Buunk, B. P.** (2001). I am not a better teacher, but others are doing worse: Burnout and perceptions of superiority among teachers. *Social Psychology of Education, 4*(3–4), 259–274.

**Bretherton, I., & Munholland, K. A.** (1999). Internal working models in attachment relationships: A construct revisited. In J. Cassidy & P. R. Shaver (Eds.), *Handbook of attachment: Theory, research and clinical applications* (pp. 89–114). New York: Guilford Press.

**Brewer, J. A., Worhunsky, P. D., Gray, J. R., Tang, Y.-Y., Weber, J., & Kober, H.** (2011). Meditation experience is associated with differences in default mode network activity and connectivity. *Proceedings of the National Academy of Sciences, 108,* 20254–20259.

Brewer, W. F. (1996). What is recollective memory? In D. C. Rubin (Ed.), *Remembering our past: Studies in autobiographical memory* (pp. 19–66). New York: Cambridge University Press.

Broadbent, D. E. (1958). *Perception and communication*. London: Pergamon Press.

Broberg, D. J., & Bernstein, I. L. (1987). Candy as a scapegoat in the prevention of food aversions in children receiving chemotherapy. *Cancer, 60,* 2344–2347.

Broca, P. (1861). Remarques sur le siège de la faculté du langage articulé; suivies d'une observation d'aphémie (perte de la parole) [Remarks on the seat of the faculty of articulated language, following an observation of aphemia (loss of speech)]. *Bulletin de la Société Anatomique de Paris, 36,* 330–357.

Broca, P. (1863). Localisation des fonction cérébrales: Siège du langage articulé [Localization of brain functions: Seat of the faculty of articulated language]. *Bulletin de la Société d'Anthropologie de Paris, 4,* 200–202.

Brock, A. (1993). Something old, something new: The "reappraisal" of Wilhelm Wundt in textbooks. *Theory & Psychology, 3*(2), 235–242.

Brody, N. (2003). Construct validation of the Sternberg Triarchic Abilities Test: Comment and reanalysis. *Intelligence, 31*(4), 319–329.

Brooks, D. (2011, July 7). The unexamined society. *New York Times.* Retrieved from http://www.nytimes.com/2011/07/08/opinion/08brooks.html

Brooks, D. (2012a, May 3). The campus tsunami. *New York Times.* Retreived from http://www.nytimes.com/2012/05/04/opinion/brooks-the-campus-tsunami.html

Brooks, D. (2012b, October 12). The personality problem. *New York Times.* Retrieved from http://www.nytimes.com/2012/10/12/opinion/brooks-the-personality-problem.html

Brooks, R., & Meltzoff, A. N. (2002). The importance of eyes: How infants interpret adult looking behavior. *Developmental Psychology, 38,* 958–966.

Brooks-Gunn, J., Graber, J. A., & Paikoff, R. L. (1994). Studying links between hormones and negative affect: Models and measures. *Journal of Research on Adolescence, 4,* 469–486.

Brosnan, S. F., & DeWaal, F. B. M. (2003). Monkeys reject unequal pay. *Nature, 425,* 297–299.

Brown, A. S. (2004). *The déjà vu experience.* New York: Psychology Press.

Brown, B. B., Mory, M., & Kinney, D. (1994). Casting crowds in a relational perspective: Caricature, channel, and context. In G. A. R. Montemayor & T. Gullotta (Eds.), *Advances in adolescent development: Personal relationships during adolescence* (Vol. 5, pp. 123–167). Newbury Park, CA: Sage.

Brown, J. D. (1993). Self-esteem and self-evaluation: Feeling is believing. In J. M. Suls (Ed.), *The self in social perspective: Psychological perspectives on the self* (Vol. 4, pp. 27–58). Hillsdale, NJ: Erlbaum.

Brown, J. D., & McGill, K. L. (1989). The cost of good fortune: When positive life events produce negative health consequences. *Journal of Personality and Social Psychology, 57,* 1103–1110.

Brown, L. E., Wilson, E. T., & Gribble, P. L. (2009). Repetitive transcranial magnetic stimulation to the primary cortex interferes with motor learning by observing. *Journal of Cognitive Neuroscience, 21,* 1013–1022.

Brown, R. (1958). *Words and things.* New York: Free Press.

Brown, R., & Hanlon, C. (1970). Derivational complexity and order of acquisition in child speech. In J. R. Hayes (Ed.), *Cognition and the development of language* (pp. 11–53). New York: Wiley.

Brown, R., & Kulik, J. (1977). Flashbulb memories. *Cognition, 5,* 73–99.

Brown, R., & McNeill, D. (1966). The "tip-of-the-tongue" phenomenon. *Journal of Verbal Learning and Verbal Behavior, 5,* 325–337.

Brown, R. P., Osterman, L. L., & Barnes, C. D. (2009). School violence and the culture of honor. *Psychological Science, 20*(11), 1400–1405.

Brown, S. C., & Craik, F. I. M. (2000). Encoding and retrieval of information. In E. Tulving & F. I. M. Craik (Eds.), *The Oxford handbook of memory* (pp. 93–107). New York: Oxford University Press.

Brown, T. A., & Barlow, D. H. (2002). Classification of anxiety and mood disorders. In D. H. Barlow (Ed.), *Anxiety and its disorders: The nature and treatment of anxiety and panic* (2nd ed.). New York: Guilford Press.

Brownell, K. D., Greenwood, M. R. C., Stellar, E., & Shrager, E. E. (1986). The effects of repeated cycles of weight loss and regain in rats. *Physiology and Behavior, 38,* 459–464.

Bruner, J. S. (1983). Education as social invention. *Journal of Social Issues, 39,* 129–141.

Brunet, A., Orr, S. P., Tremblay, J., Robertson, K., Nader, K., & Pitman, R. K. (2008). Effects of post-retrieval propranolol on psychophysiologic responding during subsequent script-driven traumatic imagery in posttraumatic stress disorder. *Journal of Psychiatric Research, 42,* 503–506.

Brunet, A., Poundjia, J., Tremblay, J., Bui, E., Thomas, E., Orr, S. P., ... Pitman, R. K. (2011). Trauma reactivation under the influence of propranolol decreases posttraumatic stress symptoms and disorder. *Journal of Clinical Psychopharmacology, 31,* 547–550.

Brunner, D. P., Dijk, D. J., Tobler, I., & Borbely, A. A. (1990). Effect of partial sleep deprivation on sleep stages and EEG power spectra. *Electroencephalography and Clinical Neurophysiology, 75,* 492–499.

Bryck, R. L., & Fisher, P. A. (2012). Training the brain: Practical applications of neural plasticity from the intersection of cognitive neuroscience, developmental psychology, and prevention science. *American Psychologist, 67,* 87–100.

Buchanan, C. M., Eccles, J. S., & Becker, J. B. (1992). Are adolescents the victims of raging hormones? Evidence for activational effects of hormones on moods and behavior at adolescence. *Psychological Bulletin, 111,* 62–107.

Buchanan, T. W. (2007). Retrieval of emotional memories. *Psychological Bulletin, 133,* 761–779.

Buckholtz, J. W., & Meyer-Lindenberg, A. (2012). Psychopathology and the human connectome: Toward a transdiagnostic model of risk for mental illness. *Neuron, 74,* 990–1003.

Buck Louis, G. M., Gray, L. E., Marcus, M., Ojeda, S. R., Pescovitz, O. H., Witchel, S. F., ... Euling, S. Y. (2008). Environmental factors and puberty timing: Expert panel research. *Pediatrics, 121*(Suppl. 3), S192–S207. doi:10.1542/peds1813E

Buckner, R. L., Andrews-Hanna, J. R., & Schacter, D. L. (2008). The brain's default network: Anatomy, function, and relevance to disease. *Annals of the New York Academy of Sciences, 1124,* 1–38.

Buckner, R. L., Petersen, S. E., Ojemann, J. G., Miezin, F. M., Squire, L. R., & Raichle, M. E. (1995). Functional anatomical studies of explicit and implicit memory retrieval tasks. *The Journal of Neuroscience, 15,* 12–29.

Bunce, D. M., Flens, E. A., & Neiles, K. Y. (2011). How long can students pay attention in class? A study of student attention decline using clickers. *Journal of Chemical Education, 87,* 1438–1443.

Burger, J. M. (1999). The foot-in-the-door compliance procedure: A multiple-process analysis and review. *Personality and Social Psychology Review, 3,* 303–325.

Burger, J. M. (2009). Replicating Milgram: Would people still obey today? *American Psychologist, 64,* 1–11.

Burger, J. M., & Burns, L. (1988). The illusion of unique invulnerability and the use of effective contraception. *Personality and Social Psychology Bulletin, 14,* 264–270.

Burger, J. M., Sanchez, J., Imberi, J. E., & Grande, L. R. (2009). The norm of reciprocity as an internalized social norm: Returning favors even when no one finds out. *Social Influence, 4*(1), 11–17.

Burke, D., MacKay, D. G., Worthley, J. S., & Wade, E. (1991). On the tip of the tongue: What causes word failure in young and older adults? *Journal of Memory and Language, 30,* 237–246.

Burke, J. D., Loeber, R., & Birmaher, B. (2002). Oppositional defiant disorder and conduct disorder: Part II. A review of the past 10 years. *Journal of the American Academy of Child and Adolescent Psychiatry, 41,* 1275–1293.

Burkham, D. T., Ready, D. D., Lee, V. E., & LoGerfo, L. F. (2004). Social-class differences in summer learning between kindergarten and first grade: Model specification and estimation. *Sociology of Education, 77,* 1–31.

Burks, S. V., Carpenter, J. P., Goette, L., & Rustichini, A. (2009). Cognitive skills affect economic preferences, strategic behavior, and job attachment. *Proceedings of the National Academy of Sciences, 106*(19), 7745–7750. doi:10.1073/pnas.0812360106

Burns, D. J., Hwang, A. J., & Burns, S. A. (2011). Adaptive memory: Determining the proximate mechanisms responsible for the memorial advantages of survival processing. *Journal of Experimental Psychology: Learning, Memory, and Cognition, 37,* 206–218.

Burnstein, E., Crandall, C., & Kitayama, S. (1994). Some neo-Darwinian decision rules for altruism: Weighing cues for inclusive fitness as a function of the biological importance of the decision. *Journal of Personality and Social Psychology, 67,* 773–789.

Burrelli, J. (2008). *Thirty-three years of women in S&E faculty positions.* Washington, DC: National Science Foundation. Retrieved from http://www.nsf.gov/statistics/infbrief/nsf08308/

Burris, C. T., & Branscombe, N. R. (2005). Distorted distance estimation induced by a self-relevant national boundary. *Journal of Experimental Social Psychology, 41,* 305–312.

Bushman, B. J., & Huesmann, L. R. (2010). Aggression. In S. T. Fiske, D. T. Gilbert, & G. Lindzey (Eds.), *The handbook of social psychology* (5th ed., Vol. 2, pp. 833–863). New York: Wiley.

Buss, D. M. (1985). Human mate selection. *American Scientist, 73,* 47–51.

Buss, D. M. (1989). Sex differences in human mate preferences: Evolutionary hypotheses tested in 37 cultures. *Behavioral and Brain Sciences, 12,* 1–49.

Buss, D. M. (1996). Social adaptation and five major factors of personality. In J. S. Wiggins (Ed.), *The five-factor model of personality: Theoretical perspectives* (pp. 180–208). New York: Guilford Press.

Buss, D. M. (1999). *Evolutionary psychology: The new science of the mind.* Boston: Allyn & Bacon.

Buss, D. M. (2000). *The dangerous passion: Why jealousy is as necessary as love and sex.* New York: Free Press.

Buss, D. M. (2007). The evolution of human mating. *Acta Psychologica Sinica, 39,* 502–512.

Buss, D. M., & Haselton, M. G. (2005). The evolution of jealousy. *Trends in Cognitive Sciences, 9,* 506–507.

Buss, D. M., Haselton, M. G., Shackelford, T. K., Bleske, A. L., & Wakefield, J. C. (1998). Adaptations, exaptations, and spandrels. *American Psychologist, 53,* 533–548.

Buss, D. M., & Schmitt, D. P. (1993). Sexual strategies theory: An evolutionary perspective on human mating. *Psychological Review, 100,* 204–232.

Butler, A. C., Chapman, J. E., Forman, E. M., & Beck, A. T. (2006). The empirical status of cognitive-behavioral therapy: A review of meta-analyses. *Clinical Psychology Review, 26,* 17–31.

Butler, M. A., Corboy, J. R., & Filley, C. M. (2009). How the conflict between American psychiatry and neurology delayed the appreciation of cognitive dysfunction in multiple sclerosis. *Neuropsychology Review, 19,* 399–410.

Byers-Heinlein, K., Burns, T. C., & Werker, J. F. (2010). The roots of bilingualism in newborns. *Psychological Science, 21*(3), 343–348. doi:10.1177/0956797609360758

Byrne, D., Allgeier, A. R., Winslow, L., & Buckman, J. (1975). The situational facilitation of interpersonal attraction: A three-factor hypothesis. *Journal of Applied Social Psychology, 5,* 1–15.

Byrne, D., & Clore, G. L. (1970). A reinforcement model of evaluative responses. *Personality: An International Journal, 1,* 103–128.

Byrne, D., Ervin, C. R., & Lamberth, J. (1970). Continuity between the experimental study of attraction and real-life computer dating. *Journal of Personality and Social Psychology, 16,* 157–165.

Byrne, D., & Nelson, D. (1965). Attraction as a linear function of proportion of positive reinforcements. *Journal of Personality and Social Psychology, 1,* 659–663.

Cabeza, R. (2002). Hemispheric asymmetry reduction in older adults: The HAROLD model. *Psychology and Aging, 17,* 85–100.

Cabeza, R., Grady, C. L., Nyberg, L., McIntosh, A. R., Tulving, E., Kapur, S., ... Craik, F. I. M. (1997). Age-related differences in neural activity during memory encoding and retrieval: A positron emission tomography study. *The Journal of Neuroscience, 17,* 391–400.

Cabeza, R., Rao, S., Wagner, A. D., Mayer, A., & Schacter, D. L. (2001). Can medial temporal lobe regions distinguish true from false? An event-related fMRI study of veridical and illusory recognition memory. *Proceedings of the National Academy of Sciences, USA, 98,* 4805–4810.

Cacioppo, J. T., & Patrick, B. (2008). *Loneliness: Human nature and the need for social connection.* New York: Norton.

Cahill, L., Haier, R. J., Fallon, J., Alkire, M. T., Tang, C., Keator, D., ... McGaugh, J. L. (1996). Amygdala activity at encoding correlated with longterm, free recall of emotional information. *Proceedings of the National Academy of Sciences, USA, 93,* 8016–8021.

Cahill, L., & McGaugh, J. L. (1998). Mechanisms of emotional arousal and lasting declarative memory. *Trends in Neurosciences, 21,* 294–299.

Calder, A. J., Young, A. W., Rowland, D., Perrett, D. I., Hodges, J. R., & Etcoff, N. L. (1996). Facial emotion recognition after bilateral amygdala damage: Differentially severe impairment of fear. *Cognitive Neuropsychology, 13,* 699–745.

Callaghan, T., Rochat, P., Lillard, A., Claux, M. L., Odden, H., Itakura, S., ... Singh, S. (2005). Synchrony in the onset of mental-state reasoning: Evidence from five cultures. *Psychological Science, 16,* 378–384.

Calvin, C. M., Deary, I. J., Fenton, C., Roberts, B. A., Der, G., Leckenby, N., & Batty, G. D. (2010). Intelligence in youth and all-cause-mortality: Systematic review with meta-analysis. *International Journal of Epidemiology, 40*(3), 626–644. doi:10.1093/ije/dyq190

Calzo, J. P., Antonucci, T. C., Mays, V. M., & Cochran, S. D. (2011). Retrospective recall of sexual orientation identity development among gay, lesbian, and bisexual adults. *Developmental Psychology, 47*(6), 1658–1673. doi:10.1037/a0025508

Cameron, C. D., & Payne, B. K. (2011). Escaping affect: How motivated emotion regulation creates insensitivity to mass suffering. *Journal of Personality and Social Psychology, 100*(1), 1–15.

Campbell, A. (1999). Staying alive: Evolution, culture, and women's intra-sexual aggression. *Behavioral & Brain Sciences, 22,* 203–252.

Canadian Mental Health Association. (n.d. 1). *Fast facts about mental illness.* Retrieved from http://www.cmha.ca/media/fast-facts-about-mental-illness/#.UrCJ8I2HnY0

Canadian Mental Health Association. (n.d. 2). *Post-traumatic stress disorder (PSTD).* Retrieved from http://www.cmha.ca/mental_health/post-traumatic-stress-disorder/#.UrHiJI2HnY0

Canadian Mental Health Association (BC Division). (2009). *Panic disorder.* Retrieved from http://www.cmha.bc.ca/get-informed/mental-health-information/panic-disorder#A

Canadian Psychological Association. (2000). *Canadian code of ethics for psychologists* (3rd ed.). Ottawa: Author.

Canadian Psychological Association. (2012a). *"Psychology works" fact sheet: Generalized anxiety disorder.* Ottawa: Author.

Canadian Psychological Association. (2012b). *"Psychology works" fact sheet: Obsessive compulsive disorder.* Ottawa: Author.

Canadian Public Health Association. (n.d.). *Alcohol and your health: Less is more when it comes to healthy living.* Retrieved from http://www.cpha.ca/en/portals/substance/article01.aspx

Cannon, W. B. (1929). *Bodily changes in pain, hunger, fear, and rage: An account of recent research into the function of emotional excitement* (2nd ed.). New York: Appleton-Century-Crofts.

Cantor, N. (1990). From thought to behavior: "Having" and "doing" in the study of personality and cognition. *American Psychologist, 45,* 735–750.

Caparelli, E. C. (2007). TMS & fMRI: A new neuroimaging combinational tool to study brain function. *Current Medical Imaging Review, 3,* 109–115.

Caprioli, M. (2003). Gender equality and state aggression: The impact of domestic gender equality on state first use of force. *International Interactions, 29*(3), 195–214. doi:10.1080/03050620304595

Carey, N. (2012). *The epigenetics revolution: How modern biology is rewriting our understanding of genetics, disease, and inheritance.* New York: Columbia University Press.

Carlson, C., & Hoyle, R. (1993). Efficacy of abbreviated progressive muscle relaxation training: A quantitative review of behavioral medicine research. *Journal of Consulting and Clinical Psychology, 61,* 1059–1067.

Carmichael Olson, H., Streissguth, A. P., Sampson, P. D., Barr, H. M., Bookstein, F. L., & Thiede, K. (1997). Association of prenatal alcohol exposure with behavioral and learning problems in early adolescence. *Journal of the American Academy of Child & Adolescent Psychiatry, 36*(9), 1187–1194.

Carolson, E. A. (1998). A prospective longitudinal study of attachment disorganization/disorientation. *Child Development, 69,* 1107–1128.

Carpenter, S. K. (2012). Testing enhances the transfer of learning. *Current Directions in Psychological Science, 21,* 279–283.

Carr, L., Iacoboni, M., Dubeau, M., Mazziotta, J. C., & Lenzi, G. L. (2003). Neural mechanisms of empathy in humans: A relay from neural systems for imitation to limbic areas. *Proceedings of the National Academy of Sciences, USA, 100,* 5497–5502.

Carroll, J. B. (1993). *Human cognitive abilities.* Cambridge, England: Cambridge University Press.

Carson, R. C., Butcher, J. N., & Mineka, S. (2000). *Abnormal psychology and modern life* (11th ed.). Boston: Allyn & Bacon.

Carstensen, L. L. (1992). Social and emotional patterns in adulthood: Support for socioemotional selectivity theory. *Psychology and Aging, 7,* 331–338.

Carstensen, L. L., & Fredrickson, B. L. (1998). Influence of HIV status and age on cognitive representations of others. *Health Psychology, 17,* 1–10.

Carstensen, L. L., Pasupathi, M., Mayr, U., & Nesselroade, J. R. (2000). Emotional experience in everyday life across the adult life span. *Journal of Personality and Social Psychology, 79,* 644–655.

Carstensen, L. L., & Turk-Charles, S. (1994). The salience of emotion across the adult life span. *Psychology and Aging, 9,* 259–264.

Carver, C. S. (2006). Approach, avoidance, and the self-regulation of affect and action. *Motivation and Emotion, 30,* 105–110.

Carver, C. S., Lehman, J. M., & Antoni, M. H. (2003). Dispositional pessimism predicts illness-related disruption of social and recreational activities among breast cancer patients. *Journal of Personality and Social Psychology, 84,* 813–821.

Carver, C. S., & White, T. L. (1994). Behavioral inhibition, behavioral activation, and affective responses to impending reward and punishment: The BIS/BAS scales. *Journal of Personality and Social Psychology, 67*(2), 319–333.

Casasanto, D., & Boroditsky, L. (2008). Time in the mind: Using space to think about time. *Cognition, 106,* 579–593.

Casazza, K., Fontaine, K. R., Astrup, A., Birch, L. L., Brown, A. W., Bohan Brown, M. M., ... Allison, D. B. (2013). Myths, presumptions, and facts about obesity. *New England Journal of Medicine, 368*(5), 446–454.

Caspi, A., & Herbener, E. S. (1990). Continuity and change: Assortative marriage and the consistency of personality in adulthood. *Journal of Personality and Social Psychology, 58,* 250–258.

Caspi, A., Lynam, D., Moffitt, T. E., & Silva, P. A. (1993). Unraveling girls' delinquency: Biological, dispositional, and contextual contributions to adolescent misbehavior. *Developmental Psychology, 29,* 19–30.

Caspi, A., Roberts, B. W., & Shiner, R. L. (2005). Personality development: Stability and change. *Annual Review of Psychology, 56,* 453–484.

Caspi, A., Sugden, K., Moffitt, T. E., Taylor, A., Craig, I. W., Harrington, H., ... Poulton, R. (2003). Influence of life stress on depression: Moderation by a polymorphism in the 5-HTT gene. *Science, 301,* 386–389.

Castel, A. D., McCabe, D. P., & Roediger, H. L. III. (2007). Illusions of competence and overestimation of associate memory for identical items: Evidence from judgments of learning. *Psychonomic Bulletin & Review, 14,* 197–111.

Castellanos, F. X., Patti, P. L., Sharp, W., Jeffries, N. O., Greenstein, D. K., Clasen, L. S., ... Rapoport, J. L. (2002). Developmental trajectories of brain volume abnormalities in children and adolescents with attention-deficit/hyperactivity disorder. *Journal of the American Medical Association, 288,* 1740–1748. doi: 10.1001/jama.288.14.1740

Catrambone, R. (2002). The effects of surface and structural feature matches on the access of story analogs. *Journal of Experimental Psychology: Learning, Memory, & Cognition, 28,* 318–334.

Cattell, R. B. (1950). *Personality: A systematic, theoretical, and factual study.* New York: McGraw-Hill.

Ceci, S. J. (1991). How much does schooling influence general intelligence and its cognitive components? A reassessment of the evidence. *Developmental Psychology, 27,* 703–722.

Ceci, S. J., DeSimone, M., & Johnson, S. (1992). Memory in context: A case study of "Bubbles P.," a gifted but uneven memorizer. In D. J. Herrmann, H. Weingartner, A. Searleman, & C. McEvoy (Eds.), *Memory improvement: Implications for memory theory* (pp. 169–186). New York: Springer-Verlag.

Ceci, S. J., & Williams, W. M. (1997). Schooling, intelligence, and income. *American Psychologist, 52,* 1051–1058.

Ceci, S. J., Williams, W. M., & Barnett, S. M. (2009). Women's underrepresentation in science: Sociocultural and biological considerations. *Psychological Bulletin, 135*(2), 218–261. doi:10.1037/a0014412

Centers for Disease Control and Prevention (CDC). (2002, June 28). Youth risk behavior surveillance. *Surveillance Summary, 51*(SS-4), 1–64. Washington, DC: Author.

Centre for Addiction and Mental Health. (2012). *Mental illness and addiction statistics.* Retrieved from http://www.camh.ca/en/hospital/about_camh/newsroom/for_reporters/Pages/addictionmentalhealthstatistics.aspx

Cepeda, N. J., Pashler, H., Vul, E., Wixted, J. T., & Rohrer, D. (2006). Distributed practice in verbal recall tests: A review and quantitative synthesis. *Psychological Bulletin, 132,* 354–380.

Chabris, C. F., Hebert, B. M., Benjamin, D. J., Beauchamp, J., Cesarini, D., van der Loos, M., & Laibson, D. (2012). Most reported genetic associations with general intelligence are probably false positives. *Psychological Science, 23*(11), 1314–1323. doi:10.1177/0956797611435528

Chabris, C., & Simons, D. (2012, November 16). Using just 10% of your brains? Think again. *Wall Street Journal Online.* Retrieved from http://online.wsj.com/article/SB10001424127887324556304578119351 87421218.html

Chaiken, S. (1980). Heuristic versus systematic information processing and the use of source versus message cues in persuasion. *Journal of Personality and Social Psychology, 39,* 752–766.

Chalmers, D. (1996). *The conscious mind: In search of a fundamental theory.* New York: Oxford University Press.

Chambless, D. L., Baker, M. J., Baucom, D. H., Beutler, L. E., Calhoun, K. S., Crits-Christoph, P., … Woody, S. R. (1998). Update on empirically validated therapies, II. *Clinical Psychologist, 51*(1), 3–14.

Chandler, J., & Schwarz, N. (2009). How extending your middle finger affects your perception of others: Learned movements influence concept accessibility. *Journal of Experimental Social Psychology, 45,* 123–128.

Chandrashekar, J., Hoon, M. A., Ryba, N. J., & Zuker, C. S. (2006). The receptors and cells for human tastes. *Nature, 444,* 288–294.

Chang, P. P., Ford, D. E., Meoni, L. A., Wang, N., & Klag, M. J. (2002). Anger in young men and subsequent premature cardiovascular disease. *Archives of Internal Medicine, 162,* 901–906.

Charles, S. T., Reynolds, C. A., & Gatz, M. (2001). Age-related differences and change in positive and negative affect over 23 years. *Journal of Personality and Social Psychology, 80,* 136–151.

Charness, N. (1981). Aging and skilled problem solving. *Journal of Experimental Psychology: General, 110,* 21–38.

Charpak, G., & Broch, H. (2004). *Debunked!: ESP, telekinesis, and other pseudoscience* (B. K. Holland, Trans.). Baltimore, MD: Johns Hopkins University Press.

Chartrand, T. L., & Bargh, J. A. (1999). The chameleon effect: The perception-behavior link and social interaction. *Journal of Personality and Social Psychology, 76,* 893–910.

Chartrand, T. L., & Kay, A. (2006). *Mystery moods and perplexing performance: Consequences of succeeding and failing at a nonconscious goal.* Unpublished manuscript.

Chen, E., Cohen, S., & Miller, G. E. (2010). How low socioeconomic status affects 2-year hormonal trajectories in children. *Psychological Science, 21*(1), 31–37.

Chen, S. X., & Bond, M. H. (2010). Two languages, two personalities? Examining language effects on the expression of personality in a bilingual context. *Personality and Social Psychology Bulletin, 36,* 1514–1528.

Cheney, D. L., & Seyfarth, R. M. (1990). *How monkeys see the world.* Chicago: University of Chicago Press.

Cheng, D. T., Disterhoft, J. F., Power, J. M., Ellis, D. A., & Desmond, J. E. (2008). Neural substrates underlying human delay and trace eyeblink conditioning. *Proceedings of the National Academy of Sciences, USA, 105,* 8108–8113.

Cherlin, A. J. (Ed.). (1992). *Marriage, divorce, remarriage* (2nd ed.). Cambridge, MA: Harvard University Press.

Cherry, C. (1953). Some experiments on the recognition of speech with one and two ears. *Journal of the Acoustical Society of America, 25,* 275–279.

Choi, I., Nisbett, R. E., & Norenzayan, A. (1999). Causal attribution across cultures: Variation and universality. *Psychological Bulletin, 125,* 47–63.

Chomsky, N. (1957). *Syntactic structures.* The Hague: Mouton.

Chomsky, N. (1959). A review of *Verbal Behavior* by B. F. Skinner. *Language, 35,* 26–58.

Chomsky, N. (1986). *Knowledge of language: Its nature, origin, and use.* New York: Praeger.

Chorover, S. L. (1980). *From Genesis to genocide: The meaning of human nature and the power of behavior control.* Cambridge, MA: MIT Press.

Choy, Y., Fyer, A. J., & Lipsitz, J. D. (2007). Treatment of specific phobia in adults. *Clinical Psychology Review, 27,* 266–286.

Christakis, N. A., & Fowler, J. H. (2007). The spread of obesity in a large social network over 32 years. *New England Journal of Medicine, 357*(4), 370–379.

Christianson, S.-Å., & Loftus, E. F. (1987). Memory for traumatic events. *Applied Cognitive Psychology, 1,* 225–239.

Chung, G. H., Flook, L., & Fuligni, A. J. (2009). Daily family conflict and emotional distress among adolescents from Latin American, Asian, and European backgrounds. *Developmental Psychology, 45,* 1406–1415.

Cialdini, R. B. (2005). Don't throw in the towel: Use social influence research. *American Psychological Society, 18,* 33–34.

Cialdini, R. B. (2013). The focus theory of normative conduct. In P. A. M. van Lange, A. W. Kruglanski, & E. T. Higgins (Eds.), *Handbook of theories of social psychology* (Vol. 3, pp. 295–312). New York: Sage.

Cialdini, R. B., & Goldstein, N. J. (2004). Social influence: Compliance and conformity. *Annual Review of Psychology, 55*(1), 591–621. doi: 10.1146/annurev.psych.55.090902.142015

Cialdini, R. B., Trost, M. R., & Newsom, J. T. (1995). Preference for consistency: The development of a valid measure and the discovery of surprising behavioral implications. *Journal of Personality and Social Psychology, 69,* 318–328.

Cialdini, R. B., Vincent, J. E., Lewis, S. K., Catalan, J., Wheeler, D., & Darby, B. L. (1975). Reciprocal concessions procedure for inducing compliance: The door-in-the-face technique. *Journal of Personality and Social Psychology, 31,* 206–215.

Ciarrochi, J. V., Chan, A. Y., & Caputi, P. (2000). A critical evaluation of the emotional intelligence concept. *Personality & Individual Differences, 28,* 539.

Cicchetti, D., & Toth, S. L. (1998). Perspectives on research and practice in developmental psychopathology. In I. E. Sigel & K. A. Renninger (Eds.), *Handbook of child psychology: Vol. 4. Child psychology in practice* (5th ed., pp. 479–583). New York: Wiley.

Clancy, S. A. (2005). *Abducted: How people come to believe they were kidnapped by aliens.* Cambridge, MA: Harvard University Press.

Clark, M. S., & Lemay, E. P. (2010). Close relationships. In S. T. Fiske, D. T. Gilbert, & G. Lindzey (Eds.), *The handbook of social psychology* (5th ed., Vol. 2). New York: Wiley.

Clark, R. D., & Hatfield, E. (1989). Gender differences in receptivity to sexual offers. *Journal of Psychology and Human Sexuality, 2,* 39–55.

Clark, R. E., Manns, J. R., & Squire, L. R. (2002). Classical conditioning, awareness and brain systems. *Trends in Cognitive Sciences, 6,* 524–531.

Clark, R. E., & Squire, L. R. (1998). Classical conditioning and brain systems: The role of awareness. *Science, 280,* 77–81.

Cleckley, H. M. (1976). *The mask of sanity* (5th ed.). St. Louis: Mosby.

Coe, C. L., & Lubach, G. R. (2008). Fetal programming prenatal origins of health and illness. *Current Directions in Psychological Science, 17,* 36–41.

Cogan, R., Cogan, D., Waltz, W., & McCue, M. (1987). Effects of laughter and relaxation on discomfort thresholds. *Journal of Behavioral Medicine, 10,* 139–144.

Coghill, R. C., McHaffie, J. G., & Yen, Y. (2003). Neural correlates of individual differences in the subjective experience of pain. *Proceedings of the National Academy of Sciences, USA, 100,* 8538–8542.

Cohen, D., Nisbett, R. E., Bowdle, B. F., & Schwarz, N. (1996). Insult, aggression, and the southern culture of honor: An "experimental ethnography." *Journal of Personality and Social Psychology, 70,* 945–960.

Cohen, G. (1990). Why is it difficult to put names to faces? *British Journal of Psychology, 81,* 287–297.

Cohen, S. (1988). Psychosocial models of the role of social support in the etiology of physical disease. *Health Psychology, 7,* 269–297.

Cohen, S. (1999). Social status and susceptibility to respiratory infections. *New York Academy of Sciences, 896,* 246–253.

Cohen, S., Frank, E., Doyle, W. J., Skoner, D. P., Rabin, B. S., & Gwaltney, J. M., Jr. (1998). Types of stressors that increase susceptibility to the common cold in healthy adults. *Health Psychology, 17,* 214–223.

Coifman, K. G., Bonanno, G. A., Ray, R. D., & Gross, J. J. (2007). Does repressive coping promote resilience? Affective-autonomic response discrepancy during bereavement. *Journal of Personality and Social Psychology, 92,* 745–758.

Colcombe, S. J., Erickson, K. I., Scalf, P. E., Kim, J. S., Prakesh, R., McAuley, E., … Kramer, A. F. (2006). Aerobic exercise training increases brain volume in aging humans. *Journals of Gerontology Series A: Biological Sciences and Medical Sciences, 61,* 1166–1170.

Colcombe, S. J., Kramer, A. F., Erickson, K. I., Scalf, P., McAuley, E., Cohen, N. J., … Elavsky, S. (2004). Cardiovascular fitness, cortical plasticity, and aging. *Proceedings of the National Academy of Sciences, USA, 101,* 3316–3321.

Cole, M. (1996). *Cultural psychology: A once and future discipline.* Cambridge, MA: Belknap Press of Harvard University Press.

Coman, A., Manier, D., & Hirst, W. (2009). Forgetting the unforgettable through conversation: Social shared retrieval-induced forgetting of September 11 memories. *Psychological Science, 20,* 627–633.

Condon, J. W., & Crano, W. D. (1988). Inferred evaluation and the relation between attitude similarity and interpersonal attraction. *Journal of Personality and Social Psychology, 54,* 789–797.

Conley, T. D. (2011). Perceived proposer personality characteristics and gender differences in acceptance of casual sex offers. *Journal of Personality and Social Psychology, 100*(2), 309–329. doi: 10.1037/a0022152

Conley, T. D., Moors, A. C., Matsick, J. L., Ziegler, A., & Valentine, B. A. (2011). Women, men, and the bedroom: Methodological and conceptual insights that narrow, reframe, and eliminate gender differences in sexuality. *Current Directions in Psychological Science, 20*(5), 296–300. doi: 10.1177/0963721411418467

Conway, M., & Ross, M. (1984). Getting what you want by revising what you had. *Journal of Personality and Social Psychology, 47,* 738–748.

Cook, M., & Mineka, S. (1989). Observational conditioning of fear to fear-relevant versus fear-irrelevant stimuli in rhesus monkeys. *Journal of Abnormal Psychology, 98*(4), 448–459.

Cook, M., & Mineka, S. (1990). Selective associations in the observational conditioning of fear in rhesus monkeys. *Journal of Experimental Psychology: Animal Behavior Process, 16,* 372–389.

Cooper, H., Nye, B., Charlton, K., Lindsay, J., & Greathouse, S. (1996). The effects of summer vacation on achievement test scores: A narrative and meta-analytic review. *Review of Educational Research, 66*(3), 227–268.

Cooper, J., & Fazio, R. H. (1984). A new look at dissonance theory. In L. Berkowitz (Ed.), *Advances in experimental social psychology* (Vol. 17, pp. 229–266). New York: Academic Press.

Cooper, J. C., Hollon, N. G., Wimmer, G. E., & Knutson, B. (2009). Available alternative incentives modulate anticipatory nucleus accumbens activation. *Social Cognitive and Affective Neuroscience, 4,* 409–416.

Cooper, J. M., & Strayer, D. L. (2008). Effects of simulator practice and real-world experience on cell-phone related driver distraction. *Human Factors, 50,* 893–902.

Cooper, J. R., Bloom, F. E., & Roth, R. H. (2003). *Biochemical basis of neuropharmacology.* New York: Oxford University Press.

Cooper, M. L. (2006). Does drinking promote risky sexual behavior? A complex answer to a simple question. *Current Directions in Psychological Science, 15,* 19–23.

Cooper, W. H., & Withey, W. J. (2009). The strong situation hypothesis. *Personality and Social Psychology Review, 13,* 62–72.

Corbetta, M., Shulman, G. L., Miezin, F. M., & Petersen, S. E. (1995). Superior parietal cortex activation during spatial attention shifts and visual feature conjunction. *Science, 270,* 802–805.

Coren, S. (1997). *Sleep thieves.* New York: Free Press.

Corkin, S. (2002). What's new with the amnesic patient HM? *Nature Reviews Neuroscience, 3,* 153–160.

Corkin, S. (2013). *Permanent present tense: The unforgettable life of the amnesic patient, H.M.* New York: Basic Books.

Correll, J., Park, B., Judd, C. M., & Wittenbrink, B. (2002). The police officer's dilemma: Using ethnicity to disambiguate potentially threatening individuals. *Journal of Personality and Social Psychology, 83,* 1314–1329.

Correll, J., Park, B., Judd, C. M., Wittenbrink, B., Sadler, M. S., & Keesee, T. (2007). Across the thin blue line: Police officers and racial bias in the decision to shoot. *Journal of Personality and Social Psychology, 92,* 1006–1023.

Corsi, P. (1991). *The enchanted loom: Chapters in the history of neuroscience.* New York: Oxford University Press.

Corti, E. (1931). *A history of smoking* (P. England, Trans.). London: Harrap.

Coryell, W., Endicott, J., Maser, J. D., Mueller, T., Lavori, P., & Keller, M. (1995). The likelihood of recurrence in bipolar affective disorder: The importance of episode recency. *Journal of Affective Disorders, 33,* 201–206.

Costa, P. T., Terracciano, A., & McCrae, R. R. (2001). Gender differences in personality traits across cultures: Robust and surprising findings. *Journal of Personality and Social Psychology, 81,* 322–331.

Costanza, A., Weber, K., Gandy, S., Bouras, C., Hof, P. R., Giannakopoulos, G., & Canuto, A. (2011). Contact sport-related chronic traumatic encephalopathy in the elderly: Clinical expression and structural substrates. *Neuropathology and Applied Neurobiology, 37,* 570–584.

**Cottrell, C. A., Neuberg, S. L., & Li, N. P.** (2007). What do people desire in others? A sociofunctional perspective on the importance of different valued characteristics. *Journal of Personality and Social Psychology, 92,* 208–231.

**Coyne, J. A.** (2000, April 3). Of vice and men: Review of R. Tornhill and C. Palmer, *A natural history of rape. The New Republic,* pp. 27–34.

**Crabb, R., & Hunsley, J.** (2011). Age related patterns in mental health-related complementary and alternative medicine utilization in Canada. *International Psychogeriatrics, 23,* 459–471.

**Craddock, N., & Jones, I.** (1999). Genetics of bipolar disorder. *Journal of Medical Genetics, 36,* 585–594.

**Craft, L.** (2012, January 2) *Japanese smoking culture proves hard to snuff out.* Retrieved from http://www.npr.org/2012/01/02/144451043/japanese-smoking-culture-proves-hard-to-snuff-out

**Craik, F. I. M., Govoni, R., Naveh-Benjamin, M., & Anderson, N. D.** (1996). The effects of divided attention on encoding and retrieval processes in human memory. *Journal of Experimental Psychology: General, 125,* 159–180.

**Craik, F. I. M., & Tulving, E.** (1975). Depth of processing and the retention of words in episodic memory. *Journal of Experimental Psychology: General, 104,* 268–294.

**Cramer, R. E., Schaefer, J. T., & Reid, S.** (1996). Identifying the ideal mate: More evidence for male–female convergence. *Current Psychology, 15,* 157–166.

**Crane, J. M., Keough, M., Murphy, P., Burrage, L., & Hutchens, D.** (2011). Effects of environmental tobacco smoke on perinatal outcomes: A retrospective cohort study. *BJOG: An International Journal of Obstetrics and Gynaecology, 118,* 865–871.

**Craske, M. G.** (1999). *Anxiety disorders: Psychological approaches to theory and treatment.* Boulder, CO: Westview Press.

**Crick, N. R., & Grotpeter, J. K.** (1995). Relational aggression, gender, and social-psychological adjustment. *Child Development, 66,* 710–722.

**Crocker, J., & Wolfe, C. T.** (2001). Contingencies of self-worth. *Psychological Review, 108*(3), 593–623.

**Crombag, H. F. M., Wagenaar, W. A., & Van Koppen, P. J.** (1996). Crashing memories and the problem of "source monitoring." *Applied Cognitive Psychology, 10,* 95–104.

**Cross, E. S., Kraemer, D. J. M., Hamilton, A. F. de C., Kelley, W. M., & Grafton, S. T.** (2009). Sensitivity of the action observation network to physical and observational learning. *Cerebral Cortex, 19,* 315–326.

**Cross, P.** (1977). Not can but will college teachers be improved? *New Directions for Higher Education, 17,* 1–15.

**Cross-Disorder Group of the Psychiatric Genomics Consortium.** (2013). Identification of risk loci with shared effects on five major psychiatric disorders: A genome-wide analysis. *Lancet, 381,* 1371–1379.

**Cruse, D., Chennu, S., Chatelle, C., Fernández-Espejo, D., Bekinschtein, T. A., Pickard, J. D., ... Owen, A. M.** (2012). Relationship between etiology and covert cognition in the minimally conscious state. *Neurology, 78,* 816–822.

**Cruse, D., Chennu, S., Fernández-Espejo, D., Payne, W. L., Young, G. B., & Owen, A. M.** (2012). Detecting awareness in the vegetative state: Electroencephalographic evidence for attempted movements to command. *PLoS One, 7*(11), e49933. doi:10.1371/journal.pone.0049933

**Csigó, K., Harsányi, A., Demeter, G., Rajkai, C., Németh, A., & Racsmány, M.** (2010). Long-term follow-up of patients with obsessive-compulsive disorder treated by anterior capsulotomy: A neuropsychological study. *Journal of Affective Disorders, 126,* 198–205.

**Csikszentmihalyi, M.** (1990). *Flow: The psychology of optimal experience.* New York: Harper & Row.

**Cuc, A., Koppel, J., & Hirst, W.** (2007). Silence is not golden: A case of socially shared retrieval-induced forgetting. *Psychological Science, 18,* 727–733.

**Cummins, D. D.** (2012). *Good thinking: Seven powerful ideas that influence the way we think.* New York: Cambridge University Press.

**Cunningham, M. R., Barbee, A. P., & Pike, C. L.** (1990). What do women want? Facial metric assessment of multiple motives in the perception of male facial physical attractiveness. *Journal of Personality and Social Psychology, 59,* 61–72.

**Cunningham, M. R., Roberts, A. R., Barbee, A. P., Druen, P. B., & Wu, C.-H.** (1995). "Their ideas of beauty are, on the whole, the same as ours": Consistency and variability in the cross-cultural perception of female physical attractiveness. *Journal of Personality and Social Psychology, 68,* 261–279.

**Cunningham, W. A., & Brosch, T.** (2012). Motivational salience: Amygdala tuning from traits, needs, values, and goals. *Current Directions in Psychological Science, 21*(1), 54–59.

**Curran, J. P., & Lippold, S.** (1975). The effects of physical attraction and attitude similarity on attraction in dating dyads. *Journal of Personality, 43,* 528–539.

**Curtiss, S.** (1977). *Genie: A psycholinguistic study of a modern-day "wildchild."* New York: Academic Press.

**Dabbs, J. M., Bernieri, F. J., Strong, R. K., Campo, R., & Milun, R.** (2001). Going on stage: Testosterone in greetings and meetings. *Journal of Research in Personality, 35,* 27–40.

**Dabbs, J. M., Carr, T. S., Frady, R. L., & Riad, J. K.** (1995). Testosterone, crime, and misbehavior among 692 male prison inmates. *Personality and Individual Differences, 18,* 627–633.

**Dael, N., Mortillaro, M., & Scherer, K. R.** (2012). Emotion expression in body action and posture. *Emotion, 12,* 1085–1101.

**D'Agostino, P. R., & Fincher-Kiefer, R.** (1992). Need for cognition and correspondence bias. *Social Cognition, 10,* 151–163.

**Dahger, A., & Robbins, T. W.** (2009). Personality, addiction, dopamine: Insights from Parkinson's disease. *Neuron, 61,* 502–510.

**Dahl, G., & Della Vigna, S.** (2009). Does movie violence increase violent crime? *The Quarterly Journal of Economics, 124,* 677–734.

**Dally, P.** (1999). *The marriage of heaven and hell: Manic depression and the life of Virginia Woolf.* New York: St. Martin's Griffin.

**Dalton, P.** (2003). Olfaction. In H. Pashler & S. Yantis (Eds.), *Stevens' handbook of experimental psychology: Vol. 1. Sensation and perception* (3rd ed., pp. 691–746). New York: Wiley.

**Daly, M., & Wilson, M.** (1988). Evolutionary social psychology and family homicide. *Science, 242,* 519–524.

**Damasio, A. R.** (1989). Time-locked multiregional retroactivation: A systems-level proposal for the neural substrates of recall and recognition. *Cognition, 33,* 25–62.

**Damasio, A. R.** (1994). *Descartes' error: Emotion, reason, and the human brain.* New York: Putnam.

**Damasio, A. R.** (2005). *Descartes' error: Emotion, reason, and the human Brain.* New York: Penguin.

**Damasio, A. R., Grabowski, T. J., Bechara, A., Damasio, H., Ponto, L. L. B., Parvisi, J., & Hichwa, R. D.** (2000). Subcortical and cortical brain activity during the feeling of self-generated emotions. *Nature Neuroscience, 3,* 1049–1056.

**Damasio, H., Grabowski, T. J., Tranel, D., Hichwa, R. D., & Damasio, A. R.** (1996). A neural basis for lexical retrieval. *Nature, 380,* 499–505.

**Damsma, G., Pfaus, J. G., Wenkstern, D., Phillips, A. G., & Fibiger, H. C.** (1992). Sexual behavior increases dopamine transmission in the nucleus accumbens and striatum of male rats: Comparison with novelty and locomotion. *Behavioral Neurosciences, 106*, 181–191.

**Daneshvar, D. H., Nowinski, C. J., McKee, A. C., & Cantu, R. C.** (2011). The epidemiology of sport-related concussion. *Clinical Sports Medicine, 30*, 1–17.

**Daniel, H. J., O'Brien, K. F., McCabe, R. B., & Quinter, V. E.** (1985). Values in mate selection: A 1984 campus survey. *College Student Journal, 19*, 44–50.

**Danner, U. N., Ouwehand, C., van Haastert, N. L., Homsveld, H., & de Ridder, D. T.** (2012). Decision-making impairments in women with binge eating disorder in comparison with obese and normal weight women. *European Eating Disorders Review, 20*, e56–e62.

**Darley, J. M., & Berscheid, E.** (1967). Increased liking caused by the anticipation of interpersonal contact. *Human Relations, 10*, 29–40.

**Darley, J. M., & Gross, P. H.** (1983). A hypothesis-confirming bias in labeling effects. *Journal of Personality and Social Psychology, 44*, 20–33.

**Darley, J. M., & Latané, B.** (1968). Bystander intervention in emergencies: Diffusion of responsibility. *Journal of Personality and Social Psychology, 8*, 377–383.

**Dar-Nimrod, I., & Heine, S. J.** (2006). Exposure to scientific theories affects women's math performance. *Science, 314*, 435.

**Darwin, C.** (2007). *The expression of the emotions in man and animals.* New York: Bibliobazaar. (Original work published 1899)

**Darwin, C.** (1998). *The expression of the emotions in man and animals* (P. Ekman, Ed.). New York: Oxford University Press. (Original work published 1872)

**Darwin, C. J., Turvey, M. T., & Crowder, R. G.** (1972). An auditory analogue of the Sperling partial report procedure: Evidence for brief auditory storage. *Cognitive Psychology, 3*, 255–267.

**Dauer, W., & Przedborski, S.** (2003). Parkinson's disease: Mechanisms and models. *Neuron, 39*, 889–909.

**Daum, I., Schugens, M. M., Ackermann, H., Lutzenberger, W., Dichgans, J., & Birbaumer, N.** (1993). Classical conditioning after cerebellar lesions in humans. *Behavioral Neuroscience, 107*, 748–756.

**Davidson, R. J., Ekman, P., Saron, C., Senulis, J., & Friesen, W. V.** (1990). Emotional expression and brain physiology I: Approach/withdrawal and cerebral asymmetry. *Journal of Personality and Social Psychology, 58*, 330–341.

**Davidson, R. J., Putnam, K. M., & Larson, C. L.** (2000). Dysfunction in the neural circuitry of emotion regulation—a possible prelude to violence. *Science, 289*, 591–594.

**Davies, G.** (1988). Faces and places: Laboratory research on context and face recognition. In G. M. Davies & D. M. Thomson (Eds.), *Memory in context: Context in memory* (pp. 35–53). New York: Wiley.

**Davies, G, Tenesa, A., Payton, A., Yang, J., Harris, S. E., Liewald, D., ... Deary, I. J.** (2011). Genome-wide association studies establish that human intelligence is highly heritable and polygenic. *Molecular Psychiatry, 16*(10), 996–1005. doi:10.1038/mp2011.85

**Davila Ross, M., Menzler, S., & Zimmermann, E.** (2008). Rapid facial mimicry in orangutan play. *Biology Letters, 4*(1), 27–30.

**Davis, C.** (2008, March 30). Simon Cowell admits to using Botox. *People Magazine.* Retrieved from http://www.people.com/people/article/0,,20181478,00.html

**Davis, J. L., Senghas, A., Brandt, F., & Ochsner, K. N.** (2010). The effects of BOTOX injections on emotional experience. *Emotion, 10*(3), 433–440. doi: 10.1037/a0018690

**Dawes, R. M.** (1994). *House of cards: Psychology and psychotherapy built on myth.* New York: Free Press.

**Dawood, K., Kirk, K. M., Bailey, J. M., Andrews, P. W., & Martin, N. G.** (2005). Genetic and environmental influences on the frequency of orgasm in women. *Twin Research, 8*, 27–33.

**Dawson, G., Rogers, S., Munson, J., Smith, M., Winter, J., Greenson, J., ... Varley, J.** (2010). Randomized, controlled trial of an intervention for toddlers with autism: The Early Start Denver Model. *Pediatrics, 125*, e17–e23.

**Dawson, G., Jones, E. J. H., Merkle, K., Venema, K., Lowry, R., Faja, S., ... Webb, S. J.** (2012). Early behavioral intervention is associated with normalized brain activity in young children with autism. *Journal of the American Academy of child and Adolescent Psychiatry, 51*, 1150–1159.

**Dawson, M., Soulieres, I., Gernsbacher, M. A., & Mottron, L.** (2007). The level and nature of autistic intelligence. *Psychological Science, 18*, 657–662.

**Day, J. J., & Sweatt, J. D.** (2011). Epigenetic mechanisms in cognition. *Neuron, 70*, 813–829.

**Dayan, P., & Huys, Q. J. M.** (2009). Serotonin in affective control. *Annual Review of Neuroscience, 32*, 95–126.

**Deák, G. O.** (2006). Do children really confuse appearance and reality? *Trends in Cognitive Sciences, 10*(12), 546–550.

**de Araujo, I. E., Rolls, E. T., Velazco, M. I., Margot, C., & Cayeux, I.** (2005). Cognitive modulation of olfactory processing. *Neuron, 46*, 671–679.

**Deary, I. J.** (2000). *Looking down on human intelligence: From psychometrics to the brain.* New York: Oxford University Press.

**Deary, I. J.** (2012). Intelligence. *Annual Review of Psychology, 63*(1), 453–482. doi:10.1146/annurev-psych-120710-100353

**Deary, I. J., Batty, G. D., & Gale, C. R.** (2008). Bright children become enlightened adults. *Psychological Science, 19*(1), 1–6.

**Deary, I. J., Batty, G. D., Pattie, A., & Gale, C. R.** (2008). More intelligent, more dependable children live longer: A 55-year longitudinal study of a representative sample of the Scottish nation. *Psychological Science, 19*, 874.

**Deary, I. J., Der, G., & Ford, G.** (2001). Reaction time and intelligence differences: A population based cohort study. *Intelligence, 29*(5), 389–399.

**Deary, I. J., Taylor, M. D., Hart, C. L., Wilson, V., Smith, G. D., Blane, D., & Starr, J. M.** (2005). Intergenerational social mobility and mid-life status attainment: Influences of childhood intelligence, childhood social factors, and education. *Intelligence, 33*(5), 455–472. doi:10.1016/j.intell.2005.06.003

**Deary, I. J., Weiss, A., & Batty, G. D.** (2011). Intelligence and personality as predictors of illness and death: How researchers in differential psychology and chronic disease epidemiology are collaborating to understand and address health inequalities. *Psychological Science in the Public Interest, 11*(2), 53–79. doi:10.1177/1529100610387081

**Deary, I. J., Whiteman, M. C., Starr, J. M., Whalley, L. J., & Fox, H. C.** (2004). The impact of childhood intelligence on later life: Following up the Scottish mental surveys of 1932 and 1947. *Journal of Personality and Social Psychology, 86*, 130–147.

**DeCasper, A. J., & Spence, M. J.** (1986). Prenatal maternal speech influences newborns' perception of speech sounds. *Infant Behavior and Development, 9*, 133–150.

**Deci, E. L.** (1971). Effects of externally mediated rewards on intrinsic motivation. *Journal of Personality and Social Psychology, 18*, 105–115.

**Deci, E. L., Koestner, R., & Ryan, R. M.** (1999). A meta-analytic review of experiments examining the effects of extrinsic rewards on intrinsic motivation. *Psychological Bulletin, 125,* 627–668.

**de Craen, A. J. M., Moerman, D. E., Heisterkamp, S. H., Tytgat, G. N. J., Tijssen, J. G. P., & Kleijnen, J.** (1999). Placebo effect in the treatment of duodenal ulcer. *British Journal of Clinical Pharmacology, 48,* 853–860.

**Deese, J.** (1959). On the prediction of occurrence of particular verbal intrusions in immediate recall. *Journal of Experimental Psychology, 58,* 17–22.

**DeFelipe, J., & Jones, E. G.** (1988). *Cajal on the cerebral cortex: An annotated translation of the complete writings.* New York: Oxford University Press.

**Degenhardt, L., Dierker, L., Chiu, W. T., Medina-Mora, M. E., Neumark, Y., Sampson, N., … Kessler, R. C.** (2010). Evaluating the drug use "gateway" theory using cross-national data: Consistency and associations of the order of initiation of drug use among participants in the WHO World Mental Health surveys. *Drug and Alcohol Dependence, 108,* 84–97.

**Dekker, M. C., & Koot, H. M.** (2003). *DSM–IV* disorders in children with borderline to moderate intellectual disability: I. Prevalence and impact. *Journal of the American Academy of Child and Adolescent Psychiatry, 42*(8), 915–922. doi:10.1097/01. CHI.0000046892.27264.1A

**Dekker, S., Lee, N. C., Howard-Jones, P., & Jolles, J.** (2012). Neuromyths in education: Prevalence and predictors of misconceptions among teachers. *Frontiers in Psychology 3: 429.* doi:10.3389/fpsyg.2012.00429

**Delgado, M. R., Frank, R. H., & Phelps, E. A.** (2005). Perceptions of moral character modulate the neural systems of reward during the trust game. *Nature Neuroscience, 8,* 1611–1618.

**Demb, J. B., Desmond, J. E., Wagner, A. D., Vaidya, C. J., Glover, G. H., & Gabrieli, J. D. E.** (1995). Semantic encoding and retrieval in the left inferior prefrontal cortex: A functional MRI study of task difficulty and process specificity. *The Journal of Neuroscience, 15,* 5870–5878.

**Dement, W. C.** (1959, November 30). Dreams. *Newsweek.*

**Dement, W. C.** (1978). *Some must watch while some must sleep.* New York: Norton.

**Dement, W. C.** (1999). *The promise of sleep.* New York: Delacorte Press.

**Dement, W. C., & Kleitman, N.** (1957). The relation of eye movements during sleep to dream activity: An objective method for the study of dreaming. *Journal of Experimental Psychology, 53,* 339–346.

**Dement, W. C., & Wolpert, E.** (1958). Relation of eye movements, body motility, and external stimuli to dream content. *Journal of Experimental Psychology, 55,* 543–553.

**Dempster, E. L., Pidsley, R., Schalkwyk, L. C., Owens, S., Georgiades, A., Kane, F., … Mill, J.** (2011). Disease-associated epigenetic changes in monozygotic twins discordant for schizophrenia and bipolar disorder. *Human Molecular Genetics, 20,* 4786–4796.

**Denison, S., Reed, C., & Xu, F.** (2013). The emergence of probabilistic reasoning in very young infants: Evidence from 4.5- and 6-month-olds. *Developmental Psychology, 49*(2), 243–249. doi:10.1037/a0028278

**Dennett, D.** (1991). *Consciousness explained.* New York: Basic Books.

**De Neve, J. E., & Oswald, A. J.** (2012). Estimating the influence of life satisfaction and positive affect on later income using sibling fixed effects. *Proceedings of the National Academy of Sciences of the United States of America, 109*(40), 19953–19958.

**DePaulo, B. M., Charlton, K., Cooper, H., Lindsay, J. J., & Muhlenbruck, L.** (1997). The accuracy–confidence correlation in the detection of deception. *Personality and Social Psychology Review, 1,* 346–357.

**DePaulo, B. M., Lindsay, J. J., Malone, B. E., Muhlenbruck, L., Charlton, K., & Cooper, H.** (2003). Cues to deception. *Psychological Bulletin, 129,* 74–118.

**DePaulo, B. M., Stone, J. I., & Lassiter, G. D.** (1985). Deceiving and detecting deceit. In B. R. Schlenker (Ed.), *The self and social life* (pp. 323–370). New York: McGraw-Hill.

**Der, G., Batty, G. D., & Deary, I. J.** (2009). The association between IQ in adolescence and a range of health outcomes at 40 in the 1979 U.S. national longitudinal study of youth. *Intelligence, 37*(6), 573–580.

**DeRosnay, M., Pons, F., Harris, P. L., & Morrell, J. M. B.** (2004). A lag between understanding false belief and emotion attribution in young children: Relationships with linguistic ability and mothers' mental-state language. *British Journal of Developmental Psychology, 24*(1), 197–218.

**DesJardin, J. L., Eisenberg, L. S., & Hodapp, R. M.** (2006). Sound beginnings: Supporting families of young deaf children with cochlear implants. *Infants and Young Children, 19,* 179–189.

**Deutsch, M.** (1949). A theory of cooperation and competition. *Human Relations, 2,* 129–152.

**DeVilliers, P.** (2005). The role of language in theory-of-mind development: What deaf children tell us. In J. W. Astington & J. A. Baird (Eds.), *Why language matters for theory of mind* (pp. 266–297). Oxford, England: Oxford University Press.

**De Vries, M. H., Barth, A. C. R., Maiworm, S., Knecht, S., Zwitserlood, P., & Flöel, A.** (2010). Electrical stimulation of Broca's area enhances implicit learning of an artificial grammar. *Journal of Cognitive Neuroscience, 22,* 2427–2436.

**de Waal, F. B. M.** (2012). The antiquity of empathy. *Science, 336*(6083), 874–876. doi:10.1126/science.1220999

**Dewhurst, D. L., & Cautela, J. R.** (1980). A proposed reinforcement survey schedule for special needs children. *Journal of Behavior Therapy and Experimental Psychiatry, 11,* 109–112.

**De Witte, P.** (1996). The role of neurotransmitters in alcohol dependency. *Alcohol & Alcoholism, 31*(Suppl. 1), 13–16.

**De Wolff, M., & van IJzendoorn, M. H.** (1997). Sensitivity and attachment: A meta-analysis on parental antecedents of infant attachment. *Child Development, 68,* 571–591.

**DeYoung, C. G., & Gray, J. R.** (2009). Personality neuroscience: Explaining individual differences in affect, behavior, and cognition. In P. J. Corr & G. Matthews (Eds.), *The Cambridge handbook of personality psychology* (pp. 323–346). New York: Cambridge University Press.

**DeYoung, C. G., Hirsh, J. B., Shane, M. S., Papademetris, X., Rajeevan, N., & Gray, J. R.** (2010). Testing predictions from personality neuroscience: Brain structure and the Big Five. *Psychological Science, 21,* 820–828.

**Diaconis, P., & Mosteller, F.** (1989). Methods for studying coincidences. *Journal of the American Statistical Association, 84,* 853–861.

**Diano, S., Farr, S. A., Benoit, S. C., McNay, E. C., da Silva, I., Horvath, B., … Horvath, T. L.** (2006). Ghrelin controls hippocampal spine synapse density and memory performance. *Nature Neuroscience, 9*(3), 381–388.

**Dibattista, D., & Holder, M. D.** (1998). Enhanced preference for a protein-containing diet in response to dietary protein restriction. *Appetite, 30,* 237–257.

**Dickens, W. T., & Flynn, J. R.** (2001). Heritability estimates versus large environmental effects: The IQ paradox resolved. *Psychological Review, 108,* 346–369.

**Dickinson, A., Watt, A., & Griffiths, J. H.** (1992). Free-operant acquisition with delayed reinforcement. *Quarterly Journal of*

*Experimental Psychology Section B: Comparative and Physiological Psychology, 45,* 241–258.

**Didden, R., Sigafoos, J., Lang, R., O'Reilly, M., Drieschner, K., & Lancioni, G. E.** (2012). Intellectual disabilities. In P. Sturmey & M. Hersen (Eds.), *Handbook of evidence-based practice in clinical psychology.* Hoboken, NJ: Wiley. Retrieved from http://doi.wiley.com/10.1002/9781118156391.ebcp001006

**DiDonato, T. E., Ullrich, J., & Krueger, J. I.** (2011). Social perception as induction and inference: An integrative model of intergroup differentiation, ingroup favoritism, and differential accuracy. *Journal of Personality and Social Psychology, 100*(1), 66–83. doi: 10.1037/a0021051

**Diederich, N. J., & Goetz, C. G.** (2008). The placebo treatments in neurosciences: New insights from clinical and neuroimaging studies. *Neurology, 71,* 677–684.

**Diekelmann, S., & Born, J.** (2010). The memory function of sleep. *Nature Reviews Neuroscience, 11,* 114–126.

**Dijksterhuis, A.** (2004). Think different: The merits of unconscious thought in preference development and decision making. *Journal of Personality and Social Psychology, 87,* 586–598.

**Dimberg, U.** (1982). Facial reactions to facial expressions. *Psychophysiology, 19,* 643–647.

**Dion, K., Berscheid, E., & Walster, E.** (1972). What is beautiful is good. *Journal of Personality and Social Psychology, 24,* 285–290.

**Disner, S. G., Beevers, C. G., Haigh, E. A., & Beck, A. T.** (2011). Neural mechanisms of the cognitive model of depression. *Nature Reviews Neuroscience, 12,* 467–477.

**DiTella, R., MacCulloch, R. J., & Oswald, A. J.** (2003). The macroeconomics of happiness. *Review of Economics and Statistics, 85,* 809–827.

**Dittrich, W. H., Troscianko, T., Lea, S., & Morgan, D.** (1996). Perception of emotion from dynamic point-light displays represented in dance. *Perception, 25,* 727–738.

**Dollard, J., Doob, L. W., Miller, N. E., Mowrer, O. H., & Sears, R. R.** (1939). *Frustration and aggression.* Oxford, England: Yale University Press.

**Domhoff, G. W.** (2007). Realistic simulation and bizarreness in dream content: Past findings and suggestions for future research. In D. B. P. McNamara (Ed.), *The new science of dreaming: Content, recall, and personality correlates* (Vol. 22, pp. 1–27). Westport, CT: Praeger.

**Domjan, M.** (2005). Pavlovian conditioning: A functional perspective. *Annual Review of Psychology, 56,* 179–206.

**Donner, T. H., Kettermann, A., Diesch, E., Ostendorf, F., Villiringer, A., & Brandt, S. A.** (2002). Visual feature and conjunction searches of equal difficulty engage only partially overlapping frontoparietal networks. *NeuroImage, 15,* 16–25.

**Dornbusch, S. M., Hastorf, A. H., Richardson, S. A., Muzzy, R. E., & Vreeland, R. S.** (1965). The perceiver and perceived: Their relative influence on categories of interpersonal perception. *Journal of Personality and Social Psychology, 1,* 434–440.

**Dorus, S., Vallender, E. J., Evans, P. D., Anderson, J. R., Gilbert, S. L., Mahowald, M., ... Lahn, B. T.** (2004). Accelerated evolution of nervous system genes in the origin of *Homo sapiens. Cell, 119,* 1027–1040.

**Dostoevsky, F.** (1988). *Winter notes on summer impressions* (D. Patterson, Trans.). Evanston, IL: Northwestern University Press. (Original work published 1863)

**Dovidio, J. F., & Gaertner, S. L.** (2010). Intergroup bias. In S. T. Fiske, D. T. Gilbert, & G. Lindzey (Eds.), *The handbook of social psychology* (5th ed., Vol. 2, pp. 1085–1121). New York: Wiley.

**Downer, J. D. C.** (1961). Changes in visual gnostic function and emotional behavior following unilateral temporal damage in the "splitbrain" monkey. *Nature, 191,* 50–51.

**Downing, P. E., Chan, A. W. Y., Peelen, M. V., Dodds, C. M., & Kanwisher, N.** (2006). Domain specificity in visual cortex. *Cerebral Cortex, 16,* 1453–1461.

**Draguns, J. G., & Tanaka-Matsumi, J.** (2003). Assessment of psychopathology across and within cultures: Issues and findings. *Behaviour Research and Therapy, 41,* 755–776.

**Dreifus, C.** (2003, May 20). Living one disaster after another, and then sharing the experience. *New York Times,* p. D2.

**Drigotas, S. M., & Rusbult, C. E.** (1992). Should I stay or should I go? A dependence model of breakups. *Journal of Personality and Social Psychology, 62,* 62–87.

**Druckman, D., & Bjork, R. A.** (1994). *Learning, remembering, believing: Enhancing human performance.* Washington, DC: National Academy Press.

**Duckworth, A. L., & Seligman, M. E. P.** (2005). Self-discipline outdoes IQ in predicting academic performance of adolescents. *Psychological Science, 16,* 939–944.

**Dudai, Y.** (2012). The restless engram: Consolidations never end. *Annual Review of Neuroscience, 35,* 227–247.

**Dudycha, G. J., & Dudycha, M. M.** (1933). Some factors and characteristics of childhood memories. *Child Development, 4,* 265–278.

**Duenwald, M.** (2002, September 12). Students find another staple of campus life: Stress. *New York Times.* Retrieved from http://www.nytimes.com/2002/09/17/health/students-find-another-staple-of-campus-life-stress.html?pagewanted=all&src=pm

**Duncan, D. E.** (2012, November 4). How science can build a better you. *The New York Times.* Retrieved from http://www.nytimes.com/2012/11/04/sunday-review/how-science-can-build-a-better-you.html_r=0

**Duncan, G. J., Yeung, W. J., Brooks-Gunn, J., & Smith, J. R.** (1998). How much does childhood poverty affect the life chances of children? *American Sociological Review, 63,* 406–423.

**Duncker, K.** (1945). On problem-solving. *Psychological Monographs, 58*(5).

**Dunham, Y., Chen, E. E., & Banaji, M. R.** (2013). Two signatures of implicit intergroup attitudes: Developmental invariance and early enculturation. *Psychological Science, 6,* 860–868. doi:10.1177/0956797612463081

**Dunlap, K.** (1919). Are there any instincts? *Journal of Abnormal Psychology, 14,* 307–311.

**Dunlop, S. A.** (2008). Activity-dependent plasticity: Implications for recovery after spinal cord injury. *Trends in Neurosciences, 31,* 410–418.

**Dunlosky, J., & Rawson, K. A.** (2012). Overconfidence produces underachievement: Inaccurate self-evaluations undermine students' learning and retention. *Learning and Instruction, 22,* 271–280.

**Dunlosky, J., Rawson, K. A., Marsh, E. J., Nathan, M. J., & Willingham, D. T.** (2013). Improving students' learning with effective learning techniques: Promising directions from cognitive and educational psychology. *Psychological Science in the Public Interest, 14*(1), 4–58.

**Dunlosky, J., & Thiede, K. W.** (2013). Four cornerstones of calibration research: Why understanding students' judgments can improve their achievement. *Learning and Instruction, 24,* 58–61.

**Dunphy, D. C.** (1963). The social structure of urban adolescent peer groups. *Sociometry, 26,* 230–246.

**Dutton, D. G., & Aron, A. P.** (1974). Some evidence for heightened sexual attraction under conditions of high anxiety. *Journal of Personality and Social Psychology, 30,* 510–517.

**Duval, S., & Wicklund, R. A.** (1972). *A theory of objective self awareness.* New York: Academic Press.

**Dyer, D., Dalzell, F., & Olegario, F.** (2004). *Rising Tide: Lessons from 165 years of brand building at Procter & Gamble.* Cambridge, MA: Harvard Business School Press.

**Eacott, M. J., & Crawley, R. A.** (1998). The offset of childhood amnesia: Memory for events that occurred before age 3. *Journal of Experimental Psychology: General, 127,* 22–33.

**Eagly, A. H., Ashmore, R. D., Makhijani, M. G., & Longo, L. C.** (1991). What is beautiful is good, but … : A meta-analytic review of research on the physical attractiveness stereotype. *Psychological Bulletin, 110,* 109–128.

**Eagly, A. H., & Steffen, V. J.** (1986). Gender and aggressive behavior: A meta-analytic review of the social psychological literature. *Psychological Bulletin, 100,* 309–330.

**Eagly, A. H., & Wood, W.** (1999). The origins of sex differences in human behavior: Evolved dispositions versus social roles. *American Psychologist, 54,* 408–423.

**Eastwick, P. W., Eagly, A. H., Finkel, E. J., & Johnson, S.E.** (2011). Implicit and explicit preferences for physical attractiveness in a romantic partner: A double dissociation in predictive validity. *Journal of Personality and Social Psychology, 101*(5), 993–1011. doi: 10.1037/a0024061

**Eastwick, P. W., Finkel, E. J., Mochon, D., & Ariely, D.** (2007). Selective versus unselective romantic desire: Not all reciprocity is created equal. *Psychological Science, 18,* 317–319.

**Eaton, W. W., Shao, H., Nestadt, G., Lee, B. H., Bienvenu, O. J., & Zandi, P.** (2008). Population-based study of first onset and chronicity of major depressive disorder. *Archives of General Psychiatry, 65,* 513–520.

**Ebbinghaus, H.** (1964). *Memory: A contribution to experimental psychology.* New York: Dover. (Original work published 1885)

**Eddy, D. M.** (1982). Probabilistic reasoning in clinical medicine: Problems and opportunities. In D. Kahneman, P. Slovic, & A. Tversky (Eds.), *Judgments under uncertainty: Heuristics and biases* (pp. 249–267). New York: Cambridge University Press.

**Edgerton, V. R., Tillakaratne, J. K. T., Bigbee, A. J., deLeon, R. D., & Roy, R. R.** (2004). Plasticity of the spinal neural circuitry after injury. *Annual Review of Neuroscience, 27,* 145–167.

**Edwards, W.** (1955). The theory of decision making. *Psychological Bulletin, 51,* 201–214.

**Efferson, C., Lalive, R., & Fehr, E.** (2008). The coevolution of cultural groups and ingroup favoritism. *Science, 321,* 1844–1849.

**Eich, J.E.** (1980). The cue-dependent nature of state-dependent retention. *Memory & Cognition, 8,* 157–173.

**Eich, J.E.** (1995). Searching for mood dependent memory. *Psychological Science, 6,* 67–75.

**Eichenbaum, H.** (2008). *Learning & memory.* New York: Norton.

**Eichenbaum, H., & Cohen, N. J.** (2001). *From conditioning to conscious recollection: Memory systems of the brain.* New York: Oxford University Press.

**Eickhoff, S. B., Dafotakis, M., Grefkes, C., Stoecker, T., Shah, N. J., Schnitzler, A., … Siebler, M.** (2008). fMRI reveals cognitive and emotional processing in a long-term comatose patient. *Experimental Neurology, 214,* 240–246.

**Eimas, P. D., Siqueland, E. R., Jusczyk, P., & Vigorito, J.** (1971). Speech perception in infants. *Science, 171,* 303–306.

**Einstein, G. O., & McDaniel, M. A.** (1990). Normal aging and prospective memory. *Journal of Experimental Psychology: Learning, Memory, and Cognition, 16,* 717–726.

**Einstein, G. O., & McDaniel, M. A.** (2005). Prospective memory: Multiple retrieval processes. *Current Direction in Psychological Science, 14,* 286–290.

**Eisenberg, M. J., Atallah, R., Grandi, S. M., Windle, S. B., & Berry, E. M.** (2011). Legislative approaches to tackling the obesity epidemic. *Canadian Medical Association Journal, 183*(13), 1496–1500.

**Eisenberg, N., Fabes, R. A., Guthrie, I. K., & Reiser, M.** (2000). Dispositional emotionality and regulation: Their role in predicting quality of social functioning. *Journal of Personality and Social Psychology, 78,* 136.

**Eisenegger, C. Haushofer, J., & Fehr, E.** (2011). The role of testosterone in social interaction. *Trends in Cognitive Sciences, 15*(6), 263–271. doi:10.1016/j.tics.2011.04.008

**Eisenegger, C., Naef, M., Snozzi, R., Heinrichs, M., & Fehr, E.** (2010). Prejudice and truth about the effect of testosterone on human bargaining behaviour. *Nature, 463,* 356–359.

**Ekman, P.** (1965). Differential communication of affect by head and body cues. *Journal of Personality and Social Psychology, 2,* 726–735.

**Ekman, P.** (1972). Universals and cultural differences in facial expressions of emotion. In J. K. Cole (Ed.), *Nebraska Symposium on Motivation, 1971* (pp. 207–283). Lincoln: University of Nebraska Press.

**Ekman, P.** (1992). *Telling lies.* New York: Norton.

**Ekman, P.** (2003). Darwin, deception, and facial expression. *Annals of the New York Academy of Sciences, 1000,* 205–221.

**Ekman, P., & Friesen, W. V.** (1968). Nonverbal behavior in psychotherapy research. In J. M. Shlien (Ed.), *Research in psychotherapy* (Vol. 3, pp. 179–216). Washington, DC: American Psychological Association.

**Ekman, P., & Friesen, W. V.** (1971). Constants across cultures in the face and emotion. *Journal of Personality and Social Psychology, 17,* 124–129.

**Ekman, P., & Friesen, W. V.** (1982). Felt, false, and miserable smiles. *Journal of Nonverbal Behavior, 6,* 238–252.

**Ekman, P., Levenson, R. W., & Friesen, W. V.** (1983). Autonomic nervous system activity distinguishes among emotions. *Science, 221,* 1208–1210.

**Elbogen, E. B., & Johnson, S. C.** (2009). The intricate link between violence and mental disorder. *Archives of General Psychiatry, 66*(2), 152–161.

**Eldar, S., Apter, A., Lotan, D., Edgar, K. P., Naim, R., Fox, N. A., … Bar-Heim, Y.** (2012). Attention bias modification treatment for pediatric anxiety disorders: A randomized controlled trial. *American Journal of Psychiatry, 169,* 213–220.

**Eldridge, L. L., Knowlton, B. J., Furmanski, C. S., Bookheimer, S. Y., & Engel, S. A.** (2000). Remembering episodes: A selective role for the hippocampus during retrieval. *Nature Neuroscience, 3,* 1149–1152.

**Eldridge, M. A., Barnard, P. J., & Bekerian, D. A.** (1994). Autobiographical memory and daily schemas at work. *Memory, 2,* 51–74.

**Elfenbein, H. A., & Ambady, N.** (2002). On the universality and cultural specificity of emotion recognition: A meta-analysis. *Psychological Bulletin, 128,* 203–235.

**Elfenbein, H. A., Der Foo, M. D., White, J., & Tan, H. H.** (2007). Reading your counterpart: The benefit of emotion recognition accuracy for effectiveness in negotiation. *Journal of Nonverbal Behavior, 31,* 205–223.

**Ellemers, N.** (2012). The group self. *Science, 336*(6083), 848–852. doi:10.10.1126/science.1220987

**Ellenbogen, J. M., Payne, J. D., & Stickgold, R.** (2006). The role of sleep in declarative memory consolidation: Passive, permissive, or none? *Current Opinion in Neurobiology, 16,* 716–722.

**Elliott, R., Sahakian, B. J., Matthews, K., Bannerjea, A., Rimmer, J., & Robbins, T. W.** (1997). Effects of methylphenidate on spatial working memory and planning in healthy young adults. *Psychopharmacology, 131,* 196–206.

**Ellis, A. (1991).** *Reason and emotion in psychotherapy.* New York: Carol.

**Ellis, B. J., & Garber, J.** (2000). Psychosocial antecedents of variation in girls' pubertal timing: Maternal depression, stepfather presence, and marital and family stress. *Child Development, 71,* 485–501.

**Ellis, E. M.** (1983). A review of empirical rape research: Victim reactions and response to treatment. *Clinical Psychology Review, 3,* 473–490.

**Ellis, L., & Ames, M. A.** (1987). Neurohormonal functioning in sexual orientation: A theory of homosexuality–heterosexuality. *Psychological Bulletin, 101,* 233–258.

**Ellman, S. J., Spielman, A. J., Luck, D., Steiner, S. S., & Halperin, R.** (1991). REM deprivation: A review. In S. J. Ellman & J. S. Antrobus (Eds.), *The mind in sleep: Psychology and psychophysiology* (2nd ed., pp. 329–376). New York: Wiley.

**Ellsworth, P. C., & Scherer, K. R.** (2003). Appraisal processes in emotion. In R. J. Davidson, K. R. Scherer, & H. H. Goldsmith (Eds.), *The handbook of affective science* (pp. 572–595). New York: Oxford University Press.

**Emerson, R. C., Bergen, J. R., & Adelson, E. H.** (1992). Directionally selective complex cells and the computation of motion energy in cat visual cortex. *Vision Research, 32,* 203–218.

**Epel, E. S., Blackburn, E. H., Lin, J., Dhabhar, F. S., Adler, N.E., Morrow, J. D., & Cawthorn, R. M.** (2004). Accelerated telomere shortening in response to life stress. *Proceedings of the National Academy of Sciences, 101,* 17312–17315.

**Enock, P. M., & McNally, R. J.** (2013). How mobile apps and other web-based interventions can transform psychological treatment and the treatment development cycle. *Behavior Therapist, 36(3),* 56–66.

**Epel, E. S., Daubenmier, J., Moskowitz, J. T., Foldman, S., & Blackburn, E. H.** (2009). Can meditation slow rate of cellular aging? Cognitive stress, mindfulness, and telomerase. *Annals of the New York Academy of Sciences, 1172,* 34–53.

**Epley, N., Savitsky, K., & Kachelski, R. A.** (1999). What every skeptic should know about subliminal persuasion. *Skeptical Inquirer, 23,* 40–45, 58.

**Epley, N., & Waytz, A.** (2010). Mind perception. In S. T. Fiske, D. T. Gilbert, & G. Lindzey (Eds.), *The handbook of social psychology* (5th ed., Vol. 1, pp. 498–541). New York: Wiley.

**Epstein, R.** (2007a). *The case against adolescence: Rediscovering the adult in every teen.* New York: Quill Driver.

**Epstein, R.** (2007b). The myth of the teen brain. *Scientific American Mind, 18,* 27–31.

**Erber, R., Wegner, D. M., & Therriault, N.** (1996). On being cool and collected: Mood regulation in anticipation of social interaction. *Journal of Personality and Social Psychology, 70,* 757–766.

**Erffmeyer, E. S.** (1984). Rule-violating behavior on the golf course. *Perceptual and Motor Skills, 59,* 591–596.

**Ericsson, K. A., & Charness, N.** (1999). Expert performance: Its structure and acquisition. In S. J. Ceci & W. M. Williams (Eds.), *The nature–nurture debate: The essential readings* (pp. 200–256). Oxford, England: Blackwell.

**Ericson, E. H.** (1959). *Identity and the life cycle.* New York: International Universities Press.

**Espy, K. A., Fang, H., Johnson, C., Stopp, C., Wiebe, S. A., & Respass, J.** (2011). Prenatal tobacco exposure: Developmental outcomes in the neonatal period. *Developmental Psychology, 47(1),* 153–169. doi:10.1037/a0020724

**Etcoff, N.** (1999). *Survival of the prettiest: The science of beauty.* New York: Doubleday.

**Evans, G. W.** (2004). The environment of childhood poverty. *American Psychologist, 59(2),* 77–92.

**Evans, G. W.** (2006). Child development and the physical environment. *Annual Review of Psychology, 57,* 423–451.

**Evans, S. W., & Kim, P.** (2012). Childhood poverty and young adults' allostatic load: The mediating role of childhood cumulative risk exposure. *Psychological Science, 23(9),* 979–983. doi:10.1177/0956797612441218

**Evans, G. W., & Stecker, R.** (2004). Motivational consequences of environmental stress. *Journal of Environmental Psychology, 24,* 143–165.

**Evans, J. St. B., Barston, J. L., & Pollard, P.** (1983), On the conflict between logic and belief in syllogistic reasoning. *Memory & Cognition, 11,* 295–306.

**Evans, P. D., Gilbert, S. L., Mekel-Bobrov, N., Vallender, E. J., Anderson, J. R., Vaez-Azizi, L. M., … Lahn, B. T.** (2005). Microcephalin, a gene regulating brain size, continues to evolve adaptively to humans. *Science, 309,* 1717–1720.

**Everson, S. A., Lynch, J. W., Chesney, M. A., Kaplan, G. A., Goldberg, D.E., Shade, S. B., … Salonen, J. T.** (1997). Interaction of workplace demands and cardiovascular reactivity in progression of carotid atherosclerosis: Population based study. *British Medical Journal, 314,* 553–558.

**Exner, J.E.** (1993). *The Rorschach: A comprehensive system: Vol. 1. Basic Foundations.* New York: Wiley.

**Eysenck, H. J.** (1957). The effects of psychotherapy: An evaluation. *Journal of Consulting Psychology, 16,* 319–324.

**Eysenck, H. J.** (1967). *The biological basis of personality.* Springfield, IL: Charles C Thomas.

**Eysenck, H. J.** (1990). Biological dimensions of personality. In L. A. Pervin (Ed.), *Handbook of personality: Theory and research* (pp. 244–276). New York: Guilford Press.

**Falk, A., & Szech, N.** (2013). Morals and markets. *Science, 340(6133),* 707–711. doi:10.1126/science.1231566

**Falk, R., & McGregor, D.** (1983). The surprisingness of coincidences. In P. Humphreys, O. Svenson, & A. Vari (Eds.), *Analysing and aiding decision processes* (pp. 489–502). New York: North Holland.

**Fancher, R. E.** (1979). *Pioneers in psychology.* New York: Norton.

**Fantz, R. L.** (1964). Visual experience in infants: Decreased attention to familiar patterns relative to novel ones. *Science, 164,* 668–670.

**Farah, M. J., Illes, J., Cook-Deegan, R., Gardner, H., Kandel, E., King, P., … Wolpe, P. R.** (2004) Neurocognitive enhancement: What can we do and what should we do? *Nature Reviews Neuroscience, 5,* 421–426.

**Farah, M. J., & Rabinowitz, C.** (2003). Genetic and environmental influences on the organization of semantic memory in the brain: Is "living things" an innate category? *Cognitive Neuropsychology, 20,* 401–408.

**Faraone, S. V., Perlis, R. H., Doyle, A. E., Smoller, J. W., Goralnick, J. J., Holmgren, M. A., & Sklar, P.** (2005). Molecular genetics of attention-deficit/hyperactivity disorder. *Biological Psychiatry, 57,* 1313–1323.

**Farivar, R.** (2009). Dorsal–ventral integration in object recognition. *Brain Research Reviews, 61,* 144–153.

**Farooqi, I. S., Bullmore, E., Keogh, J., Gillard, J., O'Rahilly, S., & Fletcher, P. C.** (2007). Leptin regulates striatal regions and human eating behavior. *Science, 317,* 1355.

**Farooqi, I. S., Matarese, G., Lord, G. M., Keogh, J. M., Lawrence, E., Agwu, C., & O'Rahilly, S.** (2002). Beneficial effects of leptin on obesity, T cell hyporesponsiveness, and neuroendocrine/metabolic dysfunction of human congenital leptin deficiency. *The Journal of Clinical Investigation, 110*(8), 1093–1103.

**Farrar, M. J.** (1990). Discourse and the acquisition of grammatical morphemes. *Journal of Child Language, 17,* 607–624.

**Favazza, A.** (2011). *Bodies under siege: Self-mutilation, nonsuicidal self-injury, and body modification in culture and psychiatry.* Baltimore, MD: Johns Hopkins University Press.

**Fazel, S., & Danesh, J.** (2002). Serious mental disorder in 23,000 prisoners: A review of 62 surveys. *Lancet, 359,* 545–550.

**Fechner, G. T.** (1966). *Elements of psychophysics* (H. E. Alder, Trans.). New York: Holt, Rinehart, & Winston. (Original work published 1860)

**Feczer, D., & Bjorklund, P.** (2009). Forever changed: Posttraumatic stress disorder in female military veterans, a case report. *Perspectives in Psychiatric Care, 45,* 278–291.

**Fehr, E., & Gaechter, S.** (2002). Altruistic punishment in humans. *Nature, 415,* 137–140.

**Fein, D., Barton, M., Eigsti, I.-M., Kelley, E., Naigles, L., Schultz, R. T., ... Tyson, K.** (2013). Optimal outcome in individuals with a history of autism. *Journal of child Psychology and Psychiatry, 54,* 195–205.

**Fein, S., Goethals, G. R., & Kugler, M. B.** (2007). Social influence on political judgments: The case of presidential debates. *Political Psychology, 28,* 165–192.

**Feinberg, T. E.** (2001). *Altered egos: How the brain creates the self.* New York: Oxford University Press.

**Feingold, A.** (1990). Gender differences in effects of physical attractiveness on romantic attraction: A comparison across five research paradigms. *Journal of Personality and Social Psychology, 59,* 981–993.

**Feingold, A.** (1992a). Gender differences in mate selection preferences: A test of the parental investment model. *Psychological Bulletin, 112,* 125–139.

**Feingold, A.** (1992b). Good-looking people are not what we think. *Psychological Bulletin, 111,* 304–341.

**Feinstein, J. S., Buzza, C., Hurlemann, R., Follmer, R. L., Dahdaleh, N. S., Coryell, W. H., ... Wemmie, J. A.** (2013). Fear and panic in humans with bilateral amygdala damage. *Nature Neuroscience, 3,* 270–272.

**Feldman, D. E.** (2009). Synaptic mechanisms for plasticity in neocortex. *Annual Review of Neuroscience, 32,* 33–55.

**Feldman, M. D.** (2004). *Playing sick.* New York: Brunner-Routledge.

**Felmlee, D., Sprecher, S., & Bassin, E.** (1990). The dissolution of intimate relationships: A hazard model. *Social Psychology Quarterly, 53,* 13–30.

**Ferguson, C. J.** (2010). Blazing angels or resident evil? Can violent video games be a force for good? *Review of General Psychology, 14*(2), 68–81. doi:10.1037/a0018941

**Fernandez-Espejo, D., Junque, C., Vendrell, P., Bernabeu, M., Roig, T., Bargallo, N., & Mercader, J. M.** (2008). Cerebral response to speech in vegetative and minimally conscious states after traumatic brain injury. *Brain Injury, 22,* 882–890.

**Fernbach, P. M., Rogers, T., Fox, C. R., & Sloman, S. A.** (2013). Political extremism is supported by an illusion of understanding. *Psychological Science, 24*(6), 939–946.

**Fernyhough, C.** (2012). *Pieces of light: The new science of memory.* London: Profile Books.

**Ferster, C. B., & Skinner, B. F.** (1957). *Schedules of reinforcement.* New York: Appleton-Century-Crofts.

**Festinger, L.** (1957). *A theory of cognitive dissonance.* Stanford, CA: Stanford University Press.

**Festinger, L., & Carlsmith, J. M.** (1959). Cognitive consequences of forced compliance. *Journal of Abnormal and Social Psychology, 58,* 203–210.

**Festinger, L., Schachter, S., & Back, K.** (1950). *Social pressures in informal groups: A study of human factors in housing.* Oxford, England: Harper & Row.

**Field, G. C.** (1921). Faculty psychology and instinct psychology. *Mind, 30,* 257–270.

**Fields, H. L., & Levine, J. D.** (1984). Placebo analgesia: A role for endorphins? *Trends in Neurosciences, 7,* 271–273.

**Finkel, E. J., & Eastwick, P. W.** (2009). Arbitrary social norms influence sex differences in romantic selectivity. *Psychological Science, 20,* 1290–1295.

**Finkelstein, K. E.** (1999, October 17). Yo-Yo Ma's lost Stradivarius is found after wild search. *New York Times,* p. 34.

**Finn, R.** (1991). Different minds. *Discover, 12,* 54–59.

**Fiore, A. T., Taylor, L. S., Zhong, X., Mendelsohn, G. A., & Cheshire, C.** (2010). Who's right and who writes: People, profiles, contacts, and replies in online dating. *Proceedings of Hawaii International Conferences on Systems Science, 43,* Persistent Conversation minitrack.

**Fiorentine, R.** (1999). After drug treatment: Are 12-step programs effective in maintaining abstinence? *American Journal of Drug and Alcohol Abuse, 25,* 93–116.

**Fiorillo, C. D., Newsome, W. T., & Schultz, W.** (2008). The temporal precision of reward prediction in dopamine neurons. *Nature Neuroscience, 11,* 966–973.

**Fisher, H. E.** (1993). *Anatomy of love: The mysteries of mating, marriage, and why we stray.* New York: Fawcett.

**Fisher, R. P., & Craik, F. I. M.** (1977). The interaction between encoding and retrieval operations in cued recall. *Journal of Experimental Psychology: Human Learning and Perception, 3,* 153–171.

**Fiske, S. T.** (1998). Stereotyping, prejudice, and discrimination. In D. T. Gilbert, S. T. Fiske, & G. Lindzey (Eds.), *The handbook of social psychology* (4th ed., Vol. 2, pp. 357–411). New York: McGraw-Hill.

**Fiske, S. T.** (2010). *Social beings: A core motives approach to social psychology.* Hoboken, NJ: Wiley.

**Fleeson, W.** (2004). Moving personality beyond the person-situation debate: The challenge and opportunity of within-person variability. *Current Directions in Psychological Science, 13,* 83–87.

**Fletcher, P. C., Shallice, T., & Dolan, R. J.** (1998). The functional roles of prefrontal cortex in episodic memory. I. Encoding. *Brain, 121,* 1239–1248.

**Flor, H., Nikolajsen, L., & Jensen, T. S.** (2006). Phantom limb pain: A case of maladaptive CNS plasticity? *Nature Reviews Neuroscience, 7,* 873–881.

**Flynn, E.** (2008). Investigating children as cultural magnets: Do young children transmit redundant information along diffusion chains? *Philosophical Transactions of the Royal Society of London Series B, 363,* 3541–3551.

**Flynn, E., & Whiten, A.** (2008). Cultural transmission of tool-use in young children: A diffusion chain study. *Social Development, 17,* 699–718.

**Flynn, J. R.** (2012). *Are we getting smarter? Rising IQ in the twenty-first century.* New York: Cambridge University Press.

**Foa, E. B.** (2010). Cognitive behavioral therapy of obsessive-compulsive disorder. *Dialogues in Clinical Neuroscience, 12,* 199–207.

Foa, E. B., Dancu, C. V., Hembree, E. A., Jaycox, L. H., Meadows, E. A., & Street, G. P. (1999). A comparison of exposure therapy, stress inoculation training, and their combination for reducing posttraumatic stress disorder in female assault victims. *Journal of Consulting and Clinical Psychology, 67*, 194–200.

Foa, E. B., Liebowitz, M. R., Kozak, M. J., Davies, S., Campeas, R., Franklin, M. E., … Tu, X. (2007). Randomized, placebo-controlled trial of exposure and ritual prevention, clomipramine, and their combination in the treatment of obsessive-compulsive disorder. *Focus, 5*, 368–380.

Foa, E. B., & Meadows, E. A. (1997). Psychosocial treatments for posttraumatic stress disorder: A critical review. *Annual Review of Psychology, 48*, 449–480.

Fogassi, L., Ferrari, P. F., Gesierich, B., Rozzi, S., Chersi, F., & Rizzolatti, G. (2005). Parietal lobe: From action organization to intention understanding. *Science, 308*, 662–667.

Folley, B. S., & Park, S. (2005). Verbal creativity and schizotypal personality in relation to prefrontal hemispheric laterality: A behavioral and near-infrared optical imaging study. *Schizophrenia Research, 80*, 271–282.

Forkstam, C., Hagoort, P., Fernández, G., Ingvar, M., & Petersson, K. M. (2006). Neural correlates of artificial syntactic structure classification. *NeuroImage, 32*, 956–967.

Foroni, F., & Semin, G. R. (2009). Language that puts you in touch with your bodily feelings: The multimodal responsiveness of affective expressions. *Psychological Science, 20*(8), 974–980.

Fournier, J. C., DeRubeis, R., Hollon, S. D., Dimidjian, S., Amsterdam, J. D., Shelton, R. C., & Fawcett, J. (2010). Antidepressant drug effects and depression severity. *Journal of the American Medical Association, 303*, 47–53.

Fouts, R. S., & Bodamer, M. (1987). Preliminary report to the National Geographic Society on "Chimpanzee intrapersonal signing." *Friends of Washoe, 7*, 4–12.

Fox, M. J. (2009). *Always looking up.* New York: Hyperion.

Fox, P. T., Mintun, M. A., Raichle, M. E., Miezin, F. M., Allman, J. M., & Van Essen, D. C. (1986). Mapping human visual cortex with positron emission tomography. *Nature, 323*, 806–809.

Fox, R. E., DeLeon, P. H., Newman, R., Sammons, M. T., Dunivin, D. L., & Baker, D. C. (2009). Prescriptive authority and psychology: A status report. *American Psychologist, 64*, 257–268.

Fragaszy, D. M., Izar, P., Visalberghi, E., Ottoni, E. B., & de Oliveria, M. G. (2004). Wild capuchin monkeys (*Cebus libidinosus*) use anvils and stone pounding tools. *American Journal of Primatology, 64*, 359–366.

Francis, D., Diorio, J., Liu, D., & Meaney, M. J. (1999). Nongenomic transmission across generations of maternal behavior and stress responses in the rat. *Science, 286*, 1155–1158.

François, C., Chobert, J., Besson, M., & Schon, D. (2013). Music training for the development of speech segmentation. *Cerebral Cortex, 9*, 2038–2043. doi:10.1093/cercor/bhs180

Frank, M. G., Ekman, P., & Friesen, W. V. (1993). Behavioral markers and recognizability of the smile of enjoyment. *Journal of Personality and Social Psychology, 64*, 83–93.

Frank, M. G., & Stennet, J. (2001). The forced-choice paradigm and the perception of facial expressions of emotion. *Journal of Personality and Social Psychology, 80*, 75–85.

Frankl, V. (2000). *Man's search for meaning.* New York: Beacon Press.

Fredman, T., & Whiten, A. (2008). Observational learning from tool using models by human-reared and mother-reared capuchin monkeys (*Cebus apella*). *Animal Cognition, 11*, 295–309.

Fredrickson, B. L. (2000). Cultivating positive emotions to optimize health and well-being. *Prevention and Treatment, 3*, Article 0001a.

doi:10.1037/1522-3736.3.1.31a. Retrieved September 21, 2013 from http://psycnet.apa.org

Freedman, J. L., & Fraser, S. C. (1966). Compliance without pressure: The foot-in-the-door technique. *Journal of Personality and Social Psychology, 4*, 195–202.

Freeman, S., Walker, M. R., Borden, R., & Latané, B. (1975). Diffusion of responsibility and restaurant tipping: Cheaper by the bunch. *Personality and Social Psychology Bulletin, 1*, 584–587.

French, H. W. (1997, February 26). In the land of the small it isn't easy being tall. *New York Times.* Retrieved from http://www.nytimes.com/1997/02/26/world/in-the-land-of-the-small-it-isn-t-easy-being-tall.html

Freud, S. (1938). The psychopathology of everyday life. In A. A. Brill (Ed.), *The basic writings of Sigmund Freud* (pp. 38–178). New York: Basic Books. (Original work published 1901)

Freud, S. (1965). *The interpretation of dreams* (J. Strachey, Trans.). New York: Avon. (Original work published 1900)

Frick, R. W. (1985). Communicating emotion: The role of prosodic features. *Psychological Bulletin, 97*, 412–429.

Fried, P. A., & Watkinson, B. (2000). Visuoperceptual functioning differs in 9- to 12-year-olds prenatally exposed to cigarettes and marijuana. *Neurotoxicology and Teratology, 22*, 11–20.

Friedlander, L., & Desrocher, M. (2006). Neuroimaging studies of obsessive-compulsive disorder in adults and children. *Clinical Psychology Review, 26*, 32–49.

Friedman, J. M. (2003). A war on obesity, not the obese. *Science, 299*(5608), 856–858.

Friedman, J. M., & Halaas, J. L. (1998). Leptin and the regulation of body weight in mammals. *Nature, 395*(6704), 763–770.

Friedman, M., & Rosenman, R. H. (1974). *Type A behavior and your heart.* New York: Knopf.

Friedman, S. L., & Boyle, D. E. (2008). Attachment in U.S. children experiencing nonmaternal care in the early 1990s. *Attachment & Human Development, 10*(3), 225–261.

Friedman-Hill, S. R., Robertson, L. C., & Treisman, A. (1995). Parietal contributions to visual feature binding: Evidence from a patient with bilateral lesions. *Science, 269*, 853–855.

Friesen, W. V. (1972). *Cultural differences in facial expressions in a social situation: An experimental test of the concept of display rules.* Unpublished doctoral dissertation, University of California, San Francisco.

Frith, C. D., & Fletcher, P. (1995). Voices from nowhere. *Critical Quarterly, 37*, 71–83.

Frith, U. (2003). *Autism: Explaining the enigma.* Oxford, England: Blackwell.

Fry, D. P. (2012). Life without war. *Science, 336*(6083), 879–884. doi:10.1126/science.1217987

Fryer, A. J., Mannuzza, S., Gallops, M. S., Martin, L. Y., Aaronson, C., Gorman, J. M., … Klein, D. F. (1990). Familial transmission of simple phobias and fears: A preliminary report. *Archives of General Psychiatry, 47*, 252–256.

Fu, F., Tarnita, C. E., Christakis, N. A., Wang, L., Rand, D. G., & Novak, M. A. (2012). Evolution of in-group favoritism. *Scientific Reports, 2*, Article 460. doi:10.1038/srep00460

Fukui, H., Murai, T., Fukuyama, H., Hayashi, T., & Hanakawa, T. (2005). Functional activity related to risk anticipation during performance of the Iowa gambling task. *NeuroImage, 24*, 253–259.

Funder, D. C. (2001). Personality. *Annual Review of Psychology, 52*, 197–221.

Furmark, T., Tillfors, M., Marteinsdottir, I., Fischer, H., Pissiota, A., Långström, B., & Fredrikson, M. (2002). Common changes in cerebral blood flow in patients with social phobia treated with citalopram or cognitive behavioral therapy. *Archives of General Psychiatry, 59*(5), 425–433.

**Fuster, J. M.** (2003). *Cortex and mind.* New York: Oxford University Press.

**Gadermann, A. M., Alonso, J., Vilagut, G., Zaslavsky, A. M., & Kessler, R. C.** (2012). Comorbidity and disease burden in the National Comorbidity Survey Replication (NCS-R). *Depression and Anxiety, 29,* 797–806.

**Gais, S., & Born, J.** (2004). Low acetylcholine during slow-wave sleep is critical for declarative memory consolidation. *Proceedings of the National Academy of Sciences, USA, 101,* 2140–2144.

**Galati, D., Scherer, K. R., & Ricci-Bitt, P. E.** (1997). Voluntary facial expression of emotion: Comparing congenitally blind with normally sighted encoders. *Journal of Personality and Social Psychology, 73,* 1363–1379.

**Gale, C. R., Batty, G. D., McIntosh, A. M., Porteous, D. J., Deary, I. J., & Rasmussen, F.** (2012). Is bipolar disorder more common in highly intelligent people? A cohort study of a million men. *Molecular Psychiatry, 18*(2), 190–194. doi:10.1038/mp.2012.26

**Gale, C. R., Batty, G. D., Tynelius, P. Deary, I. J., & Rasmussen, F.** (2010). Intelligence in early adulthood and subsequent hospitalization for mental disorders. *Epidemiology, 21*(1), 70–77. doi:10.1097/EDE.0b013e3181c17da8

**Galef, B.** (1998). Edward Thorndike: Revolutionary psychologist, ambiguous biologist. *American Psychologist, 53,* 1128–1134.

**Gallistel, C. R.** (2000). The replacement of general-purpose learning models with adaptively specialized learning modules. In M. S. Gazzaniga (Ed.), *The new cognitive neurosciences* (pp. 1179–1191). Cambridge, MA: MIT Press.

**Gallo, D. A.** (2006). *Associative illusions of memory.* New York: Psychology Press.

**Gallo, D. A.** (2010). False memories and fantastic beliefs: 15 years of the DRM illusion. *Memory & Cognition, 38,* 833–848.

**Gallup, G. G.** (1977). Self-recognition in primates: A comparative approach to the bidirectional properties of consciousness. *American Psychologist, 32,* 329–338.

**Gallup, G. G.** (1997). On the rise and fall of self-conception in primates. *Annals of the New York Academy of Sciences, 818,* 73–84.

**Gallup, G. G., & Frederick, D. A.** (2010). The science of sex appeal: An evolutionary perspective. *Review of General Psychology, 14*(3), 240–250. doi:10.1037/a0020451

**Galton, F.** (1869). *Hereditary genius: An inquiry into its laws and consequences.* London: Macmillan/Fontana.

**Ganzel, B. L., Kim, P., Glover, G. H., & Temple, E.** (2008). Resilience after 9/11: Multimodal neuroimaging evidence for stress-related change in the healthy adult brain. *NeuroImage, 40,* 788–795.

**Garb, H. N.** (1998). *Studying the clinician: Judgment research and psychological assessment.* Washington, DC: American Psychological Association.

**Garcia, J.** (1981). Tilting at the windmills of academe. *American Psychologist,36,* 149–158.

**Garcia, J., & Koelling, R. A.** (1966). Relation of cue to consequence in avoidance learning. *Psychonomic Science, 4,* 123–124.

**Gardner, R. A., & Gardner, B. T.** (1969). Teaching sign language to a chimpanzee. *Science, 165,* 664–672.

**Gardner, M., & Steinberg, L.** (2005). Peer influence on risk taking, risk preference, and risky decision making in adolescence and adulthood: An experimental study. *Developmental Psychology, 41,*(4), 625–635. doi:10.1037/0012-1649.41.4.625

**Garland, A. F., & Zigler, E.** (1999). Emotional and behavioral problems among highly intellectually gifted youth. *Roeper Review, 22*(1), 41.

**Garry, M., Manning, C., Loftus, E. F., & Sherman, S. J.** (1996). Imagination inflation: Imagining a childhood event inflates confidence that it occurred. *Psychonomic Bulletin & Review, 3,* 208–214.

**Gaser, C., & Schlaug, G.** (2003). Brain structures differ between musicians and nonmusicians. *Journal of Neuroscience, 23,* 9240–9245.

**Gathercole, S. E.** (2008). Nonword repetition and word learning: The nature of the relationship. *Applied Psycholinguistics, 27,* 513–543.

**Gazzaniga, M. S. (Ed.).** (2000). *The new cognitive neurosciences.* Cambridge, MA: MIT Press.

**Gazzaniga, M. S.** (2006). Forty-five years of split brain research and still going strong. *Nature Reviews Neuroscience, 6,* 653–659.

**Ge, D., Fellay, J., Thompson, A. J., Simon, J. S., Shianna, K. V., Urban, T. J., … Goldstein, D. B.** (2009). Genetic variation in il28b predicts hepatitis C treatment-induced viral clearance. *Nature, 461,* 399–401.

**Ge, X. J., Conger, R. D., & Elder, G. H.** (1996). Coming of age too early: Pubertal influences on girls' vulnerability to psychological distress. *Child Development, 67,* 3386–3400.

**Ge, X. J., Conger, R. D., & Elder, G. H., Jr.** (2001). Pubertal transition, stressful life events, and the emergence of gender differences in adolescent depressive symptoms. *Developmental Psychology, 37*(3), 404–417. Doi:10.1037/0012-1649.37.3.404

**Ge, X. J., & Natsuaki, M. N.** (2009). In search of explanations for early pubertal timing effects on developmental psychopathology. *Current Directions in Psychological Science, 18,* 327–331.

**Geen, R. G.** (1984). Preferred stimulation levels in introverts and extraverts: Effects on arousal and performance. *Journal of Personality and Social Psychology, 46,* 1303–1312.

**Gegenfurtner, K. R., & Kiper, D. C.** (2003). Color vision. *Annual Review of Neuroscience, 26,* 181–206.

**Geier, A., Wansink, B., & Rozin, P.** (2012). Red potato chips: Segmentation cues substantially decrease food intake. *Health Psychology, 31,* 398–401.

**Gendron, M., Roberson, D., van der Vyver, J. M., & Barrett, L. F.** (in press). Perceptions of emotion from facial expressions are not culturally universal: Evidence from a remote culture. *Emotion.*

**Gershoff, E. T.** (2002). Corporal punishment by parents and associated child behaviors and experiences: A meta-analytic and theoretical review. *Psychological Bulletin, 128,* 539–579.

**Geschwind, D. H.** (2009). Advances in autism. *Annual Review of Medicine, 60,* 67–80.

**Gibb, B. E., Alloy, L. B., & Tierney, S.** (2001). History of childhood maltreatment, negative cognitive styles, and episodes of depression in adulthood. *Cognitive Therapy and Research, 25,* 425–446.

**Gibbons, F. X.** (1990). Self-attention and behavior: A review and theoretical update. In M. P. Zanna (Ed.), *Advances in experimental social psychology* (Vol. 23, pp. 249–303). San Diego, CA: Academic Press.

**Gick, M. L., & Holyoak, K. J.** (1980). Analogical problem solving. *Cognitive Psychology, 12,* 306–355.

**Giedd, J. N., Blumenthal, J., Jeffries, N. O., Castellanos, F. X., Liu, H., Zijdenbos, A., … Rapoport, J. L.** (1999). Brain development during childhood and adolescence: A longitudinal MRI study. *Nature Neuroscience, 2,* 861–863.

**Gierlach, E., Blesher, B. E., & Beutler, L. E.** (2010). Cross-cultural differences in risk perceptions of disasters. *Risk Analysis, 30,* 1539–1549.

**Gigerenzer, G.** (1996). The psychology of good judgment: Frequency formats and simple algorithms. *Journal of Medical Decision Making, 16,* 273–280.

Gigerenzer, G., & Hoffrage, U. (1995). How to improve Bayesian reasoning without instruction: Frequency formats. *Psychological Review, 102,* 684–704.

Gigone, D., & Hastie, R. (1993). The common knowledge effect: Information sharing and group judgment. *Journal of Personality and Social Psychology, 54,* 959–974.

Gilbert, D. T. (1991). How mental systems believe. *American Psychologist, 46,* 107–119.

Gilbert, D. T. (1998). Ordinary personology. In D. T. Gilbert, S. T. Fiske, & G. Lindzey (Eds.), *The handbook of social psychology* (4th ed., Vol. 2, pp. 89–150). New York: McGraw-Hill.

Gilbert, D. T. (2006). *Stumbling on happiness.* New York: Knopf.

Gilbert, D. T., Brown, R. P., Pinel, E. C., & Wilson, T. D. (2000). The illusion of external agency. *Journal of Personality and Social Psychology, 79,* 690–700.

Gilbert, D. T., Gill, M. J., & Wilson, T. D. (2002). The future is now: Temporal correction in affective forecasting. *Organizational Behavior and Human Decision Processes, 88,* 430–444.

Gilbert, D. T., & Malone, P. S. (1995). The correspondence bias. *Psychological Bulletin, 117,* 21–38.

Gilbert, D. T., Pelham, B. W., & Krull, D. S. (1988). On cognitive busyness: When persons perceive meet persons perceived. *Journal of Personality and Social Psychology, 54,* 733–740.

Gilbert, G. M. (1951). Stereotype persistence and change among college students. *Journal of Abnormal and Social Psychology, 46,* 245–254.

Gilbertson, M. W., Shenton, M. E., Ciszewski, A., Kasai, K., Lasko, N. B., Orr, S. P., & Pitman, R. K. (2002). Smaller hippocampal volume predicts pathological vulnerability to psychological trauma. *Nature Neuroscience, 5,* 1242–1247.

Gillespie, C. F., & Nemeroff, C. B. (2007). Corticotropin-releasing factor and the psychobiology of early-life stress. *Current Directions in Psychological Science, 16,* 85–89.

Gillette, J., Gleitman, H., Gleitman, L., & Lederer, A. (1999). Human simulation of vocabulary learning. *Cognition, 73,* 135–176.

Gilligan, C. (1982). *In a different voice: Psychological theory and women's development.* Cambridge, MA: Harvard University Press.

Gilovich, T. (1991). *How we know what isn't so: The fallibility of human reason in everyday life.* New York: Free Press.

Ginzburg, K., Solomon, Z., & Bleich, A. (2002). Repressive coping style, acute stress disorder, and posttraumatic stress disorder after myocardial infarction. *Psychosomatic Medicine, 64,* 748–757.

Giovanello, K. S., Schnyer, D. M., & Verfaellie, M. (2004). A critical role for the anterior hippocampus in relational memory: Evidence from an fMRI study comparing associative and item recognition. *Hippocampus, 14,* 5–8.

Gladue, B. A. (1994). The biopsychology of sexual orientation. *Current Directions in Psychological Science, 3,* 150–154.

Glass, D. C., & Singer, J. E. (1972). *Urban stress.* New York: Academic Press.

Glenwick, D. S., Jason, L. A., & Elman, D. (1978). Physical attractiveness and social contact in the singles bar. *Journal of Social Psychology, 105,* 311–312.

Glynn, L. M., & Sandman, C. A. (2011). Prenatal origins of neurological development: A critical period for fetus and mother. *Current Directions in Psychological Science, 20*(6), 384–389. doi:10.1177/0963721411422056

Gneezy, U., & Rustichini, A. (2000). A fine is a price. *Journal of Legal Studies, 29,* 1–17.

Gobert, A., Rivet, J. M., Cistarelli, L., Melon, C., & Millan, M. J. (1999). Buspirone modulates basal and fluoxetine-stimulated dialysate levels of dopamine, noradrenaline, and serotonin in the frontal cortex of freely moving rats: Activation of serotonin 1A receptors and blockade of alpha2-adrenergic receptors underlie its actions. *Neuroscience, 93,* 1251–1262.

Goddard, H. H. (1913). *The Kallikak family: A study in the heredity of feeble-mindedness.* New York: Macmillan.

Godden, D. R., & Baddeley, A. D. (1975). Context-dependent memory in two natural environments: On land and underwater. *British Journal of Psychology, 66,* 325–331.

Goehler, L. E., Gaykema, R. P. A., Hansen, M. K., Anderson, K., Maier, S. F., & Watkins, L. R. (2000). Vagal immune-to-brain communication: A visceral chemosensory pathway. *Autonomic Neuroscience: Basic and Clinical, 85,* 49–59.

Goel, V. (2007). Anatomy of deductive reasoning. *Trends in Cognitive Sciences, 11,* 435–441.

Goel, V., & Dolan, R. J. (2003). Explaining modulation of reasoning by belief. *Cognition, 87,* 11–22.

Goetzman, E. S., Hughes, T., & Klinger, E. (1994). *Current concerns of college students in a midwestern sample.* Unpublished report, University of Minnesota, Morris.

Goff, L. M., & Roediger, H. L., III. (1998). Imagination inflation for action events—repeated imaginings lead to illusory recollections. *Memory & Cognition, 26,* 20–33.

Goldman, M. S., Brown, S. A., & Christiansen, B. A. (1987). Expectancy theory: Thinking about drinking. In H. T. Blane & K. E. Leonard (Eds.), *Psychological theories of drinking and alcoholism* (pp. 181–266). New York: Guilford Press.

Goldstein, M. H., Schwade, J. A., Briesch, J., & Syal, S. (2010). Learning while babbling: Prelinguistic object-directed vocalizations signal a readiness to learn. *Infancy, 15,* 362–391

Goldstein, R., Almenberg, J., Dreber, A., Emerson, J. W., Herschkowitsch, A., & Katz, J. (2008). Do more expensive wines taste better? Evidence from a large sample of blind tastings. *Journal of Wine Economics, 3,* 1–9.

Goldstein, R., & Herschkowitsch, A. (2008). *The wine trials.* Austin, TX: Fearless Critic Media.

Gomez, C., Argandota, E. D., Solier, R. G., Angulo, J. C., & Vazquez, M. (1995). Timing and competition in networks representing ambiguous figures. *Brain and Cognition, 29,* 103–114.

Gontier, N. (2008). Genes, brains, and language: An epistemological examination of how genes can underlie human cognitive behavior. *Review of General Psychology, 12,* 170–180.

Gonzaga, G. C., Keltner, D., Londahl, E. A., & Smith, M. D. (2001). Love and the commitment problem in romantic relations and friendship. *Journal of Personality and Social Psychology, 81,* 247–262.

Goodale, M. A., & Milner, A. D. (1992). Separate visual pathways for perception and action. *Trends in Neurosciences, 15,* 20–25.

Goodale, M. A., & Milner, A. D. (2004). *Sight unseen.* Oxford, England: Oxford University Press.

Goodale, M. A., Milner, A. D., Jakobson, L. S., & Carey, D. P. (1991). A neurological dissociation between perceiving objects and grasping them. *Nature, 349,* 154–156.

Gootman, E. (2003, March 3). Separated at birth in Mexico, united at campuses on Long Island. *New York Times,* p. A25.

Gopnik, A. (2012). Scientific thinking in young children: Theoretical advances, empirical research, and policy implications. *Science, 337*(6102), 1623–1627. doi:10.1126/science.1223416

Gopnik, A., & Astington, J. W. (1988). Children's understanding of representational change and its relation to the understanding of false belief and the appearance reality distinction. *Child Development, 59,* 26–37.

**Gopnik, M.** (1990a). Feature-blind grammar and dysphasia. *Nature, 344,* 715.

**Gopnik, M.** (1990b). Feature blindness: A case study. *Language Acquisition: A Journal of Developmental Linguistics, 1,* 139–164.

**Gorczynski, P., & Faulkner, G.** (2011). Exercise therapy for schizophrenia. *Cochrane Database of Systematic Reviews, 5,* CD004412.

**Gordon, P.** (2004). Numerical cognition without words: Evidence from Amazonia. *Science, 306,* 496–499.

**Gorno-Tempini, M. L., Price, C. J., Josephs, O., Vandenberghe, R., Cappa, S. F., Kapur, N., & Frackowiak, R. S.** (1998). The neural systems sustaining face and proper-name processing. *Brain, 121,* 2103–2118.

**Gosling, S. D.** (1998). Personality dimensions in spotted hyenas (*Crocuta crocuta*). *Journal of Comparative Psychology, 112,* 107–118.

**Gosling, S. D., & John, O. P.** (1999). Personality dimensions in nonhuman animals: A cross-species review. *Current Directions in Psychological Science, 8,* 69–75.

**Gosling, S. D., Rentfrow, P. J., & Swann, W. B., Jr.** (2003). A very brief measure of the Big-Five personality domains. *Journal of Research in Personality, 37,* 504–528.

**Gotlib, I. H., & Joormann, J.** (2010). Cognition and depression: Current status and future directions. *Annual Review of Clinical Psychology, 6,* 285–312.

**Gottesman, I. I.** (1991). *Schizophrenia genesis: The origins of madness.* New York: Freeman.

**Gottesman, I. I., & Hanson, D. R.** (2005). Human development: Biological and genetic processes. *Annual Review of Psychology, 56,* 263–286.

**Gottfredson, L. S.** (1997). Mainstream science on intelligence: An editorial with 52 signatories, history, and bibliography. *Intelligence, 24,* 13–23.

**Gottfredson, L. S.** (2003). Dissecting practical intelligence theory: Its claims and evidence. *Intelligence, 31*(4), 343–397.

**Gottfredson, L. S., & Deary, I. J.** (2004). Intelligence predicts health and longevity, but why? *Current Directions in Psychological Science, 13,* 1–4.

**Gottfried, J. A.** (2008). Perceptual and neural plasticity of odor quality coding in the human brain. *Chemosensory Perception, 1,* 127–135.

**Gouldner, A. W.** (1960). The norm of reciprocity. *American Sociological Review, 25,* 161–178.

**Government of Canada.** (2006). *The human face of mental health and mental illness in Canada 2006.* Ottawa: Minister of Public Works and Government Services Canada.

**Grady, C. L., Haxby, J. V., Horwitz, B., Schapiro, M. B., Rapoport, S. I., Ungerleider, L. G., ... Herscovitch, P.** (1992). Dissociation of object and spatial vision in human extrastriate cortex: Age-related changes in activation of regional cerebral blood flow measured with [¹⁵O] water and positiron emission tomography. *Journal of Cognitive Neuroscience, 4*(1), 23–34. doi:10.1162/jocn.1992.4.1.23

**Graf, P., & Schacter, D. L.** (1985). Implicit and explicit memory for new associations in normal subjects and amnesic patients. *Journal of Experimental Psychology: Learning, Memory, and Cognition, 11,* 501–518.

**Grandin, T.** (2006). *Thinking in pictures: My life with autism* (expanded edition). Visalia, CA: Vintage.

**Grant, A. M.** (2008). Personal life coaching for coaches-in-training enhances goal attainment, insight, and learning. *Coaching, 1*(1), 54–70.

**Grant, B. F., Hasin, D. S., Stinson, F. S., Dawson, D. A., Chou, S. P., & Ruan, W. J.** (2004). Prevalence, correlates, and disability of personality disorders in the U.S.: Results from the National Epidemiologic Survey on Alcohol and Related Conditions. *Journal of Clinical Psychiatry, 65,* 948–958.

**Grassian, S.** (2006). Psychiatric effects of solitary confinement. *Journal of Law & Policy, 22,* 325–383.

**Gray, H. M., Gray, K., & Wegner, D. M.** (2007). Dimensions of mind perception. *Science, 315,* 619.

**Gray, J. A.** (1970). The psychophysiological basis of introversion–extraversion. *Behavior Research and Therapy, 8,* 249–266.

**Gray, J. A.** (1990). Brain systems that mediate both emotion and cognition. *Cognition and Emotion, 4,* 269–288.

**Greely, H., Sahakian, B., Harris, J., Kessler, R. C., Gazzaniga, M., Campbell, P., & Farah, M. J.** (2008). Towards responsible use of cognitive-enhancing drugs by the healthy. *Nature, 456*(7223), 702–705.

**Green, C. S., & Bavelier, D.** (2007). Action video-game experience alters the spatial resolution of vision. *Psychological Science, 18,* 88–94.

**Green, D. A., & Swets, J. A.** (1966). *Signal detection theory and psychophysics.* New York: Wiley.

**Green, M. F., Kern, R. S., Braff, D. L., & Mintz, J.** (2000). Neurocognitive deficits and functional outcome in schizophrenia: Are we measuring the "right stuff"? *Schizophrenia Bulletin, 26,* 119–136.

**Green, S. K., Buchanan, D. R., & Heuer, S. K.** (1984). Winners, losers, and choosers: A field investigation of dating initiation. *Personality and Social Psychology Bulletin, 10,* 502–511.

**Greenberg, J., Pyszczynski, T., Solomon, S., Rosenblatt, A., Veeder, M., Kirkland, S., & Lyon, D.** (1990). Evidence for terror management theory II: The effects of mortality salience on reactions to those who threaten or bolster the cultural worldview. *Journal of Personality and Social Psychology, 58,* 308–318.

**Greenberg, J., Solomon, S., & Arndt, J.** (2008). A basic but uniquely human motivation: Terror management. In J. Y. Shah & W. L. Gardner (Eds.), *Handbook of motivation science* (pp. 114–134). New York: Guilford Press.

**Greene, J.** (2013). *Moral tribes: Emotion, reason, and the gap between us and them.* New York: Penguin.

**Greene, J. D., Sommerville, R. B., Nystrom, L. E., Darley, J. M., & Cohen, J. D.** (2001). An fMRI investigation of emotional engagement in moral judgment. *Science, 293,* 2105–2108.

**Greenwald, A. G.** (1992). New look 3: Unconscious cognition reclaimed. *American Psychologist, 47,* 766–779.

**Greenwald, A. G., McGhee, D. E., & Schwartz, J. L. K.** (1998). Measuring individual differences in implicit cognition: The implicit association test. *Journal of Personality and Social Psychology, 74,* 1464–1480.

**Greenwald, A. G., & Nosek, B. A.** (2001). Health of the Implicit Association Test at age 3. *Zeitschrift für Experimentelle Psychologie, 48,* 85–93.

**Gropp, E., Shanabrough, M., Borok, E., Xu, A. W., Janoschek, R., Buch, T., ... Brüning, J. C.** (2005). Agouti-related peptide-expressing neurons are mandatory for feeding. *Nature Neuroscience, 8,* 1289–1291.

**Gross, J. J.** (1998). Antecedent- and response-focused emotion regulation: Divergent consequences for experience, expression, and physiology. *Journal of Personality and Social Psychology, 74,* 224–237.

**Gross, J. J.** (2002). Emotion regulation: Affective, cognitive, and social consequences. *Psychophysiology, 39,* 281–291.

**Gross, J. J., & Munoz, R. F.** (1995). Emotion regulation and mental health. *Clinical Psychology: Science and Practice, 2,* 151–164.

**Groves, B.** (2004, August 2). Unwelcome awareness. *San Diego Union-Tribune,* p. 24.

Grün, F., & Blumberg, B. (2006). Environmental obesogens: Organotins and endocrine disruption via nuclear receptor signaling. *Endocrinology, 147,* s50–s55.

Guerin, S. A., Robbins, C. A., Gilmore, A. W., & Schacter, D. L. (2012a). Interactions between visual attention and episodic retrieval: Dissociable contributions of parietal regions during gist-based false recognition. *Neuron, 75,* 1122–1134.

Guerin, S. A., Robbins, C. A., Gilmore, A. W., & Schacter, D. L. (2012b). Retrieval failure contributes to gist-based false recognition. *Journal of Memory and Language, 66,* 68–78.

Guillery, R. W., & Sherman, S. M. (2002). Thalamic relay functions and their role in corticocortical communication: Generalizations from the visual system. *Neuron, 33,* 163–175.

Gup, T. (2013, April 3). Diagnosis: Human. *New York Times,* p. A27.

Gur, R. E., Cowell, P., Turetsky, B. I., Gallacher, F., Cannon, T., Bilker, W., & Gur, R. C. (1998). A follow-up magnetic resonance imaging study of schizophrenia: Relationship of neuroanatomical changes to clinical and neurobehavioral measures. *Archives of General Psychiatry, 55,* 145–152.

Gurwitz, J. H., McLaughlin, T. J., Willison, D. J., Guadagnoli, E., Hauptman, P. J., Gao, X., & Soumerai, S. B. (1997). Delayed hospital presentation in patients who have had acute myocardial infarction. *Annals of Internal Medicine, 126,* 593–599.

Gusnard, D. A., & Raichle, M. E. (2001). Searching for a baseline: Functional imaging and the resting human brain. *Nature Reviews: Neuroscience, 2,* 685–694.

Gustafsson, J.-E. (1984). A unifying model for the structure of intellectual abilities. *Intelligence, 8,* 179–203.

Gutchess, A. H., & Schacter, D. L. (2012). The neural correlates of gist-based true and false recognition. *NeuroImage, 59,* 3418–3426.

Haase, C. M., Heckhausen, J., & Wrosch, C. (2013). Developmental regulation across the life span: Toward a new synthesis. *Developmental Psychology, 49*(5), 964–972. doi:10.1037/a0029231

Hacking, I. (1975). *The emergence of probability.* New York: Cambridge University Press.

Hackman, D. A., & Farah, M. J. (2008). Socioeconomic status and the developing brain. *Trends in Cognitive Sciences, 13,* 65–73.

Hackman, J. R., & Katz, N. (2010). Group behavior and performance. In S. T. Fiske, D. T. Gilbert, & G. Lindzey (Eds.), *The handbook of social psychology* (5th ed., Vol. 2, pp. 1208–1251). New York: Wiley.

Haedt-Matt, A. A., & Keel, P. K. (2011). Revisiting the affect regulation model of binge eating: A meta-analysis of studies using ecological momentary assessment. *Psychological Bulletin, 137*(4), 660–681.

Haggard, P., & Tsakiris, M. (2009). The experience of agency: Feelings, judgments, and responsibility. *Current Directions in Psychological Science, 18,* 242–246.

Haidt, J. (2001). The emotional dog and its rational tail: A social intuitionist approach to moral judgment. *Psychological Review, 108,* 814–834.

Haidt, J. (2006). *The happiness hypothesis: Finding modern truth in ancient wisdom.* New York: Basic Books.

Haidt, J., & Keltner, D. (1999). Culture and facial expression: Openended methods find more expressions and a gradient of recognition. *Cognition and Emotion, 13,* 225–266.

Haines, M. M., Stansfeld, S. A., Job, R. F., Berglund, B., & Head, J. (2001). Chronic aircraft noise exposure, stress responses, mental health and cognitive performance in school children. *Psychological Medicine, 31,* 265–277.

Hallett, M. (2000). Transcranial magnetic stimulation and the human brain. *Nature, 406,* 147–150.

Halliday, R., Naylor, H., Brandeis, D., Callaway, E., Yano, L., & Herzig, K. (1994). The effect of D-amphetamine, clonidine, and yohimbine on human information processing. *Psychophysiology, 31,* 331–337.

Halpern, B. (2002). Taste. In H. Pashler & S. Yantis (Eds.), *Stevens' handbook of experimental psychology: Vol. 1. Sensation and perception* (3rd ed., pp. 653–690). New York: Wiley.

Halpern, D. F. (1997). Sex differences in intelligence: Implications for education. *American Psychologist, 52,* 1091–1102.

Halpern, D. F., Benbow, C. P., Geary, D. C., Gur, R. C., Hyde, J. S., & Gernsbacher, M. A. (2007). The science of sex differences in science and mathematics. *Psychological Science in the Public Interest, 8,* 1–51.

Hambrick, D. Z., Oswald, F. L., Altmann, E. M., Meinz, E. J., Gobet, F., & Campitelli, G. (2013). Deliberate practice: Is that all it takes to become an expert? *Intelligence.* Advance online publication. doi:10.1016/j.intell.2013.04.001

Hamermesh, D. S., & Biddle, J. E. (1994). Beauty and the labor market. *American Economic Review, 84,* 1174–1195.

Hamilton, A. F., & Grafton, S. T. (2006). Goal representation in human anterior intraparietal sulcus. *The Journal of Neuroscience, 26,* 1133–1137.

Hamilton, A. F., & Grafton, S. T. (2008). Action outcomes are represented in human inferior frontoparietal cortex. *Cerebral Cortex, 18,* 1160–1168.

Hamilton, D. L., & Gifford, R. K. (1976). Illusory correlation in interpersonal perception: A cognitive basis of stereotypic judgements. *Journal of Experimental Social Psychology, 12,* 392–407.

Hamilton, J. P., Etkin, A., Furman, D. J., Lemus, M. G., Johnson, R. F., & Gotlib, I. H. (2012). Functional neuroimaging of major depressive disorder: A meta-analysis and new integration of baseline activation and neural response data. *American Journal of Psychiatry, 169,* 693–703.

Hamilton, J. P., Glover, G. H., Hsu, J. J., Johnson, R. F., & Gotlib, I. H. (2010). Modulation of subgenual anterior cingulated cortex activity with real-time neurofeedback. *Human Brain Mapping, 32,* 22–31.

Hamilton, W. D. (1964). The genetical evolution of social behaviour. *Journal of Theoretical Biology, 7,* 1–16.

Hamlin, J. K., Mahajan, N., Liberman, Z., & Wynn, K. (2013). Not like me = bad: Infants prefer those who harm dissimilar others. *Psychological Science, 24*(4), 589–594. doi:10.1177/0956797612457785

Hamlin, J. K., Wynn, K., & Bloom, P. (2007). Social evaluation by preverbal infants. *Nature, 450*(7169), 557–559.

Hampikian, G. (2012, August 24). Men, who needs them? *New York Times.* Retrieved from http://www.nytimes.com/2012/08/25/opinion/men-who-needs-them.html

Haney, C., Banks, W. C., & Zimbardo, P. G. (1973). Study of prisoners and guards in a simulated prison. *Naval Research Reviews, 9,* 1–17.

Hannon, E. E., & Trainor, L. J. (2007). Music acquisition: Effects of enculturation and formal training on development. *Trends in Cognitive Sciences, 11,* 466–472.

Hansen, E. S., Hasselbalch, S., Law, I., & Bolwig, T. G. (2002). The caudate nucleus in obsessive-compulsive disorder. Reduced metabolism following treatment with paroxetine: A PET study. *International Journal of Neuropsychopharmacology, 5,* 1–10.

Hanson, J. D., Larson, M. E., & Snowdon, C. T. (1976). The effects of control over high intensity noise on plasma cortisol levels in rhesus monkeys. *Behavioural Biology, 16*(3), 333–340.

Happé, F. G. E. (1995). The role of age and verbal ability in the theory-of-mind performance of subjects with autism. *Child Development, 66,* 843–855.

Happé, F. G. E., & Vital, P. (2009). What aspects of autism pre-dispose to talent? *Philosophical Transactions of the Royal Society B: Biological Science, 364*, 1369–1375.

Harand, C., Bertran, F., La Joie, R., Landeau, B., Mézenge, F., ... Rauchs, G. (2012). The hippocampus remains activated over the long term for the retrieval of truly episodic memories. *PLoS ONE, 7*, e43495. doi:10.1371/journal.pone.0043495

Harding, C. M., Brooks, G. W., Ashikaga, T., Strauss, J. S., & Brier, A. (1987). The Vermont longitudinal study of persons with severe mental illness, II: Long-term outcome of subjects who retrospectively met DSM-III criteria for schizophrenia. *American Journal of Psychiatry, 144*, 727–735.

Hare, R. D. (1998). *Without conscience: The disturbing world of the psychopaths among us.* New York: Guilford Press.

Harkness, S., Edwards, C. P., & Super, C. M. (1981). Social roles and moral reasoning: A case study in a rural African community. *Developmental Psychology, 17*, 595–603.

Harlow, H. F. (1958). The nature of love. *American Psychologist, 13*, 573–685.

Harlow, H. F., & Harlow, M. L. (1965). The affectional systems. In A. M. Schrier, H. F. Harlow, & F. Stollnitz (Eds.), *Behavior of nonhuman primates* (Vol. 2, pp. 287–334). New York: Academic Press.

Harlow, J. M. (1848). Passage of an iron rod through the head. *Boston Medical and Surgical Journal, 39*, 389–393.

Harris, B. (1979). Whatever happened to Little Albert? *American Psychologist, 34*, 151–160.

Harris, P. L., de Rosnay, M., & Pons, F. (2005). Language and children's understanding of mental states. *Current Directions in Psychological Science, 14*, 69–73.

Harris, P. L., Johnson, C. N., Hutton, D., Andrews, G., & Cooke, T. (1989). Young children's theory of mind and emotion. *Cognition and Emotion, 3*, 379–400.

Hart, B. L. (1988). Biological basis of the behavior of sick animals. *Neuroscience and Biobehavioral Reviews, 12*, 123–137.

Hart, B., & Risley, T. R. (1995). *Meaningful differences in the everyday experience of young American children.* Baltimore, MD: Brookes.

Hart, W., Albarracin, D., Eagly, A. H., Lindberg, M. J., Merrill, L., & Brechan, I. (2009). Feeling validated versus being correct: A meta-analysis of selective exposure to information. *Psychological Bulletin, 135*, 555–588.

Hartshorne, H., & May, M. A. (1928). *Studies in deceit.* New York: Macmillan.

Hasher, L., & Zacks, R. T. (1984). Automatic processing of fundamental information: The case of frequency of occurrence. *American Psychologist, 39*, 1372–1388.

Haskell, E. (1869). *The trial of Ebenezer Haskell, in lunacy, and his acquittal before Judge Brewster, in November, 1868, together with a brief sketch of the mode of treatment of lunatics in different asylums in this country and in England: with illustrations, including a copy of Hogarth's celebrated painting of a scene in old Bedlam, in London, 1635.* Philadelphia, PA: Ebenezer Haskell.

Haslam, C., Wills, A. J., Haslam, S. A., Kay, J., Baron, R., & McNab, F. (2007). Does maintenance of colour categories rely on language? Evidence to the contrary from a case of semantic dementia. *Brain and Language, 103*, 251–263.

Hassabis, D., Kumaran, D., Vann, S. D., & Maguire, E. A. (2007). Patients with hippocampal amnesia cannot imagine new experiences. *Proceedings of the National Academy of Sciences, USA, 104*, 1726–1731.

Hasselmo, M. E. (2006). The role of acetylcholine in learning and memory. *Current Opinion in Neurobiology, 16*, 710–715.

Hassin, R. R., Bargh, J. A., & Zimerman, S. (2009). Automatic and flexible: The case of non-conscious goal pursuit. *Social Cognition, 27*, 20–36.

Hassmen, P., Koivula, N., & Uutela, A. (2000). Physical exercise and psychological well-being: A population study in Finland. *Preventive Medicine, 30*, 17–25.

Hasson, U., Hendler, T., Bashat, D. B., & Malach, R. (2001). Vase or face? A neural correlate of shape-selective grouping processes in the human brain. *Journal of Cognitive Neuroscience, 13*, 744–753.

Hatemi, P. K., Gillespie, N. A., Eaves, L. J., Maher, B. S., Webb, B. T., Heath, A. C., ... Martin, N. G. (2011). A genome-wide analysis of liberal and conservative political attitudes. *The Journal of Politics, 73*, 271–285.

Hatfield, E. (1988). Passionate and companionate love. In R. J. Sternberg & M. L. Barnes (Eds.), *The psychology of love* (pp. 191–217). New Haven, CT: Yale University Press.

Hatfield, E., & Rapson, R. L. (1992). Similarity and attraction in close relationships. *Communication Monographs, 59*, 209–212.

Hausser, M. (2000). The Hodgkin-Huxley theory of the action potential. *Nature Neuroscience, 3*, 1165.

Havas, D. A., Glenberg, A. M., Gutowski, K. A., Lucarelli, M. J., & Davidson, R. J. (2010). Cosmetic use of botulinum toxin-A affects processing of emotional language. *Psychological Science, 21*(7), 895–900. doi:10.1177/0956797610374742

Hawley, P. H. (2002). Social dominance and prosocial and coercive strategies of resource control in preschoolers. *International Journal of Behavioral Development, 26*, 167–176.

Haxby, J. V., Gobbini, M. I., Furey, M. L., Ishai, A., Schouten, J. L., & Pietrini, P. (2001). Distributed and overlapping representations of faces and objects in ventral temporal cortex. *Science, 293*, 2425–2430.

Hayes, J. E., Bartoshuk, L. M., Kidd, J. R., & Duffy, V. B. (2008). Supertasting and PROP bitterness depends on more than the TAS2R38 gene. *Chemical Senses, 23*, 255–265.

Hayes, K., & Hayes, C. (1951). The intellectual development of a home-raised chimpanzee. *Proceedings of the American Philosophical Society, 95*, 105–109.

Hayes, S. C., Strosahl, K., & Wilson, K. G. (1999). *Acceptance and commitment therapy: An experiential approach to behavior change.* New York: Guilford Press.

Hay-McCutcheon, M. J., Kirk, K. I., Henning, S. C., Gao, S. J., & Qi, R. (2008). Using early outcomes to predict later language ability in children with cochlear implants. *Audiology and Neuro-Otology, 13*, 370–378.

Health Canada. (2013). Canadian tobacco use monitoring survey (CTUMS) 2012: *Supplementary tables—Annual.* Retrieved from http://www.hc-sc.gc.ca/hc-ps/tobac-tabac/research-recherche/stat/_ctums-esutc_2012/ann-eng.php#t8

Heart and Stroke Foundation. (2010). *Women and heart disease: The heart truth.* Retrieved from http://www.heartandstroke.com/site/c.ikIQLcMWJtE/b.5889207/k.11DD/Women_and_heart_disease_The_Heart_Truth.htm

Heath, S. B. (1983). *Way with words: Language, life and work in communities and classrooms.* Cambridge, England: Cambridge University Press.

Heatherton, T. F., & Weinberger, J. L. (Eds.). (1994). *Can personality change?* Washington, DC: American Psychological Association.

Heaton, R., Paulsen, J. S., McAdams, L. A., Kuck, J., Zisook, S., Braff, D., ... Jeste, D. V. (1994). Neuropsychological deficits in schizophrenia: Relationship to age, chronicity, and dementia. *Archives of General Psychiatry, 51*, 469–476.

Heavey, C. L., Hurlburt, R. T., & Lefforge, N. L. (2012). Toward a phenomenology of feelings. *Emotion, 12*(4), 763–777.

**Hebb, D. O.** (1949). *The organization of behavior.* New York: Wiley.

**Hebl, M. R., & Heatherton, T. F.** (1997). The stigma of obesity in women: The difference is Black and White. *Personality and Social Psychology Bulletin, 24,* 417–426.

**Hebl, M. R., & Mannix, L. M.** (2003). The weight of obesity in evaluating others: A mere proximity effect. *Personality and Social Psychology Bulletin, 29,* 28–38.

**Hedges, L. V., & Nowell, A.** (1995). Sex differences in mental test scores, variability, and numbers of high-scoring individuals. *Science, 269*(5220), 41–45.

**Heerey, E. A., Keltner, D., & Capps, L. M.** (2003). Making sense of self-conscious emotion: Linking theory of mind and emotion in children with autism. *Emotion, 3,* 394–400.

**Heine, S. J.** (2010). Cultural psychology. In S. T. Fiske, D. T. Gilbert, & G. Lindzey (Eds.), *The handbook of social psychology* (5th ed., Vol. 2, pp. 1423– 1464). New York: Wiley.

**Heine, S. J., & Lehman, D. R.** (1995). Cultural variation in unrealistic optimism: Does the west feel more invulnerable than the east? *Journal of Peronality and Social Psychology, 68,* 595–607.

**Helt, M., Kelley, E., Kinsbourne, M., Pandey, J., Boorstein, H., Herbert, M., & Fein, D.** (2008). Can children with autism recover? If so, how? *Neuropsychology Review, 18,* 339–366.

**Henderlong, J., & Lepper, M. R.** (2002). The effects of praise on children's intrinsic motivation: A review and synthesis. *Psychological Bulletin, 128,* 774–795.

**Henrich, J., Heine, S. J., & Norenzayan, A.** (2010). Most people are not WEIRD. *Nature, 466,* 29.

**Henry, W. P., Strupp, H. H., Schacht, T. E., & Gaston, L.** (1994). Psychodynamic approaches. In A. E. Bergin & S. L. Garfield (Eds.), *Handbook of psychotherapy and behavior change* (pp. 467–508). New York: Wiley.

**Herman, C. P., & Polivy, J.** (2008). External cues in the control of food intake in humans: The sensory-normative distinction. *Physiology & Behavior, 94,* 722–728.

**Herman, C. P., Roth, D. A., & Polivy, J.** (2003). Effects of the presence of others on food intake: A normative interpretation. *Psychological Bulletin, 129,* 873–886.

**Herman-Giddens, M. E., Steffes, J., Harris, D., Slora, E., Hussey, M., Dowshen, S. A., & Reiter, E. O.** (2012). Secondary sexual characteristics in boys: Data from the pediatric research in office settings network. *Pediatrics, 130*(5), e1058–e1068. doi:10.1542/peds.2011-3291

**Herring, M. P., Puetz, T. W., O'Connor, P. J., & Dishman, R. K.** (2010). Effect of exercise training on depressive symptoms among patients with chronic illness: A systematic review and meta-analysis of randomized controlled trials. *Archives of Internal Medicine, 172,* 101–111.

**Herrnstein, R. J.** (1977). The evolution of behaviorism. *American Psychologist, 32,* 593–603.

**Hertenstein, M. J., Holmes, R., McCullough, M., & Keltner, D.** (2009). The communication of emotion via touch. *Emotion, 9,* 566–573.

**Hertig, M. M., & Nagel, B. J.** (2012). Aerobic fitness relates to learning on a virtual Morris water maze task and hippocampal volume in adolescents. *Behavioral Brain Research, 233,* 517–525.

**Hertwig, R., & Gigerenzer, G.** (1999). The "conjunction fallacy" revisited: How intelligent inferences look like reasoning errors. *Journal of Behavioral Decision Making, 12,* 275–305.

**Herz, R. S., & von Clef, J.** (2001). The influence of verbal labeling on the perception of odors. *Perception, 30,* 381–391.

**Hettema, J. M., Neale, M. C., & Kendler, K. S.** (2001). A review and meta-analysis of the genetic epidemiology of anxiety disorders. *American Journal of Psychiatry, 158,* 1568–1578.

**Heyes, C. M., & Foster, C. L.** (2002). Motor learning by observation: Evidence from a serial reaction time task. *Quarterly Journal of Experimental Psychology (A), 55,* 593–607.

**Heyman, G. M.** (2009). *Addiction: A disorder of choice.* Cambridge, MA: Harvard University Press.

**Heymsfield, S. B., Greenberg, A. S., Fujioka, K., Dixon, R. M., Kushner, R., Hunt, T., … McCarnish, M.** (1999). Recombinant leptin for weight loss in obese and lean adults: A randomized, controlled, dose-escalation trial. *Journal of the American Medical Association, 282*(16), 1568–1575.

**Hibbeln, J. R.** (1998). Fish consumption and major depression. *Lancet, 351,* 1213.

**Hickok, G.** (2009). Eight problems for the mirror neuron theory of action understanding in monkeys and humans. *Journal of Cognitive Neuroscience, 21,* 1229–1243.

**Higgins, E. T.** (1987). Self-discrepancy theory: A theory relating self and affect. *Psychological Review, 94,* 319–340.

**Higgins, E. T.** (1997). Beyond pleasure and pain. *American Psychologist, 52,* 1280–1300.

**Hilgard, E. R.** (1965). *Hypnotic susceptibility.* New York: Harcourt, Brace and World.

**Hilgard, E. R.** (1986). *Divided consciousness: Multiple controls in human thought and action.* New York: Wiley-Interscience.

**Hillman, C. H., Erickson, K. I., & Kramer, A. F.** (2008). Be smart, exercise your heart: Exercise effects on brain and cognition. *Nature Reviews Neuroscience, 9,* 58–65.

**Hilts, P.** (1995). *Memory's ghost: The strange tale of Mr. M and the nature of memory.* New York: Simon & Schuster.

**Hine, T.** (1995). *The total package: The evolution and secret meanings of boxes, bottles, cans, and tubes.* Boston: Little, Brown.

**Hintzman, D. L., Asher, S. J., & Stern, L. D.** (1978). Incidental retrieval and memory for coincidences. In M. M. Gruneberg, P. E. Morris, & R. N. Sykes (Eds.), *Practical aspects of memory* (pp. 61–68). New York: Academic Press.

**Hirschberger, G., Florian, V., & Mikulincer, M.** (2002). The anxiety buffering function of close relationships: Mortality salience effects on the readiness to compromise mate selection standards. *European Journal of Social Psychology, 32,* 609–625.

**Hirst, W., & Echterhoff, G.** (2012). Remembering in conversations: The social sharing and reshaping of memory. *Annual Review of Psychology, 63,* 55–79.

**Hirst, W., Phelps, E. A., Buckner, R. L., Budson, A. E., Cuc, A., Gabrieli, J. D. E., … Vaidya, C. J.** (2009). Long-term memory for the terrorist attack of September 11: Flashbulb memories, event memories, and the factors that influence their retention. *Journal of Experimental Psychology: General, 138,* 161–176.

**Hirstein, W., & Ramachandran, V. S.** (1997). Capgras syndrome: A novel probe for understanding the neural representation of the identity and familiarity of persons. *Proceedings: Biological Sciences, 264,* 437–444.

**Hitchcock, S. T.** (2005). *Mad Mary Lamb: Lunacy and murder in literary London.* New York: Norton.

**Hobson, J. A.** (1988). *The dreaming brain.* New York: Basic Books.

**Hobson, J. A., & McCarley, R. W.** (1977). The brain as a dream-state generator: An activation–synthesis hypothesis of the dream process. *American Journal of Psychiatry, 134,* 1335–1368.

Hockley, W. E. (2008). The effects of environmental context on recognition memory and claims of remembering. *Journal of Experimental Psychology: Learning, Memory, and Cognition, 34*, 1412–1429.

Hodgkin, A. L., & Huxley, A. F. (1939). Action potential recorded from inside a nerve fibre. *Nature, 144*, 710–712.

Hodson, G., & Sorrentino, R. M. (2001). Just who favors the ingroup? Personality differences in reactions to uncertainty in the minimal group paradigm. *Group Dynamics, 5*, 92–101.

Hoffrage, U., & Gigerenzer, G. (1996). The impact of information representation on Bayesian reasoning. In G. Cottrell (Ed.), *Proceedings of the Eighteenth Annual Conference of the Cognitive Science Society* (pp. 126–130). Mahwah, NJ: Erlbaum.

Hoffrage, U., & Gigerenzer, G. (1998). Using natural frequencies to improve diagnostic inferences. *Academic Medicine, 73*, 538–540.

Hofmann, S. G., & Asmundson, G. J. G. (2008). Acceptance and mindfulness-based therapy: New wave or old hat? *Clinical Psychology Review, 28*, 1–16.

Hofmann, W., Vohs, K. D., & Baumeister, R. F. (2012). What people desire, feel conflicted about, and try to resist in everyday life. *Psychological Science, 23*, 582–588.

Holder, M. D., Love, A. B., & Timoney, L. R. (2014). The poor subjective well-being associated with alexithymia is mediated by romantic relationships. *Journal of Happiness Studies, January, 2014*. doi: 10.1007/s10902-014-9500-0

Hollins, M. (2010). Somesthetic senses. *Annual Review of Psychology, 61*, 243–271.

Holloway, G. (2001). *The complete dream book: What your dreams tell about you and your life.* Naperville, IL: Sourcebooks.

Holman, E. A., Silver, R. C., Poulin, M., Andersen, J., Gil-Rivas, V., & McIntosh, D. N. (2008). Terrorism, acute stress, and cardiovascular health. *Archives of General Psychiatry, 65*, 73–80.

Holman, M. A., Carlson, M. L., Driscoll, C. L. W., Grim, K. J., Petersson, R., Sladen, D. P., & Flick, R. P. (2013). Cochlear implantation in children 12 months of age or younger. *Otology & Neurology, 34*, 251–258.

Holmbeck, G. N., & O'Donnell, K. (1991). Discrepancies between perceptions of decision making and behavioral autonomy. In R. L. Paikoff (Ed.), *New directions for child development: Shared views in the family during adolescence* (no. 51, pp. 51–69). San Francisco: Jossey-Bass.

Holmes, J., Gathercole, S. E., & Dunning, D. L. (2009). Adaptive training leads to sustained enhancement of poor working memory in children. *Developmental Science, 12*, F9-F15.

Holmes, T. H., & Rahe, R. H. (1967). The social readjustment rating scale. *Journal of Psychosomatic Research, 11*, 213–318.

Hölzel, B. K., Carmody, J., Vangel, M., Congleton, C., Yerramsetti, S. M., Gard, T., & Lazar, S. W. (2011). Mindfulness practice leads to increases in regained gray matter density. *Psychiatry Research: Neuroimaging, 191*(1), 36–43.

Homan, K. J., Houlihan, D., Ek, K., & Wanzek, J. (2012). Cultural differences in the level of rewards between adolescents from America, Tanzania, Denmark, Honduras, Korea, and Spain. *International Journal of Psychological Studies, 4*, 264–272.

Homans, G. C. (1961). *Social behavior.* New York: Harcourt, Brace and World.

Hooley, J. M. (2007). Expressed emotion and relapse of psychopathology. *Annual Review of Clinical Psychology, 3*, 329–352.

Hopper, L. M., Flynn, E. G., Wood, L. A. N., & Whiten, A. (2010). Observational learning of tool use in children: Investigating cultural spread through diffusion chains and learning mechanisms through ghost displays. *Journal of Experimental Child Psychology, 106*, 82–97.

Horn, J. L., & Cattell, R. B. (1966). Refinement and test of the theory of fluid and crystallized general intelligences. *Journal of Educational Psychology, 5*, 253–270.

Horner, V., Whiten, A., Flynn, E., & de Waal, F. B. M. (2006). Faithful replication of foraging techniques along cultural transmission chains by chimpanzees and children. *Proceedings of the National Academy of Sciences, USA, 103*, 13878–13883.

Horrey, W. J., & Wickens, C. D. (2006). Examining the impact of cell phone conversation on driving using meta-analytic techniques. *Human Factors, 48*, 196–205.

Horta, B. L., Victoria, C. G., Menezes, A. M., Halpern, R., & Barros, F. C. (1997). Low birthweight, preterm births and intrauterine growth retardation in relation to maternal smoking. *Pediatrics and Perinatal Epidemiology, 11*, 140–151.

Hosking, S. G., Young, K. L., & Regan, M. A. (2009). The effects of text messaging on young drivers. *Human Factors, 51*, 582–592.

Houlihan, D., Jesse, V. C., Levine, H. D., & Sombke, C. (1991). A survey of rewards for use with teenage children. *Child & Family Behavior Therapy, 13*, 1–12.

House, J. S., Landis, K. R., & Umberson, D. (1988). Social relationships and health. *Science, 241*, 540–545.

Howard, I. P. (2002). Depth perception. In S. Yantis & H. Pashler (Eds.), *Stevens' handbook of experimental psychology: Vol. 1. Sensation and perception* (3rd ed., pp. 77–120). New York: Wiley.

Howard, J. H., Jr., & Howard, D. V. (1997). Age differences in implicit learning of higher order dependencies in serial patterns. *Psychology and Aging, 12*, 634–656.

Howard, M. O., Brown, S. E., Garland, E. L., Perron, B. E., & Vaughn, M. G. (2011). Inhalant use and inhalant use disorders in the United States. *Addiction Science & Clinical Practice, 6*, 18–31.

Howard-Jones, P. A., Blakemore, S.-J., Samuel, E. A., Summers, I. R., & Claxton, G. (2005). Semantic divergence and creative story generation: An fMRI investigation. *Cognitive Brain Research, 25*, 240–250.

Howell, A. (2011). Afghanistan's price: By downplaying PTSD, our government makes soldiers and their families bear the costs of war. *Literary Review of Canada.* Retrieved from http://reviewcanada.ca/magazine/2011/11/afghanistans-price/

Howes, M., Siegel, M., & Brown, F. (1993). Early childhood memories—accuracy and affect. *Cognition, 47*, 95–119.

Huang, J., Perlis, R. H., Lee, P. H., Rush, A. J., Fava, M., Sachs, G. S., … Smoller, J. W. (2010). Cross-disorder genomewide analysis of schizophrenia, bipolar disorder, and depression. *American Journal of Psychiatry, 167*, 1254–1263.

Hubel, D. H. (1988). *Eye, brain, and vision.* New York: Freeman.

Hubel, D. H., & Wiesel, T. N. (1962). Receptive fields, binocular interaction and functional architecture in the cat's visual cortex. *Journal of Physiology, 160*, 106–154.

Hubel, D. H., & Wiesel, T. N. (1998). Early exploration of the visual cortex. *Neuron, 20*, 401–412.

Huesmann, L. R., Moise-Titus, J., Podolski, C.-L., & Eron, L. D. (2003). Longitudinal relations between children's exposure to TV violence and their aggressive and violent behavior in young adulthood: 1977–1992. *Developmental Psychology, 39*, 201–221.

Hughes, J. R. (2007). A review of sleepwalking (somnambulism): The enigma of neurophysiology and polysomnography with differential diagnosis of complex partial seizures. *Epilepsy & Behavior, 11*, 483–491.

Hughs, S., Power, T., & Francis, D. (1992). Defining patterns of drinking in adolescence: A cluster analytic approach. *Journal of Studies on Alcohol, 53*, 40–47.

Hunsley, J., & Di Giulio, G. (2002). Dodo bird, phoenix, or urban legend? The question of psychotherapy equivalence. *Scientific Review of Mental Health Practice, 1,* 13–24.

Hunsley, J., Ronson, A., & Cohen, K. R. (2013). Professional psychology in Canada: A survey of demographic and practice characteristics. *Professional Psychology, 44,* 118–126.

Hunt, E. B. (2011). *Human intelligence.* New York: Cambridge University Press.

Hunt, M. (1959). *The natural history of love.* New York: Knopf.

Hunter, J. E., & Hunter, R. F. (1984). Validity and utility of alternative predictors of job performance. *Psychological Bulletin, 96,* 72–98.

Hurvich, L. M., & Jameson, D. (1957). An opponent process theory of color vision. *Psychological Review, 64,* 384–404.

Hussey, E., & Safford, A. (2009). Perception of facial expression in somatosensory cortex supports simulationist models. *The Journal of Neuroscience, 29*(2), 301–302.

Huttenlocher, P. R. (1979). Synaptic density in human frontal cortex—developmental changes and effects of aging. *Brain Research, 163,* 195–205.

Huxley, A. (1932). *Brave new world.* London: Chatto and Windus.

Huxley, A. (1954). *The doors of perception.* New York: Harper & Row.

Hyde, J. S. (2005). The gender similarities hypothesis. *American Psychologist, 60*(6), 581–592.

Hyde, K. L., Lerch, J., Norton, A., Forgeard, M., Winner, E., Evans, A. C., & Schlaug, G. (2009). Musical training shapes structural brain development. *Journal of Neuroscience, 29,* 3019–3025.

Hyman, I. E., Jr., Boss, S. M., Wise, B. M., McKenzie, K. E., & Caggiano, J. M. (2010). Did you see the unicycling clown? Inattentional blindness while walking and talking on a cell phone. *Applied Cognitive Psychology, 24*(5), 597–607.

Hyman, I. E., Jr., & Pentland, J. (1996). The role of mental imagery in the creation of false childhood memories. *Journal of Memory and Language, 35,* 101–117.

Hypericum Depression Trial Study Group. (2002). Effect of *Hypericum perforatum* (St. John's wort) in major depressive disorder: A randomized controlled trial. *Journal of the American Medical Association, 287,* 1807–1814.

Iacoboni, M. (2009). Imitation, empathy, and mirror neurons. *Annual Review of Psychology, 60,* 653–670.

Iacoboni, M., Molnar-Szakacs, I., Gallese, V., Buccino, G., Mazziotta, J. C., & Rizzolatti, G. (2005). Grasping the intentions of others with one's own mirror neuron system. *PLoS Biology, 3,* 529–535.

Ichheiser, G. (1949). Misunderstandings in human relations: A study in false social perceptions. *American Journal of Sociology, 55* (Pt. 2):1–70.

Imbo, I., & LeFevre, J.-A. (2009). Cultural differences in complex addition: Efficient Chinese versus adaptive Belgians and Canadians. *Journal of Experimental Psychology: Learning, Memory, and Cognition, 35,* 1465–1476.

Inciardi, J. A. (2001). *The war on drugs III.* New York: Allyn & Bacon.

Ingvar, M., Ambros-Ingerson, J., Davis, M., Granger, R., Kessler, M., Rogers, G. A., ... Lynch, G. (1997). Enhancement by an ampakine of memory encoding in humans. *Experimental Neurology, 146,* 553–559.

Innocence Project. (2012). *DNA exonerations nationwide.* Retrieved from http://www.innocenceproject.org/Content/DNA_Exonerations_ Nationwide.php

Inui, A. (2001). Ghrelin: An orexigenic and somatotrophic signal from the stomach. *Nature Reviews Neuroscience, 2,* 551–560.

Ireland, M. E., Slatcher, R. B., Eastwick, P. W., Scissors, L. E., Finkel, E. J., & Pennebaker, J. W. (2010). Language style matching predicts relationship initiation and stability. *Psychological Science, 22*(1), 39–44. doi:10.1177/0956797610392928

Irvine, J. T. (1978). Wolof "magical thinking": Culture and conservation revisited. *Journal of Cross-Cultural Psychology, 9,* 300–310.

Isaacowitz, D. M. (2012). Mood regulation in real time: Age differences in the role of looking. *Current Directions in Psychological Science, 21*(4), 237–242. doi:10.1177/0963721412448651

Isaacowitz, D. M., & Blanchard-Fields, F. (2012). Linking process and outcome in the study of emotion and aging. *Perspectives on Psychological Science, 7*(1), 3–17. doi:10.1177/1745691611424750

Isabelle, R. A. (1993). Origins of attachment: Maternal interactive behavior across the first year. *Child Development, 64,* 605–621.

Isen, A. M., & Patrick, R. (1983). The effect of positive feelings on risk-taking: When the chips are down. *Organizational Behavior and Human Performance, 31,* 194–202.

Isenberg, D. J. (1986). Group polarization: A critical review and meta-analysis. *Journal of Personality and Social Psychology, 50*(6), 1141–1151. Doi:10.1037/0022-3514.50.6.1141

Ishii, K., Reyes, J. A., & Kitayama, S. (2003). Spontaneous attention to word content versus emotional tone. *Psychological Science, 14*(1), 39–46.

Ittelson, W. H. (1952). *The Ames demonstrations in perception.* Princeton, NJ: Princeton University Press.

Izard, C. E. (1971). *The face of emotion.* New York: Appleton-Century-Crofts.

Jablensky, A. (1997). The 100-year epidemiology of schizophrenia. *Schizophrenia Research, 28,* 111–125.

Jaccard, J., Dittus, P. J., & Gordon, V. V. (1998). Parent–adolescent congruency in reports of adolescent sexual behavior and in communications about sexual behavior. *Child Development, 69,* 247–261.

Jacobs, B. L. (1994). Serotonin, motor activity, and depression-related disorders. *American Scientist, 82,* 456–463.

Jacobson, E. (1932). The electrophysiology of mental activities. *American Journal of Psychology, 44,* 677–694.

Jacobson, T., & Hoffman, V. (1997). Children's attachment representations: Longitudinal relations to school behavior and academic competency in middle childhood and adolescence. *Developmental Psychology, 33,* 703–710.

Jaffee, S., & Hyde, J. S. (2000). Gender differences in moral orientation: A meta-analysis. *Psychological Bulletin, 126,* 703–726.

Jahoda, G. (1993). *Crossroads between culture and mind.* Cambridge, MA: Harvard University Press.

James, T. W., Culham, J., Humphrey, G. K., Milner, A. D., & Goodale, M. A. (2003). Ventral occipital lesions impair object recognition but not object-directed grasping: An fMRI study. *Brain, 126,* 2463–2475.

James, W. (1884). What is an emotion? *Mind, 9,* 188–205.

James, W. (1890). *The principles of psychology.* Cambridge, MA: Harvard University Press.

James, W. (1911). *Memories and studies.* New York: Longman.

Jamieson, J. P., Koslov, K., Nock, M. K., & Mendes, W. B. (2013). Experiencing discrimination increases risk-taking. *Psychological Science, 24,* 131–139.

Jamieson, J. P., Mendes, W. B., Blackstock, E., & Schmader, T. (2010). Turning the knots in your stomach into bows: Reappraising arousal improves performance on the GRE. *Journal of Experimental Social Psychology, 46,* 208–212.

**Jamieson, J. P., Mendes, W. B., & Nock, M. K.** (2013). Improving acute stress responses: The power of reappraisal. *Current Directions in Psychological Science, 22*(1), 51–56.

**Jamieson, J. P., Nock, M. K., & Mendes, W. B.** (2013). Changing the conceptualization of stress in social anxiety disorder: Affective and physiological consequences. *Clinical Psychological Science*. Advance online publication. doi:10.1177/2167702613482119

**Jamison, K. R.** (1993). *Touched with fire: Manic-depressive illness and the artistic temperament.* New York: Free Press.

**Jamison, K. R.** (1995). *An unquiet mind: A memoir of moods and madness.* New York: Random House.

**Janicak, P. G., Dowd, S. M., Martis, B., Alam, D., Beedle, D., Krasuski, J., ... Viana, M.** (2002). Repetitive transcranial magnetic stimulation versus electroconvulsive therapy for major depression: Preliminary results of a randomized trial. *Biological Psychiatry, 51,* 659–667.

**Janis, I. L.** (1982). *Groupthink: Scientific studies of policy decisions and fiascoes.* Boston: Houghton-Mifflin.

**Jarosz, A. F., Colflesh, G. J. H., & Wiley, J.** (2012). Uncorking the muse: Alcohol intoxication facilitates creative problem solving. *Consciousness and Cognition, 21,* 487–493.

**Jarvella, R. J.** (1970). Effects of syntax on running memory span for connected discourse. *Psychonomic Science, 19,* 235–236.

**Jarvella, R. J.** (1971). Syntactic processing of connected speech. *Journal of Verbal Learning and Verbal Behavior, 10,* 409–416.

**Jausovec, N., & Jausovec, K.** (2005). Differences in induced gamma and upper alpha oscillations in the human brain related to verbal performance and emotional intelligence. *International Journal of Psychophysiology, 56,* 223.

**Jausovec, N., Jausovec, K., & Gerlic, I.** (2001). Differences in even-trelated and induced electroencephalography patterns in the theta and alpha frequency bands related to human emotional intelligence. *Neuroscience Letters, 311,* 93.

**Jaynes, J.** (1976). *The origin of consciousness in the breakdown of the bicameral mind.* London: Allen Lane.

**Jenkins, H. M., Barrera, F. J., Ireland, C., & Woodside, B.** (1978). Signal-centered action patterns of dogs in appetitive classical conditioning. *Learning and Motivation, 9,* 272–296.

**Jenkins, J. G., & Dallenbach, K. M.** (1924). Obliviscence during sleep and waking. *American Journal of Psychology, 35,* 605–612.

**John, O. P., Naumann, L. P., & Soto, C. J.** (2008). Paradigm shift to the integrative Big-Five trait taxonomy: History, measurement, and conceptual issues. In O. P. John, R. W. Robins, & L. A. Pervin (Eds.), *Handbook of personality: Theory and research* (3rd ed., pp. 114–158). New York: Guilford Press.

**John, O. P., & Srivastava, S.** (1999). The Big Five trait taxonomy: History, measurement, and theoretical perspectives. In L. A. Pervin & O. P. John (Eds.), *Handbook of personality: Theory and research* (2nd ed., pp. 102–138). New York: Guilford Press.

**Johnson, C. A., Xiao, L., Palmer, P., Sun, P., Wang, Q., Wei, Y. L., ... Bechara, A.** (2008). Affective decision-making deficits, linked to dysfunctional ventromedial prefrontal cortex, revealed in 10th grade Chinese adolescent binge drinkers. *Neuropsychologia, 46,* 714–726.

**Johnson, D. H.** (1980). The relationship between spike rate and synchrony in responses of auditory-nerve fibers to single tones. *Journal of the Acoustical Society of America, 68,* 1115–1122.

**Johnson, D. R., & Wu, J.** (2002). An empirical test of crisis, social selection, and role explanations of the relationship between marital disruption and psychological distress: A pooled time-series analysis of four-wave panel data. *Journal of Marriage and the Family, 64,* 211–224.

**Johnson, J. D., Noel, N. E., & Sutter-Hernandez, J.** (2000). Alcohol and male sexual aggression: A cognitive disruption analysis. *Journal of Applied Social Psychology, 30,* 1186–1200.

**Johnson, J. S., & Newport, E. L.** (1989). Critical period effects in second language learning: The influence of maturational state on the acquisition of English as a second language. *Cognitive Psychology, 21,* 60–99.

**Johnson, K.** (2002). Neural basis of haptic perception. In H. Pashler & S. Yantis (Eds.), *Stevens' handbook of experimental psychology: Vol. 1. Sensation and perception* (3rd ed., pp. 537–583). New York: Wiley.

**Johnson, M. H., Dziurawiec, S., Ellis, H. D., & Morton, J.** (1991). Newborns' preferential tracking of face-like stimuli and its subsequent decline. *Cognition, 40,* 1–19.

**Johnson, M. K., Hashtroudi, S., & Lindsay, D. S.** (1993). Source monitoring. *Psychological Bulletin, 114,* 3–28.

**Johnson, N. J., Backlund, E., Sorlie, P. D., & Loveless, C. A.** (2000). Marital status and mortality: The National Longitudinal Mortality Study. *Annual Review of Epidemiology, 10,* 224–238.

**Johnson, S. C., Dweck, C. S., & Chen, F. S.** (2007). Evidence for infants' internal working models of attachment. *Psychological Science, 18,* 501–502.

**Johnson, S. L., Cuellar, A. K., & Miller, C.** (2009). Unipolar and bipolar depression: A comparison of clinical phenomenology, biological vulnerability, and psychosocial predictors. In I. H. Gottlib & C. L. Hammen (Eds.), *Handbook of depression* (2nd ed., pp. 142–162). New York: Guilford Press.

**Johnson, S. L., Cuellar, A. K., Ruggiero, C., Winnett-Perman, C., Goodnick, P., White, R., & Miller, I.** (2008). Life events as predictors of mania and depression in bipolar 1 disorder. *Journal of Abnormal Psychology, 117,* 268–277.

**Johnson, S. L., & Miller, I.** (1997). Negative life events and time to recover from episodes of bipolar disorder. *Journal of Abnormal Psychology, 106,* 449–457.

**Johnston, L., Bachman, J., & O'Malley, P.** (1997). *Monitoring the future.* Ann Arbor, MI: Institute for Social Research.

**Johnstone, E. C., Crow, T. J., Frith, C., Husband, J., & Kreel, L.** (1976). Cerebral ventricular size and cognitive impairment in chronic schizophrenia. *Lancet, 2,* 924–926.

**Jonas, E., Graupmann, V., Kayser, D. N., Zanna, M., Traut-Mattausch, E., & Frey, D.** (2009). Culture, self, and the emergence of reactance: Is there a "universal" freedom? *Journal of Experimental Social Psychology, 45,* 1068–1080.

**Jones, B. C., Little, A. C., Penton-Voak, I. S., Tiddeman, B. P., Burt, D. M., & Perrett, D. I.** (2001). Facial symmetry and judgements of apparent health: Support for a "good genes" explanation of the attractiveness–symmetry relationship. *Evolution and Human Behavior, 22,* 417–429.

**Jones, E. E., & Harris, V. A.** (1967). The attribution of attitudes. *Journal of Experimental Social Psychology, 3,* 1–24.

**Jones, E. E., & Nisbett, R. E.** (1972). The actor and the observer: Divergent perceptions of the causes of behavior. In E. E. Jones, D. E. Kanouse, H. H. Kelley, R. E. Nisbett, S. Valins, & B. Weiner (Eds.), *Attribution: Perceiving the causes of behavior* (pp. 79–94). Morristown, NJ: General Learning Press.

**Jones, K.** (1972). *A history of mental health services.* London: Routledge and Kegan Paul.

**Jones, L. M., & Foshay, N. N.** (1984). Diffusion of responsibility in a nonemergency situation: Response to a greeting from a stranger. *Journal of Social Psychology, 123,* 155–158.

**Jones, S. S.** (2007). Imitation in infancy. *Psychological Science, 18*(7), 593–599.

Jonsson, H., & Hougaard, E. (2008). Group cognitive behavioural therapy for obsessive-compulsive disorder: A systematic review and meta-analysis. *Acta Psychiatrica Scandinavica, 117,* 1–9.

Jordan, S. A., Cunningham, D. G., & Marles, R. J. (2010). Assessment of herbal medicinal products: Challenges and opportunities to increase the knowledge base for safety assessment. *Toxicology and Applied Pharmacology, 243,* 198–216.

Jost, J. T., Napier, J. L., Thorisdottir, H., Gosling, S. D., Palfai, T. P., & Ostafin, B. (2007). Are needs to manage uncertainty and threat associated with political conservatism or ideological extremity? *Personality & Social Psychology Bulletin, 33*(7), 989–1007.

Joyce, J. (1922/2013) *Ulysses.* London, UK: Urban Romantics.

Judd, L. L. (1997). The clinical course of unipolar major depressive disorders. *Archives of General Psychiatry, 54,* 989–991.

Jung-Beeman, M. (2005). Bilateral brain processes for comprehending natural language. *Trends in Cognitive Sciences, 9,* 512–518.

Jung-Beeman, M., Bowden, E. M., Haberman, J., Frymiare, J. L., Arambel-Liu, S., Greenblatt, R., … Kounios, J. (2004). Neural activity when people solve verbal problems with insight. *PLoS Biology, 2,* 500–510.

Jurewicz, I., Owen, R. J., & O'Donovan, M. C. (2001). Searching for susceptibility genes in schizophrenia. *European Neuropsychopharmacology, 11,* 395–398.

Kaas, J. H. (1991). Plasticity of sensory and motor maps in adult mammals. *Annual Review of Neuroscience, 14,* 137–167.

Kagan, J. (1997). Temperament and the reactions to unfamiliarity. *Child Development, 68,* 139–143.

Kahneman, D., Krueger, A. B., Schkade, D. A., Schwarz, N., & Stone, A. A. (2004). A survey method for characterizing daily life experience: The day reconstruction method. *Science, 306,* 1776–1780.

Kahneman, D., & Tversky, A. (1973). On the psychology of prediction. *Psychological Review, 80,* 237–251.

Kahneman, D., & Tversky, A. (1979). Prospect theory: An analysis of decision under risk. *Econometrica, 47,* 263–291.

Kamin, L. J. (1959). The delay-of-punishment gradient. *Journal of Comparative and Physiological Psychology, 52,* 434–437.

Kamiya, J. (1969). Operant control of the EEG alpha rhythm and some of its reported effects on consciousness. In C. S. Tart (Ed.), *Altered states of consciousness* (pp. 519–529). Garden City, NY: Anchor Books.

Kan, P. F., & Kohnert, K. (2008). Fast mapping by bilingual preschool children. *Journal of Child Language, 35,* 495–514.

Kanai, R., Feilden, T., Firth, C., & Rees, G. (2011). Political orientations are correlated with brain structure in young adults. *Current Biology, 21*(8), 677–680.

Kandel, E. R. (2000). Nerve cells and behavior. In E. R. Kandel, G. H. Schwartz, & T. M. Jessell (Eds.), *Principles of neural science* (pp. 19–35). New York. McGraw-Hill.

Kandel, E. R. (2006). *In search of memory: The emergence of a new science of mind.* New York: Norton.

Kang, S. H. K., McDermott, K. B., & Roediger, H. L. III. (2007). Test format and corrective feedback modify the effect of testing on long-term retention. *European Journal of Cognitive Psychology, 19,* 528–558.

Kanwisher, N. (2000). Domain specificity in face perception. *Nature Neuroscience, 3,* 759–763.

Kanwisher, N., McDermott, J., & Chun, M. M. (1997). The fusiform face area: A module in human extrastriate cortex specialized for face perception. *The Journal of Neuroscience, 17,* 4302–4311.

Kanwisher, N., & Yovel, G. (2006). The fusiform face area: A cortical region specialized for the perception of faces. *Philosophical Transactions of the Royal Society (B), 361,* 2109–2128.

Kaplan, R. M., & Stone, A. A. (2013). Bringing the laboratory and clinic to the community: Mobile technologies for health promotion and disease prevention. *Annual Review of Psychology, 64,* 471–498.

Kapur, S., Craik, F. I. M., Tulving, E., Wilson, A. A., Houle, S., & Brown, G. M. (1994). Neuroanatomical correlates of encoding in episodic memory: Levels of processing effects. *Proceedings of the National Academy of Sciences, USA, 91,* 2008–2011.

Karau, S. J., & Williams, K. D. (1993). Social loafing: A meta-analytic review and theoretical integration. *Journal of Personality and Social Psychology, 65,* 681–706.

Karlins, M., Coffman, T. L., & Walters, G. (1969). On the fading of social stereotypes: Studies in three generations of college students. *Journal of Personality and Social Psychology, 13,* 1–16.

Karney, B. R., & Bradbury, T. N. (1995). The longitudinal course of marital quality and stability: A review of theory, methods, and research. *Psychological Bulletin, 118,* 3–34.

Karow, A., Pajonk, F. G., Reimer, J., Hirdes, F., Osterwald, C., Naber, D., & Moritz, S. (2007). The dilemma of insight into illness in schizophrenia: Self- and expert-rated insight and quality of life. *European Archives of Psychiatry and Clinical Neuroscience, 258,* 152–159.

Karpicke, J. D. (2012). Retrieval-based learning: Active retrieval promotes meaningful learning. *Current Directions in Psychological Science, 21,* 157–163.

Karpicke, J. D., & Blunt, J. R. (2011). Retrieval practice produces more learning than elaborative studying with concept mapping. *Science, 331,* 772–775.

Karpicke, J. D., & Roediger, H. L., III. (2008). The critical importance of retrieval for learning. *Science, 319,* 966–968.

Kasser, T., & Sharma, Y. S. (1999). Reproductive freedom, educational equality, and females' preference for resource-acquisition characteristics in mates. *Psychological Science, 10,* 374–377.

Katon, W. (1994). Primary care—psychiatry panic disorder management. In B. E. Wolfe & J. D. Maser (Eds.), *Treatment of panic disorder: A consensus development conference* (pp. 41–56). Washington, DC: American Psychiatric Press.

Katz, D., & Braly, K. (1933). Racial stereotypes of one hundred college students. *Journal of Abnormal and Social Psychology, 28,* 280–290.

Kaufman, A. S. (2001). WAIS-III IQs, Horn's theory, and generational changes from young adulthood to old age. *Intelligence, 29,* 131–167.

Kaufman, L. (2009, January 30). Utilities turn their customers green, with envy. *New York Times.* Retrieved from http://www.nytimes.com/2009/01/31/science/earth/31compete.html

Kawakami, K., Dovidio, J. F., Moll, J., Hermsen, S., & Russin, A. (2000). Just say no (to stereotyping): Effects of training in the negation of stereotypic associations on stereotype activation. *Journal of Personality and Social Psychology, 78,* 871–888.

Kazdin, A. E., & Blaise, S. L. (2011). Rebooting psychotherapy research and practice to reduce the burden of mental illness. *Perspectives on Psychological Science, 6,* 21–37.

Keane, T. M., Marshall, A. D., & Taft, C. T. (2006). Posttraumatic stress disorder: Etiology, epidemiology, and treatment outcome. *Annual Review of Clinical Psychology, 2,* 161–197.

Keefe, F. J., Abernathy, A. P., & Campbell, L. C. (2005). Psychological approaches to understanding and treating disease-related pain. *Annual Review of Psychology, 56,* 601–630.

Keefe, F. J., Lumley, M., Anderson, T., Lynch, T., & Carson, K. L. (2001). Pain and emotion: New research directions. *Journal of Clinical Psychology, 57,* 587–607.

**Kelley, H. H.** (1967). Attribution theory in social psychology. In D. Levine (Ed.), *Nebraska Symposium on Motivation* (Vol. 15, pp. 192–238). Lincoln: University of Nebraska Press.

**Kelley, H. H.** (1983). Love and commitment. In H. H. Kelley, E. Berscheid, A. Christensen, & J. H. Harvey (Eds.), *Close relationships* (pp. 265–314). New York: W. H. Freeman and Company.

**Kelley, W. M., Macrae, C. N., Wyland, C. L., Caglar, S., Inati, S., & Heatherton, T. F.** (2002). Finding the self? An event-related fMRI study. *Journal of Cognitive Neuroscience, 14,* 785–794.

**Kellman, P. J., & Spelke, E. S.** (1983). Perception of partly occluded objects in infancy. *Cognitive Psychology, 15,* 483–524.

**Kelly, G.** (1955). *The psychology of personal constructs.* New York: Norton.

**Keltner, D.** (1995). Signs of appeasement: Evidence for the distinct displays of embarrassment, amusement, and shame. *Journal of Personality and Social Psychology, 68,* 441–454.

**Keltner, D., & Buswell, B. N.** (1996). Evidence for the distinctness of embarrassment, shame, and guilt: A study of recalled antecedents and facial expressions of emotion. *Cognition and Emotion, 10,* 155–171.

**Keltner, D., & Haidt, J.** (1999). Social functions of emotions at four levels of analysis. *Cognition and Emotion, 13,* 505–521.

**Keltner, D., & Harker, L. A.** (1998). The forms and functions of the nonverbal signal of shame. In P. Gilbert & B. Andrews (Eds.), *Shame: Interpersonal behavior, psychopathology, and culture* (pp. 78–98). New York: Oxford University Press.

**Keltner, D., & Shiota, M. N.** (2003). New displays and new emotions: A commentary on Rozin and Cohen (2003). *Emotion, 3,* 86–91.

**Kendler, K. S., Hettema, J. M., Butera, F., Gardner, C. O., & Prescott, C. A.** (2003). Life event dimensions of loss, humiliation, entrapment, and danger in the prediction of onsets of major depression and generalized anxiety. *Archives of General Psychiatry, 60,* 789–796.

**Kendler, K. S., Myers, J., & Prescott, C. A.** (2002). The etiology of phobias: An evaluation of the stress–diathesis model. *Archives of General Psychiatry, 59,* 242–248.

**Kenrick, D. T., Neuberg, S. L., Griskevicius, V., Becker, D. V., & Schaller, M.** (2010). Goal-driven cognition and functional behavior: The fundamental motives framework. *Current Directions in Psychological Science, 19*(1), 63–67.

**Kenrick, D. T., Sadalla, E. K., Groth, G., & Trost, M. R.** (1990). Evolution, traits, and the stages of human courtship: Qualifying the parental investment model. *Journal of Personality, 58,* 97–116.

**Kensinger, E. A., Clarke, R. J., & Corkin, S.** (2003). What neural correlates underlie successful encoding and retrieval? A functional magnetic resonance imaging study using a divided attention paradigm. *The Journal of Neuroscience, 23,* 2407–2415.

**Kensinger, E. A., & Schacter, D. L.** (2005). Emotional content and reality monitoring ability: fMRI evidence for the influence of encoding processes. *Neuropsychologia, 43,* 1429–1443.

**Kensinger, E. A., & Schacter, D. L.** (2006). Amygdala activity is associated with the successful encoding of item, but not source, information for positive and negative stimuli. *The Journal of Neuroscience, 26,* 2564–2570.

**Kershaw, T. C., & Ohlsson, S.** (2004). Multiple causes of difficulty in insight: The case of the nine-dot problem. *Journal of Experimental Psychology: Learning, Memory, and Cognition, 30,* 3–13.

**Kertai, M. D., Pal, N., Palanca, B. J., Lin, N., Searleman, S. A., Zhang, L., … B-Unaware Study Group.** (2010). Association of perioperative risk factors and cumulative duration of low bispectral index with intermediate-term mortality after cardiac surgery in the B-Unaware trial. *Anesthesiology, 112*(5), 1116–1127.

**Kessler, R. C., Adler, L., Barkley, R., Biederman, J., Connors, C. K., Demler, O., … Zaslavsky, A. M.** (2006). The prevalence and correlates of adult ADHD in the United States: Results from the National Comorbidity Study Replication. *American Journal of Psychiatry, 163,* 716–723.

**Kessler, R. C., Angermeyer, M., Anthony, J. C., deGraaf, R., Demyittenaere, K., Gasquet, I., … Üstün, T. B.** (2007). Lifetime prevalence and age-of-onset distributions of mental disorders in the World Health Organization World Mental Health Survey Initiative. *World Psychiatry, 6,* 168–176.

**Kessler, R. C., Berglund, P., Demler, M. A., Jin, R., Merikangas, K. R., & Walters, E. E.** (2005). Lifetime prevalence and age-of-onset distributions of *DSM–IV* disorders in the National Comorbidity Survey replication. *Archives of General Psychiatry, 62,* 593–602.

**Kessler, R. C., Demler, O., Frank, R. G., Olfson, M., Pincus, H. A., Walters, E. E., … Zaslavsky, A. M.** (2005). Prevalence and treatment of mental disorders, 1990 to 2003. *New England Journal of Medicine, 352*(24), 2515–2523.

**Kessler, R. C., Petukhova, M., Sampson, N. A., Zaslavsky, A. M., & Wittchen, H.U.** (2012). Twelve-month and lifetime prevalence and lifetime morbid risk of anxiety and mood disorders in the United States. *International Journal of Methods in Psychiatric Research, 21*(3), 169–184.

**Kessler, R. C., & Üstün, T. B. (Eds.).** (2008). *The WHO Mental Health surveys: Global perspectives on the epidemiology of mental health.* Cambridge, England: Cambridge University Press.

**Kessler, R. C., & Wang, P. S.** (2008). The descriptive epidemiology of commonly occurring mental disorders in the United States. *Annual Reviews of Public Health, 29,* 115–129.

**Keuler, D. J., & Safer, M. A.** (1998). Memory bias in the assessment and recall of pre-exam anxiety: How anxious was I? *Applied Cognitive Psychology, 12,* S127–S137.

**Khalid, N., Atkins, M., Tredget, J., Giles, M., Champney- Smith, K., & Kirov, G.** (2008). The effectiveness of electroconvulsive therapy in treatment-resistant depression: A naturalistic study. *The Journal of ECT, 24,* 141–145.

**Khalid, R.** (1991). Personality and academic achievement: A thematic apperception perspective. *British Journal of Projective Psychology, 36,* 25–34.

**Khan, R. M., Luk, C.-H., Flinker, A., Aggarwal, A., Lapid, H., Haddad, R., & Sobel, N.** (2007). Predicting odor pleasantness from odorant structure: Pleasantness as a reflection of the physical world. *Journal of Neuroscience, 27,* 10015–10023.

**Kiecolt-Glaser, J. K., Garner, W., Speicher, C., Penn, G., & Glaser, R.** (1984). Psychosocial modifiers of immunocompetence in medical students. *Psychosomatic Medicine, 46,* 7–14.

**Kiefer, M., Schuch, S., Schenk, W., & Fiedler, K.** (2007). Mood states modulate activity in semantic brain areas during emotional word encoding. *Cerebral Cortex, 17,* 1516–1530.

**Kiehl, K. A., Smith, A. M., Hare, R. D., Mendrek, A., Forster, B. B., Brink, J., & Liddle, P. F.** (2001). Limbic abnormalities in affective processing by criminal psychopaths as revealed by functional magnetic resonance imaging. *Biological Psychiatry, 50,* 677–684.

**Kihlstrom, J. F.** (1985). Hypnosis. *Annual Review of Psychology, 36,* 385–418.

**Kihlstrom, J. F.** (1987). The cognitive unconscious. *Science, 237,* 1445–1452.

**Kihlstrom, J. F., Beer, J. S., & Klein, S. B.** (2002). Self and identity as memory. In M. R. Leary & J. P. Tangney (Eds.), *Handbook of self and identity* (pp. 68–90). New York: Guilford Press.

**Kim, G., Walden, T. A., & Knieps, L. J.** (2010). Impact and characteristics of positive and fearful emotional messages during infant social referencing. *Infant Behavior and Development, 33,* 189–195.

**Kim, K., & Smith, P. K.** (1998). Childhood stress, behavioural symptoms and mother–daughter pubertal development. *Journal of Adolescence, 21,* 231–240.

**Kim, U. K., Jorgenson, E., Coon, H., Leppert, M., Risch, N., & Drayna, D.** (2003). Positional cloning of the human quantaitive trait locus underlying taste sensitivity to phenylthiocarbamide. *Science, 299,* 1221–1225.

**King, D. (2008).** Doctoral Graduates in Canada: Findings from the Survey of of Earned Doctorates, 2004/2005. Retrieved from http://www.statcan.gc.ca/pub/81-595-m/81-595-m2008065-eng.pdf

**Kinney, D. A.** (1993). From nerds to normals—the recovery of identity among adolescents from middle school to high school. *Sociology of Education, 66,* 21–40.

**Kirchner, W. H., & Towne, W. F.** (1994). The sensory basis of the honeybee's dance language. *Scientific American, 270*(6), 74–80.

**Kirsch, I., Cardena, E., Derbyshire, S., Dienes, Z., Heap, M., Kallio, S., ... Whalley, M.** (2011). Definitions of hypnosis and hypnotizability and their relation to suggestion and suggestibility: A consensus statement. *Contemporary Hypnosis and Integrative Therapy, 28,* 107–115.

**Kirwan, C. B., Bayley, P. J., Galvan, V. V., & Squire, L. R.** (2008). Detailed recollection of remote autobiographical memory after damage to the medial temporal lobe. *Proceedings of the National Academy of Sciences, USA, 105,* 2676–2680.

**Kish, S. J., Lerch, J., Furukawa, Y., Tong, J., McCluskey, T., Wilkins, D., ... Bioleau, I.** (2010). Decreased cerebral cortical serotonin transporter binding in ecstacy users: A positron emission tomography [$^{11}$c] DASB and structural brain imaging study. *Brain, 133,* 1779–1797.

**Kitayama, S., Duffy, S., Kawamura, T., & Larsen, J. T.** (2003). Perceiving an object and its context in different cultures: A cultural look at the new look. *Psychological Science, 14,* 201–206.

**Kitayama, S., & Uskul, A. K.** (2011). Culture, mind, and the brain: Current evidence and future directions. *Annual Review of Psychology, 62,* 419–449.

**Klein, C. T. F., & Helweg-Larsen, M.** (2002). Perceived control and the optimistic bias: A meta-analytic review. *Psychology and Health, 17,* 437–446.

**Klein, S. B.** (2004). The cognitive neuroscience of knowing one's self. In M. Gazzaniga (Ed.), *The cognitive neurosciences* (3rd ed., pp. 1007–1089). Cambridge, MA: MIT Press.

**Klein, S. B., Robertson, T. E., & Delton, A. W.** (2011). The future-orientation of memory: Planning as a key component mediating the high levels of recall found with survival processing. *Memory, 19,* 121–139.

**Klein, S. B., & Thorne, B. M.** (2007). *Biological psychology.* New York: Worth Publishers.

**Klingberg, T.** (2010). Training and plasticity of working memory. *Trends in Cognitive Sciences, 14,* 317–324.

**Klinger, E.** (1975). Consequences of commitment to and disengagement from incentives. *Psychological Review, 82,* 1–25.

**Klinger, E.** (1977). *Meaning and void.* Minneapolis: University of Minnesota Press.

**Klonsky, E. D.** (2011). Non-suicidal self-injury in United States adults: Prevalence, sociodemographics, topography, and functions. *Psychological Medicine, 41,* 1981–1986.

**Klump, K. L., & Culbert, K. M.** (2007). Molecular genetic studies of eating disorders: Current status and future directions. *Current Directions in Psychological Science, 16*(1), 37–41.

**Klüver, H., & Bucy, P. C.** (1937). "Psychic blindness" and other symptoms following bilateral temporary lobectomy in rhesus monkeys. *American Journal of Physiology, 119,* 352–353.

**Knowlton, B. J., Ramus, S. J., & Squire, L. R.** (1992). Intact artificial grammar learning in amnesia: Dissociation of classification learning and explicit memory for specific instances. *Psychological Science, 3,* 173–179.

**Knutson, B., Adams, C. M., Fong, G. W., & Hommer, D.** (2001). Anticipation of increasing monetary reward selectively recruits nucleus accumbens. *Journal of Neuroscience, 21,* 159.

**Knutson, B., Wolkowitz, O. M., Cole, S. W., Chan, T., Moore, E. A., Johnson, R. C., Reus, V. I.** (1998). Selective alteration of personality and social behavior by serotonergic intervention. *American Journal of Psychiatry, 155,* 373–379.

**Kobasa, S.** (1979). Stressful life events, personality, and health: An inquiry into hardiness. *Journal of Personality and Social Psychology, 37,* 1–11.

**Koehler, J. J.** (1993). The influence of prior beliefs on scientific judgments of evidence quality. *Organizational Behavior and Human Decision Processes, 56,* 28–55.

**Koenigs, M., Young, L., Adolphs, R., Tranel, D., Cushman, F., Hauser, M., & Damasio, A.** (2007). Damage to the prefrontal cortex increases utilitarian moral judgements. *Nature, 446,* 908–911.

**Koffka, K.** (1935). *Principles of Gestalt psychology.* New York: Harcourt, Brace and World.

**Kohlberg, L.** (1958). *The development of modes of thinking and choices in years 10 to 16.* Unpublished doctoral dissertation, University of Chicago.

**Kohlberg, L.** (1963). Development of children's orientation towards a moral order (Part I). Sequencing in the development of moral thought. *Vita Humana, 6,* 11–36.

**Kohlberg, L.** (1986). A current statement on some theoretical issues. In S. Modgil & C. Modgil (Eds.), *Lawrence Kohlberg: Concensus and controversy* (pp. 485–546). Philadelphia: Falmer.

**Kohler, P. K., Manhart, L. E., & Lafferty, E.** (2008). Abstinence-only and comprehensive sex education and the initiation of sexual activity and teen pregnancy. *Journal of Adolescent Health, 42,* 344–351.

**Kolb, B., & Whishaw, I. Q.** (2003). *Fundamentals of human neuropsychology* (5th ed.). New York: Worth Publishers.

**Koller, D.** (2011, December 5). Death knell for the lecture: Technology as a passport to personalized education. Retrieved from http://www.nytimes.com/2011/12/06/science/daphne-koller-technology-as-a-passport-to-personalized-education.html?pagewanted=all

**Kolotkin, R. L., Meter, K., & Williams, G. R.** (2001). Quality of life and obesity. *Obesity Reviews, 2,* 219–229.

**Komter, A.** (2010). The evolutionary origins of human generosity. *International Sociology, 25*(3), 443–464.

**Konen, C. S., & Kastner, S.** (2008). Two hierarchically organized neural systems for object information in human visual cortex. *Nature Neuroscience, 11,* 224–231.

**Koole, S. L., Dijksterhuis, A., & van Knippenberg, A.** (2001). What's in a name: Implicit self-esteem and the automatic self. *Journal of Personality and Social Psychology, 80,* 669–685.

**Koss, M. P.** (1990). The women's mental health research agenda: Violence against women. *American Psychologist, 45,* 374–380.

**Kosslyn, S. M., Alpert, N. M., Thompson, W. L., Chabris, C. F., Rauch, S. L., & Anderson, A. K.** (1993). Visual mental imagery activates topographically organized visual cortex: PET investigations. *Journal of Cognitive Neuroscience, 5,* 263–287.

**Kosslyn, S. M., Pascual-Leone, A., Felician, O., Camposano, S., Keenan, J. P., Thompson, W. L., ... Alpert, N. M.** (1999). The role of area 17 in visual imagery: Convergent evidence from PET and rTMS. *Science, 284,* 167–170.

Kosslyn, S. M., Thompson, W. L., Constantini-Ferrando, M. F., Alpert, N. M., & Spiegel, D. (2000). Hypnotic visual illusion alters color processing in the brain. *American Journal of Psychiatry, 157,* 1279–1284.

Kounios, J., & Beeman, M. (2009). The aha! moment. *Current Directions in Psychological Science, 18,* 210–216.

Kounios, J., Fleck, J. L., Green, D. L., Payne, L., Stevenson, J. L., Bowden, E. M., & Jung-Beeman, M. (2008). The origins of insight in resting-state brain activity. *Neuropsychologia, 46,* 281–291.

Kounios, J., Frymiare, J. L., Bowden, E. M., Fleck, J. I., Subramaniam, K., Parrish, T. B., & Jung-Beeman, M. (2006). The prepared mind: Neural activity prior to problem presentation predicts subsequent solution by sudden insight. *Psychological Science, 17,* 882–890.

Kovalevskaya, S. (1978). *A Russian childhood.* New York: Springer-Verlag.

Kraemer, H. C., Shrout, P. E., & Rubio-Stipec, M. (2007). Developing the *Diagnostic and Statistical Manual–V*: What will "statistical" mean in *DSM–V*? *Social Psychiatry and Psychiatric Epidemiology, 42,* 259–267.

Kraepelin, E. (1899). *Psychiatrie.* Leipzig, Germany: Barth.

Krantz, D. S., & McCeney, M. K. (2002). Effects of psychological and social factors on organic disease: A critical assessment of research on coronary heart disease. *Annual Review of Psychology, 53,* 341–369.

Kraus, N., & Chandrasekaran, B. (2010). Music training for the development of auditory skills. *Nature Reviews Neuroscience, 11,* 599–605.

Kravitz, D. J., Saleem, K. S., Baker, C. I., & Mishkin, M. (2011). A new neural framework for visuospatial processing. *Nature Reviews Neuroscience, 12,* 217–230.

Kravitz, D. J., Saleem, K. S., Baker, C. I., Ungerleider, L. G., & Mishkin, M. (2013). The ventral visual pathway: An expanded neural framework for the processing of object quality. *Trends in Cognitive Sciences, 17,* 26–49.

Kravitz, R. L., Epstein, R. M., Feldman, M. D., Franz, C. E., Azari, R., Wilkes, M. S., … Franks, P. (2005). Influence of patients' requests for direct-to-consumer advertised antidepressants: A randomized controlled trial. *Journal of the American Medical Association, 293,* 1995–2002.

Kreider, T. (2013, January 20). You are going to die. *New York Times.* Retrieved from http://opinionator.blogs.nytimes.com/2013/01/20/you-are-going-to-die/

Kringelbach, M. L., O'Doherty, J., Rolls, E. T., & Andrews, C. (2003). Activation of the human orbitofrontal cortex to a liquid food stimulus is correlated with its subjective pleasantness. *Cerebral Cortex, 13,* 1064–1071.

Krings, T., Topper, R., Foltys, H., Erberich, S., Sparing, R., Willmes, K., & Thron, A. (2000). Cortical activation patterns during complex motor tasks in piano players and control subjects. A functional magnetic resonance imaging study. *Neuroscience Letters, 278,* 189–193.

Krishnan, V., & Nestler, E. J. (2008). The molecular neurobiology of depression. *Nature, 455,* 894–902.

Kristensen, P., & Bjerkedal, T. (2007). Explaining the relation between birth order and intelligence. *Science, 316,* 1717.

Kroeze, W. K., & Roth, B. L. (1998). The molecular biology of serotonin receptors: Therapeutic implications for the interface of mood and psychosis. *Biological Psychiatry, 44,* 1128–1142.

Kruk, M. R., Halasz, J., Meelis, W., & Haller, J. (2004). Fast positive feedback between the adrenocortical stress response and a brain mechanism involved in aggressive behavior. *Behavioral Neuroscience, 118,* 1062–1070.

Kubovy, M. (1981). Concurrent-pitch segregation and the theory of indispensable attributes. In M. Kubovy & J. R. Pomerantz (Eds.), *Perceptual organization* (pp. 55–96). Hillsdale, NJ: Erlbaum.

Kuhl, B. A., Dudukovic, N. M., Kahn, I., & Wagner, A. D. (2007). Decreased demands on cognitive control reveal the neural processing benefits of forgetting. *Nature Neuroscience, 10,* 908–917.

Kuhl, P. K. (2010). Brain mechanisms in early language acquisition. *Neuron, 67,* 713–727.

Kuhl, P. K., & Meltzoff, A. N. (1996). Infant vocalizations in response to speech: Vocal imitation and developmental change. *Journal of the Acoustical Society of America, 100*(4), 2425. doi:10.1121/1.417951

Kuhl, P., & Rivera-Gaxiola, M. (2008). Neural substrates of language acquisition. *Annual Review of Neuroscience, 31,* 511–534.

Kuhn, S., & Gallinat, J. (2012). The neural correlates of subjective pleasantness. *NeuroImage, 61,* 289–294.

Kunda, Z. (1990). The case for motivated reasoning. *Psychological Bulletin, 108,* 480–498.

Kunda, Z., & Oleson, K. C. (1997). When exceptions prove the rule: How extremity of deviance determines the impact of deviant examples on stereotypes. *Journal of Personality and Social Psychology, 72,* 965–979.

Kunugi, H., Urushibara, T., Murray, R. M., Nanko, S., & Hirose, T. (2003). Prenatal underdevelopment and schizophrenia: A case report of monozygotic twins. *Psychiatry and Clinical Neurosciences, 57,* 271–274.

Kunz, P. R., & Woolcott, M. (1976). Season's greetings: From my status to yours. *Social Science Research, 5,* 269–278.

Kvavilashvili, L., Mirani, J., Schlagman, S., Foley, K., & Kornbrot, D. E. (2009). Consistency of flashbulb memories of September 11 over long delays: Implications for consolidation and wrong time slice hypotheses. *Journal of Memory and Language, 61,* 556–572.

LaBar, K. S., & Phelps, E. A. (1998). Arousal-mediated memory consolidation: Role of the medial temporal lobe in humans. *Psychological Science, 9,* 490–493.

Labrie, V., Pai, S., & Petronis, A. (2012). Epigenetics of major psychosis: Progress, problems, and perspectives. *Trends in Genetics, 28,* 427–435.

Lachman, R., Lachman, J. L., & Butterfield, E. C. (1979). *Cognitive psychology and information processing: An introduction.* Hillsdale, NJ: Erlbaum.

Lackner, J. R., & DiZio, P. (2005). Vestibular, proprioceptive, and haptic contributions to spatial orientation. *Annual Review of Psychology, 56,* 115–147.

LaFraniere, S. (2007, July 4). In Mauritania, seeking to end an overfed ideal. *New York Times.* Retrieved from http://www.nytimes.com/2007/07/04/world/africa/04mauritania.html?pagewanted=all

Lahkan, S. E., & Kirchgessner, A. (2012, March 12). Chronic traumatic encephalopathy: The dangers of getting "dinged." *Springer Plus,* 1:2 doi:10.1186/2193-1801-1-2

Lai, Y., & Siegal, J. (1999). Muscle atonia in REM sleep. In B. Mallick & S. Inoue (Eds.), *Rapid eye movement sleep* (pp. 69–90). New Delhi, India: Narosa Publishing House.

Lake, J. (2009). Natural products used to treat depressed mood as monotherapies and adjuvants to antidepressants: A review of the evidence. *Psychiatric Times, 26,* 1–6.

Lakin, J. M. (2013). Sex differences in reasoning abilities: Surprising evidence that male–female ratios in the tails of the quantitative reasoning distribution have increased. *Intelligence, 41*(4), 263–274. doi:10.1016/j.intell.2013.04.004

Lakshminarayanan, V. R., Chen, M. K., & Santos, L. R. (2011). The evolution of decision-making under risk: Framing effects in monkey risk preferences. *Journal of Experimental Social Psychology, 47*(3), 689–693. doi:10.1016/j.jesp.2010.12.011

**Lam, L. L., Emberly, E., Fraser, H. B., Neumann, S. M., Chen, E., Miller, G. E., … Kobor, M. S.** (2012). Factors underlying variable DNA methylation in a human community cohort. *Proceedings of the National Academy of Sciences, USA, 109*(Suppl. 2), 17253–17260.

**Lamb, M. E., Sternberg, K. J., & Prodromidis, M.** (1992). Nonmaternal care and the security of infant/mother attachment: A reanalysis of the data. *Infant Behavior & Development, 15,* 71–83.

**Lamb, M. E., Thompson, R. A., Gardner, W., & Charnov, E. L.** (1985). *Infant–mother attachment: The origins and developmental significance of individual differences in Strange Situation behavior.* Hillsdale, NJ: Erlbaum.

**Landauer, T. K., & Bjork, R. A.** (1978). Optimum rehearsal patterns and name learning. In M. M. Gruneberg, P. E. Morris, & R. N. Sykes (Eds.), *Practical aspects of memory* (pp. 625–632). New York: Academic Press.

**Lang, F. R., & Carstensen, L. L.** (1994). Close emotional relationships in late life: Further support for proactive aging in the social domain. *Psychology and Aging, 9,* 315–324.

**Langer, E. J., & Abelson, R. P.** (1974). A patient by any other name … . Clinician group difference in labeling bias. *Journal of Consulting and Clinical Psychology, 42,* 4–9.

**Langleben, D. D., Loughead, J. W., Bilker, W. B., Ruparel, K., Childress, A. R., Busch, S. I., & Gur, R. C.** (2005). Telling truth from lie in individual subjects with fast event-related fMRI. *Human Brain Mapping, 26,* 262–272.

**Langlois, J. H., Kalakanis, L., Rubenstein, A. J., Larson, A., Hallam, M., & Smoot, M.** (2000). Maxims or myths of beauty? A meta-analytic and theoretical review. *Psychological Bulletin, 126,* 390–423.

**Langlois, J. H., Ritter, J. M., Casey, R. J., & Sawin, D. B.** (1995). Infant attractiveness predicts maternal behaviors and attitudes. *Developmental Psychology, 31,* 464–472.

**LaPierre, S., Boyer, R., Desjardins, S., Dubé, M., Lorrain, D., Préville, M., & Brassard, J.** (2012). Daily hassles, physical illness, and sleep problems in older adults with wishes to die. *International Psychogeriatrics, 24,* 243–252.

**Lareau, A.** (2003). *Unequal childhoods: Class, race, and family life.* Berkeley: University of California Press.

**Laroche, M.** (2000). Health status and health service utilization of Canada's immigrant and non-immigrant populations. *Canada Public Policy, 26*(1), 51–75.

**Larrick, R. P., Timmerman, T. A., Carton, A. M., & Abrevaya, J.** (2011). Temper, temperature, and temptation: Heat-related retaliation in baseball. *Psychological Science, 22*(4), 423–428. doi:10.1177/0956797611399292

**Larsen, S. F.** (1992). Potential flashbulbs: Memories of ordinary news as baseline. In E. Winograd & U. Neisser (Eds.), *Affect and accuracy in recall: Studies of "flashbulb memories"* (pp. 32–64). New York: Cambridge University Press.

**Larson, R., & Richards, M. H.** (1991). Daily companionship in late childhood and early adolescence—changing developmental contexts. *Child Development, 62,* 284–300.

**Lashley, K. S.** (1960). In search of the engram. In F. A. Beach, D. O. Hebb, C. T. Morgan, & H. W. Nissen (Eds.), *The neuropsychology of Lashley* (pp. 478–505). New York: McGraw-Hill.

**Latané, B., & Nida, S.** (1981). Ten years of research on group size and helping. *Psychological Bulletin, 89*(2), 308–324.

**Latané, B., Williams, K., & Harkins, S.** (1979). Many hands make light the work: The causes and consequences of social loafing. *Journal of Personality and Social Psychology, 37,* 822–832.

**Lattal, K. A.** (2010). Delayed reinforcement of operant behavior. *Journal of the Experimental Analysis of Behavior, 93,* 129–139.

**Laupa, M., & Turiel, E.** (1986). Children's conceptions of adult and peer authority. *Child Development, 57,* 405–412.

**Laureys, S., Giacino, J. T., Schiff, N. D., Schabus, M., & Owen, A. M.** (2006). How should functional imaging of patients with disorders of consciousness contribute to their clinical rehabilitation needs? *Current Opinion in Neurology, 19,* 520–527.

**Lavie, P.** (2001). Sleep–wake as a biological rhythm. *Annual Review of Psychology, 52,* 277–303.

**Lawrence, N. S., Jollant, F., O'Daly, O., Zelaya, F., & Phillips, M. L.** (2009). Distinct roles of prefrontal cortical subregions in the Iowa Gambling Task. *Cerebral Cortex, 19,* 1134–1143.

**Lawton, M. P., Kleban, M. H., Rajagopal, D., & Dean, J.** (1992). The dimensions of affective experience in three age groups. *Psychology and Aging, 7,* 171–184.

**Lazarus, R. S.** (1984). On the primacy of cognition. *American Psychologist, 39,* 124–129.

**Lazarus, R. S., & Alfert, E.** (1964). Short-circuiting of threat by experimentally altering cognitive appraisal. *Journal of Abnormal and Social Psychology, 69,* 195–205.

**Lazarus, R. S., & Folkman, S.** (1984). *Stress, appraisal, and coping.* New York: Springer.

**Leader, T., Mullen, B., & Abrams, D.** (2007). Without mercy: The immediate impact of group size on lynch mob atrocity. *Personality and Social Psychology Bulletin, 33*(10), 1340–1352.

**Leary, M. R.** (1990). Responses to social exclusion: Social anxiety, jealousy, loneliness, depression, and low self-esteem. *Journal of Social and Clinical Psychology, 9,* 221–229.

**Leary, M. R.** (2010). Affiliation, acceptance, and belonging: The pursuit of interpersonal connection. In S. T. Fiske, D. T. Gilbert, & G. Lindzey (Eds.), *The handbook of social psychology* (5th ed., Vol. 2, pp. 864–897). New York: Wiley.

**Leary, M. R., & Baumeister, R. F.** (2000). The nature and function of self-esteem: Sociometer theory. In M. P. Zanna (Ed.), *Advances in experimental social psychology* (Vol. 32, pp. 1–62). San Diego: Academic Press.

**Leary, M. R., Britt, T. W., Cutlip, W. D., & Templeton, J. L.** (1992). Social blushing. *Psychological Bulletin, 112,* 446–460.

**Lecky, P.** (1945). *Self-consistency: A theory of personality.* New York: Island Press.

**Lecrubier, Y., Clerc, G., Didi, R., & Kieser, M.** (2002). Efficacy of St. John's wort extract WS 5570 in major depression: A double-blind, placebo-controlled trial. *American Journal of Psychiatry, 159,* 1361–1366.

**Lederman, S. J., & Klatzky, R. L.** (2009). Haptic perception: A tutorial. *Attention, Perception, & Psychophysics, 71,* 1439–1459.

**LeDoux, J. E.** (1992). Brain mechanisms of emotion and emotional learning. *Current Opinion in Neurobiology, 2,* 191–197.

**LeDoux, J. E.** (2000). Emotion circuits in the brain. *Annual Review of Neuroscience, 23,* 155–184.

**LeDoux, J. E., Iwata, J., Cicchetti, P., & Reis, D. J.** (1988). Different projections of the central amygdaloid nucleus mediate autonomic and behavioral correlates of conditioned fear. *Journal of Neuroscience, 8,* 2517–2529.

**Lee, D. N., & Aronson, E.** (1974). Visual proprioceptive control of standing in human infants. *Perception & Psychophysics, 15,* 529–532.

**Lee, L., Loewenstein, G., Ariely, D., Hong, J., & Young, J.** (2008). If I'm not hot, are you hot or not? Physical-attractiveness evaluations and dating preferences as a function of one's own attractiveness. *Psychological Science, 19,* 669–677.

Lee, M. H., Smyser, C. D., & Shimony, J. S. (2013). Resting-state fMRI: A review of methods and clinical applications. *American Journal of Neuroradiology, 34,* 1866–1872. doi: 10.3174/ajnr.A3263

Lefcourt, H. M. (1982). *Locus of control: Current trends in theory and research* (2nd ed.). Hillsdale, NJ: Erlbaum.

Leichsenring, F., & Rabung, S. (2008). Effectiveness of long-term psychodynamic psychotherapy: A meta-analysis. *Journal of the American Medical Association, 300,* 1551–1565.

Lempert, D. (2007). *Women's increasing wage penalties from being overweight and obese.* Washington, DC: U.S. Bureau of Labor Statistics.

Lenoir, M., Serre, F., Chantin, L., & Ahmed, S. H. (2007). Intense sweetness surpasses cocaine reward. *PLoS ONE, 2,* e698.

Lenton, A. P., & Francesconi, M. (2010). How humans cognitively manage an abundance of mate options. *Psychological Science, 21*(4), 528–533. doi: 10.1177/0956797610364958

Lentz, M. J., Landis, C. A., Rothermel, J., & Shaver, J. L. (1999). Effects of selective slow wave sleep disruption on musculoskeletal pain and fatigue in middle aged women. *Journal of Rheumatology, 26,* 1586–1592.

Leon, D. A., Lawlor, D. A., Clark, H., Batty, G. D., & Macintyre, S. (2009). The association of childhood intelligence with mortality risk from adolescence to middle age: Findings from the Aberdeen children of the 1950s cohort study. *Intelligence, 37*(6), 520–528.

Lepage, M., Ghaffar, O., Nyberg, L., & Tulving, E. (2000). Prefrontal cortex and episodic memory retrieval mode. *Proceedings of the National Academy of Sciences, USA, 97,* 506–511.

LePort, A. K. R., Mattfield, A. T., Dickinson-Anson, H., Fallon, J. H., Stark, C. E. L., Kruggel, F., ... McGaugh, J. L. (2012). Behavioral and neuroanatomical investigation of highly superior autobiographical memory (HSAM). *Neurobiology of Learning and Memory, 98,* 78–92.

Lepper, M. R., Greene, D., & Nisbett, R. E. (1973). Undermining children's intrinsic interest with extrinsic rewards: A test of the "overjustification" hypothesis. *Journal of Personality and Social Psychology, 28,* 129–137.

Lerman, D. (2006). Consumer politeness and complaining behavior. *Journal of Services Marketing, 20,* 92–100.

Lerman, D. C., & Vorndran, C. M. (2002). On the status of knowledge for using punishment: Implications for treating behavior disorders. *Journal of Applied Behavior Analysis, 35,* 4312–4464.

Lesage, A., Vasiliadis, H.-M., Gagné, M.-A., Dudgeon, S., Kasman, N., & Hay, C. (2006). *Prevalence of mental illness and related service utilization in Canada: An analysis of the Canadian community health survey.* Mississauga, ON: Canadian Collaborative Mental Health Initiative.

Leung, A. K.-Y., & Cohen, D. (2011). Within- and between-culture variation: Individual differences and the cultural logics of honor, face, and dignity cultures. *Journal of Personality and Social Psychology, 100*(3), 507–526. doi:10.1037/a0022151

Levelt Committee, Noort Committee, Drenth Committee. (2012, November 28). *Flawed science: The fraudulent research practices of social psychologist Diederik Stapel.* Retrieved from http://www.tilburguniversity.edu/nl/nieuws-en-agenda/finalreportLevelt.pdf

Levenson, J. M., & Sweatt, J. D. (2005). Epigenetic mechanisms in memory formation. *Nature Reviews Neuroscience, 6,* 108–118.

Levenson, R. W., Cartensen, L. L., Friesen, W. V., & Ekman, P. (1991). Emotion physiology, and expression in old age. *Psychology and Aging, 6,* 28–35.

Levenson, R. W., Ekman, P., & Friesen, W. V. (1990). Voluntary facial action generates emotion-specific autonomic nervous system activity. *Psychophysiology, 27,* 363–384.

Levenson, R. W., Ekman, P., Heider, K., & Friesen, W. V. (1992). Emotion and automatic nervous system activity in the Minangkabau of West Sumatra. *Journal of Personality and Social Psychology, 62,* 972–988.

Levin, D. T., & Simons, D. J. (1997). Failure to detect changes to attended objects in motion pictures. *Psychonomic Bulletin & Review, 4,* 501–506.

Levin, R., & Nielsen, T. (2009). Nightmares, bad dreams, and emotion dysregulation: A review and new neurocognitive model of dreaming. *Current Directions in Psychological Science, 18,* 84–88.

Levine, M. (1981). *History and politics of community mental health.* New York: Oxford University Press.

Levine, R. V., Norenzayan, A., & Philbrick, K. (2001). Cross-cultural differences in helping strangers. *Journal of Cross-Cultural Psychology, 32,* 543–560.

Levy, J., Trevarthen, C., & Sperry, R. W. (1972). Perception of bilateral chimeric figures following hemispheric disconnection. *Brain, 95,* 61–78.

Lewin, K. (1936). *Principles of topological psychology.* New York: McGraw-Hill.

Lewin, K. (1951). Behavior and development as a function of the total situation. In K. Lewin (Ed.), *Field theory in social science: Selected theoretical papers* (pp. 791–843). New York: Harper & Row.

Lewis, M., & Brooks-Gunn, J. (1979). *Social cognition and the acquisition of self.* New York: Plenum Press.

Lewis, M. B. (2012). Exploring the positive and negative implications of facial feedback. *Emotion, 12*(4), 852–859.

Lewis, M. D., Hibbeln, J. R., Johnson, J. E., Lin, Y. H., Hyun, D. Y., & Loewke, J. D. (2011). Suicide deaths of active duty U. S. military and omega-3 fatty acid status: A case control comparison. *Journal of Clinical Psychiatry, 72,* 1585–1590.

Lewontin, R., Rose, S., & Kamin, L. J. (1984). *Not in our genes.* New York: Pantheon.

Li, R., Polat, U., Makous, W., & Bavelier, D. (2009). Enhancing the contrast sensitivity function through action video game training. *Nature Neuroscience, 12,* 549–551.

Li, Y. J., Johnson, K. A., Cohen, A. B., Williams, M. J., Knowles, E. D., & Chen, Z. (2012). Fundamental(ist) attribution error: Protestants are dispositionally focused. *Journal of Personality and Social Psychology, 102*(2), 281–290. doi:10.1037/a0026294

Libet, B. (1985). Unconscious cerebral initiative and the role of conscious will in voluntary action. *Behavioral and Brain Sciences, 8,* 529–566.

Liebenluft, E. (1996). Women with bipolar illness: Clinical and research issues. *American Journal of Psychiatry, 153,* 163–173.

Lieberman, M. D., Inagaki, T. K., Tabibnia, G., & Crockett, M. J. (2011). Subjective responses to emotional stimuli during labeling, reappraisal, and distraction. *Emotion, 11,* 468–480.

Lieberman, M. D., & Rosenthal, R. (2001). Why introverts can't always tell who likes them: Multitasking and nonverbal decoding. *Journal of Personality and Social Psychology, 80,* 294–310.

Liebowitz, M. R., Gorman, J. M., Fyer, A. J., Levitt, M., Dillon, D., Levy, G., ... Davies, S. O. (1985). Lactate provocation of panic attacks: II. Biochemical and physiological findings. *Archives of General Psychiatry, 42,* 709–719.

Lifshitz, M., Aubert Bonn, N., Fischer, A., Kashem, I. R., & Raz, A. (2013). Using suggestion to modulate automatic processes: From Stroop to McGurk and beyond. *Cortex, 49*(2), 463–473. doi:10.1016/j.cortex.2012.08.007

Lilienfeld, S. O. (2007). Psychological treatments that cause harm. *Perspectives on Psychological Science, 2,* 53–70.

**Lilienfeld, S. O., Lynn, S. J., & Lohr, J. M. (Eds.).** (2003). *Science and pseudoscience in clinical psychology.* New York: Guilford Press.

**Lilienfeld, S. O., Wood, J. M., & Garb, H. N.** (2000). The scientific status of projective techniques. *Psychological Science in the Public Interest, 1,* 27–66.

**Lillard, L. A., & Waite, L. J.** (1995) 'Til death do us part': Marital disruption and mortality. *American Journal of Sociology, 100*(5), 1131–1156.

**Lim, K. L. L., Jacobs, P., Ohinmaa, A., Schopflocher, D., & Dewa, C. S.** (2008). A new population-based measure of the economic burden of mental illness in Canada. *Chronic Diseases and Injuries in Canada, 28*(2), 92–98.

**Linardatos, L., & Lydon, J. E.** (2011). A little reminder is all it takes: The effects of priming and relational self-construal on responses to partner transgressions. *Self and Identity, 10,* 85–100.

**Lindenberger, U., & Baltes, P. B.** (1994). Sensory functioning and intelligence in old age: A strong connection. *Psychology and Aging, 9*(3), 339–355. doi:10.1037/0882-7974.9.3.339

**Lindenberger, U., & Baltes, P. B.** (1997). Intellectual functioning in old and very old age: Cross-sectional results from the Berling aging study. *Psychology and Aging, 12,* 410–432.

**Lindquist, K., & Barrett, L. F.** (2008). Constructing emotion: The experience of fear as a conceptual act. *Psychological Science, 19,* 898–903.

**Lindquist, S. I., & McLean, J. P.** (2011). Daydreaming and its correlates in an educational environment. *Learning and Individual Differences, 21,* 158–167.

**Lindstrom, M.** (2005). *Brand sense: How to build powerful brands through touch, taste, smell, sight and sound.* London: Kogan Page.

**Liou, A. P., Paziuk, M., Luevano, J.-M., Machineni, S., Turnbaugh, P. J., & Kaplan, L. M.** (2013). Conserved shifts in the gut microbiota due to gastric bypass reduce host weight and adiposity. *Science Translational Medicine, 5*(178), 178ra41.

**Little, B. R.** (1983). Personal projects: A rationale and method for investigation. *Environment and Behavior, 15,* 273–309.

**Little, B. R.** (1993). Personal projects and the distributed self: Aspects of a conative psychology. In J. R. Suls (Ed.), *Psychological perspectives on the self* (Vol. 4, pp. 157–185). Hillsdale, NJ: Erlbaum.

**Liu, D., Diorio, J., Tannenbaum, B., Caldji, C., Francis, D., Freedman, A., … Meaney, M. J.** (1997). Maternal care, hippocampal glucocorticoid receptors, and hypothalamic–pituitary–adrenal responses to stress. *Science, 277,* 1659–1662.

**Liu, D., Wellman, H. M., Tardif, T., & Sabbagh, M. A.** (2008). Theory of mind development in Chinese children: A meta-analysis of false belief understanding across cultures and languages. *Developmental Psychology, 44,* 523–531.

**Livingstone, M., & Hubel, D.** (1988). Segregation of form, color, movement, and depth: Anatomy, physiology, and perception. *Science, 240,* 740–749.

**Locksley, A., Ortiz, V., & Hepburn, C.** (1980). Social categorization and discriminatory behavior: Extinguishing the minimal intergroup discrimination effect. *Journal of Personality and Social Psychology, 39,* 773–783.

**Loehlin, J. C.** (1973). Blood group genes and Negro–White ability differences. *Behavior Genetics, 3*(3), 263–270.

**Loehlin, J. C.** (1992). *Genes and environment in personality development.* Newbury Park, CA: Sage.

**Loftus, E. F.** (1993). The reality of repressed memories. *American Psychologist, 48,* 518–537.

**Loftus, E. F.** (2003). Make-believe memories. *American Psychologist, 58,* 867–873.

**Loftus, E. F., & Ketchum, K.** (1994). *The myth of repressed memory.* New York: St. Martin's Press.

**Loftus, E. F., & Klinger, M. R.** (1992). Is the unconscious smart or dumb? *American Psychologist, 47,* 761–765.

**Loftus, E. F., & Pickrell, J. E.** (1995). The formation of false memories. *Psychiatric Annals, 25,* 720–725.

**Lopes, P. N., Grewal, D., Kadis, J., Gall, M., & Salovey, P.** (2006). Emotional intelligence and positive work outcomes. *Psichothema, 18,* 132.

**Lord, C. G., Ross, L., & Lepper, M. R.** (1979). Biased assimilation and attitude polarization: The effects of prior theories on subsequently considered evidence. *Journal of Personality and Social Psychology, 37,* 2098–2109.

**Lorenz, K.** (1952). *King Solomon's ring.* New York: Crowell.

**Lovaas, O. I.** (1987). Behavioral treatment and normal educational and intellectual functioning in young autistic children. *Journal of Consulting and Clinical Psychology, 55,* 3–9.

**Low, J., & Watts, J.** (2013). Attributing false beliefs about object identity reveals a signature blind spot in humans' efficient mind-reading system. *Psychological Science, 24*(3), 305–311. doi:10.1177/0956797612451469

**Lozano, B. E., & Johnson, S. L.** (2001). Can personality traits predict increases in manic and depressive symptoms? *Journal of Affective Disorders, 63,* 103–111.

**Luborsky, L., Rosenthal, R., Diguer, L., Andrusyna, T. P., Berman, J. S., Levitt, J. T., … Krause, E. D.** (2002). The dodo bird verdict is alive and well—mostly. *Clinical Psychology: Science and Practice, 9,* 2–12.

**Luborsky, L., & Singer, B.** (1975). Comparative studies of psychotherapies: Is it true that "everyone has won and all must have prizes"? *Archives of General Psychiatry, 32*(8), 995–1008.

**Lucas, R. E., Clark, A. E., Georgellis, Y., & Diener, E.** (2003). Reexamining adaptation and the set point model of happiness: Reactions to changes in marital status. *Journal of Personality and Social Psychology, 84,* 527–539.

**Ludwig, A. M.** (1966). Altered states of consciousness. *Archives of General Psychiatry, 15,* 225–234.

**Lykken, D. T.** (1995). *The antisocial personalities.* Hillsdale, NJ: Erlbaum.

**Lynn, M., & Shurgot, B. A.** (1984). Responses to lonely hearts advertisements: Effects of reported physical attractiveness, physique, and coloration. *Personality and Social Psychology Bulletin, 10,* 349–357.

**Lynn, R.** (2009). What has caused the Flynn effect? Secular increases in the development quotients of infants. *Intelligence, 37*(1), 16–24.

**Lynn, R.** (2013). Who discovered the Flynn effect? A review of early studies of the secular increase of intelligence. *Intelligence.* Advance online publication. doi:10.1016/j.intell.2013.03.008

**Lyons, D. E., Young, A. G., & Keil, F. C.** (2007). The hidden structure of overimitation. *Proceedings of the National Academy of Sciences, 104*(50), 19751–19756. doi:10.1073/pnas.0704452104

**Lyubomirsky, S.** (2008). *The how of happiness: A scientific approach to getting the life you want.* New York: Penguin.

**Lyubomirsky, S., & Lepper, H. S.** (1999). A measure of subjective happiness: Preliminary reliability and construct validation. *Social Indicators Research, 46,* 137–155.

**MacDonald, S., Uesiliana, K., & Hayne, H.** (2000). Cross-cultural and gender differences in childhood amnesia. *Memory, 8,* 365–376.

**MacGregor, J. N., Ormerod, T. C., & Chronicle, E. P.** (2001). Information processing and insight: A process model of performance on the nine-dot and related problems. *Journal of Experimental Psychology: Learning, Memory, and Cognition, 27,* 176–201.

**Mack, A. H., Franklin, J. E., Jr., & Frances, R. J.** (2003). Substance use disorders. In R. E. Hales & S. C. Yudofsky (Eds.), *The American Psychiatric Publishing textbook of clinical psychiatry* (4th ed., pp. 309–377). Washington, DC: American Psychiatric Publishing.

**Maclean, P. D.** (1970). The triune brain, emotion, and scientific bias. In F. O. Schmitt (Ed.), *The neurosciences: A second study program* (pp. 336–349). New York: Rockefeller University Press.

**MacLeod, C., & Mathews, A.** (2012). Cognitive bias modification approaches to anxiety. *Annual Review of Clinical Psychology, 8,* 189–217.

**MacLeod, M. D.** (2002). Retrieval-induced forgetting in eyewitness memory: Forgetting as a consequence of remembering. *Applied Cognitive Psychology, 16,* 135–149.

**MacLeod, M. D., & Saunders, J.** (2008). Retrieval inhibition and memory distortion: Negative consequences of an adaptive process. *Current Directions in Psychological Science, 17,* 26–30.

**Macmillan, M.** (2000). *An odd kind of fame: Stories of Phineas Gage.* Cambridge, MA: MIT Press.

**Macmillan, N. A., & Creelman, C. D.** (2005). *Detection theory.* Mahwah, NJ: Erlbaum.

**Macrae, C. N., Bodenhausen, G. V., Milne, A. B., & Jetten, J.** (1994). Out of mind but back in sight: Stereotypes on the rebound. *Journal of Personality and Social Psychology, 67,* 808–817.

**Macrae, C. N., Moran, J. M., Heatherton, T. F., Banfield, J. F., & Kelley, W. M.** (2004). Medial prefrontal activity predicts memory for self. *Cerebral Cortex, 14,* 647–654.

**MADD Canada.** (2013). *The magnitude of the alcohol/drug-related crash problem in Canada: Overview.* Retrieved from http://madd.ca/madd2/en/impaired_driving/impaired_driving_statistics.html

**Maddi, S. R., Harvey, R. H., Khoshaba, D. M., Fazel, M., & Resurreccion, N.** (2009). Hardiness training facilitates performance in college. *Journal of Positive Psychology, 4,* 566–577.

**Maddi, S. R., Kahn, S., & Maddi, K. L.** (1998). The effectiveness of hardiness training. *Consulting Psychology Journal: Practice and Research, 50,* 78–86.

**Maddux, W. W., Mullen, E., & Galinsky, A. D.** (2008). Chameleons bake bigger pies and take bigger pieces: Strategic behavioral mimicry facilitates negotiation outcomes. *Journal of Experimental Social Psychology, 44,* 461–468.

**Madigan, S., Atkinson, L., Laurin, K., & Benoit, D.** (2013). Attachment and internalizing behavior in early childhood: A meta-analysis. *Developmental Psychology, 49*(4), 672–689. doi:10.1037/a0028793

**Maes, M.** (1995). Evidence for an immune response in major depression: A review and hypothesis. *Progress in Neuro-Psychopharmacology and Biological Psychiatry, 19,* 11–38.

**Maguire, E. A., Woollett, K., & Spiers, H. J.** (2006). London taxi drivers and bus drivers: A structural MRI and neuropsychological analysis. *Hippocampus, 16,* 1091–1101.

**Mahajan, N., Martinez, M. A., Gutierrez, N. L., Diesendruck, G., Banaji, M. R., & Santos, L. R.** (2011). The evolution of intergroup bias: Perceptions and attitudes in rhesus macaques. *Journal of Personality and Social Psychology, 100*(3), 387–405. doi:10.1037/a0022459

**Mahon, B. Z., Anzellotti, S., Schwarzbach, J., Zampini, M., & Caramazza, A.** (2009). Category-specific organization in the human brain does not require visual experience. *Neuron, 63,* 397–405.

**Mahon, B. Z., & Caramazza, A.** (2009). Concepts and categories: A cognitive neuropschological perspective. *Cognitive Neuropsychology, 60,* 27–51.

**Mahowald, M., & Schenck, C.** (2000). REM sleep parasomnias. In M. Kryger, T. Roth, & W. Dement (Eds.), *Principles and practices of sleep medicine* (3rd ed., pp. 724–741). Philadelphia: Saunders.

**Maier, S. F., & Watkins, L. R.** (1998). Cytokines for psychologists: Implications of bidirectional immune-to-brain communication for understanding behavior, mood, and cognition. *Psychological Review, 105,* 83–107.

**Maier, S. F., & Watkins, L. R.** (2000). The immune system as a sensory system: Implications for psychology. *Current Directions in Psychological Science, 9,* 98–102.

**Major, B., Mendes, W. B., & Dovidio, J. F.** (2013). Intergroup relations and health disparities: A social psychological perspective. *Health Psychology, 32,* 514–524.

**Makin, J. E., Fried, P. A., & Watkinson, B.** (1991). A comparison of active and passive smoking during pregnancy: Long-term effects. *Neurotoxicology and Teratology, 16,* 5–12.

**Makris, N., Biederman, J., Monuteaux, M. C., & Seidman, L. J.** (2009). Towards conceptualizing a neural systems-based anatomy of attention-deficit/hyperactivity disorder. *Developmental Neuroscience, 31,* 36–49.

**Malenfant, E. C.** (2004, March 29). Suicide in Canada's immigrant population. (Catalogue no. 82-003). *Statistics Canada Health Reports, 15*(2), 9–17.

**Malina, R. M., Bouchard, C., & Beunen, G.** (1988). Human growth: Selected aspects of current research on well-nourished children. *Annual Review of Anthropology, 17,* 187–219.

**Malooly, A. M., Genet, J. J., & Siemer, M.** (2013). Individual differences in reappraisal effectiveness: The role of affective flexibility. *Emotion, 13*(2), 302–313. doi:10.1037/a0029980

**Mampe, B., Friederici, A. D., Christophe, A., & Wermke, K.** (2009). Newborns' cry melody is shaped by their native language. *Current Biology, 19,* 1–4.

**Mandel, D. R., & Lehman, D. R.** (1998). Integration of contingency information in judgments of cause, covariation, and probability. *Journal of Experimental Psychology: General, 127,* 269–285.

**Mandle, C. L., Jacobs, S. C., Arcari, P. M., & Domar, A. D.** (1996). The efficacy of relaxation response interventions with adult patients: A review of the literature. *Journal of Cardiovascular Nursing, 10,* 4–26.

**Mandler, G.** (1967). Organization and memory. In K. W. Spence & J. T. Spence (Eds.), *The psychology of learning and motivation* (Vol. 1, pp. 327–372). New York: Academic Press.

**Mankiw, N. G., & Weinzierl, M.** (2010). The optimal taxation of height: A case study of utilitarian income redistribution. *American Economic Journal: Economic Policy, 2,* 155–176.

**Mann, J. J.** (2005). The medical management of depression. *New England Journal of Medicine, 353,* 1819–1834.

**Mann, J. J., Apter, A., Bertolote, J., Beautrais, A., Currier, D., Haas, A., … Hendin, H.** (2005). Suicide prevention strategies: A systematic review. *Journal of the American Medical Association, 294*(16), 2064–2074. doi:10.1001/jama.294.16.2064

**Marangell, L. B., Silver, J. M., Goff, D. M., & Yudofsky, S. C.** (2003). Psychopharmacology and electroconvulsive therapy. In R. E. Hales & S. C. Yudofsky (Eds.), *The American Psychiatric Publishing textbook of clinical psychiatry* (4th ed., pp. 1047–1149). Washington, DC: American Psychiatric Publishing.

**Marci, C. D., Ham, J., Moran, E., & Orr, S. P.** (2007). Physiologic correlates of perceived therapist empathy and social-emotional process during psychotherapy. *Journal of Nervous and Mental Disease, 195,* 103–111.

**Marcus, G.** (2012, December 3). Neuroscience fiction. *New Yorker.* Retrieved from http://www.newyorker.com/online/blogs/

newsdesk/2012/12/what-neuroscicnec-really-teaches-us-and-what-it-doesnt.html

**Margolis, R., & Myrskylä, M.** (2011). A global perspective on happiness and fertility. *Population and Development Review, 37,* 29–56.

**Markowitz, J. C.** (1999). Developments in interpersonal psychotherapy. *Canadian Journal of Psychiatry, 44*(6), 556–561.

**Markus, G. B.** (1986). Stability and change in political attitudes: Observe, recall, and "explain." *Political Behavior, 8,* 21–44.

**Markus, H.** (1977). Self-schemata and processing information about the self. *Journal of Personality and Social Psychology, 35,* 63–78.

**Marlatt, G. A., & Rohsenow, D.** (1980). Cognitive processes in alcohol use: Expectancy and the balanced placebo design. In N. K. Mello (Ed.), *Advances in substance abuse: Behavioral and biological research* (pp. 159–199). Greenwich, CT: JAI Press.

**Marmot, M. G., Stansfeld, S., Patel, C., North, F., Head, J., White, L., ... Feeney, A.** (1991). Health inequalities among British civil servants: The Whitehall II study. *Lancet, 337,* 1387–1393.

**Marr, D., & Nishihara, H. K.** (1978). Representation and recognition of the spatial organization of three-dimensional shapes. *Proceedings of the Royal Society B: Biological Sciences, 200,* 269–294.

**Marsolek, C. J.** (1995). Abstract visual-form representations in the left cerebral hemispheres. *Journal of Experimental Psychology: Human Perception and Performance, 21,* 375–386.

**Martin, A.** (2007). The representation of object concepts in the brain. *Annual Review of Psychology, 58,* 25–45.

**Martin, A., & Caramazza, A.** (2003). Neuropsychological and neuroimaging perspectives on conceptual knowledge: An introduction. *Cognitive Neuropsychology, 20,* 195–212.

**Martin, A., & Chao, L. L.** (2001). Semantic memory and the brain: Structure and processes. *Current Opinion in Neurobiology, 11,* 194–201.

**Martin, K. D., & Hill, R. P.** (2012). Life satisfaction, self-determination, and consumption adequacy at the bottom of the pyramid. *Journal of Consumer Research, 38,* 1155–1168.

**Martin, N. G., Eaves, L. J., Geath, A. R., Jarding, R., Feingold, L. M., & Eysenck, H. J.** (1986). Transmission of social attitudes. *Proceedings of the National Academy of Sciences, USA, 83,* 4364–4368.

**Martinez, G., Copen, C. E., & Abma, J. C.** (2011). Teenagers in the United States: Sexual activity, contraceptive use, and childbearing, 2006–2010: National Survey of Family Growth. *Vital Health Statistics, 23*(31).

**Marucha, P. T., Kiecolt-Glaser, J. K., & Favagehi, M.** (1998). Mucosal wound healing is impaired by examination stress. *Psychosomatic Medicine, 60,* 362–365.

**Marzuk, P. M., Tardiff, K., Leon, A. C., Hirsch, C., Portera, L., Iqbal, M. I., ... Hartwell, N.** (1998). Ambient temperature and mortality from unintentional cocaine overdose. *Journal of the American Medical Association, 279,* 1795–1800.

**Maslach, C.** (2003). Job burnout: New directions in research and intervention. *Current Directions in Psychological Science, 12,* 189–192.

**Maslach, C., Schaufeli, W. B., & Leiter, M. P.** (2001). Job burnout. *Annual Review of Psychology, 52,* 397–422.

**Maslow, A. H.** (1937). Dominance-feeling, behavior, and status. In R. J. Lowry (Ed.), *Dominance, self-esteem, self-actualization: Germinal papers by A. H. Maslow* (pp. 49–70). Monterey, CA: Brooks-Cole.

**Maslow, A. H.** (1954). *Motivation and personality.* New York: Harper & Row.

**Maslow, A. H.** (1970). *Motivation and personality* (2nd ed.). New York: Harper & Row.

**Mason, M. F., Magee, J. C., Kuwabara, K., & Nind, L.** (2010). Specialization in relational reasoning: The efficiency, accuracy, and neural substrates of social versus nonsocial inferences. *Social Psychological and Personality Science, 1*(4), 318–326. doi:10.1177/1948550610366166

**Mason, M. F., Norton, M. I., Van Horn, J. D., Wegner, D. M., Grafton, S. T., & Macrae, C. N.** (2007). Wandering minds: The default network and stimulus-independent thought. *Science, 3154,* 393–395.

**Masten, A. S.** (2004). Family therapy as a treatment for children: A critical review of outcome research. *Family Process, 18,* 323–335.

**Masters, W. H., & Johnson, V. E.** (1966). *Human sexual response.* Boston: Little, Brown.

**Masuda, T., & Nisbett, R. E.** (2006). Culture and change blindness. *Cognitive Science, 30,* 381–300.

**Mather, M., Canli, T., English, T., Whitfield, S., Wais, P., Ochsner, K., ... Cartensen, L. L.** (2004). Amygdala responses to emotionally valenced stimuli in older and younger adults. *Psychological Science, 15,* 259–263.

**Mather, M., & Carstensen, L. L.** (2003). Aging and attentional biases for emotional faces. *Psychological Science, 14,* 409–415.

**Mather, M., & Carstensen, L. L.** (2005). Aging and motivated cognition: The positivity effect in attention and memory. *Trends in Cognitive Sciences, 9*(10), 496–502.

**Matsuda, O., & Saito, M.** (1998). Crystallized and fluid intelligence in elderly patients with mild dementia of the Alzheimer type. *International Psychogeriatrics, 10*(2), 147–154. doi:10.1017/S1041610298005250

**Matsumoto, D., & Willingham, B.** (2009). Spontaneous facial expressions of emotion of congenitally and noncongenitally blind individuals. *Journal of Personality and Social Psychology, 96,* 1–10.

**Mattar, A. A. G., & Gribble, P. L.** (2005). Motor learning by observing. *Neuron, 46,* 153–160.

**Matthews, G., & Gilliland, K.** (1999). The personality theories of H. J. Eysenck and J. A. Gray: A comparative review. *Personality and Individual Differences, 26,* 583–626.

**Matzel, L. D., Han, Y. R., Grossman, H., Karnik, M. S., Patel, D., Scott, N., ... Gandhi, C. C.** (2003). Individual differences in the expression of a general learning ability in mice. *Journal of Neuroscience, 23*(16), 6423–6433.

**Maudsley, H.** (1886). *Natural causes and supernatural seemings.* London: Kegan Paul, Trench.

**Max, A.** (2006, September 16). Dutch reach new heights. *USA Today.* Retrieved from http://usatoday30.usatoday.com/news/offbeat/2006-09-16-dutch-tall_x.htm

**May, R.** (1983). *The discovery of being: Writings in existential psychology.* New York: Norton.

**Mayberg, H., Lozano, A., Voon, V., McNeely, H., Seminowicz, D., Hamani, C., ... Kennedy, S. H.** (2005). Deep brain stimulation for treatment resistant depresssion. *Neuron, 45,* 651–660.

**Mayer, J. D., Caruso, D. R., & Salovey, P.** (1999). Emotional intelligence meets traditional standards for an intelligence. *Intelligence, 27,* 267.

**Mayer, J. D., Caruso, D. R., Zigler, E., & Dreyden, J. I.** (1989). Intelligence and intelligence-related personality traits. *Intelligence, 13*(2), 119–133. doi:10.1016/0160-2896(89)90011-1

**Mayer, J. D., Roberts, R. D., & Barsade, S. G.** (2008). Human abilities: Emotional intelligence. *Annual Review of Psychology, 59,* 507–536.

**Maynard-Smith, J.** (1965). The evolution of alarm calls. *American Naturalist, 100,* 637–650.

**McAdams, D.** (1993). *The stories we live by: Personal myths and the making of the self.* New York: Morrow.

McCabe, S. E., Knight, J. R., Teter, C. J., & Wechsler, H. (2005). Nonmedical use of prescription stimulants among U.S. college students: Prevalence and correlates from a national survey. *Addiction, 100,* 96–106.

McCauley, J., Ruggiero, K. J., Resnick, H. S., Conoscenti, L. M., & Kilpatrick, D. G. (2009). Forcible, drug-facilitated, and incapacitated rape in relation to substance use problems: Results from a national sample of college women. *Addictive Behaviors, 34,* 458–462.

McClelland, D. C., Atkinson, J. W., Clark, R. A., & Lowell, E. L. (1953). *The achievement motive.* New York: Appleton-Century-Crofts.

McConkey, K. M., Barnier, A. J., & Sheehan, P. W. (1998). Hypnosis and pseudomemory: Understanding the findings and their implications. In S. J. Lynn & K. M. McConkey (Eds.), *Truth in memory* (pp. 227–259). New York: Guilford Press.

McCrae, R. R., & Costa, P. T. (1990). *Personality in adulthood.* New York: Guilford Press.

McCrae, R. R., & Costa, P. T. (1999). A five-factor theory of personality. In L. A. Pervin & O. P. John (Eds.), *Handbook of personality: Theory and research* (pp. 139–153). New York: Guilford Press.

McCrea, S. M., Buxbaum, L. J., & Coslett, H. B. (2006). Illusory conjunctions in simultanagnosia: Coarse coding of visual feature location? *Neuropsychologia, 44,* 1724–1736.

McDougall, W. (1930). The hormic psychology. In C. Murchison (Ed.), *Psychologies of 1930* (pp. 3–36). Worcester, MA: Clark University Press.

McElwain, N. L., Booth-LaForce, C., & Wu, X. (2011). Infant–mother attachment and children's friendship quality: Maternal mental state talk as an intervening mechanism. *Developmental Psychology, 47*(5), 1295–1311. doi:10.1037/a0024094

McEvoy, S. P., Stevenson, M. R., McCartt, A. T., Woodward, M., Haworth, C., Palamara, P., & Circarelli, R. (2005). Role of mobile phones in motor vehicle crashes resulting in hospital attendance: A casecrossover study. *British Medical Journal, 331,* 428–430.

McFall, R. M., & Treat, T. A. (1999). Quantifying the information value of clinical assessments with signal detection theory. *Annual Review of Psychology, 50,* 215–241.

McFarlane, A. H., Norman, G. R., Streiner, D. L., Roy, R., & Scott, D. J. (1980). A longitudinal study of the influence of the psychosocial environment on health status: A preliminary report. *Journal of Health and Social Behavior, 21,* 124–133.

McGarty, C., & Turner, J. C. (1992). The effects of categorization on social judgement. *British Journal of Social Psychology, 31,* 253–268.

McGaugh, J. L. (2000). Memory: A century of consolidation. *Science, 287,* 248–251.

McGaugh, J. L. (2006). Make mild moments memorable: Add a little arousal. *Trends in Cognitive Sciences, 10,* 345–347.

McGowan, P. O., Sasaki, A., D'Alessio, A. D., Dymov, S., Labonté, B., Szyf, M., ... Meaney, M. J. (2009). Epigenetic regulation of the glucocorticoid receptor in human brain associates with childhood abuse. *Nature Neuroscience, 12,* 342–348.

McGowan, P. O., Suderman, M., Sasaki, A., Huang, T. C. T., Hallett, M., Meaney, J. J., & Szyf, M. (2011). Broad epigenetic signature of maternal care in the brain of adult rats. *PLoS One, 6*(2), e14739. doi:10.1371/journal.pone.0014739

McGrath, J., Saha, S., Chant, D., & Welham, J. (2008). Schizophrenia: A concise overview of incidence, prevalence, and mortality. *Epidemiologic Reviews, 30,* 67–76.

McGraw, M. B. (1943). *Neuromuscular naturation of the human infant.* New York: Hafner.

McGue, M., & Bouchard, T. J. (1998). Genetic and environmental influences on human behavioral differences. *Annual Review of Neuroscience, 21,* 1–24.

McGuire, P. K., Shah, G. M., & Murray, R. M. (1993). Increased blood flow in Broca's area during auditory hallucinations in schizophrenia. *Lancet, 342,* 703–706.

McIntyre, S. H., & Munson, J. M. (2008). Exploring cramming: Student behaviors, beliefs, and learning retention in the principles of marketing course. *Journal of Marketing Education, 30,* 226–243.

McKee, A. C., Cantu, R. C., Nowinski, C. J., Hedley-Whyte, E. T., Gavett, B. E., Budson, A. E., ... Stern, R. A. (2009). Chronic traumatic encephalopathy in athletes: Progressive tauopathy after repetitive head injury. *Journal of Neuropathology and Experimental Neurology, 68,* 709–735.

McKee, A. C., Stein, T. D., Nowinski, C. J., Stern, R. A., Daneshvar, D. H., Alvarez, V. E., ... Cantu, R. (2012). The spectrum of disease in chronic traumatic encephalopathy. *Brain, 136*(1), 43–64. doi:10.1093/brain/aws307

McKetin, R., Ward, P. B., Catts, S. V., Mattick, R. P., & Bell, J. R. (1999). Changes in auditory selective attention and event-related potentials following oral administration of D-amphetamine in humans. *Neuropsychopharmacology, 21,* 380–390.

McKinney, C. H., Antoni, M. H., Kumar, M., Tims, F. C., & McCabe, P. M. (1997). Effects of guided imagery and music (GIM) therapy on mood and cortisol in healthy adults. *Health Psychology, 16,* 390–400.

McLaughlin, K. A., Nandi, A., Keyes, K. M., Uddin, M., Aiello, A. E., Galea, S., & Koenen, K. C. (2012). Home foreclosure and risk of psychiatric morbidity during the recent financial crisis. *Psychological Medicine, 42,* 1441–1448.

McLean, K. C. (2008). The emergence of narrative identity. *Social and Personality Psychology Compass, 2*(4), 1685–1702.

McNally, R. J. (2003). *Remembering trauma.* Cambridge, MA: Belknap Press of Harvard University Press.

McNally, R. J., & Clancy, S. A. (2005). Sleep paralysis, sexual abuse, and space alien abduction. *Transcultural Psychiatry, 42,* 113–122.

McNally, R. J., & Geraerts, E. (2009). A new solution to the recovered memory debate. *Perspective on Psychological Science, 4,* 126–134.

McNally, R. J., & Steketee, G. S. (1985). Etiology and maintenance of severe animal phobias. *Behavioral Research and Therapy, 23,* 431–435.

McNeilly, A. S., Robinson, I. C., Houston, M. J., & Howie, P. W. (1983). Release of oxytocin and prolactin in response to suckling. *British Medical Journal, 286,* 257–259.

McRae, C., Cherin, E., Yamazaki, G., Diem, G., Vo, A. H., Russell, D., ... Freed, C. R. (2004). Effects of perceived treatment on quality of life and medical outcomes in a double-blind placebo surgery trial. *Archives of General Psychiatry, 61,* 412–420.

Mead, G. H. (1934). *Mind, self, and society.* Chicago: University of Chicago Press.

Mead, M. (1968). *Sex and temperament in three primitive societies.* New York: Dell. (Original work published 1935)

Meaney, M. J., & Ferguson-Smith, A. C. (2010). Epigenetic regulation of the neural transcriptome: The meaning of the marks. *Nature Neuroscience, 13,* 1313–1318.

Mechelli, A., Crinion, J. T., Noppeney, U., O'Doherty, J., Ashburner, J., Frackowiak, R. S., & Price, C. J. (2004). Neurolinguistics: Structural plasticity in the bilingual brain. *Nature, 431,* 757.

Medin, D. L., & Schaffer, M. M. (1978). Context theory of classification learning. *Psychological Review, 85,* 207–238.

Medvec, V. H., Madey, S. F., & Gilovich, T. (1995). When less is more: Counterfactual thinking and satisfaction among Olympic medalists. *Journal of Personality and Social Psychology, 69,* 603–610.

Meeren, H. K. M., van Heijnsbergen, C. C. R. J., & de Gelder, B. (2005). Rapid perceptual integration of facial expression and emotional body language. *Proceedings of the National Academy of Sciences, USA, 102*(45), 16518–16523.

Mehl, M. R., Vazire, S., Ramirez-Esparza, N., Slatcher, R. B., & Pennebaker, J. W. (2009). Are women really more talkative than men? *Science, 317,* 82.

Mehrabian, L. (1998). Effects of poll reports on voter preferences. *Journal of Applied Social Psychology, 28*(23), 2119–2130.

Meindl, J. N., & Casey, L. B. (2012). Increasing the suppressive effect of delayed punishers: A review of basic and applied literature. *Behavioral Interventions, 27,* 129–150.

Meins, E. (2003). Emotional development and attachment relationships. In A. Slater & G. Bremner (Eds.), *An introduction to developmental psychology* (pp. 141–164). Malden, MA: Blackwell.

Meins, E., Fernyhough, C., Fradley, E., & Tuckey, M. (2001). Rethinking maternal sensitivity: Mothers' comments on infants' mental processes predict security of attachment at 12 months. *Journal of Child Psychology & Psychiatry & Allied Disciplines, 42,* 637–648.

Meisel, S. R., Dayan, K. I., Pauzner, H., Chetboun, I., Arbel, Y., & David, D. (1991). Effect of Iraqi missile war on incidence of acute myocardial infarction and sudden death in Israeli citizens. *Lancet, 338,* 660–661.

Mekel-Bobrov, N., Gilbert, S. L., Evans, P. D., Vallender, E. J., Anderson, J. R., Hudson, R. R., ... Lahn, B. T. (2005). Ongoing adaptive evolution of ASPM, a brain size determinant in *Homo sapiens. Science, 309,* 1720–1722.

Melander, E. (2005). Gender equality and intrastate armed conflict. *International Studies Quarterly, 49*(4), 695–714. doi:10.1111/j.1468-2478.2005.00384.x

Mellon, R. C. (2009). Superstitious perception: Response-independent reinforcement and punishment as determinants of recurring eccentric interpretations. *Behaviour Research and Therapy, 47,* 868–875.

Meltzer, H. Y. (2013). Update on typical and atypical antipsychotic drugs. *Annual Review of Medicine, 64,* 393–406.

Meltzoff, A. N. (1995). Understanding the intentions of others: Re-enactment of intended acts by 18-month-old children. *Developmental Psychology, 31,* 838–850.

Meltzoff, A. N. (2007). "Like me": A foundation for social cognition. *Developmental Science, 10*(1), 126–134. doi:10.1111/j.1467-7687.2007.00574x

Meltzoff, A. N., Kuhl, P. K., Movellan, J., & Sejnowski, T. J. (2009). Foundations for a new science of learning. *Science, 325,* 284–288.

Meltzoff, A. N., & Moore, M. K. (1977). Imitation of facial and manual gestures by human neonates. *Science, 198,* 75–78.

Melzack, R., & Wall, P. D. (1965). Pain mechanisms: A new theory. *Science, 150,* 971–979.

Melzack, R., & Wall, P. D. (1988). *The challenge of pain* (2nd ed.). London, UK: Penguin Books.

Mendes, W. B., Blascovich, J., Hunter, S. B., Lickel, B., & Jost, J. T. (2007). Threatened by the unexpected: Physiological responses during social interactions with expectancy-violating partners. *Journal of Personality and Social Psychology, 92,* 698–716.

Mendes, W. B., Blascovich, J., Lickel, B., & Hunter, S. (2002). Challenge and threat during social interaction with White and Black men. *Personality & Social Psychology Bulletin, 28,* 939–952.

Mendle, J., Harden, K. P., Brooks-Gunn, J., & Graber, J. A. (2010). Development's tortoise and hare: Pubertal timing, pubertal tempo, and depressive symptoms in boys and girls. *Developmental Psychology, 46*(5), 1341–1353. doi: 10.1037/a0020205

Mendle, J., Turkheimer, E., & Emery, R. E. (2007). Detrimental psychological outcomes associated with early pubertal timing in adolescent girls. *Developmental Review, 27,* 151–171.

Mennella, J. A., Johnson, A., & Beauchamp, G. K. (1995). Garlic ingestion by pregnant women alters the odor of amniotic fluid. *Chemical Senses, 20,* 207–209.

Mental Health Commission of Canada. (n.d.). *The facts.* Retrieved from http://strategy.mentalhealthcommission.ca/the-facts/#sthash.m01NndHw.dpuf

Merikangas, K. R., Wicki, W., & Angst, J. (1994). Heterogeneity of depression: Classification of depressive subtype by longitudinal course. *British Journal of Psychiatry, 164,* 342–348.

Mervis, C. B., & Bertrand, J. (1994). Acquisition of the "Novel Name" Nameless Category (N3C) principle. *Child Development, 65,* 1646–1662.

Merzenich, M. M., Recanzone, G. H., Jenkins, W. M., & Grajski, K. A. (1990). Adaptive mechanisms in cortical networks underlying cortical contributions to learning and nondeclarative memory. *Cold Spring Harbor Symposia on Quantitative Biology, 55,* 873–887.

Messick, D. M., & Cook, K. S. (1983). *Equity theory: Psychological and sociological perspectives.* New York: Praeger.

Meston, C. M., & Buss, D. M. (2007). Why humans have sex. *Archives of Sexual Behavior, 36,* 477–507.

Mestre, J. M., Guil, R., Lopes, P. N., Salovey, P., & Gil-Olarte, P. (2006). Emotional intelligence and social and academic adaptation to school. *Psicothema, 18,* 112.

Mestry, N., Donnelly, N., Meneer, T., & McCarthy, R. A. (2012). Discriminating Thatcherised from typical faces in a case of prosopagnosia. *Neuropsychologia, 50,* 3410–3418.

Metcalfe, J. (2009). Metacognitive judgments and control of study. *Current Directions in Psychological Science, 18,* 159–163.

Metcalfe, J., & Finn, B. (2008). Evidence that judgments of learning are causally related to study choice. *Psychonomic Bulletin & Review, 15,* 174–179.

Metcalfe, J., & Wiebe, D. (1987). Intuition in insight and noninsight problem solving. *Memory & Cognition, 15,* 238–246.

Methven, L., Allen, V. J., Withers, G. A., & Gosney, M. A. (2012). Ageing and taste. *Proceedings of the Nutrition Society, 71,* 556–565.

Meyer-Bahlberg, H. F. L., Ehrhardt, A. A., Rosen, L. R., & Gruen, R. S. (1995). Prenatal estrogens and the development of homosexual orientation. *Developmental Psychology, 31,* 12–21.

Michaela, R., Florian, S., Gert, G. W., & Ulman, L. (2009). Seeking pleasure and seeking pain: Differences in prohedonic and contrahedonic motivation from adolescence to old age. *Psychological Science, 20*(12), 1529–1535.

Michelson, D., Pollack, M., Lydiard, R. D., Tamura, R., Tepner, R., & Tollefson, G. (1999). Continuing treatment of panic disorder after acute responses: Randomized, placebo-controlled trial with fluoxetine. The Fluoxetine Panic Disorder Study Group. *British Journal of Psychiatry, 174,* 213–218.

Mikels, J. A., Maglio, S. J., Reed, A. E., & Kaplowitz, L. J. (2011). Should I go with my gut? Investigating the benefits of emotion-focused decision making. *Emotion, 11*(4), 743–753.

Miklowitz, D. J., & Johnson, S. L. (2006). The psychopathology and treatment of bipolar disorder. *Annual Review of Clinical Psychology, 2,* 199–235.

Milan, A. (2011). *Migration: International, 2009.* (Catalogue no. 91-209-X). Ottawa: Statistics Canada.

Milgram, S. (1963). Behavioral study of obedience. *Journal of Abnormal and Social Psychology, 67,* 371–378.

Milgram, S. (1974). *Obedience to authority.* New York: Harper & Row.

Milgram, S., Bickman, L., & Berkowitz, O. (1969). Note on the drawing power of crowds of different size. *Journal of Personality and Social Psychology, 13*, 79–82.

Miller, A. J. (1986). *The obedience experiments: A case study of controversy in social science.* New York: Praeger.

Miller, C., Seckel, E., & Ramachandran, V. S. (2012). Using mirror box therapy to treat phatom pain in Haitian earthquake victims. *Journal of Vision, 12*, article 1323. doi:10.1167/12.9.1323

Miller, D. T., & Prentice, D. A. (1996). The construction of social norms and standards. In E. T. Higgins & A. W. Kruglanski (Ed.), *Social psychology: Handbook of basic principles* (pp. 799–829). New York: Guilford Press.

Miller, D. T., & Ratner, R. K. (1998). The disparity between the actual and assumed power of self-interest. *Journal of Personality and Social Psychology, 74*, 53–62.

Miller, D. T., & Ross, M. (1975). Self-serving biases in the attribution of causality: Fact or fiction? *Psychological Bulletin, 82*, 213–225.

Miller, G. A. (1956). The magical number seven, plus or minus two: Some limits on our capacity for processing information. *Psychological Review, 63*, 81–96.

Miller, K. F., Smith, C. M., & Zhu, J. (1995). Preschool origins of cross-national differences in mathematical competence: The role of number-naming systems. *Psychological Science, 6*, 56–60.

Miller, N. E. (1960). Motivational effects of brain stimulation and drugs. *Federation Proceedings, 19*, 846–854.

Miller, T. W. (Ed.). (1996). *Theory and assessment of stressful life events.* Madison, CT: International Universities Press.

Miller, W. R., & Rollnick, S. (2012). *Motivational interviewing: Helping people change* (3rd ed.). New York: Guilford Press.

Mills, P. J., & Dimsdale, J. E. (1991). Cardiovascular reactivity to psychosocial stressors. A review of the effects of beta-blockade. *Psychosomatics, 32*, 209–220.

Milne, E., & Grafman, J. (2001). Ventromedial prefrontal cortex lesions in humans eliminate implicit gender stereotyping. *Journal of Neuroscience, 21*, 1–6.

Milner, A. D., & Goodale, M. A. (1995). *The visual brain in action.* Oxford, England: Oxford University Press.

Milner, B. (1962). Laterality effects in audition. In V. B. Mountcastle (Ed.), *Interhemispheric relations and cerebral dominance* (pp. 177–195). Baltimore: Johns Hopkins University Press.

Mineka, S., & Cook, M. (1988). Social learning and the acquisition of snake fear in monkeys. In T. Zentall & B. G. Galef, Jr. (Eds.), *Social learning* (pp. 51–73). Hillsdale, NJ: Erlbaum.

Mineka, S., & Ohman, A. (2002). Born to fear: Non-associative vs. associative factors in the etiology of phobia. *Behaviour Research and Therapy, 40*, 173–184.

Mingroni, M. A. (2007). Resolving the IQ paradox: Heterosis as a cause of the Flynn effect and other trends. *Psychological Review, 114*, 806–829.

Minsky, M. (1986). *The society of mind.* New York: Simon & Schuster.

Minson, J. A., & Mueller, J. S. (2012). The cost of collaboration: Why joint decision making exacerbates rejection of outside information. *Psychological Science, 23*(3), 219–224. doi:10.1177/0956797611429132

Miranda, J., Bernal, G., Lau, A., Kihn, L., Hwang, W. C., & LaFramboise, T. (2005). State of the science on psychological interventions for ethnic minorities. *Annual Review of Clinical Psychology, 1*, 113–142.

Mischel, W. (1968). *Personality and assessment.* New York: Wiley.

Mischel, W. (2004). Toward an integrative science of the person. *Annual Review of Psychology, 55*, 1–22.

Mischel, W., Ayduk, O., Baumeister, R. F., & Vohs, K. D. (2004). Willpower in a cognitive-affective processing system: The dynamics of delay of gratification. In *Handbook of self-regulation: Research, theory, and applications* (pp. 99–129). New York: Guilford Press.

Mischel, W., & Shoda, Y. (1999). Integrating dispositions and processing dynamics within a unified theory of personality: The cognitive-affective personality system. In L. A. Pervin & O. P. John (Eds.), *Handbook of personality: Theory and research.* New York: Guilford Press.

Mischel, W., Shoda, Y., & Rodriguez, M. L. (1989). Delay of gratification in children. *Science, 244*, 933–938.

Mishra, A., & Mishra, H. (2010). Border bias: The belief that state borders can protect against disasters. *Psychological Science, 21*(11), 1582–1586. doi:10.1177/0956797610385950

Mita, T. H., Dermer, M., & Knight, J. (1977). Reversed facial images and the mere-exposure hypothesis. *Journal of Personality and Social Psychology, 35*, 597–601.

Mitchell, J. P. (2006). Mentalizing and Marr: An information processing approach to the study of social cognition. *Brain Research, 1079*, 66–75.

Mitchell, J. P., Heatherton, T. F., & Macrae, C. N. (2002). Distinct neural systems subserve person and object knowledge. *Proceedings of the National Academy of Sciences, USA, 99*, 15238–15243.

Mitchell, K. J., & Johnson, M. K. (2009). Source monitoring 15 years later: What have we learned from fMRI about the neural mechanisms of source memory? *Psychological Bulletin, 135*, 638–677.

Miura, I. T., Okamoto, Y., Kim, C. C., & Chang, C. M. (1994). Comparisons of children's cognitive representation of number: China, France, Japan, Korea, Sweden and the United States. *International Journal of Behavioral Development, 17*, 401–411.

Moffitt, T. E. (1993). Adolescence-limited and life-course-persistent antisocial behavior: A developmental taxonomy. *Psychological Review, 100*, 674–701.

Moffitt, T. E. (2005). Genetic and environmental influences on antisocial behaviors: Evidence from behavioral-genetic research. *Advances in Genetics, 55*, 41–104.

Moghaddam, B., & Bunney, B. S. (1989). Differential effect of cocaine on extracellular dopamine levels in rat medial prefrontal cortex and nucleus accumbens: Comparison to amphetamine. *Synapse, 4*, 156–161.

Mojtabai, R., Olfson, M., Sampson, N. A., Jin, R., Druss, B., Wang, P. S., … Kessler, R. C. (2011). Barriers to mental health treatment: Results from the National Comorbidity Survey replication. *Psychological Medicine, 41*(8), 1751–1761.

Molden, D., Lee, A. Y., & Higgins, E. T. (2009). Motivations for promotion and prevention. In J. Shah & W. Gardner (Eds.), *Handbook of motivation science* (pp. 169–187). New York: Guilford Press.

Monahan, J. (1992). Mental disorder and violent behavior: Perceptions and evidence. *American Psychologist, 47*, 511–521.

Monahan, J. L., Murphy, S. T., & Zajonc, R. B. (2000). Subliminal mere exposure: Specific, general, and diffuse effects. *Psychological Science, 11*, 462–466.

Moncrieff, J. (2009). A critique of the dopamine hypothesis of schizophrenia and psychosis. *Harvard Review of Psychiatry, 17*, 214–225.

Montague, C. T., Farooqi, I. S., Whitehead, J. P., Soos, M. A., Rau, H., Wareham, N. J., … O'Rahilly, S. (1997). Congenital leptin deficiency is associated with severe early-onset obesity in humans. *Nature, 387*(6636), 903–908.

Monti, M. M. (2012). Cognition in the vegetative state. *Annual Review of Clinical Psychology, 8*, 431–454.

Monti, M. M., Coleman, M. R., & Owen, A. M. (2009). Neuroimaging and the vegetative state: Resolving the behavioral assessment dilemma? *Annals of the New York Academy of Sciences, 1157*, 81–89.

**Monti, M. M., Vanhaudenhuyse, A., Coleman, M. R., Boly, M., Pickard, J. D., Tshibanda, L., ... Laureys, S.** (2010). Willful modulation of brain activity in disorders of consciousness. *New England Journal of Medicine, 362*, 579–589.

**Mook, D. G.** (1983). In defense of external invalidity. *American Psychologist, 38*, 379–387.

**Moon, S. M., & Illingworth, A. J.** (2005). Exploring the dynamic nature of procrastination: A latent growth curve analysis of academic procrastination. *Personality and Individual Differences, 38*, 297–309.

**Moore, E. G. J.** (1986). Family socialization and the IQ test performance of traditionally and transracially adopted Black children. *Developmental Psychology, 22*, 317–326.

**Moore, K. L.** (1977). *The developing human* (2nd ed.). Philadelphia: Saunders.

**Moran, P., Klinteberg, B. A., Batty, G. D., & Vågerö, D.** (2009). Brief report: Childhood intelligence predicts hospitalization with personality disorder in adulthood: Eveidence from a population-based study in Sweden. *Journal of Personality Disorders, 23*(5), 535–540. doi:10.1521/pedi.2009.23.5.535

**Moray, N.** (1959). Attention in dichotic listening: Affective cues and the influence of instructions. *Quarterly Journal of Experimental Psychology, 11*, 56–60.

**Moreno, S., Marques, C., Santos, A., Santos, M., Castro, S. L., & Besson, M.** (2009). Musical training influences linguistic abilities in 8-year-old children: More evidence for brain plasticity. *Cerebral Cortex, 19*, 712–723.

**Morewedge, C. K., & Norton, M. I.** (2009). When dreaming is believing: The (motivated) interpretation of dreams. *Journal of Personality and Social Psychology, 96*, 249–264.

**Morgenstern, J., Labouvie, E., McCrady, B. S., Kahler, C. W., & Frey, R. M.** (1997). Affiliation with Alcoholics Anonymous after treatment: A study of its therapeutic effects and mechanisms of action. *Journal of Consulting and Clinical Psychology, 65*, 768–777.

**Morin, A.** (2002). Right hemisphere self-awareness: A critical assessment. *Consciousness & Cognition, 11*, 396–401.

**Morin, A.** (2006). Levels of consciousness and self-awareness: A comparison of various neurocognitive views. *Consciousness & Cognition, 15*, 358–371.

**Morin, C. M., Bélanger, L., LeBlanc, M., Ivers, H., Savard, J., Espie, C. A., ... Grégoire, J. P.** (2009). The natural history of insomnia: A population-based 3-year longitudinal study. *Archives of Internal Medicine, 169*, 447–453.

**Morris, C. D., Bransford, J. D., & Franks, J. J.** (1977). Levels of processing versus transfer-appropriate processing. *Journal of Verbal Learning and Verbal Behavior, 16*, 519–533.

**Morris, R. G., Anderson, E., Lynch, G. S., & Baudry, M.** (1986). Selective impairment of learning and blockade of long-term potentiation by an N-methyl-D-aspartate receptor antagonist, AP5. *Nature, 319*, 774–776.

**Morris, T. L.** (2001). Social phobia. In M. W. Vasey & M. R. Dadds (Eds.), *The developmental psychopathology of anxiety* (pp. 435–458). New York: Oxford University Press.

**Morrow, D., Leirer, V., Altiteri, P., & Fitzsimmons, C.** (1994). When expertise reduces age differences in performance. *Psychology and Aging, 9*, 134–148.

**Moruzzi, G., & Magoun, H. W.** (1949). Brain stem reticular formation and activation of the EEG. *Electroencephalography and Clinical Neurophysiology, 1*, 455–473.

**Morwitz, V. G., & Pluzinski, C.** (1996). Do polls reflect opinions or do opinions reflect polls? *Journal of Consumer Research, 23*(1), 53–67.

**Mosby, I.** (2013). Administering colonial science: Nutrition research and human biomedical experimentation in Aboriginal communities and residential schools, 1942–1952. *Social History, 46*(91), 145-172. doi: 10.1353/his.2013.0015

**Moscovitch, M.** (1994). Memory and working-with-memory: Evaluation of a component process model and comparisons with other models. In D. L. Schacter & E. Tulving (Eds.), *Memory systems 1994* (pp. 269–310). Cambridge, MA: MIT Press.

**Moscovitch, M., Nadel, L., Winocur, G., Gilboa, A., & Rosenbaum, R. S.** (2006). The cognitive neuroscience of remote episodic, semantic and spatial memory. *Current Opinion in Neurobiology, 16*, 179–190.

**Motley, M. T., & Baars, B. J.** (1979). Effects of cognitive set upon laboratory induced verbal (Freudian) slips. *Journal of Speech & Hearing Research, 22*, 421–432.

**Moulin, C. J. A., Conway, M. A., Thompson, R. G., James, N., & Jones, R. W.** (2005). Disordered memory awareness: Recollective confabulation in two cases of persistent déjà vecu. *Neuropsychologia, 43*, 1362–1378.

**Moura, A. C. A. de, & Lee, P. C.** (2004). Capuchin stone tool use in Caatinga dry forest. *Science, 306*, 1909.

**Mroczek, D. K., & Spiro, A.** (2005). Change in life satisfaction during adulthood: Findings from the Veterans Affairs Normative Aging Study. *Journal of Personality and Social Psychology, 88*, 189.

**Muehlenkamp, J. J., Claes, L., Havertape, L., & Plener, P. L.** (2012). International prevalence of adolescent non-suicidal self-injury and deliberate self-harm. *Child and Adolescent Psychiatry and Mental Health, 6*(10). doi:10.1156/1753-2000-6-10

**Mueller, T. E., Gavin, L. E., & Kulkarni, A.** (2008). The association between sex education and youth's engagement in sexual intercourse, age at first intercourse, and birth control use at first sex. *The Journal of Adolescent Health, 42*(1), 89–96.

**Mueller, T. I., Leon, A. C., Keller, M. B., Solomon, D. A., Endicott, J., Coryell, W., ... Maser, J. D.** (1999). Recurrence after recovery from major depressive disorder during 15 years of observational follow-up. *American Journal of Psychiatry, 156*, 1000–1006.

**Muenter, M. D., & Tyce, G. M.** (1971). L-dopa therapy of Parkinson's disease: Plasma L-dopa concentration, therapeutic response, and side effects. *Mayo Clinic Proceedings, 46*, 231–239.

**Mullen, M. K.** (1994). Earliest recollections of childhood: A demographic analysis. *Cognition, 52*, 55–79.

**Muller, M. N., & Wrangham, R. W.** (2004). Dominance, aggression and testosterone in wild chimpanzees: A test of the "challenge hypothesis." *Animal Behaviour, 67*, 113–123.

**Multi-Society Task Force on PVS.** (1994). Medical aspects of the persistent vegetative state. *New England Journal of Medicine, 330*, 1499–1508.

**Murphy, N. A., Hall, J. A., & Colvin, C. R.** (2003). Accurate intelligence assessments in social interactions: Mediators and gender effects. *Journal of Personality, 71*, 465–493.

**Murray, C.** (2002). *IQ and income inequality in a sample of sibling pairs from advantaged family backgrounds.* Paper presented at the 114th Annual Meeting of the American Economic Association.

**Murray, H. A.** (1943). *Thematic Apperception Test manual.* Cambridge, MA: Harvard University Press.

**Murray, H. A., & Kluckhohn, C.** (1953). Outline of a conception of personality. In C. Kluckhohn, H. A. Murray, & D. M. Schneider (Eds.), *Personality in nature, society, and culture* (2nd ed., pp. 3–52). New York: Knopf.

**Myers, D. G., & Diener, E.** (1995). Who is happy? *Psychological Science, 6*, 10–19.

**Myers, D. G., & Lamm, H.** (1975). The polarizing effect of group discussion. *American Scientist, 63*(3), 297–303.

**Myles, P. S., Leslie, K., McNell, J., Forbes, A., & Chan, M. T. V.** (2004). Bispectral index monitoring to prevent awareness during anaesthesia: The B-Aware randomized controlled trial. *Lancet, 363,* 1757–1763.

**Nadasdy, A.** (1995). Phonetics, phonology, and applied linguistics. *Annual Review of Applied Linguistics, 15,* 68–77.

**Nader, K., & Hardt, O.** (2009). A single standard for memory: The case of reconsolidation. *Nature Reviews Neuroscience, 10,* 224–234.

**Nader, K., Shafe, G., & LeDoux, J. E.** (2000). Fear memories require protein synthesis in the amygdala for reconsolidation after retrieval. *Nature, 406,* 722–726.

**Nagasako, E. M., Oaklander, A. L., & Dworkin, R. H.** (2003). Congenital insensitivity to pain: An update. *Pain, 101,* 213–219.

**Nagell, K., Olguin, R. S., & Tomasello, M.** (1993). Processes of social learning in the tool use of chimpanzees (*Pan troglodytes*) and human children (*Homo sapiens*). *Journal of Comparative Psychology, 107,* 174–186.

**Nahemow, L., & Lawton, M. P.** (1975). Similarity and propinquity in friendship formation. *Journal of Personality and Social Psychology, 32,* 205–213.

**Nairne, J. S., & Pandeirada, J. N. S.** (2008). Adaptive memory: Remembering with a stone age brain. *Current Directions in Psychological Science, 17,* 239–243.

**Nairne, J. S., Pandeirada, J. N. S., & Thompson, S. R.** (2008). Adaptive memory: The comparative value of survival processing. *Psychological Science, 19,* 176–180.

**Nairne, J. S., Thompson, S. R., & Pandeirada, J. N. S.** (2007). Adaptive memory: Survival processing enhances retention. *Journal of Experimental Psychology: Learning, Memory, and Cognition, 33,* 263–273.

**Nakazato, M., Murakami, N., Date, Y., Kojima, M., Matsuo, H., Kangawa, K., & Matsukura, S.** (2001). A role for ghrelin in the central regulation of feeding. *Nature, 409,* 194–198.

**Naqvi, N., Shiv, B., & Bechara, A.** (2006). The role of emotion in decision making: A cognitive neuroscience perspective. *Current Directions in Psychological Science, 15,* 260–264.

**Nathan, P. E., & Gorman, J. M.** (2007). *A guide to treatments that work* (3rd ed.). New York: Oxford University Press.

**Nathanson, C., Paulhus, D. L., & Williams, K. M.** (2006). Personality and misconduct correlates of body modification and other cultural deviance markers. *Journal of Research in Personality, 40,* 779–802.

**National Center for Health Statistics.** (2004). *Health, United States, 2004* (with chartbook on trends in the health of Americans). Hyattsville, MD: Author.

**National Research Council.** (2003). *The polygraph and lie detection.* Washington, DC: National Academies Press.

**National Science Foundation (NSF).** (2008). *Science and engineering indicators 2008.* Arlington, VA: National Science Foundation. Retrieved from http://www.nsf.gov/statistics/seind08/c0/c0i.htm

**Naumann, L. P., Vazire, S., Rentfrow, P. J., & Gosling, S. D.** (2009). Personality judgments based on physical appearance. *Personality & Social Psychology Bulletin, 35,* 1661–1671.

**NEDSAC.** (2012). *Findings from NEDSAC: Changes in the prevalence of autism spectrum disorders in Newfoundland and Labrador, Prince Edward Island, and Southeastern Ontario.* Retrieved from http://www.autismsocietycanada.ca/DocsAndMedia/KeyReports/NEDSAC_Report_March2012_Key_Findings.pdf

**Neihart, M.** (1999). The impact of giftedness on psychological well being: What does the empirical literature say? *Roeper Review, 22*(1), 10–17.

**Neimark, J.** (2004, July/August). The power of coincidence. *Psychology Today,* pp. 47–52.

**Neimeyer, R. A., & Mitchell, K. A.** (1988). Similarity and attraction: A longitudinal study. *Journal of Social and Personal Relationships, 5,* 131–148.

**Neisser, U.** (1967). *Cognitive psychology.* New York: Appleton-Century- Crofts.

**Neisser, U. (Ed.).** (1998). *The rising curve: Long-term gains in IQ and related measures.* Washington, DC: American Psychological Association.

**Neisser, U., Boodoo, G., Bouchard, T. J., Jr., Boykin, A. W., Brody, N., Ceci, S. J., … Loehlin, J. C.** (1996). Intelligence: Knowns and unknowns. *American Psychologist, 51,* 77–101.

**Neisser, U., & Harsch, N.** (1992). Phantom flashbulbs: False recollections of hearing the news about *Challenger.* In E. Winograd & U. Neisser (Eds.), *Affect and accuracy in recall: Studies of "flashbulb memories"* (pp. 9–31). Cambridge, England: Cambridge University Press.

**Nelson, C. A., Zeanah, C. H., Fox, N. A., Marshall, P. J., Smyke, A. T., & Guthrie, D.** (2007). Cognitive recovery in socially deprived young children: The Bucharest early intervention project. *Science, 318,* 1937–1940.

**Nemeth, C., & Chiles, C.** (1988). Modelling courage: The role of dissent in fostering independence. *European Journal of Social Psychology, 18,* 275–280.

**Neuberg, S. L., Kenrick, D. T., & Schaller, M.** (2010). Evolutionary social psychology. In S. T. Fiske, D. T. Gilbert, & G. Lindzey (Eds.), *The handbook of social psychology* (5th ed., Vol. 2, pp. 761–796). New York: Wiley.

**Neugebauer, R., Hoek, H. W., & Susser, E.** (1999). Prenatal exposure to wartime famine and development of antisocial personality in early adulthood. *Journal of the American Medical Association, 282,* 455–462.

**Newbold, B.** (2009). The short-term health of Canada's new immigrant arrivals: Evidence from the LSIC. *Ethnicity and Health, 14*(3), 315–336.

**Newbold, R. R., Padilla-Banks, E., Snyder, R. J., & Jefferson, W. N.** (2005). Developmental exposure to estrogenic compounds and obesity. *Birth Defects Research Part A: Clinical and Molecular Teratology, 73,* 478–480.

**Newell, A., Shaw, J. C., & Simon, H. A.** (1958). Elements of a theory of human problem solving. *Psychological Review, 65,* 151–166.

**Newman, A. J., Bavelier, D., Corina, D., Jezzard, P., & Neville, H. J.** (2002). A critical period for right hemisphere recruitment in American Sign Language processing. *Nature Neuroscience, 5,* 76–80.

**Newman, J. P., Wolff, W. T., & Hearst, E.** (1980). The feature-positive effect in adult human subjects. *Journal of Experimental Psychology: Human Learning and Memory, 6,* 630–650.

**Newman, M. G., & Stone, A. A.** (1996). Does humor moderate the effects of experimentally induced stress? *Annals of Behavioral Medicine, 18,* 101–109.

**Newschaffer, C. J., Croen, L. A., Daniels, J., Giarelli, E., Grether, J. K., Levy, S. E., … Windham, G. C.** (2007). The epidemiology of autism spectrum disorders. *Annual Review of Public Health, 28,* 235–258.

**Newsome, W. T., & Paré, E. B.** (1988). A selective impairment of motion perception following lesions of the middle temporal visual area (MT). *Journal of Neuroscience, 8,* 2201–2211.

**Neylan, T. C., Metzler, T. J., Best, S. R., Weiss, D. S., Fagan, J. A., Libermans, A., … Marmar, C. R.** (2002). Critical incident exposure and sleep quality in police officers. *Psychosomatic Medicine, 64,* 345–352.

**Niaura, R., Todaro, J. F., Stroud, L., Spiro, A. III, Ward, K. D., & Weiss, S.** (2002). Hostility, the metabolic syndrome, and incident coronary heart disease. *Health Psychology, 21,* 588–593.

**Nicoladis, E., & Genesee, F.** (1997). Language development in preschool bilingual children. *Journal of Speech-Language Pathology & Audiology, 21,* 258–270.

**Niedenthal, P. M., Barsalou, L. W., Winkielman, P., Krauth-Gruber, S., & Ric, F.** (2005). Embodiment in attitudes, social perception, and emotion. *Personality and Social Psychology Review, 9*(3), 184–211.

**Nikles, C. D., II, Brecht, D. L., Klinger, E., & Bursell, A. L.** (1998). The effects of current concern- and nonconcern-related waking suggestions on nocturnal dream content. *Journal of Personality and Social Psychology, 75,* 242–255.

**Nikula, R., Klinger, E., & Larson-Gutman, M. K.** (1993). Current concerns and electrodermal reactivity: Responses to words and thoughts. *Journal of Personality, 61,* 63–84.

**Nir, Y., & Tononi, G.** (2010). Dreaming and the brain: From phenomenology to neurophysiology. *Trends in Cognitive Sciences, 14*(2), 88–100.

**Nisbett, R. E.** (2009). *Intelligence and how to get it.* New York: Norton.

**Nisbett, R. E., Aronson, J., Blair, C., Dickens, W., Flynn, J., Halpern, D. F., & Turkheimer, E.** (2012). Intelligence: New findings and theoretical developments. *American Psychologist, 67*(2), 130–159. doi:10.1037/a0026699

**Nisbett, R. E., Caputo, C., Legant, P., & Maracek, J.** (1973). Behavior as seen by the actor and as seen by the observer. *Journal of Personality and Social Psychology, 27,* 154–164.

**Nisbett, R. E., & Cohen, D.** (1996). *Culture of honor: The psychology of violence in the South.* Boulder, CO: Westview Press.

**Nisbett, R. E., & Miyamoto, Y.** (2005). The influence of culture: Holistic versus analytic perception. *Trends in Cognitive Sciences, 9,* 467–473.

**Nissen, M. J., & Bullemer, P.** (1987). Attentional requirements of learning: Evidence from performance measures. *Cognitive Psychology, 19,* 1–32.

**Nitschke, J. B., Dixon, G. E., Sarianopoulos, I., Short, S. J., Cohen, J. D., Smith, E. E., ... Davidson, R. J.** (2006). Altering expectancy dampens neural response to aversive taste in primary taste cortex. *Neuroscience, 9,* 435–442.

**Nock, M. K.** (2009). Why do people hurt themselves? New insights into the nature and functions of self-injury. *Current Directions in Psychological Science, 18,* 78–83. doi:10.1111/j.1467-8721.2009.01613.x

**Nock, M. K.** (2010). Self-injury. *Annual Review of Clinical Psychology, 6,* 339–363. doi: 10.1146/annurev.clinpsy.121208.131258

**Nock, M. K., Borges, G., Bromet, E. J., Alonso, J., Angermeyer, M., Beautrais, A., ... Williams, D.** (2008). Cross-national prevalence and risk factors for suicidal ideation, plans, and attempts. *British Journal of Psychiatry, 192,* 98–105.

**Nock, M. K., Borges, G., & Ono, Y. (Eds.).** (2012). *Suicide: Global perspectives from the WHO World Mental Health Surveys.* New York: Cambridge University Press.

**Nock, M. K., Green, J. G., Hwang, I., McLaughlin, K. A., Sampson, N. A., Zaslavsky, A. M., & Kessler, R. C.** (2013). Prevalence, correlates and treatment of lifetime suicidal behavior among adolescents: Results from the National Comorbidity Survey Replication–Adolescent Supplement (NCSA–A). *Journal of the American Medical Association Psychiatry, 70*(3), 300–310. doi:10.1001/2013.jamapsychiatry.55

**Nock, M. K., Holmberg, E. G., Photos, V. I., & Michel, B. D.** (2007). Structured and semi-structured interviews. In M. Hersen & J. C. Thomas (Eds.), *Handbook of clinical interviewing with children* (pp. 30–49). Thousand Oaks, CA: Sage.

**Nock, M. K., Kazdin, A. E., Hiripi, E., & Kessler, R. C.** (2006). Prevalence, subtypes, and correlates of *DSM–IV* conduct disorder in the National Comorbidity Survey Replication. *Psychological Medicine, 36,* 699–710.

**Nolen-Hoeksema, S.** (2008). Gender differences in coping with depression across the lifespan. *Depression, 3,* 81–90.

**Norrholm, S. D., & Ressler, K. J.** (2009). Genetics of anxiety and trauma-related disorders. *Neuroscience, 164,* 272–287.

**Norton, M. I., Frost, J. H., & Ariely, D.** (2007). Less is more: The lure of ambiguity, or why familiarity breeds contempt. *Journal of Personality and Social Psychology, 92*(1), 97–105. doi:10.1037/0022-3514.92.1.97

**Nosanchuk, T. A., & Lightstone, J.** (1974). Canned laughter and public and private conformity. *Journal of Personality and Social Psychology, 29,* 153–156.

**Nowak, M. A.** (2006). Five rules for the evolution of cooperation. *Science, 314,* 1560–1563.

**Nuttin, J. M.** (1985). Narcissism beyond Gestalt and awareness: The name letter effect. *European Journal of Social Psychology, 15,* 353–361.

**Nyborg, H., & Jensen, A. R.** (2001). Occupation and income related to psychometric g. *Intelligence, 29,* 45–55.

**Oately, K., Keltner, D., & Jenkins, J. M.** (2006). *Understanding emotions* (2nd ed.). Malden, MA: Blackwell.

**Ochsner, K. N.** (2000). Are affective events richly recollected or simply familiar? The experience and process of recognizing feelings past. *Journal of Experimental Psychology: General, 129,* 242–261.

**Ochsner, K. N., Bunge, S. A., Gross, J. J., & Gabrieli, J. D. E.** (2002). Rethinking feelings: An fMRI study of the cognitive regulation of emotion. *Journal of Cognitive Neuroscience, 14,* 1215–1229.

**Ochsner, K. N., Ray, R. R., Hughes, B., McRae, K., Cooper, J. C., Weber, J., ... Gross, J. J.** (2009). Bottom-up and top-down processes in emotion generation: Common and distinct neural mechanisms. *Psychological Science, 20,* 1322–1331.

**O'Connor, T. G., & Rutter, M.** (2000). Attachment disorder following early severe deprivation: Extension and longitudinal follow-up. *Journal of the American Academy of Child and Adolescent Psychiatry, 39,* 703–712.

**O'Doherty, J. P., Dayan, P., Friston, K., Critchley, H., & Dolan, R. J.** (2003). Temporal difference models and reward-related learning in the human brain. *Neuron, 38,* 329–337.

**OECD.** (2013) Health at a glance 2013: OECD indicators. *OECD Publishing.* Retrieved from http://www.oecd.org/els/health-systems/Health-at-a-Glance-2013.pdf

**Ofshe, R. J.** (1992). Inadvertent hypnosis during interrogation: False confession due to dissociative state, misidentified multiple personality, and the satanic cult hypothesis. *International Journal of Clinical and Experimental Hypnosis, 40,* 125–126.

**Ofshe, R., & Watters, E.** (1994). *Making monsters: False memories, psychotherapy, and sexual hysteria.* New York: Scribner/Macmillan.

**Ohayon, M. M.** (2002). Epidemiology of insomnia: What we know and what we still need to learn. *Sleep Medicine, 6,* 97–111.

**Ohayon, M. M., Guilleminault, C., & Priest, R. G.** (1999). Night terrors, sleepwalking, and confusional arousals in the general population: Their frequency and relationship to other sleep and mental disorders. *Journal of Clinical Psychiatry, 60,* 268–276.

**Öhman, A.** (1996). Preferential preattentive processing of threat in anxiety: Preparedness and attentional biases. In R. M. Rapee (Ed.), *Current controversies in the anxiety disorders.* New York: Guilford Press.

Öhman, A., Dimberg, U., & Öst, L. G. (1985). Animal and social phobias: Biological constraints on learned fear responses. In S. Reiss & R. Bootzin (Eds.), *Theoretical issues in behavior therapy* (pp. 123–175). New York: Academic Press.

Okagaki, L., & Sternberg, R. J. (1993). Parental beliefs and children's school performance. *Child Development, 64,* 36–56.

Okuda, J., Fujii, T., Ohtake, H., Tsukiura, T., Tanji, K., Suzuki, K., ... Yamadori, A. (2003). Thinking of the future and the past: The roles of the frontal pole and the medial temporal lobes. *NeuroImage, 19,* 1369–1380.

Okulicz-Kozaryn, A. (2011). Europeans work to live and Americans live to work (Who is happy to work more: Americans or Europeans?) *Journal of Happiness Studies, 12*(2), 225–243.

Olatunji, B. O., & Wolitzky-Taylor, K. B. (2009). Anxiety sensitivity and the anxiety disorders: A meta-analytic review and synthesis. *Psychological Bulletin, 135,* 974–999.

O'Laughlin, M. J., & Malle, B. F. (2002). How people explain actions performed by groups and individuals. *Journal of Personality and Social Psychology, 82,* 33–48.

Olausson, P. O., Haglund, B., Weitoft, G. R., & Cnattingius, S. (2001). Teenage child-bearing and long-term socioeconomic consequences: A case study in Sweden. *Family Planning Perspectives, 33,* 70–74.

Olds, J. (1956, October). Pleasure center in the brain. *Scientific American, 195,* 105–116.

Olds, J., & Fobes, J. I. (1981). The central basis of motivation: Intracranial self-stimulation studies. *Annual Review of Psychology, 32,* 523–574.

Olds, J., & Milner, P. (1954). Positive reinforcement produced by electrical stimulation of septal areas and other regions of rat brains. *Journal of Comparative and Physiological Psychology, 47,* 419–427.

Ollers, D. K., & Eilers, R. E. (1988). The role of audition in infant babbling. *Child Development, 59,* 441–449.

Olofsson, J. K., Bowman, N. E., Khatibi, K., & Gottfried, J. A. (2012). A time-based account of the perception of odor objects and valences. *Psychological Science, 23,* 1224–1232.

Olsson, A., & Phelps, E. A. (2007). Social learning of fear. *Nature Neuroscience, 10,* 1095–1102.

Oltmanns, T. F., Neale, J. M., & Davison, G. C. (1991). *Case studies in abnormal psychology* (3rd ed.). New York: Wiley.

Olton, D. S., & Samuelson, R. J. (1976). Remembrance of places passed: Spatial memory in rats. *Journal of Experimental Psychology: Animal Behavior Processes, 2,* 97–116.

Onishi, K. H., & Baillargeon, R. (2005). Do 15-month-old infants understand false beliefs? *Science, 308,* 255–258.

Ono, K. (1987). Superstitious behavior in humans. *Journal of the Experimental Analysis of Behavior, 47,* 261–271.

Ontario Ministry of Children and Youth Services. (2010). *Review of the roots of youth violence: Literature reviews—Volume 5: Deterrence strategies.* Retrieved from http://www.children.gov.on.ca/htdocs/English/topics/youthandthelaw/roots/volume5/preventing04_deterrence.aspx

OPHEA. (2013). *Sexual health education in schools across Canada.* Toronto: Author.

Ophir, E., Nass, C., & Wagner, A. D. (2009). Cognitive control in media multitaskers. *Proceedings of the National Academy of Sciences, USA, 106,* 15583–15587.

Orban, P., Lungu, O., & Doyon, J. (2008). Motor sequence learning and developmental dyslexia. *Annals of the New York Academy of Sciences, 1145,* 151–172.

Ormel, J., Petukhova, M., Chatterji, S., Aguilar-Gaxiola, S., Alonso, J., Angermeyer, M. C., ... Kessler, R. C. (2008). Disability and treatment of specific mental and physical disorders across the world: Results from the WHO World Mental Health Surveys. *British Journal of Psychiatry, 192,* 368–375.

Ospina, M., & Harstall, C. (2002). *Prevalence of chronic pain: An overview.* (Health Technology Assessment 29). Edmonton, AB: Alberta Heritage Foundation for Medical Research.

O'Sullivan, L. F., & Allegeier, E. R. (1998). Feigning sexual desire: Consenting to unwanted sexual activity in heterosexual dating relationships. *Journal of Sex Research, 35,* 234–243.

Oswald, L., Taylor, A. M., & Triesman, M. (1960). Discriminative responses to stimulation during human sleep. *Brain, 83,* 440–453.

Otto, M. W., Henin, A., Hirshfeld-Becker, D. R., Pollack, M. H., Biederman, J., & Rosenbaum, J. F. (2007). Posttraumatic stress disorder symptoms following media exposure to tragic events: Impact of 9/11 on children at risk for anxiety disorders. *Journal of Anxiety Disorders, 21,* 888–902.

Owen, A. M., & Coleman, M. R. (2008). Functional neuroimaging of the vegetative state. *Nature Reviews Neuroscience, 9,* 235–243.

Owen, A. M., Coleman, M. R., Boly, M., Davis, M. H., Laureys, S., & Pickard, J. D. (2006). Detecting awareness in the vegetative state. *Science, 313,* 1402.

Owens, W. A. (1966). Age and mental abilities: A second adult follow-up. *Journal of Educational Psychology, 57,* 311–325.

Oztekin, I., Curtis, C. E., & McElree, B. (2009). The medial temporal lobe and left inferior prefrontal cortex jointly support interference resolution in verbal working memory. *Journal of Cognitive Neuroscience, 21,* 1967–1979.


Pagnin, D., de Queiroz, V., Pini, S., & Cassano, G. B. (2008). Efficacy of ECT in depression: A meta-analytic review. *Focus, 6,* 155–162.

Paivio, A. (1971). *Imagery and verbal processes.* New York: Holt, Rinehart and Winston.

Paivio, A. (1986). *Mental representations: A dual coding approach.* New York: Oxford University Press.

Palermo, T. M., Eccleston, C., Lewandowski, A. S., Williams, A. C., & Morley, S. (2011). Randomized controlled trials of psychological therapies for management of chronic pain in children and adolescents: An updated meta-analytic review. *Pain, 148,* 387–397.

Pantev, C., Oostenveld, R., Engelien, A., Ross, B., Roberts, L. E., & Hoke, M. (1998). Increased auditory cortical representation in musicians. *Nature, 392,* 811–814.

Papez, J. W. (1937). A proposed mechanism of emotion. *Archives of Neurology and Pathology, 38,* 725–743.

Parbery-Clark, A., Skoe, E., & Kraus, N. (2009). Musical experience limits the degradative effects of background noise on the neural processing of sound. *Journal of Neuroscience, 11,* 14100–14107.

Parbery-Clark, A., Strait, D. L., Anderson, S., Hittner, E., & Kraus, N. (2011). Musical experience and the aging auditory system: Implications for cognitive abilities and hearing speech in noise. *PLoS One, 6,* e18082.

Parbery-Clark, A., Tierney, A., Strait, D. L., & Kraus, N. (2012). Musicians have fine-tuned neural distinction of speech syllables. *Neuroscience, 219,* 111–119.

Park, B., & Hastie, R. (1987). Perception of variability in category development: Instance- versus abstraction-based stereotypes. *Journal of Personality and Social Psychology, 53*(4), 621–635. doi:10.1037/0022-3514.53.4.621

Park, D. C., & McDonough, I. M. (2013). The dynamic aging mind: Revelations from functional neuroimaging research. *Perspectives on Psychological Science, 8*(1), 62–67. doi:10.1177/1745691612469034

**Park, D. C., Polk, T. A., Park, R., Minear, M., Savage, A., & Smith, M. R.** (2004). Aging reduces neural specialization in ventral visual cortex. *Proceedings of the National Academy of Sciences, USA, 101*(35), 13091–13095. doi:10.1073/pnas.0405148101

**Parker, E. S., Cahill, L. S., & McGaugh, J. L.** (2006). A case of unusual autobiographical remembering. *Neurocase, 12,* 35–49.

**Parker, G., Gibson, N. A., Brotchie, H., Heruc, G., Rees, A. M., & Hadzi-Pavlovic, D.** (2006). Omega-3 fatty acids and mood disorders. *American Journal of Psychiatry, 163,* 969–978.

**Parker, H. A., & McNally, R. J.** (2008). Repressive coping, emotional adjustment, and cognition in people who have lost loved ones to suicide. *Suicide and Life-Threatening Behavior, 38,* 676–687.

**Parkinson, B., & Totterdell, P.** (1999). Classifying affect-regulation strategies. *Cognition and Emotion, 13,* 277–303.

**Parks, C. D., & Stone, A. B.** (2010). The desire to expel unselfish members from the group. *Journal of Personality and Social Psychology, 99*(2), 303–310. doi:10.1037/a0018403

**Parrott, A. C.** (2001). Human psychopharmacology of Ecstasy (MDMA): A review of 15 years of empirical research. *Human Psychopharmacology, 16,* 557–577.

**Parrott, A. C., Morinan, A., Moss, M., & Scholey, A.** (2005). *Understanding drugs and behavior.* Chichester, England: Wiley.

**Parrott, W. G.** (1993). Beyond hedonism: Motives for inhibiting good moods and for maintaining bad moods. In D. M. Wegner & J. W. Pennebaker (Eds.), *Handbook of mental control* (pp. 278–308). Englewood Cliffs, NJ: Prentice Hall.

**Parsons, T.** (1975). The sick role and the role of the physician reconsidered. *Milbank Memorial Fund Quarterly, Health and Society, 53*(3), 257–278.

**Pascual-Ferrá, P., Liu, Y., & Beatty, M. J.** (2012). A meta-analytic comparison of the effects of text messaging to substance-induced impairment on driving performance. *Communication Research Reports, 29,* 229–238.

**Pascual-Leone, A., Amedi, A., Fregni, F., & Merabet, L. B.** (2005). The plastic human brain cortex. *Annual Review of Neuroscience, 28,* 377–401.

**Pascual-Leone, A., Houser, C. M., Reese, K., Shotland, L. I., Grafman, J., Sato, S., ... Cohen, L. G.** (1993). Safety of rapid-rate transcranial magnetic stimulation in normal volunteers. *Electroencephalography and Clinical Neurophysiology, 89,* 120–130.

**Passini, F. T., & Norman, W. T.** (1966). A universal conception of personality structure? *Journal of Personality and Social Psychology, 4,* 44–49.

**Pasupathi, M., McLean, K. C., & Weeks, T.** (2009). To tell or not to tell: Disclosure and the narrative self. *Journal of Personality, 77,* 1–35.

**Patall, E. A., Cooper, H., & Robinson, J. C.** (2008). The effects of choice on intrinsic motivation and related outcomes: A meta-analysis of research findings. *Psychological Bulletin, 134*(2), 270–300.

**Patrick, C. J., Cuthbert, B. N., & Lang, P. J.** (1994). Emotion in the criminal psychopath: Fear image processing. *Journal of Abnormal Psychology, 103,* 523–534.

**Patterson, C. J.** (1995). Lesbian mothers, gay fathers, and their children. In A. R. D'Augelli & C. J. Patterson (Eds.), *Lesbian, gay and bisexual identities across the lifespan: Psychological perspectives* (pp. 262–290). New York: Oxford University Press.

**Paus, T.** (2005). Mapping brain maturation and cognitive development during adolescence. *Trends in Cognitive Science, 9,* 60–68.

**Paus, T., Zijdenbos, A., Worsley, K., Collins, D. L., Blumenthal, J., Giedd, J. N., ... Evans, A. C.** (1999). Structural maturation of neural pathways in children and adolescents: In vivo study. *Science, 283*(5409), 1908–1911.

**Pavlidis, I., Eberhardt, N. L., & Levine, J. A.** (2002). Human behaviour: Seeing through the face of deception. *Nature, 415,* 35.

**Pavlidou, E. V., Williams, J. M., & Kelly, L. M.** (2009). Artificial grammar learning in primary school children with and without developmental dyslexia. *Annals of Dyslexia, 59,* 55–77.

**Pavlov, I. P.** (1923a). New researches on conditioned reflexes. *Science, 58,* 359–361.

**Pavlov, I. P.** (1923b, July 23). Pavloff. *Time, 1*(21), 20–21.

**Pavlov, I. P.** (1927). *Conditioned reflexes.* Oxford, England: Oxford University Press.

**Payne, J. D., Schacter, D. L., Propper, R., Huang, L., Wamsley, E., Tucker, M. A., ... Stickgold, R.** (2009). The role of sleep in false memory formation. *Neurobiology of Learning and Memory, 92,* 327–334.

**Payne, J. D., Stickgold, R., Swanberg, K., & Kensinger, E. A.** (2008). Sleep preferentially enhances memory for emotional components of scenes. *Psychological Science, 19,* 781–788.

**Pearce, J. M.** (1987). A model of stimulus generalization for Pavlovian conditioning. *Psychological Review, 84,* 61–73.

**Peck, J., & Shu, S. B.** (2009). The effect of mere touch on perceived ownership. *Journal of Consumer Research, 36,* 434–447.

**Peelen, M. V., & Kastner, S.** (2009). A nonvisual look at the functional organization of visual cortex. *Neuron, 63,* 284–286.

**Peeters. A. L., Barendregt, J. J., Willekens, F., Mackenbach, J. P., Al Mamun, A., Bonneux, L., & Netherlands Epidemiology and Demography Compression of Morbidity Research Group (NEDCOM).** (2003). Obesity in adulthood and its consequences for life expectancy: A life table analysis. *Annals of Internal Medicine, 138,* 24–32.

**Peissig, J. J., & Tarr, M. J.** (2007). Visual object recognition: Do we know more now than we did 20 years ago? *Annual Review of Psychology, 58,* 75–96.

**Pelham, B. W.** (1985). Self-investment and self-esteem: Evidence for a Jamesian model of self-worth. *Journal of Personality and Social Psychology, 69,* 1141–1150.

**Pelham, B. W., Carvallo, M., & Jones, J. T.** (2005). Implicit egotism. *Current Directions in Psychological Science, 14,* 106–110.

**Pelham, B. W., Mirenberg, M. C., & Jones, J. T.** (2002). Why Susie sells seashells by the seashore: Implicit egotism and major life decisions. *Journal of Personality and Social Psychology, 82,* 469–487.

**Penfield, W., & Rasmussen, T.** (1950). *The cerebral cortex of man: A clinical study of localization of function.* New York: Macmillan.

**Pennebaker, J. W.** (1980). Perceptual and environmental determinants of coughing. *Basic and Applied Social Psychology, 1,* 83–91.

**Pennebaker, J. W.** (1989). Confession, inhibition, and disease. *Advances in Experimental Social Psychology, 22,* 211–244.

**Pennebaker, J. W., & Chung, C. K.** (2007). Expressive writing, emotional upheavals, and health. In H. Friedman & R. Silver (Eds.), *Handbook of health psychology* (pp. 263–284). New York: Oxford University Press.

**Pennebaker, J. W., Kiecolt-Glaser, J. K., & Glaser, R.** (1988). Disclosure of traumas and immune function: Health implications for psychotherapy. *Journal of Consulting and Clinical Psychology, 56,* 239–245.

**Pennebaker, J. W., & Sanders, D. Y.** (1976). American graffiti: Effects of authority and reactance arousal. *Personality and Social Psychology Bulletin, 2,* 264–267.

**Penner, L. A., Albrecht, T. L., Orom, H., Coleman, D. K., & Underwood, W.** (2010). Health and health care disparities. In J. F. Dovidio, M. Hewstone, P. Glick, & V. M. Esses (Eds.), *The Sage* *handbook of prejudice, stereotyping and discrimination* (pp. 472–489). Thousand Oaks, CA: Sage.

**Perenin, M.-T., & Vighetto, A.** (1988). Optic ataxia: A specific disruption in visuomotor mechanisms. I. Different aspects of the deficit in reaching for objects. *Brain, 111,* 643–674.

**Perilloux, H. K., Webster, G. D., & Gaulin, S. J. C.** (2010). Signals of genetic quality and maternal investment capacity: The dynamic effects of fluctuating asymmetry and waist-to-hip ratio on men's ratings of women's attractiveness. *Social Psychological and Personality Science, 1*(1), 34–42. doi:10.1177/1948550609349514

**Perkins, D. N., & Grotzer, T. A.** (1997). Teaching intelligence. *American Psychologist, 52,* 1125–1133.

**Perlmutter, J. S., & Mink, J. W.** (2006). Deep brain stimulation. *Annual Review of Neuroscience, 29,* 229–257.

**Perloff, L. S., & Fetzer, B. K.** (1986). Self-other judgments and perceived vulnerability to victimization. *Journal of Personality and Social Psychology, 50,* 502–510.

**Perls, F. S., Hefferkine, R., & Goodman, P.** (1951). *Gestalt therapy: Excitement and growth in the human personality.* New York: Julian Press.

**Perrett, D. I., Burt, D. M., Penton-Voak, I. S., Lee, K. J., Rowland, D. A., & Edwards, R.** (1999). Symmetry and human facial attractiveness. *Evolution and Human Behavior, 20,* 295–307.

**Perrett, D. I., Rolls, E. T., & Caan, W.** (1982). Visual neurones responsive to faces in the monkey temporal cortex. *Experimental Brain Research, 47,* 329–342.

**Perry, R., & Sibley, C. G.** (2012). Big Five personality prospectively predicts social dominance orientation and right wing authoritarianism. *Personality and Individual Differences, 52,* 3–8.

**Perry, R. B.** (1996). *The thought and character of William James.* Nashville: Vanderbilt University Press. (Original work published 1935)

**Pessiglione, M., Seymour, B., Flandin, G., Dolan, R. J., & Frith, C. D.** (2006). Dopamine-dependent prediction errors underpin reward-seeking behavior in humans. *Nature, 442,* 1042–1045.

**Petersen, A. C., & Grockett, L.** (1985). Pubertal timing and grade effects on adjustment. *Journal of Youth and Adolescence, 14,* 191–206.

**Petersen, J. L., & Hyde, J. S.** (2010). A meta-analytic review of research on gender differences in sexuality, 1993–2007. *Psychological Bulletin, 136*(1), 21–38. doi:10.1037/a0017504

**Peterson, C., & Siegal, M.** (1999). Representing inner worlds: Theory of mind in autistic, deaf and normal hearing children. *Psychological Science, 10,* 126–129.

**Peterson, C., Wang, Q., & Hou, Y.** (2009). "When I was little": Childhood recollections in Chinese and European Canadian grade school children. *Child Development, 80,* 506–518.

**Peterson, G. B.** (2004). A day of great illumination: B. F. Skinner's discovery of shaping. *Journal of the Experimental Analysis of Behavior, 82,* 317–328.

**Peterson, L. R., & Peterson, M. J.** (1959). Short-term retention of individual verbal items. *Journal of Experimental Psychology, 58,* 193–198.

**Peterson, S. E., Fox, P. T., Posner, M. I., Mintun, M. A., & Raichle, M. E.** (1989). Positron emission tomographic studies of the processing of single words. *Journal of Cognitive Neuroscience, 1,* 154–170.

**Petersson, K. M., Forkstam, C., & Ingvar, M.** (2004). Artificial syntactic violations activate Broca's region. *Cognitive Science, 28,* 383–407.

**Petitto, L. A., & Marentette, P. F.** (1991). Babbling in the manual mode: Evidence for the ontogeny of language. *Science, 251,* 1493–1496.

**Petrie, K. P., Booth, R. J., & Pennebaker, J. W.** (1998). The immunological effects of thought suppression. *Journal of Personality and Social Psychology, 75,* 1264–1272.

**Petry, N. M., Alessi, S. M., & Rash, C. J.** (2013). Contingency management treatments decrease psychiatric symptoms. *Journal of Consulting and Clinical Psychology, 81*(5), 926–931. doi:10.1037/a0032499

**Petty, R. E., & Cacioppo, J. T.** (1986). The elaboration likelihood model of persuasion. In L. Berkowitz (Ed.), *Advances in experimental social psychology* (Vol. 19, pp. 123–205). New York: Academic Press.

**Petty, R. E., Cacioppo, J. T., & Goldman, R.** (1981). Personal involvement as a determinant of argument-based persuasion. *Journal of Personality and Social Psychology, 41,* 847–855.

**Petty, R. E., & Wegener, D. T.** (1998). Attitude change: Multiple roles for persuasion variables. In D. T. Gilbert, S. T. Fiske, & G. Lindzey (Eds.), *The handbook of social psychology* (4th ed., Vol. 1, pp. 323–390). Boston: McGraw-Hill.

**Pew Research Center for People & the Press.** (1997). *Motherhood today: A tougher job, less ably done.* Washington, DC: Author.

**Pew Research Center for People & the Press.** (2009). *Growing old in America: Expectations vs. reality.* Retrieved May 3, 2010, from http://pewsocialtrends.org/pubs/736/getting-old-in-america

**Pew Research Center Global Attitudes Project.** (2013, June 4). *The global divide on homosexuality.* Retrieved from http://www.pewglobal.org/2013/06/04/the-global-divide-on-homosexuality/

**Pham, M. T., Lee, L., & Stephen, A. T.** (2012). Feeling the future: The emotional oracle effect. *Journal of Consumer Research, 39*(3), 461–477.

**Phelan, J., Link, B., Stueve, A., & Pescosolido, B.** (1997, August). *Public conceptions of mental illness in 1950 in 1996: Has sophistication increased? Has stigma declined?* Paper presented at the American Sociological Association, Toronto, Ontario.

**Phelps, E. A.** (2006). Emotion and cognition: Insights from studies of the human amygdala. *Annual Review of Psychology, 24,* 27–53.

**Phelps, E. A., & LeDoux, J. L.** (2005). Contributions of the amygdala to emotion processing: From animal models to human behavior. *Neuron, 48,* 175–187.

**Phills, C. E., Kawakami, K., Tabi, E., Nadolny, D., & Inzlicht, M.** (2011). Mind the gap: Increasing associations between the self and Blacks with approach behaviors. *Journal of Personality and Social Psychology, 100*(2), 197–210. doi:10.1037/a0022159

**Piaget, J.** (1954). *The child's conception of number.* New York: Norton.

**Piaget, J.** (1965). *The moral judgment of the child.* New York: Free Press. (Original work published 1932)

**Piaget, J.** (1977). The first year of life of the child. In H. E. Gruber & J. J. Voneche (Eds.), *The essential Piaget: An interpretative reference and guide* (pp. 198–214). New York: Basic Books. (Original work published 1927)

**Piaget, J., & Inhelder, B.** (1969). *The psychology of the child* (H. Weaver, Trans.). New York: Basic Books.

**Piazza, J. R., Charles, S. T., Sliwinski, M. J., Mogle, J., & Almeida, D. M.** (2013). Affective reactivity to daily stressors and long-term risk of reporting a chronic physical health condition. *Annals of Behavioral Medicine, 45,* 110–120.

**Pinel, J. P. J., Assanand, S., & Lehman, D. R.** (2000). Hunger, eating, and ill health. *American Psychologist, 55,* 1105–1116.

**Pines, A. M.** (1993). Burnout: An existential perspective. In W. B. Schaufeli, C. Maslach, & T. Marek (Eds.), *Professional burnout: Recent developments in theory and research* (pp. 33–51). Washington, DC: Taylor & Francis.

**Pinker, S.** (1994). *The language instinct.* New York: Morrow.

**Pinker, S.** (1997a). Evolutionary psychology: An exchange. *New York Review of Books, 44,* 55–58.

**Pinker, S.** (1997b). *How the mind works.* New York: Norton.

**Pinker, S.** (2003). *The blank slate: The modern denial of human nature.* New York: Viking.

**Pinker, S.** (2007, March 19). A history of violence. *The New Republic Online.*

**Pinker, S., & Bloom, P.** (1990). Natural language and natural selection. *Behavioral and Brain Sciences, 13,* 707–784.

**Pitcher, D., Garrido, L., Walsh, V., & Duchaine, B. C.** (2008). Transcranial magnetic stimulation disrupts the perception and embodiment of facial expressions. *Journal of Neuroscience, 28*(36), 8929–8933.

**Planty, M., Hussar, W., Snyder, T., Provasnik, S., Kena, G., Dinkes, R., ... Kemp, J.** (2008). *The condition of education, 2008.* Washington: IES, NECS, & U.S. Department of Education.

**Plassman, H., O'Doherty, J., Shiv, B., & Rangel, A.** (2008). Marketing actions can modulate neural representations of experienced pleasantness. *Proceedings of the National Academy of Sciences, USA, 105,* 1050–1054.

**Platek, S. M., Critton, S. R., Myers, T. E., & Gallup, G. G., Jr.** (2003). Contagious yawning: The role of self-awareness and mental state attribution. *Cognitive Brain Research, 17,* 223–227.

**Plato.** (1956). *Protagoras* (O. Jowett, Trans.). New York: Prentice Hall. (Original work circa 380 BCE)

**Pliner, P., Hart, H., Kohl, J., & Saari, D.** (1974). Compliance without pressure: Some further data on the foot-in-the-door technique. *Journal of Experimental Social Psychology, 19,* 17–22.

**Plomin, R., & Caspi, A.** (1999). Behavioral genetics and personality. In L. A. Pervin & O. P. John (Eds.), *Handbook of personality: Theory and research* (Vol. 2, pp. 251–276). New York: Guilford Press.

**Plomin, R., DeFries, J. C., McClearn, G. E., & Rutter, M.** (1997). *Behavioral genetics* (3rd ed.). New York: W. H. Freeman and Company.

**Plomin, R., DeFries, J. C., McClearn, G. E., & McGuffin, P.** (2001). *Behavioral genetics* (4th ed.). New York: W. H. Freeman and Company.

**Plomin, R., Haworth, C. M. A., Meaburn, E. L., Price, T. S., Wellcome Trust Case Control Consortium 2, & Davis, O. S. P.** (2013). Common DNA markers can account for more than half of the genetic influence on cognitive abilities. *Psychological Science, 24*(4), 562–568. doi:10.1177/0956797612457952

**Plomin, R., Scheier, M. F., Bergeman, C. S., Pedersen, N. L., Nesselroade, J. R., & McClearn, G. E.** (1992). Optimism, pessimism, and mental health: A twin/adoption analysis. *Personality and Individual Differences, 13,* 921–930.

**Plomin, R., & Spinath, F. M.** (2004). Intelligence: Genetics, genes, and genomics. *Journal of Personality and Social Psychology, 86,* 112–129.

**Plotnik, J. M., de Waal, F. B. M., & Reiss, D.** (2006). Self-recognition in an Asian elephant. *Proceedings of the National Academy of Sciences, USA, 103,* 17053–17057.

**Polanczyk, G., de Lima, M. S., Horta, B. L., Biederman, J., & Rohde, L. A.** (2007). The worldwide prevalence of ADHD: A systematic review and metaregression analysis. *American Journal of Psychiatry, 164,* 942–948.

**Poliak, S., & Peles, E.** (2003). The local differentiation of myelinated axons at nodes of Ranvier. *Nature Reviews Neuroscience, 4,* 968–980.

**Polivy, J., & Herman, C. P.** (1992). Undieting: A program to help people stop dieting. *International Journal of Eating Disorders, 11,* 261–268.

**Polivy, J., & Herman, C. P.** (2002). If at first you don't succeed: False hopes of self-change. *American Psychologist, 57,* 677–689.

**Pond, R. S., DeWall, C. N., Lambert, N. M., Deckman, T., Bonser, I. M., & Fincham, F. D.** (2012). Repulsed by violence: Disgust sensitivity buffers trait, behavioral, and daily aggression. *Journal of Personality and Social Psychology, 102*(1), 175–188. doi:10.1037/a0024296

**Poole, D. A., Lindsay, S. D., Memon, A., & Bull, R.** (1995). Psychotherapy and the recovery of memories of childhood sexual abuse: U.S. and British practitioners' opinions, practices, and experiences. *Journal of Consulting and Clinical Psychology, 63,* 426–487.

**Poon, S. H., Sim, K., Sum, M. Y., Kuswanto, C. N., & Baldessarini, R. J.** (2012). Evidence-based options for treatment-resistant adult bipolar disorder patients. *Bipolar Disorders, 14,* 573–584.

**Pope, A. W., & Bierman, K. L.** (1999). Predicting adolescent peer problems and antisocial activities: The relative roles of aggression and dysregulation. *Developmental Psychology, 35,* 335–346.

**Porter, S., & ten Brinke, L.** (2008). Reading between the lies: Identifying concealed and falsified emotions in universal facial expressions. *Psychological Science, 19,* 508–514.

**Portocarrero, J. S., Burright, R. G., & Donovick, P. J.** (2007). Vocabulary and verbal fluency of bilingual and monolingual college students. *Archives of Clinical Neuropsychology, 22,* 415–422.

**Posner, M. I., & Raichle, M. E.** (1994). *Images of mind.* New York: W. H. Freeman and Company.

**Post, R. M., Frye, M. A., Denicoff, G. S., Leverich, G. S., Dunn, R. T., Osuch, E. A., ... Jajodia, K.** (2008). Emerging trends in the treatment of rapid cycling bipolar disorder: A selected review. *Bipolar Disorders, 2,* 305–315.

**Posthuma, D., & de Geus, E. J. C.** (2006). Progress in the molecular-genetic study of intelligence. *Current Directions in Psychological Science, 15,* 151–155.

**Postman, L., & Underwood, B. J.** (1973). Critical issues in interference theory. *Memory & Cognition, 1,* 19–40.

**Postmes, T., & Spears, R.** (1998). Deindividuation and anti-normative behavior: A meta-analysis. *Psychological Bulletin, 123,* 238–259.

**Powell, R. A., Symbaluk, D. G., MacDonald, S. E., & Honey, P. L.** (2009). *Introduction to learning and behavior* (3rd ed.). Belmont, CA: Wadsworth Cengage Learning.

**Power, M. L., & Schulkin, J.** (2009). *The evolution of obesity.* Baltimore, MD: Johns Hopkins University Press.

**Prasada, S., & Pinker, S.** (1993). Generalizations of regular and irregular morphology. *Language and Cognitive Processes, 8,* 1–56.

**Pratkanis, A. R.** (1992). The cargo-cult science of subliminal persuasion. *Skeptical Inquirer, 16,* 260–272.

**Pressman, S. D., Cohen, S., Miller, G. E., Barkin, A., Rabin, B. S., & Treanor, J. J.** (2005). Loneliness, social network size, and immune response to influenza vaccination in college freshmen. *Health Psychology, 24,* 297–306.

**Price, J. L., & Davis, B.** (2008). *The woman who can't forget: The extraordinary story of living with the most remarkable memory known to science.* New York: Free Press.

**Prior, H., Schwartz, A., & Güntürkün, O.** (2008). Mirror-induced behavior in the magpie (*Pica pica*): Evidence of self-recognition. *PLoS Biology, 6,* e202.

**Prochaska, J. J., & Sallis, J. F.** (2004). A randomized controlled trial of single versus multiple health behavior change: Promoting physical activity and nutrition among adolescents. *Health Psychology, 23,* 314–318.

Procopio, M., & Marriott, P. (2007). Intrauterine hormonal environment and risk of developing anorexia nervosa. *Archives of General Psychiatry, 64*(12), 1402–1407.

Protzko, J., Aronson, J., & Blair, C. (2013). How to make a young child smarter: Evidence from the database of raising intelligence. *Perspectives on Psychological Science, 8*(1), 25–40. doi:10.1177/1745691612462585

Provine, R. R. (2000). *Laughter: A scientific investigation.* New York: Viking.

Pruitt, D. G. (1998). Social conflict. In D. T. Gilbert, S. T. Fiske, & G. Lindzey (Eds.), *The handbook of social psychology* (4th ed., Vol. 2, pp. 470–503). New York: McGraw-Hill.

Public Health Agency of Canada. (2002a). *A report on mental illness in Canada—Chapter 2: Mood disorders (archived).* Retrieved from http://www.phac-aspc.gc.ca/publicat/miic-mmac/chap_2-eng.php

Public Health Agency of Canada. (2002b). *A report on mental illness in Canada—Chapter 5: Personality disorders (archived).* Retrieved from http://www.phac-aspc.gc.ca/publicat/miic-mmac/chap_5-eng.php

Public Health Agency of Canada. (2009). *Obesity in Canada: A snapshot.* Ottawa: Author.

Public Health Agency of Canada. (2010). *Report on sexually transmitted infections in Canada: 2008 (archived).* Retrieved from http://www.phac-aspc.gc.ca/std-mts/report/sti-its2008/02-eng.php

Public Health Agency of Canada. (2011a). *Obesity in Canada: A joint report from the public health agency of Canada and the Canadian institute for health information.* Ottawa: Author.

Public Health Agency of Canada. (2011b, January 24). *Government of Canada supports new physical activity guidelines.* [Press release]. Ottawa: Author.

Public Health Agency of Canada. (2012). *Summary: Estimates of HIV prevalence and incidence in Canada, 2011 (archived).* Retrieved from http://www.phac-aspc.gc.ca/aids-sida/publication/survreport/estimat2011-eng.php

Punjabi, N. M. (2008). The epidemiology of adult obstructive sleep apnea. *Proceedings of the American Thoracic Society, 5,* 136–143.

Puterman, E., Lin, J., Blackburn, E. H., O'Donovan, A., Adler, N., & Epel, E. (2010). The power of exercise: Buffering the effect of chronic stress on telomere length. *PLoS ONE, 5,* e10837.

Pyc, M. A., & Rawson, K. A. (2009). Testing the retrieval effort hypothesis: Does greater difficulty correctly recalling information lead to higher levels of memory? *Journal of Memory and Language, 60,* 437–447.

Pyers, J. E., & Senghas, A. (2009). Language promotes false-belief understanding: Evidence from learners of a new sign language. *Psychological Science, 20*(7), 805–812.

Pyers, J. E., Shusterman, A., Senghas, A., Spelke, E. S., & Emmorey, K. (2010). Evidence from an emerging sign language reveals that language supports spatial cognition. *Proceedings of the National Academy of Sciences, USA,107,* 12116–12120.

Pyszczynski, T., Holt, J., & Greenberg, J. (1987). Depression, self-focused attention, and expectancy for positive and negative future life events for self and others. *Journal of Personality and Social Psychology, 52,* 994–1001.

Quattrone, G. A. (1982). Behavioral consequences of attributional bias. *Social Cognition, 1,* 358–378.

Querleu, D., Lefebvre, C., Titran, M., Renard, X., Morillon, M., & Crepin, G. (1984). Réactivité de nouveau-né de moins de deux heures de vie á la voix maternelle [Reactivity of a newborn at less than two hours of life to the mother's voice]. *Journal de Gynécologie Obstétrique et de Biologie de la Reproduction, 13,* 125–134.

Quiroga, R. Q., Reddy, L., Kreiman, G., Koch, C., & Fried, I. (2005). Invariant visual representation by single neurons in the human brain. *Nature, 435,* 1102–1107.

Quoidbach, J., Gilbert, D. T., & Wilson, T. D. (2013). The end of history illusion. *Science, 339,* 96–98.

Qureshi, A., & Lee-Chiong, T. (2004). Medications and their effects on sleep. *Medical Clinics of North America, 88,* 751–766.

Rabbitt, P., Diggle, P., Holland, F., & McInnes, L. (2004). Practice and drop-out effects during a 17-year longitudinal study of cognitive aging. *Journal of Gerontology: Psychological Sciences and Social Sciences, 59*(2), 84–97.

Race, E., Keane, M. M., & Verfaellie, M. (2011). Medial temporal lobe damage causes deficits in episodic memory and episodic future thinking not attributable to deficits in narrative construction. *Journal of Neuroscience, 31,* 10262–10269.

Radford, E., & Radford, M. A. (1949). *Encyclopedia of superstitions.* New York: Philosophical Library.

Rahe, R. H., Meyer, M., Smith, M., Klaer, G., & Holmes, T. H. (1964). Social stress and illness onset. *Journal of Psychosomatic Research, 8,* 35–44.

Raichle, M. E., & Mintun, M. A. (2006). Brain work and brain imaging. *Annual Review of Neuroscience, 29,* 449–476.

Rajaram, S. (2011). Collaboration both hurts and helps memory: A cognitive perspective. *Current Directions in Psychological Science, 20,* 76–81.

Rajaram, S., & Pereira-Pasarin, L. P. (2010). Collaborative memory: Cognitive research and theory. *Perspectives on Psychological Science, 6,* 649–663.

Ramachandran, V. S., & Altschuler, E. L. (2009). The use of visual feedback, in particular mirror visual feedback, in restoring brain function. *Brain, 132,* 1693–1710.

Ramachandran, V. S., & Blakeslee, S. (1998). *Phantoms in the brain: Probing the mysteries of the human mind.* New York: Morrow.

Ramachandran, V. S., Brang, D., & McGeoch, P. D. (2010). Dynamic reorganization of referred sensations by movements of phantom limbs. *NeuroReport, 21,* 727–730.

Ramachandran, V. S., Rodgers-Ramachandran, D., & Stewart, M. (1992). Perceptual correlates of massive cortical reorganization. *Science, 258,* 1159–1160.

Rapaport, D. (1946). *Diagnostic psychological testing: The theory, statistical evaluation, and diagnostic application of a battery of tests.* Chicago: Year Book Publishers.

Rapoport, J., Chavez, A., Greenstein, D., Addington, A., & Gogtay, N. (2009). Autism-spectrum disorders and childhood onset schizophrenia: Clinical and biological contributions to a relationship revisited. *Journal of the American Academy of Child and Adolescent Psychiatry, 48,* 10–18.

Rappoport, J. L. (1990). Obsessive-compulsive disorder and basal ganglia dysfunction. *Psychological Medicine, 20,* 465–469.

Rauschecker, J. P., & Scott, S. K. (2009). Maps and streams in the auditory cortex: Nonhuman primates illuminate human speech processing. *Nature Neuroscience, 12,* 718–724.

Raz, A., Fan, J., & Posner, M. I. (2005). Hypnotic suggestion reduces conflict in the brain. *Proceedings of the National Academy of Sciences, 102,* 9978–9983.

Raz, A., Shapiro, T., Fan, J., & Posner, M. I. (2002). Hypnotic suggestion and the modulation of Stroop interference. *Archives of General Psychiatry, 59,* 1155–1161.

Raz, N. (2000). Aging of the brain and its impact on cognitive performance: Integration of structural and functional findings. In F. I. M.

Craik & T. A. Salthouse (Eds.), *The handbook of aging and cognition* (pp. 1–90). Mahwah, NJ: Erlbaum.

Read, K. E. (1965). *The high valley.* London: Allen and Unwin.

Reason, J., & Mycielska, K. (1982). *Absent-minded?: The psychology of mental lapses and everyday errors.* Englewood Cliffs, NJ: Prentice-Hall.

Reber, A. S. (1967). Implicit learning of artificial grammars. *Journal of Verbal Learning and Verbal Behavior, 6,* 855–863.

Reber, A. S. (1996). *Implicit learning and tacit knowledge: An essay on the cognitive unconscious.* New York: Oxford University Press.

Reber, A. S., & Allen, R. (2000). Individual differences in implicit learning. In R. G. Kunzendorf & B. Wallace (Eds.), *Individual differences in conscious experience* (pp. 227–247). Philadelphia: John Benjamins.

Reber, A. S., Walkenfeld, F. F., & Hernstadt, R. (1991). Implicit learning: Individual differences and IQ. *Journal of Experimental Psychology: Learning, Memory, and Cognition, 17,* 888–896.

Reber, P. J., Gitelman, D. R., Parrish, T. B., & Mesulam, M. M. (2003). Dissociating explicit and implicit category knowledge with fMRI. *Journal of Cognitive Neuroscience, 15,* 574–583.

Recanzone, G. H., & Sutter, M. L. (2008). The biological basis of audition. *Annual Review of Psychology, 59,* 119–142.

Rechsthaffen, A., Gilliland, M. A., Bergmann, B. M., & Winter, J. B. (1983). Physiological correlates of prolonged sleep deprivation in rats. *Science, 221,* 182–184.

Redick, T. S., Shipstead, Z., Harrison, T. L., Hicks, K. L., Fried, D. E., Hambrick, D. Z., ... Engle, R. W. (2013). No evidence of intelligence improvement after working memory training: A randomized, placebo-controlled study. *Journal of Experimental Psychology: General, 142,* 359–379. doi:10.1037/a002908

Reed, C. L., Klatzky, R. L., & Halgren, E. (2005). What vs. where in touch: An fMRI study. *NeuroImage, 25,* 718–726.

Reed, D. R. (2008). Birth of a new breed of supertaster. *Chemical Senses, 33,* 489–491.

Reed, G. (1988). *The psychology of anomalous experience* (rev. ed.). Buffalo, NY: Prometheus Books.

Reeve, C. L., Heggestad, E. D., & Lievens, F. (2009). Modelling the impact of test anxiety and test familiarity on the criterion-related validity of cognitive ability tests. *Intelligence, 37,* 34–41.

Regan, P. C. (1998). What if you can't get what you want? Willingness to compromise ideal mate selection standards as a function of sex, mate value, and relationship context. *Personality and Social Psychology Bulletin, 24,* 1294–1303.

Regier, T., & Kay, P. (2009). Language, thought, and color: Whorf was half right. *Trends in Cognitive Sciences, 13,* 439–446.

Reis, H. T., Maniaci, M. R., Caprariello, P. S., Eastwick, P. W., & Finkel, E. J. (2011). Familiarity does indeed promote attraction in live interaction. *Journal of Personality and Social Psychology, 101*(3), 557–570. doi:10.1037/a0022885

Reiss, D., & Marino, L. (2001). Mirror self-recognition in the bottlenose dolphin: A case of cognitive convergence. *Proceedings of the National Academy of Sciences, USA, 98,* 5937–5942.

Reissland, N. (1988). Neonatal imitation in the first hour of life: Observations in rural Nepal. *Developmental Psychology, 24,* 464–469.

Renner, K. E. (1964). Delay of reinforcement: A historical review. *Psychological Review, 61,* 341–361.

Renner, M. J., & Mackin, R. (1998). A life stress instrument for classroom use. *Teaching of Psychology, 25,* 46–48.

Rensink, R. A. (2002). Change detection. *Annual Review of Psychology, 53,* 245–277.

Rensink, R. A., O'Regan, J. K., & Clark, J. J. (1997). To see or not to see: The need for attention to perceive changes in scenes. *Psychological Science, 8,* 368–373.

Repacholi, B. M., & Gopnik, A. (1997). Early reasoning about desires: Evidence from 14- and 18-month-olds. *Developmental Psychology, 33,* 12–21.

Rescorla, R. A. (2006). Stimulus generalization of excitation and inhibition. *Quarterly Journal of Experimental Psychology, 59,* 53–67.

Rescorla, R. A., & Wagner, A. R. (1972). A theory of Pavlovian conditioning: Variations in effectiveness of reinforcement and nonreinforcement. In A. Black & W. F. Prokasky, Jr. (Eds.), *Classical conditioning II* (pp. 64–99). New York: Appleton-Century-Crofts.

Ressler, K. J., & Mayberg, H. S. (2007). Targeting abnormal neural circuits in mood and anxiety disorders: From the laboratory to the clinic. *Nature Neuroscience, 10,* 1116–1124.

Ressler, K. J., & Nemeroff, C. B. (1999). Role of norepinephrine in the pathophysiology and treatment of mood disorders. *Biological Psychiatry, 46,* 1219–1233.

Rice, K. G., Richardson, C. M. E., & Clark, D. (2012). Perfectionism, procrastination, and psychological distress. *Journal of Counseling Psychology, 39,* 288–302.

Richards, M., Black, S., Mishra, G., Gale, C. R., Deary, I. J., & Batty, D. G. (2009). IQ in childhood and the metabolic syndrome in middle age: Extended follow-up of the 1946 British birth cohort study. *Intelligence, 37*(6), 567–572.

Richards, M. H., Crowe, P. A., Larson, R., & Swarr, A. (1998). Developmental patterns and gender differences in the experience of peer companionship during adolescence. *Child Development, 69,* 154–163.

Richert, E. S. (1997). Excellence with equity in identification and programming. In N. Colangelo & G. A. Davis (Eds.), *Handbook of gifted education* (2nd ed., pp. 75–88). Boston: Allyn & Bacon.

Richters, J., de Visser, R., Rissel, C., & Smith, A. (2006). Sexual practices at last heterosexual encounter and occurrence of orgasm in a national survey. *Journal of Sex Research, 43,* 217–226.

Ridenour, T. A., & Howard, M. O. (2012). Inhalants abuse: Status of etiology and intervention. In J. C. Verster, K. Brady, M. Galanter, & P. Conrod (Eds.), *Drug abuse and addiction in medical illness: Causes, consequences, and treatment* (pp. 189–199). New York: Springer.

Rieber, R. W. (Ed.). (1980). *Wilhelm Wundt and the making of scientific psychology.* New York: Plenum Press.

Riefer, D. M., Kevari, M. K., & Kramer, D. L. F. (1995). Name that tune: Eliciting the tip-of-the-tongue experience using auditory stimuli. *Psychological Reports, 77,* 1379–1390.

Rimer, J., Dwan, K., Lawlor, D. A., Greig, C. A., McMurdo, M., Morley, W., & Mead, G. E. (2012). Exercise for depression. *Cochrane Database of Systematic Reviews, 7,* CD004366.

Ringach, D. L., & Jentsch, J. D. (2009). We must face the threats. *The Journal of Neuroscience, 29,* 11417–11418.

Risko, E. F., Anderson, N., Sarwal, A., Engelhardt, M., & Kingstone, A. (2012). Every attention: Variation in mind wandering and memory in a lecture. *Applied Cognitive Psychology, 26,* 234–242.

Risman, J. E., Coyle, J. T., Green, R. W., Javitt, D. C., Benes, F. M., Heckers, S., & Grace, A. A. (2008). Circuit-based framework for understanding neurotransmitter and risk gene interactions in schizophrenia. *Trends in Neurosciences, 31,* 234–242.

Rizzolatti, G., & Craighero, L. (2004). The mirror-neuron system. *Annual Review of Neuroscience, 27,* 169–192.

Rizzolatti, G., & Sinigaglia, C. (2012). The functional role of the parieto-frontal mirror circuit. *Nature Reviews Neuroscience, 11,* 264–274.

**Roberson, D., Davidoff, J., Davies, I. R. L., & Shapiro, L. R.** (2004). The development of color categories in two languages: A longitudinal study. *Journal of Experimental Psychology: General, 133,* 554–571.

**Roberts, G. A.** (1991). Delusional belief and meaning in life: A preferred reality? *British Journal of Psychiatry, 159,* 20–29.

**Roberts, G. A., & McGrady, A.** (1996). Racial and gender effects on the relaxation response: Implications for the development of hypertension. *Biofeedback and Self-Regulation, 21,* 51–62.

**Robertson, L. C.** (1999). What can spatial deficits teach us about feature binding and spatial maps? *Visual Cognition, 6,* 409–430.

**Robertson, L. C.** (2003). Binding, spatial attention and perceptual awareness. *Nature Reviews Neuroscience, 4,* 93–102.

**Robins, L. N., Helzer, J. E., Hesselbrock, M., & Wish, E.** (1980). Vietnam veterans three years after Vietnam. In L. Brill & C. Winick (Eds.), *The yearbook of substance use and abuse* (Vol. 11). New York: Human Sciences Press.

**Robins, R. W., Fraley, R. C., & Krueger, R. F. (Eds.).** (2007). *Handbook of research methods in personality psychology.* New York: Guilford Press.

**Robinson, A., & Clinkenbeard, P. R.** (1998). Giftedness: An exceptionality examined. *Annual Review of Psychology, 49,* 117–139.

**Robinson, D. N.** (1995). *An intellectual history of psychology.* Madison: University of Wisconsin Press.

**Rodieck, R. W.** (1998). *The first steps in seeing.* Sunderland, MA: Sinauer.

**Roediger, H. L., III.** (2000). Why retrieval is the key process to understanding human memory. In E. Tulving (Ed.), *Memory, consciousness, and the brain: The Tallinn conference* (pp. 52–75). Philadelphia: Psychology Press.

**Roediger, H. L., III, & Karpicke, J. D.** (2006). Test-enhanced learning: Taking memory tests improves long-term retention. *Psychological Science, 17,* 249–255.

**Roediger, H. L., III, & McDermott, K. B.** (1995). Creating false memories: Remembering words not presented in lists. *Journal of Experimental Psychology: Learning, Memory, and Cognition, 21,* 803–814.

**Roediger, H. L., III, & McDermott, K. B.** (2000). Tricks of memory. *Current Directions in Psychological Science, 9,* 123–127.

**Roediger, H. L., III, Weldon, M. S., & Challis, B. H.** (1989). Explaining dissociations between implicit and explicit measures of retention: A processing account. In H. L. Roediger, III & F. I. M. Craik (Eds.), *Varieties of memory and consciousness: Essays in honor of Endel Tulving* (pp. 3–41). Hillsdale, NJ: Erlbaum.

**Rogers, C. R.** (1951). *Client-centered therapy: Its current practice, implications, and theory.* Boston: Houghton Mifflin.

**Rogers, T. B., Kuiper, N. A., & Kirker, W. S.** (1977). Self-reference and the encoding of personal information. *Journal of Personality and Social Psychology, 35,* 677–688.

**Roig, M., Skriver, K., Lundbye-Jensen, J., Kiens, B., & Nielsen, J. B.** (2012). A single bout of exercise improves motor memory. *PLoS One, 7,* e44594. doi:10.1371/journal.pone.0044594

**Romero-Corral, A., Montori, V. M., Somers, V. K., Korinek, J., Thomas, R. J., Allison, T. G., … Lopez-Jiminez, F.** (2006). Association of body weight with total mortality and with cardiovascular events in coronary artery disease: A systematic review of cohort studies. *Lancet, 368*(9536), 666–678.

**Ronay, R., & Galinsky, A. D.** (2011). Lex talionis: Testosterone and the law of retaliation. *Journal of Experimental Social Psychology, 47*(3), 702–705. doi:10.1016/j.jesp.2010.11.009

**Rosch, E. H.** (1973). Natural categories. *Cognitive Psychology, 4,* 328–350.

**Rosch, E. H.** (1975). Cognitive representations of semantic categories. *Journal of Experimental Psychology: General, 104,* 192–233.

**Rosch, E. H., & Mervis, C. B.** (1975). Family resemblances: Studies in the internal structure of categories. *Cognitive Psychology, 7,* 573–605.

**Rose, S. P. R.** (2002). Smart drugs: Do they work? Are they ethical? Will they be legal? *Nature Reviews Neuroscience, 3,* 975–979.

**Roseman, I. J.** (1984). Cognitive determinants of emotion: A structural theory. *Review of Personality and Social Psychology, 5,* 11–36.

**Roseman, I. J., & Smith, C. A.** (2001). Appraisal theory: Overview, assumptions, varieties and controversies. In K. R. Scherer, A. Schorr, & T. Johnstone (Eds.), *Appraisal processes in emotion: Theory, methods, research* (pp. 3–19). New York: Oxford University Press.

**Rosenbaum, J. E.** (2009). Patient teenagers? A comparison of the sexual behavior of virginity pledgers and matched nonpledgers. *Pediatrics, 123*(1), e110–e120.

**Rosenberg, M.** (1965). *Society and the adolescent self-image.* Princeton, NJ: Princeton University Press.

**Rosenberg, T.** (2013, March 27). The destructive influence of imaginary peers. *New York Times.* Retrieved from http://opinionator.blogs.nytimes.com/2013/03/27/the-destructive-influence-of-imaginary-peers/

**Rosenhan, D.** (1973). On being sane in insane places. *Science, 179,* 250–258.

**Rosenkranz, K., Williamon, A., & Rothwell, J. C.** (2007). Motorcortical excitability and synaptic plasticity is enhanced in professional musicians. *The Journal of Neuroscience, 27,* 5200–5206.

**Rosenstein, M. J., Milazzo-Sayre, L. J., & Manderscheid, R. W.** (1990). Characteristics of persons using specifically inpatient, outpatient, and partial care programs in 1986. In M. A. Sonnenschein (Ed.), *Mental health in the United States* (pp. 139–172). Washington, DC: U.S. Government Printing Office.

**Rosenthal, R., & Fode, K. L.** (1963). The effect of experimenter bias on the performance of the albino rat. *Behavioral Science, 8,* 183–189.

**Ross, L.** (1977). The intuitive psychologist and his shortcomings: Distortions in the attribution process. *Advances in Experimental Social Psychology, 10,* 173–220.

**Ross, L., Amabile, T. M., & Steinmetz, J. L.** (1977). Social roles, social control, and biases in social-perception processes. *Journal of Personality and Social Psychology, 35,* 485–494.

**Ross, L., & Nisbett, R. E.** (1991). *The person and the situation.* New York: McGraw-Hill.

**Ross, M., Blatz, C. W., & Schryer, E.** (2008). Social memory processes. In H. L. Roediger III (Ed.), *Learning and memory: A comprehensive reference* (Vol. 2, pp. 911–926). Oxford, England: Elsevier.

**Rossano, F., Carpenter, M., & Tomasello, M.** (2012). One-year-old infants follow others' voice direction. *Psychological Science, 23*(11), 1298–1302. doi:10.1177/0956797612450032

**Rosvall, M., & Bergstrom, C. T.** (2008). Maps of random walks on complex networks reveal community structure. *Proceedings of the National Academy of Sciences, USA, 105,* 1118–1123.

**Rotermann, M.** (2008).*Trends in teen sexual behaviour and condom use.* (Catalogue no. 82-003-X). Ottawa: Statistics Canada.

**Rotermann, M.** (2012). *Sexual behaviour and condom use of 15-to-24-year-olds in 2003 and 2009/2010.* (Catalogue no. 82-003-X). Ottawa: Statistics Canada.

**Roth, H. P., & Caron, H. S.** (1978). Accuracy of doctors' estimates and patients' statements on adherence to a drug regimen. *Clinical Pharmacology and Therapeutics, 23,* 361–370.

Rothbart, M. K., & Bates, J. E. (1998). Temperament. In W. Damon (Series Ed.) & N. Eisenberg (Vol. Ed.), *Handbook of child psychology: Vol. 3. Social, emotional and personality development* (5th ed., pp. 105–176). New York: Wiley.

Rothbaum, B. O., & Schwartz, A. C. (2002). Exposure therapy for posttraumatic stress disorder. *American Journal of Psychotherapy, 56,* 59–75.

Rothon, R. (2012, November 21). Opinion: Happily, Canadian bilingualism on the rise. *Montreal Gazette.* Retrieved from http://www.montrealgazette.com/news/Opinion+Happily+Canadian+bilingualism+rise/7589936/story.html

Rotter, J. B. (1966). Generalized expectancies for internal versus external locus of control of reinforcement. *Psychological Monographs: General and Applied, 80,* 1–28.

Rotton, L. (1992). Trait humor and longevity: Do comics have the last laugh? *Health Psychology, 11,* 262–266.

Roy-Byrne, P. P., & Cowley, D. (1998). *Pharmacological treatment of panic, generalized anxiety, and phobic disorders.* New York: Oxford University Press.

Roy-Byrne, P. P., & Cowley, D. S. (2002). Pharmacological treatments for panic disorder, generalized anxiety disorder, specific phobia, and social anxiety disorder. In P. E. Nathan & J. M. Gorman (Eds.), *A guide to treatments that work* (2nd ed., pp. 337–365). New York: Oxford University Press.

Rozenblit, L., & Keil, F. C. (2002). The misunderstood limits of folk science: An illusion of explanatory depth. *Cognitive Science, 26,* 521–562.

Rozin, P., Bauer, R., & Catanese, D. (2003). Food and life, pleasure and worry, among American college students: Gender differences and regional similarities. *Journal of Personality and Social Psychology, 85,* 132–141.

Rozin, P., Dow, S., Moscovitch, M., & Rajaram, S. (1998). What causes humans to begin and end a meal? A role for memory for what has been eaten, as evidenced by a study of multiple meal eating in amnesic patients. *Psychological Science, 9,* 392–396.

Rozin, P., Kabnick, K., Pete, E., Fischler, C., & Shields, C. (2003). The ecology of eating: Smaller portion size in France than in the United States helps to explain the French paradox. *Psychological Science, 14,* 450–454.

Rozin, P., & Kalat, J. W. (1971). Specific hungers and poison avoidance as adaptive specializations of learning. *Psychological Review, 78,* 459–486.

Rozin, P., Scott, S., Dingley, M., Urbanek, J. K., Jiang, H., & Kaltenbach, M. (2011). Nudge to nobesity: I. Minor changes in accessibility decrease food intake. *Judgment and Decision Making, 6,* 323–332.

Rozin, P., Trachtenberg, S., & Cohen, A. B. (2001). Stability of body image and body image dissatisfaction in American college students over about the last 15 years. *Appetite, 37,* 245–248.

Rubin, M., & Badea, C. (2012). They're all the same! … but for several different reasons: A review of the multicausal nature of perceived group variability. *Current Directions in Psychological Science, 21*(6), 367–372. doi:10.1177/0963721412457363

Rubin, Z. (1973). *Liking and loving.* New York: Holt, Rinehart & Winston.

Rubio-Fernandez, P., & Geurts, B. (2012). How to pass the false-belief task before your fourth birthday. *Psychological Science, 24*(1), 27–33. doi:10.1177/0956797612447819

Rudman, L. A., Ashmore, R. D., & Gary, M. L. (2001). "Unlearning" automatic biases: The malleability of implicit prejudice and stereotypes. *Journal of Personality and Social Psychology, 81,* 856–868.

Rusbult, C. E. (1983). A longitudinal test of the investment model: The development (and deterioration) of satisfaction and commitment in heterosexual involvements. *Journal of Personality and Social Psychology, 45,* 101–117.

Rusbult, C. E., & Van Lange, P. A. M. (2003). Interdependence, interaction and relationships. *Annual Review of Psychology, 54,* 351–375.

Rusbult, C. E., Verette, J., Whitney, G. A., & Slovik, L. F. (1991). Accommodation processes in close relationships: Theory and preliminary empirical evidence. *Journal of Personality and Social Psychology, 60,* 53–78.

Ruscio, A. M., Stein, D. J., Chiu, W. T., Kessler, R. C. (2010). The epidemiology of obsessive-compulsive disorder in the National Comorbidity Survey Replication. *Molecular Psychiatry, 15,* 53–63.

Rushton, J. P. (1995). Asian achievement, brain size, and evolution: Comment on A. H. Yee. *Educational Psychology Review, 7,* 373–380.

Rushton, J. P., & Templer, D. I. (2009). National differences in intelligence, crime, income, and skin color. *Intelligence, 37*(4), 341–346.

Russell, B. (1945). *A history of Western philosophy.* New York: Simon & Schuster.

Russell, J., Gee, B., & Bullard, C. (2012). Why do young children hide by closing their eyes? Self-visibility and the developing concept of self. *Journal of Cognition and Development, 13*(4), 550–576. doi:10.1108 0/15248372.2011.594826

Russell, J. A. (1980). A circumplex model of affect. *Journal of Personality and Social Psychology, 39,* 1161–1178.

Rutledge, R. B., Lazzaro, S. C., Lau, B., Myers, C. E., Gluck, M. A., & Glimcher, P. W. (2009). Dopaminergic drugs modulate learning rates and perseveration in Parkinson's patients in a dynamic foraging task. *Journal of Neuroscience, 29,* 15104–15114.

Rutter, M., O'Connor, T. G., & the English and Romanian Adoptees Study Team. (2004). Are there biological programming effects for psychological development? Findings from a study of Romanian adoptees. *Developmental Psychology, 40,* 81–94.

Rutter, M., & Silberg, J. (2002). Gene–environment interplay in relation to emotional and behavioral disturbance. *Annual Review of Psychology, 53,* 463–490.

Ryan, R. M., & Deci, E. L. (2000). Self-determination theory and the facilitation of intrinsic motivation, social development, and wellbeing. *American Psychologist, 55,* 68–78.

Ryle, G. (1949). *The Concept of Mind,* Hutchinson, London.

Sachs, J. S. (1967). Recognition of semantic, syntactic, and lexical changes in sentences. *Psychonomic Bulletin & Review, 1,* 17–18.

Sacks, O. (1995). *An anthropologist on Mars.* New York: Knopf.

Sacks, O. (1996). *An anthropologist on Mars* (ppbk). Visalia, CA: Vintage.

Saffran, J. R., Aslin, R. N., & Newport, E. I. (1996). Statistical learning by 8-month-old infants. *Science, 274,* 1926–1928.

Sahakian, B., & Morein-Zamir, S. (2007). Professor's little helper. *Nature, 450*(7173), 1157–1159.

Saks, E. R. (2013, January 25). Successful and schizophrenic. *New York Times.* Retrieved from http://www.nytimes.com/2013/01/27/opinion/sunday/schizophrenic-not-stupid.html

Sakuraba, S., Sakai, S., Yamanaka, M., Yokosawa, Y., & Hirayama, K. (2012). Does the human dorsal stream really process a category for tools? *Journal of Neuroscience, 32,* 3949–3953.

Sallet, J., Mars, R. B., Noonan, M. P., Andersson, J. L., O'Reilly, J. X., Jbabdi, S., … Rushworth, M. F. S. (2011). Social network size affects neural circuits in macaques. *Science, 334*(6056), 697–700. doi:10.1126/science.1210027

**Salmon, D. P., & Bondi, M. W.** (2009). Neuropsychological assessment of dementia. *Annual Review of Psychology, 60,* 257–282.

**Salovey, P., & Grewal, D.** (2005). The science of emotional intelligence. *Current Directions in Psychological Science, 14*(6), 281–285.

**Salthouse, T. A.** (1984). Effects of age and skill in typing. *Journal of Experimental Psychology: General, 113,* 345–371.

**Salthouse, T. A.** (1987). Age, experience, and compensation. In C. Schooler & K. W. Schaie (Eds.), *Cognitive functioning and social structure over the life course* (pp. 142–150). Norwood, NJ: Ablex.

**Salthouse, T. A.** (1996a). General and specific mediation of adult age differences in memory. *Journal of Gerontology: Series B: Psychological Sciences and Social Sciences, 51B,* P30–P42.

**Salthouse, T. A.** (1996b). The processing-speed theory of adult age differences in cognition. *Psychological Review, 103,* 403–428.

**Salthouse, T. A.** (2000). Pressing issues in cognitive aging. In D. Park & N. Schwartz (Eds.), *Cognitive aging: A primer* (pp. 43–54). Philadelphia: Psychology Press.

**Salthouse, T. A.** (2001). Structural models of the relations between age and measures of cognitive functioning. *Intelligence, 29,* 93–115.

**Salthouse, T. A.** (2006). Mental exercise and mental aging. *Perspectives on Psychological Science, 1*(1), 68–87.

**Salvatore, J. E., Kuo, S. I.-C., Steele, R. D., Simpson, J. A., & Collins, W. A.** (2011). Recovering from conflict in romantic relationships: A developmental perspective. *Psychological Science, 22*(3), 376–383. doi:10.1177/0956797610397055

**Sampson, P. D., Bookstein, F. L., Barr, H. M., & Streissguth, A. P.** (1994). Prenatal alcohol exposure, birthweight and measures of child size from birth to age fourteen years. *American Journal of Public Health, 84*(9), 1421–1428.

**Sampson, R. J., & Laub, J. H.** (1995). Understanding variability in lives through time: Contributions of life-course criminology. *Studies of Crime Prevention, 4,* 143–158.

**Sandin, R. H., Enlund, G., Samuelsson, P., & Lenmarken, C.** (2000). Awareness during anesthesia: A prospective case study. *Lancet, 355,* 707–711.

**Sapolsky, R. M., & Share, L. J.** (2004). A pacific culture among wild baboons: Its emergence and transmission. *PLoS Biology, 2,* e106.

**Sara, S. J.** (2000). Retrieval and reconsolidation: Toward a neurobiology of remembering. *Learning & Memory, 7,* 73–84.

**Sarris, V.** (1989). Max Wertheimer on seen motion: Theory and evidence. *Psychological Research, 51,* 58–68.

**Sarter, M.** (2006). Preclinical research into cognition enhancers. *Trends in Pharmacological Sciences, 27,* 602–608.

**Sasanuma, S.** (1975). Kana and kanji processing in Japanese aphasics. *Brain and Language, 2,* 369–383.

**Satcher, D.** (2001). *The Surgeon General's call to action to promote sexual health and responsible sexual behavior.* Washington, DC: U.S. Government Printing Office.

**Savage, C. R., Deckersbach, T., Heckers, S., Wagner, A. D., Schacter, D. L., Alpert, N. M., … Rauch, S. L.** (2001). Prefrontal regions supporting spontaneous and directed application of verbal learning strategies: Evidence from PET. *Brain, 124,* 219–231.

**Savage-Rumbaugh, S., & Lewin, R.** (1996). *Kanzi: The ape on the brink of the human mind.* New York: Wiley.

**Savage-Rumbaugh, S., Shanker, G., & Taylor, T. J.** (1998). *Apes, language, and the human mind.* Oxford, England: Oxford University Press.

**Savic, I., Berglund, H., & Lindstrom, P.** (2005). Brain response to putative pheromones in homosexual men. *Proceedings of the National Academy of Sciences, USA, 102,* 7356–7361.

**Savic, I., & Lindstrom, P.** (2008). PET and MRI show differences in cerebral asymmetry and functional connectivity between homo- and heterosexual subjects. *Proceedings of the National Academy of Sciences, USA, 105*(27), 9403–9408.

**Savitsky, K., & Gilovich, T.** (2003). The illusion of transparency and the alleviation of speech anxiety. *Journal of Experimental Social Psychology, 39,* 618–625.

**Sawa, A., & Snyder, S. H.** (2002). Schizophrenia: Diverse approaches to a complex disease. *Science, 295,* 692–695.

**Scarborough, E., & Furumoto, L.** (1987). *Untold lives: The first generation of American women psychologists.* New York: Columbia University Press.

**Scarr, S., Pakstis, A. J., Katz, S. H., & Barker, W. B.** (1977). Absence of a relationship between degree of White ancestry and intellectual skills within a Black population. *Human Genetics, 39*(1), 69–86.

**Schachter, S.** (1982). Recidivism and self-cure of smoking and obesity. *American Psychologist, 37,* 436–444.

**Schachter, S., & Singer, J. E.** (1962). Cognitive, social, and psychological determinants of emotional state. *Physiological Review, 69,* 379–399.

**Schacter, D. L.** (1987). Implicit memory: History and current status. *Journal of Experimental Psychology: Learning, Memory, and Cognition, 13,* 501–518.

**Schacter, D. L.** (1996). *Searching for memory: The brain, the mind, and the past.* New York: Basic Books.

**Schacter, D. L.** (1999). The seven sins of memory: Insights from psychology and cognitive neuroscience. *American Psychologist, 54*(3), 182–203.

**Schacter, D. L.** (2001a). *Forgotten ideas, neglected pioneers: Richard Semon and the story of memory.* Philadelphia: Psychology Press.

**Schacter, D. L.** (2001b). *The seven sins of memory: How the mind forgets and remembers.* Boston: Houghton Mifflin.

**Schacter, D. L.** (2012). Adaptive constructive processes and the future of memory. *American Psychologist, 67,* 603–613.

**Schacter, D. L., & Addis, D. R.** (2007). The cognitive neuroscience of constructive memory: Remembering the past and imagining the future. *Philosophical Transactions of the Royal Society of London. Series B: Biological Sciences, 362,* 773–786.

**Schacter, D. L., Addis, D. R., & Buckner, R. L.** (2008). Episodic simulation of future events: Concepts, data, and applications. *Annals of the New York Academy of Sciences, 1124,* 39–60.

**Schacter, D. L., Addis, D. R., Hassabis, D., Martin, V. C., Spreng, R. N., & Szpunar, K. K.** (2012). The future of memory: Remembering, imagining, and the brain. *Neuron, 16,* 582–583.

**Schacter, D. L., Alpert, N. M., Savage, C. R., Rauch, S. L., & Albert, M. S.** (1996). Conscious recollection and the human hippocampal formation: Evidence from positron emission tomography. *Proceedings of the National Academy of Sciences, USA, 93,* 321–325.

**Schacter, D. L., & Buckner, R. L.** (1998). Priming and the brain. *Neuron, 20,* 185–195.

**Schacter, D. L., & Curran, T.** (2000). Memory without remembering and remembering without memory: Implicit and false memories. In M. S. Gazzaniga (Ed.), *The new cognitive neurosciences* (2nd ed., pp. 829–840). Cambridge, MA: MIT Press.

**Schacter, D. L., Dobbins, I. G., & Schnyer, D. M.** (2004). Specificity of priming: A cognitive neuroscience perspective. *Nature Reviews Neuroscience, 5,* 853–862.

Schacter, D. L., Gaesser, B., & Addis, D. R. (2012). Remembering the past and imagining the future in the elderly. *Gerontologist, 59*(2), 143–151. doi:10.1159/000342198

Schacter, D. L., Guerin, S. A., & St. Jacques, P. L. (2011). Memory distortion: An adaptive perspective. *Trends in Cognitive Sciences, 15,* 467–474.

Schacter, D. L., Harbluk, J. L., & McLachlan, D. R. (1984). Retrieval without recollection: An experimental analysis of source amnesia. *Journal of Verbal Learning and Verbal Behavior, 23,* 593–611.

Schacter, D. L., Israel, L., & Racine, C. A. (1999). Suppressing false recognition in younger and older adults: The distinctiveness heuristic. *Journal of Memory and Language, 40,* 1–24.

Schacter, D. L., & Loftus, E. F. (2013). Memory and law: What can cognitive neuroscience contribute? *Nature Neuroscience, 16,* 119–123.

Schacter, D. L., Reiman, E., Curran, T., Yun, L. S., Bandy, D., McDermott, K. B., & Roediger, H. L., III. (1996). Neuroanatomical correlates of veridical and illusory recognition memory: Evidence from positron emission tomography. *Neuron, 17,* 267–274.

Schacter, D. L., & Tulving, E. (1994). *Memory systems 1994.* Cambridge, MA: MIT Press.

Schacter, D. L., Wagner, A. D., & Buckner, R. L. (2000). Memory systems of 1999. In E. Tulving & F. I. M. Craik (Eds.), *The Oxford handbook of memory* (pp. 627–643). New York: Oxford University Press.

Schacter, D. L., Wig, G. S., & Stevens, W. D. (2007). Reductions in cortical activity during priming. *Current Opinion in Neurobiology, 17,* 171–176.

Schacter, S. (1982). Recidivism and self-cure of smoking and obesity. *American Psychologist, 37,* 436–444.

Schafer, R. B., & Keith, P. M. (1980). Equity and depression among married couples. *Social Psychology Quarterly, 43,* 430–435.

Schaie, K. W. (1996). *Intellectual development in adulthood: The Seattle Longitudinal Study.* New York: Cambridge University Press.

Schaie, K. W. (2005). *Developmental influences on adult intelligence: The Seattle Longitudinal Study.* New York: Oxford University Press.

Schapira, A. H. V., Emre, M., Jenner, P., & Poewe, W. (2009). Levodopa in the treatment of Parkinson's disease. *European Journal of Neurology, 16,* 982–989.

Schatzberg, A. F., Cole, J. O., & DeBattista, C. (2003). *Manual of clinical psychopharmacology* (4th ed.). Washington, DC: American Psychiatric Publishing.

Schellenberg, E. G. (2004). Music lessons enhance IQ. *Psychological Science, 15,* 511–514.

Schenk, T., Ellison, A., Rice, N., & Milner, A. D. (2005). The role of V5/MT+ in the control of catching movements: An rTMS study. *Neuropsychologia, 43,* 189–198.

Scherer, K. R. (1999). Appraisal theory. In T. Dalgleish & M. Power (Eds.), *Handbook of cognition and emotion* (pp. 637–663). New York: Wiley.

Scherer, K. R. (2001). The nature and study of appraisal: A review of the issues. In K. R. Scherer, A. Schorr, & T. Johnstone (Eds.), *Appraisal processes in emotion: Theory, methods, research* (pp. 369–391). New York: Oxford University Press.

Schiff, M., Duyme, M., Stewart, J., Tomkiewicz, S., & Feingold, J. (1978). Intellectual status of working class children adopted early in upper middle class families. *Science, 200,* 1503–1504.

Schildkraut, J. J. (1965). The catecholamine hypothesis of affective disorders: A review of supporting evidence. *American Journal of Psychiatry, 122,* 509–522.

Schiller, D., Monfils, M. H., Raio, C. M., Johnson, D. C., LeDoux, J. E., & Phelps, E. A. (2010). Preventing the return of fear in humans using reconsolidation update mechanisms. *Nature, 463,* 49–54.

Schilling, O. K., Wahl, H.-W., & Wiegering, S. (2013). Affective development in advanced old age: Analyses of terminal change in positive and negative affect. *Developmental Psychology, 49*(5), 1011–1020. doi:10.1037/a0028775

Schlegel, A., & Barry, H., III. (1991). *Adolescence: An anthropological inquiry.* New York: Free Press.

Schlesinger, J. (2012) *The insanity hoax: Exposing the myth of the mad genius.* Ardsley-on-Hudson, NY: Shrinktunes Media.

Schmader, T., Johns, M., & Forbes, C. (2008). An integrated process model of stereotype threat effects on performance. *Psychological Review, 115,* 336–356.

Schmidt, F. L., & Hunter, J. E. (1998). The validity and utility of selection methods in personnel psychology: Practical and theoretical implications of 85 years of research findings. *Psychological Bulletin, 124,* 262–274.

Schmitt, D. P., Jonason, P. K., Byerley, G. J., Flores, S. D., Illbeck, B. E., O'Leary, K. N., & Qudrat, A. (2012). A reexamination of sex differences in sexuality: New studies reveal old truths. *Current Directions in Psychological Science, 21*(2), 135–139. doi:10.1177/0963721412436808

Schmitt, D. P., Realo, A., Voracek, M., & Allik, J. (2008). Why can't a man be more like a woman? Sex differences in personality traits across 55 cultures. *Journal of Personality and Social Psychology, 94,* 168–182.

Schneider, B. H., Atkinson, L., & Tardif, C. (2001). Child–parent attachment and children's peer relations: A quantitative review. *Developmental Psychology, 37,* 86–100.

Schnorr, J. A., & Atkinson, R. C. (1969). Repetition versus imagery instructions in the short- and long-term retention of paired associates. *Psychonomic Science, 15,* 183–184.

Schoenemann, P. T., Sheenan, M. J., & Glotzer, L. D. (2005). Prefrontal white matter volume is disproportionately larger in humans than in other primates. *Nature Neuroscience, 8,* 242–252.

Schonberg, T., O'Doherty, J. P., Joel, D., Inzelberg, R., Segev, Y., & Daw, N. D. (2010). Selective impairment of prediction error signaling in human dorsolateral but not ventral striatum in Parkinson's disease patients: Evidence from a model-based fMRI study. *NeuroImage, 49,* 772–781.

Schott, B. J., Henson, R. N., Richardson-Klavehn, A., Becker, C., Thoma, V., Heinze, H. J., & Duzel, E. (2005). Redefining implicit and explicit memory: The functional neuroanatomy of priming, remembering, and control of retrieval. *Proceedings of the National Academy of Sciences, USA, 102,* 1257–1262.

Schouwenburg, H. C. (1995). Academic procrastination: Theoretical notions, measurement, and research. In J. R. Ferrari, J. L. Johnson, & W. G. McCown (Eds.), *Procrastination and task avoidance: Theory, research, and treatment* (pp. 71–96). New York: Plenum Press.

Schreiner, C. E., Read, H. L., & Sutter, M. L. (2000). Modular organization of frequency integration in primary auditory cortex. *Annual Review of Neuroscience, 23,* 501–529.

Schreiner, C. E., & Winer, J. A. (2007). Auditory cortex mapmaking: Principles, projections, and plasticity. *Neuron, 56,* 356–365.

Schubert, T. W., & Koole, S. L. (2009). The embodied self: Making a fist enhances men's power-related self-conceptions. *Journal of Experimental Social Psychology, 45,* 828–834.

Schultz, D., Izard, C. E., & Bear, G. (2004). Children's emotion processing: Relations to emotionality and aggression. *Development and Psychopathology, 16*(2), 371–387.

**Schultz, D. P., & Schultz, S. E.** (1987). *A history of modern psychology* (4th ed.). San Diego: Harcourt Brace Jovanovich.

**Schultz, W.** (2006). Behavioral theories and the neurophysiology of reward. *Annual Review of Psychology, 57,* 87–115.

**Schultz, W.** (2007). Behavioral dopamine signals. *Trends in Neurosciences, 30,* 203–210.

**Schultz, W., Dayan, P., & Montague, P. R.** (1997). A neural substrate of prediction and reward. *Science, 275,* 1593–1599.

**Schwartz, B. L.** (2002). *Tip-of-the-tongue states: Phenomenology, mechanisms, and lexical retrieval.* Mahwah, NJ: Erlbaum.

**Schwartz, C. E., Wright, C. I., Shin, L. M., Kagan, J., & Rauch, S. L.** (2003). Inhibited and uninhibited infants "grown up": Adult amygdalar response to novelty. *Science, 300,* 1952–1953.

**Schwartz, J. H., & Westbrook, G. L.** (2000). The cytology of neurons. In E. R. Kandel, G. H. Schwartz, & T. M. Jessell (Eds.), *Principles of neural science* (pp. 67–104). New York: McGraw-Hill.

**Schwartz, S., & Maquet, P.** (2002). Sleep imaging and the neuropsychological assessment of dreams. *Trends in Cognitive Sciences, 6,* 23–30.

**Schwartzman, A. E., Gold, D., & Andres, D.** (1987). Stability of intelligence: A 40-year follow-up. *Canadian Journal of Psychology, 41,* 244–256.

**Schwarz, N., & Clore, G. L.** (1983). Mood, misattribution, and judgments of well-being: Informative and directive functions of affective states. *Journal of Personality and Social Psychology, 45,* 513–523.

**Schwarz, N., Mannheim, Z., & Clore, G. L.** (1988). How do I feel about it? The informative function of affective states. In K. Fiedler & J. Forgas (Eds.), *Affect cognition and social behavior: New evidence and integrative attempts* (pp. 44–62). Toronto: C. J. Hogrefe.

**Schweizer, T. A., Ware, J., Fischer, C. E., Craik, F. I. M., & Bialystok, E.** (2012). Bilingualism as a contributor to cognitive reserve: Evidence from brain atrophy in Alzheimer's disease. *Cortex, 48,* 991–996.

**Scoville, W. B., & Milner, B.** (1957). Loss of recent memory after bilateral hippocampal lesions. *Journal of Neurology, Neurosurgery, and Psychiatry, 20,* 11–21.

**Scribner, S.** (1975). Recall of classical syllogisms: A cross-cultural investigation of errors on logical problems. In R. J. Falmagne (Ed.), *Reasoning: Representation and process in children and adults* (pp. 153–173). Hillsdale, NJ: Erlbaum.

**Scribner, S.** (1984). Studying working intelligence. In B. Rogoff & J. Lave (Eds.), *Everyday cognition: Its development in social context* (pp. 9–40). Cambridge, MA: Harvard University Press.

**Sedlmeier, P., Eberth, J., Schwarz, M., Zimmermann, D., Haarig, F., Jaeger, S., & Kunze, S.** (2012). The psychological effects of meditation: A meta-analysis. *Psychological Bulletin, 138,* 1139–1171.

**Seeman, T. E., Dubin, L. F., & Seeman, M.** (2003). Religiosity/spirituality and health: A critical review of the evidence for biological pathways. *American Psychologist, 58,* 53–63.

**Segall, M. H., Lonner, W. J., & Berry, J. W.** (1998). Cross-cultural psychology as a scholarly discipline: On the flowering of culture in behavioral research. *American Psychologist, 53*(10), 1101–1110.

**Seidman, G.** (2013). Self-presentation and belonging on Facebook: How personality influences social media use and motivations. *Personality and Individual Differences, 54,* 402–407.

**Seligman, M. E. P.** (1971). Phobias and preparedness. *Behavior Therapy, 2,* 307–320.

**Seligman, M. E. P.** (1995). The effectiveness of psychotherapy: The consumer reports study. *American Psychologist, 48,* 966–971.

**Selikoff, I. J., Robitzek, E. H., & Ornstein, G. G.** (1952). Toxicity of hydrazine derivatives of isonicotinic acid in the chemotherapy of human tuberculosis. *Quarterly Bulletin of SeaView Hospital, 13,* 17–26.

**Selye, H., & Fortier, C.** (1950). Adaptive reaction to stress. *Psychosomatic Medicine, 12,* 149–157.

**Semenza, C.** (2009). The neuropsychology of proper names. *Mind & Language, 24,* 347–369.

**Semenza, C., & Zettin, M.** (1989). Evidence from aphasia for the role of proper names as pure referring expressions. *Nature, 342,* 678–679.

**Senghas, A., Kita, S., & Ozyurek, A.** (2004). Children create core properties of language: Evidence from an emerging sign language in Nicaragua. *Science, 305,* 1782.

**Senior, J.** (2014). *All joy and no fun: The paradox of modern parenthood.* New York: Harper-Collins.

**Senju, A., Maeda, M., Kikuchi, Y., Hasegawa, T., Tojo, Y., & Osanai, H.** (2007). Absence of contagious yawning in children with autism spectrum disorder. *Biology Letters, 3*(6), 706–708.

**Senju, A., Southgate, V., Snape, C., Leonard, M., & Csibra, G.** (2011). Do 18-month-olds really attribute mental states to others?: A critical test. *Psychological Science, 22*(7), 878–880. doi:10.1177/0956797611411584

**Senju, A., Southgate, V., White, S., & Frith, U.** (2009). Mindblind eyes: An absence of spontaneous theory of mind in Asperger syndrome. *Science, 325,* 883–885.

**Serpell, R.** (1974). Aspects of intelligence in a developing country. *African Social Research, 17,* 578–596.

**Seybold, K. S., & Hill, P. C.** (2001). The role of religion and spirituality in mental and physical health. *Current Directions in Psychological Science, 10,* 21–23.

**Seymour, K., Clifford, C. W. G., Logothetis, N. K., & Bartels, A.** (2010). Coding and binding of color and form in visual cortex. *Cerebral Cortex, 20*(8), 1946–1954. doi:10.1093/cercor/bhp265

**Shafritz, K. M., Gore, J. C., & Marois, R.** (2002). The role of the parietal cortex in visual feature binding. *Proceedings of the National Academy of Sciences, USA, 99,* 10917–10922.

**Shah, J. Y., Higgins, E. T., & Friedman, R. S.** (1998). Performance incentives and means: How regulatory focus influences goal attainment. *Journal of Personality and Social Psychology, 74,* 285–293.

**Shallcross, A. J., Ford, B. Q., Floerke, V. A., & Mauss, I. B.** (2013). Getting better with age: The relationship between age, acceptance, and negative affect. *Journal of Personality and Social Psychology, 104*(4), 734–749. doi:10.1037/a0031180

**Shallice, T., Fletcher, P., Frith, C. D., Grasby, P., Frackowiak, R. S. J., & Dolan, R. J.** (1994). Brain regions associated with acquisition and retrieval of verbal episodic memory. *Nature, 368,* 633–635.

**Shariff, A. F., & Tracy, J. L.** (2011). What are emotion expressions for? *Current Directions in Psychological Science, 20*(6), 395–399.

**Sharot, T.** (2011). *The optimism bias: A tour of the irrationally positive brain.* New York: Pantheon Books.

**Shaw, J. S., Bjork, R. A., & Handal, A.** (1995). Retrieval-induced forgetting in an eyewitness paradigm. *Psychonomic Bulletin & Review, 13,* 1023–1027.

**Shedler, J.** (2010). The efficacy of psychodynamic psychotherapy. *American Psychologist, 65,* 98–109.

**Sheehan, P.** (1979). Hypnosis and the process of imagination. In E. Fromm & R. S. Shor (Eds.), *Hypnosis: Developments in research and new perspectives* (pp. 293–319). Chicago: Aldine.

**Sheese, B. E., & Graziano, W. G.** (2005). Deciding to defect: The effects of video-game violence on cooperative behavior. *Psychological Science, 16,* 354–357.

Shen, H., Wan, F., & Wyer, R. S. (2011). Cross-cultural differences in the refusal to accept a small gift: The differential influence of reciprocity norms on Asians and North Americans. *Journal of Personality and Social Psychology, 100*(2), 271–281. doi:10.1037/a0021201

Shenton, M. E., Dickey, C. C., Frumin, M., & McCarley, R. W. (2001). A review of MRI findings in schizophrenia. *Schizophrenia Research, 49,* 1–52.

Shepherd, G. M. (1988). *Neurobiology.* New York: Oxford University Press.

Shepperd, J., Malone, W., & Sweeny, K. (2008). Exploring the causes of the self-serving bias. *Social and Personality Psychology Compass, 2*(2), 895–908.

Sherry, D. F., & Schacter, D. L. (1987). The evolution of multiple memory systems. *Psychological Review, 94,* 439–454.

Sherry, S. B., & Hall, P. A. (2009). The perfectionism model of binge eating: Tests of an integrative model. *Journal of Personality and Social Psychology, 96*(3), 690–709.

Shiffman, S., Gnys, M., Richards, T. J., Paty, J. A., & Hickcox, M. (1996). Temptations to smoke after quitting: A comparison of lapsers and maintainers. *Health Psychology, 15,* 455–461.

Shih, M., Pittinsky, T. L., & Ambady, N. (1999). Stereotype susceptibility: Identity salience and shifts in quantitative performance. *Psychological Science, 10,* 80–83.

Shimamura, A. P., & Squire, L. R. (1987). A neuropsychological study of fact memory and source amnesia. *Journal of Experimental Psychology: Learning, Memory, and Cognition, 13,* 464–473.

Shin, L. M., Rauch, S. L., & Pitman, R. K. (2006). Amygdale, medial prefrontal cortex, and hippocampal function in PTSD. *Annals of the New York Academy of Science, 1071,* 67–79.

Shinskey, J. L., & Munakata, Y. (2005). Familiarity breeds searching. *Psychological Science, 16*(8), 596–600.

Shipstead, Z., Redick, T. S., & Engle, R. W. (2012). Is working memory training effective? *Psychological Bulletin, 138,* 628–654.

Shiv, B., Loewenstein, G., Bechara, A., Damasio, H., & Damasio, A. R. (2005). Investment behavior and the negative side of emotion. *Psychological Science, 16,* 435–439.

Shomstein, S., & Yantis, S. (2004). Control of attention shifts between vision and audition in human cortex. *Journal of Neuroscience, 24,* 10702–10706.

Shore, C. (1986). Combinatorial play: Conceptual development and early multiword speech. *Developmental Psychology, 22,* 184–190.

Shultz, S., & Dunbar, R. (2010). Encephalization is not a universal macroevolutionary phenomenon in mammals but is associated with sociality. *Proceedings of the National Academy of Sciences,107,* 21582–21586.

Shweder, R. A. (1991). *Thinking through cultures: Expeditions in cultural psychology.* Cambridge, MA: Harvard University Press.

Shweder, R. A., & Sullivan, M. A. (1993). Cultural psychology: Who needs it? *Annual Review of Psychology, 44,* 497–523.

Siegel, A., Roeling, T. A. P., Gregg, T. R., & Kruk, M. R. (1999). Neuropharmacology of brain-stimulation-evoked aggression. *Neuroscience and Biobehavioral Reviews, 23,* 359–389.

Siegel, S. (1976). Morphine analgesia tolerance: Its situational specificity supports a Pavlovian conditioning model. *Science, 193,* 323–325.

Siegel, S. (1984). Pavlovian conditioning and heroin overdose: Reports by overdose victims. *Bulletin of the Psychonomic Society, 22,* 428–430.

Siegel, S. (2005). Drug tolerance, drug addiction, and drug anticipation. *Current Directions in Psychological Science, 14,* 296–300.

Siegel, S., Baptista, M. A. S., Kim, J. A., McDonald, R. V., & Weise- Kelly, L. (2000). Pavlovian psychopharmacology: The associative basis of tolerance. *Experimental and Clinical Psychopharmacology, 8,* 276–293.

Siegler, R. S. (1992). The other Alfred Binet. *Developmental Psychology, 28*(2), 179–190. doi:10.1037/0012-1649.28.2.179

Sigman, M., Spence, S. J., & Wang, T. (2006). Autism from developmental and neuropsychological perspectives. *Annual Review of Clinical Psychology, 2,* 327–355.

Sigurdsson, T., Doyere, V., Cain, C. K., & LeDoux, J. E. (2007). Longterm potentiation in the amygdala: A cellular mechanism of fear learning and memory. *Neuropharmacology, 52,* 215–227.

Silver, R. L., Boon, C., & Stones, M. H. (1983). Searching for meaning in misfortune: Making sense of incest. *Journal of Social Issues, 39,* 81–102.

Simon, L. (1998). *Genuine reality: A life of William James.* New York: Harcourt Brace.

Simon, R. W. (2008). The joys of parenthood reconsidered. *Contexts, 7,* 40–45.

Simons, D. J., & Chabris, C. F. (1999). Gorillas in our midst: Sustained inattentional blindness for dynamic events. *Perception, 28,* 1059–1074.

Simons, D. J., & Levin, D. T. (1998). Failure to detect changes to people during a real-world interaction. *Psychonomic Bulletin & Review, 5,* 644–649.

Simons, D. J., & Rensink, R. A. (2005). Change blindness: Past, present, and future. *Trends in Cognitive Sciences, 9,* 16–20.

Simpson, A., & Riggs, K. J. (2011). Three- and 4-year-olds encode modeled actions in two ways leading to immediate imitation and delayed emulation. *Developmental Psychology, 47*(3), 834–840. doi:10.1037/a0023270

Simpson, E. L. (1974). Moral development research: A case study of scientific cultural bias. *Human Development, 17,* 81–106.

Simpson, J. A., Collins, W. A., & Salvatore, J. E. (2011). The impact of early interpersonal experience on adult romantic relationship functioning: Recent findings from the Minnesota Longitudinal Study of Risk and Adaptation. *Current Directions in Psychological Science, 20*(6), 355–359. doi:10.1177/0963721411418468

Simpson, J. A., Collins, W. A., Tran, S., & Haydon, K. C. (2007). Attachment and the experience and expression of emotions in romantic relationships: A developmental perspective. *Journal of Personality and Social Psychology, 92*(2), 355–367. doi:10.1037/0022-3514.92.2.355

Singer, P. (1975). *Animal liberation: A new ethics for our treatment of animals.* New York: Random House.

Singer, T., Seymour, B., O'Doherty, J., Kaube, H., Dolan, R. J., & Frith, C. D. (2004). Empathy for pain involves the affective but not sensory components of pain. *Science, 303,* 1157–1162.

Singh, D. (1993). Adaptive significance of female physical attractiveness: Role of waist-to-hip ratio. *Journal of Personality and Social Psychology, 65,* 293–307.

Skinner, B. F. (1938). *The behavior of organisms: An experimental analysis.* New York: Appleton-Century-Crofts.

Skinner, B. F. (1948). "Superstition" in the pigeon. *Journal of Experimental Psychology, 38,* 168–172.

Skinner, B. F. (1950). Are theories of learning necessary? *Psychological Review, 57,* 193–216.

Skinner, B. F. (1953). *Science and human behavior.* New York: Macmillan.

Skinner, B. F. (1957). *Verbal behavior.* New York: Appleton-Century- Crofts.

Skinner, B. F. (1958). Teaching machines. *Science, 129,* 969–977.

**Skinner, B. F.** (1971). *Beyond freedom and dignity.* New York: Bantam Books.

**Skinner, B. F.** (1972). The operational analysis of psychological terms. In B. F. Skinner, *Cumulative record* (3rd ed., pp. 370–384). New York: Appleton-Century-Crofts. (Original work published 1945)

**Skinner, B. F.** (1979). *The shaping of a behaviorist: Part two of an autobiography.* New York: Knopf.

**Skinner, B. F.** (1986). *Walden II.* Englewood Cliffs, NJ: Prentice Hall. (Original work published 1948)

**Skoe, E., & Kraus, N.** (2012). A little goes a long way: How the adult brain is shaped by musical training in adulthood. *Journal of Neuroscience, 32,* 11507–11510.

**Skotko, B. G., Levine, S. P., & Goldstein, R.** (2011). Self- perceptions from people with Down syndrome. *American Journal of Medical Genetics Part A, 155*(10), 2360–2369. doi:10.1002/ajmg.a.34235

**Slagter, H. A.** (2012). Conventional working memory training may not improve intelligence. *Trends in Cognitive Sciences, 16,* 582–583.

**Slater, A., Morison, V., & Somers, M.** (1988). Orientation discrimination and cortical function in the human newborn. *Perception, 17,* 597–602.

**Slotnick, S. D., & Schacter, D. L.** (2004). A sensory signature that distinguished true from false memories. *Nature Neuroscience, 7,* 664–672.

**Smart, E., Smart, L, & Morton, L.** (2003). *Bringing Elizabeth home: A journey of faith and hope.* New York: Doubleday.

**Smetacek, V.** (2002). Balance: Mind-grasping gravity. *Nature, 415,* 481.

**Smetana, J. G.** (1981). Preschool children's conceptions of moral and social rules. *Child Development, 52,* 1333–1336.

**Smetana, J. G., & Braeges, J. L.** (1990). The development of toddlers' moral and conventional judgments. *Merrill-Palmer Quarterly, 36,* 329–346.

**Smetanin, P., Stiff, D., Briante, C., Adair, C. E., Ahmad, S., & Khan, M.** (2011). *The life and economic impact of major mental illnesses in Canada.* Ottawa: RiskAnalytica, on behalf of the Mental Health Commission of Canada.

**Smith, A. R., Seid, M. A., Jimanez, L. C., & Wcislo, W. T.** (2010). Socially induced brain development in a facultatively eusocial sweat bee *Megalopta genalis* (Halictidae). *Proceedings of the Royal Society B: Biological Sciences.*

**Smith, E. E., & Jonides, J.** (1997). Working memory: A view from neuroimaging. *Cognitive Psychology, 33,* 5–42.

**Smith, M. L., Glass, G. V., & Miller, T. I.** (1980). *The benefits of psychotherapy.* Baltimore: Johns Hopkins University Press.

**Smith, N., & Tsimpli, I.-M.** (1995). *The mind of a savant.* Oxford, England: Oxford University Press.

**Snedeker, J., Geren, J., & Shafto, C.** (2007). Starting over: International adoption as a natural experiment in language development. *Psychological Science, 18,* 79–87.

**Snedeker, J., Geren, J., & Shafto, C.** (2012). Disentangling the effects of cognitive development and linguistic expertise: A longitudinal study of the acquisition of English in internationally adopted children. *Cognitive Psychology, 65,* 39–76.

**Society, the Individual, and Medicine (SIM).** (2013). *Mental health: Suicide in Canada—Facts and figures.* Retrieved from http://www.med.uottawa.ca/sim/data/Suicide_e.htm

**Solomon, J., & George, C.** (1999). The measurement of attachment security in infancy and childhood. In J. Cassidy & P. R. Shaver (Eds.), *Handbook of attachment: Theory, research and clinical applications* (pp. 287–316). New York: Guilford Press.

**Solomon, S., Greenberg, J., & Pyszczynski, T.** (1991). A terror management theory of social behavior: The psychological functions of self-esteem and cultural worldviews. In M. P. Zanna (Ed.), *Advances in experimental social psychology* (Vol. 24, pp. 93–159). New York: Academic Press.

**Solomon, S., Greenberg, J., & Pyszczynski, T.** (2004). The cultural animal: Twenty years of terror management theory and research. In J. Greenberg, S. L. Koole, & T. Pyszczynski (Eds.), *Handbook of experimental existential psychology* (pp. 13–34). New York: Guilford Press.

**Son, L. K., & Metcalfe, J.** (2000). Metacognitive and control strategies in study-time allocation. *Journal of Experimental Psychology: Learning, Memory, and Cognition, 26,* 204–221.

**Sonnby-Borgstrom, M., Jonsson, P., & Svensson, O.** (2003). Emotional empathy as related to mimicry reactions at different levels of information processing. *Journal of Nonverbal Behavior, 27,* 3–23.

**Southgate, V., Senju, A., & Csibra, G.** (2007). Action anticipation through attribution of false belief by two-year-olds. *Psychological Science, 18,* 587–592.

**Sparrow, B., Liu, J., & Wegner, D. M.** (2011). Google effects on memory: Cognitive consequence of having information at our fingertips. *Science, 333,* 776–778.

**Spearman, C.** (1904). "General intelligence," objectively determined and measured. *American Journal of Psychology, 15,* 201–293.

**Speisman, J. C., Lazarus, R. S., Moddkoff, A., & Davison, L.** (1964). Experimental reduction of stress based on ego-defense theory. *Journal of Abnormal and Social Psychology, 68,* 367–380.

**Spelke, E. S.** (2005). Sex differences in intrinsic aptitude for mathematics and science: A critical review. *The American Psychologist, 60*(9), 950–958. doi:10.1037/0003-066X.60.9.950

**Spellman, B. A.** (1996). Acting as intuitive scientists: Contingency judgments are made while controlling for alternative potential causes. *Psychological Science, 7,* 337–342.

**Sperling, G.** (1960). The information available in brief visual presentations. *Psychological Monographs, 74* (Whole No. 48).

**Sperry, R. W.** (1964). The great cerebral commissure. *Scientific American, 210,* 42–52.

**Spinoza, B.** (1982). *The ethics and selected letters* (S. Feldman, Ed., & S. Shirley, Trans.). Indianapolis, IN: Hackett. (Original work published 1677)

**Spiro, H. M., McCrea Curnan, M. G., Peschel, E., & St. James, D.** (1994). *Empathy and the practice of medicine: Beyond pills and the scalpel.* New Haven, CT: Yale University Press.

**Spitz, R. A.** (1949). Motherless infants. *Child Development, 20,* 145–155.

**Sprecher, S.** (1999). "I love you more today than yesterday": Romantic partners' perceptions of changes in love and related affect over time. *Journal of Personality and Social Psychology, 76,* 46–53.

**Square, D.** (1997). Fetal alcohol syndrome endemic on Manitoba reserve. *Canadian Medical Association Journal, 157,* 59–60.

**Squire, L. R.** (1992). Memory and the hippocampus: A synthesis from findings with rats, monkeys, and humans. *Psychological Review, 99,* 195–231.

**Squire, L. R.** (2009). The legacy of patient HM for neuroscience. *Neuron, 61,* 6–9.

**Squire, L. R., & Kandel, E. R.** (1999). *Memory: From mind to molecules.* New York: Scientific American Library.

**Squire, L. R., Knowlton, B., & Musen, G.** (1993). The structure and organization of memory. *Annual Review of Psychology, 44,* 453–495.

**Squire, L. R., & Wixted, J. T.** (2011). The cognitive neuroscience of memory since HM. *Annual Review of Neuroscience, 34,* 259–288.

Srivistava, S., John, O. P., Gosling, S. D., & Potter, J. (2003). Development of personality in early and middle adulthood: Set like plaster or persistent change? *Journal of Personality and Social Psychology, 84,* 1041–1053.

Sroufe, L. A., Egeland, B., & Kruetzer, T. (1990). The fate of early experience following developmental change: Longitudinal approaches to individual adaptation in childhood. *Child Development, 61,* 1363–1373.

Staddon, J. E. R., & Simmelhag, V. L. (1971). The "superstition" experiment: A reexamination of its implications for the principles of adaptive behavior. *Psychological Review, 78,* 3–43.

Stafford, M., Newbold, B. K., & Ross, N. A. (2011). Psychological distress among immigrants and visible minorities in Canada: A contextual analysis. *International Journal of Social Psychiatry, 57*(4), 428–441.

Stanovich, K. E. (2009). *What intelligence tests miss: The psychology of rational thought.* New Haven, CT: Yale University Press.

Starkey, P., Spelke, E. S., & Gelman, R. (1983). Detection of inter-modal numerical correspondences by human infants. *Science, 222,* 179–181.

Starkey, P., Spelke, E. S., & Gelman, R. (1990). Numerical abstraction by human infants. *Cognition, 36,* 97–127.

Statistics Canada. (2004, June 15). Canadian community health survey (2003). *The Daily.* Retrieved from http://www.statcan.gc.ca/daily-quotidien/040615/dq040615b-eng.htm

Statistics Canada. (2010). Canadian community health survey (2009, 2010). In Childhood Obesity Foundation, (n.d.), *Facts: Statistics.* Retrieved from http://www.childhoodobesityfoundation.ca/statistics

Statistics Canada. (2012a, October 24). 2011 Census of population: Linguistic characteristics of Canadians. *The Daily.* Retrieved from http://www.statcan.gc.ca/daily-quotidien/121024/dq121024a-eng.htm

Statistics Canada. (2012b). *Father's Day … By the Numbers 2011.* Retrieved from http://www42.statcan.gc.ca/smr08/2012/smr08_165_2012-eng.htm

Statistics Canada. (2013a). *Heavy drinking, 2012.* Retrieved from http://www.statcan.gc.ca/pub/82-625-x/2013001/article/11838-eng.htm

Statistics Canada. (2013b). *Overweight and obese adults (self-reported), 2012.* Retrieved from http://www.statcan.gc.ca/pub/82-625-x/2013001/article/11840-eng.htm

Statistics Canada. (2013c). *Section B—Anxiety disorders.* Retrieved from http://www.statcan.gc.ca/pub/82-619-m/2012004/sections/sectionb-eng.htm

Statistics Canada. (2013d, September 18). Canadian community health survey: Mental health, 2012. *The Daily.* Retrieved from http://www.statcan.gc.ca/daily-quotidien/130918/dq130918a-eng.pdf

Statistics Canada. (2014). *Suicides and suicide rate, by sex and by age group (both sexes no.).* (CANSIM table 102-0551). Retrieved from http://www.statcan.gc.ca/tables-tableaux/sum-som/l01/cst01/hlth66a-eng.htm

Steele, C. M., & Aronson, J. (1995). Stereotype threat and the intellectual test performance of African Americans. *Journal of Personality and Social Psychology, 69,* 797–811.

Steele, C. M., & Josephs, R. A. (1990). Alcohol myopia: Its prized and dangerous effects. *American Psychologist, 45,* 921–933.

Steele, H., Steele, M., Croft, C., & Fonagy, P. (1999). Infant-mother attachment at one year predicts children's understanding of mixed emotions at six years. *Social Development, 8,* 161–178.

Stein, D. J., Phillips, K. A., Bolton, D., Fulford, K. W. M., Sadler, J. Z., & Kendler, K. S. (2010). What is a mental/psychiatric disorder? From *DSM–IV* to *DSM–V. Psychological Medicine, 40*(11), 1759–1765. doi:10.1017/S0033291709992261.

Stein, M., Federspiel, A., Koenig, T., Wirth, M., Lehmann, C., Wiest, … Dierks, T. (2009). Reduced frontal activation with increasing second language proficiency. *Neuropsychologia,47,* 2712–2720.

Stein, M. B. (1998). Neurobiological perspectives on social phobia: From affiliation to zoology. *Biological Psychiatry, 44,* 1277–1285.

Stein, M. B., Chavira, D. A., & Jang, K. L. (2001). Bringing up bashful baby: Developmental pathways to social phobia. *Psychiatric Clinics of North America, 24,* 661–675.

Stein, Z., Susser, M., Saenger, G., & Marolla, F. (1975). *Famine and development: The Dutch hunger winter of 1944–1945.* Oxford, England: Oxford University Press.

Steinbaum, E. A., & Miller, N. E. (1965). Obesity from eating elicited by daily stimulation of hypothalamus. *American Journal of Physiology, 208,* 1–5.

Steinberg, L. (1999). *Adolescence* (5th ed.). Boston: McGraw-Hill.

Steinberg, L. (2007). Risk taking in adolescence: New perspectives from brain and behavioral science. *Current Directions in Psychological Science, 16*(2), 55–59. doi:10.1111/j.1467-8721.2007.00475x

Steinberg, L., & Monahan, K. C. (2007). Age differences in resistance to peer influence. *Developmental Psychology, 43,* 1531–1543.

Steinberg, L., & Morris, A. S. (2001). Adolescent development. *Annual Review of Psychology, 52,* 83–110.

Steiner, F. (1986). Differentiating smiles. In E. Branniger-Huber & F. Steiner (Eds.), *FACS in psychotherapy research* (pp.139–148). Zurich: Universität Zürich, Department of Clinical Psychology.

Steiner, J. E. (1973). The gustofacial response: Observation on normal and anencephalic newborn infants. In J. F. Bosma (Ed.), *Fourth symposium on oral sensation and perception: Development in the fetus and infant* (DHEW 73–546; pp. 254–278). Bethesda, MD: U.S. Department of Heath, Education, and Welfare.

Steiner, J. E. (1979). Human facial expressions in response to taste and smell stimulation. *Advances in Child Development and Behavior, 13,* 257–295.

Stellar, J. R., Kelley, A. E., & Corbett, D. (1983). Effects of peripheral and central dopamine blockade on lateral hypothalamic self- stimulation: Evidence for both reward and motor deficits. *Pharmacology, Biochemistry, and Behavior, 18,* 433–442.

Stellar, J. R., & Stellar, E. (1985). *The neurobiology of motivation and reward.* New York: Springer-Verlag.

Stelmack, R. M. (1990). Biological bases of extraversion: Psychophysiological evidence. *Journal of Personality, 58,* 293–311.

Stephens, R. S. (1999). Cannabis and hallucinogens. In B. S. McCrady & E. E. Epstein (Eds.), *Addictions: A comprehensive guidebook* (pp. 121–140). New York: Oxford University Press.

Sterelny, K., & Griffiths, P. E. (1999). *Sex and death: An introduction to philosophy of biology.* Chicago: University of Chicago Press.

Stern, J. A., Brown, M., Ulett, A., & Sletten, I. (1977). A comparison of hypnosis, acupuncture, morphine, Valium, aspirin, and placebo in the management of experimentally induced pain. In W. E. Edmonston (Ed.), *Conceptual and investigative approaches to hypnosis and hypnotic phenomena* (Vol. 296, pp. 175–193). New York: Annals of the New York Academy of Sciences.

Stern, W. (1914). *The psychological methods of testing intelligence* (G. M. Whipple, Trans.). Baltimore: Warwick & York.

Sternberg, R. J. (1986). A triangular theory of love. *Psychological Review, 93,* 119–135.

Sternberg, R. J. (1999). The theory of successful intelligence. *Review of General Psychology, 3*(4), 292–316. doi:10.1037/1089-2680.3.4.292

Stevens, J. (1988). An activity approach to practical memory. In M. M. Gruneberg, P. E. Morris, & R. N. Sykes (Eds.), *Practical aspects of memory: Current research and issues* (Vol. 1, pp. 335–341). New York: Wiley.

**Stevens, L. A.** (1971). *Explorers of the brain.* New York: Knopf.

**Stevenson, R. J., & Boakes, R. A.** (2003). A mnemonic theory of odor perception. *Psychological Review, 110,* 340–364.

**Stevenson, R. J., & Wilson, D. A.** (2007). Odour perception: An object-recognition approach. *Perception, 36,* 1821–1833.

**Stewart-Williams, S.** (2004). The placebo puzzle: Putting together the pieces. *Health Psychology, 23,* 198–206.

**Stickgold, R., Hobson, J. A., Fosse, R., & Fosse, M.** (2001). Sleep, learning, and dreams: Off-line memory reprocessing. *Science, 294,* 1052–1057.

**Stickgold, R., Malia, A., Maguire, D., Roddenberry, D., & O'Connor, M.** (2000). Replaying the game: Hypnagogic images in normals and anmesics. *Science, 290,* 350–353.

**Stigler, J. W., Shweder, R., & Herdt, G. (Eds.).** (1990). *Cultural psychology: Essays on comparative human development.* Cambridge, England: Cambridge University Press.

**St. Jacques, P. L., & Schacter, D. L.** (2013). Modifying memory: Selectively enhancing and updating personal memories for a museum tour by reactivating them. *Psychological Science, 24,* 537–543.

**Stone, A. A., Schwartz, J. E., Broderick, J. E., & Deaton, A.** (2010). A snapshot of the age distribution of psychological well-being in the United States. *Proceedings of the National Academy of Sciences, USA, 107*(22), 9985–9990. doi:10.1073/pnas.1003744107

**Stone, J., Perry, Z. W., & Darley, J. M.** (1997). "White men can't jump": Evidence for the perceptual confirmation of racial stereotypes following a basketball game. *Basic and Applied Social Psychology, 19,* 291–306.

**Stoodley, C. J., Ray, N., J., Jack, A., & Stein, J. F.** (2008). Implicit learning in control, dyslexic, and garden-variety poor readers. *Annals of the New York Academy of Sciences, 1145,* 173–183.

**Storm, B. C., Bjork, E. L., Bjork, R. A., & Nestojko, J. F.** (2006). Is retrieval success a necessary condition for retrieval-induced forgetting? *Psychonomic Bulletin & Review, 2,* 249–253.

**Storms, M. D.** (1973). Videotape and the attribution process: Reversing actors' and observers' points of view. *Journal of Personality and Social Psychology, 27,* 165–175.

**Strack, F., Martin, L. L., & Stepper, S.** (1988). Inhibiting and facilitating conditions of the human smile: A nonobtrusive test of the facial feedback hypothesis. *Journal of Personality and Social Psychology, 54,* 768–777.

**Strayer, D. L., Drews, F. A., & Johnston, W. A.** (2003). Cell phone induced failures of visual attention during simulated driving. *Journal of Experimental Psychology: Applied, 9,* 23–32.

**Streissguth, A. P., Barr, H. M., Bookstein, F. L., Sampson, P. D., & Carmichael Olson, H.** (1999). The long-term neurocognitive consequences of prenatal alcohol exposure: A 14-year study. *Psychological Science, 10,* 186–190.

**Striano, T., & Reid, V. M.** (2006). Social cognition in the first year. *Trends in Cognitive Sciences, 10*(10), 471–476.

**Strickland, L. H.** (1991). Russian and Soviet social psychology. *Canadian Psychology, 32,* 580–595.

**Striegel-Moore, R. H., & Bulik, C. M.** (2007). Risk factors for eating disorders. *American Psychologist, 62,* 181–198.

**Strohmetz, D. B., Rind, B., Fisher, R., & Lynn, M.** (2002). Sweetening the till: The use of candy to increase restaurant tipping. *Journal of Applied Social Psychology, 32,* 300–309.

**Stroop, J. P.** (1935). Studies of interference in serial verbal reactions. *Journal of Experimental Psychology, 18,* 643–661.

**Stuss, D. T., & Benson, D. F.** (1986). *The frontal lobes.* New York: Raven Press.

**Subramaniam, K., Kounios, J., Parrish, T. B., & Jung-Beeman, M.** (2009). A brain mechanism for facilitation of insight by positive affect. *Journal of Cognitive Neuroscience, 21,* 415–432.

**Substance Abuse and Mental Health Services Administration.** (2005). *Results from the 2004 National Survey on Drug Use and Health: National findings* (DHHS Publication No. SMA 05–4062, NSDUH Series H-28). Rockville, MD: U. S. Department of Health and Human Services.

**Suchman, A. L., Markakis, K., Beckman, H. B., & Frankel, R.** (1997). A model of empathic communication in the medical interview. *Journal of the American Medical Association, 277,* 678–682.

**Suddendorf, T., & Corballis, M. C.** (2007). The evolution of foresight: What is mental time travel and is it unique to humans? *Behavioral and Brain Sciences, 30,* 299–313.

**Suderman, M., McGowan, P. O., Sasaki, A., Huang, T. C. T., Hallett, M. T., Meaney, M. J., ... Szyf, M.** (2012). Conserved epigenetic sensitivity to early life experiences in the rat and human hippocampus. *Proceedings of the National Academy of Sciences, USA, 109*(Suppl. 2), 17266–17272.

**Sulloway, F. J.** (1992). *Freud, biologist of the mind.* Cambridge, MA: Harvard University Press.

**Sundet, J. M., Eriksen, W., & Tambs, K.** (2008). Intelligence correlations between brothers decrease with increasing age difference: Evidence for shared environmental effects in young adults. *Psychological Science, 19,* 843–847.

**Susman, S., Dent, C., McAdams, L., Stacy, A., Burton, D., & Flay, B.** (1994). Group self-identification and adolescent cigarette smoking: A 1-year prospective study. *Journal of Abnormal Psychology, 103,* 576–580.

**Susser, E. B., Brown, A., & Matte, T. D.** (1999). Prenatal factors and adult mental and physical health. *Canadian Journal of Psychiatry, 44*(4), 326–334.

**Suthana, N., & Fried, I.** (2012). Percepts to recollections: Insights from single neuron recordings in the human brain. *Trends in Cognitive Sciences, 16,* 427–436.

**Suzuki, L. A., & Valencia, R. R.** (1997). Race-ethnicity and measured intelligence: Educational implications. *American Psychologist, 52,* 1103–1114.

**Swann, W. B., Jr.** (1983). Self-verification: Bringing social reality into harmony with the self. In J. M. Suls & A. G. Greenwald (Ed.), *Psychological perspectives on the self* (Vol. 2, pp. 33–66). Hillsdale, NJ: Erlbaum.

**Swann, W. B., Jr.** (2012). Self-verification theory. In P. Van Lang, A. Kruglanski, & E. T. Higgins (Eds.), *Handbook of theories of social psychology* (pp. 23–42). London: Sage.

**Swann, W. B., Jr., & Rentfrow, P. J.** (2001). Blirtatiousness: Cognitive, behavioral, and physiological consequences of rapid responding. *Journal of Personality and Social Psychology, 181*(6), 1160–1175.

**Swayze, V. W. II.** (1995). Frontal leukotomy and related psychosurgical procedures before antipsychotics (1935–1954): A historical overview. *American Journal of Psychiatry, 152,* 505–515.

**Swednsen, J., Hammen, C., Heller, T., & Gitlin, M.** (1995). Correlates of stress reactivity in patients with bipolar disorder. *American Journal of Psychiatry, 152,* 795–797.

**Swets, J. A., Dawes, R. M., & Monahan, J.** (2000). Psychological science can improve diagnostic decisions. *Psychological Science in the Public Interest, 1,* 1–26.

**Swinkels, A.** (2003). An effective exercise for teaching cognitive heuristics. *Teaching of Psychology, 30,* 120–122.

Szechtman, H., & Woody, E. Z. (2006). Obsessive-compulsive disorder as a disturbance of security motivation: Constraints on comorbidity. *Neurotoxicity Research, 10*, 103–112.

Szpunar, K. K. (2010). Episodic future thought: An emerging concept. *Perspectives on Psychological Science, 5*, 142–162.

Szpunar, K. K., Khan, N. Y., & Schacter, D. L. (2013). Interpolated memory tests reduce mind wandering and improve learning of online lectures. *Proceedings of the National Academy of Sciences, USA, 110*, 6313–6317.

Szpunar, K. K., Watson, J. M., & McDermott, K. B. (2007). Neural substrates of envisioning the future. *Proceedings of the National Academy of Sciences, USA, 104*, 642–647.

Tajfel, H., Billig, M. G., Bundy, R. P., & Flament, C. (1971). Social categorization and intergroup behaviour. *European Journal of Social Psychology, 1*, 149–178.

Tajfel, H., & Turner, J. C. (1986). The social identity theory of intergroup behavior. In S. Worchel & W. G. Austin (Eds.), *Psychology of intergroup relations* (pp. 7–24). Chicago: Nelson.

Tajfel, H., & Wilkes, A. L. (1963). Classification and quantitative judgement. *British Journal of Psychology, 54*, 101–114.

Takahashi, K. (1986). Examining the Strange Situation procedure with Japanese mothers and 12-month-old infants. *Developmental Psychology, 22*, 265–270.

Tamir, M., & Ford, B. Q. (2012). Should people pursue feelings that feel good or feelings that do good? Emotional preferences and well-being. *Emotion, 12*, 1061–1070.

Tamis-LeMonda, C. S., Adolph, K. E., Lobo, S. A., Karasik, L. B., Ishak, S., & Dimitropoulou, K. A. (2008). When infants take mothers' advice: 18-month-olds integrate perceptual and social information to guide motor action. *Developmental Psychology, 44*, 734–746.

Tamminga, C. A., Nemeroff, C. B., Blakely, R. D., Brady, L., Carter, C. S., Davis, K. L., … Suppes, T. (2002). Developing novel treatments for mood disorders: Accelerating discovery. *Biological Psychiatry, 52*, 589–609.

Tanaka, F., Cicourel, A., & Movellan, J. R. (2007). Socialization between toddlers and robots at an early childhood education center. *Proceedings of the National Academy of Sciences, USA, 104*(46), 17954–17958.

Tang, Y.-P., Shimizu, E., Dube, G. R., Rampon, C., Kerchner, G. A., Zhuo, M., … Tsien, J. Z. (1999). Genetic enhancement of learning and memory in mice. *Nature, 401*, 63–69.

Tang, Y. Y., Lu, Q., Fan, M., Yang, Y., & Posner, M. I. (2012). Mechanisms of white matter changes induced by meditation. *Proceedings of the National Academy of Sciences,109*, 10570–10574.

Tarr, M. J., & Vuong, Q. C. (2002). Visual object recognition. In S. Yantis & H. Pashler (Eds.), *Stevens' handbook of experimental psychology: Vol. 1. Sensation and perception* (3rd ed., pp. 287–314). New York: Wiley.

Tart, C. T. (Ed.). (1969). *Altered states of consciousness.* New York: Wiley.

Task Force on Empirically Supported Treatments. (1998). Empirically supported treatments in psychology: Recommendations for Canadian professional psychology. (Discussion document). Retrieved from http://www.cpa.ca/documents/empiric_toc.html

Task Force on Promotion and Dissemination of Psychological Procedures. (1995). Training in and dissemination of empirically-validated psychological treatments: Report and recommendations. *Clinical Psychologist, 48*, 3–23.

Taylor, D., & Lambert, W. (1990). *Language and culture in the lives of immigrants and refugees.* Austin, TX: Hogg Foundation for Mental Health.

Taylor, E. (2001). *William James on consciousness beyond the margin.* Princeton, NJ: Princeton University Press.

Taylor, S. E. (1986). *Health psychology.* New York: Random House.

Taylor, S. E. (1989). *Positive illusions.* New York: Basic Books.

Taylor, S. E. (2002). *The tending instinct: How nurturing is essential to who we are and how we live.* New York: Times Books.

Taylor, S. E., & Brown, J. D. (1988). Illusion and well-being: A social psychological perspective on mental health. *Psychological Bulletin, 103*, 193–210.

Taylor, S. E., & Fiske, S. T. (1975). Point-of-view and perceptions of causality. *Journal of Personality and Social Psychology, 32*, 439–445.

Taylor, S. E., & Fiske, S. T. (1978). Salience, attention, and attribution: Top of the head phenomenon. In L. Berkowitz (Ed.), *Advances in experimental social psychology* (Vol. 11, pp. 249–288). New York: Academic Press.

Teasdale, J. D., Segal, Z. V., & Williams, J. M. G. (2000). Prevention of relapse/recurrence in major depression by mindfulness-based cognitive therapy. *Journal of Consulting and Clinical Psychology, 68*, 615–623.

Telch, M. J., Lucas, J. A., & Nelson, P. (1989). Non-clinical panic in college students: An investigation of prevalence and symptomology. *Journal of Abnormal Psychology, 98*, 300–306.

Tellegen, A., & Atkinson, G. (1974). Openness to absorbing and self-altering experiences ("absorption"), a trait related to hypnotic susceptibility. *Journal of Abnormal Psychology, 83*, 268–277.

Tellegen, A., Lykken, D. T., Bouchard, T. J., Wilcox, K., Segal, N., & Rich, A. (1988). Personality similarity in twins reared together and apart. *Journal of Personality and Social Psychology, 54*, 1031–1039.

Temerlin, M. K., & Trousdale, W. W. (1969). The social psychology of clinical diagnosis. *Psychotherapy: Theory, Research & Practice, 6*, 24–29.

ten Brinke, L., & Porter, S. (2012). Cry me a river: Identifying the behavioural consequences of extremely high-stakes interpersonal deception. *Law and Human Behavior, 36*, 469–477.

ten Brinke, L., Porter, S., & Baker, A. (2012). Darwin the detective: Observable facial muscle contractions reveal emotional high-stakes lies. *Evolution and Human Behavior, 33*, 411–416.

Terman, L. M. (1916). *The measurement of intelligence.* Boston: Houghton Mifflin.

Terman, L. M., & Oden, M. H. (1959). *Genetic studies of genius: Vol. 5. The gifted group at mid-life.* Stanford, CA: Stanford University Press.

Tesser, A. (1991). Emotion in social comparison and reflection processes. In J. Suls & T. A. Wills (Ed.), *Social comparison: Contemporary theory and research* (pp. 117–148). Hillsdale, NJ: Erlbaum.

Teyler, T. J., & DiScenna, P. (1986). The hippocampal memory indexing theory. *Behavioral Neuroscience, 100*, 147–154.

Thaker, G. K. (2002). Current progress in schizophrenia research. Search for genes of schizophrenia: Back to defining valid phenes. *Journal of Nervous and Mental Disease, 190*, 411–412.

Thaler, K., Delivuk, M., Chapman, A., Gaynes, B. N., Kaminski, A., & Gartlehner, G. (2011). Second-generation antidepressants for seasonal affective disorder. *Cochrane Database of Systematic Reviews,* CD008591.

Thaler, R. H. (1988). The ultimatum game. *Journal of Economic Perspectives, 2*, 195–206.

Thase, M. E., & Howland, R. H. (1995). Biological processes in depression: An updated review and integration. In E. E. Beckham &

W. R. Leber (Eds.), *Handbook of depression* (2nd ed., pp. 213–279). New York: Guilford Press.

**Thelen, E., Corbetta, D., Kamm, K., Spencer, J. P., Schneider, K., & Zernicke, R. F.** (1993). The transition to reaching: Mapping intention and intrinsic dynamics. *Child Development, 64,* 1058–1098.

**Thibaut, J. W., & Kelley, H. H.** (1959). *The social psychology of groups.* New Brunswick, NJ: Transaction Publishers.

**Thoma, S. J., Narvaez, D., Rest, J., & Derryberry, P.** (1999). Does moral judgment development reduce to political attitudes or verbal ability? Evidence using the defining issues test. *Educational Psychology Review, 11,* 325–341.

**Thomaes, S., Bushman, B. J., Stegge, H., & Olthof, T.** (2008). Trumping shame by blasts of noise: Narcissism, self-esteem, shame, and aggression in young adolescents. *Child Development, 79*(6), 1792–1801.

**Thomas, A., & Chess, S.** (1977). *Temperament and development.* New York: Brunner/Mazel.

**Thomason, M., & Thompson, P. M.** (2011). Diffusion imaging, white matter, and psychopathology. *Annual Review of Clinical Psychology, 7,* 63–85.

**Thompson, C. P., Skowronski, J., Larsen, S. F., & Betz, A.** (1996). *Autobiographical memory: Remembering what and remembering when.* Mahwah, NJ: Erlbaum.

**Thompson, P. M., Giedd, J. N., Woods, R. P., MacDonald, D., Evans, A. C., & Toga, A. W.** (2000). Growth patterns in the developing brain detected by using continuum mechanical tensor maps. *Nature, 404,* 190–193.

**Thompson, P. M., Vidal, C., Giedd, J. N., Gochman, P., Blumenthal, J., Nicolson, R., … Rapoport, J. L.** (2001). Accelerated gray matter loss in very early-onset schizophrenia. *Proceedings of the National Academy of Sciences, USA, 98,* 11650–11655.

**Thompson, R. F.** (2005). In search of memory traces. *Annual Review of Psychology, 56,* 1–23.

**Thomson, D. M.** (1988). Context and false recognition. In G. M. Davies & D. M. Thomson (Eds.), *Memory in context: Context in memory* (pp. 285–304). Chichester, England: Wiley.

**Thorndike, E. L.** (1898). Animal intelligence: An experimental study of associative processes in animals. *Psychological Review Monograph Supplements, 2,* 4–160.

**Thornhill, R., & Gangestad, S. W.** (1993). Human facial beauty: Averageness, symmetry, and parasite resistance. *Human Nature, 4,* 237–269.

**Thornhill, R., & Gangestad, S. W.** (1999). The scent of symmetry: A human sex pheromone that signals fitness? *Evolution and Human Behavior, 20,* 175–201.

**Thurber, J.** (1956). *Further fables of our time.* New York: Simon & Schuster.

**Thurstone, L. L.** (1938). *Primary mental abilities.* Chicago: University of Chicago Press.

**Tice, D. M., & Baumeister, R. F.** (1997). Longitudinal study of procrastination, performance, stress, and health: The costs and benefits of dawdling. *Psychological Science, 8*(6), 454–458.

**Tienari, P., Wynne, L. C., Sorri, A., Lahti, I., Läksy, K., Moring, J., … Wahlberg, K. E.** (2004). Genotype–environment interaction in schizophrenia-spectrum disorder: Long-term follow-up study of Finnish adoptees. *British Journal of Psychiatry, 184,* 216–222.

**Timmerman, T. A.** (2007). "It was a thought pitch": Personal, situational, and target influences on hit-by-pitch events across time. *Journal of Applied Psychology, 92,* 876–884.

**Todd, A. R., Bodenhausen, G. V., Richeson, J. A., & Galinsky, A. D.** (2011). Perspective taking combats automatic expressions of racial bias. *Journal of Personality and Social Psychology, 100*(6), 1027–1042. doi:10.1037/a0022308

**Todd, J. T., & Morris, E. K.** (1992). Case histories in the great power of steady misrepresentation. *American Psychologist, 47*(11), 1441–1453.

**Toga, A. W., Clark, K. A., Thompson, P. M., Shattuck, D. W., & Van Horn, J. D.** (2012). Mapping the human connectome. *Neurosurgery, 71,* 1–5.

**Tolman, E. C., & Honzik, C. H.** (1930a). "Insight" in rats. *University of California Publications in Psychology, 4,* 215–232.

**Tolman, E. C., & Honzik, C. H.** (1930b). Introduction and removal of reward and maze performance in rats. *University of California Publications in Psychology, 4,* 257–275.

**Tolman, E. C., Ritchie, B. F., & Kalish, D.** (1946). Studies in spatial learning: I: Orientation and short cut. *Journal of Experimental Psychology, 36,* 13–24.

**Tomasello, M., & Call, J.** (2004). The role of humans in the cognitive development of apes revisited. *Animal Cognition, 7,* 213–215.

**Tomasello, M., Davis-Dasilva, M., Camak, L., & Bard, K.** (1987). Observational learning of tool use by young chimpanzees. *Human Evolution, 2,* 175–183.

**Tomasello, M., Savage-Rumbaugh, S., & Kruger, A. C.** (1993). Imitative learning of actions on objects by children, chimpanzees, and enculturated chimpanzees. *Child Development, 64,* 1688–1705.

**Tomkins, S. S.** (1981). The role of facial response in the experience of emotion. *Journal of Personality and Social Psychology, 40,* 351–357.

**Tooby, J., & Cosmides, L.** (2000). Mapping the evolved functional organization of mind and brain. In M. S. Gazzaniga (Ed.), *The cognitive neurosciences* (pp. 1185–1198). Cambridge, MA: MIT Press.

**Tootell, R. B. H., Reppas, J. B., Dale, A. M., Look, R. B., Sereno, M. I., Malach, R., … Rosen, B. R.** (1995). Visual-motion aftereffect in human cortical area MT revealed by functional magnetic resonance imaging. *Nature, 375,* 139–141.

**Torgensen, S.** (1986). Childhood and family characteristics in panic and generalized anxiety disorder. *American Journal of Psychiatry, 143,* 630–639.

**Torrey, E. F., Bower, A. E., Taylor, E. H., & Gottesman, I. I.** (1994). *Schizophrenia and manic-depressive disorder: The biological roots of mental illness as revealed by the landmark study of identical twins.* New York: Basic Books.

**Tracy, J. L., & Beall, A. T.** (2011). Happy guys finish last: The impact of emotion expressions on sexual attraction. *Emotion, 11*(6), 1379–1387. doi:10.1037/a0022902

**Tracy, J. L., Shariff, A. F., Zhao, W., & Henrich, J.** (2013). Cross-cultural evidence that the noverbal expression of pride is an automatic status signal. *Journal of Experimental Psychology: General, 142*(1), 163–180.

**Treede, R. D., Kenshalo, D. R., Gracely, R. H., & Jones, A. K.** (1999). The cortical representation of pain. *Pain, 79,* 105–111.

**Treisman, A.** (1998). Feature binding, attention and object perception. *Philosophical Transactions of the Royal Society (B), 353,* 1295–1306.

**Treisman, A.** (2006). How the deployment of attention determines what we see. *Visual Cognition, 14,* 411–443.

**Treisman, A., & Gelade, G.** (1980). A feature integration theory of attention. *Cognitive Psychology, 12,* 97–136.

**Treisman, A., & Schmidt, H.** (1982). Illusory conjunctions in the perception of objects. *Cognitive Psychology, 14,* 107–141.

**Trivers, R. L.** (1972). Parental investment and sexual selection. In B. Campbell (Ed.), *Sexual selection and the descent of man, 1871–1971* (pp. 139–179). Chicago: Aldine.

Trompeter, S. E., Bettencourt, R., & Barrett-Connor, E. (2012). Sexual activity and satisfaction in healthy community-dwelling older women. *American Journal of Medicine, 125*(1), 37–43. doi:10.1016/j.amjmed.2011.07.036

Trull, T. J., & Durrett, C. A. (2005). Categorical and dimensional models of personality disorder. *Annual Review of Clinical Psychology, 1,* 355–380.

Tucker, E. (2003, June 25). Move over, Fido! Chickens are becoming hip suburban pets. *USA Today.* Retrieved from http://usatoday30.usatoday.com/money/2003-06-25-pet-chickens_x.htm

Tucker-Drob, E. M., Rhemtulla, M., Harden, K. P., Turkheimer, E., & Fask, D. (2010). Emergence of a Gene × Socioeconomic Status interaction on infant mental ability between 10 months and 2 years. *Psychological Science, 22*(1), 125–133. doi:10.1177/0956797610392926

Tuerlinckx, F., De Boeck, P., & Lens, W. (2002). Measuring needs with the Thematic Apperception Test: A psychometric study. *Journal of Personality and Social Psychology, 82,* 448–461.

Tulving, E. (1972). Episodic and semantic memory. In E. Tulving & W. Donaldson (Eds.), *Organization of memory* (pp. 381–403). New York: Academic Press.

Tulving, E. (1983). *Elements of episodic memory.* Oxford, England: Clarendon Press.

Tulving, E. (1985). Memory and consciousness. *Canadian Psychologist, 25,* 1–12.

Tulving, E. (1998). Neurocognitive processes of human memory. In C. von Euler, I. Lundberg, & R. Llins (Eds.), *Basic mechanisms in cognition and language* (pp. 261–281). Amsterdam: Elsevier.

Tulving, E., Kapur, S., Craik, F. I. M., Moscovitch, M., & Houle, S. (1994). Hemispheric encoding/retrieval asymmetry in episodic memory: Positron emission tomography findings. *Proceedings of the National Academy of Sciences, USA, 91,* 2016–2020.

Tulving, E., & Pearlstone, Z. (1966). Availability versus accessibility of information in memory for words. *Journal of Verbal Learning and Verbal Behavior, 5,* 381–391.

Tulving, E., & Schacter, D. L. (1990). Priming and human memory systems. *Science, 247,* 301–306.

Tulving, E., Schacter, D. L., & Stark, H. (1982). Priming effects in word-fragment completion are independent of recognition memory. *Journal of Experimental Psychology: Learning, Memory, and Cognition, 8,* 336–342.

Tulving, E., & Thompson, D. M. (1973). Encoding specificity and retrieval processes in episodic memory. *Psychological Review, 80,* 352–373.

Turiel, E. (1998). The development of morality. In N. Eisenberg (Ed.), *Handbook of child psychology: Vol. 3. Social, emotional and personality development* (pp. 863–932). New York: Wiley.

Turkheimer, E. (2000). Three laws of behavior genetics and what they mean. *Current Directions in Psychological Science, 9,* 160–164.

Turkheimer, E., Haley, A., Waldron, M., D'Onofrio, B., & Gottesman, I. I. (2003). Socioeconomic status modifies heritability of IQ in young children. *Psychological Science, 14,* 623–628.

Turkheimer, E., & Waldron, M. (2000). Nonshared environment: A theoretical, methodological, and quantitative review. *Psychological Bulletin, 126,* 78–108.

Turner, D. C., Robbins, T. W., Clark, L., Aron, A. R., Dowson, J., & Sahakian, B. J. (2003). Cognitive enhancing effects of modafinil in healthy volunteers. *Psychopharmacology, 165,* 260–269.

Turner, D. C., & Sahakian, B. J. (2006). Neuroethics of cognitive enhancement. *BioSocieties, 1,* 113–123.

Turner, M. E., & Pratkanis, A. R. (1998). Twenty-five years of group-think theory and research: Lessons from the evaluation of a theory. *Organizational Behavior and Human Decision Processes, 73*(2–3), 105–115. doi:10.1006/obhd.1998.2756

Tversky, A., & Kahneman, D. (1973). Availability: A heuristic for judging frequency and probability. *Cognitive Psychology, 5,* 207–232.

Tversky, A., & Kahneman, D. (1974). Judgment under uncertainty: Heuristics and biases. *Science, 185,* 1124–1131.

Tversky, A., & Kahneman, D. (1981). The framing of decisions and the psychology of choice. *Science, 211,* 453–458.

Tversky, A., & Kahneman, D. (1983). Extensional versus intuitive reasoning: The conjunction fallacy in probability judgment. *Psychological Review, 90,* 293–315.

Tversky, A., & Kahneman, D. (1992). Advances in prospect theory: Cumulative representation of uncertainty. *Journal of Risk and Uncertainty, 5,* 297–323.

Twenge, J. M., Campbell, W. K., & Foster, C. A. (2003). Parenthood and marital satisfaction: A meta-analytic review. *Journal of Marriage and Family, 65,* 574–583.

Tyler, T. R. (1990). *Why people obey the law.* New Haven, CT: Yale University Press.

Umberson, D., Williams, K., Powers, D. A., Liu, H., & Needham, B. (2006). You make me sick: Marital quality and health over the life course. *Journal of Health and Social Behavior, 47,* 1–16.

Uncapher, M. R., & Rugg, M. D. (2008). Fractionation of the component processes underlying successful episodic encoding: A combined fMRI and divided-attention study. *Journal of Cognitive Neuroscience, 20,* 240–254.

Ungerleider, L. G., & Mishkin, M. (1982). Two cortical visual systems. In D. J. Ingle, M. A. Goodale, & R. J. W. Mansfield (Eds.), *Analysis of visual behavior* (pp. 549–586). Cambridge, MA: MIT Press.

Urban, N. B. L., Girgis, R. R., Talbot, P. S., Kegeles, L. S., Xu, X., Frankie, W. G., … Laruelle, M. (2012). Sustained recreational use of ecstasy is associated with altered pre- and postsynaptic markers of serotonin transmission in neocortical areas: A PET study with [11c] DASB and [11c] MDL 100907. *Neuropsychopharmacology, 37,* 1465–1473.

Ursano, R. J., & Silberman, E. K. (2003). Psychoanalysis, psychoanalytic psychotherapy, and supportive psychotherapy. In R. E. Hales & S. C. Yudofsky (Eds.), *The American Psychiatric Publishing textbook of clinical psychiatry* (4th ed., pp. 1177–1203). Washington, DC: American Psychiatric Publishing.

U.S. Department of State. (2013, January). *FY 2012 annual report on intercountry adoption.* Washington, DC: Bureau of Consular Affairs, Office of Children's Issues. Retrieved from http://adoption.state.gov/content/pdf/fy2012_annual_report.pdf

Vacha, E., & McBride, M. (1993). Cramming: A barrier to student success, a way to beat the system, or an effective strategy? *College Student Journal, 27,* 2–11.

Valentine, T., Brennen, T., & Brédart, S. (1996). *The cognitive psychology of proper names: On the importance of being Ernest.* London: Routledge.

Valins, S. (1966). Cognitive effects of false heart-rate feedback. *Journal of Personality and Social Psychology, 4,* 400–408.

Vallacher, R. R., & Wegner, D. M. (1985). *A theory of action identification.* Hillsdale, NJ: Erlbaum.

Vallacher, R. R., & Wegner, D. M. (1987). What do people think they're doing? Action identification and human behavior. *Psychological Review, 94,* 3–15.

Vallender, E. J., Mekel-Bobrov, N., & Lahn, B. T. (2008). Genetic basis of human brain evolution. *Trends in Neurosciences, 31,* 637–644.

van den Boom, D. C. (1994). The influence of temperament and mothering on attachment and exploration: An experimental manipulation of sensitive responsiveness among lower-class mothers with irritable infants. *Child Development, 65,* 1457–1477.

van den Boom, D. C. (1995). Do first year intervention effects endure? Follow-up during toddlerhood of a sample of Dutch irritable infants. *Child Development, 66,* 1798–1816.

van Dis, I., Kromhout, D., Geleijnse, J. M., Boer, J. M. A., & Verschuren, W. M. M. (2009). Body mass index and waist circumference predict both 10-year nonfatal and fatal cardiovascular disease risk: Study conducted in 20,000 Dutch men and women aged 20–65 years. *European Journal of Cardiovascular Prevention & Rehabilitation, 16*(6), 729–734.

van Dongen, E. V., Thielen, J.-W., Takashima, A., Barth, M., & Fernandez, G. (2012). Sleep supports selective retention of associative memories based on relevance for future utilization. *PLoS One, 7,* e43426. doi:10.1371/journal.pone.0043426

van Honk, J., & Schutter, D. J. L. G. (2007). Testosterone reduces conscious detection of signals serving social correction: Implications for antisocial behavior. *Psychological Science, 18,* 663–667.

van IJzendoorn, M. H. (1995). Adult attachment representations, parental responsiveness, and infant attachment: A meta-analysis on the predictive validity of the Adult Attachment Interview. *Psychological Bulletin, 117,* 387–403.

van IJzendoorn, M. H., Juffer, F., & Klein Poelhuis, C. W. (2005). Adoption and cognitive development: A meta-analytic comparison of adopted and nonadopted children's IQ and school performance. *Psychological Bulletin, 131,* 301–316.

van IJzendoorn, M. H., & Kroonenberg, P. M. (1988). Cross-cultural patterns of attachment: A meta-analysis of the Strange Situation. *Child Development, 59,* 147–156.

van IJzendoorn, M. H., & Sagi, A. (1999). Cross-cultural patterns of attachment: Universal and contextual dimensions. In J. Cassidy & P. R. Shaver (Eds.), *Handbook of attachment: Theory, research and clinical applications* (pp. 713–734). New York: Guilford Press.

van Ittersum, K., & Wansink, B. (2012). Plate size and color suggestibility: The Delboeuf illusion's bias on serving and eating behavior. *Journal of Consumer Research, 39,* 121–130.

van Praag, H. (2009). Exercise and the brain: Something to chew on. *Trends in Neuroscience, 32,* 283–290.

van Stegeren, A. H., Everaerd, W., Cahill, L., McGaugh, J. L., & Gooren, L. J. G. (1998). Memory for emotional events: Differential effects of centrally versus peripherally acting blocking agents. *Psychopharmacology, 138,* 305–310.

van Vliet, I. M., van Well, E. P., Bruggeman, R., Campo, J. A., Hijman, R., Van Megen, H. J., ... Van Rijen, P. C. (2013). An evaluation of irreversible psychosurgical treatment of patients with obsessive-compulsive disorder in the Netherlands, 2001–2008. *Journal of Nervous and Mental Disease, 201,* 226–228.

Vargha-Khadem, F., Gadian, D. G., Copp, A., & Mishkin, M. (2005). FOXP2 and the neuroanatomy of speech and language. *Nature Reviews Neuroscience, 6,* 131–138.

Vargha-Khadem, F., Gadian, D. G., Watkins, K. E., Connelly, A., Van Paesschen, W., & Mishkin, M. (1997). Differential effects of early hippocampal pathology on episodic and semantic memory. *Science, 277,* 376–380.

Vazire, S., & Mehl, M. R. (2008). Knowing me, knowing you: The relative accuracy and unique predictive validity of self-ratings and other-ratings of daily behavior. *Journal of Personality and Social Psychology, 95,* 1202–1216.

Veldhuizen, M. G., Douglas, D., Aschenbrenner, K., Gitelman, D. R., & Small, D. M. (2011). The anterior insular cortex represents breaches of taste identity expectation. *Journal of Neuroscience, 31,* 14735–14744.

Vinter, A., & Perruchet, P. (2002). Implicit motor learning through observational training in adults and children. *Memory & Cognition, 30,* 256–261.

Vitkus, J. (1999). *Casebook in abnormal psychology* (4th ed.). New York: McGraw-Hill.

Vondra, J. I., Shaw, D. S., Swearingen, L., Cohen, M., & Owens, E. B. (2001). Attachment stability and emotional and behavioral regulation from infancy to preschool age. *Development and Psychopathology, 13,* 13–33.

Von Frisch, K. (1974). Decoding the language of the bee. *Science, 185,* 663–668.

Voon, V., Pessiglione, M., Brezing, C., Gallea, C., Fernandez, H. H., Dolan, R. J., & Hallett, M. (2011). Mechanisms underlying dopamine-mediated reward bias in compulsive behaviors. *Neuron, 65,* 135–142.

Vortac, O. U., Edwards, M. B., & Manning, C. A. (1995). Functions of external cues in prospective memory. *Memory, 3,* 201–219.

Vrij, A., Granhag, P. A., Mann, S., & Leal, S. (2011). Outsmarting the liars: Toward a cognitive lie detection approach. *Current Directions in Psychological Science, 20*(1), 28–32.

Vygotsky, L. S. (1978). *Mind in society: The development of higher psychological processes.* Cambridge, MA: Harvard University Press.


Wade, N. J. (2005). *Perception and illusion: Historical perspectives.* New York: Springer.

Wade, S. E., Trathen, W., & Schraw, G. (1990). An analysis of spontaneous study strategies. *Reading Research Quarterly, 25,* 147–166.

Wadhwa, P. D., Sandman, C. A., & Garite, T. J. (2001). The neurobiology of stress in human pregnancy: Implications for prematurity and development of the fetal central nervous system. *Progress in Brain Research, 133,* 131–142.

Wager, T. D., Rilling, J., K., Smith, E. E., Sokolik, A., Casey, K. L., Davidson, R. J., ... Cohen, J. D. (2004). Placebo-induced changes in fMRI in the anticipation and experience of pain. *Science, 303,* 1162–1167.

Wagner, A. D., Schacter, D. L., Rotte, M., Koutstaal, W., Maril, A., Dale, A. M., ... Buckner, R. L. (1998). Remembering and forgetting of verbal experiences as predicted by brain activity. *Science, 281,* 1188–1190.

Wagner, G., & Morris, E. (1987). Superstitious behavior in children. *Psychological Record, 37,* 471–488.

Wai, J., Putallaz, M., & Makel, M. C. (2012). Studying intellectual outliers: Are there sex differences, and are the smart getting smarter? *Current Directions in Psychological Science, 21*(6), 382–390. doi:10.1177/0963721412455052

Waite, L. J. (1995). Does marriage matter? *Demography, 32,* 483–507.

Wakefield, J. C. (2007). The concept of mental disorder: Diagnostic implications of the harmful dysfunction analysis. *World Psychiatry, 6,* 149-56.

Walden, T. A., & Ogan, T. A. (1988). The development of social referencing. *Child Development, 59,* 1230–1240.

Waldfogel, S. (1948). The frequency and affective character of childhood memories. *Psychological Monographs, 62* (Whole No. 291).

Waldmann, M. R. (2000). Competition among causes but not effects in predictive and diagnostic learning. *Journal of Experimental Psychology: Learning, Memory, and Cognition, 26,* 53–76.

Walker, C. (1977). Some variations in marital satisfaction. In R. C. J. Peel (Ed.), *Equalities and inequalities in family life* (pp. 127–139). London: Academic Press.

Walker, L. J. (1988). The development of moral reasoning. *Annals of Child Development, 55*, 677–691.

Walker, N. P., McConville, P. M., Hunter, D., Deary, I. J., & Whalley, L. J. (2002). Childhood mental ability and lifetime psychiatric contact. *Intelligence, 30*(3), 233–245. doi:10.1016/S0160-2896(01)00098-8

Wallace, J., Schnieder, T., & McGuffin, P. (2002). Genetics of depression. In I. H. Gottlib & C. L. Hammen (Eds.), *Handbook of depression* (pp. 169–191). New York: Guilford Press.

Wallbott, H. G. (1998). Bodily expression of emotion. *European Journal of Social Psychology, 28*, 879–896.

Walster, E., Aronson, V., Abrahams, D., & Rottmann, L. (1966). Importance of physical attractiveness in dating behavior. *Journal of Personality and Social Psychology, 4*, 508–516.

Walster, E., Walster, G. W., & Berscheid, E. (1978). *Equity: Theory and research*. Boston: Allyn & Bacon.

Walton, D. N. (1990). What is reasoning? What is an argument? *Journal of Philosophy, 87*, 399–419.

Walton, G. M., & Spencer, S. J. (2009). Latent ability: Grades and test scores systematically underestimate the intellectual ability of negatively stereotyped students. *Psychological Science, 20*, 1132–1139.

Waltzman, S. B. (2006). Cochlear implants: Current status. *Expert Review of Medical Devices, 3*, 647–655.

Wamsley, E. J., & Stickgold, R. (2011). Memory, sleep, and dreaming: Experiencing consolidation. *Sleep Medicine Clinics, 6*, 97–108.

Wang, J. L., Jackson, L. A., Zhang, D. J., & Su, Z. Q. (2012). The relationships among the Big Five personality factors, self-esteem, narcissism, and sensation seeking to Chinese university students' uses of social networking sites (SNSs). *Computers in Human Behavior, 28*, 2313–2319.

Wang, L. H., McCarthy, G., Song, A. W., & LaBar, K. S. (2005). Amygdala activation to sad pictures during high-field (4 tesla) functional magnetic resonance imaging. *Emotion, 5*, 12–22.

Wang, P. S., Aguilar-Gaxiola, S., Alonso, J., Angermeyer, M. C., Borges, G., Bromet, E. J., ... Wells, J. E. (2007). Use of mental health services for anxiety, mood, and substance disorders in 17 countries in the WHO World Mental Health Surveys. *Lancet, 370*, 841–850.

Wang, P. S., Berglund, P. A., Olfson, M., & Kessler, R. C. (2004). Delays in initial treatment contact after first onset of a mental disorder. *Health Services Research, 39*, 393–415.

Wang, P. S., Berglund, P., Olfson, M., Pincus, H. A., Wells, K. B., & Kessler, R. C. (2005). Failure and delay ininitial treatment contact after first onset of mental disorders in the National Comorbidity Survey Replication. *Archives of General Psychiatry, 62*(6), 629–640.

Wang, S.-H., & Baillargeon, R. (2008). Detecting impossible changes in infancy: A three-system account. *Trends in Cognitive Sciences, 12*(1), 17–23.

Wansink, B., & Linder, L. R. (2003). Interactions between forms of fat consumption and restaurant bread consumption. *International Journal of Obesity, 27*, 866–868.

Wansink, B., Painter, J. E., & North, J. (2005). Bottomless bowls: Why visual cues of portion size may influence intake. *Obesity Research, 13*, 93–100.

Wansink, B., & Wansink, C. S. (2010). The largest last supper: Depictions of food portions and plate size increased over the millennium. *International Journal of Obesity, 34*, 943–944.

Ward, J., Parkin, A. J., Powell, G., Squires, E. J., Townshend, J., & Bradley, V. (1999). False recognition of unfamiliar people: "Seeing film stars everywhere." *Cognitive Neuropsychology, 16*, 293–315.

Warneken, F., & Tomasello, M. (2009). Varieties of altruism in children and chimpanzees. *Trends in Cognitive Sciences, 13*, 397–402.

Warrington, E. K., & McCarthy, R. A. (1983). Category specific access dysphasia. *Brain, 106*, 859–878.

Warrington, E. K., & Shallice, T. (1984). Category specific semantic impairments. *Brain, 107*, 829–854.

Warrington, E. K., & Weiskrantz, L. (1968). New method of testing long-term retention with special reference to amnesic patients, *Nature, 217*, 972–974.

Wasylenki, D. (2001). The paradigm shift from institution to community. In Q. Dae-Grant (Ed.), *Psychiatry in Canada: 50 years, 1951–2000* (p. 96). Ottawa: Canadian Psychiatric Association.

Watanabe, S., Sakamoto, J., & Wakita, M. (1995). Pigeons' discrimination of painting by Monet and Picasso. *Journal of the Experimental Analysis of Behavior, 63*, 165–174.

Watkins, L. R., & Maier, S. F. (2005). Immune regulation of central nervous system functions: From sickness responses to pathological pain. *Journal of Internal Medicine, 257*, 139–155.

Watson, D., & Pennebaker, J. W. (1989). Health complaints, stress, and distress: Exploring the central role of negative affectivity. *Psychological Review, 96*, 234–254.

Watson, D., & Tellegen, A. (1985). Toward a consensual structure of mood. *Psychological Bulletin, 98*, 219–235.

Watson, J. B. (1913). Psychology as the behaviorist views it. *Psychological Review, 20*, 158–177.

Watson, J. B. (1924). *Behaviorism.* New York: People's Institute.

Watson, J. B. (1928). *Psychological care of infant and child.* New York: Norton.

Watson, J. B., & Rayner, R. (1920). Conditioned emotional reactions. *Journal of Experimental Psychology, 3*, 1–14.

Watson, R. I. (1978). *The great psychologists.* New York: Lippincott.

Watt, H. J. (1905). Experimentelle Beitraege zu einer Theorie des Denkens [Experimental contributions to a theory of thinking]. *Archiv fuer die gesamte Psychologie, 4*, 289–436.

Watzke, B., Rüddel, H., Jürgensen, R., Koch, U., Kristen, L., Grothgar, B., & Schulz, H. (2012). Longer term outcome of cognitive-behavioural and psychodynamic psychotherapy in routine mental health care: Randomised controlled trial. *Behaviour Research and Therapy, 50*, 580–387.

Weaver, I. C. G., Cervoni, N., Champagne, F. A., D'Alessio, A. C., Sharma, S., Seckl, J. R., ... Meaney, M. J. (2004). Epigenetic programming by maternal behavior. *Nature Neuroscience, 7*, 847–854.

Webb, T. L., Miles, E., & Sheeran, P. (2012). Dealing with feeling: A meta-analysis of the effectiveness of strategies derived from the process model of emotion regulation. *Psychological Bulletin, 138*(4), 775–808.

Weber, R., & Crocker, J. (1983). Cognitive processes in the revision of stereotypic beliefs. *Journal of Personality and Social Psychology, 45*, 961–977.

Webster Marketon, J. I., & Glaser, R. (2008). Stress hormones and immune function. *Cellular Immunology, 252*, 16–26.

Wechsler, H., & Nelson, T. F. (2001). Binge drinking and the American college students: What's five drinks? *Psychology of Addictive Behaviors, 15*(4), 287–291. doi:10.1037/0893-164X.15.4.287

Wegner, D. M. (1989). *White bears and other unwanted thoughts.* New York: Viking.

Wegner, D. M. (1994a). Ironic processes of mental control. *Psychological Review, 101*, 34–52.

**Wegner, D. M.** (1994b). *White bears and other unwanted thoughts: Suppression, obsession, and the psychology of mental control.* New York: Guilford Press.

**Wegner, D. M.** (1997). Why the mind wanders. In J. D. Cohen & J. W. Schooler (Eds.), *Scientific approaches to consciousness* (pp. 295–315). Mahwah, NJ: Erlbaum.

**Wegner, D. M.** (2002). *The illusion of conscious will.* Cambridge, MA: MIT Press.

**Wegner, D. M.** (2009). How to think, say, or do precisely the worst thing for any occasion. *Science, 325,* 48–51.

**Wegner, D. M., Ansfield, M., & Pilloff, D.** (1998). The putt and the pendulum: Ironic effects of the mental control of action. *Psychological Science, 9,* 196–199.

**Wegner, D. M., Broome, A., & Blumberg, S. J.** (1997). Ironic effects of trying to relax under stress. *Behavior Research and Therapy, 35,* 11–21.

**Wegner, D. M., Erber, R., & Raymond, P.** (1991). Transactive memory in close relationships. *Journal of Personality and Social Psychology, 61,* 923–929.

**Wegner, D. M., Erber, R. E., & Zanakos, S.** (1993). Ironic processes in the mental control of mood and mood-related thought. *Journal of Personality and Social Psychology, 65,* 1093–1104.

**Wegner, D. M., & Gilbert, D. T.** (2000). Social psychology: The science of human experience. In H. Bless & J. Forgas (Eds.), *The message within: Subjective experience in social cognition and behavior* (pp. 1–9). Philadelphia: Psychology Press.

**Wegner, D. M., Schneider, D. J., Carter, S. R., & White, T. L.** (1987). Paradoxical effects of thought suppression. *Journal of Personality and Social Psychology, 53,* 5–13.

**Wegner, D. M., Vallacher, R. R., Macomber, G., Wood, R., & Arps, K.** (1984). The emergence of action. *Journal of Personality and Social Psychology, 46,* 269–279.

**Wegner, D. M., & Wenzlaff, R. M.** (1996). Mental control. In E. T. Higgins & A. Kruglanski (Eds.), *Social psychology: Handbook of basic mechanisms and processes* (pp. 466–492). New York: Guilford Press.

**Wegner, D. M., Wenzlaff, R. M., & Kozak, M.** (2004). Dream rebound: The return of suppressed thoughts in dreams. *Psychological Science, 15,* 232–236.

**Wegner, D. M., & Zanakos, S.** (1994). Chronic thought suppression. *Journal of Personality, 62,* 615–640.

**Weinstein, N. D.** (1980). Unrealistic optimism about future life events. *Journal of Personality and Social Psychology, 39,* 806–820.

**Weintraub, D., Papay, K., & Siderowf, A.** (2013). Screening for impulse control symptoms in patients with de novo Parkinson disease: A case-control study. *Neurology, 80,* 176–180.

**Weir, C., Toland, C., King, R. A., & Martin, L. M.** (2005). Infant contingency/extinction performance after observing partial reinforcement. *Infancy, 8,* 63–80.

**Weiser, M., Zarka, S., Werbeloff, N., Kravitz, E., & Lubin, G.** (2010). Cognitive test scores in male adolescent cigarette smokers compared to non-smokers: A population-based study. *Addiction, 105*(2), 358–363. doi:10.1111/j.1360-0443.2009.02740.x

**Weisfeld, G.** (1999). *Evolutionary principles of human adolescence.* New York: Basic Books.

**Weissenborn, R.** (2000). State-dependent effects of alcohol on explicit memory: The role of semantic associations. *Psychopharmacology, 149,* 98–106.

**Weissman, M. M., Markowitz, J. C., & Klerman, G. L.** (2000). *Comprehensive guide to interpersonal psychotherapy.* New York: Basic Books.

**Weldon, M. S.** (2001). Remembering as a social process. In D. L. Medin (Ed.), *The psychology of learning and motivation: Advances in research and theory* (Vol. 40, pp. 67–120). San Diego, CA: Academic Press.

**Wenzlaff, R. M., & Wegner, D. M.** (2000). Thought suppression. In S. T. Fiske (Ed.), *Annual review of psychology* (Vol. 51, pp. 51–91). Palo Alto, CA: Annual Reviews.

**Wernicke, K.** (1874). *Der Aphasische Symptomenkomplex* [The aphasic symptom complex]. Breslau: Cohn and Weigart.

**Wertheimer, M.** (1982). *Productive thinking.* Chicago: University of Chicago Press. (Originally published 1945)

**Wesch, N. N., Law, B., & Hall, C. R.** (2007). The use of observational learning by athletes. *Journal of Sport Behavior, 30,* 219–231.

**Westrin, A., & Lam, R. W.** (2007). Seasonal affective disorder: A clinical update. *Journal of Clinical Psychiatry, 19,* 239–246.

**Wexler, K.** (1999). Maturation and growth of grammar. In W. C. Ritchie & T. K. Bhatia (Eds.), *Handbook of child language acquisition* (pp. 55–110). San Diego: Academic Press.

**Whalen, P. J., Rauch, S. L., Etcoff, N. L., McInerney, S. C., Lee, M. B., & Jenike, M. A.** (1998). Masked presentations of emotional facial expressions modulate amygdala activity without explicit knowledge. *The Journal of Neuroscience, 18,* 411–418.

**Whalley, L. J., & Deary, I. J.** (2001). Longitudinal cohort study of childhood IQ and survival up to age 76. *British Medical Journal, 322,* 1–5.

**Wheatley, T., & Haidt, J.** (2005). Hypnotic disgust makes moral judgments more severe. *Psychological Science, 16,* 780–784.

**Wheeler, M. A., Petersen, S. E., & Buckner, R. L.** (2000). Memory's echo: Vivid recollection activates modality-specific cortex. *Proceedings of the National Academy of Sciences, USA, 97,* 11125–11129.

**White, B. L., & Held, R.** (1966). Plasticity of motor development in the human infant. In J. F. Rosenblith & W. Allinsmith (Eds.), *The cause of behavior* (pp. 60–70). Boston: Allyn & Bacon.

**White, F. J.** (1996). Synaptic regulation of mesocorticolimbic dopamine neurons. *Annual Review of Neuroscience, 19,* 405–436.

**White, G. M., & Kirkpatrick, J. (Eds.).** (1985). *Person, self, and experience: Exploring pacific ethnopsychologies.* Berkeley: University of California Press.

**White, N. M., & Milner, P. M.** (1992). The psychobiology of reinforcers. *Annual Review of Psychology, 41,* 443–471.

**Whitney, D., Ellison, A., Rice, N. J., Arnold, D., Goodale, M., Walsh, V., & Milner, D.** (2007). Visually guided reaching depends on motion area MT+. *Cerebral Cortex, 17,* 2644–2649.

**Whorf, B.** (1956). *Language, thought, and reality.* Cambridge, MA: MIT Press.

**Whybrow, P. C.** (1997). *A mood apart.* New York: Basic Books.

**Wicker, B., Keysers, C., Plailly, J., Royet, J.-P., Gallese, V., & Rizzolatti, G.** (2003). Both of us disgusted in *my* insula: The common neural basis of seeing and feeling disgust. *Neuron, 40,* 655–664.

**Wicklund, R.** (1975). Objective self-awareness. In L. Berkowitz (Ed.), *Advances in experimental social psychology* (Vol. 8, pp. 233–275). New York: Academic Press.

**Wiederman, M. W.** (1997). Pretending orgasm during sexual intercourse: Correlates in a sample of young adult women. *Journal of Sex & Marital Therapy, 23,* 131–139.

**Wiener, D. N.** (1996). *B. F. Skinner: Benign anarchist.* Boston: Allyn & Bacon.

**Wiesenthal, D. L., Austrom, D., & Silverman, I.** (1983). Diffusion of responsibility in charitable donations. *Basic and Applied Social Psychology, 4,* 17–27.

**Wig, G. S., Buckner, R. L., & Schacter, D. L.** (2009). Repetition priming influences distinct brain systems: Evidence from task-evoked data and resting-state correlations. *Journal of Neurophysiology, 101,* 2632–2648.

**Wiggs, C. L., & Martin, A.** (1998). Properties and mechanisms of perceptual priming. *Current Opinion in Neurobiology, 8,* 227–233.

**Wilcoxon, H. C., Dragoin, W. B., & Kral, P. A.** (1971). Illness-induced aversions in rats and quail: Relative salience of visual and gustatory cues. *Science, 171,* 826–828.

**Wiley, J. L.** (1999). Cannabis: Discrimination of "internal bliss"? *Pharmacology, Biochemistry, & Behavior, 64,* 257–260.

**Wilhelm, I., Dieckelmann, S., Molzow, I., Ayoub, A., Molle, M., & Born, J.** (2011). Sleep selectively enhances memories expected to be of future relevance. *Journal of Neuroscience, 31,* 1563–1569.

**Wilkinson, L., Teo, J. T., Obeso, I., Rothwell, J. C., & Jahanshahi, M.** (2010). The contribution of primary motor cortex is essential for probabilistic implicit sequence learning: Evidence from theta burst magnetic stimulation. *Journal of Cognitive Neuroscience, 22,* 427–436.

**Williams, A. C.** (2002). Facial expression of pain: An evolutionary account. *Behavioral and Brain Sciences, 25,* 439–488.

**Williams, C. M., & Kirkham, T. C.** (1999). Anandamide induces overeating: Mediation by central cannabinoid (CB1) receptors. *Psychopharmacology, 143,* 315–317.

**Williams, K. D., Nida, S. A., Baca, L. D., & Latané, B.** (1989). Social loafing and swimming: Effects of identifiability on individual and relay performance of intercollegiate swimmers. *Basic and Applied Social Psychology, 10,* 73–81.

**Willingham, D. T.** (2007). Critical thinking: Why is it so hard to teach? *American Educator, 31*(2), 8–19.

**Wilson, K., & Korn, J. H.** (2007). Attention during lectures: Beyond ten minutes. *Teaching of Psychology, 34,* 85–89.

**Wilson, T. D.** (2002). *Strangers to ourselves: Discovering the adaptive unconscious.* Cambridge, MA: Harvard University Press.

**Wilson, T. D.** (2009). Know thyself. *Perspectives on Psychological Science, 4,* 384–389.

**Wilson, T. D.** (2012, July 12). Stop bullying the "soft" sciences. *Los Angeles Times.* Retrieved from http://articles.latimes.com/2012/jul/12/opinion/la-oe-wilson-social-sciences-20120712

**Wilson, T. D., & Lassiter, G. D.** (1982). Increasing intrinsic interest with superfluous extrinsic constraints. *Journal of Personality and Social Psychology, 42,* 811–819.

**Wilson, T. D., Meyers, J., & Gilbert, D. T.** (2003). "How happy was I, anyway?" A retrospective impact bias. *Social Cognition, 21,* 421–446.

**Wimber, M., Rutschmann, R. N., Greenlee, M. W., & Bauml, K.-H.** (2009). Retrieval from episodic memory: Neural mechanisms of interference resolution. *Journal of Cognitive Neuroscience, 21,* 538–549.

**Wimmer, H., & Perner, J.** (1983). Beliefs about beliefs: Representations and constraining function of wrong beliefs in young children's understanding of deception. *Cognition, 13,* 103–128.

**Winawer, J., Witthoft, N., Frank, M. C., Wu, L., Wade, A. R., & Boroditsky, L.** (2007). Russian blues reveal effects of language on color discrimination. *Proceedings of the National Academy of Sciences, USA, 104,* 7780–7785.

**Windeler, J., & Kobberling, J.** (1986). Empirische Untersuchung zur Einschatzung diagnostischer Verfahren am Beispiel des Haemoccult-Tests [An empirical study of the value of diagnostic procedures using the example of the hemoccult test]. *Klinische Wochenscrhrift, 64,* 1106–1112.

**Windham, G. C., Eaton, A., & Hopkins, B.** (1999). Evidence for an association between environmental tobacco smoke exposure and birthweight: A meta-analysis and new data. *Pediatrics and Perinatal Epidemiology, 13,* 35–57.

**Winner, E.** (2000). The origins and ends of giftedness. *American Psychologist, 55,* 159–169.

**Winocur, G., Moscovitch, M., & Bontempi, B.** (2010). Memory formation and long-term retention in humans and animals: Convergence towards a transformation account of hippocampal–neocortical interactions. *Neuropsychologia, 48,* 2339–2356.

**Winter, L., & Uleman, J. S.** (1984). When are social judgments made? Evidence for the spontaneousness of trait inferences. *Journal of Personality and Social Psychology, 47,* 237–252.

**Winterer, G., & Weinberger, D. R.** (2004). Genes, dopamine and cortical signal-to-noise ratio in schizophrenia. *Trends in Neuroscience, 27,* 683–690.

**Wise, R. A.** (1989). Brain dopamine and reward. *Annual Review of Psychology, 40,* 191–225.

**Wise, R. A.** (2005). Forebrain substrates of reward and motivation. *Journal of Comparative Neurology, 493,* 115–121.

**Wittgenstein, L.** (1999). *Philosophical investigations.* Upper Saddle River, NJ: Prentice Hall. (Originally published 1953)

**Wixted, J. T., & Ebbensen, E.** (1991). On the form of forgetting. *Psychological Science, 2,* 409–415.

**Wolf, J. R., Arkes, H. R., & Muhanna, W. A.** (2008). The power of touch: An examination of the effect of duration of physical contact on the valuation of objects. *Judgment and Decision Making, 3,* 476–482.

**Wolff, P., & Holmes, K. J.** (2011). Linguistic relativity. *WIRES Cognitive Science, 2,* 253–265.

**Wong, D. T., Bymaster, F. P., & Engleman, E. A.** (1995). Prozac (fluoxetine, Lilly 110140), the first selective serotonin uptake inhibitor and an antidepressant drug: Twenty years since its first publication. *Life Sciences, 57,* 411–441.

**Wood, J. M., & Bootzin, R. R.** (1990). Prevalence of nightmares and their independence from anxiety. *Journal of Abnormal Psychology, 99,* 64–68.

**Wood, J. M., Bootzin, R. R., Rosenhan, D., Nolen-Hoeksema, S., & Jourden, F.** (1992). Effects of the 1989 San Francisco earthquake on frequency and content of nightmares. *Journal of Abnormal Psychology, 101,* 219–224.

**Woodley, M. A., te Nijenhuis, J., & Murphy, R.** (2013). Were the Victorians cleverer than us? The decline in general intelligence estimated from a meta-analysis of the slowing of simple reaction time. *Intelligence.* Advance online publication. doi:10.1016/j.intell.2013.04.006

**Woods, S. C., Seeley, R. J., Porte, D., Jr., & Schwartz, M. W.** (1998). Signals that regulate food intake and energy homeostasis. *Science, 280,* 1378–1383.

**Woody, S. R., & Nosen, E.** (2008). Psychological models of phobic disorders and panic. In M. M. Anthony & M. B. Stein (Eds.), *Oxford handbook of anxiety and related disorders* (pp. 209–224). New York: Oxford University Press.

**Woody, S. R., & Sanderson, W. C.** (1998). Manuals for empirically supported treatments: 1998 update. *Clinical Psychologist, 51,* 17–21.

**Wrangham, R., & Peterson, D.** (1997). *Demonic males: Apes and the origin of human violence.* New York: Mariner.

**Wren, A. M., Seal, L. J., Cohen, M. A., Brynes, A. E., Frost, G. S., Murphy, K. G., … Bloom, S. R.** (2001). Ghrelin enhances appetite and increases food intake in humans. *Journal of Clinical Endocrinology and Metabolism, 86,* 5992–5995.

**Wrenn, C. C., Turchi, J. N., Schlosser, S., Dreiling, J. L., Stephenson, D. A., & Crawley, J. N.** (2006). Performance of galanin transgenic mice in the 5-choice serial reaction time attentional task. *Pharmacology Biochemistry and Behavior, 83,* 428–440.

**Wundt, W.** (1900–1920). *Völkerpsychologie. Eine untersuchung der entwicklungsgesetze von sprache, mythos und sitte* [Völkerpsychologie: An examination of the developmental laws of language, myth, and custom]. Leipzig, Germany: Engelmann & Kroner.


**Yamaguchi, S.** (1998). Basic properties of umami and its effects in humans. *Physiology and Behavior, 49,* 833–841.

**Yang, S., & Sternberg, R. J.** (1997). Conceptions of intelligence in ancient Chinese philosophy. *Journal of Theoretical and Philosophical Psychology, 17,* 101–119.

**Yawching, D.** (2013, October 27). The silent racism of 'post racial' Canada: Canada's multicultural rhetoric is a skin-deep illusion. *Toronto Star.* Retrieved from http://www.thestar.com/opinion/commentary/2013/10/27/the_silent_racism_of_post_racial_canada.html

**Yeo, B. T. T., Krienen, F. M., Sepulcre, J., Sabuncu, M. R., Lashkari, D., Hollinshead, M., ... Buckner, R. L.** (2011). The organization of the human cerebral cortex estimated by intrinsic functional connectivity. *Journal of Neurophysiology, 106,* 1125–1165.

**Yeshurun, Y., & Sobel, N.** (2010). An odor is not worth a thousand words: From multidimensional odors to unidimensional odor objects. *Annual Review of Psychology, 61,* 219–241.

**Yik, M., Russell, J. A., & Steiger, J. H.** (2011). A 12-point circumplex structure of core affect. *Emotion, 11*(4), 705–731.

**Young, R. M.** (1990). *Mind, brain, and adaptation in the nineteenth century: Cerebral localization and its biological context from Gall to Ferrier.* New York: Oxford University Press.

**Yucha, C., & Gilbert, C. D.** (2004). *Evidence-based practice in biofeedback and neurofeedback.* Colorado Springs, CO: Association for Applied Psychophysiology and Biofeedback.

**Yuill, N., & Perner, J.** (1988). Intentionality and knowledge in children's judgments of actor's responsibility and recipient's emotional reaction. *Developmental Psychology, 24,* 358–365.

**Yzerbyt, V., & Demoulin, S.** (2010). Intergroup relations. In S. T. Fiske, D. T. Gilbert, & G. Lindzey (Eds.), *The handbook of social psychology* (5th ed., Vol. 2, pp. 1024–1083). New York: Wiley.


**Zahn-Waxler, C., Radke-Yarrow, M., Wagner, E., & Chapman, M.** (1992). Development of concern for others. *Developmental Psychology, 28,* 126–136.

**Zajonc, R. B.** (1968). Attitudinal effects of mere exposure. *Journal of Personality and Social Psychology, 9,* 1–27.

**Zajonc, R. B.** (1989). Feeling the facial efference: Implications of the vascular theory of emotion. *Psychological Review, 96,* 395–416.

**Zebrowitz, L. A., Hall, J. A., Murphy, N. A., & Rhodes, G.** (2002). Looking smart and looking good: Facial cues to intelligence and their origins. *Personality and Social Psychology Bulletin, 28,* 238–249.

**Zebrowitz, L. A., & Montepare, J. M.** (1992). Impressions of baby-faced individuals across the life span. *Developmental Psychology, 28,* 1143–1152.

**Zeki, S.** (1993). *A vision of the brain.* London: Blackwell Scientific.

**Zeki, S.** (2001). Localization and globalization in conscious vision. *Annual Review of Neuroscience, 24,* 57–86.

**Zelazo, P. R.** (1972). Smiling and vocalizing: A cognitive emphasis. *Merrill-Palmer Quarterly, 18,* 349–365.

**Zelazo, P. R.** (1976). From reflexive to instrumental behavior. In L. P. Lipsitt (Ed.), *Developmental psychology: The significance of infancy.* Hillsdale, NJ: Erlbaum.

**Zelazo, P. R.** (1983). The development of walking: New findings and old assumptions. *Journal of Motor Behavior, 15,* 99–137.

**Zelazo, P. R., Zelazo, N. A., & Kolb, S.** (1972). "Walking" in the newborn. *Science, 176*(4032), 314–315.

**Zentall, T. R., Sutton, J. E., & Sherburne, L. M.** (1996). True imitative learning in pigeons. *Psychological Science, 7,* 343–346.

**Zentner, M., & Mitura, K.** (2012). Stepping out of the caveman's shadow: Nations' gender gap predicts degree of sex differentiation in mate preferences. *Psychological Science, 23*(10), 1176–1185. doi:10.1177/0956797612441004

**Zernike, K.** (2012, August 25). After gay son's suicide, mother finds blame in herself and in her church. *New York Times,* p. A14.

**Zhang, T. Y., & Meaney, M. J.** (2010). Epigenetics and the environmental regulation of the genome and its function. *Annual Review of Psychology, 61,* 439–466.

**Zhong, C.-B., Bohns, V. K., & Gino, F.** (2010). Good lamps are the best police: Darkness increases dishonesty and self-interested behavior. *Psychological Science, 21*(3), 311–314. doi:10.1177/0956797609360754

**Zihl, J., von Cramon, D., & Mai, N.** (1983). Selective disturbance of movement vision after bilateral brain damage. *Brain, 106,* 313–340.

**Zillmann, D., Katcher, A. H., & Milavsky, B.** (1972). Excitation transfer from physical exercise to subsequent aggressive behavior. *Journal of Experimental Psychology, 8,* 247–259.

**Zimprich, D., & Martin, M.** (2002). Can longitudinal changes in processing speed explain longitudinal age changes in fluid intelligence? *Psychology and Aging, 17,* 690–695.

**Zuckerman, M., DePaulo, B. M., & Rosenthal, R.** (1981). Verbal and nonverbal communication of deception. In L. Berkowitz (Ed.), *Advances in experimental social psychology* (Vol. 14, pp. 1–59). New York: Academic Press.

**Zuckerman, M., & Driver, R. E.** (1985). Telling lies: Verbal and nonverbal correlates of deception. In W. Seigman & S. Feldstein (Eds.), *Multichannel integrations of nonverbal behavior* (pp. 129–147). Hillsdale, NJ: Erlbaum.

# Name Index

## A

Aarts, H., 344
Abel, T., 235
Abelson, J., 656
Abelson, R. P., 592
Abernathy, A. P., 166
Abrams, D., 515
Abrams, M., 302
Abramson, L. Y., 604
Acevedo, B. P., 524
Acevedo-Garcia, D., 419
Achter, J. A., 417
Acocella, J., 661
Adam, patient, 372, 373
Addis, D. R., 107, 245, 246, 260
Adelmann, P. K., 324
Adelson, E. H., 153
Adler, A., 14
Adler, L., 616
Adolph, K. E., 432, 433
Adolphs, R., 99, 326
Adorno, T. W., 477
Aggleton, J., 99
Agin, D., 74
Agren, T., 234
Agthe, M., 521
Aharon, I., 291
Ahlskog, J. E., 292
Ainslie, G., 207
Ainsworth, M. D. S., 444, 445
Ainsworth, S. E., 510
Ainsworth-Vincze, C., 420
Aksglaede, L., 453
Al-Anon, 644
Alasaari, J. S., 111
al-Assad, B., 477
Albarracín, D., 534
Albee, E., 583
Albert, prince consort of England, 215
Alcoholics Anonymous, 644, 645
Aleman, A., 655
Alessi, S. M., 638
Alfert, E., 321
al-Haytham, I., 41
Alicke, M. D., 500
Allegeier, E. R., 342
Allen, P., 156
Allen, R., 302
Allison, D. B., 337
Alloway, T. P., 230
Alloy, L. B., 604

Allport, G. W., 28, 476, 477, 538
Al-Sahab, B., 430
Alt, K. W., 646
Altschuler, E. L., 104
Alvarez, L., 61
Amabile, T. M., 68, 544
Amanda de Jesus, Sister, 541
Ambady, N., 323, 327, 419
American Academy of Pediatrics, 64
American National Academy of Sciences, 328
American National Institute of Mental Health, 590
American National Institutes of Health, 120
American Psychiatric Association, 587, 588, 619
American Psychological Association, 31, 71, 456, 578, 660, 661
American Psychological Society, 31, 578
Ames, A., 152
Ames, M. A., 456
Anand, S., 125
Anderson, C. A., 55, 508, 509
Anderson, J., 510
Anderson, J. R., 259
Anderson, M. C., 238, 240, 241
Anderson, R. C., 237
Andreasen, N. C., 605
Andres, D., 411
Andrewes, D., 114
Andrews, I., 363
Andrews-Hanna, J. R., 121, 537
Angelone, B., 154
Angst, J., 602
Annis, D. B., 304
Annis, L. F., 304
Ansfield, M., 189, 199
Antoni, M. H., 575
AnxietyBC, 594
Apicella, C. L., 26
Apperly, I. A., 438
Arellano, D., 323
Ariely, D., 520
Aristotle, 5, 6, 332, 334
Ariyasu, H., 335
Arkes, H. R., 165
Armstrong, D. M., 184
Arndt, J., 347
Arnold, M. B., 319
Arnold, S. E., 611
Aron, A., 524, 525

Aron, A. P., 318, 520
Aronson, E., 167, 343, 524, 536, 541
Aronson, J., 418, 420, 541
Asante, K. O., 430
Asch, S. E., 27, 28, 529, 530
Aschoff, J., 195
Aserinsky, E., 196
Ashby, F. G., 372
Ashcraft, M. H., 22
Asher, S. J., 61
Ashmore, R. D., 542
Aslin, R. N., 302
Asmundson, G. J. G., 641
Assanand, S., 577
Associated Press, 631
Association for Psychological Science, 31
Astington, J. W., 438, 439
Atance, C. M., 438
Atkinson, G., 215
Atkinson, J. W., 344
Atkinson, L., 446
Atkinson, R. C., 224
Aunt Polly, 574
Aurora, monkey, 319
Austrom, D., 515
Avery, D., 655
Aviezer, H., 325
Avoilio, A. M., 433
Avolio, B. J., 412
Axelrod, R., 512
Ayduk, O., 343
Ayres, C. E., 333
Azuma, H., 406

## B

Baars, B. J., 20, 190
Baca-Motes, K., 536
Bachman, J., 454
Back, K., 518
Back, M. D., 479, 519
Backlund, E., 565
Backman, C. W., 524
Bäckman, L., 461
Bacon, F., 66–68
Baddeley, A. D., 229, 230, 237
Badea, C., 540
Bagby, R. M., 480
Bahrick, H. P., 231, 249, 257
Bai, D. L., 167
Bailey, J. M., 456

Baillargeon, R., 434, 435, 438, 440
Baird, J., 439
Baker, A., 329
Baker, E., 445
Baker, T. B., 212, 659
Baldwin, J. M., 12, 14
Baldwin, M. W., 499
Baler, R. D., 88
Baltes, P. B., 412, 414, 462
Banaji, M. R., 513, 542
Bandura, A., 295, 296, 490
Banks, M. S., 431
Banks, W. C., 532
Banse, R., 322
Barbee, A. P., 522
Barber, J. P., 635
Barber, S. J., 247
Bard, P., 316, 317, 318
Bargh, J. A., 191, 325, 344, 526
Barker, A. T., 123
Barkow, J., 499
Barlow, D. H., 593, 652, 660
Barnard, P. J., 250
Barnes, C. D., 511
Barnett, S. M., 416
Barnier, A. J., 256, 561
Baron-Cohen, S., 439, 615
Barondes, S., 646
Barrett, L. F., 318, 324
Barrett-Connor, E., 464
Barrientos, R. M., 569
Barry, H., III, 454
Barsade, S. G., 406
Barston, J. L., 390, 391
Bartal, I. B.-A., 517
Bartlett, F. C., 21, 22, 250
Bartol, C. R., 483
Bartoshuk, L. M., 172, 173
Barzee, W. I., 549
Basden, B. H., 247
Basquiat, J.-M., 494
Bassin, E., 525
Bates, E., 358
Bates, J. E., 445
Bateson, G., 29
Bateson, M., 515
Batson, C. D., 517
Batty, G. D., 398, 400, 412
Bauby, J.-D., 185, 217
Bauer, R., 336
Baumeister, R. F., 4, 340, 342, 498, 500, 510, 528, 566, 576
Bavelier, D., 136

Baxter, L. R., 599
Bayley, P. J., 232, 303
Beall, A. T., 523
Bean, D., 417
Bear, G., 406
Beard, C., 642
Beatles, The, 213
Beatty, M. J., 146
Beauchamp, G. K., 172, 428
Bechara, A., 380, 381
Beck, A. T., 604, 639, 640
Becker, J. B., 454
Beckers, G., 125
Bednarczyk, R. A., 457
Bedny, M., 373
Beek, M. R., 154
Beeman, M., 386
Beer, J. S., 497
Beesdo, K., 593
Bekerian, D. A., 250
Bekinschtein, T. A., 274
Belak, W., 79
Bélanger, M., 438
Bell, A. P., 456
Bellotto, B., 182
Belluck, P., 590
Belmonte, M. K., 615
Belsky, J., 445, 454
Bem, S. L., 481
Ben-Porath, Y. S., 474
Benbow, C. P., 417
Benedetti, F., 571
Benenson, J. F., 510
Bennett, I. J., 302
Benoit, R. G., 240
Benoit, S. C., 338
Benson, D. F., 102, 320
Benson, H., 564, 567
Bergen, J. R., 153
Berger, H., 195
Berger, S. A., 257
Bergeron, P., 566
Berglund, H., 171
Berglund, P. A., 592, 594, 597, 599,
    600, 614, 628
Bergstrom, C. T., 35
Bering, J., 298, 299
Berkowitz, A., 531
Berkowitz, L., 509
Berkowitz, O., 533
Bernard, L. L., 333
Bernat, J. L., 123
Bernstein, I. L., 276
Berridge, K. C., 291
Berry, D. S., 522
Berry, J. W., 29
Berscheid, E., 518, 519, 521, 523,
    525
Bertelsen, B., 602
Bertenthal, B. I., 167
Berthoud, H.-R., 98
Bertrand, J., 356
Best, J. B., 23
Bettencourt, B. A., 510
Bettencourt, R., 464
Beunen, G., 453
Beutler, L. E., 378, 659
Bhargava, S., 200
Bialystok, E., 363, 365
Bickerton, D., 355

Bickman, L., 533
Biddle, J. E., 521
Bieber, J., 327
Biederman, I., 150
Biederman, J., 616
Bierman, K. L., 459
Billet, E., 599
bin Laden, O., 190
Binet, A., 397, 398, 411, 414, 417,
    418
Binswanger, L., 490
Bjerkedal, T., 411
Bjork, D. W., 2, 10, 12, 13, 19
Bjork, E. L., 10, 238, 259, 306, 308,
    309
Bjork, R. A., 10, 216, 238, 239, 259,
    306, 308, 309
Bjorklund, P., 265
Blackburn, E., 556
Blackburn, E. H., 557
Blair, C., 405, 420
Blair, I. V., 542
Blair, J., 620
Blakeslee, S., 104
Blanchard-Fields, F., 463
Blascovich, J., 559
Blase, S., 642
Blasi, A., 449
Blatt, S. J., 604
Blatz, C. W., 247
Bleich, A., 561
Blesch, A., 95
Blesher, B. E., 378
Bliss, T. V. P., 235
Bloch, C., 361
Bloom, B., 308
Bloom, C. M., 288
Bloom, F. E., 89
Bloom, M., 183
Bloom, P., 359, 450
Blumberg, S. J., 189, 337
Blumen, H. M., 247
Blunt, J. R., 306
Boakes, R. A., 169
Bodamer, M., 365
Boden, J. M., 510, 617
Boecker, H., 89
Boehm, J. K., 575
Boergers, J., 622
Bogaert, A. F., 456
Bohan, J. S., 456
Bohns, V. K., 515
Boinski, S., 298
Boisvert, C. M., 660
Bolger, N., 187
Bolton, G. E., 525
Bond, M. H., 492
Bondi, M. W., 88
Bonnet, C., 156
Bontempi, B., 232
Boogaard, D., 79
Boomsma, D., 109
Boon, C., 562
Booth, R. J., 563
Booth-LaForce, C., 446
Bootzin, R. R., 199, 202
Borges, G., 622
Borghol, N., 111
Borkenau, P., 400
Borkevec, T. D., 199

Born, J., 88, 233
Born, R. T., 153
Börner, K., 35
Bornstein, R. F., 519
Boroditsky, L., 368
Bosco, J., 406
Bostic, B., 520
Botwin, M. D., 523
Bouazizi, M., 342
Bouchard, C., 453
Bouchard, S. M., 381
Bouchard, T. J., 408, 480, 482
Bouton, M. E., 273
Bower, B., 191
Bower, G. H., 225, 226, 256
Bowers, K. S., 384, 385
Bowlby, J., 443–444
Bowser, R., 199
Boyack, K. W., 34
Boyce, J., 509
Boyd, R., 124
Boyle, D. E., 447
Bozarth, M. A., 206, 207
Brackett, M. A., 406
Bradbury, T. N., 525
Bradford, D., 648
Bradley, D. C., 153
Bradmetz, J., 438
Brady, T., 521
Braeges, J. L., 451
Braet, W., 145
Braly, K., 539
Bramlett, M. D., 525
Brandon, T. H., 212
Brandt, K. R., 245
Brang, D., 104
Branscombe, N. R., 540
Bransford, J. D., 237
Braun, A. R., 204
Breazeal, C., 314, 322
Breckler, S. J., 257
Brédart, S., 252
Bredy, T. W., 111
Breggin, P. R., 611, 660
Brehm, S. S., 524
Breivik, H., 165
Breland, K., 293–294
Breland, M., 293–294
Brennan, P. A., 171
Brennen, T., 252
Brenninkmeijer, V., 560
Bretherton, I., 446
Breuer, J., 13
Brewer, J. A., 563
Brewer, W. F., 250
Bright, C., 417
Broadbent, D., 23
Broberg, D. J., 276
Broca, P., 7, 114–115, 362
Broch, H., 61
Brock, A., 9
Brody, N., 406
Brooks, D., 75, 309, 503
Brooks, R., 441
Brooks-Gunn, J., 187, 454
Broome, A., 189
Brosch, T., 319
Brosnan, S. F., 513
Brown, A., 428
Brown, A. S., 252

Brown, B. B., 459
Brown, F., 240
Brown, J. D., 498, 501, 551
Brown, L. E., 300
Brown, R., 252, 253, 258, 359, 361
Brown, R. P., 511
Brown, S. A., 210
Brown, S. C., 224
Brown, T. A., 593
Brown, T. G., 381
Brownell, K. D., 339
Bruner, J. S., 361
Brunet, A., 234
Brunner, D. P., 198
Brunson, D., 327
Bryck, R. L., 105
Bubbles P., 223
Bublé, M., 537
Buchanan, C. M., 454, 455
Buchanan, D. R., 520
Buchanan, T. W., 256
Buckholtz, J. W., 591
Buck Louis, G. M., 454
Buckner, R. L., 121, 240, 241, 244,
    246, 537
Bucy, P. C., 319
Bulik, C. M., 336
Bull, C. L., 250
Bullard, C., 437
Bullemer, P., 302
Bunce, D. M., 307
Bunchen, G., 521
Bunney, B. S., 291
Burger, J. M., 517, 532, 535, 577
Burke, D., 252
Burke, J. D., 617
Burkham, D. T., 414
Burks, S. V., 399
Burns, D. J., 227
Burns, L., 577
Burns, S. A., 277
Burns, T. C., 430
Burnstein, E., 517
Burright, R. G., 365
Burris, C. T., 540
Bush, G. W., 256
Bushman, B. J., 55, 508, 509
Busjahn, A., 109
Buss, D. M., 26, 341, 342, 481,
    483, 518, 522, 523
Buswell, B. N., 324
Butcher, J. N., 594
Butler, A. C., 642
Butler, M. A., 82
Butterfield, E. C., 22
Butterfill, S. A., 438
Buunk, B. P., 560
Buxbaum, L. J., 145
Byers-Heinlein, K., 430
Bymaster, F. P., 91
Byrne, D., 318, 520, 523

C

Caan, W., 119
Cabeza, R., 254, 462
Cacioppo, J. T., 507, 515, 534, 535
Cage, N., 164
Cahill, L., 259
Cahill, L. S., 221
Cajal, S. R., 80, 81, 82

Calder, A. J., 319
Call, J., 299
Callaghan, T., 437
Calvin, C. M., 400
Calzo, J. P., 455
Cameron, C. D., 321
Campbell, A., 481
Campbell, C. M., 166
Campbell, L. C., 166
Campbell, W. K., 465
Canada Public Health Association, 454
Canadian Association for Neuroscience–association canadienne de neuroscience, 31
Canadian Council on Animal Care, 72
Canadian Institute of Health Research, 79
Canadian Mental Health Association, 596, 600, 628
Canadian Parents for French, 364
Canadian Psychological Association, 31, 71, 74, 597, 599, 660, 661
Canadian Register of Health Service Providers in Psychology, 630
Canadian Society for Brain, Behaviour and Cognitive Science, 31
Cannon, W. B., 316, 317, 318, 554, 555
Cantanese, K. R., 340
Cantor, N., 493
Caparelli, E. C., 125
Capps, L. M., 439
Caprioli, M., 511
Caputi, P., 406
Caramazza, A., 372
Carey, B., 590
Carey, N., 110
Carlsmith, J. M., 537
Carlson, C., 564
Carmichael Olson, H., 429
Carolson, E. A., 446
Caron, H. S., 573
Carpenter, M., 441
Carpenter, S. K., 306
Carr, L., 450
Carrell, S. E., 499
Carroll, J. B., 403, 404–405
Carson, R. C., 594, 608
Carstensen, L. L., 463, 464
Caruso, D. R., 406
Carvallo, M., 501
Carver, C. S., 345, 346, 575
Casasanto, D., 368
Casazza, K., 339
Casey, L. B., 281
Caspi, A., 459, 480, 482, 523, 603
Castel, A. D., 307
Castellanos, F. X., 616
Catanese, D., 336, 340
Catherine (Kate), duchess of Cambridge, 316
Catrambone, R., 384
Cattell, R. B., 405, 478
Cautela, J. R., 281
Ceci, S. J., 223, 414, 416
Centre for Addiction and Mental Health, 628

Cepeda, N. J., 306
Chabris, C. F., 124, 155, 409
Chaiken, S., 534
Challis, B. H., 237
Chalmers, D., 179
Chamberlain, N., 329
Chambless, D. L., 660
Chan, A. Y., 406
Chandler, J., 325
Chandrashekar, J., 172
Chandrashekaran, B., 163
Chang, P. P., 558
Chao, L. L., 372
Charcot, J.-M., 13
Charles, S. T., 463
Charness, N., 417, 461
Charpak, G., 61
Chartrand, T. L., 191, 325, 344
Chassin, L., 212
Chavira, D. A., 595
Chen, E., 413
Chen, E. E., 513
Chen, F. S., 446
Chen, M. K., 345
Chen, S. X., 492
Cheney, D. L., 352
Cheng, D. T., 274
Cherlin, A. J., 525
Cherry, C., 182
Cherry, D., 472
Chess, S., 445
Chestnut, J., 57
Chiles, C., 530
Choi, I., 545
Chomsky, N., 23, 354, 359, 360
Chorover, S. L., 396
Choy, Y., 638
Chrétien, J., 556
Christakis, N. A., 529
Christiansen, B. A., 210
Christianson, S.-Å., 258
Christine, patient, 627, 628, 638, 656
Christopher, patient, 351–352, 360, 368
Chronicle, E. P., 386
Chun, M. M., 122, 147
Chung, C. K., 563
Chung, G. H., 459
Churchill, W., 69, 606
Cialdini, R. B., 526, 528, 529, 530, 535
Ciarrochi, J. V., 406
Cicchetti, D., 446
Cicourel, A., 444
Clancy, S. A., 200, 661
Clark, D., 4
Clark, J. J., 155
Clark, M. S., 524
Clark, R. D., 518
Clark, R. E., 274
Clarke, R. J., 251
Cleckley, H. M., 620
Clementi, J., 456
Clementi, T., 456
Clinkenbeard, P. R., 417
Clore, G. L., 331, 523
Coe, C. L., 428
Coffman, T. L., 539
Cogan, R., 568

Coghill, R. C., 570
Cohen, A. B., 336
Cohen, D., 511, 512
Cohen, G., 252
Cohen, N. J., 241
Cohen, S., 413, 515, 557
Coifman, K. G., 561
Colcombe, S. J., 105
Cole, J. O., 649
Cole, M., 30
Coleman, M. R., 123, 185
Colflesh, G. J., 387
College of Psychologists of BC, 630
Collette, U., 408
Collins, W. A., 446
Colvin, C. R., 400
Coman, A., 239, 246
Condon, J. W., 524
Conger, R. D., 455
Conley, T. D., 518
Conrad, J., 467
Conway, M., 658
Cook, K. S., 525
Cook, M., 297, 594
Cooper, H., 343, 414
Cooper, J., 536
Cooper, J. C., 291
Cooper, J. M., 146
Cooper, J. R., 89
Cooper, M. L., 210
Cooper, T. D., 503
Cooper, W. H., 491
Coppola, A., 164
Coppola, F. F., 164
Corballis, M. C., 102, 227, 246
Corbett, D., 291
Corbetta, M., 145
Corboy, J. R., 82
Coren, S., 198
Corkin, S., 232, 251
Correll, J., 542, 543
Corsi, P., 80
Corti, E., 208
Coryell, W., 605
Coslett, H. B., 145
Cosmides, L., 26
Costa, P. T., 478, 481
Costanza, A., 79
Costello, N., 483
Cotter, A., 509
Cottrell, C. A., 513
Cowell, S., 326
Cowley, D. S., 597, 649
Coyne, J. A., 26
Crabb, R., 651
Craddock, N., 606
Craft, L., 212
Craighero, L., 103, 299
Craik, F. I. M., 223, 224, 237, 251, 363
Cramer, R. E., 523
Crandall, C., 517
Crane, J. M., 430
Crano, W. D., 524
Craske, M. G., 595
Crawley, R. A., 261
Creelman, C. D., 134
Crick, N. R., 481, 510
Crnic, K., 445
Crocker, J., 499, 541

Crombag, H. F. M., 255
Cromwell, O., 68
Cross, E. S., 299
Cross, P., 501
Cross-Disorder Group of the Psychiatric Genomics Consortium, 606
Crowder, R. G., 228
Cruikshank, G., 601
Cruse, D., 123, 185
Csibra, G., 438
Csigó, K., 656
Csikszentmihalyi, M., 489
Cuc, A., 239, 246
Cuellar, A. K., 605, 606
Culbert, K. M., 335
Cummins, D. D., 384
Cunningham, D. G., 651
Cunningham, M. R., 29, 521, 522
Cunningham, W. A., 319
Curran, J. P., 521
Curran, T., 243
Curtis, C. E., 239
Curtiss, S., 360
Custers, R., 344
Cuthbert, B. N., 620
Cyrus, M., 472
Czerny, V., 295

D
D'Agostino, P. R., 545
Dabbs, J. M., 510
DaCosta, L. A., 257
Dael, N., 322
Dahger, A., 292
Dahl, G., 64
Dalí, S., 494
Dallenbach, K. M., 233
Dally, P., 583, 584
Dalton, P., 168
Daly, M., 510
Dalzell, F., 129
Damasio, A. R., 3, 115, 232, 252, 320, 332, 480
Damasio, H., 372, 381
Damon, M., 635
Damsma, G., 292
Danes, C., 110, 615
Danesh, J., 620
Daneshvar, D. H., 79
Daniel, Old Testament prophet, 202
Daniel, H. J., 523
Danner, U. N., 381
Dar-Nimrod, I., 419
Darley, J. M., 66, 515, 519, 541
Darwin, C., 11–12, 25, 226, 323, 327, 407, 472
Darwin, C. J., 228
Dauer, W., 100
Daum, I., 274
Davidson, R. J., 321, 322, 345
Davies, G., 253, 420
Davila Ross, M., 326
Davis, A., 186
Davis, B., 221
Davis, C., 326
Davis, J. L., 326
Davison, G. C., 598
Dawes, R. M., 134, 659
Dawood, K., 341

Dawson, G., 615
Dawson, M., 439
Day, C., 164
Day, J. J., 111
Dayan, P., 88, 292
Deák, G. O., 436
de Araujo, I. E., 169
Deary, I. J., 398, 399, 400, 402, 412, 413, 414, 420
Deb, S., 417
DeBattista, C., 649
De Boeck, P., 344
DeCasper, A. J., 430
Decety, J., 517
Deci, E. L., 343, 489, 527
de Craen, A. J. M., 571
Deese, J., 254
DeFelipe, J., 81
Degenhardt, L., 214
de Gelder, B., 324
de Geus, E. J. C., 415
Dekker, M. C., 416
Dekker, S., 124
Delgado, M. R., 290
Della Vigna, S., 64
Delton, A. W., 227
Demb, J. B., 224
Dement, W. C., 118, 196, 197, 200, 201
Demler, O., 592
Demoulin, S., 514
de Moura, A. C. A., 298
Dempster, E. L., 606
De Neve, J. E., 401
Denison, S., 435
Dennett, D., 182
DePaulo, B. M., 327, 328
Depp, J., 147
Der, G., 398, 414
Dermer, M., 520
de Rosnay, M., 439
Descartes, R., 6, 180–181
DeSimone, M., 223
DesJardin, J. L., 162
Deskey, D., 129
Desrocher, M., 599
Deuenwald, M., 561
Deutsch, M., 512
DeVilliers, P., 439
De Vries, M. H., 304
de Waal, F. B. M., 186, 451, 513
Dewey, T., 65
Dewhurst, D. L., 281
De Witte, P., 209
De Wolff, M., 445
DeYoung, C. G., 484
D.F., patient, 142–143
Diaconis, P., 61
Diana, princess of Wales, 221
Diano, S., 334
Dibattista, D., 335
DiCaprio, L., 110, 117
Dickens, W. T., 412, 415
Dickinson, A., 280
Didden, R., 416
DiDonato, T. E., 513
Diederich, N. J., 571
Diekelmann, S., 233
Diener, E., 515
Di Giulio, G., 659

Dijksterhuis, A., 192, 193, 501
Dimberg, U., 325, 594
Dimsdale, J. E., 91
Dion, K., 521
DiScenna, P., 232
Disner, S. G., 604
DiTella, R., 465
Dittrich, W. H., 322
Dixon, R. A., 461
DiZio, P., 167
Dobbins, I. G., 244
Dolan, R. J., 226, 391
Dollard, J., 509
Domhoff, G. W., 201
Domjan, M., 276
Donaldson, D., 622
Donner, T. H., 145
Donovick, P. J., 365
Doohan, J., 405
Dornbusch, S. M., 472
Dorus, S., 108
Dostoyevsky, F., 188
Dovidio, J. F., 513, 552
Downer, J. D. C., 319
Downing, P. E., 147
Doyon, J., 302
Dragoin, W. B., 276
Draguns, J. G., 29
Dreifus, C., 517
Drenth Committee, 74
Drews, F. A., 146
Drigotas, S. M., 525
Driver, R. E., 328
Druckman, D., 216
Dubin, L. F., 567
Duckworth, A. L., 343, 401
Dudai, Y., 234
Dudycha, G. J., 240
Dudycha, M. M., 240
Duenwald, M., 561
Dunbar, R., 538
Dunbar, R. I. M., 508
Duncan, D. E., 421
Duncan, G. J., 413
Duncker, K., 382–383
Dunham, Y., 513
Dunlap, K., 333
Dunlop, S. A., 95, 105
Dunlosky, J., 305, 306, 307, 308, 309
Dunning, D. L., 230
Dunphy, D. C., 459
Durrett, C. A., 618
Dutton, D. G., 318, 520
Duval, S., 184
Dweck, C. S., 446
Dworkin, R. H., 165
Dyer, D., 129

**E**

Eacott, M. J., 261
Eagly, A. H., 481, 510, 518, 521
Eastwick, P. W., 519, 521, 524
Eaton, A., 430
Eaton, W. W., 602
Ebbensen, E., 249
Ebbinghaus, H., 21, 249–250, 306
Eberhardt, N. L., 328
Eccles, J. S., 454
Echterhoff, G., 239, 246, 247

Eddy, D. M., 374
Edgerton, V. R., 95
Edwards, C. P., 389
Edwards, M. B., 251
Edwards, W., 374
Efferson, C., 513
Egeland, B., 447
Egloff, B., 519
Eich, J. E., 237, 256
Eichenbaum, H., 241, 301
Eickhoff, S. B., 123
Eilers, R. E., 356
Eimas, P. D., 355
Einstein, A., 41, 69, 124
Einstein, G. O., 251
Eisenberg, L. S., 162
Eisenberg, M. J., 336
Eisenberg, N., 406
Eisenegger, C., 510
Ekman, P., 318, 322, 323, 326, 327, 328
Elbogen, E. B., 593
Eldar, S., 642
Elder, G. H., Jr., 455
Eldridge, L. L., 239
Eldridge, M. A., 250
Elfenbein, H. A., 323, 327, 406
Ell, S. W., 372
Ellemers, N., 515
Ellenbogen, J. M., 233
Elliot, patient, 3, 5, 380
Elliott, R., 420
Ellis, A., 638, 639
Ellis, B. J., 454
Ellis, E. M., 561
Ellis, L., 456
Ellman, S. J., 198
Ellsworth, P. C., 319
Elman, D., 45
Emerson, R. C., 153
Emery, R. E., 455
Eminem, 559
Engle, R. W., 230
Engleman, E. A., 91
English and Romanian Adoptees Study Team, 444
Enock, P. M., 642
Epel, E. S., 556, 557
Epictetus, 604
Epley, N., 191, 543
Epstein, D. R., 199
Epstein, R., 454
Erber, R., 247, 320
Erber, R. E., 188
Erffmeyer, E. S., 45
Erickson, K. I., 105
Ericsson, K. A., 417
Eriksen, W., 411
Erikson, E., 458, 503
Ervin, C. R., 523
Espy, K. A., 430
Etcoff, N., 521
Etoff, N., 521
Euclid, 41
Evans, G. W., 413, 552, 553
Evans, J. St. B., 390, 391
Evans, P. D., 108
Evans, S. W., 414
Everson, S. A., 558
Exner, J. E., 474
Eysenck, H. J., 478, 480, 483, 659

**F**

Fahlman, S., 322
Falk, A., 516
Falk, R., 61
Faulkner, G., 565
Fan, J., 216
Fancher, R. E., 7, 8, 9, 18, 20
Fantz, R. L., 435
Farah, M. J., 372, 413, 421
Faraone, S. V., 616
Farivar, R., 143
Farooqi, I. S., 335
Farrar, M. J., 361
Faust, D., 660
Favagehi, M., 557
Favazza, A., 623
Fazel, S., 620
Fazio, R. H., 536
Fechner, G. T., 132
Feczer, D., 265
Fehr, E., 510, 513
Fein, D., 615
Fein, S., 534
Feinberg, D. R., 26
Feinberg, T. E., 480, 494
Feingold, A., 517, 521
Feinstein, J. S., 319
Feldman, D. E., 103
Feldman, M. D., 573
Felmlee, D., 525
Ferguson, C. J., 512
Ferguson-Smith, A. C., 112
Fernandez-Espejo, D., 123
Fernbach, P. M., 390
Fernyhough, C., 261
Ferster, C. B., 283
Festinger, L., 518, 535, 537
Fetzer, B. K., 577
Field, G. C., 333
Fields, H. L., 571
Filley, C. M., 82
Fincher-Kiefer, R., 545
Finkel, E. J., 519
Finkelstein, K. E., 250
Finn, B., 307
Finn, R., 395
Fiore, A. T., 517
Fiorentine, R., 645
Fiorillo, C. D., 291
Fisher, C., 545
Fisher, H. E., 524
Fisher, P. A., 105
Fisher, R. P., 237
Fiske, S. T., 526, 541, 545
Fleeson, W., 491
Fletcher, P., 608
Fletcher, P. C., 226
Flens, E. A., 307
Flook, L., 459
Flor, H., 104
Florian, V., 523
Flourens, M. J. P., 7
Floyd, J., 524
Flynn, E., 295, 296, 297
Flynn, J. R., 412, 414, 415
Foa, E. B., 562, 627, 639
Fobes, J. I., 291
Fode, K. L., 46
Fogassi, L., 299
Folkman, S., 559

Folley, B. S., 387
Forbes, C., 541
Ford, B. Q., 320
Ford, D., 411
Ford, G., 414
Ford, R., 411
Forkstam, C., 304
Foroni, F., 326
Fortier, C., 99
Foshay, N. N., 515
Foster, C. A., 465
Foster, C. L., 297
Fournier, J. C., 657, 658
Fouts, R. S., 365
Fowler, J. H., 529
Fox, E. B., 247
Fox, M. J., 89–90, 292
Fox, P. T., 122
Fox, R. E., 654
Fox, T., 345
Fragaszy, D. M., 298
Fraley, R. C., 475
Frances, R. J., 645
Francesconi, M., 523
Francis, D., 112, 454
François, C., 163
Frank, M. G., 323
Frank, R. H., 290
Frankl, V., 489, 503
Franklin, J. E., Jr., 645
Franks, J. J., 237
Frascino, J. C., 303
Fraser, S. C., 535
Frederick, D. A., 522
Fredman, T., 298
Fredrickson, B. L., 464, 551
Freedman, J. L., 535
Freeman, S., 45, 515
Freeston, I. L., 123
French, H. W., 521
Freud, S., 13–15, 190, 191, 202–
   203, 272, 458, 466, 484–488,
   503, 637, 642
Frick, R. W., 322
Fried, I., 147
Fried, P. A., 430
Friedlander, L., 599
Friedman, J. M., 336, 337
Friedman, M., 33, 558
Friedman, R. S., 346
Friedman, S. L., 447
Friedman-Hill, S. R., 145
Friesen, W. V., 318, 322, 323, 326
Frith, C. D., 608
Frith, U., 439
Fromm, E., 503
Frost, J. H., 520
Fry, D. P., 512
Fryer, A. J., 595
Fu, F., 513
Fukui, H., 381
Fuligni, A. J., 459
Funder, D. C., 491
Furmark, T., 654
Furumoto, L., 16
Fuseli, H., 202
Fuster, J. M., 100
Fyer, A. J., 638

## G

Gadermann, A. M., 587
Gaechter, S., 513
Gaertner, S. L., 513
Gaesser, B., 245
Gage, P., 115, 122, 480
Gais, S., 88
Galanter, E., 133
Galati, D., 323
Gale, C. R., 398, 412, 416
Galef, B., 278
Galilei, G., 40
Galinsky, A. D., 326, 510
Gall, F. J., 6–7
Gallinat, J., 170
Gallistel, C. R., 294
Gallo, D. A., 254
Gallup, G. G., 186, 522
Galton, F., 407, 414
Gamblers Anonymous, 644
Gangestad, S. W., 522
Ganzel, B. L., 554
Garb, H. N., 344, 592
Garber, J., 454
Garcia, J., 25, 276
Gardner, B. T., 365
Gardner, M., 454
Gardner, R., 197
Gardner, R. A., 365
Garite, T. J., 428
Garland, A. F., 416
Garry, M., 256
Gary, M. L., 542
Gaser, C., 163
Gathercole, S. E., 230
Gatz, M., 463
Gaulin, S. J. C., 522
Gauss, F., 384
Gavin, L. E., 457
Gazzaley, A., 421
Gazzaniga, M. S., 25, 117
Ge, D., 419
Ge, X. J., 455
Gee, B., 437
Geen, R. G., 483
Gegenfurtner, K. R., 140
Geier, A., 339
Gelade, G., 145
Gelman, R., 380
Gendron, M., 324
Genesee, F., 363
Genet, J. J., 321
Genie, 360–361
George, C., 445
Geraerts, E., 256
Geren, J., 358
Gerlic, I., 406
Germanotta, S. J. A., 471
Gershoff, E. T., 279
Geschwind, D. H., 614
Geurts, B., 438
Gibb, B. E., 604
Gibbons, F. X., 184
Gibson, N. A., 652
Gick, M. L., 384
Giedd, J. N., 453
Gierlach, E., 378
Gifford, R. K., 539
Gigerenzer, G., 374, 375, 379, 380
Gigone, D., 514

Gijselaar, P., 411
Gilbert, C. D., 564
Gilbert, D. T., 45, 256, 288, 328,
   343, 490, 543, 544, 545
Gilbert, G. M., 539
Gilbertson, M. W., 600
Gill, M. J., 45
Gillespie, C. F., 444
Gillette, J., 358
Gilligan, C., 449
Gilliland, K., 483
Gilovich, T., 45, 67, 330, 499
Gino, F., 515
Ginzburg, K., 561
Giovanello, K. S., 239
Gjernes, M., 425
Gladue, B. A., 456
Glaser, R., 557, 563
Glass, D. C., 553
Glass, G. V., 659
Glenwick, D. S., 45
Glotzer, L. D., 102
Glynn, L. M., 428
Gneezy, U., 344
Gobert, A., 597
Goddard, H. H., 396
Godden, D. R., 237
Goehler, L. E., 569
Goel, V., 391
Goethals, G. R., 534
Goetz, C. G., 571
Goetzman, E. S., 186, 187
Goff, L. M., 255
Gold, D., 411
Goldman, M. S., 210
Goldman, R., 534, 535
Goldstein, M. H., 356
Goldstein, N. J., 526
Goldstein, R., 170, 417
Gollwitzer, P. M., 526
Gomez, C., 183
Gontier, N., 360
Gonzaga, G. C., 525
Goodale, M. A., 142, 143
Goodman, J. C., 358
Goodman, P., 637
Gootman, E., 409
Gopnik, A., 435, 438, 440
Gopnik, M., 360
Gorczynski, P., 565
Gordon, P., 441
Gore, A., 256
Gore, J. C., 145
Gorman, J. M., 659
Gorno-Tempini, M. L., 252
Gotlib, I. H., 604
Gottesman, I. I., 108, 609, 610
Gottfredson, L. S., 396, 398, 406
Gottfried, J. A., 169
Gouldner, A. W., 529
Government of Canada, 335
Graber, J. A., 454
Grady, C. L., 462
Graf, P., 242
Grafman, J., 542
Grafton, S. T., 103
Graham, R., 420
Grandin, T., 615
Grant, A. M., 637

Grant, B. F., 620
Grassian, S., 507
Gray, H. M., 179, 180
Gray, J. A., 345, 483
Gray, J. R., 484
Gray, K., 179
Graziano, W. G., 512
Greely, H., 420
Green, C. S., 136
Green, D. A., 134
Green, M. F., 609
Green, S. K., 520
Greenberg, J., 184, 347, 500, 523
Greenburg, J., 64
Greene, D., 343, 527
Greene, J., 449
Greene, J. D., 449, 450
Greenwald, A. G., 192, 542
Greg, patient, 241, 242, 243, 245
Gretzky, W., 328
Grewal, D., 406
Gribble, P. L., 297, 300
Griffiths, J. H., 280
Griffiths, P. E., 26
Grimaldi, J., 331
Grockett, L., 455
Groom, R. W., 509
Gropp, E., 334
Gross, J. J., 320, 321
Gross, P. H., 66
Grotpeter, J. K., 481, 510
Grotzer, T. A., 415
Groves, B., 177
Grün, F., 337
Guerin, S. A., 254, 260
Guilleminault, C., 200
Guillery, R. W., 98
Güntürkün, O., 186
Gup, D., 653
Gup, T., 653
Gur, R. E., 611
Gurwitz, J. H., 570
Gusnard, D. A., 121, 188
Gustafsson, J.-E., 403
Gutchess, A. H., 254
Gutting, G., 17

## H

Haase, C. M., 463
Hacking, I., 380
Hackman, D. A., 413
Hackman, J. R., 514
Hadfield, C., 472
Haedt-Matt, A. A., 335
Haggard, P., 181
Haidt, J., 323, 324, 449, 450, 508
Haines, M. M., 531, 552
Halaas, J. L., 337
Halbrooks, D., 256
Halgren, E., 165
Hall, C. R., 297
Hall, G. S., 12, 14, 26, 31
Hall, J. A., 400
Hall, L. K., 257
Hall, P. A., 335
Hallett, M., 123
Halliday, R., 420
Halpern, B., 172
Halpern, D. F., 418
Hambrick, D. Z., 417

Hamelin, C., 96
Hamermesh, D. S., 521
Hamilton, A. F., 103
Hamilton, D. L., 539
Hamilton, J. P., 564, 603
Hamilton, W. D., 512, 516
Hamlin, J. K., 450, 451
Hammersmith, S. K., 456
Hampikian, G., 429
Handal, A., 239
Haney, C., 532
Hankins, H., 399
Hanlon, C., 359
Hannon, E. E., 163
Hansen, E. S., 599
Hanson, D. R., 108
Hanson, J. D., 553
Happé, F. G. E., 439, 614
Haraguchi, A., 64
Harand, C., 232
Harbluk, J. L., 253
Harding, C. M., 593
Hardt, O., 234
Hare, R. D., 620
Harker, L. A., 324
Harkins, S., 515
Harkness, S., 389
Harlow, H. F., 442, 443
Harlow, J. M., 115
Harlow, M. L., 442
Harper, S., 379, 556
Harris, B., 272
Harris, P. L., 438, 439
Harris, V. A., 544
Harrison, G., 253
Harsch, N., 258
Harstall, C., 165
Hart, B., 413
Hart, B. L., 569
Hart, W., 67
Hartshorne, H., 491
Harvald, B., 602
Haselton, M. G., 26
Hasher, L., 380
Hashtroudi, S., 253
Haskell, E., 632
Haslam, C., 369
Haslet, A., 574
Hassabis, D., 245
Hasselmo, M. E., 88
Hassin, R. R., 344
Hassmen, P., 565
Hasson, U., 149
Hastie, R., 514, 540
Hatemi, P. K., 482
Hatfield, E., 518, 523, 524
Hauge, M., 602
Hauser, G., 430
Haushofer, J., 510
Hausser, M., 86
Havas, D. A., 326
Hawley, P. H., 508
Haxby, J. V., 147
Hay, L., 39–40, 59
Hayes, C., 365
Hayes, J. E., 173
Hayes, K., 365
Hayes, S. C., 562
Hay-McCutcheon, M. J., 162
Hayne, H., 29, 240

He, Z., 438
Health Canada, 337, 576, 578, 651
Heart and Stroke Foundation, 574
Hearst, E., 68
Heath, S. B., 413
Heatherton, T. F., 336, 496, 537, 575, 576
Heaton, R., 611
Heavey, C. L., 314
Hebb, D. O., 32, 235
Hebl, M. R., 336
Heckhausen, J., 463
Hedges, L. V., 416
Heerey, E. A., 439
Hefferkine, R., 637
Heggestad, E. D., 418
Heine, S. J., 65, 378, 419, 524
Heiphetz, L., 542
Held, R., 432
Helt, M., 615
Helweg-Larsen, M., 378
Hemingway, E., 606
Henderlong, J., 343
Henderson, P., 258
Henrich, J., 65
Henry, W. P., 635
Hepburn, C., 513
Herbener, E. S., 523
Herdt, G., 29
Herman, C. P., 337, 338, 577
Herman-Giddens, M. E., 453
Hernstadt, R., 302
Herring, M. P., 565
Herrnstein, R. J., 19
Herschkowitsch, A., 170
Hertenstein, M. J., 322
Hertig, M. M., 105
Hertwig, R., 380
Herz, R. S., 169
Hettema, J. M., 596, 597
Heuer, S. K., 520
Heyes, C. M., 297
Heyman, G. M., 208
Heymsfield, S. B., 337
Hibbeln, J. R., 652
Hickok, G., 299
Higgins, E. T., 346, 499, 577
Hilgard, E. R., 215
Hill, P. C., 567
Hill, R. P., 335
Hillman, C. H., 105
Hilts, P., 232
Hine, T., 129
Hintzman, D. L., 61
Hippocrates, 573
Hirschberger, G., 523
Hirst, W., 99, 239, 246, 247, 258
Hirstein, W., 331
Hitch, G. J., 229
Hitchcock, S. T., 647
Hitler, A., 425
Hobbes, T., 6
Hobson, J. A., 201, 203
Hockley, W. E., 236
Hodapp, R. M., 162
Hodgkin, A. L., 84, 86
Hodson, G., 513
Hoek, H. W., 428
Hoffman, V., 446
Hoffrage, U., 374, 375, 379, 380

Hofman, A., 213
Hofmann, S. G., 641, 642
Hofmann, W., 342
Holder, M., 335, 406
Hollins, M., 164
Holloway, G., 201
Holman, E. A., 554
Holman, M. A., 162
Holmbeck, G. N., 458
Holmes, J., 230
Holmes, K. J., 368
Holmes, T. H., 550
Holt, J., 184
Holyoak, K. J., 384
Hölzel, B. K., 563
Homan, K. J., 281
Homann, E., 604
Homans, G. C., 525
Honzik, C. H., 288, 289
Hooley, J. M., 607
Hopkins, B., 430
Hopper, L. M., 297
Horn, J. L., 405
Horner, V., 297
Horney, K., 503
Horrey, W. J., 146
Horta, B. L., 430
Hosking, S. G., 146
Hotson, J., 125
Hou, Y., 240
Hougaard, E., 644
Houlihan, D., 281
House, J., 507
Howard, D. V., 302
Howard, I. P., 150
Howard, J. H., Jr., 302
Howard, L., 110
Howard, M. O., 211
Howard-Jones, P. A., 387
Howell, A., 600
Howes, M., 240
Howland, R. H., 602
Hoyle, R., 564
Huang, J., 606
Hubel, D. H., 118, 142
Huesmann, L. R., 55, 509
Hughes, J. R., 649
Hughes, L., 467
Hughes, T., 186, 187
Hughs, S., 454
Hull, C., 333–334
Humphreys, G. W., 145
Hunsley, J., 633, 651, 659
Hunt, E. B., 413
Hunt, M., 524
Hunter, J. E., 400
Hunter, R. F., 400
Hurlburt, R. T., 314
Hurvich, L. M., 141
Hussey, E., 326
Huttenlocher, P. R., 453
Huxley, A., 205, 206
Huxley, A. F., 84, 86
Huys, Q. J. M., 88
Hwang, A. J., 227
Hyde, J. S., 449, 481, 518
Hyde, K. L., 163
Hyman, I. E., Jr., 155–156, 256
Hypericum Depression Trial Study Group, 651

**I**
Iacoboni, M., 103
ibn Tulun, A., 647
Ichheiser, G., 544
Illingworth, A. J., 4
Imbo, I., 441
Inciardi, J. A., 208
Ingram, P., 215
Ingvar, M., 304, 420
Inhelder, B., 22
Innocence Project, 253
Insel, T. R., 590
Inui, A., 334
Ireland, M. E., 523
Irvine, J. T., 406
Isaacowitz, D. M., 463
Isabelle, R. A., 446
Isen, A. M., 331
Isenberg, D. J., 514
Ishii, K., 330
Israel, L., 254
Ittelson, W. H., 152
Iverson, L. L., 610
Izard, C. E., 324, 406

**J**
Jablensky, A., 609
Jacobs, B. L., 565
Jacobson, E., 563–564
Jacobson, T., 446
Jaffee, S., 449
Jahoda, G., 29
Jalinous, R., 123
James, T. W., 143
James, W., 1–5, 7, 10–12, 13, 14, 20, 26, 31, 124, 183, 184, 316–317, 318, 333, 480, 495, 499, 511
Jameson, D., 141
Jamieson, J. P., 321, 552, 559, 595
Jamison, K. R., 416, 605
Janet, P., 13
Jang, K. L., 595
Janicak, P. G., 655
Janis, I. L., 514
Jarosz, A. F., 387
Jarvella, R. J., 355
Jason, L. A., 45
Jausovec, K., 406
Jausovec, N., 406
Jaynes, J., 184, 189
J.B., patient, 369
Jenkins, doctor, 627
Jenkins, H. M., 273
Jenkins, J. G., 233
Jenkins, J. M., 318
Jennifer, 265–266, 272
Jennings, K., 401
Jensen, A. R., 399
Jensen, T. S., 104
Jentsch, J. D., 72
Jesus Christ, 608
Joan of Arc, 608
John, O. P., 478, 479, 482
Johns, M., 541
Johnson, A., 428
Johnson, C. A., 381
Johnson, D., 467
Johnson, D. H., 161
Johnson, D. R., 465

Johnson, J. D., 210
Johnson, J. S., 361
Johnson, K., 164
Johnson, M. H., 431
Johnson, M. K., 253
Johnson, N. J., 565
Johnson, S., 223
Johnson, S. C., 446, 593
Johnson, S. L., 605, 606, 607
Johnson, V. E., 340
Johnston, L., 454
Johnston, W. A., 146
Johnstone, E. C., 611
Jonas, E., 528
Jones, B. C., 522
Jones, E. E., 544, 545
Jones, E. G., 81
Jones, I., 606
Jones, J. T., 501
Jones, K., 647
Jones, L. M., 515
Jones, S. S., 441
Jonides, J., 462
Jonsson, H., 644
Jonsson, P., 326
Joormann, J., 604
Jordan, S. A., 651
Josephs, R. A., 210
Joyce, J., 183
Judd, L. L., 602
Juffer, F., 413
Jung, C. G., 14, 503
Jung-Beeman, M., 363, 386
Jurewicz, I., 610

**K**

Kaas, J. H., 103
Kabnick, K., 577
Kachelski, R. A., 191
Kagan, J., 445
Kahlo, F., 494
Kahn, R. S., 655
Kahn, S., 576
Kahneman, D., 187, 345, 375, 376,
      377, 378–379, 466
Kalat, J. W., 335
Kalish, D., 289
Kamin, L. J., 281, 396
Kamiya, J., 564
Kan, P. F., 356
Kandel, E. R., 84, 232, 235, 241,
      266, 301
Kang, S. H. K., 306
Kanzi, chimp, 366
Kanwisher, N., 119, 122, 147
Kaplan, R. M., 642
Kapur, S., 224
Karau, S. J., 247
Karg-Palerio, C., 517
Karlins, M., 539
Karney, B. R., 525
Karow, A., 608
Karpicke, J. D., 238, 306
Kashiwagi, K., 406
Kasser, T., 518
Kastner, S., 143, 373
Katcher, A. H., 318
Katon, W., 596
Katz, D., 539
Katz, N., 514

Kaufman, A. S., 412
Kaufman, L., 530
Kawakami, K., 542
Kay, A., 344
Kay, P., 368
Kazdin, A. E., 642
K.C., patient, 245
Keane, M. M., 245
Keane, T. M., 600
Keefe, F. J., 89, 166
Keel, P. K., 335
Keil, F. C., 390, 441
Keith, P. M., 525
Kelley, A. E., 291
Kelley, H. H., 525, 543
Kelley, W. M., 496, 497
Kellman, P. J., 435
Kellogg, A., 1
Kelly, G., 492
Kelly, L. M., 302
Keltner, D., 318, 322, 323, 324, 439
Kendler, K. S., 595, 596, 597
Kennedy, J., 599
Kenrick, D. T., 334, 518, 522
Kensinger, E. A., 99, 251, 259
Kepler, J., 40
Kershaw, T. C., 386
Kertai, M. D., 178
Kessler, R. C., 589, 592, 594, 597,
      599, 600, 602, 605, 614, 616,
      628
Ketchum, K., 216
Keuler, D. J., 257
Kevari, M. K., 252
Khalid, N., 654
Khalid, R., 344
Khan, N. Y., 306
Khan, R. M., 169
Khan, S., 308
Kidman, N., 48
Kiecolt-Glaser, J. K., 557, 563, 566
Kiefer, H. M., 73
Kiefer, M., 237
Kiehl, K. A., 620
Kihlstrom, J. F., 191, 216, 497
Kim, G., 441
Kim, K., 454
Kim, P., 414
Kim, U. K., 173
King, M. L., Jr., 543
King, R., 507
Kinney, D., 459
Kinney, D. A., 459
Kiper, D. C., 141
Kirchgessner, A., 79
Kirchner, W. H., 352
Kirker, W. S., 496
Kirkham, T. C., 213
Kirkpatrick, J., 406
Kirsch, I., 214
Kirwan, C. B., 232, 233
Kish, S. J., 212
Kita, S., 361
Kitayama, S., 30, 157, 330, 517
Klatzky, R. L., 165
Klein Poelhuis, C. W., 413
Klein, C. T. F., 378
Klein, S. B., 85, 227, 497
Kleitman, N., 196
Klerman, G. L., 635

Klingberg, T., 230
Klinger, E., 186, 187, 493
Klinger, M. R., 192
Klonsky, E. D., 623
Kluckhohn, C., 477
Klump, K. L., 335
Klüver, H., 319
Knieps, L. J., 441
Knight, J., 520
Knowlton, B., 99
Knowlton, B. J., 302
Knutson, B., 291, 480
Kobasa, S., 575
Kobberling, J., 375
Koehler, J. J., 67
Koelling, R. A., 276
Koenigs, M., 450
Koestner, R., 343, 527
Koffka, K., 148
Kohlberg, L., 448–449
Kohnert, K., 356
Koivula, N., 565
Kolb, B., 114
Kolb, S., 432
Koller, D., 308–309
Kolotkin, R. L., 336
Komter, A., 517
Konen, C. S., 143
Koole, S. L., 325, 501
Koot, H. M., 416
Koppel, J., 239
Korn, J. H., 307
Kornell, N., 309
Koslov, K., 552
Koss, M. P., 597
Kosslyn, S. M., 216, 225
Kounios, J., 386, 387
Kovalevskaya, S., 418
Kozak, M., 202
Kraemer, H. C., 586
Kraepelin, E., 609
Kral, P. A., 276
Kramer, A. F., 105
Kramer, D. L. F., 252
Krantz, D. S., 558
Kraus, N., 163
Kravitz, D. J., 142
Kravitz, R. L., 649
Kreider, T., 467
Kringelbach, M. L., 170
Krings, T., 2
Krishnan, V., 603
Kristensen, P., 411
Kroeze, W. K., 88
Kroonenberg, P. M., 445
Krueger, A. B., 187
Krueger, J. I., 513
Krueger, R. F., 475
Kruetzer, T., 447
Kruger, A. C., 298
Kruglinski, S., 156
Kruk, M. R., 509
Krull, D. S., 545
Kubovy, M., 159
Kugler, M. B., 533
Kuhl, B. A., 240, 241
Kuhl, P., 362
Kuhl, P. K., 362, 431
Kuhn, S., 170
Kuiper, N. A., 496

Kulik, J., 258
Kulkarni, A., 457
Kubzansky, L. D., 575
Kunda, Z., 67, 541
Kunugi, H., 611
Kunz, P. R., 529
Kvavilashvil, L., 258

**L**

LaBar, K. S., 319
Labrie, V., 606
Lachman, J. L., 22
Lachman, R., 22
Lackner, J. R., 167
Lady Gaga, 471, 472–473, 508
LaFraniere, S., 521
Lahkan, S. E., 79
Lahn, B. T., 108
Lai, Y., 205
Lake, J., 651
Lakin, J. M., 416
Lakshminarayanan, V. R., 345
Lalive, R., 513
Lam, L. L., 111
Lam, R. W., 602
Lamb, M. E., 445, 447
Lambert, W., 365
Lamberth, J., 523
Lamm, H., 514
Landauer, T. K., 10
Landis, K., 507
Landru, H. D., 619–620
Lane, C., 17
Lang, F. R., 464
Lang, P. J., 620
Lange, C., 316–317, 318
Langer, E. J., 592
Langleben, D. D., 328
Langlois, J. H., 521
LaPierre, S., 552
Lareau, A., 413
Laroche, M., 566
Larrick, R. P., 509
Larsen, S. F., 258
Larson, C. L., 321
Larson, M. E., 553
Larson, R., 458, 459
Larson-Gutman, M. K., 187
Lashley, K. S., 24
Lassiter, G. D., 328, 343
Latané, B., 515
Lattal, K. A., 280
Laub, J. H., 454
Laupa, M., 451
Laureys, S., 123
Lavie, P., 195
Lavoisier, A., 41
Law, B., 297
Lawrence, N. S., 381
Lawton, M. P., 463, 518
Lazarus, R. S., 319, 321, 559
Leader, T., 515
Leary, M. R., 318, 500, 515, 528,
      566
Leary, T., 213
Lecky, P., 497
Lecrubier, Y., 651
Lederman, S. J., 165
LeDoux, J. E., 99, 234, 275, 319,
      320

LeDoux, J. L., 275
Lee, A. Y., 577
Lee, B., 417
Lee-Chiong, T., 199
Lee, D. N., 167
Lee, L., 332, 523
Lee, M. H., 121
Lee, P. C., 298
Lefcourt, H. M., 493
LeFevre, J.-A., 441
Lefforge, N. L., 314
Lehman, D. R., 378, 380, 577
Lehman, J. M., 575
Leichsenring, F., 635
Leiter, M. P., 560
Lemay, E. P., 524
Lempert, D., 336
Lenoir, M., 206
Lens, W., 344
Lenton, A. P., 523
Lentz, M. J., 198
Leon, D. A., 398
Leonardo, robot, 313–314, 322
Lepage, M., 239
LePort, A. K. R., 222
Lepper, H. S., 473
Lepper, M. R., 67, 343, 527
Lerman, D., 474
Lerman, D. C., 281
Lesage, A., 628
Leslie, A., 439
Leung, A. K.-Y., 512
Levelt Committee, 74
Levenson, J. M., 111
Levenson, R. W., 318
Levin, D. T., 154, 155
Levin, K., 561
Levin, R., 202
Levine, J. A., 328
Levine, J. D., 571
Levine, M., 647
Levine, R. V., 45
Levine, S. P., 417
Levy, J., 117
Lewin, K., 22, 27, 28, 490
Lewin, R., 366
Lewis, I., 338
Lewis, M., 187
Lewis, M. B., 325
Lewis, M. D., 652
Lewontin, R., 396
Li, N. P., 513
Li, R., 136
Li, Y. J., 545
Libet, B., 181
Liebenluft, E., 605
Lieberman, J., 648
Lieberman, M. D., 320, 483
Liebler, A., 400
Liebowitz, M. R., 596
Lievens, F., 418
Lifshitz, M., 216
Lightstone, J., 533
Lilienfeld, S. O., 344, 475, 661
Lillard, L. A., 465
Lim, K. L., 628
Linardatos, L., 526
Lincoln, A., 1, 2, 606
Lindenberger, U., 412, 462
Linder, L. R., 338

Lindquist, K., 318
Lindquist, S. I., 307
Lindsay, D. S., 253
Lindstrom, M., 129
Lindstrom, P., 171, 456
Liou, A. P., 337
Lippmann, W., 538
Lippold, S., 521
Lipsitz, J. D., 638
Lisiecki, J., 489
Little Albert, 18, 272, 273, 595
Little, B. R., 187, 493
Liu, D., 112, 437
Liu, J., 248
Liu, Y., 146
Livingstone, M., 119
Locksley, A., 513
Loehlin, J. C., 419, 480
Loftus, E. F., 122, 191, 216, 255, 258
Lohr, J. M., 475
Lømo, W. T., 235
Lonner, W. J., 29
Lopes, P. N., 406
Lopez, D. F., 499
Lopiano, L., 571
Lord, C. G., 67
Lorenz, K., 443
Loulis, chimp, 365, 366
Lovaas, I., 615
Love, A. B., 406
Low, J., 438
Lozano, B. E., 607
Lubach, G. R., 428
Lubinski, D., 417
Luborsky, L., 659
Lucas G., 421
Lucas, J. A., 596
Lucas, R. E., 465
Lucy, chimp, 365
Ludwig, A. M., 194
Luk, G., 363
Lungu, O., 302
Lydon, J., 526
Lykken, D. T., 620
Lynn, M., 520
Lynn, R., 412
Lynn, S. J., 475
Lyons, D. E., 441
Lyubomirsky, S., 473

**M**

Ma, Y.-Y., 250, 251
MacArthur Foundation, 613
MacCulloch, R. J., 465
MacDonald, S., 29, 240
MacGregor, J. N., 386
Mack, A. H., 645
Mackin, R., 550, 551
Maclean, P. D., 99
MacLeod, C., 642
MacLeod, M. D., 239
Macmillan, M., 115
Macmillan, N. A., 134
Macrae, C. N., 496, 497, 537, 542
MADD Canada, 211
Maddi, K. L., 576
Maddi, S. R., 576
Maddux, W. W., 326
Madey, S. F., 45, 499

Madigan, S., 446
Madoff, B., 290–291
Maes, M., 569
Maggi, G., 571
Magnani, F., 230
Magoun, H. W., 96
Maguire, E. A., 105
Mahajan, N., 513
Maher, A., 561
Mahon, B. Z., 372, 373
Mahowald, M., 205
Mai, N., 153
Maier, S. F., 569
Major, B., 552
Makel, M. C., 416
Makin, J. E., 430
Makris, N., 616
Malina, R. M., 453
Malle, B. F., 595
Mallory, G. L., 338
Malone, P. S., 544
Malone, W., 500
Malooly, A. M., 321
Mampe, B., 430
Mandel, D. R., 380
Mandel, H., 599
Mandela, N., 309
Manderscheid, R. W., 609
Mandle, C. L., 564
Mandler, G., 225
Maner, J. K., 510, 521
Manier, D., 239
Mankiw, N. G., 521
Mann, J. J., 91, 623
Mannheim, Z., 331
Manning, C. A., 251
Mannix, L. M., 336
Manns, J. R., 274
Maquet, P., 204
Marangell, L. B., 648, 650, 655
Marci, C. D., 636
Marcus, G., 122
Marentette, P. F., 356
Margolis, R., 458
Marien, H., 344
Marino, L., 185
Markowitz, J. C., 633, 635
Markus, G. B., 257
Markus, H., 496
Marlatt, G. A., 210
Marles, R. J., 651
Marlowe, F. W., 26
Marmot, M. G., 557
Marois, R., 145
Marr, D., 150
Marriott, P., 336
Marsolek, C. J., 371
Martin, A., 102, 244, 372
Martin, K. D., 335
Martin, L. L., 324
Martin, M., 412
Martin, N. G., 482
Martin, P., 556
Marucha, P. T., 557
Marzuk, P. M., 212
Maslach, C., 560
Maslow, A. H., 15, 334, 335, 489, 499, 503
Mason, A., 568

Mason, M. F., 188, 538
Mason, P., 517
Masten, A. S., 643
Masters, W. H., 340
Masuda, T., 157
Mather, M., 463
Mathews, A., 642
Matisse, H., 283
Matsuda, O., 405
Matsumoto, D., 323
Mattar, A. A. G., 297, 300
Matte, T. D., 428
Matthews, G., 483
Matzel, L. D., 402
Maudsley, H., 608
Max, A., 411
May, E., 379
May, M. A., 491
May, R., 489, 490
Mayberg, H. S., 656
Mayer, J. D., 406, 417
Maynard-Smith, J., 516
McAdams, D., 496
McArthur, L. Z., 522
McBride, M., 305
McCabe, D. P., 307
McCabe, S. E., 420
McCain, J., 507
McCarley, R. W., 203
McCarthy, R. A., 372
McCauley, J., 211
McCeney, M. K., 558
McClelland, D. C., 344, 475
McConkey, K. M., 256
McCrae, R. R., 478, 481
McCrea, S. M., 145
McDaniel, M. A., 251
McDermott, J., 122, 147
McDermott, K. B., 107, 246, 254, 306
McDonough, I. M., 461
McDougall, W., 334
McElree, B., 239
McElwain, N. L., 446
McEvoy, S. P., 146
McFall, R. M., 134, 659
McFarlane, A. H., 551
McGarrah, A., 395–396
McGarty, C., 540
McGaugh, J. L., 99, 221, 222, 232, 259
McGeoch, P. D., 104
McGhee, D. E., 542
McGill, K. L., 551
McGowan, P. O., 112
McGrady, A., 564
McGrath, J., 609
McGraw, M. B., 432
McGregor, D., 61
McGue, M., 408, 482
McGuffin, P., 602
McGuire, P. K., 608
McHaffie, J. G., 570
McIntyre, S. H., 305
McKee, A. C., 79, 80
McKetin, R., 420
McKinney, C. H., 564
McLachlan, D. R., 253
McLanahan, S. S., 429
McLaughlin, K. A., 597

McLean, J. P., 307
McLean, K. C., 246, 496
McNally, R. J., 200, 256, 561, 595, 642, 661
McNeill, D., 252
McNeilly, A. S., 99
McRae, C., 571
Mead, G. H., 497
Mead, M., 29
Meadows, E. A., 562
Meaney, M. J., 108, 111, 112, 113
Mechelli, A., 364, 365
Medin, D. L., 371
Medvec, V. H., 45, 499
Meeren, H. K., 324
Mehl, M. R., 476, 495
Mehood, W., 400
Mehrabian, L., 533
Meindl, J. N., 281
Meins, E., 446
Meisel, S. R., 557
Mekel-Bobrov, N., 108
Melander, E., 511
Mellon, R. C., 288
Meltzer, H. Y., 648
Meltzoff, A. N., 431, 438, 441
Melzack, R., 165, 166
Mendes, W. B., 321, 552, 559, 595
Mendle, J., 455
Mennella, J. A., 428
Mental Health Commission of Canada, 632
Menzler, S., 326
Merikangas, K. R., 602
Merkel, A., 472
Mervis, C. B., 356, 370
Merzenich, M. M., 103
Messick, D. M., 525
Meston, C. M., 341, 342
Mestre, J. M., 406
Mestry, N., 122
Metcalfe, J., 307, 384
Meter, K., 336
Methven, L., 172
Meyer-Bahlberg, H. F. L., 456
Meyer-Lindenberg, A., 591
Meyers, J., 256
Michaela, R., 320
Michelson, D., 597
Midas, king, 217
Mikels, J. A., 332
Miklowitz, D. J., 607
Mikulincer, M., 523
Milan, A., 566
Milavsky, B., 318
Milazzo-Sayre, L. J., 609
Miles, E., 320
Milgram, S., 531–533
Miller, A. J., 533
Miller, C., 104, 605
Miller, D. T., 500, 517, 528
Miller, G. A., 23, 229
Miller, G. E., 413
Miller, I., 606
Miller, K. F., 441
Miller, N., 510
Miller, N. E., 335
Miller, T. I., 659
Miller, T. W., 550
Miller, W. R., 573

Mills, J., 536
Mills, P. J., 91
Milne, E., 542
Milner, A. D., 142, 143
Milner, B., 24, 32, 99, 231, 241, 302
Milner, P., 98–99
Milner, P. M., 291
Minaj, N., 483
Mineka, S., 297, 594
Mingroni, M. A., 412
Mink, J. W., 656
Minsky, M., 180
Minson, J. A., 514
Mintun, M. A., 119
Miranda, J., 660
Mirenberg, M. C., 501
Mischel, W., 343, 401, 490, 491
Mishkin, M., 142
Mishra, A., 540
Mishra, H., 540
Mita, T. H., 520
Mitura, K., 518
Mitchell, B. D., 549
Mitchell, D. R., 620
Mitchell, J. P., 188, 243, 496, 537
Mitchell, K. A., 523
Mitchell, K. J., 253
Miura, I. T., 440
Miyamoto, Y., 30, 157
Moffitt, T. E., 113, 454
Moghaddam, B., 291
Mojtabai, R., 629
Molaison, H., 231–232, 235, 241, 242, 243, 302
Molden, D., 577
Monahan, J., 134, 593
Monahan, J. L., 519
Monahan, K. C., 459
Moncrieff, J., 610
Monet, C., 282–283
Moniz, E., 655
Montag, H., 317
Montague, C. T., 335
Montague, P. R., 292
Montepare, J. M., 522
Monti, M. M., 123, 185, 193
Mook, D. G., 63
Moon, S. M., 4
Moon, S. M., Rev., 28
Moore, A. J., 195
Moore, E. G. J., 419
Moore, K. L., 106
Moore, M. K., 431
Moran, P., 416
Moray, N., 182
Morein-Zamir, S., 420
Moreno, S., 163
Morewedge, C. K., 203
Morgenstern, J., 645
Morin, A., 184, 497
Morin, C. M., 199
Morison, V., 431
Morris, A. S., 454
Morris, C. D., 237
Morris, E., 288
Morris, E. K., 18
Morris, R. G., 235
Morris, T. L., 595
Morrison, C., 98
Morrow, D., 461

Morsella, E., 191
Mortillaro, M., 322
Morton, L., 555
Moruzzi, G., 96
Morwitz, V. G., 533
Mory, M., 459
Mosby, I., 70
Moscovitch, M., 232, 233, 239
Mosher, W. D., 525
Mosteller, F., 61
Motley, M. T., 190
Moulin, C. J. A., 253, 254
Movellan, J. R., 444
M.R., patient, 253
Mroczek, D. K., 463
Muehlenkamp, J. J., 623
Mueller, J. S., 515
Mueller, T. E., 457
Mueller, T. I., 602
Muenter, M. D., 89
Muhanna, W. A., 165
Mullainathan, S., 75
Mullen, B., 515
Mullen, E., 326
Mullen, M. K., 240
Muller, M. N., 510
Multi-Society Task Force on PVS, 185
Munakata, Y., 434
Munholland, K. A., 446
Munoz, R. F., 321
Munson, J. M., 305
Murphy, N. A., 400
Murphy, R., 414
Murphy, S. T., 519
Murray, C., 398
Murray, H. A., 475, 477
Murray, R. M., 608
Murray, T. H., 421
Musen, G., 99
Muybridge, E., 42
Mycielska, K., 4
Myers, D. G., 514, 515
Myers, J., 595
Myles, P. S., 178
Myrskylä, M., 458

## N

Nadasdy, A., 353
Nadeau, L., 381
Nader, K., 234
Nagasako, E. M., 165
Nagel, B. J., 105
Nagell, K., 298
Nahemow, L., 518
Nairne, J. S., 226, 227
Nakazato, M., 334
Napoleon, 608
Naqvi, N., 380
Nash, J., 608
Nass, C., 146
Nathan, P. E., 659
Nathanson, C., 479
National Center for Health Statistics, 419
National Safety Council, 565
National Science Foundation, 75
Natsuaki, M. N., 455

Natural Science and Engineering Research Council of America, 75
Natural Science and Engineering Research Council of Canada, 70
Naumann, L. P., 478, 479
Neale, J. M., 598
Neale, M. C., 596
Nebuchadnezzar, king, 202
NEDSAC, 614
Neihart, M., 416
Neiles, K. Y., 307
Neimark, J., 61
Neimeyer, R. A., 523
Neisser, U., 20, 23, 258, 412, 414, 418
Nelms-Matzke, J., 430
Nelson, C. A., 413
Nelson, D., 523
Nelson, P., 596
Nelson, T. F., 531
Nemeroff, C. B., 88, 444
Nemeth, C., 530
Nestler, E. J., 603
Nettle, D., 515
Neuberg, S. L., 513, 522
Neugebauer, R., 428
Newbold, B., 566
Newbold, R. R., 337
Newell, A., 23
Newman, A. J., 25
Newman, J. P., 68
Newman, M. G., 568
Newport, E. I., 302
Newport, E. L., 361
Newschaffer, C. J., 614
Newsom, J. T., 535
Newsome, W. T., 153, 291
Newton, I., 140, 606
Neylan, T. C., 202
Niaura, R., 558
Nicoladis, E., 363
Nida, S., 515
Niedenthal, P. M., 326
Nielsen, T., 202
Nietzsche, F., 555
Nikles, C. D., II, 201
Nikolajsen, L., 104
Nikula, R., 187
Nir, Y., 204
Nisbett, R. E., 30, 157, 343, 411, 413, 414, 415, 416, 420, 490, 511, 527, 545
Nishihara, H. K., 150
Nissen, M. J., 302
Nitschke, J. B., 170
Nock, M. K., 321, 592, 595, 617, 622, 623
Noel, N. E., 210
Nolen-Hoeksema, S., 602
Noor-Eldeen, N., 542
Noort Committee, 74
Norenzayan, A., 45, 65, 545
Norman, W. T., 479
Norrholm, S. D., 597
Norton, M. I., 203, 520
Nosanchuk, T. A., 533
Nosek, B. A., 542
Nosen, E., 595

Nowak, M. A., 512
Nowell, A., 416
Nuttin, J. M., 501
Nyborg, H., 399
Nye, B., 299

## O

Oaklander, A. L., 165
Oately, K., 318
Obama, B., 190
O'Brien, J. B., 372
Ochsner, K. N., 258, 320, 321
Ockenfels, A., 525
Ockham, W., 41
O'Connor, T. G., 444
Odbert, H. S., 477
Oden, M. H., 417
O'Doherty, J. P., 292
O'Donnell, K., 458
O'Donovan, M. C., 610
OECD. See Organisation for
    Economic Co-operation and
    Development
Oettingen, G., 526
Ofshe, R., 215, 661
Ogan, T. A., 441
Ohayon, M. M., 199, 200
Ohlsson, S., 386
Ohman, A., 297
Öhman, A., 594, 595
Okagagi, L., 407
Okuda, J., 246
Olatunji, B. O., 596
O'Laughlin, M. J., 595
Olds, J., 98–99, 291
Olegario, F., 129
Oleson, K. C., 541
Olguin, R. S., 298
Ollers, D. K., 356
Olofsson, J., 169
Olofsson, J. K., 168
Olsson, A., 275
Oltmanns, T. F., 598, 607
Olton, D. S., 293
O'Malley, P., 454
Onishi, K. H., 438
Ono, K., 288
Ono, Y., 622
Ontario College of Psychologist, 630
Ontario Ministry of Children and
    Youth Services, 661
Ophir, E., 146
Orban, P., 302
O'Regan, J. K., 155
Organisation for Economic
    Co-operation and Development
    (OECD), 646
Ormel, J., 628
Ormerod, T. C., 386
Ornstein, G. G., 649
Ortiz, V., 513
Orwell, G., 503
Ospina, M., 165
Öst, L. G., 594
Osterman, L. L., 511
O'Sullivan, L. F., 342
Oswald, A. J., 401, 465
Oswald, L., 183
Otto, M. W., 554
Owen, A. M., 123, 185, 192

Owen, R. J., 610
Owens, W. A., 411
Oztekin, I., 239
Ozyurek, A., 361

## P

Pagnin, D., 655
Pai, S., 606
Paikoff, R. L., 454
Paivio, A., 225
Palermo, T. M., 564
Pandeirada, J. N. S., 226
Pantev, C., 163
Papay, K., 292
Papez, J. W., 99
Parbery-Clark, A., 163
Paré, E. B., 153
Park, B., 540
Park, D. C., 461, 462
Park, S., 387
Parker, E. S., 221, 222
Parker, G., 652
Parker, H. A., 561
Parkinson, B., 320
Parks, C. D., 525
Parrott, A. C., 208, 212
Parrott, W. G., 320
Parsons, T., 572
Pascual-Ferrá, P., 146
Pascual-Leone, A., 104, 125
Passini, F. T., 479
Pasteur, L., 386
Pasupathi, M., 246
Patall, E. A., 343
Patrick, B., 507, 515
Patrick, C. J., 620
Patrick, R., 331
Patterson, C. J., 456
Pattie, A., 398, 412
Paulhus, D. L., 479
Paulos, J. A., 61
Paus, T., 452, 453
Pavlidis, I., 328
Pavlidou, E. V., 302
Pavlov, I. P., 16, 18, 267–268, 271–
    272, 273, 274, 286, 325
Payne, B. K., 321
Payne, J. D., 233
Pearce, J. M., 271
Pearlstone, Z., 236
Peck, J., 165
Peelen, M. V., 373
Peeters, A. I., 336
Peissig, J. J., 150
Peles, E., 87
Pelham, B. W., 499, 501, 545
Peltonen, L., 109
Penfield, W., 32, 101, 249
Pennebaker, J. W., 528, 562–563,
    570
Penner, L. A., 552
Pentland, J., 256
Perales, F., 323
Pereira-Pasarin, L. P., 247
Perenin, M.-T., 143
Perilloux, H. K., 522
Perkins, D. N., 415
Perkins, W., 531
Perlmutter, J. S., 656

Perls, F. S., 637–638
Perner, J., 437, 448
Perrett, D. I., 119, 522
Perruchet, P., 297
Perry, R., 477
Perry, R. B., 5
Perry, Z. W., 541
Peschardt, K., 620
Pessiglione, M., 292
Petersen, A. C., 455
Petersen, J. L., 518
Petersen, S. E., 240
Peterson, C., 240, 439
Peterson, D., 509
Peterson, G. B., 286
Peterson, L. R., 229
Peterson, M. J., 229
Peterson, O., 2
Peterson, S. E., 24
Petersson, K. M., 304
Petitto, L. A., 356
Petrie, K. P., 563
Petronis, A., 606
Petry, N. M., 638
Petty, R. E., 534, 535
Pew Research Center for People &
    the Press, 463, 464, 465
Pew Research Center Global
    Attitudes Project, 455
Pham, M. T., 332
Phelan, J., 592
Phelps, E. A., 122, 275, 290, 319
Philbrick, K., 45
Phills, C. E., 543
Piaget, J., 21–22, 433–434, 435,
    436, 438, 439–440, 447–448
Piazza, J. R., 552
Picasso, P., 282–283, 494
Pickrell, J. E., 255
Pike, C. L., 522
Pillard, R. C., 456
Pilloff, D., 189
Pinel, J. P. J., 577, 647
Pines, A. M., 560
Pinker, S., 26, 357, 359, 367, 411,
    511
Pitcher, D., 326
Pitman, R. K., 600
Pitt, B., 117
Pittinsky, T. L., 419
Plassman, H., 170
Platek, S. M., 439
Plato, 5, 6, 332, 334, 407
Pleis, J. R., 576
Pliner, P., 535
Plomin, R., 111, 409, 415, 482,
    574, 602
Plotnik, J. M., 186
Pluzinski, C., 533
Polanczyk, G., 616
Poliak, S., 87
Polivy, J., 337, 338, 579
Pollard, P., 390, 391
Pollo, A., 571
Pollock, J., 487
Pollyanna, 574
Pond, R. S., 509
Pons, F., 439
Poole, D. A., 256
Poon, S. H., 654

Pope, A. W., 459
Porter, E. H., 574
Porter, S., 327, 329
Portocarrero, J. S., 365
Posner, M. I., 119, 216
Post, R. M., 605
Posthuma, D., 415
Postman, L., 250
Postmes, T., 514
Potter, H., 236, 343
Powell, R. A., 280
Power, M. L., 338
Power, T., 454
Prasada, S., 357
Pratkanis, A. R., 191, 514
Pratt, S., 317
Prentice, D. A., 528
Prescott, C. A., 595
Presley, E. A., 221
Pressman, S. D., 566
Price, J. L., 221–222, 259
Priest, R. G., 200
Prior, H., 186
Prochaska, J. J., 577
Procopio, M., 336
Prodromidis, M., 445
Protzko, J., 420
Provine, R. R., 568
Pruitt, D. G., 512
Przedborski, S., 100
Ptolemy, 41
Public Health Agency of Canada,
    336, 337, 565, 576, 602, 618
Punjabi, N. M., 199
Putallaz, M., 416
Puterman, E., 557
Putin, V., 12, 538
Putnam, K. M., 321
Pyc, M. A., 306
Pyers, J. E., 361, 439
Pyszczynski, T., 184, 500

## Q

Quatrone, R. P., 298
Quattrone, G. A., 544
Querleu, D., 430
Quiroga, R. Q., 147
Quoidbach, J., 460
Qureshi, A., 199

## R

Rabbitt, P., 412
Rabi, T., 409
Rabinowitz, C., 372
Rabung, S., 636
Race, E., 245
Racine, C. A., 254
Radford, E., 288
Radford, M. A., 288
Rafaeli, E., 186
Rahe, R. H., 550
Raichle, M. E., 119, 121, 188
Rajaram, S., 246, 247
Ralston, A., 166
Ramachandran, V. S., 104, 156, 331
Ramus, S. J., 302
Ranvier, L.-A., 87
Raonic, M., 167
Rapaport, D., 474

Raphael, 334
Rapoport, J., 609
Rappoport, J. L., 599
Rapson, R. L., 523
Rash, C. J., 638
Rasmussen, T., 101
Ratner, R. K., 517
Rauch, S. L., 600
Rauschecker, J. P., 161
Rawson, K. A., 306, 308
Raymond, P., 247
Rayner, R., 18, 272
Raz, A., 216, 217
Raz, N., 461
Read, H. L., 161
Read, K. E., 29
Reason, J., 4
Reber, A. S., 301, 303
Reber, P. J., 302
Recanzone, G. H., 102, 161
Rechtshaffen, A., 198
Redick, T. S., 230
Reed, C., 435
Reed, C. L., 165
Reed, D. R., 173
Reed, G., 253
Reeve, C., 95
Reeve, C. L., 418
Refaeili, B., 336
Regan, M. A., 146
Regan, P. C., 523
Regier, T., 368
Reid, S., 523
Reid, V. M., 441
Reiman, E., 254
Reinert, G., 414
Reis, H. T., 520
Reiss, D., 186
Reissland, N., 431
Renner, K. E., 280
Renner, M. J., 550, 551
Renoir, A., 283
Rensink, R. A., 154, 155
Rentfrow, P. J., 473, 474
Repacholi, B. M., 438
Rescorla, R. A., 271, 273
Reshatdardhi, B. H. D., 449
Ressler, K. J., 88, 597, 656
Reyes, J. A., 330
Reynolds, C. A., 463
Reynolds, D., 545
Ricci-Bitt, P. E., 323
Rice, K. G., 4
Richards, M., 398
Richards, M. H., 458, 459
Richardson, C. M., 4
Richert, E. S., 417
Richeson, J., 402
Richter, J., 599
Richters, J., 341
Ridenour, T. A., 211
Rieber, R. W., 8, 9
Riefer, D. M., 252
Rieff, P., 503
Riggs, K. J., 441
Rihanna, 332
Ringach, D. L., 72
Risko, E. F., 307
Riskin, B., 177, 178
Risley, T. R., 413

Risman, J. E., 610
Ritchie, B. F., 289
Rivera-Gaxiola, M., 362
Rizzolatti, G., 103, 299
R.M., patient, 145
Robbins, T. W., 292
Roberson, D., 367
Roberts, B. W., 480
Roberts, G., 515
Roberts, G. A., 564, 608
Roberts, R. D., 406
Robertson, L. C., 145
Robertson, T. E., 227
Robins, L. N., 207, 208
Robins, R. W., 475
Robinson, A., 417
Robinson, D. N., 5
Robinson, J. C., 343
Robitzek, E. H., 649
Rochette, J., 242
Rodgers-Ramachandran, D., 104
Rodieck, R. W., 136
Rodriguez, M. L., 343
Roediger, H. L., III, 236, 237, 238, 254, 255, 306, 307
Rogers, C. R., 15, 503, 636
Rogers, T. B., 496
Rohsenow, D., 210
Roig, M., 105
Rolls, E. T., 119
Rollnick, S., 573
Romero-Corral, A., 336
Ronay, R., 510
Roosevelt, T., 606
Rosa Elena, Sister 541
Rosch, E. H., 367, 370
Rose, J. L., 167
Rose, S., 396
Rose, S. P. R., 421
Roseman, I. J., 319
Rosenberg, M., 498
Rosenberg, T., 531
Rosenhan, D., 593
Rosenkranz, K., 105, 163
Rosenman, R. H., 558
Rosenstein, M. J., 609
Rosenthal, R., 46, 328, 483
Ross, D., 295, 296
Ross, L., 67, 68, 490, 544
Ross, M., 247, 500, 658
Ross, N. A., 566
Ross, S., 295, 296
Rossano, F., 441
Rosvall, M., 35
Rotermann, M., 457
Roth, B. L., 88, 89
Roth, D. A., 337
Roth, H. P., 573
Roth, R. H., 89
Rothbart, M. K., 445
Rothbaum, B. O., 273
Rothon, R., 364
Rothwell, J. C., 105
Rotter, J. B., 493
Rotton, L., 568
Routley, S., 192–193
Roy, P., 288
Roy-Byrne, P. P., 597, 649
Rozenblit, L., 390
Rozin, P., 335, 336, 337, 339, 577

Rubin, E., 149
Rubin, M., 540
Rubin, Z., 524
Rubio-Fernandez, P., 438
Rubio-Stipec, M., 586
Rudman, L. A., 542
Rugg, M. D., 251
Rusbult, C. E., 525
Ruscio, A. M., 599
Rush, B., 647
Rushton, J. P., 398, 418
Russell, B., 40
Russell, J., 437
Russell, J. A., 316, 326
Rustichini, A., 344
Rutledge, R. B., 292
Rutter, M., 108, 444
Ryan, R. M., 343, 489, 527
Rypien, R., 79

## S

Sachs, J. S., 355
Sacks, O., 230, 241, 615
Safer, M. A., 257
Safford, A., 326
Saffran, J. R., 302
Sagi, A., 446
Sahakian, B. J., 420, 421
Saito, M., 405
Sakamoto, J., 282
Saks, E. R., 613
Sakuraba, S., 143
Salapatek, P., 431
Sallet, J., 508
Sallis, J. F., 577
Salmon, D. P., 88
Salovey, P., 406
Salthouse, T. A., 405, 412, 461
Salvatore, J. E., 446, 447
Sampson, R. J., 454
Sampson, P. D., 429
Samuelson, R. J., 293
Sanders, D. Y., 528
Sanderson, W. C., 660
Sandin, R. H., 177
Sandler, B., 56
Sandman, C. A., 428
Santos, L. R., 345
Sapolsky, R. M., 512
Saqib, M., 430
Sara, S. J., 234
Sarris, V., 20
Sarter, M., 89
Sasanuma, S., 363
Satcher, D., 457
Saunders, J., 239
Savage, C. R., 226
Savage-Rumbaugh, S., 298, 365, 366
Savic, I., 171, 456
Savitsky, K., 191, 330
Sawa, A., 610
Sawyer, A. T., 642
Saxe, R., 373
Scarborough, E., 16
Scarr, S., 419
Schachter, S., 317–318, 518, 520, 578

Schacter, D. L., 99, 107, 121, 122, 222, 226, 227, 230, 232, 236, 239, 241, 242, 243, 244, 245, 246, 249, 253, 254, 256, 257, 259, 260, 306, 537
Schachter, S., 207
Schaefer, J. T., 523
Schafer, R. B., 525
Schaffer, M. M., 371
Schaie, K. W., 411, 412
Schaller, M., 522
Schapira, A. H. V., 89
Schatzberg, A. F., 649, 651
Schaufeli, W. B., 560
Schellenberg, E. G., 163
Schenck, C., 205
Schenk, T., 125
Scherer, K. R., 319, 322, 323
Schiavo, T., 123
Schiff, M., 413
Schildkraut, J. J., 602
Schiller, D., 234
Schilling, O. K., 463
Schkade, D. A., 187
Schlaug, G., 163
Schlegel, A., 454
Schlesinger, J., 416
Schmader, T., 541
Schmidt, F. L., 400
Schmidt, H., 145
Schmitt, D. P., 481, 518
Schmukle, S. C., 519
Schneider, B. H., 446
Schneider, R., 438
Schnieder, S., 602
Schnorr, J. A., 224
Schnyer, D. M., 239, 244
Schryer, E., 247
Schoenemann, P. T., 102
Schön, J. H., 74
Schonberg, T., 292
Schooler, L. J., 259
Schott, B. J., 244
Schouwenburg, H. C., 4
Schraw, G., 304
Schreiner, C. E., 161
Schubert, T. W., 325
Schulkin, J., 338
Schultz, D., 406
Schultz, D. P., 9, 10, 12
Schultz, S. E., 9, 10, 12
Schultz, W., 291, 292
Schutter, D. J. L. G., 510
Schwartz, A., 186
Schwartz, A. C., 273
Schwartz, B. L., 252
Schwartz, C. E., 445
Schwartz, J. H., 82
Schwartz, J. L. K., 542
Schwartz, S., 204
Schwartzenberg, S., 230
Schwartzman, A. E., 411
Schwarz, C. E., 445
Schwarz, N., 325, 331
Schweizer, T. A., 364
Scopes, J., 26
Scott, A., 409
Scott, R. M., 438
Scott, S. K., 161
Scoville, W. B., 24, 99, 231

Scribner, S., 389, 406
Seckel, E., 104
Secord, P. F., 524
Sedlmeier, P., 563
Seeman, T. E., 567
Seeman, M., 567
Segal, Z. V., 641
Segall, M. H., 29, 30
Seidman, G., 479
Seligman, M. E. P., 343, 401, 594, 604, 659
Selikoff, I. J., 649
Selye, H., 99, 554–555
Semenza, C., 252
Semin, G. R., 326
Sendak, M., 156
Senghas, A., 361, 439
Senior, J., 465
Senju, A., 438, 439
Serpell, R., 406
Seybold, K. S., 567
Seyfarth, R. M., 352
Seymour, K., 145
Shackelford, T. K., 523
Shafe, G., 234
Shafir, E., 75
Shafritz, K. M., 145
Shafto, C., 358
Shah, G. M., 608
Shah, J., 346
Shakespeare, W., 110, 198, 404
Shallcross, A. J., 463
Shallice, T., 226, 251, 372
Shanker, S. G., 365
Share, L. J., 512
Sharma, Y. S., 518
Sharot, T., 378
Shaw, J. C., 23
Shaw, J. S., 239
Shearer, N., 110
Shedler, J., 659
Sheehan, P., 215
Sheehan, P. W., 256
Sheenan, M. J., 102
Sheeran, P., 320
Sheese, B. E., 512
Shen, H., 529
Shenton, M. E., 611
Shepherd, G. M., 107
Shepperd, J., 500
Sherburne, L. M., 297
Sherman, S. M., 98
Sherry, D. F., 226
Sherry, S. B., 335
Shields, B., 602
Shiffman, S., 578
Shih, M., 419
Shimamura, A. P., 253
Shimony, J. S., 121
Shin, L. M., 600
Shiner, R. L., 480
Shinskey, J. L., 434
Shiota, M. N., 322
Shipstead, Z., 230
Shiv, B., 332, 380
Shoda, Y., 343, 490
Shoham, V., 659
Shomstein, S., 146
Shore, C., 358
Shrout, P. E., 586
Shu, S. B., 165

Shultz, S., 508, 538
Shurgot, B. A., 520
Shweder, R. A., 28, 29
Sibley, C. G., 477
Siddartha Gautama, 467
Siderowf, A., 292
Siegal, J., 205
Siegal, M., 439
Siegel, A., 98
Siegel, M., 240
Siegel, S., 270
Siegler, R. S., 397
Siemer, M., 321
Sigman, M., 615
Sigurdsson, T., 99
Silberg, J., 108
Silberman, E. K., 634
Silver, R. L., 562
Silverman, I., 515
SIM. See Society, the Individual, and Medicine
Simmelhag, V. L., 288
Simon, H. A., 23
Simon, L., 2
Simon, R. W., 465
Simon, T., 397, 398, 417, 418
Simonides, 224
Simons, D. J., 124, 154, 155
Simpson, A., 441
Simpson, E. L., 449
Simpson, J. A., 446
Singer, B., 659
Singer, J. E., 317–318, 520, 553
Singer, P., 72
Singer, T., 451
Singh, D., 521, 522
Sinigaglia, C., 102
Skinner, B. F., 10, 18–19, 20, 23, 278–279, 282, 283, 286–288, 295, 359
Skoe, E., 163
Skotko, B. G., 417
Slagter, H. A., 230
Slater, A., 431
Slotnick, S. D., 254
Smart, E., 549–550, 555, 561
Smart, L., 510, 555
Smart, M. K., 549
Smetacek, V., 96
Smetana, J. G., 451
Smetanin, P., 628
Smith, A. R., 508
Smith, C. A., 319
Smith, C. M., 441
Smith, E. E., 462
Smith, M. L., 659
Smith, N., 351
Smith, P. K., 454
Smyser, C. D., 121
Snedeker, J., 358, 359
Snellen, H., 135
Snowdon, C. T., 553
Snyder, S. H., 610
Sobel, N., 169
Social Sciences and Humanities Research Council, 70
Solomon, J., 445
Solomon, S., 347, 500
Solomon, Z., 561
Somers, M., 431
Sommer, I. E., 655
Son, L. K., 307

Sonnby-Borgstrom, M., 326
Sonne, L., 439
Sonne, T., 439
Suu Kyi, A. S., 563
Society, the Individual, and Medicine (SIM), 621
Sorrentino, R. M., 513
Soto, C. J., 478
Southgate, V., 438
Soyinka, W., 407
Sparrow, B., 248
Spearman, C., 401–403, 404
Spears, R., 514
Speisman, J. C., 559
Spelke, E. S., 380, 416, 434, 435
Spellman, B. A., 380
Spence, K., 333–334
Spence, M. J., 430
Spence, S. J., 615
Spencer, S. J., 541
Sperling, G., 228
Sperry, R. W., 116, 117
Spiers, H. J., 105
Spinath, F. M., 409
Spinoza, B., 19
Spirito, A., 622
Spiro, A., 463
Spiro, H. M., 573
Spitz, R. A., 442
Spörrle, M., 521
Sprecher, S., 257, 525
Spritz, B., 445
Square, D., 430
Squire, L. R., 99, 232, 233, 235, 241, 253, 274, 301, 302, 303
Srivastava, S., 478, 479, 480, 481
Sroufe, L. A., 447
Staddon, J. E. R., 288
Stafford, M., 566
Stanovich, K. E., 405
Stapel, D., 74
Stark, H., 242
Starkey, P., 380
Statistics Canada, 209, 336, 363, 364, 455, 576, 596, 621, 629
Stecker, R., 553
Stecklein, T., 299
Steele, C. M., 210, 418, 541
Steele, H., 446
Steffen, V. J., 510
Stiegler, J. H., 316
Stein, D. J., 584
Stein, M., 364
Stein, M. B., 595
Stein, Z., 428
Steinbaum, E. A., 335
Steinberg, L., 454, 459
Steiner, F., 323
Steiner, J. E., 323
Steinmetz, J. L., 68, 544
Steketee, G. S., 595
Stellar, E., 335
Stellar, J. R., 291, 335
Stelmack, R. M., 483
Stennet, J., 323
Stephen, A. T., 332
Stephens, R. S., 213
Stepper, S., 324
Sterelny, K., 26
Stern, J. A., 216
Stern, L. D., 61

Stern, W., 397
Sternberg, K. J., 445
Sternberg, R. J., 405, 406, 407, 524
Stevens, B., 33
Stevens, J., 225
Stevens, L. A., 84
Stevens, W. D., 244
Stevenson, R. J., 169
Stewart, M., 104
Stewart-Williams, S., 571
Stibbard, J., 565
Stickgold, R., 197, 198, 201, 233
Stickney-Gibson, M., 257–258
Stigler, J. W., 29
St. Jacques, P. L., 239, 260
Stone, A. A., 187, 464, 568, 642
Stone, A. B., 525
Stone, J., 541
Stone, J. I., 328
Stones, M. H., 562
Stoodley, C. J., 302
Storm, B. C., 238
Storms, M. D., 545
Stowens, D., 156
Strack, F., 324
Strayer, D. L., 146
Streissguth, A. P., 429
Striano, T., 441
Strickland, L. H., 597
Striegel-Moore, R. H., 336
Strohmetz, D. B., 529
Stroop, J. P., 216
Strosahl, K., 562
Stroup, S., 648
Stuss, D. T., 102, 320
Subramaniam, K., 386
Substance Abuse and Mental Health
    Services Administration, 430
Suchman, A. L., 573
Suddendorf, T., 102, 227, 246
Suderman, M., 112
Sullenberger, C., 462
Sullivan, M. A., 28
Sulloway, F. J., 14
Sundet, J. M., 411
Super, C. M., 389
Susman, S., 459
Susser, E. B., 428
Susser, M., 428
Suthana, N., 147
Sutherland, D., 545
Sutherland, K., 545
Sutter, M. L., 102, 161
Sutter-Hernandez, J., 210
Sutton, J. E., 297
Suzuki, L. A., 418
Svensson, O., 326
Swann, W. B., Jr., 473, 474, 497
Swartz, H., 298
Swayze, V. W., II, 655
Sweatt, J. D., 111
Swednsen, J., 606
Sweeny, K., 500
Swets, J. A., 134
Swinkels, A., 375
Szech, N., 516
Szechtman, H., 599
Szpunar, K. K., 107, 246, 306, 307,
    309

**T**
Taft, C. T., 600
Tajfel, H., 513, 515, 540
Takahashi, K., 445
Tambs, K., 411
Tamim, H., 430
Tamir, M., 320
Tamis-LeMonda, C. S., 442
Tamminga, C. A., 88
Tanaka, F., 444
Tanaka-Matsumi, J., 29
Tang, Y.-P., 421
Tang, Y. Y., 563
Tardif, C., 446
Tarr, M. J., 149, 150
Tart, C. T., 206
Task Force on Empirically Supported
    Treatments, 633, 660
Task Force on Promotion and
    Dissemination of Psychological
    Procedures, 660
Tavares, R., 510
Taylor, A. M., 183
Taylor, D., 365
Taylor, E., 13
Taylor, S. E., 260, 501, 545, 567,
    573
Taylor, T. J., 365
Teasdale, J. D., 604, 641
Telch, M. J., 596
Tellegen, A., 215, 316, 474, 482
Temerlin, M. K., 592
Templer, D. I., 398
ten Brinke, L., 327, 329
te Nijenhuis, J., 414
Terman, L. M., 397, 398, 417–418
Terracciano, A., 481
Tesser, A., 524
Teyler, T. J., 232
Thaker, G. K., 610
Thaler, K., 655
Thaler, R. H., 513
Thase, M. E., 602
Thelen, E., 433
Therriault, N., 320
Thibaut, J. W., 525
Thiede, K. W., 307
Thoma, S. J., 449
Thomaes, S., 501
Thomas, A., 445
Thomas, M., 417
Thomason, M., 120
Thompson, C. P., 250
Thompson, D. M., 236
Thompson, P. M., 120, 452, 611,
    612
Thompson, R. F., 274
Thompson, S. R., 226
Thomson, D. M., 253
Thorndike, E. L., 277–278, 286, 295
Thorne, B. M., 85
Thornhill, R., 522
Thurber, J., 345
Thurstone, L. L., 402–403, 404
Tice, D. M., 4, 576
Tienari, P., 612
Tierney, S., 604
Timmerman, T. A., 511
Timoney, L. R., 406

Titchener, E., 9–10, 13, 14, 132,
    190
Todd, A. R., 543
Todd, J. T., 18
Toga, A. W., 120
Tolman, E. C., 288–289
Tomaka, J., 559
Tomasello, M., 297, 298, 299, 441,
    451, 517
Tomkins, S. S., 324
Todorov, A., 325
Tooby, J., 26
Tootell, R. B. H., 154
Torgensen, S., 597
Torrey, E. F., 609, 610
Tononi, G., 204
Toth, S. L., 446
Totterdell, P., 320
Towne, W. F., 352
Trachtenberg, S., 336
Tracy, J. L., 323, 324, 523
Trainor, L. J., 163
Tranel, D., 326, 381
Trathen, W., 304
Treat, T. A., 134
Trebek, A., 68
Treede, R. D., 166
Treisman, A., 144, 145, 183
Trevarthen, C., 117
Triesman, M., 183
Triplett, N., 27
Trivers, R. L., 517
Trompeter, S. E., 464
Trope, Y., 325
Trost, M. R., 535
Trousdale, W. W., 592
Trudeau, J., 379, 452
Trull, T. J., 618
Truman, H., 65
Tsakiris, M., 181
Tsimpli, I.-M., 351
Tsujii, N., 324
Tucker, E., 482
Tucker-Drob, E. M., 410
Tuerlinckx, F., 344
Tuke, W., 647
Tulving, E., 223, 224, 236, 239,
    241, 242, 243, 244, 245
Turiel, E., 449, 451
Turk-Charles, S., 463
Turkheimer, E., 410, 411, 455
Turner, D. C., 420, 421
Turner, J. C., 515, 540
Turner, M. E., 514
Turvey, M. T., 228
Tuszynski, M. H., 95
Tversky, A., 345, 375, 376, 377,
    378–379
Twain, M., 576
Twenge, J. M., 465
Tyce, G. M., 89
Tyler, T. R., 531

**U**
U.S. Department of State, 358
U.S. Food and Drug Administration,
    651
Uesiliana, K., 29, 240
Uleman, J. S., 545
Ullrich, J., 513

Umberson, D., 507, 565
Uncapher, M. R., 251
Underwood, B. J., 250
Ungerleider, L. G., 142
Urban, K., 48
Urban, N. B. L., 212
Ursano, R. J., 634
Usher, 520
Uskul, A. K., 30
Üstün, T. B., 589
Uutela, V., 565

**V**
Vacha, E., 305
Valencia, R. R., 418
Valentine, T., 252
Valins, S., 318
Vallacher, R. R., 344–345, 493
Vallender, E. J., 108
van den Boom, D. C., 446
van Dis, I., 336
van Dongen, E. V., 233
van Gogh, V., 416, 606
van Heijnsbergen, C. C., 324
van Honk, J., 510
van IJzendoorn, M. H., 413, 445,
    446
van Ittersum, K., 339
van Knippenberg, A., 501
Van Koppen, P. J., 255
Van Lange, P. A. M., 525
van Praag, H., 105
van Stegeren, A. H., 319
van Vliet, I. M., 656
Vanyperen, N. W., 560
Vargas, P., 534
Vargha-Khadem, F., 245, 360
Varona, J., 323
Vazire, S., 495
Veldhuizen, M. G., 170
Venter, J. C., 429
Verfaellie, M., 239, 245
Vicary, J., 191
Vighetto, A., 143
Vinter, A., 297
Vital, P., 614
Vitkus, J., 605
Vohs, K. D., 340, 342, 576
Volkow, N. D., 88
von Békésy, G., 161
von Clef, J., 169
von Cramon, D., 153
Vondra, J. I., 446
Von Frisch, K., 352
von Helmholtz, H., 7–9
Voon, V., 292
Vorndran, C. M., 281
Vortac, O. U., 251
Vrij, A., 328
Vuong, Q. C., 149
Vygotsky, L. S., 440

**W**
Wade, N. J., 152
Wade, S. E., 304
Wadhwa, P. D., 428
Wagenaar, W. A., 255
Wager, T. D., 571
Wagner, A. D., 146, 224, 241

Wagner, A. R., 273
Wagner, G., 288
Wahl, H.-W., 463
Wai, J., 416
Waite, L. J., 465
Waite, T., 507
Wakefield, J. C., 584
Wakita, M., 282
Walden, T. A., 441
Waldfogel, S., 240
Waldman, D. A., 412
Waldmann, M. R., 380
Waldron, M., 411
Walkenfeld, F. F., 302
Walker, C., 466
Walker, L. J., 449
Walker, N. P., 416
Wall, P. D., 165, 166
Wallace, J., 602
Wallbott, H. G., 322
Wallenhorst, S., 89
Walster, E., 520, 521, 525
Walster, G. W., 525
Walters, G., 539
Walton, D. N., 388
Walton, G. M., 541
Waltzman, S. B., 162
Wamsley, E. J., 201
Wan, F., 529
Wang, L. H., 122
Wang, P. S., 479, 592, 614, 629,
        630, 632
Wang, Q., 240
Wang, S., 33
Wang, S.-H., 435
Wang, T., 615
Wansink, B., 338, 339
Wansink, C. S., 339
Ward, J., 253
Warneken, F., 451, 517
Warner, R. M., 406
Warrington, E. K., 243, 372
Washburn, M. F., 16
Washoe, chimp, 365, 366
Wasserman, S., 434, 435
Wasylenki, D., 647
Watanabe, S., 282
Watkins, L. R., 569
Watkinson, B., 430
Watson, D., 316, 570
Watson, E., 236
Watson, J. B., 16, 18, 20, 24, 267,
        268–269, 272, 273, 333, 595
Watson, J. M., 107, 246
Watson, R. I., 133
Watt, A., 280
Watt, H. J., 190
Watters, E., 661
Watts, J., 438
Watzke, B., 635
Waytz, A., 543
Weaver, I. C. G., 112
Webb, T. L., 320
Weber, E., 133
Weber, R., 541

Webster, G. D., 522
Webster Marketon, J. I., 557
Wechsler, D., 398
Wechsler, H., 531
Weeks, T., 246
Wegener, D. T., 534
Wegner, D. M., 179, 181, 183, 188,
        189, 199, 202, 214, 247, 248,
        320, 344–345, 490, 493, 542,
        561, 577, 598
Weinberg, M. S., 456
Weinberger, D. R., 88
Weinberger, J. L., 575
Weinstein, N. D., 378
Weintraub, D., 292
Weinzierl, M., 521
Weir, C., 286
Weiser, M., 400
Weisfeld, G., 459
Weiskrantz, L., 243
Weiss, A., 400
Weissenborn, R., 237
Weissman, M. M., 635
Weldon, M. S., 237, 247
Wenzlaff, R. M., 202, 577, 598
Werker, J. F., 430
Wernicke, K., 115, 362
Wertheimer, M., 20–21, 22, 384
Wesch, N. N., 297
Weschler, D., 398
West, K., 343
Westbrook, G. L., 82
Westrin, A., 602
Wexler, K., 358
Whalen, P. J., 319
Whalley, L. J., 398
Wheatley, T., 450
Wheatstone, C., 152
Wheeler, M. A., 240
Whishaw, I. Q., 114
White, B. L., 432
White, F. J., 97
White, G. M., 406
White, N. M., 291
White, T. L., 345, 346
Whiten, A., 295, 296, 297, 298
Whitney, D., 125
Whorf, B., 367, 368
Whybrow, P. C., 605
Wickenheiser, H., 401, 403
Wickens, C. D., 146
Wicker, B., 451
Wicki, W., 602
Wicklund, R. A., 184, 514
Wiebe, D., 384
Wiederman, M. W., 341
Wiegering, S., 463
Wiener, D. N., 18
Wiesel, T. N., 118, 142
Wiesenthal, D. L., 515
Wig, G. S., 244
Wiggs, C. L., 244
Wightman, L., 631
Wilcoxon, H. C., 276
Wiley, J., 387

Wiley, J. L., 213
Wilhelm, I., 233
Wilkes, A. L., 540
Wilkinson, L., 304
Willemse, L., 579
Willerman, B., 524
William, duke of Cambridge, 316
Williamon, A., 105
Williams, A. C., 572
Williams, C. M., 213
Williams, G. R., 336
Williams, J. M., 302
Williams, J. M. G., 641
Williams, K., 515
Williams, K. D., 247, 515
Williams, K. M., 479
Williams, R., 635
Williams, W. M., 414, 416
Willingham, B., 323
Willingham, D. T., 66
Wilson, D. A., 167
Wilson, E. O., 26
Wilson, E. T., 300
Wilson, K., 307
Wilson, K. G., 562
Wilson, M., 510
Wilson, T. D., 17, 45, 191, 256, 343,
        460, 474
Wimber, M., 240
Wimmer, H., 437
Winawer, J., 368
Windeler, J., 375
Windham, G. C., 430
Winer, J. A., 161
Winner, E., 417
Winocur, G., 232
Winter, L., 545
Winterer, G., 88
Wise, R. A., 206, 207, 291
Withey, W. J., 491
Wittgenstein, L., 370
Wixted, J. T., 232, 233, 249
Woite, R. S., 457
Wolf, J. R., 165
Wolfe, C. T., 499
Wolff, P., 68, 368
Wolitzky-Taylor, K. B., 596
Wolpert, E., 201
Wong, A. T., 107, 245, 246
Wong, D. T., 91
Wood, J. M., 202, 344
Wood, W., 481, 518
Woodley, M. A., 414
Woods, S. C., 335
Woody, E. Z., 599
Woody, S. R., 595, 660
Woolcott, M., 529
Woolf, L., 583
Woolf, V., 583–584, 585–586, 601,
        604–605, 606
Woollett, K., 105
Worchel, P., 524
World Bank, 632
World Health Organization, 587
Wrangham, R. W., 509

Wren, A. M., 334
Wrenn, C. C., 88
Wright, S., 199
Wrosch, C., 463
Wu, J., 465
Wu, X., 446
Wulz, W., 494
Wundt, W., 7–9, 11, 12, 13, 14, 20,
        28–29, 401
Wyer, R. S., 529
Wynn, K., 450

### X

Xiao, L., 381
Xu, F., 435

### Y

Yamaguchi, S., 172
Yang, S., 406
Yantis, S., 146
Yen, Y., 570
Yeo, B. T. T., 121
Yeshurun, Y., 169
Yik, M., 316
Young, A. G., 441
Young, K. L., 146
Young, R. M., 115
Yousafzai, M., 526
Yovel, G., 147
Yucha, C., 564
Yuill, N., 448
Yzerbyt, V., 514

### Z

Zacks, R. T., 380
Zahn-Waxler, C., 451
Zajonc, R. B., 324, 325, 519
Zanakos, S., 189, 561
Zebrowitz, L. A., 400, 522
Zeki, S., 101, 118, 125
Zelazo, N. A., 432
Zelazo, P. R., 432
Zentall, T. R., 297
Zentner, M., 518
Zerg, N., 401
Zernike, K., 456
Zettin, M., 252
Zhang, T. Y., 108, 111, 113
Zhong, C.-B., 515
Zhu, J., 441
Zigler, E., 416
Zihl, J., 153
Zillmann, D., 318
Zimbardo, P. G., 532
Zimerman, S., 344
Zimmermann, E., 326
Zimprich, D., 412
Zuckerberg, M., 49–50
Zuckerman, M., 328
Zufall, F., 171
Zych, L., 520

# Subject Index

Note: Page numbers followed by *f* indicate figures; those followed by *t* indicate tables.

AA. *See* Alcoholics Anonymous
Abilities
    attraction and, 523
    changing in adulthood, 460–462
    intelligence as hierarchy of, 401–403, 402*t*, 403*f*
    middle-level, 403–407
    primary, 402, 402*t*
Absentmindedness, 250–252, 259
Absolute threshold, 132, 132*f*, 133*t*
Absolutism, 29
Abstract concepts, in formal operational stage, 437
Abstract thought, frontal lobe and, 102
Academic performance, procrastination and, 4
ACC. *See* Anterior cingulate cortex
Acceptance, in rational coping, 562
Accommodation
    in cognitive development, 434
    visual, 137, 138*f*
Accuracy motive for social influence, 527, 533–537
Acetylcholine, 88
    drug effects on functioning of, 206
Achievement, need for, 344
ACTH. *See* Adrenocorticotropic hormone
Action potential, 85*f*, 86–87, 87*f*
Activation-synthesis model, of dreams, 203
Actor-observer effect, 545
Adaptation
    evolutionary, 26
    in psychological processes, 3
    sensory, 134–135
Adderall (mixed amphetamine salts), 420
Addiction
    DRD2 gene and, 591–592
    to drugs, 206–208
A-delta fibres, 165
ADHD. *See* Attention-deficit/hyperactivity disorder
Adolescence, 452–459
    brain in, 452–453, 453*f*
    culture and, 454
    definition of, 452
    mental disorders of, 614–617
    parent–child relationships during, 458–459
    peer relationships during, 454, 454*f*, 458–459
    protraction of, 453–455, 454*f*
    psychosocial development during, 458, 458*t*
    puberty and, 452, 453–454, 455
    sexuality during, 455–457, 455*f*, 456*f*, 457*f*
Adrenocorticotropic hormone (ACTH), 99
Adulthood, 460–466. *See also* Aging
    abilities in, 460–462
    definition of, 460

    goals in, 463*f*, 463–464, 464*f*
    roles in, 465*f*, 465–466, 466*f*
    segregation of the old and, 467
    sleep need in, 197
Advertisements, social influence in, 533–534
Advice, parental, in infancy, 442, 442*f*
Aerobic exercise, for stress management, 564–565
Affect labelling, 320
Affordability of science research, 75
Afterimages, colour, 141, 141*f*
Age. *See also* Adolescence; Adulthood; Aging;
    Childhood; Infancy
    attractiveness and, 522
    mental, 398
    sleep needs and, 197
Aggression, 508–512, 509*f*
    coronary heart disease and, 558, 558*f*
    culture and, 511*f*, 511–512
    definition of, 508
    gender and, 509–510, 510*f*
    media violence and, 64
Aging. *See also* Adulthood
    of brain, 462, 462*f*
    of cells, 556–557
    stress effects on, 555–557
Agonists, 89, 90*f*
Agoraphobia, 596
Agreeableness, 478, 478*t*
AIDS/HIV, 576, 578
Akrasia, 578
Alarm phase of general adaptation syndrome, 555, 555*f*
Alcohol myopia, 210–211
Alcohol use/abuse, 206, 208
    alcohol myopia and, 210–211
    driving and, 210–211, 381
    expectancy theory of effects of, 210–211
    neurotransmitter balance in brain and, 89
    rape and, 211
    social norming and, 531
    teratogenic effects of, 417, 428–430
Alcoholics Anonymous (AA), 644, 645
Alexithymia, 406
Algorithms, 375
Alpha waves, 195, 196*f*
Alprazolam (Xanax), 211, 649
Altered states of consciousness, 194, 205–206
Altruism, 516–517
    in animals, 516–517
    reciprocal, 517
Alzheimer's disease,
    crystallized intelligence and, 405

    treatment of mental disorders in, 660*t*
Ambien (zolpidem), 649
Ambitions, attraction and, 523
Ambivalent attachment style, 444–447
American civil rights movement, social psychology and, 28
American Psychological Association (APA), 31–32
    on effectiveness of psychotherapy, 660
    *Ethical Principles of Psychologists and Code of Conduct of*, 71, 72
    founding of, 31
    women and minorities in, 31–32
American Psychological Society (APS), 31
American Sign Language (ASL)
    in animals, 365
    babbling and, 356
    brain areas and learning of, 24–25
Ames room, 152, 153*f*
Amitriptyline (Elavil), 649–650
Amnesia. *See also* Forgetting; Memory failures
    anterograde, 232
    childhood, 240
    implicit learning and, 303
    posthypnotic, 215
    retrograde, 232
Amphetamines, 206, 209*t*
    mixed (Adderall), 420
    neurotransmitters and, 90, 91
    use/abuse of, 211
Amplitude
    of light waves, 136, 137*t*
    of sound waves, 158, 159*t*
Amputation, phantom limb syndrome and, 104
Amusement, 324
Amygdala, 7, 98*f*, 99–100, 122
    classical conditioning and, 274–275
    dreaming and, 204, 204*f*
    emotion and, 99, 122, 319*f*, 319–320, 320*f*
    memory and, 99, 234, 258–259, 259*f*
    in social phobia, 654, 654*f*
Anal stage, 487
Analgesia, hypnotic, 216, 216*f*
Analogical problem solving, 383*f*, 383–384
Analytic intelligence, 405–406
Analytic, style of information processing, 30
Anandamide, 213
Androgens. *See* Testosterone
Androgyny, 481
Anesthesia, for surgery, 177
Anger, 323*f*, 324. *See also* Aggression
    physiological arousal and, 317
*The Animal Mind* (Washburn), 16

Animals. *See also* Birds; Primates
anthropomorphization of, 482–483
brain development in, 107–108
conditioning in. *See* Classical conditioning;
  Operant conditioning
emotional expression in, 323
observational learning in, 297
personality in, 482–483
as research subjects, 72–73
self-recognition in, 186
social behaviour in, 508
*Animals in Translation* (Grandin), 615
Anonymity, avoiding demand characteristics with,
  46
Anorexia nervosa, 335–336
Anorexigenic signals, 335
ANS. *See* Autonomic nervous system
Antagonists (drugs), 89, 90f
Anterior capsulotomy, 656
Anterior cingulate cortex (ACC)
  pain and, 570, 570f
  placebo effect and, 571
  Stroop effect and, 216
Anterograde amnesia, 232
Anthropomorphize, 482–483
Anti-anxiety drugs
  for generalized anxiety disorder, 597
  risks of, 211, 649
Antidepressant drugs
  for depression, 602–603, 650–651
  for generalized anxiety disorder, 597
  growing use of, 646, 646f
  monoamine oxidase inhibitors, 649, 650f
  personality and, 480
  placebos vs., 657–658, 658f
  selective serotonin reuptake inhibitors, 650f,
    650–651
  tricyclic, 649–650, 650f
Antipsychotic drugs, 646, 648
Antisocial personality disorder (APD), 619t,
  619–620
Anvil, of ear, 159, 160f
Anxiety, in psychodynamic approach, 485
Anxiety disorders, 593–597
  definition of, 593
  drug therapy for, 211, 597, 649
  generalized, 596–597
  panic, 595–596
  phobic, 594–595
APA. *See* American Psychological Association
APD. *See* Antisocial personality disorder
Aphasia, 362
*Aplysia*
  habituation in, 300
  memory studies on, 235
Apparent motion, 154
Appearance, attraction and, 520–523, 521f
Appetite. *See also* Hunger
  leptin and, 334–335
  sickness response and, 569
Appraisal, 319
Approach motivation, 345–346, 346t
Approval motive for social influence, 526, 528–
  533
APS. *See* Association for Psychological Science;
  American Psychological Society
Aptitudes, measurement of, 397–398. *See also*
  Intelligence
Area A1, 160–161, 161f
Area VI, 142

Arousal
  physiological and emotion, 317f, 317–318, 318f
  tegmentum and, 97
Artificial grammar, implicit learning and, 301f,
  301–302
Asch's conformity experiment, 529–530, 530f
ASD. *See* Autism spectrum disorder
ASL. *See* American Sign Language
Assimilation, in cognitive development, 434
Association areas, 102–103
Association for Psychological Science (APS), 31
Asylum, 646, 647
Asylum movement, 647
Atherosclerosis, stress and, 558
Ativan (lorazepam), 649
Attachment
  becoming attached and, 443–445, 445f
  day care and, 444, 447
  definition of, 444
  memory and, 445, 445f
  significance of attachment styles and, 446–447
  sources of attachment styles and, 445–446, 446f
  temperaments and, 445
Attention
  divided, 251
  inattentional blindness and, 155
  joint, 441, 441f
  lapse in, 250–251
  selective, 146
  testing and, 306–307
  vision and, 144–145
  visual perception and, 154–155, 155f
Attention-deficit/hyperactivity disorder (ADHD),
  586, 616
  biological factors in, 606
Attitudes. *See also* Beliefs
  attraction and, 523
  definition of, 533
Attraction, 518–524
  physical factors and, 520–523, 521f
  psychological factors and, 523–524
  sexual behaviour and, 341–342, 342t
  situational factors and, 518–520
Attractiveness, culture and, 521–522
Attributions, 543–545, 544f
Atypical antipsychotics, 648
Audition. *See* Hearing; Hearing loss
Auditory cortex, primary, 102, 103, 160–161, 161f
Auditory nerve, temporal code and, 161
Auditory processing, musical training and, 163
Auditory transduction, 159–160, 160f
Authoritarianism, 477
Autism, 439
  crystalized intelligence and, 405
Autism spectrum disorder (ASD), 614–615
  biological factors in, 606
  treatment for, 615
Autobiographical memory, 495
Autonomic nervous system (ANS), 92f, 93–94
  classical conditioning and, 275
Autonomy vs. shame and doubt stage, 458t
Autoreceptors, 87f, 88
Availability bias, 375, 375f
Aversions, learned, 275–276
Avoidance motivation, 345–347, 346t
Avoidant attachment style, 444–447
Axons, 82, 81f
  myelin sheath around. *See* Myelin sheath
  of squid, study of, 84
  terminal buttons of, 87

Babbling
  in deaf infants, 356, 360
  language development and, 356
Babies. *See* Infancy
Baconian Method. *See* Scientific method
Bacteria, obesity and, 337
Balance, sense of, 167
Balanced placebo design, 210
Barbiturates, 206, 209, 209t, 2011
BAS. *See* Behavioural activation system
Basal ganglia, 98f, 100
  concepts and categories and, 372
Basilar membrane, 159, 160f
  place code and, 161
Beauty, culture and, 521–522
Bedlam, 647
Behaviour, 2
*The Behavior of Organisms: An Experimental
  Analysis* (Skinner), 19
Behavioural therapy, 637–639, 638t
  mirror box therapy as, 104
Behavioural activation system (BAS), 483
Behavioural inhibition system (BIS), 483
Behavioural neuroscience, 24–25. *See also*
  Neuroimaging
Behaviourism, 16, 18–20
  conditioning and. *See* Classical conditioning;
    Operant conditioning
  definition of, 16
  development of, 18–19
  emergence of, 16, 18
  language development and, 359
  replacement by cognitive psychology, 20
Belief bias, 389–390
Beliefs. *See also* Attitudes
  attraction and, 523
  cognitive development and, 437–438
  definition of, 533
  false, in schizophrenia, 608
  irrational, cognitive therapy for, 639t, 639–641
  observations and, 67–68
  reasoning and. *See* Reasoning
Bell curve, 48, 48f
  of intelligence, 416, 416f
Bem Sex Role Inventory, 481
Benzodiazepines
  for generalized anxiety disorder, 597
  risks of, 211, 649
Beta blockers, neurotransmitters and, 91
Beta waves, 195, 196f
*Beyond Freedom and Dignity* (Skinner), 19
Bias
  availability, 375, 375f
  belief, 389–390
  change, 257
  cognitive modification for, 642
  consistency, 257
  correspondence, 544–545
  egocentric, 257
  intelligence tests and, 396, 418–419
  as memory failure, 256–257, 260
  observer, 46–47
  optimism, culture and, 378
  self-serving, 500–501
Big Five factor model, 478t, 478–480
Bilateral asymmetry, aging and, 462, 462f
Bilingualism
  brain and, 363–365, 365f
  need for, 364
Binding problem, 144

Binge drinking, social norming and, 531
Binocular depth cues, 151–152, 151f
Binocular disparity, 151–152, 152f
Biofeedback, 564
Biological preparedness, 276
Biological treatments
    deep brain stimulation, 656
    drug therapy. See Drug therapy
    electroconvulsive therapy, 654–655
    phototherapy, 655
    psychosurgery, 655–656
    transcranial magnetic stimulation, 655
    trephining as, 646
Biopsychosocial perspective, 589
Bipolar cells, 83, 83f, 138f, 139
Bipolar disorder, 604–607
    drug therapy for, 651
Birds
    learning to sing in, 360
    self-recognition in, 186
Birth control, during adolescence, 457
Birth order, intelligence and, 411
BIS. See Behavioural inhibition system
Blind spot, 137f, 139, 140f
Blindness
    change, 154–155, 155f
    colour, 141
    inattentional, 155
Blocking, 252
BMI. See Body mass index
Body management, for stress, 563–565
Body mass index (BMI), 336, 337f, 337t
Body position sense, 167
Body senses, 164–167. See also Pain; Touch
Body shape, attractiveness and, 521–522
Body surface, neural representation of, 164–165
Body temperature, hypothalamus and, 98
Body weight. See also Obesity
    eating wisely and, 576, 577
    loss of, 577
Bonding. See Attachment
Boot-camp interventions, 661, 661t
Botox injections, 326
Bottom-up control, 166, 169, 170
Brain, 95–105
    adolescent, 452–453, 453f
    aging, 462, 462f
    amygdala of. See Amygdala
    anterior cingulate cortex of. See Anterior
        cingulate cortex
    attention and, 251
    basal ganglia of, 98f, 100, 372
    bilingualism and, 363–365, 365f
    Broca's area of, 7, 115, 304, 362, 362f
    cerebellum of, 96, 97f, 274
    cerebral cortex of. See Cerebral cortex
    cerebral hemispheres of. See Cerebral
        hemispheres
    chronic traumatic encephalopathy and, 79–80
    cognitive neuroscience and, 24–25, 25f
    collaboration with spinal cord, 94–95, 95f
    compensatory response to drugs, 270
    concepts and categories and, 371–373, 373f
    consciousness and. See Consciousness
    corpus callosum of, 101, 101f, 115–117, 116f,
        117f
    damage to. See Brain damage
    decision making and, 380–381, 381f
    deep brain stimulation of, 656
    depression and, 603, 603f

dreaming and, 204f, 204–205
electrical activity of, 118f, 118–119
embryonic, 106, 106f
emotion and, 316–317, 317f, 318, 319f, 319–
    320, 320f, 332
evolutionary development of, 107f, 107–108
exercise and, 105
forebrain of. See Forebrain
frontal lobe of. See Frontal lobe
fusiform gyrus of, 122
hindbrain of, 96, 96f, 97f, 106, 107
hippocampus of. See Hippocampus
hunger and, 335
hypothalamus of. See Hypothalamus
imaging of. See Neuroimaging
implicit vs. explicit learning and, 303–304
insight and, 386–387
language areas of, 7, 24–25, 115, 304, 362f,
    362–363
language development and, 362–366
lateral geniculate nucleus of, 141, 142f
limbic system of. See Amygdala; Hippocampus;
    Hypothalamus; Limbic system
long-term memory and, 231f, 231–232
medial forebrain bundle of, 291, 291f
meditation and, 563
medulla of, 96, 97f
memory and, 245–246, 246f, 251, 254, 254f,
    258–259, 259f
midbrain of, 96f, 96–97, 97f, 106, 107
mind and. See Mind
motor cortex of. See Motor cortex
musical training and, 163
myths about, 124
nucleus accumbens of, 291, 291f
observational learning and, 299–300
occipital cortex of, 142, 143f
occipital lobe of, 100f, 101
ontogeny of, 106
operant conditioning and, 291f, 291–292
pain and, 166, 570f, 570–571
parietal cortex of, 303
parietal lobe of, 100f, 101, 142, 143f, 145
periaqueductal grey of, 166
personality and, 115, 115f, 483–484
phylogeny of, 106–107
placebo effect and, 571
plasticity of, 103–105
pleasure centres of, 291f, 291–292
political orientation and, 482
pons of, 96, 97f
post-traumatic stress disorder and, 600, 600f
prefrontal cortex of. See Prefrontal cortex
prenatal development of, 106f, 106–107
primary auditory cortex of, 102, 103, 160–161,
    161f
priming and, 244
reasoning and, 391, 391f
reticular formation of, 96, 97f
retrieval and, 240
in schizophrenia, 610–611, 611f, 612f, 648
self-concept and, 496f, 496–497
sickness response and, 569
smell sense and, 168f, 168–169
in social phobia, 654, 654f
socioeconomic status and, 413–414
somatosensory cortex of, 101–102, 103, 570,
    570f
Stroop effect and, 216, 217f
subcortical structures of, 97–100, 98f

substantia nigra of, 100
surgery to, 655–656
tectum of, 96–97, 97f
tegmentum of, 97, 97f
temporal lobe of, 100f, 102, 115
thalamus of, 98, 98f
types of judgments and, 225f
ventricles of, in schizophrenia, 611, 611f
vision and, 141–144, 142f
visual cortex of. See Visual cortex
Wernicke's area of, 115, 362f, 362–363
Brain damage
    cerebral hemispheres and, 115–117, 116f, 117f
    chronic traumatic encephalopathy and, 79–80
    emotion and, 115
    studies of, 114–117
Brain death, 123
Brain networks, 121
Brave New World (Huxley), 205
Broca's aphasia, 362
Broca's area, 7, 115, 304, 362, 362f
    implicit learning and, 304
Bulimia nervosa, 335
Burnout, 559–560
Buspirone (Buspar), 649
    for generalized anxiety disorder, 597
Bystander intervention, 515, 515f


C fibres, 165
Caffeine, 206, 207, 208, 209, 211
Canadian Association for Neuroscience–
    association canadienne de neuroscience
    (CAN-ACN), 31
Canadian government food and nutrition
    experiments, 70
Canadian Psychological Association (CPA), 31
    on effectiveness of psychotherapy, 660
    Ethical Principles of Psychologists and Code of
        Conduct of, 71, 72, 74, 661
Canadian Society for Brain, Behaviour and
    Cognitive Science (CSBBCS), 31
Cancer treatment, food aversions and, 276
Cannabis, 208f, 213–214
Cannon-Bard theory, 316–317, 317f, 318
Capgras syndrome, 331, 331f
Cardiovascular disease, stress and, 557–558, 558f
Careers in psychology, 33–34
Caregivers. See also Parents
    infants' ways of keeping close, 443–444
    primary, attachment and, 443–446
    responsiveness of, 445–446, 446f
Case method, 64
Catatonic behaviour, 609
Catecholamines, stress and, 554, 554f
Categories
    brain and, 371–373, 373f
    exemplar theory of, 371, 371f
    family resemblance theory of, 370, 370f
    prototype theory of, 370, 370f, 371f
    psychological theories of, 369–371
Categorization
    memory and, 225–226, 226f
    racism and, 28
    warping of perception by, 539–540, 540f
Category-specific deficit, 372–373, 373f
Causation, 54–62
CBM. See Cognitive bias modification
CBT. See Cognitive behavioural therapy
Celexa (Citalopram), 650, 654, 654f
Cell body, of neurons, 81, 81f

[Cell] phones, driving while using, 146, 251
*[The] Center Cannot Hold: My Journey Through Madness* (Saks), 613
[Cent]ral nervous system (CNS), 92, 92f. *See also* Brain; Spinal cord
components of, 94f, 94–95, 95f
[de]pressants and, 209–211
[ev]olutionary development of, 107f, 107–108
[pre]natal development of, 106f, 106–107
[Cent]ral nucleus, classical conditioning and, 274
[Cent]ral tendency, statistics describing, 49, 49f
[Cent]ration, 436
[Cep]halocaudal rule, 432
[Cer]ebellum, 96, 97f
[cla]ssical conditioning and, 274
[Cer]ebral cortex, 97, 98f, 100f, 100–103
[de]finition of, 97
[he]mispheres of. *See* Cerebral hemispheres
[or]ganization within specific lobes, 102–103
[in] social phobia, 654, 654f
[Cer]ebral hemispheres, 97, 100–102, 101f
[or]ganization across, 100–101, 101f
[or]ganization within, 101–102, 102f
[rig]ht, language development and, 363
[spe]cialization of, 115–117, 116f, 117f
[Cert]ainty effect, 379
[CFI.] *See* Cultural Formulation Interview
[Chal]lenges
[har]diness and, 575
[thr]eats vs., 559
[Chan]ge bias, 257
[Chan]ge blindness, 154–155, 155f
[Char]les Bonnet syndrome, 156
[Chem]ical senses. *See* Smell sense; Taste sense
[Chem]ical signalling. *See* Neurotransmitters
[Chil]dhood
[ave]rsion to watching others' suffering in, 451
[birt]h order and intelligence and, 411
[cog]nitive development in. *See* Cognitive development
[Eri]kson's stages of psychosocial development in, 458, 458t
[gift]ed children and, 416–417
[men]tal disorders in, 614–617
[mor]al development in. *See* Moral development
[par]ental intelligence and, 408, 409t
[per]ceptual and motor development in, 431–433, 432f
[slee]p need in, 197
[Chil]dhood abuse, suicide and, 112
[Chil]dhood amnesia, culture and, 240
[Chim]eric faces, 117, 117f
[Chlo]ride ions, 85
[Chlo]rpromazine, 646
[Chro]mosomes, 108, 109f
[sex,] 108, 427
[tel]omerase and, 556–557
[zyg]ote, 427
[Chro]nic stressors, 551–552
[Chro]nic traumatic encephalopathy (CTE), 79–80
[Chu]nking, 229
[Ciga]rette smoking. *See* Nicotine; Smoking
[Cilia,] 107
[Cing]ulate cortex. *See* Anterior cingulate cortex
[Cing]ulotomy, 656
[Circa]dian rhythm, 195
[CISD.] *See* Critical-incident stress debriefing
[Cital]opram (Celexa), 650, 654, 654f
[Class]ical conditioning, 267–276
[acq]uisition in, 269, 269f

basic principles of, 268–271
cognitive elements of, 273f, 273–274
definition of, 267
discrimination in, 271
of emotional responses, 272–273
evolutionary elements of, 275–276
extinction in, 269f, 270–271
of fear, 272–273, 274–275
generalization in, 271
neural elements of, 274–275
Pavlov's experiments on, 267f, 267–270, 268f
second-order, 269–270
spontaneous recovery in, 269f, 271
Classroom learning, 304–309. *See also* Education
control of learning and, 307–309
techniques for, 304–306, 305t
testing and attention and, 306–307
Claustrophobia, 594
Client-centred therapy, 636
Clinical psychologists, 33, 33f
Clinical psychology, development of, 13–15
Cliques, adolescent, 459
Closure, perceptual organization and, 148, 149f
Clozapine (Clozaril), 648
CNS. *See* Central nervous system
Coca-Cola, 212
Cocaine, 206, 207, 208, 209t, 211–212
neurotransmitters and, 90
Cochlea, 159, 160f
Cochlear implants, 162
Codeine, 211
Coercion, freedom from, 71
Cognition. *See also* Cognitive development; Reasoning; Thought
bilingualism and, 363–364
classical conditioning and, 273f, 273–274
depression and, 604
implicit learning and, 301f, 301–302
operant conditioning and, 288–291
social. *See* Social cognition
Cognitive behavioural therapy (CBT), 641–642
drug therapy and, 652, 652f
drug therapy vs., 654, 654f
Cognitive bias modification (CBM), 642
Cognitive development, 433–442. *See also* Cognition; Reasoning; Thought
culture and, 440–441, 441f
definition of, 433
desires and emotions and, 438
egocentrism and, 437, 438
language development and, 358–359
perceptions and beliefs and, 437–438
Piaget's stages of, 433t, 433–441, 434f, 435f
theory of mind and, 438–439
Cognitive dissonance, 535–537, 536f
Cognitive enhancers, 420–421
Cognitive maps, 289–290, 290f
Cognitive neuroscience, 25
Cognitive psychology, 20–23
*Cognitive Psychology* (Neisser), 23
Cognitive restructuring, 639t, 639–641
Cognitive symptoms of schizophrenia, 609
Cognitive therapy, 639t, 639–641
Cognitive unconscious, 191–193, 193f
Collaborative inhibition, 247
Collaborative memory, 246–247, 248
College Undergraduate Stress Scale (CUSS), 550–551, 551t
Colour afterimages, 141, 141f
Colour blindness, 141

Colour deficiency, 141
Colour-opponent system, 141
Colour, perception of, 140–141
Colour processing, language and, 367f, 367–368
Colour vision, 140f, 140–141, 141f
Coma, 185
Combustion, phlogiston theory of, 41
Commissures, 101
Commitment, hardiness and, 575
Common fate, perceptual organization and, 148, 149f
Common knowledge effect, 514
Communication. *See* Language; Language development; Speech
Community mental health centres, 647
Comorbidity, 587
Companionate love, 524–525, 525f
Comparison level, 525
Comparison level for alternatives, 525
Complexity
empirical method and, 42
of sound waves, 158, 159t
Compound remote associates, 386–387
Computers. *See* Technology
Computerized axial tomography scans (CT scans), of brain, 119, 119f
Concept
abstract, in formal operational stage, 437
brain and, 371–373, 373f
definition of, 369
exemplar theory of, 371, 371f
family resemblance theory of, 370, 370f
prototype theory of, 370, 370f, 371f
psychological theories of, 369–371
of time, language and, 368
Conceptual priming, 244
Concorde, sunk-cost fallacy and, 377
Concrete operational stage, 433, 433t, 436–437
Conditioned response (CR), 268, 268f, 269, 269f, 271, 275
Conditioned stimulus (CS), 268f, 268–270, 269f, 275
Conditioning. *See* Classical conditioning; Operant conditioning
Conditioning chamber, 18, 19
Conduct disorder, 616–617, 620
Conduction, in neurons, 84–87
Conductive hearing loss, 162
Cones, in retina, 138f, 139, 140–141, 141f
Confidentiality, in research, 71
Confirmation, perceptual, 541
Confirmatory factor analysis, 402–403, 403f
Conformity, 529–530, 530f
Congenital abnormalities, teratogens causing, 428–430
Conjunction fallacy, 375–376, 376f
Conscientiousness, 478, 478t
Conscious motivations, 344–345
Consciousness, 177–217
anesthesia for surgery and, 177
basic properties of, 182f, 182–183, 183f
contents of, 186–189, 187t
daydreaming and, 188, 188f
decision making and, 192–193, 193f
definition of, 8, 178
detection of, 185, 192–193
dream, 200–205. *See also* Dreams
disorders of, 185, 192–193
drugs and, 205–214
full, 184

hypnosis and. *See* Hypnosis
intentionality of, 182
levels of, 177–178, 183–186
mind and, *See* Mind.
mind-body problem and, 180f, 180–181, 181f
minimal, 184, 185
nature of, 181–189
of others, perceiving, 179–180, 180f
phenomenology and, 179
problem of other minds and, 179–180, 180f
selectivity of, 182–183
self-, 184, 186
sleep and. *See* Sleep
thought suppression and, 188f, 188–189
transience of, 183
unconscious mind and, 189–192
unity of, 182
Consent, informed, 71
Conservation, in cognitive development, 436
Consistency bias, 257
Consistency, social influence and, 535–537, 536f
Consolidation, of memories, 232–234
Content morphemes, 353–354
Context, drug overdoses and, 270
Continuity, perceptual organization and, 148, 149f
Contralateral control, 101
Control
contralateral, 101
hardiness and, 575
locus of, 493, 493t
perceived, over stressful events, 553
Control group, 58, 59f
Conventional antipsychotics, 648
Conventional stage of moral development, 448
Cooperation, 512–517
definition of, 512
groups and favouritism and, 513–515, 515f
risk and trust and, 512f, 512–513
Coping
rational, 561–562
repressive, 561
Cornea, 137f
Corpus callosum, 101, 101f
crossing of, by seizures, 115–116
severing of, 116f, 116–117, 117f
Correlation, 51t, 51–57
causation and, 54–62
factor analysis and, 401–402
natural, 54–55
patterns of variation and, 52
strength and direction of, 52–54, 53f, 54f
third-variable problem and, 55f, 55–57, 56f
Correlation coefficients, 53
Correspondence bias, 544–545
Cortex, cerebral. *See* Cerebral cortex
Cortisol, stress and, 259, 554, 554f
Counselling psychologists, 33
Counsellor, 631
Couples therapy, 643
Covariation model of attributions, 543–544, 544f
Cover stories, observation and, 46
CPA. *See* Canadian Psychological Association
CR. *See* Conditioned response
Crack cocaine, 212
Cramming, 305–306
Creative intelligence, 405–406
Creativity, 384–388
Critical-incident stress debriefing (CISD), 661, 661t
Critical thinking, in research, 66–69

Crystallized intelligence, 405
CS. *See* Conditioned stimulus
CSBBCS. *See* Canadian Society for Brain, Behaviour and Cognitive Science
CT scans. *See* Computerized axial tomography
CTE. *See* Chronic traumatic encephalopathy
Cue exposure therapies, 270
Cues
depth, 150–152
retrieval, 236–237
Cultural Formulation Interview (CFI), 589
Cultural psychology, 28–30
Culture
adolescence and, 454
aggression and, 511f, 511–512
anorexia nervosa and, 335–336
beauty and, 521–522
behaviour and, 30
change blindness and, 157
childhood amnesia and, 240
cognitive development and, 440–441, 441f
emotional expression and, 323f, 323–324
immigrants, social support and, 566
intelligence concept and, 406–407
mental disorders and, 29, 589
moral development and, 449
optimism bias and, 378
pain intensity and, 166
personality and, 481, 492
reinforcers and, 281
social influence and, 528
tone of voice and, 330
treatment for mental disorders and, 632
CUSS. *See* College Undergraduate Stress Scale
Cytokines, 569

DARE program, 661, 661t
Darwin's theory of natural selection, 11
Data-based approach, 403–405, 404f, 405f, 406
Day care, attachment and, 444, 447
Daydreaming, 188, 188f
DBS. *See* Deep brain stimulation
Deafness. *See* Hearing loss
Debriefing, 71
Deception
in experiments, 71
insincere facial expressions and, 327, 327f
lie detection and, 327–330, 328f
Decision making, 374–381
availability bias and, 375, 375f
brain and, 380–381, 381f
conjunction fallacy and, 375–376, 376f
errors in, reasons for, 378–380
framing effects and, 377
joint decisions and, 516
judging frequencies and probabilities and, 374–375
rational choice theory of, 374
representativeness heuristic and, 376–377
Declaration of Helsinki, 70
Deep brain stimulation (DBS), 656
Deep structure, of language, 354–355
Defense mechanisms, 486, 486t
Definitions, operational, 44
Degree of relatedness, 109
Dehydroepiandrosterone (DHEA), sexual desire and, 339
Deindividuation, 514
Deinstitutionalization movement, 646–648

De-intensification, emotional expression and, 326
Delayed reinforcement and punishment, 280f, 280–281
Delta waves, 195, 196f
Delusions, in schizophrenia, 608
Demand characteristics, 45–46
Demerol, 211
Demyelinating diseases, 82
Dendrites, 81, 81f
receptors of, 87, 88
Dependent variable, 58
Depressants, 209–211
Depression
bipolar disorder vs., 604–607, 651
brain and, 603, 603f
cognitive model of, 604
culture and, 29
double, 601–602
postpartum, 602
treatment of, 650–651, 657–658, 658f, 660t. *See also* Antidepressant drugs
in twins, 602
unipolar, 601–604
Depressive disorders, 601–604
biological factors in, 602–603, 603f, 606
psychological factors in, 604
Depth cues
binocular, 151–152, 152f
monocular, 150–151, 151f
pictorial, 150–151, 151f
Depth, illusions of, 152, 153f
Description, 47–50
graphic representations as, 47–48, 48f
statistics and, 48–50, 49f, 50f
Descriptive statistics, 48–50, 49f, 50f
Desire, cognitive development and, 438
Development, 425–467
in adolescence. *See* Adolescence
in adulthood. *See* Adulthood
in childhood. *See* Childhood
cognitive. *See* Cognitive development
in infancy. *See* Infancy
moral, 447–451
motor, 431–433, 432f
perceptual, 431
prenatal, 426–430, 427f
psychosocial, Erikson's stages of, 458, 458t
social, 442–447
Developmental psychologists, 12
Developmental psychology, 426
Deviation IQ, 398
Dexedrine, 211
DHEA. *See* Dehydroepiandrosterone
Diagnoses, 586
*Diagnostic and Statistical Manual of Mental Disorders (DSM)*, 587, 588t, 590, 592
Diathesis-stress model, 589–590
Diazepam (Valium)
for generalized anxiety disorder, 211, 597, 649
effects on consciousness, 206
for sleep problems, 211
Dichotic listening, 182
Dieting
ineffectiveness of, 577
psychology of, 579
Diffusion chain, 296–297
Diffusion of responsibility, 514–515, 515f
Diffusion tensor imaging (DTI), of brain, 120, 120f
Digit memory test, 223, 223f
Discrimination (against people)

definition of, 513
stress and illness related to, 552
Discrimination (process)
in classical conditioning, 271
in operant conditioning, 282–283
Discriminative stimulus, 282
Discursive reasoning, 388–389
Disease, 586
Disgust, 323f, 324
Disorder, 586
Disorganized attachment style, 444–447
Disorganized speech, in schizophrenia, 608
Displacement, 486t
Display rules, 326–327
Dispositional attributions, 543–544, 544f
Distributed practice, 305t, 305–306
Distributed representation, 147
Divided attention, 251
*The Diving Bell and the Butterfly* (Bauby), 217
Divorce, 525–526
Dizygotic twins, 109–110
DNA, 108
epigenetic marks and, 110
DNA methylation, 110–111, 112
Doctor–patient interaction, 573, 573f
Door-in-the-face technique, 529
*The Doors of Perception* (Huxley), 205
Dopamine, 88
drug effects on functioning of, 206
hypothesis of schizophrenia, 610, 648
Parkinson's disease and, 89–90, 100, 292
receptors and DRD2 gene, 591–592
Dopaminergic neurons, operant conditioning and, 291–292
Dorsal visual stream, 142, 143, 143f
Double-blind experiment, 659
Double-blind observation, 47
Double depression, 601–602
Down syndrome, 417
DRD2 gene, 591
Dreams, 200–205
activation-synthesis model of, 203
brain and, 204f, 204–205
dream consciousness and, 201–202
Freudian theory of, 202–203
latent content of, 202
manifest content of, 202
theories of, 202–203
Dream analysis, in psychoanalysis, 634
Drinking. *See* Alcohol use/abuse
Drives, 333–334
Driving
cell phone use during, 146, 251
cost of speeding and, 527f
drinking and, 210–211, 381
road rage and, 558
Drugs
addiction to, 206–208. *See also* Alcohol use/abuse; Substance abuse
agonist and antagonist, 89, 90f
balance of neurotransmitters in brain and, 89
cognitive enhancers, 420–421
gateway, 214
overdoses of, 270
psychoactive. *See* Drug therapy; Psychoactive drugs
tolerance to, 209–207, 270, 649
Drug therapy, 646, 648–654
anti-anxiety drugs for, 211, 597, 649

antidepressant drugs for, 480, 597, 602–603, 646, 646f, 649–651, 650f
antipsychotic drugs for, 646, 648
natural remedies for, 651–652, 652f
psychologists prescribing and, 654
mood stabilizers for, 651
overuse of, 653
placebos vs., 657–658, 658f
psychotherapy and, 652, 652f
psychotherapy vs., 654, 654f
DSM. *See Diagnostic and Statistical Manual of Mental Disorders*
DTI. *See* Diffusion tensor imaging
Dualism, 6
Ducklings, imprinting in, 443
Duration, facial expressions and, 327
Dynamic unconscious, 190–191, 485
Dysgenic fertility, 414
Dysphasia, genetic, 360
Dysthymia, 601–602

EAR (electronically activated recorder), 476
Ear, 159–160, 160f
vestibular system of, 167
Early experience, persisting effects of, 112
Early memories, 261
Early Start Denver Model (ESDM), 615
Eating disorders, 335–339, 336f, 337f, 337t
Eating wisely, 576, 577
Ebbinghaus's studies of memory, 249–250, 250f
Echoic memory, 228
Ecstasy (MDMA), 206, 209t, 211–212
ECT. *See* Electroconvulsive therapy
Edge assignment, 148–149
Education. *See also* Classroom learning
for careers in psychology, 33
intelligence and, 414–415
sex, 457, 578
EEG. *See* Electroencephalograph
Effect, law of, 277f, 277–278, 278f
Effexor (Venlafaxine), 650
Ego, 485
Egocentric bias, 257
Egocentrism, cognitive development and, 437, 438
Ego integrity vs. despair stage, 458t
Egotism, implicit, 501–502
Elaborative interrogation, effectiveness as study technique, 305, 305t
Elavil (amitriptyline), 649–650
Electric signalling
action potential and, 85f, 86–87, 87f
resting potential and, 84–85, 85f
Electrical activity, of brain, 118f, 118–119
Electroconvulsive therapy (ECT), 654–655
Electroencephalograph (EEG), 118, 118f
biofeedback and, 564
sleep and, 195–197, 196f
Electromagnetic spectrum, 136, 136f
Electromyography (EMG), relaxation therapy and, 563–564
Electronically activated recorder. *See* EAR
Electrooculograph (EOG), during sleep, 195–197
Embarrassment, 324
Embryonic brain, 106, 106f
Embryonic stage, 427, 427f
EMG. *See* Electromyography
Emotion, 3, 314–330
amygdala and, 99, 122, 319f, 319–320, 320f
appraisal and, 319
assessing, 187, 187t

basic, 323f, 323–324
brain and, 99, 122, 319f, 319–320, 320f, 332
Cannon-Bard theory of, 316–317, 317f, 318
cognitive development and, 438
definition of, 314–316, 315f
dream consciousness and, 201–202
expressed, 607
James-Lange theory of, 316–317, 317f, 318
limbic system and, 99
motivation and, 331f, 331–332
multidimensional scaling and, 314–316, 315f
physiological responses and, 315–318, 317f, 318f
regulation of, 320–321
sexual behaviour and, 341–342, 342t
two-factor theory of, 317f, 317–318
Emotion regulation, 320–321
Emotional expression, 322–330
cause and effect of, 324–326, 326f
communicative, 323–326
culture and, 323f, 323–324, 330
deceptive, 326–330, 327f, 328f
definition of, 322
facial expressions and. *See* Facial expressions
suppression of, 320
universality of, 323f, 323–324
Emotional intelligence, 406
alexithymia and, 406
Empathy, in childhood, 451
Empirical method, 42–43
Empiricism, 40–43
definition of, 40
observation and, 42–43
scientific method and, 40–42
Encephalopathy, traumatic, chronic, 79–80
Encoding, 222, 223f, 223–227
organizational, 225f, 225–226, 226f
semantic, 223–224, 225f
of survival-related information, 226–227, 227f
of visual imagery, 224–225, 225f
Encoding specificity principle, 236–237
Enculturation hypothesis, 298
End of history illusion, 460
Endocrine system. *See also* Hormones *and specific hormones by name*
hypothalamic-pituitary-adrenocortical axis and, 554, 554f
Endogenous opioids, 212–213, 571
Endorphins, 89
Environment
gene expression and, 110–111, 111f
intelligence and, 411–415, 412f, 413f, 413t, 419–420
nonshared, 410–411
phobias and, 595
prenatal, 428–430
shared, 410–411
Environmental psychology, 552
Enzyme deactivation, 87f, 88
EOG. *See* Electrooculograph
Epidemiology, 589
Epigenetic marks, 110
Epigenetic writers, 110
Epigenetics, 110–112, 111f
Epinephrine, stress and, 554, 554f, 567
Episodic memory, 244–247, 246f
imagining the future and, 245–246, 246f
Equity, in relationships, 525
Erikson's stages of psychosocial development, 458, 458t

Erotogenic zones, 487
Errors, in decision making, reasons for, 378–380
ESDM. *See* Early Start Denver Model
ESP. *See* Extrasensory perception
Estrogen
    odour related to, 171
    sexual desire and, 339–340
Estrus, 340
*Ethical Principles of Psychologists and Code of Conduct* (CPA), 71, 72, 74, 661
Ethics. *See also* Moral development
    in research, 70–74
    in psychiatric treatment, 661
Etiology, 587
Evolution
    altruism in, 516–517
    classical conditioning and, 275–276
    operant conditioning and, 293f, 293–294
    self-esteem and, 499–500
Evolutionary psychology, 25–26
Exams, studying for, 305–306
Excitement phase of human sexual response cycle, 341, 341f
Excitement, physiological arousal and, 317
Exemplar theory of concepts, 371, 371f
Exercise
    aerobic, for stress management, 564–565
    brain function and, 105
Exhaustion phase of general adaptation syndrome, 555, 555f
Existential approach, 489–490
Existential therapy, 636–637
Existentialist psychologists, 488
Expectancies, outcome, 493
Expectancy theory, of alcohol effects, 210–211
Expectations
    in classical conditioning, 273f, 273–274
    influence on observations, 47
    influence on reality, 47
    observations and, 67–68
    placebo effect and, 657–658, 658f
    reward learning in Parkinson's disease and, 292
Experience-sampling technique, 186–187, 187t
Experiments, 57–69
    animal subjects in, 72–73
    beliefs and, 67–68
    critical steps in, 58
    critical thinking and, 66–69
    definition of, 57
    double-blind, 659
    ethics and, 70–74
    food and nutrition, 70
    human subjects in, 70–72
    manipulation and, 57–58, 59f
    random assignment and, 59–61, 60f
    sampling and, 64–66
    significance and, 61–62
    subjects for, 63–66
    validity and, 62–63
Experimental group, 58, 59f
Explicit learning
    implicit learning vs., 302
    neural pathways and, 303f, 303–304
Explicit memory, 242f, 242–244, 243f, 244f
Exposure and response prevention, 639
Exposure, in rational coping, 562
Exposure therapy, 638t, 638–639
Expressed emotion, 607
*The Expression of the Emotions in Man and Animals* (Darwin), 323

Expressive writing, as reframing technique, 562–563
External forces, 28
External locus of control, 493, 493t
External validity, 62–63
Extinction
    in behavioural therapy, 638t, 638–639
    in classical conditioning, 270–271
    in operant conditioning, 283
    resistance to, intermittent reinforcement effect and, 286
Extrasensory perception (ESP), 61
Extraversion, 478, 478t, 483
Extrinsic motivation, 343–344, 344f
Eye, 136–137, 137f, 138f
Eyeblink, conditioning of, 274
Eysenck's personality theory, 478

Facebook, personality judgments and, 479
Faces, chimeric, 117, 117f
Facial expressions
    ambiguity of, 325
    facial feedback hypothesis and, 324–326, 326f
    infant mimicry of, 431
    muscle movements and, 322–323, 324, 326
    sincerity of, 327, 327f
    universality of, 323f, 323–324
Facial feedback hypothesis, 324–326, 326f
Factor analysis, 401–403
    confirmatory, 402–403, 403f
    personality traits and, 477–478
Fallacies
    conjunction, 375–376, 376f
    sunk-cost, 377
False-belief task, 437–438
False hope syndrome, 579
False memories, 255–256
False recognition, 253
Familiar size, as depth cue, 150, 151f
Family resemblance theory of concepts, 370, 370f
Family therapy, 643
Farsightedness, 137, 138f
FASD. *See* Fetal alcohol spectrum disorder
Fast mapping, 356
Favouritism, 513–515, 515f
Fear, 323f, 324. *See also* Anxiety disorders
    amygdala and, 99
    conditioning of, 272–273, 274–275
    observational learning of, 297
    phobic disorders, 594–595
    physiological arousal and, 317
Feature detectors
    single-neuron, 142, 143f
    in visual cortex, 118–119
Feature-integration theory, 145
Fertility, dysgenic, 414
Fetal alcohol spectrum disorder (FASD), 417, 428–430
Fetal stage, 427f, 427–428
Fetus, hearing in, 430
FI. *See* Fixed-interval schedule
Field theory, 28
Fight-or-flight response
    to stress, 554f, 554–555, 555f
    gender and, 567
Figure-ground relationship, 148–149, 149f
Filler items, observation and, 46
Five-factor personality model, 478t, 478–480
Fixation, 487

Fixed-interval schedule (FI), 284
Fixed-ratio schedule (FR), 285
Flashbulb memories, 258
Flavour, 168, 173
Fluid intelligence, 405
Fluoxetine (Prozac)
    for depression, 602, 650
    for generalized anxiety disorder, 597
    neurotransmitters and, 91
Flynn effect, 412
fMRI. *See* functional magnetic resonance imaging
Food and nutrition experiments, 70
Food aversions, 275–276
Food intake
    appetite and, 334–335, 569
    eating disorders and, 335–339, 336f, 337f, 337t
    eating wisely and, 576, 577
    hunger and, 334–335, 335f
    obesity and, 336f, 336–339, 337f, 337t, 576
    portion size and, 338, 339f, 577
Foot-in-the-door technique, 535
Forebrain, 96f, 97–103, 98f. *See also* Cerebral cortex
    development of, 107, 107f, 108
    formation of, 106
    limbic system of, 99–100. *See also* Amygdala; Hippocampus; Hypothalamus
    subcortical structures of, 97–100, 98f
Forgetting. *See also* Amnesia; Memory failures
    dream consciousness and, 201
    retrieval-induced, 238–239, 240
Form agnosia, visual, 142–143, 143f
Formal operational stage, 433, 433t, 437
Fovea, 137f, 138f, 139
FR. *See* Fixed-ratio schedule
Framed-line test, 30
Framing effects, 377
    functional fixedness and, 385f, 385–386, 386f, 387f, 388f
Fraternal twins, 109–110
Fraud, in research, 73–74
Free association, in psychoanalysis, 634
Freedom, from coercion, 71
Freezing, 274–275
Frequencies, judging, 374–375
Frequency distributions, 48, 48f
    positively skewed, 49–50, 50f
Frequency format hypothesis of decision-making errors, 379–380
Frequency, of sound waves, 158, 159t
Freudian slips, 190
Freudian theory. *See* Psychoanalysis; Psychoanalytic theory; Psychodynamic approach
Friendships, in adolescence, 454, 454f, 459
Frontal lobes, 100f, 102
    attention and, 251
    Broca's area in, 115
    DRD2 gene and, 591
    personality and, 115, 115f, 480
    retrieval and, 240
Frustration–aggression hypothesis, 509
Full consciousness, 184
Function morphemes, 354
Functional brain imaging, 2, 120–123, 121f
Functional fixedness, 385f, 385–386, 386f, 387f, 388f
functional magnetic resonance imaging (fMRI), 2, 120–122, 121f
Functionalism, 10–12
Fundamental attribution error, 544

Fusiform gyrus, 122

GABA. *See* Gamma-aminobutyric acid
GAD. *See* Generalized anxiety disorder
Gamma-aminobutyric acid (GABA), 88
    alcohol and, 209
    anti-anxiety medications and, 649
    drug effects on functioning of, 206
Ganglion cells, retinal, 138*f*, 139, 141
GAS. *See* General adaptation syndrome
Gate-control theory of pain, 166
Gateway drugs, 214
Gaussian distribution, 48, 48*f*
Gender
    aggression and, 509–510, 510*f*
    intelligence and, 418
    moral development and, 448
    personality and, 481
    selection of sexual partners and, 517–518, 519
    social support and, 567
Genes, 108–110, 109*f*. *See also* Genetic factors;
        Heritability
    environmental influence on expression of,
        110–111, 111*f*
    obesity and, 337
General adaptation syndrome (GAS), 554–555,
        555*f*
General factor, 403, 403*f*
Generalization, 64–65
    in classical conditioning, 271
    in operant conditioning, 282–283
Generalized anxiety disorder (GAD), 596–597
General motivations, 345
Generativity vs. stagnation stage, 458*t*
Genetic dysphasia, 360
Genetic factors. *See also* Genes; Heritability
    intelligence and, 407–411, 415, 419–420
    personality and, 480, 480*t*, 482
Genital stage, 488
Genius, insight and, 384*f*, 384–385, 385*f*
Geography
    aggression and, 511*f*, 511–512
    attraction and, 520
Geons, 150, 150*f*
Germinal stage, 427
Gestalt perceptual grouping rules, 148, 149*f*
Gestalt psychology, 21
Gestalt therapy, 637
Ghrelin, 334
Glial cells, 82
Glucocorticoids, 557
Glutamate, 88
Goals
    in adulthood, 463*f*, 463–464, 464*f*
    personal, in social-cognitive approach, 493, 493*t*
Grammar
    artificial, implicit learning and, 301*f*, 301–302
    definition of, 352
Grammatical rules, emergence of, 357–358
Graphic representations, 47–48, 48*f*
Grossly disorganized behaviour, in schizophrenia,
        608–609
Group
    cooperation in, 512–517
    definition of, 513
    favouritism in, 513–515, 515*f*
Group factors, 403, 403*f*
Grouping, memory and, 225–226, 226*f*
Group polarization, 514
Groups, support, 644–645

Group therapy, 643–644
Groupthink, 514
Guilt, 324
Gustation. *See* Taste sense
Gyri, 100, 100*f*
    fusiform, 122

Habituation
    definition of, 266
    implicit learning and, 300
    in infants, 431
Hair cells, of ear, 159–160, 160*f*
Hallucinations
    hypnagogic, 200
    hypnopompic, 200
    in schizophrenia, 608
    visual, 156
Hallucinogens, 213
Haloperidol (Haldol), 646
Hammer, of ear, 159, 160*f*
Happiness, 323*f*, 324
    marriage and parenthood and, 465–466, 466*f*
    physiological arousal and, 317
Haptic perception, 164
Hardiness, health and, 575–576
Harlow's attachment studies, 442–443
Harm, protection from, 71
Head trauma. *See* Brain damage
Health. *See* Illness; Psychology of health;
        Psychology of illness; Stress
Health psychology, 550
Hear the World Foundation, 158
Hearing, 158–163
    absolute threshold for, 133*t*
    ear and, 159–160, 160*f*
    fetal, 430
    localizing sound sources and, 161–162
    loss of. *See* Hearing loss
    pitch perception and, 160–161, 161*f*
    sound sensation and, 158–159, 159*t*
    stereophonic, 161
    temporal lobe and, 102
    transduction and, 131*t*
Hearing loss
    cochlear implants for, 162
    conductive, 162
    language development and, 360, 361–362
    language use and, 24–25
    sensorineural, 162
    sign language for. *See* Sign language
    theory of mind and, 439
Hedonic motive for social influence, 526, 527*f*,
        527–528
Hedonic principle, 332
Helping behaviours, observation of, 45
Helplessness theory, 604
Hemispheres, cerebral. *See* Cerebral hemispheres
Herbal remedies, for mental disorders, 651–652,
        652*f*
*Hereditary Genius* (Galton), 407
Heritability, 111, 113. *See also* Genes; Genetic
        factors
    of bipolar disorder, 606
    of depression, 602
    of intelligence, 409*f*, 409–411, 410*f*
    of obesity, 337
    of schizophrenia, 609–610
Heritability coefficient, 409–410
Heroin, 206, 208, 209*t*, 212
    overdose of, 270

Heuristic, 375
Heuristic persuasion, 534–535, 535*f*
Heuristic, representativeness, 376–377
Hierarchy of needs, 489
Highlighting, effectiveness as study technique,
        304–305, 305*t*
Hindbrain, 96, 96*f*, 97*f*, 107
    formation of, 106
Hippocampus, 7, 98*f*, 99
    implicit vs. explicit learning and, 303
    memory and, 99, 231*f*, 231–232, 245–246,
        246*f*, 251, 254, 254*f*
    post-traumatic stress disorder and, 600, 600*f*
    in social phobia, 654, 654*f*
Histone modification, 110–111
HIV/AIDS, 576, 578
Hockey, chronic traumatic encephalopathy and,
        79–80
Holistic style of information processing, 30
Holocaust, social psychology and, 28
Homeostasis, 333–334
Homunculus, 101
Hormones. *See also specific hormones by name*
    aggression and, 509–510, 510*f*
    hunger and, 334–335
    odour related to, 171
    sexual desire and, 339–340
    stress and, 554, 554*f*, 567
Hostility. *See* Aggression
HPA axis. *See* Hypothalamic-pituitary-
        adrenocortical axis
Human Connectome Project, 120, 120*f*, 121
Humanistic-existential approach, 488–490
Humanistic psychologists, 488
Humanistic psychology, 15, 488–489, 489*f*
Humanistic therapy, 636–637
Human papillomavirus vaccine, 457
Human sexual response cycle, 340–341, 341*f*
Human subjects, ethical treatment of, 70–72
Humour, for stress management, 568
Hunger, 334–335, 335*f*. *See also* Appetite
    hypothalamus and, 98
Hyperopia, 137, 138*f*
Hypnagogic hallucinations, 200
Hypnagogic state, 194
Hypnic jerk, 194
Hypnopompic hallucinations, 200
Hypnopompic state, 194
Hypnosis, 214–216
    definition of, 214
    effects of, 215–216, 216*f*
    induction and susceptibility to, 214–215
Hypnotic analgesia, 216, 216*f*
Hypothalamic-pituitary-adrenocortical (HPA) axis,
        stress and, 554
Hypothalamus, 98*f*, 98–99
    hunger and, 335, 335*f*
    operant conditioning and, 291, 291*f*
Hypotheses, 41
    generation of, 63
Hysteria, 13

Iatrogenic illness, 660–661, 661*t*
Iconic memory, 228, 228*f*
Id, 485
Identical twins, 109–110
Identification, 486*t*
Identity vs. role confusion stage, 458*t*
Illness
    discrimination related to, 551, 552

faking and, 572–573
mental. *See* Mental disorders
patient–practitioner interaction and, 573, 573*f*
psychology of. *See* Psychology of health; Psychology of illness
psychosomatic, 572
recognizing and treating, 569–571, 570*f*
sick role and, 572
sickness response and, 569
stress and. *See* Stress
Illusion, 20
end of history, 460
of depth and size, 152, 153*f*
of explanatory depth, 390
of unique invulnerability, 577–578
Illusory conjunctions, 145
Image-based object recognition theories, 149
Imagery, effectiveness as study technique, 304–305, 305*t*
Imaging studies. *See* Neuroimaging
Imipramine (Tofranil), 649–650, 652, 652*f*
Imitation, in infancy, 441
Immediate reinforcement and punishment, 280*f*, 280–281
Immune response
sickness response and, 569
stress and, 557
Immune system, 557
Implicit egotism, 501–502
Implicit learning, 300–304
cognitive approaches to, 301*f*, 301–302
definition of, 300
explicit learning vs., 302
habituation and, 300
neural pathways and, 303*f*, 303–304
Implicit memory, 242–244, 242*f*, 243*f*, 244*f*
Imprinting, 443
Inattentional blindness, 155
Independent variable, 58
Individual differences, in intelligence, 416*f*, 416–417
Induction, of hypnosis, 214–215
Industrial/organizational psychologists, 34
Industry vs. inferiority stage, 458*t*
Infancy
babbling in, 356, 360
cognitive development in. *See* Cognitive development
imitation in, 441
language development in, 355–356
parental advice in, 442, 442*f*
perceptual and motor development in, 431–433, 432*f*
self-recognition in, 186
sleep need in, 197
social development in, 442–447
Inferential statistics, 62
Influence. *See* Social influence
Information processing. *See also* Processing
analytic style of, 30
conduction within neurons and, 84–87
functional neuroimaging and, 122–123
holistic style of, 30
transmission between neurons and, 87*f*, 87–91
Informational influence, 533–534
Informed consent, 71
Inhalants, toxic, 211
Inhibition, collaborative, 247
Initiative vs. guilt stage, 458*t*
Inner ear, 159–160, 160*f*

Insight
brain and, 386–387
in cognitive development, 436
developing, in psychoanalysis, 634–635
genius and, 384*f*, 384–385, 385*f*
Insomnia, 199
treatment of, 660*t*
Instincts, 332–333, 334
Instruction. *See* Classroom learning; Education
Instruments
definition of, 44
power of, 44, 44*f*
reliability of, 44, 44*f*
Insula, placebo effect and, 571
Intellectual disability, 416, 417
Intellectual giftedness, 416–417
Intelligence, 395–421
analytic, 405–406
birth order and, 411
creative, 405–406
crystallized, 405
culture and concept of, 406–407
data-based approach to, 403–405, 404*f*, 405*f*, 406
definition of, 396
education and, 414–415
emotional, 406
environmental influences on, 411–415, 412*f*, 413*f*, 413*t*, 419–420
ethnicity and, 417–420
fluid, 405
gender and, 418
genetic influences on, 407–411, 415
group differences in, 417–420
heritability of, 409*f*, 409–411, 410*f*
as hierarchy of abilities, 401–403, 402*t*, 403*f*
improving, 420–421
individual differences in, 416*f*, 416–417
judging of, in job interviews, 400
measurement of. *See* Intelligence tests
mental illness and, 416
middle-level abilities and, 403–407
normal curve of, 416, 416*f*
practical, 405–406
socioeconomic status and, 413–414
trends in, 414
theory-based approach to, 405–407
two-factor theory of, 402
Intelligence quotient, 397–398
Intelligence tests, 396–401
bias in, 396, 418–419
intelligence quotient and, 397–398
prediction made from scores on, 398–401, 399*f*
Stanford-Binet, 398
Wechsler Adult Intelligence Scale (WAIS), 398–399, 399*t*
Intensification, emotional expression and, 326
Intensity
of pain, 166
of sounds, 158, 159*t*
Intentionality, of consciousness, 182
Interference, proactive and retroactive, 250
Interleaved practice, effectiveness as study technique, 305*t*
Intermittent reinforcement, 285–286
Intermittent reinforcement effect, 286
Internal forces, 28
Internal locus of control, 493, 493*t*
Internal validity, 62
Internal working model of relationships, 446, 446*f*

Interneurons, 83
specialization by location, 83, 83*f*
Interpersonal psychotherapy (IPT), 635
Interposition, as depth cue, 150–151, 151*f*
Interpretation, in psychoanalysis, 634
Interrogation, elaborative, effectiveness as study technique, 305, 305*t*
Interval schedules of reinforcement, 283, 284
Intimacy vs. isolation stage, 458*t*
Intrinsic motivation, 342–344
Introspection, 9
Introversion, 478, 478*t*, 483
Ions, 84, 85
Iproniazid, 649
IPT. *See* Interpersonal psychotherapy
IQ score, 398
Iris, of eye, 137*f*
Ironic processes of mental control, 189

James-Lange theory, 316–317, 317*f*, 318
Jealousy, evolutionary psychology's view of, 26
JND. *See* Just noticeable difference
Job interviews, judging of intelligence in, 400
Joint attention, 441, 441*f*
Judgment
frontal lobe and, 102
of learning (JOLs), 307–309
rhyme, 223
semantic, 223
visual, 223–224
Just noticeable difference (JND), 132–133

K complexes, 195, 196*f*
Ketamine, 213
Keyword mnemonics, effectiveness as study technique, 305*t*
Kin selection, 516–517
Kohlberg's theory of moral development, 448–449

Labelling, in psychiatry, 592–593
LAD. *See* Language acquisition device
Language, 352–368. *See also* Speech
animal use of, 365–366
basic characteristics of, 353*f*, 353–354, 354*f*
behaviourist analysis of, 23
and bilingualism, benefits of, 364
brain and, 7, 24–25, 102, 115, 304, 362*f*, 362–363
Broca's area and, 7, 115, 304, 362, 362*f*
colour processing and, 367*f*, 367–368
deep vs. surface structure of, 354–355
definition of, 352
development of. *See* Language development
evolution of, 352
frontal lobe and, 115
morphological rules of, 353–354
of mother, fetal hearing and, 430
personality traits and, 477–478, 478*f*, 481, 492
phonological rules of, 353
structure of, 353–355
syntactical rules of, 354, 354*f*
temporal lobe and, 102, 115
thought and, 3, 367–368
time concept and, 368
Wernicke's area and, 115, 362*f*, 362–363
Language acquisition device (LAD), 360
Language development, 355–366
active vs. passive, 355

in animals, 365–366
behaviourist theories of, 359
bilingualism and, 363–365, 365f
brain and, 362–366
cognitive development and, 358–359
distinguishing speech sounds and, 355–356
emergence of grammatical rules and, 357–358
interactionist theories of, 361–362
milestones in, 356–357, 357t
nativist theories of, 360–361
Latency stage, 487–488
Latent content, of dreams, 202
Latent learning, 288–289, 289f
Lateral geniculate nucleus (LGN), 141, 142f
Lateral hypothalamus, hunger and, 335, 335f
Law of effect, 277f, 277–278, 278f
L-Dopa, 89–90
Learned aversions, 275–276
Learning, 265–309
in *Aplysia*, 266, 274
behaviourism and. *See* Behaviourism
classical conditioning and. *See* Classical conditioning
in classroom. *See* Classroom learning
control of, 307–309
definition of, 266
habituation and, 266
implicit. *See* Implicit learning
judgments of, 307–309
latent, 288–289, 289f
limbic system and, 99
observational. *See* Observational learning
online, 308–309
operant conditioning and. *See* Operant conditioning
sensitization and, 266
transfer of, 306
to trust, 290–291
Learning styles, myths about, 124
Lens, of eye, 137f
Leptin, 334–335
LGN. *See* Lateral geniculate nucleus
Librium, for generalized anxiety disorder, 597
Lie detection, 327–330, 328f
Light
sensation of, 136f, 136–139, 137t
visible spectrum of, 140, 140f
wavelength of, 136, 136t, 139–140, 140f
Limbic system, 99–100. *See also* Amygdala; Hippocampus; Hypothalamus
Linear perspective, as depth cue, 150, 151f
Linguistic relativity hypothesis, 367
Listening, dichotic, 182
Lithium, 651
Little Albert experiments, 18, 272–273
Lobotomy, 655
Locked-in syndrome, 185, 217
Locus of control, 493, 493t
Long-term memory
hippocampus and, 231f, 231–232
memory consolidation and, 232–234
Long-term potentiation (LPT), 235
Long-term storage, 230–234, 231f
Lorazepam (Ativan), 649
Loudness, 158, 159t
Love, 524–525, 525f. *See also* Attachment
LSD (lysergic acid diethylamide), 213
balance of neurotransmitters in brain and, 89
LTP. *See* Long-term potentiation
Lying. *See* Deception

Lymphocytes, 557

Magnetic resonance imaging (MRI)
of brain, 119–120, 119f
functional, 2, 120–122, 121f
Major depressive disorder, 586, 601–604
Males, role in reproduction, 429
Malingering, 572–573
Manifest content, of dreams, 202
Manipulation, in experiments, 57–58, 59f
Mantra, 563
MAOIs. *See* Monoamine oxidase inhibitors
Marijuana, 208f, 213–214
Marriage, 465, 465f, 524–525
couples therapy and, 643
divorce and, 525–526
mate selection and, 517–518, 519
Masking, emotional expression and, 326
Maslow's hierarchy of needs, 489
Massed practice, 306
Master gland, 99
Matched pairs technique, 56–57
Matched samples technique, 55–57, 56f
Mate, selection of, 517–518, 519
MDMA (ecstasy), 206, 209t, 211–212
Mean, 49, 49f
Means-end analysis, 382–383
Means-end relationships, 288
Measurement, 43–47
demand characteristics and, 45–46
instruments for, 44
observer bias and, 46–47
operational definitions and, 44
reliability and, 44, 44f
of strength and direction of correlations, 52–54, 53f, 54f
validity and, 44
Media violence, aggression and, 64
Medial forebrain bundle, operant conditioning and, 291, 291f
Medial prefrontal cortex (MPFC), self-concept and, 496f, 496–497
Median, 49, 49f
Medical model of mental disorders, 585
Meditation, 563
mindfulness, 641
Medulla, 96, 97f
Mellaril (thioridazine), 646
Memory, 3, 221–261
amygdala and, 99, 234, 258–259, 259f
attachment style and, 445, 445f
autobiographical, 495
collaborative, 246–247, 248
construction of, 223
definition of, 222
degradation of, 249
early, 261
Ebbinghaus's studies of, 21, 249–250, 250f
echoic, 228
encoding in, 222, 223f, 223–227
episodic, 244–246, 246f
explicit, 242f, 242–244, 243f, 244f
failure of. *See* Amnesia; Forgetting; Memory failure
false, 255–256
flashbulb, 258
fMRI and, 122–123
frontal lobes and, 102
hippocampus and, 99, 231f, 231–232, 245–246, 246f, 251, 254, 254f

iconic, 228, 228f
implicit, 242f, 242–244, 243f, 244f
long-term, 230–234, 231f
neurons and, 234–235
procedural, 242, 242f
prospective, 251
reconstructive, 658
retrieval in, 222, 236–241
semantic, 244–245
sensory, 228, 228f
short-term, 229f, 229–230
sleep and, 197–198, 233
source, 253
storage in, 222, 228–236
subsequent, consequences of retrieval for, 237–239, 238f
tip-of-the-tongue experience and, 252
total, 221–222
working, 229–230
Memory failure, 249–260. *See also* Amnesia; Forgetting
absentmindedness, 250–252, 259
bias, 256–257, 260
blocking, 252
memory misattribution, 253–255, 253f, 254f, 254t, 260
persistence, 257–259, 259f, 260
pros and cons of, 259–260
suggestibility, 255–256, 260
transience, 249–250, 250f, 259
Memory misattribution, 253f, 253–255, 254f, 254t, 260
Mental abilities. *See* Abilities; Intelligence
Mental age, 398
Mental control, 188
ironic processes of, 189
Mental disorders, 583–623
anxiety, 593–597
bipolar, 604–607
causes of, 587, 589–590
in childhood and adolescence, 614–617
classifying, 586–587, 588t
conceptualizing, 585–586
culture and, 29, 589
definition of, 584–585
depressive, 601–604
*DSM* and, 587, 588t, 590, 592
financial costs associated with, 628
iatrogenic, 660–661, 661t
intelligence and, 416
labelling and, 592–593
medical model of, 585
obsessive-compulsive, 598–599
overdiagnosis of, 653
personal and social burdens associated with, 628
personality, 618–620
post-traumatic stress, 599–600, 600f
psychotic, 607–613
Research Domain Criteria Project and, 590–592, 591t
schizophrenia, 607–613
self-injurious, 621–623, 622f
treatment of. *See* Biological treatments; Drug therapy; Psychotherapy; Treatment of psychological disorders
twin studies of, 590, 595, 597, 599, 600, 602, 606, 609, 610f, 611
Mental imagery tasks, 192–193
Mental placeholders, 224–225
Mental representations, 436
Mere exposure effect, 519–520

Mescaline, 213
Messenger RNA (mRNA), 108
Metabolism, 338
Methadone, 212
Methedrine, 211
Methylphenidate (Ritalin), 420
Micro-expressions, 327
Microvilli, on taste buds, 172, 172f
Midbrain, 96f, 96–97, 97f, 107
    formation of, 106
Middle ear, 159, 160f
Middle-level abilities, 403–407
Milgram's obedience studies, 531–533, 532f
Mind
    brain and, 6–7, 7f
    consciousness and. See Consciousness
    cultural influences on, 30
    definition of, 2
    fundamental questions about, 2–5
    ineffective functioning of, 3–5
    of others, discovery of, 437–440
    problem of other minds and, 179–180, 180f
    stress management and, 561–563
    structuralism and, 7–10
    structure of, psychodynamic approach to,
        485–486, 486t
    theory of. See Theory of mind
Mind-body problem, 180f, 180–181, 181f
Mindfulness meditation, 641
Mind management, for stress, 561–563
Minimal consciousness, 184, 185
Minnesota Multiphasic Personality Inventory
        (MMPI), 474
Minorities, in psychology, 31–32
Minor tranquilizers, 211
Mirror box therapy, 104
Mirror neurons, 103
    observational learning and, 299, 299f
Misattributions, memory, 253f, 253–255, 254f,
        254t, 260
Missing evidence, 68–69
MMPI. See Minnesota Multiphasic Personality
        Inventory
Modafinil, 211
Mode, 49, 49f
Models, in observational learning, 295–297
Modular view, 147
Monoamine oxidase inhibitors (MAOIs), 649, 650f
Monocular depth cues, 150–151, 151f
Monosodium glutamate (MSG), 172
Monozygotic twins, 109–110
Mood disorders, 601–607
    bipolar, 604–607
    depressive, 601–604
Mood stabilizers, 651
Moral development, 447–451
    culture and, 449
    gender and, 448
    stages of, 448
    ways of feeling and, 449–451, 450f
    ways of thinking and, 447–449
Moral intuitionist perspective, 450
Morphemes, 353f, 353–354
Morphine, 206, 207, 209t, 212–213
Morphological rules, 353–354
Morphology, facial expressions and, 327, 327f
Mortality-salience hypothesis, 347
Motion. See Movement
Motivation, 331–347. See also Needs
    approach vs. avoidance, 345–347, 346t

conscious vs. unconscious, 344–345
    definition of, 331
    drives and, 333–334
    emotion and, 331f, 331–332
    for food, 334–339, 335f, 336f, 337f, 337t
    general, 345
    instincts and, 332–333, 334
    intrinsic vs. extrinsic, 342–344, 344f
    limbic system and, 99
    for sex, 339–342, 341f, 342t
Motor cortex, 101–102, 102f
    dreaming and, 204f, 204–205
    implicit learning and, 304
    musical training and, 163
    observational learning and, 300
Motor development
    in infancy and childhood, 431–433, 432f
    timetable of, 432, 432f
Motor neurons, 82–83
Motor skills, cerebellum and, 96
Movement
    apparent, 154
    basal ganglia and, 100
    during dreams, 204–205
    perception of, 153–154
    sense of, 167
    tegmentum and, 97
    voluntary, timing of conscious will and, 181,
        181f
MPFC. See Medial prefrontal cortex
MRI. See Magnetic resonance imaging
mRNA. See Messenger RNA
MSG. See Monosodium glutamate
Multidimensional scaling, emotion and, 314–316,
        315f
Multiple sclerosis, 82
Multitasking, 146
Muscles, relaxation therapy and, 563–564
Musical training, auditory processing and, 163
Myelin sheath, 81f, 82
    action potential and, 86–87, 87f
    formation of, 428
Myelination, 428
Myopia, 137, 138f

Name-letter effect, 501
Narcissism, 501
Narcolepsy, 200
Narcotics, 206, 212–213
    endogenous, 212–213, 571
    overdoses of, 270
Nativism, 6
Nativist theory, of language development, 360–361
Natural correlations, 54–55
Natural improvement, of mental disorders, 657
Natural remedies, for mental disorders, 651–652,
        652f
Natural selection, 11
Naturalistic observation, 45–46
Nearsightedness, 137, 138f
Necker cube, 183, 183f
Needs. See also Motivation
    for achievement, 344
    hierarchy of, 334, 334f, 335f, 489
    for sleep, 197–199, 198f
Negative correlation, 53, 53f
Negative punishment, 279, 279t
Negative reinforcement, 279, 279t
Negative symptoms of schizophrenia, 609, 648

Nembutal, 211
Nerves, 92
Nervous system
    autonomic, 92f, 93–94
    central. See Brain; Central nervous system;
        Spinal cord
    definition of, 92
    parasympathetic, 92f, 94
    peripheral, 92f, 92–94, 93f
    somatic, 92f, 92–93
    sympathetic, 92f, 93, 94
Neural pathways
    emotion and, 319–320, 320f
    mapping connectivity of, 120f, 120–122
    pain, 165–166
    visual, 142–143, 143f
Neural tube, 106
Neurobiological factors, phobias and, 595
Neurofeedback, 564
Neuroimaging, 119–125
    classical conditioning and, 274
    functional, 2, 120–123, 121f
    mirror neurons and, 103
    structural, 119f, 119–120
Neurons, 80–84
    action potential of, 85f, 86–87, 87f
    axons of, 81f, 82
    bipolar cells, 83, 83f
    cell body (soma) of, 81, 81f
    components of, 80–82, 81f, 82f
    conduction in, 84–87
    definition of, 80
    dendrites of, 81, 81f
    electrochemical actions of, 84–91
    interneurons, 83
    memory and, 234–235
    mirror, 103, 299, 299f
    motor, 82–83
    neurotransmitters and, 87f, 87–91
    number of, 80
    postsynaptic, 87, 87f
    presynaptic, 87, 87f
    Purkinje cells, 83, 83f
    pyramidal cells, 83, 83f
    resting potential of, 84–85, 85f
    sensory, 82
    synapses between, 82, 82f
    transmission between, 87f, 87–91
Neuroscience
    behavioural, 24–25, 25f
    cognitive, 25
    early development of, 114–115
Neuroticism, 478, 478t
Neurotransmitters, 87f, 87–91. See also specific
        neurotransmitters by name
    altering balance of, 89
    depression and, 602–603
    drug effects on functioning of, 206
    drug mimicry of, 89–91, 90f
    endogenous opioids as, 212–213
Neutralizing, emotional expression and, 326, 327f
Nicaraguan sign language, 361–362
Nicotine, 206, 209t, 211, 212. See also Smoking
Night terrors, 200
Nodes of Ranvier, 87, 87f
Noise (sound)
    as chronic stressor, 552
    perceived control and, 553
Noise (interference), signal detection and,
        133–134

Nonrandom sampling, 65–66
Nonsense syllables, 21
Nonshared environment, 410–411
Nonspecific treatment effect, 657–658, 658f
Non-suicidal self-injury (NSSI), 622–623
Nontasters, 173
Norepinephrine, 88
  stress and, 554, 554f, 567
  tricyclic antidepressants and, 649–650
Normal curve, 48, 48f
  of intelligence, 416, 416f
Normal distribution, 48, 48f
Normative influence, 529, 529f
Norm of reciprocity, 529
Norms, 528–529, 529f
Novum Organum (Bacon), 66
NSSI. See Non-suicidal self-injury
Nucleus accumbens, operant conditioning and, 291, 291f
Nuremburg Code of 1957, 70

Obedience, 530–533, 532f
Obesity, 336f, 336–339, 337f, 337t
  avoiding, 339, 576
  causes of, 337–339, 429
  psychology of, 579
Object-centred approach, to smell sense, 169
Object permanence, 434f, 434–435, 435f
Object recognition, image-based theories of, 149
Observation, 42–50
  description and, 47–50
  double-blind, 47
  as empirical method, 42–43
  measurement and, 43–47
  naturalistic, 45–46
Observational learning, 295–300
  in animals, 297–299, 298f
  definition of, 295
  diffusion chain in, 296–297
  of fear, in animals, 297
  in humans, 295–297, 296f
  models and, 295
  neural elements of, 299f, 299–300
  of tool use, in animals, 297–299, 298f
Observer bias, 46–47
Obsessive-compulsive disorder (OCD), 598–599
  treatment of, 655–656
Occipital cortex, lateral, vision and, 142–143, 143f
Occipital lobe, 100f, 101
OCD. See Obsessive-compulsive disorder
Odorant molecules, 168, 168f
Oedipus conflict, 487
Olanzepine (Zyprexa), 648
Olfaction. See Smell sense
Olfactory bulb, 168f, 169
Olfactory epithelium, 168, 168f
Olfactory receptor neurons (ORNs), 168f, 168–169
Omega-3 fatty acids, 651–652, 652f
On the Origin of Species by Means of Natural Selection (Darwin), 11
Online learning, 308–309
Ontogeny, of brain, 106
Openness to experience, 478, 478t
Operant behaviour, 278–281, 279f, 279t
Operant conditioning, 277–294
  basic principles of, 280–288
  cognitive elements of, 288–291
  context and, 282–283

definition of, 277
discrimination in, 282–283
evolutionary elements of, 293f, 293–294
extinction in, 283
generalization in, 282–283
law of effect and, 277f, 277–278, 278f
neural elements of, 291f, 291–292
reinforcement and punishment in, 18–19, 278–281, 279f, 279t
reinforcement schedules and, 283–286, 284f
shaping and, 286–287
stimulus control and, 282–283
superstitious behaviour and, 287–288
Operant conditioning chamber, 18, 19, 278–279, 279f
Operational definitions, 44
Opiates, 206, 212–213
  endogenous, 212–213, 571
  overdoses of, 270
Opium, 212
Optic nerve, 137f, 138f, 139, 141
Optimism bias, culture and, 378
Optimism, health and, 574–575
Oral stage, 487
Orbicularis oculi, 323
Orexigenic signals, 335
Organizational encoding, 225f, 225–226, 226f
Orgasm phase of human sexual response cycle, 341, 341f
ORNs. See Olfactory receptor neurons
Orphanages, development impairment in, 442
Ossicles, 159, 160f
Outcome expectancies, 493
Outer ear, 159, 160f
An Outline of Psychology (Titchener), 9–10
Overdiagnosis of mental disorders, 653
Overgeneralization, in language development, 357
Oxycontin, 212
Oxytocin, 99, 567

PAG. See Periaqueductal grey
Pain, 165–166
  brain and, 165–166, 570f, 570–571
  gate-control theory of, 166
  intensity of, 166
  referred, 166
Pain pathways, 165–166
Pain withdrawal reflex, 94, 94f, 165
Panic disorder, 595–596
  treatment of, 660t
Papillae, on tongue, 172, 172f
Parasympathetic nervous system, 92f, 94
Parents. See also Caregivers
  happiness and, 465–466, 466f
  intelligence of, children and, 408, 409t
Parent–child relationships
  in adolescence, 458t, 458–459
  in infancy, 442, 442f. See also Attachment
Parietal cortex, implicit vs. explicit learning and, 303
Parietal lobe, 100f, 101
  vision and, 143, 145
Parkinson's disease, 89–90, 100
  dopamine and, 292
Paroxetine (Paxil), 650
Parsimony, rule of, 41
Parts-based object recognition, 150, 150f
Passionate love, 524–525, 525f
Patient–practitioner interaction, 573, 573f
Patterns of variation, 52

Pavlovian conditioning. See Classical conditioning
Pavlov's experiments, 267f, 267–270, 268f
Paxil (paroxetine), 650
PCP. See Phencyclidine
Peer relationships, in adolescence, 454, 454f, 459
People for the Ethical Treatment of Animals, 72–73
Pepsi-Cola, 212
Perceived control, over stressful events, 553
Perception, 3
  auditory. See Hearing; Hearing loss
  cognitive development and, 437–438
  of colour, 140–141
  of consciousness of others, 179–180, 180f
  definition of, 130
  figure-ground relationship and, 148–149, 149f
  Gestalt perceptual grouping rules and, 148, 149f
  haptic, 164
  of motion, 153–154
  of shape, 142, 143f
  subliminal, 191
  visual. See Visual perception
  warping of, by categorization, 539–540, 540f
Perceptual confirmation, 541
Perceptual constancy, 147
Perceptual development, in infancy and childhood, 431
Perceptual priming, 244
Perceptual sensitivity, measurement of, 134
Perfect correlation, 53, 53f
Periaqueductal grey (PAG), 166
Peripheral nervous system (PNS), 92f, 92–94, 93f
Persistence, as memory failure, 257–259, 259f, 260
Persistent vegetative state, 123, 185
Personal constructs, 491–492
Personality, 471–503
  in animals, 482–483
  assessment of. See Personality assessment
  attraction and, 523
  bipolar disorder and, 606–607
  brain and, 115, 115f, 483–484
  changing study of, 503
  consistency across situations, 491
  culture and, 481, 492
  definition of, 472
  describing and explaining, 472–473
  existential approach to, 489–490
  Eysenck's theory of, 478
  frontal lobes and, 115, 115f
  gender and, 481
  health and, 574–576
  humanistic approach to, 488–489, 489f
  measuring, 472–476
  psychodynamic approach to. See Psychodynamic approach
  psychosexual stages and, 487–488
  self and. See Self; Self-concept; Self-esteem
  social-cognitive approach to, 490–494
  trait approach to. See Personality traits
Personality assessment, 473–476
  newer methods for, 475–476
  personality inventories for, 473t, 473–474
  projective techniques for, 474f, 474–476, 475f
  superficial cues and, 479
Personality disorders, 618–620
  antisocial, 619t, 619–620
  types of, 618–619, 619t
Personality inventories, 473t, 473–474
Personality traits, 476–484

as behavioural dispositions and motives, 476–477
Big Five, 478t, 478–480
in brain, 483–484
core, 477–480
definition of, 476
genetic factors and, 480, 480t, 482
self-concept and, 496
Person-centred therapy, 636
Person–situation controversy, 491
Persuasion, 534–535, 535f
Pessimism, health and, 574–575
PET. See Positron emission tomography
Phallic stage, 487
Phantom limb syndrome, brain plasticity and, 104
Phencyclidine, 206, 213
Phenomenology, 179
Pheromones, 171
Philosophers, 5–6
Philosophical empiricism, 6
Phlogiston, 41
Phobic disorders, 594–595
Phonemes, 353, 353f
Phonological rules, 353
Phototherapy, 655
Phrenology, 6–7, 7f
Phylogeny, of brain, 106–107
Physical dependence, 206–207
Physiological psychology, 24
Physiological responses
emotions and, 315–318, 317f, 318f
to stress, 554f, 554–558, 555f
Physiology, 7
Piaget's stages of cognitive development, 433t, 433–441, 434f, 435f
Pictorial depth cues, 150–151, 151f
Pinna, 159, 160f
Pitch, 158, 159t
perception of, 160–161, 161f
wavelength and, 158, 159t
Pituitary gland, 98f, 99
Place code, 161
Placebo, 657
Placebo effect, 571
mental disorder treatment and, 657–658, 658f
Placeholders, mental, 224–225
Places of Light (Fernyhough), 261
Planning, frontal lobe and, 102
Plasticity, of brain, 103–105
Plateau phase of human sexual response cycle, 341, 341f
Pleasure centres, of brain, 291f, 291–292
Pleiotropic effects, 606
PNS. See Peripheral nervous system
Polio, third-variable problem and, 56
Political orientation, brain and, 482
Political views, illusion of explanatory depth and, 390
Pollutants, obesity and, 337
Polygraph, 328f, 328–329
Pons, 96, 97f
Population, 63–66
Portion size, 338, 339f, 577
Position, sound localization and, 161–162
Positive correlation, 53, 53f
Positive punishment, 279, 279t
Positive reinforcement, 279, 279t
Positive symptoms of schizophrenia, 608–609, 648
Positively skewed frequency distributions, 49–50, 50f

Positron emission tomography (PET), 120, 121, 121f
Postconventional stage of moral development, 448
Posthypnotic amnesia, 215
Postpartum depression, 602
Postsynaptic neurons, 87, 87f
Post-traumatic stress disorder (PTSD), 599–600, 600f
treatment of, 660t
Potassium ions
action potential and, 85f, 86, 87
resting potential and, 85, 85f, 87
Poverty, intelligence and, 413–414
Power, of instruments, 44, 44f
Practical intelligence, 405–406
Practical reasoning, 388
Practice, distributed, 305–306
Practice testing, effectiveness as study technique, 205t, 305, 306
Prayer, for stress management, 567, 567f
Preconventional stage of moral development, 448
Prefrontal cortex
concepts and categories and, 372
implicit vs. explicit learning and, 303
pain and, 570, 570f
Prefrontal lobe
decision making and, 380–381, 381f
dreaming and, 204, 204f
Prejudice, 513
social psychology and, 28
Prenatal development, 426–430, 427f
prenatal environment and, 428–430
stages of, 427f, 427–428
Pre-operational stage, 433, 433t, 436, 437–438
Preparedness theory of phobias, 594–595
Presynaptic neurons, 87, 87f
Pride, 324
Primary appraisal, 559
Primary auditory cortex, 102, 103, 160–161, 161f
Primary mental abilities, 402, 402t
Primary reinforcement, 279–280
Primary sex characteristics, 452
Primary visual cortex, 102–103
Primates
altruism in, 516–517
brains of, 108
language development in, 365–366
non-aggression in, 512
observational learning in, 297–299, 298f
self-recognition in, 186
sexual behaviour in, 340
social development in, 442–443
Priming, 243f, 243–244
Principles of Physiological Psychology (Wundt), 8
The Principles of Psychology (James), 2, 4, 12
Prisoner's dilemma, 512f, 512–513
Proactive interference, 250
Probabilities, judging, 374–375
Probability theory, extrasensory perception and, 61
Problem of other minds, 179–180, 180f
Problem solving, 382–388. See also Reasoning
analogical, 383f, 383–384
creativity and insight and, 384–388
functional fixedness and, 385f, 385–386, 386f, 387f, 388f
ill-defined and well-defined problems and, 382
means-end analysis and, 382–383
Procedural memory, 242, 242f
Processing. See also Information processing
auditory, musical training and, 163

bottom-up, taste sense and, 170
colour, language and, 367f, 367–368
top-down, taste sense and, 170
transfer-appropriate, 237
Procrastination, 4
Prognosis, 587
Projection, 486t
Projective tests, for personality assessment, 474f, 474–476, 475f
Prolonged exposure, in rational coping, 562
Propranolol, neurotransmitters and, 91
Prospect theory of decision-making errors, 378–379
Prospective memory, 251
Protection, from harm, 71
Protein ions, 85
Prototype theory of concepts, 370, 370f, 371f
Proximity
attraction and, 518–520
perceptual organization and, 148, 149f
Proximodistal rule, 432
Prozac (fluoxetine)
for depression, 602, 650
for generalized anxiety disorder, 597
neurotransmitters and, 91
Psilocybin, 213
Psychiatric hospitals, 646–648
Psychiatric illness. See Mental disorders
Psychiatric labelling, 592–593
Psychiatrist, 630
Psychoactive drugs, 205–214. See also Drug therapy; Substance abuse
definition of, 205
depressant, 209–211
hallucinogenic, 213
marijuana as, 213–214
narcotic, 212–213
stimulant, 211–212
types of, 209t, 209–214
use and abuse of, 206–208
withdrawal symptoms and, 207
Psychoanalysis
definition of, 14
influence of, 15
process of, 634–635
Psychoanalytic theory
definition of, 13–14
of dreams, 202–203
origins of, 13–14
of unconscious, 190–191
Psychodynamic approach, 484–488
defense mechanisms in, 486, 486t
psychosexual stages and, 487–488
structure of mind and, 485–486, 486t
Psychodynamic psychotherapies, 634–635
Psychological dependence, 207
Psychological disorders. See Mental disorders
Psychologist, 630
clinical, 33, 33f
counselling, 33
industrial/organizational, 34
prescribing medications, 654
school, 34
Psychology
in Canada, 32
careers in, 33–34
clinical, development of, 13–15
cognitive, 20–23
cultural, 28–30
definition of, 2

developmental, 426
environmental, 552
evolutionary, 25–26
first laboratories for, 12
Gestalt, 21
as hub science, 34–35
humanistic, 15, 488–489, 489f
of obesity, 579
physiological, 24
profession of, 31–34
roots of, 5–12
as science, 17
social. See Aggression; Attribution; Social
    behaviour; Social cognition; Social
    influence; Social psychology; Stereotyping
stimulus-response. See Behaviourism
subfields in, 33, 33f
Psychology of health, 574–578
avoiding sexual risks and, 576, 577–578
cardiovascular disease and, 557–558, 558f
eating wisely and, 576, 577
hardiness and, 575–576
optimism and, 574–575
self-regulation and, 576–577
smoking and, 578
stress effects on, 555–557
Psychology of illness, 568–573
patient–practitioner interaction and, 573, 573f
placebo effect and, 571
recognizing and treating, 569–571, 570f
sick role and, 572–573
sickness response and, 569
somatic symptom disorders and, 572
stressful events and, 550–551, 551t
Psychoneuroimmunology, 557
Psychopath, 620
The Psychopathology of Everyday Life (Freud), 191
Psychopharmacology, 648. See also Drug therapy
Psychophysics, 131–135
sensory adaptation and, 134–135
signal detection and, 133–134
thresholds and, 132f, 132–133, 133t
Psychoses, 607. See also Schizophrenia
treatment of, 646, 648
Psychosexual stages, 487–488
Psychosocial development, Erikson's stages of,
    458, 458t
Psychosomatic illness, 572
Psychosurgery, 655–656
Psychotherapists, types of, 630–631
Psychotherapy, 633f, 633–645
behavioural, 637–639
childhood memories recalled during, 256
cognitive, 639t, 639–641
cognitive behavioural, 641–642, 652, 652f, 654,
    654f
couples, 643
dangers of, 660–661, 661t
definition of, 633
drug therapy and, 652, 652f
drug therapy vs., 654, 654f
family, 643
Gestalt, 637
group, 643–644
interpersonal, 635
person-centred, 636
psychodynamic, 634–635
self-help and support groups and, 644–645
technology for, 642
Psychoticism, 478

PTSD. See Post-traumatic stress disorder
Puberty, 339, 452, 453–454, 455
Punishers, 279
Punishment
avoidance of, 345–347, 346t
in behavioural therapy, 638
hedonic motive for social influence and, 527f,
    527–528
immediate vs. delayed, 280f, 280–281
motivation and, 343–344, 344f
negative, 279, 279t
in operant conditioning, 278–279
positive, 279, 279t
primary and secondary, 279–280
Pupil, of eye, 137f
Pure tones, 158
Purkinje cells, 83, 83f
Puzzle box, 277f, 277–278, 278f
Pyramidal cells, 83, 83f


Race
intelligence and, 417–420
stereotyping and, 539, 541, 541f, 542
Random assignment, 59–61, 60f
Random sampling, 64–65
Range, 50
Ranvier, nodes of, 87, 87f
Rape trauma
repressive coping and, 561
rational coping and, 562
Rapid cycling bipolar disorder, 605
Ratio IQ, 398
Ratio schedules of reinforcement, 283, 285–286
Rational choice theory, 374
Rational coping, 561–562
Rationalization, 486t
Raven's Progressive Matrices Test, 405, 405f, 418
RDoC. See Research Domain Criteria Project
Reaction formation, 486t
Reaction time, 8, 414
Reactivity, empirical method and, 43
Re-appraisal, emotion regulation and, 320–321
Reasoning, 388–391. See also Cognition; Cognitive
    development; Thought
brain and, 391, 391f
definition of, 388
illusion of explanatory depth and, 390
moral, 447–449
practical, 388
syllogistic, 390–391
theoretical (discursive), 388–389
REB. See Research ethics boards
Rebound effect of thought suppression, 188f,
    188–189
Receptors
auditory, 159–160, 160f
body position, movement, and balance and, 167
of dendrites, 87, 88
olfactory, 168f, 168–169
pain, 166
taste, 170, 172f, 172–173
thermo-, 164
touch, 164f, 164–165
visual, 138f, 139, 140f, 141
Reciprocal altruism, 517
Reciprocity, norm of, 529
Recognition
false, 254
of illness, 569–571, 570f

of self, 186
theories of, 149–150, 150f
visual, 146–150
Reconsolidation, of memories, 234
Reconstructive memory, 658
Recreational drugs. See Substance abuse
Referred pain, 166
Reflex, 107, 431
in infancy, 431–432
pain withdrawal, 94, 94f, 165
rooting, 431
spinal, 94, 94f
sucking, 431
Refractory period, 86, 341
Reframing, 562–563
Regression, 486t
Rehearsal, 229
Reinforcement
in behavioural therapy, 638
definition of, 19
immediate vs. delayed, 280f, 280–281
intermittent, 285–286
negative, 279, 279t
in operant conditioning, 18–19, 278–279
positive, 279, 279t
primary and secondary, 279–280
schedules of, 283–286, 284f
Reinforcers, 279
culture and, 281
Relatedness, degree of, 109
Relationships, 524–525
chronic stressors related to, 551–552
couples therapy and, 643
ending, 525–526
in infancy. See Attachment
internal working model of, 446, 446f
love and, 524–525, 525f
marriage, 465, 465f, 524–525
parent–child. See Parent–child relationships
peer, in adolescence, 454, 454f, 459
social exchange and, 525
Relative height, as depth cue, 151, 151f
Relative size, as depth cue, 150, 151f
Relatives, intelligence in, 408–409, 409t
Relativism, 29
Relaxation response, 564
Relaxation therapy, 564
Reliability, 44, 44f
Religiosity, for stress management, 567, 567f
REM sleep, 195–196, 196f
deprivation of, 198
dreaming and, 204f, 204–205
Remembering. See Amnesia; Forgetting; Memory;
    Memory failure
Representativeness heuristic, 376–377
Repression, 190, 486t
Repressive coping, 561
Reproduction, male role in, 429
Re-reading, effectiveness as study technique,
    304–305, 305t
Research, 39–75
affordability of, 75
animal subjects in, 72–73
causation and, 54–62
correlation and, 51t, 51–54
description and, 47–50
drawing conclusions and, 62–66
empiricism and, 40–43
ethics and, 70–74
experiments in. See Experiments

explanation and, 51–69
fraud in, 73–74
measurement and, 43–47
observation and. *See* Observation
scientific method and, 40–42, 66
Research Domain Criteria Project (RDoC), 590–592, 591*t*
Research ethics boards (RES), 71–72
Resistance, in psychoanalysis, 634–635
Resistance phase of general adaptation syndrome, 555, 555*f*
Resolution phase of human sexual response cycle, 341, 341*f*
Response
conditioned, 268, 268*f*, 269, 269*f*, 271, 275
definition of, 18
unconditioned, 267, 268*f*, 275
Responsibility
diffusion of, 514–515, 515*f*
joint decisions and, 516
Resting potentials, 84–87, 85*f*
Resting state functional connectivity, 121
Reticular formation, 96, 97*f*
personality and, 483
Retina, 137, 137*f*, 138*f*
Retinal ganglion cells (RGCs), 138*f*, 139
Retinal surface, 137*f*, 138*f*
Retirement communities, 467
Retrieval, 222
components of, 239–241, 240*f*
consequences for subsequent memory, 237–239, 238*f*
state-dependent, 237
Retrieval cues, 236–237
Retrieval-induced forgetting, 238–239, 240
Retroactive interference, 250
Retrograde amnesia, 232
Reuptake, 87*f*, 88
Reversibility, in cognitive development, 436
Reward. *See also* Reinforcement
hedonic motive for social influence and, 527*f*, 527–528
intrinsic vs. extrinsic motivation and, 342–344, 344*f*
Reward prediction error, 292
RGCs. *See* Retinal ganglion cells
Rhyme judgments, 223
Risk and trust, 512*f*, 512–513
Risk-benefit analysis, ethics of research and, 71
Risperidone (Risperidal), 648
Ritalin (methylphenidate), 420
Road rage, 558
Rods, in retina, 138*f*, 139, 140, 140*f*
Romantic relationships. *See* Love; Marriage
Rooting reflex, 431
Rorschach Inkblot Test, 474, 474*f*
Rubin vase, 149, 149*f*
Rule of parsimony, 41
Runner's high, 212–213

SAD. *See* Seasonal affective disorder
Sadness, 323*f*, 324
St. John's wort, 651
St. Mary's of Bethlehem Hospital, 647
Saltatory conduction, 87
Samples, 64
Sampling
nonrandom, 65–66
random, 64–65
*Scared Straight*, 661, 661*t*

Schachter and Singer's two-factor theory of emotion, 317*f*, 317–318
Schedules of reinforcement, 283–286, 284*f*
Schizophrenia, 607–613
biochemical factors in, 610
biological factors in, 606, 609–611, 610*f*, 611*f*
brain in, 610–611, 611*f*, 612*f*, 648
cognitive symptoms of, 609
definition of, 607
favourable outcomes in, 613
genetic factors in, 609–610, 610*f*
negative symptoms of, 609, 648
neuroanatomy of, 611, 611*f*, 612*f*
positive symptoms of, 608–609, 648
psychological factors in, 611–612
treatment of, 646, 648
twin studies of, 110, 609–610
School psychologists, 34
Scientific method, 40–42, 66
SCL. *See* Skin conductance level
Scopes trial, 26
Sea slug (*Aplysia*)
habituation in, 300
memory studies on, 235
Seasonal affective disorder (SAD), 602
Seconal, 211
Secondary appraisal, 559
Secondary reinforcement, 279–280
Secondary sex characteristics, 452
Second-order conditioning, 269–270
Secure attachment style, 444–447
Security, self-esteem and, 500
Sedatives, for insomnia, 199
Seizures, crossing of corpus callosum by, 115–116
Selective attention, 146
Selective serotonin reuptake inhibitors (SSRIs), 91, 650, 650*f*
Selectivity
of consciousness, 182–183
of sexual partners, 517–518, 519
Self, 494–502
theory of, 495
Self-actualizing tendency, 488–489, 489*f*
Self-concept, 495–497
brain and, 496*f*, 496–497
causes and effects of, 497
definition of, 495
organization of, 495–497, 496*f*
self-narrative and, 497
Self-consciousness, 184, 186
Self-esteem, 498*t*, 498–502
aggression and, 510
definition of, 498
desire for, 499–501
implicit egotism and, 501–502
sources of, 498–499
Self-explanation, effectiveness as study technique, 305, 305*t*
Self-help groups, 644–645
Self-injury, mental disorders of, 621–623, 622*f*
Self-narrative, 495–496
self-concept and, 497
Self-recognition, 494–495
Self-regulation, health and, 576–577
Self-relevance, 496
Self-reports, 473*t*, 473–474
Self-schemas, 496
Self-selection, 59
Self-serving bias, 500–501
Self-verification, 497

Selye's general adaptation syndrome, 554–555, 555*f*
Semantic encoding, 223–224, 225*f*
Semantic judgments, 223
Semantic memory, 244–245
Semantics, 354
Seniors. *See* Adulthood; Aging
Sensation. *See also* Psychophysics *and individual senses by name*
definition of, 130
dream consciousness and, 201
of sound, 158–159, 159*t*
Sensitization, 266
Sensorimotor stage, 433*t*, 433–435
Sensorineural hearing loss, 162
Sensory adaptation, 134–135
Sensory branding, 129
Sensory memory, 228, 228*f*
Sensory neurons, 82
Sensory receptors, transduction and, 130–131, 131*t*
Sensory storage, 228, 228*f*
Serial reaction time task, implicit learning and, 302
Serotonin, 88, 91
drug effects on functioning of, 206
tricyclic antidepressants and, 650, 650*f*
Serotonin and norepinephrine reuptake inhibitors (SNRIs), 650
SES. *See* Socioeconomic status
Sex characteristics, primary and secondary, 452
Sex chromosomes, 108, 427
of zygote, 427
Sex determination, 108
Sex education, 457, 578
Sexual behaviour
during adolescence, 455*f*, 455–457, 456*f*, 457*f*
human sexual response cycle and, 340–341, 341*f*
hypothalamus and, 98
motivation for, 339 340
reasons for, 341–342, 342*t*
risky, avoiding, 576, 577–578
selection of sexual partners and, 517–518, 519
Sexual intercourse, during adolescence, 457
Sexual orientation
during adolescence, 455–456, 456*f*
determinants of, 456
odour perception and, 171
tolerance of, 455–456, 456*f*
Sexually transmitted diseases (STDs), 457, 576, 577–578
Shame, 324
Shape, perception of, 142, 143*f*
Shaping, 286–287
Shared environment, 410–411
Shock therapy, 654–655
Short-term storage, 229*f*, 229–230
Siblings, intelligence in, 408, 409*t*
Sick role, 572
Sickness response, 569
Signal detection theory, 133–134
Sign language
animal use of, 365
babbling and, 356
Nicaraguan, 361–362
Signs
in mental disorders, 585
symbols vs., 324
Significance, statistical, 61–62

Similarity
attraction and, 523–524
perceptual organization and, 148, 149f
Simplicity, perceptual organization and, 148, 149f
Sincerity, of facial expressions, 327, 327f
Single-neuron feature detectors, 142, 143f
SIT. See Stress inoculation training
Situation management, for stress, 565–568
Situational attributions, 543–544, 544f
Size, illusions of, 152, 153f
Skepticism, 69
Skewed frequency distributions, 49–50, 50f
Skin conductance level (SCL), 187
Skinner box, 18, 19, 278–279, 279f
Skinner's experiments, 278–282, 279f, 279t
Sleep, 194–200
cycle of, 195–197, 196f, 197f
deprivation of, 198
disorders of, 199–200
dreaming and. See Dreams
memory and, 197–198, 233
need for, 197–199, 198f
REM. See REM sleep
reticular formation and, 96
Sleep apnea, 199–200
Sleeping pills, 199
Sleep paralysis, 200
Sleep spindles, 195, 196f
Sleep terrors, 200
Sleepwalking, 200
Smell sense, 168f, 168–169, 171, 171f
absolute threshold for, 133t
social behaviour and, 171, 171f
transduction and, 131t
Smiling, 326
Smoking. See also Nicotine
neurotransmitter balance in brain and, 89
during pregnancy, 430
quitting, 578
Snellen chart, 135
Snoring, sleep apnea and, 199–200
SNRIs. See Serotonin and norepinephrine
reuptake inhibitors
Social anxiety disorder, 586
Social behaviour, 508–526
aggression and. See Aggression
altruism and, 516–517
in animals, 508
attraction and, 518–524
cooperation and, 512–517
divorce and, 525–526
relationships and, 524–525
sexual partner selection and, 517–518, 519
smell sense and, 171, 171f
Social brain hypothesis, 538
Social cognition, 537–545
attribution and, 543–545, 544f
definition of, 537
stereotyping and, 538–543
Social-cognitive approach, 490–493
consistency of personality across situations, 491
personal constructs and, 491–492
personal goals and expectancies and, 493, 493t
Social development, 442–447. See also Attachment
Social exchange, 525
Social influence, 526–537
accuracy motive for, 527, 533–537
approval motive for, 527, 528–533
conformity and, 529–530, 530f
consistency and, 535–537, 536f

culture and, 528
definition of, 526
hedonic motive for, 526, 527f, 527–528
informational, 533–534
normative, 528–529, 529f
obedience and, 530–533, 532f
persuasion and, 534–535, 535f
on remembering, 246–247
social norming and, 531
Social loafing, 514–515
Social norming, 531
Social phobia, 594
exposure therapy for, 638, 638t
treatment of, 654, 654f
Social psychology, 27–28, 507–545. See also
Aggression; Attribution; Social behaviour;
Social cognition; Social influence;
Stereotyping
American civil rights movement and, 28
definition of, 508
historical forces shaping, 28
Social referencing, 441
Social role theory, 481
Social stimuli, in infancy, 431
Social support, for stress management, 565–567
Social worker, 630–631
Sociobiology (Wilson), 26
Socioeconomic status (SES)
intelligence and, 413–414
stress and, 557
Socioemotional selectivity theory, 463f, 463–464,
464f
Sociopath, 620
Sodium ion
action potential and, 85f, 86, 87
resting potential and, 85, 85f, 87
Sodium lactate, panic disorder and, 596
Soma, of neurons, 81, 81f
Somatic nervous system, 92f, 92–93
Somatic symptom disorders, 572
Somatoform disorders, 572
Somatosenses, 164–167. See also Pain; Touch
Somatosensory cortex, 101–102, 102f, 103
pain and, 570, 570f
Somnambulism, 200
Sound, localizing sources of, 161–162
Sound waves, 158–159, 159t
Source memory, 253
Spatial navigation imagery task, 192–193
Specific factors, 403, 403f
Specific phobias, 594
Speech. See also Language; Language development
culture and tone of voice and, 330
detection of, musical training and, 163
disorganized, in schizophrenia, 608
distinguishing sounds of, 355–356
of mother, fetal hearing and, 430
telegraphic, 356–357
Speed. See Amphetamines
Spinal cord, 107
collaboration with brain, 94–95, 95f
hindbrain and, 96
pain withdrawal reflex and, 94, 94f, 165
regions of, 95f
Spinal reflexes, 94, 94f, 165
Spirituality, for stress management, 567, 567f
Split-brain procedure, 116f, 116–117, 117f
Spontaneous recovery, 271
Sports, chronic traumatic encephalopathy and,
79–80

S-R psychology. See Behaviourism
SSRIs. See Selective serotonin reuptake inhibitors
Standard deviation, 50, 50f
Stanford-Binet Intelligence Scale, 398
State-dependent retrieval, 237
Statistical significance, 61–62
Statistics
descriptive, 48–50, 49f, 50f
inferential, 62
STDs. See Sexually transmitted diseases
Stereophonic hearing, 161
Stereoscope, 152
Stereotype threat, 541, 541f
Stereotyping, 538–543
automatic, 542–543
definition of, 538
inaccuracy of, 539, 539f
intelligence tests and, 396, 418–419
overuse of, 539–540, 540f
self-perpetuating, 541, 541f
Sterilization laws, 396
Stimulants, 211–212
Stimulus
conditioned, 268, 268f, 269f, 269–271, 275–
276
construal of, 22
discriminative, 282–283
just noticeable difference and, 132–133
psychophysics and. See Psychophysics
reaction time and, 8
sensory adaptation and, 134–135
signal detection and, 133–134
social, in infancy, 431
thresholds and, 132f, 132–133, 133t
unconditioned, 267, 269f, 269–271, 275–276
Stimulus control, in operant conditioning, 282–
283
Stimulus-response psychology. See Behaviourism
Stirrup, of ear, 159, 160f
Storage, 222
long-term, 230–234, 231f
neurons and synapses and, 234–235
sensory, 228, 228f
short-term, 229f, 229–230
Strange Situation, 444
Stress, 549–568
aging and, 555–557
bipolar disorder and, 606
cardiovascular disease and, 557–558, 558f
chronic stressors and, 551–552
definition of, 550
discrimination related to, 551, 552
events causing, 550–551, 551t
generalized anxiety disorder and, 597
health and. See Psychology of health
illness and. See Psychology of illness
immigrants and, 566
immune response and, 557
interpretation of, 559
management of. See Stress management
perceived control and, 553
physical reactions to, 554f, 554–558, 555f
post-traumatic, 599–600, 600f, 660t
psychological reactions to, 558–560
sources of, 550–553
Stress inoculation training (SIT), 562
Stress management, 561–568
aerobic exercise for, 564–565
biofeedback for, 564
body and, 563–565

humour for, 568
meditation for, 563
mind and, 561–563
rational coping for, 561–562
reframing for, 562–563
relaxation for, 563–564
religious experiences for, 567, 567f
repressive coping for, 561
situation and, 565–568
social support for, 565–567
Stressors, 550
chronic, 551–552
Striatum, 100
DRD2 gene and, 591
Stroop task, 216, 217f
Structural brain imaging, 119f, 119–120
Structuralism, 7–10
Study skills, improving, 10–11
Study techniques, 304–306, 305t
Subcortical structures, 97–100, 98f
Sublimation, 486t
Subliminal perception, 191
Substance abuse. *See also specific substances by name*
of cognitive enhancers, 420–421
context and drug overdoses and, 270
Substantia nigra, 100
Subtyping, 541
Successive approximations, 287
Sucking reflex, 431
Suggestibility, 255–256, 260
Suicide, 621–622, 622f
attempted, 621
childhood abuse and, 112
Sulci, 100, 100f
Summarization, effectiveness as study technique, 304–305, 305t
Sunk-cost fallacy, 377
Superego, 485
Superstitious behaviour, operant conditioning of, 287 288
Supertaster, 173
Support groups, 644–645
Suppression, of emotional expression, 320
Surface structure, of language, 354–355
Surgery
anesthesia for, 177
of brain, 655–656
Surprise, 323f, 324
Survival-related information, encoding of, 226–227, 227f
Susceptibility, to hypnosis, 215
Syllogistic reasoning, 390–391
Symbols, signs vs., 324
Symmetry
attractiveness and, 522
facial expressions and, 327
Sympathetic nervous system, 92f, 93, 94
Symptoms
insensitivity to, 570–571
in mental disorders, 585–586
of schizophrenia, 608–609, 648
withdrawal, psychoactive drugs and, 207
Synapses, 82, 82f
memory and, 234–235
Synaptic proliferation, during adolescence, 452–453, 453f
Synaptic pruning, during adolescence, 453, 453f
Synaptic transmission, 87, 87f
Syntactical rules, 354, 354f

Systematic persuasion, 534–535, 535f

Tactile perception. *See* Touch sense
Tardive dyskinesia, 648
Tastant molecules, 172
Taste buds, 171–172, 172f
Tasters, 173
Taste sense, 170–173, 172f
absolute threshold for, 133t
bottom-up and top-down influences on, 170
transduction and, 131t
TAT. *See* Thematic Apperception Test
TCPS. *See* Tri-Council Policy Statement
Teaching machines, 19
Technology
computer impact on psychological thinking and, 23
driving while using cell phones and, 146, 251
for psychotherapy, 642
Tectum, 96–97, 97f
Teenagers. *See* Adolescence
Tegmentum, 97, 97f
Telegraphic speech, 356–357
Telomerase, 556–557
Telomeres, 556–557
Temperament
attachment and, 445
phobias and, 595
Templates, 149
Temporal codes, 161
Temporal lobe, 100f, 102
Wernicke's area in, 115
Tend-and-befriend response, 567
Ten-Item Personality Inventory (TIPI), 473t
Tennis imagery task, 192–193
Teratogens, 428–430
Terminal buttons, 87
Terror management theory, 347
Terrorist attack of 9/11
altruism and, 517
stress caused by, 553–554
Tests, studying for, 305–306
Testing, attention and, 306–307. *See also* Intelligence tests; Personality assessment
Testosterone
aggression and, 509–510, 510f
odour related to, 171
sexual desire and, 339–340
sexual orientation and, 456
Tetrahydrocannabinol (THC), 206, 213
Texture gradient, as depth cue, 150, 151f
Thalamus, 98, 98f
placebo effect and, 571
THC. *See* Tetrahydrocannabinol
Thematic Apperception Test (TAT), 475, 475f
Theoretical reasoning, 388–389
Theory, 40–43
Theory-based approach, 405–407
Theory of mind, 438–439
cognitive development and, 438–439
Therapy. *See* Biological treatments; Drug therapy; Psychotherapy; Treatment of psychological disorders
Thermoreceptors, 164
Theta waves, 195, 196f
Third-variable problem, 55f, 55–57, 56f
Thirst, hypothalamus and, 98
Thought, 367–391. *See also* Cognition; Cognitive development; Reasoning
abstract, frontal lobe and, 102

concepts and categories and, 369–373
decision making and. *See* Decision making
dream consciousness and, 201–202
language and, 367–368
moral, 447–449
problem solving and. *See* Problem solving
reasoning and. *See* Reasoning
thinking aloud and, 186–187, 187t
time concept and, 368
Thought suppression, 188f, 188–189
Threats, challenges vs., 559
Thresholds, 132f, 132–133, 133t
absolute, 132, 132f, 133t
action potential and, 86
Timbre, 158, 159t
Time concept, language and, 368
Timing
of conscious will, 181, 181f
facial expressions and, 327
of reinforcement and punishment, 280f, 280–281
sound localization and, 161–162
TIPI. *See* Ten-Item Personality Inventory
Tip-of-the-tongue experience, 252
TMS. *See* Transcranial magnetic stimulation
Tobacco use. *See* Nicotine; Smoking
Tofranil (imipramine), 649–650, 652, 652f
Token economy, 638
Tolerance to drugs, 206–207, 270, 649
Tolman's means-end relationships, 288
Tone of voice, culture and, 330
Tongue, papillae on, 172, 172f
Tools, use in animals, observational learning of, 297–299, 298f
Top-down control, 166, 169, 170
Topology, 22
Touch sense
absolute threshold for, 133t
parietal lobe and, 101
sensation of, 164f, 164–165
transduction and, 131t
Tourette's disorder, treatment of, 660t
Toxic inhalants, 211
Traits. *See* Personality traits
Tranquilizers, minor, 211
Transcranial magnetic stimulation (TMS), 123–125, 655
Transduction
auditory, 131t, 159–160, 160f
sensory receptors and, 130–131, 131t
Transfer-appropriate processing, 237
Transference, in psychoanalysis, 635–636
Transfer, of learning, 306
Transience
of consciousness, 183
of memory, 249–250, 250f, 259
Trauma. *See* Brain damage; Stress
Treatment of psychological disorders, 627–661
access to, 628–629
approaches to, 631–632
biological. *See* Biological treatments
culture and, 632
drug therapy. *See* Drug therapy
effectiveness of, 659–661, 660t, 661t
ethical standards for, 661
failure to seek, 629–630
illusions about, 657–658, 658f
studies of, 658–659
psychotherapy. *See* Psychotherapy.
Treatment outcome studies, 658–659

Trephining, 646
Tri-Council Policy Statement: Ethical Conduct for Research Involving Humans (TCPS), 70
Tricyclic antidepressants, 649–650, 650f
Trust and risk, 512f, 512–513
Trust, learning to, 290–291
Trust vs. mistrust stage, 458t
Trustworthiness, 513
Twins
    depression in, 602
    fraternal (dizygotic), 109–110
    identical (monozygotic), 109–110
    intelligence in, 408, 409t
    mental disorders in, 590, 595, 597, 599, 600, 602, 606, 609, 610f, 611
    personality of, 480, 482
    schizophrenia in, 110, 609–610
    sexual orientation of, 456
Two-factor theory of emotion, 317f, 317–318
Two-factor theory of intelligence, 402
Type A behaviour pattern, 558
Type B behaviour pattern, 558
Typical antipsychotics, 648

Ultimatum game, 513
Ultrasocial species, 508
Umami, 172
Unconditioned response (UR), 267, 268f, 275
Unconditioned stimulus (US), 267, 268f, 269f, 269–271, 275–276
Unconscious, 13–14, 189–192
    cognitive, 191–193, 193f
    definition of, 485
    dynamic, 190–191
    Freudian, 190–191
    modern view of, 191–193, 193f
Unconscious motivations, 344–345
Unconscious stereotyping, 542–543
Unconsciousness, during surgery, 177
Uncorrelated variables, 53, 53f
Uncritical acceptance, dream consciousness and, 201
Underlining, effectiveness as study technique, 304, 305t
Understanding, in rational coping, 562
Unipolar depression, 601–604
Unity, of consciousness, 182
Universality hypothesis, 323f, 323–324
An Unquiet Mind: A Memoir of Moods and Madness (Jamison), 605
UR. See Unconditioned response
US. See Unconditioned stimulus

Valence-centred approach, to smell sense, 169

Validity
    external, 62–63
    internal, 62
Validity scales, of MMPI, 474
Valium (diazepam)
    for generalized anxiety disorder, 211, 597, 649
    effects on consciousness, 206
    for sleep problems, 211
Valproate, 651
Values, attraction and, 523
Variability
    empirical method and, 42
    statistics describing, 49f, 49–50, 50f
Variable-interval (VI) schedule, 284
Variable-ratio (VR) schedule, 285
Variables, 52
    correlation of, 51t, 51–54
    dependent, 58
    independent, 58
    third-variable problem and, 55f, 55–57, 56f
Variation, patterns of, 52
Vegetative state, 123, 185
Venlafaxine (Effexor), 650
Ventral visual stream, 142, 143, 143f
Ventricles, of brain, in schizophrenia, 611, 611f
Ventromedial hypothalamus, hunger and, 335, 335f
Verbal Behavior (Skinner), 23
Vestibular system, 167
VI. See Variable-interval schedule
View-Master, 152
Violence. See also Aggression
    media, aggression and, 64
Visible spectrum, 140, 140f
Vision. See Visual perception; Visual sensation
Visual acuity, 135–136
Visual cortex
    concepts and categories and, 372
    feature detectors in, 118–119
    primary, 102–103
Visual form agnosia, 142–143, 143f
Visual imagery encoding, 224–225, 225f
Visual judgments, 223–224
Visual pathways, 142f, 142–143
Visual perception, 144–155
    attention and, 144–145
    binding problem and, 144
    of change, 154–155, 155f
    of depth and size, 150–153
    feature-integration theory and, 145
    hallucinations and, 156
    illusory conjunctions and, 145
    loss of. See Blindness
    of motion, 153–154
    occipital lobe and, 101
    recognizing objects and, 146–150

transduction and, 131t
Visual sensation, 135–144
    absolute threshold for, 133t
    acuity and, 135–136
    brain and, 141–144, 142f
    of colour, 140f, 140–141
    eye and, 137, 137f, 138f
    light and, 136f, 136–139, 137t
    loss of. See Blindness
    parietal lobe and, 142
    photoreceptors and, 138f, 139, 140f
Visual streaming, 142–143, 143f
Voice, tone of, culture and, 330
VR. See Variable-ratio schedule

WAIS. See Wechsler Adult Intelligence Scale
Walden II (Skinner), 19
Wavelength
    of light waves, 136, 137t, 139–141, 140f
    of sound waves, 158, 159t
Weber's law, 133
Wechsler Adult Intelligence Scale (WAIS), 398–399, 399f
Wellbutrin (bupropion), 650
Wernicke's aphasia, 362
Wernicke's area, 115, 362f, 362–363
"What" pathway
    in touch, 164–165
    visual, 142, 143, 143f, 145
What-the-hell-effect, 579
"Where" pathway
    in touch, 164–165
    visual, 142, 143, 143f, 145
Williams syndrome, 395
Wine, price of, taste and, 170
Withdrawal, from drugs, 207
Women, in psychology, 31–32
Working memory, 229–230

X chromosome, 108, 427
Xanax (alprazolam), 211, 649

Y chromosome, 108, 427
Yawning, contagious, 439

Zimbardo's prisoner study, 532
Zoloft, for depression, 602
Zolpidem (Ambien), 649
Zombie, 179
Zygomatic major, 323, 324, 326, 327
Zygote, 427
Zyprexa (olanzepine), 648